# Webster's New Dictionary of the English Language

## New Edition

# Webster's
# New Dictionary
# of the
# English Language

## New Edition

Created in Cooperation with the Editors of
MERRIAM-WEBSTER

THE
**POPULAR**
GROUP

This edition published by arrangement with
Federal Street Press,
a division of Merriam-Webster, Incorporated
P.O. Box 281
Springfield, MA 01102


The Popular Group LLC
1700 Broadway
New York, NY 10019


ISBN-13 978-1-59027-084-4
ISBN-10 1-59027-084-3

Printed in the United States of America

06 07 08 09 10    5 4 3 2 1

# PREFACE

This new edition contains new words and senses that have become established in the language since publication of the previous edition. It remains an extremely concise reference to those words that form the very core of the English vocabulary. It is intended to serve as a quick reference, especially for questions of spelling, pronunciation, and hyphenation of the most common words in everyday use.

Though small, this work shares many details of presentation with more comprehensive dictionaries. However, conciseness of presentation necessarily requires special treatment of entries, and this book has a number of special features uniquely its own. Users need to be familiar with the following major features of this dictionary.

**Main entries** follow one another in alphabetical order. Centered periods within the entries show points at which a hyphen may be put when the word is broken at the end of a line.

**Homographs** (words spelled the same but having different meanings) are run in to a single main entry when they are closely related. Second and succeeding homographs are represented by a swung dash: ～ Homographs of distinctly different origin (as **¹perch** and **²perch**) are given separate entries with preceding raised numerals.

**Variant spellings** that are quite common appear at the main entry following a comma (as **the·ater, the·atre**) and following other boldface entry words, such as inflected forms and run-on entries.

**Inflected forms** of nouns, verbs, adjectives, and adverbs are shown when they are irregular—as when requiring the dropping of a final *e* or changing a final *y* to *i* before the suffix: (as **prat·ed; prat·ing** at **prate**) or when the form of the base word itself changes: (as **swam...; swum** at **swim**)—or when there might be doubt about their spelling: (as *pl* **twos** at **two**). They are given either in full (as **worse...; worst** at **bad**) or cut back to a convenient point of division (as **-mat·ed; -mat·ing** at **es·ti·mate**). Common variants of inflected forms are shown even if they are regular (as **bused** *or* **bussed** at **bus**). When the inflected forms of a verb involve no irregularity except the doubling of a final consonant, the double consonant is shown instead of full or cutback inflected forms (as *vb* **-gg-** at **hug**). A variant or inflected form whose alphabetical place is distant from the main entry is entered at its own place with a cross-reference in small capital letters to the main entry (as **laid** *past of* LAY).

Several other kinds of entries are also found in this dictionary. A **run-in entry** is a term related to a main entry that appears within a definition (as **cacao beans** at **ca·cao**). It is essentially defined within the context of the definition and is set off by parentheses. Derivative words, made up usually of the main entry and a common word element, such as a suffix, are shown as **undefined run-on entries** following all definitions of a main entry. These are set off by a dash (as — **man·u·al·ly** at **man·u·al** or — **hill·top** at **hill**). The meaning of an undefined run-on entry can be inferred from the meaning of the main entry where it appears and that of the added word element, shown elsewhere in the book. A **run-on phrase** is a group of two or more words having the main entry as a major element and having a special meaning of its own (as **knock out** at **knock** or **set forth** at **set**). Run-on phrases are always defined.

**Lists of undefined words** formed by the addition of a common English prefix to a word entered in the dictionary and having meanings that can be inferred from the meaning of the root word and that of the prefix will be found in a separate section at the bottom of the page at entries for the following prefixes: *anti-, bi-, co-, counter-, extra-, hyper-, in-, inter-, mini-, multi-, non-, over-, post-, pre-, re-, self-, sub-, super-, un-,* and *vice-*.

**Pronunciation** information is either given explicitly or implied for every entry in the dictionary. Pronunciation respellings are placed within reversed slanted lines (as \ˌjenəˈralətē\ at **ge·ner·al·i·ty**). Where the pronunciation is not indicated at a particular entry, or is indicated in a cutback form, the full pronunciation is to be inferred from an earlier indicated pronunciation. A full list of the pronunciation symbols used is shown on the page following this Preface.

The grammatical function of entry words is indicated by an italic **functional label** (as *vb, n,* or *prefix*).

A **hyphen** that is a fixed part of a hyphenated expression (such as *self-conscious*) is converted to a special "double hyphen" (⸗) when the compound expression appears in lightface type and when the fixed hyphen comes at the end of a line in this dictionary. This indicates to you that the hyphen is to be retained when the word is not at the end of a line. Fixed hyphens in boldface entry words are shown as short boldface dashes, which are a bit larger than ordinary hyphens. These short dashes or long hyphens in boldface words are retained at the end of a line in this dictionary.

**Guide words** are used at the top of pages to indicate the range of entries on those pages. In choosing guide words for a page, we select the alphabetically first and last spelled-out boldface words or phrases on that page. This means that any boldface entry—main entry, variant spelling, inflected form, run-in or run-on entry—can be used as a guide word. Please keep this in mind if the word used as a guide word does not happen to be the first or last main entry on the page. The guide words themselves are in alphabetical order throughout the book, so occasionally it has been necessary to modify this rule. When the alphabetically last entry on one page would come later than the alphabetically first entry on the following page, a different word is chosen as guide word. On pages that contain a substantial number of undefined words derived from a prefix entry, the undefined words are not considered when choosing guide words.

All **abbreviations** used in this book are listed, along with a number of other common abbreviations, in a special section immediately following the dictionary proper.

# Pronunciation Symbols

ə  banana, collide, abut; raised \ᵊ\ in \ᵊl, ᵊn\ as in battle, cotton; in \lᵊ, mᵊ, rᵊ\ as in French table, prisme, titre

ˈə, ˌə  humbug, abut

ər  operation, further

a  map, patch

ā  day, fate

ä  bother, cot, father

à  father as pronounced by those who do not rhyme it with *bother*

aù  now, out

b  baby, rib

ch  chin, catch

d  did, adder

e  set, red

ē  beat, nosebleed, easy

f  fifty, cuff

g  go, big

h  hat, ahead

hw  whale

i  tip, banish

ī  site, buy

j  job, edge

k  kin, cook

ḵ  German ich, Buch

l  lily, cool

m  murmur, dim

n  nine, own; raised \ⁿ\ indicates that a preceding vowel or diphthong is pronounced through both nose and mouth, as in French bon \bōⁿ\

ŋ  sing, singer, finger, ink

ō  bone, hollow

ȯ  saw, cork

œ  French bœuf, German Hölle

œ̄  French feu, German Höhle

ȯi  toy, sawing

p  pepper, lip

r  rarity

s  source, less

sh  shy, mission

t  tie, attack

th  thin, ether

th̲  then, either

ü  boot, few \ˈfyü\

ù  put, pure \ˈpyùr\

ᵫ  German füllen

ᵫ̄  French rue, German fühlen

v  vivid, give

w  we, away

y  yard, cue \ˈkyü\; raised \ʸ\ indicates that a preceding \l\, \n\, or \w\ is modified by the placing of the tongue tip against the lower front teeth, as in French digne \dēnʸ\

z  zone, raise

zh  vision, pleasure

\  slant line used in pairs to mark the beginning and end of a transcription

ˈ  mark at the beginning of a syllable that has primary (strongest) stress: \ˈpenmənˌship\

ˌ  mark at the beginning of a syllable that has secondary (next-strongest) stress: \ˈpenmənˌship\

# A

**¹a** \'ā\ *n, pl* **a's** *or* **as** \'āz\ : 1st letter of the alphabet

**²a** \ə, 'ā\ *indefinite article* : one or some — used to indicate an unspecified or unidentified individual

**aard·vark** \'ärd,värk\ *n* : ant-eating African mammal

**aback** \ə'bak\ *adv* : by surprise

**aba·cus** \'abəkəs\ *n, pl* **aba·ci** \'abə-,sī, -,kē\ *or* **aba·cus·es** : calculating instrument using rows of beads

**abaft** \ə'baft\ *adv* : toward or at the stern

**ab·a·lo·ne** \,abə'lōnē\ *n* : large edible shellfish

**¹aban·don** \ə'bandən\ *vb* : give up without intent to reclaim — **aban·don·ment** *n*

**²abandon** *n* : thorough yielding to impulses

**aban·doned** \ə'bandənd\ *adj* : morally unrestrained

**abase** \ə'bās\ *vb* **abased; abas·ing** : lower in dignity — **abase·ment** *n*

**abash** \ə'bash\ *vb* : embarrass — **abashment** *n*

**abate** \ə'bāt\ *vb* **abat·ed; abat·ing** : decrease or lessen

**abate·ment** \ə'bātmənt\ *n* : tax reduction

**ab·at·toir** \'abə,twär\ *n* : slaughterhouse

**ab·bess** \'abəs\ *n* : head of a convent

**ab·bey** \'abē\ *n, pl* **-beys** : monastery or convent

**ab·bot** \'abət\ *n* : head of a monastery

**ab·bre·vi·ate** \ə'brēvē,āt\ *vb* **-at·ed; -at·ing** : shorten — **ab·bre·vi·a·tion** \ə,brēvē'āshən\ *n*

**ab·di·cate** \'abdi,kāt\ *vb* **-cat·ed; -cat·ing** : renounce — **ab·di·ca·tion** \,abdi'kāshən\ *n*

**ab·do·men** \'abdəmən, ab'dōmən\ *n* **1** : body area between chest and pelvis **2** : hindmost part of an insect — **ab·dom·i·nal** \ab'dämən²l\ *adj* — **ab·dom·i·nal·ly** *adv*

**ab·duct** \ab'dəkt\ *vb* : kidnap — **ab-**

**duc·tion** \-'dəkshən\ *n* — **ab·duc·tor** \-tər\ *n*

**abed** \ə'bed\ *adv or adj* : in bed

**ab·er·ra·tion** \,abə'rāshən\ *n* : deviation or distortion — **ab·er·rant** \a'berənt\ *adj*

**abet** \ə'bet\ *vb* **-tt-** : incite or encourage — **abet·tor, abet·ter** \-ər\ *n*

**abey·ance** \ə'bāəns\ *n* : state of inactivity

**ab·hor** \əb'hȯr, ab-\ *vb* **-rr-** : hate — **ab·hor·rence** \-əns\ *n* — **ab·hor·rent** \-ənt\ *adj*

**abide** \ə'bīd\ *vb* **abode** \-'bōd\ *or* **abid·ed; abid·ing** **1** : endure **2** : remain, last, or reside

**ab·ject** \'ab,jekt, ab'-\ *adj* : low in spirit or hope — **ab·jec·tion** \ab-'jekshən\ *n* — **ab·ject·ly** *adv* — **ab·ject·ness** *n*

**ab·jure** \ab'jùr\ *vb* **1** : renounce **2** : abstain from — **ab·ju·ra·tion** \,abjə-'rāshən\ *n*

**ablaze** \ə'blāz\ *adj or adv* : on fire

**able** \'ābəl\ *adj* **abler** \-blər\; **ablest** \-bləst\ **1** : having sufficient power, skill, or resources **2** : skilled or efficient — **abil·i·ty** \ə'bilətē\ *n* — **ably** \'āblē\ *adv*

**-able, -ible** \əbəl\ *adj suffix* **1** : capable of, fit for, or worthy of **2** : tending, given, or liable to

**ab·lu·tion** \ə'blüshən, a'blü-\ *n* : washing of one's body

**ab·ne·gate** \'abni,gāt\ *vb* **-gat·ed; -gat·ing** **1** : relinquish **2** : renounce — **ab·ne·ga·tion** \,abni'gāshən\ *n*

**ab·nor·mal** \ab'nȯrməl\ *adj* : deviating from the normal or average — **ab·nor·mal·i·ty** \,abnər'malətē, -nȯr-\ *n* — **ab·nor·mal·ly** *adv*

**aboard** \ə'bōrd\ *adv* : on, onto, or within a car, ship, or aircraft **~** *prep* : on or within

**abode** \ə'bōd\ *n* : residence

**abol·ish** \ə'bälish\ *vb* : do away with — **ab·o·li·tion** \,abə'lishən\ *n*

**abom·i·na·ble** \ə'bämənəbəl\ *adj*
: thoroughly unpleasant or revolting

**abom·i·nate** \ə'bämə,nāt\ *vb* **-nat·ed;**
**-nat·ing** : hate — **abom·i·na·tion**
\ə,bämə'nāshən\ *n*

**ab·orig·i·nal** \,abə'rijənəl\ *adj* **1**
: original **2** : primitive

**ab·orig·i·ne** \-'rijənē\ *n* : original inhabitant

**abort** \ə'bórt\ *vb* : terminate prematurely — **abor·tive** \-'bórtiv\ *adj*

**abor·tion** \ə'bórshən\ *n* : spontaneous
or induced termination of pregnancy

**abound** \ə'baùnd\ *vb* : be plentiful

**about** \ə'baùt\ *adv* : around ∼ *prep* **1**
: on every side of **2** : on the verge of
**3** : having as a subject

**above** \ə'bəv\ *adv* : in or to a higher
place ∼ *prep* **1** : in or to a higher
place than **2** : more than

**above·board** *adv or adj* : without deception

**abrade** \ə'brād\ *vb* **abrad·ed; abrad-**
**ing** : wear away by rubbing — **abra-**
**sion** \-'brāzhən\ *n*

**abra·sive** \ə'brāsiv\ *n* : substance for
grinding, smoothing, or polishing ∼
*adj* **1** : tending to abrade **2** : causing
irritation — **abra·sive·ly** *adv* —
**abra·sive·ness** *n*

**abreast** \ə'brest\ *adv or adj* **1** : side by
side **2** : up to a standard or level

**abridge** \ə'brij\ *vb* **abridged; abridg-**
**ing** : shorten or condense — **abridg-**
**ment, abridge·ment** *n*

**abroad** \ə'bród\ *adv or adj* **1** : over a
wide area **2** : outside one's country

**ab·ro·gate** \'abrəgāt\ *vb* **-gat·ed; -gat-**
**ing** : annul or revoke — **ab·ro·ga-**
**tion** \,abrə'gāshən\ *n*

**abrupt** \ə'brəpt\ *adj* **1** : sudden **2** : so
quick as to seem rude — **abrupt·ly**
*adv*

**ab·scess** \'ab,ses\ *n* : collection of pus
surrounded by inflamed tissue — **ab-**
**scessed** \-,sest\ *adj*

**ab·scond** \ab'skänd\ *vb* : run away
and hide

**ab·sent** \'absənt\ *adj* : not present ∼
**ab·sent** \ab'sent\ *vb* : keep oneself
away — **ab·sence** \'absəns\ *n* —
**absen·tee** \,absən'tē\ *n*

**ab·sent·mind·ed** \,absənt'mīndəd\
*adj* : unaware of one's surroundings
or action — **ab·sent·mind·ed·ly** *adv*
— **ab·sent·mind·ed·ness** *n*

**ab·so·lute** \'absə,lüt, ,absə'-\ *adj* **1**

: pure **2** : free from restriction **3**
: definite — **ab·so·lute·ly** *adv*

**ab·so·lu·tion** \,absə'lüshən\ *n* : remis-
sion of sins

**ab·solve** \əb'zälv, -'sälv\ *vb* **-solved;**
**-solv·ing** : set free of the consequences of guilt

**ab·sorb** \əb'sórb, -'zórb\ *vb* **1** : suck
up or take in as a sponge does **2** : engage (one's attention) — **ab·sor·ben-**
**cy** \-'sórbənsē, -'zór-\ *n* — **ab·sor-**
**bent** \-bənt\ *adj or n* — **ab·sorb·ing**
*adj*

**ab·sorp·tion** \əb'sórpshən, -'zórp-\ *n*
: process of absorbing — **ab·sorp-**
**tive** \-tiv\ *adj*

**ab·stain** \əb'stān\ *vb* : refrain from doing something — **ab·stain·er** *n* — **ab-**
**sten·tion** \-'stenchən\ *n* — **ab·sti-**
**nence** \'abstənəns\ *n*

**ab·ste·mi·ous** \ab'stēmēəs\ *adj* : sparing in use of food or drink — **ab·ste-**
**mi·ous·ly** *adv* — **ab·ste·mi·ous-**
**ness** *n*

**ab·stract** \ab'strakt, 'ab,-\ *adj* **1** : expressing a quality apart from an ob-
ject **2** : not representing something
specific ∼ \'ab,-\ *n* : summary ∼
\ab'-, 'ab,-\ *vb* **1** : remove or separate **2** : make an abstract of — **ab-**
**stract·ly** *adv* — **ab·stract·ness** *n*

**ab·strac·tion** \ab'strakshən\ *n* **1** : act
of abstracting **2** : abstract idea or
work of art

**ab·struse** \əb'strüs, ab-\ *adj* : hard to
understand — **ab·struse·ly** *adv* —
**ab·struse·ness** *n*

**ab·surd** \əb'sərd, -'zərd\ *adj* : ridiculous or unreasonable — **ab·sur·di·ty**
\-ətē\ *n* — **ab·surd·ly** *adv*

**abun·dant** \ə'bəndənt\ *adj* : more than
enough — **abun·dance** \-dəns\ *n* —
**abun·dant·ly** *adv*

**abuse** \ə'byüz\ *vb* **abused; abus·ing**
**1** : misuse **2** : mistreat **3** : attack with
words ∼ \-'byüs\ *n* **1** : corrupt
practice **2** : improper use **3** : mis-
treatment **4** : coarse and insulting
speech — **abus·er** *n* — **abu·sive**
\-'byüsiv\ *adj* — **abu·sive·ly** *adv* —
**abu·sive·ness** *n*

**abut** \ə'bət\ *vb* **-tt-** : touch along a border — **abut·ter** *n*

**abut·ment** \ə'bətmənt\ *n* : part of a
bridge that supports weight

**abys·mal** \ə'bizməl\ *adj* **1** : immeasurably deep **2** : wretched — **abys-**
**mal·ly** *adv*

**abyss** \ə'bis\ *n* : immeasurably deep gulf

**-ac** \ˌak\ *n suffix* : one affected with

**aca·cia** \ə'kāshə\ *n* : leguminous tree or shrub

**ac·a·dem·ic** \ˌakə'demik\ *adj* **1** : relating to schools or colleges **2** : theoretical — **academic** *n* — **ac·a·dem·i·cal·ly** \-iklē\ *adv*

**acad·e·my** \ə'kadəmē\ *n, pl* **-mies 1** : private high school **2** : society of scholars or artists

**acan·thus** \ə'kanthəs\ *n, pl* **acan·thus 1** : prickly Mediterranean herb **2** : ornament representing acanthus leaves

**ac·cede** \ak'sēd\ *vb* **-ced·ed; -ced·ing 1** : become a party to an agreement **2** : express approval **3** : enter upon an office

**ac·cel·er·ate** \ik'seləˌrāt, ak-\ *vb* **-at·ed; -at·ing 1** : bring about earlier **2** : speed up — **ac·cel·er·a·tion** \-ˌselə'rāshən\ *n*

**ac·cel·er·a·tor** \ik'seləˌrātər, ak-\ *n* : pedal for controlling the speed of a motor vehicle

**ac·cent** \'akˌsent\ *n* **1** : distinctive manner of pronunciation **2** : prominence given to one syllable of a word **3** : mark (as ´, `, ˆ) over a vowel in writing or printing to indicate pronunciation ~ \'akˌ-, ak'-\ *vb* : emphasize — **ac·cen·tu·al** \ak'senchəwəl\ *adj*

**ac·cen·tu·ate** \ak'senchəˌwāt\ *vb* **-at·ed; -at·ing** : stress or show off by a contrast — **ac·cen·tu·a·tion** \-ˌsenchə'wāshən\ *n*

**ac·cept** \ik'sept, ak-\ *vb* **1** : receive willingly **2** : agree to — **ac·cept·abil·i·ty** \ikˌseptə'bilətē, ak-\ *n* — **ac·cept·able** \-'septəbəl\ *adj* — **ac·cep·tance** \-'septəns\ *n*

**ac·cess** \'akˌses\ *n* : capability or way of approaching — **ac·ces·si·bil·i·ty** \ikˌsesə'bilətē, ak-\ *n* — **ac·ces·si·ble** \-'sesəbəl\ *adj*

**ac·ces·sion** \ik'seshən, ak-\ *n* **1** : something added **2** : act of taking office

**ac·ces·so·ry** \ik'sesərē, ak-\ *n, pl* **-ries 1** : nonessential addition **2** : one guilty of aiding a criminal — **accessory** *adj*

**ac·ci·dent** \'aksədənt\ *n* **1** : event occurring by chance or unintentionally **2** : chance — **ac·ci·den·tal** \ˌaksə'dent°l\ *adj* — **ac·ci·den·tal·ly** *adv*

**ac·claim** \ə'klām\ *vb or n* : praise

**ac·cla·ma·tion** \ˌaklə'māshən\ *n* **1** : eager applause **2** : unanimous vote

**ac·cli·mate** \'akləˌmāt, ə'klīmət\ *vb* **-mat·ed; -mat·ing** : acclimatize — **ac·cli·ma·tion** \ˌaklə'māshən, -ˌklī-\ *n*

**ac·cli·ma·tize** \ə'klīməˌtīz\ *vb* **-tized; -tiz·ing** : accustom to a new climate or situation — **ac·cli·ma·ti·za·tion** \-ˌklīmətə'zāshən\ *n*

**ac·co·lade** \'akəˌlād\ *n* : expression of praise

**ac·com·mo·date** \ə'käməˌdāt\ *vb* **-dat·ed; -dat·ing 1** : adapt **2** : provide with something needed **3** : hold without crowding

**ac·com·mo·da·tion** \əˌkämə'dāshən\ *n* **1** : quarters — usu. pl. **2** : act of accommodating

**ac·com·pa·ny** \ə'kəmpənē\ *vb* **-nied; -ny·ing 1** : go or occur with **2** : play supporting music — **ac·com·pa·ni·ment** \-nəmənt\ *n* — **ac·com·pa·nist** \-nist\ *n*

**ac·com·plice** \ə'kämpləs, -'kəm-\ *n* : associate in crime

**ac·com·plish** \ə'kämplish, -'kəm-\ *vb* : do, fulfill, or bring about — **ac·com·plished** *adj* — **ac·com·plish·er** *n* — **ac·com·plish·ment** *n*

**ac·cord** \ə'kórd\ *vb* **1** : grant **2** : agree ~ *n* **1** : agreement **2** : willingness to act — **ac·cor·dance** \-'kórd°ns\ *n* — **ac·cor·dant** \-°nt\ *adj*

**ac·cord·ing·ly** \ə'kórdiŋlē\ *adv* : consequently

**according to** *prep* **1** : in conformity with **2** : as stated by

**ac·cor·di·on** \ə'kórdēən\ *n* : keyboard instrument with a bellows and reeds ~ *adj* : folding like an accordion bellows — **ac·cor·di·on·ist** \-nist\ *n*

**ac·cost** \ə'kóst\ *vb* : approach and speak to esp. aggressively

**ac·count** \ə'kaúnt\ *n* **1** : statement of business transactions **2** : credit arrangement with a vendor **3** : report **4** : worth **5** : sum deposited in a bank ~ *vb* : give an explanation

**ac·count·able** \ə'kaúntəbəl\ *adj* : responsible — **ac·count·abil·i·ty** \-ˌkaúntə'bilətē\ *n*

**ac·coun·tant** \ə'kaúnt°nt\ *n* : one skilled in accounting — **ac·coun·tan·cy** \-°nsē\ *n*

**ac·count·ing** \ə'kau̇ntiŋ\ *n* : financial record keeping

**ac·cou·tre, ac·cou·ter** \ə'kütər\ *vb* **-tred** *or* **-tered; -tring** *or* **-ter·ing** \-'kütəriŋ, -'kütriŋ\ : equip

**ac·cou·tre·ment, ac·cou·ter·ment** \ə'kütrəmənt, -'kütər-\ *n* **1** : accessory item — usu. pl. **2** : identifying characteristic

**ac·cred·it** \ə'kredət\ *vb* **1** : approve officially **2** : attribute — **ac·cred·i·ta·tion** \-,kredə'tāshən\ *n*

**ac·crue** \ə'krü\ *vb* **-crued; -cru·ing** : be added by periodic growth — **ac·cru·al** \-əl\ *n*

**ac·cu·mu·late** \ə'kyümyə,lāt\ *vb* **-lat·ed; -lat·ing** : collect or pile up — **ac·cu·mu·la·tion** \-,kyümyə'lāshən\ *n*

**ac·cu·rate** \'akyərət\ *adj* : free from error — **ac·cu·ra·cy** \-rəsē\ *n* **1** : **ac·cu·rate·ly** *adv* — **ac·cu·rate·ness** *n*

**ac·cursed** \ə'kərst, -'kərsəd\ **ac·curst** \ə'kərst\ *adj* **1** : being under a curse **2** : damnable

**ac·cuse** \ə'kyüz\ *vb* **-cused; -cus·ing** : charge with an offense — **ac·cu·sa·tion** \,akyə'zāshən\ *n* — **ac·cus·er** *n*

**ac·cused** \ə'kyüzd\ *n, pl* **-cused** : defendant in a criminal case

**ac·cus·tom** \ə'kəstəm\ *vb* : make familiar through use or experience

**ace** \'ās\ *n* : one that excels

**acer·bic** \ə'sərbik, a-\ *adj* : sour or biting in temper, mood, or tone

**acet·amin·o·phen** \ə,sētə'minəfən\ *n* : pain reliever

**ac·e·tate** \'asə,tāt\ *n* : fabric or plastic derived from acetic acid

**ace·tic acid** \ə'sētik-\ *n* : acid found in vinegar

**acet·y·lene** \ə'set²lən, -²l,ēn\ *n* : colorless gas used as a fuel in welding

**ache** \'āk\ *vb* **ached; ach·ing 1** : suffer a dull persistent pain **2** : yearn — **ache** *n*

**achieve** \ə'chēv\ *vb* **achieved; achiev·ing** : gain by work or effort — **achieve·ment** *n* — **achiev·er** *n*

**ac·id** \'asəd\ *adj* **1** : sour or biting to the taste **2** : sharp in manner **3** : of or relating to an acid ∼ *n* : sour water-soluble chemical compound that reacts with a base to form a salt — **acid·ic** \ə'sidik\ *adj* — **acid·i·fy** \ə'sidə,fī\ *vb* — **acid·i·ty** \-ətē\ *n* — **acid·ly** *adv*

**ac·knowl·edge** \ik'nälij, ak-\ *vb* **-edged; -edg·ing 1** : admit as true **2** : admit the authority of **3** : express thanks for — **ac·knowl·edg·ment** *n*

**ac·me** \'akmē\ *n* : highest point

**ac·ne** \'aknē\ *n* : skin disorder marked esp. by pimples

**ac·o·lyte** \'akə,līt\ *n* : assistant to a member of clergy in a religious service

**acorn** \'ā,kȯrn, -kərn\ *n* : nut of the oak

**acous·tic** \ə'küstik\ *adj* : relating to hearing or sound — **acous·ti·cal** \-stikəl\ *adj* — **acous·ti·cal·ly** \-klē\ *adv*

**acous·tics** \ə'küstiks\ *n sing or pl* **1** : science of sound **2** : qualities in a room that affect how sound is heard

**ac·quaint** \ə'kwānt\ *vb* **1** : inform **2** : make familiar

**ac·quain·tance** \ə'kwānt²ns\ *n* **1** : personal knowledge **2** : person with whom one is acquainted — **ac·quain·tance·ship** *n*

**ac·qui·esce** \,akwē'es\ *vb* **-esced; -esc·ing** : consent or submit — **ac·qui·es·cence** \-'es²ns\ *n* — **ac·qui·es·cent** \-²nt\ *adj* — **ac·qui·es·cent·ly** *adv*

**ac·quire** \ə'kwīr\ *vb* **-quired; -quir·ing** : gain

**ac·qui·si·tion** \,akwə'zishən\ *n* : a gaining or something gained — **ac·qui·si·tive** \ə'kwizətiv\ *adj*

**ac·quit** \ə'kwit\ *vb* **-tt- 1** : pronounce not guilty **2** : conduct (oneself) usu. well — **ac·quit·tal** \-²l\ *n*

**acre** \'ākər\ *n* **1** *pl* : lands **2** : 4840 square yards

**acre·age** \'ākərij\ *n* : area in acres

**ac·rid** \'akrəd\ *adj* : sharp and biting — **acrid·i·ty** \a'kridətē, ə-\ *n* — **ac·rid·ly** *adv* — **ac·rid·ness** *n*

**ac·ri·mo·ny** \'akrə,mōnē\ *n, pl* **-nies** : harshness of language or feeling — **ac·ri·mo·ni·ous** \,akrə'mōnēəs\ *adj* — **ac·ri·mo·ni·ous·ly** *adv*

**ac·ro·bat** \'akrə,bat\ *n* : performer of tumbling feats — **ac·ro·bat·ic** \,akrə'batik\ *adj*

**across** \ə'krȯs\ *adv* : to or on the opposite side ∼ *prep* **1** : to or on the opposite side of **2** : on so as to cross

**acryl·ic** \ə'krilik\ *n* **1** : plastic used for molded parts or in paints **2** : synthetic textile fiber

**act** \'akt\ *n* **1** : thing done **2** : law **3** : main division of a play ∼ *vb* **1**

: perform in a play **2** : conduct oneself **3** : operate **4** : produce an effect

**ac·tion** \'akshən\ n **1** : legal proceeding **2** : manner or method of performing **3** : activity **4** : thing done over a period of time or in stages **5** : combat **6** : events of a literary plot **7** : operating mechanism

**ac·ti·vate** \'aktə‚vāt\ vb **-vat·ed; -vat·ing** : make active or reactive — **ac·ti·va·tion** \‚aktə'vāshən\ n

**ac·tive** \'aktiv\ adj **1** : causing action or change **2** : lively, vigorous, or energetic **3** : erupting or likely to erupt **4** : now in operation — **active** n — **ac·tive·ly** adv

**ac·tiv·i·ty** \ak'tivətē\ n, pl **-ties** **1** : quality or state of being active **2** : what one is actively doing

**ac·tor** \'aktər\ n : one that acts

**ac·tress** \'aktrəs\ n : woman who acts in plays

**ac·tu·al** \'akchəwəl\ adj : really existing — **ac·tu·al·i·ty** \‚akchə'walətē\ n — **ac·tu·al·iza·tion** \‚akchəwələ-'zāshən\ n — **ac·tu·al·ize** \'ak-chəwə‚līz\ vb — **ac·tu·al·ly** adv

**ac·tu·ary** \'akchə‚werē\ n, pl **-ar·ies** : one who calculates insurance risks and premiums — **ac·tu·ar·i·al** \‚ak-chə'werēəl\ adj

**ac·tu·ate** \'akchə‚wāt\ vb **-at·ed; -at·ing** : put into action — **ac·tu·a·tor** \-‚wātər\ n

**acu·men** \ə'kyümən\ n : mental keenness

**acu·punc·ture** \'akyu‚pəŋkchər\ n : treatment by puncturing the body with needles — **acu·punc·tur·ist** \‚akyu'pəŋkchərist\ n

**acute** \ə'kyüt\ adj **acut·er; acut·est** **1** : sharp **2** : containing less than 90 degrees **3** : mentally alert **4** : severe — **acute·ly** adv — **acute·ness** n

**ad** \'ad\ n : advertisement

**ad·age** \'adij\ n : old familiar saying

**ad·a·mant** \'adəmənt, -‚mant\ adj : insistent — **ad·a·mant·ly** adv

**adapt** \ə'dapt\ vb : adjust to be suitable for a new use or condition — **adapt·abil·i·ty** \ə‚daptə'bilətē\ n — **adapt·able** adj — **ad·ap·ta·tion** \‚ad‚ap-'tāshən, -əp-\ n — **adap·ter** n — **adap·tive** \ə'daptiv\ adj

**add** \'ad\ vb **1** : join to something else so as to increase in amount **2** : say further **3** : find a sum — **ad·di·tion** \ə'dishən\ n

**ad·der** \'adər\ n **1** : poisonous European snake **2** : No. American snake

**ad·dict** \'adikt\ n : one who is psychologically or physiologically dependent (as on a drug) ~ \ə'dikt\ vb : cause to become an addict — **ad·dic·tion** \ə'dikshən\ n — **ad·dic·tive** \-'diktiv\ adj

**ad·di·tion·al** \ə'dishənəl\ adj : existing as a result of adding — **ad·di·tion·al·ly** adv

**ad·di·tive** \'adətiv\ n : substance added to another

**ad·dle** \'ad°l\ vb **-dled; -dling** : confuse

**ad·dress** \ə'dres\ vb **1** : direct one's remarks to **2** : mark an address on ~ \ə'dres, 'ad‚res\ n **1** : formal speech **2** : place where a person may be reached or mail may be delivered

**ad·duce** \ə'düs, -'dyüs\ vb **-duced; -duc·ing** : offer as proof

**ad·e·noid** \'ad‚nóid, -°nóid\ n : enlarged tissue near the opening of the nose into the throat — usu. pl. — **ade·noid, ad·e·noi·dal** \-əl\ adj

**adept** \ə'dept\ adj : highly skilled — **adept·ly** adv — **adept·ness** n

**ad·e·quate** \'adikwət\ adj : good or plentiful enough — **ad·e·qua·cy** \-kwəsē\ n — **ad·e·quate·ly** adv

**ad·here** \ad'hir, əd-\ vb **-hered; -her·ing** **1** : remain loyal **2** : stick fast — **ad·her·ence** \-'hirəns\ n — **ad·her·ent** \-ənt\ adj or n

**ad·he·sion** \ad'hēzhən, əd-\ n : act or state of adhering

**ad·he·sive** \-'hēsiv, -ziv\ adj : tending to adhere ~ n : adhesive substance

**adieu** \ə'dü, -dyü\ n, pl **adieus** or **adieux** \-'düz,-'dyüz\ : farewell

**ad·ja·cent** \ə'jās°nt\ adj : situated near or next

**ad·jec·tive** \'ajiktiv\ n : word that serves as a modifier of a noun — **ad·jec·ti·val** \‚ajik'tīvəl\ adj — **ad·jec·ti·val·ly** adv

**ad·join** \ə'jóin\ vb : be next to

**ad·journ** \ə'jərn\ vb : end a meeting — **ad·journ·ment** n

**ad·judge** \ə'jəj\ vb **-judged; -judg·ing** **1** : think or pronounce to be **2** : award by judicial decision

**ad·ju·di·cate** \ə'jüdi‚kāt\ vb **-cat·ed; -cat·ing** : settle judicially — **ad·ju·di·ca·tion** \ə‚jüdi'kāshən\ n

**ad·junct** \'aj‚əŋkt\ n : something joined or added but not essential

**ad·just** \ə'jəst\ vb : fix, adapt, or set right — **ad·just·able** adj — **ad·just·er, ad·jus·tor** \ə'jəstər\ n — **ad·just·ment** \-mənt\ n

**ad·ju·tant** \'ajətənt\ n : aide esp. to a commanding officer

**ad–lib** \'ad'lib\ vb **-bb-** : speak without preparation — **ad–lib** n or adj

**ad·min·is·ter** \əd'minəstər\ vb **1** : manage **2** : give out esp. in doses — **ad·min·is·tra·ble** \-strəbəl\ adj

**ad·min·is·tra·tion** \əd,minə'strāshən, ad-\ n **1** : process of managing **2** : persons responsible for managing **3** : persons responsible for managing — **ad·min·is·tra·tive** \əd'minə,strātiv\ adj — **ad·min·is·tra·tive·ly** adv

**ad·min·is·tra·tor** \əd'minə,strātər\ n : one that manages

**ad·mi·ra·ble** \'admərəbəl\ adj : worthy of admiration — **ad·mi·ra·bly** \-blē\ adv

**ad·mi·ral** \'admərəl\ n : commissioned officer in the navy ranking next below a fleet admiral

**ad·mire** \əd'mīr\ vb **-mired; -mir·ing** : have high regard for — **ad·mi·ra·tion** \admə'rāshən\ n — **ad·mir·er** n — **ad·mir·ing·ly** adv

**ad·mis·si·ble** \əd'misəbəl\ adj : that can be permitted — **ad·mis·si·bil·i·ty** \-,misə'bilətē\ n

**ad·mis·sion** \əd'mishən\ n **1** : act of admitting **2** : admittance or a fee paid for this **3** : acknowledgment of a fact

**ad·mit** \əd'mit\ vb **-tt-** **1** : allow to enter **2** : permit **3** : recognize as genuine — **ad·mit·ted·ly** adv

**ad·mit·tance** \əd'mit'ns\ n : permission to enter

**ad·mix·ture** \ad'mikschər\ n **1** : thing added in mixing **2** : mixture

**ad·mon·ish** \ad'mänish\ vb : rebuke — **ad·mon·ish·ment** \-mənt\ n — **ad·mo·ni·tion** \admə'nishən\ n — **ad·mon·i·to·ry** \ad'mänə,tōrē\ adj

**ado** \ə'dü\ n **1** : fuss **2** : trouble

**ado·be** \ə'dōbē\ n : sun-dried building brick

**ad·o·les·cence** \,ad'l'es'ns\ n : period of growth between childhood and maturity — **ad·o·les·cent** \-'nt\ adj or n

**adopt** \ə'däpt\ vb **1** : take (a child of other parents) as one's own child **2** : take up and practice as one's own — **adop·tion** \-'däpshən\ n

**adore** \ə'dōr\ vb **adored; ador·ing** **1** : worship **2** : be extremely fond of —

**ador·able** adj — **ador·ably** adv — **ad·o·ra·tion** \,adə'rāshən\ n

**adorn** \ə'dórn\ vb : decorate with ornaments — **adorn·ment** n

**adrift** \ə'drift\ adv or adj **1** : afloat without motive power or moorings **2** : without guidance or purpose

**adroit** \ə'dróit\ adj : dexterous or shrewd — **adroit·ly** adv — **adroit·ness** n

**adult** \ə'dəlt, 'ad,əlt\ adj : fully developed and mature ～ n : grown-up person — **adult·hood** n

**adul·ter·ate** \ə'dəltə,rāt\ vb **-at·ed; -at·ing** : make impure by mixture — **adul·ter·a·tion** \-,dəltə'rāshən\ n

**adul·tery** \ə'dəltərē\ n, pl **-ter·ies** : sexual unfaithfulness of a married person — **adul·ter·er** \-tərər\ n — **adul·ter·ess** \-tərəs\ n — **adul·ter·ous** \-tərəs\ adj

**ad·vance** \əd'vans\ vb **-vanced; -vancing** **1** : bring or move forward **2** : promote **3** : lend ～ n **1** : forward movement **2** : improvement **3** : offer ～ adj : being ahead of time — **ad·vance·ment** n

**ad·van·tage** \əd'vantij\ n **1** : superiority of position **2** : benefit or gain — **ad·van·ta·geous** \,ad,van'tājəs, -vən-\ adj — **ad·van·ta·geous·ly** adv

**ad·vent** \'ad,vent\ n **1** cap : period before Christmas **2** : a coming into being or use

**ad·ven·ti·tious** \,advən'tishəs\ adj : accidental — **ad·ven·ti·tious·ly** adv

**ad·ven·ture** \əd'venchər\ n **1** : risky undertaking **2** : exciting experience — **ad·ven·tur·er** \-chərər\ n — **ad·ven·ture·some** \-chərsəm\ adj — **ad·ven·tur·ous** \-chərəs\ adj

**ad·verb** \'ad,vərb\ n : word that modifies a verb, an adjective, or another adverb — **ad·ver·bi·al** \ad'vərbēəl\ adj — **ad·ver·bi·al·ly** adv

**ad·ver·sary** \'advər,serē\ n, pl **-sar·ies** : enemy or rival — **adversary** adj

**ad·verse** \ad'vərs, 'ad-,\ adj : opposing or unfavorable — **ad·verse·ly** adv

**ad·ver·si·ty** \ad'vərsətē\ n, pl **-ties** : hard times

**ad·vert** \ad'vərt\ vb : refer

**ad·ver·tise** \'advər,tīz\ vb **-tised; -tis·ing** : call public attention to — **ad·ver·tise·ment** \,advər'tīzmənt, əd'vərtəzmənt\ n — **ad·ver·tis·er** n

**ad·ver·tis·ing** \'advər,tīziŋ\ n : business of preparing advertisements

**ad·vice** \əd'vīs\ *n* : recommendation with regard to a course of action

**ad·vis·able** \əd'vīzəbəl\ *adj* : wise or prudent — **ad·vis·abil·i·ty** \-ˌvīzə-'bilətē\ *n*

**ad·vise** \əd'vīz\ *vb* **-vised; -vis·ing** : give advice to — **ad·vis·er, ad·vis·or** \-'vīzər\ *n*

**ad·vise·ment** \əd'vīzmənt\ *n* : careful consideration

**ad·vi·so·ry** \əd'vīzərē\ *adj* : having power to advise

**ad·vo·cate** \'advəkət, -ˌkāt\ *n* : one who argues or pleads for a cause or proposal ∼ \-ˌkāt\ *vb* **-cat·ed; -cat·ing** : recommend — **ad·vo·ca·cy** \-vəkəsē\ *n*

**adze** \'adz\ *n* : tool for shaping wood

**ae·gis** \'ējəs\ *n* : protection or sponsorship

**ae·on** \'ēən, 'ē,än\ *var of* EON

**aer·ate** \'ar,āt\ *vb* **-at·ed; -at·ing** : supply or impregnate with air — **aer·a·tion** \ˌar'āshən\ *n* — **aer·a·tor** \'ar,ātər\ *n*

**ae·ri·al** \'arēəl\ *adj* : inhabiting, occurring in, or done in the air ∼ *n* : antenna

**ae·rie** \'arē, 'irē\ *n* : eagle's nest

**aer·o·bic** \ˌar'ōbik\ *adj* : using or needing oxygen

**aer·o·bics** \-biks\ *n sing or pl* : exercises that produce a marked increase in respiration and heart rate

**aero·dy·nam·ics** \ˌarōdī'namiks\ *n* : science of bodies in motion in a gas — **aero·dy·nam·ic** \-ik\ *adj* — **aero·dy·nam·i·cal·ly** \-iklē\ *adv*

**aero·nau·tics** \ˌarə'nótiks\ *n* : science dealing with aircraft — **aero·nau·ti·cal** \-ikəl\ *adj*

**aero·sol** \'arə,säl, -,sòl\ *n* 1 : liquid or solid particles suspended in a gas 2 : substance sprayed as an aerosol

**aero·space** \'arō,spās\ *n* : earth's atmosphere and the space beyond — **aerospace** *adj*

**aes·thet·ic** \es'thetik\ *adj* : relating to beauty — **aes·thet·i·cal·ly** \-iklē\ *adv*

**aes·thet·ics** \-'thetiks\ *n* : branch of philosophy dealing with beauty

**afar** \ə'fär\ *adv* : from, at, or to a great distance — **afar** *n*

**af·fa·ble** \'afəbəl\ *adj* : easy to talk to — **af·fa·bil·i·ty** \ˌafə'bilətē\ *n* — **af·fa·bly** \'afəblē\ *adv*

**af·fair** \ə'far\ *n* : something that relates to or involves one

¹**af·fect** \ə'fekt, a-\ *vb* : assume for effect — **af·fec·ta·tion** \ˌaf,ek'tā-shən\ *n*

²**affect** *vb* : produce an effect on

**af·fect·ed** \ə'fektəd, a-\ *adj* 1 : pretending to some trait 2 : artificially assumed to impress — **af·fect·ed·ly** *adv*

**af·fect·ing** \ə'fektiŋ, a-\ *adj* : arousing pity or sorrow — **af·fect·ing·ly** *adv*

**af·fec·tion** \ə'fekshən\ *n* : kind or loving feeling — **af·fec·tion·ate** \-shənət\ *adj* — **af·fec·tion·ate·ly** *adv*

**af·fi·da·vit** \ˌafə'dāvət\ *n* : sworn statement

**af·fil·i·ate** \ə'filē,āt\ *vb* **-at·ed; -at·ing** : become a member or branch — **af·fil·i·ate** \-ēət\ *n* — **af·fil·i·a·tion** \-ˌfilē'āshən\ *n*

**af·fin·i·ty** \ə'finətē\ *n, pl* **-ties** : close attraction or relationship

**af·firm** \ə'fərm\ *vb* : assert positively — **af·fir·ma·tion** \ˌafər'māshən\ *n*

**af·fir·ma·tive** \ə'fərmətiv\ *adj* : asserting the truth or existence of something ∼ *n* : statement of affirmation or agreement

**af·fix** \ə'fiks\ *vb* : attach

**af·flict** \ə'flikt\ *vb* : cause pain and distress to — **af·flic·tion** \-'flikshən\ *n*

**af·flu·ence** \'af,lüəns; a'flü-, ə-\ *n* : wealth — **af·flu·ent** \-ənt\ *adj*

**af·ford** \ə'fōrd\ *vb* 1 : manage to bear the cost of 2 : provide

**af·fray** \ə'frā\ *n* : fight

**af·front** \ə'frənt\ *vb or n* : insult

**af·ghan** \'af,gan, -gən\ *n* : crocheted or knitted blanket

**afire** \ə'fīr\ *adj or adv* : being on fire

**aflame** \ə'flām\ *adj or adv* : flaming

**afloat** \ə'flōt\ *adj or adv* : floating

**afoot** \ə'füt\ *adv or adj* 1 : on foot 2 : in progress

**afore·said** \ə'fōr,sed\ *adj* : said or named before

**afraid** \ə'frād, *South also* ə'fred\ *adj* : filled with fear

**afresh** \ə'fresh\ *adv* : anew

**aft** \'aft\ *adv* : to or toward the stern or tail

**af·ter** \'aftər\ *adv* : at a later time ∼ *prep* 1 : behind in place or time 2 : in pursuit of ∼ *conj* : following the time when ∼ *adj* 1 : later 2 : located toward the back

**af·ter·life** \'aftər,līf\ *n* : existence after death

**af·ter·math** \-,math\ *n* : results

**af·ter·noon** \,aftər'nün\ *n* : time between noon and evening

**af·ter·thought** *n* : later thought

**af·ter·ward** \'aftərwərd\, **af·ter·wards** \-wərdz\ *adv* : at a later time

**again** \ə'gen, -'gin\ *adv* **1** : once more **2** : on the other hand **3** : in addition

**against** \ə'genst\ *prep* **1** : directly opposite to **2** : in opposition to **3** : so as to touch or strike

**agape** \ə'gāp, -'gap\ *adj or adv* : having the mouth open in astonishment

**ag·ate** \'agət\ *n* : quartz with bands or masses of various colors

**age** \'āj\ *n* **1** : length of time of life or existence **2** : particular time in life (as majority or the latter part) **3** : quality of being old **4** : long time **5** : period in history ~ *vb* : become old or mature

**-age** \ij\ *n suffix* **1** : aggregate **2** : action or process **3** : result of **4** : rate of **5** : place of **6** : state or rank **7** : fee

**aged** *adj* **1** \'ājəd\ : old **2** \'ājd\ : allowed to mature

**age·less** \'ājləs\ *adj* : eternal

**agen·cy** \'ājənsē\ *n, pl* **-cies 1** : one through which something is accomplished **2** : office or function of an agent **3** : government administrative division

**agen·da** \ə'jendə\ *n* : list of things to be done

**agent** \'ājənt\ *n* **1** : means **2** : person acting or doing business for another

**ag·gran·dize** \ə'gran,dīz, 'agrən-\ *vb* **-dized; -diz·ing** : make great or greater — **ag·gran·dize·ment** \ə'grandəzmənt, -,dīz-; ,agrən'dīz-\ *n*

**ag·gra·vate** \'agrə,vāt\ *vb* **-vat·ed; -vat·ing 1** : make more severe **2** : irritate — **ag·gra·va·tion** \,agrə'vāshən\ *n*

**ag·gre·gate** \'agrigət\ *adj* : formed into a mass ~ \-,gāt\ *vb* **-gat·ed; -gat·ing** : collect into a mass ~ \-gət\ *n* **1** : mass **2** : whole amount

**ag·gres·sion** \ə'greshən\ *n* **1** : unprovoked attack **2** : hostile behavior — **ag·gres·sor** \-'gresər\ *n*

**ag·gres·sive** \ə'gresiv\ *adj* **1** : easily provoked to fight **2** : hard working and enterprising — **ag·gres·sive·ly** *adv* — **ag·gres·sive·ness** *n*

**ag·grieve** \ə'grēv\ *vb* **-grieved; -griev-ing 1** : cause grief to **2** : inflict injury on

**aghast** \ə'gast\ *adj* : struck with amazement or horror

**ag·ile** \'ajəl\ *adj* : able to move quickly and easily — **agil·i·ty** \ə'jilətē\ *n*

**ag·i·tate** \'ajə,tāt\ *vb* **-tat·ed; -tat·ing 1** : shake or stir back and forth **2** : excite or trouble the mind of **3** : try to arouse public feeling — **ag·i·ta·tion** \,ajə'tāshən\ *n* — **ag·i·ta·tor** \'ajə-,tātər\ *n*

**ag·nos·tic** \ag'nästik, əg-\ *n* : one who doubts the existence of God

**ago** \ə'gō\ *adj or adv* : earlier than the present

**agog** \ə'gäg\ *adj* : full of excitement

**ag·o·nize** \'agə,nīz\ *vb* **-nized; -niz-ing** : suffer mental agony — **ag·o·niz·ing·ly** *adv*

**ag·o·ny** \'agənē\ *n, pl* **-nies** : extreme pain or mental distress

**agrar·i·an** \ə'grerēən\ *adj* : relating to land ownership or farming interests — **agrarian** *n* — **agrar·i·an·ism** *n*

**agree** \ə'grē\ *vb* **agreed; agree·ing 1** : be of the same opinion **2** : express willingness **3** : get along together **4** : be similar **5** : be appropriate, suitable, or healthful

**agree·able** \-əbəl\ *adj* **1** : pleasing **2** : willing to give approval — **agree·able·ness** *n* — **agree·ably** *adv*

**agree·ment** \-mənt\ *n* **1** : harmony of opinion or purpose **2** : mutual understanding or arrangement

**ag·ri·cul·ture** \'agri,kəlchər\ *n* : farming — **ag·ri·cul·tur·al** \,agri'kəlchərəl\ *adj* — **ag·ri·cul·tur·ist** \-rist\, **ag·ri·cul·tur·al·ist** \-rəlist\ *n*

**aground** \ə'graúnd\ *adv or adj* : on or onto the bottom or shore

**ague** \'āgyü\ *n* **1** : fever with recurrent chills and sweating **2** : malaria

**ahead** \ə'hed\ *adv or adj* **1** : in or toward the front **2** : into or for the future **3** : in a more advantageous position

**ahead of** *prep* **1** : in front or advance of **2** : in excess of

**ahoy** \ə'hói\ *interj* — used in hailing

**aid** \'ād\ *vb* : provide help or support ~ *n* : help

**aide** \'ād\ *n* : helper

**AIDS** \'ādz\ *n* : serious disease of the human immune system

**ail** \'āl\ *vb* **1** : trouble **2** : be ill

**ai·le·ron** \'ālə‚rän\ *n* : movable part of an airplane wing

**ail·ment** \'ālmənt\ *n* : bodily disorder

**aim** \'ām\ *vb* **1** : point or direct (as a weapon) **2** : direct one's efforts ~ *n* **1** : an aiming or the direction of aiming **2** : object or purpose — **aim·less** *adj* — **aim·less·ly** *adv* — **aim·less·ness** *n*

**air** \'ar\ *n* **1** : mixture of gases surrounding the earth **2** : melody **3** : outward appearance **4** : artificial manner **5** : compressed air **6** : travel by or use of aircraft **7** : medium of transmission of radio waves ~ *vb* **1** : expose to the air **2** : broadcast — **air·borne** \-‚bōrn\ *adj*

**air–condition** *vb* : equip with an apparatus (**air conditioner**) for filtering and cooling the air

**air·craft** *n, pl* **aircraft** : craft that flies

**Aire·dale terrier** \'ar‚dāl-\ *n* : large terrier with a hard wiry coat

**air·field** *n* : airport or its landing field

**air force** *n* : military organization for conducting warfare by air

**air·lift** *n* : a transporting of esp. emergency supplies by aircraft — **airlift** *vb*

**air·line** *n* : air transportation system — **air·lin·er** *n*

**air·mail** *n* : system of transporting mail by airplane — **airmail** *vb*

**air·man** \-mən\ *n* **1** : aviator **2** : enlisted man in the air force in one of the 3 ranks below sergeant

**airman basic** *n* : enlisted man of the lowest rank in the air force

**airman first class** *n* : enlisted man in the air force ranking just below sergeant

**air·plane** *n* : fixed-wing aircraft heavier than air

**air·port** *n* : place for landing aircraft and usu. for receiving passengers

**air·ship** *n* : powered lighter-than-air aircraft

**air·strip** *n* : airfield runway

**air·tight** *adj* : tightly sealed to prevent flow of air

**air·waves** \'ar‚wāvz\ *n pl* : medium of transmission of radio waves

**airy** \'arē\ *adj* **air·i·er; -est** **1** : delicate **2** : breezy

**aisle** \'īl\ *n* : passage between sections or rows

**ajar** \ə'jär\ *adj or adv* : partly open

**akim·bo** \ə'kimbō\ *adj or adv* : having the hand on the hip and the elbow turned outward

**akin** \ə'kin\ *adj* **1** : related by blood **2** : similar in kind

**-al** \əl\ *adj suffix* : of, relating to, or characterized by

**al·a·bas·ter** \'alə‚bastər\ *n* : white or translucent mineral

**alac·ri·ty** \ə'lakrətē\ *n* : cheerful readiness

**alarm** \ə'lärm\ *n* **1** : warning signal or device **2** : fear at sudden danger ~ *vb* **1** : warn **2** : frighten

**alas** \ə'las\ *interj* — used to express unhappiness, pity, or concern

**al·ba·tross** \'albə‚tròs, -‚träs\ *n, pl* **-tross** *or* **-tross·es** : large seabird

**al·be·it** \òl'bēət, al-\ *conj* : even though

**al·bi·no** \al'bīnō\ *n, pl* **-nos** : person or animal with abnormally white skin — **al·bi·nism** \'albə‚nizəm\ *n*

**al·bum** \'albəm\ *n* **1** : book for displaying a collection (as of photographs) **2** : collection of recordings

**al·bu·men** \al'byümən\ *n* **1** : white of an egg **2** : albumin

**al·bu·min** \-mən\ *n* : protein found in blood, milk, egg white, and tissues

**al·che·my** \'alkəmē\ *n* : medieval chemistry — **al·che·mist** \'alkəmist\ *n*

**al·co·hol** \'alkə‚hòl\ *n* **1** : intoxicating agent in liquor **2** : liquor — **al·co·hol·ic** *adj*

**al·co·hol·ic** \‚alkə'hòlik, -'häl-\ *n* : person affected with alcoholism

**al·co·hol·ism** \'alkə‚hòl‚izəm\ *n* : addiction to alcoholic beverages

**al·cove** \'al‚kōv\ *n* : recess in a room or wall

**al·der·man** \'òldərmən\ *n* : city official

**ale** \'āl\ *n* : beerlike beverage — **ale·house** *n*

**alert** \ə'lərt\ *adj* **1** : watchful **2** : quick to perceive and act ~ *n* : alarm ~ *vb* : warn — **alert·ly** *adv* — **alert·ness** *n*

**ale·wife** *n* : fish of the herring family

**al·fal·fa** \al'falfə\ *n* : cloverlike forage plant

**al·ga** \'algə\ *n, pl* **-gae** \'al‚jē\ : any of a group of lower plants that includes seaweed — **al·gal** \-gəl\ *adj*

**al·ge·bra** \'aljəbrə\ *n* : branch of mathematics — **al·ge·bra·ic** \‚aljə'brāik\ *adj* — **al·ge·bra·i·cal·ly** \-'brāəklē\ *adv*

**alias** \'ālēəs, 'ālyəs\ *adv* : otherwise called ∼ *n* : assumed name

**al·i·bi** \'alə‚bī\ *n* **1** : defense of having been elsewhere when a crime was committed **2** : justification ∼ *vb* **-bied; -bi·ing** : offer an excuse

**alien** \'ālēən, 'ālyən\ *adj* : foreign ∼ *n* **1** : foreign-born resident **2** : extraterrestrial

**alien·ate** \'ālēə‚nāt, 'ālyə-\ *vb* **-at·ed; -at·ing** : cause to be no longer friendly — **alien·ation** \‚ālēə'nā-shən, ‚ālyə-\ *n*

**alight** \ə'līt\ *vb* : dismount

**align** \ə'līn\ *vb* : bring into line — **align·er** *n* — **align·ment** *n*

**alike** \ə'līk\ *adj* : identical or very similar ∼ *adv* : equally

**al·i·men·ta·ry** \‚alə'mentərē\ *adj* : relating to or functioning in nutrition

**al·i·mo·ny** \'alə‚mōnē\ *n, pl* **-nies** : money paid to a separated or divorced spouse

**alive** \ə'līv\ *adj* **1** : having life **2** : lively or animated

**al·ka·li** \'alkə‚lī\ *n, pl* **-lies** *or* **-lis** : strong chemical base — **al·ka·line** \-kələn, -‚līn\ *adj* — **al·ka·lin·i·ty** \‚alkə'linətē\ *n*

**all** \'ȯl\ *adj* **1** : the whole of **2** : greatest possible **3** : every one of ∼ *adv* **1** : wholly **2** : so much **3** : for each side ∼ *pron* **1** : whole number or amount **2** : everything or everyone

**Al·lah** \'älə, 'al-\ *n* : God of Islam

**all–around** *adj* : versatile

**al·lay** \ə'lā\ *vb* **1** : alleviate **2** : calm

**al·lege** \ə'lej\ *vb* **-leged; -leg·ing** : assert without proof — **al·le·ga·tion** \‚ali'gāshən\ *n* — **al·leg·ed·ly** \ə'lejədlē\ *adv*

**al·le·giance** \ə'lējəns\ *n* : loyalty

**al·le·go·ry** \'alə‚gōrē\ *n, pl* **-ries** : story in which figures and actions are symbols of general truths — **al·le·gor·i·cal** \‚alə'gȯrikəl\ *adj*

**al·le·lu·ia** \‚alə'lüyə\ *interj* : hallelujah

**al·ler·gen** \'alərjən\ *n* : something that causes allergy — **al·ler·gen·ic** \‚alər-'jenik\ *adj*

**al·ler·gy** \'alərjē\ *n, pl* **-gies** : abnormal reaction to a substance — **al·ler·gic** \ə'lərjik\ *adj* — **al·ler·gist** \'alərjist\ *n*

**al·le·vi·ate** \ə'lēvē‚āt\ *vb* **-at·ed; -at·ing** : relieve or lessen — **al·le·vi·a·tion** \ə‚lēvē'āshən\ *n*

**al·ley** \'alē\ *n, pl* **-leys** **1** : place for bowling **2** : narrow passage between buildings

**al·li·ance** \ə'līəns\ *n* : association

**al·li·ga·tor** \'alə‚gātər\ *n* : large aquatic reptile related to the crocodiles

**al·lit·er·a·tion** \ə‚litə'rāshən\ *n* : repetition of initial sounds of words — **al·lit·er·a·tive** \-'litə‚rātiv\ *adj*

**al·lo·cate** \'alə‚kāt\ *vb* **-cat·ed; -cat·ing** : assign — **al·lo·ca·tion** \‚alə'kā-shən\ *n*

**al·lot** \ə'lät\ *vb* **-tt-** : distribute as a share — **al·lot·ment** *n*

**al·low** \ə'laů\ *vb* **1** : admit or concede **2** : permit — **al·low·able** *adj*

**al·low·ance** \-əns\ *n* **1** : allotted share **2** : money given regularly for expenses

**al·loy** \'al‚ȯi\ *n* : metals melted together — **al·loy** \ə'lȯi\ *vb*

**all right** *adv or adj* **1** : satisfactorily **2** : yes **3** : certainly

**all·spice** \'ȯl‚spīs\ *n* : berry of a West Indian tree made into a spice

**al·lude** \ə'lüd\ *vb* **-lud·ed; -lud·ing** : refer indirectly — **al·lu·sion** \-'lü-zhən\ *n* — **al·lu·sive** \-'lüsiv\ *adj*

**al·lure** \ə'lůr\ *vb* **-lured; -lur·ing** : entice ∼ *n* : attractive power

**al·ly** \ə'lī, 'al‚ī\ *vb* **-lied; -ly·ing** : enter into an alliance — **al·ly** \'al‚ī, ə'lī\ *n*

**-al·ly** \əlē\ *adv suffix* : -ly

**al·ma·nac** \'ȯlmə‚nak, 'al-\ *n* : annual information book

**al·mighty** \ȯl'mītē\ *adj* : having absolute power

**al·mond** \'ämənd , 'am-, 'alm-, 'älm-\ *n* : tree with nutlike fruit kernels

**al·most** \'ȯl‚mōst, ȯl'-\ *adv* : very nearly

**alms** \'ämz, 'älmz, 'almz\ *n, pl* **alms** : charitable gift

**aloft** \ə'lȯft\ *adv* : high in the air

**alo·ha** \ä'lōhä\ *interj* — used to greet or bid farewell

**alone** \ə'lōn\ *adj* **1** : separated from others **2** : not including anyone or anything else — **alone** *adv*

**along** \ə'lȯŋ\ *prep* **1** : in line with the direction of **2** : at a point on or during ∼ *adv* **1** : forward **2** : as a companion

**along·side** *adv or prep* : along or by the side

**alongside of** *prep* : alongside

**aloof** \ə'lüf\ *adj* : indifferent and reserved — **aloof·ness** *n*

**aloud** \ə'laůd\ *adv* : so as to be heard

**al·pac·a** \al'pakǝ\ *n* **1** : So. American mammal related to the llama **2** : alpaca wool or cloth made of this

**al·pha·bet** \'alfǝ,bet, -bǝt\ *n* : ordered set of letters of a language — **al·pha·bet·i·cal** \,alfǝ'betikǝl\, **al·pha·bet·ic** \-'betik\ *adj* — **al·pha·bet·i·cal·ly** \-klē\ *adv*

**al·pha·bet·ize** \'alfǝbǝ,tīz\ *vb* **-ized; -iz·ing** : arrange in alphabetical order — **al·pha·bet·iz·er** *n*

**al·ready** \ȯl'redē\ *adv* : by a given time

**al·so** \'ȯlsō\ *adv* : in addition

**al·tar** \'ȯltǝr\ *n* : structure for rituals

**al·ter** \'ȯltǝr\ *vb* : make different — **al·ter·a·tion** \,ȯltǝ'rāshǝn\ *n*

**al·ter·ca·tion** \,ȯltǝr'kāshǝn\ *n* : dispute

**al·ter·nate** \'ȯltǝrnǝt, 'al-\ *adj* **1** : arranged or succeeding by turns **2** : every other ~ \-,nāt\ *vb* **-nat·ed; -nat·ing** : occur or cause to occur by turns ~ \-nǝt\ *n* : substitute — **al·ter·nate·ly** *adv* — **al·ter·na·tion** \,ȯltǝr'nāshǝn, ,al-\ *n*

**alternating current** *n* : electric current that regularly reverses direction

**al·ter·na·tive** \ȯl'tǝrnǝtiv, al-\ *adj* : offering a choice — **alternative** *n*

**al·ter·na·tor** \'ȯltǝr,nātǝr, 'al-\ *n* : alternating-current generator

**al·though** \ȯl'thō\ *conj* : even though

**al·tim·e·ter** \al'timǝtǝr, 'altǝ,mētǝr\ *n* : instrument for measuring altitude

**al·ti·tude** \'altǝ,tüd, -,tyüd\ *n* **1** : distance up from the ground **2** : angular distance above the horizon

**al·to** \'altō\ *n, pl* **-tos** : lower female choral voice

**al·to·geth·er** \,ȯltǝ'gethǝr\ *adv* **1** : wholly **2** : on the whole

**al·tru·ism** \'altrú,izǝm\ *n* : concern for others — **al·tru·ist** \-ist\ *n* — **al·tru·is·tic** \,altrú'istik\ *adj* — **al·tru·is·ti·cal·ly** \-tiklē\ *adv*

**al·um** \'alǝm\ *n* : crystalline compound containing aluminum

**alu·mi·num** \ǝ'lümǝnǝm\ *n* : silver-white malleable ductile light metallic element

**alum·na** \ǝ'lǝmnǝ\ *n, pl* **-nae** \-,nē\ : woman graduate

**alum·nus** \ǝ'lǝmnǝs\ *n, pl* **-ni** \-,nī\ : graduate

**al·ways** \'ȯlwēz, -wāz\ *adv* **1** : at all times **2** : forever

**am** *pres 1st sing of* BE

**amal·gam** \ǝ'malgǝm\ *n* **1** : mercury alloy **2** : mixture

**amal·gam·ate** \ǝ'malgǝ,māt\ *vb* **-at·ed; -at·ing** : unite — **amal·ga·ma·tion** \-,malgǝ'māshǝn\ *n*

**am·a·ryl·lis** \,amǝ'rilǝs\ *n* : bulbous herb with clusters of large colored flowers like lilies

**amass** \ǝ'mas\ *vb* : gather

**am·a·teur** \'amǝ,tǝr, -,tùr, -,tyùr, -,chùr, -chǝr\ *n* **1** : person who does something for pleasure rather than for pay **2** : person who is not expert — **am·a·teur·ish** \,amǝ'tǝrish, -'tùr-, -'tyùr-\ *adj* — **ama·teur·ism** \'amǝ,tǝr,izǝm, -,tùr-, -,tyùr-, -,chùr-, -chǝr-\ *n*

**am·a·to·ry** \'amǝ,tōrē\ *adj* : of or expressing sexual love

**amaze** \ǝ'māz\ *vb* **amazed; amaz·ing** : fill with wonder — **amaze·ment** *n* — **amaz·ing·ly** *adv*

**am·a·zon** \'amǝ,zän, -zǝn\ *n* : tall strong woman — **am·a·zo·ni·an** \,amǝ'zōnēǝn\ *adj*

**am·bas·sa·dor** \am'basǝdǝr\ *n* : representative esp. of a government — **am·bas·sa·do·ri·al** \-,basǝ'dō-rēǝl\ *adj* — **am·bas·sa·dor·ship** *n*

**am·ber** \'ambǝr\ *n* : yellowish fossil resin or its color

**am·ber·gris** \'ambǝr,gris, -,grēs\ *n* : waxy substance from certain whales used in making perfumes

**am·bi·dex·trous** \,ambi'dekstrǝs\ *adj* : equally skilled with both hands — **am·bi·dex·trous·ly** *adv*

**am·bi·ence, am·bi·ance** \'ambēǝns, 'ämbē,äns\ *n* : pervading atmosphere

**am·big·u·ous** \am'bigyǝwǝs\ *adj* : having more than one interpretation — **am·bi·gu·i·ty** \,ambǝ'gyüǝtē\ *n*

**am·bi·tion** \am'bishǝn\ *n* : eager desire for success or power — **am·bi·tious** \-shǝs\ *adj* — **am·bi·tious·ly** *adv*

**am·biv·a·lence** \am'bivǝlǝns\ *n* : simultaneous attraction and repulsion — **am·biv·a·lent** \-lǝnt\ *adj*

**am·ble** \'ambǝl\ *vb* **-bled; -bling** : go at a leisurely gait — **amble** *n*

**am·bu·lance** \'ambyǝlǝns\ *n* : vehicle for carrying injured or sick persons

**am·bu·la·to·ry** \'ambyǝlǝ,tōrē\ *adj* **1** : relating to or adapted to walking **2** : able to walk about

**am·bush** \'am,bùsh\ *n* : trap by which

a surprise attack is made from a place of hiding — **ambush** *vb*

**ame·lio·rate** \ə'mēlyə,rāt\ *vb* **-rat·ed; -rat·ing** : make or grow better — **ame·lio·ra·tion** \-,mēlyə'rāshən\ *n*

**amen** \'ā'men, 'ä-\ *interj* — used for affirmation esp. at the end of prayers

**ame·na·ble** \ə'mēnəbəl, -'men-\ *adj* : ready to yield or be influenced

**amend** \ə'mend\ *vb* **1** : improve **2** : alter in writing

**amend·ment** \-mənt\ *n* : change made in a formal document (as a law)

**amends** \ə'mendz\ *n sing or pl* : compensation for injury or loss

**ame·ni·ty** \ə'menətē, -'mē-\ *n, pl* **-ties 1** : agreeableness **2** *pl* : social conventions **3** : something serving to comfort or accommodate

**am·e·thyst** \'aməthəst\ *n* : purple gemstone

**ami·a·ble** \'āmēəbəl\ *adj* : easy to get along with — **ami·a·bil·i·ty** \,āmēə-'bilətē\ *n* — **ami·a·bly** \'āmēəblē\ *adv*

**am·i·ca·ble** \'amikəbəl\ *adj* : friendly — **am·i·ca·bly** \-blē\ *adv*

**amid** \ə'mid\, **amidst** \-'midst\ *prep* : in or into the middle of

**amino acid** \ə'mēnō-\ *n* : nitrogen‑containing acid

**amiss** \ə'mis\ *adv* : in the wrong way ～ *adj* : wrong

**am·me·ter** \'am,ētər\ *n* : instrument for measuring electric current

**am·mo·nia** \ə'mōnyə\ *n* **1** : colorless gaseous compound of nitrogen and hydrogen **2** : solution of ammonia in water

**am·mu·ni·tion** \,amyə'nishən\ *n* **1** : projectiles fired from guns **2** : explosive items used in war

**am·ne·sia** \am'nēzhə\ *n* : sudden loss of memory — **am·ne·si·ac** \-zē,ak, -zhē-\, **am·ne·sic** \-zik, -sik\ *adj or n*

**am·nes·ty** \'amnəstē\ *n, pl* **-ties** : a pardon for a group — **amnesty** *vb*

**amoe·ba** \ə'mēbə\ *n, pl* **-bas** *or* **-bae** \-,bē\ : tiny one‑celled animal that occurs esp. in water — **amoe·bic** \-bik\ *adj*

**amok** \ə'mək, -'mäk\ *adv* : in a violent or uncontrolled way

**among** \ə'məŋ\ *prep* **1** : in or through **2** : in the number or class of **3** : in shares to each of

**am·o·rous** \'amərəs\ *adj* **1** : inclined to love **2** : being in love **3** : indicative

of love — **am·o·rous·ly** *adv* — **am·o·rous·ness** *n*

**amor·phous** \ə'mórfəs\ *adj* : shapeless

**am·or·tize** \'amər,tīz, ə'mór-\ *vb* **-tized; -tiz·ing** : get rid of (as a debt) gradually with periodic payments — **amor·ti·za·tion** \,amərtə'zāshən, ə,mórt-\ *n*

**amount** \ə'maúnt\ *vb* **1** : be equivalent **2** : reach a total ～ *n* : total number or quantity

**amour** \ə'múr, ä-, a-\ *n* **1** : love affair **2** : lover

**am·pere** \'am,pir\ *n* : unit of electric current

**am·per·sand** \'ampər,sand\ *n* : character & used for the word *and*

**am·phib·i·ous** \am'fibēəs\ *adj* **1** : able to live both on land and in water **2** : adapted for both land and water — **am·phib·i·an** \-ən\ *n*

**am·phi·the·ater** \'amfə,thēətər\ *n* : oval or circular structure with rising tiers of seats around an arena

**am·ple** \'ampəl\ *adj* **-pler** \-plər\; **-plest** \-pləst\ **1** : large **2** : sufficient — **am·ply** \-plē\ *adv*

**am·pli·fy** \'amplə,fī\ *vb* **-fied; -fy·ing** : make louder, stronger, or more thorough — **am·pli·fi·ca·tion** \,am-pləfə'kāshən\ *n* — **am·pli·fi·er** \'amplə,fīər\ *n*

**am·pli·tude** \-,tüd, -,tyüd\ *n* **1** : fullness **2** : extent of a vibratory movement

**am·pu·tate** \'ampyə,tāt\ *vb* **-tat·ed; -tat·ing** : cut off (a body part) — **am·pu·ta·tion** \,ampyə'tāshən\ *n* — **am·pu·tee** \,ampyə'tē\ *n*

**amuck** \ə'mək\ *var of* AMOK

**am·u·let** \'amyələt\ *n* : ornament worn as a charm against evil

**amuse** \ə'myüz\ *vb* **amused; amus·ing 1** : engage the attention of in an interesting and pleasant way **2** : make laugh — **amuse·ment** *n*

**an** \ən, 'an\ *indefinite article* : a — used before words beginning with a vowel sound

**-an** \ən\, **-ian** \ēən\, **-ean** \ēən\ *n suffix* **1** : one that belongs to **2** : one skilled in ～ *adj suffix* **1** : of or belonging to **2** : characteristic of or resembling

**anach·ro·nism** \ə'nakrə,nizəm\ *n* : one that is chronologically out of place — **anach·ro·nis·tic** \ə͵nakrə-ˈnistik\ *adj*

**an·a·con·da** \͵anəˈkändə\ *n* : large So. American snake

**ana·gram** \ˈanə͵gram\ *n* : word or phrase made by transposing the letters of another word or phrase

**anal** \ˈānˀl\ *adj* : relating to the anus

**an·al·ge·sic** \͵anˀlˈjēzik, -sik\ *n* : pain reliever

**anal·o·gy** \əˈnaləjē\ *n, pl* **-gies 1** : similarity between unlike things **2** : example of something similar — **an·a·log·i·cal** \͵anˀlˈäjikəl\ *adj* — **an·a·log·i·cal·ly** \-iklē\ *adv* — **anal·o·gous** \əˈnaləgəs\ *adj*

**anal·y·sis** \əˈnaləsəs\ *n, pl* **-y·ses** \-͵sēz\ **1** : examination of a thing to determine its parts **2** : psychoanalysis — **an·a·lyst** \ˈanˀlist\ *n* — **an·a·lyt·ic** \͵anˀlˈitik\, **an·a·lyt·i·cal** \-ikəl\ *adj* — **an·a·lyt·i·cal·ly** \-iklē\ *adv*

**an·a·lyze** \ˈanˀl͵īz\ *vb* **-lyzed; -lyz·ing** : make an analysis of

**an·ar·chism** \ˈanər͵kizəm, -͵när-\ *n* : theory that all government is undesirable — **an·ar·chist** \-kist\ *n or adj* — **an·ar·chis·tic** \͵anərˈkistik\ *adj*

**an·ar·chy** \ˈanərkē, -͵när-\ *n* : lack of government or order — **an·ar·chic** \aˈnärkik\ *adj* — **an·ar·chi·cal·ly** \-iklē\ *adv*

**anath·e·ma** \əˈnathəmə\ *n* **1** : solemn curse **2** : person or thing accursed or intensely disliked

**anat·o·my** \əˈnatəmē\ *n, pl* **-mies** : science dealing with the structure of organisms — **an·a·tom·ic** \͵anə-ˈtämik\, **an·a·tom·i·cal** \-ikəl\ *adj* — **an·a·tom·i·cal·ly** *adv* — **anat·o·mist** \əˈnatəmist\ *n*

**-ance** \əns\ *n suffix* **1** : action or process **2** : quality or state **3** : amount or degree

**an·ces·tor** \ˈan͵sestər\ *n* : one from whom an individual is descended

**an·ces·tress** \-trəs\ *n* : female ancestor

**an·ces·try** \-trē\ *n* **1** : line of descent **2** : ancestors — **an·ces·tral** \anˈsestrəl\ *adj*

**an·chor** \ˈaŋkər\ *n* **1** : heavy device that catches in the sea bottom to hold a ship in place **2** : anchorperson — *vb* : hold or become held in place by or as if by an anchor — **an·chor·age** \-kərij\ *n*

**an·chor·per·son** \ˈaŋkər͵pərsən\ *n* : news broadcast coordinator

**an·cho·vy** \ˈan͵chōvē, anˈchō-\ *n, pl* **-vies** *or* **-vy** : small herringlike fish

**an·cient** \ˈānshənt\ *adj* **1** : having existed for many years **2** : belonging to times long past — **ancient** *n*

**-ancy** \ənsē\ *n suffix* : quality or state

**and** \ənd, ˈand\ *conj* — used to indicate connection or addition

**and·iron** \ˈan͵dīərn\ *n* : one of 2 metal supports for wood in a fireplace

**an·drog·y·nous** \anˈdräjənəs\ *adj* **1** : having characteristics of both male and female **2** : suitable for either sex

**an·ec·dote** \ˈanik͵dōt\ *n* : brief story — **an·ec·dot·al** \͵anikˈdōtˀl\ *adj*

**ane·mia** \əˈnēmēə\ *n* : blood deficiency — **ane·mic** \əˈnēmik\ *adj*

**anem·o·ne** \əˈnemənē\ *n* : small herb with showy usu. white flowers

**an·es·the·sia** \͵anəsˈthēzhə\ *n* : loss of bodily sensation

**an·es·thet·ic** \͵anəsˈthetik\ *n* : agent that produces anesthesia — **anesthetic** *adj* — **anes·the·tist** \əˈnesthətist\ *n* — **anes·the·tize** \-thə-͵tīz\ *vb*

**an·eu·rysm, an·eu·rism** \ˈanyə-͵rizəm\ : blood-filled bulge of a blood vessel

**anew** \əˈnü, -ˈnyü\ *adv* : over again

**an·gel** \ˈānjəl\ *n* : spiritual being superior to humans — **an·gel·ic** \anˈjelik\, **an·gel·i·cal** \-ikəl\ *adj* — **an·gel·i·cal·ly** *adv*

**an·ger** \ˈaŋgər\ *n* : strong feeling of displeasure ∼ *vb* : make angry

**an·gi·na** \anˈjīnə\ *n* : painful disorder of heart muscles — **an·gi·nal** \anˈjīnˀl\ *adj*

**¹an·gle** \ˈaŋgəl\ *n* **1** : figure formed by the meeting of 2 lines in a point **2** : sharp corner **3** : point of view ∼ *vb* **-gled; -gling** : turn or direct at an angle

**²angle** *vb* **an·gled; an·gling** : fish with a hook and line — **an·gler** \-glər\ *n* — **an·gle·worm** *n* — **an·gling** *n*

**an·go·ra** \aŋˈgōrə, an-\ *n* : yarn or cloth made from the hair of an Angora goat or rabbit

**an·gry** \ˈaŋgrē\ *adj* **-gri·er; -est** : feeling or showing anger — **an·gri·ly** \-grəlē\ *adv*

**an·guish** \ˈaŋgwish\ *n* : extreme pain or distress of mind — **an·guished** \-gwisht\ *adj*

**an•gu•lar** \'aŋgyələr\ *adj* **1** : having many or sharp angles **2** : thin and bony — **an•gu•lar•i•ty** \ˌaŋgyə'larətē\ *n*

**an•i•mal** \'anəməl\ *n* **1** : living being capable of feeling and voluntary motion **2** : lower animal as distinguished from humans

**an•i•mate** \'anəmət\ *adj* : having life ~ \-ˌmāt\ *vb* **-mat•ed; -mat•ing 1** : give life or vigor to **2** : make appear to move — **an•i•mat•ed** *adj*

**an•i•ma•tion** \ˌanə'māshən\ *n* **1** : liveliness **2** : animated cartoon

**an•i•ma•tron•ic** \ˌanəmə'tränik\ : relating to an electrically animated mechanical figure

**an•i•mos•i•ty** \ˌanə'mäsətē\ *n, pl* **-ties** : resentment

**an•i•mus** \'anəməs\ *n* : deep-seated hostility

**an•ise** \'anəs\ *n* : herb related to the carrot with aromatic seeds (**ani•seed** \-ˌsēd\) used in flavoring

**an•kle** \'aŋkəl\ *n* : joint or region between the foot and the leg — **an•kle•bone** *n*

**an•nals** \'an°lz\ *n pl* : chronological record of history — **an•nal•ist** \-°list\ *n*

**an•neal** \ə'nēl\ *vb* **1** : make less brittle by heating and then cooling **2** : strengthen or toughen

**an•nex** \ə'neks, 'an,eks\ *vb* : assume political control over (a territory) ~ \'an,eks, -iks\ *n* : added building — **an•nex•a•tion** \ˌan,ek'sāshən\ *n*

**an•ni•hi•late** \ə'nīə,lāt\ *vb* **-lat•ed; -lat•ing** : destroy — **an•ni•hi•la•tion** \-ˌnīə-'lāshən\ *n*

**an•ni•ver•sa•ry** \ˌanə'vərsərē\ *n, pl* **-ries** : annual return of the date of a notable event or its celebration

**an•no•tate** \'anə,tāt\ *vb* **-tat•ed; -tat•ing** : furnish with notes — **an•no•ta•tion** \ˌanə'tāshən\ *n* — **an•no•ta•tor** \'anə,tātər\ *n*

**an•nounce** \ə'naúns\ *vb* **-nounced; -nounc•ing** : make known publicly — **an•nounce•ment** *n* — **an•nounc•er** *n*

**an•noy** \ə'nói\ *vb* : disturb or irritate — **an•noy•ance** \-əns\ *n* — **an•noy•ing•ly** \-'nóiiŋlē\ *adv*

**an•nu•al** \'anyəwəl\ *adj* **1** : occurring once a year **2** : living only one year — **annual** *n* — **an•nu•al•ly** *adv*

**an•nu•i•ty** \ə'nüətē, -'nyü-\ *n, pl* **-ties**

: amount payable annually or the right to such a payment

**an•nul** \ə'nəl\ *vb* **-ll-** : make legally void — **an•nul•ment** *n*

**an•ode** \'an,ōd\ *n* **1** : positive electrode **2** : negative battery terminal — **an•od•ic** \a'nädik\ *adj*

**anoint** \ə'nóint\ *vb* : apply oil to as a rite — **anoint•ment** *n*

**anom•a•ly** \ə'näməlē\ *n, pl* **-lies** : something abnormal or unusual — **anom•a•lous** \ə'nämələs\ *adj*

**anon•y•mous** \ə'nänəməs\ *adj* : of unknown origin — **an•o•nym•i•ty** \ˌanə'nimətē\ *n* — **anon•y•mous•ly** *adv*

**an•oth•er** \ə'nəthər\ *adj* **1** : any or some other **2** : one more ~ *pron* **1** : one more **2** : one different

**an•swer** \'ansər\ *n* **1** : something spoken or written in reply to a question **2** : solution to a problem ~ *vb* **1** : reply to **2** : be responsible **3** : be adequate — **an•swer•er** *n*

**an•swer•able** \-rəbəl\ *adj* : responsible

**ant** \'ant\ *n* : small social insect — **ant•hill** *n*

**-ant** \ənt\ *n suffix* **1** : one that performs or causes an action **2** : thing that is acted upon — *adj suffix* **1** : performing an action or being in a condition **2** : causing an action or process

**ant•ac•id** \'ant'asəd\ : agent that counteracts acidity

**an•tag•o•nism** \an'tagə,nizəm\ *n* : active opposition or hostility — **an•tag•o•nist** \-ənist\ *n* — **an•tag•o•nis•tic** \-ˌtagə'nistik\ *adj*

**an•tag•o•nize** \an'tagə,nīz\ *vb* **-nized; -niz•ing** : cause to be hostile

**ant•arc•tic** \ant'ärktik, -'ärtik\ *adj* : relating to the region near the south pole

**antarctic circle** *n* : circle parallel to the equator approximately 23°27' from the south pole

**an•te•bel•lum** \ˌanti'beləm\ *adj* : existing before the U.S. Civil War

**an•te•ced•ent** \ˌantə'sēd°nt\ *n* : one that comes before — **antecedent** *adj*

**an•te•lope** \'ant°l,ōp\ *n, pl* **-lope** *or* **-lopes** : deerlike mammal related to the ox

**an•ten•na** \an'tenə\ *n, pl* **-nae** \-ˌnē\ *or* **-nas 1** : one of the long slender paired sensory organs on the head of an arthropod **2** *pl* **-nas** : metallic device for sending or receiving radio waves

**an·te·ri·or** \an'tirēər\ *adj* : located before in place or time

**an·them** \'anthəm\ *n* : song or hymn of praise or gladness

**an·ther** \'anthər\ *n* : part of a seed plant that contains pollen

**an·thol·o·gy** \an'thäləjē\ *n, pl* **-gies** : literary collection

**an·thra·cite** \'anthrə,sīt\ *n* : hard coal

**an·thro·poid** \'anthrə,pȯid\ *n* : large ape — **anthropoid** *adj*

**an·thro·pol·o·gy** \,anthrə'pälejē\ *n* : science dealing with humans — **an·thro·po·log·i·cal** \-pə'läjikəl\ *adj* — **an·thro·pol·o·gist** \-'päləjist\ *n*

**anti-** \,antē, -,tī\ **ant-, anth-** *prefix* **1** : opposite in kind, position, or action **2** : opposing or hostile toward **3** : defending against **4** : curing or treating

**an·ti·bi·ot·ic** \,antēbī'ätik, -bē-\ *n* : substance that inhibits harmful microorganisms — **antibiotic** *adj*

**an·ti·body** \'anti,bädē\ *n* : bodily substance that counteracts the effects of a foreign substance or organism

**an·tic** \'antik\ *n* : playful act ~ *adj* : playful

**an·tic·i·pate** \an'tisə,pāt\ *vb* **-pat·ed; -pat·ing 1** : be prepared for **2** : look forward to — **an·tic·i·pa·tion** \-,tisə'pāshən\ *n* — **an·tic·i·pa·to·ry** \-'tisəpə,tōrē\ *adj*

**an·ti·cli·max** \,antē'klī,maks\ *n* : something strikingly less important than what has preceded it — **an·ti·cli·mac·tic** \-klī'maktik\ *adj*

**an·ti·dote** \'anti,dōt\ *n* : remedy for poison

**an·ti·freeze** \'anti,frēz\ *n* : substance to prevent a liquid from freezing

**an·ti·his·ta·mine** \,anti'histə,mēn\ *n* : drug for treating allergies and colds

**an·ti·mo·ny** \'antə,mōnē\ *n* : brittle white metallic chemical element

**an·tip·a·thy** \an'tipəthē\ *n, pl* **-thies** : strong dislike

---

**List of self-explanatory words with the prefix *anti-***

| | | |
|---|---|---|
| antiabortion | anticigarette | antifatigue |
| antiacademic | anticlerical | antifemale |
| antiadministration | anticollision | antifeminine |
| antiaggression | anticolonial | antifeminism |
| antiaircraft | anticommunism | antifeminist |
| antialien | anticommunist | antifertility |
| antiapartheid | anticonservation | antiforeign |
| antiaristocratic | anticonservationist | antiforeigner |
| antiart | anticonsumer | antifraud |
| antiauthoritarian | anticonventional | antigambling |
| antiauthority | anticorrosion | antiglare |
| antibacterial | anticorrosive | antigovernment |
| antibias | anticorruption | antiguerrilla |
| antiblack | anticrime | antigun |
| antibourgeois | anticruelty | antihijack |
| antiboycott | anticult | antihomosexual |
| antibureaucratic | anticultural | antihuman |
| antiburglar | antidandruff | antihumanism |
| antiburglary | antidemocratic | antihumanistic |
| antibusiness | antidiscrimination | antihunting |
| anticancer | antidrug | anti—imperialism |
| anticapitalism | antidumping | anti—imperialist |
| anticapitalist | antiestablishment | anti—inflation |
| anti—Catholic | antievolution | anti—inflationary |
| anticensorship | antievolutionary | anti—institutional |
| anti—Christian | antifamily | anti—integration |
| anti—Christianity | antifascism | anti—intellectual |
| antichurch | antifascist | anti—intellectualism |

an·ti·quar·i·an \,antə'kwerēən\ *adj*
: relating to antiquities or old books
— **antiquarian** *n*

an·ti·quary \'antə,kwerē\ *n*, *pl* **-quar-
ies** : one who collects or studies
antiquities

an·ti·quat·ed \'antə,kwātəd\ *adj* : out-
of-date

an·tique \an'tēk\ *adj* : very old or out-
of-date — **antique** *n*

an·tiq·ui·ty \an'tikwətē\ *n*, *pl* **-ties 1**
: ancient times **2** *pl* : relics of ancient
times

an·ti·sep·tic \,antə'septik\ *adj* : killing
or checking the growth of germs —
**antiseptic** *n* — **an·ti·sep·ti·cal·ly**
\-tiklē\ *adv*

an·tith·e·sis \an'tithəsəs\ *n*, *pl* **-e·ses**
\-,sēz\ : direct opposite

ant·ler \'antlər\ *n* : solid branched
horn of a deer — **ant·lered** \-lərd\ *adj*

ant·onym \'antə,nim\ *n* : word of opposite meaning

anus \'ānəs\ *n* : the rear opening of the
alimentary canal

an·vil \'anvəl\ *n* : heavy iron block on
which metal is shaped

anx·i·ety \aŋ'zīətē\ *n*, *pl* **-eties** : uneasiness usu. over an expected misfortune

anx·ious \'aŋkshəs\ *adj* **1** : uneasy **2**
: earnestly wishing — **anx·ious·ly**
*adv*

any \'enē\ *adj* **1** : one chosen at random **2** : of whatever number or quantity ~ *pron* **1** : any one or ones **2**
: any amount ~ *adv* : to any extent or
degree

any·body \-bədē, -,bäd-\ *pron* : anyone

any·how \-,haù\ *adv* **1** : in any way **2**
: nevertheless

any·more \,enē'mōr\ *adv* : at the present time

any·one \-'enē,wən\ *pron* : any person

any·place *adv* : anywhere

any·thing *pron* : any thing whatever

any·time *adv* : at any time whatever

any·way *adv* : anyhow

---

| | | |
|---|---|---|
| antijamming | antiprofiteering | antisuicide |
| anti–Jewish | antiprogressive | antitank |
| antilabor | antiprostitution | antitax |
| antiliberal | antirabies | antitechnological |
| antiliberalism | antiracketeering | antitechnology |
| antilitter | antiradical | antiterrorism |
| antilittering | antirape | antiterrorist |
| antilynching | antirealism | antitheft |
| antimale | antirecession | antitobacco |
| antimanagement | antireform | antitotalitarian |
| antimaterialism | antireligious | antitoxin |
| antimaterialist | antirevolutionary | antitraditional |
| antimicrobial | antiriot | antitrust |
| antimilitarism | antiromantic | antituberculosis |
| antimilitarist | antirust | antitumor |
| antimilitary | antisegregation | antityphoid |
| antimiscegenation | antisex | antiulcer |
| antimonopolist | antisexist | antiunemployment |
| antimonopoly | antisexual | antiunion |
| antimosquito | antishoplifting | antiuniversity |
| antinoise | antislavery | antiurban |
| antiobesity | antismoking | antiviolence |
| antiobscenity | antismuggling | antiviral |
| antipapal | antismut | antivivisection |
| antipersonnel | antispending | antiwar |
| antipolice | antistrike | anti–West |
| antipollution | antistudent | anti–Western |
| antipornographic | antisubmarine | antiwhite |
| antipornography | antisubversion | antiwoman |
| antipoverty | antisubversive | |

**any·where** \adv\ : in or to any place

**aor·ta** \ā'ȯrtə\ n, pl **-tas** or **-tae** \-ē\ : main artery from the heart — **aor·tic** \ā'ȯrtik\ adj

**apart** \ə'pärt\ adv **1** : separately in place or time **2** : aside **3** : to pieces

**apart·heid** \ə'pär,tāt, -,tīt\ n : racial segregation

**apart·ment** \ə'pärtmənt\ n : set of usu. rented rooms

**ap·a·thy** \'apəthē\ n : lack of emotion or interest — **ap·a·thet·ic** \,apə-'thetik\ adj — **ap·a·thet·i·cal·ly** \-iklē\ adv

**ape** \'āp\ n : large tailless primate ~ vb **aped**; **ap·ing** : imitate

**ap·er·ture** \'apər,chůr, -chər\ n : opening

**apex** \'ā,peks\ n, pl **apex·es** or **api·ces** \'āpə,sēz, 'apə-\ : highest point

**aphid** \'āfid, 'a-\ n : small insect that sucks plant juices

**aph·o·rism** \'afə,rizəm\ n : short saying stating a general truth — **aph·oris·tic** \,afə'ristik\ adj

**aph·ro·di·si·ac** \,afrə'dēzē,ak, 'diz-\ n : substance that excites sexual desire

**api·a·rist** \'āpēərist\ n : beekeeper — **api·ary** \-pē,erē\ n

**apiece** \ə'pēs\ adv : for each one

**aplen·ty** \ə'plentē\ adj : plentiful or abundant

**aplomb** \ə'pläm, -'pləm\ n : complete calmness or self-assurance

**apoc·a·lypse** \ə'päkə,lips\ n : writing prophesying a cataclysm in which evil forces are destroyed — **apoc·a·lyp·tic** \-,päkə'liptik\ adj

**apoc·ry·pha** \ə'päkrəfə\ n : writings of dubious authenticity — **apocry·phal** \-fəl\ adj

**apol·o·get·ic** \ə,pälə'jetik\ adj : expressing apology — **apol·o·get·i·cal·ly** \-iklē\ adv

**apol·o·gize** \ə'pälə,jīz\ vb **-gized**; **-giz·ing** : make an apology — **apol·o·gist** \-jist\ n

**apol·o·gy** \ə'päləjē\ n, pl **-gies 1** : formal justification **2** : expression of regret for a wrong

**ap·o·plexy** \'apə,pleksē\ n : sudden loss of consciousness caused by rupture or obstruction of an artery of the brain — **ap·o·plec·tic** \,apə'plektik\ adj

**apos·ta·sy** \ə'pästəsē\ n, pl **-sies** : abandonment of a former loyalty — **apos·tate** \ə'päs,tāt\ adj or n

**apos·tle** \ə'päsəl\ n : disciple or advocate — **apos·tle·ship** n — **ap·os·tolic** \,apə'stälik\ adj

**apos·tro·phe** \ə'pästrə,fē\ n : punctuation mark ' to indicate the possessive case or the omission of a letter or figure

**apoth·e·cary** \ə'päthə,kerē\ n, pl **-car·ies** : druggist

**ap·pall** \ə'pȯl\ vb : fill with horror or dismay

**ap·pa·ra·tus** \,apə'ratəs, -'rāt-\ n, pl **-tus·es** or **-tus 1** : equipment **2** : complex machine or device

**ap·par·el** \ə'parəl\ n : clothing

**ap·par·ent** \ə'parənt\ adj **1** : visible **2** : obvious **3** : seeming — **ap·par·ent·ly** adv

**ap·pa·ri·tion** \,apə'rishən\ n : ghost

**ap·peal** \ə'pēl\ vb **1** : try to have a court case reheard **2** : ask earnestly **3** : have an attraction — **appeal** n

**ap·pear** \ə'pir\ vb **1** : become visible or evident **2** : come into the presence of someone **3** : seem

**ap·pear·ance** \ə'pirəns\ n **1** : act of appearing **2** : outward aspect

**ap·pease** \ə'pēz\ vb **-peased**; **-peas·ing** : pacify with concessions — **ap·pease·ment** n

**ap·pel·late** \ə'pelət\ adj : having power to review decisions

**ap·pend** \ə'pend\ vb : attach

**ap·pend·age** \ə'pendij\ n : something attached

**ap·pen·dec·to·my** \,apən'dektəmē\ n, pl **-mies** : surgical removal of the appendix

**ap·pen·di·ci·tis** \ə,pendə'sītəs\ n : inflammation of the appendix

**ap·pen·dix** \ə'pendiks\ n, pl **-dix·es** or **-di·ces** \-də,sēz\ **1** : supplementary matter **2** : narrow closed tube extending from lower right intestine

**ap·pe·tite** \'apə,tīt\ n **1** : natural desire esp. for food **2** : preference

**ap·pe·tiz·er** \-,tīzər\ n : food or drink to stimulate the appetite

**ap·pe·tiz·ing** \-ziŋ\ adj : tempting to the appetite — **ap·pe·tiz·ing·ly** adv

**ap·plaud** \ə'plȯd\ vb : show approval esp. by clapping

**ap·plause** \ə'plȯz\ n : a clapping in approval

**ap·ple** \'apəl\ *n* : rounded fruit with firm white flesh

**ap·ple·jack** \-ˌjak\ *n* : brandy made from cider

**ap·pli·ance** \ə'plīəns\ *n* : household machine or device

**ap·pli·ca·ble** \'aplikəbəl, ə'plikə-\ *adj* : capable of being applied — **ap·pli·ca·bil·i·ty** \ˌaplikə'bilətē, əˌplikə-\ *n*

**ap·pli·cant** \'aplikənt\ *n* : one who applies

**ap·pli·ca·tion** \ˌaplə'kāshən\ *n* 1 : act of applying or thing applied 2 : constant attention 3 : request 4 : computer program that performs a major task

**ap·pli·ca·tor** \'aplə,kātər\ *n* : device for applying a substance

**ap·pli·qué** \ˌaplə'kā\ *n* : cut-out fabric decoration — **appliqué** *vb*

**ap·ply** \ə'plī\ *vb* **-plied; -ply·ing** 1 : place in contact 2 : put to practical use 3 : devote (one's) attention or efforts to something 4 : submit a request 5 : have reference or a connection

**ap·point** \ə'pȯint\ *vb* 1 : set or assign officially 2 : equip or furnish — **ap·poin·tee** \əˌpȯin'tē, ˌa-\ *n*

**ap·point·ment** \ə'pȯintmənt\ *n* 1 : act of appointing 2 : nonelective political job 3 : arrangement for a meeting

**ap·por·tion** \ə'pōrshən\ *vb* : distribute proportionately — **ap·por·tion·ment** *n*

**ap·po·site** \'apəzət\ *adj* : suitable — **ap·po·site·ly** *adv* — **ap·po·site·ness** *n*

**ap·praise** \ə'prāz\ *vb* **-praised; -prais·ing** : set value on — **ap·prais·al** \-'prāzəl\ *n* — **ap·prais·er** *n*

**ap·pre·cia·ble** \ə'prēshəbəl\ *adj* : considerable — **ap·pre·cia·bly** \-blē\ *adv*

**ap·pre·ci·ate** \ə'prēshē,āt\ *vb* **-ated; -at·ing** 1 : value justly 2 : be grateful for 3 : increase in value — **ap·pre·cia·tion** \-ˌprēshē'āshən\ *n*

**ap·pre·cia·tive** \ə'prēshətiv, -shē,āt-\ *adj* : showing appreciation

**ap·pre·hend** \ˌapri'hend\ *vb* 1 : arrest 2 : look forward to in dread 3 : understand — **ap·pre·hen·sion** \-'hen·chən\ *n*

**ap·pre·hen·sive** \-'hensiv\ *adj* : fear-ful — **ap·pre·hen·sive·ly** *adv* — **ap·pre·hen·sive·ness** *n*

**ap·pren·tice** \ə'prentəs\ *n* : person learning a craft ~ *vb* **-ticed; -tic·ing** : employ or work as an apprentice — **ap·pren·tice·ship** *n*

**ap·prise** \ə'prīz\ *vb* **-prised; -pris·ing** : inform

**ap·proach** \ə'prōch\ *vb* 1 : move nearer or be close to 2 : make initial advances or efforts toward — **approach** *n* — **ap·proach·able** *adj*

**ap·pro·ba·tion** \ˌaprə'bāshən\ *n* : approval

**ap·pro·pri·ate** \ə'prōprē,āt\ *vb* **-at·ed; -at·ing** 1 : take possession of 2 : set apart for a particular use ~ \-prēət\ *adj* : suitable — **ap·pro·pri·ate·ly** *adv* — **ap·pro·pri·ate·ness** *n* — **ap·pro·pria·tion** \ə,prōprē-'āshən\ *n*

**ap·prov·al** \ə'prüvəl\ *n* : act of approving

**ap·prove** \ə'prüv\ *vb* **-proved; -prov·ing** : accept as satisfactory

**ap·prox·i·mate** \ə'präksəmət\ *adj* : nearly correct or exact ~ \-ˌmāt\ *vb* **-mat·ed; -mat·ing** : come near — **ap·prox·i·mate·ly** *adv* — **ap·prox·i·ma·tion** \-ˌpräksə'māshən\ *n*

**ap·pur·te·nance** \ə'pərtnəns\ *n* : accessory — **ap·pur·te·nant** \-'pərt-nənt\ *adj*

**apri·cot** \'aprə,kät, 'ā-\ *n* : peachlike fruit

**April** \'āprəl\ *n* : 4th month of the year having 30 days

**apron** \'āprən\ *n* : protective garment

**ap·ro·pos** \ˌaprə'pō, 'aprə,pō\ *adv* : suitably ~ *adj* : being to the point

**apropos of** *prep* : with regard to

**apt** \'apt\ *adj* 1 : suitable 2 : likely 3 : quick to learn — **apt·ly** *adv* — **apt·ness** *n*

**ap·ti·tude** \'aptə,tüd, -tyüd\ *n* 1 : capacity for learning 2 : natural ability

**aqua** \'akwə, 'äk-\ *n* : light greenish blue color

**aquar·i·um** \ə'kwareəm\ *n*, *pl* **-i·ums** *or* **-ia** \-ēə\ : glass container for aquatic animals and plants

**aquat·ic** \ə'kwätik, -'kwat-\ *adj* : of or relating to water — **aquatic** *n*

**aq·ue·duct** \'akwə,dəkt\ *n* : conduit for carrying running water

**aqui·line** \'akwə,līn, -lən\ *adj* : curved like an eagle's beak

**-ar** \ər\ *adj suffix* **1** : of, relating to, or being **2** : resembling

**ar·a·besque** \ˌarə'besk\ *n* : intricate design

**ar·a·ble** \'arəbəl\ *adj* : fit for crops

**ar·bi·ter** \'ärbətər\ *n* : final authority

**ar·bi·trary** \'ärbəˌtrerē\ *adj* **1** : selected at random **2** : autocratic — **ar·bi·trari·ly** \ˌärbə'trerəlē\ *adv* — **ar·bi·trari·ness** \'ärbəˌtrerēnəs\ *n*

**ar·bi·trate** \'ärbəˌtrāt\ *vb* **-trat·ed;** **-trat·ing** : settle a dispute as arbitrator — **ar·bi·tra·tion** \ˌärbə'trāshən\ *n*

**ar·bi·tra·tor** \'ärbəˌtrātər\ *n* : one chosen to settle a dispute

**ar·bor** \'ärbər\ *n* : shelter under branches or vines

**ar·bo·re·al** \är'bōrēəl\ *adj* : living in trees

**arc** \'ärk\ *n* **1** : part of a circle **2** : bright sustained electrical discharge ~ *vb* **arced** \'ärkt\; **arc·ing** \'ärkiŋ\ : form an arc

**ar·cade** \är'kād\ *n* : arched passageway between shops

**ar·cane** \är'kän\ *adj* : mysterious or secret

**¹arch** \'ärch\ *n* : curved structure spanning an opening ~ *vb* : cover with or form into an arch

**²arch** *adj* **1** : chief — usu. in combination **2** : mischievous — **arch·ly** *adv* — **arch·ness** *n*

**ar·chae·ol·o·gy, ar·che·ol·o·gy** \ˌärkē'äləjē\ *n* : study of past human life — **ar·chae·o·log·i·cal** \-kēə'läjikəl\ *adj* — **ar·chae·ol·o·gist** \-kē'äləjist\ *n*

**ar·cha·ic** \är'kāik\ *adj* : belonging to an earlier time — **ar·cha·i·cal·ly** \-iklē\ *adv*

**arch·an·gel** \'ärkˌānjəl\ *n* : angel of high rank

**arch·bish·op** \ärch'bishəp\ *n* : chief bishop — **arch·bish·op·ric** \-ˌprik\ *n*

**arch·di·o·cese** \-'dīəsəs, -ˌsēz, -ˌsēs\ *n* : diocese of an archbishop

**ar·chery** \'ärchərē\ *n* : shooting with bow and arrows — **ar·cher** \-chər\ *n*

**ar·che·type** \'ärkiˌtīp\ *n* : original pattern or model

**ar·chi·pel·a·go** \ˌärkə'peləˌgō, ˌärchə-\ *n, pl* **-goes** or **-gos** : group of islands

**ar·chi·tect** \'ärkəˌtekt\ *n* : building designer

**ar·chi·tec·ture** \'ärkəˌtekchər\ *n* **1**

: building design **2** : style of building **3** : manner of organizing elements — **ar·chi·tec·tur·al** \ˌärkə'tekchərəl, -'tekshrəl\ *adj* — **ar·chi·tec·tur·al·ly** *adv*

**ar·chives** \'ärˌkīvz\ *n pl* : public records or their storage place — **archi·vist** \'ärkəvist, -ˌkī-\ *n*

**arch·way** *n* : passageway under an arch

**arc·tic** \'ärktik, 'ärt-\ *adj* **1** : relating to the region near the north pole **2** : frigid

**arctic circle** *n* : circle parallel to the equator approximately 23°27′ from the north pole

**-ard** \ərd\ *n suffix* : one that is

**ar·dent** \'ärd°nt\ *adj* : characterized by warmth of feeling — **ar·dent·ly** *adv*

**ar·dor** \'ärdər\ *n* : warmth of feeling

**ar·du·ous** \'ärjəwəs\ *adj* : difficult — **ar·du·ous·ly** *adv* — **ar·du·ous·ness** *n*

**are** *pres 2d sing or pres pl of* BE

**ar·ea** \'arēə\ *n* **1** : space for something **2** : amount of surface included **3** : region **4** : range covered by a thing or concept

**area code** *n* : 3-digit area-identifying telephone number

**are·na** \ə'rēnə\ *n* **1** : enclosed exhibition area **2** : sphere of activity

**ar·gon** \'ärˌgän\ *n* : colorless odorless gaseous chemical element

**ar·got** \'ärgət, -ˌgō\ *n* : special language (as of the underworld)

**argu·able** \'ärgyəwəbəl\ *adj* : open to dispute

**ar·gue** \'ärgyü\ *vb* **-gued; -gu·ing 1** : give reasons for or against something **2** : disagree in words

**ar·gu·ment** \'ärgyəmənt\ *n* **1** : reasons given to persuade **2** : dispute with words

**ar·gu·men·ta·tive** \ˌärgyə'mentətiv\ *adj* : inclined to argue

**ar·gyle** \'ärˌgīl\ *n* : colorful diamond pattern in knitting

**aria** \'ärēə\ *n* : opera solo

**ar·id** \'arəd\ *adj* : very dry — **arid·i·ty** \ə'ridətē\ *n*

**arise** \ə'rīz\ *vb* **arose** \-'rōz\; **aris·en** \-'riz°n\; **aris·ing** \-'rīziŋ\ **1** : get up **2** : originate

**ar·is·toc·ra·cy** \ˌarə'stäkrəsē\ *n, pl* **-cies** : upper class — **aris·to·crat** \ə'ristəˌkrat\ *n* — **aris·to·crat·ic** \əˌristə'kratik\ *adj*

**arith·me·tic** \ə'rithməˌtik\ *n* : mathematics that deals with numbers — **ar‑ith‑met‑ic** \‚arith'metik\, **ar‑ith‑met‑i‑cal** \‑ikəl\ *adj*

**ark** \'ärk\ *n* : big boat

**¹arm** \'ärm\ *n* **1** : upper limb **2** : branch — **armed** \'ärmd\ *adj* — **arm‑less** *adj*

**²arm** *vb* : furnish with weapons ∼ *n* **1** : weapon **2** : branch of the military forces **3** *pl* : family's heraldic designs

**ar‑ma‑da** \är'mädə, ‑'mäd‑\ *n* : naval fleet

**ar‑ma‑dil‑lo** \‚ärmə'dilō\ *n, pl* **‑los** : burrowing mammal covered with bony plates

**ar‑ma‑ment** \'ärməmənt\ *n* : military arms and equipment

**ar‑ma‑ture** \'ärmə‚chủr, ‑chər\ *n* : rotating part of an electric generator or motor

**armed forces** *n pl* : military

**ar‑mi‑stice** \'ärməstəs\ *n* : truce

**ar‑mor** \'ärmər\ *n* : protective covering — **ar‑mored** \‑mərd\ *adj*

**ar‑mory** \'ärmərē\ *n, pl* **‑mor‑ies** : factory or storehouse for arms

**arm‑pit** *n* : hollow under the junction of the arm and shoulder

**ar‑my** \'ärmē\ *n, pl* **‑mies 1** : body of men organized for war esp. on land **2** : great number

**aro‑ma** \ə'rōmə\ *n* : usu. pleasing odor — **ar‑o‑mat‑ic** \‚arə'matik\ *adj*

**around** \ə'raúnd\ *adv* **1** : in or along a circuit **2** : on all sides **3** : near **4** : in an opposite direction ∼ *prep* **1** : surrounding **2** : along the circuit of **3** : to or on the other side of **4** : near

**arouse** \ə'raúz\ *vb* **aroused; arous‑ing 1** : awaken from sleep **2** : stir up — **arous‑al** \‑'raúzəl\ *n*

**ar‑raign** \ə'rān\ *vb* **1** : call before a court to answer to an indictment **2** : accuse — **ar‑raign‑ment** *n*

**ar‑range** \ə'rānj\ *vb* **‑ranged; ‑rang‑ing 1** : put in order **2** : settle or agree on **3** : adapt (a musical composition) for voices or instruments — **ar‑range‑ment** *n* — **ar‑rang‑er** *n*

**ar‑ray** \ə'rā\ *vb* **1** : arrange in order **2** : dress esp. splendidly ∼ *n* **1** : arrangement **2** : rich clothing **3** : imposing group

**ar‑rears** \ə'rirz\ *n pl* : state of being behind in paying debts

**ar‑rest** \ə'rest\ *vb* **1** : stop **2** : take into legal custody — **arrest** *n*

**ar‑rive** \ə'rīv\ *vb* **‑rived; riv‑ing 1**

: reach a destination, point, or stage **2** : come near in time — **ar‑riv‑al** \‑əl\ *n*

**ar‑ro‑gant** \'arəgənt\ *adj* : showing an offensive sense of superiority — **ar‑ro‑gance** \‑gəns\ *n* — **ar‑ro‑gant‑ly** *adv*

**ar‑ro‑gate** \‑‚gāt\ *vb* **‑gat‑ed; ‑gat‑ing** : to claim without justification

**ar‑row** \'arō\ *n* : slender missile shot from a bow — **ar‑row‑head** *n*

**ar‑royo** \ə'róiō, ‑ə\ *n, pl* **‑royos 1** : watercourse **2** : gully

**ar‑se‑nal** \'ärs°nəl\ *n* **1** : place where arms are made or stored **2** : store

**ar‑se‑nic** \'ärs°nik\ *n* : solid grayish poisonous chemical element

**ar‑son** \'ärs°n\ *n* : willful or malicious burning of property — **ar‑son‑ist** \‑ist\ *n*

**art** \'ärt\ *n* **1** : skill **2** : branch of learning **3** : creation of things of beauty or works so produced **4** : ingenuity

**ar‑te‑rio‑scle‑ro‑sis** \är‚tirēōsklə‑'rōsəs\ *n* : hardening of the arteries — **ar‑te‑rio‑scle‑rot‑ic** \‑'rätik\ *adj or n*

**ar‑tery** \'ärtərē\ *n, pl* **‑ter‑ies 1** : tubular vessel carrying blood from the heart **2** : thoroughfare — **ar‑te‑ri‑al** \är'tirēəl\ *adj*

**art‑ful** \‑fəl\ *adj* **1** : ingenious **2** : crafty — **art‑ful‑ly** *adv* — **art‑ful‑ness** *n*

**ar‑thri‑tis** \är'thrītəs\ *n, pl* **‑ti‑des** \‑'thritə‚dēz\ : inflammation of the joints — **ar‑thrit‑ic** \‑'thritik\ *adj or n*

**ar‑thro‑pod** \'ärthrə‚päd\ *n* : invertebrate animal (as an insect or crab) with segmented body and jointed limbs — **arthropod** *adj*

**ar‑ti‑choke** \'ärtə‚chōk\ *n* : tall thistlelike herb or its edible flower head

**ar‑ti‑cle** \'ärtikəl\ *n* **1** : distinct part of a written document **2** : nonfictional published piece of writing **3** : word (as *an, the*) used to limit a noun **4** : item or piece

**ar‑tic‑u‑late** \är'tikyələt\ *adj* : able to speak effectively ∼ \‑‚lāt\ *vb* **‑lated; ‑lat‑ing 1** : utter distinctly **2** : unite by joints — **ar‑tic‑u‑late‑ly** *adv* — **ar‑tic‑u‑late‑ness** *n* — **ar‑tic‑u‑la‑tion** \‑‚tikyə'lāshən\ *n*

**ar‑ti‑fact** \'ärtə‚fakt\ *n* : object of esp. prehistoric human workmanship

**ar•ti•fice** \'ärtəfəs\ n 1 : trick or trickery 2 : ingenious device or ingenuity

**ar•ti•fi•cial** \ˌärtə'fishəl\ adj 1 : manmade 2 : not genuine — **ar•ti•fi•ci•al•i•ty** \-ˌfishē'alətē\ n — **ar•ti•fi•cial•ly** adv — **ar•ti•fi•cial•ness** n

**ar•til•lery** \är'tilərē\ n, pl **-ler•ies** : large caliber firearms

**ar•ti•san** \'ärtəzən, -sən\ n : skilled craftsman

**art•ist** \'ärtist\ n : one who creates art — **ar•tis•tic** \är'tistik\ adj — **ar•tis•ti•cal•ly** \-iklē\ adv — **ar•tis•try** \'ärtəstrē\ n

**art•less** \'ärtləs\ adj : sincere or natural — **art•less•ly** adv — **art•less•ness** n

**arty** \'ärtē\ adj **art•i•er; -est** : pretentiously artistic — **art•i•ly** \'ärt°lē\ adv — **art•i•ness** n

**-ary** \ˌerē\ adj suffix : of, relating to, or connected with

**as** \əz, ˌaz\ adv 1 : to the same degree 2 : for example ∼ conj 1 : in the same way or degree as 2 : while 3 : because 4 : though ∼ pron — used after same or such ∼ prep : in the capacity of

**as•bes•tos** \as'bestəs, az-\ n : fibrous incombustible mineral

**as•cend** \ə'send\ vb : move upward — **as•cen•sion** \-'senchən\ n

**as•cen•dan•cy** \ə'sendənsē\ n : domination

**as•cen•dant** \ə'sendənt\ n : dominant position ∼ adj 1 : moving upward 2 : dominant

**as•cent** \ə'sent\ n 1 : act of moving upward 2 : degree of upward slope

**as•cer•tain** \ˌasər'tān\ vb : determine — **as•cer•tain•able** adj

**as•cet•ic** \ə'setik\ adj : self-denying — **ascetic** n — **as•cet•i•cism** \-'setəˌsizəm\ n

**as•cribe** \ə'skrīb\ vb **-cribed; -crib•ing** : attribute — **as•crib•able** adj — **as•crip•tion** \-'skripshən\ n

**asep•tic** \ā'septik\ adj : free of disease germs

**¹ash** \'ash\ n : tree related to the olives

**²ash** n : matter left when something is burned — **ash•tray** n

**ashamed** \ə'shāmd\ adj : feeling shame — **asham•ed•ly** \-'shāmədlē\ adv

**ash•en** \'ashən\ adj : deadly pale

**ashore** \ə'shōr\ adv : on or to the shore

**aside** \ə'sīd\ adv 1 : toward the side 2 : out of the way

**aside from** prep 1 : besides 2 : except for

**as•i•nine** \'as°nˌīn\ adj : foolish — **as•i•nin•i•ty** \ˌas°n'inətē\ n

**ask** \'ask\ vb 1 : call on for an answer or help 2 : utter (a question or request) 3 : invite

**askance** \ə'skans\ adv 1 : with a side glance 2 : with mistrust

**askew** \ə'skyü\ adv or adj : out of line

**asleep** \ə'slēp\ adv or adj 1 : sleeping 2 : numbed 3 : inactive

**as long as** conj 1 : on condition that 2 : because

**as of** prep : from the time of

**as•par•a•gus** \ə'sparəgəs\ n : tall herb related to the lilies or its edible stalks

**as•pect** \'asˌpekt\ n 1 : way something looks to the eye or mind 2 : phase

**as•pen** \'aspən\ n : poplar

**as•per•i•ty** \a'sperətē, ə-\ n, pl **-ties** 1 : roughness 2 : harshness

**as•per•sion** \ə'spərzhən\ n : remark that hurts someone's reputation

**as•phalt** \'asˌfolt\ n : dark tarlike substance used in paving

**as•phyx•ia** \as'fiksēə\ n : lack of oxygen causing unconsciousness

**as•phyx•i•ate** \-se͟ˌāt\ vb **-at•ed; -at•ing** : suffocate — **as•phyx•i•a•tion** \-ˌfiksē'āshən\ n

**as•pi•ra•tion** \ˌaspə'rāshən\ n : strong desire to achieve a goal

**as•pire** \ə'spīr\ vb **-pired; -pir•ing** : have an ambition — **as•pir•ant** \'aspərənt, ə'spīrənt\ n

**as•pi•rin** \'aspərən\ n, pl **aspirin** or **as•pirins** : pain reliever

**ass** \'as\ n 1 : long-eared animal related to the horse 2 : stupid person

**as•sail** \ə'sāl\ vb : attack violently — **as•sail•able** adj — **as•sail•ant** n

**as•sas•si•nate** \ə'sas°nˌāt\ vb **-nat•ed; -nat•ing** : murder esp. for political reasons — **as•sas•sin** \-'sas°n\ n — **as•sas•si•na•tion** \-ˌsas°n'āshən\ n

**as•sault** \ə'sólt\ n or vb : attack

**as•say** \'asˌā, a'sā\ n : analysis (as of an ore) to determine quality or properties — **as•say** \a'sā, 'asˌā\ vb

**as•sem•ble** \ə'sembəl\ vb **-bled; -bling** 1 : collect into one place 2 : fit together the parts of

**as•sem•bly** \-blē\ n, pl **-blies** 1 : meeting 2 cap : legislative body 3 : a fitting together of parts

**as·sem·bly·man** \-mən\ *n* : member of a legislative assembly

**as·sem·bly·wom·an** \-ˌwu̇-mən\ *n* : woman who is a member of a legislative assembly

**as·sent** \ə'sent\ *vb or n* : consent

**as·sert** \ə'sərt\ *vb* **1** : declare **2** : defend — **as·ser·tion** \-'sərshən\ *n* — **as·sert·ive** \-'sərtiv\ *adj* — **as·sert·ive·ness** *n*

**as·sess** \ə'ses\ *vb* **1** : impose (as a tax) **2** : evaluate for taxation — **as·sess·ment** *n* — **as·ses·sor** \-ər\ *n*

**as·set** \'as,et\ *n* **1** *pl* : individually owned property **2** : advantage or resource

**as·sid·u·ous** \ə'sijəwəs\ *adj* : diligent — **as·si·du·i·ty** \,asə'düətē, -'dyü-\ *n* — **as·sid·u·ous·ly** *adv* — **as·sid·u·ous·ness** *n*

**as·sign** \ə'sīn\ *vb* **1** : transfer to another **2** : appoint to a duty **3** : designate as a task **4** : attribute — **as·sign·able** *adj* — **as·sign·ment** *n*

**as·sim·i·late** \ə'simə,lāt\ *vb* **-lat·ed**; **-lat·ing 1** : absorb as nourishment **2** : understand — **as·sim·i·la·tion** \-ˌsimə'lāshən\ *n*

**as·sist** \ə'sist\ *vb* : help — **assist** *n* — **as·sis·tance** \-'sistəns\ *n* — **as·sis·tant** \-tənt\ *n*

**as·so·ci·ate** \ə'sōshē,āt, -sē-\ *vb* **-at·ed**; **-at·ing 1** : join in companionship or partnership **2** : connect in thought — **as·so·ci·ate** \-shēət, -sēət\ *n* — **as·so·ci·a·tion** \-ˌsō-shē'āshən, -sē-\ *n*

**as soon as** *conj* : when

**as·sort·ed** \ə'sórtəd\ *adj* : consisting of various kinds

**as·sort·ment** \-mənt\ *n* : assorted collection

**as·suage** \ə'swāj\ *vb* **-suaged**; **-suag·ing** : ease or satisfy

**as·sume** \ə'süm\ *vb* **-sumed**; **-sum·ing 1** : take upon oneself **2** : pretend to have or be **3** : take as true

**as·sump·tion** \ə'səmpshən\ *n* : something assumed

**as·sure** \ə'shu̇r\ *vb* **-sured**; **-sur·ing 1** : give confidence or conviction to **2** : guarantee — **as·sur·ance** \-əns\ *n*

**as·ter** \'astər\ *n* : herb with daisylike flowers

**as·ter·isk** \'astə,risk\ *n* : a character * used as a reference mark or as an indication of omission of words

**astern** \ə'stərn\ *adv or adj* **1** : behind **2** : at or toward the stern

**as·ter·oid** \'astə,ròid\ *n* : small planet between Mars and Jupiter

**asth·ma** \'azmə\ *n* : disorder marked by difficulty in breathing — **asth·mat·ic** \az'matik\ *adj or n*

**astig·ma·tism** \ə'stigmə,tizəm\ *n* : visual defect — **as·tig·mat·ic** \,astig'matik\ *adj*

**as to** *prep* **1** : concerning **2** : according to

**as·ton·ish** \ə'stänish\ *vb* : amaze — **as·ton·ish·ing·ly** *adv* — **as·ton·ish·ment** *n*

**as·tound** \ə'staund\ *vb* : fill with confused wonder — **as·tound·ing·ly** *adv*

**astrad·dle** \ə'strad⁰l\ *adv or prep* : so as to straddle

**as·tral** \'astrəl\ *adj* : relating to or coming from the stars

**astray** \ə'strā\ *adv or adj* : off the right path

**astride** \ə'strīd\ *adv* : with legs apart or one on each side ∼ *prep* : with one leg on each side of

**as·trin·gent** \ə'strinjənt\ *adj* : causing shrinking or puckering of tissues — **as·trin·gen·cy** \-jənsē\ *n* — **as·trin·gent** *n*

**as·trol·o·gy** \ə'sträləjē\ *n* : prediction of events by the stars — **as·trol·o·ger** \-əjər\ *n* — **as·tro·log·i·cal** \,astrə'läjikəl\ *adj*

**as·tro·naut** \'astrə,nót\ *n* : space traveler

**as·tro·nau·tics** \,astrə'nótiks\ *n* : construction and operation of spacecraft — **as·tro·nau·tic** \-ik\, **as·tro·nau·ti·cal** \-ikəl\ *adj*

**as·tro·nom·i·cal** \,astrə'nämikəl\ *adj* **1** : relating to astronomy **2** : extremely large

**as·tron·o·my** \ə'stränəmē\ *n, pl* **-mies** : study of the celestial bodies — **as·tron·o·mer** \-əmər\ *n*

**as·tute** \ə'stüt, -'styüt\ *adj* : shrewd — **as·tute·ly** *adv* — **as·tute·ness** *n*

**asun·der** \ə'səndər\ *adv or adj* **1** : into separate pieces **2** : separated

**asy·lum** \ə'sīləm\ *n* **1** : refuge **2** : institution for care esp. of the insane

**asym·met·ri·cal** \ˌāsə'metrikəl\, **asym·met·ric** \-trik\ *adj* : not symmetrical — **asym·me·try** \ˌā'simə-trē\ *n*

**at** \ət, 'at\ *prep* **1** — used to indicate a point in time or space **2** — used to indicate a goal **3** — used to indicate condition, means, cause, or manner

**at all** *adv* : without restriction or under any circumstances

**ate** *past of* EAT

**-ate** \ət, ˌāt\ *n suffix* **1** : office or rank **2** : group of persons holding an office or rank ∼ *adj suffix* **1** : brought into or being in a state **2** : marked by having

**athe•ist** \ˈāthēist\ *n* : one who denies the existence of God — **athe•ism** \-ˌizəm\ *n* — **athe•is•tic** \ˌāthē-ˈistik\ *adj*

**ath•ero•scle•ro•sis** \ˌathərōsklə-ˈrō-səs\ *n* : arteriosclerosis with deposition of fatty substances in the arteries — **ath•ero•scle•rot•ic** \-ˈrätik\ *adj*

**ath•lete** \ˈathˌlēt\ *n* : one trained to compete in athletics

**ath•let•ics** \athˈletiks\ *n sing or pl* : exercises and games requiring physical skill — **ath•let•ic** \-ik\ *adj*

**-a•tion** \ˈāshən\ *n suffix* : action or process

**-a•tive** \ˌātiv, ətiv\ *adj suffix* **1** : of, relating to, or connected with **2** : tending to

**atlas** \ˈatləs\ *n* : book of maps

**ATM** \ˌāˌtēˈem\ *n* : computerized machine for performing basic bank functions

**at•mo•sphere** \ˈatməˌsfir\ *n* **1** : mass of air surrounding the earth **2** : surrounding influence — **at•mo•spher•ic** \ˌatməˈsfirik, -ˈsfer-\ *adj* — **at•mo•spher•i•cal•ly** \-ikˈlē\ *adv*

**atoll** \ˈaˌtȯl, ˈä-, -ˌtäl\ *n* : ring-shaped coral island

**at•om** \ˈatəm\ *n* **1** : tiny bit **2** : smallest particle of a chemical element that can exist alone or in combination

**atom•ic** \əˈtämik\ *adj* **1** : relating to atoms **2** : nuclear

**atomic bomb** *n* : bomb utilizing the energy released by splitting the atom

**at•om•iz•er** \ˈatəˌmīzər\ *n* : device for dispersing a liquid as a very fine spray

**atone** \əˈtōn\ *vb* **atoned; aton•ing** : make amends — **atone•ment** *n*

**atop** \əˈtäp\ *prep* : on top of ∼ *adv or adj* : on, to, or at the top

**atri•um** \ˈātrēəm\ *n, pl* **atria** \-trēə\ *or* **atriums 1** : open central room or court **2** : heart chamber that receives blood from the veins

**atro•cious** \əˈtrōshəs\ *adj* : appalling or abominable — **atro•cious•ly** *adv* — **atro•cious•ness** *n*

**atroc•i•ty** \əˈträsətē\ *n, pl* **-ties** : savage act

**at•ro•phy** \ˈatrəfē\ *n, pl* **-phies** : wasting away of a bodily part or tissue — **at•ro•phy** *vb*

**at•ro•pine** \ˈatrəˌpēn\ *n* : drug used esp. to relieve spasms

**at•tach** \əˈtach\ *vb* **1** : seize legally **2** : bind by personalities **3** : join — **attach•ment** *n*

**at•ta•ché** \ˌatəˈshā, ˌaˌta-, əˌta-\ *n* : technical expert on a diplomatic staff

**at•tack** \əˈtak\ *vb* **1** : try to hurt or destroy with violence or words **2** : set to work on ∼ *n* **1** : act of attacking **2** : fit of sickness

**at•tain** \əˈtān\ *vb* **1** : achieve or accomplish **2** : reach — **at•tain•abil•i•ty** \əˌtānəˈbilətē\ *n* — **at•tain•able** *adj* — **at•tain•ment** *n*

**at•tempt** \əˈtempt\ *vb* : make an effort toward — **attempt** *n*

**at•tend** \əˈtend\ *vb* **1** : handle or provide for the care of something **2** : accompany **3** : be present at **4** : pay attention — **at•ten•dance** \-ˈtendəns\ *n* — **at•ten•dant** \-dənt\ *adj or n*

**at•ten•tion** \əˈtenchən\ *n* **1** : concentration of the mind on something **2** : notice or awareness — **at•ten•tive** \-ˈtentiv\ *adj* — **at•ten•tive•ly** *adv* — **at•ten•tive•ness** *n*

**at•ten•u•ate** \əˈtenyəˌwāt\ *vb* **-at•ed; -at•ing 1** : make or become thin **2** : weaken — **at•ten•u•a•tion** \-ˌtenyə-ˈwāshən\ *n*

**at•test** \əˈtest\ *vb* : certify or bear witness — **at•tes•ta•tion** \ˌaˌtesˈtāshən\ *n*

**at•tic** \ˈatik\ *n* : space just below the roof

**at•tire** \əˈtīr\ *vb* **-tired; -tir•ing** : dress — **attire** *n*

**at•ti•tude** \ˈatəˌtüd, -ˌtyüd\ *n* **1** : posture or relative position **2** : feeling, opinion, or mood

**at•tor•ney** \əˈtərnē\ *n, pl* **-neys** : legal agent

**at•tract** \əˈtrakt\ *vb* **1** : draw to oneself **2** : have emotional or aesthetic appeal for — **at•trac•tion** \-ˈtrakshən\ *n* — **at•trac•tive** \-ˈtraktiv\ *adj* — **at•trac•tive•ly** *adv* — **at•trac•tive•ness** *n*

**at·tri·bute** \'atrə‚byüt\ n : inherent characteristic ~ \ə'tribyət\ vb -trib·ut·ed; -trib·ut·ing 1 : regard as having a specific cause or origin 2 : regard as a characteristic — **at·trib·ut·able** adj — **at·tri·bu·tion** \‚atrə'byüshən\ n

**at·tune** \ə'tün, -'tyün\ vb : bring into harmony

**au·burn** \'óbərn\ adj : reddish brown

**auc·tion** \'ókshən\ n : public sale of property to the highest bidder — **auc·tion** vb — **auc·tion·eer** \‚ókshə'nir\ n

**au·dac·i·ty** \ó'dasətē\ n : boldness or insolence — **au·da·cious** \ó'dāshəs\ adj

**au·di·ble** \'ódəbəl\ adj : capable of being heard — **au·di·bly** \-blē\ adv

**au·di·ence** \'ódēəns\ n 1 : formal interview 2 : group of listeners or spectators

**au·dio** \'ódē‚ō\ adj : relating to sound or its reproduction ~ n : television sound

**au·dio·vi·su·al** \‚ódēō'vizhəwəl\ adj : relating to both hearing and sight

**au·dit** \'ódət\ vb : examine financial accounts — **audit** n — **au·di·tor** \'ódətər\ n

**au·di·tion** \ó'dishən\ n : tryout performance — **audition** vb

**au·di·to·ri·um** \‚ódə'tórēəm\ n, pl -ri·ums or -ria \-'rēə\ : room or building used for public performances

**au·di·to·ry** \'ódə‚tórē\ adj : relating to hearing

**au·ger** \'ógər\ n : tool for boring

**aug·ment** \ óg'ment\ vb : enlarge or increase — **aug·men·ta·tion** \‚ógmən'tāshən\ n

**au·gur** \'ógər\ n : prophet ~ vb : predict — **au·gu·ry** \'ógyərē, -gər-\ n

**au·gust** \ó'gəst\ adj : majestic

**Au·gust** \'ógəst\ n : 8th month of the year having 31 days

**auk** \'ók\ n : stocky diving seabird

**aunt** \'ant, 'ȧnt\ n 1 : sister of one's father or mother 2 : wife of one's uncle

**au·ra** \'órə\ n 1 : distinctive atmosphere 2 : luminous radiation

**au·ral** \'órəl\ adj : relating to the ear or to hearing

**au·ri·cle** \'órikəl\ n : atrium or ear-shaped pouch in the atrium of the heart

**au·ro·ra bo·re·al·is** \ə'rórə‚bórē'aləs\ n : display of light in the night sky of northern latitudes

**aus·pic·es** \'óspəsəz, -‚sēz\ n pl : patronage and protection

**aus·pi·cious** \ó'spishəs\ adj : favorable

**aus·tere** \ó'stir\ adj : severe — **aus·tere·ly** adv — **aus·ter·i·ty** \ó'sterətē\ n

**au·then·tic** \ə'thentik, ó-\ adj : genuine — **au·then·ti·cal·ly** \-iklē\ adv — **au·then·tic·i·ty** \‚ó‚then'tisətē\ n

**au·then·ti·cate** \ə'thenti‚kāt, ó-\ vb -cat·ed; -cat·ing : prove genuine — **au·then·ti·ca·tion** \-‚thenti'kāshən\ n

**au·thor** \'óthər\ n 1 : writer 2 : creator — **au·thor·ship** n

**au·thor·i·tar·i·an** \ə‚thärə'terēən, ə-, -‚thór-\ adj : marked by blind obedience to authority

**au·thor·i·ta·tive** \ə'thärə‚tātiv, ó-, -'thór-\ adj : being an authority — **au·thor·i·ta·tive·ly** adv — **au·thor·i·ta·tive·ness** n

**au·thor·i·ty** \ə'thärətē, ó-, -'thór-\ n, pl -ties 1 : expert 2 : right, responsibility, or power to influence 3 pl : persons in official positions

**au·tho·rize** \'óthə‚rīz\ vb -rized; -riz·ing : permit or give official approval for — **au·tho·ri·za·tion** \‚óthərə'zāshən\ n

**au·tism** \'ó‚tizəm\ n : mental disorder marked by impaired ability to communicate and form social relationships and by repetitive behavior patterns

**au·to** \'ótō\ n, pl **autos** : automobile

**au·to·bi·og·ra·phy** \‚ótəbī'ägrəfē, -bē-\ n : writer's own life story — **au·to·bi·og·ra·pher** \-fər\ n — **au·to·bio·graph·i·cal** \-‚bīə'grafikəl\ adj

**au·toc·ra·cy** \ó'täkrəsē\ n, pl -cies : government by one person having unlimited power — **au·to·crat** \'ótə‚krat\ n — **au·to·crat·ic** \‚ótə'kratik\ adj — **au·to·crat·i·cal·ly** \-iklē\ adv

**au·to·graph** \'ótə‚graf\ n : signature ~ vb : write one's name on

**au·to·mate** \'ótə‚māt\ vb -mat·ed; -mat·ing : make automatic — **au·to·ma·tion** \‚ótə'māshən\ n

**au·to·mat·ic** \‚ótə'matik\ adj 1 : involuntary 2 : designed to function without human intervention ~ n

: automatic device (as a firearm) —
**au·to·mat·i·cal·ly** \-ik(ə)lē\ *adv*
**au·tom·a·ton** \ȯ'tämətən, -,tän\ *n, pl*
**-a·tons** *or* **-a·ta** \-tə, -,tä\ : robot
**au·to·mo·bile** \,ȯtəmō'bēl, -'mō,bēl\
*n* : 4-wheeled passenger vehicle with
its own power source
**au·to·mo·tive** \,ȯtə'mōtiv\ *adj* : relating to automobiles
**au·ton·o·mous** \ȯ'tänəməs\ *adj* : self-
governing — **au·ton·o·mous·ly** *adv*
— **au·ton·o·my** \-mē\ *n*
**au·top·sy** \'ȯ,täpsē, 'ȯtəp-\ *n, pl* **-sies**
: medical examination of a corpse
**au·tumn** \'ȯtəm\ *n* : season between
summer and winter — **au·tum·nal**
\ȯ'təmnəl\ *adj*
**aux·il·ia·ry** \ȯg'zilyərē, -lərē\ *adj* **1**
: being a supplement or reserve **2**
: accompanying a main verb form to
express person, number, mood, or
tense — **auxiliary** *n*
**avail** \ə'vāl\ *vb* : be of use or make use
~ *n* : use
**avail·able** \ə'vāləbəl\ *adj* **1** : usable **2**
: accessible — **avail·abil·i·ty** \-,vālə-
'bilətē\ *n*
**av·a·lanche** \'avə,lanch\ *n* : mass of
sliding or falling snow or rock
**av·a·rice** \'avərəs\ *n* : greed — **av·a·ri·
cious** \,avə'rishəs\ *adj*
**avenge** \ə'venj\ *vb* **avenged; aveng-
ing** : take vengeance for — **aveng·er**
*n*
**av·e·nue** \'avə,nü, -,nyü\ *n* **1** : way of
approach **2** : broad street
**av·er·age** \'avrij\ *adj* **1** : being about
midway between extremes **2** : ordinary ~ *vb* **1** : be usually **2** : find the
mean of ~ *n* : mean
**averse** \ə'vərs\ *adj* : feeling dislike
or reluctance — **aver·sion** \-'vər-
zhən\ *n*
**avert** \ə'vərt\ *vb* : turn away
**avi·ary** \'āvē,erē\ *n, pl* **-ar·ies** : place
where birds are kept
**avi·a·tion** \,āvē'āshən, ,av-\ *n* : operation or manufacture of airplanes —
**avi·a·tor** \'āvē,ātər, 'av-\ *n*
**av·id** \'avəd\ *adj* **1** : greedy **2** : enthusiastic — **avid·i·ty** \ə'vidətē, a-\ *n*
— **av·id·ly** *adv*
**av·o·ca·do** \,avə'kädō, ,äv-\ *n, pl*
**-dos** : tropical fruit with green pulp
**av·o·ca·tion** \,avə'kāshən\ *n* : hobby
**avoid** \ə'vȯid\ *vb* **1** : keep away from **2**

: prevent the occurrence of **3** : refrain
from — **avoid·able** *adj* — **avoidance** \-ᵊns\ *n*
**av·oir·du·pois** \,avərdə'pȯiz\ *n* : system of weight based on the pound of
16 ounces
**avow** \ə'vau̇\ *vb* : declare openly —
**avow·al** \-'vau̇əl\ *n*
**await** \ə'wāt\ *vb* : wait for
**awake** \ə'wāk\ *vb* **awoke** \-'wōk\;
**awok·en** \-'wōkən\ *or* **awaked;
awak·ing** : wake up — **awake** *adj*
**awak·en** \ə'wākən\ *vb* **-ened; -en·ing**
: wake up
**award** \ə'wȯrd\ *vb* : give (something
won or deserved) ~ *n* **1** : judgment
**2** : prize
**aware** \ə'war\ *adj* : having realization
or consciousness — **aware·ness** *n*
**awash** \ə'wȯsh, -'wäsh\ *adv or adj*
: flooded
**away** \ə'wā\ *adv* **1** : from this or that
place or time **2** : out of the way **3** : in
another direction **4** : from one's
possession ~ *adj* **1** : absent **2** : distant
**awe** \'ȯ\ *n* : respectful fear or wonder
~ *vb* **awed; aw·ing** : fill with awe —
**awe·some** \-səm\ *adj* — **awe-
struck** *adj*
**aw·ful** \'ȯfəl\ *adj* **1** : inspiring awe **2**
: extremely disagreeable **3** : very
great — **aw·ful·ly** *adv*
**awhile** \ə'hwīl\ *adv* : for a while
**awk·ward** \'ȯkwərd\ *adj* **1** : clumsy **2**
: embarrassing — **awk·ward·ly** *adv*
— **awk·ward·ness** *n*
**awl** \'ȯl\ *n* : hole-making tool
**aw·ning** \'ȯniŋ\ *n* : window cover
**awry** \ə'rī\ *adv or adj* : wrong
**ax, axe** \'aks\ *n* : chopping tool
**ax·i·om** \'aksēəm\ *n* : generally accepted truth — **ax·i·om·at·ic** \,ak-
sēə'matik\ *adj*
**ax·is** \'aksəs\ *n, pl* **ax·es** \-,sēz\ : center of rotation — **ax·i·al** \-sēəl\ *adj*
— **ax·i·al·ly** *adv*
**ax·le** \'aksəl\ *n* : shaft on which a
wheel revolves
**aye** \'ī\ *adv* : yes ~ *n* : a vote of yes
**aza·lea** \ə'zālyə\ *n* : rhododendron
with funnel-shaped blossoms
**az·i·muth** \'azəməth\ *n* : horizontal direction expressed as an angle
**azure** \'azhər\ *n* : blue of the sky —
**azure** *adj*

# B

**b** \'bē\ *n, pl* **b's** *or* **bs** \'bēz\ : 2d letter of the alphabet

**bab•ble** \'babəl\ *vb* **-bled; -bling** 1 : utter meaningless sounds 2 : talk foolishly or too much — **babble** *n* — **bab•bler** *n*

**babe** \'bāb\ *n* : baby

**ba•bel** \'bābəl, 'bab-\ *n* : noisy confusion

**ba•boon** \ba'bün\ *n* : large Asian or African ape with a doglike muzzle

**ba•by** \'bābē\ *n, pl* **-bies** : very young child ∼ *vb* **-bied; -by•ing** : pamper — **baby** *adj* — **ba•by•hood** *n* — **ba•by•ish** *adj*

**ba•by–sit** *vb* **-sat; -sit•ting** : care for children while parents are away — **baby–sit•ter** *n*

**bac•ca•lau•re•ate** \,bakə'lòrēət\ *n* : bachelor's degree

**bac•cha•na•lia** \,bakə'nālyə\ *n, pl* **-lia** : drunken orgy — **bac•cha•na•lian** \-yən\ *adj or n*

**bach•e•lor** \'bachələr\ *n* 1 : holder of lowest 4-year college degree 2 : unmarried man — **bach•e•lor•hood** *n*

**ba•cil•lus** \bə'siləs\ *n, pl* **-li** \-ˌī\ : rod-shaped bacterium — **bac•il•lary** \'basəˌlerē\ *adj*

**back** \'bak\ *n* 1 : part of a human or animal body nearest the spine 2 : part opposite the front 3 : player farthest from the opponent's goal ∼ *adv* 1 : to or at the back 2 : ago 3 : to or in a former place or state 4 : in reply ∼ *adj* 1 : located at the back 2 : not paid on time 3 : moving or working backward 4 : not current ∼ *vb* 1 : support 2 : go or cause to go back 3 : form the back of — **back•ache** *n* — **back•er** *n* — **back•ing** *n* — **back•less** *adj* — **back•rest** *n*

**back•bite** *vb* **-bit; -bit•ten; -bit•ing** : say spiteful things about someone absent — **back•bit•er** *n*

**back•bone** *n* 1 : bony column in the back that encloses the spinal cord 2 : firm character

**back•drop** *n* : painted cloth hung across the rear of a stage

**back•fire** *n* : loud noise from the wrongly timed explosion of fuel in an engine ∼ *vb* 1 : make or undergo a backfire 2 : have a result opposite of that intended

**back•gam•mon** \'bak,gamən\ *n* : board game

**back•ground** *n* 1 : scenery behind something 2 : sum of a person's experience or training

**back•hand** *n* : stroke (as in tennis) made with the back of the hand turned forward — **backhand** *adj or vb* — **back•hand•ed** *adj*

**back•lash** *n* : adverse reaction

**back•log** *n* : accumulation of things to be done — **backlog** *vb*

**back•pack** *n* : camping pack carried on the back ∼ *vb* : hike with a backpack — **back•pack•er** *n*

**back•slide** *vb* **-slid; -slid** *or* **-slid•den** \-ˌslidᵊn\; **-slid•ing** : lapse in morals or religious practice — **back•slid•er** *n*

**back•stage** *adv or adj* : in or to an area behind a stage

**back–up** *n* : substitute

**back•ward** \'bakwərd\, **back•wards** *adv* 1 : toward the back 2 : with the back foremost 3 : in a reverse direction 4 : toward an earlier or worse state ∼ *adj* 1 : directed, turned, or done backward 2 : retarded in development — **back•ward•ness** *n*

**back•woods** *n pl* : remote or isolated place

**ba•con** \'bākən\ *n* : salted and smoked meat from a pig

**bac•te•ri•um** \bak'tirēəm\ *n, pl* **-ria** \-ēə\ : microscopic plant — **bac•te•ri•al** \-ēəl\ *adj* — **bac•te•ri•o•log•i•cal** \-,tirēə'läjik\, **bac•te•ri•o•log•i•cal** \-əl\ *adj* — **bac•te•ri•ol•o•gist** \-ē-'äləjist\ *n* — **bac•te•ri•ol•o•gy** \-jē\ *n*

**bad** \'bad\ *adj* **worse** \'wərs\; **worst** \'wərst\ 1 : not good 2 : naughty 3 : faulty 4 : spoiled — **bad** *n or adv* — **bad•ly** *adv* — **bad•ness** *n*

**bade** *past of* BID

**badge** \'baj\ n : symbol of status

**bad·ger** \'bajər\ n : burrowing mammal ~ vb : harass

**bad·min·ton** \'bad,mint³n\ n : tennislike game played with a shuttlecock

**bad-mouth** \'bad,maủth\ vb : criticize severely

**baf·fle** \'bafəl\ vb **-fled; -fling** : perplex ~ n : device to alter flow (as of liquid or sound) — **baf·fle·ment** n

**bag** \'bag\ n : flexible usu. closable container ~ vb **-gg-** 1 : bulge out 2 : put in a bag 3 : catch in hunting

**bag·a·telle** \,bagə'tel\ n : trifle

**ba·gel** \'bāgəl\ n : hard doughnut-shaped roll

**bag·gage** \'bagij\ n : traveler's bags and belongings

**bag·gy** \'bagē\ adj **-gi·er; -est** : puffed out like a bag — **bag·gi·ness** n

**bag·pipe** n : musical instrument with a bag, a tube with valves, and sounding pipes — often pl.

¹**bail** \'bāl\ n : container for scooping water out of a boat — **bail** vb — **bail·er** n

²**bail** n 1 : security given to guarantee a prisoner's appearance in court 2 : release secured by bail ~ vb : bring about the release of by giving bail

**bai·liff** \'bāləf\ n 1 : British sheriff's aide 2 : minor officer of a U.S. court

**bai·li·wick** \'bāli,wik\ n : one's special field or domain

**bail·out** \'bā,laủt\ n : rescue from financial distress

**bait** \'bāt\ vb 1 : harass with dogs usu. for sport 2 : furnish (a hook or trap) with bait ~ n : lure esp. for catching animals

**bake** \'bāk\ vb **baked; bak·ing** : cook in dry heat esp. in an oven ~ n : party featuring baked food — **bak·er** n — **bak·ery** \'bākərē\ n — **bake·shop** n

**bal·ance** \'baləns\ n 1 : weighing device 2 : counteracting weight, force, or influence 3 : equilibrium 4 : that which remains ~ vb **-anced; -anc·ing** 1 : compute the balance 2 : equalize 3 : bring into harmony or proportion — **bal·anced** adj

**bal·co·ny** \'balkənē\ n, pl **-nies** : platform projecting from a wall

**bald** \'bóld\ adj 1 : lacking a natural or usual covering (as of hair) 2 : plain — **bald·ing** adj — **bald·ly** adv — **bald·ness** n

**bal·der·dash** \'bóldər,dash\ n : nonsense

**bale** \'bāl\ n : large bundle ~ vb **baled; bal·ing** : pack in a bale — **bal·er** n

**bale·ful** \'bālfəl\ adj 1 : deadly 2 : ominous

**balk** \'bók\ n : hindrance ~ vb 1 : thwart 2 : stop short and refuse to go on — **balky** adj

¹**ball** \'ból\ n 1 : rounded mass 2 : game played with a ball ~ vb : form into a ball

²**ball** n : large formal dance — **ballroom** n

**bal·lad** \'baləd\ n 1 : narrative poem 2 : slow romantic song — **bal·lad·eer** \,balə'dir\ n

**bal·last** \'baləst\ n : heavy material to steady a ship or balloon ~ vb : provide with ballast

**bal·le·ri·na** \,balə'rēnə\ n : female ballet dancer

**bal·let** \'ba,lā, ba'lā\ n : theatrical dancing

**bal·lis·tics** \bə'listiks\ n sing or pl : science of projectile motion — **ballistic** adj

**bal·loon** \bə'lün\ n : inflated bag ~ vb 1 : travel in a balloon 2 : swell out — **bal·loon·ist** n

**bal·lot** \'balət\ n 1 : paper used to cast a vote 2 : system of voting ~ vb : vote

**bal·ly·hoo** \'balē,hü\ n : publicity — **ballyhoo** vb

**balm** \'bäm, 'bälm\ n 1 : fragrant healing or soothing preparation 2 : spicy fragrant herb

**balmy** \'bämē, 'bälmē\ adj **balm·i·er; -est** : gently soothing — **balm·i·ness** n

**ba·lo·ney** \bə'lōnē\ n : nonsense

**bal·sa** \'bólsə\ n : very light wood of a tropical tree

**bal·sam** \-səm\ n 1 : aromatic resinous plant substance 2 : balsam-yielding plant — **bal·sam·ic** \ból'samik\ adj

**bal·us·ter** \'baləstər\ n : upright support for a rail

**bal·us·trade** \-,strād\ n : row of balusters topped by a rail

**bam·boo** \bam'bü\ n : tall tropical grass with strong hollow stems

**bam·boo·zle** \bam'büzəl\ vb **-zled; -zling** : deceive

**ban** \'ban\ vb **-nn-** : prohibit ~ n : legal prohibition

**ba·nal** \bə'näl, -'nal; 'bān³l\ *adj* : ordinary and uninteresting — **ba·nal·ity** \bə'nalətē\ *n*

**ba·nana** \bə'nanə\ *n* : elongated fruit of a treelike tropical plant

¹**band** \'band\ *n* **1** : something that ties or binds **2** : strip or stripe different (as in color) from nearby matter **3** : range of radio wavelengths ∼ *vb* **1** : enclose with a band **2** : unite for a common end — **band·ed** *adj* — **band·er** *n*

²**band** *n* **1** : group **2** : musicians playing together

**ban·dage** \'bandij\ *n* : material used esp. in dressing wounds ∼ *vb* : dress or cover with a bandage

**ban·dan·na, ban·dana** \ban'danə\ *n* : large colored figured handkerchief

**ban·dit** \'bandət\ *n* : outlaw or robber — **ban·dit·ry** \-dətrē\ *n*

**band·stand** *n* : stage for band concerts

**band·wag·on** *n* : candidate, side, or movement gaining support

¹**ban·dy** \'bandē\ *vb* **-died; -dy·ing** : exchange in rapid succession

²**bandy** *adj* : curved outward

**bane** \'bān\ *n* **1** : poison **2** : cause of woe — **bane·ful** *adj*

¹**bang** \'baŋ\ *vb* : strike, thrust, or move usu. with a loud noise ∼ *n* **1** : blow **2** : sudden loud noise ∼ *adv* : directly

²**bang** *n* : fringe of short hair over the forehead — usu. pl. ∼ *vb* : cut in bangs

**ban·gle** \'baŋgəl\ *n* : bracelet

**ban·ish** \'banish\ *vb* **1** : force by authority to leave a country **2** : expel — **ban·ish·ment** *n*

**ban·is·ter** \-əstər\ *n* **1** : baluster **2** : handrail

**ban·jo** \'ban,jō\ *n, pl* **-jos** : stringed instrument with a drumlike body — **banjo·ist** *n*

¹**bank** \'baŋk\ *n* **1** : piled-up mass **2** : rising ground along a body of water **3** : sideways slope along a curve ∼ *vb* **1** : form a bank **2** : cover (as a fire) to keep inactive **3** : incline (an airplane) laterally

²**bank** *n* : tier of objects

³**bank** *n* **1** : money institution **2** : reserve supply ∼ *vb* : conduct business in a bank — **bank·book** *n* — **bank·er** *n* — **bank·ing** *n*

**bank·rupt** \'baŋ,krəpt\ *n* : one required by law to forfeit assets to pay off debts ∼ *adj* **1** : legally a bankrupt **2** : lacking something essential — **bankrupt** *vb* — **bank·rupt·cy** \-,krəpsē\ *n*

**ban·ner** \'banər\ *n* : flag ∼ *adj* : excellent

**banns** \'banz\ *n pl* : announcement in church of a proposed marriage

**ban·quet** \'baŋkwət\ *n* : ceremonial dinner — **banquet** *vb*

**ban·shee** \'banshē\ *n* : wailing female spirit that foretells death

**ban·tam** \'bantəm\ *n* : miniature domestic fowl

**ban·ter** \'bantər\ *n* : good-natured joking — **banter** *vb*

**ban·yan** \'banyən\ *n* : large tree that grows new trunks from the limbs

**bap·tism** \'bap,tizəm\ *n* : Christian rite signifying spiritual cleansing — **bap·tis·mal** \bap'tizməl\ *adj*

**bap·tize** \bap'tīz, 'bap,tīz\ *vb* **-tized; -tiz·ing** : administer baptism to

**bar** \'bär\ *n* **1** : long narrow object used esp. as a lever, fastening, or support **2** : barrier **3** : body of practicing lawyers **4** : wide stripe **5** : food counter **6** : place where liquor is served **7** : vertical line across the musical staff ∼ *vb* **1** : obstruct with a bar **2** : shut out **3** : prohibit ∼ *prep* : excluding — **barred** *adj* — **bar·room** *n* — **bar·tend·er** *n*

**barb** \'bärb\ *n* : sharp projection pointing backward — **barbed** *adj*

**bar·bar·ian** \bär'barēən\ *adj* **1** : relating to people considered backward **2** : not refined — **barbarian** *n*

**bar·bar·ic** \-'barik\ *adj* : barbarian

**bar·ba·rous** \'bärbərəs\ *adj* **1** : lacking refinement **2** : mercilessly cruel — **bar·bar·ism** \-bə,rizəm\ *n* — **bar·bar·i·ty** \bär'barətē\ *n* — **bar·ba·rous·ly** *adv*

**bar·be·cue** \'bärbi,kyü\ *n* : gathering at which barbecued food is served ∼ *vb* **-cued; -cu·ing** : cook over hot coals or on a spit often with a highly seasoned sauce

**bar·ber** \'bärbər\ *n* : one who cuts hair

**bar·bi·tu·rate** \bär'bichərət\ *n* : sedative or hypnotic drug

**bard** \'bärd\ *n* : poet

**bare** \'bar\ *adj* **bar·er; bar·est** **1** : naked **2** : not concealed **3** : empty **4** : leaving nothing to spare **5** : plain ∼ *vb* **bared; bar·ing** : make or lay bare — **bare·foot, bare·foot·ed** *adv or adj* — **bare–hand·ed** *adv or adj*

— **bare·head·ed** adv or adj — **bare·ly** adv — **bare·ness** n

**bare·back, bare·backed** adv or adj : without a saddle

**bare·faced** adj : open and esp. brazen

**bar·gain** \'bärgən\ n 1 : agreement 2 : something bought for less than its value ~ vb 1 : negotiate 2 : barter

**barge** \'bärj\ n : broad flat-bottomed boat ~ vb **barged; barg·ing** : move rudely or clumsily — **barge·man** n

**bari·tone** \'barə₁tōn\ n : male voice between bass and tenor

**bar·i·um** \'barēəm\ n : silver-white metallic chemical element

¹**bark** \'bärk\ vb 1 : make the sound of a dog 2 : speak in a loud curt tone ~ n : sound of a barking dog

²**bark** n : tough corky outer covering of a woody stem or root ~ vb : remove bark or skin from

³**bark** n : sailing ship with a fore-and-aft rear sail

**bark·er** \'bärkər\ n : one who calls out to attract people to a show

**bar·ley** \'bärlē\ n : cereal grass or its seeds

**barn** \'bärn\ n : building for keeping hay or livestock — **barn·yard** n

**bar·na·cle** \'bärnikəl\ n : marine crustacean

**barn·storm** vb : tour through rural districts giving performances

**ba·rom·e·ter** \bə'rämətər\ n : instrument for measuring atmospheric pressure — **baro·met·ric** \₁barə-'metrik\ adj

**bar·on** \'barən\ n : British peer — **bar·on·age** \-ij\ n — **ba·ro·ni·al** \bə-'rōnēəl\ adj — **bar·ony** \'barənē\ n

**bar·on·ess** \-ənəs\ n 1 : baron's wife 2 : woman holding a baronial title

**bar·on·et** \-ənət\ n : man holding a rank between a baron and a knight — **bar·on·et·cy** \-sē\ n

**ba·roque** \bə'rōk, -'räk\ adj : elaborately ornamented

**bar·racks** \'barəks\ n sing or pl : soldiers' housing

**bar·ra·cu·da** \₁barə'küdə\ n, pl -da or -das : large predatory sea fish

**bar·rage** \bə'räzh, -'räj\ n : heavy artillery fire

**bar·rel** \'barəl\ n 1 : closed cylindrical container 2 : amount held by a barrel 3 : cylindrical part ~ vb -reled or -relled; -rel·ing or -rel·ling 1 : pack in a barrel 2 : move at high speed

**bar·ren** \'barən\ adj 1 : unproductive of life 2 : uninteresting — **bar·ren·ness** n

**bar·rette** \bä'ret, bə-\ n : clasp for a woman's hair

**bar·ri·cade** \'barə₁kād, ₁barə¹-\ n : barrier — **barricade** vb

**bar·ri·er** \'barēər\ n : something that separates or obstructs

**bar·ring** \'bäriŋ\ prep : omitting

**bar·ris·ter** \'barəstər\ n : British trial lawyer

**bar·row** \'barō\ n : wheelbarrow

**bar·ter** \'bärtər\ vb : trade by exchange of goods — **barter** n

**ba·salt** \bə'sȯlt, 'bā₁-\ n : dark fine-grained igneous rock — **ba·sal·tic** \bə'sȯltik\ adj

¹**base** \'bās\ n, pl **bas·es** 1 : bottom 2 : fundamental part 3 : beginning point 4 : supply source of a force 5 : compound that reacts with an acid to form a salt ~ vb **based; bas·ing** : establish — **base·less** adj

²**base** adj **bas·er; bas·est** 1 : inferior 2 : contemptible — **base·ly** adv — **base·ness** n

**base·ball** n : game played with a bat and ball by 2 teams

**base·ment** \-mənt\ n : part of a building below ground level

**bash** \'bash\ vb : strike violently ~ n : heavy blow

**bash·ful** \-fəl\ adj : self-conscious — **bash·ful·ness** n

**ba·sic** \'bāsik\ adj 1 : relating to or forming the base or essence 2 : relating to a chemical base — **ba·si·cally** adv — **ba·sic·i·ty** \bā'sisətē\ n

**ba·sil** \'bazəl, 'bās-, 'bāz-\ n : aromatic mint

**ba·sil·i·ca** \bə'silikə\ n : important church or cathedral

**ba·sin** \'bās³n\ n 1 : large bowl or pan 2 : region drained by a river

**ba·sis** \'bāsəs\ n, pl **ba·ses** \-₁sēz\ 1 : something that supports 2 : fundamental principle

**bask** \'bask\ vb : enjoy pleasant warmth

**bas·ket** \'baskət\ n : woven container — **bas·ket·ful** n

**bas·ket·ball** n : game played with a ball on a court by 2 teams

**bas–re·lief** \₁bäri'lēf\ n : flat sculpture with slightly raised design

¹**bass** \'bas\ n, pl **bass** or **bass·es** : spiny-finned sport and food fish

²**bass** \'bās\ *n* **1** : deep tone **2** : lowest choral voice

**bas·set hound** \'baset-\ *n* : short-legged dog with long ears

**bas·si·net** \ˌbasə'net\ *n* : baby's bed

**bas·soon** \bə'sün, ba-\ *n* : low-pitched wind instrument

**bas·tard** \'bastərd\ *n* **1** : illegitimate child **2** : offensive person ~ *adj* **1** : illegitimate **2** : inferior — **bas·tard·ize** *vb* — **bas·tardy** *n*

¹**baste** \'bāst\ *vb* **bast·ed; bast·ing** : sew temporarily with long stitches

²**baste** *vb* **bast·ed; bast·ing** : moisten at intervals while cooking

**bas·tion** \'baschən\ *n* : fortified position

¹**bat** \'bat\ *n* **1** : stick or club **2** : sharp blow ~ *vb* **-tt-** : hit with a bat

²**bat** *n* : small flying mammal

³**bat** *vb* **-tt-** : wink or blink

**batch** \'bach\ *n* : quantity used or produced at one time

**bate** \'bāt\ *vb* **bat·ed; bat·ing** : moderate or reduce

**bath** \'bath, 'bath\ *n, pl* **baths** \'bathz, 'baths, 'bảthz, 'bảths\ **1** : a washing of the body **2** : water for washing the body **3** : liquid in which something is immersed **4** : bathroom **5** : large financial loss — **bath·tub** *n*

**bathe** \'bāth\ *vb* **bathed; bath·ing 1** : wash in liquid **2** : flow against so as to wet **3** : shine light over **4** : take a bath or a swim — **bath·er** *n*

**bath·robe** *n* : robe worn around the house

**bath·room** *n* : room with a bathtub or shower and usu. a sink and toilet

**ba·tiste** \bə'tēst\ *n* : fine sheer fabric

**ba·ton** \bə'tän\ *n* : musical conductor's stick

**bat·tal·ion** \bə'talyən\ *n* : military unit composed of a headquarters and two or more companies

**bat·ten** \'batᵊn\ *n* : strip of wood used to seal or reinforce ~ *vb* : furnish or fasten with battens

¹**bat·ter** \'batər\ *vb* : beat or damage with repeated blows

²**batter** *n* : mixture of flour and liquid

³**batter** *n* : player who bats

**bat·tery** \'batərē\ *n, pl* **-ter·ies 1** : illegal beating of a person **2** : group of artillery guns **3** : group of electric cells

**bat·ting** \'batiŋ\ *n* : layers of cotton or wool for stuffing

**bat·tle** \'batᵊl\ *n* : military fighting ~ *vb* **-tled; -tling** : engage in battle — **battle·field** *n*

**bat·tle–ax** *n* : long-handled ax formerly used as a weapon

**bat·tle·ment** \-mənt\ *n* : parapet on top of a wall

**bat·tle·ship** *n* : heavily armed warship

**bat·ty** \'batē\ *adj* **-ti·er; -est** : crazy

**bau·ble** \'bóbəl\ *n* : trinket

**bawdy** \'bódē\ *adj* **bawd·i·er; -est** : obscene or lewd — **bawd·i·ly** *adv* — **bawd·i·ness** *n*

**bawl** \'ból\ *vb* : cry loudly ~ *n* : long loud cry

¹**bay** \'bā\ *adj* : reddish brown ~ *n* : bay-colored animal

²**bay** *n* : European laurel

³**bay** *n* **1** : compartment **2** : area projecting out from a building and containing a window (**bay window**)

⁴**bay** *vb* : bark with deep long tones ~ *n* **1** : position of one unable to escape danger **2** : baying of dogs

⁵**bay** *n* : body of water smaller than a gulf and nearly surrounded by land

**bay·ber·ry** \-ˌberē\ *n* : shrub bearing small waxy berries

**bay·o·net** \'bāənət, ˌbāə'net\ *n* : dagger that fits on the end of a rifle ~ *vb* **-net·ed; -net·ing** : stab with a bayonet

**bay·ou** \'bīü, -ō\ *n* : creek flowing through marshy land

**ba·zaar** \bə'zär\ *n* **1** : market **2** : fair for charity

**ba·zoo·ka** \-'zükə\ *n* : weapon that shoots armor-piercing rockets

**BB** *n* : small shot pellet

**be** \'bē\ *vb* was \'wəz, 'wäz\, were \'wər\, been \'bin\; be·ing \'bēiŋ\; am \əm, 'am\, is \'iz, əz\, are \ər, 'är\ **1** : equal **2** : exist **3** : occupy a certain place **4** : occur ~ *verbal auxiliary* — used to show continuous action or to form the passive voice

**beach** \'bēch\ *n* : sandy shore of a sea, lake, or river ~ *vb* : drive ashore

**beach·comb·er** \-ˌkōmər\ *n* : one who searches the shore for useful objects

**beach·head** *n* : shore area held by an attacking force in an invasion

**bea·con** \'bēkən\ *n* : guiding or warning light or signal

**bead** \'bēd\ *n* : small round body esp. strung on a thread ~ *vb* : form into a bead — **bead·ing** *n* — **beady** *adj*

**bea·gle** \'bēgəl\ n : small short-legged hound

**beak** \'bēk\ n : bill of a bird — **beaked** adj

**bea·ker** \'bēkər\ n 1 : large drinking cup 2 : laboratory vessel

**beam** \'bēm\ n 1 : large long piece of timber or metal 2 : ray of light 3 : directed radio signals for the guidance of pilots ~ vb 1 : send out light 2 : smile 3 : aim a radio broadcast

**bean** \'bēn\ n : edible plant seed borne in pods

¹**bear** \'bar\ n, pl bears 1 or pl bear : large heavy mammal with shaggy hair 2 : gruff or sullen person — **bear·ish** adj

²**bear** vb bore \'bōr\; borne \'bōrn\; **bear·ing** 1 : carry 2 : give birth to or produce 3 : endure 4 : press 5 : go in an indicated direction — **bear·able** adj — **bear·er** n

**beard** \'bird\ n 1 : facial hair on a man 2 : tuft like a beard ~ vb : confront boldly — **beard·ed** adj — **beard·less** adj

**bear·ing** n 1 : way of carrying oneself 2 : supporting object or purpose 3 : significance 4 : machine part in which another part turns 5 : direction with respect esp. to compass points

**beast** \'bēst\ n 1 : animal 2 : brutal person — **beast·li·ness** n — **beast·ly** adj

**beat** \'bēt\ vb beat; beat·en \'bēt³n\ or beat; **beat·ing** 1 : strike repeatedly 2 : defeat 3 : act or arrive before 4 : throb ~ n 1 : single stroke or pulsation 2 : rhythmic stress in poetry or music ~ adj : exhausted — **beat·er** n

**be·atif·ic** \,bēə'tifik\ adj : blissful

**be·at·i·fy** \bē'atə,fī\ vb -fied; -fy·ing : make happy or blessed — **be·at·i·fi·ca·tion** \-,atəfə'kāshən\ n

**be·at·i·tude** \-'atə,tüd, -,tyüd\ n : saying in the Sermon on the Mount (Matthew 5:3-12) beginning "Blessed are"

**beau** \'bō\ n, pl beaux \'bōz\ or beaus : suitor

**beau·ty** \'byütē\ n, pl -ties : qualities that please the senses or mind — **beau·te·ous** \-ēəs\ adj — **beau·te·ously** adv — **beau·ti·fi·ca·tion** \,byütəfə'kāshən\ n — **beau·ti·fi·er** \'byütə,fīər\ n — **beau·ti·ful** \-ifəl\

adj — **beau·ti·ful·ly** adv — **beau·ti·fy** \-ə,fī\ vb

**bea·ver** \'bēvər\ n : large fur-bearing rodent

**be·cause** \bi'kòz, -'kəz\ conj : for the reason that

**because of** prep : by reason of

**beck** \'bek\ n : summons

**beck·on** \'bekən\ vb : summon esp. by a nod or gesture

**be·come** \bi'kəm\ vb -came \-'kām\; -come; -com·ing 1 : come to be 2 : be suitable — **be·com·ing** adj — **be·com·ing·ly** adv

**bed** \'bed\ n 1 : piece of furniture to sleep on 2 : flat or level surface ~ vb -dd- : put or go to bed — **bed·spread** n

**bed·bug** n : wingless bloodsucking insect

**bed·clothes** n pl : bedding

**bed·ding** n 1 : sheets and blankets for a bed 2 : soft material (as hay) for an animal's bed

**be·deck** \bi'dek\ vb : adorn

**be·dev·il** \-'devəl\ vb : harass

**bed·lam** \'bedləm\ n : uproar and confusion

**be·drag·gled** \bi'dragəld\ adj : dirty and disordered

**bed·rid·den** \'bed,rid³n\ adj : kept in bed by illness

**bed·rock** n : solid subsurface rock — **bedrock** adj

¹**bee** \'bē\ n : 4-winged honey-producing insect — **bee·hive** n — **bee·keep·er** n — **bees·wax** n

²**bee** n : neighborly work session

**beech** \'bēch\ n, pl beech·es or beech : tree with smooth gray bark and edible nuts (**beech·nuts**) — **beech·en** \-ən\ adj

**beef** \'bēf\ n, pl beefs \'bēfs\ or beeves \'bēvz\ : flesh of a steer, cow, or bull ~ vb : strengthen — used with up — **beef·steak** n

**bee·line** n : straight course

**been** past part of BE

**beep** \'bēp\ n : short usu. high-pitched warning sound — **beep** vb — **beep·er** n

**beer** \'bir\ n : alcoholic drink brewed from malt and hops — **beery** adj

**beet** \'bēt\ n : garden root vegetable

**bee·tle** \'bētəl\ n : 4-winged insect

**be·fall** \bi'fòl\ vb -fell; -fall·en : happen to

**be·fit** \bi'fit\ vb : be suitable to

**be·fore** \bi'fōr\ adv **1** : in front **2** : earlier ~ prep **1** : in front of **2** : earlier than ~ conj : earlier than

**be·fore·hand** adv or adj : in advance

**be·friend** \bi'frend\ vb : act as friend to

**be·fud·dle** \-'fəd°l\ vb : confuse

**beg** \'beg\ vb **-gg-** : ask earnestly

**be·get** \bi'get\ vb **-got; -got·ten** or **-got; -get·ting** : become the father of

**beg·gar** \'begər\ n : one that begs ~ vb : make poor — **beg·gar·ly** adj — **beg·gary** n

**be·gin** \bi'gin\ vb **-gan** \-'gan\; **-gun** \-'gən\; **-gin·ning 1** : start **2** : come into being — **be·gin·ner** n

**be·gone** \bi'gón\ vb : go away

**be·go·nia** \-'gōnyə\ n : tropical herb with waxy flowers

**be·grudge** \-'grəj\ vb **1** : concede reluctantly **2** : look upon disapprovingly

**be·guile** \-'gīl\ vb **-guiled; -guil·ing 1** : deceive **2** : amuse

**be·half** \-'haf, -'háf\ n : benefit

**be·have** \-'hāv\ vb **-haved; -hav·ing** : act in a certain way

**be·hav·ior** \-'hāvyər\ n : way of behaving — **be·hav·ior·al** \-əl\ adj

**be·head** \-'hed\ vb : cut off the head of

**be·hest** \-'hest\ n : command

**be·hind** \bi'hīnd\ adv : at the back ~ prep **1** : in back of **2** : less than **3** : supporting

**be·hold** \-'hōld\ vb **-held; -hold·ing** : see — **be·hold·er** n

**be·hold·en** \-'hōldən\ adj : indebted

**be·hoove** \-'hüv\ vb **-hooved; -hoov·ing** : be necessary for

**beige** \'bāzh\ n : yellowish brown — **beige** adj

**be·ing** \'bēiŋ\ n **1** : existence **2** : living thing

**be·la·bor** \bi'lābər\ vb : carry on to absurd lengths

**be·lat·ed** \-'lātəd\ adj : delayed

**belch** \'belch\ vb **1** : expel stomach gas orally **2** : emit forcefully — **belch** n

**be·lea·guer** \bi'lēgər\ vb **1** : besiege **2** : harass

**bel·fry** \'belfrē\ n, pl **-fries** : bell tower

**be·lie** \bi'lī\ vb **-lied; -ly·ing 1** : misrepresent **2** : prove false

**be·lief** \bə'lēf\ n **1** : trust **2** : something believed

**be·lieve** \-'lēv\ vb **-lieved; -liev·ing 1** : trust in **2** : accept as true **3** : hold as

an opinion — **be·liev·able** adj — **be·liev·ably** adv — **be·liev·er** n

**be·lit·tle** \bi'lit°l\ vb **-lit·tled; -lit·tling 1** : disparage **2** : make seem less

**bell** \'bel\ n : hollow metallic device that rings when struck ~ vb : provide with a bell

**bel·la·don·na** \,belə'dänə\ n : poisonous herb yielding a drug

**belle** \'bel\ n : beautiful woman

**bel·li·cose** \'beli,kōs\ adj : pugnacious — **bel·li·cos·i·ty** \,beli'käsətē\ n

**bel·lig·er·ent** \bə'lijərənt\ adj **1** : waging war **2** : truculent — **bel·lig·er·ence** \-rəns\ n — **bel·lig·er·en·cy** \-rənsē\ n — **belligerent** n

**bel·low** \'belō\ vb : make a loud deep roar or shout — **bellow** n

**bel·lows** \-ōz, -əz\ n sing or pl : device with sides that can be compressed to expel air

**bell·weth·er** \'bel'wethər, -,weth-\ n : leader

**bel·ly** \'belē\ n, pl **-lies** : abdomen ~ vb **-lied; -ly·ing** : bulge

**be·long** \bi'lóŋ\ vb **1** : be suitable **2** : be owned **3** : be a part of

**be·long·ings** \-iŋz\ n pl : possessions

**be·loved** \bi'ləvəd, -'ləvd\ adj : dearly loved — **beloved** n

**be·low** \-'lō\ adv : in or to a lower place ~ prep : lower than

**belt** \'belt\ n **1** : strip (as of leather) worn about the waist **2** : endless band to impart motion **3** : distinct region ~ vb **1** : put a belt around **2** : thrash

**be·moan** \bi'mōn\ vb : lament

**be·muse** \-'myüz\ vb : confuse

**bench** \'bench\ n **1** : long seat **2** : judge's seat **3** : court

**bend** \'bend\ vb **bent** \'bent\; **bend·ing 1** : curve or cause a change of shape in **2** : turn in a certain direction ~ n **1** : act of bending **2** : curve

**be·neath** \bi'nēth\ adv or prep : below

**bene·dic·tion** \,benə'dikshən\ n : closing blessing

**bene·fac·tor** \'benə,faktər\ n : one who gives esp. charitable aid

**be·nef·i·cence** \bə'nefəsəns\ n : quality of doing good — **be·nef·i·cent** \-sənt\ adj

**ben·e·fi·cial** \,benə'fishəl\ adj : being of benefit — **ben·e·fi·cial·ly** adv

**ben·e·fi·cia·ry** \-'fishē,erē, -'fishərē\ n, pl **-ries** : one who receives benefits

**ben·e·fit** \'benə,fit\ n **1** : something

that does good **2** : help **3** : fund-
raising event — **benefit** vb
**be•nev•o•lence** \bə'nevələns\ n **1**
: charitable nature **2** : act of kindness
— **be•nev•o•lent** \-lənt\ adj — be-
nev•o•lent•ly adv
**be•night•ed** \bi'nītəd\ adj : ignorant
**be•nign** \bi'nīn\ adj **1** : gentle or
kindly **2** : not malignant — **be•nig-
ni•ty** \-'nignətē\ n
**be•nig•nant** \-'nignənt\ adj : benign
**bent** \'bent\ n : aptitude or interest
**be•numb** \bi'nəm\ vb : make numb
esp. by cold
**ben•zene** \'ben,zēn\ n : colorless flammable liquid
**be•queath** \bi'kwēth, -'kwēth\ vb **1**
: give by will **2** : hand down
**be•quest** \bi'kwest\ n : something be-
queathed
**be•rate** \-'rāt\ vb : scold harshly
**be•reaved** \-'rēvd\ adj : suffering the
death of a loved one — n, pl bereaved : one who is bereaved — be-
reave•ment n
**be•reft** \-'reft\ adj : deprived of or
lacking something
**be•ret** \bə'rā\ n : round soft visorless
cap
**beri•beri** \,berē'berē\ n : thiamine-
deficiency disease
**berm** \'bərm\ n : bank of earth
**ber•ry** \'berē\ n, pl -ries : small pulpy
fruit
**ber•serk** \bər'sərk, -'zərk\ adj : crazed
— **berserk** adv
**berth** \'bərth\ n **1** : place where a ship
is anchored **2** : place to sit or sleep
esp. on a ship **3** : job ~ vb : to bring
or come into a berth
**ber•yl** \'berəl\ n : light-colored silicate
mineral
**be•seech** \bi'sēch\ vb -sought \-'sot\
or -seeched; -seech•ing : entreat
**be•set** \-'set\ vb **1** : harass **2** : hem in
**be•side** \-'sīd\ prep **1** : by the side of
**2** : besides
**be•sides** \-'sīdz\ adv **1** : in addition **2**
: moreover ~ prep **1** : other than **2**
: in addition to
**be•siege** \-'sēj\ vb : lay siege to — be-
sieg•er n
**be•smirch** \-'smərch\ vb : soil
**be•sot** \-'sät\ vb -tt- : become drunk
**be•speak** \bi'spēk\ vb -spoke; -spo-
ken; -speak•ing **1** : address **2** : indicate
**best** \'best\ adj, superlative of GOOD

**1** : excelling all others **2** : most pro-
ductive **3** : largest ~ adv superlative
of WELL **1** : in the best way **2** : most
~ n : one that is best ~ vb : outdo
**bes•tial** \'beschəl, 'bēs-\ adj **1** : relating to beasts **2** : brutish — **bes•ti•al-
i•ty** \,beschē'alətē, ,bēs-\ n
**be•stir** \bi'stər\ vb : rouse to action
**best man** n : chief male attendant at a
wedding
**be•stow** \bi'stō\ vb : give — **be•stow-
al** \-əl\ n
**bet** \'bet\ n **1** : something risked or
pledged on the outcome of a contest
**2** : the making of a bet ~ vb bet;
**bet•ting 1** : risk (as money) on an
outcome **2** : make a bet with
**be•tide** \bi'tīd\ vb : happen to
**be•to•ken** \bi'tōkən\ vb : give an indication of
**be•tray** \bi'trā\ vb **1** : seduce **2** : report or reveal to an enemy by treach-
ery **3** : abandon **4** : prove unfaithful
to **5** : reveal unintentionally — be-
tray•al n — be•tray•er n
**be•troth** \-'träth, -'trōth, -'troth, or
with th\ vb : promise to marry — be-
troth•al n — be•trothed n
**bet•ter** \'betər\ adj, comparative of
GOOD **1** : more than half **2** : im-
proved in health **3** : of higher quality
~ adv comparative of WELL **1** : in a
superior manner **2** : more ~ n **1**
: one that is better **2** : advantage ~
vb **1** : improve **2** : surpass — **bet•ter-
ment** \-mənt\ n
**bet•tor, bet•ter** \'betər\ n : one who
bets
**be•tween** \bi'twēn\ prep **1** — used to
show two things considered together
**2** : in the space separating **3** — used
to indicate a comparison or choice ~
adv : in an intervening space or interval
**bev•el** \'bevəl\ n : slant on an edge ~
vb -eled or -elled; -el•ing or -el•ling
**1** : cut or shape to a bevel **2** : incline
**bev•er•age** \'bevrij\ n : drink
**bevy** \'bevē\ n, pl bev•ies : large group
**be•wail** \bi'wāl\ vb : lament
**be•ware** \-'war\ vb : be cautious
**be•wil•der** \-'wildər\ vb : confuse —
**be•wil•der•ment** n
**be•witch** \-'wich\ vb **1** : affect by
witchcraft **2** : charm — **be•witch-
ment** n
**be•yond** \bē'yänd\ adv **1** : farther **2**
: besides ~ prep **1** : on or to the far-

ther side of **2** : out of the reach of **3** : besides

**bi-** \'bī, ,bī\ *prefix* **1** : two **2** : coming or occurring every two **3** : twice, doubly, or on both sides

**bi·an·nu·al** \,bī'anyəwəl\ *adj* : occurring twice a year — **bi·an·nu·al·ly** *adv*

**bi·as** \'bīəs\ *n* **1** : line diagonal to the grain of a fabric **2** : prejudice ~ *vb* -**ased** *or* -**assed; -as·ing** *or* -**as·sing** : prejudice

**bib** \'bib\ *n* : shield tied under the chin to protect the clothes while eating

**Bi·ble** \'bībəl\ *n* **1** : sacred scriptures of Christians **2** : sacred scriptures of Judaism or of some other religion — **bib·li·cal** \'biblikəl\ *adj*

**bib·li·og·ra·phy** \,biblē'ägrəfē\ *n, pl* -**phies** : list of writings on a subject or of an author — **bib·li·og·ra·pher** \-fər\ *n* — **bib·li·o·graph·ic** \-lēə-'grafik\ *adj*

**bi·cam·er·al** \'bī'kamərəl\ *adj* : having 2 legislative chambers

**bi·car·bon·ate** \-'kärbə,nāt, -nət\ *n* : acid carbonate

**bi·cen·ten·ni·al** \,bīsen'tenēəl\ *n* : 200th anniversary — **bicentennial** *adj*

**bi·ceps** \'bī,seps\ *n* : large muscle of the upper arm

**bick·er** \'bikər\ *vb or n* : squabble

**bi·cus·pid** \bī'kəspəd\ *n* : double-pointed tooth

**bi·cy·cle** \'bī,sikəl\ *n* : 2-wheeled vehicle moved by pedaling ~ *vb* -**cled; -cling** : ride a bicycle — **bi·cy·cler** \-klər\ *n* — **bi·cy·clist** \-list\ *n*

**bid** \'bid\ *vb* **bade** \'bad, 'bād\ *or* **bid; bid·den** \'bid²n\ *or* **bid; bid·ding 1** : order **2** : invite **3** : express **4** : make a bid ~ *n* **1** : act of bidding **2** : buyer's proposed price — **bid·da·ble** \-əbəl\ *adj* — **bid·der** *n*

**bide** \'bīd\ *vb* **bode** \'bōd\ *or* **bid·ed; bided; bid·ing 1** : wait **2** : dwell

**bi·en·ni·al** \bī'enēəl\ *adj* **1** : occurring

once in 2 years **2** : lasting 2 years — **biennial** *n* — **bi·en·ni·al·ly** *adv*

**bier** \'bir\ *n* : stand for a coffin

**bifocals** \'bī,fōkəlz\ *n pl* : eyeglasses that correct for near and distant vision

**big** \'big\ *adj* -**gg-** : large in size, amount, or scope — **big·ness** *n*

**big·a·my** \'bigəmē\ *n* : marrying one person while still married to another — **big·a·mist** \-mist\ *n* — **big·a·mous** \-məs\ *adj*

**big·horn** *n, pl* -**horn** *or* -**horns** : wild mountain sheep

**bight** \'bīt\ *n* **1** : loop of a rope **2** : bay

**big·ot** \'bigət\ *n* : one who is intolerant of others — **big·ot·ed** \-ətəd\ *adj* — **big·ot·ry** \-ətrē\ *n*

**big shot** *n* : important person

**big·wig** *n* : big shot

**bike** \'bīk\ *n* : bicycle or motorcycle

**bi·ki·ni** \bə'kēnē\ *n* : woman's brief 2-piece bathing suit

**bi·lat·er·al** \bī'latərəl\ *adj* : involving 2 sides — **bi·lat·er·al·ly** *adv*

**bile** \'bīl\ *n* **1** : greenish liver secretion that aids digestion **2** : bad temper

**bi·lin·gual** \bī'lingwəl\ *adj* : using 2 languages

**bil·ious** \'bilyəs\ *adj* : irritable — **bil·ious·ness** *n*

**bilk** \'bilk\ *vb* : cheat

**¹bill** \'bil\ *n* : jaws of a bird together with their horny covering ~ *vb* : caress fondly — **billed** *adj*

**²bill** *n* **1** : draft of a law **2** : list of things to be paid for **3** : printed advertisement **4** : piece of paper money ~ *vb* : submit a bill or account to

**bill·board** *n* : surface for displaying advertising bills

**bil·let** \'bilət\ *n* : soldiers' quarters ~ *vb* : lodge in a billet

**bill·fold** *n* : wallet

**bil·liards** \'bilyərdz\ *n* : game of driving balls into one another or into pockets on a table

**bil·lion** \'bilyən\ *n, pl* **billions** *or*

---

**List of self-explanatory words with the prefix** *bi-*

| | | |
|---|---|---|
| bicolored | bicultural | binational |
| biconcave | bidirectional | biparental |
| biconcavity | bifunctional | bipolar |
| biconvex | bimetal | biracial |
| biconvexity | bimetallic | |

**billion** : 1000 millions — **billion** adj — **bil·lionth** \-yənth\ adj or n

**bil·low** \'bilō\ n **1** : great wave **2** : rolling mass ∼ vb : swell out — **billowy** \'biləwē\ adj

**billy goat** n : male goat

**bin** \'bin\ n : storage box

**bi·na·ry** \'bīnərē\ adj : consisting of 2 things — **binary** n

**bind** \'bīnd\ vb **bound** \'baùnd\; **bind·ing 1** : tie **2** : obligate **3** : unite into a mass **4** : bandage — **bind·er** n — **binding** n

**binge** \'binj\ n : spree

**bin·go** \'biŋgō\ n, pl **-gos** : game of covering numbers on a card

**bin·oc·u·lar** \bī'näkyələr, bə-\ adj : of or relating to both eyes ∼ n : binocular optical instrument —usu. pl.

**bio·chem·is·try** \,bīō'keməstrē\ n : chemistry dealing with organisms — **bio·chemi·cal** adj or n — **bio·chem·ist** n

**bio·de·grad·able** \,bīōdi'grādəbəl\ adj : able to be reduced to harmless products by organisms — **bio·de·grad·abil·i·ty** n — **bio·deg·ra·da·tion** n — **bio·de·grade** vb

**bi·og·ra·phy** \bī'ägrəfē, bē-\ n, pl **-phies** : written history of a person's life — **bi·og·ra·pher** \-fər\ n — **bio·graph·i·cal** \,bīə'grafikəl\ adj

**bi·ol·o·gy** \bī'äləjē\ n : science of living beings and life processes — **bio·log·ic** \,bīə'läjik\, **bio·log·i·cal** \-əl\ adj — **bi·ol·o·gist** \bī'äləjist\ n

**bi·on·ic** \bī'änik\ adj : having normal biological capabilities enhanced by electronic or mechanical devices

**bio·phys·ics** \,bīō'fiziks\ n : application of physics to biological problems — **bio·phys·i·cal** adj — **bio·phys·i·cist** n

**bi·op·sy** \'bī,äpsē\ n, pl **-sies** : removal of live bodily tissue for examination

**bio·tech·nol·o·gy** \,bīōtek'näləjē\ n : manufacture of products using techniques involving the manipulation of DNA

**bi·par·ti·san** \bī'pärtəzən, -sən\ adj : involving members of 2 parties

**bi·ped** \'bī,ped\ n : 2-footed animal

**birch** \'bərch\ n : deciduous tree with close-grained wood — **birch, birch·en** \-ən\ adj

**bird** \'bərd\ n : warm-blooded egg‌laying vertebrate with wings and feathers — **bird·bath** n — **bird·house** n — **bird·seed** n

**bird's-eye** \'bərdz,ī\ adj **1** : seen from above **2** : cursory

**birth** \'bərth\ n **1** : act or fact of being born or of producing young **2** : origin — **birth·day** n — **birth·place** n — **birth·rate** n

**birth·mark** n : unusual blemish on the skin at birth

**birth·right** n : something one is entitled to by birth

**bis·cuit** \'biskət\ n : small bread made with leavening other than yeast

**bi·sect** \'bī,sekt\ vb : divide into 2 parts — **bi·sec·tion** \'bī,sekshən\ n — **bi·sec·tor** \-tər\ n

**bish·op** \'bishəp\ n : clergy member higher than a priest

**bish·op·ric** \-shə,prik\ n **1** : diocese **2** : office of bishop

**bis·muth** \'bizməth\ n : heavy brittle metallic chemical element

**bi·son** \'bīs°n, 'bīz-\ n, pl **-son** : large shaggy wild ox of central U.S.

**bis·tro** \'bēstrō, 'bis-\ n, pl **-tros** : small restaurant or bar

¹**bit** \'bit\ n **1** : part of a bridle that goes in a horse's mouth **2** : drilling tool

²**bit** n **1** : small piece or quantity **2** : small degree

**bitch** \'bich\ n : female dog ∼ vb : complain

**bite** \'bīt\ vb **bit** \'bit\; **bit·ten** \'bit°n\; **bit·ing** \'bītiŋ\ **1** : to grip or cut with teeth or jaws **2** : dig in or grab and hold **3** : sting **4** : take bait ∼ n **1** : act of biting **2** : bit of food **3** : wound made by biting — **bit·ing** adj

**bit·ter** \'bitər\ adj **1** : having an acrid lingering taste **2** : intense or severe **3** : extremely harsh or resentful — **bit·ter·ly** adv — **bit·ter·ness** n

**bit·tern** \'bitərn\ n : small heron

**bi·tu·mi·nous coal** \bə'tümənəs-, -'tyü-\ n : coal that yields volatile waste matter when heated

**bi·valve** \'bī,valv\ n : animal (as a clam) with a shell of 2 parts — **bi·valve** adj

**biv·ouac** \'bivə,wak\ n : temporary camp ∼ vb **-ouacked; -ouack·ing** : camp

**bi·zarre** \bə'zär\ adj : very strange — **bi·zarre·ly** adv

**blab** \'blab\ vb **-bb-** : talk too much

**black** \'blak\ adj **1** : of the color black

2 : dark-skinned 3 : soiled 4 : lacking light 5 : wicked or evil 6 : gloomy ~ n 1 : black pigment or dye 2 : something black 3 : color of least lightness 4 : person of a dark-skinned race ~ vb : blacken — **black•ing** n — **black•ish** adj — **black•ly** adv — **black•ness** n

**black–and–blue** adj : darkly discolored from bruising

**black•ball** \'blak,bȯl\ vb 1 : ostracize 2 : boycott — **blackball** n

**black•ber•ry** \'blak,berē\ n : black or purple fruit of a bramble

**black•bird** n : bird of which the male is largely or wholly black

**black•board** n : dark surface for writing on with chalk

**black•en** \'blakən\ vb 1 : make or become black 2 : defame

**black•guard** \'blagərd, -,ärd\ n : scoundrel

**black•head** n : small dark oily mass plugging the outlet of a skin gland

**black hole** n : invisible extremely massive celestial object

**black•jack** n 1 : flexible leather-covered club 2 : card game ~ vb : hit with a blackjack

**black•list** n : list of persons to be punished or boycotted — **blacklist** vb

**black•mail** n 1 : extortion by threat of exposure 2 : something extorted by blackmail — **blackmail** vb — **black•mail•er** n

**black•out** n 1 : darkness due to electrical failure 2 : brief fainting spell — **black out** vb

**black•smith** n : one who forges iron

**black•top** n : dark tarry material for surfacing roads — **blacktop** vb

**blad•der** \'bladər\ n : sac into which urine passes from the kidneys

**blade** \'blād\ n 1 : leaf esp. of grass 2 : something resembling the flat part of a leaf 3 : cutting part of an instrument or tool — **blad•ed** \'blādəd\ adj

**blame** \'blām\ vb **blamed; blam•ing** 1 : find fault with 2 : hold responsible or responsible for — **blam•able** adj — **blame** n — **blame•less** adj — **blame•less•ly** adv — **blame•worthy** adj

**blanch** \'blanch\ vb : make or become white or pale

**bland** \'bland\ adj 1 : smooth in manner 2 : soothing 3 : tasteless — **bland•ly** adv — **bland•ness** n

**blan•dish•ment** \'blandishmənt\ n : flattering or coaxing speech or act

**blank** \'blaŋk\ adj 1 : showing or causing a dazed look 2 : lacking expression 3 : empty 4 : free from writing 5 : downright ~ n 1 : an empty space 2 : form with spaces to write in 3 : unfinished form (as of a key) 4 : cartridge with no bullet ~ vb : cover or close up — **blank•ly** adv — **blank•ness** n

**blan•ket** \'blaŋkət\ n 1 : heavy covering for a bed 2 : covering layer ~ vb : cover ~ adj : applying to a group

**blare** \'blar\ vb **blared; blar•ing** : make a loud harsh sound — **blare** n

**blar•ney** \'blärnē\ n : skillful flattery

**bla•sé** \blä'zā\ adj : indifferent to pleasure or excitement

**blas•pheme** \blas'fēm\ vb **-phemed; -phem•ing** : speak blasphemy — **blas•phem•er** n

**blas•phe•my** \'blasfəmē\ n, pl **-mies** : irreverence toward God or anything sacred — **blas•phe•mous** adj

**blast** \'blast\ n 1 : violent gust of wind 2 : explosion ~ vb : shatter by or as if by explosive — **blast off** vb : take off esp. in a rocket

**bla•tant** \'blāt⁰nt\ adj : offensively showy — **bla•tan•cy** \-⁰nsē\ n — **bla•tant•ly** adv

¹**blaze** \'blāz\ n 1 : fire 2 : intense direct light 3 : strong display ~ vb **blazed; blaz•ing** : burn or shine brightly

²**blaze** n 1 : white stripe on an animal's face 2 : trail marker esp. on a tree ~ vb **blazed; blaz•ing** : mark with blazes

**blaz•er** \-ər\ n : sports jacket

**bleach** \'blēch\ vb : whiten — **bleach** n

**bleach•ers** \-ərz\ n sing or pl : uncovered stand for spectators

**bleak** \'blēk\ adj 1 : desolately barren 2 : lacking cheering qualities — **bleak•ish** adj — **bleak•ly** adv — **bleak•ness** n

**bleary** \'blirē\ adj : dull or dimmed esp. from fatigue

**bleat** \'blēt\ n : cry of a sheep or goat or a sound like it — **bleat** vb

**bleed** \'blēd\ vb **bled** \'bled\; **bleed•ing** 1 : lose or shed blood 2 : feel distress 3 : flow from a wound 4

: draw fluid from **5** : extort money from — **bleed•er** n

**blem•ish** \'blemish\ vb : spoil by a flaw ~ n : noticeable flaw

¹**blench** \'blench\ vb : flinch

²**blench** vb : grow or make pale

**blend** \'blend\ vb **1** : mix thoroughly **2** : combine into an integrated whole — **blend** n — **blend•er** n

**bless** \'bles\ vb **blessed** \'blest\; **bless•ing 1** : consecrate by religious rite **2** : invoke divine care for **3** : make happy — **bless•ed** \'blesəd\, **blest** \'blest\ adj — **bless•ed•ly** \'blesədlē\ adv — **bless•ed•ness** \'blesədnəs\ n — **bless•ing** n

**blew** past of BLOW

**blight** \'blīt\ n **1** : plant disorder marked by withering or an organism causing it **2** : harmful influence **3** : deteriorated condition ~ vb : affect with or suffer from blight

**blimp** \'blimp\ n : airship holding form by pressure of contained gas

**blind** \'blīnd\ adj **1** : lacking or quite deficient in ability to see **2** : not intelligently controlled **3** : having no way out ~ vb **1** : to make blind **2** : dazzle ~ n **1** : something to conceal or darken **2** : place of concealment — **blind•ly** adv — **blind•ness** n

**blind•fold** vb : cover the eyes of — **blindfold** n

**blink** \'bliŋk\ vb **1** : wink **2** : shine intermittently ~ n : wink

**blink•er** n : a blinking light

**bliss** \'blis\ n **1** : complete happiness **2** : heaven or paradise — **bliss•ful** adj — **bliss•ful•ly** adv

**blis•ter** \'blistər\ n **1** : raised area of skin containing watery fluid **2** : raised or swollen spot ~ vb : develop or cause blisters

**blithe** \'blīth, 'blīth\ adj **blith•er**; **blith•est** : cheerful — **blithe•ly** adv — **blithe•some** \-səm\ adj

**blitz** \'blits\ n **1** : series of air raids **2** : fast intensive campaign — **blitz** vb

**bliz•zard** \'blizərd\ n : severe snowstorm

**bloat** \'blōt\ vb : swell

**blob** \'bläb\ n : small lump or drop

**bloc** \'bläk\ n : group working together

**block** \'bläk\ n **1** : solid piece **2** : frame enclosing a pulley **3** : quantity considered together **4** : large building divided into separate units **5** : a city square or the distance along

one of its sides **6** : obstruction **7** : interruption of a bodily or mental function ~ vb : obstruct or hinder

**block•ade** \blä'kād\ n : isolation of a place usu. by troops or ships — **blockade** vb — **block•ad•er** n

**block•head** n : stupid person

**blond, blonde** \'bländ\ adj **1** : fair in complexion **2** : of a light color — **blond, blonde** n

**blood** \'bləd\ n **1** : red liquid that circulates in the heart, arteries, and veins of animals **2** : lifeblood **3** : lineage — **blood•ed** adj — **blood•less** adj — **blood•stain** n — **blood-stained** adj — **blood•suck•er** n — **blood•suck•ing** adj — **bloody** adj

**blood•cur•dling** adj : terrifying

**blood•hound** n : large hound with a keen sense of smell

**blood•mo•bile** \-mō,bēl\ n : truck for collecting blood from donors

**blood•shed** n : slaughter

**blood•shot** adj : inflamed to redness

**blood•stream** n : blood in a circulatory system

**blood•thirsty** adj : eager to shed blood — **blood•thirst•i•ly** adv — **blood-thirst•i•ness** n

**bloom** \'blüm\ n **1** : flower **2** : period of flowering **3** : fresh or healthy look ~ vb **1** : yield flowers **2** : mature — **bloomy** adj

**bloo•mers** \'blümərz\ n pl : woman's underwear of short loose trousers

**bloop•er** \'blüpər\ n : public blunder

**blos•som** \'bläsəm\ n or vb : flower

**blot** \'blät\ n **1** : stain **2** : blemish ~ vb **-tt- 1** : spot **2** : dry with absorbent paper — **blot•ter** n

**blotch** \'bläch\ n : large spot — **blotch** vb — **blotchy** adj

**blouse** \'blaús, 'blaúz\ n : loose garment reaching from the neck to the waist

¹**blow** \'blō\ vb **blew** \'blü\; **blown** \'blōn\; **blow•ing 1** : move forcibly **2** : send forth a current of air **3** : sound **4** : shape by blowing **5** : explode **6** : bungle ~ n **1** : gale **2** : act of blowing — **blow•er** n — **blowy** adj

²**blow** n **1** : forcible stroke **2** pl : fighting **3** : calamity

**blow•out** n : bursting of a tire

**blow•torch** n : small torch that uses a blast of air

¹**blub•ber** \'bləbər\ n : fat of whales

²**blubber** *vb* : cry noisily

**blud·geon** \'bləjən\ *n* : short club ∼ *vb* : hit with a bludgeon

**blue** \'blü\ *adj* **blu·er; blu·est** **1** : of the color blue **2** : melancholy ∼ *n* : color of the clear sky — **blu·ish** \-ish\ *adj*

**blue·bell** *n* : plant with blue bell-shaped flowers

**blue·ber·ry** \-,berē\ *n* : edible blue or blackish berry

**blue·bird** *n* : small bluish songbird

**blue·fish** *n* : bluish marine food fish

**blue jay** *n* : American crested jay

**blue·print** *n* **1** : photographic print in white on blue of a mechanical drawing **2** : plan of action — **blueprint** *vb*

**blues** \'blüz\ *n pl* **1** : depression **2** : music in a melancholy style

¹**bluff** \'bləf\ *adj* **1** : rising steeply with a broad flat front **2** : frank ∼ *n* : cliff

²**bluff** *vb* : deceive by pretense ∼ *n* : act of bluffing — **bluff·er** \-ər\ *n*

**blu·ing, blue·ing** \'blüiŋ\ *n* : laundry preparation to keep fabrics white

**blun·der** \'bləndər\ *vb* **1** : move clumsily **2** : make a stupid mistake ∼ *n* : bad mistake

**blun·der·buss** \-,bəs\ *n* : obsolete short-barreled firearm

**blunt** \'blənt\ *adj* **1** : not sharp **2** : tactless ∼ *vb* : make dull — **blunt·ly** *adv* — **blunt·ness** *n*

**blur** \'blər\ *n* **1** : smear **2** : something perceived indistinctly ∼ *vb* **-rr-** : cloud or obscure — **blur·ry** \-ē\ *adj*

**blurb** \'blərb\ *n* : short publicity notice

**blurt** \'blərt\ *vb* : utter suddenly

**blush** \'bləsh\ *n* : reddening of the face — **blush** *vb* — **blush·ful** *adj*

**blus·ter** \'bləstər\ *vb* **1** : blow violently **2** : talk or act with boasts or threats — **blus·ter** *n* — **blus·tery** *adj*

**boa** \'bōə\ *n* **1** : a large snake (as the **boa con·stric·tor** \-kən'striktər\) that crushes its prey **2** : fluffy scarf

**boar** \'bōr\ *n* : male swine

**board** \'bōrd\ *n* **1** : long thin piece of sawed lumber **2** : flat thin sheet esp. for games **3** : daily meals furnished for pay **4** : official body ∼ *vb* **1** : go aboard **2** : cover with boards **3** : supply meals to — **board·er** *n*

**board·walk** *n* : wooden walk along a beach

**boast** \'bōst\ *vb* : praise oneself or one's possessions — **boast** *n* —

**boast·er** *n* — **boast·ful** *adj* — **boast·ful·ly** *adv*

**boat** \'bōt\ *n* : small vessel for traveling on water — **boat** *vb* — **boat·man** \-mən\ *n*

**boat·swain** \'bōsᵊn\ *n* : ship's officer in charge of the hull

¹**bob** \'bäb\ *vb* **-bb-** **1** : move up and down **2** : appear suddenly

²**bob** *n* **1** : float **2** : woman's short haircut ∼ *vb* : cut hair in a bob

**bob·bin** \'bäbən\ *n* : spindle for holding thread

**bob·ble** \'bäbəl\ *vb* **-bled; -bling** : fumble — **bobble** *n*

**bob·cat** *n* : small American lynx

**bob·o·link** \'bäbə,liŋk\ *n* : American songbird

**bob·sled** \'bäb,sled\ *n* : racing sled — **bobsled** *vb*

**bob·white** \'bäb'hwīt\ *n* : quail

**bock** \'bäk\ *n* : dark beer

¹**bode** \'bōd\ *vb* **bod·ed; bod·ing** : indicate by signs

²**bode** *past of* BIDE

**bod·ice** \'bädəs\ *n* : close-fitting top of dress

**bod·i·ly** \'bädᵊlē\ *adj* : relating to the body ∼ *adv* **1** : in the flesh **2** : as a whole

**body** \'bädē\ *n, pl* **bod·ies** **1** : the physical whole of an organism **2** : human being **3** : main part **4** : mass of matter **5** : group — **bod·ied** *adj* — **bod·i·less** \-iləs, -ᵊləs\ *adj* — **body·guard** *n*

**bog** \'bäg, 'bȯg\ *n* : swamp ∼ *vb* **-gg-** : sink in or as if in a bog — **bog·gy** *adj*

**bo·gey** \'bu̇gē, 'bō-\ *n, pl* **-geys** : someone or something frightening

**bog·gle** \'bägəl\ *vb* **-gled; -gling** : overwhelm with amazement

**bo·gus** \'bōgəs\ *adj* : fake

**bo·he·mi·an** \bō'hēmēən\ *n* : one living unconventionally — **bohemian** *adj*

¹**boil** \'bȯil\ *n* : inflamed swelling

²**boil** *vb* **1** : heat to a temperature (**boiling point**) at which vapor forms **2** : cook in boiling liquid **3** : be agitated — **boil** *n*

**boil·er** \'bȯilər\ *n* : tank holding hot water or steam

**bois·ter·ous** \'bȯistərəs\ *adj* : noisily turbulent — **bois·ter·ous·ly** *adv*

**bold** \'bōld\ *adj* **1** : courageous **2** : insolent **3** : daring — **bold•ly** adv — **bold•ness** n

**bo•le•ro** \bə'lerō\ n, pl **-ros 1** : Spanish dance **2** : short open jacket

**boll** \'bōl\ n : seed pod

**boll weevil** n : small grayish weevil that infests the cotton plant

**bo•lo•gna** \bə'lōnē\ n : large smoked sausage

**bol•ster** \'bōlstər\ n : long pillow ~ vb **-stered; -ster•ing** : support

**bolt** \'bōlt\ n **1** : flash of lightning **2** : sliding bar used to fasten a door **3** : roll of cloth **4** : threaded pin used with a nut ~ vb **1** : move suddenly **2** : fasten with a bolt **3** : swallow hastily

**bomb** \'bäm\ n : explosive device ~ vb : attack with bombs — **bomb•proof** adj

**bom•bard** \bäm'bärd, bəm-\ vb : attack with or as if with artillery — **bom•bard•ment** n

**bom•bar•dier** \‚bämbə'dir\ n : one who releases the bombs from a bomber

**bom•bast** \'bäm‚bast\ n : pretentious language — **bom•bas•tic** \bäm'bastik\ adj

**bomb•er** n **1** : one that bombs **2** : airplane for dropping bombs

**bomb•shell** n **1** : bomb **2** : great surprise

**bona fide** \'bōnə‚fīd, 'bän-; ‚bōnə-'fīdē\ adj **1** : made in good faith **2** : genuine

**bo•nan•za** \bə'nanzə\ n : something yielding a rich return

**bon•bon** \'bän‚bän\ n : piece of candy

**bond** \'bänd\ n **1** pl : fetters **2** : uniting force **3** : obligation made binding by money **4** : interest-bearing certificate ~ vb **1** : insure **2** : cause to adhere — **bond•hold•er** n

**bond•age** \'bändij\ n : slavery

[1]**bonds•man** \'bändzmən\ n : slave

[2]**bondsman** n : surety

**bone** \'bōn\ n : skeletal material ~ vb **boned; bon•ing** : to free from bones — **bone•less** adj — **bony** \'bōnē\ adj

**bon•er** \'bōnər\ n : blunder

**bon•fire** \'bän‚fīr\ n : outdoor fire

**bo•ni•to** \bə'nētō\ n, pl **-tos** or **-to** : medium-sized tuna

**bon•net** \'bänət\ n : hat for a woman or infant

**bo•nus** \'bōnəs\ n : extra payment

**boo** \'bü\ n, pl **boos** : shout of disapproval — **boo** vb

**boo•by** \'bübē\ n, pl **-bies** : dunce

**book** \'búk\ n **1** : paper sheets bound into a volume **2** : long literary work or a subdivision of one ~ vb : reserve — **book•case** n — **book•let** \-lət\ n — **book•mark** n — **book•sell•er** n — **book•shelf** n

**book•end** n : support to hold up a row of books

**book•ie** \-ē\ n : bookmaker

**book•ish** \-ish\ adj : fond of books and reading

**book•keep•er** n : one who keeps business accounts — **book•keep•ing** n

**book•mak•er** n : one who takes bets — **book•mak•ing** n

**book•worm** n : one devoted to reading

[1]**boom** \'büm\ n **1** : long spar to extend the bottom of a sail **2** : beam projecting from the pole of a derrick

[2]**boom** vb **1** : make a deep hollow sound **2** : grow rapidly esp. in value ~ n **1** : booming sound **2** : rapid growth

**boo•mer•ang** \'bümə‚raŋ\ n : angular club that returns to the thrower

[1]**boon** \'bün\ n : benefit

[2]**boon** adj : congenial

**boon•docks** \'bün‚däks\ n pl : rural area

**boor** \'búr\ n : rude person — **boor•ish** adj

**boost** \'büst\ vb **1** : raise **2** : promote — **boost** n — **boost•er** n

**boot** \'büt\ n **1** : covering for the foot and leg **2** : kick ~ vb : kick

**boo•tee, boo•tie** \'bütē\ n : infant's knitted sock

**booth** \'büth\ n, pl **booths** \'büthz, 'büths\ : small enclosed stall or seating area

**boot•leg** \'büt‚leg\ vb : make or sell liquor illegally — **bootleg** adj or n — **boot•leg•ger** n

**boo•ty** \'bütē\ n, pl **-ties** : plunder

**booze** \'büz\ vb **boozed; booz•ing** : drink liquor to excess ~ n : liquor — **booz•er** n — **boozy** adj

**bo•rax** \'bōr‚aks\ n : crystalline compound of boron

**bor•der** \'bórdər\ n **1** : edge **2** : boundary ~ vb **1** : put a border on **2** : be close

[1]**bore** \'bōr\ vb **bored; bor•ing 1** : pierce **2** : make by piercing ~ n : cylindrical hole or its diameter — **bor•er** n

[2]**bore** past of BEAR

³**bore** *n* : one that is dull ∼ *vb* **bored;** **bor·ing** : tire with dullness — **bore·dom** \'bōrdəm\ *n*

**born** \'bôrn\ *adj* **1** : brought into life **2** : being such by birth

**borne** *past part of* BEAR

**bo·ron** \'bōr‚än\ *n* : dark-colored chemical element

**bor·ough** \'bərō\ *n* : incorporated town or village

**bor·row** \'bärō\ *vb* **1** : take as a loan **2** : take into use

**bo·som** \'büzəm, 'büs-\ *n* : breast ∼ *adj* : intimate — **bo·somed** *adj*

**boss** \'bós\ *n* : employer or supervisor ∼ *vb* : supervise — **bossy** *adj*

**bot·a·ny** \'bätᵊnē\ *n* : plant biology — **bo·tan·i·cal** \bə'tanikəl\ *adj* — **bot·a·nist** \'bätᵊnist\ *n* — **bot·a·nize** \-ᵊn‚īz\ *vb*

**botch** \'bäch\ *vb* : do clumsily — **botch** *n*

**both** \'bōth\ *adj or pron* : the one and the other ∼ *conj* — used to show each of two is included

**both·er** \'bäthər\ *vb* **1** : annoy or worry **2** : take the trouble — **bother** *n* — **both·er·some** \-səm\ *adj*

**bot·tle** \'bätᵊl\ *n* : container with a narrow neck and no handles ∼ *vb* **bot·tled; bot·tling** : put into a bottle

**bot·tle·neck** : place or cause of congestion

**bot·tom** \'bätəm\ *n* **1** : supporting surface **2** : lowest part or place — **bottom** *adj* — **bot·tom·less** *adj*

**bot·u·lism** \'bächə‚lizəm\ *n* : acute food poisoning

**bou·doir** \'bü‚dwär, 'bü-, ‚bü'-, ‚bü'-\ *n* : woman's private room

**bough** \'baù\ *n* : large tree branch

**bought** *past of* BUY

**bouil·lon** \'bü‚yän; 'bul‚yän, -yən\ *n* : clear soup

**boul·der** \'bōldər\ *n* : large rounded rock — **boul·dered** *adj*

**bou·le·vard** \'bùlə‚värd, 'bü-\ *n* : broad thoroughfare

**bounce** \'baùns\ *vb* **bounced; bouncing 1** : spring back **2** : make bounce — **bounce** *n* — **bouncy** \'baùnsē\ *adj*

¹**bound** \'baùnd\ *adj* : intending to go

²**bound** *n* : limit or boundary ∼ *vb* : be a boundary of — **bound·less** *adj* — **bound·less·ness** *n*

³**bound** *adj* **1** : obliged **2** : having a binding **3** : determined **4** : incapable of failing

⁴**bound** *n* : leap ∼ *vb* : move by springing

**bound·ary** \'baùndrē\ *n, pl* **-aries** : line marking extent or separation

**boun·ty** \'baùntē\ *n, pl* **-ties 1** : generosity **2** : reward — **boun·te·ous** \-ēəs\ *adj* — **boun·te·ous·ly** *adv* — **boun·ti·ful** \-ifəl\ *adj* — **boun·ti·ful·ly** *adv*

**bou·quet** \bō'kā, bü-\ *n* **1** : bunch of flowers **2** : fragrance

**bour·bon** \'bərbən\ *n* : corn whiskey

**bour·geoi·sie** \‚bùrzh‚wä'zē\ *n* : middle class of society — **bour·geois** \'bùrzh‚wä, bùrzh'wä\ *n or adj*

**bout** \'baùt\ *n* **1** : contest **2** : outbreak

**bou·tique** \bü'tēk\ *n* : specialty shop

**bo·vine** \'bō‚vīn, -‚vēn\ *adj* : relating to cattle — **bovine** *n*

¹**bow** \'baù\ *vb* **1** : submit **2** : bend the head or body ∼ *n* : act of bowing

²**bow** \'bō\ *n* **1** : bend or arch **2** : weapon for shooting arrows **3** : knot with loops **4** : rod with stretched horsehairs for playing a stringed instrument ∼ *vb* : curve or bend — **bow·man** \-mən\ *n* — **bow·string** *n*

³**bow** \'baù\ *n* : forward part of a ship — **bow** *adj*

**bow·els** \'baùəls\ *n pl* **1** : intestines **2** : inmost parts

**bow·er** \'baùər\ *n* : arbor

¹**bowl** \'bōl\ *n* : concave vessel or part — **bowl·ful** \-‚fùl\ *n*

²**bowl** *n* : round ball for bowling ∼ *vb* : roll a ball in bowling — **bowl·er** *n*

**bowl·ing** *n* : game in which balls are rolled to knock down pins

¹**box** \'bäks\ *n, pl* **box** *or* **box·es** : evergreen shrub — **box·wood** \-‚wùd\ *n*

²**box** *n* **1** : container usu. with 4 sides and a cover **2** : small compartment ∼ *vb* : put in a box

³**box** *n* : slap ∼ *vb* **1** : slap **2** : fight with the fists — **box·er** *n* — **box·ing** *n*

**box·car** *n* : roofed freight car

**box office** *n* : theater ticket office

**boy** \'bói\ *n* : male child — **boy·hood** *n* — **boy·ish** *adj* — **boy·ish·ly** *adv* — **boy·ish·ness** *n*

**boy·cott** \-‚kät\ *vb* : refrain from dealing with — **boycott** *n*

**boy·friend** \'bói‚frend\ *n* **1** : male friend **2** : woman's regular male companion

**brace** \'brās\ *n* **1** : crank for turning a

bit **2** : something that resists weight or supports **3** : punctuation mark { or } ∼ vb **braced; brac•ing 1** : make taut or steady **2** : invigorate **3** : strengthen

**brace•let** \'brāslət\ n : ornamental band for the wrist or arm

**brack•et** \'brakət\ n **1** : projecting support **2** : punctuation mark [ or ] **3** : class ∼ vb **1** : furnish or fasten with brackets **2** : place within brackets **3** : group

**brack•ish** \-ish\ adj : salty

**brad** \'brad\ n : nail with a small head

**brag** \'brag\ vb **-gg-** : boast — **brag** n

**brag•gart** \'bragərt\ n : boaster

**braid** \'brād\ vb : interweave ∼ n : something braided

**braille** \'brāl\ n : system of writing for the blind using raised dots

**brain** \'brān\ n **1** : organ of thought and nervous coordination enclosed in the skull **2** : intelligence ∼ vb : smash the skull of — **brained** adj — **brain•less** adj — **brainy** adj

**braise** \'brāz\ vb **braised; brais•ing** : cook (meat) slowly in a covered dish

**brake** \'brāk\ n : device for slowing or stopping ∼ vb **braked; brak•ing** : slow or stop by a brake

**bram•ble** \'brambəl\ n : prickly shrub

**bran** \'bran\ n : edible cracked grain husks

**branch** \'branch\ n **1** : division of a plant stem **2** : part ∼ vb **1** : develop branches **2** : diverge — **branched** adj

**brand** \'brand\ n **1** : identifying mark made by burning **2** : stigma **3** : distinctive kind (as of goods from one firm) ∼ vb : mark with a brand

**bran•dish** \'brandish\ vb : wave

**brand–new** adj : unused

**bran•dy** \'brandē\ n, pl **-dies** : liquor distilled from wine

**brash** \'brash\ adj **1** : impulsive **2** : aggressively self-assertive

**brass** \'bras\ n **1** : alloy of copper and zinc **2** : brazen self-assurance **3** : high-ranking military officers — **brassy** adj

**bras•siere** \brə'zir\ n : woman's undergarment to support the breasts

**brat** \'brat\ n : ill-behaved child — **brat•ti•ness** n — **brat•ty** adj

**bra•va•do** \brə'vädō\ n, pl **-does** or **-dos** : false bravery

**¹brave** \'brāv\ adj **brav•er; brav•est**

: showing courage ∼ vb **braved; brav•ing** : face with courage — **brave•ly** adv — **brav•ery** \-ərē\ n

**²brave** n : American Indian warrior

**bra•vo** \'brävō\ n, pl **-vos** : shout of approval

**brawl** \'brȯl\ n : noisy quarrel or violent fight — **brawl** vb — **brawl•er** n

**brawn** \'brȯn\ n : muscular strength — **brawny** \-ē\ adj — **brawn•i•ness** n

**bray** \'brā\ n : harsh cry of a donkey — **bray** vb

**bra•zen** \'brāzᵊn\ adj **1** : made of brass **2** : bold — **bra•zen•ly** adv — **bra•zen•ness** n

**bra•zier** \'brāzhər\ n : charcoal grill

**breach** \'brēch\ n **1** : breaking of a law, obligation, or standard **2** : gap ∼ vb : make a breach in

**bread** \'bred\ n : baked food made of flour ∼ vb : cover with bread crumbs

**breadth** \'bredth\ n : width

**bread•win•ner** n : wage earner

**break** \'brāk\ vb **broke** \'brōk\; **broken** \'brōkən\; **break•ing 1** : knock into pieces **2** : transgress **3** : force a way into or out of **4** : exceed **5** : interrupt **6** : fail ∼ n **1** : act or result of breaking **2** : stroke of good luck — **break•able** adj or n — **break•age** \'brākij\ n — **break•er** n — **break in** vb **1** : enter by force **2** : interrupt **3** : train — **break out** vb **1** : erupt with force **2** : develop a rash

**break•down** n **1** : physical or mental failure — **break down** vb

**break•fast** \'brekfəst\ n : first meal of the day — **breakfast** vb

**breast** \'brest\ n **1** : milk-producing gland esp. of a woman **2** : front part of the chest

**breast•bone** n : sternum

**breath** \'breth\ n **1** : slight breeze **2** : air breathed in or out — **breath•less** adj — **breath•less•ly** adv — **breath•less•ness** n — **breathy** \'brethē\ adj

**breathe** \'brēth\ vb **breathed; breathing 1** : draw air into the lungs and expel it **2** : live **3** : utter

**breath•tak•ing** adj : exciting

**breech•es** \'brichəz\ n pl : trousers ending near the knee

**breed** \'brēd\ vb **bred** \'bred\; **breeding 1** : give birth to **2** : propagate **3** : raise ∼ n **1** : kind of plant or animal usu. developed by humans **2** : class — **breed•er** n

**breeze** \'brēz\ *n* : light wind ～ *vb* **breezed; breez·ing** : move fast — **breezy** *adj*

**breth·ren** \'brethrən, -ərn\ *pl of* BROTHER

**bre·via·ry** \'brēvərē, 'bre-, -vyərē, -vē,erē\ *n, pl* **-ries** : prayer book used by Roman Catholic priests

**brev·i·ty** \'brevətē\ *n, pl* **-ties** : shortness or conciseness

**brew** \'brü\ *vb* : make by fermenting or steeping — **brew** *n* — **brew·er** *n* — **brew·ery** \'brüərē, 'brürē\ *n*

**bri·ar** *var of* BRIER

**bribe** \'brīb\ *vb* **bribed; brib·ing** : corrupt or influence by gifts ～ *n* : something offered or given in bribing — **brib·able** *adj* — **brib·ery** \-ərē\ *n*

**bric-a-brac** \'brikə,brak\ *n pl* : small ornamental articles

**brick** \'brik\ *n* : building block of baked clay — **brick** *vb* — **brick·lay·er** *n* — **brick·lay·ing** *n*

**bride** \'brīd\ *n* : woman just married or about to be married — **brid·al** \-ᵊl\ *adj*

**bride·groom** *n* : man just married or about to be married

**brides·maid** *n* : woman who attends a bride at her wedding

¹**bridge** \'brij\ *n* **1** : structure built for passage over a depression or obstacle **2** : upper part of the nose **3** : compartment from which a ship is navigated **4** : artificial replacement for missing teeth ～ *vb* : build a bridge over — **bridge·able** *adj*

²**bridge** *n* : card game for 4 players

**bri·dle** \'brīdᵊl\ *n* : headgear to control a horse ～ *vb* **-dled; -dling 1** : put a bridle on **2** : restrain **3** : show hostility or scorn

**brief** \'brēf\ *adj* : short or concise ～ *n* : concise summary (as of a legal case) ～ *vb* : give final instructions or essential information to — **brief·ly** *adv* — **brief·ness** *n*

**brief·case** *n* : case for papers

¹**bri·er** \'brīər\ *n* : thorny plant

²**brier** *n* : heath of southern Europe

¹**brig** \'brig\ *n* : 2-masted ship

²**brig** *n* : jail on a naval ship

**bri·gade** \brig'ād\ *n* **1** : large military unit **2** : group organized for a special activity

**brig·a·dier general** \,brigə'dir-\ *n* : officer ranking next below a major general

**brig·and** \'brigənd\ *n* : bandit — **brig·and·age** \-ij\ *n*

**bright** \'brīt\ *adj* **1** : radiating or reflecting light **2** : cheerful **3** : intelligent — **bright·en** \-ᵊn\ *vb* — **bright·en·er** \'brītᵊnər\ *n* — **bright·ly** *adv* — **bright·ness** *n*

**bril·liant** \'brilyənt\ *adj* **1** : very bright **2** : splendid **3** : very intelligent — **bril·liance** \-yəns\ *n* — **bril·lian·cy** \-yənsē\ *n* — **bril·liant·ly** *adv*

**brim** \'brim\ *n* : edge or rim ～ *vb* : be or become full — **brim·less** *adj* — **brimmed** *adj*

**brim·ful** \-'fủl\ *adj* : full to the brim

**brim·stone** *n* : sulfur

**brin·dled** \'brindᵊld\ *adj* : gray or tawny with dark streaks or flecks

**brine** \'brīn\ *n* **1** : salt water **2** : ocean — **brin·i·ness** *n* — **briny** *adj*

**bring** \'briŋ\ *vb* **brought** \'brȯt\; **bring·ing 1** : cause to come with one **2** : persuade **3** : produce **4** : sell for — **bring·er** *n* — **bring about** *vb* : make happen — **bring up** *vb* **1** : care for and educate **2** : cause to be noticed

**brink** \'briŋk\ *n* : edge

**bri·quette, bri·quet** \bri'ket\ *n* : pressed mass (as of charcoal)

**brisk** \'brisk\ *adj* **1** : lively **2** : invigorating — **brisk·ly** *adv* — **brisk·ness** *n*

**bris·ket** \'briskət\ *n* : breast or lower chest of a quadruped

**bris·tle** \'brisəl\ *n* : short stiff hair ～ *vb* **-tled; -tling 1** : stand erect **2** : show angry defiance **3** : appear as if covered with bristles — **bris·tly** *adj*

**brit·tle** \'britᵊl\ *adj* **-tler; -tlest** : easily broken — **brit·tle·ness** *n*

**broach** \'brōch\ *n* : pointed tool (as for opening casks) ～ *vb* **1** : pierce (as a cask) to open **2** : introduce for discussion

**broad** \'brȯd\ *adj* **1** : wide **2** : spacious **3** : clear or open **4** : obvious **5** : tolerant in outlook **6** : widely applicable **7** : dealing with essential points — **broad·en** \-ᵊn\ *vb* — **broad·ly** *adv* — **broad·ness** *n*

**broad·cast** *n* **1** : transmission by radio waves **2** : radio or television program ～ *vb* **-cast; -cast·ing 1** : scatter or sow in all directions **2** : make widely known **3** : send out on a broadcast — **broad·cast·er** *n*

**broad·cloth** *n* : fine cloth

**broad·loom** *adj* : woven on a wide loom esp. in solid color

**broad–mind·ed** *adj* : tolerant of varied opinions — **broad–mind·ed·ly** *adv* — **broad–mind·ed·ness** *n*

**broad·side** *n* 1 : simultaneous firing of all guns on one side of a ship 2 : verbal attack

**bro·cade** \brō'kād\ *n* : usu. silk fabric with a raised design

**broc·co·li** \'bräkəlē\ *n* : green vegetable akin to cauliflower

**bro·chure** \brō'shùr\ *n* : pamphlet

**brogue** \'brōg\ *n* : Irish accent

**broil** \'bròil\ *vb* : cook by radiant heat — **broil** *n*

**broil·er** *n* 1 : utensil for broiling 2 : chicken fit for broiling

**¹broke** \'brōk\ *past of* BREAK

**²broke** *adj* : out of money

**bro·ken** \'brōkən\ *adj* : imperfectly spoken — **bro·ken·ly** *adv*

**bro·ken·heart·ed** \-'härtəd\ *adj* : overcome by grief or despair

**bro·ker** \'brōkər\ *n* : agent who buys and sells for a fee — **broker** *vb* — **bro·ker·age** \-kərij\ *n*

**bro·mine** \'brō,mēn\ *n* : deep red liquid corrosive chemical element

**bron·chi·tis** \brän'kītəs, bräŋ-\ *n* : inflammation of the bronchi

**bron·chus** \'bräŋkəs\ *n, pl* **-chi** \-,kī, -,kē\ : division of the windpipe leading to a lung — **bron·chi·al** \-kēəl\ *adj*

**bronze** \'bränz\ *vb* **bronzed; bronzing** : make bronze in color ~ *n* 1 : alloy of copper and tin 2 : yellowish brown — **bronzy** \-ē\ *adj*

**brooch** \'brōch, 'brüch\ *n* : ornamental clasp or pin

**brood** \'brüd\ *n* : family of young ~ *vb* 1 : sit on eggs to hatch them 2 : ponder ~ *adj* : kept for breeding — **brood·er** *n* — **brood·ing·ly** *adv*

**¹brook** \'brùk\ *vb* : tolerate

**²brook** *n* : small stream

**broom** \'brüm, 'brùm\ *n* 1 : flowering shrub 2 : implement for sweeping — **broom·stick** *n*

**broth** \'bròth\ *n, pl* **broths** \'bròths, 'bròthz\ : liquid in which meat has been cooked

**broth·el** \'bräthəl, 'bròth-\ *n* : house of prostitutes

**broth·er** \'brəthər\ *n, pl* **brothers** *also* **breth·ren** \'brethrən, -ərn\ 1 : male sharing one or both parents

with another person 2 : kinsman — **broth·er·hood** *n* — **broth·er·li·ness** *n* — **broth·er·ly** *adj*

**broth·er–in–law** *n, pl* **brothers–in–law** : brother of one's spouse or husband of one's sister or of one's spouse's sister

**brought** *past of* BRING

**brow** \'braù\ *n* 1 : eyebrow 2 : forehead 3 : edge of a steep place

**brow·beat** *vb* **-beat; -beat·en** *or* **-beat; -beat·ing** : intimidate

**brown** \'braùn\ *adj* 1 : of the color brown 2 : of dark or tanned complexion ~ *n* : a color like that of coffee ~ *vb* : make or become brown — **brown·ish** *adj*

**browse** \'braùz\ *vb* **browsed; browsing** 1 : graze 2 : look over casually — **brows·er** *n*

**brows·er** \'braùzər\ *n* : computer program for accessing Web sites

**bru·in** \'brüən\ *n* : bear

**bruise** \'brüz\ *vb* **bruised; bruis·ing** 1 : make a bruise on 2 : become bruised ~ *n* : surface injury to flesh

**brunch** \'brənch\ *n* : late breakfast, early lunch, or combination of both

**bru·net, bru·nette** \brü'net\ *adj* : having dark hair and usu. dark skin — **bru·net, brunette** *n*

**brunt** \'brənt\ *n* : main impact

**¹brush** \'brəsh\ *n* 1 : small cut branches 2 : coarse shrubby vegetation

**²brush** *n* 1 : bristles set in a handle used esp. for cleaning or painting 2 : light touch ~ *vb* 1 : apply a brush to 2 : remove with or as if with a brush 3 : dismiss in an offhand way 4 : touch lightly — **brush up** *vb* : renew one's skill

**³brush** *n* : skirmish

**brush–off** *n* : curt dismissal

**brusque** \'brəsk\ *adj* : curt or blunt in manner — **brusque·ly** *adv*

**bru·tal** \'brüt²l\ *adj* : like a brute and esp. cruel — **bru·tal·i·ty** \brü'talətē\ *n* — **bru·tal·ize** \'brüt²l,īz\ *vb* — **bru·tal·ly** \-²lē\ *adv*

**brute** \'brüt\ *adj* 1 : relating to beasts 2 : unreasoning 3 : purely physical ~ *n* 1 : beast 2 : brutal person — **brut·ish** \-ish\ *adj*

**bub·ble** \'bəbəl\ *vb* **-bled; -bling** : form, rise in, or give off bubbles ~ *n* : globule of gas in or covered with a liquid — **bub·bly** \-əlē\ *adj*

**bu•bo** \'bübō, 'byü-\ n, pl **buboes** : inflammatory swelling of a lymph gland — **bu•bon•ic** \bü'bänik, 'byü-\ adj

**buc•ca•neer** \ˌbəkə'nir\ n : pirate

**buck** \'bək\ n, pl **buck** or **bucks** 1 : male animal (as a deer) 2 : dollar ~ vb 1 : jerk forward 2 : oppose

**buck•et** \'bəkət\ n : pail — **buck•et•ful** n

**buck•le** \'bəkəl\ n 1 : clasp (as on a belt) for two loose ends 2 : bend or fold ~ vb -**led; -ling** 1 : fasten with a buckle 2 : apply oneself 3 : bend or crumple

**buck•ler** \'bəklər\ n : shield

**buck•shot** n : coarse lead shot

**buck•skin** n : soft leather (as from the skin of a buck) — **buckskin** adj

**buck•tooth** n : large projecting front tooth — **buck–toothed** adj

**buck•wheat** n : herb whose seeds are used as a cereal grain or the seeds themselves

**bu•col•ic** \byü'kälik\ adj : pastoral

**bud** \'bəd\ n 1 : undeveloped plant shoot 2 : partly opened flower ~ vb -**dd-** 1 : form or put forth buds 2 : be or develop like a bud

**Bud•dhism** \'bü,dizəm, 'bu-\ n : religion of eastern and central Asia — **Bud•dhist** \'büdist, 'bud-\ n or adj

**bud•dy** \'bədē\ n, pl -**dies** : friend

**budge** \'bəj\ vb **budged; budg•ing** : move from a place

**bud•get** \'bəjət\ n 1 : estimate of income and expenses 2 : plan for coordinating income and expenses 3 : money available for a particular use — **budget** vb or adj — **bud•get•ary** \-ə,terē\ adj

**buff** \'bəf\ n 1 : yellow to orange yellow color 2 : enthusiast ~ adj : of the color buff ~ vb : polish

**buf•fa•lo** \'bəfə,lō\ n, pl -**lo** or -**loes** : wild ox (as a bison)

¹**buff•er** \'bəfər\ n : shield or protector

²**buffer** n : one that buffs

¹**buf•fet** \'bəfət\ n : blow or slap ~ vb : hit esp. repeatedly

²**buf•fet** \ˌbə'fā, bü-\ n 1 : sideboard 2 : meal at which people serve themselves

**buf•foon** \ˌbə'fün\ n : clown — **buf•foon•ery** \-ərē\ n

**bug** \'bəg\ n 1 : small usu. obnoxious crawling creature 2 : 4-winged sucking insect 3 : unexpected imperfec-

tion 4 : disease-producing germ 5 : hidden microphone ~ vb -**gg-** 1 : pester 2 : conceal a microphone in

**bug•a•boo** \'bəgə,bü\ n, pl -**boos** : bogey

**bug•bear** n : source of dread

**bug•gy** \'bəgē\ n, pl -**gies** : light carriage

**bu•gle** \'byügəl\ n : trumpetlike brass instrument — **bu•gler** \-glər\ n

**build** \'bild\ vb **built** \'bilt\; **build•ing** 1 : put together 2 : establish 3 : increase ~ n : physique — **build•er** n

**build•ing** \'bildiŋ\ n 1 : roofed and walled structure 2 : art or business of constructing buildings

**bulb** \'bəlb\ n 1 : large underground plant bud 2 : rounded or pear-shaped object — **bul•bous** \-əs\ adj

**bulge** \'bəlj\ n : swelling projecting part ~ vb **bulged; bulg•ing** : swell out

**bulk** \'bəlk\ n 1 : magnitude 2 : indigestible food material 3 : large mass 4 : major portion ~ vb : cause to swell or bulge — **bulky** \-ē\ adj

**bulk•head** n : ship's partition

¹**bull** \'bul\ n : large adult male animal (as of cattle) ~ adj : male

²**bull** n 1 : papal letter 2 : decree

**bull•dog** n : compact short-haired dog

**bull•doze** \-,dōz\ vb 1 : move or level with a tractor (**bull•doz•er**) having a broad blade 2 : force

**bul•let** \'bulət\ n : missile to be shot from a gun — **bul•let•proof** adj

**bul•le•tin** \'bulətən\ n 1 : brief public report 2 : periodical

**bull•fight** n : sport of taunting and killing bulls — **bull•fight•er** n

**bull•frog** n : large deep-voiced frog

**bull•head•ed** adj : stupidly stubborn

**bul•lion** \'bulyən\ n : gold or silver esp. in bars

**bull•ock** \'bulək\ n 1 : young bull 2 : steer

**bull's–eye** n, pl **bull's–eyes** : center of a target

**bul•ly** \'bulē\ n, pl -**lies** : one who hurts or intimidates others ~ vb -**lied; -ly•ing** : act like a bully toward

**bul•rush** \'bul,rəsh\ n : tall coarse rush or sedge

**bul•wark** \'bul,wərk, -,wȯrk; 'bəl-,wərk\ n 1 : wall-like defense 2 : strong support or protection

**bum** \'bəm\ vb -**mm-** 1 : wander as a

tramp **2** : get by begging ∼ *n* : idle worthless person ∼ *adj* : bad

**bum·ble·bee** \'bəmbəl,bē\ *n* : large hairy bee

**bump** \'bəmp\ *vb* : strike or knock forcibly ∼ *n* **1** : sudden blow **2** : small bulge or swelling — **bumpy** *adj*

¹**bum·per** \'bəmpər\ *adj* : unusually large

²**bump·er** \'bəmpər\ *n* : shock-absorbing bar at either end of a car

**bump·kin** \'bəmpkən\ *n* : awkward country person

**bun** \'bən\ *n* : sweet biscuit or roll

**bunch** \'bənch\ *n* : group ∼ *vb* : form into a group — **bunchy** *adj*

**bun·dle** \'bənd²l\ *n* **1** : several items bunched together **2** : something wrapped for carrying **3** : large amount ∼ *vb* -**dled; -dling** : gather into a bundle

**bun·ga·low** \'bəngə,lō\ *n* : one-story house

**bun·gle** \'bəngəl\ *vb* -**gled; -gling** : do badly — **bungle** *n* — **bun·gler** *n*

**bun·ion** \'bənyən\ *n* : inflamed swelling of the first joint of the big toe

¹**bunk** \'bəŋk\ *n* : built-in bed that is often one of a tier ∼ *vb* : sleep

²**bunk** *n* : nonsense

**bun·ker** \-ər\ *n* **1** : storage compartment **2** : protective embankment

**bun·kum, bun·combe** \'bəŋkəm\ *n* : nonsense

**bun·ny** \'bənē\ *n, pl* -**nies** : rabbit

¹**bun·ting** \'bəntiŋ\ *n* : small finch

²**bunting** *n* : flag material

**buoy** \'büē, 'boi\ *n* : floating marker anchored in water ∼ *vb* **1** : keep afloat **2** : raise the spirits of — **buoy·an·cy** \'bóiənsē, 'büyən-\ *n* — **buoy·ant** \-yənt\ *adj*

**bur, burr** \'bər\ *n* : rough or prickly covering of a fruit — **bur·ry** *adj*

**bur·den** \'bərd²n\ *n* **1** : something carried **2** : something oppressive **3** : cargo ∼ *vb* : load or oppress — **bur·den·some** \-səm\ *adj*

**bur·dock** \'bər,däk\ *n* : tall coarse herb with prickly flower heads

**bu·reau** \'byùrō\ *n* **1** : chest of drawers **2** : administrative unit **3** : business office

**bu·reau·cra·cy** \byù'räkrəsē\ *n, pl* -**cies** **1** : body of government officials **2** : unwieldy administrative system — **bu·reau·crat** \'byùrə,krat\ *n*

— **bu·reau·crat·ic** \,byùrə'kratik\ *adj*

**bur·geon** \'bərjən\ *vb* : grow

**bur·glary** \'bərglərē\ *n, pl* -**glar·ies** : forcible entry into a building to steal — **bur·glar** \-glər\ *n* — **bur·glar·ize** \'bərglə,rīz\ *vb*

**bur·gle** \'bərgəl\ *vb* -**gled; -gling** : commit burglary on or in

**Bur·gun·dy** \'bərgəndē\ *n, pl* -**dies** : kind of table wine

**buri·al** \'berēəl\ *n* : act of burying

**bur·lap** \'bər,lap\ *n* : coarse fabric usu. of jute or hemp

**bur·lesque** \bər'lesk\ *n* **1** : witty or derisive imitation **2** : broadly humorous variety show ∼ *vb* -**lesqued; -lesqu·ing** : mock

**bur·ly** \'bərlē\ *adj* -**li·er; -est** : strongly and heavily built

**burn** \'bərn\ *vb* **burned** \'bərnd, 'bərnt\ *or* **burnt** \'bərnt\; **burn·ing** **1** : be on fire **2** : feel or look as if on fire **3** : alter or become altered by or as if by fire or heat **4** : cause or make by fire ∼ *n* : injury or effect produced by burning — **burn·er** *n*

**bur·nish** \'bərnish\ *vb* : polish

**burp** \'bərp\ *n or vb* : belch

**bur·ro** \'bərō, 'bùr-\ *n, pl* -**os** : small donkey

**bur·row** \'bərō\ *n* : hole in the ground made by an animal ∼ *vb* : make a burrow — **bur·row·er** *n*

**bur·sar** \'bərsər\ *n* : treasurer esp. of a college

**bur·si·tis** \,bər'sītəs\ *n* : inflammation of a sac (**bur·sa** \'bərsə\) in a joint

**burst** \'bərst\ *vb* **burst** *or* **burst·ed; burst·ing** **1** : fly apart or into pieces **2** : enter or emerge suddenly ∼ *n* : sudden outbreak or effort

**bury** \'berē\ *vb* **bur·ied; bury·ing** **1** : deposit in the earth **2** : hide

**bus** \'bəs\ *n, pl* **bus·es** *or* **bus·ses** : large motor-driven passenger vehicle ∼ *vb* **bused** *or* **bussed; bus·ing** *or* **bus·sing** : travel or transport by bus

**bus·boy** *n* : waiter's helper

**bush** \'bùsh\ *n* **1** : shrub **2** : rough uncleared country **3** : a thick tuft or mat — **bushy** *adj*

**bush·el** \'bùshəl\ *n* : 4 pecks

**bush·ing** \'bùshiŋ\ *n* : metal lining used as a guide or bearing

**busi·ness** \'biznəs, -nəz\ *n* **1** : vocation **2** : commercial or industrial

enterprise **3** : personal concerns —
**busi•ness•man** \-ˌman\ *n* — **busi•ness•wom•an** \-ˌwùmən\ *n*

¹**bust** \'bəst\ *n* **1** : sculpture of the head and upper torso **2** : breasts of a woman

²**bust** *vb* **1** : burst or break **2** : tame ~ *n* **1** : punch **2** : failure

¹**bus•tle** \'bəsəl\ *vb* **-tled; -tling** : move or work briskly ~ *n* : energetic activity

²**bustle** *n* : pad or frame formerly worn under a woman's skirt

**busy** \'bizē\ *adj* **busi•er; -est 1** : engaged in action **2** : being in use **3** : full of activity ~ *vb* **bus•ied; busy•ing** : make or keep busy — **busi•ly** *adv*

**busy•body** *n* : meddler

**but** \'bət\ *conj* **1** : if not for the fact **2** : that **3** : without the certainty that **4** : rather **5** : yet ~ *prep* : other than

**butch•er** \'bùchər\ *n* **1** : one who slaughters animals or dresses their flesh **2** : brutal killer **3** : bungler — **butcher** *vb* — **butch•ery** \-ərē\ *n*

**but•ler** \'bətlər\ *n* : chief male household servant

¹**butt** \'bət\ *vb* : strike with a butt ~ *n* : blow with the head or horns

²**butt** *n* **1** : target **2** : victim

³**butt** *vb* : join edge to edge

⁴**butt** *n* : large end or bottom

⁵**butt** *n* : large cask

**butte** \'byüt\ *n* : isolated steep hill

**but•ter** \'bətər\ *n* : solid edible fat churned from cream ~ *vb* : spread with butter — **but•tery** *adj*

**but•ter•cup** *n* : yellow-flowered herb

**but•ter•fat** *n* : natural fat of milk and of butter

**but•ter•fly** *n* : insect with 4 broad wings

**but•ter•milk** *n* : liquid remaining after butter is churned

**but•ter•nut** *n* : edible nut of a tree related to the walnut or this tree

**but•ter•scotch** \-ˌskäch\ *n* : candy made from sugar, corn syrup, and water

**but•tocks** \'bətəks\ *n pl* : rear part of the hips

**but•ton** \'bətⁿn\ *n* **1** : small knob for fastening clothing **2** : buttonlike object ~ *vb* : fasten with buttons

**but•ton•hole** *n* : hole or slit for a button ~ *vb* : hold in talk

**but•tress** \'bətrəs\ *n* **1** : projecting structure to support a wall **2** : support — **buttress** *vb*

**bux•om** \'bəkəm\ *adj* : full-bosomed

**buy** \'bī\ *vb* **bought** \'bòt\; **buy•ing** : purchase ~ *n* : bargain — **buy•er** *n*

**buzz** \'bəz\ *vb* : make a low humming sound ~ *n* : act or sound of buzzing

**buz•zard** \'bəzərd\ *n* : large bird of prey

**buzz•er** *n* : signaling device that buzzes

**buzz•word** \'bəzˌwərd\ *n* : word or phrase in vogue

**by** \'bī\ *prep* **1** : near **2** : through **3** : beyond **4** : throughout **5** : no later than ~ *adv* **1** : near **2** : farther

**by•gone** \'bīˌgòn\ *adj* : past — **bygone** *n*

**by•law, bye•law** *n* : organization's rule

**by–line** *n* : writer's name on an article

**by•pass** *n* : alternate route ~ *vb* : go around

**by–prod•uct** *n* : product in addition to the main product

**by•stand•er** *n* : spectator

**by•way** \'bīˌwā\ *n* : side road

**by•word** *n* : proverb

# C

**c** \'sē\ *n, pl* **c's** *or* **cs** \'sēz\ : 3d letter of the alphabet

**cab** \'kab\ *n* **1** : light closed horse-drawn carriage **2** : taxicab **3** : compartment for a driver — **cab•bie, cab•by** *n* — **cab•stand** *n*

**ca•bal** \kə'bal\ *n* : group of conspirators

**ca•bana** \kə'banə, -nyə\ *n* : shelter at a beach or pool

**cab•a•ret** \ˌkabə'rā\ *n* : nightclub

**cab•bage** \'kabij\ *n* : vegetable with a dense head of leaves

**cab•in** \'kabn\ *n* **1** : private room on a ship **2** : small house **3** : airplane compartment

**cab•i•net** \'kabnət\ *n* **1** : display case or cupboard **2** : advisory council of a head of state — **cab•i•net•mak•er** *n* — **cab•i•net•mak•ing** *n* — **cab•i•net•work** *n*

**ca·ble** \'kābəl\ *n* **1** : strong rope, wire, or chain **2** : cablegram **3** : bundle of electrical wires ~ *vb* **-bled; -bling** : send a cablegram to

**ca·ble·gram** \-ˌgram\ *n* : message sent by a submarine telegraph cable

**ca·boose** \kə'büs\ *n* : crew car on a train

**ca·cao** \kə'kaủ, -'kāō\ *n, pl* **cacaos** : So. American tree whose seeds (**cacao beans**) yield cocoa and chocolate

**cache** \'kash\ *n* **1** : hiding place **2** : something hidden — **cache** *vb*

**ca·chet** \ka'shā\ *n* : prestige or a feature conferring this

**cack·le** \'kakəl\ *vb* **-led; -ling** : make a cry or laugh like the sound of a hen — **cackle** *n* — **cack·ler** *n*

**ca·coph·o·ny** \ka'käfənē\ *n, pl* **-nies** : harsh noise — **ca·coph·o·nous** \-nəs\ *adj*

**cac·tus** \'kaktəs\ *n, pl* **cac·ti** \-ˌtī\ *or* **-tus·es** : drought-resistant flowering plant with scales or prickles

**cad** \'kad\ *n* : ungentlemanly person — **cad·dish** \-ish\ *adj* — **cad·dish·ly** *adv*

**ca·dav·er** \kə'davər\ *n* : dead body — **ca·dav·er·ous** \-ərəs\ *adj*

**cad·die, cad·dy** \'kadē\ *n, pl* **-dies** : golfer's helper — **caddie, caddy** *vb*

**cad·dy** \'kadē\ *n, pl* **-dies** : small tea chest

**ca·dence** \'kādᵊns\ *n* : measure of a rhythmical flow — **ca·denced** \-ᵊnst\ *adj*

**ca·det** \kə'det\ *n* : student in a military academy

**cadge** \'kaj\ *vb* **cadged; cadg·ing** : beg — **cadg·er** *n*

**cad·mi·um** \'kadmēəm\ *n* : grayish metallic chemical element

**cad·re** \-rē\ *n* : nucleus of highly trained people

**ca·fé** \ka'fā, kə-\ *n* : restaurant

**caf·e·te·ria** \ˌkafə'tirēə\ *n* : self-service restaurant

**caf·feine** \ka'fēn, 'kaˌfēn\ *n* : stimulating alkaloid in coffee and tea

**cage** \'kāj\ *n* : box of wire or bars for confining an animal ~ *vb* **caged; cag·ing** : put or keep in a cage

**ca·gey** \-ē\ *adj* **-gi·er; -est** : shrewd — **ca·gi·ly** *adv* — **ca·gi·ness** *n*

**cais·son** \'kāˌsän, -sən\ *n* **1** : ammunition carriage **2** : watertight chamber for underwater construction

**ca·jole** \kə'jōl\ *vb* **-joled; -jol·ing** : persuade or coax — **ca·jol·ery** \-ərē\ *n*

**cake** \'kāk\ *n* **1** : food of baked or fried usu. sweet batter **2** : compacted mass ~ *vb* **caked; cak·ing** **1** : form into a cake **2** : encrust

**cal·a·bash** \'kaləˌbash\ *n* : gourd

**cal·a·mine** \'kaləˌmīn\ *n* : lotion of oxides of zinc and iron

**ca·lam·i·ty** \kə'lamətē\ *n, pl* **-ties** : disaster — **ca·lam·i·tous** \-ətəs\ *adj* — **ca·lam·i·tous·ly** *adv*

**cal·ci·fy** \'kalsəˌfī\ *vb* **-fied; -fy·ing** : harden — **cal·ci·fi·ca·tion** \ˌkalsəfə'kāshən\ *n*

**cal·ci·um** \'kalsēəm\ *n* : silver-white soft metallic chemical element

**cal·cu·late** \'kalkyəˌlāt\ *vb* **-lat·ed; -lat·ing** **1** : determine by mathematical processes **2** : judge — **cal·cu·lable** \-ləbəl\ *adj* — **cal·cu·la·tion** \ˌkalkyə'lāshən\ *n* — **cal·cu·la·tor** \'kalkyəˌlātər\ *n*

**cal·cu·lat·ing** *adj* : shrewd

**cal·cu·lus** \'kalkyələs\ *n, pl* **-li** \-ˌlī\ : higher mathematics dealing with rates of change

**cal·dron** *var of* CAULDRON

**cal·en·dar** \'kaləndər\ *n* : list of days, weeks, and months

¹**calf** \'kaf, 'káf\ *n, pl* **calves** \'kavz, 'kávz\ : young cow or related mammal — **calf·skin** *n*

²**calf** *n, pl* **calves** : back part of the leg below the knee

**cal·i·ber, cal·i·bre** \'kaləbər\ *n* **1** : diameter of a bullet or shell or of a gun bore **2** : degree of mental or moral excellence

**cal·i·brate** \'kaləˌbrāt\ *vb* **-brat·ed; -brat·ing** : adjust precisely — **cal·ibra·tion** \ˌkalə'brāshən\ *n*

**cal·i·co** \'kaliˌkō\ *n, pl* **-coes** *or* **-cos** **1** : printed cotton fabric **2** : animal with fur having patches of different colors

**cal·i·pers** \'kaləpərz\ *n* : measuring instrument with two adjustable legs

**ca·liph** \'kāləf, 'kal-\ *n* : title of head of Islam — **ca·liph·ate** \-ˌāt, -ət\ *n*

**cal·is·then·ics** \ˌkaləs'theniks\ *n sing or pl* : stretching and jumping exercises — **cal·is·then·ic** *adj*

**calk** \'kȯk\ *var of* CAULK

**call** \'kȯl\ *vb* **1** : shout **2** : summon **3** : demand **4** : telephone **5** : make a visit **6** : name — **call** *n* — **call·er** *n*

— **call down** vb : reprimand — **call off** vb : cancel

**call•ing** n : vocation

**cal•li•ope** \kə'līə‚pē, 'kalē‚ōp\ n : musical instrument of steam whistles

**cal•lous** \'kaləs\ adj 1 : thickened and hardened 2 : unfeeling ～ vb : make callous — **cal•los•i•ty** \ka'läsətē\ n — **cal•lous•ly** adv — **cal•lous•ness** n

**cal•low** \'kalō\ adj : inexperienced or innocent — **cal•low•ness** n

**cal•lus** \'kaləs\ n : callous area on skin or bark ～ vb : form a callus

**call–waiting** n : telephone service by which during a call in progress an incoming call is signaled

**calm** \'käm, 'kälm\ n 1 : period or condition of peacefulness or stillness ～ adj : still or tranquil ～ vb : make calm — **calm•ly** adv — **calm•ness** n

**ca•lor•ic** \kə'lórik\ adj : relating to heat or calories

**cal•o•rie** \'kalərē\ n : unit for measuring heat and energy value of food

**ca•lum•ni•ate** \kə'ləmnē‚āt\ vb -at-ed; -at•ing : slander — **ca•lum•ni•a•tion** \-‚ləmnē'āshən\ n

**cal•um•ny** \'kaləmnē\ n, pl -nies : false and malicious charge — **ca•lum•ni•ous** \kə'ləmnēəs\ adj

**calve** \'kav, 'kàv\ vb calved; calv•ing : give birth to a calf

**calves** pl of CALF

**ca•lyp•so** \kə'lipsō\ n, pl -sos : West Indian style of music

**ca•lyx** \'kāliks, 'kal-\ n, pl -lyx•es or -ly•ces \-lə‚sēz\ : sepals of a flower

**cam** \'kam\ n : machine part that slides or rotates irregularly to transmit linear motion

**ca•ma•ra•de•rie** \‚käm'rädərē, ‚kam-, -mə²-, -'rad-\ n : fellowship

**cam•bric** \'kāmbrik\ n : fine thin linen or cotton fabric

**came** past of COME

**cam•el** \'kaməl\ n : large hoofed mammal of desert areas

**ca•mel•lia** \kə'mēlyə\ n : shrub or tree grown for its showy roselike flowers or the flower itself

**cam•eo** \'kamē‚ō\ n, pl -eos : gem carved in relief

**cam•era** \'kamrə\ n : box with a lens for taking pictures — **cam•era•man** \-‚man, -mən\ n

**cam•ou•flage** \'kaməˌfläzh, -‚fläj\ vb : hide by disguising — **camouflage** n

**camp** \'kamp\ n 1 : place to stay temporarily esp. in a tent 2 : group living in a camp ～ vb : make or live in a camp — **camp•er** n — **camp•ground** n — **camp•site** n

**cam•paign** \kam'pān\ n : series of military operations or of activities meant to gain a result — **campaign** vb

**cam•pa•ni•le** \‚kampə'nēlē, -'nēl\ n, pl -ni•les or -ni•li \-'nēlē\ : bell tower

**cam•phor** \'kamfər\ n : gummy volatile aromatic compound from an evergreen tree (**cam•phor tree**)

**cam•pus** \'kampəs\ n : grounds and buildings of a college or school

¹**can** \kən, 'kan\ vb, past **could** \kəd, 'kúd\; pres sing & pl **can** 1 : be able to 2 : be permitted to by conscience or feeling 3 : have permission or liberty to

²**can** \'kan\ n : metal container ～ vb -nn- : preserve by sealing in airtight cans or jars — **can•ner** n — **can•nery** \-ərē\ n

**ca•nal** \kə'nal\ n 1 : tubular passage in the body 2 : channel filled with water

**can•a•pé** \'kanəpē, -‚pā\ n : appetizer

**ca•nard** \kə'närd\ n : false report

**ca•nary** \-'nerē\ n, pl -nar•ies : yellow or greenish finch often kept as a pet

**can•cel** \'kansəl\ vb -celed or -celled; -cel•ing or -cel•ling 1 : cross out 2 : destroy, neutralize, or match the force or effect of — **cancel** n — **can•cel•la•tion** \‚kansə'läshən\ n — **can•cel•er, can•cel•ler** n

**can•cer** \'kansər\ n 1 : malignant tumor that tends to spread 2 : slowly destructive evil — **can•cer•ous** \-sərəs\ adj — **can•cer•ous•ly** adv

**can•de•la•bra** \‚kandə'läbrə, -'lab-\ n : candelabrum

**can•de•la•brum** \-rəm\ n, pl -bra \-rə\ : ornamental branched candlestick

**can•did** \'kandəd\ adj 1 : frank 2 : unposed — **can•did•ly** adv — **can•did•ness** n

**can•di•date** \'kandə‚dāt, -dət\ n : one who seeks an office or membership — **can•di•da•cy** \-dəsē\ n

**can•dle** \'kand³l\ n : tallow or wax molded around a wick and burned to give light — **can•dle•light** n — **can•dle•stick** n

**can•dor** \'kandər\ n : frankness

**can•dy** \-dē\ n, pl -dies : food made

from sugar ~ *vb* **-died; -dy·ing** : encrust in sugar

**cane** \'kān\ *n* **1** : slender plant stem **2** : a tall woody grass or reed **3** : stick for walking or beating ~ *vb* **caned; can·ing 1** : beat with a cane **2** : weave or make with cane — **can·er** *n*

**ca·nine** \'kā,nīn\ *adj* : relating to dogs ~ *n* **1** : pointed tooth next to the incisors **2** : dog

**can·is·ter** \'kanəstər\ *n* : cylindrical container

**can·ker** \'kaŋkər\ *n* : mouth ulcer — **can·ker·ous** \-kərəs\ *adj*

**can·na·bis** \'kanəbəs\ *n* : preparation derived from hemp

**can·ni·bal** \'kanəbəl\ *n* : human or animal that eats its own kind — **can·ni·bal·ism** \-bə,lizəm\ *n* — **can·ni·bal·is·tic** \,kanəbə'listik\ *adj*

**can·ni·bal·ize** \'kanəbə,līz\ *vb* **-ized; -iz·ing 1** : take usable parts from **2** : practice cannibalism

**can·non** \'kanən\ *n, pl* **-nons** *or* **-non 1** : large heavy gun — **can·non·ball** *n* — **can·non·eer** \,kanə'nir\ *n*

**can·non·ade** \,kanə'nād\ *n* : heavy artillery fire ~ *vb* **-ad·ed; -ad·ing** : bombard

**can·not** \'kan,ät; kə'nät\ : can not — **cannot but** : be bound to

**can·ny** \'kanē\ *adj* **-ni·er; -est** : shrewd — **can·ni·ly** *adv* — **can·ni·ness** *n*

**ca·noe** \kə'nü\ *n* : narrow sharp-ended boat propelled by paddles — **canoe** *vb* — **ca·noe·ist** *n*

**¹can·on** \'kanən\ *n* **1** : regulation governing a church **2** : authoritative list **3** : an accepted principle

**²canon** *n* : clergy member in a cathedral

**ca·non·i·cal** \kə'nänikəl\ *adj* **1** : relating to or conforming to a canon **2** : orthodox — **ca·non·i·cal·ly** *adv*

**can·on·ize** \'kanə,nīz\ *vb* **-ized; -iz·ing** : recognize as a saint — **can·on·iza·tion** \,kanənə-'zāshən\ *n*

**can·o·py** \'kanəpē\ *n, pl* **-pies** : overhanging cover — **canopy** *vb*

**¹cant** \'kant\ *n* **1** : slanting surface **2** : slant ~ *vb* **1** : tip up **2** : lean to one side

**²cant** *vb* : talk hypocritically ~ *n* **1** : jargon **2** : insincere talk

**can't** \'kant, 'kånt\ : can not

**can·ta·loupe** \'kant³l,ōp\ *n* : muskmelon with orange flesh

**can·tan·ker·ous** \kan'taŋkərəs\ *adj* : hard to deal with — **can·tan·ker·ous·ly** *adv* — **can·tan·ker·ous·ness** *n*

**can·ta·ta** \kən'tätə\ *n* : choral work

**can·teen** \kan'tēn\ *n* **1** : place of recreation for service personnel **2** : water container

**can·ter** \'kantər\ *n* : slow gallop — **can·ter** *vb*

**can·ti·cle** \'kantikəl\ *n* : liturgical song

**can·ti·le·ver** \'kant³l,ēvər, -,ev-\ *n* : beam or structure supported only at one end

**can·to** \'kan,tō\ *n, pl* **-tos** : major division of a long poem

**can·tor** \'kantər\ *n* : synagogue official who sings liturgical music

**can·vas** \'kanvəs\ *n* **1** : strong cloth orig. used for making tents and sails **2** : set of sails **3** : oil painting

**can·vass** \-vəs\ *vb* : solicit votes, orders, or opinions from ~ *n* : act of canvassing — **can·vass·er** *n*

**can·yon** \'kanyən\ *n* : deep valley with steep sides

**cap** \'kap\ *n* **1** : covering for the head **2** : top or cover like a cap **3** : upper limit ~ *vb* **-pp- 1** : provide or protect with a cap **2** : climax — **cap·ful** \-,fúl\ *n*

**ca·pa·ble** \'kāpəbəl\ *adj* : able to do something — **ca·pa·bil·i·ty** \,kāpə-'bilətē\ *n* — **ca·pa·bly** \'kāpəblē\ *adv*

**ca·pa·cious** \kə'pāshəs\ *adj* : able to contain much

**ca·pac·i·tance** \kə'pasətəns\ *n* : ability to store electrical energy

**ca·pac·i·tor** \-sətər\ *n* : device for storing electrical energy

**ca·pac·i·ty** \-sətē\ *n, pl* **-ties 1** : ability to contain **2** : volume **3** : ability **4** : role or job ~ *adj* : equaling maximum capacity

**¹cape** \'kāp\ *n* : point of land jutting out into water

**²cape** *n* : garment that drapes over the shoulders

**¹ca·per** \'kāpər\ *n* : flower bud of a shrub pickled for use as a relish

**²caper** *vb* : leap or prance about ~ *n* **1** : frolicsome leap **2** : escapade

**cap·il·lary** \'kapə,lerē\ *adj* **1** : resembling a hair **2** : having a very small bore ~ *n, pl* **-lar·ies** : tiny thin-walled blood vessel

¹**cap·i·tal** \'kapət³l\ *adj* **1** : punishable by death **2** : being in the series A, B, C rather than a, b, c **3** : relating to capital **4** : excellent ~ *n* **1** : capital letter **2** : seat of government **3** : wealth **4** : total face value of a company's stock **5** : investors as a group

²**capital** *n* : top part of a column

**cap·i·tal·ism** \-,izəm\ *n* : economic system of private ownership of capital

**cap·i·tal·ist** \-ist\ *n* **1** : person with capital invested in business **2** : believer in capitalism — *adj* **1** : owning capital **2** : practicing, advocating, or marked by capitalism — **cap·i·tal·is·tic** \,kapət³l'istik\ *adj*

**cap·i·tal·ize** \-,īz\ *vb* -ized; -iz·ing **1** : write or print with a capital letter **2** : use as capital **3** : supply capital for **4** : turn something to advantage — **cap·i·tal·iza·tion** \,kapət³lə-'zāshən\ *n*

**cap·i·tol** \'kapət³l\ *n* : building in which a legislature sits

**ca·pit·u·late** \kə'pichə,lāt\ *vb* -lat·ed; -lat·ing : surrender — **ca·pit·u·la·tion** \-,pichə'lāshən\ *n*

**ca·pon** \'kā,pän, -pən\ *n* : castrated male chicken

**ca·price** \kə'prēs\ *n* : whim — **ca·pri·cious** \-'prishəs\ *adj* — **ca·pri·cious·ly** *adv* — **ca·pri·cious·ness** *n*

**cap·size** \'kap,sīz, kap'sīz\ *vb* -sized; -siz·ing : overturn

**cap·stan** \'kapstən, -,stan\ *n* : upright winch

**cap·sule** \'kapsəl, -sül\ *n* **1** : enveloping cover (as for medicine) **2** : small pressurized compartment for astronauts ~ *adj* : very brief or compact — **cap·su·lar** \-sələr\ *adj* — **cap·su·lat·ed** \-sə,lātəd\ *adj*

**cap·tain** \'kaptən\ *n* **1** : commander of a body of troops **2** : officer in charge of a ship **3** : commissioned officer in the navy ranking next below a rear admiral or a commodore **4** : commissioned officer (as in the army) ranking next below a major **5** : leader ~ *vb* : be captain of — **cap·tain·cy** *n*

**cap·tion** \'kapshən\ *n* **1** : title **2** : explanation with an illustration — **caption** *vb*

**cap·tious** \'kapshəs\ *adj* : tending to find fault — **cap·tious·ly** *adv*

**cap·ti·vate** \'kaptə,vāt\ *vb* -vat·ed; -vat·ing : attract and charm — **cap·ti·va·tion** \,kaptə'vāshən\ *n* — **cap·ti·va·tor** \'kaptə,vātər\ *n*

**cap·tive** \-tiv\ *adj* **1** : made prisoner **2** : confined or under control — **captive** *n* — **cap·tiv·i·ty** \kap'tivətē\ *n*

**cap·tor** \'kaptər\ *n* : one that captures

**cap·ture** \-chər\ *n* : seizure by force or trickery ~ *vb* -tured; -tur·ing : take captive

**car** \'kär\ *n* **1** : vehicle moved on wheels **2** : cage of an elevator

**ca·rafe** \kə'raf, -'räf\ *n* : decanter

**car·a·mel** \'karəməl, 'kärməl\ *n* **1** : burnt sugar used for flavoring and coloring **2** : firm chewy candy

¹**carat** *var of* KARAT

²**car·at** \'karət\ *n* : unit of weight for precious stones

**car·a·van** \'karə,van\ *n* : travelers journeying together (as in a line)

**car·a·way** \'karə,wā\ *n* : aromatic herb with seeds used in seasoning

**car·bine** \'kär,bēn, -,bīn\ *n* : short-barreled rifle

**car·bo·hy·drate** \,kärbō'hī,drāt, -drət\ *n* : compound of carbon, hydrogen, and oxygen

**car·bon** \'kärbən\ *n* **1** : chemical element occurring in nature esp. as diamond and graphite **2** : piece of carbon paper or a copy made with it

¹**car·bon·ate** \'kärbə,nāt, -nət\ *n* : salt or ester of a carbon-containing acid

²**car·bon·ate** \-,nāt\ *vb* -at·ed; -at·ing : impregnate with carbon dioxide — **car·bon·ation** \,kärbə'nāshən\ *n*

**carbon paper** *n* : thin paper coated with a pigment for making copies

**car·bun·cle** \'kär,bəŋkəl\ *n* : painful inflammation of the skin and underlying tissue

**car·bu·re·tor** \'kärbə,rātər, -byə-\ *n* : device for mixing fuel and air

**car·cass** \'kärkəs\ *n* : dead body

**car·cin·o·gen** \kär'sinəjən\ *n* : agent causing cancer — **car·ci·no·gen·ic** \,kärs³nō'jenik\ *adj*

**car·ci·no·ma** \,kärs³n'ōmə\ *n, pl* -mas *or* -ma·ta \-mətə\ : malignant tumor

¹**card** \'kärd\ *vb* : comb (fibers) before spinning ~ *n* : device for carding fibers — **card·er** *n*

²**card** *n* **1** : playing card **2** *pl* : game played with playing cards **3** : small flat piece of paper

**card·board** *n* : stiff material like paper

**car·di·ac** \'kärdē,ak\ *adj* : relating to the heart

**car·di·gan** \'kärdigən\ *n* : sweater with an opening in the front

¹**car·di·nal** \'kärd°nəl\ *n* 1 : official of the Roman Catholic Church 2 : bright red songbird

²**cardinal** *adj* : of basic importance

**cardinal number** *n* : number (as 1, 82, 357) used in counting

**car·di·ol·o·gy** \,kärdē'äləjē\ *n* : study of the heart — **car·di·ol·o·gist** \-jist\ *n*

**car·dio·vas·cu·lar** \-ō'vaskyələr\ *adj* : relating to the heart and blood vessels

**care** \'ker\ *n* 1 : anxiety 2 : watchful attention 3 : supervision ~ *vb* **cared; car·ing** 1 : feel anxiety or concern 2 : like 3 : provide care — **care·free** *adj* — **care·ful** \-fəl\ *adj* — **care·ful·ly** *adv* — **care·ful·ness** *n* — **care·giv·er** \-,givər\ *n* — **care·less** *adj* — **care·less·ly** *adv* — **care·less·ness** *n*

**ca·reen** \kə'rēn\ *vb* 1 : sway from side to side 2 : career

**ca·reer** \kə'rir\ *n* : vocation ~ *vb* : go at top speed

**ca·ress** \kə'res\ *n* : tender touch ~ *vb* : touch lovingly or tenderly

**car·et** \'karət\ *n* : mark ∧ showing where something is to be inserted

**care·tak·er** *n* : one in charge for another or temporarily

**car·go** \'kärgō\ *n, pl* **-goes** *or* **-gos** : transported goods

**car·i·bou** \'karə,bü\ *n, pl* **-bou** *or* **-bous** : large No. American deer

**car·i·ca·ture** \'karikə,chùr\ *n* : distorted representation for humor or ridicule — **caricature** *vb* — **car·i·ca·tur·ist** \-ist\ *n*

**car·ies** \'karēz\ *n, pl* **caries** : tooth decay

**car·il·lon** \'karə,län\ *n* : set of tuned bells

**car·jack·ing** \'kär,jakiŋ\ *n* : theft of an automobile by force or intimidation — **car·jack·er** *n*

**car·mine** \'kärmən, -,mīn\ *n* : vivid red

**car·nage** \'kärnij\ *n* : slaughter

**car·nal** \'kärn°l\ *adj* : sensual — **car·nal·i·ty** \kär'nalətē\ *n* — **car·nal·ly** *adv*

**car·na·tion** \kär'nāshən\ *n* : showy flower

**car·ni·val** \'kärnəvəl\ *n* 1 : festival 2 : traveling enterprise offering amusements

**car·ni·vore** \-,vōr\ *n* : flesh-eating animal — **car·niv·o·rous** \kär'nivərəs\ *adj* — **car·niv·o·rous·ly** *adv* — **car·niv·o·rous·ness** *n*

**car·ol** \'karəl\ *n* : song of joy — **carol** *vb* — **car·ol·er, car·ol·ler** \-ələr\ *n*

**car·om** \-əm\ *n or vb* : rebound

**ca·rouse** \kə'raùz\ *vb* **-roused; -rousing** : drink and be boisterous — **carouse** *n* — **ca·rous·er** *n*

**car·ou·sel, car·rou·sel** \,karə'sel, 'karə,-\ *n* : merry-go-round

¹**carp** \'kärp\ *vb* : find fault

²**carp** *n, pl* **carp** *or* **carps** : freshwater fish

**car·pel** \'kärpəl\ *n* : modified leaf forming part of the ovary of a flower

**car·pen·ter** \'kärpəntər\ *n* : one who builds with wood — **carpenter** *vb* — **car·pen·try** \-trē\ *n*

**car·pet** \'kärpət\ *n* : fabric floor covering ~ *vb* : cover with a carpet — **car·pet·ing** \-iŋ\ *n*

**car·port** *n* : open-sided automobile shelter

**car·riage** \'karij\ *n* 1 : conveyance 2 : manner of holding oneself 3 : wheeled vehicle

**car·ri·on** \'karēən\ *n* : dead and decaying flesh

**car·rot** \'karət\ *n* : orange root vegetable

**car·ry** \'karē\ *vb* **-ried; -ry·ing** 1 : move while supporting 2 : hold (oneself) in a specified way 3 : support 4 : keep in stock 5 : reach to a distance 6 : win — **car·ri·er** \-ēər\ *n* — **carry on** *vb* 1 : conduct 2 : behave excitedly — **carry out** *vb* : put into effect

**cart** \'kärt\ *n* : wheeled vehicle ~ *vb* : carry in a cart — **cart·age** \-ij\ *n* — **cart·er** *n*

**car·tel** \kär'tel\ *n* : business combination designed to limit competition

**car·ti·lage** \'kärt°lij\ *n* : elastic skeletal tissue — **car·ti·lag·i·nous** \,kärt°l'ajənəs\ *adj*

**car·tog·ra·phy** \kär'tägrəfē\ *n* : making of maps — **car·tog·ra·pher** \-fər\ *n*

**car·ton** \'kärt°n\ *n* : cardboard box

**car·toon** \kär'tün\ *n* 1 : humorous drawing 2 : comic strip — **cartoon** *vb* — **car·toon·ist** *n*

**car·tridge** \'kärtrij\ *vb* 1 : tube containing powder and a bullet or shot for a firearm 2 : container of material for insertion into an apparatus

**carve** \'kärv\ *vb* **carved; carv·ing** 1 : cut with care 2 : cut into pieces or slices — **carv·er** *n*

**cas·cade** \kas'kād\ *n* : small steep waterfall ∼ *vb* **-cad·ed; -cad·ing** : fall in a cascade

¹**case** \'kās\ *n* 1 : particular instance 2 : convincing argument 3 : inflectional form esp. of a noun or pronoun 4 : fact 5 : lawsuit 6 : instance of disease — **in case** : as a precaution — **in case of** : in the event of

²**case** *n* 1 : box 2 : outer covering ∼ *vb* **cased; cas·ing** 1 : enclose 2 : inspect

**case·ment** \-mənt\ *n* : window that opens like a door

**cash** \'kash\ *n* 1 : ready money 2 : money paid at the time of purchase ∼ *vb* : give or get cash for

**ca·shew** \'kashü, kə'shü\ *n* : tropical American tree or its nut

¹**ca·shier** \ka'shir\ *vb* : dismiss in disgrace

²**cash·ier** *n* : person who receives and records payments

**cash·mere** \'kazh₁mir, 'kash-\ *n* : fine goat's wool or a fabric of this

**ca·si·no** \kə'sēnō\ *n, pl* **-nos** : place for gambling

**cask** \'kask\ *n* : barrel-shaped container for liquids

**cas·ket** \'kaskət\ *n* : coffin

**cas·se·role** \'kasə₁rōl\ *n* : baking dish or the food cooked in this

**cas·sette** \kə'set, ka-\ *n* : case containing magnetic tape

**cas·sock** \'kasək\ *n* : long clerical garment

**cast** \'kast\ *vb* **cast; cast·ing** 1 : throw 2 : deposit (a ballot) 3 : assign parts in a play 4 : mold ∼ *n* 1 : throw 2 : appearance 3 : rigid surgical dressing 4 : actors in a play

**cas·ta·nets** \₁kastə'nets\ *n pl* : shells clicked together in the hand

**cast·away** \'kastə₁wā\ *n* : survivor of a shipwreck — **castaway** *adj*

**caste** \'kast\ *n* : social class or rank

**cast·er** \'kastər\ *n* : small wheel on furniture

**cas·ti·gate** \'kastə₁gāt\ *vb* **-gat·ed; -gat·ing** : chastise severely — **cas·ti-**

**ga·tion** \₁kastə'gāshən\ *n* — **cas·ti·ga·tor** \'kastə₁gātər\ *n*

**cast iron** *n* : hard brittle alloy of iron

**cas·tle** \'kasəl\ *n* : fortified building

**cast–off** *adj* : thrown away — **cast·off** *n*

**cas·trate** \'kas₁trāt\ *vb* **-trat·ed; -trat·ing** : remove the testes of — **cas·tra·tion** \ka'strāshən\ *n*

**ca·su·al** \'kazhəwəl\ *adj* 1 : happening by chance 2 : showing little concern 3 : informal — **ca·su·al·ly** \-ē\ *adv* — **ca·su·al·ness** *n*

**ca·su·al·ty** \-tē\ *n, pl* **-ties** 1 : serious or fatal accident 2 : one injured, lost, or destroyed

**ca·su·ist·ry** \'kazhəwəstrē\ *n, pl* **-ries** : rationalization — **ca·su·ist** \-wist\ *n*

**cat** \'kat\ *n* 1 : small domestic mammal 2 : related animal (as a lion) — **cat·like** *adj*

**cat·a·clysm** \'katə₁klizəm\ *n* : violent change — **cat·a·clys·mal** \₁katə'klizməl\, **cat·a·clys·mic** \-'klizmik\ *adj*

**cat·a·comb** \'katə₁kōm\ *n* : underground burial place

**cat·a·log, cat·a·logue** \'kat³l₁óg\ *n* 1 : list 2 : book containing a description of items ∼ *vb* **-loged** *or* **-logued; -log·ing** *or* **-logu·ing** : make a catalog of 2 : enter in a catalog — **cat·a·log·er, cat·a·logu·er** *n*

**ca·tal·pa** \kə'talpə\ *n* : tree with broad leaves and long pods

**ca·tal·y·sis** \kə'taləsəs\ *n, pl* **-y·ses** \-₁sēz\ : increase in the rate of chemical reaction caused by a substance (**cat·a·lyst** \'kat³list\) that is itself unchanged — **cat·a·lyt·ic** \₁kat³l-'itik\ *adj*

**cat·a·ma·ran** \₁katəmə'ran\ *n* : boat with twin hulls

**cat·a·mount** \'katə₁maúnt\ *n* : cougar

**cat·a·pult** \'katə₁pəlt, -₁púlt\ *n* : device for hurling or launching — **catapult** *vb*

**cat·a·ract** \'katə₁rakt\ *n* 1 : large waterfall 2 : cloudiness of the lens of the eye

**ca·tarrh** \kə'tär\ *n* : inflammation of the nose and throat

**ca·tas·tro·phe** \kə'tastrə₁fē\ *n* 1 : great disaster or misfortune 2 : utter failure — **cat·a·stroph·ic** \₁katə-'sträfik\ *adj* — **cat·a·stroph·i·cal·ly** \-iklē\ *adv*

**cat·bird** *n* : American songbird

**cat·call** *n* : noise of disapproval

**catch** \'kach, 'kech\ *vb* **caught** \'kȯt\; **catch·ing 1** : capture esp. after pursuit **2** : trap **3** : detect esp. by surprise **4** : grasp **5** : get entangled **6** : become affected with or by **7** : seize and hold firmly ∼ *n* **1** : act of catching **2** : something caught **3** : something that fastens **4** : hidden difficulty — **catch·er** *n*

**catch·ing** \-iŋ\ *adj* : infectious

**catch·up** \'kechəp, 'kach-; 'katsəp\ *var of* KETCHUP

**catch·word** *n* : slogan

**catchy** \-ē\ *adj* **catch·i·er; -est** : likely to catch interest

**cat·e·chism** \'katə,kizəm\ *n* : set of questions and answers esp. to teach religious doctrine

**cat·e·gor·i·cal** \,katə'górikəl\ *adj* : absolute — **cat·e·gor·i·cal·ly** \-klē\ *adv*

**cat·e·go·ry** \'katə,gōrē\ *n, pl* **-ries** : group or class — **cat·e·go·ri·za·tion** \,katigərə'zāshən\ *n* — **cat·e·go·rize** \'katigə,rīz\ *vb*

**ca·ter** \'kātər\ *vb* **1** : provide food for **2** : supply what is wanted — **ca·ter·er** *n*

**cat·er·cor·ner** \,katē'kȯrnər, ,katə-, ,kitē-\, **cat·er—cor·nered** *adv or adj* : in a diagonal position

**cat·er·pil·lar** \'katər,pilər\ *n* : butterfly or moth larva

**cat·er·waul** \'katər,wȯl\ *vb* : make the harsh cry of a cat — **caterwaul** *n*

**cat·fish** *n* : big-headed fish with feelers about the mouth

**cat·gut** *n* : tough cord made usu. from sheep intestines

**ca·thar·sis** \kə'thärsəs\ *n, pl* **ca·thar·ses** \-,sēz\ : a purging — **ca·thar·tic** \kə'thärtik\ *adj or n*

**ca·the·dral** \-'thēdrəl\ *n* : principal church of a diocese

**cath·e·ter** \'kathətər\ *n* : tube for insertion into a body cavity

**cath·ode** \'kath,ōd\ *n* **1** : negative electrode **2** : positive battery terminal — **ca·thod·ic** \ka'thädik\ *adj*

**cath·o·lic** \'kathəlik\ *adj* **1** : universal **2** *cap* : relating to Roman Catholics

**Cath·o·lic** *n* : member of the Roman Catholic Church — **Ca·thol·i·cism** \kə'thälə,sizəm\ *n*

**cat·kin** \'katkən\ *n* : long dense flower cluster

**cat·nap** *n* : short light nap — **catnap** *vb*

**cat·nip** \-,nip\ *n* : aromatic mint relished by cats

**cat's—paw** *n, pl* **cat's—paws** : person used as if a tool

**cat·sup** \'kechəp, 'kach-; 'katsəp\ *var of* KETCHUP

**cat·tail** *n* : marsh herb with furry brown spikes

**cat·tle** \'katᵊl\ *n pl* : domestic bovines — **cat·tle·man** \-mən, -,man\ *n*

**cat·ty** \'katē\ *adj* **-ti·er; -est** : mean or spiteful — **cat·ti·ly** *adv* — **cat·ti·ness** *n*

**cat·walk** *n* : high narrow walk

**Cau·ca·sian** \kȯ'kāzhən\ *adj* : relating to the white race — **Caucasian** *n*

**cau·cus** \'kȯkəs\ *n* : political meeting — **caucus** *vb*

**caught** *past of* CATCH

**cauldron** \'kȯldrən\ *n* : large kettle

**cau·li·flow·er** \'kȯli,flaůər, 'käl-\ *n* : vegetable having a compact head of usu. white undeveloped flowers

**caulk** \'kȯk\ *vb* : make seams watertight — **caulk** *n* — **caulk·er** *n*

**caus·al** \'kȯzəl\ *adj* : relating to or being a cause — **cau·sal·i·ty** \kȯ'zalətē\ *n* — **caus·al·ly** \'kȯzəlē\ *adv*

**cause** \'kȯz\ *n* **1** : something that brings about a result **2** : reason **3** : lawsuit **4** : principle or movement to support ∼ *vb* **caused; caus·ing** : be the cause of — **cau·sa·tion** \kȯ'zāshən\ *n* — **caus·ative** \'kȯzətiv\ *adj* — **cause·less** *adj* — **caus·er** *n*

**cause·way** *n* : raised road esp. over water

**caus·tic** \'kȯstik\ *adj* **1** : corrosive **2** : sharp or biting — **caustic** *n*

**cau·ter·ize** \'kȯtə,rīz\ *vb* **-ized; -iz·ing** : burn to prevent infection or bleeding — **cau·ter·i·za·tion** \,kȯtərə'zāshən\ *n*

**cau·tion** \'kȯshən\ *n* **1** : warning **2** : care or prudence ∼ *vb* : warn — **cau·tion·ary** \-shə,nerē\ *adj*

**cau·tious** \'kȯshəs\ *adj* : taking caution — **cau·tious·ly** *adv* — **cau·tious·ness** *n*

**cav·al·cade** \,kavəl'kād, 'kavəl,-\ *n* **1** : procession on horseback **2** : series

**cav·a·lier** \,kavə'lir\ *n* : mounted soldier ∼ *adj* : disdainful or arrogant — **cav·a·lier·ly** *adv*

**cav·al·ry** \'kavəlrē\ *n, pl* **-ries** : troops on horseback or in vehicles — **cav·al·ry·man** \-mən, -,man\ *n*

**cave** \'kāv\ *n* : natural underground chamber — **cave in** *vb* : collapse

**cav·ern** \'kavərn\ *n* : large cave — **cav·ern·ous** *adj* — **cav·ern·ous·ly** *adv*

**cav·i·ar, cav·i·are** \'kavē,är, 'käv-\ *n* : salted fish roe

**cav·il** \'kavəl\ *vb* **-iled** *or* **-illed; -il·ing** *or* **-il·ling** : raise trivial objections — **cavil** *n* — **cav·il·er, cav·il·ler** *n*

**cav·i·ty** \'kavətē\ *n, pl* **-ties** **1** : unfilled place within a mass **2** : decay in a tooth

**ca·vort** \kə'vȯrt\ *vb* : prance or caper

**caw** \'kȯ\ *vb* : utter the harsh call of the crow — **caw** *n*

**cay·enne pepper** \,kī'en-, ,kā-\ *n* : ground dried fruits of a hot pepper

**CD** \,sē'dē\ *n* : compact disc

**cease** \'sēs\ *vb* **ceased; ceas·ing** : stop

**cease·less** \-ləs\ *adj* : continuous

**ce·dar** \'sēdər\ *n* : cone-bearing tree with fragrant durable wood

**cede** \'sēd\ *vb* **ced·ed; ced·ing** : surrender — **ced·er** *n*

**ceil·ing** \'sēliŋ\ *n* **1** : overhead surface of a room **2** : upper limit

**cel·e·brate** \'selə,brāt\ *vb* **-brat·ed; -brat·ing** **1** : perform with appropriate rites **2** : honor with ceremonies **3** : extol — **cel·e·brant** \-brənt\ *n* — **cel·e·bra·tion** \,selə'brāshən\ *n* — **cel·e·bra·tor** \'selə,brātər\ *n*

**cel·e·brat·ed** \-əd\ *adj* : renowned

**ce·leb·ri·ty** \sə'lebrətē\ *n, pl* **-ties** **1** : renown **2** : well-known person

**ce·ler·i·ty** \sə'lerətē\ *n* : speed

**cel·ery** \'selərē\ *n, pl* **-er·ies** : herb grown for crisp edible stalks

**ce·les·ta** \si'lestə\ **ce·leste** \sə'lest\ *n* : keyboard musical instrument

**ce·les·tial** \sə'leschəl\ *adj* **1** : relating to the sky **2** : heavenly

**cel·i·ba·cy** \'seləbəsē\ *n* **1** : state of being unmarried **2** : abstention from sexual intercourse — **cel·i·bate** \'seləbət\ *n or adj*

**cell** \'sel\ *n* **1** : small room **2** : tiny mass of protoplasm that forms the fundamental unit of living matter **3** : container holding an electrolyte for generating electricity — **celled** *adj*

**cel·lar** \'selər\ *n* : room or area below ground

**cel·lo** \'chelō\ *n, pl* **-los** : bass member of the violin family — **cel·list** \-ist\ *n*

**cel·lo·phane** \'selə,fān\ *n* : thin transparent cellulose wrapping

**cell phone** *n* : portable cordless telephone for use in a system of radio transmitters

**cel·lu·lar** \'selyələr\ *adj* : relating to or consisting of cells

**cel·lu·lose** \'selyə,lōs\ *n* : complex plant carbohydrate

**Cel·sius** \'selsēəs\ *adj* : relating to a thermometer scale on which the freezing point of water is 0° and the boiling point is 100°

**ce·ment** \si'ment\ *n* **1** : powdery mixture of clay and limestone that hardens when wetted **2** : binding agent ~ *vb* : unite or cover with cement

**cem·e·tery** \'semə,terē\ *n, pl* **-ter·ies** : burial ground

**cen·ser** \'sensər\ *n* : vessel for burning incense

**cen·sor** \'sensər\ *n* : one with power to suppress anything objectionable (as in printed matter) ~ *vb* : be a censor of — **cen·so·ri·al** \sen'sōrēəl\ *adj* — **cen·sor·ship** \-,ship\ *n*

**cen·so·ri·ous** \sen'sōrēəs\ *adj* : critical — **cen·so·ri·ous·ly** *adv* — **cen·so·ri·ous·ness** *n*

**cen·sure** \'senchər\ *n* : official reprimand ~ *vb* **-sured; -sur·ing** : find blameworthy — **cen·sur·able** *adj*

**cen·sus** \'sensəs\ *n* : periodic population count — **census** *vb*

**cent** \'sent\ *n* : monetary unit equal to $\frac{1}{100}$ of a basic unit of value

**cen·taur** \'sen,tȯr\ *n* : mythological creature that is half man and half horse

**cen·ten·ni·al** \sen'tenēəl\ *n* : 100th anniversary — **centennial** *adj*

**cen·ter** \'sentər\ *n* **1** : middle point **2** : point of origin or greatest concentration **3** : region of concentrated population **4** : player near the middle of the team ~ *vb* **1** : place, fix, or concentrate at or around a center **2** : have a center — **cen·ter·piece** *n*

**cen·ti·grade** \'sentə,grād, 'sänt-\ *adj* : Celsius

**cen·ti·me·ter** \'sentə,mētər, 'sänt-\ *n* : $\frac{1}{100}$ meter

**cen·ti·pede** \'sentə,pēd\ *n* : long flat many-legged arthropod

**cen·tral** \'sentrəl\ *adj* **1** : constituting or being near a center **2** : essential or principal — **cen·tral·ly** *adv*

**cen·tral·ize** \-trə,līz\ *vb* **-ized; -iz·ing**

: bring to a central point or under central control — **cen·tral·i·za·tion** \ˌsentrələ'zāshən\ n — **cen·tral·iz·er** n

**cen·tre** chiefly Brit var of CENTER

**cen·trif·u·gal** \sen'trifyəgəl, -'trifigəl\ adj : acting in a direction away from a center or axis

**cen·tri·fuge** \'sentrə,fyüj\ n : machine that separates substances by spinning

**cen·trip·e·tal** \sen'tripət°l\ adj : acting in a direction toward a center or axis

**cen·tu·ri·on** \sen'chu̇rēən, -'tu̇r-\ n : Roman military officer

**cen·tu·ry** \'senchərē\ n, pl -ries : 100 years

**ce·ram·ic** \sə'ramik\ n 1 pl : art or process of shaping and hardening articles from clay 2 : product of ceramics — **ceramic** adj

**ce·re·al** \'sirēəl\ adj : made of or relating to grain or to the plants that produce it ~ n 1 : grass yielding edible grain 2 : food prepared from a cereal grain

**cer·e·bel·lum** \ˌserə'beləm\ n, pl -bel·lums or -bel·la \-'belə\ : part of the brain controlling muscular coordination — **cer·e·bel·lar** \-ər\ adj

**ce·re·bral** \sə'rēbrəl, 'serə-\ adj 1 : relating to the brain, intellect, or cerebrum 2 : appealing to the intellect

**cerebral palsy** n : disorder caused by brain damage and marked esp. by defective muscle control

**cer·e·brate** \'serə,brāt\ vb -brat·ed; -brat·ing : think — **cer·e·bra·tion** \ˌserə'brāshən\ n

**ce·re·brum** \sə'rēbrəm, 'serə-\ n, pl -brums or -bra \-brə\ : part of the brain that contains the higher nervous centers

**cer·e·mo·ny** \'serə,mōnē\ n, pl -nies 1 : formal act prescribed by law, ritual, or convention 2 : prescribed procedures — **cer·e·mo·ni·al** \ˌserə'mōnēəl\ adj or n — **cer·e·mo·ni·ous** \-nēəs\ adj

**ce·rise** \sə'rēs\ n : moderate red

**cer·tain** \'sərt°n\ adj 1 : settled 2 : true 3 : specific but not named 4 : bound 5 : assured ~ pron : certain ones — **cer·tain·ly** adv — **cer·tain·ty** \-tē\ n

**cer·tif·i·cate** \sər'tifikət\ n : document establishing truth or fulfillment

**cer·ti·fy** \'sərtə,fī\ vb -fied; -fy·ing 1

: verify 2 : endorse — **cer·ti·fi·able** \-ˌfīəbəl\ adj — **cer·ti·fi·ably** \-blē\ adv — **cer·ti·fi·ca·tion** \ˌsərtəfə'kāshən\ n — **cer·ti·fi·er** n

**cer·ti·tude** \'sərtə,tüd, -,tyüd\ n : state of being certain

**cer·vix** \'sərviks\ n, pl -vi·ces \-və,sēz\ or -vix·es 1 : neck 2 : narrow end of the uterus — **cer·vi·cal** \-vikəl\ adj

**ce·sar·e·an** \si'zarēən\ n : surgical operation to deliver a baby — **cesarean** adj

**ce·si·um** \'sēzēəm\ n : silver-white soft ductile chemical element

**ces·sa·tion** \se'sāshən\ n : a halting

**ces·sion** \'seshən\ n : a yielding

**cess·pool** \'ses,pül\ n : underground sewage pit

**Cha·blis** \'shab,lē; sha'blē\ n, pl Cha·blis \-,lēz, -'blēz\ : dry white wine

**chafe** \'chāf\ vb **chafed**; **chaf·ing** 1 : fret 2 : make sore by rubbing

**chaff** \'chaf\ n 1 : debris separated from grain 2 : something worthless

**chaf·ing dish** \'chāfiŋ-\ n : utensil for cooking at the table

**cha·grin** \shə'grin\ n : embarrassment or humiliation ~ vb : cause to feel chagrin

**chain** \'chān\ n 1 : flexible series of connected links 2 pl : fetters 3 : linked series ~ vb : bind or connect with a chain

**chair** \'cher\ n 1 : seat with a back 2 : position of authority or dignity 3 : chairman ~ vb : act as chairman of

**chair·man** \-mən\ n : presiding officer — **chair·man·ship** n

**chair·wom·an** \-ˌwu̇mən\ n : woman who is a presiding officer

**chaise longue** \'shāz'lȯŋ\ n, pl **chaise longues** \-lȯŋ, -'lȯŋz\ : long chair for reclining

**cha·let** \sha'lā\ n : Swiss mountain cottage with overhanging roof

**chal·ice** \'chaləs\ n : eucharistic cup

**chalk** \'chȯk\ n 1 : soft limestone 2 : chalky material used as a crayon ~ vb : mark with chalk — **chalky** adj — **chalk up** vb 1 : credit 2 : achieve

**chalk·board** n : blackboard

**chal·lenge** \'chalənj\ vb -lenged; -leng·ing 1 : dispute 2 : invite or dare to act or compete — **challenge** n — **chal·leng·er** n

**cham·ber** \'chāmbər\ n 1 : room 2 : enclosed space 3 : legislative meeting place or body **4** *pl* : judge's consultation room — **cham·bered** *adj*

**cham·ber·maid** *n* : bedroom maid

**chamber music** *n* : music by a small group for a small audience

**cha·me·leon** \kə'mēlyən\ *n* : small lizard whose skin changes color

**cham·ois** \'shamē\ *n, pl* **cham·ois** \-ē, -ēz\ **1** : goatlike antelope **2** : soft leather

**¹champ** \'champ, 'chämp\ *vb* : chew noisily

**²champ** \'champ\ *n* : champion

**cham·pagne** \sham'pān\ *n* : sparkling white wine

**cham·pi·on** \'champēən\ *n* **1** : advocate or defender **2** : winning contestant ∼ *vb* : protect or fight for

**cham·pi·on·ship** \-,ship\ *n* **1** : title of a champion **2** : contest to pick a champion

**chance** \'chans\ *n* **1** : unpredictable element of existence **2** : opportunity **3** : probability **4** : risk **5** : raffle ticket ∼ *vb* **chanced; chanc·ing 1** : happen **2** : encounter unexpectedly **3** : risk — **chance** *adj*

**chan·cel** \'chansəl\ *n* : part of a church around the altar

**chan·cel·lery, chan·cel·lory** \'chansələrē\ *n, pl* **-ler·ies** *or* **-lor·ies 1** : position of a chancellor **2** : chancellor's office

**chan·cel·lor** \-ələr\ *n* **1** : chief or high state official **2** : head of a university — **chan·cel·lor·ship** *n*

**chan·cre** \'shaŋkər\ *n* : skin ulcer esp. from syphilis

**chancy** \'chansē\ *adj* **chanc·i·er; -est** : risky

**chan·de·lier** \,shandə'lir\ *n* : hanging lighting fixture

**chan·dler** \'chandlər\ *n* : provisions dealer — **chan·dlery** *n*

**change** \'chānj\ *vb* **changed; changing 1** : make or become different **2** : exchange **3** : give or receive change for ∼ *n* **1** : a changing **2** : excess from a payment **3** : money in smaller denominations **4** : coins — **changeable** *adj* — **change·less** *adj* — **chang·er** *n*

**chan·nel** \'chanᵊl\ *n* **1** : deeper part of a waterway **2** : means of passage or communication **3** : strait **4** : broadcast frequency ∼ *vb* **-neled** *or* **-nelled; -nel·ing** *or* **-nel·ling** : make or direct through a channel

**chant** \'chant\ *vb* : sing or speak in one tone — **chant** *n* — **chant·er** *n*

**chan·tey, chan·ty** \'shantē, 'chant-\ *n, pl* **-teys** *or* **-ties** : sailors' work song

**Cha·nu·kah** \'känəkə, 'hän-\ *var of* HANUKKAH

**cha·os** \'kā,äs\ *n* : complete disorder — **cha·ot·ic** \kā'ätik\ *adj* — **cha·ot·i·cal·ly** \-iklē\ *adv*

**¹chap** \'chap\ *n* : fellow

**²chap** *vb* **-pp-** : dry and crack open usu. from wind and cold

**cha·pel** \'chapəl\ *n* : private or small place of worship

**chap·er·on, chap·er·one** \'shapə,rōn\ *n* : older person who accompanies young people at a social gathering ∼ *vb* **-oned; -on·ing** : act as chaperon at or for — **chap·er·on·age** \-ij\ *n*

**chap·lain** \'chaplən\ *n* : clergy member in a military unit or a prison — **chap·lain·cy** \-sē\ *n*

**chap·ter** \'chaptər\ *n* **1** : main book division **2** : branch of a society

**char** \'chär\ *vb* **-rr- 1** : burn to charcoal **2** : scorch

**char·ac·ter** \'kariktər\ *n* **1** : letter or graphic mark **2** : trait or distinctive combination of traits **3** : peculiar person **4** : fictional person — **char·ac·ter·i·za·tion** \,kariktərə'zāshən\ *n* — **char·ac·ter·ize** \'kariktə,rīz\ *vb*

**char·ac·ter·is·tic** \,kariktə'ristik\ *adj* : typical ∼ *n* : distinguishing quality — **char·ac·ter·is·ti·cal·ly** \-tiklē\ *adv*

**cha·rades** \shə'rādz\ *n sing or pl* : pantomime guessing game

**char·coal** \'chär,kōl\ *n* : porous carbon prepared by partial combustion

**chard** \'chärd\ *n* : leafy vegetable

**charge** \'chärj\ *vb* **charged; charging 1** : give an electric charge to **2** : impose a task or responsibility on **3** : command **4** : accuse **5** : rush forward in assault **6** : assume a debt for **7** : fix as a price ∼ *n* **1** : excess or deficiency of electrons in a body **2** : tax **3** : responsibility **4** : accusation **5** : cost **6** : attack — **charge·able** *adj*

**charg·er** \-ər\ *n* : horse ridden in battle

**char·i·ot** \'charēət\ *n* : ancient 2-wheeled vehicle — **char·i·o·teer** \,charēə'tir\ *n*

**cha·ris·ma** \kə'rizmə\ *n* : special abil-

ity to lead — **char·is·mat·ic** \,karəz-
'matik\ *adj*

**char·i·ty** \'charətē\ *n, pl* **-ties 1** : love
for mankind **2** : generosity or leniency **3** : alms **4** : institution for relief of the needy — **char·i·ta·ble**
\-əbəl\ *adj* — **char·i·ta·ble·ness** *n*
— **char·i·ta·bly** \-blē\ *adv*

**char·la·tan** \'shärlətən\ *n* : impostor

**charm** \'chärm\ *n* **1** : something with
magic power **2** : appealing trait **3**
: small ornament ~ *vb* : fascinate —
**charm·er** *n* — **charm·ing** *adj* —
**charm·ing·ly** *adv*

**char·nel house** \'chärnᵊl-\ *n* : place
for dead bodies

**chart** \'chärt\ *n* **1** : map **2** : diagram
~ *vb* **1** : make a chart of **2** : plan

**char·ter** \-ər\ *n* **1** : document granting
rights **2** : constitution ~ *vb* **1** : establish by charter **2** : rent — **char·
ter·er** *n*

**char·treuse** \shär'trüz, -'trüs\ *n*
: brilliant yellow green

**char·wom·an** \'chär,wumən\ *n* : cleaning woman

**chary** \'charē\ *adj* **chari·er; -est** : cautious — **char·i·ly** \'charəlē\ *adv*

**¹chase** \'chās\ *vb* **chased; chas·ing 1**
: follow trying to catch **2** : drive away
— **chase** *n* — **chas·er** *n*

**²chase** *vb* **chased; chas·ing** : decorate
(metal) by embossing or engraving

**chasm** \'kazəm\ *n* : gorge

**chas·sis** \'chasē, 'shasē\ *n, pl* **chas·
sis** \-ēz\ : supporting structural
frame

**chaste** \'chāst\ *adj* **chast·er; chast·
est 1** : abstaining from all or unlawful sexual relations **2** : modest or decent **3** : severely simple — **chaste·ly**
*adv* — **chaste·ness** *n* — **chas·ti·ty**
\'chastətē\

**chas·ten** \'chāsᵊn\ *vb* : discipline

**chas·tise** \chas'tīz\ *vb* **-tised; -tis·ing
1** : punish **2** : censure — **chas·tise·
ment** \-mənt, 'chastəz-\ *n*

**chat** \'chat\ *n* : informal talk — **chat**
*vb* — **chat·ty** \-ē\ *adj*

**châ·teau** \sha'tō\ *n, pl* **-teaus** \-'tōz\
*or* **-teaux** \-'tō, -'tōz\ **1** : large country house **2** : French vineyard estate

**chat·tel** \'chatᵊl\ *n* : item of tangible
property other than real estate

**chat·ter** \'chatər\ *vb* **1** : utter rapidly
succeeding sounds **2** : talk fast or too
much — **chatter** *n* — **chat·ter·er** *n*

**chat·ter·box** *n* : incessant talker

**chauf·feur** \'shōfər, shō'fər\ *n* : hired
car driver ~ *vb* : work as a chauffeur

**chau·vin·ism** \'shōvə,nizəm\ *n* : excessive patriotism — **chau·vin·ist**
\-vənist\ *n* — **chau·vin·is·tic**
\,shōvə'nistik\ *adj*

**cheap** \'chēp\ *adj* **1** : inexpensive **2**
: shoddy — **cheap** *adv* — **cheap·en**
\'chēpən\ *vb* — **cheap·ly** *adv* —
**cheap·ness** *n*

**cheap·skate** *n* : stingy person

**cheat** \'chēt\ *n* **1** : act of deceiving **2**
: one that cheats ~ *vb* **1** : deprive
through fraud or deceit **2** : violate
rules dishonestly — **cheat·er** *n*

**check** \'chek\ *n* **1** : sudden stoppage **2**
: restraint **3** : test or standard for testing **4** : written order to a bank to pay
money **5** : ticket showing ownership
**6** : slip showing an amount due **7**
: pattern in squares or fabric in such a
pattern **8** : mark placed beside an
item noted ~ *vb* **1** : slow down or
stop **2** : restrain **3** : compare or correspond with a source or original **4**
: inspect or test for condition **5**
: mark with a check **6** : leave or accept for safekeeping or shipment **7**
: checker — **check in** *vb* : report
one's arrival — **check out** *vb* : settle
one's account and leave

**¹check·er** \-ər\ *n* : piece in checkers ~
*vb* : mark with different colors or into
squares

**²checker** *n* : one that checks

**check·er·board** \-,bōrd\ *n* : board of
64 squares of alternate colors

**check·ers** \'chekərz\ *n* : game for 2
played on a checkerboard

**check·mate** *vb* : thwart completely —
**checkmate** *n*

**check·point** *n* : place where traffic is
checked

**check·up** *n* : physical examination

**ched·dar** \'chedər\ *n* : hard smooth
cheese

**cheek** \'chēk\ *n* **1** : fleshy side part of
the face **2** : impudence — **cheeked**
\'chēkt\ *adj* — **cheeky** *adj*

**cheep** \'chēp\ *vb* : utter faint shrill
sounds — **cheep** *n*

**cheer** \'chir\ *n* **1** : good spirits **2**
: food and drink for a feast **3** : shout
of applause or encouragement ~ *vb*
**1** : give hope or courage to **2** : make
or become glad **3** : urge on or applaud with shouts — **cheer·er** *n* —
**cheer·ful** \-fəl\ *adj* — **cheer·ful·ly**

*adv* — **cheer·ful·ness** *n* — **cheer·lead·er** *n* — **cheer·less** *adj* — **cheer·less·ly** *adv* — **cheer·less·ness** *n*

**cheery** \'chirē\ *adj* **cheer·i·er; -est** : cheerful — **cheer·i·ly** *adv* — **cheer·i·ness** *n*

**cheese** \'chēz\ *n* : curd of milk usu. pressed and cured — **cheesy** *adj*

**cheese·cloth** *n* : lightweight coarse cotton gauze

**chee·tah** \'chētə\ *n* : spotted swift-moving African cat

**chef** \'shef\ *n* : chief cook

**chem·i·cal** \'kemikəl\ *adj* **1** : relating to chemistry **2** : working or produced by chemicals ~ *n* : substance obtained by chemistry — **chem·i·cal·ly** \-klē\ *adv*

**che·mise** \shə'mēz\ *n* **1** : woman's one-piece undergarment **2** : loose dress

**chem·ist** \'kemist\ *n* **1** : one trained in chemistry **2** *Brit* : pharmacist

**chem·is·try** \-istrē\ *n, pl* **-tries** : science that deals with the composition and properties of substances

**che·mo·ther·a·py** \ˌkēmō'therəpē, ˌkemō-\ *n* : use of chemicals in the treatment of disease — **che·mo·ther·a·peu·tic** *adj*

**che·nille** \shə'nēl\ *n* : yarn with protruding pile or fabric of such yarn

**cheque** \'chek\ *chiefly Brit var of* CHECK 4

**cher·ish** \'cherish\ *vb* : hold dear

**cher·ry** \'cherē\ *n, pl* **-ries** : small fleshy fruit of a tree related to the roses or the tree or its wood

**cher·ub** \'cherəb\ *n* **1** *pl* **-u·bim** \-ə̩bim, -yə-\ : angel **2** *pl* **-ubs** : chubby child — **che·ru·bic** \chə-'rübik\ *adj*

**chess** \'ches\ *n* : game for 2 played on a checkerboard — **chess·board** *n* — **chess·man** *n*

**chest** \'chest\ *n* **1** : boxlike container **2** : part of the body enclosed by the ribs and breastbone — **chest·ed** *adj*

**chest·nut** \'ches̩nət\ *n* : nut of a tree related to the beech or the tree

**chev·i·ot** \'shevēət\ *n* **1** : heavy rough wool fabric **2** : soft-finished cotton fabric

**chev·ron** \'shevrən\ *n* : V-shaped insignia

**chew** \'chü\ *vb* : crush or grind with the teeth ~ *n* : something to chew —

**chew·able** *adj* — **chew·er** *n* — **chewy** *adj*

**chic** \'shēk\ *n* : smart elegance of dress or manner ~ *adj* **1** : stylish **2** : currently fashionable

**chi·ca·nery** \shik'ānərē\ *n, pl* **-ner·les** : trickery

**chick** \'chik\ *n* : young chicken or bird

**chick·a·dee** \-ə̩dē\ *n* : small grayish American bird

**chick·en** \'chikən\ *n* **1** : common domestic fowl or its flesh used as food **2** : coward

**chicken pox** *n* : acute contagious virus disease esp. of children

**chi·cle** \'chikəl\ *n* : gum from a tropical evergreen tree

**chic·o·ry** \'chikərē\ *n, pl* **-ries** : herb used in salad or its dried ground root used to adulterate coffee

**chide** \'chīd\ *vb* **chid** \'chid\ *or* **chid·ed** \'chīdəd\; **chid** *or* **chid·den** \'chid³n\ *or* **chided; chid·ing** \'chīdiŋ\ : scold

**chief** \'chēf\ *n* : leader ~ *adj* **1** : highest in rank **2** : most important — **chief·dom** *n* — **chief·ly** *adv*

**chief·tain** \'chēftən\ *n* : chief

**chif·fon** \shif'än, 'shif̩-\ *n* : sheer fabric

**chig·ger** \'chigər\ *n* : bloodsucking mite

**chi·gnon** \'shēn̩yän\ *n* : knot of hair

**chil·blain** \'chil̩blān\ *n* : sore or inflamed swelling caused by cold

**child** \'chīld\ *n, pl* **chil·dren** \'childrən\ **1** : unborn or recently born person **2** : son or daughter — **child·bear·ing** *n or adj* — **child·birth** *n* — **child·hood** *n* — **child·ish** *adj* — **child·ish·ly** *adv* — **child·ish·ness** *n* — **child·less** *adj* — **child·less·ness** *n* — **child·like** *adj* — **child·proof** \-̩prüf\ *adj*

**chili, chile, chil·li** \'chilē\ *n, pl* **chil·ies** *or* **chil·es** *or* **chil·lies** **1** : hot pepper **2** : spicy stew of ground beef, chilies, and beans

**chill** \'chil\ *vb* : make or become cold or chilly ~ *adj* : moderately cold ~ *n* **1** : feeling of coldness with shivering **2** : moderate coldness

**chilly** \-ē\ *adj* **chil·li·er; -est** : noticeably cold — **chill·i·ness** *n*

**chime** \'chīm\ *n* : set of tuned bells or their sound ~ *vb* : make bell-like sounds — **chime in** *vb* : break into or join in a conversation

**chi·me·ra, chi·mae·ra** \kī'mirə, kə-\ *n* **1** : imaginary monster **2** : illusion — **chi·mer·i·cal** \-'merikəl\ *adj*

**chim·ney** \'chimnē\ *n, pl* **-neys 1** : passage for smoke **2** : glass tube around a lamp flame

**chimp** \'chimp, 'shimp\ *n* : chimpanzee

**chim·pan·zee** \ˌchimˌpanˈzē, ˌshim-; chimˈpanzē, shim-\ *n* : small ape

**chin** \'chin\ *n* : part of the face below the mouth — **chin·less** *adj*

**chi·na** \'chīnə\ *n* **1** : porcelain ware **2** : domestic pottery

**chin·chil·la** \chin'chilə\ *n* : small So. American rodent with soft pearl-gray fur or this fur

**chink** \'chiŋk\ *n* : small crack ～ *vb* : fill chinks of

**chintz** \'chints\ *n* : printed cotton cloth

**chip** \'chip\ *n* **1** : small thin flat piece cut or broken off **2** : thin crisp morsel of food **3** : counter used in games **4** : flaw where a chip came off **5** : small slice of semiconductor containing electronic circuits ～ *vb* **-pp-** : cut or break chips from — **chip in** *vb* : contribute

**chip·munk** \-ˌməŋk\ *n* : small striped ground-dwelling rodent

**chip·per** \-ər\ *adj* : lively and cheerful

**chi·rop·o·dy** \kə'räpədē, shə-\ *n* : podiatry — **chi·rop·o·dist** \-ədist\ *n*

**chi·ro·prac·tic** \'kīrəˌpraktik\ *n* : system of healing based esp. on manipulation of body structures — **chi·ro·prac·tor** \-tər\ *n*

**chirp** \'chərp\ *n* : short sharp sound like that of a bird or cricket — **chirp** *vb*

**chis·el** \'chizəl\ *n* : sharp-edged metal tool ～ *vb* **-eled** *or* **-elled; -el·ing** *or* **-el·ling 1** : work with a chisel **2** : cheat — **chis·el·er** \-ələr\ *n*

**chit** \'chit\ *n* : signed voucher for a small debt

**chit·chat** \-ˌchat\ *n* : casual conversation — **chitchat** *vb*

**chiv·al·rous** \'shivəlrəs\ *adj* **1** : relating to chivalry **2** : honest, courteous, or generous — **chiv·al·rous·ly** *adv* — **chiv·al·rous·ness** *n*

**chiv·al·ry** \-rē\ *n, pl* **-ries 1** : system or practices of knighthood **2** : spirit or character of the ideal knight — **chi·val·ric** \shə'valrik\ *adj*

**chive** \'chīv\ *n* : herb related to the onion

**chlo·ride** \'klōrˌīd\ *n* : compound of chlorine

**chlo·ri·nate** \-əˌnāt\ *vb* **-nat·ed; -nat·ing** : treat or combine with chlorine — **chlo·ri·na·tion** \ˌklōrə'nāshən\ *n*

**chlo·rine** \'klōrˌēn\ *n* : chemical element that is a heavy strong-smelling greenish yellow irritating gas

**chlo·ro·form** \'klōrəˌfôrm\ *n* : etherlike colorless heavy fluid ～ *vb* : anesthetize or kill with chloroform

**chlo·ro·phyll** \'klōrəˌfil\ *n* : green coloring matter of plants

**chock** \'chäk\ *n* : wedge for blocking the movement of a wheel — **chock** *vb*

**chock–full** \'chək'fûl, 'chäk-\ *adj* : full to the limit

**choc·o·late** \'chäkələt, 'chôk-\ *n* **1** : ground roasted cacao beans or a beverage made from them **2** : candy made of or with chocolate **3** : dark brown

**choice** \'chòis\ *n* **1** : act or power of choosing **2** : one selected **3** : variety offered for selection — *adj* **choic·er; choic·est 1** : worthy of being chosen **2** : selected with care **3** : of high quality

**choir** \'kwīr\ *n* : group of singers esp. in church — **choir·boy** *n* — **choir·mas·ter** *n*

**choke** \'chōk\ *vb* **choked; chok·ing 1** : hinder breathing **2** : clog or obstruct ～ *n* **1** : a choking or sound of choking **2** : valve for controlling air intake in a gasoline engine

**chok·er** \-ər\ *n* : tight necklace

**cho·ler** \'kälər, 'kō-\ *n* : bad temper — **cho·ler·ic** \'kälərik, kə'ler-\ *adj*

**chol·era** \'kälərə\ *n* : disease marked by severe vomiting and dysentery

**cho·les·ter·ol** \kə'lestəˌról, -ˌrōl\ *n* : waxy substance in animal tissues

**choose** \'chüz\ *vb* **chose** \'chōz\; **cho·sen** \'chōzᵊn\; **choos·ing 1** : select after consideration **2** : decide **3** : prefer — **choos·er** *n*

**choosy, choos·ey** \'chüzē\ *adj* **choos·i·er; -est** : fussy in making choices

**chop** \'chäp\ *vb* **-pp- 1** : cut by repeated blows **2** : cut into small pieces ～ *n* **1** : sharp downward blow **2** : small cut of meat often with part of a rib

**chop•per** \-ər\ n 1 : one that chops 2 : helicopter

**chop•py** \-ē\ adj **-pi•er; -est 1** : rough with small waves **2** : jerky or disconnected — **chop•pi•ly** adv — **chop•pi•ness** n

**chops** \'chäps\ n pl : fleshy covering of the jaws

**chop•sticks** n pl : pair of sticks used in eating in oriental countries

**cho•ral** \'kōrəl\ adj : relating to or sung by a choir or chorus or in chorus — **cho•ral•ly** adv

**cho•rale** \kə'ral, -'räl\ n 1 : hymn tune or harmonization of a traditional melody **2** : chorus or choir

**¹chord** \'kòrd\ n : harmonious tones sounded together

**²chord** n 1 : cordlike anatomical structure **2** : straight line joining 2 points on a curve

**chore** \'chōr\ n 1 pl : daily household or farm work **2** : routine or disagreeable task

**cho•re•og•ra•phy** \ˌkōrē'ägrəfē\ n, pl **-phies** : art of composing and arranging dances — **cho•reo•graph** \'kōrēəˌgraf\ vb — **cho•re•og•ra•pher** \ˌkōrē'ägrəfər\ n — **cho•reo•graph•ic** \-ēə'grafik\ adj

**cho•ris•ter** \'kōrəstər\ n : choir singer

**chor•tle** \'chòrtᵊl\ vb **-tled; -tling** : laugh or chuckle — **chortle** n

**cho•rus** \'kōrəs\ n 1 : group of singers or dancers **2** : part of a song repeated at intervals **3** : composition for a chorus ~ vb : sing or utter together

**chose** past of CHOOSE

**cho•sen** \'chōzᵊn\ adj : favored

**¹chow** \'chaù\ n : food

**²chow** n : thick-coated muscular dog

**chow•der** \'chaùdər\ n : thick soup usu. of seafood and milk

**chow mein** \'chaù'mān\ n : thick stew of shredded vegetables and meat

**chris•ten** \'krisᵊn\ vb **1** : baptize **2** : name — **chris•ten•ing** n

**Chris•ten•dom** \-dəm\ n : areas where Christianity prevails

**Chris•tian** \'krischən\ n : adherent of Christianity ~ adj : relating to or professing a belief in Christianity or Jesus Christ — **Chris•tian•ize** \'krischəˌnīz\ vb

**Chris•ti•an•i•ty** \ˌkrischē'anətē\ n : religion derived from the teachings of Jesus Christ

**Christian name** n : first name

**Christ•mas** \'krisməs\ n : December 25 celebrated as the birthday of Christ

**chro•mat•ic** \krō'matik\ adj **1** : relating to color **2** : proceeding by half steps of the musical scale

**chrome** \'krōm\ n : chromium or something plated with it

**chro•mi•um** \-ēəm\ n : a bluish white metallic element used esp. in alloys

**chro•mo•some** \'krōməˌsōm, -ˌzōm\ n : part of a cell nucleus that contains the genes — **chro•mo•som•al** \ˌkrōmə'sōməl, -'zō-\ adj

**chron•ic** \'kränik\ adj : frequent or persistent — **chron•i•cal•ly** \-iklē\ adv

**chron•i•cle** \'känikəl\ n : history ~ vb **-cled; -cling** : record — **chron•i•cler** \-iklər\ n

**chro•nol•o•gy** \krə'näləjē\ n, pl **-gies** : list of events in order of their occurrence — **chron•o•log•i•cal** \ˌkränᵊl-'äjikəl\ adj — **chron•o•log•i•cal•ly** \-iklē\ adv

**chro•nom•e•ter** \krə'nämətər\ n : very accurate timepiece

**chrys•a•lis** \'krisələs\ n, pl **chry•sal•i•des** \kris'aləˌdēz\ or **chrys•a•lis•es** : insect pupa enclosed in a shell

**chry•san•the•mum** \kris'anthəməm\ n : plant with showy flowers

**chub•by** \'chəbē\ adj **-bi•er; -est** : fat — **chub•bi•ness** n

**¹chuck** \'chək\ vb **1** : tap **2** : toss ~ n **1** : light pat under the chin **2** : toss

**²chuck** n 1 : cut of beef **2** : machine part that holds work or another part

**chuck•le** \'chəkəl\ vb **-led; -ling** : laugh quietly — **chuckle** n

**chug** \'chəg\ n : sound of a laboring engine ~ vb **-gg-** : work or move with chugs

**chum** \'chəm\ n : close friend ~ vb **-mm-** : be chums — **chum•my** \-ē\ adj

**chump** \'chəmp\ n : fool

**chunk** \'chəŋk\ n 1 : short thick piece **2** : sizable amount

**chunky** \-ē\ adj **chunk•i•er; -est** **1** : stocky **2** : containing chunks

**church** \'chərch\ n 1 : building esp. for Christian public worship **2** : whole body of Christians **3** : denomination **4** : congregation — **church•go•er** n — **church•go•ing** adj or n

**church•yard** n : cemetery beside a church

**churl** \'chərl\ *n* : rude ill-bred person — **churl·ish** *adj*

**churn** \'chərn\ *n* : container in which butter is made ∼ *vb* **1** : agitate in a churn **2** : shake violently

**chute** \'shüt\ *n* : trough or passage

**chut·ney** \'chətnē\ *n, pl* **-neys** : sweet and sour relish

**chutz·pah** \'hùtspə, 'kùt-, -ˌspä\ *n* : nerve or insolence

**ci·ca·da** \sə'kādə\ *n* : stout-bodied insect with transparent wings

**ci·der** \'sīdər\ *n* : apple juice

**ci·gar** \sig'är\ *n* : roll of leaf tobacco for smoking

**cig·a·rette** \ˌsigə'ret, 'sigəˌret\ *n* : cut tobacco rolled in paper for smoking

**cinch** \'sinch\ *n* **1** : strap holding a saddle or pack in place **2** : sure thing — **cinch** *vb*

**cin·cho·na** \sin'kōnə\ *n* : So. American tree that yields quinine

**cinc·ture** \'siŋkchər\ *n* : belt or sash

**cin·der** \'sindər\ *n* **1** *pl* : ashes **2** : piece of partly burned wood or coal

**cin·e·ma** \'sinəmə\ *n* : movies or a movie theater — **cin·e·mat·ic** \ˌsinə'matik\ *adj*

**cin·na·mon** \'sinəmən\ *n* : spice from an aromatic tree bark

**ci·pher** \'sīfər\ *n* **1** : zero **2** : code

**cir·ca** \'sərkə\ *prep* : about

**cir·cle** \'sərkəl\ *n* **1** : closed symmetrical curve **2** : cycle **3** : group with a common tie ∼ *vb* **-cled; -cling 1** : enclose in a circle **2** : move or revolve around

**cir·cuit** \'sərkət\ *n* **1** : boundary **2** : regular tour of a territory **3** : complete path of an electric current **4** : group of electronic components

**cir·cu·itous** \ˌsər'kyüətəs\ *adj* : circular or winding

**cir·cuit·ry** \'sərkətrē\ *n, pl* **-ries** : arrangement of an electric circuit

**cir·cu·lar** \'sərkyələr\ *adj* **1** : round **2** : moving in a circle ∼ *n* : advertising leaflet — **cir·cu·lar·i·ty** \ˌsərkyə'larətē\ *n*

**cir·cu·late** \'sərkyəˌlāt\ *vb* **-lat·ed; -lat·ing** : move or cause to move in a circle or from place to place or person to person — **cir·cu·la·tion** \ˌsərkyə'lāshən\ *n* — **cir·cu·la·to·ry** \'sərkyələˌtōrē\ *adj*

**cir·cum·cise** \'sərkəmˌsīz\ *vb* **-cised; -cis·ing** : cut off the foreskin of — **cir·cum·ci·sion** \ˌsərkəm'sizhən\ *n*

**cir·cum·fer·ence** \sər'kəmfrəns\ *n* : perimeter of a circle

**cir·cum·flex** \'sərkəmˌfleks\ *n* : phonetic mark (as ^)

**cir·cum·lo·cu·tion** \ˌsərkəmlō'kyüshən\ *n* : excessive use of words

**cir·cum·nav·i·gate** \ˌsərkəm'navəˌgāt\ *vb* : sail completely around — **cir·cum·nav·i·ga·tion** *n*

**cir·cum·scribe** \'sərkəmˌskrīb\ *vb* **1** : draw a line around **2** : limit

**cir·cum·spect** \'sərkəmˌspekt\ *adj* : careful — **cir·cum·spec·tion** \ˌsərkəm'spekshən\ *n*

**cir·cum·stance** \'sərkəmˌstans\ *n* **1** : fact or event **2** *pl* : surrounding conditions **3** *pl* : financial situation — **cir·cum·stan·tial** \ˌsərkəm'stanchəl\ *adj*

**cir·cum·vent** \ˌsərkəm'vent\ *vb* : get around esp. by trickery — **cir·cum·ven·tion** \-'venchən\ *n*

**cir·cus** \'sərkəs\ *n* : show with feats of skill, animal acts, and clowns

**cir·rho·sis** \sə'rōsəs\ *n, pl* **-rho·ses** \-ˌsēz\ : fibrosis of the liver — **cir·rhot·ic** \-'rätik\ *adj or n*

**cir·rus** \'sirəs\ *n, pl* **-ri** \-ˌī\ : wispy white cloud

**cis·tern** \'sistərn\ *n* : underground water tank

**cit·a·del** \'sitəd°l, -əˌdel\ *n* : fortress

**cite** \'sīt\ *vb* **cit·ed; cit·ing 1** : summon before a court **2** : quote **3** : refer to esp. in commendation — **ci·ta·tion** \sī'tāshən\ *n*

**cit·i·zen** \'sitəzən\ *n* : member of a country — **cit·i·zen·ry** \-rē\ *n* — **cit·i·zen·ship** *n*

**cit·ron** \'sitrən\ *n* : lemonlike fruit

**cit·rus** \'sitrəs\ *n, pl* **-rus** *or* **-rus·es** : evergreen tree or shrub grown for its fruit (as the orange or lemon)

**city** \'sitē\ *n, pl* **cit·ies** : place larger or more important than a town

**civ·ic** \'sivik\ *adj* : relating to citizenship or civil affairs

**civ·ics** \-iks\ *n* : study of citizenship

**civ·il** \'sivəl\ *adj* **1** : relating to citizens **2** : polite **3** : relating to or being a lawsuit — **civ·il·ly** *adv*

**ci·vil·ian** \sə'vilyən\ *n* : person not in a military, police, or fire-fighting force

**ci·vil·i·ty** \sə'vilətē\ *n, pl* **-ties** : courtesy

**civ·i·li·za·tion** \ˌsivələ'zāshən\ *n* **1**

: high level of cultural development **2**
: culture of a time or place

**civ·i·lize** \'sivə‚līz\ vb **-lized; -liz·ing**
: raise from a primitive stage of cultural development — **civ·i·lized** adj

**civil liberty** n : freedom from arbitrary governmental interference — usu. pl.

**civil rights** n pl : nonpolitical rights of a citizen

**civil service** n : government service

**civil war** n : war among citizens of one country

**clack** \'klak\ vb : make or cause a clatter — **clack** n

**clad** \'klad\ adj : covered

**claim** \'klām\ vb **1** : demand or take as the rightful owner **2** : maintain ~ n **1** : demand of right or ownership **2** : declaration **3** : something claimed — **claim·ant** \-ənt\ n

**clair·voy·ant** \klar'vȯiənt\ adj : able to perceive things beyond the senses — **clair·voy·ance** \-əns\ n — **clair·voy·ant** n

**clam** \'klam\ n : bivalve mollusk

**clam·ber** \'klambər\ vb : climb awkwardly

**clam·my** \'klamē\ adj **-mi·er; -est** : being damp, soft, and usu. cool — **clam·mi·ness** n

**clam·or** \-ər\ n **1** : uproar **2** : protest — **clamor** vb — **clam·or·ous** adj

**clamp** \'klamp\ n : device for holding things together — **clamp** vb

**clan** \'klan\ n : group of related families — **clan·nish** adj — **clan·nish·ness** n

**clan·des·tine** \klan'destən\ adj : secret

**clang** \'klaŋ\ n : loud metallic ringing — **clang** vb

**clan·gor** \-ər, -gər\ n : jumble of clangs

**clank** \'klaŋk\ n : brief sound of struck metal — **clank** vb

**clap** \'klap\ vb **-pp- 1** : strike noisily **2** : applaud ~ n **1** : loud crash **2** : noise made by clapping the hands

**clap·board** \'klabərd, 'klap-, -‚bȯrd\ n : narrow tapered board used for siding

**clap·per** \'klapər\ n : tongue of a bell

**claque** \'klak\ n **1** : group hired to applaud at a performance **2** : group of sycophants

**clar·et** \'klarət\ n : dry red wine

**clar·i·fy** \'klarə‚fī\ vb **-fied; -fy·ing** : make or become clear — **clar·i·fi·ca·tion** \‚klarəfə'kāshən\ n

**clar·i·net** \‚klarə'net\ n : woodwind instrument shaped like a tube — **clar·i·net·ist, clar·i·net·tist** \-ist\ n

**clar·i·on** \'klarēən\ adj : loud and clear

**clar·i·ty** \'klarətē\ n : clearness

**clash** \'klash\ vb **1** : make or cause a clash **2** : be in opposition or disharmony ~ n **1** : crashing sound **2** : hostile encounter

**clasp** \'klasp\ n **1** : device for holding things together **2** : embrace or grasp ~ vb **1** : fasten **2** : embrace or grasp

**class** \'klas\ n **1** : group of the same status or nature **2** : social rank **3** : course of instruction **4** : group of students ~ vb : classify — **class·less** adj — **class·mate** n — **class·room** n

**clas·sic** \'klasik\ adj **1** : serving as a standard of excellence **2** : classical ~ n : work of enduring excellence and esp. of ancient Greece or Rome — **clas·si·cal** \-ikəl\ adj — **clas·si·cal·ly** \-klē\ adv — **clas·si·cism** \'klasə‚sizəm\ n — **clas·si·cist** \-sist\ n

**clas·si·fied** \'klasə‚fīd\ adj : restricted for security reasons

**clas·si·fy** \-‚fī\ vb **-fied; -fy·ing** : arrange in or assign to classes — **clas·si·fi·ca·tion** \‚klasəfə'kāshən\ n — **clas·si·fi·er** \'klasə‚fīər\ n

**clat·ter** \'klatər\ n : rattling sound — **clatter** vb

**clause** \'klȯz\ n **1** : separate part of a document **2** : part of a sentence with a subject and predicate

**claus·tro·pho·bia** \‚klȯstrə'fōbēə\ n : fear of closed or narrow spaces — **claus·tro·pho·bic** \-bik\ adj

**clav·i·chord** \'klavə‚kȯrd\ n : early keyboard instrument

**clav·i·cle** \'klavikəl\ n : collarbone

**claw** \'klȯ\ n : sharp curved nail or process (as on the toe of an animal) ~ vb : scratch or dig — **clawed** adj

**clay** \'klā\ n : plastic earthy material — **clay·ey** \-ē\ adj

**clean** \'klēn\ adj **1** : free from dirt or disease **2** : pure or honorable **3** : thorough ~ vb : make or become clean — **clean** adv — **clean·er** n — **clean·ly** \-lē\ adv — **clean·ness** n

**clean·ly** \'klenlē\ adj **-li·er; -est** : clean — **clean·li·ness** n

**cleanse** \'klenz\ vb **cleansed; cleans·ing** : make clean — **cleans·er** n

**clear** \'klir\ adj **1** : bright **2** : free from

clouds **3** : transparent **4** : easily heard, seen or understood **5** : free from doubt **6** : free from restriction or obstruction ～ *vb* **1** : make or become clear **2** : go away **3** : free from accusation or blame **4** : explain or settle **5** : net **6** : jump or pass without touching ～ *n* : clear space or part — **clear** *adv* — **clear•ance** \'klirəns\ *n*

**clear•ing** \'klirin\ *n* : land cleared of wood

**clear•ly** *adv* **1** : in a clear manner **2** : it is obvious that

**cleat** \'klēt\ *n* : projection that strengthens or prevents slipping

**cleav•age** \'klēvij\ *n* **1** : a splitting apart **2** : depression between a woman's breasts

**¹cleave** \'klēv\ *vb* **cleaved** \'klēvd\ *or* **clove** \'klōv\; **cleav•ing** : adhere

**²cleave** *vb* **cleaved** \'klēvd\; **cleav•ing** : split apart

**cleav•er** \'klēvər\ *n* : heavy chopping knife

**clef** \'klef\ *n* : sign on the staff in music to show pitch

**cleft** \'kleft\ *n* : crack

**clem•ent** \'klemənt\ *adj* **1** : merciful **2** : temperate or mild — **clem•en•cy** \-ənsē\ *n*

**clench** \'klench\ *vb* **1** : hold fast **2** : close tightly

**cler•gy** \'klərjē\ *n* : body of religious officials — **cler•gy•man** \-jimən\ *n*

**cler•ic** \'klerik\ *n* : member of the clergy

**cler•i•cal** \-ikəl\ *adj* **1** : relating to the clergy **2** : relating to a clerk or office worker

**clerk** \'klərk, *Brit* 'klärk\ *n* **1** : official responsible for record-keeping **2** : person doing general office work **3** : salesperson in a store — **clerk** *vb* — **clerk•ship** *n*

**clev•er** \'klevər\ *adj* **1** : resourceful **2** : marked by wit or ingenuity — **clev•er•ly** *adv* — **clev•er•ness** *n*

**clew** *var of* CLUE

**cli•ché** \kli'shā\ *n* : trite phrase — **cli•chéd** \-'shād\ *adj*

**click** \'klik\ *n* : slight sharp noise ～ *vb* : make or cause to make a click

**cli•ent** \'klīənt\ *n* **1** : person who engages professional services **2** : customer

**cli•en•tele** \ˌklīən'tel, ˌklē-\ *n* : body of customers

**cliff** \'klif\ *n* : high steep face of rock

**cli•mate** \'klīmət\ *n* : average weather conditions over a period of years — **cli•mat•ic** \klī'matik\ *adj*

**cli•max** \'klīˌmaks\ *n* : the highest point ～ *vb* : come to a climax — **cli•mac•tic** \klī'maktik\ *adj*

**climb** \'klīm\ *vb* **1** : go up or down by use of hands and feet **2** : rise ～ *n* : a climbing — **climb•er** *n*

**clinch** \'klinch\ *vb* **1** : fasten securely **2** : settle **3** : hold fast or firmly — **clinch** *n* — **clinch•er** *n*

**cling** \'klin\ *vb* **clung** \'klən\; **cling•ing** **1** : adhere firmly **2** : hold on tightly

**clin•ic** \'klinik\ *n* : facility for diagnosis and treatment of outpatients — **clin•i•cal** \-əl\ *adj* — **clin•i•cal•ly** \-klē\ *adv*

**clink** \'klink\ *vb* : make a slight metallic sound — **clink** *n*

**clin•ker** \'klinkər\ *n* : fused stony matter esp. in a furnace

**¹clip** \'klip\ *vb* **-pp-** : fasten with a clip ～ *n* : device to hold things together

**²clip** *vb* **-pp-** **1** : cut or cut off **2** : hit ～ *n* **1** : clippers **2** : sharp blow **3** : rapid pace

**clip•per** \'klipər\ *n* **1** *pl* : implement for clipping **2** : fast sailing ship

**clique** \'klēk, 'klik\ *n* : small exclusive group of people

**cli•to•ris** \'klitərəs, kli'tōrəs\ *n, pl* **cli•to•ri•des** \-'tōrəˌdēz\ : small organ at the front of the vulva

**cloak** \'klōk\ *n* **1** : loose outer garment **2** : something that conceals ～ *vb* : cover or hide with a cloak

**clob•ber** \'kläbər\ *vb* : hit hard

**clock** \'kläk\ *n* : timepiece not carried on the person ～ *vb* : record the time of

**clock•wise** \-ˌwīz\ *adv or adj* : in the same direction as a clock's hands move

**clod** \'kläd\ *n* **1** : lump esp. of earth **2** : dull insensitive person

**clog** \'kläg\ *n* **1** : restraining weight **2** : thick-soled shoe ～ *vb* **-gg-** **1** : impede with a clog **2** : obstruct passage through **3** : become plugged up

**clois•ter** \'klòistər\ *n* **1** : monastic establishment **2** : covered passage ～ *vb* : shut away from the world

**clone** \'klōn\ *n* **1** : offspring produced from a single organism **2** : copy

**¹close** \'klōz\ *vb* **closed; clos•ing** **1**

: shut **2** : cease operation **3** : terminate **4** : bring or come together ~ *n* : conclusion or end

**²close** \'klōs\ *adj* **clos•er; clos•est 1** : confining **2** : secretive **3** : strict **4** : stuffy **5** : having little space between items **6** : fitting tightly **7** : near **8** : intimate **9** : accurate **10** : nearly even — **close** *adv* — **close•ly** *adv* — **close•ness** *n*

**clos•et** \'kläzət, 'klóz-\ *n* : small compartment for household utensils or clothing ~ *vb* : take into a private room for a talk

**clo•sure** \'klōzhər\ *n* **1** : act of closing **2** : something that closes

**clot** \'klät\ *n* : dried mass of a liquid — **clot** *vb*

**cloth** \'klóth\ *n, pl* **cloths** \'klóthz, 'klóths\ **1** : fabric **2** : tablecloth

**clothe** \'klōth\ *vb* **clothed** *or* **clad** \'klad\; **cloth•ing** : dress

**clothes** \'klōthz, 'klōz\ *n pl* **1** : clothing **2** : bedclothes

**cloth•ier** \'klōthyər, -thēər\ *n* : maker or seller of clothing

**cloth•ing** \'klōthiŋ\ *n* : covering for the human body

**cloud** \'klaúd\ *n* **1** : visible mass of particles in the air **2** : something that darkens, hides, or threatens ~ *vb* : darken or hide — **cloud•i•ness** *n* — **cloud•less** *adj* — **cloudy** *adj*

**cloud•burst** *n* : sudden heavy rain

**clout** \'klaút\ *n* **1** : blow **2** : influence ~ *vb* : hit forcefully

**¹clove** \'klōv\ *n* : section of a bulb

**²clove** *past of* CLEAVE

**³clove** *n* : dried flower bud of an East Indian tree used as a spice

**clo•ver** \'klōvər\ *n* : leguminous herb with usu. 3-part leaves

**clo•ver•leaf** *n, pl* **-leafs** *or* **-leaves** : highway interchange

**clown** \'klaún\ *n* : funny costumed entertainer esp. in a circus ~ *vb* : act like a clown — **clown•ish** *adj* — **clown•ish•ly** *adv* — **clown•ish•ness** *n*

**cloy** \'klói\ *vb* : disgust with excess — **cloy•ing•ly** \-iŋlē\ *adv*

**club** \'kləb\ *n* **1** : heavy wooden stick **2** : playing card of a suit marked with a black figure like a clover leaf **3** : group associated for a common purpose ~ *vb* **-bb-** : hit with a club

**club•foot** *n* : misshapen foot twisted out of position from birth — **club•foot•ed** \-,fútəd\ *adj*

**cluck** \'klək\ *n* : sound made by a hen — **cluck** *vb*

**clue** \'klü\ *n* : piece of evidence that helps solve a problem ~ *vb* **clued; clue•ing** *or* **clu•ing** : provide with a clue

**clump** \'kləmp\ *n* **1** : cluster **2** : heavy tramping sound ~ *vb* : tread heavily

**clum•sy** \'kləmzē\ *adj* **-si•er; -est 1** : lacking dexterity, nimbleness, or grace **2** : tactless — **clum•si•ly** *adv* — **clum•si•ness** *n*

**clung** *past of* CLING

**clunk•er** \'kləŋkər\ *n* : old automobile

**clus•ter** \'kləstər\ *n* : group ~ *vb* : grow or gather in a cluster

**clutch** \'kləch\ *vb* : grasp ~ *n* **1** : grasping hand or claws **2** : control or power **3** : coupling for connecting two working parts in machinery

**clut•ter** \'klətər\ *vb* : fill with things that get in the way — **clutter** *n*

**co-** *prefix* : with, together, joint, or jointly

---

**List of self-explanatory words with the prefix** *co-*

| | | |
|---|---|---|
| coact | codesign | coexist |
| coactor | codevelop | coexistence |
| coauthor | codeveloper | coexistent |
| coauthorship | codirect | cofeature |
| cocaptain | codirector | cofinance |
| cochairman | codiscoverer | cofound |
| cochampion | codrive | cofounder |
| cocomposer | codriver | coheir |
| coconspirator | coedit | coheiress |
| cocreator | coeditor | cohost |
| codefendant | coexecutor | cohostess |

**coach** \'kōch\ *n* **1** : closed 2-door 4-wheeled carriage **2** : railroad passenger car **3** : bus **4** : 2d-class air travel **5** : one who instructs or trains performers ~ *vb* : instruct or direct as a coach

**co·ag·u·late** \kō'agyə,lāt\ *vb* **-lat·ed; -lat·ing** : clot — **co·ag·u·lant** \-lənt\ *n* — **co·ag·u·la·tion** \-,agyə'lāshən\ *n*

**coal** \'kōl\ *n* **1** : ember **2** : black solid mineral used as fuel — **coal·field** *n*

**co·alesce** \,kōə'les\ *vb* **-alesced; -alesc·ing** : grow together — **co·ales·cence** \-'les°ns\ *n*

**co·ali·tion** \-'lishən\ *n* : temporary alliance

**coarse** \'kōrs\ *adj* **coars·er; coars·est** **1** : composed of large particles **2** : rough or crude — **coarse·ly** *adv* — **coars·en** \-°n\ *vb* — **coarse·ness** *n*

**coast** \'kōst\ *n* : seashore ~ *vb* : move without effort — **coast·al** \-°l\ *adj*

**coast·er** \-ər\ *n* **1** : one that coasts **2** : plate or tray to protect a surface

**coast guard** *n* : military force that guards or patrols a coast — **coastguards·man** \'kōst,gärdzmən\ *n*

**coast·line** *n* : shape of a coast

**coat** \'kōt\ *n* **1** : outer garment for the upper body **2** : external growth of fur or feathers **3** : covering layer ~ *vb* : cover with a coat — **coat·ed** *adj* — **coat·ing** *n*

**coax** \'kōks\ *vb* : move to action or achieve by gentle urging or flattery

**cob** \'käb\ *n* : corncob

**co·balt** \'kō,bolt\ *n* : shiny silver-white magnetic metallic chemical element

**cob·ble** \'käbəl\ *vb* **cob·bled; cob·bling** : make or put together hastily

**cob·bler** \'käblər\ *n* **1** : shoemaker **2** : deep-dish fruit pie

**cob·ble·stone** *n* : small round paving stone

**co·bra** \'kōbrə\ *n* : venomous snake

**cob·web** \'käb,web\ *n* : network spun by a spider or a similar filament

**co·caine** \kō'kān, 'kō,kān\ *n* : drug obtained from the leaves of a So. American shrub (**co·ca** \'kōkə\)

**co·chlea** \'kōklēə, 'käk-\ *n, pl* **-chle·as** *or* **-chle·ae** \-lē,ē, -,ī\ : the usu. spiral part of the inner ear — **coch·le·ar** \-lēər\ *adj*

**cock** \'käk\ *n* **1** : male fowl **2** : valve or faucet ~ *vb* **1** : draw back the hammer of a firearm **2** : tilt to one side — **cock·fight** *n*

**cock·a·too** \'käkə,tü\ *n, pl* **-toos** : large Australian crested parrot

**cock·eyed** \'käk'īd\ *adj* **1** : tilted to one side **2** : slightly crazy

**cock·le** \'käkəl\ *n* : edible shellfish

**cock·pit** \'käk,pit\ *n* : place for a pilot, driver, or helmsman

**cock·roach** *n* : nocturnal insect often infesting houses

**cock·tail** \'käk,tāl\ *n* **1** : iced drink of liquor and flavorings **2** : appetizer

**cocky** \'käkē\ *adj* **cock·i·er; -est** : overconfident — **cock·i·ly** \-əlē\ *adv* — **cock·i·ness** *n*

**co·coa** \'kōkō\ *n* **1** : cacao **2** : powdered chocolate or a drink made from this

**co·co·nut** \'kōkə,nət\ *n* : large nutlike fruit of a tropical palm (**coconut palm**)

**co·coon** \kə'kün\ *n* : case protecting an insect pupa

**cod** \'käd\ *n, pl* **cod** : food fish of the No. Atlantic

**cod·dle** \'käd°l\ *vb* **-dled; -dling** : pamper

---

| | | |
|---|---|---|
| coinvent | copartnership | copublisher |
| coinventor | copresident | corecipient |
| coinvestigator | coprincipal | coresident |
| coleader | coprisoner | cosignatory |
| comanagement | coproduce | cosigner |
| comanager | coproducer | cosponsor |
| co-organizer | coproduction | costar |
| co-own | copromoter | cowinner |
| co-owner | coproprietor | coworker |
| copartner | copublish | cowrite |

**code** \'kōd\ *n* **1** : system of laws or rules **2** : system of signals

**co·deine** \'kō,dēn\ *n* : narcotic drug used in cough remedies

**cod·ger** \'käjər\ *n* : odd fellow

**cod·i·cil** \'kädəsəl, -,sil\ *n* : postscript to a will

**cod·i·fy** \'kädə,fī, 'kōd-\ *vb* **-fied; -fy·ing** : arrange systematically — **cod·i·fi·ca·tion** \,kädəfə'kāshən, ,kōd-\ *n*

**co·ed** \'kō,ed\ *n* : female student in a coeducational institution — **coed** *adj*

**co·ed·u·ca·tion** \,kō-\ *n* : education of the sexes together — **co·ed·u·ca·tion·al** *adj*

**co·ef·fi·cient** \,kōə'fishənt\ *n* **1** : number that is a multiplier of another **2** : number that serves as a measure of some property

**co·erce** \kō'ərs\ *vb* **-erced; -erc·ing** : force — **co·er·cion** \-'ərzhən, -shən\ *n* — **co·er·cive** \-'ərsiv\ *adj*

**cof·fee** \'kófē\ *n* : drink made from the roasted and ground seeds (**coffee beans**) of a tropical shrub — **cof·fee·house** *n* — **cof·fee·pot** *n*

**cof·fer** \'kófər\ *n* : box for valuables

**cof·fin** \-fən\ *n* : box for burial

**cog** \'käg\ *n* : tooth on the rim of a gear — **cogged** \'kägd\ *adj* — **cog·wheel** *n*

**co·gent** \'kōjənt\ *adj* : compelling or convincing — **co·gen·cy** \-jənsē\ *n*

**cog·i·tate** \'käjə,tāt\ *vb* **-tat·ed; -tat·ing** : think over — **cog·i·ta·tion** \,käjə'tāshən\ *n* — **cog·i·ta·tive** \'käjə,tātiv\ *adj*

**co·gnac** \'kōn,yak\ *n* : French brandy

**cog·nate** \'käg,nāt\ *adj* : related — **cog·nate** *n*

**cog·ni·tion** \käg'nishən\ *n* : act or process of knowing — **cog·ni·tive** \'kägnətiv\ *adj*

**cog·ni·zance** \'kägnəzəns\ *n* : notice or awareness — **cog·ni·zant** \'kägnəzənt\ *adj*

**co·hab·it** \kō'habət\ *vb* : live together as husband and wife — **co·hab·i·ta·tion** \-,habə'tāshən\ *n*

**co·here** \kō'hir\ *vb* **-hered; -her·ing** : stick together

**co·her·ent** \-'hirənt\ *adj* **1** : able to stick together **2** : logically consistent — **co·her·ence** \-əns\ *n* — **co·her·ent·ly** *adv*

**co·he·sion** \-'hēzhən\ *n* : a sticking together — **co·he·sive** \-siv\ *adj* —

**co·he·sive·ly** *adv* — **co·he·sive·ness** *n*

**co·hort** \'kō,hórt\ *n* **1** : group of soldiers **2** : companion

**coif·fure** \kwä'fyur\ *n* : hair style

**coil** \'kóil\ *vb* : wind in a spiral — *n* : series of loops (as of rope)

**coin** \'kóin\ *n* : piece of metal used as money — *vb* **1** : make (a coin) by stamping **2** : create — **coin·age** \-ij\ *n* — **coin·er** *n*

**co·in·cide** \,kōən'sīd, 'kōən,sīd\ *vb* **-cid·ed; -cid·ing** **1** : be in the same place **2** : happen at the same time **3** : be alike — **co·in·ci·dence** \kō'in-sədəns\ *n* — **co·in·ci·dent** \-dənt\ *adj* — **co·in·ci·den·tal** \-,insə'dent°l\ *adj*

**co·itus** \'kōətəs\ *n* : sexual intercourse — **co·ital** \-ət°l\ *adj*

**coke** \'kōk\ *n* : fuel made by heating soft coal

**co·la** \'kōlə\ *n* : carbonated soft drink

**col·an·der** \'kələndər, 'käl-\ *n* : perforated utensil for draining food

**cold** \'kōld\ *adj* **1** : having a low or below normal temperature **2** : lacking warmth of feeling **3** : suffering from lack of warmth — *n* **1** : low temperature **2** : minor respiratory illness — **cold·ly** *adv* — **cold·ness** *n* — **in cold blood** : with premeditation

**cold–blood·ed** *adj* **1** : cruel or merciless **2** : having a body temperature that varies with the temperature of the environment

**cole·slaw** \'kōl,sló\ *n* : cabbage salad

**col·ic** \'kälik\ *n* : sharp abdominal pain — **col·icky** *adj*

**col·i·se·um** \,kälə'sēəm\ *n* : arena

**col·lab·o·rate** \kə'labə,rāt\ *vb* **-rat·ed; -rat·ing** **1** : work jointly with others **2** : help the enemy — **col·lab·o·ra·tion** \-,labə'rāshən\ *n* — **col·lab·o·ra·tor** \-'labə,rātər\ *n*

**col·lapse** \kə'laps\ *vb* **-lapsed; -laps·ing** **1** : fall in **2** : break down physically or mentally **3** : fold down — *n* : breakdown — **col·laps·ible** *adj*

**col·lar** \'kälər\ *n* : part of a garment around the neck — *vb* **1** : seize by the collar **2** : grab — **col·lar·less** *adj*

**col·lar·bone** *n* : bone joining the breastbone and the shoulder blade

**col·lards** \'kälərdz\ *n pl* : kale

**col·late** \kə'lāt; 'käl,āt, 'kōl-\ *vb* **-lat-**

ed; **-lat·ing 1** : compare carefully **2** : assemble in order

**col·lat·er·al** \kə'latərəl\ *adj* **1** : secondary **2** : descended from the same ancestors but not in the same line **3** : similar ~ *n* : property used as security for a loan

**col·league** \'käl‚ēg\ *n* : associate

**col·lect** \kə'lekt\ *vb* **1** : bring, come, or gather together **2** : receive payment of ~ *adv or adj* : to be paid for by the receiver — **col·lect·ible, col·lect·able** *adj* — **col·lec·tion** \-'lekshən\ *n* — **col·lec·tor** \-'lektər\ *n*

**col·lec·tive** \-tiv\ *adj* : denoting or shared by a group ~ *n* : a cooperative unit — **col·lec·tive·ly** *adv*

**col·lege** \'kälij\ *n* : institution of higher learning granting a bachelor's degree — **col·le·gian** \kə'lējan\ *n* — **col·le·giate** \kə'lējət\ *adj*

**col·lide** \kə'līd\ *vb* **-lid·ed; -lid·ing** : strike together — **col·li·sion** \-'lizhən\ *n*

**col·lie** \'kälē\ *n* : large long-haired dog

**col·loid** \'käl‚óid\ *n* : tiny particles in suspension in a fluid — **col·loi·dal** \kə'lóid°l\ *adj*

**col·lo·qui·al** \kə'lōkwēəl\ *adj* : used in informal conversation — **col·lo·qui·al·ism** \-ə‚lizəm\ *n*

**col·lu·sion** \kə'lüzhən\ *n* : secret cooperation for deceit — **col·lu·sive** \-'lüsiv\ *adj*

**co·logne** \kə'lōn\ *n* : perfumed liquid

¹**co·lon** \'kōlən\ *n, pl* **colons** *or* **co·la** \-lə\ : lower part of the large intestine — **co·lon·ic** \kō'länik\ *adj*

²**colon** *n, pl* **colons** : punctuation mark : used esp. to direct attention to following matter

**col·o·nel** \'kərn°l\ *n* : commissioned officer (as in the army) ranking next below a brigadier general

**col·o·nize** \'kälə‚nīz\ *vb* **-nized; -niz·ing 1** : establish a colony in **2** : settle — **col·o·ni·za·tion** \‚kälənə'zāshən\ *n* — **col·o·niz·er** *n*

**col·on·nade** \‚kälə'nād\ *n* : row of supporting columns

**col·o·ny** \'kälənē\ *n, pl* **-nies 1** : people who inhabit a new territory or the territory itself **2** : animals of one kind (as bees) living together — **co·lo·nial** \kə'lōnēəl\ *adj or n* — **col·o·nist** \'kälənist\ *n*

**col·or** \'kələr\ *n* **1** : quality of visible things distinct from shape that results

from light reflection **2** *pl* : flag **3** : liveliness ~ *vb* **1** : give color to **2** : blush — **col·or·fast** *adj* — **col·or·ful** *adj* — **col·or·less** *adj*

**col·or–blind** *adj* : unable to distinguish colors — **color blindness** *n*

**col·ored** \'kələrd\ *adj* **1** : having color **2** : of a race other than the white ~ *n, pl* **colored** *or* **coloreds** : colored person

**co·los·sal** \kə'läsəl\ *adj* : very large or great

**co·los·sus** \-səs\ *n, pl* **-si** \-'läs‚ī\ : something of great size or scope

**colt** \'kōlt\ *n* : young male horse — **colt·ish** *adj*

**col·umn** \'käləm\ *n* **1** : vertical section of a printed page **2** : regular feature article (as in a newspaper) **3** : pillar **4** : row (as of soldiers) — **co·lum·nar** \kə'ləmnər\ *adj* — **col·um·nist** \'käləmnist\ *n*

**co·ma** \'kōmə\ *n* : deep prolonged unconsciousness — **co·ma·tose** \-‚tōs, 'kämə-\ *adj*

**comb** \'kōm\ *n* **1** : toothed instrument for arranging the hair **2** : crest on a fowl's head — **comb** *vb* — **combed** \'kōmd\ *adj*

**com·bat** \kəm'bat, 'käm‚bat\ *vb* **-bat·ed** *or* **-bat·ted; -bat·ing** *or* **-bat·ting** : fight — **com·bat** \'käm‚bat\ *n* — **com·bat·ant** \kəm'bat°nt\ *n* — **com·bat·ive** \kəm'bativ\ *adj*

**com·bi·na·tion** \‚kämbə'nāshən\ *n* **1** : process or result of combining **2** : code for opening a lock

**com·bine** \kəm'bīn\ *vb* **-bined; -bin·ing** : join together ~ \'käm‚bīn\ *n* **1** : association for business or political advantage **2** : harvesting machine

**com·bus·ti·ble** \kəm'bəstəbəl\ *adj* : apt to catch fire — **com·bus·ti·bil·i·ty** \-‚bəstə'bilətē\ *n* — **combustible** *n*

**com·bus·tion** \-'bəschən\ *n* : process of burning

**come** \'kəm\ *vb* **came** \'kām\; **come; com·ing 1** : move toward or arrive at something **2** : reach a state **3** : originate or exist **4** : amount — **come clean** *vb* : confess — **come into** *vb* : acquire, achieve — **come off** *vb* : succeed — **come to** *vb* : regain consciousness — **come to pass** : happen — **come to terms** : reach an agreement

**come·back** \n\ **1** : retort **2** : return to a former position — **come back** vb

**co·me·di·an** \kə'mēdēən\ n **1** : comic actor **2** : funny person **3** : entertainer specializing in comedy

**co·me·di·enne** \-,mēdē'en\ n : a woman who is a comedian

**com·e·dy** \'kämədē\ n, pl **-dies** **1** : an amusing play **2** : humorous entertainment

**come·ly** \'kəmlē\ adj **-li·er; -est** : attractive — **come·li·ness** n

**com·et** \'kämət\ n : small bright celestial body having a tail

**com·fort** \'kəmfərt\ n **1** : consolation **2** : well-being or something that gives it ~ vb **1** : give hope to **2** : console — **com·fort·able** \'kəmftəbəl, 'kəmfərt-\ adj — **com·fort·ably** \-blē\ adv

**com·fort·er** \'kəmfərtər\ n **1** : one that comforts **2** : quilt

**com·ic** \'kämik\ adj **1** : relating to comedy **2** : funny ~ n **1** : comedian **2** : sequence of cartoons — **com·i·cal** adj

**com·ing** \'kəmiŋ\ adj : next

**com·ma** \'kämə\ n : punctuation mark , used esp. to separate sentence parts

**com·mand** \kə'mand\ vb **1** : order **2** : control ~ n **1** : act of commanding **2** : an order given **3** : mastery **4** : troops under a commander — **com·man·dant** \'kämən,dant, -,dänt\ n

**com·man·deer** \,kämən'dir\ vb : seize by force

**com·mand·er** \kə'mandər\ n **1** : officer commanding an army or subdivision of an army **2** : commissioned officer in the navy ranking next below a captain

**com·mand·ment** \-'mandmənt\ n : order

**command sergeant major** n : noncommissioned officer in the army ranking above a first sergeant

**com·mem·o·rate** \kə'memə,rāt\ vb **-rat·ed; -rat·ing** : celebrate or honor — **com·mem·o·ra·tion** \-,memə'rāshən\ n — **com·mem·o·ra·tive** \-'memrətiv, -'memə,rāt-\ adj

**com·mence** \kə'mens\ vb **-menced; -menc·ing** : start

**com·mence·ment** \-mənt\ n **1** : beginning **2** : graduation ceremony

**com·mend** \kə'mend\ vb **1** : entrust **2** : recommend **3** : praise — **com-** **mend·able** \-əbəl\ adj — **com·men·da·tion** \,kämən'dāshən, -,en-\ n

**com·men·su·rate** \kə'mensərət, -'mench-\ adj : equal in measure or extent

**com·ment** \'käm,ent\ n : statement of opinion or remark — **comment** vb

**com·men·tary** \-ən,terē\ n, pl **-tar·ies** : series of comments

**com·men·ta·tor** \-ən,tātər\ n : one who discusses news

**com·merce** \'kämərs\ n : business

**com·mer·cial** \kə'mərshəl\ adj : designed for profit or for mass appeal ~ n : broadcast advertisement — **com·mer·cial·ize** \-,īz\ vb — **com·mer·cial·ly** \-ē\ adv

**com·min·gle** \kə'miŋgəl\ vb : mix

**com·mis·er·ate** \kə'mizə,rāt\ vb **-at·ed; -at·ing** : sympathize — **com·mis·er·a·tion** \-,mizə'rāshən\ n

**com·mis·sary** \'kämə,serē\ n, pl **-sar·ies** : store esp. for military personnel

**com·mis·sion** \kə'mishən\ n **1** : order granting power or rank **2** : panel to judge, approve, or act **3** : the doing of an act **4** : agent's fee ~ vb **1** : confer rank or authority to or for **2** : request something be done

**com·mis·sion·er** \-shənər\ n **1** : member of a commission **2** : head of a government department

**com·mit** \kə'mit\ vb **-tt-** **1** : turn over to someone for safekeeping or confinement **2** : perform or do **3** : pledge — **com·mit·ment** n

**com·mit·tee** \kə'mitē\ n : panel that examines or acts on something

**com·mo·di·ous** \kə'mōdēəs\ adj : spacious

**com·mod·i·ty** \kə'mädətē\ n, pl **-ties** : article for sale

**com·mo·dore** \'kämə,dōr\ n **1** : former commissioned officer in the navy ranking next below a rear admiral **2** : officer commanding a group of merchant ships

**com·mon** \'kämən\ adj **1** : public **2** : shared by several **3** : widely known, found, or observed **4** : ordinary ~ n : community land — **com·mon·ly** adv — **in common** : shared together

**com·mon·place** \'kämən,plās\ n : cliché ~ adj : ordinary

**common sense** n : good judgment

**com·mon·weal** \-,wēl\ n : general welfare

**com·mon·wealth** \-,welth\ n : state

**com·mo·tion** \kə'mōshən\ *n* : disturbance

¹**com·mune** \kə'myün\ *vb* **-muned; -mun·ing** : communicate intimately

²**com·mune** \'käm,yün; kə'myün\ : community that shares all ownership and duties — **com·mu·nal** \-ᵊl\ *adj*

**com·mu·ni·cate** \kə'myünə,kāt\ *vb* **-cat·ed; -cat·ing 1** : make known **2** : transmit **3** : exchange information or opinions — **com·mu·ni·ca·ble** \-'myünikəbəl\ *adj* — **com·mu·ni·ca·tion** \-,myünə'kāshən\ *n* — **com·mu·ni·ca·tive** \-'myüni,kātiv, -kət-\ *adj*

**Com·mu·nion** \kə'myünyən\ *n* : Christian sacrament of partaking of bread and wine

**com·mu·ni·qué** \kə'myünə,kā, -,myünə'kā\ *n* : official bulletin

**com·mu·nism** \'kämyə,nizəm\ *n* **1** : social organization in which goods are held in common **2** *cap* : political doctrine based on revolutionary Marxist socialism — **com·mu·nist** \-nist\ *n or adj, often cap* — **com·mu·nis·tic** \,kämyə'nistik\ *adj, often cap*

**com·mu·ni·ty** \kə'myünətē\ *n, pl* **-ties** : body of people living in the same place under the same laws

**com·mute** \kə'myüt\ *vb* **-mut·ed; -mut·ing 1** : reduce (a punishment) **2** : travel back and forth regularly ⁓ *n* : trip made in commuting — **com·mu·ta·tion** \,kämyə'tāshən\ *n* — **com·mut·er** *n*

¹**com·pact** \kəm'pakt, 'käm,pakt\ *adj* **1** : hard **2** : small or brief ⁓ *vb* : pack together ⁓ \'käm,pakt\ *n* **1** : cosmetics case **2** : small car — **com·pact·ly** *adv* — **com·pact·ness** *n*

²**com·pact** \'käm,pakt\ *n* : agreement

**compact disc** *n* : plastic-coated disc with laser-readable recorded music

**com·pan·ion** \kəm'panyən\ *n* **1** : close friend **2** : one of a pair — **com·pan·ion·able** *adj* — **com·pan·ion·ship** *n*

**com·pa·ny** \'kəmpənē\ *n, pl* **-nies 1** : business organization **2** : group of performers **3** : guests **4** : infantry unit

**com·par·a·tive** \kəm'parətiv\ *adj* **1** : relating to or being an adjective or adverb form that denotes increase **2** : relative — **comparative** *n* — **com·par·a·tive·ly** *adv*

**com·pare** \kəm'par\ *vb* **-pared; -par-**ing **1** : represent as similar **2** : check for likenesses or differences ⁓ *n* : comparison — **com·pa·ra·ble** \'kämprəbəl\ *adj*

**com·par·i·son** \kəm'parəsən\ *n* **1** : act of comparing **2** : change in the form and meaning of an adjective or adverb to show different levels of quality, quantity, or relation

**com·part·ment** \kəm'pärtmənt\ *n* : section or room

**com·pass** \'kəmpəs, 'käm-\ *n* **1** : scope **2** : device for drawing circles **3** : device for determining direction

**com·pas·sion** \kəm'pashən\ *n* : pity — **com·pas·sion·ate** \-ənət\ *adj*

**com·pat·i·ble** \-'patəbəl\ *adj* : harmonious — **com·pat·i·bil·i·ty** \-,patə'bilətē\ *n*

**com·pa·tri·ot** \kəm'pātrēət, -trē,ät\ *n* : fellow countryman

**com·pel** \kəm'pel\ *vb* **-ll-** : cause through necessity

**com·pen·di·ous** \kam'pendēəs\ *adj* **1** : concise and comprehensive **2** : comprehensive

**com·pen·di·um** \-'pendēəm\ *n, pl* **-di·ums** *or* **-dia** \-dēə\ : summary

**com·pen·sate** \'kämpən,sāt\ *vb* **-sat·ed; -sat·ing 1** : offset or balance **2** : repay — **com·pen·sa·tion** \,kämpən'sāshən\ *n* — **com·pen·sa·to·ry** \kəm'pensə,tōrē\ *adj*

**com·pete** \kəm'pēt\ *vb* **-pet·ed; -pet·ing** : strive to win — **com·pe·ti·tion** \,kämpə'tishən\ *n* — **com·pet·i·tive** \kəm'petətiv\ *adj* — **com·pet·i·tive·ness** *n* — **com·pet·i·tor** \kəm'petətər\ *n*

**com·pe·tent** \'kämpətənt\ *adj* : capable — **com·pe·tence** \-əns\ *n* — **com·pe·ten·cy** \-ənsē\ *n*

**com·pile** \kəm'pīl\ *vb* **-piled; -pil·ing** : collect or compose from several sources — **com·pi·la·tion** \,kämpə'lāshən\ *n* — **com·pil·er** \kəm'pīlər\ *n*

**com·pla·cen·cy** \kəm'plās°nsē\ *n* : self-satisfaction — **com·pla·cent** \-ᵊnt\ *adj*

**com·plain** \kəm'plān\ *vb* **1** : express grief, pain, or discontent **2** : make an accusation — **com·plain·ant** *n* — **com·plain·er** *n*

**com·plaint** \-'plānt\ *n* **1** : expression of grief or discontent **2** : ailment **3** : formal accusation

**com·ple·ment** \'kämpləmənt\ *n* **1**

: something that completes **2** : full number or amount ~ \-ˌment\ *vb* : complete — **com·ple·men·ta·ry** \ˌkämplə'mentərē\ *adj*

**com·plete** \kəm'plēt\ *adj* **-plet·er; -est 1** : having all parts **2** : finished **3** : total ~ *vb* **-plet·ed; -plet·ing 1** : make whole **2** : finish — **com·plete·ly** *adv* — **com·plete·ness** *n* — **com·ple·tion** \-'plēshən\ *n*

**com·plex** \käm'pleks, kəm-; 'kämˌpleks\ *adj* **1** : having many parts **2** : intricate ~ \'kämˌpleks\ *n* : psychological problem — **com·plex·i·ty** \kəm'pleksətē, käm-\ *n*

**com·plex·ion** \kəm'plekshən\ *n* : hue or appearance of the skin esp. of the face — **com·plex·ioned** *adj*

**com·pli·cate** \'kämplə,kāt\ *vb* **-cat·ed; -cat·ing** : make complex or hard to understand — **com·pli·cat·ed** \-əd\ *adj* — **com·pli·ca·tion** \ˌkämplə'kāshən\ *n*

**com·plic·i·ty** \kəm'plisətē\ *n, pl* **-ties** : participation in guilt

**com·pli·ment** \'kämpləmənt\ *n* **1** : flattering remark **2** *pl* : greeting ~ \-ˌment\ *vb* : pay a compliment to

**com·pli·men·ta·ry** \ˌkämplə'mentərē\ *adj* **1** : praising **2** : free

**com·ply** \kəm'plī\ *vb* **-plied; -ply·ing** : conform or yield — **com·pli·ance** \-əns\ *n* — **com·pli·ant** \-ənt\ *n*

**com·po·nent** \kəm'pōnənt, 'käm,pō-\ *n* : part of something larger ~ *adj* : serving as a component

**com·port** \kəm'pōrt\ *vb* **1** : agree **2** : behave — **com·port·ment** \-mənt\ *n*

**com·pose** \kəm'pōz\ *vb* **-posed; -pos·ing 1** : create (as by writing) or put together **2** : calm **3** : set type — **com·pos·er** *n* — **com·po·si·tion** \ˌkämpə'zishən\ *n*

**com·pos·ite** \käm'päzət, kəm-\ *adj* : made up of diverse parts — **composite** *n*

**com·post** \'käm,pōst\ *n* : decayed organic fertilizing material

**com·po·sure** \kəm'pōzhər\ *n* : calmness

**com·pote** \'käm,pōt\ *n* : fruits cooked in syrup

¹**com·pound** \'käm,pau̇nd, käm'pau̇nd\ *vb* **1** : combine or add **2** : pay (interest) on principal and accrued interest ~ \'käm,pau̇nd\ *adj* : made up of 2

or more parts ~ \'käm,pau̇nd\ *n* : something that is compound

²**com·pound** \'käm,pau̇nd\ *n* : enclosure

**com·pre·hend** \ˌkämpri'hend\ *vb* **1** : understand **2** : include — **com·pre·hen·si·ble** \-'hensəbəl\ *adj* — **com·pre·hen·sion** \-'henchən\ *n* — **com·pre·hen·sive** \-siv\ *adj*

**com·press** \kəm'pres\ *vb* : squeeze together ~ \'käm,pres\ *n* : pad for pressing on a wound — **com·pres·sion** \-'preshən\ *n* — **com·pres·sor** \-'presər\ *n*

**compressed air** *n* : air under pressure greater than that of the atmosphere

**com·prise** \kəm'prīz\ *vb* **-prised; -pris·ing 1** : contain or cover **2** : be made up of

**com·pro·mise** \'kämprə,mīz\ *vb* **-mised; -mis·ing** : settle differences by mutual concessions — **compromise** *n*

**comp·trol·ler** \kən'trōlər, 'kämp,trō-\ *n* : financial officer

**com·pul·sion** \kəm'pəlshən\ *n* **1** : coercion **2** : irresistible impulse — **com·pul·sive** \-siv\ *adj* — **com·pul·so·ry** \-'pəlsərē\ *adj*

**com·punc·tion** \-'pənkshən\ *n* : remorse

**com·pute** \-'pyüt\ *vb* **-put·ed; -put·ing** : calculate — **com·pu·ta·tion** \ˌkämpyü'tāshən\ *n*

**com·put·er** \kəm'pyütər\ *n* : electronic data processing machine — **com·put·er·i·za·tion** \-ˌpyütərə'zāshən\ *n* — **com·put·er·ize** \-'pyütə-ˌrīz\ *vb*

**com·rade** \'käm,rad, -rəd\ *n* : companion — **com·rade·ship** *n*

¹**con** \'kän\ *adv* : against ~ *n* : opposing side or person

²**con** *vb* **-nn-** : swindle

**con·cave** \kän'kāv, 'kän,kāv\ *adj* : curved like the inside of a sphere — **con·cav·i·ty** \kän'kavətē\ *n*

**con·ceal** \kən'sēl\ *vb* : hide — **con·ceal·ment** *n*

**con·cede** \-'sēd\ *vb* **-ced·ed; -ced·ing** : grant

**con·ceit** \-'sēt\ *n* : excessively high opinion of oneself — **con·ceit·ed** \-əd\ *adj*

**con·ceive** \-'sēv\ *vb* **-ceived; -ceiv·ing 1** : become pregnant **2** : think of — **con·ceiv·able** \-'sēvəbəl\ *adj* — **con·ceiv·ably** \-blē\ *adv* con·cen·trate \'känsən,trāt\ vb -trat-ed; -trat·ing 1 : gather together 2 : make stronger 3 : fix one's attention ~ n : something concentrated — con·cen·tra·tion \,känsən'trāshən\ n

con·cen·tric \kən'sentrik\ adj : having a common center

con·cept \'kän,sept\ n : thought or idea

con·cep·tion \kən'sepshən\ n 1 : act of conceiving 2 : idea

con·cern \kən'sərn\ vb 1 : relate to 2 : involve ~ n 1 : affair 2 : worry 3 : business — con·cerned \-'sərnd\ adj — con·cern·ing \-'sərniŋ\ prep

con·cert \'kän,sərt\ n 1 : agreement or joint action 2 : public performance of music — con·cert·ed \kən-'sərtəd\ adj

con·cer·ti·na \,känsər'tēnə\ n : accordionlike instrument

con·cer·to \kən'chertō\ n, pl -ti \-tē\ or -tos : orchestral work with solo instruments

con·ces·sion \-'seshən\ n 1 : act of conceding 2 : something conceded 3 : right to do business on a property

conch \'käŋk, 'känch\ n, pl conchs \'käŋks\ or conch·es \'känchəz\ : large spiral-shelled marine mollusk

con·cil·ia·to·ry \kən'silēə,tōrē\ adj : mollifying

con·cise \kən'sīs\ adj : said in few words — con·cise·ly adv — con·cise·ness n — con·ci·sion \kən-'sizhən\ n

con·clave \'kän,klāv\ n : private meeting

con·clude \kən'klüd\ vb -clud·ed; -clud·ing 1 : end 2 : decide — con·clu·sion \-'klüzhən\ n — con·clu·sive \-siv\ adj — con·clu·sive·ly adv

con·coct \kən'käkt, kän-\ vb : prepare or devise — con·coc·tion \-'käkshən\ n

con·com·i·tant \-'kämətənt\ adj : accompanying — concomitant n

con·cord \'kän,kórd, 'käŋ-\ n : agreement

con·cor·dance \kən'kórdᵊns\ n 1 : agreement 2 : index of words — con·cor·dant \-ᵊnt\ adj

con·course \'kän,kōrs\ n : open space where crowds gather

con·crete \kän'krēt, 'kän,krēt\ adj 1 : naming something real 2 : actual or

substantial 3 : made of concrete ~ \'kän,krēt, kän'krēt\ n : hard building material made of cement, sand, gravel, and water

con·cre·tion \kän'krēshən\ n : hard mass

con·cu·bine \'käŋkyú,bīn\ n : mistress

con·cur \kən'kər\ vb -rr- : agree — con·cur·rence \-'kərəns\ n

con·cur·rent \-ənt\ adj : happening at the same time

con·cus·sion \kən'kəshən\ n 1 : shock 2 : brain injury from a blow

con·demn \-'dem\ vb 1 : declare to be wrong, guilty, or unfit for use 2 : sentence — con·dem·na·tion \,kän-,dem'nāshən\ n

con·dense \kən'dens\ vb -densed; -dens·ing 1 : make or become more compact 2 : change from vapor to liquid — con·den·sa·tion \,kän-,den'sāshən, -dən-\ n — con·dens·er n

con·de·scend \,kändi'send\ vb 1 : lower oneself 2 : act haughtily — con·de·scen·sion \-'senchən\ n

con·di·ment \'kändəmənt\ n : pungent seasoning

con·di·tion \kən'dishən\ n 1 : necessary situation or stipulation 2 pl : state of affairs 3 : state of being ~ vb : put into proper condition — con·di·tion·al \kən'dishənəl\ adj — con·di·tion·al·ly \-ē\ adv

con·do·lence \kən'dōləns\ n : expression of sympathy — usu. pl.

con·do·min·i·um \,kändə'minēəm\ n, pl -ums : individually owned apartment

con·done \kən'dōn\ vb -doned; -don·ing : overlook or forgive

con·dor \'kändər, -,dór\ n : large western American vulture

con·du·cive \kən'düsiv, -'dyü-\ adj : tending to help or promote

con·duct \'kän,dəkt\ n 1 : management 2 : behavior ~ \kən'dəkt\ vb 1 : guide 2 : manage or direct 3 : be a channel for 4 : behave — con·duc·tion \-'dəkshən\ n — con·duc·tive \-'dəktiv\ adj — con·duc·tiv·i·ty \,kän,dək'tivətē\ n — con·duc·tor \-'dəktər\ n

con·duit \'kän,düət, -,dyü-\ n : channel (as for conveying fluid)

cone \'kōn\ n 1 : scaly fruit of pine

and related trees **2** : solid figure having a circular base and tapering sides

**con·fec·tion** \kən'fekshən\ n : sweet dish or candy — **con·fec·tion·er** \-shənər\ n

**con·fed·er·a·cy** \kən'fedərəsē\ n, pl **-cies 1** : league **2** cap : 11 southern states that seceded from the U.S. in 1860 and 1861

**con·fed·er·ate** \-rət\ adj **1** : united in a league **2** cap : relating to the Confederacy ~ n **1** : ally **2** cap : adherent of the Confederacy ~ \-'fedə,rāt\ vb **-at·ed; -at·ing** : unite — **con·fed·er·a·tion** \-,fedə'rāshən\ n

**con·fer** \kən'fər\ vb **-rr- 1** : give **2** : meet to exchange views — **con·fer·ee** \,känfə'rē\ n — **con·fer·ence** \'känfərəns\ n

**con·fess** \kən'fes\ vb **1** : acknowledge or disclose one's misdeed, fault, or sin **2** : declare faith in — **con·fes·sion** \-'feshən\ n — **con·fes·sion·al** \-'feshənəl\ n or adj

**con·fes·sor** \kən'fesər, 2 also ' kän,fes-\ n **1** : one who confesses **2** : priest who hears confessions

**con·fet·ti** \kən'fetē\ n : bits of paper or ribbon thrown in celebration

**con·fi·dant** \'känfə,dant, -,dänt\ n : one to whom secrets are confided

**con·fide** \kən'fīd\ vb **-fid·ed; -fid·ing 1** : share private thoughts **2** : reveal in confidence

**con·fi·dence** \'känfədəns\ n **1** : trust **2** : self-assurance **3** : something confided — **con·fi·dent** \-dənt\ adj — **con·fi·den·tial** \,känfə'denchəl\ adj — **con·fi·den·tial·ly** \-ē\ adv — **con·fi·dent·ly** adv

**con·fig·u·ra·tion** \kən,figyə'rāshən\ n : arrangement

**con·fine** \kən'fīn\ vb **-fined; -fin·ing 1** : restrain or restrict to a limited area **2** : imprison — **con·fine·ment** n — **con·fin·er** n

**confines** \'kän,fīnz\ n pl : bounds

**con·firm** \kən'fərm\ vb **1** : ratify **2** : verify **3** : admit as a full member of a church or synagogue — **con·fir·ma·tion** \,känfər'māshən\ n

**con·fis·cate** \'känfə,skāt\ vb **-cat·ed; -cat·ing** : take by authority — **con·fis·ca·tion** \,känfə'skāshən\ n — **con·fis·ca·to·ry** \kən'fiskə,tōrē\ adj

**con·fla·gra·tion** \,känflə'grāshən\ n : great fire

**con·flict** \'kän,flikt\ n **1** : war **2** : clash of ideas ~ \kən'flikt\ vb : clash

**con·form** \kən'fórm\ vb **1** : make or be like **2** : obey — **con·for·mi·ty** \kən'fórmətē\ n

**con·found** \kən'faúnd, kän-\ vb : confuse

**con·front** \kən'frənt\ vb : oppose or face — **con·fron·ta·tion** \,känfrən-'tāshən\ n

**con·fuse** \kən'fyüz\ vb **-fused; -fus·ing 1** : make mentally uncertain **2** : jumble — **con·fu·sion** \-'fyüzhən\ n

**con·fute** \-'fyüt\ vb **-fut·ed; -fut·ing** : overwhelm by argument

**con·geal** \kən'jēl\ vb **1** : freeze **2** : become thick and solid

**con·ge·nial** \kən'jēnēəl\ adj : kindred or agreeable — **con·ge·ni·al·i·ty** n

**con·gen·i·tal** \kən'jenət³l\ adj : existing from birth

**con·gest** \kən'jest\ vb : overcrowd or overfill — **con·ges·tion** \-'jeschən\ n — **con·ges·tive** \-'jestiv\ adj

**con·glom·er·ate** \kən'glämərət\ adj : made up of diverse parts ~ \-ə,rāt\ vb **-at·ed; -at·ing** : form into a mass ~ \-ərət\ n : diversified corporation — **con·glom·er·a·tion** \-,glämə'rāshən\ n

**con·grat·u·late** \kən'grachə,lāt, -'graj-\ vb **-lat·ed; -lat·ing** : express pleasure to for good fortune — **con·grat·u·la·tion** \-,grachə'lāshən, -,graj-\ n — **con·grat·u·la·to·ry** \-'grachələ,tōrē, -'graj-\ adj

**con·gre·gate** \'kängri,gāt\ vb **-gat·ed; -gat·ing** : assemble

**con·gre·ga·tion** \,kängri'gāshən\ n **1** : assembly of people at worship **2** : religious group — **con·gre·ga·tion·al** \-shənəl\ adj

**con·gress** \'kängrəs\ n : assembly of delegates or of senators and representatives — **con·gres·sio·nal** \kən-'greshənəl, kän-\ adj — **con·gress·man** \'kängrəsmən\ n — **con·gress·wom·an** n

**con·gru·ence** \kən'grüəns, 'kängrəw-əns\ n : likeness — **con·gru·ent** \-ənt\ adj

**con·gru·ity** \kən'grüətē, kän-\ n : correspondence between things — **con·gru·ous** \'kängrəwəs\ adj

**con·ic** \'känik\ adj : relating to or like a cone — **con·i·cal** \-ikəl\ adj

**con·ni·fer** \'känəfər, 'kōn-\ *n* : cone-bearing tree — **co·nif·er·ous** \kō-'nifərəs\ *adj*

**con·jec·ture** \kən'jekchər\ *n or vb* : guess — **con·jec·tur·al** \-əl\ *adj*

**con·join** \kən'jóin\ *vb* : join together — **con·joint** \-'jóint\ *adj*

**con·ju·gal** \'känjigəl, kən'jü-\ *adj* : relating to marriage

**con·ju·gate** \'känjə,gāt\ *vb* -**gat·ed**; -**gat·ing** : give the inflected forms of (a verb) — **con·ju·ga·tion** \,känjə-'gāshən\ *n*

**con·junc·tion** \kən'jəŋkshən\ *n* 1 : combination 2 : occurrence at the same time 3 : a word that joins other words together — **con·junc·tive** \-tiv\ *adj*

**con·jure** \'känjər, 'kən-\ *vb* -**jured**; -**jur·ing** 1 : summon by sorcery 2 : practice sleight of hand 3 : entreat — **con·jur·er, con·ju·ror** \'känjərər, 'kən-\ *n*

**con·nect** \kə'nekt\ *vb* : join or associate — **con·nect·able** *adj* — **con·nec·tion** \-'nekshən\ *n* — **con·nec·tive** \-tiv\ *n or adj* — **con·nec·tor** *n*

**con·nive** \kə'nīv\ *vb* -**nived**; -**niv·ing** 1 : pretend ignorance of wrongdoing 2 : cooperate secretly — **con·niv·ance** *n*

**con·nois·seur** \,känə'sər, -'súr\ *n* : expert judge esp. of art

**con·note** \kə'nōt\ *vb* -**not·ed**; -**not·ing** : suggest additional meaning — **con·no·ta·tion** \,känə'tāshən\ *n*

**con·nu·bi·al** \kə'nübēəl, -'nyü-\ *adj* : relating to marriage

**con·quer** \'käŋkər\ *vb* : defeat or overcome — **con·quer·or** \-kərər\ *n*

**con·quest** \'kän,kwest, 'käŋ-\ *n* 1 : act of conquering 2 : something conquered

**con·science** \'känchəns\ *n* : awareness of right and wrong

**con·sci·en·tious** \,känchē'enchəs\ *adj* : honest and hard-working — **con·sci·en·tious·ly** *adv*

**con·scious** \'känchəs\ *adj* 1 : aware 2 : mentally awake or alert 3 : intentional — **con·scious·ly** *adv* — **con·scious·ness** *n*

**con·script** \kən'skript\ *vb* : draft for military service — **con·script** \'kän,skript\ *n* — **con·scrip·tion** \kən'skripshən\ *n*

**con·se·crate** \'känsə,krāt\ *vb* -**crat·ed**; -**crat·ing** 1 : declare sacred 2

: devote to a solemn purpose — **con·se·cra·tion** \,känə'krāshən\ *n*

**con·sec·u·tive** \kən'sekyətiv\ *adj* : following in order — **con·sec·u·tive·ly** *adv*

**con·sen·sus** \-'sensəs\ *n* 1 : agreement in opinion 2 : collective opinion

**con·sent** \-'sent\ *vb* : give permission or approval — **consent** *n*

**con·se·quence** \'känsə,kwens\ *n* 1 : result or effect 2 : importance — **con·se·quent** \-kwənt, -,kwent\ *adj* — **con·se·quent·ly** *adv*

**con·se·quen·tial** \,känsə'kwenchəl\ *adj* : important

**con·ser·va·tion** \,känsər'vāshən\ *n* : planned management of natural resources — **con·ser·va·tion·ist** \-shən-ist\ *n*

**con·ser·va·tive** \kən'sərvətiv\ *adj* 1 : disposed to maintain the status quo 2 : cautious — **con·ser·va·tism** \-və,tizəm\ *n* — **conservative** *n* — **con·ser·va·tive·ly** *adv*

**con·ser·va·to·ry** \kən'sərvə,tōrē\ *n*, *pl* -**ries** : school for art or music

**con·serve** \-'sərv\ *vb* -**served**; -**serv·ing** : keep from wasting ~ \'kän-,sərv\ *n* : candied fruit or fruit preserves

**con·sid·er** \kən'sidər\ *vb* 1 : think about 2 : give thoughtful attention to 3 : think that — **con·sid·er·ate** \-'sidərət\ *adj* — **con·sid·er·ation** \-,sidə'rāshən\ *n*

**con·sid·er·able** \-'sidərəbəl\ *adj* 1 : significant 2 : noticeably large — **con·sid·er·a·bly** \-blē\ *adv*

**con·sid·er·ing** *prep* : taking notice of

**con·sign** \kən'sīn\ *vb* 1 : transfer 2 : send to an agent for sale — **con·sign·ee** \,känsə'nē, -,sī-; kən,sī-\ *n* — **con·sign·ment** \kən'sīnmənt\ *n* — **con·sign·or** \,känsə'nór, -,sī-; kən,sī-\ *n*

**con·sist** \kən'sist\ *vb* 1 : be inherent — used with *in* 2 : be made up — used with *of*

**con·sis·ten·cy** \-'sistənsē\ *n*, *pl* -**cies** 1 : degree of thickness or firmness 2 : quality of being consistent

**con·sis·tent** \-tənt\ *adj* : being steady and regular — **con·sis·tent·ly** *adv*

¹**con·sole** \kən'sōl\ *vb* -**soled**; -**sol·ing** : soothe the grief of — **con·so·la·tion** \,känsə'lāshən\ *n*

²**con·sole** \'kän,sōl\ *n* : cabinet or part with controls

**con·sol·i·date** \kən'sälə‚dāt\ vb -dat-ed; -dat·ing : unite or compact — **con·sol·i·da·tion** \-‚sälə'dāshən\ n

**con·som·mé** \‚känsə'mā\ n : clear soup

**con·so·nance** \'känsənəns\ n : agreement or harmony — **con·so·nant** \-nənt\ adj — **con·so·nant·ly** adv

**con·so·nant** \-nənt\ n 1 : speech sound marked by constriction or closure in the breath channel 2 : letter other than a, e, i, o and u — **con·so·nan·tal** \‚känsə'nant²l\ adj

**con·sort** \'kän‚sòrt\ n : spouse ~ \kən'sòrt\ vb : keep company

**con·spic·u·ous** \kən'spikyəwəs\ adj : very noticeable — **con·spic·u·ous·ly** adv

**con·spire** \kən'spīr\ vb -spired; -spir-ing : secretly plan an unlawful act — **con·spir·a·cy** \-'spirəsē\ n — **con·spir·a·tor** \-'spirətər\ n — **con·spir·a·to·ri·al** \-‚spirə'tōrēəl\ adj

**con·sta·ble** \'känstəbəl, 'kən-\ n : police officer

**con·stab·u·lary** \kən'stabyə‚lerē\ n, pl -lar·ies : police force

**con·stant** \'känstənt\ adj 1 : steadfast or faithful 2 : not varying 3 : continually recurring ~ n : something unchanging — **con·stan·cy** \-stənsē\ n — **con·stant·ly** adv

**con·stel·la·tion** \‚känstə'lāshən\ n : group of stars

**con·ster·na·tion** \-stər'nāshən\ n : amazed dismay

**con·sti·pa·tion** \-stə'pāshən\ n : difficulty of defecation — **con·sti·pate** \'känstə‚pāt\ vb

**con·stit·u·ent** \kən'stichəwənt\ adj 1 : component 2 : having power to elect ~ n 1 : component part 2 : one who may vote for a representative — **con·stit·u·en·cy** \-wənsē\ n

**con·sti·tute** \'känstə‚tüt, -‚tyüt\ vb -tut·ed; -tut·ing 1 : establish 2 : be all or a basic part of

**con·sti·tu·tion** \‚känstə'tüshən, -'tyü-\ n 1 : physical composition or structure 2 : the basic law of an organized body or the document containing it — **con·sti·tu·tion·al** \-əl\ adj — **con·sti·tu·tion·al·i·ty** \-‚tüshə'nalətē, -‚tyü-\ n

**con·strain** \kən'strān\ vb 1 : compel 2 : confine 3 : restrain — **con·straint** \-'strānt\ n

**con·strict** \-'strikt\ vb : draw or squeeze together — **con·stric·tion** \-'strikshən\ n — **con·stric·tive** \-'striktiv\ adj

**con·struct** \kən'strəkt\ vb : build or make — **con·struc·tion** \-'strək-shən\ n — **con·struc·tive** \-tiv\ adj

**con·strue** \kən'strü\ vb -strued; -stru·ing : explain or interpret

**con·sul** \'känsəl\ n 1 : Roman magistrate 2 : government commercial official in a foreign country — **con·sul·ar** \-ələr\ adj — **con·sul·ate** \-lət\ n

**con·sult** \kən'səlt\ vb 1 : ask the advice or opinion of 2 : confer — **con·sul·tant** \-ənt\ n — **con·sul·ta·tion** \‚känsəl'tāshən\ n

**con·sume** \kən'süm\ vb -sumed; -sum·ing : eat or use up — **con·sum·able** adj — **con·sum·er** n

**con·sum·mate** \kən'səmət\ adj : complete or perfect ~ \'känsə‚māt\ vb -mat·ed; -mat·ing : make complete — **con·sum·ma·tion** \‚känsə'mā-shən\ n

**con·sump·tion** \kən'səmpshən\ n 1 : act of consuming 2 : use of goods 3 : tuberculosis — **con·sump·tive** \-tiv\ adj or n

**con·tact** \'kän‚takt\ n 1 : a touching 2 : association or relationship 3 : connection or communication ~ vb 1 : come or bring into contact 2 : communicate with

**con·ta·gion** \kən'tājən\ n 1 : spread of disease by contact 2 : disease spread by contact — **con·ta·gious** \-jəs\ adj

**con·tain** \-'tān\ vb 1 : enclose or include 2 : have or hold within 3 : restrain — **con·tain·er** n — **con·tain·ment** n

**con·tam·i·nate** \kən'tamə‚nāt\ vb -nat·ed; -nat·ing : soil or infect by contact or association — **con·tam·i·na·tion** \-‚tamə'nāshən\ n

**con·tem·plate** \'käntəm‚plāt\ vb -plat·ed; -plat·ing : view or consider thoughtfully — **con·tem·pla·tion** \‚käntəm'plāshən\ n — **con·tem·pla·tive** \kən'templətiv; 'käntəm‚plāt-\ adj

**con·tem·po·ra·ne·ous** \kən‚tempə-'rānēəs\ adj : contemporary

**con·tem·po·rary** \-'tempə‚rerē\ adj 1 : occurring or existing at the same time 2 : of the same age — **contemporary** n

**con·tempt** \kən'tempt\ n 1 : feeling

of scorn **2** : state of being despised **3** : disobedience to a court or legislature — **con·tempt·ible** \-'tempt-əbəl\ adj

**con·temp·tu·ous** \-'tempchəwəs\ adj : feeling or expressing contempt — **con·temp·tu·ous·ly** adv

**con·tend** \kən'tend\ vb **1** : strive against rivals or difficulties **2** : argue **3** : maintain or claim — **con·tend·er** n

**¹con·tent** \kən'tent\ adj : satisfied ~ vb : satisfy ~ n : ease of mind — **con·tent·ed** adj — **con·tent·ed·ly** adv — **con·tent·ed·ness** n — **content·ment** n

**²con·tent** \'kän,tent\ n **1** pl : something contained **2** pl : subject matter (as of a book) **3** : essential meaning **4** : proportion contained

**con·ten·tion** \kən'tenchən\ n : state of contending — **con·ten·tious** \-chəs\ adj — **con·ten·tious·ly** adv

**con·test** \kən'test\ vb : dispute or challenge ~ \'kän,test\ n **1** : struggle **2** : game — **con·test·able** \kən-'testəbəl\ adj — **con·tes·tant** \-'testənt\ n

**con·text** \'kän,tekst\ n : words surrounding a word or phrase

**con·tig·u·ous** \kən'tigyəwəs\ adj : connected to or adjoining — **con·ti·gu·i·ty** \,käntə'gyüətē\ n

**con·ti·nence** \'känt°nəns\ n : self-restraint — **con·ti·nent** \-nənt\ adj

**con·ti·nent** \'känt°nənt\ n : great division of land on the globe — **con·ti·nen·tal** \,känt°n'ent°l\ adj

**con·tin·gen·cy** \kən'tinjənsē\ n, pl **-cies** : possible event

**con·tin·gent** \-jənt\ adj : dependent on something else ~ n : a quota from an area or group

**con·tin·u·al** \kən'tinyəwəl\ adj **1** : continuous **2** : steadily recurring — **con·tin·u·al·ly** \-ē\ adv

**con·tin·ue** \kən'tinyü\ vb **-tin·ued; -tin·u·ing 1** : remain in a place or condition **2** : endure **3** : resume after an intermission **4** : extend — **con·tin·u·ance** \-yəwəns\ n — **con·tin·u·ation** \-,tinyə'wāshən\ n

**con·tin·u·ous** \-'tinyəwəs\ adj : continuing without interruption — **con·ti·nu·i·ty** \,känt°n'üətē, -'yü-\ n — **con·tin·u·ous·ly** adv

**con·tort** \kən'tort\ vb : twist out of shape — **con·tor·tion** \-'torshən\ n

**con·tour** \'kän,túr\ n **1** : outline **2** pl : shape

**con·tra·band** \'käntrə,band\ n : illegal goods

**con·tra·cep·tion** \,käntrə'sepshən\ n : prevention of conception — **con·tra·cep·tive** \-'septiv\ adj or n

**con·tract** \'kän,trakt\ n : binding agreement ~ \kən'trakt; *1* usu 'kän,trakt\ vb **1** : establish or undertake by contract **2** : become ill with **3** : make shorter — **con·trac·tion** \kən'trakshən\ n — **con·trac·tor** \'kän,traktər, kən'trak-\ n — **con·trac·tu·al** \kən'trakchəwəl\ adj — **con·trac·tu·al·ly** adv

**con·tra·dict** \,käntrə'dikt\ vb : state the contrary of — **con·tra·dic·tion** \-'dikshən\ n — **con·tra·dic·to·ry** \-'diktərē\ adj

**con·tral·to** \kən'traltō\ n, pl **-tos** : lowest female singing voice

**con·trap·tion** \kən'trapshən\ n : device or contrivance

**con·trary** \'kän,trerē; *4 often* kən-'trerē\ adj **1** : opposite in character, nature, or position **2** : mutually opposed **3** : unfavorable **4** : uncooperative or stubborn — **con·trar·i·ly** \-,trerəlē, -'trer-\ adv — **con·trari·wise** \-,wīz\ adv — **contrary** \'kän,trerē\ n

**con·trast** \'kän,trast\ n **1** : unlikeness shown by comparing **2** : unlike color or tone of adjacent parts ~ \kən-'trast\ vb **1** : show differences **2** : compare so as to show differences

**con·tra·vene** \,käntrə'vēn\ vb **-vened; -ven·ing** : go or act contrary to

**con·trib·ute** \kən'tribyət\ vb **-ut·ed; -ut·ing** : give or help along with others — **con·tri·bu·tion** \,käntrə-'byüshən\ n — **con·trib·u·tor** \kən-'tribyətər\ n — **con·trib·u·to·ry** \-yə,tōrē\ adj

**con·trite** \'kän,trīt, kən'trīt\ adj : repentant — **con·tri·tion** \kən'trishən\ n

**con·trive** \kən'trīv\ vb **-trived; -triv·ing 1** : devise or make with ingenuity **2** : bring about — **con·triv·ance** \-'trīvəns\ n — **con·triv·er** n

**con·trol** \-'trōl\ vb **-ll- 1** : exercise power over **2** : dominate or rule ~ n **1** : power to direct or regulate **2** : restraint **3** : regulating device — **con·trol·la·ble** adj — **con·trol·ler** \-'trōlər, 'kän,-\ n

**con·tro·ver·sy** \'kän·trə₁vərsē\ *n, pl* **-sies** : clash of opposing views — **con·tro·ver·sial** \₁käntrə'vərshəl, -sēəl\ *adj*

**con·tro·vert** \'käntrə₁vərt, ₁käntrə'-\ *vb* : contradict — **con·tro·vert·ible** *adj*

**con·tu·ma·cious** \₁käntə'māshəs, -tyə-\ *adj* : rebellious

**con·tu·me·ly** \kən'tüməlē, 'käntü-₁mēlē, -tyü-\ *n* : rudeness

**con·tu·sion** \kən'tüzhən, -tyü-\ *n* : bruise — **con·tuse** \-'tüz, -'tyüz\ *vb*

**co·nun·drum** \kə'nəndrəm\ *n* : riddle

**con·va·lesce** \₁känvə'les\ *vb* **-lesced; -lesc·ing** : gradually recover health — **con·va·les·cence** \-ᵊns\ *n* — **con·va·les·cent** \-ᵊnt\ *adj or n*

**con·vec·tion** \kən'vekshən\ *n* : circulation in fluids due to warmer portions rising and colder ones sinking — **con·vec·tion·al** \-'vekshənəl\ *adj* — **con·vec·tive** \-'vektiv\ *adj*

**con·vene** \kən'vēn\ *vb* **-vened; -ven·ing** : assemble or meet

**con·ve·nience** \-'vēnyəns\ *n* 1 : personal comfort or ease 2 : device that saves work

**con·ve·nient** \-nyənt\ *adj* 1 : suited to one's convenience 2 : near at hand — **con·ve·nient·ly** *adv*

**con·vent** \'känvənt, -₁vent\ *n* : community of nuns

**con·ven·tion** \kən'venchən\ *n* 1 : agreement esp. between nations 2 : large meeting 3 : body of delegates 4 : accepted usage or way of behaving — **con·ven·tion·al** \-'venchənəl\ *adj* — **con·ven·tion·al·ly** *adv*

**con·verge** \kən'vərj\ *vb* **-verged; -verg·ing** : approach a single point — **con·ver·gence** \-'vərjəns\ *n* — **con·ver·gent** \-jənt\ *adj*

**con·ver·sant** \-'vərsᵊnt\ *adj* : having knowledge and experience

**con·ver·sa·tion** \₁känvər'sāshən\ *n* : an informal talking together — **con·ver·sa·tion·al** \-shənəl\ *adj*

¹**con·verse** \kən'vərs, 'kän₁vərs\ *vb* **-vers·ing** : engage in conversation — **con·verse** \'kän₁vərs\ *n*

²**con·verse** \kən'vərs, 'kän₁vərs\ *adj* : opposite — **con·verse** \'kän₁vərs\ *n* — **con·verse·ly** *adv*

**con·ver·sion** \kən'vərzhən\ *n* 1 : change 2 : adoption of religion

**con·vert** \kən'vərt\ *vb* 1 : turn from one belief or party to another 2 : change ~ \'kän₁vərt\ *n* : one who has undergone religious conversion — **con·vert·er, con·ver·tor** \kən-'vərtər\ *n* — **con·vert·ible** *adj*

**con·vert·ible** \kən'vərtəbəl\ *n* : automobile with a removable top

**con·vex** \kän'veks, 'kän₁-, kən'-\ *adj* : curved or rounded like the outside of a sphere — **con·vex·i·ty** \kən'veksətē, kän-\ *n*

**con·vey** \kən'vā\ *vb* **-veyed; -vey·ing** : transport or transmit — **con·vey·ance** \-'vāəns\ *n* — **con·vey·or** \-ər\ *n*

**con·vict** \kən'vikt\ *vb* : find guilty ~ \'kän₁vikt\ *n* : person in prison

**con·vic·tion** \kən'vikshən\ *n* 1 : act of convicting 2 : strong belief

**con·vince** \-'vins\ *vb* **-vinced; -vinc·ing** : cause to believe — **con·vinc·ing·ly** *adv*

**con·viv·ial** \-'vivyəl, -'vivēəl\ *adj* : cheerful or festive — **con·viv·i·al·i·ty** \-₁vivē'alətē\ *n*

**con·voke** \kən'vōk\ *vb* **-voked; -vok·ing** : call together to a meeting — **con·vo·ca·tion** \₁känvə'kāshən\ *n*

**con·vo·lut·ed** \'känvə₁lütəd\ *adj* 1 : intricately folded 2 : intricate

**con·vo·lu·tion** \₁känvə'lüshən\ *n* : convoluted structure

**con·voy** \'kän₁vȯi, kən'vȯi\ *vb* : accompany for protection ~ \'kän₁vȯi\ *n* : group of vehicles or ships moving together

**con·vul·sion** \kən'vəlshən\ *n* : violent involuntary muscle contraction — **con·vulse** \-'vəls\ *vb* — **con·vul·sive** \-'vəlsiv\ *adj*

**coo** \'kü\ *n* : sound of a pigeon — **coo** *vb*

**cook** \'kük\ *n* : one who prepares food ~ *vb* : prepare food — **cook·book** *n* — **cook·er** *n* — **cook·ery** \-ərē\ *n* — **cook·ware** *n*

**cook·ie, cooky** \'kükē\ *n, pl* **-ies** : small sweet flat cake

**cool** \'kül\ *adj* 1 : moderately cold 2 : not excited 3 : unfriendly ~ *vb* : make or become cool ~ *n* 1 : cool time or place 2 : composure — **cool·ant** \-ənt\ *n* — **cool·er** *n* — **cool·ly** *adv* — **cool·ness** *n*

**coo·lie** \'külē\ *n* : unskilled laborer in or from the Far East

**coop** \'küp, 'kůp\ *n* : enclosure usu.

for poultry ~ *vb* : confine in or as if in a coop

**co·op** \'kō̩äp\ *n* : cooperative

**coo·per** \'küpər, 'kup-\ *n* : barrel maker — **cooper** *vb*

**co·op·er·ate** \kō'äpə̩rāt\ *vb* : act jointly — **co·op·er·a·tion** \-̩äpə-'rāshən\ *n*

**co·op·er·a·tive** \kō'äpərətiv, -'äpə̩rāt-\ *adj* : willing to work with others ~ *n* : enterprise owned and run by those using its services

**co·opt** \kō'äpt\ *vb* 1 : elect as a colleague 2 : take over

**co·or·di·nate** \-'órd³nət\ *adj* : equal esp. in rank ~ *n* : any of a set of numbers used in specifying the location of a point on a surface or in space ~ \-³n̩āt\ *vb* **-nat·ed; -nat·ing** 1 : make or become coordinate 2 : work or act together harmoniously — **co·or·di·nate·ly** *adv* — **co·or·di·na·tion** \-̩órd³n'āshən\ *n* — **co·or·di·na·tor** \-³n̩ātər\ *n*

**coot** \'küt\ *n* 1 : dark-colored ducklike bird 2 : harmless simple person

**cop** \'käp\ *n* : police officer

**¹cope** \'kōp\ *n* : cloaklike ecclesiastical vestment

**²cope** *vb* **coped; cop·ing** : deal with difficulties

**co·pi·lot** \'kō̩pīlət\ *n* : assistant airplane pilot

**cop·ing** \'kōpiŋ\ *n* : top layer of a wall

**co·pi·ous** \'kōpēəs\ *adj* : very abundant — **co·pi·ous·ly** *adv* — **co·pi·ous·ness** *n*

**cop·per** \'käpər\ *n* 1 : malleable reddish metallic chemical element 2 : penny — **cop·pery** *adj*

**cop·per·head** *n* : largely coppery brown venomous snake

**co·pra** \'kōprə\ *n* : dried coconut meat

**copse** \'käps\ *n* : thicket

**cop·u·la** \'käpyələ\ *n* : verb linking subject and predicate — **cop·u·la·tive** \-̩lātiv\ *adj*

**cop·u·late** \'käpyə̩lāt\ *vb* **-lat·ed; -lat·ing** : engage in sexual intercourse — **cop·u·la·tion** \̩käpyə'lāshən\ *n*

**copy** \'käpē\ *n, pl* **cop·ies** 1 : imitation or reproduction of an original 2 : writing to be set for printing ~ *vb* **cop·ied; copy·ing** 1 : make a copy of 2 : imitate — **copi·er** \-ər\ *n* — **copyist** *n*

**copy·right** *n* : sole right to a literary or artistic work ~ *vb* : get a copyright on

**co·quette** \kō'ket\ *n* : flirt

**cor·al** \'kórəl\ *n* 1 : skeletal material of colonies of tiny sea polyps 2 : deep pink — **coral** *adj*

**cord** \'kórd\ *n* 1 : usu. heavy string 2 : long slender anatomical structure 3 : measure of firewood equal to 128 cu. ft. 4 : small electrical cable ~ *vb* 1 : tie or furnish with a cord 2 : pile (wood) in cords

**cor·dial** \'kórjəl\ *adj* : warmly welcoming ~ *n* : liqueur — **cor·di·al·i·ty** \̩kórjē'alətē, kórd'yal-\ *n* — **cor·dial·ly** \'kórjəlē\ *adv*

**cor·don** \'kórd³n\ *n* : encircling line of troops or police — **cordon** *vb*

**cor·do·van** \'kórdəvən\ *n* : soft fine=grained leather

**cor·du·roy** \'kórdə̩rói\ *n* 1 : heavy ribbed fabric 2 *pl* : trousers of corduroy

**core** \'kōr\ *n* 1 : central part of some fruits 2 : inmost part ~ *vb* **cored; cor·ing** : take out the core of — **cor·er** *n*

**cork** \'kórk\ *n* 1 : tough elastic bark of a European oak (**cork oak**) 2 : stopper of cork ~ *vb* : stop up with a cork — **corky** *adj*

**cork·screw** *n* : device for drawing corks from bottles

**cor·mo·rant** \'kórmərənt, -̩rant\ *n* : dark seabird

**¹corn** \'kórn\ *n* : cereal grass or its seeds ~ *vb* : cure or preserve in brine — **corn·meal** *n* — **corn·stalk** *n* — **corn·starch** *n*

**²corn** *n* : local hardening and thickening of skin

**corn·cob** *n* : axis on which the kernels of Indian corn are arranged

**cor·nea** \'kórnēə\ *n* : transparent part of the coat of the eyeball — **cor·ne·al** *adj*

**cor·ner** \'kórnər\ *n* 1 : point or angle formed by the meeting of lines or sides 2 : place where two streets meet 3 : inescapable position 4 : control of the supply of something ~ *vb* 1 : drive into a corner 2 : get a corner on 3 : turn a corner

**cor·ner·stone** *n* 1 : stone at a corner of a wall 2 : something basic

**cor·net** \kór'net\ *n* : trumpetlike instrument

**cor·nice** \\'kórnəs\ *n* : horizontal wall projection

**cor·nu·co·pia** \\,kórnə'kōpēə, -nyə-\ *n* : goat's horn filled with fruits and grain emblematic of abundance

**co·rol·la** \kə'rälə\ *n* : petals of a flower

**cor·ol·lary** \'kórə,lerē\ *n, pl* **-lar·ies** **1** : logical deduction **2** : consequence or result

**co·ro·na** \kə'rōnə\ *n* : shining ring around the sun seen during eclipses

**cor·o·nary** \'kórə,nerē\ *adj* : relating to the heart or its blood vessels ~ *n* **1** : thrombosis of an artery supplying the heart **2** : heart attack

**cor·o·na·tion** \,kórə'nāshən\ *n* : crowning of a monarch

**cor·o·ner** \'kórənər\ *n* : public official who investigates causes of suspicious deaths

¹**cor·po·ral** \'kórpərəl\ *adj* : bodily

²**corporal** *n* : noncommissioned officer ranking next below a sergeant

**cor·po·ra·tion** \,kórpə'rāshən\ *n* : legal creation with the rights and liabilities of a person — **cor·po·rate** \'kórpərət\ *adj*

**cor·po·re·al** \kór'pōrēəl\ *adj* : physical or material — **cor·po·re·al·ly** *adv*

**corps** \'kór\ *n, pl* **corps** \'kórz\ **1** : subdivision of a military force **2** : working group

**corpse** \'kórps\ *n* : dead body

**cor·pu·lence** \'kórpyələns\ *n* : obesity — **cor·pu·lent** \-lənt\ *adj*

**cor·pus** \'kórpəs\ *n, pl* **-po·ra** \-pərə\ **1** : corpse **2** : body of writings

**cor·pus·cle** \'kór,pəsəl\ *n* : blood cell

**cor·ral** \kə'ral\ *n* : enclosure for animals — **corral** *vb*

**cor·rect** \kə'rekt\ *vb* **1** : make right **2** : chastise ~ *adj* **1** : true or factual **2** : conforming to a standard — **cor·rec·tion** \-'rekshən\ *n* — **cor·rec·tive** \-'rektiv\ *adj* — **cor·rect·ly** *adv* — **cor·rect·ness** *n*

**cor·re·late** \'kórə,lāt\ *vb* **-lat·ed; -lat·ing** : show a connection between — **cor·re·late** \-lət, -,lāt\ *n* — **cor·re·la·tion** \,kórə'lāshən\ *n*

**cor·rel·a·tive** \kə'relətiv\ *adj* : regularly used together — **correlative** *n*

**cor·re·spond** \,kórə'spänd\ *vb* **1** : match **2** : communicate by letter — **cor·re·spon·dence** \-'spändəns\ *n* — **cor·re·spond·ing·ly** \-'spändiŋlē\ *adv*

**cor·re·spon·dent** \-'spändənt\ *n* **1** : person one writes to **2** : reporter

**cor·ri·dor** \'kórədər, -,dòr\ *n* : passageway connecting rooms

**cor·rob·o·rate** \kə'räbə,rāt\ *vb* **-rat·ed; -rat·ing** : support with evidence — **cor·rob·o·ra·tion** \-,räbə'rāshən\ *n*

**cor·rode** \kə'rōd\ *vb* **-rod·ed; -rod·ing** : wear away by chemical action — **cor·ro·sion** \-'rōzhən\ *n* — **cor·ro·sive** \-'rōsiv\ *adj or n*

**cor·ru·gate** \'kórə,gāt\ *vb* **-gat·ed; -gat·ing** : form into ridges and grooves — **cor·ru·gat·ed** *adj* — **cor·ru·ga·tion** \,kórə'gāshən\ *n*

**cor·rupt** \kə'rəpt\ *vb* **1** : change from good to bad **2** : bribe ~ *adj* : morally debased — **cor·rupt·ible** *adj* — **cor·rup·tion** \-'rəpshən\ *n*

**cor·sage** \kór'säzh, -'säj\ *n* : bouquet worn by a woman

**cor·set** \'kórsət\ *n* : woman's stiffened undergarment

**cor·tege** \kór'tezh, 'kór,-\ *n* : funeral procession

**cor·tex** \'kór,teks\ *n, pl* **-ti·ces** \'kórtə-,sēz\ *or* **-tex·es** : outer or covering layer of an organism or part (as the brain) — **cor·ti·cal** \'kórtikəl\ *adj*

**cor·ti·sone** \'kórtə,sōn, -zōn\ *n* : adrenal hormone

**cos·met·ic** \käz'metik\ *n* : beautifying preparation ~ *adj* : relating to beautifying

**cos·mic** \'käzmik\ *adj* **1** : relating to the universe **2** : vast or grand

**cos·mo·naut** \'käzmə,nót\ *n* : Soviet or Russian astronaut

**cos·mo·pol·i·tan** \,käzmə'pälətᵊn\ *adj* : belonging to all the world — **cosmopolitan** *n*

**cos·mos** \'käzməs, -,mōs, -,mäs\ *n* : universe

**Cos·sack** \'käs,ak, -ək\ *n* : Russian cavalryman

**cost** \'kóst\ *n* **1** : amount paid for something **2** : loss or penalty ~ *vb* **cost; cost·ing** **1** : require so much in payment **2** : cause to pay, suffer, or lose — **cost·li·ness** \-lēnəs\ *n* — **cost·ly** \-lē\ *adj*

**cos·tume** \'käs,tüm, -,tyüm\ *n* : clothing

**co·sy** \'kōzē\ *var of* **COZY**

**cot** \'kät\ *n* : small bed

**cote** \'kōt, 'kät\ *n* : small shed or coop

**co·te·rie** \'kōtə,rē, ,kōtə'-\ *n* : exclusive group of persons

**co·til·lion** \kō'tilyən\ n : formal ball

**cot·tage** \'kätij\ n : small house

**cot·ton** \'kät³n\ n : soft fibrous plant substance or thread or cloth made of it — **cot·ton·seed** n — **cot·tony** adj

**cot·ton·mouth** n : poisonous snake

**couch** \'kau̇ch\ vb 1 : lie or place on a couch 2 : phrase ～ n : bed or sofa

**couch potato** n : one who spends a great deal of time watching television

**cou·gar** \'kügər, -ˌgär\ n : large tawny wild American cat

**cough** \'kȯf\ vb : force air from the lungs with short sharp noises — **cough** n

**could** \'ku̇d\ past of CAN

**coun·cil** \'kau̇nsəl\ n 1 : assembly or meeting 2 : body of lawmakers — **coun·cil·lor, coun·cil·or** \-sələr\ n — **coun·cil·man** \-mən\ n — **coun·cil·wom·an** n

**coun·sel** \'kau̇nsəl\ n 1 : advice 2 : deliberation together 3 pl -sel : lawyer ～ vb -seled or -selled; -sel·ing or -sel·ling 1 : advise 2 : consult together — **coun·sel·or, coun·sel·lor** \-sələr\ n

¹**count** \'kau̇nt\ vb 1 : name or indicate one by one to find the total number 2 : recite numbers in order 3 : rely 4 : be of value or account ～ n 1 : act of counting or the total obtained by counting 2 : charge in an indictment — **count·able** adj

²**count** n : European nobleman

**coun·te·nance** \'kau̇nt³nəns\ n : face or facial expression ～ vb -nanced; -nanc·ing : allow or encourage

¹**count·er** \'kau̇ntər\ n 1 : piece for reckoning or games 2 : surface over which business is transacted

²**count·er** n : one that counts

³**coun·ter** vb : oppose ～ adv : in an opposite direction ～ n : offsetting force or move ～ adj : contrary

**counter-** prefix 1 : contrary or opposite 2 : opposing 3 : retaliatory

**coun·ter·act** vb : lessen the force of — **coun·ter·ac·tive** adj

**coun·ter·bal·ance** n : balancing influence or weight ～ vb : oppose or balance

**coun·ter·clock·wise** adv or adj : opposite to the way a clock's hands move

**coun·ter·feit** \'kau̇ntər,fit\ vb 1 : copy in order to deceive 2 : pretend ～ adj : spurious ～ n : fraudulent copy — **coun·ter·feit·er** n

**coun·ter·mand** \-ˌmand\ vb : supersede with a contrary order

**coun·ter·pane** \-ˌpān\ n : bedspread

**coun·ter·part** n : one that is similar or corresponds

**coun·ter·point** n : music with interwoven melodies

**coun·ter·sign** n : secret signal ～ vb : add a confirming signature to

**count·ess** \'kau̇ntəs\ n : wife or widow of a count or an earl or a woman holding that rank in her own right

---

**List of self-explanatory words with the prefix counter-**

| | | |
|---|---|---|
| counteraccusation | counterevidence | counterreform |
| counteraggression | counterguerrilla | counterresponse |
| counterargue | counterinflationary | counterretaliation |
| counterassault | counterinfluence | counterrevolution |
| counterattack | countermeasure | counterrevolutionary |
| counterbid | countermove | counterstrategy |
| counterblockade | countermovement | counterstyle |
| counterblow | counteroffer | countersue |
| countercampaign | counterpetition | countersuggestion |
| countercharge | counterploy | countersuit |
| counterclaim | counterpower | countertendency |
| countercomplaint | counterpressure | counterterror |
| countercoup | counterpropaganda | counterterrorism |
| countercriticism | counterproposal | counterterrorist |
| counterdemand | counterprotest | counterthreat |
| counterdemonstration | counterquestion | counterthrust |
| counterdemonstrator | counterraid | countertrend |
| countereffort | counterrally | |

**count·less** \-ləs\ *adj* : too many to be numbered

**coun·try** \'kəntrē\ *n, pl* **-tries 1** : nation **2** : rural area — *adj* : rural — **coun·try·man** \-mən\ *n*

**coun·try·side** *n* : rural area or its people

**coun·ty** \'kaùntē\ *n, pl* **-ties** : local government division esp. of a state

**coup** \'kü\ *n, pl* **coups** \'küz\ **1** : brilliant sudden action or plan **2** : sudden overthrow of a government

**coupe** \'küp\ *n* : 2-door automobile with an enclosed body

**cou·ple** \'kəpəl\ *vb* **-pled; -pling** : link together — *n* **1** : pair **2** : two persons closely associated or married

**cou·pling** \'kəpliŋ\ *n* : connecting device

**cou·pon** \'kü,pän, 'kyü-\ *n* : certificate redeemable for goods or a cash discount

**cour·age** \'kərij\ *n* : ability to conquer fear or despair — **cou·ra·geous** \kə'rājəs\ *adj*

**cou·ri·er** \'kürēər, 'kərē-\ *n* : messenger

**course** \'kōrs\ *n* **1** : progress **2** : ground over which something moves **3** : part of a meal served at one time **4** : method of procedure **5** : subject taught in a series of classes — *vb* **coursed; cours·ing 1** : hunt with dogs **2** : run speedily — **of course** : as might be expected

**court** \'kōrt\ *n* **1** : residence of a sovereign **2** : sovereign and his or her officials and advisers **3** : area enclosed by a building **4** : space marked for playing a game **5** : place where justice is administered — *vb* : woo — **court·house** *n* — **court·room** *n* — **court·ship** \-,ship\ *n*

**cour·te·ous** \'kərtēəs\ *adj* : showing politeness and respect for others — **cour·te·ous·ly** *adv*

**cour·te·san** \'kōrtəzən, 'kərt-\ *n* : prostitute

**cour·te·sy** \'kərtəsē\ *n, pl* **-sies** : courteous behavior

**court·ier** \'kōrtēər, 'kōrtyər\ *n* : person in attendance at a royal court

**court·ly** \'kōrtlē\ *adj* **-li·er; -est** : polite or elegant — **court·li·ness** *n*

**court–mar·tial** *n, pl* **courts–martial** : military trial court — **court–martial** *vb*

**court·yard** *n* : enclosure open to the sky that is attached to a house

**cous·in** \'kəz°n\ *n* : child of one's uncle or aunt

**cove** \'kōv\ *n* : sheltered inlet or bay

**co·ven** \'kəvən\ *n* : group of witches

**cov·e·nant** \'kəvənənt\ *n* : binding agreement — **cov·e·nant** \-nənt, -,nant\ *vb*

**cov·er** \'kəvər\ *vb* **1** : place something over or upon **2** : protect or hide **3** : include or deal with — *n* : something that covers — **cov·er·age** \-ərij\ *n*

**cov·er·let** \-lət\ *n* : bedspread

**co·vert** \'kō,vərt, 'kəvərt\ *adj* : secret — *n* \'kəvərt, 'kō-\ : thicket that shelters animals

**cov·et** \'kəvət\ *vb* : desire enviously — **cov·et·ous** *adj*

**cov·ey** \'kəvē\ *n, pl* **-eys 1** : bird with her young **2** : small flock (as of quail)

¹**cow** \'kaù\ *n* : large adult female animal (as of cattle) — **cow·hide** *n*

²**cow** *vb* : intimidate

**cow·ard** \'kaùərd\ *n* : one who lacks courage — **cow·ard·ice** \-əs\ *n* — **cow·ard·ly** *adv or adj*

**cow·boy** *n* : a mounted ranch hand who tends cattle

**cow·er** \'kaùər\ *vb* : shrink from fear or cold

**cow·girl** *n* : woman ranch hand who tends cattle

**cowl** \'kaùl\ *n* : monk's hood

**cow·lick** \'kaù,lik\ *n* : turned-up tuft of hair that resists control

**cow·slip** \-,slip\ *n* : yellow flower

**cox·swain** \'käkən, -,swän\ *n* : person who steers a boat

**coy** \'kòi\ *adj* : shy or pretending shyness

**coy·ote** \'kī,ōt, kī'ōtē\ *n, pl* **coy·otes** *or* **coyote** : small No. American wolf

**coz·en** \'kəz°n\ *vb* : cheat

**co·zy** \'kōzē\ *adj* **-zi·er; -est** : snug

**crab** \'krab\ *n* : short broad shellfish with pincers

**crab·by** \'krabē\ *adj* **-bi·er; -est** : cross

¹**crack** \'krak\ *vb* **1** : break with a sharp sound **2** : fail in tone **3** : break without completely separating — *n* **1** : sudden sharp noise **2** : witty remark **3** : narrow break **4** : sharp blow **5** : try

²**crack** *adj* : extremely proficient

**crack·down** *n* : disciplinary action — **crack down** *vb*

**crack·er** \-ər\ *n* : thin crisp bakery product

**crack·le** \'krakəl\ *vb* **-led; -ling 1** : make snapping noises **2** : develop fine cracks in a surface — **crackle** *n*

**crack·pot** \'krak,pät\ *n* : eccentric

**crack–up** *n* : crash

**cra·dle** \'krād³l\ *n* : baby's bed ~ *vb* **-dled; -dling 1** : place in a cradle **2** : hold securely

**craft** \'kraft\ *n* **1** : occupation requiring special skill **2** : craftiness **3** *pl usu* **craft** : structure designed to provide transportation **4** *pl usu* **craft** : small boat — **crafts·man** \'kraftsmən\ *n* — **crafts·man·ship** \-,ship\ *n*

**crafty** \'kraftē\ *adj* **craft·i·er; -est** : sly — **craft·i·ness** *n*

**crag** \'krag\ *n* : steep cliff — **crag·gy** \-ē\ *adj*

**cram** \'kram\ *vb* **-mm- 1** : eat greedily **2** : pack in tight **3** : study intensely for a test

**cramp** \'kramp\ *n* **1** : sudden painful contraction of muscle **2** *pl* : sharp abdominal pains ~ *vb* **1** : affect with cramp **2** : restrain

**cran·ber·ry** \'kran,berē\ *n* : red acid berry of a trailing plant

**crane** \'krān\ *n* **1** : tall wading bird **2** : machine for lifting heavy objects ~ *vb* **craned; cran·ing** : stretch one's neck to see

**cra·ni·um** \'krānēəm\ *n, pl* **-ni·ums** *or* **-nia** \-nēə\ : skull — **cra·ni·al** \-əl\ *adj*

**crank** \'kraŋk\ *n* **1** : bent lever turned to operate a machine **2** : eccentric ~ *vb* : start or operate by turning a crank

**cranky** \'kraŋkē\ *adj* **crank·i·er; -est** : irritable

**cran·ny** \'kranē\ *n, pl* **-nies** : crevice

**craps** \'kraps\ *n* : dice game

**crash** \'krash\ *vb* **1** : break noisily **2** : fall and hit something with noise and damage ~ *n* **1** : loud sound **2** : action of crashing **3** : failure

**crass** \'kras\ *adj* : crude or unfeeling

**crate** \'krāt\ *n* : wooden shipping container — **crate** *vb*

**cra·ter** \'krātər\ *n* : volcanic depression

**cra·vat** \krə'vat\ *n* : necktie

**crave** \'krāv\ *vb* **craved; crav·ing** : long for — **crav·ing** *n*

**cra·ven** \'krāvən\ *adj* : cowardly — **cra·ven** *n*

**craw·fish** \'krȯ,fish\ *n* : crayfish

**crawl** \'krȯl\ *vb* **1** : move slowly (as by drawing the body along the ground) **2** : swarm with creeping things ~ *n* : very slow pace

**cray·fish** \'krā,fish\ *n* : lobsterlike freshwater crustacean

**cray·on** \'krā,än, -ən\ *n* : stick of chalk or wax used for drawing or coloring — **crayon** *vb*

**craze** \'krāz\ *vb* **crazed; craz·ing** : make or become insane ~ *n* : fad

**cra·zy** \'krāzē\ *adj* **cra·zi·er; -est 1** : mentally disordered **2** : wildly impractical — **cra·zi·ly** *adv* — **cra·zi·ness** *n*

**creak** \'krēk\ *vb or n* : squeak — **creaky** *adj*

**cream** \'krēm\ *n* **1** : yellowish fat-rich part of milk **2** : thick smooth sauce, confection, or cosmetic **3** : choicest part ~ *vb* : beat into creamy consistency — **creamy** *adj*

**cream·ery** \-ərē\ *n, pl* **-er·ies** : place where butter and cheese are made

**crease** \'krēs\ *n* : line made by folding — **crease** *vb*

**cre·ate** \krē'āt\ *vb* **-at·ed; -at·ing** : bring into being — **cre·ation** \krē'āshən\ *n* — **cre·ative** \-'ātiv\ *adj* — **cre·ativ·i·ty** \,krēā'tivətē\ *n* — **cre·a·tor** \krē'ātər\ *n*

**crea·ture** \'krēchər\ *n* : lower animal or human being

**cre·dence** \'krēd³ns\ *n* : belief

**cre·den·tials** \kri'denchəlz\ *n pl* : evidence of qualifications or authority

**cred·i·ble** \'kredəbəl\ *adj* : believable — **cred·i·bil·i·ty** \,kredə'bilətē\ *n*

**cred·it** \'kredət\ *n* **1** : balance in a person's favor **2** : time given to pay for goods **3** : belief **4** : esteem **5** : source of honor ~ *vb* **1** : believe **2** : give credit to

**cred·it·able** \-əbəl\ *adj* : worthy of esteem or praise — **cred·it·ably** \-əblē\ *adv*

**cred·i·tor** \-ər\ *n* : person to whom money is owed

**cred·u·lous** \'krejələs\ *adj* : easily convinced — **cre·du·li·ty** \kri'dülətē, -'dyü-\ *n*

**creed** \'krēd\ *n* : statement of essential beliefs

**creek** \'krēk, 'krik\ *n* : small stream

**creel** \'krēl\ *n* : basket for carrying fish

**creep** \'krēp\ *vb* **crept** \'krept\; **creep·ing 1** : crawl **2** : grow over

a surface like ivy — **creep** n —
**creep·er** n

**cre·mate** \'krē‚māt\ vb **-mat·ed;
-mat·ing** : burn up (a corpse) — **cre·
ma·tion** \kri'māshən\ n — **cre·ma·
to·ry** \'krēmə‚tōrē, 'krem-\ n

**cre·o·sote** \'krēə‚sōt\ n : oily wood
preservative

**crepe, crêpe** \'krāp\ n : light crinkled
fabric

**cre·scen·do** \krə'shendō\ adv or adj
: growing louder — **crescendo** n

**cres·cent** \'kres²nt\ n : shape of the
moon between new moon and first
quarter

**crest** \'krest\ n  **1** : tuft on a bird's head
**2** : top of a hill or wave  **3** : part of a
coat of arms ⁓ vb : rise to a crest —
**crest·ed** \-təd\ adj

**crest·fall·en** adj : sad

**cre·tin** \'krēt²n\ n : stupid person

**cre·vasse** \kri'vas\ n : deep fissure esp.
in a glacier

**crev·ice** \'krevəs\ n : narrow fissure

**crew** \'krü\ n : body of workers (as on
a ship) — **crew·man** \-mən\ n

**crib** \'krib\ n  **1** : manger  **2** : grain
storage bin  **3** : baby's bed ⁓ vb **-bb-**
: put in a crib

**crib·bage** \'kribij\ n : card game
scored by moving pegs on a board
(**cribbage board**)

**crick** \'krik\ n : muscle spasm

¹**crick·et** \'krikət\ n : insect noted for
the chirping of the male

²**cricket** n : bat and ball game played on a
field with wickets

**cri·er** \'krīər\ n : one who calls out an-
nouncements

**crime** \'krīm\ n : serious violation of
law

**crim·i·nal** \'krimən²l\ adj : relating to
or being a crime or its punishment ⁓
n : one who commits a crime

**crimp** \'krimp\ vb : cause to become
crinkled, wavy, or bent — **crimp** n

**crim·son** \'krimzən\ n : deep red —
**crimson** adj

**cringe** \'krinj\ vb **cringed; cring·ing**
: shrink in fear

**crin·kle** \'kriŋkəl\ vb **-kled; -kling**
: wrinkle — **crinkle** n — **crin·kly**
\-klē\ adj

**crin·o·line** \'krin²lən\ n  **1** : stiff cloth
**2** : full stiff skirt or petticoat

**crip·ple** \'kripəl\ n : disabled person
⁓ vb **-pled; -pling** : disable

**cri·sis** \'krīsəs\ n, pl **cri·ses** \-‚sēz\
: decisive or critical moment

**crisp** \'krisp\ adj  **1** : easily crumbled
**2** : firm and fresh  **3** : lively  **4** : invigorating — **crisp** vb — **crisp·ly** adv
— **crisp·ness** n — **crispy** adj

**criss·cross** \'kris‚krós\ n : pattern of
crossed lines ⁓ vb : mark with or follow a crisscross

**cri·te·ri·on** \krī'tirēən\ n, pl **-ria** \-ēə\
: standard

**crit·ic** \'kritik\ n : judge of literary or
artistic works

**crit·i·cal** \-ikəl\ adj  **1** : inclined to criticize  **2** : being a crisis  **3** : relating to
criticism or critics — **crit·i·cal·ly**
\-iklē\ adv

**crit·i·cize** \'kritə‚sīz\ vb **-cized; -ciz·
ing  1** : judge as a critic  **2** : find fault
— **crit·i·cism** \-ə‚sizəm\ n

**cri·tique** \krə'tēk\ n : critical estimate

**croak** \'krōk\ n : hoarse harsh cry (as
of a frog) — **croak** vb

**cro·chet** \krō'shā\ n : needlework
done with a hooked needle — **cro·
chet** vb

**crock** \'kräk\ n : thick earthenware pot
or jar — **crock·ery** \-ərē\ n

**croc·o·dile** \'kräkə‚dīl\ n : large reptile of tropical waters

**cro·cus** \'krōkəs\ n, pl **-cus·es** : herb
with spring flowers

**crone** \'krōn\ n : ugly old woman

**cro·ny** \'krōnē\ n, pl **-nies** : chum

**crook** \'krúk\ n  **1** : bent or curved tool
or part  **2** : thief ⁓ vb : curve sharply

**crook·ed** \'krúkəd\ adj  **1** : bent  **2**
: dishonest — **crook·ed·ness** n

**croon** \'krün\ vb : sing softly —
**croon·er** n

**crop** \'kräp\ n  **1** : pouch in the throat
of a bird or insect  **2** : short riding
whip  **3** : something that can be har-
vested ⁓ vb **-pp-  1** : trim  **2** : appear
unexpectedly — used with up

**cro·quet** \krō'kā\ n : lawn game of
driving balls through wickets

**cro·quette** \-'ket\ n : mass of minced
food deep-fried

**cro·sier** \'krōzhər\ n : bishop's staff

**cross** \'krós\ n  **1** : figure or structure
consisting of an upright and a cross
piece  **2** : interbreeding of unlike
strains ⁓ vb  **1** : intersect  **2** : cancel
**3** : go or extend across  **4** : interbreed
⁓ adj  **1** : going across  **2** : contrary
**3** : marked by bad temper — **cross·
ing** n — **cross·ly** adv

**cross•bow** \-,bō\ *n* : short bow mounted on a rifle stock

**cross•breed** *vb* **-bred; -breed•ing** : hybridize

**cross•ex•am•ine** *vb* : question about earlier testimony — **cross•ex•am•i•na•tion** *n*

**cross•eyed** *adj* : having the eye turned toward the nose

**cross•re•fer** *vb* : refer to another place (as in a book) — **cross•ref•er•ence** *n*

**cross•roads** *n* : place where 2 roads cross

**cross section** *n* : representative portion

**cross•walk** *n* : path for pedestrians crossing a street

**cross•ways** *adv* : crosswise

**cross•wise** \-,wīz\ *adv* : so as to cross something — **crosswise** *adj*

**crotch** \'kräch\ *n* : angle formed by the parting of 2 legs or branches

**crotch•ety** \'krächətē\ *adj* : cranky, ill-natured

**crouch** \'kraùch\ *vb* : stoop over — **crouch** *n*

**croup** \'krüp\ *n* : laryngitis of infants

**crou•ton** \'krü,tän\ *n* : bit of toast

¹**crow** \'krō\ *n* : large glossy black bird

²**crow** *vb* **1** : make the loud sound of the cock **2** : gloat ~ *n* : cry of the cock

**crow•bar** *n* : metal bar used as a pry or lever

**crowd** \'kraùd\ *vb* : collect or cram together ~ *n* : large number of people

**crown** \'kraùn\ *n* **1** : wreath of honor or victory **2** : royal headdress **3** : top or highest part ~ *vb* **1** : place a crown on **2** : honor — **crowned** \'kraùnd\ *adj*

**cru•cial** \'krüshəl\ *adj* : vitally important

**cru•ci•ble** \'krüsəbəl\ *n* : heat-resisting container

**cru•ci•fix** \'krüsə,fiks\ *n* : representation of Christ on the cross

**cru•ci•fix•ion** \,krüsə'fikshən\ *n* : act of crucifying

**cru•ci•fy** \'krüsə,fī\ *vb* **-fied; -fy•ing 1** : put to death on a cross **2** : persecute

**crude** \'krüd\ *adj* **crud•er; -est 1** : not refined **2** : lacking grace or elegance ~ *n* : unrefined petroleum — **crude•ly** *adv* — **cru•di•ty** \-ətē\ *n*

**cru•el** \'krüəl\ *adj* **-el•er** *or* **-el•ler; -el•est** *or* **-el•lest** : causing suffering to others — **cru•el•ly** \-ē\ *adv* — **cru•el•ty** \tē\ *n*

**cru•et** \'krüət\ *n* : bottle for salad dressings

**cruise** \'krüz\ *vb* **cruised; cruis•ing 1** : sail to several ports **2** : travel at the most efficient speed — **cruise** *n*

**cruis•er** \'krüzər\ *n* **1** : warship **2** : police car

**crumb** \'krəm\ *n* : small fragment

**crum•ble** \'krəmbəl\ *vb* **-bled; -bling** : break into small pieces — **crum•bly** \-blē\ *adj*

**crum•ple** \'krəmpəl\ *vb* **-pled; -pling 1** : crush together **2** : collapse

**crunch** \'krənch\ *vb* : chew or press with a crushing noise ~ *n* : crunching sound — **crunchy** *adj*

**cru•sade** \krü'sād\ *n* **1** *cap* : medieval Christian expedition to the Holy Land **2** : reform movement — **crusade** *vb* — **cru•sad•er** *n*

**crush** \'krəsh\ *vb* **1** : squeeze out of shape **2** : grind or pound to bits **3** : suppress ~ *n* **1** : severe crowding **2** : infatuation

**crust** \'krəst\ *n* **1** : hard outer part of bread or a pie **2** : hard surface layer — **crust•al** *adj* — **crusty** *adj*

**crus•ta•cean** \,krəs'tāshən\ *n* : aquatic arthropod having a firm shell

**crutch** \'krəch\ *n* : support for use by the disabled in walking

**crux** \'krəks, 'krùks\ *n, pl* **crux•es 1** : hard problem **2** : crucial point

**cry** \'krī\ *vb* **cried; cry•ing 1** : call out **2** : weep ~ *n, pl* **cries 1** : shout **2** : fit of weeping **3** : characteristic sound of an animal

**crypt** \'kript\ *n* : underground chamber

**cryp•tic** \'kriptik\ *adj* : enigmatic

**cryp•tog•ra•phy** \krip'tägrəfē\ *n* : coding and decoding of messages — **cryp•tog•ra•pher** \-fər\ *n*

**crys•tal** \'krist²l\ *n* **1** : transparent quartz **2** : something (as glass) like crystal **3** : body formed by solidification that has a regular repeating atomic arrangement — **crys•tal•line** \-tələn\ *adj*

**crys•tal•lize** \-tə,līz\ *vb* **-lized; -liz•ing** : form crystals or a definite shape — **crys•tal•li•za•tion** \,kristələ'zāshən\ *n*

**cub** \'kəb\ *n* : young animal

**cub•by•hole** \'kəbē,hōl\ *n* : small confined space

**cube** \'kyüb\ *n* **1** : solid having 6 equal square sides **2** : product obtained by taking a number 3 times as a factor

~ *vb* **cubed; cub·ing 1** : raise to the 3d power **2** : form into a cube **3** : cut into cubes — **cu·bic** \'kyübik\ *adj*

**cu·bi·cle** \-bikəl\ *n* : small room

**cu·bit** \'kyübət\ *n* : ancient unit of length equal to about 18 inches

**cuck·old** \'kəkəld, 'kuk-\ *n* : man whose wife is unfaithful — **cuckold** *vb*

**cuck·oo** \'kükü, 'kuk-\ *n, pl* **-oos** : brown European bird ~ *adj* : silly

**cu·cum·ber** \'kyü,kəmbər\ *n* : fleshy fruit related to the gourds

**cud** \'kəd\ *n* : food chewed again by ruminating animals

**cud·dle** \'kəd³l\ *vb* **-dled; -dling** : lie close

**cud·gel** \'kəjəl\ *n or vb* : club

¹**cue** \'kyü\ *n* : signal — **cue** *vb*

²**cue** *n* : stick used in pool

¹**cuff** \'kəf\ *n* **1** : part of a sleeve encircling the wrist **2** : folded trouser hem

²**cuff** *vb or n* : slap

**cui·sine** \kwi'zēn\ *n* : manner of cooking

**cu·li·nary** \'kələ,nerē, 'kyülə-\ *adj* : of or relating to cookery

**cull** \'kəl\ *vb* : select

**cul·mi·nate** \'kəlmə,nāt\ *vb* **-nat·ed; -nat·ing** : rise to the highest point — **cul·mi·na·tion** \,kəlmə'nāshən\ *n*

**cul·pa·ble** \'kəlpəbəl\ *adj* : deserving blame

**cul·prit** \'kəlprət\ *n* : guilty person

**cult** \'kəlt\ *n* **1** : religious system **2** : faddish devotion — **cult·ist** *n*

**cul·ti·vate** \'kəltə,vāt\ *vb* **-vat·ed; -vat·ing 1** : prepare for crops **2** : foster the growth of **3** : refine — **cul·ti·va·tion** \,kəltə'vāshən\ *n*

**cul·ture** \'kəlchər\ *n* **1** : cultivation **2** : refinement of intellectual and artistic taste **3** : particular form or stage of civilization — **cul·tur·al** \'kəlchərəl\ *adj* — **cul·tured** \'kəlchərd\ *adj*

**cul·vert** \'kəlvərt\ *n* : drain crossing under a road or railroad

**cum·ber·some** \'kəmbərsəm\ *adj* : awkward to handle due to bulk

**cu·mu·la·tive** \'kyümyələtiv, -,lāt-\ *adj* : increasing by additions

**cu·mu·lus** \'kyümyələs\ *n, pl* **-li** \-,lī, -,lē\ : massive rounded cloud

**cun·ning** \'kəniŋ\ *adj* **1** : crafty **2** : clever **3** : appealing ~ *n* **1** : skill **2** : craftiness

**cup** \'kəp\ *n* **1** : small drinking vessel **2** : contents of a cup **3** : a half pint ~ *vb* **-pp-** : shape like a cup — **cup·ful** *n*

**cup·board** \'kəbərd\ *n* : small storage closet

**cup·cake** *n* : small cake

**cu·pid·i·ty** \kyü'pidətē\ *n, pl* **-ties** : excessive desire for money

**cu·po·la** \'kyüpələ, -,lō\ *n* : small rooftop structure

**cur** \'kər\ *n* : mongrel dog

**cu·rate** \'kyúrət\ *n* : member of the clergy — **cu·ra·cy** \-əsē\ *n*

**cu·ra·tor** \kyú'rātər\ *n* : one in charge of a museum or zoo

**curb** \'kərb\ *n* **1** : restraint **2** : raised edging along a street ~ *vb* : hold back

**curd** \'kərd\ *n* : coagulated milk

**cur·dle** \'kərd³l\ *vb* **-dled; -dling 1** : form curds **2** : sour

**cure** \'kyúr\ *n* **1** : recovery from disease **2** : remedy ~ *vb* **cured; cur·ing 1** : restore to health **2** : process for storage or use — **cur·able** *adj*

**cur·few** \'kər,fyü\ *n* : requirement to be off the streets at a set hour

**cu·rio** \'kyúrē,ō\ *n, pl* **-ri·os** : rare or unusual article

**cu·ri·ous** \'kyúrēəs\ *adj* **1** : eager to learn **2** : strange — **cu·ri·os·i·ty** \,kyúrē'äsətē\ *n* — **cu·ri·ous·ness** *n*

**curl** \'kərl\ *vb* **1** : form into ringlets **2** : curve ~ *n* **1** : ringlet of hair **2** : something with a spiral form — **curl·er** *n* — **curly** *adj*

**cur·lew** \'kərlü, -lyü\ *n, pl* **-lews** *or* **-lew** : long-legged brownish bird

**curli·cue** \'kərli,kyü\ *n* : fanciful curve

**cur·rant** \'kərənt\ *n* **1** : small seedless raisin **2** : berry of a shrub

**cur·ren·cy** \'kərənsē\ *n, pl* **-cies 1** : general use or acceptance **2** : money

**cur·rent** \'kərənt\ *adj* : occurring in or belonging to the present ~ *n* **1** : swiftest part of a stream **2** : flow of electricity

**cur·ric·u·lum** \kə'rikyələm\ *n, pl* **-la** \-lə\ : course of study

¹**cur·ry** \'kərē\ *vb* **-ried; -ry·ing** : brush (a horse) with a horse brush (**cur·ry·comb** \-,kōm\) — **curry fa·vor** : seek favor by flattery

²**curry** *n, pl* **-ries** : blend of pungent spices or a food seasoned with this

**curse** \\'kərs\ *n* **1** : a calling down of evil or harm upon one **2** : affliction ~ *vb* **cursed; curs·ing 1** : call down injury upon **2** : swear at **3** : afflict

**cur·sor** \\'kərsər\ *n* : indicator on a computer screen

**cur·so·ry** \\'kərsərē\ *adj* : hastily done

**curt** \\'kərt\ *adj* : rudely abrupt — **curt·ly** *adv* — **curt·ness** *n*

**cur·tail** \kər'tāl\ *vb* : shorten — **cur·tail·ment** *n*

**cur·tain** \\'kərtᵊn\ *n* : hanging screen that can be drawn back or raised — **curtain** *vb*

**curt·sy, curt·sey** \\'kərtsē\ *n, pl* **-sies** *or* **-seys** : courteous bow made by bending the knees — **curtsy, curtsey** *vb*

**cur·va·ture** \\'kərvə,chùr\ *n* : amount or state of curving

**curve** \\'kərv\ *vb* **curved; curv·ing** : bend from a straight line or course ~ *n* **1** : a bending without angles **2** : something curved

**cush·ion** \\'kùshən\ *n* **1** : soft pillow **2** : something that eases or protects ~ *vb* **1** : provide with a cushion **2** : soften the force of

**cusp** \\'kəsp\ *n* : pointed end

**cus·pid** \\'kəspəd\ *n* : a canine tooth

**cus·pi·dor** \\'kəspə,dȯr\ *n* : spittoon

**cus·tard** \\'kəstərd\ *n* : sweetened cooked mixture of milk and eggs

**cus·to·dy** \\'kəstədē\ *n, pl* **-dies** : immediate care or charge — **cus·to·di·al** \,kəs'tōdēəl\ *adj* — **cus·to·di·an** \-dēən\ *n*

**cus·tom** \\'kəstəm\ *n* **1** : habitual course of action **2** *pl* : import taxes — *adj* : made to personal order — **cus·tom·ar·i·ly** \,kəstə'merəlē\ *adv* — **cus·tom·ary** \\'kəstə,merē\ *adj* — **custom–built** *adj* — **cus·tom–made** *adj*

**cus·tom·er** \\'kəstəmər\ *n* : buyer

**cut** \\'kət\ *vb* **cut; cut·ting 1** : penetrate or divide with a sharp edge **2** : experience the growth of (a tooth) through the gum **3** : shorten **4** : remove by severing **5** : intersect ~ *n* **1** : something separated by cutting **2** : reduction — **cut in** *vb* : thrust oneself between others

**cu·ta·ne·ous** \kyú'tānēəs\ *adj* : relating to the skin

**cute** \\'kyüt\ *adj* **cut·er; -est** : pretty

**cu·ti·cle** \\'kyütikəl\ *n* : outer layer (as of skin)

**cut·lass** \\'kətləs\ *n* : short heavy curved sword

**cut·lery** \-lərē\ *n* : cutting utensils

**cut·let** \-lət\ *n* : slice of meat

**cut·ter** \\'kətər\ *n* **1** : tool or machine for cutting **2** : small armed motorboat **3** : light sleigh

**cut·throat** *n* : murderer ~ *adj* : ruthless

**-cy** \sē\ *n suffix* **1** : action or practice **2** : rank or office **3** : body **4** : state or quality

**cy·a·nide** \\'sīə,nīd, -nəd\ *n* : poisonous chemical salt

**cy·ber-** *comb form* : computer : computer network

**cy·ber·space** \\'sībər,spās\ *n* : online world of the Internet

**cy·cle** \\'sīkəl, 4 also 'sikəl\ *n* **1** : period of time for a series of repeated events **2** : recurring round of events **3** : long period of time **4** : bicycle or motorcycle ~ *vb* **-cled; -cling** : ride a cycle — **cy·clic** \\'sīklik, 'sik-\, **cy·cli·cal** \-əl\ *adj* — **cy·clist** \\'sīklist, 'sik-\ *n*

**cy·clone** \\'sī,klōn\ *n* : tornado — **cy·clon·ic** \sī'klänik\ *adj*

**cy·clo·pe·dia, cy·clo·pae·dia** \,sīklə-'pēdēə\ *n* : encyclopedia

**cyl·in·der** \\'siləndər\ *n* **1** : long round body or figure **2** : rotating chamber in a revolver **3** : piston chamber in an engine — **cy·lin·dri·cal** \sə'lindrikəl\ *adj*

**cym·bal** \\'simbəl\ *n* : one of 2 concave brass plates clashed together

**cyn·ic** \\'sinik\ *n* : one who attributes all actions to selfish motives — **cyn·i·cal** \-ikəl\ *adj* — **cyn·i·cism** \-ə,sizəm\ *n*

**cy·no·sure** \\'sīnə,shùur, 'sin-\ *n* : center of attraction

**cy·press** \\'sīprəs\ *n* : evergreen tree related to the pines

**cyst** \\'sist\ *n* : abnormal bodily sac — **cys·tic** \\'sistik\ *adj*

**czar** \\'zär\ *n* : ruler of Russia until 1917 — **czar·ist** *n or adj*

# D

**d** \'dē\ *n, pl* **d's** *or* **ds** \'dēz\ : 4th letter of the alphabet

**¹dab** \'dab\ *n* : gentle touch or stroke ~ *vb* **-bb-** : touch or apply lightly

**²dab** *n* : small amount

**dab·ble** \'dabəl\ *vb* **-bled; -bling** 1 : splash 2 : work without serious effort — **dab·bler** \-blər\ *n*

**dachs·hund** \'däks,hu̇nt\ *n* : small dog with a long body and short legs

**dad** \'dad\ *n* : father

**dad·dy** \'dadē\ *n, pl* **-dies** : father

**daf·fo·dil** \'dafə,dil\ *n* : narcissus with trumpetlike flowers

**daft** \'daft\ *adj* : foolish — **daft·ness** *n*

**dag·ger** \'dagər\ *n* : knife for stabbing

**dahl·ia** \'dalyə, 'däl-\ *n* : tuberous herb with showy flowers

**dai·ly** \'dālē\ *adj* 1 : occurring, done, or used every day or every weekday 2 : computed in terms of one day ~ *n, pl* **-lies** : daily newspaper — **daily** *adv*

**dain·ty** \'dāntē\ *n, pl* **-ties** : something delicious ~ *adj* **-ti·er; -est** : delicately pretty — **dain·ti·ly** *adv* — **dain·ti·ness** *n*

**dairy** \'darē\ *n, pl* **-ies** : farm that produces or company that processes milk — **dairy·maid** *n* — **dairy·man** \-mən, -,man\ *n*

**da·is** \'dāəs\ *n* : raised platform (as for a speaker)

**dai·sy** \'dāzē\ *n, pl* **-sies** : tall leafy-stemmed plant bearing showy flowers

**dale** \'dāl\ *n* : valley

**dal·ly** \'dalē\ *vb* **-lied; -ly·ing** 1 : flirt 2 : dawdle — **dal·li·ance** \-əns\ *n*

**dal·ma·tian** \dal'māshən\ *n* : large dog having a spotted white coat

**¹dam** \'dam\ *n* : female parent of a domestic animal

**²dam** *n* : barrier to hold back water — **dam** *vb*

**dam·age** \'damij\ *n* 1 : loss or harm due to injury 2 *pl* : compensation for loss or injury ~ *vb* **-aged; -ag·ing** : do damage to

**dam·ask** \'daməsk\ *n* : firm lustrous figured fabric

**dame** \'dām\ *n* : woman of rank or authority

**damn** \'dam\ *vb* 1 : condemn to hell 2 : curse — **dam·na·ble** \-nəbəl\ *adj* — **dam·na·tion** \dam'nāshən\ *n* — **damned** *adj*

**damp** \'damp\ *n* : moisture ~ *vb* 1 : reduce the draft in 2 : restrain 3 : moisten ~ *adj* : moist — **damp·ness** *n*

**damp·en** \'dampən\ *vb* 1 : diminish in activity or vigor 2 : make or become damp

**damp·er** \'dampər\ *n* : movable plate to regulate a flue draft

**dam·sel** \'damzəl\ *n* : young woman

**dance** \'dans\ *vb* **danced; danc·ing** : move rhythmically to music ~ *n* : act of dancing or a gathering for dancing — **danc·er** *n*

**dan·de·li·on** \'dand°l,īən\ *n* : common yellow-flowered herb

**dan·der** \'dandər\ *n* : temper

**dan·druff** \'dandrəf\ *n* : whitish thin dry scales of skin on the scalp

**dan·dy** \'dandē\ *n, pl* **-dies** 1 : man too concerned with clothes 2 : something excellent ~ *adj* **-di·er; -est** : very good

**dan·ger** \'dānjər\ *n* 1 : exposure to injury or evil 2 : something that may cause injury — **dan·ger·ous** \'dānjərəs\ *adj*

**dan·gle** \'daŋgəl\ *vb* **-gled; -gling** 1 : hang and swing freely 2 : be left without support or connection 3 : allow or cause to hang 4 : offer as an inducement

**dank** \'daŋk\ *adj* : unpleasantly damp

**dap·per** \'dapər\ *adj* : neat and stylishly dressed

**dap·ple** \'dapəl\ *vb* **-pled; -pling** : mark with colored spots

**dare** \'dar\ *vb* **dared; dar·ing** 1 : have sufficient courage 2 : urge or provoke to contend — **dare** *n* — **dar·ing** \'dariŋ\ *n or adj*

**dare·dev·il** *n* : recklessly bold person

**dark** \'därk\ *adj* 1 : having little or no light 2 : not light in color 3 : gloomy

~ n : absence of light — **dark·en** \-ən\ vb — **dark·ly** adv — **dark·ness** n

**dar·ling** \'därliŋ\ n 1 : beloved 2 : favorite ~ adj 1 : dearly loved 2 : very pleasing

**darn** \'därn\ vb : mend with interlacing stitches — **darn·er** n

**dart** \'därt\ n 1 : small pointed missile 2 pl : game of throwing darts at a target 3 : tapering fold in a garment 4 : quick movement ~ vb : move suddenly or rapidly

**dash** \'dash\ vb 1 : smash 2 : knock or hurl violently 3 : ruin 4 : perform or finish hastily 5 : move quickly ~ n 1 : sudden burst, splash, or stroke 2 : punctuation mark — 3 : tiny amount 4 : showiness or liveliness 5 : sudden rush 6 : short race 7 : dashboard

**dash·board** n : instrument panel

**dash·ing** \'dashiŋ\ adj : dapper and charming

**das·tard** \'dastərd\ n : one who sneakingly commits malicious acts

**das·tard·ly** \-lē\ adj : base or malicious

**da·ta** \'dātə, 'dat-, 'dät-\ n sing or pl : factual information

**da·ta·base** \-ˌbās\ n : data organized for computer search

¹**date** \'dāt\ n : edible fruit of a palm

²**date** n 1 : day, month, or year when something is done or made 2 : historical time period 3 : social engagement or the person one goes out with ~ vb **dat·ed; dat·ing** 1 : determine or record the date of 2 : have a date with 3 : originate — **to date** : up to now

**dat·ed** \-əd\ adj : old-fashioned

**da·tum** \'dātəm, 'dat-, 'dät-\ n, pl **-ta** \-ə\ or **-tums** : piece of data

**daub** \'dób\ vb : smear ~ n : something daubed on — **daub·er** n

**daugh·ter** \'dótər\ n : human female offspring

**daugh·ter–in–law** n, pl **daughters–in–law** : wife of one's son

**daunt** \'dónt\ vb : lessen the courage of

**daunt·less** \-ləs\ adj : fearless

**dav·en·port** \'davənˌpórt\ n : sofa

**daw·dle** \'dódᵊl\ vb **-dled; -dling** 1 : waste time 2 : loiter

**dawn** \'dón\ vb 1 : grow light as the sun rises 2 : begin to appear, develop, or be understood ~ n : first appearance (as of daylight)

**day** \'dā\ n 1 : period of light between one night and the next 2 : 24 hours 3 : specified date 4 : particular time or age 5 : period of work for a day — **day·light** n — **day·time** n

**day·break** n : dawn

**day·dream** n : fantasy of wish fulfillment — **daydream** vb

**daylight saving time** n : time one hour ahead of standard time

**daze** \'dāz\ vb **dazed; daz·ing** 1 : stun by a blow 2 : dazzle — **daze** n

**daz·zle** \'dazəl\ vb **-zled; -zling** 1 : overpower with light 2 : impress greatly — **dazzle** n

**DDT** \ˌdēˌdēˈtē\ n : long-lasting insecticide

**dea·con** \'dēkən\ n : subordinate church officer

**dea·con·ess** \'dēkənəs\ n : woman who assists in church ministry

**dead** \'ded\ adj 1 : lifeless 2 : unresponsive or inactive 3 : exhausted 4 : obsolete 5 : precise ~ n, pl **dead** 1 : one that is dead — usu. with the 2 : most lifeless time — adv 1 : completely 2 : directly — **dead·en** \'dedᵊn\ vb

**dead·beat** n : one who will not pay debts

**dead end** n : end of a street with no exit — **dead–end** adj

**dead heat** n : tie in a contest

**dead·line** n : time by which something must be finished

**dead·lock** n : struggle that neither side can win — **deadlock** vb

**dead·ly** \'dedlē\ adj **-li·er; -est** 1 : capable of causing death 2 : very accurate 3 : fatal to spiritual progress 4 : suggestive of death 5 : very great ~ adv : extremely — **dead·li·ness** n

**dead·pan** adj : expressionless — **deadpan** n or vb or adv

**dead·wood** n : something useless

**deaf** \'def\ adj : unable or unwilling to hear — **deaf·en** \-ən\ vb — **deaf·ness** n

**deaf–mute** n : deaf person unable to speak

**deal** \'dēl\ n 1 : indefinite quantity 2 : distribution of playing cards 3 : negotiation or agreement 4 : treatment received 5 : bargain ~ vb **dealt** \'delt\; **deal·ing** \'dēliŋ\ 1 : distribute playing cards 2 : be concerned with 3 : administer or deliver 4 : take action **5** : sell **6** : reach a state of acceptance — **deal•er** n — **deal•ing** n

**dean** \'dēn\ n **1** : head of a group of clergy members **2** : university or school administrator **3** : senior member

**dear** \'dir\ adj **1** : highly valued or loved **2** : expensive ~ n : loved one — **dear•ly** adv — **dear•ness** n

**dearth** \'dərth\ n : scarcity

**death** \'deth\ n **1** : end of life **2** : cause of loss of life **3** : state of being dead **4** : destruction or extinction — **death•less** adj — **death•ly** adj or adv

**de•ba•cle** \di'bäkəl, -'bakəl\ n : disaster or fiasco

**de•bar** \di'bär\ vb : bar from something

**de•bark** \-'bärk\ vb : disembark — **de•bar•ka•tion** \,dē,bär'kāshən\ n

**de•base** \di'bās\ vb : disparage — **de•base•ment** n

**de•bate** \-'bāt\ vb -bat•ed; -bat•ing : discuss a question by argument — **de•bat•able** adj — **debate** n — **de•bat•er** n

**de•bauch** \-'bóch\ vb : seduce or corrupt — **de•bauch•ery** \-ərē\ n

**de•bil•i•tate** \-'bilə,tāt\ vb -tat•ed; -tat•ing : make ill or weak

**de•bil•i•ty** \-'bilətē\ n, pl -ties : physical weakness

**deb•it** \'debət\ n : account entry of a payment or debt ~ vb : record as a debit

**deb•o•nair** \,debə'nar\ adj : suave

**de•bris** \də'brē, dā-; 'dā,brē\ n, pl -bris \-'brēz, -,brēz\ : remains of something destroyed

**debt** \'det\ n **1** : sin **2** : something owed **3** : state of owing — **debt•or** \-ər\ n

**de•bunk** \dē'bəŋk\ vb : expose as false

**de•but** \'dā,byü, dā'byü\ n **1** : first public appearance **2** : formal entrance into society — **debut** vb — **deb•u•tante** \'debyù,tänt\ n

**de•cade** \'dek,ād, -əd; de'kād\ n : 10 years

**dec•a•dence** \'dekədəns, di'kād³ns\ n : deterioration — **dec•a•dent** \-ənt, -³nt\ adj or n

**de•cal** \'dē,kal, di'kal, 'dekəl\ n : picture or design for transfer from prepared paper

**de•camp** \di'kamp\ vb : depart suddenly

**de•cant** \di'kant\ vb : pour gently

**de•cant•er** \-ər\ n : ornamental bottle

**de•cap•i•tate** \di'kapə,tāt\ vb -tat•ed; -tat•ing : behead — **de•cap•i•ta•tion** \-,kapə'tāshən\ n

**de•cay** \di'kā\ vb **1** : decline in condition **2** : decompose — **decay** n

**de•cease** \-'sēs\ n : death — **decease** vb

**de•ceit** \-'sēt\ n **1** : deception **2** : dishonesty — **de•ceit•ful** \-fəl\ adj — **de•ceit•ful•ly** adv — **de•ceit•ful•ness** n

**de•ceive** \-'sēv\ vb -ceived; -ceiv•ing : trick or mislead — **de•ceiv•er** n

**de•cel•er•ate** \dē'selə,rāt\ vb -at•ed; -at•ing : slow down

**De•cem•ber** \di'sembər\ n : 12th month of the year having 31 days

**de•cent** \'dēs³nt\ adj **1** : good, right, or just **2** : clothed **3** : not obscene **4** : fairly good — **de•cen•cy** \-³nsē\ n — **de•cent•ly** adv

**de•cep•tion** \di'sepshən\ n **1** : act or fact of deceiving **2** : fraud — **de•cep•tive** \-'septiv\ adj — **de•cep•tive•ly** adv — **de•cep•tive•ness** n

**de•cide** \di'sīd\ vb -cid•ed; -cid•ing **1** : make a choice or judgment **2** : bring to a conclusion **3** : cause to decide

**de•cid•ed** adj **1** : unquestionable **2** : resolute — **de•cid•ed•ly** adv

**de•cid•u•ous** \di'sijəwəs\ adj : having leaves that fall annually

**dec•i•mal** \'desəməl\ n : fraction in which the denominator is a power of 10 expressed by a point (**decimal point**) placed at the left of the numerator — **decimal** adj

**de•ci•pher** \di'sīfər\ vb : make out the meaning of — **de•ci•pher•able** adj

**de•ci•sion** \-'sizhən\ n **1** : act or result of deciding **2** : determination

**de•ci•sive** \-'sīsiv\ adj **1** : having the power to decide **2** : conclusive **3** : showing determination — **de•ci•sive•ly** adv — **de•ci•sive•ness** n

**deck** \'dek\ n **1** : floor of a ship **2** : pack of playing cards ~ vb **1** : array or dress up **2** : knock down

**de•claim** \di'klām\ vb : speak loudly or impressively — **dec•la•ma•tion** \,deklə'māshən\ n

**de•clare** \di'klar\ vb -clared; -clar•ing **1** : make known formally **2** : state emphatically — **dec•la•ra•tion** \,deklə'rāshən\ n — **de•clar•a•tive** \di'klarətiv\ adj — **de•clar•a•to•ry** \di'klarə,tōrē\ adj — **de•clar•er** n

**de·clen·sion** \di'klenchən\ *n* : inflectional forms of a noun, pronoun, or adjective

**de·cline** \di'klīn\ *vb* **-clined; -clin·ing** 1 : turn or slope downward 2 : wane 3 : refuse to accept 4 : inflect ~ *n* 1 : gradual wasting away 2 : change to a lower state or level 3 : a descending slope — **dec·li·na·tion** \,dek-lə'nāshən\ *n*

**de·code** \dē'kōd\ *vb* : decipher (a coded message) — **de·cod·er** *n*

**de·com·mis·sion** \,dēkə'mishən\ *vb* : remove from service

**de·com·pose** \,dēkəm'pōz\ *vb* 1 : separate into parts 2 : decay — **de·com·po·si·tion** \dē,kämpə'zishən\ *n*

**de·con·ges·tant** \,dēkən'jestənt\ *n* : agent that relieves congestion

**de·cor, dé·cor** \dā'kór, 'dā,kór\ *n* : room design or decoration

**dec·o·rate** \'dekə,rāt\ *vb* **-rat·ed; -rat·ing** 1 : add something attractive to 2 : honor with a medal — **dec·o·ra·tion** \,dekə'rāshən\ *n* — **dec·o·ra·tive** \'dekərətiv\ *adj* — **dec·o·ra·tor** \'dekə,rātər\ *n*

**de·co·rum** \di'kōrəm\ *n* : proper behavior — **dec·o·rous** \'dekərəs, di-'kōrəs\ *adj*

**de·coy** \'dē,kói, di'-\ *n* : something that tempts or draws attention from another ~ *vb* : tempt

**de·crease** ~ \di'krēs\ *vb* **-creased; -creas·ing** : grow or cause to grow less — **decrease** \'dē,krēs\ *n*

**de·cree** \di'krē\ *n* : official order — **decree** *vb*

**de·crep·it** \di'krepət\ *adj* : impaired by age

**de·cre·scen·do** \,dākrə'shendō\ *adv or adj* : with a decrease in volume

**de·cry** \di'krī\ *vb* : express strong disapproval of

**ded·i·cate** \'dedi,kāt\ *vb* **-cat·ed; -cat·ing** 1 : set apart for a purpose (as honor or worship) 2 : address to someone as a compliment — **ded·i·ca·tion** \,dedi'kāshən\ *n* — **ded·i·ca·to·ry** \'dedika,tōrē\ *adj*

**de·duce** \di'düs, -'dyüs\ *vb* **-duced; -duc·ing** : derive by reasoning — **de·duc·ible** *adj*

**de·duct** \-'dəkt\ *vb* : subtract — **de·duct·ible** *adj*

**de·duc·tion** \-'dəkshən\ *n* 1 : subtrac-

tion 2 : reasoned conclusion — **de·duc·tive** \-'dəktiv\ *adj*

**deed** \'dēd\ *n* 1 : exploit 2 : document showing ownership ~ *vb* : convey by deed

**deem** \'dēm\ *vb* : think

**deep** \'dēp\ *adj* 1 : extending far or a specified distance down, back, within, or outward 2 : occupied 3 : dark and rich in color 4 : low in tone ~ *adv* 1 : deeply 2 : far along in time ~ *n* : deep place — **deep·en** \'dēpən\ *vb* — **deep·ly** *adv*

**deep–seat·ed** \-'sētəd\ *adj* : firmly established

**deer** \'dir\ *n, pl* **deer** : ruminant mammal with antlers in the male — **deer·skin** *n*

**de·face** \di'fās\ *vb* : mar the surface of — **de·face·ment** *n* — **de·fac·er** *n*

**de·fame** \di'fām\ *vb* **-famed; -fam·ing** : injure the reputation of — **def·a·ma·tion** \,defə'māshən\ *n* — **de·fam·a·to·ry** \di'famə,tōrē\ *adj*

**de·fault** \di'fólt\ *n* : failure in a duty — **default** *vb* — **de·fault·er** *n*

**de·feat** \di'fēt\ *vb* 1 : frustrate 2 : win victory over ~ *n* : loss of a battle or contest

**def·e·cate** \'defi,kāt\ *vb* **-cat·ed; -cat·ing** : discharge feces from the bowels — **def·e·ca·tion** \,defi'kāshən\ *n*

**de·fect** \'dē,fekt, di'fekt\ *n* : imperfection ~ \di'-\ *vb* : desert — **de·fec·tion** \-'fekshən\ *n* — **de·fec·tor** \-'fektər\ *n*

**de·fec·tive** \di'fektiv\ *adj* : faulty or deficient — **defective** *n*

**de·fend** \-'fend\ *vb* 1 : protect from danger or harm 2 : take the side of — **de·fend·er** *n*

**de·fen·dant** \-'fendənt\ *n* : person charged or sued in a court

**de·fense** \-'fens\ *n* 1 : act of defending 2 : something that defends 3 : party, group, or team that opposes another — **de·fense·less** *adj* — **de·fen·si·ble** *adj* — **de·fen·sive** *adj or n*

¹**de·fer** \di'fər\ *vb* **-rr-** : postpone — **de·fer·ment** \di'fərmənt\ *n* — **de·fer·ra·ble** \-əbəl\ *adj*

²**defer** *vb* **-rr-** : yield to the opinion or wishes of another — **def·er·ence** \'defrəns\ *n* — **def·er·en·tial** \,defə'renchəl\ *adj*

**de·fi·ance** \di'fīəns\ *n* : disposition to resist — **de·fi·ant** \-ənt\ *adj*

**de·fi·cient** \di'fishənt\ *adj* 1 : lacking

something necessary **2** : not up to standard — **de·fi·cien·cy** \-'fishən-sē\ *n*

**def·i·cit** \'defəsət\ *n* : shortage esp. in money

**de·file** \di'fīl\ *vb* **-filed; -fil·ing 1** : make filthy or corrupt **2** : profane or dishonor — **de·file·ment** *n*

**de·fine** \di'fīn\ *vb* **-fined; -fin·ing 1** : fix or mark the limits of **2** : clarify in outline **3** : set forth the meaning of — **de·fin·able** *adj* — **de·fin·ably** *adv* — **de·fin·er** *n* — **def·i·ni·tion** \ˌdefə'nishən\ *n*

**def·i·nite** \'defənət\ *adj* **1** : having distinct limits **2** : clear in meaning, intent, or identity **3** : typically designating an identified or immediately identifiable person or thing — **def·i·nite·ly** *adv*

**de·fin·i·tive** \di'finitiv\ *adj* **1** : conclusive **2** : authoritative

**de·flate** \di'flāt\ *vb* **-flat·ed; -flat·ing 1** : release air or gas from **2** : reduce — **de·fla·tion** \-'flāshən\ *n*

**de·flect** \-'flekt\ *vb* : turn aside — **de·flec·tion** \-'flekshən\ *n*

**de·fog** \-'fȯg, -'fäg\ *vb* : remove condensed moisture from — **de·fog·ger** *n*

**de·fo·li·ate** \dē'fōlē,āt\ *vb* **-at·ed; -at·ing** : deprive of leaves esp. prematurely — **de·fo·li·ant** \-lēənt\ *n* — **de·fo·li·a·tion** \-ˌfōlē'āshən\ *n*

**de·form** \di'fȯrm\ *vb* **1** : distort **2** : disfigure — **de·for·ma·tion** \ˌdē-ˌfȯr'māshən, ˌdefər-\ *n* — **de·for·mi·ty** \di'fȯrmətē\ *n*

**de·fraud** \di'frȯd\ *vb* : cheat

**de·fray** \-'frā\ *vb* : pay

**de·frost** \-'frȯst\ *vb* **1** : thaw out **2** : free from ice — **de·frost·er** *n*

**deft** \'deft\ *adj* : quick and skillful — **deft·ly** *adv* — **deft·ness** *n*

**de·funct** \di'fəŋkt\ *adj* : dead

**de·fy** \-'fī\ *vb* **-fied; -fy·ing 1** : challenge **2** : boldly refuse to obey

**de·gen·er·ate** \di'jenərət\ *adj* : degraded or corrupt — *n* : degenerate person — \-ə,rāt\ *vb* : become degenerate — **de·gen·er·a·cy** \-ərəsē\ *n* — **de·gen·er·a·tion** \-ˌjenə'rāshən\ *n* — **de·gen·er·a·tive** \-'jenə-ˌrātiv\ *adj*

**de·grade** \di'grād\ *vb* **1** : reduce from a higher to a lower rank or degree **2** : debase **3** : decompose — **de·grad-**

**able** \-əbəl\ *adj* — **deg·ra·da·tion** \ˌdegrə'dāshən\ *n*

**de·gree** \di'grē\ *n* **1** : step in a series **2** : extent, intensity, or scope **3** : title given to a college graduate **4** : a 360th part of the circumference of a circle **5** : unit for measuring temperature

**de·hy·drate** \dē'hī,drāt\ *vb* **1** : remove water from **2** : lose liquid — **de·hy·dra·tion** \ˌdēhī'drāshən\ *n*

**de·i·fy** \'dēə,fī, 'dā-\ *vb* **-fied; -fy·ing** : make a god of — **de·i·fi·ca·tion** \ˌdēəfə'kāshən, ˌdā-\ *n*

**deign** \'dān\ *vb* : condescend

**de·i·ty** \'dēətē, 'dā-\ *n, pl* **-ties 1** *cap* : God **2** : a god or goddess

**de·ject·ed** \di'jektəd\ *adj* : sad — **de·jec·tion** \-shən\ *n*

**de·lay** \di'lā\ *n* : a putting off of something ~ *vb* **1** : postpone **2** : stop or hinder for a time

**de·lec·ta·ble** \di'lektəbəl\ *adj* : delicious

**del·e·gate** \'deligət, -ˌgāt\ *n* : representative ~ \-ˌgāt\ *vb* **-gat·ed; -gat·ing 1** : entrust to another **2** : appoint as one's delegate — **del·e·ga·tion** \ˌdeli'gāshən\ *n*

**de·lete** \di'lēt\ *vb* **-let·ed; -let·ing** : eliminate something written — **de·le·tion** \-'lēshən\ *n*

**del·e·te·ri·ous** \ˌdelə'tirēəs\ *adj* : harmful

**de·lib·er·ate** \di'libərət\ *adj* **1** : determined after careful thought **2** : intentional **3** : not hurried ~ \-ə,rāt\ *vb* **-at·ed; -at·ing** : consider carefully — **de·lib·er·ate·ly** *adv* — **de·lib·er·ate·ness** *n* — **de·lib·er·a·tion** \-ˌlibə'rāshən\ *n* — **de·lib·er·a·tive** \-'libə,rātiv, -rət-\ *adj*

**del·i·ca·cy** \'delikəsē\ *n, pl* **-cies 1** : something special and pleasing to eat **2** : fineness **3** : frailty

**del·i·cate** \'delikət\ *adj* **1** : subtly pleasing to the senses **2** : dainty and charming **3** : sensitive or fragile **4** : requiring fine skill or tact — **del·i·cate·ly** *adv*

**del·i·ca·tes·sen** \ˌdelikə'tes?n\ *n* : store that sells ready-to-eat food

**de·li·cious** \di'lishəs\ *adj* : very pleasing esp. in taste or aroma — **de·li·cious·ly** *adv* — **de·li·cious·ness** *n*

**de·light** \di'līt\ *n* **1** : great pleasure **2** : source of great pleasure ~ *vb* **1** : take great pleasure **2** : satisfy greatly — **de·light·ful** \-fəl\ *adj* — **de·light·ful·ly** *adv*

**de·lin·eate** \di'linē,āt\ *vb* **-eat·ed; -eat·ing** : sketch or portray — **de·lin·ea·tion** \-,linē'āshən\ *n*

**de·lin·quent** \-'liŋkwənt\ *n* : delinquent person ~ *adj* **1** : violating duty or law **2** : overdue in payment — **de·lin·quen·cy** \-kwənsē\ *n*

**de·lir·i·um** \di'lirēəm\ *n* : mental disturbance — **de·lir·i·ous** \-ēəs\ *adj*

**de·liv·er** \di'livər\ *vb* **1** : set free **2** : hand over **3** : assist in birth **4** : say or speak **5** : send to an intended destination — **de·liv·er·ance** \-ərəns\ *n* — **de·liv·er·er** *n* — **de·liv·ery** \-ərē\ *n*

**dell** \'del\ *n* : small secluded valley

**del·ta** \'deltə\ *n* : triangle of land at the mouth of a river

**de·lude** \di'lüd\ *vb* **-lud·ed; -lud·ing** : mislead or deceive

**del·uge** \'delyüj\ *n* **1** : flood **2** : drenching rain ~ *vb* **-uged; -ug·ing 1** : flood **2** : overwhelm

**de·lu·sion** \di'lüzhən\ *n* : false belief

**de·luxe** \di'lùks, -'ləks, -'lüks\ *adj* : very luxurious or elegant

**delve** \'delv\ *vb* **delved; delv·ing 1** : dig **2** : seek information in records

**dem·a·gogue, dem·a·gog** \'demə,gäg\ *n* : politician who appeals to emotion and prejudice — **dem·a·gogu·ery** \-,gägərē\ *n* — **dem·a·gogy** \-,gägē, -,gäjē\ *n*

**de·mand** \di'mand\ *n* **1** : act of demanding **2** : something claimed as due **3** : ability and desire to buy **4** : urgent need ~ *vb* **1** : ask for with authority **2** : require

**de·mar·cate** \di'mär,kāt, 'dē,mär-\ *vb* **-cat·ed; -cat·ing** : mark the limits of — **de·mar·ca·tion** \,dē,mär'kāshən\ *n*

**de·mean** \di'mēn\ *vb* : degrade

**de·mean·or** \-'mēnər\ *n* : behavior

**de·ment·ed** \-'mentəd\ *adj* : crazy

**de·mer·it** \-'merət\ *n* : mark given an offender

**demi·god** \'demi,gäd\ *n* : mythological being less powerful than a god

**de·mise** \di'mīz\ *n* **1** : death **2** : loss of status

**demi·tasse** \'demi,tas\ *n* : small cup of coffee

**de·mo·bi·lize** \di'mōbə,līz, dē-\ *vb* : disband from military service — **de·mo·bi·li·za·tion** \-,mōbələ'zāshən\ *n*

**de·moc·ra·cy** \di'mäkrəsē\ *n, pl* **-cies 1** : government in which the supreme power is held by the people **2** : political unit with democratic government

**dem·o·crat** \'demə,krat\ *n* : adherent of democracy

**dem·o·crat·ic** \,demə'kratik\ *adj* : relating to or favoring democracy — **dem·o·crat·i·cal·ly** \-tiklē\ *adv* — **de·moc·ra·tize** \di'mäkrə,tīz\ *vb*

**de·mol·ish** \di'mälish\ *vb* **1** : tear down or smash **2** : put an end to — **de·mo·li·tion** \,demə'lishən, ,dē-\ *n*

**de·mon** \'dēmən\ *n* : evil spirit — **de·mon·ic** \di'mänik\ *adj*

**dem·on·strate** \'demən,strāt\ *vb* **-strat·ed; -strat·ing 1** : show clearly or publicly **2** : prove **3** : explain — **de·mon·stra·ble** \di'mänstrəbəl\ *adj* — **de·mon·stra·bly** \-blē\ *adv* — **dem·on·stra·tion** \,demən'strāshən\ *n* — **de·mon·stra·tive** \di-'mänstrətiv\ *adj or n* — **dem·on·stra·tor** \'demən,strātər\ *n*

**de·mor·al·ize** \di'mórə,līz\ *vb* : destroy the enthusiasm of

**de·mote** \di'mōt\ *vb* **-mot·ed; -mot·ing** : reduce to a lower rank — **de·mo·tion** \-'mōshən\ *n*

**de·mur** \di'mər\ *vb* **-rr-** : object — **de·mur** *n*

**de·mure** \di'myùr\ *adj* : modest — **de·mure·ly** *adv*

**den** \'den\ *n* **1** : animal's shelter **2** : hiding place **3** : cozy private little room

**de·na·ture** \dē'nāchər\ *vb* **-tured; -tur·ing** : make (alcohol) unfit for drinking

**de·ni·al** \di'nīəl\ *n* : rejection of a request or of the validity of a statement

**den·i·grate** \'deni,grāt\ *vb* **-grat·ed; -grat·ing** : speak ill of

**den·im** \'denəm\ *n* **1** : durable twilled cotton fabric **2** *pl* : pants of denim

**den·i·zen** \'denəzən\ *n* : inhabitant

**de·nom·i·na·tion** \di,nämə'nāshən\ *n* **1** : religious body **2** : value or size in a series — **de·nom·i·na·tion·al** \-shənəl\ *adj*

**de·nom·i·na·tor** \-'nämə,nātər\ *n* : part of a fraction below the line

**de·note** \di'nōt\ *vb* **1** : mark out plainly **2** : mean — **de·no·ta·tion** \,dēnō'tāshən\ *n* — **de·no·ta·tive** \'dēnō,tātiv, di'nōtətiv\ *adj*

**de·noue·ment** \ˌdā₁nü'mäⁿ\ *n* : final outcome (as of a drama)

**de·nounce** \di'naůns\ *vb* **-nounced; -nounc·ing** 1 : pronounce blameworthy or evil 2 : inform against

**dense** \'dens\ *adj* **dens·er; -est** 1 : thick, compact, or crowded 2 : stupid — **dense·ly** *adv* — **dense·ness** *n* — **den·si·ty** \'densətē\ *n*

**dent** \'dent\ *n* : small depression — **dent** *vb*

**den·tal** \'dentᵊl\ *adj* : relating to teeth or dentistry

**den·ti·frice** \'dentəfrəs\ *n* : preparation for cleaning teeth

**den·tin** \'dentᵊn\, **den·tine** \'den₁tēn, ₁den'-\ *n* : bonelike component of teeth

**den·tist** \'dentist\ *n* : one who cares for and replaces teeth — **den·tist·ry** *n*

**den·ture** \'denchər\ *n* : artificial teeth

**de·nude** \di'nüd, -'nyüd\ *vb* **-nud·ed; -nud·ing** : strip of covering

**de·nun·ci·a·tion** \di₁nənsē'āshən\ *n* : act of denouncing

**de·ny** \-'nī\ *vb* **-nied; -ny·ing** 1 : declare untrue 2 : disavow 3 : refuse to grant

**de·odor·ant** \dē'ōdərənt\ *n* : preparation to prevent unpleasant odors — **de·odor·ize** \-₁rīz\ *vb*

**de·part** \di'pärt\ *vb* 1 : go away or away from 2 : die — **de·par·ture** \-'pärchər\ *n*

**de·part·ment** \di'pärtmənt\ *n* 1 : area of responsibility or interest 2 : functional division — **de·part·men·tal** \di₁pärt'mentᵊl, ₁dē-\ *adj*

**de·pend** \di'pend\ *vb* 1 : rely for support 2 : be determined by or based on something else — **de·pend·abil·i·ty** \-₁pendə'bilətē\ *n* — **de·pend·able** *adj* — **de·pen·dence** \di'pendəns\ *n* — **de·pen·den·cy** \-dənsē\ *n* — **de·pen·dent** \-ənt\ *adj or n*

**de·pict** \di'pikt\ *vb* : show by or as if by a picture — **de·pic·tion** \-'pikshən\ *n*

**de·plete** \di'plēt\ *vb* **-plet·ed; -plet·ing** : use up resources of — **de·ple·tion** \-'plēshən\ *n*

**de·plore** \-'plōr\ *vb* **-plored; -plor·ing** : regret strongly — **de·plor·able** \-əbəl\ *adj*

**de·ploy** \-'plȯi\ *vb* : spread out for battle — **de·ploy·ment** \-mənt\ *n*

**de·port** \di'pōrt\ *vb* 1 : behave 2 : send out of the country — **de·por-**

**ta·tion** \ˌdē₁pȯr'tāshən\ *n* — **de·port·ment** \di'pȯrtmənt\ *n*

**de·pose** \di-'pōz\ *vb* **-posed; -pos·ing** 1 : remove (a ruler) from office 2 : testify — **de·po·si·tion** \ˌdepə-'zishən, ₁dē-\ *n*

**de·pos·it** \di'päzət\ *vb* **-it·ed; -it·ing** : place esp. for safekeeping ∼ *n* 1 : state of being deposited 2 : something deposited 3 : act of depositing 4 : natural accumulation — **de·pos·i·tor** \-'päzətər\ *n*

**de·pos·i·to·ry** \di'päzə₁tōrē\ *n, pl* **-ries** : place for deposit

**de·pot** \*1 usu* 'depō, *2 usu* 'dēp-\ *n* 1 : place for storage 2 : bus or railroad station

**de·prave** \di'prāv\ *vb* **-praved; -prav·ing** : corrupt morally — **de·praved** *adj* — **de·prav·i·ty** \-'pravətē\ *n*

**dep·re·cate** \'depri₁kāt\ *vb* **-cat·ed; -cat·ing** 1 : express disapproval of 2 : belittle — **dep·re·ca·tion** \ˌdepri-'kāshən\ *n* — **dep·re·ca·to·ry** \'deprikə₁tōrē\ *adj*

**de·pre·ci·ate** \di'prēshē₁āt\ *vb* **-at·ed; -at·ing** 1 : lessen in value 2 : belittle — **de·pre·ci·a·tion** \-₁prēshē'āshən\ *n*

**dep·re·da·tion** \ˌdeprə'dāshən\ *n* : a laying waste or plundering — **dep·re·date** \'deprə₁dāt\ *vb*

**de·press** \di'pres\ *vb* 1 : press down 2 : lessen the activity or force of 3 : discourage 4 : decrease the market value of — **de·pres·sant** \-ᵊnt\ *n or adj* — **de·pressed** *adj* — **de·pres·sive** \-iv\ *adj or n* — **de·pres·sor** \-ər\ *n*

**de·pres·sion** \di'preshən\ *n* 1 : act of depressing or state of being depressed 2 : depressed place 3 : period of low economic activity

**de·prive** \-'prīv\ *vb* **-prived; -priv·ing** : take or keep something away from — **de·pri·va·tion** \ˌdeprə'vāshən\ *n*

**depth** \'depth\ *n, pl* **depths** 1 : something that is deep 2 : distance down from a surface 3 : distance from front to back 4 : quality of being deep

**dep·u·ta·tion** \ˌdepyə'tāshən\ *n* : delegation

**dep·u·ty** \'depyətē\ *n, pl* **-ties** : person appointed to act for another — **dep·u·tize** \-yə₁tīz\ *vb*

**de·rail** \di'rāl\ *vb* : leave the rails — **de·rail·ment** *n*

**de·range** \-'rānj\ *vb* **-ranged; -rang-**

**ing 1** : disarrange or upset **2** : make insane — **de·range·ment** n

**der·by** \'dərbē, *Brit* 'där-\ n, pl **-bies 1** : horse race **2** : stiff felt hat with dome-shaped crown

**de·reg·u·late** \dē'regyu̇‚lāt\ vb : remove restrictions on — **de·reg·u·la·tion** \-‚regyu̇'lāshən\ n

**der·e·lict** \'derə‚likt\ adj **1** : abandoned **2** : negligent ~ n **1** : something abandoned **2** : bum — **der·e·lic·tion** \‚derə'likshən\ n

**de·ride** \di'rīd\ vb **-rid·ed; -rid·ing** : make fun of — **de·ri·sion** \-'ri-zhən\ n — **de·ri·sive** \-'rīsiv\ adj — **de·ri·sive·ly** adv — **de·ri·sive·ness** n

**de·rive** \di'rīv\ vb **-rived; -riv·ing 1** : obtain from a source or parent **2** : come from a certain source **3** : infer or deduce — **der·i·va·tion** \‚derə-'vāshən\ n — **de·riv·a·tive** \di'rivə-tiv\ adj or n

**der·ma·tol·o·gy** \‚dərmə'täləjē\ n : study of the skin and its disorders — **der·ma·tol·o·gist** \-jist\ n

**de·rog·a·tive** \di'rägətiv\ adj : derogatory

**de·rog·a·to·ry** \di'rägə‚tōrē\ adj : intended to lower the reputation

**der·rick** \'derik\ n **1** : hoisting apparatus **2** : framework over an oil well

**de·scend** \di'send\ vb **1** : move or climb down **2** : derive **3** : extend downward **4** : appear suddenly (as in an attack) — **de·scen·dant, de·scen·dent** \-ənt\ adj or n — **de·scent** \di'sent\ n

**de·scribe** \di'skrīb\ vb **-scribed; -scrib·ing** : represent in words — **de·scrib·able** adj — **de·scrip·tion** \-'skripshən\ n — **de·scrip·tive** \-'skriptiv\ adj

**de·scry** \di'skrī\ vb **-scried; -scry·ing** : catch sight of

**des·e·crate** \'desi‚krāt\ vb **-crat·ed; -crat·ing** : treat (something sacred) with disrespect — **des·e·cra·tion** \‚desi'krāshən\ n

**de·seg·re·gate** \dē'segrə‚gāt\ vb : eliminate esp. racial segregation in — **de·seg·re·ga·tion** n

**¹des·ert** \'dezərt\ n : dry barren region — **desert** adj

**²de·sert** \di'zərt\ n : what one deserves

**³de·sert** \di'zərt\ vb : abandon — **de·sert·er** n — **de·ser·tion** \-'zərshən\ n

**de·serve** \-'zərv\ vb **-served; -serv·ing** : be worthy of

**des·ic·cate** \'desi‚kāt\ vb **-cat·ed; -cat·ing** : dehydrate — **des·ic·ca·tion** \‚desi'kāshən\ n

**de·sign** \di'zīn\ vb **1** : create and work out the details of **2** : make a pattern or sketch of ~ n **1** : mental project or plan **2** : purpose **3** : preliminary sketch **4** : underlying arrangement of elements **5** : decorative pattern — **de·sign·er** n

**des·ig·nate** \'dezig‚nāt\ vb **-nat·ed; -nat·ing 1** : indicate, specify, or name **2** : appoint — **des·ig·na·tion** \‚dezig'nāshən\ n

**de·sire** \di'zīr\ vb **-sired; -sir·ing 1** : feel desire for **2** : request ~ n **1** : strong conscious impulse to have, be, or do something **2** : something desired — **de·sir·abil·i·ty** \-‚zīrə'-bilətē\ n — **de·sir·able** \-'zīrəbəl\ adj — **de·sir·able·ness** n — **de·sir·ous** \-'zīrəs\ adj

**de·sist** \di'zist, -'sist\ vb : stop

**desk** \'desk\ n : table esp. for writing and reading

**des·o·late** \'desələt, 'dez-\ adj **1** : lifeless **2** : disconsolate ~ \-‚lāt\ vb **-lat·ed; -lat·ing** : lay waste — **des·o·la·tion** \‚desə'lāshən, ‚dez-\ n

**de·spair** \di'spar\ vb : lose all hope ~ n : loss of hope

**des·per·a·do** \‚despə'rädō, -'räd-\ n, pl **-does** or **-dos** : desperate criminal

**des·per·ate** \'desprət\ adj **1** : hopeless **2** : rash **3** : extremely intense — **des·per·ate·ly** adv — **des·per·a·tion** \‚despə'rāshən\ n

**des·pi·ca·ble** \di'spikəbəl, 'despik-\ adj : deserving scorn

**de·spise** \di'spīz\ vb **-spised; -spis·ing** : feel contempt for

**de·spite** \-'spīt\ prep : in spite of

**de·spoil** \-'spȯil\ vb : strip of possessions or value

**de·spon·den·cy** \-'spändənsē\ n : dejection — **de·spon·dent** \-dənt\ adj

**des·pot** \'despət, -‚pät\ n : tyrant — **des·pot·ic** \des'pätik\ adj — **des·po·tism** \'despə‚tizəm\ n

**des·sert** \di'zərt\ n : sweet food, fruit, or cheese ending a meal

**des·ti·na·tion** \‚destə'nāshən\ n : place where something or someone is going

**des·tine** \'destən\ vb **-tined; -tin·ing** 1 : designate, assign, or determine in advance 2 : direct

**des·ti·ny** \'destənē\ n, pl **-nies** : that which is to happen in the future

**des·ti·tute** \'destə₁tüt, -₁tyüt\ adj 1 : lacking something 2 : very poor — **des·ti·tu·tion** \₁destə'tüshən, -'tyü-\ n

**de·stroy** \di'stròi\ vb : kill or put an end to

**de·stroy·er** \-'stròiər\ n 1 : one that destroys 2 : small speedy warship

**de·struc·tion** \-'strəkshən\ n 1 : action of destroying 2 : ruin — **de·struc·ti·bil·i·ty** \-₁strəktə'bilətē\ n — **de·struc·ti·ble** \-'strəktəbəl\ adj — **de·struc·tive** \-'strəktiv\ adj

**des·ul·to·ry** \'desəl₁tōrē\ adj : aimless

**de·tach** \di'tach\ vb : separate

**de·tached** \-'tacht\ adj 1 : separate 2 : aloof or impartial

**de·tach·ment** \-'tachmənt\ n 1 : separation 2 : troops or ships on special service 3 : aloofness 4 : impartiality

**de·tail** \di'tāl, 'dē₁tāl\ n : small item or part ~ vb : give details of

**de·tain** \di'tān\ vb 1 : hold in custody 2 : delay

**de·tect** \di'tekt\ vb : discover — **de·tect·able** adj — **de·tec·tion** \-'tekshən\ n — **de·tec·tor** \-tər\ n

**de·tec·tive** \-'tektiv\ n : one who investigates crime

**dé·tente** \dā'tä$^n$t\ n : relaxation of tensions between nations

**de·ten·tion** \di'tenchən\ n : confinement

**de·ter** \-'tər\ vb **-rr-** : discourage or prevent — **de·ter·rence** \-əns\ n — **de·ter·rent** \-ənt\ adj or n

**de·ter·gent** \di'tərjənt\ n : cleansing agent

**de·te·ri·o·rate** \-'tirēə₁rāt\ vb **-rat·ed; -rat·ing** : make or become worse — **de·te·ri·o·ra·tion** \-₁tirēə'rāshən\ n

**de·ter·mi·na·tion** \di₁tərmə'nāshən\ n 1 : act of deciding or fixing 2 : firm purpose

**de·ter·mine** \-'tərmən\ vb **-mined; -min·ing** 1 : decide on, establish, or settle 2 : find out 3 : bring about as a result

**de·test** \-'test\ vb : hate — **de·test·able** adj — **de·tes·ta·tion** \₁dē₁tes·'tāshən\ n

**det·o·nate** \'det³n₁āt\ vb **-nat·ed; -nat·ing** : explode — **det·o·na·tion** \₁det³n'āshən\ n — **det·o·na·tor** \'det³n₁ātər\ n

**de·tour** \'dē₁túr\ n : temporary indirect route — **detour** vb

**de·tract** \di'trakt\ vb : take away — **de·trac·tion** \-'trakshən\ n — **de·trac·tor** \-'traktər\ n

**det·ri·ment** \'detrəmənt\ n : damage — **det·ri·men·tal** \₁detrə'ment³l\ adj — **det·ri·men·tal·ly** adv

**deuce** \'düs, 'dyüs\ n 1 : 2 in cards or dice 2 : tie in tennis 3 : devil — used as an oath

**deut·sche mark** \'dòichə-\ n : monetary unit of Germany

**de·val·ue** \dē'val₁yü\ vb : reduce the value of — **de·val·u·a·tion** n

**dev·as·tate** \'devə₁stāt\ vb **-tat·ed; -tat·ing** : ruin — **dev·as·ta·tion** \₁devə'stāshən\ n

**de·vel·op** \di'veləp\ vb 1 : grow, increase, or evolve gradually 2 : cause to grow, increase, or reach full potential — **de·vel·op·er** n — **de·vel·op·ment** n — **de·vel·op·men·tal** \-₁veləp'ment³l\ adj

**de·vi·ate** \'dēvē₁āt\ vb **-at·ed; -at·ing** : change esp. from a course or standard — **de·vi·ant** \-vēənt\ adj or n — **de·vi·ate** \-vēət, -vē₁āt\ n — **de·vi·a·tion** \₁dēvē'āshən\ n

**de·vice** \di'vīs\ n 1 : specialized piece of equipment or tool 2 : design

**dev·il** \'devəl\ n 1 : personified supreme spirit of evil 2 : demon 3 : wicked person ~ vb **-iled** or **-illed; -il·ing** or **-il·ling** 1 : season highly 2 : pester — **dev·il·ish** \'devəlish\ adj — **dev·il·ry** \'devəlrē\, **dev·il·try** \-trē\ n

**de·vi·ous** \'dēvēəs\ adj : tricky

**de·vise** \di'vīz\ vb **-vised; -vis·ing** 1 : invent 2 : plot 3 : give by will

**de·void** \-'vòid\ adj : entirely lacking

**de·vote** \di'vōt\ vb **-vot·ed; -vot·ing** : set apart for a special purpose

**de·vot·ed** adj : faithful

**dev·o·tee** \₁devə'tē, -'tā\ n : ardent follower

**de·vo·tion** \di'vōshən\ n 1 : prayer — usu. pl. 2 : loyalty and dedication — **de·vo·tion·al** \-shənəl\ adj

**de·vour** \di'vaúər\ vb : consume ravenously — **de·vour·er** n

**de·vout** \-'vaút\ adj 1 : devoted to religion 2 : serious — **de·vout·ly** adv — **de·vout·ness** n

**dew** \\'dü, 'dyü\ *n* : moisture condensed at night — **dew-drop** *n* — **dewy** *adj*

**dex-ter-ous** \\'dekstrəs\ *adj* : skillful with the hands — **dex-ter-i-ty** \dek-'sterətē\ *n* — **dex-ter-ous-ly** *adv*

**dex-trose** \\'dek,strōs\ *n* : plant or blood sugar

**di-a-be-tes** \,dīə'bētēz, -'bētəs\ *n* : disorder in which the body has too little insulin and too much sugar — **di-a-bet-ic** \-'betik\ *adj or n*

**di-a-bol-ic** \-'bälik\, **di-a-bol-i-cal** \-ikəl\ *adj* : fiendish

**di-a-crit-ic** \-'kritik\ *n* : mark accompanying a letter and indicating a specific sound value — **di-a-crit-i-cal** \-'kritikəl\ *adj*

**di-a-dem** \\'dīə,dem\ *n* : crown

**di-ag-no-sis** \,dīig'nōsəs, -əg-\ *n, pl* **-no-ses** \-,sēz\ : identifying of a disease from its symptoms — **di-ag-nose** \\'dīig,nōs, -əg-\ *vb* — **di-ag-nos-tic** \,dīig'nästik, -əg-\ *adj*

**di-ag-o-nal** \dī'agənəl\ *adj* : extending from one corner to the opposite corner ~ *n* : diagonal line, direction, or arrangement — **di-ag-o-nal-ly** *adv*

**di-a-gram** \\'dīə,gram\ *n* : explanatory drawing or plan ~ *vb* **-gramed** *or* **-grammed; -gram-ing** *or* **-gram-ming** : represent by a diagram — **di-a-gram-mat-ic** \,dīəgrə'matik\ *adj*

**di-al** \\'dīəl\ *n* **1** : face of a clock, meter, or gauge **2** : control knob or wheel ~ *vb* **-aled** *or* **-alled; -al-ing** *or* **-al-ling** : turn a dial to call, operate, or select

**di-a-lect** \\'dīə,lekt\ *n* : variety of language confined to a region or group

**di-a-logue** \-,lóg\ *n* : conversation

**di-am-e-ter** \dī'amətər\ *n* **1** : straight line through the center of a circle **2** : thickness

**di-a-met-ric** \,dīə'metrik\ **di-a-met-ri-cal** \-trikəl\ *adj* : completely opposite — **di-a-met-ri-cal-ly** \-iklē\ *adv*

**di-a-mond** \\'dīmənd, 'dīə-\ *n* **1** : hard brilliant mineral that consists of crystalline carbon **2** : flat figure having 4 equal sides, 2 acute angles, and 2 obtuse angles **3** : playing card of a suit marked with a red diamond **4** : baseball field

**di-a-per** \\'dīpər\ *n* : baby's garment for receiving bodily wastes ~ *vb* : put a diaper on

**di-a-phragm** \\'dīə,fram\ *n* **1** : sheet of

muscle between the chest and abdominal cavity **2** : contraceptive device

**di-ar-rhea** \,dīə'rēə\ *n* : abnormally watery discharge from bowels

**di-a-ry** \\'dīərē\ *n, pl* **-ries** : daily record of personal experiences — **di-a-rist** \\'dīərist\ *n*

**di-a-tribe** \\'dīə,trīb\ *n* : biting or abusive denunciation

**dice** \\'dīs\ *n, pl* **dice** : die or a game played with dice ~ *vb* **diced; dic-ing** : cut into small cubes

**dick-er** \\'dikər\ *vb* : bargain

**dic-tate** \\'dik,tāt\ *vb* **-tat-ed; -tat-ing** **1** : speak for a person or a machine to record **2** : command ~ *n* : order — **dic-ta-tion** \dik'tāshən\ *n*

**dic-ta-tor** \\'dik,tātər\ *n* : person ruling absolutely and often brutally — **dic-ta-to-ri-al** \,diktətōrēəl\ *adj* — **dic-ta-tor-ship** \dik'tātər,ship, 'dik,-\ *n*

**dic-tion** \\'dikshən\ *n* **1** : choice of the best word **2** : precise pronunciation

**dic-tio-nary** \-shə,nerē\ *n, pl* **-nar-ies** : reference book of words with information about their meanings

**dic-tum** \\'diktəm\ *n, pl* **-ta** \-tə\ : authoritative or formal statement

**did** *past of* DO

**di-dac-tic** \dī'daktik\ *adj* : intended to teach a moral lesson

¹**die** \\'dī\ *vb* **died; dy-ing** \\'dīiŋ\ **1** : stop living **2** : pass out of existence **3** : stop or subside **4** : long

²**die** \\'dī\ *n* **1** *pl* **dice** \\'dīs\ : small marked cube used in gambling **2** *pl* **dies** \\'dīz\ : form for stamping or cutting

**die-sel** \\'dēzəl, -səl\ *n* : engine in which high compression causes ignition of the fuel

**di-et** \\'dīət\ *n* : food and drink regularly consumed (as by a person) ~ *vb* : eat less or according to certain rules — **di-etary** \\'dīə,terē\ *adj or n* — **di-et-er** *n*

**di-etet-ics** \,dīə'tetiks\ *n sing or pl* : science of nutrition — **di-etet-ic** *adj* — **di-eti-tian, di-eti-cian** \-'tishən\ *n*

**dif-fer** \\'difər\ *vb* **1** : be unlike **2** : vary **3** : disagree — **dif-fer-ence** \\'difrəns\ *n*

**dif-fer-ent** \-rənt\ *adj* : not the same — **dif-fer-ent-ly** *adv*

**dif-fer-en-ti-ate** \,difə'renchē,āt\ *vb* **-at-ed; -at-ing** **1** : make or become different **2** : attain a specialized adult form during development **3** : distinguish — **dif·fer·en·ti·a·tion** \-ˌren-chē'āshən\ n

**dif·fi·cult** \'difikəlt\ adj : hard to do, understand, or deal with

**dif·fi·cul·ty** \-kəltē\ n, pl **-ties 1** : difficult nature **2** : great effort **3** : something hard to do, understand, or deal with

**dif·fi·dent** \'difədənt\ adj : reserved — **dif·fi·dence** \-əns\ n

**dif·fuse** \dif'yüs\ adj **1** : wordy **2** : not concentrated ~ \-'yüz\ vb **-fused; -fus·ing** : pour out or spread widely — **dif·fu·sion** \-'yüzhən\ n

**dig** \'dig\ vb **dug** \'dəg\; **dig·ging 1** : turn up soil **2** : hollow out or form by removing earth **3** : uncover by turning up earth ~ n **1** : thrust **2** : cutting remark — **dig in** vb **1** : establish a defensive position **2** : begin working or eating — **dig up** vb : discover

**¹di·gest** \'dīˌjest\ n : body of information in shortened form

**²di·gest** \dī'jest, də-\ vb **1** : think over **2** : convert (food) into a form that can be absorbed **3** : summarize — **di·gest·ible** adj — **di·ges·tion** \-'jeschən\ n — **di·ges·tive** \-'jestiv\ adj

**dig·it** \'dijət\ n **1** : any of the figures 1 to 9 inclusive and usu. the symbol 0 **2** : finger or toe

**dig·i·tal** \-ᵊl\ adj : providing information in numerical digits — **dig·i·tal·ly** adv

**digital camera** n : camera that records images as digital data instead of on film

**dig·ni·fy** \'dignəˌfī\ vb **-fied; -fy·ing** : give dignity or attention to

**dig·ni·tary** \-ˌterē\ n, pl **-taries** : person of high position

**dig·ni·ty** \'dignətē\ n, pl **-ties 1** : quality or state of being worthy or honored **2** : formal reserve (as of manner)

**di·gress** \dī'gres, də-\ vb : wander from the main subject — **di·gres·sion** \-'greshən\ n

**dike** \'dīk\ n : earth bank or dam

**di·lap·i·dat·ed** \də'lapəˌdātəd\ adj : fallen into partial ruin — **di·lap·i·da·tion** \-ˌlapə'dāshən\ n

**di·late** \dī'lāt, 'dīˌlāt\ vb **-lat·ed; -lat·ing** : swell or expand — **dil·a·ta·tion**

\ˌdilə'tāshən\ n — **di·la·tion** \dī'lā-shən\ n

**dil·a·to·ry** \'diləˌtōrē\ adj **1** : delaying **2** : tardy or slow

**di·lem·ma** \də'lemə\ n **1** : undesirable choice **2** : predicament

**dil·et·tante** \'diləˌtänt, -ˌtant; ˌdilə'tänt, -'tant\ n, pl **-tantes** or **-tan·ti** \-'täntē, -'tantē\ : one who dabbles in a field of interest

**dil·i·gent** \'diləjənt\ adj : attentive and busy — **dil·i·gence** \-jəns\ n — **dil·i·gent·ly** adv

**dill** \'dil\ n : herb with aromatic leaves and seeds

**dil·ly·dal·ly** \'dilēˌdalē\ vb : waste time by delay

**di·lute** \dī'lüt, də-\ vb **-lut·ed; -lut·ing** : lessen the consistency or strength of by mixing with something else ~ adj : weak — **di·lu·tion** \-'lüshən\ n

**dim** \'dim\ adj **-mm- 1** : not bright or distinct **2** : having no luster **3** : not seeing or understanding clearly — **dim** vb — **dim·ly** adv — **dim·mer** n — **dim·ness** n

**dime** \'dīm\ n : U.S. coin worth ¹⁄₁₀ dollar

**di·men·sion** \də'menchən, dī-\ n **1** : measurement of extension (as in length, height, or breadth) **2** : extent — **di·men·sion·al** \-'menchənəl\ adj

**di·min·ish** \də'minish\ vb **1** : make less or cause to appear less **2** : dwindle

**di·min·u·tive** \də'minyətiv\ adj : extremely small

**dim·ple** \'dimpəl\ n : small depression esp. in the cheek or chin

**din** \'din\ n : loud noise

**dine** \'dīn\ vb **dined; din·ing** : eat dinner

**din·er** \'dīnər\ n **1** : person eating dinner **2** : railroad dining car or restaurant resembling one

**din·ghy** \'dinē, -gē, -kē\ n, pl **-ghies** : small boat

**din·gy** \'dinjē\ adj **-gi·er; -est 1** : dirty **2** : shabby — **din·gi·ness** n

**din·ner** \'dinər\ n : main daily meal

**di·no·saur** \'dīnəˌsȯr\ n : extinct often huge reptile

**dint** \'dint\ n : force — in the phrase by **dint of**

**di·o·cese** \'dīəsəs, -ˌsēz, -ˌsēs\ n, pl **-ces·es** \-səz, 'dīəˌsēz\ : territorial jurisdiction of a bishop — **di·oc·e·san** \dī'äsəsən, ˌdī·ə'sēz·ᵊn\ adj or n

**dip** \'dip\ vb **-pp-** **1** : plunge into a liquid **2** : take out with a ladle **3** : lower and quickly raise again **4** : sink or slope downward suddenly ～ n **1** : plunge into water for sport **2** : sudden downward movement or incline — **dip·per** n

**diph·the·ria** \dif'thirēə\ n : acute contagious disease

**diph·thong** \'dif,thoṅ\ n : two vowel sounds joined to form one speech sound (as ou in out)

**di·plo·ma** \də'plōmə\ n, pl **-mas** : record of graduation from a school

**di·plo·ma·cy** \-məsē\ n **1** : business of conducting negotiations between nations **2** : tact — **dip·lo·mat** \'diplə-ˌmat\ n — **dip·lo·mat·ic** \ˌdiplə-'matik\ adj

**dire** \'dīr\ adj **dir·er; -est** **1** : very horrible **2** : extreme

**di·rect** \də'rekt, dī-\ vb **1** : address **2** : cause to move or to follow a certain course **3** : show (someone) the way **4** : regulate the activities or course of **5** : request with authority ～ adj **1** : leading to or coming from a point without deviation or interruption **2** : frank — **direct** adv — **di·rect·ly** adv — **di·rect·ness** n — **di·rec·tor** \-tər\ n

**direct current** : electric current flowing in one direction only

**di·rec·tion** \də'rekshən, dī-\ n **1** : supervision **2** : order **3** : course along which something moves — **di·rec·tion·al** \-shənəl\ adj

**di·rec·tive** \-tiv\ n : order

**di·rec·to·ry** \-tərē\ n, pl **-ries** : alphabetical list of names and addresses

**dirge** \'dərj\ n : funeral hymn

**di·ri·gi·ble** \'dirəjəbəl, də'rijə-\ n : airship

**dirt** \'dərt\ n **1** : mud, dust, or grime that makes something unclean **2** : soil

**dirty** \-ē\ adj **dirt·i·er; -est** **1** : not clean **2** : unfair **3** : indecent ～ vb **dirt·ied; dirty·ing** : make or become dirty — **dirt·i·ness** n

**dis·able** \dis'ābəl\ vb **-abled; -abling** : make unable to function — **dis·abil·i·ty** \ˌdisə'bilətē\ n

**dis·abuse** \ˌdisə'byüz\ vb : free from error or misconception

**dis·ad·van·tage** \ˌdisəd'vantij\ n : something that hinders success — **dis·ad·van·ta·geous** adj

**dis·af·fect** \ˌdisə'fekt\ vb : cause discontent in — **dis·af·fec·tion** n

**dis·agree** \ˌdisə'grē\ vb **1** : fail to agree **2** : differ in opinion — **dis·agree·ment** n

**dis·agree·able** \-əbəl\ adj : unpleasant

**dis·al·low** \ˌdisə'laủ\ vb : refuse to admit or recognize

**dis·ap·pear** \ˌdisə'pir\ vb **1** : pass out of sight **2** : cease to be — **dis·ap·pear·ance** n

**dis·ap·point** \ˌdisə'point\ vb : fail to fulfill the expectation or hope of — **dis·ap·point·ment** n

**dis·ap·prove** \-ə'prüv\ vb **1** : condemn or reject **2** : feel or express dislike or rejection — **dis·ap·prov·al** n — **dis·ap·prov·ing·ly** adv

**dis·arm** \dis'ärm\ vb **1** : take weapons from **2** : reduce armed forces **3** : make harmless or friendly — **dis·ar·ma·ment** \-'ärməmənt\ n

**dis·ar·range** \ˌdisə'rānj\ vb : throw into disorder — **dis·ar·range·ment** n

**dis·ar·ray** \ˌdisə'rā\ n : disorder

**di·sas·ter** \diz'astər, dis-\ n : sudden great misfortune — **di·sas·trous** \-'astrəs\ adj

**dis·avow** \ˌdisə'vaủ\ vb : deny responsibility for — **dis·avow·al** \-'vaủəl\ n

**dis·band** \dis'band\ vb : break up the organization of

**dis·bar** \dis'bär\ vb : expel from the legal profession — **dis·bar·ment** n

**dis·be·lieve** \ˌdisbi'lēv\ vb : hold not worthy of belief — **dis·be·lief** n

**dis·burse** \dis'bərs\ vb **-bursed; -burs·ing** : pay out — **dis·burse·ment** n

**disc** var of DISK

**dis·card** \dis'kärd, 'dis,kärd\ vb : get rid of as unwanted — **dis·card** \'dis,kärd\ n

**dis·cern** \dis'ərn, diz-\ vb : discover with the eyes or the mind — **dis·cern·ible** adj — **dis·cern·ment** n

**dis·charge** \dis'chärj, 'dis,chärj\ vb **1** : unload **2** : shoot **3** : set free **4** : dismiss from service **5** : let go or let off **6** : give forth fluid ～ \'dis,-, dis'-\ n **1** : act of discharging **2** : a flowing out (as of blood) **3** : dismissal

**dis·ci·ple** \di'sīpəl\ n : one who helps spread another's teachings

**dis·ci·pli·nar·i·an** \ˌdisəplə'nerēən\ *n* : one who enforces order

**dis·ci·pline** \'disəplən\ *n* **1** : field of study **2** : training that corrects, molds, or perfects **3** : punishment **4** : control gained by obedience or training ~ *vb* **-plined; -plin·ing** **1** : punish **2** : train in self-control — **dis·ci·plin·ary** \'disəplə,nerē\ *adj*

**dis·claim** \dis'klām\ *vb* : disavow

**dis·close** \-'klōz\ *vb* : reveal — **dis·clo·sure** \-'klōzhər\ *n*

**dis·col·or** \dis'kələr\ *vb* : change the color of esp. for the worse — **dis·col·or·ation** \dis,kələ'rāshən\ *n*

**dis·com·fit** \dis'kəmfət\ *vb* : upset — **dis·com·fi·ture** \dis'kəmfə,chŭr\ *n*

**dis·com·fort** \dis'kəmfərt\ *n* : uneasiness

**dis·con·cert** \ˌdiskən'sərt\ *vb* : upset

**dis·con·nect** \ˌdiskə'nekt\ *vb* : undo the connection of

**dis·con·so·late** \dis'känsələt\ *adj* : hopelessly sad

**dis·con·tent** \ˌdiskən'tent\ *n* : uneasiness of mind — **dis·con·tent·ed** *adj*

**dis·con·tin·ue** \ˌdiskən'tinyü\ *vb* : end — **dis·con·tin·u·ance** *n* — **dis·con·ti·nu·i·ty** \dis,käntə'nüətē, -'nyü-\ *n* — **dis·con·tin·u·ous** \diskən'tinyəwəs\ *adj*

**dis·cord** \'dis,kȯrd\ *n* : lack of harmony — **dis·cor·dant** \dis'kȯrdᵊnt\ *adj* — **dis·cor·dant·ly** *adv*

**dis·count** \'dis,kaůnt\ *n* : reduction from a regular price ~ \'dis,-, dis'-\ *vb* **1** : reduce the amount of **2** : disregard — **discount** *adj* — **dis·count·er** *n*

**dis·cour·age** \dis'kərij\ *vb* **-aged; -ag·ing** **1** : deprive of courage, confidence, or enthusiasm **2** : dissuade — **dis·cour·age·ment** *n*

**dis·course** \'dis,kōrs\ *n* **1** : conversation **2** : formal treatment of a subject ~ \dis'-\ *vb* **-coursed; -cours·ing** : talk at length

**dis·cour·te·ous** \dis'kərtēəs\ *adj* : lacking courtesy — **dis·cour·te·ous·ly** *adv* — **dis·cour·te·sy** *n*

**dis·cov·er** \dis'kəvər\ *vb* **1** : make known **2** : obtain the first sight or knowledge of **3** : find out — **dis·cov·er·er** *n* — **dis·cov·ery** \-ərē\ *n*

**dis·cred·it** \dis'kredət\ *vb* **1** : disbelieve **2** : destroy confidence in ~ *n* **1** : loss of reputation **2** : disbelief — **dis·cred·it·able** *adj*

**dis·creet** \dis'krēt\ *adj* : capable of keeping a secret — **dis·creet·ly** *adv*

**dis·crep·an·cy** \dis'krepənsē\ *n, pl* **-cies** : difference or disagreement

**dis·crete** \dis'krēt, 'dis,-\ *adj* : individually distinct

**dis·cre·tion** \dis'kreshən\ *n* **1** : discreet quality **2** : power of decision or choice — **dis·cre·tion·ary** *adj*

**dis·crim·i·nate** \dis'krimə,nāt\ *vb* **-nat·ed; -nat·ing** **1** : distinguish **2** : show favor or disfavor unjustly — **dis·crim·i·na·tion** \-,krimə'nāshən\ *n* — **dis·crim·i·na·to·ry** \-'krimənə,tōrē\ *adj*

**dis·cur·sive** \dis'kərsiv\ *adj* : passing from one topic to another — **dis·cur·sive·ly** *adv* — **dis·cur·sive·ness** *n*

**dis·cus** \'diskəs\ *n, pl* **-cus·es** : disk hurled for distance in a contest

**dis·cuss** \dis'kəs\ *vb* : talk about or present — **dis·cus·sion** \-'kəshən\ *n*

**dis·dain** \dis'dān\ *n* : feeling of contempt ~ *vb* : look upon or reject with disdain — **dis·dain·ful** \-fəl\ *adj* — **dis·dain·ful·ly** *adv*

**dis·ease** \di'zēz\ *n* : condition of a body that impairs its functioning — **dis·eased** \-'zēzd\ *adj*

**dis·em·bark** \ˌdisəm'bärk\ *vb* : get off a ship — **dis·em·bar·ka·tion** \dis-,em,bär'kāshən\ *n*

**dis·em·bod·ied** \ˌdisəm'bädēd\ *adj* : having no substance or reality

**dis·en·chant** \ˌdisᵊn'chant\ *vb* : to free from illusion — **dis·en·chant·ment** *n*

**dis·en·chant·ed** \-'chantəd\ *adj* : disappointed

**dis·en·gage** \-ᵊn'gāj\ *vb* : release — **dis·en·gage·ment** *n*

**dis·en·tan·gle** \-ᵊn'taŋgəl\ *vb* : free from entanglement

**dis·fa·vor** \dis'fāvər\ *n* : disapproval

**dis·fig·ure** \dis'figyər\ *vb* : spoil the appearance of — **dis·fig·ure·ment** *n*

**dis·fran·chise** \dis'fran,chīz\ *vb* : deprive of the right to vote — **dis·fran·chise·ment** *n*

**dis·gorge** \dis'gȯrj\ *vb* : spew forth

**dis·grace** \dis'grās\ *vb* : bring disgrace to ~ *n* **1** : shame **2** : cause of shame — **dis·grace·ful** \-fəl\ *adj* — **dis·grace·ful·ly** *adv*

**dis·grun·tle** \dis'grəntᵊl\ *vb* **-tled; -tling** : put in bad humor

**dis·guise** \dis'gīz\ *vb* **-guised; -guis-**

ing : hide the true identity or nature of ~ *n* : something that conceals

**dis·gust** \dis'gəst\ *n* : strong aversion ~ *vb* : provoke disgust in — **dis·gust·ed·ly** *adv* — **dis·gust·ing·ly** *adv*

**dish** \'dish\ *n* **1** : vessel for serving food or the food it holds **2** : food prepared in a particular way ~ *vb* : put in a dish — **dish·cloth** *n* — **dish·rag** *n* — **dish·wash·er** *n* — **dish·wa·ter** *n*

**dis·har·mo·ny** \dis'härmənē\ *n* : lack of harmony — **dis·har·mo·ni·ous** \ˌdishär'mōnēəs\ *adj*

**dis·heart·en** \dis'härt³n\ *vb* : discourage

**di·shev·el** \di'shevəl\ *vb* **-eled** *or* **-elled; -el·ing** *or* **-el·ling** : throw into disorder — **di·shev·eled, di·shev·elled** *adj*

**dis·hon·est** \dis'änəst\ *adj* : not honest — **dis·hon·est·ly** *adv* — **dis·hon·es·ty** *n*

**dis·hon·or** \dis'änər\ *n or vb* : disgrace — **dis·hon·or·able** *adj* — **dis·hon·or·ably** *adv*

**dis·il·lu·sion** \ˌdisə'lüzhən\ *vb* : to free from illusion — **dis·il·lu·sion·ment** *n*

**dis·in·cli·na·tion** \dis,inklə'nāshən\ *n* : slight aversion — **dis·in·cline** \ˌdis³n'klīn\ *vb*

**dis·in·fect** \ˌdis³n'fekt\ *vb* : destroy disease germs in or on — **dis·in·fec·tant** \-'fektənt\ *adj or n* — **dis·in·fec·tion** \-'fekshən\ *n*

**dis·in·gen·u·ous** \ˌdis³n'jenyəwəs\ *adj* : lacking in candor

**dis·in·her·it** \-³n'herət\ *vb* : prevent from inheriting property

**dis·in·te·grate** \dis'intə,grāt\ *vb* : break into parts or small bits — **dis·in·te·gra·tion** \dis,intə'grāshən\ *n*

**dis·in·ter·est·ed** \dis'intərəstəd, -,res-\ *adj* **1** : not interested **2** : not prejudiced — **dis·in·ter·est·ed·ness** *n*

**dis·joint·ed** \dis'jóintəd\ *adj* **1** : separated at the joint **2** : incoherent

**disk** \'disk\ *n* : something round and flat

**dis·like** \dis'līk\ *vb* : regard with dislike ~ *n* : feeling that something is unpleasant and to be avoided

**dis·lo·cate** \'dislō,kāt, dis'-\ *vb* : move out of the usual or proper place — **dis·lo·ca·tion** \ˌdislō'kāshən\ *n*

**dis·lodge** \dis'läj\ *vb* : force out of a place

**dis·loy·al** \dis'lóiəl\ *adj* : not loyal — **dis·loy·al·ty** *n*

**dis·mal** \'dizməl\ *adj* : showing or causing gloom — **dis·mal·ly** *adv*

**dis·man·tle** \dis'mant³l\ *vb* **-tled; -tling** : take apart

**dis·may** \dis'mā\ *vb* **-mayed; -may·ing** : discourage — **dismay** *n*

**dis·mem·ber** \dis'membər\ *vb* : cut into pieces — **dis·mem·ber·ment** *n*

**dis·miss** \dis'mis\ *vb* **1** : send away **2** : remove from service **3** : put aside or out of mind — **dis·miss·al** *n*

**dis·mount** \dis'maúnt\ *vb* **1** : get down from something **2** : take apart

**dis·obey** \ˌdisə'bā\ *vb* : refuse to obey — **dis·obe·di·ence** \-'bēdēəns\ *n* — **dis·obe·di·ent** \-ənt\ *adj*

**dis·or·der** \dis'órdər\ *n* **1** : lack of order **2** : breach of public order **3** : abnormal state of body or mind — **disorder** *vb* — **dis·or·der·li·ness** *n* — **dis·or·der·ly** *adj*

**dis·or·ga·nize** \dis'órgə,nīz\ *vb* : throw into disorder — **dis·or·ga·ni·za·tion** *n*

**dis·own** \dis'ōn\ *vb* : repudiate

**dis·par·age** \-'parij\ *vb* **-aged; -ag·ing** : say bad things about — **dis·par·age·ment** *n*

**dis·pa·rate** \dis'parət, 'dispərət\ *adj* : different in quality or character — **dis·par·i·ty** \dis'parətē\ *n*

**dis·pas·sion·ate** \dis'pashənət\ *adj* : not influenced by strong feeling — **dis·pas·sion·ate·ly** *adv*

**dis·patch** \dis'pach\ *vb* **1** : send **2** : kill **3** : attend to rapidly **4** : defeat ~ *n* **1** : message **2** : news item from a correspondent **3** : promptness and efficiency — **dis·patch·er** *n*

**dis·pel** \dis'pel\ *vb* **-ll-** : clear away

**dis·pen·sa·ry** \-'pensərē\ *n, pl* **-ries** : place where medical or dental aid is provided

**dis·pen·sa·tion** \ˌdispən'sāshən\ *n* **1** : system of principles or rules **2** : exemption from a rule **3** : act of dispensing

**dis·pense** \dis'pens\ *vb* **-pensed; -pens·ing** **1** : portion out **2** : make up and give out (remedies) — **dis·pens·er** *n* — **dispense with** : do without

**dis·perse** \-'pərs\ *vb* **-persed; -pers-**

ing : scatter — **dis·per·sal** \-'pərsəl\ n — **dis·per·sion** \-'pərzhən\ n

**dis·place** \-'plās\ vb 1 : expel or force to flee from home or native land 2 : take the place of — **dis·place·ment** \-mənt\ n

**dis·play** \-'plā\ vb : present to view — **display** n

**dis·please** \-'plēz\ vb : arouse the dislike of — **dis·plea·sure** \-'plezhər\ n

**dis·port** \dis'pōrt\ vb 1 : amuse 2 : frolic

**dis·pose** \dis'pōz\ vb -posed; -pos·ing 1 : give a tendency to 2 : settle — **dis·pos·able** \-'pōzəbəl\ adj — **dis·pos·al** \-'pōzəl\ n — **dis·pos·er** n — **dispose of** 1 : determine the fate, condition, or use of 2 : get rid of

**dis·po·si·tion** \ˌdispə'zishən\ n 1 : act or power of disposing of 2 : arrangement 3 : natural attitude

**dis·pos·sess** \ˌdispə'zes\ vb : deprive of possession or occupancy — **dis·pos·ses·sion** \-'zeshən\ n

**dis·pro·por·tion** \ˌdisprə'pōrshən\ n : lack of proportion — **dis·pro·por·tion·ate** \-shənət\ adj

**dis·prove** \dis'prüv\ vb : prove false

**dis·pute** \dis'pyüt\ vb -put·ed; -put·ing 1 : argue 2 : deny the truth or rightness of 3 : struggle against or over ~ n : debate or quarrel — **dis·put·able** \-əbəl, 'dispyət-\ adj — **dis·pu·ta·tion** \ˌdispyə'tāshən\ n

**dis·qual·i·fy** \dis'kwälə,fī\ vb : make ineligible — **dis·qual·i·fi·ca·tion** n

**dis·qui·et** \dis'kwīət\ vb : make uneasy or restless ~ n : anxiety

**dis·re·gard** \ˌdisri'gärd\ vb : pay no attention to ~ n : neglect

**dis·re·pair** \ˌdisri'par\ n : need of repair

**dis·rep·u·ta·ble** \dis'repyətəbəl\ adj : having a bad reputation

**dis·re·pute** \ˌdisri'pyüt\ n : low regard

**dis·re·spect** \ˌdisri'spekt\ n : lack of respect — **dis·re·spect·ful** adj

**dis·robe** \dis'rōb\ vb : undress

**dis·rupt** \dis'rəpt\ vb : throw into disorder — **dis·rup·tion** \-'rəpshən\ n — **dis·rup·tive** \-'rəptiv\ adj

**dis·sat·is·fac·tion** \dis,satəs'fakshən\ n : lack of satisfaction

**dis·sat·is·fy** \dis'satəs,fī\ vb : fail to satisfy

**dis·sect** \di'sekt\ vb : cut into parts esp. to examine — **dis·sec·tion** \-'sekshən\ n

**dis·sem·ble** \di'sembəl\ vb -bled; -bling : disguise feelings or intention — **dis·sem·bler** n

**dis·sem·i·nate** \di'semə,nāt\ vb -nat·ed; -nat·ing : spread around — **dis·sem·i·na·tion** \-,semə'nāshən\ n

**dis·sen·sion** \di'senchən\ n : discord

**dis·sent** \di'sent\ vb : object or disagree ~ n : difference of opinion — **dis·sent·er** n

**dis·ser·ta·tion** \ˌdisər'tāshən\ n : long written study of a subject

**dis·ser·vice** \dis'sərvəs\ n : injury

**dis·si·dent** \'disədənt\ n : one who differs openly with an establishment — **dis·si·dence** \-əns\ n — **dissident** adj

**dis·sim·i·lar** \di'simələr\ adj : different — **dis·sim·i·lar·i·ty** \di,simə'larətē\ n

**dis·si·pate** \'disə,pāt\ vb -pat·ed; -pat·ing 1 : break up and drive off 2 : squander — **dis·si·pa·tion** \ˌdisə'pāshən\ n

**dis·so·ci·ate** \dis'ōsē,āt, -shē-\ vb -at·ed; -at·ing : separate from association — **dis·so·ci·a·tion** \dis,ōsē'āshən, -shē-\ n

**dis·so·lute** \'disə,lüt\ adj : loose in morals or conduct

**dis·so·lu·tion** \ˌdisə'lüshən\ n : act or process of dissolving

**dis·solve** \di'zälv\ vb 1 : break up or bring to an end 2 : pass or cause to pass into solution

**dis·so·nance** \'disənəns\ n : discord — **dis·so·nant** \-nənt\ adj

**dis·suade** \di'swād\ vb -suad·ed; -suad·ing : persuade not to do something — **dis·sua·sion** \-'swāzhən\ n

**dis·tance** \'distəns\ n 1 : measure of separation in space or time 2 : reserve

**dis·tant** \-tənt\ adj 1 : separate in space 2 : remote in time, space, or relationship 3 : reserved — **dis·tant·ly** adv

**dis·taste** \dis'tāst\ n : dislike — **dis·taste·ful** adj

**dis·tem·per** \dis'tempər\ n : serious virus disease of dogs

**dis·tend** \dis'tend\ vb : swell out — **dis·ten·sion, dis·ten·tion** \-'tenchən\ n

**dis·till** \di'stil\ vb : obtain by distillation — **dis·til·late** \'distə,lāt, -lət\ n

— **dis·till·er** n — **dis·till·ery** \di-'stilərē\ n

**dis·til·la·tion** \,distə'lāshən\ n : purification of liquid by evaporating then condensing

**dis·tinct** \dis'tiŋkt\ adj 1 : distinguishable from others 2 : readily discerned — **dis·tinc·tive** \-tiv\ adj — **dis·tinc·tive·ly** adv — **dis·tinc·tive·ness** n — **dis·tinct·ly** adv — **dis·tinct·ness** n

**dis·tinc·tion** \-'tiŋkshən\ n 1 : act of distinguishing 2 : difference 3 : special recognition

**dis·tin·guish** \-'tiŋgwish\ vb 1 : perceive as different 2 : set apart 3 : discern 4 : make outstanding — **dis·tin·guish·able** adj — **dis·tin·guished** \-gwisht\ adj

**dis·tort** \dis'tort\ vb : twist out of shape, condition, or true meaning — **dis·tor·tion** \-'torshən\ n

**dis·tract** \di'strakt\ vb : divert the mind or attention of — **dis·trac·tion** \-'strakshən\ n

**dis·traught** \dis'trot\ adj : agitated with mental conflict

**dis·tress** \-'tres\ n 1 : suffering 2 : misfortune 3 : state of danger or great need ~ vb : subject to strain or distress — **dis·tress·ful** adj

**dis·trib·ute** \-'tribyət\ vb -ut·ed; -ut·ing 1 : divide among many 2 : spread or hand out — **dis·tri·bu·tion** \,distrə'byüshən\ n — **dis·trib·u·tive** \dis'tribyətiv\ adj — **dis·trib·u·tor** \-ər\ n

**dis·trict** \'dis,trikt\ n : territorial division

**dis·trust** \dis'trəst\ vb or n : mistrust — **dis·trust·ful** \-fəl\ adj

**dis·turb** \dis'tərb\ vb 1 : interfere with 2 : destroy the peace, composure, or order of — **dis·tur·bance** \-'tərbəns\ n — **dis·turb·er** n

**dis·use** \dis'yüs\ n : lack of use

**ditch** \'dich\ n : trench ~ vb 1 : dig a ditch in 2 : get rid of

**dith·er** \'dithər\ n : highly nervous or excited state

**dit·to** \'ditō\ n, pl -tos : more of the same

**dit·ty** \'ditē\ n, pl -ties : short simple song

**di·uret·ic** \,dīyù'retik\ adj : tending to increase urine flow — **diuretic** n

**di·ur·nal** \dī'ərn°l\ adj 1 : daily 2 : of or occurring in the daytime

**di·van** \'dī,van, di'-\ n : couch

**dive** \'dīv\ vb dived \'dīvd\ or dove \'dōv\; dived; div·ing 1 : plunge into water headfirst 2 : submerge 3 : descend quickly ~ n 1 : act of diving 2 : sharp decline — **div·er** n

**di·verge** \də'vərj, dī-\ vb -verged; -verg·ing 1 : move in different directions 2 : differ — **di·ver·gence** \-'vərjəns\ n — **di·ver·gent** \-jənt\ adj

**di·vers** \'dīvərz\ adj : various

**di·verse** \dī'vərs, də-, 'dī,vərs\ adj : involving different forms — **di·ver·si·fi·ca·tion** \də,vərsəfə'kāshən, dī-\ n — **di·ver·si·fy** \-'vərsə,fī\ vb — **di·ver·si·ty** \-sətē\ n

**di·vert** \də'vərt, dī-\ vb 1 : turn from a course or purpose 2 : distract 3 : amuse — **di·ver·sion** \-'vərzhən\ n

**di·vest** \dī'vest, də-\ vb : strip of clothing, possessions, or rights

**di·vide** \də'vīd\ vb -vid·ed; -vid·ing 1 : separate 2 : distribute 3 : share 4 : subject to mathematical division ~ n : watershed — **di·vid·er** n

**div·i·dend** \'divə,dend\ n 1 : individual share 2 : bonus 3 : number to be divided

**div·i·na·tion** \,divə'nāshən\ n : practice of trying to foretell future events

**di·vine** \də'vīn\ adj -vin·er; -est 1 : relating to or being God or a god 2 : supremely good ~ n : clergy member ~ vb -vined; -vin·ing 1 : infer 2 : prophesy — **di·vine·ly** adv — **di·vin·er** n — **di·vin·i·ty** \də'vinətē\ n

**di·vis·i·ble** \-'vizəbəl\ adj : capable of being divided — **di·vis·i·bil·i·ty** \-,vizə'bilətē\ n

**di·vi·sion** \-'vizhən\ n 1 : distribution 2 : part of a whole 3 : disagreement 4 : process of finding out how many times one number is contained in another

**di·vi·sive** \də'vīsiv, -'vi-, -ziv\ adj : creating dissension

**di·vi·sor** \-'vīzər\ n : number by which a dividend is divided

**di·vorce** \də'vōrs\ n : legal breaking up of a marriage — **divorce** vb

**di·vor·cée** \-,vōr'sā, -'sē\ n : divorced woman

**di·vulge** \də'vəlj, dī-\ vb -vulged; -vulg·ing : reveal

**diz·zy** \'dizē\ adj -zi·er; -est 1 : having a sensation of whirling 2 : causing or

caused by giddiness — **diz·zi·ly** *adv*
— **diz·zi·ness** *n*

**DNA** \ˌdēˌenˈā\ *n* : compound in cell nuclei that is the basis of heredity

**do** \ˈdü\ *vb* **did** \ˈdid\; **done** \ˈdən\; **do·ing** \ˈdüiŋ\; **does** \ˈdəz\ **1** : work to accomplish (an action or task) **2** : behave **3** : prepare or fix up **4** : fare **5** : finish **6** : serve the needs or purpose of **7** — used as an auxiliary verb — **do·er** \ˈdüər\ *n* — **do away with 1** : get rid of **2** : destroy — **do by** : deal with — **do in** *vb* **1** : ruin **2** : kill

**doc·ile** \ˈdäsəl\ *adj* : easily managed — **do·cil·i·ty** \däˈsilətē\ *n*

¹**dock** \ˈdäk\ *vb* **1** : shorten **2** : reduce

²**dock** *n* **1** : berth between 2 piers to receive ships **2** : loading wharf or platform ∼ *vb* : bring or come into dock — **dock·work·er** *n*

³**dock** *n* : place in a court for a prisoner

**dock·et** \ˈdäkət\ *n* **1** : record of the proceedings in a legal action **2** : list of legal causes to be tried — **docket** *vb*

**doc·tor** \ˈdäktər\ *n* **1** : person holding one of the highest academic degrees **2** : one (as a surgeon) skilled in healing arts ∼ *vb* **1** : give medical treatment to **2** : repair or alter — **doc·tor·al** \-tərəl\ *adj*

**doc·trine** \ˈdäktrən\ *n* : something taught — **doc·tri·nal** \-trən°l\ *adj*

**doc·u·ment** \ˈdäkyəmənt\ *n* : paper that furnishes information or legal proof — **doc·u·ment** \-ˌment\ *vb* — **doc·u·men·ta·tion** \ˌdäkyəmənˈtāshən\ *n* — **doc·u·ment·er** *n*

**doc·u·men·ta·ry** \ˌdäkyəˈmentərē\ *adj* **1** : of or relating to documents **2** : giving a factual presentation — **documentary** *n*

**dod·der** \ˈdädər\ *vb* : become feeble usu. from age

**dodge** \ˈdäj\ *vb* **dodged; dodg·ing 1** : move quickly aside or out of the way of **2** : evade — **dodge** *n*

**do·do** \ˈdōdō\ *n, pl* **-does** *or* **-dos 1** : heavy flightless extinct bird **2** : stupid person

**doe** \ˈdō\ *n, pl* **does** *or* **doe** : adult female deer — **doe·skin** \-ˌskin\ *n*

**does** *pres 3d sing of* DO

**doff** \ˈdäf\ *vb* : remove

**dog** \ˈdȯg\ *n* : flesh-eating domestic mammal ∼ *vb* **1** : hunt down or track like a hound **2** : harass — **dog·catch·er** *n* — **dog·gy** \-ē\ *n or adj* — **dog·house** *n*

**dog–ear** \ˈdȯgˌir\ *n* : turned-down corner of a page — **dog–ear** *vb* — **dog–eared** \-ˌird\ *adj*

**dog·ged** \ˈdȯgəd\ *adj* : stubbornly determined

**dog·ma** \ˈdȯgmə\ *n* : tenet or code of tenets

**dog·ma·tism** \-ˌtizəm\ *n* : unwarranted stubbornness of opinion — **dog·ma·tic** \dȯgˈmatik\ *adj*

**dog·wood** *n* : flowering tree

**doi·ly** \ˈdȯilē\ *n, pl* **-lies** : small decorative mat

**do·ings** \ˈdüiŋz\ *n pl* : events

**dol·drums** \ˈdōldrəmz, ˈdäl-\ *n pl* : spell of listlessness, despondency, or stagnation

**dole** \ˈdōl\ *n* : distribution esp. of money to the needy or unemployed — **dole out** *vb* : give out esp. in small portions

**dole·ful** \ˈdōlfəl\ *adj* : sad — **dole·ful·ly** *adv*

**doll** \ˈdäl, ˈdȯl\ *n* : small figure of a person used esp. as a child's toy

**dol·lar** \ˈdälər\ *n* : any of various basic monetary units (as in the U.S. and Canada)

**dol·ly** \ˈdälē\ *n, pl* **-lies** : small cart or wheeled platform

**dol·phin** \ˈdälfən\ *n* **1** : sea mammal related to the whales **2** : saltwater food fish

**dolt** \ˈdōlt\ *n* : stupid person — **dolt·ish** *adj*

**-dom** \dəm\ *n suffix* **1** : office or realm **2** : state or fact of being **3** : those belonging to a group

**do·main** \dōˈmān, də-\ *n* **1** : territory over which someone reigns **2** : sphere of activity or knowledge

**dome** \ˈdōm\ *n* **1** : large hemispherical roof **2** : roofed stadium

**do·mes·tic** \dəˈmestik\ *adj* **1** : relating to the household or family **2** : relating and limited to one's own country **3** : tame ∼ *n* : household servant — **do·mes·ti·cal·ly** \-tiklē\ *adv*

**do·mes·ti·cate** \-tiˌkāt\ *vb* **-cat·ed; -cat·ing** : tame — **do·mes·ti·ca·tion** \-ˌmestiˈkāshən\ *n*

**dom·i·cile** \ˈdäməˌsīl, ˈdō-; ˈdäməsəl\ *n* : home — **domicile** *vb*

**dom·i·nance** \ˈdämənəns\ *n* : control — **dom·i·nant** \-nənt\ *adj*

**dom·i·nate** \-ˌnāt\ *vb* **-nat·ed; -nat·ing** **1** : have control over **2** : rise high above — **dom·i·na·tion** \ˌdämə'nā-shən\ *n*

**dom·i·neer** \ˌdämə'nir\ *vb* : exercise arbitrary control

**do·min·ion** \də'minyən\ *n* **1** : supreme authority **2** : governed territory

**dom·i·no** \'däməˌnō\ *n, pl* **-noes** or **-nos** : flat rectangular block used as a piece in a game (**dominoes**)

**don** \'dän\ *vb* **-nn-** : put on (clothes)

**do·nate** \'dōˌnāt\ *vb* **-nat·ed; -nat·ing** : make a gift of — **do·na·tion** \dō'nāshən\ *n*

¹**done** \'dən\ *past part of* DO

²**done** *adj* **1** : finished or ended **2** : cooked sufficiently

**don·key** \'däŋkē, 'dəŋ-\ *n, pl* **-keys** : sturdy domestic ass

**do·nor** \'dōnər\ *n* : one that gives

**doo·dle** \'düdəl\ *vb* **-dled; -dling** : draw or scribble aimlessly — **doo·dle** *n*

**doom** \'düm\ *n* **1** : judgment **2** : fate **3** : ruin — **doom** *vb*

**door** \'dōr\ *n* : passage for entrance or a movable barrier that can open or close such a passage — **door·jamb** *n* — **door·knob** *n* — **door·mat** *n* — **door·step** *n* — **door·way** *n*

**dope** \'dōp\ **1** : narcotic preparation **2** : stupid person **3** : information ~ *vb* **doped; dop·ing** : drug

**dor·mant** \'dórmənt\ *adj* : not actively growing or functioning — **dor·man·cy** \-mənsē\ *n*

**dor·mer** \'dórmər\ *n* : window built upright in a sloping roof

**dor·mi·to·ry** \'dórməˌtōrē\ *n, pl* **-ries** : residence hall (as at a college)

**dor·mouse** \'dórˌmaùs\ *n* : squirrel-like rodent

**dor·sal** \'dórsəl\ *adj* : relating to or on the back — **dor·sal·ly** *adv*

**do·ry** \'dōrē\ *n, pl* **-ries** : flat-bottomed boat

**dose** \'dōs\ *n* : quantity (as of medicine) taken at one time ~ *vb* **dosed; dos·ing** : give medicine to — **dos·age** \'dōsij\ *n*

**dot** \'dät\ *n* **1** : small spot **2** : small round mark made with or as if with a pen ~ *vb* **-tt-** : mark with dots

**dot·age** \'dōtij\ *n* : senility

**dote** \'dōt\ *vb* **dot·ed; dot·ing** **1** : act feebleminded **2** : be foolishly fond

**dou·ble** \'dəbəl\ *adj* **1** : consisting of 2 members or parts **2** : being twice as great or as many **3** : folded in two ~ *n* **1** : something twice another **2** : one that resembles another ~ *adv* : doubly ~ *vb* **-bled; -bling** **1** : make or become twice as great **2** : fold or bend **3** : clench

**dou·ble–cross** *vb* : deceive by trickery — **dou·ble–cross·er** *n*

**dou·bly** \'dəblē\ *adv* : to twice the degree

**doubt** \'daùt\ *vb* **1** : be uncertain about **2** : mistrust **3** : consider unlikely ~ *n* **1** : uncertainty **2** : mistrust **3** : inclination not to believe — **doubt·ful** \-fəl\ *adj* — **doubt·ful·ly** *adv* — **doubt·less** \-ləs\ *adv*

**douche** \'düsh\ *n* : jet of fluid for cleaning a body part

**dough** \'dō\ *n* : stiff mixture of flour and liquid — **doughy** \'dōē\ *adj*

**dough·nut** \-ˌnət\ *n* : small fried ring-shaped cake

**dough·ty** \'daùtē\ *adj* **-ti·er; -est** : able, strong, or valiant

**dour** \'daùər, 'dùr\ *adj* **1** : severe **2** : gloomy or sullen — **dour·ly** *adv*

**douse** \'daùs, 'daùz\ *vb* **doused; dous·ing** **1** : plunge into or drench with water **2** : extinguish

¹**dove** \'dəv\ *n* : small wild pigeon

²**dove** \'dōv\ *past of* DIVE

**dove·tail** \'dəvˌtāl\ *vb* : fit together neatly

**dow·a·ger** \'daùijər\ *n* **1** : widow with wealth or a title **2** : dignified elderly woman

**dowdy** \'daùdē\ *adj* **dowd·i·er; -est** : lacking neatness and charm

**dow·el** \'daùəl\ *n* **1** : peg used for fastening two pieces **2** : wooden rod

**dow·er** \'daùər\ *n* : property given a widow for life ~ *vb* : supply with a dower

¹**down** \'daùn\ *adv* **1** : toward or in a lower position or state **2** : to a lying or sitting position **3** : as a cash deposit **4** : on paper ~ *adj* **1** : lying on the ground **2** : directed or going downward **3** : being at a low level ~ *prep* : toward the bottom of ~ *vb* **1** : cause to go down **2** : defeat

²**down** *n* : fluffy feathers

**down·cast** *adj* **1** : sad **2** : directed down

**down·fall** *n* : ruin or cause of ruin

**down•grade** *n* : downward slope ~ *vb* : lower in grade or position

**down•heart•ed** *adj* : sad

**down•pour** *n* : heavy rain

**down•right** *adv* : thoroughly ~ *adj* : absolute or thorough

**downs** \'daùnz\ *n pl* : rolling treeless uplands

**down•size** \'daùn,sīz\ *vb* : reduce in size

**down•stairs** *adv* : on or to a lower floor and esp. the main floor — **down-stairs** *adj or n*

**down-to-earth** *adj* : practical

**down•town** *adv* : to, toward, or in the business center of a town — **down-town** *n or adj*

**down•trod•den** \'daùn,träd°n\ *adj* : suffering oppression

**down•ward** \'daùnwərd\, **down•wards** \-wərdz\ *adv* : to a lower place or condition — **downward** *adj*

**down•wind** *adv or adj* : in the direction the wind is blowing

**downy** \'daùnē\ *adj* **-i•er; -est** : resembling or covered with down

**dow•ry** \'daùrē\ *n, pl* **-ries** : property a woman gives her husband in marriage

**dox•ol•o•gy** \däk'säləjē\ *n, pl* **-gies** : hymn of praise to God

**doze** \'dōz\ *vb* **dozed; doz•ing** : sleep lightly — **doze** *n*

**doz•en** \'dəz°n\ *n, pl* **-ens** *or* **-en** : group of 12 — **doz•enth** \-°nth\ *adj*

**drab** \'drab\ *adj* **-bb-** : dull — **drab•ly** *adv* — **drab•ness** *n*

**dra•co•ni•an** \drā'kōnēən, dra-\ *adj, often cap* : harsh, cruel

**draft** \'draft, 'dràft\ *n* **1** : act of drawing or hauling **2** : act of drinking **3** : amount drunk at once **4** : preliminary outline or rough sketch **5** : selection from a pool or the selection process **6** : order for the payment of money **7** : air current ~ *vb* **1** : select usu. on a compulsory basis **2** : make a preliminary sketch, version, or plan of ~ *adj* : drawn from a container — **draft•ee** \draf'tē, dràf-\ *n* — **drafty** \'draftē\ *adj*

**drafts•man** \'draftsmən, 'dràft-\ *n* : person who draws plans

**drag** \'drag\ *n* **1** : something dragged over a surface or through water **2** : something that hinders progress or is boring **3** : act or an instance of dragging ~ *vb* **-gg- 1** : haul **2** : move or

work with difficulty **3** : pass slowly **4** : search or fish with a drag — **drag-ger** *n*

**drag•net** \-,net\ *n* **1** : trawl **2** : planned actions for finding a criminal

**dra•gon** \'dragən\ *n* : fabled winged serpent

**drag•on•fly** *n* : large 4-winged insect

**drain** \'drān\ *vb* **1** : draw off or flow off gradually or completely **2** : exhaust ~ *n* : means or act of draining — **drain•age** \-ij\ *n* — **drain•er** *n* — **drain•pipe** *n*

**drake** \'drāk\ *n* : male duck

**dra•ma** \'drämə, 'dram-\ *n* **1** : composition for theatrical presentation esp. on a serious subject **2** : series of events involving conflicting forces — **dra•mat•ic** \drə'matik\ *adj* — **dra•mat•i•cal•ly** \-iklē\ *adv* — **dram-a•tist** \'dramətist, 'dräm-\ *n* — **dram•a•ti•za•tion** \,dramətə'zāshən, ,dräm-\ *n* — **dra•ma•tize** \'dramə-,tīz, 'dräm-\ *vb*

**drank** *past of* DRINK

**drape** \'drāp\ *vb* **draped; drap•ing 1** : cover or adorn with folds of cloth **2** : cause to hang in flowing lines or folds ~ *n* : curtain

**drap•ery** \'drāpərē\ *n, pl* **-er•ies** : decorative fabric hung esp. as a heavy curtain

**dras•tic** \'drastik\ *adj* : extreme or harsh — **dras•ti•cal•ly** \-tiklē\ *adv*

**draught** \'draft\, **draughty** \'draftē\ *chiefly Brit var of* DRAFT, DRAFTY

**draw** \'drò\ *vb* **drew** \'drü\; **drawn** \'dròn\; **draw•ing 1** : move or cause to move (as by pulling) **2** : attract or provoke **3** : extract **4** : take or receive (as money) **5** : bend a bow in preparation for shooting **6** : leave a contest undecided **7** : sketch **8** : write out **9** : deduce ~ *n* **1** : act, process, or result of drawing **2** : tie — **draw out** : cause to speak candidly — **draw up 1** : write out **2** : pull oneself erect **3** : bring or come to a stop

**draw•back** *n* : disadvantage

**draw•bridge** *n* : bridge that can be raised

**draw•er** \'dròr, 'dròər\ *n* **1** : one that draws **2** : sliding boxlike compartment **3** *pl* : underpants

**draw•ing** \'dròin\ *n* **1** : occasion of choosing by lot **2** : act or art of making a figure, plan, or sketch with lines **3** : something drawn

**drawl** \'dról\ vb : speak slowly — **drawl** n

**dread** \'dred\ vb : feel extreme fear or reluctance ~ n : great fear ~ adj : causing dread — **dread·ful** \-fəl\ adj — **dread·ful·ly** adv

**dream** \'drēm\ n 1 : series of thoughts or visions during sleep 2 : dreamlike vision 3 : something notable 4 : ideal ~ vb **dreamed** \'dremt, 'drēmd\ or **dreamt** \'dremt\; **dream·ing** 1 : have a dream 2 : imagine — **dream·er** n — **dream·like** adj — **dreamy** adj

**drea·ry** \'drirē\ adj -ri·er; -est : dismal — **drea·ri·ly** \'drirəlē\ adv

**¹dredge** \'drej\ n : machine for removing earth esp. from under water ~ vb **dredged; dredg·ing** : dig up or search with a dredge — **dredg·er** n

**²dredge** vb **dredged; dredg·ing** : coat (food) with flour

**dregs** \'dregz\ n pl 1 : sediment 2 : most worthless part

**drench** \'drench\ vb : wet thoroughly

**dress** \'dres\ vb 1 : put clothes on 2 : decorate 3 : prepare (as a carcass) for use 4 : apply dressings, remedies, or fertilizer to ~ n 1 : apparel 2 : single garment of bodice and skirt ~ adj : suitable for a formal event — **dress·mak·er** n — **dress·mak·ing** n

**dress·er** \'dresər\ n : bureau with a mirror

**dress·ing** n 1 : act or process of dressing 2 : sauce or a seasoned mixture 3 : material to cover an injury

**dressy** \'dresē\ adj **dress·i·er; -est** 1 : showy in dress 2 : stylish

**drew** past of DRAW

**drib·ble** \'dribəl\ vb -bled; -bling 1 : fall or flow in drops 2 : drool — **dribble** n

**drier** comparative of DRY

**driest** superlative of DRY

**drift** \'drift\ n 1 : motion or course of something drifting 2 : mass piled up by wind 3 : general intention or meaning ~ vb 1 : float or be driven along (as by a current) 2 : wander without purpose 3 : pile up under force — **drift·er** n — **drift·wood** n

**¹drill** \'dril\ vb 1 : bore with a drill 2 : instruct by repetition ~ n 1 : tool for boring holes 2 : regularly practiced exercise — **drill·er** n

**²drill** n : seed-planting implement

**³drill** n : twill-weave cotton fabric

**drily** var of DRYLY

**drink** \'drink\ vb **drank** \'drank\; **drunk** \'drəŋk\ or **drank; drink·ing** 1 : swallow liquid 2 : absorb 3 : drink alcoholic beverages esp. to excess ~ n 1 : beverage 2 : alcoholic liquor — **drink·able** adj — **drink·er** n

**drip** \'drip\ vb -pp- : fall or let fall in drops ~ n 1 : a dripping 2 : sound of falling drops

**drive** \'drīv\ vb **drove** \'drōv\; **driv·en** \'drivən\; **driv·ing** 1 : urge or force onward 2 : direct the movement or course of 3 : compel 4 : cause to become 5 : propel forcefully ~ n 1 : trip in a vehicle 2 : intensive campaign 3 : aggressive or dynamic quality 4 : basic need — **driv·er** n

**drive–in** adj : accommodating patrons in cars — **drive–in** n

**driv·el** \'drivəl\ vb -eled or -elled; -el·ing or -el·ling 1 : drool 2 : talk stupidly ~ n : nonsense

**drive·way** n : usu. short private road from the street to a house

**driz·zle** \'drizəl\ n : fine misty rain — **drizzle** vb

**droll** \'drōl\ adj : humorous or whimsical — **droll·ery** n — **drol·ly** adv

**drom·e·dary** \'drämə,derē\ n, pl **-dar·ies** : speedy one-humped camel

**drone** \'drōn\ n 1 : male honeybee 2 : deep hum or buzz ~ vb **droned; dron·ing** : make a dull monotonous sound

**drool** \'drül\ vb : let liquid run from the mouth

**droop** \'drüp\ vb 1 : hang or incline downward 2 : lose strength or spirit — **droop** n — **droopy** \-ē\ adj

**drop** \'dräp\ n 1 : quantity of fluid in one spherical mass 2 pl : medicine used by drops 3 : decline or fall 4 : distance something drops ~ vb -pp- 1 : fall in drops 2 : let fall 3 : convey 4 : go lower or become less strong or less active — **drop·let** \-lət\ n — **drop back** vb : move toward the rear — **drop behind** : fail to keep up — **drop in** vb : pay an unexpected visit

**drop·per** n : device that dispenses liquid by drops

**drop·sy** \'dräpsē\ n : edema

**dross** \'dräs\ n : waste matter

**drought** \'draut\ n : long dry spell

**¹drove** \'drōv\ n : crowd of moving people or animals

**²drove** past of DRIVE

**drown** \'draún\ *vb* **1** : suffocate in water **2** : overpower or become overpowered

**drowse** \'draúz\ *vb* **drowsed; drowsing** : doze — **drowse** *n*

**drowsy** \'draúzē\ *adj* **drows·i·er; -est** : sleepy — **drows·i·ly** *adv* — **drows·i·ness** *n*

**drub** \'drəb\ *vb* **-bb-** : beat severely

**drudge** \'drəj\ *vb* **drudged; drudg·ing** : do hard or boring work — **drudge** *n* — **drudg·ery** \-ərē\ *n*

**drug** \'drəg\ *n* **1** : substance used as or in medicine **2** : narcotic ~ *vb* **-gg-** : affect with drugs — **drug·gist** \-ist\ *n* — **drug·store** *n*

**dru·id** \'drüəd\ *n* : ancient Celtic priest

**drum** \'drəm\ *n* **1** : musical instrument that is a skin-covered cylinder beaten usu. with sticks **2** : drum-shaped object (as a container) ~ *vb* **-mm-** **1** : beat a drum **2** : drive, force, or bring about by steady effort — **drum·beat** *n* — **drum·mer** *n*

**drum·stick** *n* **1** : stick for beating a drum **2** : lower part of a fowl's leg

**drunk** \'drəŋk\ *adj* : having the faculties impaired by alcohol ~ *n* : one who is drunk — **drunk·ard** \'drəŋkərd\ *n* — **drunk·en** \-kən\ *adj* — **drunk·en·ly** *adv* — **drunk·en·ness** *n*

**dry** \'drī\ *adj* **dri·er** \'drīər\; **dri·est** \'drīəst\ **1** : lacking water or moisture **2** : thirsty **3** : marked by the absence of alcoholic beverages **4** : uninteresting **5** : not sweet ~ *vb* **dried; dry·ing** : make or become dry — **dry·ly** *adv* — **dry·ness** *n*

**dry–clean** *vb* : clean (fabrics) chiefly with solvents other than water — **dry cleaning** *n*

**dry·er** \'drīər\ *n* : device for drying

**dry goods** *n pl* : textiles, clothing, and notions

**dry ice** *n* : solid carbon dioxide

**du·al** \'düəl, 'dyü-\ *adj* : twofold — **du·al·ism** \-ə₁lizəm\ *n* — **du·al·i·ty** \dü'alətē, dyü-\ *n*

**dub** \'dəb\ *vb* **-bb-** : name

**du·bi·ous** \'dübēəs, 'dyü-\ *adj* **1** : uncertain **2** : questionable — **du·bi·ous·ly** *adv* — **du·bi·ous·ness** *n*

**du·cal** \'dükəl, 'dyü-\ *adj* : relating to a duke or dukedom

**duch·ess** \'dəchəs\ *n* **1** : wife of a duke **2** : woman holding a ducal title

**duchy** \-ē\ *n, pl* **-ies** : territory of a duke or duchess

**¹duck** \'dək\ *n* : swimming bird related to the goose and swan ~ *vb* **1** : thrust or plunge under water **2** : lower the head or body suddenly **3** : evade — **duck·ling** \-liŋ\ *n*

**²duck** *n* : cotton fabric

**duct** \'dəkt\ *n* : canal for conveying a fluid — **duct·less** \-ləs\ *adj*

**duc·tile** \'dəkt²l\ *adj* : able to be drawn out or shaped — **duc·til·i·ty** \₁dək-'tilətē\ *n*

**dude** \'düd, 'dyüd\ *n* **1** : dandy **2** : guy

**dud·geon** \'dəjən\ *n* : ill humor

**due** \'dü, 'dyü\ *adj* **1** : owed **2** : appropriate **3** : attributable **4** : scheduled ~ *n* **1** : something due **2** *pl* : fee ~ *adv* : directly

**du·el** \'düəl, 'dyü-\ *n* : combat between 2 persons — **duel** *vb* — **du·el·ist** *n*

**du·et** \dü'et, dyü-\ *n* : musical composition for 2 performers

**due to** *prep* : because of

**dug** *past of* DIG

**dug·out** \'dəg₁aút\ *n* **1** : boat made by hollowing out a log **2** : shelter made by digging

**duke** \'dük, 'dyük\ *n* : nobleman of the highest rank — **duke·dom** *n*

**dull** \'dəl\ *adj* **1** : mentally slow **2** : blunt **3** : not brilliant or interesting — **dull** *vb* — **dul·lard** \'dələrd\ *n* — **dull·ness** *n* — **dul·ly** *adv*

**du·ly** \'dülē, 'dyü-\ *adv* : in a due manner or time

**dumb** \'dəm\ *adj* **1** : mute **2** : stupid — **dumb·ly** *adv*

**dumb·bell** \'dəm₁bel\ *n* **1** : short bar with weights on the ends used for exercise **2** : stupid person

**dumb·found, dum·found** \₁dəm-'faúnd\ *vb* : amaze

**dum·my** \'dəmē\ *n, pl* **-mies 1** : stupid person **2** : imitative substitute

**dump** \'dəmp\ *vb* : let fall in a pile ~ *n* : place for dumping something (as refuse) — **in the dumps** : sad

**dump·ling** \'dəmpliŋ\ *n* : small mass of boiled or steamed dough

**dumpy** \'dəmpē\ *adj* **dump·i·er; -est** : short and thick in build

**¹dun** \'dən\ *adj* : brownish gray

**²dun** *vb* **-nn-** : hound for payment of a debt

**dunce** \'dəns\ *n* : stupid person

**dune** \'dün, 'dyün\ *n* : hill of sand

**dung** \'dəŋ\ *n* : manure

**dun·ga·ree** \ˌdəŋgə'rē\ *n* **1** : blue denim **2** *pl* : work clothes made of dungaree

**dun·geon** \'dənjən\ *n* : underground prison

**dunk** \'dəŋk\ *vb* : dip or submerge temporarily in liquid

**duo** \'düō, 'dyüō\ *n*, *pl* **du·os** : pair

**du·o·de·num** \ˌdüə'dēnəm, ˌdyü-; dù·'äd°nəm, dyù-\ *n*, *pl* **-na** \-'dēnə, -°nə\ *or* **-nums** : part of the small intestine nearest the stomach — **du·o·de·nal** \-'dēn°l, -°nəl\ *adj*

**dupe** \'düp, dyüp\ *n* : one easily deceived or cheated — **dupe** *vb*

**du·plex** \'dü,pleks, 'dyü-\ *adj* : double ~ *n* : 2-family house

**du·pli·cate** \'düplikət, 'dyü-\ *adj* **1** : consisting of 2 identical items **2** : being just like another ~ *n* : exact copy ~ \-ˌkāt\ *vb* **-cat·ed; -cat·ing** **1** : make an exact copy of **2** : repeat or equal — **du·pli·ca·tion** \ˌdüpli-'kāshən, ˌdyü-\ *n* — **du·pli·ca·tor** \'düpliˌkātər, dyü-\ *n*

**du·plic·i·ty** \dù'plisətē, ˌdyü-\ *n*, *pl* **-ties** : deception

**du·ra·ble** \'dùrəbəl, 'dyùr-\ *adj* : lasting a long time — **du·ra·bil·i·ty** \ˌdùrə'bilətē, ˌdyùr-\ *n*

**du·ra·tion** \dù'rāshən, dyù-\ *n* : length of time something lasts

**du·ress** \dù'res, dyù-\ *n* : coercion

**dur·ing** \'dùriŋ, 'dyùr-\ *prep* **1** : throughout **2** : at some point in

**dusk** \'dəsk\ *n* : twilight — **dusky** *adj*

**dust** \'dəst\ *n* : powdered matter ~ *vb* **1** : remove dust from **2** : sprinkle with fine particles — **dust·er** *n* — **dust·pan** *n* — **dusty** *adj*

**du·ty** \'dütē, 'dyü-\ *n*, *pl* **-ties** **1** : ac- tion required by one's occupation or position **2** : moral or legal obligation **3** : tax — **du·te·ous** \-əs\ *adj* — **du·ti·able** \-əbəl\ *adj* — **du·ti·ful** \'dütifəl, 'dyü-\ *adj*

**DVD** \ˌdē,vē'dē\ *n* : digital video disk

**dwarf** \'dwórf\ *n*, *pl* **dwarfs** \'dwórfs\ *or* **dwarves** \'dwórvz\ : one that is much below normal size ~ *vb* **1** : stunt **2** : cause to seem smaller — **dwarf·ish** *adj*

**dwell** \'dwel\ *vb* **dwelt** \'dwelt\ *or* **dwelled** \'dweld, 'dwelt\; **dwell·ing** **1** : reside **2** : keep the attention directed — **dwell·er** *n* — **dwell·ing** *n*

**dwin·dle** \'dwind°l\ *vb* **-dled; -dling** : become steadily less

**dye** \'dī\ *n* : coloring material ~ *vb* **dyed; dye·ing** : give a new color to

**dying** *pres part of* DIE

**dyke** *var of* DIKE

**dy·nam·ic** \dī'namik\ *adj* **1** : relating to physical force producing motion **2** : energetic or forceful

**dy·na·mite** \'dīnə,mīt\ *n* : explosive made of nitroglycerin — **dynamite** *vb*

**dy·na·mo** \-ˌmō\ *n*, *pl* **-mos** : electrical generator

**dy·nas·ty** \'dīnəstē, -ˌnas-\ *n*, *pl* **-ties** : succession of rulers of the same family — **dy·nas·tic** \dī'nastik\ *adj*

**dys·en·tery** \'dis°nˌterē\ *n*, *pl* **-ter·ies** : disease marked by diarrhea

**dys·lex·ia** \dis'leksēə\ *n* : disturbance of the ability to read — **dys·lex·ic** \-sik\ *adj*

**dys·pep·sia** \-'pepshə, -sēə\ *n* : indigestion — **dys·pep·tic** \-'peptik\ *adj or n*

**dys·tro·phy** \'distrəfē\ *n*, *pl* **-phies** : disorder involving nervous and muscular tissue

# E

**e** \'ē\ *n*, *pl* **e's** *or* **es** \'ēz\ : 5th letter of the alphabet

**e-** *comb form* : electronic

**each** \'ēch\ *adj* : being one of the class named ~ *pron* : every individual one ~ *adv* : apiece

**ea·ger** \'ēgər\ *adj* : enthusiastic or anx- ious — **ea·ger·ly** *adv* — **ea·ger·ness** *n*

**ea·gle** \'ēgəl\ *n* : large bird of prey

**-ean** — see -AN

**¹ear** \'ir\ *n* : organ of hearing or the outer part of this — **ear·ache** *n* — **eared** *adj* — **ear·lobe** \-ˌlōb\ *n*

**²ear** *n* : fruiting head of a cereal

**ear·drum** *n* : thin membrane that receives and transmits sound waves in the ear

**earl** \'ərl\ *n* : British nobleman — **earl·dom** \-dəm\ *n*

**ear·ly** \'ərlē\ *adj* **-li·er; -est 1** : relating to or occurring near the beginning or before the usual time **2** : ancient — **early** *adv*

**ear·mark** *vb* : designate for a specific purpose

**earn** \'ərn\ *vb* **1** : receive as a return for service **2** : deserve

**ear·nest** \'ərnəst\ *n* : serious state of mind — **earnest** *adj* — **ear·nest·ly** *adv* — **ear·nest·ness** *n*

**earn·ings** \'ərniŋz\ *n pl* : something earned

**ear·phone** *n* : device that reproduces sound and is worn over or in the ear

**ear·ring** *n* : earlobe ornament

**ear·shot** *n* : range of hearing

**earth** \'ərth\ *n* **1** : soil or land **2** : planet inhabited by man — **earth·li·ness** *n* — **earth·ly** *adj* — **earth·ward** \-wərd\ *adv*

**earth·en** \'ərthən\ *adj* : made of earth or baked clay — **earth·en·ware** \-₁war\ *n*

**earth·quake** *n* : shaking or trembling of the earth

**earth·worm** *n* : long segmented worm

**earthy** \'ərthē\ *adj* **earth·i·er; -est 1** : relating to or consisting of earth **2** : practical **3** : coarse — **earth·i·ness** *n*

**ease** \'ēz\ *n* **1** : comfort **2** : naturalness of manner **3** : freedom from difficulty ~ *vb* **eased; eas·ing 1** : relieve from distress **2** : lessen the tension of **3** : make easier

**ea·sel** \'ēzəl\ *n* : frame to hold a painter's canvas

**east** \'ēst\ *adv* : to or toward the east ~ *adj* : situated toward or at or coming from the east ~ *n* **1** : direction of sunrise **2** *cap* : regions to the east — **east·er·ly** \'ēstərlē\ *adv or adj* — **east·ward** *adv or adj* — **east·wards** *adv*

**Eas·ter** \'ēstər\ *n* : church feast celebrating Christ's resurrection

**east·ern** \'ēstərn\ *adj* **1** *cap* : relating to a region designated East **2** : lying toward or coming from the east — **East·ern·er** *n*

**easy** \'ēzē\ *adj* **eas·i·er; -est 1**
: marked by ease **2** : lenient — **eas·i·ly** \'ēzəlē\ *adv* — **eas·i·ness** \-ēnəs\ *n*

**easy·go·ing** *adj* : relaxed and casual

**eat** \'ēt\ *vb* **ate** \'āt\; **eat·en** \'ēt°n\; **eat·ing 1** : take in as food **2** : use up or corrode — **eat·able** *adj or n* — **eat·er** *n*

**eaves** \'ēvz\ *n pl* : overhanging edge of a roof

**eaves·drop** *vb* : listen secretly — **eaves·drop·per** *n*

**ebb** \'eb\ *n* **1** : outward flow of the tide **2** : decline ~ *vb* **1** : recede from the flood state **2** : wane

**eb·o·ny** \'ebənē\ *n, pl* **-nies** : hard heavy wood of tropical trees ~ *adj* **1** : made of ebony **2** : black

**ebul·lient** \i'bulyənt, -'bəl-\ *adj* : exuberant — **ebul·lience** \-yəns\ *n*

**ec·cen·tric** \ik'sentrik\ *adj* **1** : odd in behavior **2** : being off center — **eccentric** *n* — **ec·cen·tri·cal·ly** \-triklē\ *adv* — **ec·cen·tric·i·ty** \₁ek₁sen'trisətē\ *n*

**ec·cle·si·as·tic** \ik₁lēzē'astik\ *n* : clergyman

**ec·cle·si·as·ti·cal** \-tikəl\, **ecclesias·tic** *adj* : relating to a church — **ec·cle·si·as·ti·cal·ly** \-tiklē\ *adv*

**ech·e·lon** \'eshə₁län\ *n* **1** : steplike arrangement **2** : level of authority

**echo** \'ekō\ *n, pl* **ech·oes** : repetition of a sound caused by a reflection of the sound waves — **echo** *vb*

**èclair** \ā'klar\ *n* : custard-filled pastry

**eclec·tic** \e'klektik, i-\ *adj* : drawing or drawn from varied sources

**eclipse** \i'klips\ *n* : total or partial obscuring of one celestial body by another — **eclipse** *vb*

**ecol·o·gy** \i'käləjē, e-\ *n, pl* **-gies** : science concerned with the interaction of organisms and their environment — **eco·log·i·cal** \₁ēkə'läjikəl, ₁ek-\ *adj* — **eco·log·i·cal·ly** *adv* — **ecol·o·gist** \i'kälɔjist, e-\ *n*

**eco·nom·ic** \₁ekə'nämik, ₁ēkə-\ *adj* : relating to the producing and the buying and selling of goods and services

**eco·nom·ics** \-'nämiks\ *n* : branch of knowledge dealing with goods and services — **econ·o·mist** \i'känəmist\ *n*

**econ·o·mize** \i'känə₁mīz\ *vb* **-mized; -miz·ing** : be thrifty — **econ·o·miz·er** *n*

**econ·o·my** \-əmē\ *n, pl* **-mies** **1** : thrifty use of resources **2** : economic system — **eco·nom·i·cal** \‚ekə'nämikəl, ‚ēkə-\ *adj* — **eco·nom·i·cal·ly** *adv* — **economy** *adj*

**ecru** \'ekrü, 'ākrü\ *n* : beige

**ec·sta·sy** \'ekstəsē\ *n, pl* **-sies** : extreme emotional excitement — **ec·stat·ic** \ek'statik, ik-\ *adj* — **ec·stat·i·cal·ly** \-iklē\ *adv*

**ec·u·men·i·cal** \‚ekyə'menikəl\ *adj* : promoting worldwide Christian unity

**ec·ze·ma** \ig'zēmə, 'egzəmə, 'eksə-\ *n* : itching skin inflammation

**¹-ed** \d *after a vowel or* b, g, j, l, m, n, ŋ, r, <u>th</u>, v, z, zh; əd, id *after* d, t; t *after other sounds*\ *vb suffix or adj suffix* **1** — used to form the past participle of regular verbs **2** : having or having the characteristics of

**²-ed** *vb suffix* — used to form the past tense of regular verbs

**ed·dy** \'edē\ *n, pl* **-dies** : whirlpool — **eddy** *vb*

**ede·ma** \i'dēmə\ *n* : abnormal accumulation of fluid in the body tissues — **edem·a·tous** \-'demətəs\ *adj*

**Eden** \'ēd²n\ *n* : paradise

**edge** \'ej\ *n* **1** : cutting side of a blade **2** : line where something begins or ends ~ *vb* **edged; edg·ing 1** : give or form an edge **2** : move gradually **3** : narrowly defeat — **edg·er** *n*

**edge·wise** \-‚wīz\ *adv* : sideways

**edgy** \'ejē\ *adj* **edg·i·er; -est** : nervous — **edg·i·ness** *n*

**ed·i·ble** \'edəbəl\ *adj* : fit or safe to be eaten — **ed·i·bil·i·ty** \‚edə'bilətē\ *n* — **edible** *n*

**edict** \'ē‚dikt\ *n* : order or decree

**ed·i·fi·ca·tion** \‚edəfə'kāshən\ *n* : instruction or information — **ed·i·fy** \'edə‚fī\ *vb*

**ed·i·fice** \'edəfəs\ *n* : large building

**ed·it** \'edət\ *vb* **1** : revise and prepare for publication **2** : delete — **ed·i·tor** \-ər\ *n* — **ed·i·tor·ship** *n*

**edi·tion** \i'dishən\ *n* **1** : form in which a text is published **2** : total number published at one time

**ed·i·to·ri·al** \‚edə'tōrēəl\ *adj* **1** : relating to an editor or editing **2** : expressing opinion ~ *n* : article (as in a newspaper) expressing the views of an editor — **ed·i·to·ri·al·ize** \-ē‚līz\ *vb* — **ed·i·to·ri·al·ly** *adv*

**ed·u·cate** \'ejə‚kāt\ *vb* **-cat·ed; -cat-**ing **1** : give instruction to **2** : develop mentally and morally **3** : provide with information — **ed·u·ca·ble** \'ejəkəbəl\ *adj* — **ed·u·ca·tion** \‚ejə'kāshən\ *n* — **ed·u·ca·tion·al** \-shənəl\ *adj* — **ed·u·ca·tor** \-ər\ *n*

**eel** \'ēl\ *n* : snakelike fish

**ee·rie** \'irē\ *adj* **-ri·er; -est** : weird — **ee·ri·ly** \'irəlē\ *adv*

**ef·face** \i'fās, e-\ *vb* **-faced; -fac·ing** : obliterate by rubbing out — **ef·face·ment** *n*

**ef·fect** \i'fekt\ *n* **1** : result **2** : meaning **3** : influence **4** *pl* : goods or possessions ~ *vb* : cause to happen — **in effect** : in substance

**ef·fec·tive** \i'fektiv\ *adj* **1** : producing a strong or desired effect **2** : being in operation — **ef·fec·tive·ly** *adv* — **ef·fec·tive·ness** *n*

**ef·fec·tu·al** \i'fekchəwəl\ *adj* : producing an intended effect — **ef·fec·tu·al·ly** *adv* — **ef·fec·tu·al·ness** *n*

**ef·fem·i·nate** \ə'femənət\ *adj* : having qualities more typical of women than men — **ef·fem·i·na·cy** \-nəsē\ *n*

**ef·fer·vesce** \‚efər'ves\ *vb* **-vesced; -vesc·ing 1** : bubble and hiss as gas escapes **2** : show exhilaration — **ef·fer·ves·cence** \-'ves²ns\ *n* — **ef·fer·ves·cent** \-²nt\ *adj* — **ef·fer·ves·cent·ly** *adv*

**ef·fete** \e'fēt\ *adj* **1** : worn out **2** : weak or decadent **3** : effeminate

**ef·fi·ca·cious** \‚efə'kāshəs\ *adj* : effective — **ef·fi·ca·cy** \'efikəsē\ *n*

**ef·fi·cient** \i'fishənt\ *adj* : working well with little waste — **ef·fi·cien·cy** \-ənsē\ *n* — **ef·fi·cient·ly** *adv*

**ef·fi·gy** \'efəjē\ *n, pl* **-gies** : usu. crude image of a person

**ef·flu·ent** \'e‚flüənt, e'flü-\ *n* : something that flows out — **effluent** *adj*

**ef·fort** \'efərt\ *n* **1** : a putting forth of strength **2** : use of resources toward a goal **3** : product of effort — **ef·fort·less** *adj* — **ef·fort·less·ly** *adv*

**ef·fron·tery** \i'frəntərē\ *n, pl* **-ter·ies** : insolence

**ef·fu·sion** \i'fyüzhən, e-\ *n* : a gushing forth — **ef·fu·sive** \-'fyüsiv\ *adj* — **ef·fu·sive·ly** *adv*

**¹egg** \'eg, 'āg\ *vb* : urge to action

**²egg** *n* **1** : rounded usu. hard-shelled reproductive body esp. of birds and reptiles from which the young hatches **2** : ovum — **egg·shell** *n*

**egg·nog** \-,näg\ *n* : rich drink of eggs and cream

**egg·plant** *n* : edible purplish fruit of a plant related to the potato

**ego** \'ēgō\ *n, pl* **egos** : self-esteem

**ego·cen·tric** \,ēgō'sentrik\ *adj* : self-centered

**ego·tism** \'ēgə,tizəm\ *n* : exaggerated sense of self-importance — **ego·tist** \-tist\ *n* — **ego·tis·tic** \,ēgə'tistik\, **ego·tis·ti·cal** \-tikəl\ *adj* — **ego·tis·ti·cal·ly** *adv*

**egre·gious** \i'grējəs\ *adj* : notably bad — **egre·gious·ly** *adv*

**egress** \'ē,gres\ *n* : a way out

**egret** \'ēgrət, i'gret, 'egrət\ *n* : long-plumed heron

**ei·der·down** \'īdər,daùn\ *n* : soft down obtained from a northern sea duck (**eider**)

**eight** \'āt\ *n* **1** : one more than 7 **2** : 8th in a set or series **3** : something having 8 units — **eight** *adj or pron* — **eighth** \'āteth\ *adj or adv or n*

**eigh·teen** \āt'tēn\ *n* : one more than 17 — **eigh·teen** *adj or pron* — **eigh·teenth** \-'tēnth\ *adj or n*

**eighty** \'ātē\ *n, pl* **eight·ies** : 8 times 10 — **eight·i·eth** \'āteəth\ *adj or n* — **eighty** *adj or pron*

**ei·ther** \'ēthər, 'ī-\ *adj* **1** : both **2** : being the one or the other of two *~ pron* : one of two or more *~ conj* : one or the other

**ejac·u·late** \i'jakyə,lāt\ *vb* **-lat·ed; -lat·ing 1** : say suddenly **2** : eject a fluid (as semen) — **ejac·u·la·tion** \-,jakyə'lāshən\ *n*

**eject** \i'jekt\ *vb* : drive or throw out — **ejec·tion** \-'jekshən\ *n*

**eke** \'ēk\ *vb* **eked; ek·ing** : barely gain with effort — usu. with *out*

**elab·o·rate** \i'labərət\ *adj* **1** : planned in detail **2** : complex and ornate *~* \-ə,rāt\ *vb* **-rat·ed; -rat·ing** : work out in detail — **elab·o·rate·ly** *adv* — **elab·o·rate·ness** *n* — **elab·o·ra·tion** \-,labə'rāshən\ *n*

**elapse** \i'laps\ *vb* **elapsed; elaps·ing** : slip by

**elas·tic** \i'lastik\ *adj* **1** : springy **2** : flexible *~ n* **1** : elastic material **2** : rubber band — **elas·tic·i·ty** \-,las-'tisətē, ,ē,las-\ *n*

**elate** \i'lāt\ *vb* **elat·ed; elat·ing** : fill with joy — **ela·tion** \-'lāshən\ *n*

**el·bow** \'el,bō\ *n* **1** : joint of the arm **2** : elbow-shaped bend or joint *~ vb* : push aside with the elbow

**el·der** \'eldər\ *adj* : older *~ n* **1** : one who is older **2** : church officer

**el·der·ber·ry** \'eldər,berē\ *n* : edible black or red fruit or a tree or shrub bearing these

**el·der·ly** \'eldərlē\ *adj* : past middle age

**el·dest** \'eldəst\ *adj* : oldest

**elect** \i'lekt\ *adj* : elected but not yet in office *~ n* **elect** *pl* : exclusive group *~ vb* : choose esp. by vote — **elec·tion** \i'lekshən\ *n* — **elec·tive** \i'lektiv\ *n or adj* — **elec·tor** \i'lektər\ *n* — **elec·tor·al** \-tərəl\ *adj*

**elec·tor·ate** \i'lektərət\ *n* : body of persons entitled to vote

**elec·tric** \i'lektrik\ *adj* **1** *or* **elec·tri·cal** \-trikəl\ : relating to or run by electricity **2** : thrilling — **elec·tri·cal·ly** *adv*

**elec·tri·cian** \i,lek'trishən\ *n* : person who installs or repairs electrical equipment

**elec·tric·i·ty** \-'trisətē\ *n, pl* **-ties 1** : fundamental form of energy occurring naturally (as in lightning) or produced artificially **2** : electric current

**elec·tri·fy** \i'lektrə,fī\ *vb* **-fied; -fy·ing 1** : charge with electricity **2** : equip for use of electric power **3** : thrill — **elec·tri·fi·ca·tion** \-,lektrəfə'kā-shən\ *n*

**elec·tro·car·dio·gram** \i,lektrō-'kärdēə,gram\ *n* : tracing made by an electrocardiograph

**elec·tro·car·dio·graph** \-,graf\ *n* : instrument for monitoring heart function

**elec·tro·cute** \i'lektrə,kyüt\ *vb* **-cut·ed; -cut·ing** : kill by an electric shock — **elec·tro·cu·tion** \-,lektrə'kyü-shən\ *n*

**elec·trode** \i'lek,trōd\ *n* : conductor at a nonmetallic part of a circuit

**elec·trol·y·sis** \i,lek'träləsəs\ *n* **1** : production of chemical changes by passage of an electric current through a substance **2** : destruction of hair roots with an electric current — **elec·tro·lyt·ic** \-trə'litik\ *adj*

**elec·tro·lyte** \i'lektrə,līt\ *n* : nonmetallic electric conductor

**elec·tro·mag·net** \i,lektrō'magnət\ *n* : magnet made using electric current

**elec·tro·mag·ne·tism** \-nə,tizəm\ *n* : natural force responsible for interac-

tions between charged particles —
**elec·tro·mag·net·ic** \-mag'netik\
*adj* — **elec·tro·mag·net·i·cal·ly**
\-iklē\ *adv*

**elec·tron** \i'lek,trän\ *n* : negatively
charged particle within the atom

**elec·tron·ic** \i,lek'tränik\ *adj* : relating to electrons or electronics —
**elec·tron·i·cal·ly** \-iklē\ *adv*

**elec·tron·ics** \-iks\ *n* : physics of electrons and their use esp. in devices

**elec·tro·plate** \i'lektrə,plāt\ *vb* : coat
(as with metal) by electrolysis

**el·e·gance** \'eligəns\ *n* : refined grace-
fulness — **el·e·gant** \-gənt\ *adj* —
**el·e·gant·ly** *adv*

**el·e·gy** \'eləjē\ *n, pl* **-gies** : poem expressing grief for one who is dead —
**ele·gi·ac** \,elə'jīək, -,ak\ *adj*

**el·e·ment** \'eləmənt\ *n* 1 *pl* : weather
conditions 2 : natural environment 3
: constituent part 4 *pl* : simplest principles 5 : substance that has atoms of
only one kind — **el·e·men·tal** \,elə'-
mentʰl\ *adj*

**el·e·men·ta·ry** \,elə'mentrē\ *adj* 1
: simple 2 : relating to the basic subjects of education

**el·e·phant** \'eləfənt\ *n* : huge mammal
with a trunk and 2 ivory tusks

**el·e·vate** \'elə,vāt\ *vb* **-vat·ed; -vat·ing**
1 : lift up 2 : exalt

**el·e·va·tion** \,elə'vāshən\ *n* : height or
a high place

**el·e·va·tor** \'elə,vātər\ *n* 1 : cage or
platform for raising or lowering
something 2 : grain storehouse

**elev·en** \i'levən\ *n* 1 : one more than
10 2 : 11th in a set or series 3
: something having 11 units —
**eleven** *adj or pron* — **elev·enth**
\-ənth\ *adj or n*

**elf** \'elf\ *n, pl* **elves** \'elvz\ : mischievous fairy — **elf·in** \'elfən\ *adj* —
**elf·ish** \'elfish\ *adj*

**elic·it** \i'lisət\ *vb* : draw forth

**el·i·gi·ble** \'eləjəbəl\ *adj* : qualified to
participate or to be chosen — **el·i·gi·**
**bil·i·ty** \,eləjə'bilətē\ *n*

**elim·i·nate** \i'limə,nāt\ *vb* **-nat·ed;**
**-nat·ing** : get rid of — **elim·i·na·tion**
\i,limə'nāshən\ *n*

**elite** \ā'lēt\ *n* : choice or select group

**elix·ir** \i'liksər\ *n* : medicinal solution

**elk** \'elk\ *n* : large deer

**el·lipse** \i'lips, e-\ *n* : oval

**el·lip·sis** \-'lipsəs\ *n, pl* **-lip·ses**
\-,sēz\ 1 : omission of a word 2
: marks (as ...) to show omission

**el·lip·ti·cal** \-'tikəl\, **el·lip·tic** \-'tik\
*adj* 1 : relating to or shaped like an
ellipse 2 : relating to or marked by
ellipsis

**elm** \'elm\ *n* : tall shade tree

**el·o·cu·tion** \,elə'kyūshən\ *n* : art of
public speaking

**elon·gate** \i'lòn,gāt\ *vb* **-gat·ed; -gat-**
**ing** : make or grow longer — **elon·**
**ga·tion** \,ē,lòn'gāshən\ *n*

**elope** \i'lōp\ *vb* **eloped; elop·ing** : run
away esp. to be married — **elope-**
**ment** *n* — **elop·er** *n*

**el·o·quent** \'eləkwənt\ *adj* : forceful
and persuasive in speech — **el·o·**
**quence** \-kwəns\ *n* — **el·o·quent·ly**
*adv*

**else** \'els\ *adv* 1 : in a different way,
time, or place 2 : otherwise ∼ *adj* 1
: other 2 : more

**else·where** *adv* : in or to another place

**elu·ci·date** \i'lüsə,dāt\ *vb* **-dat·ed;**
**-dat·ing** : explain — **elu·ci·da·tion**
\i,lüsə'dāshən\ *n*

**elude** \ē'lüd\ *vb* **elud·ed; elud·ing**
: evade — **elu·sive** \ē'lüsiv\ *adj* —
**elu·sive·ly** *adv* — **elu·sive·ness** *n*

**elves** *pl of* ELF

**ema·ci·ate** \i'māshē,āt\ *vb* **-at·ed; -at-**
**ing** : become or make very thin —
**ema·ci·a·tion** \i,māsē'āshən, -shē-\
*n*

**e-mail** \'ē,māl\ *n* : message sent or received via computers

**em·a·nate** \'emə,nāt\ *vb* **-nat·ed;**
**-nat·ing** : come forth — **em·a·na·**
**tion** \,emə'nāshən\ *n*

**eman·ci·pate** \i'mansə,pāt\ *vb* **-pat·ed;**
**-pat·ing** : set free — **eman·ci·pa·**
**tion** \i,mansə'pāshən\ *n* — **eman·**
**ci·pa·tor** \i'mansə,pātər\ *n*

**emas·cu·late** \i'maskyə,lāt\ *vb* **-lat·ed;**
**-lat·ing** 1 : castrate 2 : weaken —
**emas·cu·la·tion** \i,maskyə'lāshən\
*n*

**em·balm** \im'bäm, -'bälm\ *vb* : preserve (a corpse) — **em·balm·er** *n*

**em·bank·ment** \im'baŋkmənt\ *n*
: protective barrier of earth

**em·bar·go** \im'bärgō\ *n, pl* **-goes**
: ban on trade — **embargo** *vb*

**em·bark** \-'bärk\ *vb* 1 : go on board a
ship or airplane 2 : make a start —
**em·bar·ka·tion** \,em,bär'kāshən\ *n*

**em·bar·rass** \im'barəs\ *vb* : cause distress and self-consciousness — **em·bar·rass·ment** *n*

**em·bas·sy** \'embəsē\ *n, pl* **-sies** : residence and offices of an ambassador

**em·bed** \im'bed\ *vb* **-dd-** : fix firmly

**em·bel·lish** \-'belish\ *vb* : decorate — **em·bel·lish·ment** *n*

**em·ber** \'embər\ *n* : smoldering fragment from a fire

**em·bez·zle** \im'bezəl\ *vb* **-zled; -zling** : steal (money) by falsifying records — **em·bez·zle·ment** *n* — **em·bez·zler** \-ələr\ *n*

**em·bit·ter** \im'bitər\ *vb* : make bitter

**em·bla·zon** \-'blāz°n\ *vb* : display conspicuously

**em·blem** \'embləm\ *n* : symbol — **em·blem·at·ic** \‚emblə'matik\ *adj*

**em·body** \im'bädē\ *vb* **-bod·ied; -body·ing** : give definite form or expression to — **em·bod·i·ment** \-'bädimənt\ *n*

**em·boss** \-'bäs, -'bȯs\ *vb* : ornament with raised work

**em·brace** \-'brās\ *vb* **-braced; -bracing** **1** : clasp in the arms **2** : welcome **3** : include — **embrace** *n*

**em·broi·der** \-'brȯidər\ *vb* : ornament with or do needlework — **em·broidery** \-ərē\ *n*

**em·broil** \im'brȯil\ *vb* : involve in conflict or difficulties

**em·bryo** \'embrē‚ō\ *n* : living being in its earliest stages of development — **em·bry·on·ic** \‚embrē'änik\ *adj*

**emend** \ē'mend\ *vb* : correct — **emen·da·tion** \‚ē‚men'dāshən\ *n*

**em·er·ald** \'emrəld, 'emə-\ *n* : green gem ~ *adj* : bright green

**emerge** \i'mərj\ *vb* **emerged; emerging** : rise, come forth, or appear — **emer·gence** \-'mərjəns\ *n* — **emergent** \-jənt\ *adj*

**emer·gen·cy** \i'mərjənsē\ *n, pl* **-cies** : condition requiring prompt action

**em·ery** \'emərē\ *n, pl* **-er·ies** : dark granular mineral used for grinding

**emet·ic** \i'metik\ *n* : agent that induces vomiting — **emetic** *adj*

**em·i·grate** \'emə‚grāt\ *vb* **-grat·ed; -grat·ing** : leave a country to settle elsewhere — **em·i·grant** \-igrənt\ *n* — **em·i·gra·tion** \‚emə'grāshən\ *n*

**em·i·nence** \'emənəns\ *n* **1** : prominence or superiority **2** : person of high rank

**em·i·nent** \-nənt\ *adj* : prominent — **em·i·nent·ly** *adv*

**em·is·sary** \'emə‚serē\ *n, pl* **-sar·ies** : agent

**emis·sion** \ē'mishən\ *n* : substance discharged into the air

**emit** \ē'mit\ *vb* **-tt-** : give off or out

**emol·u·ment** \i'mälyəmənt\ *n* : salary or fee

**emote** \i'mōt\ *vb* **emot·ed; emot·ing** : express emotion

**emo·tion** \i'mōshən\ *n* : intense feeling — **emo·tion·al** \-shənəl\ *adj* — **emo·tion·al·ly** *adv*

**em·per·or** \'empərər\ *n* : ruler of an empire

**em·pha·sis** \'emfəsəs\ *n, pl* **-pha·ses** \-‚sēz\ : stress

**em·pha·size** \-‚sīz\ *vb* **-sized; -siz·ing** : stress

**em·phat·ic** \im'fatik, em-\ *adj* : uttered with emphasis — **em·phat·i·cal·ly** \-iklē\ *adv*

**em·pire** \'em‚pīr\ *n* : large state or a group of states

**em·pir·i·cal** \im'pirikəl\ *adj* : based on observation — **em·pir·i·cal·ly** \-iklē\ *adv*

**em·ploy** \im'plȯi\ *vb* **1** : use **2** : occupy ~ *n* : paid occupation — **employ·ee, em·ploye** \im‚plȯi'ē, -'plȯi‚ē\ *n* — **em·ploy·er** *n* — **em·ploy·ment** \-mənt\ *n*

**em·pow·er** \im'pau̇ər\ *vb* : give power to — **em·pow·er·ment** *n*

**em·press** \'emprəs\ *n* **1** : wife of an emperor **2** : woman emperor

**emp·ty** \'emptē\ *adj* **1** : containing nothing **2** : not occupied **3** : lacking value, sense, or purpose ~ *vb* **-tied; -ty·ing** : make or become empty — **emp·ti·ness** \-tēnəs\ *n*

**emu** \'ēmyü\ *n* : Australian bird related to the ostrich

**em·u·late** \'emyə‚lāt\ *vb* **-lat·ed; -lat·ing** : try to equal or excel — **em·u·la·tion** \‚emyə'lāshən\ *n*

**emul·si·fy** \i'məlsə‚fī\ *vb* **-fied; -fy·ing** : convert into an emulsion — **emul·si·fi·ca·tion** \i‚məlsəfə'kāshən\ *n* — **emul·si·fi·er** \-'məlsə‚fīər\ *n*

**emul·sion** \i'məlshən\ *n* **1** : mixture of mutually insoluble liquids **2** : light-sensitive coating on photographic film

**-en** \ən,°n\ *vb suffix* **1** : become or cause to be **2** : cause or come to have

**en·able** \in'ābəl\ *vb* **-abled; -abling** : give power, capacity, or ability to

**en·act** \in'akt\ *vb* **1** : make into law **2** : act out — **en·act·ment** *n*

**enam·el** \in'aməl\ *n* **1** : glasslike substance used to coat metal or pottery **2** : hard outer layer of a tooth **3** : glossy paint — **enamel** *vb*

**en·am·or** \in'amər\ *vb* : excite with love

**en·camp** \in'kamp\ *vb* : make camp — **en·camp·ment** *n*

**en·case** \in'kās\ *vb* : enclose in or as if in a case

**-ence** \əns,²ns\ *n suffix* **1** : action or process **2** : quality or state

**en·ceph·a·li·tis** \in₁sefə'lītəs\ *n, pl* **-lit·i·des** \-'litə₁dēz\ : inflammation of the brain

**en·chant** \in'chant\ *vb* **1** : bewitch **2** : fascinate — **en·chant·er** *n* — **en·chant·ment** *n* — **en·chant·ress** \-'chantrəs\ *n*

**en·cir·cle** \in'sərkəl\ *vb* : surround

**en·close** \in'klōz\ *vb* **1** : shut up or surround **2** : include — **en·clo·sure** \in'klōzhər\ *n*

**en·co·mi·um** \en'kōmēəm\ *n, pl* **-mi·ums** *or* **-mia** \-mēə\ : high praise

**en·com·pass** \in'kəmpəs, -'käm-\ *vb* : surround or include

**en·core** \'än₁kōr\ *n* : further performance

**en·coun·ter** \in'kaùntər\ *vb* **1** : fight **2** : meet unexpectedly — **encounter** *n*

**en·cour·age** \in'kərij\ *vb* **-aged; -ag·ing** **1** : inspire with courage and hope **2** : foster — **en·cour·age·ment** *n*

**en·croach** \in'krōch\ *vb* : enter upon another's property or rights — **en·croach·ment** *n*

**en·crust** \in'krəst\ *vb* : form a crust on

**en·cum·ber** \in'kəmbər\ *vb* : burden — **en·cum·brance** \-brəns\ *n*

**-en·cy** \ənsē,²n-\ *n suffix* : -ence

**en·cyc·li·cal** \in'siklikəl, en-\ *n* : papal letter to bishops

**en·cy·clo·pe·dia** \in₁sīklə'pēdēə\ *n* : reference work on many subjects — **en·cy·clo·pe·dic** \-'pēdik\ *adj*

**end** \'end\ *n* **1** : point at which something stops or no longer exists **2** : cessation **3** : purpose ⁓ *vb* **1** : stop or finish **2** : be at the end of — **end·less** *adj* — **end·less·ly** *adv*

**en·dan·ger** \in'dānjər\ *vb* : bring into danger

**en·dear** \in'dir\ *vb* : make dear — **en·dear·ment** \-mənt\ *n*

**en·deav·or** \in'devər\ *vb or n* : attempt

**end·ing** \'endiŋ\ *n* : end

**en·dive** \'en₁dīv\ *n* : salad plant

**en·do·crine** \'endəkrən, -₁krīn, -₁krēn\ *adj* : producing secretions distributed by the bloodstream

**en·dorse** \in'dórs\ *vb* **-dorsed; -dors·ing** **1** : sign one's name to **2** : approve — **en·dorse·ment** *n*

**en·dow** \in'daù\ *vb* **1** : furnish with funds **2** : furnish naturally — **en·dow·ment** *n*

**en·dure** \in'dùr, -'dyùr\ *vb* **-dured; -dur·ing** **1** : last **2** : suffer patiently **3** : tolerate — **en·dur·able** *adj* — **en·dur·ance** \-əns\ *n*

**en·e·ma** \'enəmə\ *n* : injection of liquid into the rectum

**en·e·my** \-mē\ *n, pl* **-mies** : one that attacks or tries to harm another

**en·er·get·ic** \₁enər'jetik\ *adj* : full of energy or activity — **en·er·get·i·cal·ly** \-iklē\ *adv*

**en·er·gize** \'enər₁jīz\ *vb* **-gized; -giz·ing** : give energy to

**en·er·gy** \'enərjē\ *n, pl* **-gies** **1** : capacity for action **2** : vigorous action **3** : capacity for doing work

**en·er·vate** \'enər₁vāt\ *vb* **-vat·ed; -vat·ing** : make weak or listless — **en·er·va·tion** \₁enər'vāshən\ *n*

**en·fold** \in'fōld\ *vb* : surround or embrace

**en·force** \-'fōrs\ *vb* **1** : compel **2** : carry out — **en·force·able** \-əbəl\ *adj* — **en·force·ment** *n*

**en·fran·chise** \-'fran₁chīz\ *vb* **-chised; -chis·ing** : grant voting rights to — **en·fran·chise·ment** \-₁chīzmənt, -chəz-\ *n*

**en·gage** \in'gāj\ *vb* **-gaged; -gag·ing** **1** : participate or cause to participate **2** : bring or come into working contact **3** : bind by a pledge to marry **4** : hire **5** : bring or enter into conflict — **en·gage·ment** \-mənt\ *n*

**en·gag·ing** *adj* : attractive

**en·gen·der** \in'jendər\ *vb* **-dered; -der·ing** : create

**en·gine** \'enjən\ *n* **1** : machine that converts energy into mechanical motion **2** : locomotive

**en·gi·neer** \₁enjə'nir\ *n* **1** : one trained in engineering **2** : engine operator ⁓ *vb* : lay out or manage as an engineer

**en·gi·neer·ing** \-iŋ\ *n* : practical application of science and mathematics

**en·grave** \in'grāv\ vb **-graved; -graving** : cut into a surface — **engrav·er** n — **en·grav·ing** n

**en·gross** \-'grōs\ vb : occupy fully

**en·gulf** \-'gəlf\ vb : swallow up

**en·hance** \-'hans\ vb **-hanced; -hancing** : improve in value — **en·hancement** n

**enig·ma** \i'nigmə\ n : puzzle or mystery — **enig·mat·ic** \,enig'matik, ,ē-\ adj — **enig·mat·i·cal·ly** adv

**en·join** \in'jȯin\ vb **1** : command **2** : forbid

**en·joy** \-'jȯi\ vb : take pleasure in — **en·joy·able** adj — **en·joy·ment** n

**en·large** \-'lärj\ vb **-larged; -larging** : make or grow larger — **en·largement** n — **en·larg·er** n

**en·light·en** \-'līt³n\ vb : give knowledge or spiritual insight to — **en·light·en·ment** n

**en·list** \-'list\ vb **1** : join the armed forces **2** : get the aid of — **en·list·ee** \-,lis'tē\ n — **en·list·ment** \-'listmənt\ n

**en·liv·en** \in'līvən\ vb : give life or spirit to

**en·mi·ty** \'enmətē\ n, pl **-ties** : mutual hatred

**en·no·ble** \in'ōbəl\ vb **-bled; -bling** : make noble

**en·nui** \,än'wē\ n : boredom

**enor·mi·ty** \i'nȯrmətē\ n, pl **-ties 1** : great wickedness **2** : huge size

**enor·mous** \i'nȯrməs\ adj : great in size, number, or degree — **enor·mous·ly** adv — **enor·mous·ness** n

**enough** \i'nəf\ adj : adequate ~ adv **1** : in an adequate manner **2** : in a tolerable degree ~ pron : adequate number, quantity, or amount

**en·quire** \in'kwīr\, **en·qui·ry** \'in-,kwīrē, in'-; 'inkwərē, 'iŋ-\ var of INQUIRE, INQUIRY

**en·rage** \in'rāj\ vb : fill with rage

**en·rich** \-'rich\ vb : make rich — **en·rich·ment** n

**en·roll, en·rol** \-'rōl\ vb **-rolled; -rolling 1** : enter on a list **2** : become enrolled — **en·roll·ment** n

**en route** \än'rüt, en-, in-\ adv or adj : on or along the way

**en·sconce** \in'skäns\ vb **-sconced; -sconc·ing** : settle snugly

**en·sem·ble** \än'sämbəl\ n **1** : small group **2** : complete costume

**en·shrine** \in'shrīn\ vb **1** : put in a shrine **2** : cherish

**en·sign** \'ensən, 1 also 'en,sīn\ n **1** : flag **2** : lowest ranking commissioned officer in the navy

**en·slave** \in'slāv\ vb : make a slave of — **en·slave·ment** n

**en·snare** \-'snar\ vb : trap

**en·sue** \-'sü\ vb **-sued; -su·ing** : follow as a consequence

**en·sure** \-'shu̇r\ vb **-sured; -sur·ing** : guarantee

**en·tail** \-'tāl\ vb : involve as a necessary result

**en·tan·gle** \-'taŋgəl\ vb : tangle — **en·tan·gle·ment** n

**en·ter** \'entər\ vb **1** : go or come in or into **2** : start **3** : set down (as in a list)

**en·ter·prise** \'entər,prīz\ n **1** : an undertaking **2** : business organization **3** : initiative

**en·ter·pris·ing** \-,prīziŋ\ adj : showing initiative

**en·ter·tain** \,entər'tān\ vb **1** : treat or receive as a guest **2** : hold in mind **3** : amuse — **en·ter·tain·er** n — **en·ter·tain·ment** n

**en·thrall, en·thral** \in'thrȯl\ vb **-thralled; -thrall·ing** : hold spellbound

**en·thu·si·asm** \-'thüzē,azəm, -'thyü-\ n : strong excitement of feeling or its cause — **en·thu·si·ast** \-,ast, -əst\ n — **en·thu·si·as·tic** \-,thüzē'astik, -,thyü-\ adj — **en·thu·si·as·ti·cal·ly** \-tiklē\ adv

**en·tice** \-'tīs\ vb **-ticed; -tic·ing** : tempt — **en·tice·ment** n

**en·tire** \in'tīr\ adj : complete or whole — **en·tire·ly** adv — **en·tire·ty** \-'tīrətē, -'tīrtē\ n

**en·ti·tle** \-'tīt³l\ vb **-tled; -tling 1** : name **2** : give a right to

**en·ti·ty** \'entətē\ n, pl **-ties** : something with separate existence

**en·to·mol·o·gy** \,entə'mäləjē\ n : study of insects — **en·to·mo·log·i·cal** \-mə'läjikəl\ adj — **en·to·mol·o·gist** \-'mäləjist\ n

**en·tou·rage** \,äntu̇'räzh\ n : retinue

**en·trails** \'entrəlz, -,trālz\ n pl : intestines

¹**en·trance** \'entrəns\ n **1** : act of entering **2** : means or place of entering — **en·trant** \'entrənt\ n

²**en·trance** \in'trans\ vb **-tranced; -tranc·ing** : fascinate or delight

**en·trap** \in'trap\ vb : trap — **en·trap·ment** n

**en·treat** \-'trēt\ vb : ask urgently — **en·treaty** \-'trētē\ n

**en·trée, en·tree** \'än₁trā\ n : principal dish of the meal

**en·trench** \in'trench\ vb : establish in a strong position — **en·trench·ment** n

**en·tre·pre·neur** \₁äntrəprə'nər\ n : organizer or promoter of an enterprise

**en·trust** \in'trəst\ vb : commit to another with confidence

**en·try** \'entrē\ n, pl **-tries** 1 : entrance 2 : an entering in a record or an item so entered

**en·twine** \in'twīn\ vb : twine together or around

**enu·mer·ate** \i'nümə₁rāt, -'nyü-\ vb **-at·ed; -at·ing** 1 : count 2 : list — **enu·mer·a·tion** \i₁nümə'rāshən, -₁nyü-\ n

**enun·ci·ate** \ē'nənsē₁āt\ vb **-at·ed; -at·ing** 1 : announce 2 : pronounce — **enun·ci·a·tion** \-₁nənsē'āshən\ n

**en·vel·op** \in'veləp\ vb : surround — **en·vel·op·ment** n

**en·ve·lope** \'envə₁lōp, 'än-\ n : paper container for a letter

**en·vi·ron·ment** \in'vīrənmənt\ n : surroundings — **en·vi·ron·men·tal** \-₁vīrən'ment³l\ adj

**en·vi·ron·men·tal·ist** \-³list\ n : person concerned about the environment

**en·vi·rons** \in'vīrənz\ n pl : vicinity

**en·vis·age** \in'vizij\ vb **-aged; -ag·ing** : have a mental picture of

**en·vi·sion** \-'vizhən\ vb : picture to oneself

**en·voy** \'en₁vȯi, 'än-\ n : diplomat

**en·vy** \'envē\ n 1 : resentful awareness of another's advantage 2 : object of envy ~ vb **-vied; -vy·ing** : feel envy toward or on account of — **en·vi·able** \-vēəbəl\ adj — **en·vi·ous** \-vēəs\ adj — **en·vi·ous·ly** adv

**en·zyme** \'en₁zīm\ n : biological catalyst

**eon** \'ēən, ē₁än\ n : indefinitely long time

**ep·au·let** \₁epə'let\ n : shoulder ornament on a uniform

**ephem·er·al** \i'femərəl\ adj : short-lived

**ep·ic** \'epik\ n : long poem about a hero — **epic** adj

**ep·i·cure** \'epi₁kyu̇r\ n : person with fastidious taste esp. in food and wine — **ep·i·cu·re·an** \₁epikyu̇'rēən, -'kyu̇rē-\ n or adj

**ep·i·dem·ic** \₁epə'demik\ adj : affecting many persons at one time — **epidemic** n

**epi·der·mis** \₁epə'dərməs\ n : outer layer of skin

**ep·i·gram** \'epə₁gram\ n : short witty poem or saying

**ep·i·lep·sy** \'epə₁lepsē\ n, pl **-sies** : nervous disorder marked by convulsive attacks — **ep·i·lep·tic** \₁epə'leptik\ adj or n

**epis·co·pal** \i'piskəpəl\ adj : governed by bishops

**ep·i·sode** \'epə₁sōd, -₁zōd\ n : occurrence — **ep·i·sod·ic** \₁epə'sädik, -'zäd-\ adj

**epis·tle** \i'pisəl\ n : letter

**ep·i·taph** \'epə₁taf\ n : inscription in memory of a dead person

**ep·i·thet** \'epə₁thet, -thət\ n : characterizing often abusive word or phrase

**epit·o·me** \i'pitəmē\ n 1 : summary 2 : ideal example — **epit·o·mize** \-₁mīz\ vb

**ep·och** \'epək, 'ep₁äk\ n : extended period — **ep·och·al** \'epəkəl, 'ep₁äkəl\ adj

**ep·oxy** \'ep₁äksē, ep'äksē\ n : synthetic resin used esp. in adhesives ~ vb **-ox·ied** or **-oxyed; -oxy·ing** : glue with epoxy

**equa·ble** \'ekwəbəl, 'ēkwə-\ adj : free from unpleasant extremes — **equa·bil·i·ty** \₁ekwə'bilətē, ₁ē-\ n — **equa·bly** \-blē\ adv

**equal** \'ēkwəl\ adj : of the same quantity, value, quality, number, or status as another ~ n : one that is equal ~ vb **equaled** or **equalled; equal·ing** or **equal·ling** : be or become equal to — **equal·i·ty** \i'kwälətē\ n — **equal·ize** \'ēkwə₁līz\ vb — **equal·ly** \'ēkwəlē\ adv

**equa·nim·i·ty** \₁ēkwə'nimətē, ek-\ n, pl **-ties** : calmness

**equate** \i'kwāt\ vb **equat·ed; equat·ing** : treat or regard as equal

**equa·tion** \i'kwāzhən, -shən\ n : mathematical statement that two things are equal

**equa·tor** \i'kwātər\ n : imaginary circle that separates the northern and southern hemispheres — **equa·to·ri·al** \₁ēkwə'tōrēəl, ₁ek-\ adj

**eques·tri·an** \i'kwestrēən\ adj : relating to horseback riding ~ n : horseback rider

**equi·lat·er·al** \ˌēkwə'latərəl\ *adj* : having equal sides

**equi·lib·ri·um** \-'librēəm\ *n*, *pl* **-ri·ums** *or* **-ria** \-rēə\ : state of balance

**equine** \'ēˌkwīn, 'ekˌwīn\ *adj* : relating to the horse — **equine** *n*

**equi·nox** \'ēkwəˌnäks, 'ek-\ *n* : time when day and night are everywhere of equal length

**equip** \i'kwip\ *vb* **-pp-** : furnish with needed resources — **equip·ment** \-mənt\ *n*

**eq·ui·ta·ble** \'ekwətəbəl\ *adj* : fair

**eq·ui·ty** \'ekwətē\ *n*, *pl* **-ties** 1 : justice 2 : value of a property less debt

**equiv·a·lent** \i'kwivələnt\ *adj* : equal — **equiv·a·lence** \-ləns\ *n* — **equivalent** *n*

**equiv·o·cal** \i'kwivəkəl\ *adj* : ambiguous or uncertain

**equiv·o·cate** \i'kwivəˌkāt\ *vb* **-cat·ed; -cat·ing** 1 : use misleading language 2 : avoid answering definitely — **equiv·o·ca·tion** \-ˌkwivə'kāshən\ *n*

**¹-er** \ər\ *adj suffix or adv suffix* — used to form the comparative degree of adjectives and adverbs and esp. those of one or two syllables

**²-er** \ər\, **-ier** \ēər, yər\, **-yer** \yər\ *n suffix* 1 : one that is associated with 2 : one that performs or is the object of an action 3 : one that is

**era** \'irə, 'erə, 'ērə\ *n* : period of time associated with something

**erad·i·cate** \i'radəˌkāt\ *vb* **-cat·ed; -cat·ing** : do away with

**erase** \i'rās\ *vb* **erased; eras·ing** : rub or scratch out — **eras·er** *n* — **era·sure** \i'rāshər\ *n*

**ere** \'er\ *prep or conj* : before

**erect** \i'rekt\ *adj* : not leaning or lying down ~ *vb* 1 : build 2 : bring to an upright position — **erec·tion** \i'rek-shən\ *n*

**er·mine** \'ərmən\ *n* : weasel with white winter fur or its fur

**erode** \i'rōd\ *vb* **erod·ed; erod·ing** : wear away gradually

**ero·sion** \i'rōzhən\ *n* : process of eroding

**erot·ic** \i'rätik\ *adj* : sexually arousing — **erot·i·cal·ly** \-iklē\ *adv* — **erot·i·cism** \i'rätəˌsizəm\ *n*

**err** \'er, 'ər\ *vb* : be or do wrong

**er·rand** \'erənd\ *n* : short trip taken to do something often for another

**er·rant** \-ənt\ *adj* 1 : traveling about 2 : going astray

**er·rat·ic** \ir'atik\ *adj* 1 : eccentric 2 : inconsistent — **er·rat·i·cal·ly** \-iklē\ *adv*

**er·ro·ne·ous** \ir'ōnēəs, e'rō-\ *adj* : wrong — **er·ro·ne·ous·ly** *adv*

**er·ror** \'erər\ *n* 1 : something that is not accurate 2 : state of being wrong

**er·satz** \'erˌsäts\ *adj* : phony

**erst·while** \'ərstˌhwīl\ *adv* : in the past ~ *adj* : former

**er·u·di·tion** \ˌerə'dishən, ˌeryə-\ *n* : great learning — **er·u·dite** \'erəˌdīt, 'eryə-\ *adj*

**erupt** \i'rəpt\ *vb* : burst forth esp. suddenly and violently — **erup·tion** \i'rəpshən\ *n* — **erup·tive** \-tiv\ *adj*

**-ery** \ərē\ *n suffix* 1 : character or condition 2 : practice 3 : place of doing

**¹-es** \əz, iz *after* s, z, sh, ch; z *after* v *or* a *vowel*\ *n pl suffix* — used to form the plural of some nouns

**²-es** *vb suffix* — used to form the 3d person singular present of some verbs

**es·ca·late** \'eskəˌlāt\ *vb* **-lat·ed; -lat·ing** : become quickly larger or greater — **es·ca·la·tion** \ˌeskə'lāshən\ *n*

**es·ca·la·tor** \'eskəˌlātər\ *n* : moving stairs

**es·ca·pade** \'eskəˌpād\ *n* : mischievous adventure

**es·cape** \is'kāp\ *vb* **-caped; -cap·ing** : get away or get away from ~ *n* 1 : flight from or avoidance of something unpleasant 2 : leakage 3 : means of escape ~ *adj* : providing means of escape — **es·cap·ee** \isˌkā'pē, ˌes-\ *n*

**es·ca·role** \'eskəˌrōl\ *n* : salad green

**es·carp·ment** \is'kärpmənt\ *n* : cliff

**es·chew** \is'chü\ *vb* : shun

**es·cort** \'esˌkȯrt\ *n* : one accompanying another — **es·cort** \is'kȯrt, es-\ *vb*

**es·crow** \'esˌkrō\ *n* : deposit to be delivered upon fulfillment of a condition

**esoph·a·gus** \i'säfəgəs\ *n*, *pl* **-gi** \-ˌgī, -ˌjī\ : muscular tube connecting the mouth and stomach

**es·o·ter·ic** \ˌesə'terik\ *adj* : mysterious or secret

**es·pe·cial·ly** \is'peshəlē\ *adv* : particularly or notably

**es·pi·o·nage** \'espēəˌnäzh, -nij\ *n* : practice of spying

**es·pous·al** \is'pauzəl\ *n* 1 : betrothal 2 : wedding 3 : a taking up as a supporter — **es·pouse** \-'pauz\ *vb*

**espres·so** \e'spresō\ n, pl **-sos** : strong steam-brewed coffee

**es·py** \is'pī\ vb **-pied; -py·ing** : catch sight of

**es·quire** \'es¸kwīr\ n — used as a title of courtesy

**-ess** \əs, ¸es\ n suffix : female

**es·say** \'es¸ā\ n : literary composition ∼ vb \e'sā, 'es¸ā\ : attempt — **es·say·ist** \'es¸āist\ n

**es·sence** \'es²ns\ n **1** : fundamental nature or quality **2** : extract **3** : perfume

**es·sen·tial** \i'senchəl\ adj : basic or necessary — **essential** n — **es·sen·tial·ly** adv

**-est** \əst, ist\ adj suffix or adv suffix — used to form the superlative degree of adjectives and adverbs and esp. those of 1 or 2 syllables

**es·tab·lish** \is'tablish\ vb **1** : bring into existence **2** : put on a firm basis **3** : cause to be recognized

**es·tab·lish·ment** \-mənt\ n **1** : business or a place of business **2** : an establishing or being established **3** : controlling group

**es·tate** \is'tāt\ n **1** : one's possessions **2** : large piece of land with a house

**es·teem** \is'tēm\ n or vb : regard

**es·ter** \'estər\ n : organic chemical compound

**esthetic** var of AESTHETIC

**es·ti·ma·ble** \'estəməbəl\ adj : worthy of esteem

**es·ti·mate** \'estə¸māt\ vb **-mat·ed; -mat·ing** : judge the approximate value, size, or cost ∼ \-mət\ n **1** : rough or approximate calculation **2** : statement of the cost of a job — **es·ti·ma·tion** \¸estə'māshən\ n — **es·ti·ma·tor** \'estə¸mātər\ n

**es·trange** \is'trānj\ vb **-tranged; -trang·ing** : make hostile — **es·trange·ment** n

**es·tro·gen** \'estrəjən\ n : hormone that produces female characteristics

**es·tu·ary** \'eschə¸werē\ n, pl **-ar·ies** : arm of the sea at a river's mouth

**et cet·era** \et'setərə, -'setrə\ : and others esp. of the same kind

**etch** \'ech\ vb : produce by corroding parts of a surface with acid — **etch·er** n — **etch·ing** n

**eter·nal** \i'tərn²l\ adj : lasting forever — **eter·nal·ly** adv

**eter·ni·ty** \-nətē\ n, pl **-ties** : infinite duration

**eth·ane** \'eth¸ān\ n : gaseous hydrocarbon

**eth·a·nol** \'ethə¸nòl, -¸nōl\ n : alcohol

**ether** \'ēthər\ n : light flammable liquid used as an anesthetic

**ethe·re·al** \i'thirēəl\ adj **1** : celestial **2** : exceptionally delicate

**eth·i·cal** \'ethikəl\ adj **1** : relating to ethics **2** : honorable — **eth·i·cal·ly** adv

**eth·ics** \-iks\ n sing or pl **1** : study of good and evil and moral duty **2** : moral principles or practice

**eth·nic** \'ethnik\ adj : relating to races or groups of people with common customs ∼ n : member of a minority ethnic group

**eth·nol·o·gy** \eth'näləjē\ n : study of the races of human beings — **eth·no·log·i·cal** \¸ethnə'läjikəl\ adj — **eth·nol·o·gist** \eth'näləjist\ n

**et·i·quette** \'etikət, -¸ket\ n : good manners

**et·y·mol·o·gy** \¸etə'mäləjē\ n, pl **-gies** **1** : history of a word **2** : study of etymologies — **et·y·mo·log·i·cal** \-¸mä-'läjikəl\ adj — **et·y·mol·o·gist** \-'mäləjist\ n

**eu·ca·lyp·tus** \¸yükə'liptəs\ n, pl **-ti** \-¸tī\ or **-tus·es** : Australian evergreen tree

**Eu·cha·rist** \'yükərəst\ n : Communion — **eu·cha·ris·tic** \¸yükə'ristik\ adj

**eu·lo·gy** \'yüləjē\ n, pl **-gies** : speech in praise — **eu·lo·gis·tic** \¸yülə'jistik\ adj — **eu·lo·gize** \'yülə¸jīz\ vb

**eu·nuch** \'yünək\ n : castrated man

**eu·phe·mism** \'yüfə¸mizəm\ n : substitution of a pleasant expression for an unpleasant or offensive one — **eu·phe·mis·tic** \¸yüfə'mistik\ adj

**eu·pho·ni·ous** \yü'fōnēəs\ adj : pleasing to the ear — **eu·pho·ny** \'yüfənē\ n

**eu·pho·ria** \yü'fōrēə\ n : elation — **eu·phor·ic** \-'fòrik\ adj

**eu·ro** \'yürō\ n, pl **euros** : commmon monetary unit of most of the European Union

**eu·tha·na·sia** \¸yüthə'nāzhə, -zhēə\ n : mercy killing

**evac·u·ate** \i'vakyə¸wāt\ vb **-at·ed; -at·ing** **1** : discharge wastes from the body **2** : remove or withdraw from — **evac·u·a·tion** \i¸vakyə'wāshən\ n

**evade** \i'vād\ vb **evad·ed; evad·ing** : manage to avoid

**eval·u·ate** \i'valyə,wāt\ *vb* **-at·ed; -at·ing** : appraise — **eval·u·a·tion** \i,valyə'wāshən\ *n*

**evan·gel·i·cal** \,ē,van'jelikəl, ,evən-\ *adj* : relating to the Christian gospel

**evan·ge·lism** \i'vanjə,lizəm\ *n* : the winning or revival of personal commitments to Christ — **evan·ge·list** \i'vanjəlist\ *n* — **evan·ge·lis·tic** \i,vanjə'listik\ *adj*

**evap·o·rate** \i'vapə,rāt\ *vb* **-rat·ed; -rat·ing** **1** : pass off in or convert into vapor **2** : disappear quickly — **evap·o·ra·tion** \i,vapə'rāshən\ *n* — **evap-ora·tor** \i'vapə,rātər\ *n*

**eva·sion** \i'vāzhən\ *n* : act or instance of evading — **eva·sive** \i'vāsiv\ *adj* — **eva·sive·ness** *n*

**eve** \'ēv\ *n* : evening

**even** \'ēvən\ *adj* **1** : smooth **2** : equal or fair **3** : fully revenged **4** : divisible by 2 ～ *adv* **1** : already **2** — used for emphasis ～ *vb* : make or become even — **even·ly** *adv* — **even·ness** *n*

**eve·ning** \'ēvniŋ\ *n* : early part of the night

**event** \i'vent\ *n* **1** : occurrence **2** : noteworthy happening **3** : eventuality — **event·ful** *adj*

**even·tu·al** \i'venchəwəl\ *adj* : later — **even·tu·al·ly** *adv*

**even·tu·al·i·ty** \i,venchə'walətē\ *n, pl* **-ties** : possible occurrence or outcome

**ev·er** \'evər\ *adv* **1** : always **2** : at any time **3** : in any case

**ev·er·green** *adj* : having foliage that remains green — **evergreen** *n*

**ev·er·last·ing** \,evər'lastiŋ\ *adj* : lasting forever

**every** \'evrē\ *adj* **1** : being each one of a group **2** : all possible

**ev·ery·body** \'evri,bädē, -bəd-\ *pron* : every person

**ev·ery·day** *adj* : ordinary

**ev·ery·one** \-,wən\ *pron* : every person

**ev·ery·thing** *pron* : all that exists

**ev·ery·where** *adv* : in every place or part

**evict** \i'vikt\ *vb* : force (a person) to move from a property — **evic·tion** \i'vikshən\ *n*

**ev·i·dence** \'evədəns\ *n* **1** : outward sign **2** : proof or testimony

**ev·i·dent** \-ənt\ *adj* : clear or obvious — **ev·i·dent·ly** \-ədəntlē, -ə,dent-\ *adv*

**evil** \'ēvəl\ *adj* **evil·er** *or* **evil·ler; evil·**est *or* **evil·lest** : wicked ～ *n* **1** : sin **2** : source of sorrow or distress — **evil·do·er** \,ēvəl'düər\ *n* — **evil·ly** *adv*

**evince** \i'vins\ *vb* **evinced; evinc·ing** : show

**evis·cer·ate** \i'visə,rāt\ *vb* **-at·ed; -at·ing** : remove the viscera of — **evis·cer·a·tion** \i,visə'rāshən\ *n*

**evoke** \i'vōk\ *vb* **evoked; evok·ing** : call forth or up — **evo·ca·tion** \,ēvō'kāshən, ,evə-\ *n* — **evoc·a·tive** \i'väkətiv\ *adj*

**evo·lu·tion** \,evə'lüshən\ *n* : process of change by degrees — **evo·lu·tion·ary** \-shə,nerē\ *adj*

**evolve** \i'välv\ *vb* **evolved; evolv·ing** : develop or change by degrees

**ewe** \'yü\ *n* : female sheep

**ew·er** \'yüər\ *n* : water pitcher

**ex·act** \ig'zakt\ *vb* : compel to furnish ～ *adj* : precisely correct — **ex·act·ing** *adj* — **ex·ac·tion** \-'zakshən\ *n* — **ex·ac·ti·tude** \-'zaktə,tüd, -,tyüd\ *n* — **ex·act·ly** *adv* — **ex·act·ness** *n*

**ex·ag·ger·ate** \ig'zajə,rāt\ *vb* **-at·ed; -at·ing** : say more than is true — **ex·ag·ger·at·ed·ly** *adv* — **ex·ag·ger·a·tion** \-,zajə'rāshən\ *n* — **ex·ag·ger·a·tor** \-'zajərātər\ *n*

**ex·alt** \ig'zȯlt\ *vb* : glorify — **ex·al·ta·tion** \,eg,zȯl'tāshən, ,ek,sȯl-\ *n*

**ex·am** \ig'zam\ *n* : examination

**ex·am·ine** \-ən\ *vb* **-ined; -in·ing** **1** : inspect closely **2** : test by questioning — **ex·am·i·na·tion** \-,zamə'nāshən\ *n*

**ex·am·ple** \ig'zampəl\ *n* **1** : representative sample **2** : model **3** : problem to be solved for teaching purposes

**ex·as·per·ate** \ig'zaspə,rāt\ *vb* **-at·ed; -at·ing** : thoroughly annoy — **ex·as·per·a·tion** \-,zaspə'rāshən\ *n*

**ex·ca·vate** \'ekskə,vāt\ *vb* **-vat·ed; -vat·ing** : dig or hollow out — **ex·ca·va·tion** \,ekskə'vāshən\ *n* — **ex·ca·va·tor** \'ekskə,vātər\ *n*

**ex·ceed** \ik'sēd\ *vb* **1** : go or be beyond the limit of **2** : do better than

**ex·ceed·ing·ly** *adv* : extremely

**ex·cel** \ik'sel\ *vb* **-ll-** : do extremely well or far better than

**ex·cel·lence** \'eksələns\ *n* : quality of being excellent

**ex·cel·len·cy** \-lənsē\ *n, pl* **-cies** — used as a title of honor

**ex·cel·lent** \'eksələnt\ *adj* : very good — **ex·cel·lent·ly** *adv*

**ex·cept** \ik'sept\ *vb* : omit ~ *prep* : excluding ~ *conj* : but — **ex·cep·tion** \-'sepshən\ *n*

**ex·cep·tion·al** \-'sepshənəl\ *adj* : superior — **ex·cep·tion·al·ly** *adv*

**ex·cerpt** \'ek,sərpt, 'eg,zərpt\ *n* : brief passage ~ \ek'-, eg'-, 'ek,-, 'eg,-\ *vb* : select an excerpt

**ex·cess** \ik'ses, 'ek,ses\ *n* : amount left over — **excess** *adj* — **ex·ces·sive** \ik'sesiv\ *adj* — **ex·ces·sive·ly** *adv*

**ex·change** \iks'chānj, 'eks,chānj\ *n* 1 : the giving or taking of one thing in return for another 2 : marketplace esp. for securities ~ *vb* -**changed; -chang·ing** : transfer in return for some equivalent — **ex·change·able** \iks'chānjəbəl\ *adj*

¹**ex·cise** \'ek,sīz, -,sīs\ *n* : tax

²**ex·cise** \ik'sīz\ *vb* -**cised; -cis·ing** : cut out — **ex·ci·sion** \-'sizhən\ *n*

**ex·cite** \ik'sīt\ *vb* -**cit·ed; -cit·ing** 1 : stir up 2 : kindle the emotions of — **ex·cit·abil·i·ty** \-,sītə'bilətē\ *n* — **ex·cit·able** \-'sītəbəl\ *adj* — **ex·ci·ta·tion** \,ek,sī'tāshən, -ə-\ *n* — **ex·cit·ed·ly** *adv* — **ex·cite·ment** \ik'sītmənt\ *n*

**ex·claim** \iks'klām\ *vb* : cry out esp. in delight — **ex·cla·ma·tion** \,eks-klə'māshən\ *n* — **ex·clam·a·to·ry** \iks'klamə,tōrē\ *adj*

**exclamation point** *n* : punctuation mark ! used esp. after an interjection or exclamation

**ex·clude** \iks'klüd\ *vb* -**clud·ed; -clud·ing** : leave out — **ex·clu·sion** \-'klüzhən\ *n*

**ex·clu·sive** \-'klüsiv\ *adj* 1 : reserved for particular persons 2 : stylish 3 : sole — **exclusive** *n* — **ex·clu·sive·ly** *adv* — **ex·clu·sive·ness** *n*

**ex·com·mu·ni·cate** \,ekskə'myünə,kāt\ *vb* : expel from a church — **ex·com·mu·ni·ca·tion** \-,myünə'kā-shən\ *n*

**ex·cre·ment** \'ekskrəmənt\ *n* : bodily waste

**ex·crete** \ik'skrēt\ *vb* -**cret·ed; -cret·ing** : eliminate wastes from the body — **ex·cre·tion** \-'skrēshən\ *n* — **ex·cre·to·ry** \'ekskrə,tōrē\ *adj*

**ex·cru·ci·at·ing** \ik'skrüshē,ātiŋ\ *adj* : intensely painful — **ex·cru·ci·at·ing·ly** *adv*

**ex·cul·pate** \'ekskəl,pāt\ *vb* -**pat·ed; -pat·ing** : clear from alleged fault

**ex·cur·sion** \ik'skərzhən\ *n* : pleasure trip

**ex·cuse** \ik'skyüz\ *vb* -**cused; -cus·ing** 1 : pardon 2 : release from an obligation 3 : justify ~ \-'skyüs\ *n* 1 : justification 2 : apology

**ex·e·cute** \'eksi,kyüt\ *vb* -**cut·ed; -cut·ing** 1 : carry out fully 2 : enforce 3 : put to death — **ex·e·cu·tion** \,eksi'kyüshən\ *n* — **ex·e·cu·tion·er** \-shənər\ *n*

**ex·ec·u·tive** \ig'zekyətiv\ *adj* : relating to the carrying out of decisions, plans, or laws ~ *n* 1 : branch of government with executive duties 2 : administrator

**ex·ec·u·tor** \-yətər\ *n* : person named in a will to execute it

**ex·ec·u·trix** \ig'zekyə,triks\ *n, pl* **ex·ec·u·tri·ces** \-,zekyə'trī,sēz\ *or* **ex·ec·u·trix·es** : woman executor

**ex·em·pla·ry** \ig'zemplərē\ *adj* : so commendable as to serve as a model

**ex·em·pli·fy** \-plə,fī\ *vb* -**fied; -fy·ing** : serve as an example of — **ex·em·pli·fi·ca·tion** \-,zempləfə'kāshən\ *n*

**ex·empt** \ig'zempt\ *adj* : being free from some liability ~ *vb* : make exempt — **ex·emp·tion** \-'zempshən\ *n*

**ex·er·cise** \'eksər,sīz\ *n* 1 : a putting into action 2 : exertion to develop endurance or a skill 3 *pl* : public ceremony ~ *vb* -**cised; -cis·ing** 1 : exert 2 : engage in exercise — **ex·er·cis·er** *n*

**ex·ert** \ig'zərt\ *vb* : put into action — **ex·er·tion** \-'zərshən\ *n*

**ex·hale** \eks'hāl\ *vb* -**haled; -hal·ing** : breathe out — **ex·ha·la·tion** \eks-shə'lāshən\ *n*

**ex·haust** \ig'zòst\ *vb* 1 : draw out or develop completely 2 : use up 3 : tire or wear out ~ *n* : waste steam or gas from an engine or a system for removing it — **ex·haus·tion** \-'zò-schən\ *n* — **ex·haus·tive** \-'zóstiv\ *adj*

**ex·hib·it** \ig'zibət\ *vb* : display esp. publicly ~ *n* 1 : act of exhibiting 2 : something exhibited — **ex·hi·bi·tion** \,eksə'bishən\ *n* — **ex·hib·i·tor** \ig'zibətər\ *n*

**ex·hil·a·rate** \ig'zilə,rāt\ *vb* -**rat·ed; -rat·ing** : thrill — **ex·hil·a·ra·tion** \-,zilə'rāshən\ *n*

**ex·hort** \-'zȯrt\ *vb* : urge earnestly — **ex·hor·ta·tion** \ˌeks.ȯr'tāshən, ˌegz-, -ər-\ *n*

**ex·hume** \igz'üm, -'yüm; iks'yüm, -'hyüm\ *vb* **-humed; -hum·ing** : dig up (a buried corpse) — **ex·hu·ma·tion** \ˌeksyü'māshən, -hyü-; ˌegzü-, -zyü-\ *n*

**ex·i·gen·cies** \'eksəjənsēz, ig'zijən-\ *n pl* : requirements (as of a situation)

**ex·ile** \'eg,zīl, 'ek,sīl\ *n* **1** : banishment **2** : person banished from his or her country — **exile** *vb*

**ex·ist** \ig'zist\ *vb* **1** : have real or actual being **2** : live — **ex·is·tence** \-əns\ *n* — **ex·is·tent** \-ənt\ *adj*

**ex·it** \'egzət, 'eksət\ *n* **1** : departure **2** : way out of an enclosed space **3** : way off an expressway — **exit** *vb*

**ex·o·dus** \'eksədəs\ *n* : mass departure

**ex·on·er·ate** \ig'zänə,rāt\ *vb* **-at·ed; -at·ing** : free from blame — **ex·on·er·a·tion** \-ˌzänə'rāshən\ *n*

**ex·or·bi·tant** \ig'zȯrbətənt\ *adj* : exceeding what is usual or proper

**ex·or·cise** \'ek,sȯr,sīz, -,sȯr\ *vb* **-cised; -cis·ing** : drive out (as an evil spirit) — **ex·or·cism** \-,sizəm\ *n* — **ex·or·cist** \-,sist\ *n*

**ex·ot·ic** \ig'zätik\ *adj* : foreign or strange — **exotic** *n* — **ex·ot·i·cal·ly** \-iklē\ *adv*

**ex·pand** \ik'spand\ *vb* : enlarge

**ex·panse** \-'spans\ *n* : very large area

**ex·pan·sion** \-'spanchən\ *n* **1** : act or process of expanding **2** : expanded part

**ex·pan·sive** \-'spansiv\ *adj* **1** : tending to expand **2** : warmly benevolent **3** : of large extent — **ex·pan·sive·ly** *adv* — **ex·pan·sive·ness** *n*

**ex·pa·tri·ate** \ek'spātrē,āt, -ət\ *n* : exile — **expatriate** \-,āt\ *adj or vb*

**ex·pect** \ik'spekt\ *vb* **1** : look forward to **2** : consider probable or one's due — **ex·pec·tan·cy** \-ənsē\ *n* — **ex·pec·tant** \-ənt\ *adj* — **ex·pec·tant·ly** *adv* — **ex·pec·ta·tion** \ˌek,spek-'tāshən\ *n*

**ex·pe·di·ent** \ik'spēdēənt\ *adj* : convenient or advantageous rather than right or just — ~ *n* : convenient often makeshift means to an end

**ex·pe·dite** \'ekspə,dīt\ *vb* **-dit·ed; -dit·ing** : carry out or handle promptly — **ex·pe·dit·er** *n*

**ex·pe·di·tion** \ˌekspə'dishən\ *n* : long journey for work or research or the people making this

**ex·pe·di·tious** \-əs\ *adj* : prompt and efficient

**ex·pel** \ik'spel\ *vb* **-ll-** : force out

**ex·pend** \-'spend\ *vb* **1** : pay out **2** : use up — **ex·pend·able** *adj*

**ex·pen·di·ture** \-'spendichər, -də,chùr\ *n* : act of using or spending

**ex·pense** \ik'spens\ *n* : cost — **ex·pen·sive** \-'spensiv\ *adj* — **ex·pen·sive·ly** *adv*

**ex·pe·ri·ence** \ik'spirēəns\ *n* **1** : a participating in or living through an event **2** : an event that affects one **3** : knowledge from doing ~ *vb* **-enced; -enc·ing** : undergo

**ex·per·i·ment** \ik'sperəmənt\ *n* : test to discover something — ~ *vb* : make experiments — **ex·per·i·men·tal** \-ˌsperə'mentᵊl\ *adj* — **ex·per·i·men·ta·tion** \-mən'tāshən\ *n* — **ex·per·i·men·ter** \-'sperə,mentər\ *n*

**ex·pert** \'ek,spərt\ *adj* : thoroughly skilled ~ *n* : person with special skill — **ex·pert·ly** *adv* — **ex·pert·ness** *n*

**ex·per·tise** \ˌekspər'tēz\ *n* : skill

**ex·pi·ate** \'ekspē,āt\ *vb* : make amends for — **ex·pi·a·tion** \ˌekspē'āshən\ *n*

**ex·pire** \ik'spīr, ek-\ *vb* **-pired; -pir·ing** **1** : breathe out **2** : die **3** : end — **ex·pi·ra·tion** \ˌekspə'rāshən\ *n*

**ex·plain** \ik'splān\ *vb* **1** : make clear **2** : give the reason for — **ex·plain·able** \-əbəl\ *adj* — **ex·pla·na·tion** \ˌeksplə'nāshən\ *n* — **ex·plan·a·to·ry** \ik'splanə,tōrē\ *adj*

**ex·ple·tive** \'eksplətiv\ *n* : usu. profane exclamation

**ex·pli·ca·ble** \ek'splikəbəl, 'eksplik-\ *adj* : capable of being explained

**ex·plic·it** \ik'splisət\ *adj* : absolutely clear or precise — **ex·plic·it·ly** *adv* — **ex·plic·it·ness** *n*

**ex·plode** \ik'splōd\ *vb* **-plod·ed; -plod·ing** **1** : discredit **2** : burst or cause to burst violently **3** : increase rapidly

**ex·ploit** \'ek,splȯit\ *n* : heroic act ~ \ik'splȯit\ *vb* **1** : utilize **2** : use unfairly — **ex·ploi·ta·tion** \ˌek,splȯi-'tāshən\ *n*

**ex·plore** \ik'splōr\ *vb* **-plored; -plor·ing** : examine or range over thoroughly — **ex·plo·ra·tion** \ˌeksplə-

'rāshən\ *n* — **ex•plor•a•to•ry** \ik-'splōrə‚tōrē\ *adj* — **ex•plor•er** *n*

**ex•plo•sion** \ik'splōzhən\ *n* : process or instance of exploding

**ex•plo•sive** \-siv\ *adj* **1** : able to cause explosion **2** : likely to explode — **explosive** *n* — **ex•plo•sive•ly** *adv*

**ex•po•nent** \ik'spōnənt, 'ek‚spō-\ *n* **1** : mathematical symbol showing how many times a number is to be repeated as a factor **2** : advocate — **ex•po•nen•tial** \‚ekspə'nenchəl\ *adj* — **ex•po•nen•tial•ly** *adv*

**ex•port** \ek'spōrt, 'ek‚spōrt\ *vb* : send to foreign countries — **export** \'ek‚-\ *n* — **ex•por•ta•tion** \‚ek‚spōr'tāshən\ *n* — **ex•port•er** \ek'spōrtər, 'ek‚spōrt-\ *n*

**ex•pose** \ik'spōz\ *vb* **-posed; -posing 1** : deprive of shelter or protection **2** : subject (film) to light **3** : make known — **ex•po•sure** \-'spōzhər\ *n*

**ex•po•sé, ex•po•se** \‚ekspō'zā\ *n* : exposure of something discreditable

**ex•po•si•tion** \‚ekspə'zishən\ *n* : public exhibition

**ex•pound** \ik'spaùnd\ *vb* : set forth or explain in detail

¹**ex•press** \-'spres\ *adj* **1** : clear **2** : specific **3** : traveling at high speed with few stops — **express** *adv or n* — **ex•press•ly** *adv*

²**express** *vb* **1** : make known in words or appearance **2** : press out (as juice)

**ex•pres•sion** \-'spreshən\ *n* **1** : utterance **2** : mathematical symbol **3** : significant word or phrase **4** : look on one's face — **ex•pres•sive** \-'spresiv\ *adj* — **ex•pres•sive•ness** *n*

**ex•press•way** \ik'spres‚wā\ *n* : high-speed divided highway with limited access

**ex•pul•sion** \ik'spəlshən\ *n* : an expelling or being expelled

**ex•pur•gate** \'ekspər‚gāt\ *vb* **-gat•ed; -gat•ing** : censor — **ex•pur•ga•tion** \‚ekspər'gāshən\ *n*

**ex•qui•site** \ek'skwizət, 'ekskwiz-\ *adj* **1** : flawlessly beautiful and delicate **2** : keenly discriminating

**ex•tant** \'ekstənt, ek'stant\ *adj* : existing

**ex•tem•po•ra•ne•ous** \‚ek‚stempə'rānēəs\ *adj* : impromptu — **ex•tem•po•ra•ne•ous•ly** *adv*

**ex•tend** \ik'stend\ *vb* **1** : stretch forth

or out **2** : prolong **3** : enlarge — **ex•tend•able** \-'stendəbəl\ *adj*

**ex•ten•sion** \-'stenchən\ *n* **1** : an extending or being extended **2** : additional part **3** : extra telephone line

**ex•ten•sive** \-'stensiv\ *adj* : of considerable extent — **ex•ten•sive•ly** *adv*

**ex•tent** \-'stent\ *n* : range, space, or degree to which something extends

**ex•ten•u•ate** \ik'stenyə‚wāt\ *vb* **-at•ed; -at•ing** : lessen the seriousness of — **ex•ten•u•a•tion** \-‚stenyə'wāshən\ *n*

**ex•te•ri•or** \ek'stirēər\ *adj* : external ~ *n* : external part or surface

**ex•ter•mi•nate** \ik'stərmə‚nāt\ *vb* **-nat•ed; -nat•ing** : destroy utterly — **ex•ter•mi•na•tion** \-‚stərmə'nāshən\ *n* — **ex•ter•mi•na•tor** \-'stərmə‚nātər\ *n*

**ex•ter•nal** \ek'stərnᵊl\ *adj* : relating to or on the outside — **ex•ter•nal•ly** *adv*

**ex•tinct** \ik'stiŋkt\ *adj* : no longer existing — **ex•tinc•tion** \-'stiŋkshən\ *n*

**ex•tin•guish** \-'stiŋgwish\ *vb* : cause to stop burning — **ex•tin•guish•able** *adj* — **ex•tin•guish•er** *n*

**ex•tir•pate** \'ekstər‚pāt\ *vb* **-pat•ed; -pat•ing** : destroy

**ex•tol** \ik'stōl\ *vb* **-ll-** : praise highly

**ex•tort** \-'stòrt\ *vb* : obtain by force or improper pressure — **ex•tor•tion** \-'stòrshən\ *n* — **ex•tor•tion•er** *n* — **ex•tor•tion•ist** *n*

**ex•tra** \'ekstrə\ *adj* **1** : additional **2** : superior — **extra** *n or adv*

**extra-** *prefix* : outside or beyond

**ex•tract** \ik'strakt\ *vb* **1** : pull out forcibly **2** : withdraw (as a juice) ~ \'ek‚-\ *n* **1** : excerpt **2** : product (as a juice) obtained by extracting — **ex•tract•able** *adj* — **ex•trac•tion** \ik's-trakshən\ *n* — **ex•trac•tor** \-tər\ *n*

**ex•tra•cur•ric•u•lar** \‚ekstrəkə'rikyələr\ *adj* : lying outside the regular curriculum

**ex•tra•dite** \'ekstrə‚dīt\ *vb* **-dit•ed; -dit•ing** : bring or deliver a suspect to a different jurisdiction for trial — **ex•tra•di•tion** \‚ekstrə'dishən\ *n*

**ex•tra•mar•i•tal** \‚ekstrə'marətᵊl\ *adj* : relating to sexual relations of a married person outside of the marriage

**ex•tra•ne•ous** \ek'strānēəs\ *adj* : not essential or relevant — **ex•tra•ne•ous•ly** *adv*

**ex•traor•di•nary** \ik'strórdᵊn‚erē, ‚ekstrə'ȯrd-\ *adj* : notably unusual or exceptional — **ex·traor·di·nari·ly** \ik,strȯrd³n'eralē, ,ekstrə,ȯrd-\ *adv*

**ex·tra·sen·so·ry** \,ekstrə'sensərē\ *adj* : outside the ordinary senses

**ex·tra·ter·res·tri·al** \,ekstrətə'restrēəl\ *n* : one existing or coming from outside the earth ~ *adj* : relating to an extraterrestrial

**ex·trav·a·gant** \ik'stravigənt\ *adj* : wildly excessive, lavish, or costly — **ex·trav·a·gance** \-gəns\ *n* — **ex·trav·a·gant·ly** *adv*

**ex·trav·a·gan·za** \-,stravə'ganzə\ *n* : spectacular event

**ex·tra·ve·hic·u·lar** \,ekstrəvē'hik-yələr\ *adj* : occurring outside a spacecraft

**ex·treme** \ik'strēm\ *adj* 1 : very great or intense 2 : very severe 3 : not moderate 4 : most remote ~ *n* 1 : extreme state 2 : something located at one end or the other of a range — **ex·treme·ly** *adv*

**ex·trem·i·ty** \-'stremətē\ *n, pl* **-ties** 1 : most remote part 2 : human hand or foot 3 : extreme degree or state (as of need)

**ex·tri·cate** \'ekstrə,kāt\ *vb* **-cat·ed; -cat·ing** : set or get free from an entanglement or difficulty — **ex·tri·ca·ble** \ik'strikəbəl, ek-; 'ekstrik-\ *adj* — **ex·tri·ca·tion** \,ekstrə'kā-shən\ *n*

**ex·tro·vert** \'ekstrə,vərt\ *n* : gregarious person — **ex·tro·ver·sion** \,ek-strə'vərzhən\ *n* — **ex·tro·vert·ed** \'ekstrə,vərtəd\ *adj*

**ex·trude** \ik'strüd\ *vb* **-trud·ed; -trud·ing** : to force or push out

**ex·u·ber·ant** \ig'zübərənt\ *adj* : joyously unrestrained — **ex·u·ber·ance** \-rəns\ *n* — **ex·u·ber·ant·ly** *adv*

**ex·ude** \ig'züd\ *vb* **-ud·ed; -ud·ing** 1 : discharge slowly through pores 2 : display conspicuously

**ex·ult** \ig'zəlt\ *vb* : rejoice — **ex·ul·tant** \-'zəlt³nt\ *adj* — **ex·ul·tant·ly** *adv* — **ex·ul·ta·tion** \,eksəl'tāshən, ,egzəl-\ *n*

**-ey** — see **-Y**

**eye** \'ī\ *n* 1 : organ of sight consisting of a globular structure (**eye·ball**) in a socket of the skull with thin movable covers (**eye·lids**) bordered with hairs (**eye·lash·es**) 2 : vision 3 : judgment 4 : something suggesting an eye ~ *vb* **eyed; eye·ing** *or* **ey·ing** : look at — **eye·brow** \-,brau\ *n* — **eyed** \'īd\ *adj* — **eye·strain** *n*

**eye·drop·per** *n* : dropper

**eye·glass·es** *n pl* : glasses

**eye·let** \'īlət\ *n* : hole (as in cloth) for a lacing or rope

**eye–open·er** *n* : something startling — **eye–open·ing** *adj*

**eye·piece** *n* : lens at the eye end of an optical instrument

**eye·sight** *n* : sight

**eye·sore** *n* : unpleasant sight

**eye·tooth** *n* : upper canine tooth

**eye·wit·ness** *n* : person who actually sees something happen

**ey·rie** \'īrē\ *n, or like* AERIE\ *var of* AERIE

# F

**f** \'ef\ *n, pl* **f's** *or* **fs** \'efs\ : 6th letter of the alphabet

**fa·ble** \'fābəl\ *n* 1 : legendary story 2 : story that teaches a lesson — **fa·bled** \-bəld\ *adj*

**fab·ric** \'fabrik\ *n* 1 : structure 2 : material made usu. by weaving or knitting fibers

**fab·ri·cate** \'fabri,kāt\ *vb* **-cat·ed; -cat·ing** 1 : construct 2 : invent — **fab·ri·ca·tion** \,fabri'kāshən\ *n*

**fab·u·lous** \'fabyələs\ *adj* 1 : like, told in, or based on fable 2 : incredible or marvelous — **fab·u·lous·ly** *adv*

**fa·cade** \fə'säd\ *n* 1 : principal face of a building 2 : false or superficial appearance

**face** \'fās\ *n* 1 : front or principal surface (as of the head) 2 : presence 3 : facial expression 4 : grimace 5 : outward appearance ~ *vb* **faced; fac·ing** 1 : challenge or resist firmly or brazenly 2 : cover with different material 3 : sit or stand with the face toward **4** : have the front oriented toward — **faced** \'fāst\ adj — **face•less** adj — **fa•cial** \'fāshəl\ adj or n

**face•down** adv : with the face downward

**face–lift** \'fās,lift\ n **1** : cosmetic surgery on the face **2** : modernization

**fac•et** \'fasət\ n **1** : surface of a cut gem **2** : phase — **fac•et•ed** adj

**fa•ce•tious** \fə'sēshəs\ adj : jocular — **fa•ce•tious•ly** adv — **fa•ce•tious•ness** n

**fac•ile** \'fasəl\ adj **1** : easy **2** : fluent

**fa•cil•i•tate** \fə'silə,tāt\ vb **-tat•ed; -tat•ing** : make easier

**fa•cil•i•ty** \fə'silətē\ n, pl **-ties 1** : ease in doing or using **2** : something built or installed to serve a purpose or facilitate an activity

**fac•ing** \'fāsiŋ\ n : lining or covering or material for this

**fac•sim•i•le** \fak'siməlē\ n : exact copy

**fact** \'fakt\ n **1** : act or action **2** : something that exists or is real **3** : piece of information — **fac•tu•al** \'fakchəwəl\ adj — **fac•tu•al•ly** adv

**fac•tion** \'fakshən\ n : part of a larger group — **fac•tion•al•ism** \-shənə,l-izəm\ n

**fac•tious** \'fakshəs\ adj : causing discord

**fac•ti•tious** \fak'tishəs\ adj : artificial

**fac•tor** \'faktər\ n **1** : something that has an effect **2** : gene **3** : number used in multiplying

**fac•to•ry** \'faktərē\ n, pl **-ries** : place for manufacturing

**fac•to•tum** \fak'tōtəm\ n : person (as a servant) with varied duties

**fac•ul•ty** \'fakəltē\ n, pl **-ties 1** : ability to act **2** : power of the mind or body **3** : body of teachers or department of instruction

**fad** \'fad\ n : briefly popular practice or interest — **fad•dish** adj — **fad•dist** n

**fade** \'fād\ vb **fad•ed; fad•ing 1** : wither **2** : lose or cause to lose freshness or brilliance **3** : grow dim **4** : vanish

**fag** \'fag\ vb **-gg- 1** : drudge **2** : tire or exhaust

**fag•ot, fag•got** \'fagət\ n : bundle of twigs

**Fahr•en•heit** \'farən,hīt\ adj : relating to a thermometer scale with the boiling point at 212 degrees and the freezing point at 32 degrees

**fail** \'fāl\ vb **1** : decline in health **2** : die away **3** : stop functioning **4** : be unsuccessful **5** : become bankrupt **6** : disappoint **7** : neglect ⁓ n : act of failing

**fail•ing** n : slight defect in character or conduct ⁓ prep : in the absence or lack of

**faille** \'fīl\ n : closely woven ribbed fabric

**fail•ure** \'fālyər\ n **1** : absence of expected action or performance **2** : bankruptcy **3** : deficiency **4** : one that has failed

**faint** \'fānt\ adj **1** : cowardly or spiritless **2** : weak and dizzy **3** : lacking vigor **4** : indistinct ⁓ vb : lose consciousness ⁓ n : act or condition of fainting — **faint•heart•ed** adj — **faint•ly** adv — **faint•ness** n

¹**fair** \'far\ adj **1** : pleasing in appearance **2** : not stormy or cloudy **3** : just or honest **4** : conforming with the rules **5** : open to legitimate pursuit or attack **6** : light in color **7** : adequate — **fair•ness** n

²**fair** adv chiefly Brit : FAIRLY

³**fair** n : exhibition for judging or selling — **fair•ground** n

**fair•ly** \'farlē\ adv **1** : in a manner of speaking **2** : without bias **3** : somewhat

**fairy** \'farē\ n, pl **fair•ies** : usu. small imaginary being — **fairy tale** n

**fairy•land** \-,land\ n **1** : land of fairies **2** : beautiful or charming place

**faith** \'fāth\ n, pl **faiths** \'fāths, 'fāthz\ **1** : allegiance **2** : belief and trust in God **3** : confidence **4** : system of religious beliefs — **faith•ful** \-fəl\ adj — **faith•ful•ly** adv — **faith•ful•ness** n — **faith•less** adj — **faith•less•ly** adv — **faith•less•ness** n

**fake** \'fāk\ vb **faked; fak•ing 1** : falsify **2** : counterfeit ⁓ n : copy, fraud, or impostor ⁓ adj : not genuine — **fak•er** n

**fa•kir** \fə'kir\ n : wandering beggar of India

**fal•con** \'falkən, 'fol-\ n : small long-winged hawk used esp. for hunting — **fal•con•ry** \-rē\ n

**fall** \'fol\ vb **fell** \'fel\; **fall•en** \'fólən\; **fall•ing 1** : go down by gravity **2** : hang freely **3** : go lower **4** : be defeated or ruined **5** : commit a sin **6** : happen at a certain time **7** : become gradually ⁓ n **1** : act of falling **2**

: autumn **3** : downfall **4** *pl* : waterfall **5** : distance something falls

**fal·la·cy** \\'faləsē\ *n, pl* **-cies 1** : false idea **2** : false reasoning — **fal·la·cious** \fə'lāshəs\ *adj*

**fal·li·ble** \\'faləbəl\ *adj* : capable of making a mistake — **fal·li·bly** \-blē\ *adv*

**fall·out** *n* **1** : radioactive particles from a nuclear explosion **2** : secondary effects

**fal·low** \\'falō\ *adj* **1** : plowed but not planted **2** : dormant — **fallow** *n or vb*

**false** \\'fóls\ *adj* **fals·er; fals·est 1** : not genuine, true, faithful, or permanent **2** : misleading — **false·ly** *adv* — **false·ness** *n* — **fal·si·fi·ca·tion** \,fólsəfə'kāshən\ *n* — **fal·si·fy** \\'fólsə,fī\ *vb* — **fal·si·ty** \\'fólsətē\ *n*

**false·hood** \\'fóls,húd\ *n* : lie

**fal·set·to** \fól'setō\ *n, pl* **-tos** : artificially high singing voice

**fal·ter** \\'fóltər\ *vb* **-tered; -ter·ing 1** : move unsteadily **2** : hesitate — **fal·ter·ing·ly** *adv*

**fame** \\'fām\ *n* : public reputation — **famed** \\'fāmd\ *adj*

**fa·mil·ial** \fə'milyəl\ *adj* : relating to a family

**¹fa·mil·iar** \fə'milyər\ *n* **1** : companion **2** : guardian spirit

**²familiar** *adj* **1** : closely acquainted **2** : forward **3** : frequently seen or experienced — **fa·mil·iar·i·ty** \fə,mil'-yarətē, -,milē'yar-\ *n* — **fa·mil·iar·ize** \fə'milyə,rīz\ *vb* — **fa·mil·iar·ly** *adv*

**fam·i·ly** \\'famlē\ *n, pl* **-lies 1** : persons of common ancestry **2** : group living together **3** : parents and children **4** : group of related individuals

**fam·ine** \\'famən\ *n* : extreme scarcity of food

**fam·ish** \\'famish\ *vb* : starve

**fa·mous** \\'fāməs\ *adj* : widely known or celebrated

**fa·mous·ly** *adv* : very well

**¹fan** \\'fan\ *n* : device for producing a current of air *~ vb* **-nn- 1** : move air with a fan **2** : direct a current of air upon **3** : stir to activity

**²fan** *n* : enthusiastic follower or admirer

**fa·nat·ic** \fə'natik\, **fa·nat·i·cal** \-ikəl\ *adj* : excessively enthusiastic or devoted — **fanatic** *n* — **fa·nat·i·cism** \-'natə,sizəm\ *n*

**fan·ci·er** \\'fansēər\ *n* : one devoted to raising a particular plant or animal

**fan·cy** \\'fansē\ *n, pl* **-cies 1** : liking **2** : whim **3** : imagination *~ vb* **-cied; -cy·ing 1** : like **2** : imagine *~ adj* **-cier; -est 1** : not plain **2** : of superior quality — **fan·ci·ful** \-sifəl\ *adj* — **fan·ci·ful·ly** \-fəlē\ *adv* — **fan·ci·ly** *adv*

**fan·dan·go** \fan'daŋgō\ *n, pl* **-gos** : lively Spanish dance

**fan·fare** \\'fan,far\ *n* **1** : a sounding of trumpets **2** : showy display

**fang** \\'faŋ\ *n* : long sharp tooth

**fan·light** *n* : semicircular window

**fan·ta·sia** \fan'tāzhə, -zēə; ,fan-tə'zēə\ *n* : music written to fancy rather than to form

**fan·tas·tic** \fan'tastik\ *adj* **1** : imaginary or unrealistic **2** : exceedingly or unbelievably great — **fan·tas·ti·cal·ly** \-tiklē\ *adv*

**fan·ta·sy** \\'fantəsē\ *n* **1** : imagination **2** : product (as a daydream) of the imagination **3** : fantasia — **fan·ta·size** \\'fantə,sīz\ *vb*

**FAQ** *abbr* frequently asked questions

**far** \\'fär\ *adv* **far·ther** \-thər\ *or* **fur·ther** \\'fər-\; **far·thest** *or* **fur·thest** \-thəst\ **1** : at or to a distance **2** : much **3** : to a degree **4** : to an advanced point or extent *~ adj* **farther** *or* **further; far·thest** *or* **furthest 1** : remote **2** : long **3** : being more distant

**far·away** *adj* : distant

**farce** \\'färs\ *n* **1** : satirical comedy with an improbable plot **2** : ridiculous display — **far·ci·cal** \-sikəl\ *adj*

**¹fare** \\'far\ *vb* **fared; far·ing** : get along

**²fare** *n* **1** : price of transportation **2** : range of food

**fare·well** \far'wel\ *n* **1** : wish of welfare at parting **2** : departure — **farewell** *adj*

**far–fetched** \\'fär'fecht\ *adj* : improbable

**fa·ri·na** \fə'rēnə\ *n* : fine meal made from cereal grains

**farm** \\'färm\ *n* : place where something is raised for food *~ vb* **1** : use (land) as a farm **2** : raise plants or animals for food — **farm·er** *n* — **farm·hand** \-,hand\ *n* — **farm·house** *n* — **farm·ing** *n* — **farm·land** \-,land\ *n* — **farm·yard** *n*

**far–off** *adj* : remote in time or space

**far·ri·er** \\'farēər\ *n* : blacksmith who shoes horses

**far·row** \'farō\ *vb* : give birth to a litter of pigs — **farrow** *n*

**far·sight·ed** *adj* **1** : better able to see distant things than near **2** : judicious or shrewd — **far·sight·ed·ness** *n*

**far·ther** \'färthər\ *adv* **1** : at or to a greater distance or more advanced point **2** : to a greater degree or extent ~ *adj* : more distant

**far·ther·most** *adj* : most distant

**far·thest** \'färthəst\ *adj* : most distant ~ *adv* **1** : to or at the greatest distance **2** : to the most advanced point **3** : by the greatest extent

**fas·ci·cle** \'fasikəl\ *n* **1** : small bundle **2** : division of a book published in parts — **fas·ci·cled** \-kəld\ *adj*

**fas·ci·nate** \'fasⁿ,āt\ *vb* **-nat·ed; -nat·ing** : transfix and hold spellbound — **fas·ci·na·tion** \,fasⁿ-'āshən\ *n*

**fas·cism** \'fash,izəm\ *n* : dictatorship that exalts nation and race — **fas·cist** \-ist\ *n or adj* — **fas·cis·tic** \fa'shistik\ *adj*

**fash·ion** \'fashən\ *n* **1** : manner **2** : prevailing custom or style ~ *vb* : form or construct — **fash·ion·able** \-ənəbəl\ *adj* — **fash·ion·ably** \-blē\ *adv*

¹**fast** \'fast\ *adj* **1** : firmly fixed, bound, or shut **2** : faithful **3** : moving or acting quickly **4** : indicating ahead of the correct time **5** : deep and undisturbed **6** : permanently dyed **7** : wild or promiscuous ~ *adv* **1** : so as to be secure or bound **2** : soundly or deeply **3** : swiftly

²**fast** *vb* : abstain from food or eat sparingly ~ *n* : act or time of fasting

**fas·ten** \'fasⁿn\ *vb* : attach esp. by pinning or tying — **fas·ten·er** *n* — **fas·ten·ing** *n*

**fas·tid·i·ous** \fas'tidēəs\ *adj* : hard to please — **fas·tid·i·ous·ly** *adv* — **fas·tid·i·ous·ness** *n*

**fat** \'fat\ *adj* **-tt- 1** : having much fat **2** : thick ~ *n* : animal tissue rich in greasy or oily matter — **fat·ness** *n* — **fat·ten** \'fatⁿn\ *vb* — **fat·ty** *adj or n*

**fa·tal** \'fātⁿl\ *adj* : causing death or ruin — **fa·tal·i·ty** \fā'talətē, fə-\ *n* — **fa·tal·ly** *adv*

**fa·tal·ism** \'fātⁿl,izəm\ *n* : belief that fate determines events — **fa·tal·ist** \-ist\ *n* — **fa·tal·is·tic** \,fātⁿl'istik\ *adj* — **fa·tal·is·ti·cal·ly** \-tiklē\ *adv*

**fate** \'fāt\ *n* **1** : principle, cause, or will held to determine events **2** : end or outcome — **fat·ed** *adj* — **fate·ful** \-fəl\ *adj* — **fate·ful·ly** *adv*

**fa·ther** \'fäthər, 'fáth-\ *n* **1** : male parent **2** *cap* : God **3** : originator — **fa·ther** *vb* — **fa·ther·hood** \-,hùd\ *n* — **fa·ther·land** \-,land\ *n* — **fa·ther·less** *adj* — **fa·ther·ly** *adj*

**father–in–law** *n, pl* **fa·thers–in–law** : father of one's spouse

**fath·om** \'fathəm\ *n* : nautical unit of length equal to 6 feet ~ *vb* : understand — **fath·om·able** *adj* — **fath·om·less** *adj*

**fa·tigue** \fə'tēg\ *n* **1** : weariness from labor or use **2** : tendency to break under repeated stress ~ *vb* **-tigued; -tigu·ing** : tire out

**fat·u·ous** \'fachəwəs\ *adj* : foolish or stupid — **fat·u·ous·ly** *adv* — **fat·u·ous·ness** *n*

**fau·cet** \'fòsət, 'fäs-\ : fixture for drawing off a liquid

**fault** \'fòlt\ *n* **1** : weakness in character **2** : something wrong or imperfect **3** : responsibility for something wrong **4** : fracture in the earth's crust ~ *vb* : find fault in or with — **fault·find·er** *n* — **fault·find·ing** *n* — **fault·i·ly** \'fòltəlē\ *adv* — **fault·less** *adj* — **fault·less·ly** *adv* — **faulty** *adj*

**fau·na** \'fònə\ *n* : animals or animal life esp. of a region — **fau·nal** \-ⁿl\ *adj*

**faux pas** \'fō'pä\ *n, pl* **faux pas** \*same or* -'päz\ : social blunder

**fa·vor** \'fāvər\ *n* **1** : approval **2** : partiality **3** : act of kindness ~ *vb* : regard or treat with favor — **fa·vor·able** \'fāvərəbəl\ *adj* — **fa·vor·ably** \-blē\ *adv*

**fa·vor·ite** \'fāvərət\ *n* : one favored — **favorite** *adj* — **fa·vor·it·ism** \-,izəm\ *n*

¹**fawn** \'fòn\ *vb* : seek favor by groveling

²**fawn** *n* : young deer

**faze** \'fāz\ *vb* **fazed; faz·ing** : disturb the composure of

**fear** \'fir\ *n* : unpleasant emotion caused by expectation or awareness of danger ~ *vb* : be afraid of — **fear·ful** \-fəl\ *adj* — **fear·ful·ly** *adv* — **fear·less** *adj* — **fear·less·ly** *adv* — **fear·less·ness** *n* — **fear·some** \-səm\ *adj*

**fea·si·ble** \'fēzəbəl\ *adj* : capable of being done — **fea·si·bil·i·ty** \,fēzə'bilətē\ *n* — **fea·si·bly** \'fēzəblē\ *adv*

**feast** \'fēst\ *n* **1** : large or fancy meal **2**

: religious festival ∼ *vb* : eat plentifully

**feat** \'fēt\ *n* : notable deed

**feath·er** \'fethər\ *n* : one of the light horny outgrowths that form the external covering of a bird's body — **feather** *vb* — **feath·ered** \-ərd\ *adj* — **feath·er·less** *adj* — **feath·ery** *adj*

**fea·ture** \'fēchər\ *n* **1** : shape or appearance of the face **2** : part of the face **3** : prominent characteristic **4** : special attraction ∼ *vb* : give prominence to — **fea·ture·less** *adj*

**Feb·ru·ary** \'febyə,werē, 'febə-, 'febrə-\ *n* : 2d month of the year having 28 and in leap years 29 days

**fe·ces** \'fē,sēz\ *n pl* : intestinal body waste — **fe·cal** \-kəl\ *adj*

**feck·less** \'fekləs\ *adj* : irresponsible

**fe·cund** \'fekənd, 'fē-\ *adj* : prolific — **fe·cun·di·ty** \fi'kəndətē, fe-\ *n*

**fed·er·al** \'fedrəl, -dərəl\ *adj* : of or constituting a government with power distributed between a central authority and constituent units — **fed·er·al·ism** \-rə,lizəm\ *n* — **fed·er·al·ist** \-list\ *n or adj* — **fed·er·al·ly** *adv*

**fed·er·ate** \'fedə,rāt\ *vb* **-at·ed; -at·ing** : join in a federation

**fed·er·a·tion** \,fedə'rāshən\ *n* : union of organizations

**fe·do·ra** \fi'dōrə\ *n* : soft felt hat

**fed up** *adj* : out of patience

**fee** \'fē\ *n* : fixed charge

**fee·ble** \'fēbəl\ *adj* **-bler; -blest** : weak or ineffective — **fee·ble·mind·ed** \,fēbəl'mīndəd\ *adj* — **fee·ble·mind·ed·ness** *n* — **fee·ble·ness** *n* — **fee·bly** \-blē\ *adv*

**feed** \'fēd\ *vb* **fed** \'fed\; **feed·ing** **1** : give food to **2** : eat **3** : furnish ∼ *n* : food for livestock — **feed·er** *n*

**feel** \'fēl\ *vb* **felt** \'felt\; **feel·ing** **1** : perceive or examine through physical contact **2** : think or believe **3** : be conscious of **4** : seem **5** : have sympathy ∼ *n* **1** : sense of touch **2** : quality of a thing imparted through touch — **feel·er** *n*

**feel·ing** \'fēliŋ\ *n* **1** : sense of touch **2** : state of mind **3** *pl* : sensibilities **4** : opinion

**feet** *pl of* FOOT

**feign** \'fān\ *vb* : pretend

**feint** \'fānt\ *n* : mock attack intended to distract attention — **feint** *vb*

**fe·lic·i·tate** \fi'lisə,tāt\ *vb* **-tat·ed; -tat-**

ing : congratulate — **fe·lic·i·ta·tion** \-,lisə'tāshən\ *n*

**fe·lic·i·tous** \fi'lisətəs\ *adj* : aptly expressed — **fe·lic·i·tous·ly** *adv*

**fe·lic·i·ty** \-'lisətē\ *n, pl* **-ties 1** : great happiness **2** : pleasing faculty esp. in art or language

**fe·line** \'fē,līn\ *adj* : relating to cats — **feline** *n*

¹**fell** \'fel\ *vb* : cut or knock down

²**fell** *past of* FALL

**fel·low** \'felō\ *n* **1** : companion or associate **2** : man or boy — **fel·low·ship** \-,ship\ *n*

**fel·low·man** \,felō'man\ *n* : kindred human being

**fel·on** \'felən\ *n* : one who has committed a felony

**fel·o·ny** \'felənē\ *n, pl* **-nies** : serious crime — **fe·lo·ni·ous** \fə'lōnēəs\ *adj*

¹**felt** \'felt\ *n* : cloth made of pressed wool and fur

²**felt** *past of* FEEL

**fe·male** \'fē,māl\ *adj* : relating to or being the sex that bears young — **female** *n*

**fem·i·nine** \'femənən\ *adj* : relating to the female sex — **fem·i·nin·i·ty** \,femə'ninətē\ *n*

**fem·i·nism** \'femə,nizəm\ *n* : organized activity on behalf of women's rights — **fem·i·nist** \-nist\ *n or adj*

**fe·mur** \'fēmər\ *n, pl* **fe·murs** *or* **fem·o·ra** \'femərə\ : long bone of the thigh — **fem·o·ral** \'femərəl\ *adj*

**fence** \'fens\ *n* : enclosing barrier esp. of wood or wire ∼ *vb* **fenced; fencing** **1** : enclose with a fence **2** : practice fencing — **fenc·er** *n*

**fenc·ing** \'fensiŋ\ *n* **1** : combat with swords for sport **2** : material for building fences

**fend** \'fend\ *vb* : ward off

**fend·er** \'fendər\ *n* : guard over an automobile wheel

**fen·nel** \'fen°l\ *n* : herb related to the carrot

**fer·ment** \fər'ment\ *vb* : cause or undergo fermentation ∼ \'fər,ment\ *n* : agitation

**fer·men·ta·tion** \,fərmən'tāshən, -,men-\ *n* : chemical decomposition of an organic substance in the absence of oxygen

**fern** \'fərn\ *n* : flowerless seedless green plant

**fe·ro·cious** \fə'rōshəs\ *adj* : fierce or savage — **fe·ro·cious·ly** *adv* — **fe·ro-**

cious•ness *n* — fe•roc•i•ty \-'räs-
ətē\ *n*

fer•ret \'ferət\ *n* : white European polecat ∼ *vb* : find out by searching

fer•ric \'ferik\, fer•rous \'ferəs\ *adj*
: relating to or containing iron

fer•rule \'ferəl\ *n* : metal band or ring

fer•ry \'ferē\ *vb* -ried; -ry•ing : carry
by boat over water ∼ *n, pl* -ries
: boat used in ferrying — fer•ry•boat
*n*

fer•tile \'fərt°l\ *adj* 1 : producing plentifully 2 : capable of developing or
reproducing — fer•til•i•ty \fər'tilətē\
*n*

fer•til•ize \'fərt°l,īz\ *vb* -ized; -iz•ing
: make fertile — fer•til•iza•tion
\,fərt°lə'zāshən\ *n* — fer•til•iz•er *n*

fer•vid \'fərvəd\ *adj* : ardent or zealous
— fer•vid•ly *adv*

fer•vor \'fərvər\ *n* : passion — fer-
ven•cy \-vənsē\ *n* — fer•vent
\-vənt\ *adj* — fer•vent•ly *adv*

fes•ter \'festər\ *vb* 1 : form pus 2 : become more bitter or malignant

fes•ti•val \'festəvəl\ *n* : time of celebration

fes•tive \-tiv\ *adj* : joyous or happy —
fes•tive•ly *adv* — fes•tiv•i•ty \fes-
'tivətē\ *n*

fes•toon \fes'tün\ *n* : decorative chain
or strip hanging in a curve — fes-
toon *vb*

fe•tal \'fēt°l\ *adj* : of, relating to, or being a fetus

fetch \'fech\ *vb* 1 : go or come after
and bring or take back 2 : sell for

fetch•ing \'fechiŋ\ *adj* : attractive —
fetch•ing•ly *adv*

fête \'fāt, 'fet\ *n* : lavish party ∼ *vb*
fêt•ed; fêt•ing : honor or commemo-
rate with a fête

fet•id \'fetəd\ *adj* : having an offensive
smell

fe•tish \'fetish\ *n* 1 : object believed to
have magical powers 2 : object of
unreasoning devotion or concern

fet•lock \'fet,läk\ *n* : projection on the
back of a horse's leg above the hoof

fet•ter \'fetər\ *n* : chain or shackle for
the feet — fetter *vb*

fet•tle \'fet°l\ *n* : state of fitness

fe•tus \'fētəs\ *n* : vertebrate not yet
born or hatched

feud \'fyüd\ *n* : prolonged quarrel —
feud *vb*

feu•dal \'fyüd°l\ *adj* : of or relating to
feudalism

feu•dal•ism \-,izəm\ *n* : medieval political order in which land is granted in
return for service — feu•dal•is•tic
\,fyüd°l'istik\ *adj*

fe•ver \'fēvər\ *n* 1 : abnormal rise in
body temperature 2 : state of height-
ened emotion — fe•ver•ish *adj* — fe-
ver•ish•ly *adv*

few \'fyü\ *pron* : not many ∼ *adj*
: some but not many — often with *a*
∼ *n* : small number — often with *a*

few•er \-ər\ *pron* : smaller number of
things

fez \'fez\ *n, pl* fez•zes : round flat-
crowned hat

fi•an•cé \,fē,än'sā\ *n* : man one is engaged to

fi•an•cée \,fē,än'sā\ *n* : woman one is
engaged to

fi•as•co \fē'askō\ *n, pl* -coes : ridiculous failure

fi•at \'fēat, -,at, -,ät; 'fīət, -,at\ *n* : decree

fib \'fib\ *n* : trivial lie — fib *vb* — fib-
ber *n*

fi•ber, fi•bre \'fībər\ *n* 1 : threadlike
substance or structure (as a muscle
cell or fine root) 2 : indigestible material in food 3 : element that gives
texture or substance — fi•brous
\-brəs\ *adj*

fi•ber•board *n* : construction material
made of compressed fibers

fi•ber•glass *n* : glass in fibrous form in
various products (as insulation)

fi•bril•la•tion \,fibrə'lāshən, ,fīb-\ *n*
: rapid irregular contractions of heart
muscle — fib•ril•late \'fibrə,lāt,
'fīb-\ *vb*

fib•u•la \'fibyələ\ *n, pl* -lae \-lē, -lī\ *or*
-las : outer of the two leg bones below the knee — fib•u•lar \-lər\ *adj*

fick•le \'fikəl\ *adj* : unpredictably
changeable — fick•le•ness *n*

fic•tion \'fikshən\ *n* : a made-up story
or literature consisting of these —
fic•tion•al \-shənəl\ *adj*

fic•ti•tious \fik'tishəs\ *adj* : made up or
pretended

fid•dle \'fid°l\ *n* : violin ∼ *vb* -dled;
-dling 1 : play on the fiddle 2 : move
the hands restlessly — fid•dler
\'fidlər, -°lər\ *n*

fid•dle•sticks *n* : nonsense — used as
an interjection

fi•del•i•ty \fə'delətē, fī-\ *n, pl* -ties 1
: quality or state of being faithful 2
: quality of reproduction

**fid·get** \'fijət\ *n* **1** *pl* : restlessness **2** : one that fidgets ~ *vb* : move restlessly — **fid·gety** *adj*

**fi·du·cia·ry** \fə'düshē,erē, -'dyü-, -shərē\ *adj* : held or holding in trust — **fiduciary** *n*

**field** \'fēld\ *n* **1** : open country **2** : cleared land **3** : land yielding some special product **4** : sphere of activity **5** : area for sports **6** : region or space in which a given effect (as magnetism) exists ~ *vb* : put into the field — **field** *adj* — **field·er** *n*

**fiend** \'fēnd\ *n* **1** : devil **2** : extremely wicked person — **fiend·ish** *adj* — **fiend·ish·ly** *adv*

**fierce** \'firs\ *adj* **fierc·er; -est** **1** : violently hostile or aggressive **2** : intense **3** : menacing looking — **fierce·ly** *adv* — **fierce·ness** *n*

**fi·ery** \'fīərē\ *adj* **fi·er·i·er; -est** **1** : burning **2** : hot or passionate — **fi·eri·ness** \'fīərēnəs\ *n*

**fi·es·ta** \fē'estə\ *n* : festival

**fife** \'fīf\ *n* : small flute

**fif·teen** \fif'tēn\ *n* : one more than 14 — **fifteen** *adj or pron* — **fif·teenth** \-'tēnth\ *adj or n*

**fifth** \'fifth\ *n* **1** : one that is number 5 in a countable series **2** : one of 5 equal parts of something — **fifth** *adj or adv*

**fif·ty** \'fiftē\ *n, pl* **-ties** : 5 times 10 — **fif·ti·eth** \-tēəth\ *adj or n* — **fifty** *adj or pron*

**fif·ty–fif·ty** *adv or adj* : shared equally

**fig** \'fig\ *n* : pear-shaped edible fruit

**fight** \'fīt\ *vb* **fought** \'fót\; **fight·ing** **1** : contend against another in battle **2** : box **3** : struggle ~ *n* **1** : hostile encounter **2** : boxing match **3** : verbal disagreement — **fight·er** *n*

**fig·ment** \'figmənt\ *n* : something imagined or made up

**fig·u·ra·tive** \'figyərətiv, -gə-\ *adj* : metaphorical — **fig·u·ra·tive·ly** *adv*

**fig·ure** \'figyər, -gər\ *n* **1** : symbol representing a number **2** *pl* : arithmetical calculations **3** : price **4** : shape or outline **5** : illustration **6** : pattern or design **7** : prominent person ~ *vb* **-ured; -ur·ing** **1** : be important **2** : calculate — **fig·ured** *adj*

**fig·u·rine** \,figyə'rēn\ *n* : small statue

**fil·a·ment** \'filəmənt\ *n* : fine thread or threadlike part — **fil·a·men·tous** \,filə'mentəs\ *adj*

**fil·bert** \'filbərt\ *n* : edible nut of a European hazel

**filch** \'filch\ *vb* : steal furtively

¹**file** \'fīl\ *n* : tool for smoothing or sharpening ~ *vb* **filed; fil·ing** : rub or smooth with a file

²**file** *vb* **filed; fil·ing** **1** : arrange in order **2** : enter or record officially ~ *n* : device for keeping papers in order

³**file** *n* : row of persons or things one behind the other ~ *vb* **filed; fil·ing** : march in file

**fil·ial** \'filēəl, 'filyəl\ *adj* : relating to a son or daughter

**fil·i·bus·ter** \'filə,bəstər\ *n* : long speeches to delay a legislative vote — **filibuster** *vb* — **fil·i·bus·ter·er** *n*

**fil·i·gree** \'filə,grē\ *n* : ornamental designs of fine wire — **fil·i·greed** \-,grēd\ *adj*

**fill** \'fil\ *vb* **1** : make or become full **2** : stop up **3** : feed **4** : satisfy **5** : occupy fully **6** : spread through ~ *n* **1** : full supply **2** : material for filling — **fill·er** *n* — **fill in** *vb* **1** : provide information to or for **2** : substitute

**fil·let** \'filət, fi'lā, 'fil,ā\ *n* : piece of boneless meat or fish ~ *vb* : cut into fillets

**fill·ing** *n* : material used to fill something

**fil·ly** \'filē\ *n, pl* **-lies** : young female horse

**film** \'film\ *n* **1** : thin skin or membrane **2** : thin coating or layer **3** : strip of material used in taking pictures **4** : movie ~ *vb* : make a movie of — **filmy** *adj*

**film·strip** *n* : strip of film with photographs for still projection

**fil·ter** \'filtər\ *n* **1** : device for separating matter from a fluid **2** : device (as on a camera lens) that absorbs light ~ *vb* **1** : pass through a filter **2** : remove by means of a filter — **fil·ter·able** *adj* — **fil·tra·tion** \fil'trāshən\ *n*

**filth** \'filth\ *n* : repulsive dirt or refuse — **filth·i·ness** *n* — **filthy** \'filthē\ *adj*

**fin** \'fin\ *n* **1** : thin external process controlling movement in an aquatic animal **2** : fin-shaped part (as on an airplane) **3** : flipper — **finned** \'find\ *adj*

**fi·na·gle** \fə'nāgəl\ *vb* **-gled; -gling** : get by clever or tricky means — **fi·na·gler** *n*

**fi·nal** \'fīnʲl\ *adj* **1** : not to be changed

**2** : ultimate **3** : coming at the end — **final** n — **fi•nal•ist** \'fīn°list\ n — **fi•nal•i•ty** \fī'nalətē, fə-\ n — **fi•nal•ize** \-,īz\ vb — **fi•nal•ly** adv

**fi•na•le** \fə'nalē, fī'näl-\ n : last or climactic part

**fi•nance** \fə'nans, 'fī,nans\ n **1** pl : money resources **2** : management of money affairs ∼ vb **-nanced; -nanc•ing 1** : raise funds for **2** : give necessary funds to **3** : sell on credit

**fi•nan•cial** \fə'nanchəl, fī-\ adj : relating to finance — **fi•nan•cial•ly** adv

**fi•nan•cier** \,finən'sir, ,fī,nan-\ n : person who invests large sums of money

**finch** \'finch\ n : songbird (as a sparrow or linnet) with a strong bill

**find** \'fīnd\ vb **found** \'faůnd\; **find•ing 1** : discover or encounter **2** : obtain by effort **3** : experience or feel **4** : gain or regain the use of **5** : decide on (a verdict) ∼ n **1** : act or instance of finding **2** : something found — **find•er** n — **find•ing** n — **find out** vb : learn, discover, or verify something

**fine** \'fīn\ n : money paid as a penalty ∼ vb **fined; fin•ing** : impose a fine on ∼ adj **fin•er; -est 1** : free from impurity **2** : small or thin **3** : not coarse **4** : superior in quality or appearance ∼ adv : finely — **fine•ly** adv — **fine•ness** n

**fin•ery** \'fīnərē\ n, pl **-er•ies** : showy clothing and jewels

**fi•nesse** \fə'nes\ n **1** : delicate skill **2** : craftiness — **finesse** vb

**fin•ger** \'fiŋgər\ n **1** : one of the 5 divisions at the end of the hand and esp. one other than the thumb **2** : something like a finger **3** : part of a glove for a finger ∼ vb **1** : touch with the fingers **2** : identify as if by pointing — **fin•gered** adj — **fin•ger•nail** n — **fin•ger•tip** n

**fin•ger•ling** \-gərliŋ\ n : small fish

**fin•ger•print** n : impression of the pattern of marks on the tip of a finger — **fingerprint** vb

**fin•icky** \'finikē\ adj : excessively particular in taste or standards

**fin•ish** \'finish\ vb **1** : come or bring to an end **2** : use or dispose of entirely **3** : put a final coat or surface on ∼ n **1** : end **2** : final treatment given a surface — **fin•ish•er** n

**fi•nite** \'fī,nīt\ adj : having definite limits

**fink** \'fiŋk\ n : contemptible person

**fiord** var of FJORD

**fir** \'fər\ n : evergreen tree or its wood

**fire** \'fīr\ n **1** : light or heat and esp. the flame of something burning **2** : destructive burning (as of a house) **3** : enthusiasm **4** : the shooting of weapons ∼ vb **fired; fir•ing 1** : kindle **2** : stir up or enliven **3** : dismiss from employment **4** : shoot **5** : bake — **fire•bomb** n or vb — **fire•fight•er** n — **fire•less** adj — **fire•proof** adj or vb — **fire•wood** n

**fire•arm** n : weapon (as a rifle) that works by an explosion of gunpowder

**fire•ball** n **1** : ball of fire **2** : brilliant meteor

**fire•boat** n : boat equipped for fighting fire

**fire•box** n **1** : chamber (as of a furnace) that contains a fire **2** : fire-alarm box

**fire•break** n : cleared land for checking a forest fire

**fire•bug** n : person who deliberately sets destructive fires

**fire•crack•er** n : small firework that makes noise

**fire•fight•er** \'fīr,fītər\ n : a person who fights fires

**fire•fly** n : night-flying beetle that produces a soft light

**fire•place** n : opening made in a chimney to hold an open fire

**fire•plug** n : hydrant

**fire•side** n **1** : place near the fire or hearth **2** : home ∼ adj : having an informal quality

**fire•trap** n : place apt to catch on fire

**fire•work** n : device that explodes to produce noise or a display of light

**¹firm** \'fərm\ adj **1** : securely fixed in place **2** : strong or vigorous **3** : not subject to change **4** : resolute ∼ vb : make or become firm — **firm•ly** adv — **firm•ness** n

**²firm** n : business enterprise

**fir•ma•ment** \'fərməmənt\ n : sky

**first** \'fərst\ adj **1** : being number one **2** : foremost ∼ adv **1** : before any other **2** : for the first time ∼ n **1** : number one **2** : one that is first — **first class** n — **first–class** adj or adv — **first•ly** adv — **first–rate** adj or adv

**first aid** n : emergency care

**first lieutenant** n : commissioned officer ranking next below a captain

**first sergeant** n **1** : noncommissioned

officer serving as the chief assistant to the commander of a military unit 2 : rank in the army below a sergeant major and in the marine corps below a master gunnery sergeant

**firth** \'fərth\ *n* : estuary

**fis·cal** \'fiskəl\ *adj* : relating to money — **fis·cal·ly** *adv*

**fish** \'fish\ *n, pl* **fish** *or* **fish·es** : water animal with fins, gills, and usu. scales ~ *vb* 1 : try to catch fish 2 : grope — **fish·er** *n* — **fish·hook** *n* — **fish·ing** *n*

**fish·er·man** \-mən\ *n* : one who fishes

**fish·ery** \'fishərē\ *n, pl* **-er·ies** : fishing business or a place for this

**fishy** \'fishē\ *adj* **fish·i·er; -est** 1 : relating to or like fish 2 : questionable

**fis·sion** \'fishən, 'fizh-\ *n* : splitting of an atomic nucleus — **fis·sion·able** \-ənəbəl\ *adj*

**fis·sure** \'fishər\ *n* : crack

**fist** \'fist\ *n* : hand doubled up — **fist·ed** \'fistəd\ *adj* — **fist·ful** \-,ful\ *n*

**fist·i·cuffs** \'fisti,kəfs\ *n pl* : fist fight

¹**fit** \'fit\ *n* : sudden attack of illness or emotion

²**fit** *adj* **-tt-** 1 : suitable 2 : qualified 3 : sound in body ~ *vb* **-tt-** 1 : be suitable to 2 : insert or adjust correctly 3 : make room for 4 : supply or equip 5 : belong ~ *n* : state of fitting or being fitted — **fit·ly** *adv* — **fit·ness** *n* — **fit·ter** *n*

**fit·ful** \'fitfəl\ *adj* : restless — **fit·ful·ly** *adv*

**fit·ting** *adj* : suitable ~ *n* : a small part

**five** \'fīv\ *n* 1 : one more than 4 2 : 5th in a set or series 3 : something having 5 units — **five** *adj or pron*

**fix** \'fiks\ *vb* 1 : attach 2 : establish 3 : make right 4 : prepare 5 : improperly influence ~ *n* 1 : predicament 2 : determination of location — **fix·er** *n*

**fix·a·tion** \fik'sāshən\ *n* : obsessive attachment — **fix·ate** \'fik,sāt\ *vb*

**fixed** \'fikst\ *adj* 1 : stationary 2 : settled — **fixed·ly** \'fiksədlē\ *adv* — **fixed·ness** \-nəs\ *n*

**fix·ture** \'fikschər\ *n* : permanent part of something

**fizz** \'fiz\ *vb* : make a hissing sound ~ *n* : effervescence

**fiz·zle** \'fizəl\ *vb* **-zled; -zling** 1 : fizz 2 : fail ~ *n* : failure

**fjord** \fē'ȯrd\ *n* : inlet of the sea between cliffs

**flab** \'flab\ *n* : flabby flesh

**flab·ber·gast** \'flabər,gast\ *vb* : astound

**flab·by** \'flabē\ *adj* **-bi·er; -est** : not firm — **flab·bi·ness** *n*

**flac·cid** \'flaksəd, 'flasəd\ *adj* : not firm

¹**flag** \'flag\ *n* : flat stone

²**flag** *n* 1 : fabric that is a symbol (as of a country) 2 : something used to signal ~ *vb* **-gg-** : signal with a flag — **flag·pole** *n* — **flag·staff** *n*

³**flag** *vb* **-gg-** : lose strength or spirit

**flag·el·late** \'flajə,lāt\ *vb* **-lat·ed; -lat·ing** : whip — **flag·el·la·tion** \,flajə'lāshən\ *n*

**flag·on** \'flagən\ *n* : container for liquids

**fla·grant** \'flāgrənt\ *adj* : conspicuously bad — **fla·grant·ly** *adv*

**flag·ship** *n* : ship carrying a commander

**flag·stone** *n* : flag

**flail** \'flāl\ *n* : tool for threshing grain ~ *vb* : beat with or as if with a flail

**flair** \'flar\ *n* : natural aptitude

**flak** \'flak\ *n, pl* **flak** 1 : antiaircraft fire 2 : criticism

**flake** \'flāk\ *n* : small flat piece ~ *vb* **flaked; flak·ing** : separate or form into flakes

**flam·boy·ant** \flam'bȯiənt\ *adj* : showy — **flam·boy·ance** \-əns\ *n* — **flam·boy·ant·ly** *adv*

**flame** \'flām\ *n* 1 : glowing part of a fire 2 : state of combustion 3 : burning passion — **flame** *vb* — **flam·ing** *adj*

**fla·min·go** \flə'miŋgō\ *n, pl* **-gos** : long-legged long-necked tropical water bird

**flam·ma·ble** \'flaməbəl\ *adj* : easily ignited

**flange** \'flanj\ *n* : rim

**flank** \'flaŋk\ *n* : side of something ~ *vb* 1 : attack or go around the side of 2 : be at the side of

**flan·nel** \'flanᵊl\ *n* : soft napped fabric

**flap** \'flap\ *n* 1 : slap 2 : something flat that hangs loose ~ *vb* **-pp-** 1 : move (wings) up and down 2 : swing back and forth noisily

**flap·jack** \-,jak\ *n* : pancake

**flare** \'flar\ *vb* **flared; flar·ing** : become suddenly bright or excited ~ *n* : blaze of light

**flash** \'flash\ *vb* 1 : give off a sudden flame or burst of light 2 : appear or pass suddenly ~ *n* 1 : sudden burst of light or inspiration **2** : instant ~ *adj* : coming suddenly

**flash•light** *n* : small battery-operated light

**flashy** \'flashē\ *adj* **flash•i•er; -est** : showy — **flash•i•ly** *adv* — **flash•i•ness** *n*

**flask** \'flask\ *n* : flattened bottle

**flat** \'flat\ *adj* **-tt- 1** : smooth **2** : broad and thin **3** : definite **4** : uninteresting **5** : deflated **6** : below the true pitch ~ *n* **1** : level surface of land **2** : flat note in music **3** : apartment **4** : deflated tire ~ *adv* **-tt- 1** : exactly **2** : below the true pitch ~ *vb* **-tt-** : make flat — **flat•ly** *adv* — **flat•ness** *n* — **flat•ten** \-ᵊn\ *vb*

**flat•car** *n* : railroad car without sides

**flat•fish** *n* : flattened fish with both eyes on the upper side

**flat•foot** *n, pl* **flat•feet** : foot condition in which the arch is flattened — **flat–foot•ed** *adj*

**flat–out** *adj* **1** : being maximum effort or speed **2** : downright

**flat•ter** \'flatər\ *vb* **1** : praise insincerely **2** : judge or represent too favorably — **flat•ter•er** *n* — **flat•tery** \'flatərē\ *n*

**flat•u•lent** \'flachələnt\ *adj* : full of gas — **flat•u•lence** \-ləns\ *n*

**flat•ware** *n* : eating utensils

**flaunt** \'flȯnt\ *vb* : display ostentatiously — **flaunt** *n*

**fla•vor** \'flāvər\ *n* **1** : quality that affects the sense of taste **2** : something that adds flavor ~ *vb* : give flavor to — **fla•vor•ful** *adj* — **fla•vor•ing** *n* — **fla•vor•less** *adj*

**flaw** \'flȯ\ *n* : fault — **flaw•less** *adj* — **flaw•less•ly** *adv* — **flaw•less•ness** *n*

**flax** \'flaks\ *n* : plant from which linen is made

**flax•en** \'flaksən\ *adj* : made of or like flax

**flay** \'flā\ *vb* **1** : strip off the skin of **2** : criticize harshly

**flea** \'flē\ *n* : leaping bloodsucking insect

**fleck** \'flek\ *vb or n* : streak or spot

**fledg•ling** \'flejliŋ\ *n* : young bird

**flee** \'flē\ *vb* **fled** \'fled\; **flee•ing** : run away

**fleece** \'flēs\ *n* : sheep's wool ~ *vb* **fleeced; fleec•ing 1** : shear **2** : get money from dishonestly — **fleecy** *adj*

¹**fleet** \'flēt\ *vb* : pass rapidly ~ *adj*

: swift — **fleet•ing** *adj* — **fleet•ness** *n*

²**fleet** *n* : group of ships

**fleet admiral** *n* : commissioned officer of the highest rank in the navy

**flesh** \'flesh\ *n* **1** : soft parts of an animal's body **2** : soft plant tissue (as fruit pulp) — **fleshed** \'flesht\ *adj* — **fleshy** *adj* — **flesh out** *vb* : make fuller

**flesh•ly** \'fleshlē\ *adj* : sensual

**flew** *past of* FLY

**flex** \'fleks\ *vb* : bend

**flex•i•ble** \'fleksəbəl\ *adj* **1** : capable of being flexed **2** : adaptable — **flex•i•bil•i•ty** \ˌfleksə'bilətē\ *n* — **flex•i•bly** \-səblē\ *adv*

**flick** \'flik\ *n* : light jerky stroke ~ *vb* **1** : strike lightly **2** : flutter

**flick•er** \'flikər\ *vb* **1** : waver **2** : burn unsteadily ~ *n* **1** : sudden movement **2** : wavering light

**fli•er** \'flīər\ *n* **1** : aviator **2** : advertising circular

¹**flight** \'flīt\ *n* **1** : act or instance of flying **2** : ability to fly **3** : a passing through air or space **4** : series of stairs — **flight•less** *adj*

²**flight** *n* : act or instance of running away

**flighty** \-ē\ *adj* **flight•i•er; -est** : capricious or silly — **flight•i•ness** *n*

**flim•flam** \'flim,flam\ *n* : trickery

**flim•sy** \-zē\ *adj* **-si•er; -est 1** : not strong or well made **2** : not believable — **flim•si•ly** *adv* — **flim•si•ness** *n*

**flinch** \'flinch\ *vb* : shrink from pain

**fling** \'fliŋ\ *vb* **flung** \'fləŋ\; **fling•ing 1** : move brusquely **2** : throw ~ *n* **1** : act or instance of flinging **2** : attempt **3** : period of self-indulgence

**flint** \'flint\ *n* : hard quartz that gives off sparks when struck with steel — **flinty** *adj*

**flip** \'flip\ *vb* **-pp- 1** : cause to turn over quickly or many times **2** : move with a quick push ~ *adj* : insolent — **flip** *n*

**flip•pant** \'flipənt\ *adj* : not serious enough — **flip•pan•cy** \-ənsē\ *n*

**flip•per** \'flipər\ *n* : paddlelike limb (as of a seal) for swimming

**flirt** \'flərt\ *vb* **1** : be playfully romantic **2** : show casual interest ~ *n* : one who flirts — **flir•ta•tion** \ˌflər'tāshən\ *n* — **flir•ta•tious** \-shəs\ *adj*

**flit** \'flit\ *vb* **-tt-** : dart

**float** \'flōt\ *n* **1** : something that floats **2** : vehicle carrying an exhibit ~ *vb*

1 : rest on or in a fluid without sinking 2 : wander 3 : finance by issuing stock or bonds — **float·er** n

**flock** \\'fläk\ n : group of animals (as birds) or people ∼ vb : gather or move as a group

**floe** \\'flō\ n : mass of floating ice

**flog** \\'fläg\ vb **-gg-** : beat with a rod or whip — **flog·ger** n

**flood** \\'fləd\ n 1 : great flow of water over the land 2 : overwhelming volume ∼ vb : cover or fill esp. with water — **flood·wa·ter** n

**floor** \\'flōr\ n 1 : bottom of a room on which one stands 2 : story of a building 3 : lower limit ∼ vb 1 : furnish with a floor 2 : knock down 3 : amaze — **floor·board** n — **floor·ing** \-iŋ\ n

**floo·zy, floo·zie** \\'flüzē\ n, pl **-zies** : promiscuous young woman

**flop** \\'fläp\ vb **-pp-** 1 : flap 2 : slump heavily 3 : fail — **flop** n

**flop·py** \\'fläpē\ adj **-pi·er; -est** : soft and flexible

**flo·ra** \\'flōrə\ n : plants or plant life of a region

**flo·ral** \\'flōrəl\ adj : relating to flowers

**flor·id** \\'flòrəd\ adj 1 : very flowery in style 2 : reddish

**flo·rist** \\'flòrist\ n : flower dealer

**floss** \\'fläs\ n 1 : soft thread for embroidery 2 : thread used to clean between teeth — **floss** vb

**flo·ta·tion** \flō'tāshən\ n : process or instance of floating

**flo·til·la** \flō'tilə\ n : small fleet

**flot·sam** \\'flätsəm\ n : floating wreckage

¹**flounce** \\'flaúns\ vb **flounced; flounc·ing** : move with exaggerated jerky motions — **flounce** n

²**flounce** n : fabric border or wide ruffle

¹**floun·der** \\'flaúndər\ n, pl **flounder** or **flounders** : flatfish

²**flounder** vb 1 : struggle for footing 2 : proceed clumsily

**flour** \\'flaúər\ n : finely ground meal ∼ vb : coat with flour — **floury** adj

**flour·ish** \\'flərish\ vb 1 : thrive 2 : wave threateningly ∼ n 1 : embellishment 2 : fanfare 3 : wave 4 : showiness of action

**flout** \\'flaút\ vb : treat with disdain

**flow** \\'flō\ vb 1 : move in a stream 2 : proceed smoothly and readily ∼ n : uninterrupted stream

**flow·er** \\'flaúər\ n 1 : showy plant

shoot that bears seeds 2 : state of flourishing ∼ vb 1 : produce flowers 2 : flourish — **flow·ered** adj — **flow·er·less** adj — **flow·er·pot** n — **flow·ery** \-ē\ adj

**flown** past part of FLY

**flu** \\'flü\ n 1 : influenza 2 : minor virus ailment

**flub** \\'fləb\ vb **-bb-** : bungle — **flub** n

**fluc·tu·ate** \\'fləkchə,wāt\ vb **-at·ed; -at·ing** : change rapidly esp. up and down — **fluc·tu·a·tion** \,fləkchə-'wāshən\ n

**flue** \\'flü\ n : smoke duct

**flu·ent** \\'flüənt\ adj : speaking with ease — **flu·en·cy** \-ənsē\ n — **flu·ent·ly** adv

**fluff** \\'fləf\ n 1 : something soft and light 2 : blunder ∼ vb 1 : make fluffy 2 : make a mistake — **fluffy** \-ē\ adj

**flu·id** \\'flüəd\ adj : flowing ∼ n : substance that can flow — **flu·id·i·ty** \flü'idətē\ n — **flu·id·ly** adv

**fluid ounce** n : unit of liquid measure equal to $\frac{1}{16}$ pint

**fluke** \\'flük\ n : stroke of luck

**flume** \\'flüm\ n : channel for water

**flung** past of FLING

**flunk** \\'fləŋk\ vb : fail in school work

**flun·ky, flun·key** \\'fləŋkē\ n, pl **-kies** or **-keys** : lackey

**flu·o·res·cence** \,flùr'es³ns, ,flòr-\ n : emission of light after initial absorption — **flu·o·resce** \-'es\ vb — **flu·o·res·cent** \-'es³nt\ adj

**flu·o·ri·date** \\'flòrə,dāt, 'flùr-\ vb **-dat·ed; -dat·ing** : add fluoride to — **flu·o·ri·da·tion** \,flòrə'dāshən, ,flùr-\ n

**flu·o·ride** \\'flòr,īd, 'flùr-\ n : compound of fluorine

**flu·o·rine** \\'flùr,ēn, -ən\ n : toxic gaseous chemical element

**flu·o·ro·car·bon** \,flòrō'kärbən, ,flùr-\ n : compound containing fluorine and carbon

**flu·o·ro·scope** \\'flùrə,skōp\ n : instrument for internal examination — **flu·o·ro·scop·ic** \,flùrə'skäpik\ adj — **flu·o·ros·co·py** \,flùr'äskəpē\ n

**flur·ry** \\'flərē\ n, pl **-ries** 1 : light snowfall 2 : bustle 3 : brief burst of activity — **flurry** vb

¹**flush** \\'fləsh\ vb : cause (a bird) to fly from cover

²**flush** n 1 : sudden flow (as of water) 2 : surge of emotion 3 : blush ∼ vb 1

: blush **2** : wash out with a rush of liquid ~ *adj* **1** : filled to overflowing **2** : of a reddish healthy color **3** : smooth or level **4** : abutting — **flush** *adv*

³**flush** *n* : cards of the same suit

**flus·ter** \'fləstər\ *vb* : upset — **fluster** *n*

**flute** \'flüt\ *n* **1** : pipelike musical instrument **2** : groove — **flut·ed** *adj* — **flut·ing** *n* — **flut·ist** \-ist\ *n*

**flut·ter** \'flətər\ *vb* **1** : flap the wings rapidly **2** : move with quick wavering or flapping motions **3** : behave in an agitated manner ~ *n* **1** : a fluttering **2** : state of confusion — **flut·tery** \-ərē\ *adj*

**flux** \'fləks\ *n* : state of continuous change

¹**fly** \'flī\ *vb* **flew** \'flü\; **flown** \'flōn\; **fly·ing** **1** : move through the air with wings **2** : float or soar **3** : flee **4** : move or pass swiftly **5** : operate an airplane

²**fly** *n, pl* **flies** : garment closure

³**fly** *n, pl* **flies** : winged insect

**fly·er** *var of* FLIER

**fly·pa·per** *n* : sticky paper for catching flies

**fly·speck** *n* **1** : speck of fly dung **2** : something tiny

**fly·wheel** *n* : rotating wheel that regulates the speed of machinery

**foal** \'fōl\ *n* : young horse — **foal** *vb*

**foam** \'fōm\ *n* **1** : mass of bubbles on top of a liquid **2** : material of cellular form ~ *vb* : form foam — **foamy** *adj*

**fob** \'fäb\ *n* : short chain for a pocket watch

**fo·c·sle** *var of* FORECASTLE

**fo·cus** \'fōkəs\ *n, pl* **-ci** \-,sī\ **1** : point at which reflected or refracted rays meet **2** : adjustment (as of eyeglasses) for clear vision **3** : central point ~ *vb* : bring to a focus — **fo·cal** \-kəl\ *adj* — **fo·cal·ly** *adv*

**fod·der** \'fädər\ *n* : food for livestock

**foe** \'fō\ *n* : enemy

**fog** \'fȯg, 'fäg\ *n* **1** : fine particles of water suspended near the ground **2** : mental confusion ~ *vb* **-gg-** : obscure or be obscured with fog — **fog·gy** *adj*

**fog·horn** *n* : warning horn sounded in a fog

**fo·gy** \'fōgē\ *n, pl* **-gies** : person with old-fashioned ideas

**foi·ble** \'fȯibəl\ *n* : minor character fault

¹**foil** \'fȯil\ *vb* : defeat ~ *n* : light fencing sword

²**foil** *n* **1** : thin sheet of metal **2** : one that sets off another by contrast

**foist** \'fȯist\ *vb* : force another to accept

¹**fold** \'fōld\ *n* **1** : enclosure for sheep **2** : group with a common interest

²**fold** *vb* **1** : lay one part over another **2** : embrace ~ *n* : part folded

**fold·er** \'fōldər\ *n* **1** : one that folds **2** : circular **3** : folded cover or envelope for papers

**fol·de·rol** \'fäldə,räl\ *n* : nonsense

**fo·liage** \'fōlēij, -lij\ *n* : plant leaves

**fo·lio** \'fōlē,ō\ *n, pl* **-li·os** : sheet of paper folded once

**folk** \'fōk\ *n, pl* **folk** *or* **folks** **1** : people in general **2** *folks pl* : one's family ~ *adj* : relating to the common people

**folk·lore** *n* : customs and traditions of a people — **folk·lor·ist** *n*

**folksy** \'fōksē\ *adj* **folks·i·er; -est** : friendly and informal

**fol·li·cle** \'fälikəl\ *n* : small anatomical cavity or gland

**fol·low** \'fälō\ *vb* **1** : go or come after **2** : pursue **3** : obey **4** : proceed along **5** : keep one's attention fixed on **6** : result from — **fol·low·er** *n*

**fol·low·ing** \'fäləwiŋ\ *adj* : next ~ *n* : group of followers ~ *prep* : after

**fol·ly** \'fälē\ *n, pl* **-lies** : foolishness

**fo·ment** \fō'ment\ *vb* : incite

**fond** \'fänd\ *adj* **1** : strongly attracted **2** : affectionate **3** : dear — **fond·ly** *adv* — **fond·ness** *n*

**fon·dle** \'fänd³l\ *vb* **-dled; -dling** : touch lovingly

**fon·due** \fän'dü, -'dyü\ *n* : preparation of melted cheese

**font** \'fänt\ *n* **1** : baptismal basin **2** : fountain

**food** \'füd\ *n* : material eaten to sustain life

**fool** \'fül\ *n* **1** : stupid person **2** : jester ~ *vb* **1** : waste time **2** : meddle **3** : deceive — **fool·ery** \'fülərē\ *n* — **fool·ish** \'fülish\ *adj* — **fool·ish·ly** *adv* — **fool·ish·ness** *n* — **fool·proof** *adj*

**fool·har·dy** \'fül,härdē\ *adj* : rash — **fool·har·di·ness** *n*

**foot** \'fut\ *n, pl* **feet** \'fēt\ **1** : end part of a leg **2** : unit of length equal to ⅓ yard **3** : unit of verse meter **4** : bottom — **foot·age** \-ij\ *n* — **foot·ed** *adj* — **foot·path** *n* — **foot·print** *n* —

**foot·race** n — **foot·rest** n — **foot·wear** n

**foot·ball** n : ball game played by 2 teams on a rectangular field

**foot·bridge** n : bridge for pedestrians

**foot·hill** n : hill at the foot of higher hills

**foot·hold** n : support for the feet

**foot·ing** n 1 : foothold 2 : basis

**foot·lights** n pl : stage lights along the floor

**foot·lock·er** n : small trunk

**foot·loose** adj : having no ties

**foot·man** \'fútmən\ n : male servant

**foot·note** n : note at the bottom of a page

**foot·step** n 1 : step 2 : distance covered by a step 3 : footprint

**foot·stool** n : stool to support the feet

**foot·work** n : skillful movement of the feet (as in boxing)

**fop** \'fäp\ n : dandy — **fop·pery** \-ərē\ n — **fop·pish** adj

**for** \'fȯr\ prep 1 — used to show preparation or purpose 2 : because of 3 — used to show a recipient 4 : in support of 5 : so as to support or help cure 6 : so as to be equal to 7 : concerning 8 : through the period of ∼ conj : because

**for·age** \'fȯrij\ n : food for animals ∼ vb **-aged; -ag·ing** 1 : hunt food 2 : search for provisions

**for·ay** \'fȯr‚ā\ n or vb : raid

¹**for·bear** \fȯr'bar\ vb **-bore** \-'bȯr\; **-borne** \-'bȯrn\; **-bear·ing** 1 : refrain from 2 : be patient — **for·bear·ance** \-'barəns\ n

²**forbear** var of FOREBEAR

**for·bid** \fər'bid\ vb **-bade** \-'bad, -'bād\ or **-bad** \-'bad\; **-bid·den** \-'bid°n\; **-bid·ding** 1 : prohibit 2 : order not to do something

**for·bid·ding** adj : tending to discourage

**force** \'fȯrs\ n 1 : exceptional strength or energy 2 : military strength 3 : body (as of persons) available for a purpose 4 : violence 5 : influence (as a push or pull) that causes motion ∼ vb **forced; forc·ing** 1 : compel 2 : gain against resistance 3 : break open — **force·ful** \-fəl\ adj — **force·ful·ly** adv — **in force** 1 : in great numbers 2 : valid

**for·ceps** \'fȯrsəps\ n, pl **forceps** : surgical instrument for grasping objects

**forc·ible** \'fȯrsəbəl\ adj 1 : done by force 2 : showing force — **forc·i·bly** \-blē\ adv

**ford** \'fȯrd\ n : place to wade across a stream ∼ vb : wade across

**fore** \'fȯr\ adv 1 : in or toward the front ∼ adj : being or coming before in time, place, or order ∼ n : front

**fore-and-aft** adj : lengthwise

**fore·arm** \'fȯr‚ärm\ n : part of the arm between the elbow and the wrist

**fore·bear** \'fȯr‚bar\ n : ancestor

**fore·bod·ing** \fȯr'bōdiŋ\ n : premonition of disaster — **fore·bod·ing** adj

**fore·cast** \'fȯr‚kast\ vb **-cast; -cast·ing** : predict — **forecast** n — **fore·cast·er** n

**fore·cas·tle** \'fōksəl\ n : forward part of a ship

**fore·close** \fȯr'klōz\ vb : take legal measures to terminate a mortgage — **fore·clo·sure** \-'klōzhər\ n

**fore·fa·ther** \'fȯr‚fäthər\ n : ancestor

**fore·fin·ger** \'fȯr‚fiŋgər\ n : finger next to the thumb

**fore·foot** \'fȯr‚fùt\ n : front foot of a quadruped

**fore·front** \'fȯr‚frənt\ n : foremost position or place

¹**fore·go** \fȯr'gō\ vb **-went; -gone; -go·ing** : precede

²**forego** var of FORGO

**fore·go·ing** adj : preceding

**fore·gone** adj : determined in advance

**fore·ground** \'fȯr‚graúnd\ n : part of a scene nearest the viewer

**fore·hand** \'fȯr‚hand\ n : stroke (as in tennis) made with the palm of the hand turned forward — **forehand** adj

**fore·head** \'fȯrəd, 'fȯr‚hed\ n : part of the face above the eyes

**for·eign** \'fȯrən\ adj 1 : situated outside a place or country and esp. one's own country 2 : belonging to a different place or country 3 : not pertinent 4 : related to or dealing with other nations — **for·eign·er** \-ər\ n

**fore·know** \fȯr'nō\ vb **-knew; -known; -know·ing** : know beforehand — **fore·knowl·edge** n

**fore·leg** \'fȯr‚leg\ n : front leg

**fore·lock** \'fȯr‚läk\ n : front lock of hair

**fore·man** \'fōrmən\ n 1 : spokesman of a jury 2 : workman in charge

**fore·most** \'fȯr‚mōst\ adj : first in time, place, or order — **foremost** adv

**fore·noon** \'fȯr‚nün\ n : morning

**fo·ren·sic** \fə'rensik\ adj : relating to courts or public speaking or debate

**fo·ren·sics** \-siks\ *n pl* : art or study of speaking or debating

**fore·or·dain** \ˌfōrôr'dān\ *vb* : decree beforehand

**fore·quar·ter** \'fōrˌkwȯrtər\ *n* : front half on one side of the body of a quadruped

**fore·run·ner** \'fōrˌrənər\ *n* : one that goes before

**fore·see** \fōr'sē\ *vb* **-saw; -seen; -see·ing** : see or realize beforehand — **fore·see·able** *adj*

**fore·shad·ow** \fōr'shadō\ *vb* : hint or suggest beforehand

**fore·sight** \'fōrˌsīt\ *n* : care or provision for the future — **fore·sight·ed** *adj* — **fore·sight·ed·ness** *n*

**for·est** \'fȯrəst\ *n* : large thick growth of trees and underbrush — **for·est·ed** \'fȯrəstəd\ *adj* — **for·est·er** \-əstər\ *n* — **for·est·land** \-ˌland\ *n* — **for·est·ry** \-əstrē\ *n*

**fore·stall** \fōr'stȯl, fȯr-\ *vb* : prevent by acting in advance

**foreswear** *var of* FORSWEAR

**fore·taste** \'fōrˌtāst\ *n* : advance indication or notion ~ *vb* : anticipate

**fore·tell** \fōr'tel\ *vb* **-told; -tell·ing** : predict

**fore·thought** \'fōrˌthȯt\ *n* : foresight

**for·ev·er** \fōr'evər\ *adv* **1** : for a limitless time **2** : always

**for·ev·er·more** \-ˌevər'mōr\ *adv* : forever

**fore·warn** \fōr'wȯrn\ *vb* : warn beforehand

**fore·word** \'fōrwərd\ *n* : preface

**for·feit** \'fȯrfət\ *n* : something forfeited ~ *vb* : lose or lose the right to by an error or crime — **for·fei·ture** \-fəˌchür\ *n*

**¹forge** \'fōrj\ *n* : smithy ~ *vb* **forged; forg·ing 1** : form (metal) by heating and hammering **2** : imitate falsely esp. to defraud — **forg·er** *n* — **forg·ery** \-ərē\ *n*

**²forge** *vb* **forged; forg·ing** : move ahead steadily

**for·get** \fər'get\ *vb* **-got** \-'gät\; **-got·ten** \-'gät'n\ *or* **-got; -get·ting 1** : be unable to think of or recall **2** : fail to think of at the proper time — **for·get·ta·ble** *adj* — **for·get·ful** \-fəl\ *adj* — **for·get·ful·ly** *adv*

**forget–me–not** *n* : small herb with blue or white flowers

**for·give** \fər'giv\ *vb* **-gave** \-'gāv\; **-giv·en** \-'givən\; **-giv·ing** : pardon

— **for·giv·able** *adj* — **for·give·ness** *n*

**for·giv·ing** *adj* **1** : able to forgive **2** : allowing room for error or weakness

**for·go, fore·go** \fōr'gō\ *vb* **-went; -gone; -go·ing** : do without

**fork** \'fȯrk\ *n* **1** : implement with prongs for lifting, holding, or digging **2** : forked part **3** : a dividing into branches or a place where something branches ~ *vb* **1** : divide into branches **2** : move with a fork — **forked** \'fȯrkt, 'fȯrkəd\ *adj*

**fork·lift** *n* : machine for lifting with steel fingers

**for·lorn** \fər'lȯrn\ *adj* **1** : deserted **2** : wretched — **for·lorn·ly** *adv*

**form** \'fȯrm\ *n* **1** : shape **2** : set way of doing or saying something **3** : document with blanks to be filled in **4** : manner of performing with respect to what is expected **5** : mold **6** : kind or variety **7** : one of the ways in which a word is changed to show difference in use ~ *vb* **1** : give form or shape to **2** : train **3** : develop **4** : constitute — **for·ma·tive** \'fȯrmətiv\ *adj* — **form·less** \-ləs\ *adj*

**for·mal** \'fȯrməl\ *adj* : following established custom ~ *n* : formal social event — **for·mal·i·ty** \fȯr'malətē\ *n* — **for·mal·ize** \'fȯrməˌlīz\ *vb* — **for·mal·ly** *adv*

**form·al·de·hyde** \fȯr'maldəˌhīd\ *n* : colorless pungent gas used as a preservative and disinfectant

**for·mat** \'fȯrˌmat\ *n* : general style or arrangement of something — **format** *vb*

**for·ma·tion** \fȯr'māshən\ *n* **1** : a giving form to something **2** : something formed **3** : arrangement

**for·mer** \'fȯrmər\ *adj* : coming before in time — **for·mer·ly** *adv*

**for·mi·da·ble** \'fȯrmədəbəl, fȯr'mid-\ *adj* **1** : causing fear or dread **2** : very difficult — **for·mi·da·bly** \-blē\ *adv*

**for·mu·la** \'fȯrmyələ\ *n, pl* **-las** *or* **-lae** \-ˌlē, -ˌlī\ **1** : set form of words for ceremonial use **2** : recipe **3** : milk mixture for a baby **4** : group of symbols or figures briefly expressing information **5** : set form or method

**for·mu·late** \-ˌlāt\ *vb* **-lat·ed; -lat·ing** : design, devise — **for·mu·la·tion** \ˌfȯrmyə'lāshən\ *n*

**for·ni·ca·tion** \ˌfȯrnə'kāshən\ *n* : illicit sexual intercourse — **for·ni·cate** \'fȯrnə,kāt\ *vb* — **for·ni·ca·tor** \-,kātər\ *n*

**for·sake** \fər'sāk\ *vb* **-sook** \-'sùk\; **-sak·en** \-'sākən\; **-sak·ing** : renounce completely

**for·swear** \fȯr'swar\ *vb* **-swore; -sworn; -swear·ing** 1 : renounce under oath 2 : perjure

**for·syth·ia** \fər'sithēə\ *n* : shrub grown for its yellow flowers

**fort** \'fȯrt\ *n* 1 : fortified place 2 : permanent army post

**forte** \'fȯrt, 'fȯr,tā\ *n* : something at which a person excels

**forth** \'fȯrth\ *adv* : forward

**forth·com·ing** *adj* 1 : coming or available soon 2 : open and direct

**forth·right** *adj* : direct — **forth·right·ly** *adv* — **forth·right·ness** *n*

**forth·with** *adv* : immediately

**for·ti·fy** \'fȯrtə,fī\ *vb* **-fied; -fy·ing** : make strong — **for·ti·fi·ca·tion** \,fȯrtəfə'kāshən\ *n*

**for·ti·tude** \'fȯrtə,tüd, -,tyüd\ *n* : ability to endure

**fort·night** \'fȯrt,nīt\ *n* : 2 weeks — **fort·night·ly** *adj or adv*

**for·tress** \'fȯrtrəs\ *n* : strong fort

**for·tu·itous** \fȯr'tüətəs, -'tyü-\ *adj* : accidental

**for·tu·nate** \'fȯrchənət\ *adj* 1 : coming by good luck 2 : lucky — **for·tu·nate·ly** *adv*

**for·tune** \'fȯrchən\ *n* 1 : prosperity attained partly through luck 2 : good or bad luck 3 : destiny 4 : wealth

**for·tune–tel·ler** \-,telər\ *n* : one who foretells a person's future — **for·tune–tell·ing** \-,iŋ\ *n or adj*

**for·ty** \'fȯrtē\ *n, pl* **forties** : 4 times 10 — **for·ti·eth** \-ēəth\ *adj or n* — **forty** *adj or pron*

**fo·rum** \'fȯrəm\ *n, pl* **-rums** 1 : Roman marketplace 2 : medium for open discussion

**for·ward** \'fȯrwərd\ *adj* 1 : being near or at or belonging to the front 2 : brash ~ *adv* : toward what is in front ~ *n* : player near the front of his team ~ *vb* 1 : help onward 2 : send on — **for·ward·er** \-wərdər\ *n* — **for·ward·ness** *n*

**for·wards** \'fȯrwərdz\ *adv* : forward

**fos·sil** \'fäsəl\ *n* : preserved trace of an ancient plant or animal — *adj* : being or originating from a fossil — **fos·sil·ize** *vb*

**fos·ter** \'fȯstər\ *adj* : being, having, or relating to substitute parents ~ *vb* : help to grow or develop

**fought** *past of* FIGHT

**foul** \'faùl\ *adj* 1 : offensive 2 : clogged with dirt 3 : abusive 4 : wet and stormy 5 : unfair ~ *n* : a breaking of the rules in a game ~ *adv* : foully ~ *vb* 1 : make or become foul or filthy 2 : tangle — **foul·ly** *adv* — **foul–mouthed** \-'maùthd, -'maùtht\ *adj* — **foul·ness** *n*

**fou·lard** \fù'lärd\ *n* : lightweight silk

**foul–up** *n* : error or state of confusion — **foul up** *vb* : bungle

[1]**found** \'faùnd\ *past of* FIND

[2]**found** *vb* : establish — **found·er** *n*

**foun·da·tion** \faùn'dāshən\ *n* 1 : act of founding 2 : basis for something 3 : endowed institution 4 : supporting structure — **foun·da·tion·al** \-shənəl\ *adj*

**foun·der** \'faùndər\ *vb* : sink

**found·ling** \'faùndliŋ\ *n* : abandoned infant that is found

**found·ry** \'faùndrē\ *n, pl* **-dries** : place where metal is cast

**fount** \'faùnt\ *n* : fountain

**foun·tain** \'faùnt°n\ *n* 1 : spring of water 2 : source 3 : artificial jet of water

**four** \'fȯr\ *n* 1 : one more than 3 2 : 4th in a set or series 3 : something having 4 units — **four** *adj or pron*

**four·fold** *adj* : quadruple — **four·fold** *adv*

**four·score** *adj* : 80

**four·some** \'fȯrsəm\ *n* : group of 4

**four·teen** \fȯr'tēn\ *n* : one more than 13 — **fourteen** *adj or pron* — **four·teenth** \-'tēnth\ *adj or n*

**fourth** \'fȯrth\ *n* 1 : one that is 4th 2 : one of 4 equal parts of something — **fourth** *adj or adv*

**fowl** \'faùl\ *n, pl* **fowl** *or* **fowls** 1 : bird 2 : chicken

**fox** \'fäks\ *n, pl* **fox·es** 1 : small mammal related to wolves 2 : clever person ~ *vb* : trick — **foxy** \'fäksē\ *adj*

**fox·glove** *n* : flowering plant that provides digitalis

**fox·hole** \'fäks,hōl\ *n* : pit for protection against enemy fire

**foy·er** \'fȯiər, 'fȯi,yā\ *n* : entrance hallway

**fra·cas** \'frākəs, 'frak-\ *n, pl* **-cas·es** \-əsəz\ : brawl

**frac·tion** \'frakshən\ *n* 1 : number indicating one or more equal parts of a whole **2** : portion — **frac·tion·al** \-shənəl\ adj — **frac·tion·al·ly** adv

**frac·tious** \'frakshəs\ adj : hard to control

**frac·ture** \'frakchər\ n : a breaking of something — **fracture** vb

**frag·ile** \'frajəl, -ˌīl\ adj : easily broken — **fra·gil·i·ty** \frə'jilətē\ n

**frag·ment** \'fragmənt\ n : part broken off ~ \-ˌment\ vb : break into parts — **frag·men·tary** \'fragmənˌterē\ adj — **frag·men·ta·tion** \ˌfragmən'tāshən, -ˌmen-\ n

**fra·grant** \'frāgrənt\ adj : sweet-smelling — **fra·grance** \-grəns\ n — **fra·grant·ly** adv

**frail** \'frāl\ adj : weak or delicate — **frail·ty** \-tē\ n

**frame** \'frām\ vb **framed; fram·ing** **1** : plan **2** : formulate **3** : construct or arrange **4** : enclose in a frame **5** : make appear guilty ~ n **1** : makeup of the body **2** : supporting or enclosing structure **3** : state or disposition (as of mind) — **frame·work** n

**franc** \'fraŋk\ n : monetary unit (as of France)

**fran·chise** \'franˌchīz\ n **1** : special privilege **2** : the right to vote — **fran·chi·see** \ˌfranˌchī'zē, -chə-\ n

**fran·gi·ble** \'franjəbəl\ adj : breakable — **fran·gi·bil·i·ty** \ˌfranjə'bilətē\ n

¹**frank** \'fraŋk\ adj : direct and sincere — **frank·ly** adv — **frank·ness** n

²**frank** vb : mark (mail) with a sign showing it can be mailed free ~ n : sign on franked mail

**frank·furt·er** \'fraŋkfərtər, -ˌfərt-\, **frank·furt** \-fərt\ n : cooked sausage

**frank·in·cense** \'fraŋkən̩sens\ n : incense resin

**fran·tic** \'frantik\ adj : wildly excited — **fran·ti·cal·ly** \-iklē\ adv

**fra·ter·nal** \frə'tərnᵊl\ adj **1** : brotherly **2** : of a fraternity — **fra·ter·nal·ly** adv

**fra·ter·ni·ty** \frə'tərnətē\ n, pl **-ties** : men's student social group

**frat·er·nize** \'fratər̩nīz\ vb **-nized; -niz·ing 1** : mingle as friends **2** : associate with members of a hostile group — **frat·er·ni·za·tion** \ˌfratərnə'zāshən\ n

**frat·ri·cide** \'fratrəˌsīd\ n : killing of a sibling — **frat·ri·cid·al** \ˌfratrə'sīdᵊl\ adj

**fraud** \'frȯd\ n : trickery — **fraud·u·lent** \'frȯjələnt\ adj — **fraud·u·lent·ly** adv

**fraught** \'frȯt\ adj : full of or accompanied by something specified

¹**fray** \'frā\ n : fight

²**fray** vb **1** : wear by rubbing **2** : separate the threads of **3** : irritate

**fraz·zle** \'frazəl\ vb **-zled; -zling** : wear out ~ n : exhaustion

**freak** \'frēk\ n **1** : something abnormal or unusual **2** : enthusiast — **freak·ish** adj — **freak out** vb **1** : experience nightmarish hallucinations from drugs **2** : distress or become distressed

**freck·le** \'frekəl\ n : brown spot on the skin — **freckle** vb

**free** \'frē\ adj **fre·er; fre·est 1** : having liberty or independence **2** : not taxed **3** : given without charge **4** : voluntary **5** : not in use **6** : not fastened ~ adv : without charge ~ vb **freed; free·ing** : set free — **free** adv — **free·born** adj — **free·dom** \'frēdəm\ n — **free·ly** adv

**free·boo·ter** \-ˌbütər\ n : pirate

**free–for–all** n : fight with no rules

**free·load** vb : live off another's generosity — **free·load·er** n

**free·stand·ing** adj : standing without support

**free·way** \'frēˌwā\ n : expressway

**free will** n : independent power to choose — **free–will** adj

**freeze** \'frēz\ vb **froze** \'frōz\; **fro·zen** \'frōzᵊn\; **freez·ing 1** : harden into ice **2** : become chilled **3** : damage by frost **4** : stick fast **5** : become motionless **6** : fix at one stage or level ~ n **1** : very cold weather **2** : state of being frozen — **freez·er** n

**freeze–dry** vb : preserve by freezing then drying — **freeze–dried** adj

**freight** \'frāt\ n **1** : carrying of goods or payment for this **2** : shipped goods ~ vb : load or ship goods — **freight·er** n

**french fry** vb : fry in deep fat — **french fry** n

**fre·net·ic** \fri'netik\ adj : frantic — **fre·net·i·cal·ly** \-iklē\ adv

**fren·zy** \'frenzē\ n, pl **-zies** : violent agitation — **fren·zied** \-zēd\ adj

**fre·quen·cy** \'frēkwənsē\ n, pl **-cies 1** : frequent or regular occurrence **2** : number of cycles or sound waves per second

**fre·quent** \'frēkwənt\ adj : happening

often ～ \frē'kwent, 'frēkwənt\ vb
: go to habitually — **fre•quent•er** n
— **fre•quent•ly** adv

**fres•co** \'freskō\ n, pl **-coes** : painting
on fresh plaster

**fresh** \'fresh\ adj **1** : not salt **2** : pure
**3** : not preserved **4** : not stale **5** : like
new **6** : insolent — **fres•hen** \-ən\
vb — **fresh•ly** adv — **fresh•ness** n

**fresh•et** \-ət\ n : overflowing stream

**fresh•man** \-mən\ n : first-year student

**fresh•wa•ter** n : water that is not salty

**fret** \'fret\ vb **-tt-** **1** : worry or become
irritated **2** : fray **3** : agitate ～ n **1**
: worn spot **2** : irritation — **fret•ful**
\-fəl\ adj — **fret•ful•ly** adv

**fri•a•ble** \'frīəbəl\ adj : easily pulverized

**fri•ar** \'frīər\ n : member of a religious
order

**fri•ary** \-ē\ n, pl **-ar•ies** : monastery of
friars

**fric•as•see** \'frikə‚sē, ‚frikə'-\ n
: meat stewed in a gravy ～ vb **-seed;**
**-see•ing** : stew in gravy

**fric•tion** \'frikshən\ n **1** : a rubbing
between 2 surfaces **2** : clash of opinions — **fric•tion•al** adj

**Fri•day** \'frīdā\ n : 6th day of the week

**friend** \'frend\ n : person one likes —
**friend•less** \-ləs\ adj — **friend•li-**
**ness** \-lēnəs\ n — **friend•ly** adj —
**friend•ship** \-‚ship\ n

**frieze** \'frēz\ n : ornamental band
around a room

**frig•ate** \'frigət\ n : warship smaller
than a destroyer

**fright** \'frīt\ n : sudden fear — **frigh•ten**
\-ᵊn\ vb — **fright•ful** \-fəl\ adj —
**fright•ful•ly** adv — **fright•ful•ness** n

**frig•id** \'frijəd\ adj : intensely cold —
**fri•gid•i•ty** \frij'idətē\ n

**frill** \'fril\ n **1** : ruffle **2** : pleasing but
nonessential addition — **frilly** adj

**fringe** \'frinj\ n **1** : ornamental border
of short hanging threads or strips **2**
: edge — **fringe** vb

**frisk** \'frisk\ vb **1** : leap about **2**
: search (a person) esp. for weapons

**frisky** \'friskē\ adj **frisk•i•er; -est**
: playful — **frisk•i•ly** adv — **frisk•i-**
**ness** n

¹**frit•ter** \'fritər\ n : fried batter containing fruit or meat

²**fritter** vb : waste little by little

**friv•o•lous** \'frivələs\ adj : not important or serious — **fri•vol•i•ty** \friv-
'älətē\ n — **friv•o•lous•ly** adv

**frizz** \'friz\ vb : curl tightly — **frizz** n —
**frizzy** adj

**fro** \'frō\ adv : away

**frock** \'fräk\ n **1** : loose outer garment
**2** : dress

**frog** \'frȯg, 'fräg\ n **1** : leaping amphibian **2** : hoarseness **3** : ornamental braid fastener **4** : small holder for
flowers

**frog•man** \-‚man, -mən\ n : underwater swimmer

**frol•ic** \'frälik\ vb **-icked; -ick•ing**
: romp ～ n : fun — **frol•ic•some**
\-səm\ adj

**from** \'frəm, 'främ\ prep — used to
show a starting point

**frond** \'fränd\ n : fern or palm leaf

**front** \'frənt\ n **1** : face **2** : behavior **3**
: main side of a building **4** : forward
part **5** : boundary between air masses
～ vb **1** : have the main side adjacent
to something **2** : serve as a front —
**fron•tal** \-ᵊl\ adj

**front•age** \'frəntij\ n : length of
boundary line on a street

**fron•tier** \‚frən'tir\ n : outer edge of
settled territory — **fron•tiers•man**
\-'tirzmən\ n

**fron•tis•piece** \'frəntə‚spēs\ n : illustration facing a title page

**frost** \'frȯst\ n **1** : freezing temperature
**2** : ice crystals on a surface ～ vb **1**
: cover with frost **2** : put icing on (a
cake) — **frosty** adj

**frost•bite** \-‚bīt\ n : partial freezing of
part of the body — **frost•bit•ten**
\-‚bitᵊn\ adj

**frost•ing** n : icing

**froth** \'frȯth\ n, pl **froths** \'frȯths,
'frȯthz\ : bubbles on a liquid —
**frothy** adj

**fro•ward** \'frōwərd\ adj : willful

**frown** \'fraùn\ vb or n : scowl

**frow•sy, frow•zy** \'fraùzē\ adj **-si•er** or
**-zi•er; -est** : untidy

**froze** past of FREEZE

**frozen** past part of FREEZE

**fru•gal** \'frügəl\ adj : thrifty — **fru•gal-**
**i•ty** \frü'galətē\ n — **fru•gal•ly** adv

**fruit** \'früt\ n **1** : usu. edible and sweet
part of a seed plant **2** : result ～ vb
: bear fruit — **fruit•cake** n — **fruit•ed**
\-əd\ adj — **fruit•ful** adj — **fruit•ful-**
**ness** n — **fruit•less** adj — **fruit-**
**less•ly** adv — **fruity** adj

**fru•ition** \frü'ishən\ n : completion

**frumpy** \'frəmpē\ adj **frump•i•er; -est**
: dowdy

**frus•trate** \'frəs,trāt\ *vb* **-trat•ed; -trat•ing** 1 : block 2 : cause to fail — **frus•trat•ing•ly** *adv* — **frus•tra•tion** \,frəs'trāshən\ *n*

¹**fry** \'frī\ *vb* **fried; fry•ing** 1 : cook esp. with fat or oil 2 : be cooked by frying ∼ *n, pl* **fries** 1 : something fried 2 : social gathering with fried food

²**fry** *n, pl* **fry** : recently hatched fish

**fud•dle** \'fəd°l\ *vb* **-dled; -dling** : muddle

**fud•dy–dud•dy** \'fədē,dədē\ *n, pl* **-dies** : one who is old-fashioned or unimaginative

**fudge** \'fəj\ *vb* **fudged; fudg•ing** : cheat or exaggerate ∼ *n* : creamy candy

**fu•el** \'fyüəl\ *n* : material burned to produce heat or power ∼ *vb* **-eled** *or* **-elled; -el•ing** *or* **-el•ling** : provide with or take in fuel

**fu•gi•tive** \'fyüjətiv\ *adj* 1 : running away or trying to escape 2 : not lasting — **fugitive** *n*

**-ful** \'fəl\ *adj suffix* 1 : full of 2 : having the qualities of 3 : -able ∼ *n suffix* : quantity that fills

**ful•crum** \'fulkrəm, 'fəl-\ *n, pl* **-crums** *or* **-cra** \-krə\ : support on which a lever turns

**ful•fill, ful•fil** \fu̇l'fil\ *vb* **-filled; -fill•ing** 1 : perform 2 : satisfy — **ful•fill•ment** *n*

¹**full** \'fu̇l\ *adj* 1 : filled 2 : complete 3 : rounded 4 : having an abundance of something ∼ *adv* : entirely ∼ *n* : utmost degree — **full•ness** *n* — **ful•ly** *adv*

²**full** *vb* : shrink and thicken woolen cloth — **full•er** *n*

**full–fledged** \'fu̇l'flejd\ *adj* : fully developed

**ful•some** \'fu̇lsəm\ *adj* : copious verging on excessive

**fum•ble** \'fəmbəl\ *vb* **-bled; -bling** : fail to hold something properly — **fumble** *n*

**fume** \'fyüm\ *n* : irritating gas ∼ *vb* **fumed; fum•ing** 1 : give off fumes 2 : show annoyance

**fu•mi•gate** \'fyümə,gāt\ *vb* **-gat•ed; -gat•ing** : treat with pest-killing fumes — **fu•mi•gant** \'fyümigənt\ *n* — **fu•mi•ga•tion** \,fyümə'gāshən\ *n*

**fun** \'fən\ *n* 1 : something providing amusement or enjoyment 2 : enjoyment ∼ *adj* : full of fun

**func•tion** \'fəŋkshən\ *n* 1 : special purpose 2 : formal ceremony or social affair ∼ *vb* : have or carry on a function — **func•tion•al** \-shənəl\ *adj* — **func•tion•al•ly** *adv*

**func•tion•ary** \-shə,nerē\ *n, pl* **-ar•ies** : official

**fund** \'fənd\ *n* 1 : store 2 : sum of money intended for a special purpose 3 *pl* : available money ∼ *vb* : provide funds for

**fun•da•men•tal** \,fəndə'ment°l\ *adj* 1 : basic 2 : of central importance or necessity — **fundamental** *n* — **fun•da•men•tal•ly** *adv*

**fu•ner•al** \'fyünərəl\ *n* : ceremony for a dead person — **funeral** *adj* — **fu•ne•re•al** \fyü'nirēəl\ *adj*

**fun•gi•cide** \'fənjə,sīd, 'fəŋgə-\ *n* : agent that kills fungi — **fun•gi•cid•al** \,fənjə'sīd°l, ,fəŋgə-\ *adj*

**fun•gus** \'fəŋgəs\ *n, pl* **fun•gi** \'fən,jī, 'fəŋ,gī\ : lower plant that lacks chlorophyll — **fun•gal** \'fəŋgəl\ *adj* — **fun•gous** \-gəs\ *adj*

**funk** \'fəŋk\ *n* : state of depression

**funky** \'fəŋkē\ *adj* **funk•i•er; -est** : unconventional and unsophisticated

**fun•nel** \'fən°l\ *n* 1 : cone-shaped utensil with a tube for directing the flow of a liquid 2 : ship's smokestack ∼ *vb* **-neled; -nel•ing** : move to a central point or into a central channel

**fun•nies** \'fənēz\ *n pl* : section of comic strips

**fun•ny** \'fənē\ *adj* **-ni•er; -est** 1 : amusing 2 : strange

**fur** \'fər\ *n* 1 : hairy coat of a mammal 2 : article of clothing made with fur — **fur** *adj* — **furred** \'fərd\ *adj* — **fur•ry** \-ē\ *adj*

**fur•bish** \'fərbish\ *vb* : make lustrous or new looking

**fu•ri•ous** \'fyu̇rēəs\ *adj* : fierce or angry — **fu•ri•ous•ly** *adv*

**fur•long** \'fər,lȯŋ\ *n* : a unit of distance equal to 220 yards

**fur•lough** \'fərlō\ *n* : authorized absence from duty — **furlough** *vb*

**fur•nace** \'fərnəs\ *n* : enclosed structure in which heat is produced

**fur•nish** \'fərnish\ *vb* 1 : provide with what is needed 2 : make available for use

**fur•nish•ings** \-iŋs\ *n pl* 1 : articles or accessories of dress 2 : furniture

**fur•ni•ture** \'fərnichər\ *n* : movable articles for a room

**fu·ror** \\'fyur̯‚òr\ *n* 1 : anger 2 : sensational craze

**fur·ri·er** \\'fərēər\ *n* : dealer in furs

**fur·row** \\'fərō\ *n* 1 : trench made by a plow 2 : wrinkle or groove — **furrow** *vb*

**fur·ther** \\'fərthər\ *adv* 1 : at or to a more advanced point 2 : more ~ *adj* : additional ~ *vb* : promote — **fur·ther·ance** \-ərəns\ *n*

**fur·ther·more** \\'fərthər‚mōr\ *adv* : in addition

**fur·ther·most** \-‚mōst\ *adj* : most distant

**fur·thest** \\'fərthəst\ *adv or adj* : farthest

**fur·tive** \\'fərtiv\ *adj* : slyly or secretly done — **fur·tive·ly** *adv* — **fur·tive·ness** *n*

**fu·ry** \\'fyurē\ *n, pl* **-ries** 1 : intense rage 2 : violence

**¹fuse** \\'fyüz\ *n* 1 : cord lighted to transmit fire to an explosive 2 *usu* **fuze** : device for exploding a charge ~ *or* **fuze** *vb* **fused** *or* **fuzed; fus·ing** *or* **fuz·ing** : equip with a fuse

**²fuse** *vb* **fused; fus·ing** 1 : melt and run together 2 : unite ~ *n* : electrical safety device — **fus·ible** *adj*

**fu·se·lage** \\'fyüsə‚läzh, -zə-\ *n* : main body of an aircraft

**fu·sil·lade** \\'fyüsə‚läd, -‚läd, ‚fyüsə'-, -zə-\ *n* : volley of fire

**fu·sion** \\'fyüzhən\ *n* 1 : process of merging by melting 2 : union of atomic nuclei

**fuss** \\'fəs\ *n* 1 : needless bustle or excitement 2 : show of attention 3 : objection or protest ~ *vb* : make a fuss

**fuss·bud·get** \-‚bəjət\ *n* : one who fusses or is fussy about trifles

**fussy** \\'fəsē\ *adj* **fuss·i·er; -est** 1 : irritable 2 : paying very close attention to details — **fuss·i·ly** *adv* — **fuss·i·ness** *n*

**fu·tile** \\'fyüt²l, 'fyü‚tīl\ *adj* : useless or vain — **fu·til·i·ty** \fyü'tilətē\ *n*

**fu·ton** \\'fü‚tän\ *n* : a cotton-filled mattress

**fu·ture** \\'fyüchər\ *adj* : coming after the present ~ *n* 1 : time yet to come 2 : what will happen — **fu·tur·is·tic** \‚fyüchə'ristik\ *adj*

**fuze** *var of* FUSE

**fuzz** \\'fəz\ *n* : fine particles or fluff

**fuzzy** \-ē\ *adj* **fuzz·i·er; -est** 1 : covered with or like fuzz 2 : indistinct — **fuzz·i·ness** *n*

**-fy** \‚fī\ *vb suffix* : make — **-fi·er** \‚fīər\ *n suffix*

# G

**g** \\'jē\ *n, pl* **g's** *or* **gs** \\'jēz\ 1 : 7th letter of the alphabet 2 : unit of gravitational force

**gab** \\'gab\ *vb* **-bb-** : chatter — **gab** *n* — **gab·by** \\'gabē\ *adj*

**gab·ar·dine** \\'gabər‚dēn\ *n* : durable twilled fabric

**ga·ble** \\'gābəl\ *n* : triangular part of the end of a building — **ga·bled** \-bəld\ *adj*

**gad** \\'gad\ *vb* **-dd-** : roam about

**gad·fly** *n* : persistently critical person

**gad·get** \\'gajət\ *n* : device — **gad·get·ry** \\'gajətrē\ *n*

**gaff** \\'gaf\ *n* : metal hook for lifting fish — **gaff** *vb*

**gaffe** \\'gaf\ *n* : social blunder

**gag** \\'gag\ *vb* **-gg-** 1 : prevent from speaking or crying out by stopping up the mouth 2 : retch or cause to retch

~ *n* 1 : something that stops up the mouth 2 : laugh-provoking remark or act

**gage** *var of* GAUGE

**gag·gle** \\'gagəl\ *n* : flock of geese

**gai·ety** \\'gāətē\ *n, pl* **-eties** : high spirits

**gai·ly** \\'gālē\ *adv* : in a gay manner

**gain** \\'gān\ *n* 1 : profit 2 : obtaining of profit or possessions 3 : increase ~ *vb* 1 : get possession of 2 : win 3 : arrive at 4 : increase or increase in 5 : profit — **gain·er** *n* — **gain·ful** *adj* — **gain·ful·ly** *adv*

**gain·say** \gān'sā\ *vb* **-said** \-'sād, -'sed\; **-say·ing; -says** \-'sāz, -'sez\ : deny or dispute — **gain·say·er** *n*

**gait** \\'gāt\ *n* : manner of walking or running — **gait·ed** *adj*

**gal** \\'gal\ *n* : girl

**ga·la** \'gālə, 'galə, 'gälə\ *n* : festive celebration — **gala** *adj*

**gal·axy** \'galəksē\ *n, pl* **-ax·ies** : very large group of stars — **ga·lac·tic** \gə'laktik\ *adj*

**gale** \'gāl\ *n* **1** : strong wind **2** : outburst

**¹gall** \'gȯl\ *n* **1** : bile **2** : insolence

**²gall** *n* **1** : skin sore caused by chafing **2** : swelling of plant tissue caused by parasites ~ *vb* **1** : chafe **2** : irritate or vex

**gal·lant** \gə'lant, -'länt; 'galənt\ *n* : man very attentive to women ~ \'galənt; gə'lant, -'länt\ *adj* **1** : splendid **2** : brave **3** : polite and attentive to women — **gal·lant·ly** *adv* — **gal·lant·ry** \'galəntrē\ *n*

**gall·blad·der** *n* : pouch attached to the liver in which bile is stored

**gal·le·on** \'galyən\ *n* : large sailing ship formerly used esp. by the Spanish

**gal·lery** \'galərē\ *n, pl* **-ler·ies** **1** : outdoor balcony **2** : long narrow passage or hall **3** : room or building for exhibiting art **4** : spectators — **gal·ler·ied** \-rēd\ *adj*

**gal·ley** \'galē\ *n, pl* **-leys** **1** : old ship propelled esp. by oars **2** : kitchen of a ship or airplane

**gal·li·um** \'galēəm\ *n* : bluish white metallic chemical element

**gal·li·vant** \'galə͵vant\ *vb* : travel or roam about for pleasure

**gal·lon** \'galən\ *n* : unit of liquid measure equal to 4 quarts

**gal·lop** \'galəp\ *n* : fast 3-beat gait of a horse — **gallop** *vb* — **gal·lop·er** *n*

**gal·lows** \'galōz\ *n, pl* **-lows** *or* **-lows·es** : upright frame for hanging criminals

**gall·stone** *n* : abnormal concretion in the gallbladder or bile passages

**ga·lore** \gə'lōr\ *adj* : in abundance

**ga·losh** \gə'läsh\ *n* : overshoe — usu. pl.

**gal·va·nize** \'galvə͵nīz\ *vb* **-nized; -niz·ing** **1** : shock into action **2** : coat (iron or steel) with zinc — **gal·va·ni·za·tion** \͵galvənə'zāshən\ *n* — **gal·va·niz·er** *n*

**gam·bit** \'gambit\ *n* **1** : opening tactic in chess **2** : stratagem

**gam·ble** \'gambəl\ *vb* **-bled; -bling** **1** : play a game for stakes **2** : bet **3** : take a chance ~ *n* : risky undertaking — **gam·bler** \-blər\ *n*

**gam·bol** \'gambəl\ *vb* **-boled** *or* **-bolled; -bol·ing** *or* **-bol·ling** : skip about in play — **gambol** *n*

**game** \'gām\ *n* **1** : playing activity **2** : competition according to rules **3** : animals hunted for sport or food ~ *vb* **gamed; gam·ing** : gamble ~ *adj* **1** : plucky **2** : lame — **game·ly** *adv* — **game·ness** *n*

**game·cock** *n* : fighting cock

**game·keep·er** *n* : person in charge of game animals or birds

**gam·ete** \gə'mēt, 'gam͵ēt\ *n* : mature germ cell — **ga·met·ic** \gə'metik\ *adj*

**ga·mine** \ga'mēn\ *n* : charming tomboy

**gam·ut** \'gamət\ *n* : entire range or series

**gamy** *or* **gam·ey** \'gāmē\ *adj* **gam·i·er; -est** : having the flavor of game esp. when slightly tainted — **gam·i·ness** *n*

**¹gan·der** \'gandər\ *n* : male goose

**²gander** *n* : glance

**gang** \'gaŋ\ *n* **1** : group of persons working together **2** : group of criminals ~ *vb* : attack in a gang — with *up*

**gan·gling** \'gaŋgliŋ\ *adj* : lanky

**gan·gli·on** \'gaŋglēən\ *n, pl* **-glia** \-glēə\ : mass of nerve cells

**gang·plank** *n* : platform used in boarding or leaving a ship

**gan·grene** \'gaŋ͵grēn, gaŋ'-, 'gan-, gan-\ *n* : local death of body tissue — **gangrene** *vb* — **gan·gre·nous** \'gaŋgrənəs\ *adj*

**gang·ster** \'gaŋstər\ *n* : member of criminal gang

**gang·way** \-͵wā\ *n* : passage in or out

**gan·net** \'ganət\ *n* : large fish-eating marine bird

**gan·try** \'gantrē\ *n, pl* **-tries** : frame structure supported over or around something

**gap** \'gap\ *n* **1** : break in a barrier **2** : mountain pass **3** : empty space

**gape** \'gāp\ *vb* **gaped; gap·ing** **1** : open widely **2** : stare with mouth open — **gape** *n*

**ga·rage** \gə'räzh, -'räj\ *n* : shelter or repair shop for automobiles ~ *vb* **-raged; -rag·ing** : put or keep in a garage

**garb** \'gärb\ *n* : clothing ~ *vb* : dress

**gar·bage** \'gärbij\ *n* **1** : food waste **2** : trash — **gar·bage·man** *n*

**gar·ble** \'gärbəl\ vb **-bled; -bling** : distort the meaning of

**gar·den** \'gärd°n\ n **1** : plot for growing fruits, flowers, or vegetables **2** : public recreation area ~ vb : work in a garden — **gar·den·er** \'gärd°nər\ n

**gar·de·nia** \gär'dēnyə\ n : tree or shrub with fragrant white or yellow flowers or the flower

**gar·gan·tuan** \gär'ganchəwən\ adj : having tremendous size or volume

**gar·gle** \'gärgəl\ vb **-gled; -gling** : rinse the throat with liquid — **gargle** n

**gar·goyle** \'gär.ɡȯil\ n : waterspout in the form of a grotesque human or animal

**gar·ish** \'garish\ adj : offensively bright or gaudy

**gar·land** \'gärlənd\ n : wreath ~ vb : form into or deck with a garland

**gar·lic** \'gärlik\ n : herb with pungent bulbs used in cooking — **gar·licky** \-likē\ adj

**gar·ment** \'gärmənt\ n : article of clothing

**gar·ner** \'gärnər\ vb : acquire by effort

**gar·net** \'gärnət\ n : deep red mineral

**gar·nish** \'gärnish\ vb : add decoration to (as food) — **garnish** n

**gar·nish·ee** \ˌgärnə'shē\ vb **-eed; -ee·ing** : take (as a debtor's wages) by legal authority

**gar·nish·ment** \'gärnishmənt\ n : attachment of property to satisfy a creditor

**gar·ret** \'garət\ n : attic

**gar·ri·son** \'garəsən\ n : military post or the troops stationed there — **garrison** vb

**gar·ru·lous** \'garələs\ adj : talkative — **gar·ru·li·ty** \gə'rülətē\ n — **gar·ru·lous·ly** adv — **gar·ru·lous·ness** n

**gar·ter** \'gärtər\ n : band to hold up a stocking or sock

**gas** \'gas\ n, pl **gas·es 1** : fluid (as hydrogen or air) that tends to expand indefinitely **2** : gasoline ~ vb **gassed; gas·sing 1** : treat with gas **2** : fill with gasoline — **gas·eous** \'gasēəs, 'gashəs\ adj

**gash** \'gash\ n : deep long cut — **gash** vb

**gas·ket** \'gaskət\ n : material or a part used to seal a joint

**gas·light** n : light of burning illuminating gas

**gas·o·line** \'gasəˌlēn, ˌgasə'-\ n : flammable liquid from petroleum

**gasp** \'gasp\ vb **1** : catch the breath audibly **2** : breathe laboriously — **gasp** n

**gas·tric** \'gastrik\ adj : relating to or located near the stomach

**gas·tron·o·my** \gas'tränəmē\ n : art of good eating — **gas·tro·nom·ic** \ˌgastrə'nämik\ adj

**gate** \'gāt\ n : an opening for passage in a wall or fence — **gate·keep·er** n — **gate·post** n

**gate·way** n : way in or out

**gath·er** \'gathər\ vb **1** : bring or come together **2** : harvest **3** : pick up little by little **4** : deduce — **gath·er·er** n — **gath·er·ing** n

**gauche** \'gōsh\ adj : crude or tactless

**gaudy** \'gȯdē\ adj **gaud·i·er; -est** : tastelessly showy — **gaud·i·ly** \'gȯd°lē\ adv — **gaud·i·ness** n

**gauge** \'gāj\ n : instrument for measuring ~ vb **gauged; gaug·ing** : measure

**gaunt** \'gȯnt\ adj : thin or emaciated — **gaunt·ness** n

**¹gaunt·let** \-lət\ n **1** : protective glove **2** : challenge to combat

**²gauntlet** n : ordeal

**gauze** \'gȯz\ n : thin often transparent fabric — **gauzy** adj

**gave** past of GIVE

**gav·el** \'gavəl\ n : mallet of a presiding officer, auctioneer, or judge

**gawk** \'gȯk\ vb : stare stupidly

**gawky** \-ē\ adj **gawk·i·er; -est** : clumsy

**gay** \'gā\ adj **1** : merry **2** : bright and lively **3** : homosexual — **gay** n

**gaze** \'gāz\ vb **gazed; gaz·ing** : fix the eyes in a steady intent look — **gaze** n — **gaz·er** n

**ga·zelle** \gə'zel\ n : small swift antelope

**ga·zette** \-'zet\ n : newspaper

**gaz·et·teer** \ˌgazə'tir\ n : geographical dictionary

**gear** \'gir\ n **1** : clothing **2** : equipment **3** : toothed wheel — **gear** vb

**gear·shift** n : mechanism by which automobile gears are shifted

**geek** \'gēk\ n : socially inept person

**geese** pl of GOOSE

**gei·sha** \'gāshə, 'gē-\ n, pl **-sha** or **-shas** : Japanese girl or woman trained to entertain men

**gel·a·tin** \'jelət°n\ n : sticky substance

obtained from animal tissues by boiling — **ge·lat·i·nous** \jə'lat³nəs\ adj

**geld** \'geld\ vb : castrate

**geld·ing** \-iŋ\ n : castrated horse

**gem** \'jem\ n : cut and polished valuable stone — **gem·stone** n

**gen·der** \'jendər\ n **1** : sex **2** : division of a class of words (as nouns) that determines agreement of other words

**gene** \'jēn\ n : segment of DNA that controls inheritance of a trait

**ge·ne·al·o·gy** \jēnē'äləjē, jen-, -'al-\ n, pl -**gies** : study of family pedigrees — **ge·ne·a·log·i·cal** \-ēə'läjikəl\ adj — **ge·ne·a·log·i·cal·ly** adv — **ge·ne·al·o·gist** \-ē'äləjist, -'al-\ n

**genera** pl of GENUS

**gen·er·al** \'jenrəl, 'jenə-\ adj **1** : relating to the whole **2** : applicable to all of a group **3** : common or widespread ~ n **1** : something that involves or is applicable to the whole **2** : commissioned officer in the army, air force, or marine corps ranking above a lieutenant general — **gen·er·al·ly** adv — **in general** : for the most part

**gen·er·al·i·ty** \jenə'ralətē\ n, pl -**ties** : general statement

**gen·er·al·ize** \'jenrə,līz, 'jenə-\ vb -**ized; -iz·ing** : reach a general conclusion esp. on the basis of particular instances — **gen·er·al·iza·tion** \jenrələ'zāshən, jenə-\ n

**general of the air force** : commissioned officer of the highest rank in the air force

**general of the army** : commissioned officer of the highest rank in the army

**gen·er·ate** \'jenə,rāt\ vb -**at·ed; -at·ing** : create or produce

**gen·er·a·tion** \jenə'rāshən\ n **1** : living beings constituting a single step in a line of descent **2** : production — **gen·er·a·tive** \'jenə,rātiv, -rət-\ adj

**gen·er·a·tor** \'jenə,rātər\ n **1** : one that generates **2** : machine that turns mechanical into electrical energy

**ge·ner·ic** \jə'nerik\ adj **1** : general **2** : not protected by a trademark **3** : relating to a genus — **generic** n

**gen·er·ous** \'jenərəs\ adj : freely giving or sharing — **gen·er·os·i·ty** \jenə'räsətē\ n — **gen·er·ous·ly** adv — **gen·er·ous·ness** n

**ge·net·ics** \jə'netiks\ n : biology dealing with heredity and variation — **ge-**

**net·ic** \-ik\ adj — **ge·net·i·cal·ly** adv — **ge·net·i·cist** \-'netəsist\ n

**ge·nial** \'jēnēəl\ adj : cheerful — **ge·nial·i·ty** \jēnē'alətē\ n — **ge·nial·ly** adv

**ge·nie** \'jēnē\ n : supernatural spirit that often takes human form

**gen·i·tal** \'jenət³l\ adj : concerned with reproduction — **gen·i·tal·ly** \-təlē\ adv

**gen·i·ta·lia** \jenə'tālyə\ n pl : external genital organs

**gen·i·tals** \'jenət³lz\ n pl : genitalia

**ge·nius** \'jēnyəs\ n **1** : single strongly marked capacity **2** : extraordinary intellectual power or a person having such power

**geno·cide** \'jenə,sīd\ n : systematic destruction of a racial or cultural group

**genre** \'zhänrə, 'zhä**ⁿ**rə\ n : category esp. of literary composition

**gen·teel** \jen'tēl\ adj : polite or refined

**gen·tile** \'jen,tīl\ n : person who is not Jewish — **gentile** adj

**gen·til·i·ty** \jen'tilətē\ n, pl -**ties 1** : good birth and family **2** : good manners

**gen·tle** \'jent³l\ adj -**tler; -tlest 1** : of a family of high social station **2** : not harsh, stern, or violent **3** : soft or delicate ~ vb -**tled; -tling** : make gentle — **gen·tle·ness** n — **gen·tly** adv

**gen·tle·man** \-mən\ n : man of good family or manners — **gen·tle·man·ly** adv

**gen·tle·wom·an** \-,wùmən\ n : woman of good family or breeding

**gen·try** \'jentrē\ n, pl -**tries** : people of good birth or breeding

**gen·u·flect** \'jenyə,flekt\ vb : bend the knee in worship — **gen·u·flec·tion** \jenyə'flekshən\ n

**gen·u·ine** \'jenyəwən\ adj : being the same in fact as in appearance — **gen·u·ine·ly** adv — **gen·u·ine·ness** n

**ge·nus** \'jēnəs\ n, pl **gen·era** \'jenərə\ : category of biological classification

**ge·ode** \'jē,ōd\ n : stone having a mineral-lined cavity

**geo·de·sic** \jēə'desik, -'dēs-\ adj : made of a framework of linked polygons

**ge·og·ra·phy** \jē'ägrəfē\ n **1** : study of the earth and its climate, products, and inhabitants **2** : natural features of a region — **ge·og·ra·pher** \-fər\ n — **geo·graph·ic** \jēə-

'grafik\, **geo•graph•i•cal** \-ikəl\ *adj*
— **geo•graph•i•cal•ly** *adv*

**ge•ol•o•gy** \jē'äləjē\ *n* : study of the history of the earth and its life esp. as recorded in rocks — **geo•log•ic** \ˌjēə'läjik\, **geo•log•i•cal** \-ikəl\ — **geo•log•i•cal•ly** *adv* — **ge•ol•o•gist** \jē'äləjist\ *n*

**ge•om•e•try** \jē'ämətrē\ *n, pl* **-tries** : mathematics of the relations, properties, and measurements of solids, surfaces, lines, and angles — **geo•met•ric** \ˌjēə'metrik\, **geo•met•ri•cal** \-rikəl\ *adj*

**geo•ther•mal** \ˌjēo'thərməl\ *adj* : relating to or derived from the heat of the earth's interior

**ge•ra•ni•um** \jə'rānēəm\ *n* : garden plant with clusters of white, pink, or scarlet flowers

**ger•bil** \'jərbəl\ *n* : burrowing desert rodent

**ge•ri•at•ric** \jerē'atrik\ *adj* 1 : relating to aging or the aged 2 : old

**ge•ri•at•rics** \-triks\ *n* : medicine dealing with the aged and aging

**germ** \'jərm\ *n* 1 : microorganism 2 : source or rudiment

**ger•mane** \jər'mān\ *adj* : relevant

**ger•ma•ni•um** \-'mānēəm\ *n* : grayish white hard chemical element

**ger•mi•cide** \'jərmə,sīd\ *n* : agent that destroys germs — **ger•mi•cid•al** \ˌjərmə'sīdᵊl\ *adj*

**ger•mi•nate** \'jərmə,nāt\ *vb* **-nat•ed; -nat•ing** : begin to develop — **ger•mi•na•tion** \ˌjərmə'nāshən\ *n*

**ger•ry•man•der** \'jerē'mandər, 'jerē-, ˌgerē-, 'gerē-\ *vb* : divide into election districts so as to give one political party an advantage — **gerrymander** *n*

**ger•und** \'jerənd\ *n* : word having the characteristics of both verb and noun

**ge•sta•po** \gə'stäpō\ *n, pl* **-pos** : secret police

**ges•ta•tion** \je'stāshən\ *n* : pregnancy or incubation — **ges•tate** \'jes,tāt\ *vb*

**ges•ture** \'jeschər\ *n* 1 : movement of the body or limbs that expresses something 2 : something said or done for its effect on the attitudes of others — **ges•tur•al** \-chərəl\ *adj* — **gesture** *vb*

**ge•sund•heit** \gə'zùnt,hīt\ *interj* : used to wish good health to one who has just sneezed

**get** \'get\ *vb* **got** \'gät\; **got** *or* **got•ten** \'gätᵊn\; **get•ting** 1 : gain or be in possession of 2 : succeed in coming or going 3 : cause to come or go or to be in a certain condition or position 4 : become 5 : be subjected to 6 : understand 7 : be obliged — **get along** *vb* 1 : get by 2 : be on friendly terms — **get by** *vb* : meet one's needs

**get•away** \'getə,wā\ *n* 1 : escape 2 : a starting or getting under way

**gey•ser** \'gīzər\ *n* : spring that intermittently shoots up hot water and steam

**ghast•ly** \'gastlē\ *adj* **-li•er; -est** : horrible or shocking

**gher•kin** \'gərkən\ *n* : small pickle

**ghet•to** \'getō\ *n, pl* **-tos** *or* **-toes** : part of a city in which members of a minority group live

**ghost** \'gōst\ *n* : disembodied soul — **ghost•ly** *adv*

**ghost•write** *vb* **-wrote; -writ•ten** : write for and in the name of another — **ghost•writ•er** *n*

**ghoul** \'gül\ *n* : legendary evil being that feeds on corpses — **ghoul•ish** *adj*

**GI** \ˌjē'ī\ *n, pl* **GI's** *or* **GIs** : member of the U.S. armed forces

**gi•ant** \'jīənt\ *n* 1 : huge legendary being 2 : something very large or very powerful — **giant** *adj*

**gib•ber** \'jibər\ *vb* **-bered; -ber•ing** : speak rapidly and foolishly

**gib•ber•ish** \'jibərish\ *n* : unintelligible speech or language

**gib•bon** \'gibən\ *n* : manlike ape

**gibe** \'jīb\ *vb* **gibed; gib•ing** : jeer at — **gibe** *n*

**gib•lets** \'jibləts\ *n pl* : edible fowl viscera

**gid•dy** \'gidē\ *adj* **-di•er; -est** 1 : silly 2 : dizzy — **gid•di•ness** *n*

**gift** \'gift\ *n* 1 : something given 2 : talent — **gift•ed** *adj*

**gi•gan•tic** \jī'gantik\ *adj* : very big

**gig•gle** \'gigəl\ *vb* **-gled; -gling** : laugh in a silly manner — **giggle** *n* — **gig•gly** \-əlē\ *adj*

**gig•o•lo** \'jigə,lō\ *n, pl* **-los** : man living on the earnings of a woman

**Gi•la monster** \'hēlə-\ *n* : large venomous lizard

**gild** \'gild\ *vb* **gild•ed** \'gildəd\ *or* **gilt** \'gilt\; **gild•ing** : cover with or as if with gold

**gill** \'gil\ *n* : organ of a fish for obtaining oxygen from water

**gilt** \'gilt\ *adj* : gold-colored ~ *n* : gold or goldlike substance on the surface of an object

**gim·bal** \'gimbəl, 'jim-\ *n* : device that allows something to incline freely

**gim·let** \'gimlət\ *n* : small tool for boring holes

**gim·mick** \'gimik\ *n* : new and ingenious scheme, feature, or device — **gim·mick·ry** *n* — **gim·micky** \-ikē\ *adj*

**gimpy** \'gimpē\ *adj* : lame

**¹gin** \'jin\ *n* : machine to separate seeds from cotton — **gin** *vb*

**²gin** *n* : clear liquor flavored with juniper berries

**gin·ger** \'jinjər\ *n* : pungent aromatic spice from a tropical plant — **gin·ger·bread** *n*

**gin·ger·ly** *adv* : very cautiously

**ging·ham** \'giŋəm\ *n* : cotton clothing fabric

**gin·gi·vi·tis** \,jinjə'vītəs\ *n* : inflammation of the gums

**gink·go** \'giŋkō\ *n, pl* -goes *or* -gos : tree of eastern China

**gin·seng** \'jin,siŋ, -,seŋ, -saŋ\ *n* : aromatic root of a Chinese herb

**gi·raffe** \jə'raf\ *n* : African mammal with a very long neck

**gird** \'gərd\ *vb* **gird·ed** \'gərdəd\ *or* **girt** \'gərt\; **gird·ing** 1 : encircle or fasten with or as if with a belt 2 : prepare

**gird·er** \'gərdər\ *n* : horizontal supporting beam

**gir·dle** \'gərd³l\ *n* : woman's supporting undergarment ~ *vb* : surround

**girl** \'gərl\ *n* 1 : female child 2 : young woman 3 : sweetheart — **girl·hood** \-,hùd\ *n* — **girl·ish** *adj*

**girl·friend** *n* : frequent or regular female companion of a boy or man

**girth** \'gərth\ *n* : measure around something

**gist** \'jist\ *n* : main point or part

**give** \'giv\ *vb* **gave** \'gāv\; **giv·en** \'givən\; **giv·ing** 1 : put into the possession or keeping of another 2 : pay 3 : perform 4 : contribute or donate 5 : produce 6 : utter 7 : yield to force, strain, or pressure ~ *n* : capacity or tendency to yield to force or strain — **give in** *vb* : surrender — **give out** *vb* : become used up or exhausted — **give up** *vb* 1 : let out of one's control 2 : cease from trying, doing, or hoping

**give·away** *n* 1 : unintentional betrayal 2 : something given free

**giv·en** \'givən\ *adj* 1 : prone or disposed 2 : having been specified

**giz·zard** \'gizərd\ *n* : muscular usu. horny-lined enlargement following the crop of a bird

**gla·cial** \'glāshəl\ *adj* 1 : relating to glaciers 2 : very slow — **gla·cial·ly** *adv*

**gla·cier** \'glāshər\ *n* : large body of ice moving slowly

**glad** \'glad\ *adj* -dd- 1 : experiencing or causing pleasure, joy, or delight 2 : very willing — **glad·den** \-³n\ *vb* — **glad·ly** *adv* — **glad·ness** *n*

**glade** \'glād\ *n* : grassy open space in a forest

**glad·i·a·tor** \'gladē,ātər\ *n* : one who fought to the death for the entertainment of ancient Romans — **glad·i·a·to·ri·al** \,gladēə'tōrēəl\ *adj*

**glad·i·o·lus** \,gladē'ōləs\ *n, pl* -li \-lē, -,lī\ : plant related to the irises

**glam·our, glam·or** \'glamər\ *n* : romantic or exciting attractiveness — **glam·or·ize** \-ə,rīz\ *vb* — **glam·or·ous** \-ərəs\ *adj*

**glance** \'glans\ *vb* **glanced; glanc·ing** 1 : strike and fly off to one side 2 : give a quick look ~ *n* : quick look

**gland** \'gland\ *n* : group of cells that secretes a substance — **glan·du·lar** \'glanjələr\ *adj*

**glans** \'glanz\ *n, pl* **glan·des** \'glan-,dēz\ : conical vascular body forming the end of the penis or clitoris

**glare** \'glar\ *vb* **glared; glar·ing** 1 : shine with a harsh dazzling light 2 : stare angrily ~ *n* 1 : harsh dazzling light 2 : angry stare

**glar·ing** \'glariŋ\ *adj* : painfully obvious — **glar·ing·ly** *adv*

**glass** \'glas\ *n* 1 : hard usu. transparent material made by melting sand and other materials 2 : something made of glass 3 *pl* : lenses used to correct defects of vision — **glass** *adj* — **glass·ful** \-,fùl\ *n* — **glass·ware** \-,war\ *n* — **glassy** *adj*

**glass·blow·ing** *n* : art of shaping a mass of molten glass by blowing air into it — **glass·blow·er** *n*

**glau·co·ma** \glaù'kōmə, glò-\ *n* : state of increased pressure within the eyeball

**glaze** \'glāz\ *vb* **glazed; glaz·ing** 1

: furnish with glass **2** : apply glaze to ~ *n* : glassy surface or coating

**gla·zier** \'glāzhər\ *n* : one who sets glass in window frames

**gleam** \'glēm\ *n* **1** : transient or partly obscured light **2** : faint trace ~ *vb* : send out gleams

**glean** \'glēn\ *vb* : collect little by little — **glean·able** *adj* — **glean·er** *n*

**glee** \'glē\ *n* : joy — **glee·ful** *adj*

**glen** \'glen\ *n* : narrow hidden valley

**glib** \'glib\ *adj* **-bb-** : speaking or spoken with ease — **glib·ly** *adv*

**glide** \'glīd\ *vb* **glid·ed; glid·ing** : move or descend smoothly and effortlessly — **glide** *n*

**glid·er** \'glīdər\ *n* **1** : winged aircraft having no engine **2** : swinging porch seat

**glim·mer** \'glimər\ *vb* : shine faintly or unsteadily ~ *n* **1** : faint light **2** : small amount

**glimpse** \'glimps\ *vb* **glimpsed; glimps·ing** : take a brief look at — **glimpse** *n*

**glint** \'glint\ *vb* : gleam or sparkle — **glint** *n*

**glis·ten** \'glis°n\ *vb* : shine or sparkle by reflection — **glisten** *n*

**glit·ter** \'glitər\ *vb* : shine with brilliant or metallic luster ~ *n* : small glittering ornaments — **glit·tery** *adj*

**glitz** \'glits\ *n* : extravagant showiness — **glitzy** \'glitsē\ *adj*

**gloat** \'glōt\ *vb* : think of something with triumphant delight

**glob** \'gläb\ *n* : large rounded lump

**glob·al** \'glōbəl\ *adj* : worldwide — **glob·al·ly** *adv*

**globe** \'glōb\ *n* **1** : sphere **2** : the earth or a model of it

**glob·u·lar** \'gläbyələr\ *adj* **1** : round **2** : made up of globules

**glob·ule** \'gläbyül\ *n* : tiny ball

**glock·en·spiel** \'gläkən,shpēl\ *n* : portable musical instrument consisting of tuned metal bars

**gloom** \'glüm\ *n* **1** : darkness **2** : sadness — **gloom·i·ly** *adv* — **gloom·i·ness** *n* — **gloomy** *adj*

**glop** \'gläp\ *n* : messy mass or mixture

**glo·ri·fy** \'glōrə,fī\ *vb* **-fied; -fy·ing** **1** : make to seem glorious **2** : worship — **glo·ri·fi·ca·tion** \,glōrəfə-'kāshən\ *n*

**glo·ry** \'glōrē\ *n, pl* **-ries 1** : praise or honor offered in worship **2** : cause for praise or renown **3** : magnificence

**4** : heavenly bliss ~ *vb* **-ried; -ry·ing** : rejoice proudly — **glo·ri·ous** \'glōrēəs\ *adj* — **glo·ri·ous·ly** *adv*

**¹gloss** \'gläs, 'glós\ *n* : luster — **gloss·i·ly** \-əlē\ *adv* — **gloss·i·ness** \-ēnəs\ *n* — **glossy** \-ē\ *adj* **gloss over** *vb* **1** : mask the true nature of **2** : deal with only superficially

**²gloss** *n* : brief explanation or translation ~ *vb* : translate or explain

**glos·sa·ry** \'gläsərē, 'glós-\ *n, pl* **-ries** : dictionary — **glos·sar·i·al** \glä-'sarēəl, glo-\ *adj*

**glove** \'gləv\ *n* : hand covering with sections for each finger

**glow** \'glō\ *vb* **1** : shine with or as if with intense heat **2** : show exuberance ~ *n* : brightness or warmth of color or feeling

**glow·er** \'glauər\ *vb* : stare angrily — **glower** *n*

**glow·worm** *n* : insect or insect larva that emits light

**glu·cose** \'glü,kōs\ *n* : sugar found esp. in blood, plant sap, and fruits

**glue** \'glü\ *n* : substance used for sticking things together — **glue** *vb* — **glu·ey** \'glüē\ *adj*

**glum** \'gləm\ *adj* **-mm-** **1** : sullen **2** : dismal

**glut** \'glət\ *vb* **-tt-** : fill to excess — **glut** *n*

**glu·ten** \'glüt°n\ *n* : gluey protein substance in flour

**glu·ti·nous** \'glüt°nəs\ *adj* : sticky

**glut·ton** \'glət°n\ *n* : one who eats to excess — **glut·ton·ous** \'glət°nəs\ *adj* — **glut·tony** \'glət°nē\ *n*

**gnarled** \'närld\ *adj* **1** : knotty **2** : gloomy or sullen

**gnash** \'nash\ *vb* : grind (as teeth) together

**gnat** \'nat\ *n* : small biting fly

**gnaw** \'nó\ *vb* : bite or chew on

**gnome** \'nōm\ *n* : dwarf of folklore — **gnom·ish** *adj*

**gnu** \'nü, 'nyü\ *n, pl* **gnu** *or* **gnus** : large African antelope

**go** \'gō\ *vb* **went** \'went\; **gone** \'gón, 'gän\; **go·ing** \'góiŋ\; **goes** \'gōz\ **1** : move, proceed, run, or pass **2** : leave **3** : extend or lead **4** : sell or amount — with *for* **5** : happen **6** — used in present participle to show intent or imminent action **7** : become **8** : fit or harmonize **9** : belong ~ *n, pl* **goes 1** : act or manner of going **2** : vigor **3** : attempt — **go back on** : betray — **go by the board** : be discarded — **go for** : favor — **go off** : explode — **go one better** : outdo — **go over 1** : examine **2** : study — **go to town** : be very successful — **on the go** : constantly active

**goad** \'gōd\ *n* : something that urges — **goad** *vb*

**goal** \'gōl\ *n* **1** : mark to reach in a race **2** : purpose **3** : object in a game through which a ball is propelled

**goal•ie** \'gōlē\ *n* : player who defends the goal

**goal•keep•er** *n* : goalie

**goat** \'gōt\ *n* : horned ruminant mammal related to the sheep — **goat•skin** *n*

**goa•tee** \gō'tē\ *n* : small pointed beard

**gob** \'gäb\ *n* : lump

¹**gob•ble** \'gäbəl\ *vb* **-bled; -bling** : eat greedily

²**gobble** *vb* **-bled; -bling** : make the noise of a turkey (**gobbler**)

**gob•ble•dy•gook** \'gäbəldē,gúk, -'gük\ *n* : nonsense

**gob•let** \'gäblət\ *n* : large stemmed drinking glass

**gob•lin** \'gäblən\ *n* : ugly mischievous sprite

**god** \'gäd, 'gód\ *n* **1** *cap* : supreme being **2** : being with supernatural powers — **god•like** *adj* — **god•ly** *adj*

**god•child** *n* : person one sponsors at baptism — **god•daugh•ter** *n* — **god•son** *n*

**god•dess** \'gädəs, 'gód-\ *n* : female god

**god•less** \-ləs\ *adj* : not believing in God — **god•less•ness** *n*

**god•par•ent** *n* : sponsor at baptism — **god•fa•ther** *n* — **god•moth•er** *n*

**god•send** \-,send\ *n* : something needed that comes unexpectedly

**goes** *pres 3d sing of* GO

**go-get•ter** \'gō,getər\ *n* : enterprising person — **go-get•ting** \-iŋ\ *adj or n*

**gog•gle** \'gägəl\ *vb* **-gled; -gling** : stare wide-eyed

**gog•gles** \-əlz\ *n pl* : protective glasses

**go•ings-on** \,gōiŋz'òn, -'än\ *n pl* : events

**goi•ter** \'gòitər\ *n* : abnormally enlarged thyroid gland

**gold** \'gōld\ *n* : malleable yellow metallic chemical element — **gold•smith** \-,smith\ *n*

**gold-brick** \-,brik\ *n* : person who shirks duty — **goldbrick** *vb*

**gold•en** \'gōldən\ *adj* **1** : made of, containing, or relating to gold **2** : having the color of gold **3** : precious or favorable

**gold•en•rod** \'gōldən,räd\ *n* : herb having tall stalks with tiny yellow flowers

**gold•finch** \'gōld,finch\ *n* : yellow American finch

**gold•fish** \-,fish\ *n* : small usu. orange or golden carp

**golf** \'gälf, 'gólf\ *n* : game played by hitting a small ball (**golf ball**) with clubs (**golf clubs**) into holes placed in a field (**golf course**) — **golf** *vb* — **golf•er** *n*

**go•nad** \'gō,nad\ *n* : sex gland

**gon•do•la** \'gändələ (*usual for 1*), gän'dō-\ *n* **1** : long narrow boat used on the canals of Venice **2** : car suspended from a cable

**gon•do•lier** \,gändə'lir\ *n* : person who propels a gondola

**gone** \'gón\ *adj* **1** : past **2** : involved

**gon•er** \'gónər\ *n* : hopeless case

**gong** \'gäŋ, 'góŋ\ *n* : metallic disk that makes a deep sound when struck

**gon•or•rhea** \,gänə'rēə\ *n* : bacterial inflammatory venereal disease of the genital tract

**goo** \'gü\ *n* : thick or sticky substance — **goo•ey** \-ē\ *adj*

**good** \'gúd\ *adj* **bet•ter** \'betər\; **best** \'best\ **1** : satisfactory **2** : salutary **3** : considerable **4** : desirable **5** : well-behaved, kind, or virtuous ∼ *n* **1** : something good **2** : benefit **3** *pl* : personal property **4** *pl* : wares ∼ *adv* : well — **good-heart•ed** \-'härtəd\ *adj* — **good-look•ing** *adj* — **good-na•tured** *adj* — **good•ness** *n* — **for good** : forever

**good-bye, good-by** \gúd'bī\ *n* : parting remark

**good-for-noth•ing** *n* : idle worthless person

**Good Friday** *n* : Friday before Easter observed as the anniversary of the crucifixion of Christ

**good•ly** *adj* **-li•er; -est** : considerable

**good•will** *n* **1** : good intention **2** : kindly feeling

**goody** \'gúdē\ *n, pl* **good•ies** : something that is good esp. to eat

**goody-goody** *adj* : affectedly or annoyingly sweet or self-righteous — **goody-goody** *n*

**goof** \'güf\ *vb* **1** : blunder **2** : waste time — usu. with *off* or *around* — **goof** *n* — **goof-off** *n*

**goofy** \'güfē\ adj goof•i•er; -est : crazy — **goof•i•ness** n

**goose** \'güs\ n, pl **geese** \'gēs\ : large bird with webbed feet

**goose•ber•ry** \'güs₁berē, 'güz-\ n : berry of a shrub related to the currant

**goose bumps** n pl : roughening of the skin caused by fear, excitement, or cold

**goose•flesh** n : goose bumps

**goose pimples** n pl : goose bumps

**go•pher** \'gōfər\ n : burrowing rodent

¹**gore** \'gōr\ n : blood

²**gore** vb **gored; gor•ing** : pierce or wound with a horn or tusk

¹**gorge** \'górj\ n : narrow ravine

²**gorge** vb **gorged; gorg•ing** : eat greedily

**gor•geous** \'górjəs\ adj : supremely beautiful

**go•ril•la** \gə'rilə\ n : African manlike ape

**gory** \'gōrē\ adj **gor•i•er; -est** : bloody

**gos•hawk** \'gäs₁hók\ n : long-tailed hawk with short rounded wings

**gos•ling** \'gäzliŋ, 'góz-\ n : young goose

**gos•pel** \'gäspəl\ n **1** : teachings of Christ and the apostles **2** : something accepted as infallible truth — **gospel** adj

**gos•sa•mer** \'gäsəmər, gäz-\ n **1** : film of cobweb **2** : light filmy substance

**gos•sip** \'gäsəp\ n **1** : person who reveals personal information **2** : rumor or report of an intimate nature ∼ vb : spread gossip — **gos•sipy** \-ē\ adj

**got** past of GET

**Goth•ic** \'gäthik\ adj : relating to a medieval style of architecture

**gotten** past part of GET

**gouge** \'gaúj\ n **1** : rounded chisel **2** : cavity or groove scooped out ∼ vb **gouged; goug•ing 1** : cut or scratch a groove in **2** : overcharge

**gou•lash** \'gü₁läsh, -₁lash\ n : beef stew with vegetables and paprika

**gourd** \'gōrd, 'gúrd\ n **1** : any of a group of vines including the cucumber, squash, and melon **2** : inedible hard-shelled fruit of a gourd

**gour•mand** \'gúr₁mänd\ n : person who loves good food and drink

**gour•met** \'gúr₁mā, gúr'mā\ n : connoisseur of food and drink

**gout** \'gaút\ n : disease marked by painful inflammation and swelling of the joints — **gouty** adj

**gov•ern** \'gəvərn\ vb **1** : control and direct policy in **2** : guide or influence strongly **3** : restrain — **gov•ern•ment** \-ərmənt\ n — **gov•ern•men•tal** \₁gəvər'ment⁽ᵊ⁾l\ adj

**gov•ern•ess** \'gəvərnəs\ n : female teacher in a private home

**gov•er•nor** \'gəvənər, 'gəvər-\ n **1** : head of a political unit **2** : automatic speed-control device — **gov•er•nor•ship** n

**gown** \'gaún\ n **1** : loose flowing outer garment **2** : woman's formal evening dress — **gown** vb

**grab** \'grab\ vb **-bb-** : take by sudden grasp — **grab** n

**grace** \'grās\ n **1** : unmerited divine assistance **2** : short prayer before or after a meal **3** : respite **4** : ease of movement or bearing ∼ vb **graced; grac•ing 1** : honor **2** : adorn — **graceful** \-fəl\ adj — **grace•ful•ly** adv — **grace•ful•ness** n — **grace•less** adj

**gra•cious** \'grāshəs\ adj : marked by kindness and courtesy or charm and taste — **gra•cious•ly** adv — **gra•cious•ness** n

**grack•le** \'grakəl\ n : American blackbird

**gra•da•tion** \grā'dāshən, grə-\ n : step, degree, or stage in a series

**grade** \'grād\ n **1** : stage in a series, order, or ranking **2** : division of school representing one year's work **3** : mark of accomplishment in school **4** : degree of slope ∼ vb **grad•ed; grad•ing 1** : arrange in grades **2** : make level or evenly sloping **3** : give a grade to — **grad•er** n

**grade school** n : school including the first 4 or 8 grades

**gra•di•ent** \'grādēənt\ n : slope

**grad•u•al** \'grajəwəl\ adj : going by steps or degrees — **grad•u•al•ly** adv

**grad•u•ate** \'grajəwət\ n : holder of a diploma ∼ adj : of or relating to studies beyond the bachelor's degree ∼ \-ə₁wāt\ vb **-at•ed; -at•ing 1** : grant or receive a diploma **2** : mark with degrees of measurement — **grad•u•a•tion** \₁grajə'wāshən\ n

**graf•fi•to** \grə'fētō, grä-\ n, pl **-ti** \-ē\ : inscription on a wall

**graft** \'graft\ vb : join one thing to another so that they grow together ∼ n

**1** : grafted plant **2** : the getting of money dishonestly or the money so gained — **graft·er** *n*

**grain** \'grān\ *n* **1** : seeds or fruits of cereal grasses **2** : small hard particle **3** : arrangement of fibers in wood — **grained** \'grānd\ *adj* — **grainy** *adj*

**gram** \'gram\ *n* : metric unit of weight equal to 1/1000 kilogram

**gram·mar** \'gramər\ *n* : study of words and their functions and relations in the sentence — **gram·mar·i·an** \grə-'marēən\ *n* — **gram·mat·i·cal** \-'matikəl\ *adj* — **gram·mat·i·cal·ly** *adv*

**grammar school** *n* : grade school

**gra·na·ry** \'grānərē, 'gran-\ *n, pl* **-ries** : storehouse for grain

**grand** \'grand\ *adj* **1** : large or striking in size or scope **2** : fine and imposing **3** : very good — **grand·ly** *adv* — **grand·ness** *n*

**grand·child** \-,chīld\ *n* : child of one's son or daughter — **grand·daugh·ter** *n* — **grand·son** *n*

**gran·deur** \'granjər\ *n* : quality or state of being grand

**gran·dil·o·quence** \gran'diləkwəns\ *n* : pompous speaking — **gran·dil·o·quent** \-kwənt\ *adj*

**gran·di·ose** \'grandē,ōs, ,grandē-'\ *adj* **1** : impressive **2** : affectedly splendid — **gran·di·ose·ly** *adv*

**grand·par·ent** \'grand,parənt\ *n* : parent of one's father or mother — **grand·fa·ther** \-,fäthər, -,fath-\ *n* — **grand·moth·er** \-,məthər\ *n*

**grand·stand** \-,stand\ *n* : usu. roofed stand for spectators

**grange** \'grānj\ *n* : farmers association

**gran·ite** \'granət\ *n* : hard igneous rock

**grant** \'grant\ *vb* **1** : consent to **2** : give **3** : admit as true ~ *n* **1** : act of granting **2** : something granted — **grant·ee** \grant'ē\ *n* — **grant·er** \'grantər\ *n* — **grant·or** \-ər, -,ȯr\ *n*

**gran·u·late** \'granyə,lāt\ *vb* **-lat·ed; -lat·ing** : form into grains or crystals — **gran·u·la·tion** \,granyə'lāshən\ *n*

**gran·ule** \'granyül\ *n* : small particle — **gran·u·lar** \-yələr\ *adj* — **gran·u·lar·i·ty** \,granyə'larətē\ *n*

**grape** \'grāp\ *n* : smooth juicy edible berry of a woody vine (**grape·vine**)

**grape·fruit** *n* : large edible yellow-skinned citrus fruit

**graph** \'graf\ *n* : diagram that shows relationships between things — **graph** *vb*

**graph·ic** \'grafik\ *adj* **1** : vividly described **2** : relating to the arts (**graphic arts**) of representation and printing on flat surfaces ~ *n* **1** : picture used for illustration **2** *pl* : computer screen display — **graph·i·cal·ly** \-iklē\ *adv*

**graph·ite** \'graf,īt\ *n* : soft carbon used for lead pencils and lubricants

**grap·nel** \'grapnəl\ *n* : small anchor with several claws

**grap·ple** \'grapəl\ *vb* **-pled; -pling 1** : seize or hold with or as if with a hooked implement **2** : wrestle

**grasp** \'grasp\ *vb* **1** : take or seize firmly **2** : understand ~ *n* **1** : one's hold or control **2** : one's reach **3** : comprehension

**grass** \'gras\ *n* : plant with jointed stem and narrow leaves — **grassy** *adj*

**grass·hop·per** \-,häpər\ *n* : leaping plant-eating insect

**grass·land** *n* : land covered with grasses

¹**grate** \'grāt\ *n* **1** : grating **2** : frame of iron bars to hold burning fuel

²**grate** *vb* **grat·ed; -ing 1** : pulverize by rubbing against something rough **2** : irritate — **grat·er** *n* — **grat·ing·ly** *adv*

**grate·ful** \'grātfəl\ *adj* : thankful or appreciative — **grate·ful·ly** *adv* — **grate·ful·ness** *n*

**grat·i·fy** \'gratə,fī\ *vb* **-fied; -fy·ing** : give pleasure to — **grat·i·fi·ca·tion** \,gratəfə'kāshən\ *n*

**grat·ing** \'grātiŋ\ *n* : framework with bars across it

**gra·tis** \'gratəs, 'grāt-\ *adv or adj* : free

**grat·i·tude** \'gratə,tüd, -,tyüd\ *n* : state of being grateful

**gra·tu·itous** \grə'tüətəs, -'tyü-\ *adj* **1** : free **2** : uncalled-for

**gra·tu·ity** \-ətē\ *n, pl* **-ities** : tip

¹**grave** \'grāv\ *n* : place of burial — **grave·stone** *n* — **grave·yard** *n*

²**grave** *adj* **grav·er; grav·est 1** : threatening great harm or danger **2** : solemn — **grave·ly** *adv* — **grave·ness** *n*

**grav·el** \'gravəl\ *n* : loose rounded fragments of rock — **grav·el·ly** *adj*

**grav·i·tate** \'gravə,tāt\ *vb* **-tat·ed; -tat·ing** : move toward something

**grav·i·ta·tion** \,gravə'tāshən\ *n* : natural force of attraction that tends to draw bodies together — **grav·i·ta·tion·al** \-shənəl\ *adj*

**grav·i·ty** \\'gravətē\\ *n, pl* **-ties** 1 : serious importance 2 : gravitation

**gra·vy** \\'grāvē\\ *n, pl* **-vies** : sauce made from thickened juices of cooked meat

**gray** \\'grā\\ *adj* 1 : of the color gray 2 : having gray hair ~ *n* : neutral color between black and white ~ *vb* : make or become gray — **gray·ish** \\-ish\\ *adj* — **gray·ness** *n*

¹**graze** \\'grāz\\ *vb* **grazed; graz·ing** : feed on herbage or pasture — **graz·er** *n*

²**graze** *vb* **grazed; graz·ing** : touch lightly in passing

**grease** \\'grēs\\ *n* : thick oily material or fat ~ \\'grēs, 'grēz\\ *vb* **greased; greas·ing** : smear or lubricate with grease — **greasy** \\'grēsē, -zē\\ *adj*

**great** \\'grāt\\ *adj* 1 : large in size or number 2 : larger than usual — **great·ly** *adv* — **great·ness** *n*

**grebe** \\'grēb\\ *n* : diving bird related to the loon

**greed** \\'grēd\\ *n* : selfish desire beyond reason — **greed·i·ly** \\-ᵊlē\\ *adv* — **greed·i·ness** \\-ēnəs\\ *n* — **greedy** \\'grēdē\\ *adj*

**green** \\'grēn\\ *adj* 1 : of the color green 2 : unripe 3 : inexperienced ~ *vb* : become green ~ *n* 1 : color between blue and yellow 2 *pl* : leafy parts of plants — **green·ish** *adj* — **green·ness** *n*

**green·ery** \\'grēnərē\\ *n, pl* **-er·ies** : green foliage or plants

**green·horn** *n* : inexperienced person

**green·house** *n* : glass structure for the growing of plants

**greet** \\'grēt\\ *vb* 1 : address with expressions of kind wishes 2 : react to — **greet·er** *n*

**greet·ing** *n* 1 : friendly address on meeting 2 *pl* : best wishes

**gre·gar·i·ous** \\gri'garēəs\\ *adj* : social or companionable — **gre·gar·i·ous·ly** *adv* — **gre·gar·i·ous·ness** *n*

**grem·lin** \\'gremlən\\ *n* : small mischievous gnome

**gre·nade** \\grə'nād\\ *n* : small missile filled with explosive or chemicals

**grew** *past of* GROW

**grey** *var of* GRAY

**grey·hound** \\'grā,haund\\ *n* : tall slender dog noted for speed

**grid** \\'grid\\ *n* 1 : grating 2 : evenly spaced horizontal and vertical lines (as on a map)

**grid·dle** \\'gridᵊl\\ *n* : flat metal surface for cooking

**grid·iron** \\'grid,īərn\\ *n* 1 : grate for broiling 2 : football field

**grief** \\'grēf\\ *n* 1 : emotional suffering caused by or as if by bereavement 2 : disaster

**griev·ance** \\'grēvəns\\ *n* : complaint

**grieve** \\'grēv\\ *vb* **grieved; griev·ing** : feel or cause to feel grief or sorrow

**griev·ous** \\'grēvəs\\ *adj* 1 : oppressive 2 : causing grief or sorrow — **griev·ous·ly** *adv*

**grill** \\'gril\\ *vb* 1 : cook on a grill 2 : question intensely ~ *n* 1 : griddle 2 : informal restaurant

**grille, grill** \\'gril\\ *n* : grating forming a barrier or screen — **grill·work** *n*

**grim** \\'grim\\ *adj* **-mm-** 1 : harsh and forbidding in appearance 2 : relentless — **grim·ly** *adv* — **grim·ness** *n*

**gri·mace** \\'griməs, grim'ās\\ *n* : facial expression of disgust — **grimace** *vb*

**grime** \\'grīm\\ *n* : embedded or accumulated dirt — **grimy** *adj*

**grin** \\'grin\\ *vb* **-nn-** : smile so as to show the teeth — **grin** *n*

**grind** \\'grīnd\\ *vb* **ground** \\'graund\\; **grind·ing** 1 : reduce to powder 2 : wear down or sharpen by friction 3 : operate or produce by turning a crank ~ *n* : monotonous labor or routine — **grind·er** *n* — **grind·stone** \\'grīn,stōn\\ *n*

**grip** \\'grip\\ *vb* **-pp-** : seize or hold firmly ~ *n* 1 : grasp 2 : control 3 : device for holding

**gripe** \\'grīp\\ *vb* **griped; grip·ing** 1 : cause pains in the bowels 2 : complain — **gripe** *n*

**grippe** \\'grip\\ *n* : influenza

**gris·ly** \\'grizlē\\ *adj* **-li·er; -est** : horrible or gruesome

**grist** \\'grist\\ *n* : grain to be ground or already ground — **grist·mill** *n*

**gris·tle** \\'grisəl\\ *n* : cartilage — **gris·tly** \\-lē\\ *adj*

**grit** \\'grit\\ *n* 1 : hard sharp granule 2 : material composed of granules 3 : unyielding courage ~ *vb* **-tt-** : press with a grating noise — **grit·ty** *adj*

**grits** \\'grits\\ *n pl* : coarsely ground hulled grain

**griz·zled** \\'grizəld\\ *adj* : streaked with gray

**groan** \\'grōn\\ *vb* 1 : moan 2 : creak under a strain — **groan** *n*

**gro·cer** \\'grōsər\\ *n* : food dealer — **gro·cery** \\'grōsrē, 'grōsh-, -ərē\\ *n*

**grog** \\'gräg\\ *n* : rum diluted with water

**grog•gy** \-ē\ *adj* **-gi•er; -est** : dazed and unsteady on the feet — **grog•gi•ly** *adv* — **grog•gi•ness** *n*

**groin** \'gròin\ *n* : juncture of the lower abdomen and inner thigh

**grom•met** \'grämət, 'grəm-\ *n* : eyelet

**groom** \'grüm, 'grùm\ *n* **1** : one who cares for horses **2** : bridegroom ~ *vb* **1** : clean and care for (as a horse) **2** : make neat or attractive **3** : prepare

**groove** \'grüv\ *n* **1** : long narrow channel **2** : fixed routine — **groove** *vb*

**grope** \'grōp\ *vb* **groped; grop•ing** : search for by feeling

**gros•beak** \'grōs₁bēk\ *n* : finch with large conical bill

¹**gross** \'grōs\ *adj* **1** : glaringly noticeable **2** : bulky **3** : consisting of an overall total exclusive of deductions **4** : vulgar ~ *n* : the whole before any deductions ~ *vb* : earn as a total — **gross•ly** *adv* — **gross•ness** *n*

²**gross** *n, pl* **gross** : 12 dozen

**gro•tesque** \grō'tesk\ *adj* **1** : absurdly distorted or repulsive **2** : ridiculous — **gro•tesque•ly** *adv*

**grot•to** \'grätō\ *n, pl* **-toes** : cave

**grouch** \'graùch\ *n* : complaining person — **grouch** *vb* — **grouchy** *adj*

¹**ground** \'graùnd\ *n* **1** : bottom of a body of water **2** *pl* : sediment **3** : basis for something **4** : surface of the earth **5** : conductor that makes electrical connection with the earth or a framework ~ *vb* **1** : force or bring down to the ground **2** : give basic knowledge to **3** : connect with an electrical ground — **ground•less** *adj*

²**ground** *past of* GRIND

**ground•hog** *n* : woodchuck

**ground•wa•ter** *n* : underground water

**ground•work** *n* : foundation

**group** \'grüp\ *n* : number of associated individuals ~ *vb* : gather or collect into groups

**grou•per** \'grüpər\ *n* : large fish of warm seas

**grouse** \'graùs\ *n, pl* **grouse** *or* **grouses** : ground-dwelling game bird

**grout** \'graùt\ *n* : mortar for filling cracks — **grout** *vb*

**grove** \'grōv\ *n* : small group of trees

**grov•el** \'grävəl, 'grəv-\ *vb* **-eled** *or* **-elled; -el•ing** *or* **-el•ling** : abase oneself

**grow** \'grō\ *vb* **grew** \'grü\; **grown** \'grōn\; **grow•ing** **1** : come into existence and develop to maturity **2** : be

able to grow **3** : advance or increase **4** : become **5** : cultivate — **grow•er** *n*

**growl** \'graùl\ *vb* : utter a deep threatening sound — **growl** *n*

**grown–up** \'grōn₁əp\ *n* : adult — **grown–up** *adj*

**growth** \'grōth\ *n* **1** : stage in growing **2** : process of growing **3** : result of something growing

**grub** \'grəb\ *vb* **-bb-** **1** : root out by digging **2** : search about ~ *n* **1** : thick wormlike larva **2** : food

**grub•by** \'grəbē\ *adj* **-bi•er; -est** : dirty — **grub•bi•ness** *n*

**grub•stake** *n* : supplies for a prospector

**grudge** \'grəj\ *vb* **grudged; grudg•ing** : be reluctant to give ~ *n* : feeling of ill will

**gru•el** \'grüəl\ *n* : thin porridge

**gru•el•ing, gru•el•ling** \-əliŋ\ *adj* : requiring extreme effort

**grue•some** \'grüsəm\ *adj* : horribly repulsive

**gruff** \'grəf\ *adj* : rough in speech or manner — **gruff•ly** *adv*

**grum•ble** \'grəmbəl\ *vb* **-bled; -bling** : mutter in discontent — **grum•bler** \-blər\ *n*

**grumpy** \-pē\ *adj* **grump•i•er; -est** : cross — **grump•i•ly** *adv* — **grump•i•ness** *n*

**grunge** \'grənj\ *n* **1** : something shabby, tattered, or dirty **2** : rock music expressing alienation and discontent — **grun•gy** \'grənjē\ *adj*

**grun•ion** \'grənyən\ *n* : fish of the California coast

**grunt** \'grənt\ *n* : deep guttural sound — **grunt** *vb*

**gua•no** \'gwänō\ *n* : excrement of seabirds used as fertilizer

**guar•an•tee** \₁garən'tē\ *n* **1** : assurance of the fulfillment of a condition **2** : something given or held as a security ~ *vb* **-teed; -tee•ing** **1** : promise to be responsible for **2** : state with certainty — **guar•an•tor** \₁garən'tòr\ *n*

**guar•an•ty** \'garəntē\ *n, pl* **-ties** **1** : promise to answer for another's failure to pay a debt **2** : guarantee **3** : pledge ~ *vb* **-tied; -ty•ing** : guarantee

**guard** \'gärd\ *n* **1** : defensive position **2** : act of protecting **3** : an individual or group that guards against danger **4** : protective or safety device ~ *vb* **1** : protect or watch over **2** : take precautions — **guard·house** $n$ — **guard-room** $n$

**guard·ian** \'gärdēən\ $n$ : one who has responsibility for the care of the person or property of another — **guardian·ship** $n$

**gua·va** \'gwävə\ $n$ : shrubby tropical tree or its mildly acid fruit

**gu·ber·na·to·ri·al** \gübənə'tōrēəl, gyü-\ $adj$ : relating to a governor

**guer·ril·la, gue·ril·la** \gə'rilə\ $n$ : soldier engaged in small-scale harassing tactics

**guess** \'ges\ $vb$ **1** : form an opinion from little evidence **2** : state correctly solely by chance **3** : think or believe — **guess** $n$

**guest** \'gest\ $n$ **1** : person to whom hospitality (as of a house) is extended **2** : patron of a commercial establishment (as a hotel) **3** : person not a regular cast member who appears on a program

**guf·faw** \gə'fò, 'gəf,ò\ $n$ : loud burst of laughter — **guf·faw** \gə'fò\ $vb$

**guide** \'gīd\ $n$ **1** : one that leads or gives direction to another **2** : device on a machine to direct motion $\sim$ $vb$ **guid·ed; guid·ing 1** : show the way to **2** : direct — **guid·able** $adj$ — **guid·ance** \'gīd°ns\ $n$ — **guide·book** $n$

**guide·line** \-,līn\ $n$ : summary of procedures regarding policy or conduct

**guild** \'gild\ $n$ : association

**guile** \'gīl\ $n$ : craftiness — **guile·ful** $adj$ — **guile·less** $adj$ — **guile·less·ness** $n$

**guil·lo·tine** \'gilə,tēn, ,gēyə'tēn, 'gēyə,-\ $n$ : machine for beheading persons — **guillotine** $vb$

**guilt** \'gilt\ $n$ **1** : fact of having committed an offense **2** : feeling of responsibility for offenses — **guilt·i·ly** $adv$ — **guilt·i·ness** $n$ — **guilty** \'giltē\ $adj$

**guin·ea** \'ginē\ $n$ **1** : old gold coin of United Kingdom **2** : 21 shillings

**guinea pig** $n$ : small So. American rodent

**guise** \'gīz\ $n$ : external appearance

**gui·tar** \gə'tär, gi-\ $n$ : 6-stringed musical instrument played by plucking

**gulch** \'gəlch\ $n$ : ravine

**gulf** \'gəlf\ $n$ **1** : extension of an ocean or a sea into the land **2** : wide gap

¹**gull** \'gəl\ $n$ : seabird with webbed feet

²**gull** $vb$ : make a dupe of $\sim$ $n$ : dupe — **gull·ible** $adj$

**gul·let** \'gələt\ $n$ : throat

**gul·ly** \'gəlē\ $n$, $pl$ **-lies** : trench worn by running water

**gulp** \'gəlp\ $vb$ : swallow hurriedly or greedily — **gulp** $n$

¹**gum** \'gəm\ $n$ : tissue along the jaw at the base of the teeth

²**gum** $n$ **1** : sticky plant substance **2** : gum usu. of sweetened chicle prepared for chewing — **gum·my** $adj$

**gum·bo** \'gəmbō\ $n$ : thick soup

**gum·drop** $n$ : gumlike candy

**gump·tion** \'gəmpshən\ $n$ : initiative

**gun** \'gən\ $n$ **1** : cannon **2** : portable firearm **3** : discharge of a gun **4** : something like a gun $\sim$ $vb$ **-nn-** : hunt with a gun — **gun·fight** $n$ — **gun·fight·er** $n$ — **gun·fire** $n$ — **gun·man** \-mən\ $n$ — **gun·pow·der** $n$ — **gun·shot** $n$ — **gun·smith** $n$

**gun·boat** $n$ : small armed ship

**gun·ner** \'gənər\ $n$ : person who uses a gun

**gun·nery sergeant** \'gənərē-\ $n$ : noncommissioned officer in the marine corps ranking next below a master sergeant

**gun·ny·sack** \'gənē,sak\ $n$ : burlap sack

**gun·sling·er** \'gən,slinər\ $n$ : skilled gunman in the old West

**gun·wale** \'gən°l\ $n$ : upper edge of a boat's side

**gup·py** \'gəpē\ $n$, $pl$ **-pies** : tiny tropical fish

**gur·gle** \'gərgəl\ $vb$ **-gled; -gling** : make a sound like that of a flowing and gently splashing liquid — **gurgle** $n$

**gu·ru** \'gü,rü\ $n$, $pl$ **-rus 1** : personal religious teacher in Hinduism **2** : expert

**gush** \'gəsh\ $vb$ : pour forth violently or enthusiastically — **gush·er** \'gəshər\ $n$

**gushy** \-ē\ $adj$ **gush·i·er; -est** : effusively sentimental

**gust** \'gəst\ $n$ **1** : sudden brief rush of wind **2** : sudden outburst — **gust** $vb$ — **gusty** $adj$

**gus·ta·to·ry** \'gəstə,tōrē\ $adj$ : relating to the sense of taste

**gus·to** \'gəstō\ $n$ : zest

**gut** \'gət\ $n$ **1** $pl$ : intestines **2** : digestive canal **3** $pl$ : courage $\sim$ $vb$ **-tt-** : eviscerate

**gut·ter** \'gətər\ $n$ : channel for carrying off rainwater

**gut·tur·al** \'gətərəl\ $adj$ : sounded in the throat — **guttural** $n$

**¹guy** \'gī\ *n* : rope, chain, or rod attached to something to steady it — **guy** *vb*
**²guy** *n* : person
**guz·zle** \'gəzəl\ *vb* **-zled; -zling** : drink greedily
**gym** \'jim\ *n* : gymnasium
**gym·na·si·um** \jim'nāzēəm, -zhəm\ *n, pl* **-si·ums** *or* **-sia** \-zēə, -zhə\ : place for indoor sports
**gym·nas·tics** \jim'nastiks\ *n* : physical exercises performed in a gymnasium — **gym·nast** \'jim,nast\ *n* — **gym·nas·tic** *adj*
**gy·ne·col·o·gy** \,gīnə'käləjē, ,jin-\ *n* : branch of medicine dealing with the diseases of women — **gy·ne·co·log·ic** \-ikə'läjik\, **gy·ne·co·log·i·cal** \-ikəl\ *adj* — **gy·ne·col·o·gist** \-ə'käləjist\ *n*
**gyp** \'jip\ *n* **1** : cheat **2** : trickery — **gyp** *vb*
**gyp·sum** \'jipsəm\ *n* : calcium-containing mineral
**gy·rate** \'jī,rāt\ *vb* **-rat·ed; -rat·ing** : revolve around a center — **gy·ra·tion** \jī'rāshən\ *n*
**gy·ro·scope** \'jīro,skōp\ *n* : wheel mounted to spin rapidly about an axis that is free to turn in various directions

# H

**h** \'āch\ *n, pl* **h's** *or* **hs** \'āchəz\ : 8th letter of the alphabet
**hab·er·dash·er** \'habər,dashər\ *n* : men's clothier — **hab·er·dash·ery** \-ərē\ *n*
**hab·it** \'habət\ *n* **1** : monk's or nun's clothing **2** : usual behavior **3** : addiction — **hab·it–form·ing** *adj*
**hab·it·able** \-əbəl\ *adj* : capable of being lived in
**hab·i·tat** \'habə,tat\ *n* : place where a plant or animal naturally occurs
**hab·i·ta·tion** \,habə'tāshən\ *n* **1** : occupancy **2** : dwelling place
**ha·bit·u·al** \hə'bichəwəl\ *adj* **1** : commonly practiced or observed **2** : doing, practicing, or acting by habit — **ha·bit·u·al·ly** *adv*
**ha·bit·u·ate** \hə'bichə,wāt\ *vb* **-at·ed; -at·ing** : accustom
**ha·ci·en·da** \,häsē'endə\ *n* : ranch house
**¹hack** \'hak\ *vb* **1** : cut with repeated irregular blows **2** : cough in a short dry manner **3** : manage successfully — **hack** *n* — **hack·er** *n*
**²hack** *n* **1** : horse or vehicle for hire **2** : saddle horse **3** : writer for hire — **hack** *adj* — **hack·man** \-mən\ *n*
**hack·le** \'hakəl\ *n* **1** : long feather on the neck or back of a bird **2** *pl* : hairs that can be erected **3** *pl* : temper
**hack·ney** \-nē\ *n, pl* **-neys 1** : horse for riding or driving **2** : carriage for hire
**hack·neyed** \-nēd\ *adj* : trite
**hack·saw** *n* : saw for metal
**had** *past of* HAVE
**had·dock** \'hadək\ *n, pl* **haddock** : Atlantic food fish
**Ha·des** \'hādēz\ *n* **1** : mythological abode of the dead **2** *often not cap* : hell
**haft** \'haft\ *n* : handle of a weapon or tool
**hag** \'hag\ *n* **1** : witch **2** : ugly old woman
**hag·gard** \'hagərd\ *adj* : worn or emaciated — **hag·gard·ly** *adv*
**hag·gle** \'hagəl\ *vb* **-gled; -gling** : argue in bargaining — **hag·gler** *n*
**¹hail** \'hāl\ *n* **1** : precipitation in small lumps of ice **2** : something like a rain of hail ~ *vb* : rain hail — **hail·stone** *n* — **hail·storm** *n*
**²hail** *vb* **1** : greet or salute **2** : summon ~ *n* : expression of greeting or praise — often used as an interjection
**hair** \'har\ *n* : threadlike growth from the skin — **hair·brush** *n* — **hair·cut** *n* — **hair·dress·er** *n* — **haired** *adj* — **hair·i·ness** *n* — **hair·less** *adj* — **hair·pin** *n* — **hair·style** *n* — **hair·styl·ing** *n* — **hair·styl·ist** *n* — **hairy** *adj*
**hair·breadth** \-,bredth\, **hairs·breadth** \'harz-\ *n* : tiny distance or margin
**hair·do** \-,dü\ *n, pl* **-dos** : style of wearing hair
**hair·line** *n* **1** : thin line **2** : outline of the hair on the head

**hair·piece** n : toupee

**hair–rais·ing** adj : causing terror or astonishment

**hake** \'hāk\ n : marine food fish

**hal·cy·on** \'halsēən\ adj : prosperous or most pleasant

¹**hale** \'hāl\ adj : healthy or robust

²**hale** vb **haled; hal·ing** 1 : haul 2 : compel to go

**half** \'haf, 'håf\ n, pl **halves** \'havz, 'håvz\ : either of 2 equal parts ~ adj 1 : being a half or nearly a half 2 : partial — **half** adv

**half brother** n : brother related through one parent only

**half–heart·ed** \-'härtəd\ adj : without enthusiasm — **half–heart·ed·ly** adv

**half–life** n : time for half of something to undergo a process

**half sister** n : sister related through one parent only

**half–way** adj : midway between 2 points — **half–way** adv

**half–wit** \-,wit\ n : foolish person — **half–wit·ted** \-,witəd\ adj

**hal·i·but** \'haləbət\ n, pl **halibut** : large edible marine flatfish

**hal·i·to·sis** \,halə'tōsəs\ n : bad breath

**hall** \'hól\ n 1 : large public or college or university building 2 : lobby 3 : auditorium

**hal·le·lu·jah** \,halə'lüyə\ interj — used to express praise, joy, or thanks

**hall·mark** \'hól,märk\ n : distinguishing characteristic

**hal·low** \'halō\ vb : consecrate — **hallowed** \-ōd, -əwəd\ adj

**Hal·low·een** \,halə'wēn, ,häl-\ n : evening of October 31 observed esp. by children in merrymaking and masquerading

**hal·lu·ci·na·tion** \hə,lüs⁰n'āshən\ n : perception of objects that are not real — **hal·lu·ci·nate** \ha'lüs⁰n,āt\ vb — **hal·lu·ci·na·to·ry** \-'lüs⁰nə,tōrē\ adj

**hal·lu·ci·no·gen** \hə'lüs⁰nəjən\ n : substance that induces hallucinations — **hal·lu·ci·no·gen·ic** \-,lüs⁰nə'jenik\ adj

**hall·way** n : entrance hall

**ha·lo** \'hālō\ n, pl **-los** or **-loes** : circle of light appearing to surround a shining body

¹**halt** \'hólt\ adj : lame

²**halt** vb : stop or cause to stop — **halt** n

**hal·ter** \'hóltər\ n 1 : rope or strap for leading or tying an animal 2 : brief blouse held up by straps ~ vb : catch (an animal) with a halter

**halt·ing** \'hóltiŋ\ adj : uncertain — **halt·ing·ly** adv

**halve** \'hav, 'håv\ vb **halved; halv·ing** 1 : divide into halves 2 : reduce to half

**halves** pl of HALF

**ham** \'ham\ n 1 : thigh — usu. pl. 2 : cut esp. of pork from the thigh 3 : showy actor 4 : amateur radio operator ~ vb **-mm-** : overplay a part — **ham** adj

**ham·burg·er** \'ham,bərgər\, **ham·burg** \-,bərg\ n : ground beef or a sandwich made with this

**ham·let** \'hamlət\ n : small village

**ham·mer** \'hamər\ n 1 : hand tool for pounding 2 : gun part whose striking explodes the charge ~ vb : beat, drive, or shape with a hammer — **hammer out** vb : produce with effort

**ham·mer·head** n 1 : striking part of a hammer 2 : shark with a hammerlike head

**ham·mock** \'hamək\ n : swinging bed hung by cords at each end

¹**ham·per** \'hampər\ vb : impede

²**hamper** n : large covered basket

**ham·ster** \'hamstər\ n : stocky short-tailed rodent

**ham·string** \'ham,striŋ\ vb **-strung** \-,strəŋ\; **-string·ing** \-,striŋiŋ\ 1 : cripple by cutting the leg tendons 2 : make ineffective or powerless

**hand** \'hand\ n 1 : end of a front limb adapted for grasping 2 : side 3 : promise of marriage 4 : handwriting 5 : assistance or participation 6 : applause 7 : cards held by a player 8 : worker ~ vb : lead, assist, give, or pass with the hand — **hand·clasp** n — **hand·craft** vb — **hand·ful** n — **hand·gun** n — **hand·less** adj — **hand·made** adj — **hand·rail** n — **hand·saw** n — **hand·wo·ven** adj — **hand·writ·ing** n — **hand·writ·ten** adj

**hand·bag** n : woman's purse

**hand·ball** n : game played by striking a ball with the hand

**hand·bill** n : printed advertisement or notice distributed by hand

**hand·book** n : concise reference book

**hand·cuffs** n pl : locking bracelets that bind the wrists together — **handcuff** vb

**hand·i·cap** \'handē,kap\ n 1 : advantage given or disadvantage imposed to equalize a competition **2** : disadvantage — **handicap** vb — **hand•i•capped** adj — **hand•i•cap•per** n

**hand•i•craft** \'handē,kraft\ n **1** : manual skill **2** : article made by hand — **hand•i•craft•er** n

**hand•i•work** \-,wərk\ n : work done personally or by the hands

**hand•ker•chief** \'haŋkərchəf, -,chēf\ n, pl **-chiefs** \-chəfs, -,chēfs\ : small piece of cloth carried for personal use

**han•dle** \'hand°l\ n : part to be grasped ~ vb **-dled; -dling 1** : touch, hold, or manage with the hands **2** : deal with **3** : deal or trade in — **han•dle•bar** n — **han•dled** \-d°ld\ adj — **han•dler** \'handlər\ n

**hand•maid•en** n : female attendant

**hand•out** n : something given out

**hand•pick** vb : select personally

**hand•shake** n : clasping of hands (as in greeting)

**hand•some** \'hansəm\ adj **-som•er; -est 1** : sizable **2** : generous **3** : nice-looking — **hand•some•ly** adv — **hand•some•ness** n

**hand•spring** n : somersault on the hands

**hand•stand** n : a balancing upside down on the hands

**handy** \'handē\ adj **hand•i•er; -est 1** : conveniently near **2** : easily used **3** : dexterous — **hand•i•ly** adv — **hand•i•ness** n

**handy•man** \-,man\ n : one who does odd jobs

**hang** \'haŋ\ vb **hung** \'həŋ\; **hang•ing 1** : fasten or remain fastened to an elevated point without support from below **2** : suspend by the neck until dead — past tense often **hanged 3** : droop ~ n **1** : way a thing hangs **2** : an understanding of something — **hang•er** n — **hang•ing** n

**han•gar** \'haŋər\ n : airplane shelter

**hang•dog** \'haŋ,dȯg\ adj : ashamed or guilty

**hang•man** \-mən\ n : public executioner

**hang•nail** n : loose skin near a fingernail

**hang•out** n : place where one likes to spend time

**hang•over** n : sick feeling following heavy drinking

**hank** \'haŋk\ n : coil or loop

**han•ker** \'haŋkər\ vb : desire strongly — **han•ker•ing** n

**han•ky–pan•ky** \,haŋkē'paŋkē\ n : questionable or underhanded activity

**han•som** \'hansəm\ n : 2-wheeled covered carriage

**Ha•nuk•kah** \'känəkə, 'hän-\ n : 8-day Jewish holiday commemorating the rededication of the Temple of Jerusalem after its defilement by Antiochus of Syria

**hap•haz•ard** \hap'hazərd\ adj : having no plan or order — **hap•haz•ard•ly** adv

**hap•less** \'hapləs\ adj : unfortunate — **hap•less•ly** adv — **hap•less•ness** n

**hap•pen** \'hapən\ vb **1** : take place **2** : be fortunate to encounter something unexpectedly — often used with infinitive

**hap•pen•ing** \-əniŋ\ n : occurrence

**hap•py** \'hapē\ adj **-pi•er; -est 1** : fortunate **2** : content, pleased, or joyous — **hap•pi•ly** \'hapəlē\ adv — **hap•pi•ness** n

**ha•rangue** \hə'raŋ\ n : ranting or scolding speech — **harangue** vb — **ha•rangu•er** \-'raŋər\ n

**ha•rass** \hə'ras, 'harəs\ vb **1** : disturb and impede by repeated raids **2** : annoy continually — **ha•rass•ment** n

**har•bin•ger** \'härbənjər\ n : one that announces or foreshadows what is coming

**har•bor** \-bər\ n : protected body of water suitable for anchorage ~ vb **1** : give refuge to **2** : hold as a thought or feeling

**hard** \'härd\ adj **1** : not easily penetrated **2** : firm or definite **3** : close or searching **4** : severe or unfeeling **5** : strenuous or difficult **6** : physically strong or intense — **hard** adv — **hard•ness** n

**hard•en** \'härd°n\ vb : make or become hard or harder — **hard•en•er** n

**hard•head•ed** \,härd'hedəd\ adj **1** : stubborn **2** : realistic — **hard•head•ed•ly** adv — **hard•head•ed•ness** n

**hard•heart•ed** \-'härtəd\ adj : lacking sympathy — **hard•heart•ed•ly** adv — **hard•heart•ed•ness** n

**hard•ly** \'härdlē\ adv **1** : only just **2** : certainly not

**hard–nosed** \-,nōzd\ adj : tough or uncompromising

**hard•ship** \-,ship\ n : suffering or privation

**hard•tack** \-,tak\ n : hard biscuit

**hard•ware** n **1** : cutlery or tools made

of metal **2** : physical components of a vehicle or apparatus

**hard•wood** *n* : wood of a broad-leaved usu. deciduous tree — **hardwood** *adj*

**har•dy** \'härdē\ *adj* **-di•er; -est** : able to withstand adverse conditions — **har•di•ly** *adv* — **har•di•ness** *n*

**hare** \'har\ *n, pl* **hare** *or* **hares** : long=eared mammal related to the rabbit

**hare•brained** \-,brānd\ *adj* : foolish

**hare•lip** *n* : deformity in which the upper lip is vertically split — **hare•lipped** \-,lipt\ *adj*

**ha•rem** \'harəm\ *n* : house or part of a house allotted to women in a Muslim household or the women and servants occupying it

**hark** \'härk\ *vb* : listen

**har•le•quin** \'härlikən, -kwən\ *n* : clown

**har•lot** \'härlət\ *n* : prostitute

**harm** \'härm\ *n* **1** : physical or mental damage **2** : mischief ~ *vb* : cause harm — **harm•ful** \-fəl\ *adj* — **harm•ful•ly** *adv* — **harm•ful•ness** *n* — **harm•less** *adj* — **harm•less•ly** *adv* — **harm•less•ness** *n*

**har•mon•ic** \här'mänik\ *adj* **1** : of or relating to musical harmony **2** : pleasing to hear — **har•mon•i•cal•ly** \-iklē\ *adv*

**har•mon•i•ca** \här'mänikə\ *n* : small wind instrument with metallic rccds

**har•mo•ny** \'härmənē\ *n, pl* **-nies 1** : musical combination of sounds **2** : pleasing arrangement of parts **3** : lack of conflict **4** : internal calm — **har•mo•ni•ous** \här'mōnēəs\ *adj* — **har•mo•ni•ous•ly** *adv* — **har•mo•ni•ous•ness** *n* — **har•mo•ni•za•tion** \,härmənə'zāshən\ *n* — **har•mo•nize** \'härmə,nīz\ *vb*

**har•ness** \'härnəs\ *n* : gear of a draft animal ~ *vb* **1** : put a harness on **2** : put to use

**harp** \'härp\ *n* : musical instrument with many strings plucked by the fingers ~ *vb* **1** : play on a harp **2** : dwell on a subject tiresomely — **harp•er** *n* — **harp•ist** *n*

**har•poon** \här'pün\ *n* : barbed spear used in hunting whales — **harpoon** *vb* — **har•poon•er** *n*

**harp•si•chord** \'härpsi,kȯrd\ *n* : keyboard instrument with strings that are plucked

**har•py** \'härpē\ *n, pl* **-pies** : shrewish woman

**har•row** \'harō\ *n* : implement used to break up soil ~ *vb* **1** : cultivate with a harrow **2** : distress

**har•ry** \'harē\ *vb* **-ried; -ry•ing** : torment by or as if by constant attack

**harsh** \'härsh\ *adj* **1** : disagreeably rough **2** : severe — **harsh•ly** *adv* — **harsh•ness** *n*

**har•um—scar•um** \,harəm'skarəm\ *adv* : recklessly

**har•vest** \'härvəst\ *n* **1** : act or time of gathering in a crop **2** : mature crop — **harvest** *vb* — **har•vest•er** *n*

**has** *pres 3d sing of* HAVE

**hash** \'hash\ *vb* : chop into small pieces ~ *n* : chopped meat mixed with potatoes and browned

**hasp** \'hasp\ *n* : hinged strap fastener esp. for a door

**has•sle** \'hasəl\ *n* **1** : quarrel **2** : struggle **3** : cause of annoyance — **has•sle** *vb*

**has•sock** \'hasək\ *n* : cushion used as a seat or leg rest

**haste** \'hāst\ *n* **1** : rapidity of motion **2** : rash action **3** : excessive eagerness — **hast•i•ly** \'hāstəlē\ *adv* — **hast•i•ness** \-stēnəs\ *n* — **hasty** \-stē\ *adj*

**has•ten** \'hāsᵊn\ *vb* : hurry

**hat** \'hat\ *n* : covering for the head

¹**hatch** \'hach\ *n* : small door or opening — **hatch•way** *n*

²**hatch** *vb* : emerge from an egg — **hatch•ery** \-ərē\ *n*

**hatch•et** \'hachət\ *n* : short-handled ax

**hate** \'hāt\ *n* : intense hostility and aversion ~ *vb* **hat•ed; hat•ing 1** : express or feel hate **2** : dislike — **hate•ful** \-fəl\ *adj* — **hate•ful•ly** *adv* — **hate•ful•ness** *n* — **hat•er** *n*

**ha•tred** \'hātrəd\ *n* : hate

**hat•ter** \'hatər\ *n* : one that makes or sells hats

**haugh•ty** \'hȯtē\ *adj* **-ti•er; -est** : disdainfully proud — **haugh•ti•ly** *adv* — **haugh•ti•ness** *n*

**haul** \'hȯl\ *vb* **1** : draw or pull **2** : transport or carry ~ *n* **1** : amount collected **2** : load or the distance it is transported — **haul•er** *n*

**haunch** \'hȯnch\ *n* : hip or hindquarter — usu. pl.

**haunt** \'hȯnt\ *vb* **1** : visit often **2** : visit or inhabit as a ghost ~ *n* : place frequented — **haunt•er** *n* — **haunt•ing•ly** *adv*

**have** \'hav, *in sense 2 before* "to" *usu*

**'haf\** *vb* **had** \'had\; **hav•ing**
\'havin\; **has** \'haz, *in sense 2 be-*
*fore "to" usu* 'has\ **1** : hold in possession, service, or affection **2** : be
compelled or forced to **3** — used
as an auxiliary with the past participle
to form the present perfect, past perfect, or future perfect **4** : obtain or receive **5** : undergo **6** : cause to **7**
: bear — **have to do with** : have in the
way of connection or relation with or
effect on

**ha•ven** \'hāvən\ *n* : place of safety

**hav•oc** \'havək\ *n* **1** : wide destruction
**2** : great confusion

**'hawk** \'hòk\ *n* : bird of prey with a
strong hooked bill and sharp talons

**²hawk** *vb* : offer for sale by calling out in
the street — **hawk•er** *n*

**haw•ser** \'hòzər\ *n* : large rope

**haw•thorn** \'hò,thòrn\ *n* : spiny shrub
or tree with pink or white fragrant
flowers

**hay** \'hā\ *n* : herbs (as grass) cut and
dried for use as fodder — **hay** *vb* —
**hay•loft** *n* — **hay•mow** \-,maù\ *n* —
**hay•stack** *n*

**hay•cock** \'hā,käk\ *n* : small pile of
hay

**hay•rick** \-,rik\ *n* : large outdoor stack
of hay

**hay•seed** \'hā,sēd\ *n* : bumpkin

**hay•wire** *adj* : being out of order

**haz•ard** \'hazərd\ *n* **1** : source of danger **2** : chance ∼ *vb* : venture or risk
— **haz•ard•ous** *adj*

**'haze** \'hāz\ *n* : fine dust, smoke, or light
vapor in the air that reduces visibility

**²haze** *vb* **hazed; haz•ing** : harass by abusive and humiliating tricks

**ha•zel** \'hāzəl\ *n* **1** : shrub or small tree
bearing edible nuts (**ha•zel•nuts**) **2**
: light brown color

**hazy** \'hāzē\ *adj* **haz•i•er; -est** **1** : obscured by haze **2** : vague or indefinite
— **haz•i•ly** *adv* — **haz•i•ness** *n*

**he** \'hē\ *pron* **1** : that male one **2** : a or
the person

**head** \'hed\ *n* **1** : front or upper part of
the body **2** : mind **3** : upper or higher
end **4** : director or leader **5** : place of
leadership or honor ∼ *adj* : principal
or chief ∼ *vb* **1** : provide with or
form a head **2** : put, stand, or be at
the head **3** : point or proceed in a certain direction — **head•ache** *n* —
**head•band** *n* — **head•dress** *n* —
**head•ed** *adj* — **head•first** *adv or adj*

— **head•gear** *n* — **head•less** *adj*
— **head•rest** *n* — **head•ship** *n* —
**head•wait•er** *n*

**head•ing** \-in\ *n* **1** : direction in which
a plane or ship heads **2** : something
(as a title) standing at the top or beginning

**head•land** \'hedlənd, -,land\ *n*
: promontory

**head•light** *n* : light on the front of a vehicle

**head•line** *n* : introductory line of a
newspaper story printed in large type

**head•long** \-'lòn\ *adv* **1** : head foremost **2** : in a rash or reckless manner
— **head•long** \-,lòn\ *adj*

**head•mas•ter** *n* : man who is head of a
private school

**head•mis•tress** *n* : woman who is head
of a private school

**head—on** *adj* : having the front facing in
the direction of initial contact —
**head—on** *adv*

**head•phone** *n* : an earphone held on by
a band over the head — usu. pl.

**head•quar•ters** *n sing or pl* : command
or administrative center

**head•stone** *n* : stone at the head of a
grave

**head•strong** *adj* : stubborn or willful

**head•wa•ters** *n pl* : source of a stream

**head•way** *n* : forward motion

**heady** \'hedē\ *adj* **head•i•er; -est** **1**
: intoxicating **2** : shrewd

**heal** \'hēl\ *vb* : make or become sound
or whole — **heal•er** *n*

**health** \'helth\ *n* : sound physical or
mental condition

**health•ful** \-fəl\ *adj* : beneficial to health
— **health•ful•ly** *adv* — **health•ful•-
ness** *n*

**healthy** \'helthē\ *adj* **health•i•er; -est**
: enjoying or typical of good health
— **health•i•ly** *adv* — **health•i•ness** *n*

**heap** \'hēp\ *n* : pile ∼ *vb* : throw or lay
in a heap

**hear** \'hir\ *vb* **heard** \'hərd\; **hear•ing**
\'hirin\ **1** : perceive by the ear **2**
: heed **3** : learn

**hear•ing** *n* **1** : process or power of perceiving sound **2** : earshot **3** : session
in which witnesses are heard

**hear•ken** \'härkən\ *vb* : give attention

**hear•say** *n* : rumor

**hearse** \'hərs\ *n* : vehicle for carrying
the dead to the grave

**heart** \'härt\ *n* **1** : hollow muscular organ that keeps up the circulation of

the blood **2** : playing card of a suit marked with a red heart **3** : whole personality or the emotional or moral part of it **4** : courage **5** : essential part — **heart·beat** n — **heart·ed** adj

**heart·ache** n : anguish of mind

**heart·break** n : crushing grief — **heart·break·er** n — **heart·break·ing** adj — **heart·bro·ken** adj

**heart·burn** n : burning distress in the heart area after eating

**heart·en** \'härt°n\ vb : encourage

**hearth** \'härth\ n **1** : area in front of a fireplace **2** : home — **hearth·stone** n

**heart·less** \'härtləs\ adj : cruel

**heart·rend·ing** \-ˌrendiŋ\ adj : causing intense grief or anguish

**heart·sick** adj : very despondent

**heart·strings** n pl : deepest emotions

**heart·throb** n : sweetheart

**heart·warm·ing** adj : inspiring sympathetic feeling

**heart·wood** n : central portion of wood

**hearty** \'härtē\ adj **heart·i·er**; **-est 1** : vigorously healthy **2** : nourishing — **heart·i·ly** adv — **heart·i·ness** n

**heat** \'hēt\ vb : make or become warm or hot ~ n **1** : condition of being hot **2** : form of energy that causes a body to rise in temperature **3** : intensity of feeling — **heat·ed·ly** adv — **heat·er** n

**heath** \'hēth\ n **1** : often evergreen shrubby plant of wet acid soils **2** : tract of wasteland — **heathy** adj

**hea·then** \'hēthən\ n, pl **-thens** or **-then** : uncivilized or godless person — **heathen** adj

**heath·er** \'hethər\ n : evergreen heath with lavender flowers — **heath·ery** adj

**heat·stroke** n : disorder that follows prolonged exposure to excessive heat

**heave** \'hēv\ vb **heaved** or **hove** \'hōv\; **heav·ing 1** : rise or lift upward **2** : throw **3** : rise and fall ~ n **1** : an effort to lift or raise **2** : throw

**heav·en** \'hevən\ n **1** pl : sky **2** : abode of the Deity and of the blessed dead **3** : place of supreme happiness — **heav·en·ly** adj — **heav·en·ward** adv or adj

**heavy** \'hevē\ adj **heav·i·er**; **-est 1** : having great weight **2** : hard to bear **3** : greater than the average — **heav·i·ly** adv — **heav·i·ness** n — **heavy·weight** n

**heavy–du·ty** adj : able to withstand unusual strain

**heavy·set** adj : stocky and compact in build

**heck·le** \'hekəl\ vb **-led**; **-ling** : harass with gibes — **heck·ler** \'heklər\ n

**hec·tic** \'hektik\ adj : filled with excitement, activity, or confusion — **hec·ti·cal·ly** \-tiklē\ adv

**hedge** \'hej\ n **1** : fence or boundary of shrubs or small trees **2** : means of protection ~ vb **hedged**; **hedg·ing 1** : protect oneself against loss **2** : evade the risk of commitment — **hedg·er** n

**hedge·hog** n : spiny mammal (as a porcupine)

**he·do·nism** \'hēd°nˌizəm\ n : way of life devoted to pleasure — **he·do·nist** \-°nist\ n — **he·do·nis·tic** \ˌhēd°n-'istik\ adj

**heed** \'hēd\ vb : pay attention ~ n : attention — **heed·ful** \-fəl\ adj — **heed·ful·ly** adv — **heed·ful·ness** n — **heed·less** adj — **heed·less·ly** adv — **heed·less·ness** n

¹**heel** \'hēl\ n **1** : back of the foot **2** : crusty end of a loaf of bread **3** : solid piece forming the back of the sole of a shoe — **heel·less** \'hēlləs\ adj

²**heel** vb : tilt to one side

**heft** \'heft\ n : weight ~ vb : judge the weight of by lifting

**hefty** \'heftē\ adj **heft·i·er**; **-est** : big and bulky

**he·ge·mo·ny** \hi'jemənē\ n : preponderant influence over others

**heif·er** \'hefər\ n : young cow

**height** \'hīt, 'hītth\ n **1** : highest part or point **2** : distance from bottom to top **3** : altitude

**height·en** \'hīt°n\ vb : increase in amount or degree

**hei·nous** \'hānəs\ adj : shockingly evil — **hei·nous·ly** adv — **hei·nous·ness** n

**heir** \'ar\ n : one who inherits or is entitled to inherit property

**heir·ess** \'arəs\ n : female heir esp. to great wealth

**heir·loom** \'arˌlüm\ n : something handed on from one generation to another

**held** past of HOLD

**he·li·cal** \'helikəl, 'hē-\ adj : spiral

**he·li·cop·ter** \'heləˌkäptər, 'hē-\ n : aircraft supported in the air by rotors

**he·lio·trope** \'hēlyəˌtrōp\ n : garden

herb with small fragrant white or purple flowers

**he•li•um** \'hēlēəm\ n : very light non-flammable gaseous chemical element

**he•lix** \'hēliks\ n, pl **-li•ces** \'helə,sēz, 'hē-\ : something spiral

**hell** \'hel\ n 1 : nether world in which the dead continue to exist 2 : realm of the devil 3 : place or state of torment or destruction — **hell•ish** adj

**hell•gram•mite** \'helgrə,mīt\ n : aquatic insect larva

**hel•lion** \'helyən\ n : troublesome person

**hel•lo** \hə'lō, he-\ n, pl **-los** : expression of greeting

**helm** \'helm\ n : lever or wheel for steering a ship — **helms•man** \'helmzmən\ n

**hel•met** \'helmət\ n : protective covering for the head

**help** \'help\ vb 1 : supply what is needed 2 : be of use 3 : refrain from or prevent ~ n 1 : something that helps or a source of help 2 : one who helps another — **help•er** n — **help•ful** \-fəl\ adj — **help•ful•ly** adv — **help•ful•ness** n — **help•less** adj — **help•less•ly** adv — **help•less•ness** n

**help•ing** \'helpiŋ\ n : portion of food

**help•mate** n 1 : helper 2 : wife

**help•meet** \-,mēt\ n : helpmate

**hel•ter–skel•ter** \,heltər'skeltər\ adv : in total disorder

**hem** \'hem\ n : border of an article of cloth doubled back and stitched down ~ vb **-mm-** 1 : sew a hem 2 : surround restrictively — **hem•line** n

**he•ma•tol•o•gy** \,hēmə'täləjē\ n : study of the blood and blood-forming organs — **hema•to•log•ic** \-mət°l-'äjik\ adj — **he•ma•tol•o•gist** \-'täləjist\ n

**hemi•sphere** \'hemə,sfir\ n : one of the halves of the earth divided by the equator into northern and southern parts (**northern hemisphere, southern hemisphere**) or by a meridian into eastern and western parts (**eastern hemisphere, western hemisphere**) — **hemi•spher•ic** \,hemə'sfirik, -'sfer-\, **hemi•spher•i•cal** \-'sfirikəl, -'sfer-\ adj

**hem•lock** \'hem,läk\ n 1 : poisonous herb related to the carrot 2 : evergreen tree related to the pines

**he•mo•glo•bin** \'hēmə,glōbən\ n : iron-containing compound found in red blood cells

**he•mo•phil•ia** \,hēmə'filēə\ n : hereditary tendency to severe prolonged bleeding — **he•mo•phil•i•ac** \-ē,ak\ adj or n

**hem•or•rhage** \'hemərij\ n : large discharge of blood — **hemorrhage** vb — **hem•or•rhag•ic** \,hemə'rajik\ adj

**hem•or•rhoids** \'hemə,rȯidz\ n pl : swollen mass of dilated veins at or just within the anus

**hemp** \'hemp\ n : tall Asian herb grown for its tough fiber

**hen** \'hen\ n : female domestic fowl

**hence** \'hens\ adv 1 : away 2 : therefore 3 : from this source or origin

**hence•forth** adv : from this point on

**hence•for•ward** adv : henceforth

**hench•man** \'henchmən\ n : trusted follower

**hen•na** \'henə\ n : reddish brown dye from a tropical shrub used esp. on hair

**hen•peck** \'hen,pek\ vb : subject (one's husband) to persistent nagging

**he•pat•ic** \hi'patik\ adj : relating to or resembling the liver

**hep•a•ti•tis** \,hepə'tītəs\ n, pl **-tit•i•des** \-'titə,dēz\ : disease in which the liver becomes inflamed

**her** \'hər\ adj : of or relating to her or herself ~ \ər, (')hər\ pron objective case of SHE

**her•ald** \'herəld\ n 1 : official crier or messenger 2 : harbinger ~ vb : give notice

**her•ald•ry** \'herəldrē\ n, pl **-ries** : practice of devising and granting stylized emblems (as for a family) — **he•ral•dic** \he'raldik, hə-\ adj

**herb** \'ərb, 'hərb\ n 1 : seed plant that lacks woody tissue 2 : plant or plant part valued for medicinal or savory qualities — **her•ba•ceous** \,ər'bāshəs, ,hər-\ adj — **herb•age** \'ərbij, 'hər-\ n — **herb•al** \-bəl\ n or adj — **herb•al•ist** \-bəlist\ n

**her•bi•cide** \'ərbə,sīd, 'hər-\ n : agent that destroys plants — **her•bi•cid•al** \,ərbə'sīd°l, ,hər-\ adj

**her•biv•o•rous** \,ər'bivərəs, ,hər-\ adj : feeding on plants — **her•bi•vore** \'ərbə,vȯr, 'hər-\ n

**her•cu•le•an** \,hərkyə'lēən, ,hər'kyü-lēən\ adj : of extraordinary power, size, or difficulty

**herd** \'hərd\ n : group of animals of

one kind ~ vb : assemble or move in a herd — **herd·er** n — **herds·man** \'hərdzmən\ n

**here** \'hir\ adv **1** : in, at, or to this place **2** : now **3** : at or in this point or particular **4** : in the present life or state ~ n : this place — **here·abouts** \'hirə,baủts\, **here·about** \-,baủt\ adv

**here·af·ter** adv : in some future time or state ~ n : existence beyond earthly life

**here·by** adv : by means of this

**he·red·i·tary** \hə'redə,terē\ adj **1** : genetically passed or passable from parent to offspring **2** : passing by inheritance

**he·red·i·ty** \-ətē\ n : the passing of characteristics from parent to offspring

**here·in** adv : in this

**here·of** adv : of this

**here·on** adv : on this

**her·e·sy** \'herəsē\ n, pl **-sies** : opinion or doctrine contrary to church dogma — **her·e·tic** \-,tik\ n — **he·re·ti·cal** \hə'retikəl\ adj

**here·to** adv : to this document

**here·to·fore** \'hirtü,fōr\ adv : up to this time

**here·un·der** adv : under this

**here·un·to** adv : to this

**here·upon** adv : on this

**here·with** adv **1** : with this **2** : hereby

**her·i·tage** \'herətij\ n **1** : inheritance **2** : birthright

**her·maph·ro·dite** \hər'mafrə,dīt\ n : animal or plant having both male and female reproductive organs — **hermaphrodite** adj — **her·maph·ro·dit·ic** \-,mafrə'ditik\ adj

**her·met·ic** \hər'metik\ adj : sealed airtight — **her·met·i·cal·ly** \-iklē\ adv

**her·mit** \'hərmət\ n : one who lives in solitude

**her·nia** \'hərnēə\ n, pl **-ni·as** or **-ni·ae** \-nē,ē, -nē,ī\ : protrusion of a bodily part through the weakened wall of its enclosure — **her·ni·ate** \-nē,āt\ vb

**he·ro** \'hērō, 'hirō\ n, pl **-roes** : one that is much admired or shows great courage — **he·ro·ic** \hi'rōik\ adj — **he·ro·i·cal·ly** \-iklē\ adv — **he·ro·ics** \-iks\ n pl — **he·ro·ism** \'herə,wizəm\ n

**her·o·in** \'herəwən\ n : strongly addictive narcotic

**her·o·ine** \'herəwən\ n : woman of heroic achievements or qualities

**her·on** \'herən\ n : long-legged long-billed wading bird

**her·pes** \'hərpēz\ n : virus disease characterized by the formation of blisters

**her·pe·tol·o·gy** \,hərpə'täləjē\ n : study of reptiles and amphibians — **her·pe·tol·o·gist** \-pə'täləjist\ n

**her·ring** \'heriŋ\ n, pl **-ring** or **-rings** : narrow-bodied Atlantic food fish

**hers** \'hərz\ pron : one or the ones belonging to her

**her·self** \hər'self\ pron : she, her — used reflexively or for emphasis

**hertz** \'herts, 'hərts\ n, pl **hertz** : unit of frequency equal to one cycle per second

**hes·i·tant** \'hezətənt\ adj : tending to hesitate — **hes·i·tance** \-təns\ n — **hes·i·tan·cy** \-tənsē\ n — **hes·i·tant·ly** adv

**hes·i·tate** \'hezə,tāt\ vb **-tat·ed; -tat·ing** **1** : hold back esp. in doubt **2** : pause — **hes·i·ta·tion** \,hezə'tāshən\ n

**het·er·o·ge·neous** \,hetərə'jēnēəs, -nyəs\ adj : consisting of dissimilar ingredients or constituents — **het·er·o·ge·ne·i·ty** \-jə'nēətē\ n — **het·er·o·ge·neous·ly** adv

**het·ero·sex·u·al** \,hetərō'sekshəwəl\ adj : oriented toward the opposite sex — **heterosexual** n — **het·ero·sex·u·al·i·ty** \-,sekshə'walətē\ n

**hew** \'hyü\ vb **hewed; hewed** or **hewn** \'hyün\; **hew·ing** **1** : cut or shape with or as if with an ax **2** : conform strictly — **hew·er** n

**hex** \'heks\ vb : put an evil spell on — **hex** n

**hexa·gon** \'heksə,gän\ n : 6-sided polygon — **hex·ag·o·nal** \hek'sagən³l\ adj

**hey·day** \'hā,dā\ n : time of flourishing

**hi·a·tus** \hī'ātəs\ n : lapse in continuity

**hi·ba·chi** \hi'bächē\ n : brazier

**hi·ber·nate** \'hībər,nāt\ vb **-nat·ed; -nat·ing** : pass the winter in a torpid or resting state — **hi·ber·na·tion** \,hībər'nāshən\ n — **hi·ber·na·tor** \'hībər,nātər\ n

**hic·cup** \'hikəp\ vb **-cuped; -cup·ing** : to inhale spasmodically and make a peculiar sound ~ n pl : attack of hiccuping

**hick** \'hik\ n : awkward provincial person — **hick** adj

**hick·o·ry** \'hikərē\ n, pl **-ries** : No.

American hardwood tree — **hickory**
*adj*

¹**hide** \'hīd\ *vb* **hid** \'hid\; **hid·den**
\'hid²n\ *or* **hid**; **hid·ing** : put or remain out of sight — **hid·er** *n*

²**hide** *n* : animal skin

**hide·bound** \'hīd,baund\ *adj* : inflexible or conservative

**hid·eous** \'hidēəs\ *adj* : very ugly —
**hid·eous·ly** *adv* — **hid·eous·ness** *n*

**hie** \'hī\ *vb* **hied; hy·ing** *or* **hie·ing**
: hurry

**hi·er·ar·chy** \'hīə,rärkē\ *n, pl* **-chies**
: persons or things arranged in a
graded series — **hi·er·ar·chi·cal** \,hīə-
'rärkikəl\ *adj*

**hi·er·o·glyph·ic** \,hīərə'glifik\ *n* : character in the picture writing of the ancient Egyptians

**high** \'hī\ *adj* **1** : having large extension upward **2** : elevated in pitch **3**
: exalted in character **4** : of greater
degree or amount than average **5**
: expensive **6** : excited or stupefied by
alcohol or a drug ~ *adv* : at or to a
high place or degree ~ *n* **1** : elevated
point or level **2** : automatic gear giving the highest speed — **high·ly** *adv*

**high·boy** *n* : high chest of drawers on
legs

**high·brow** \-,braù\ *n* : person of superior learning or culture — **highbrow**
*adj*

**high–definition** *adj* : being or relating
to a television system with twice as
many scan lines per frame as a conventional system

**high–flown** *adj* : pretentious

**high–hand·ed** *adj* : willful and arrogant
— **high–hand·ed·ly** *adv* — **high–
hand·ed·ness** *n*

**high·land** \'hīlənd\ *n* : hilly country —
**high·land·er** \-ləndər\ *n*

**high·light** *n* : event or detail of major
importance ~ *vb* **1** : emphasize **2**
: be a highlight of

**high·ness** \-nəs\ *n* **1** : quality or degree of being high **2** — used as a title (as for kings)

**high–rise** *adj* : having several stories

**high school** *n* : school usu. including
grades 9 to 12 or 10 to 12

**high–spir·it·ed** *adj* : lively

**high–strung** \,hī'strəŋ\ *adj* : very nervous or sensitive

**high·way** *n* : public road

**high·way·man** \-mən\ *n* : one who robs
travelers on a road

**hi·jack** \'hī,jak\ *vb* : steal esp. by com-
mandeering a vehicle — **hijack** *n* —
**hi·jack·er** *n*

**hike** \'hīk\ *vb* **hiked; hik·ing** **1** : raise
quickly **2** : take a long walk ~ *n* **1**
: long walk **2** : increase — **hik·er** *n*

**hi·lar·i·ous** \hi'lareəs, hī'-\ *adj* : extremely funny — **hi·lar·i·ous·ly** *adv*
— **hi·lar·i·ty** \-ətē\ *n*

**hill** \'hil\ *n* : place where the land rises
— **hill·side** *n* — **hill·top** *n* — **hilly** *adj*

**hill·bil·ly** \'hil,bilē\ *n, pl* **-lies** : person
from a backwoods area

**hill·ock** \'hilək\ *n* : small hill

**hilt** \'hilt\ *n* : handle of a sword

**him** \'him\ *pron, objective case of* HE

**him·self** \him'self\ *pron* : he, him —
used reflexively or for emphasis

¹**hind** \'hīnd\ *n* : female deer

²**hind** *adj* : back

**hin·der** \'hindər\ *vb* : obstruct or hold
back

**hind·most** *adj* : farthest to the rear

**hind·quar·ter** *n* : back half of a complete side of a carcass

**hin·drance** \'hindrəns\ *n* : something
that hinders

**hind·sight** *n* : understanding of an
event after it has happened

**Hin·du·ism** \'hindü,izəm\ *n* : body of
religious beliefs and practices native
to India — **Hin·du** *n or adj*

**hinge** \'hinj\ *n* : jointed piece on which
a swinging part (as a door) turns ~
*vb* **hinged; hing·ing 1** : attach by or
furnish with hinges **2** : depend

**hint** \'hint\ *n* **1** : indirect suggestion **2**
: clue **3** : very small amount — **hint** *vb*

**hin·ter·land** \'hintər,land\ *n* : remote
region

**hip** \'hip\ *n* : part of the body on either
side just below the waist — **hip·bone** *n*

**hip·po·pot·a·mus** \,hipə'pätəməs\ *n,
pl* **-mus·es** *or* **-mi** \-,mī\ : large
thick-skinned African river animal

**hire** \'hīr\ *n* **1** : payment for labor **2**
: employment **3** : one who is hired ~
*vb* **hired; hir·ing** : employ for pay

**hire·ling** \-liŋ\ *n* : one who serves another only for gain

**hir·sute** \'hər,süt, 'hir-\ *adj* : hairy

**his** \'hiz\ *adj* : of or belonging to him
~ *pron* : ones belonging to him

**hiss** \'his\ *vb* **1** : make a sibilant sound
**2** : show dislike by hissing — **hiss** *n*

**his·to·ri·an** \his'tōrēən\ *n* : writer of
history

**his·to·ry** \'histərē\ *n, pl* **-ries 1** : chronological record of significant events **2** : study of past events **3** : an established record — **his·tor·ic** \his-'tòrik\, **his·tor·i·cal** \-ikəl\ *adj* — **his·tor·i·cal·ly** \-klē\ *adv*

**his·tri·on·ics** \ˌhistrē'äniks\ *n pl* : exaggerated display of emotion

**hit** \'hit\ *vb* **hit; hit·ting** **1** : reach with a blow **2** : come or cause to come in contact **3** : affect detrimentally ∼ *n* **1** : blow **2** : great success — **hit·ter** *n*

**hitch** \'hich\ *vb* **1** : move by jerks **2** : catch by a hook **3** : hitchhike ∼ *n* **1** : jerk **2** : sudden halt

**hitch·hike** \'hich,hīk\ *vb* : travel by securing free rides from passing vehicles — **hitch·hik·er** *n*

**hith·er** \'hithər\ *adv* : to this place

**hith·er·to** \-ˌtü\ *adv* : up to this time

**hive** \'hīv\ *n* **1** : container housing honeybees **2** : colony of bees — **hive** *vb*

**hives** \'hīvz\ *n sing or pl* : allergic disorder with itchy skin patches

**HMO** \ˌäch,em'ō\ *n* : comprehensive health-care organization financed by clients

**hoard** \'hòrd\ *n* : hidden accumulation — **hoard** *vb* — **hoard·er** *n*

**hoar·frost** \'hòr,fròst\ *n* : frost

**hoarse** \'hòrs\ *adj* **hoars·er; -est** **1** : harsh in sound **2** : speaking in a harsh strained voice — **hoarse·ly** *adv* — **hoarse·ness** *n*

**hoary** \'hòrē\ *adj* **hoar·i·er; -est** : gray or white with age — **hoar·i·ness** *n*

**hoax** \'hōks\ *n* : act intended to trick or dupe — **hoax** *vb* — **hoax·er** *n*

**hob·ble** \'häbəl\ *vb* **-bled; -bling** : limp along ∼ *n* : hobbling movement

**hob·by** \'häbē\ *n, pl* **-bies** : interest engaged in for relaxation — **hob·by·ist** \-ēist\ *n*

**hob·gob·lin** \'häb,gäblən\ *n* **1** : mischievous goblin **2** : bogey

**hob·nail** \-ˌnāl\ *n* : short nail for studding shoe soles — **hob·nailed** \-ˌnāld\ *adj*

**hob·nob** \-ˌnäb\ *vb* **-bb-** : associate socially

**ho·bo** \'hōbō\ *n, pl* **-boes** : tramp

**¹hock** \'häk\ *n* : joint or region in the hind limb of a quadruped corresponding to the human ankle

**²hock** *n or vb* : pawn

**hock·ey** \'häkē\ *n* : game played on ice or a field by 2 teams

**hod** \'häd\ *n* : carrier for bricks or mortar

**hodge·podge** \'häj,päj\ *n* : heterogeneous mixture

**hoe** \'hō\ *n* : long-handled tool for cultivating or weeding — **hoe** *vb*

**hog** \'hòg, 'häg\ *n* **1** : domestic adult swine **2** : glutton ∼ *vb* : take selfishly — **hog·gish** *adj*

**hogs·head** \'hògz,hed, 'hägz-\ *n* : large cask or barrel

**hog·wash** *n* : nonsense

**hoist** \'hòist\ *vb* : lift ∼ *n* **1** : lift **2** : apparatus for hoisting

**hok·ey** \'hōkē\ *adj* **hok·i·er; -est** **1** : tiresomely simple or sentimental **2** : phony

**¹hold** \'hōld\ *vb* **held** \'held\; **hold·ing** **1** : possess **2** : restrain **3** : have a grasp on **4** : remain or keep in a particular situation or position **5** : contain **6** : regard **7** : cause to occur **8** : occupy esp. by appointment or election ∼ *n* **1** : act or manner of holding **2** : restraining or controlling influence — **hold·er** *n* — **hold forth** : speak at length — **hold to** : adhere to — **hold with** : agree with

**²hold** *n* : cargo area of a ship

**hold·ing** \'hōldiŋ\ *n* : property owned — usu. pl.

**hold·up** *n* **1** : robbery at the point of a gun **2** : delay

**hole** \'hōl\ *n* **1** : opening into or through something **2** : hollow place (as a pit) **3** : den — **hole** *vb*

**hol·i·day** \'hälə,dā\ *n* **1** : day of freedom from work **2** : vacation — **holiday** *vb*

**ho·li·ness** \'hōlēnəs\ *n* : quality or state of being holy — used as a title for a high religious official

**ho·lis·tic** \hō'listik\ *adj* : relating to a whole (as the body)

**hol·ler** \'hälər\ *vb* : cry out — **holler** *n*

**hol·low** \'hälō\ *adj* **-low·er** \-əwər\; **-est** **1** : sunken **2** : having a cavity within **3** : sounding like a noise made in an empty place **4** : empty of value or meaning ∼ *vb* : make or become hollow ∼ *n* **1** : surface depression **2** : cavity — **hol·low·ness** *n*

**hol·ly** \'hälē\ *n, pl* **-lies** : evergreen tree or shrub with glossy leaves

**hol·ly·hock** \-ˌhäk, -ˌhòk\ *n* : tall perennial herb with showy flowers

**ho·lo·caust** \'hälə,kòst, 'hō-, 'hò-\ *n* : thorough destruction esp. by fire

**hol·stein** \'hōl,stēn, -,stīn\ *n* : large black-and-white dairy cow

**hol·ster** \'hōlstər\ *n* : case for a pistol

**ho·ly** \'hōlē\ *adj* **-li·er; -est** 1 : sacred 2 : spiritually pure

**hom·age** \'ämij, 'hä-\ *n* : reverent regard

**home** \'hōm\ *n* 1 : residence 2 : congenial environment 3 : place of origin or refuge ~ *vb* **homed; hom·ing** : go or return home — **home·bred** *adj* — **home·com·ing** *n* — **home-grown** *adj* — **home·land** \-,land\ *n* — **home·less** *adj* — **home·made** \-'mād\ *adj*

**home·ly** \-lē\ *adj* **-li·er; -est** : plain or unattractive — **home·li·ness** *n*

**home·mak·er** *n* : one who manages a household — **home·mak·ing** *n*

**home·sick** *adj* : longing for home — **home·sick·ness** *n*

**home·spun** \-,spən\ *adj* : simple

**home·stead** \-,sted\ *n* : home and land occupied and worked by a family — **home·stead·er** \-ər\ *n*

**home·stretch** *n* 1 : last part of a racetrack 2 : final stage

**home·ward** \-wərd\, **home·wards** \-wərdz\ *adv* : toward home — **homeward** *adj*

**home·work** *n* : school lessons to be done outside the classroom

**hom·ey** \'hōmē\ *adj* **hom·i·er; -est** : characteristic of home

**ho·mi·cide** \'hämə,sīd, 'hō-\ *n* : the killing of one human being by another — **hom·i·cid·al** \,hämə'sīd⁰l, ,hō-\ *adj*

**hom·i·ly** \'häməlē\ *n, pl* **-lies** : sermon

**hom·i·ny** \'hämənē\ *n* : type of processed hulled corn

**ho·mo·ge·neous** \,hōmə'jēnēəs, -nyəs\ *adj* : of the same or a similar kind — **ho·mo·ge·ne·i·ty** \-jə'nēətē\ *n* — **ho·mo·ge·neous·ly** *adv*

**ho·mog·e·nize** \hō'mäjə,nīz, hə-\ *vb* **-nized; -niz·ing** : make the particles in (as milk) of uniform size and even distribution — **ho·mog·e·ni·za·tion** \-,mäjənə'zāshən\ *n* — **ho·mog·e·niz·er** *n*

**ho·mo·graph** \'hämə,graf, 'hō-\ *n* : one of 2 or more words (as the noun *conduct* and the verb *conduct*) spelled alike but different in origin or meaning or pronunciation

**hom·onym** \'hämə,nim, 'hō-\ *n* 1 : homophone 2 : homograph 3 : one of 2 or more words (as *pool* of water and *pool* the game) spelled and pronounced alike but different in meaning

**ho·mo·phone** \'hämə,fōn, 'hō-\ *n* : one of 2 or more words (as *to, too,* and *two*) pronounced alike but different in origin or meaning or spelling

**Ho·mo sa·pi·ens** \,hōmō'sapēənz, -'sä-\ *n* : humankind

**ho·mo·sex·u·al** \,hōmə'sekshəwəl\ *adj* : oriented toward one's own sex — **homosexual** *n* — **ho·mo·sex·u·al·i·ty** \-,seksha'walətē\ *n*

**hone** \'hōn\ *vb* : sharpen with or as if with an abrasive stone

**hon·est** \'änəst\ *adj* 1 : free from deception 2 : trustworthy 3 : frank — **hon·est·ly** *adv* — **hon·esty** \-əstē\ *n*

**hon·ey** \'hənē\ *n, pl* **-eys** : sweet sticky substance made by bees (**hon·ey-bees**) from the nectar of flowers

**hon·ey·comb** *n* : mass of 6-sided wax cells built by honeybees or something like it ~ *vb* : make or become full of holes like a honeycomb

**hon·ey·moon** *n* : holiday taken by a newly married couple — **honeymoon** *vb*

**hon·ey·suck·le** \-,səkəl\ *n* : shrub or vine with flowers rich in nectar

**honk** \'häŋk, 'hȯŋk\ *n* : cry of a goose or a similar sound — **honk** *vb* — **honk·er** *n*

**hon·or** \'änər\ *n* 1 : good name 2 : outward respect or symbol of this 3 : privilege 4 : person of superior rank or position — used esp. as a title 5 : something or someone worthy of respect 6 : integrity ~ *vb* 1 : regard with honor 2 : confer honor on 3 : fulfill the terms of — **hon·or·able** \'änərəbəl\ *adj* — **hon·or·ably** \-blē\ *adv* — **hon·or·ari·ly** \,änə'rerəlē\ *adv* — **hon·or·ary** \'änə,rerē\ *adj* — **hon·or·ee** \,änə'rē\ *n*

**hood** \'hůd\ *n* 1 : part of a garment that covers the head 2 : covering over an automobile engine compartment — **hood·ed** *adj*

**-hood** \,hůd\ *n suffix* 1 : state, condition, or quality 2 : individuals sharing a state or character

**hood·lum** \'hůdləm, 'hüd-\ *n* : thug

**hood·wink** \'hůd,wiŋk\ *vb* : deceive

**hoof** \'hůf, 'hüf\ *n, pl* **hooves** \'hůvz, 'hüvz\ *or* **hoofs** : horny covering of the toes of some mammals (as horses or cattle) — **hoofed** \'hůft, 'hüft\ *adj*

**hook** \'hůk\ *n* : curved or bent device for catching, holding, or pulling ~ *vb* : seize or make fast with a hook — **hook•er** *n*

**hook•worm** *n* : parasitic intestinal worm

**hoo•li•gan** \'hüligən\ *n* : thug

**hoop** \'hüp\ *n* : circular strip, figure, or object

**hoot** \'hüt\ *vb* 1 : shout in contempt 2 : make the cry of an owl — **hoot** *n* — **hoot•er** *n*

¹**hop** \'häp\ *vb* -pp- : move by quick springy leaps — **hop** *n*

²**hop** *n* : vine whose ripe dried flowers are used to flavor malt liquors

**hope** \'hōp\ *vb* **hoped; hop•ing** : desire with expectation of fulfillment ~ *n* 1 : act of hoping 2 : something hoped for — **hope•ful** \-fəl\ *adj* — **hope•ful•ly** *adv* — **hope•ful•ness** *n* — **hope•less** *adj* — **hope•less•ly** *adv* — **hope•less•ness** *n*

**hop•per** \'häpər\ *n* : container that releases its contents through the bottom

**horde** \'hōrd\ *n* : throng or swarm

**ho•ri•zon** \hə'rīz°n\ *n* : apparent junction of earth and sky

**hor•i•zon•tal** \,hȯrə'zänt°l\ *adj* : parallel to the horizon — **hor•i•zon•tal•ly** *adv*

**hor•mone** \'hȯr,mōn\ *n* : cell product in body fluids that has a specific effect on other cells — **hor•mon•al** \hȯr'mōn°l\ *adj*

**horn** \'hȯrn\ *n* 1 : hard bony projection on the head of a hoofed animal 2 : brass wind instrument — **horned** *adj* — **horn•less** *adj*

**hor•net** \'hȯrnət\ *n* : large social wasp

**horny** \'hȯrnē\ *adj* **horn•i•er; -est** 1 : made of horn 2 : hard or callous 3 : sexually aroused

**horo•scope** \'hȯrə,skōp\ *n* : astrological forecast

**hor•ren•dous** \hȯ'rendəs\ *adj* : horrible

**hor•ri•ble** \'hȯrəbəl\ *adj* 1 : having or causing horror 2 : highly disagreeable — **hor•ri•ble•ness** *n* — **hor•ri•bly** \-blē\ *adv*

**hor•rid** \'hȯrəd\ *adj* : horrible — **hor•rid•ly** *adv*

**hor•ri•fy** \'hȯrə,fī\ *vb* **-fied; -fy•ing** : cause to feel horror

**hor•ror** \'hȯrər\ *n* 1 : intense fear, dread, or dismay 2 : intense repugnance 3 : something horrible

**hors d'oeuvre** \ȯr'dərv\ *n, pl* **hors d'oeuvres** \-'dərvz\ : appetizer

**horse** \'hȯrs\ *n* : large solid-hoofed domesticated mammal — **horse•back** *n or adv* — **horse•hair** *n* — **horse-hide** *n* — **horse•less** *adj* — **horse-man** \-mən\ *n* — **horse•man•ship** *n* — **horse•wom•an** *n* — **hors•ey, horsy** *adj*

**horse•fly** *n* : large fly with bloodsucking female

**horse•play** *n* : rough boisterous play

**horse•pow•er** *n* : unit of mechanical power

**horse•rad•ish** *n* : herb with a pungent root used as a condiment

**horse•shoe** *n* : U-shaped protective metal plate fitted to the rim of a horse's hoof

**hor•ti•cul•ture** \'hȯrtə,kəlchər\ *n* : science of growing fruits, vegetables, and flowers — **hor•ti•cul•tur•al** \,hȯrtə'kəlchərəl\ *adj* — **hor•ti-cul•tur•ist** \-rist\ *n*

**ho•san•na** \hō'zanə, -'zän-\ *interj* : used as a cry of acclamation and adoration — **hosanna** *n*

**hose** \'hōz\ *n* 1 *pl* **hose** : stocking or sock 2 *pl* **hos•es** : flexible tube for conveying fluids ~ *vb* **hosed; hos•ing** : spray, water, or wash with a hose

**ho•siery** \'hōzhərē, 'hōzə-\ *n* : stockings or socks

**hos•pice** \'häspəs\ *n* 1 : lodging (as for travelers) maintained by a religious order 2 : facility or program for caring for dying persons

**hos•pi•ta•ble** \hä'spitəbəl, 'häs,pit-\ *adj* : given to generous and cordial reception of guests — **hos•pi•ta•bly** \-blē\ *adv*

**hos•pi•tal** \'häs,pit°l\ *n* : institution where the sick or injured receive medical care — **hos•pi•tal•i•za•tion** \,häs,pit°lə'zāshən\ *n* — **hos•pi•tal-ize** \'häs,pit°l,īz\ *vb*

**hos•pi•tal•i•ty** \,häspə'talətē\ *n, pl* **-ties** : hospitable treatment, reception, or disposition

¹**host** \'hōst\ *n* 1 : army 2 : multitude

²**host** *n* : one who receives or entertains guests — **host** *vb*

³**host** *n* : eucharistic bread

**hos•tage** \'hästij\ *n* : person held to guarantee that promises be kept or demands met

**hos·tel** \'häst°l\ *n* : lodging for youth — **hos·tel·er** *n*

**hos·tel·ry** \-rē\ *n, pl* **-ries** : hotel

**host·ess** \'hōstəs\ *n* : woman who is host

**hos·tile** \'häst°l, -ˌtīl\ *adj* : openly or actively unfriendly or opposed to someone or something — **hostile** *n* — **hos·tile·ly** *adv* — **hos·til·i·ty** \häs'tilətē\ *n*

**hot** \'hät\ *adj* **-tt-** **1** : having a high temperature **2** : giving a sensation of heat or burning **3** : ardent **4** : pungent — **hot** *adv* — **hot·ly** *adv* — **hot·ness** *n*

**hot·bed** *n* : environment that favors rapid growth

**hot dog** *n* : frankfurter

**ho·tel** \hō'tel\ *n* : building where lodging and personal services are provided

**hot·head·ed** *adj* : impetuous — **hot·head** *n* — **hot·head·ed·ly** *adv* — **hot·head·ed·ness** *n*

**hot·house** *n* : greenhouse

**hound** \'haund\ *n* : long-eared hunting dog ~ *vb* : pursue relentlessly

**hour** \'aůər\ *n* **1** : 24th part of a day **2** : time of day — **hour·ly** *adv or adj*

**hour·glass** *n* : glass vessel for measuring time

**house** \'haůs\ *n, pl* **hous·es** \'haůzəz\ **1** : building to live in **2** : household **3** : legislative body **4** : business firm ~ \'haůz\ *vb* **housed; hous·ing** : provide with or take shelter — **house·boat** \'haůsˌbōt\ *n* — **house·clean** \'haůsˌklēn\ *vb* — **house·clean·ing** *n* — **house·ful** \-ˌfůl\ *n* — **house·maid** *n* — **house·wares** *n pl* — **house·work** *n*

**house·bro·ken** \-ˌbrōkən\ *adj* : trained in excretory habits acceptable in indoor living

**house·fly** *n* : two-winged fly common about human habitations

**house·hold** \-ˌhōld\ *n* : those who dwell as a family under the same roof ~ *adj* **1** : domestic **2** : common or familiar — **house·hold·er** *n*

**house·keep·ing** \-ˌkēpiŋ\ *n* : care and management of a house or institution — **house·keep·er** *n*

**house·warm·ing** *n* : party to celebrate moving into a house

**house·wife** \'haůsˌwīf\ *n* : married woman in charge of a household — **house·wife·ly** *adj* — **house·wif·ery** \-ˌwīfərē\ *n*

**hous·ing** \'haůziŋ\ *n* **1** : dwellings for people **2** : protective covering

**hove** *past of* HEAVE

**hov·el** \'həvəl, 'häv-\ *n* : small wretched house

**hov·er** \'həvər, 'häv-\ *vb* **1** : remain suspended in the air **2** : move about in the vicinity

**how** \'haů\ *adv* **1** : in what way or condition **2** : for what reason **3** : to what extent ~ *conj* : the way or manner in which

**how·ev·er** \haů'evər\ *conj* : in whatever manner ~ *adv* **1** : to whatever degree or in whatever manner **2** : in spite of that

**how·it·zer** \'haůtsər\ *n* : short cannon

**howl** \'haůl\ *vb* : emit a loud long doleful sound like a dog — **howl** *n* — **howl·er** *n*

**hoy·den** \'hóid°n\ *n* : girl or woman of saucy or carefree behavior

**hub** \'həb\ *n* : central part of a circular object (as of a wheel) — **hub·cap** *n*

**hub·bub** \'həbˌəb\ *n* : uproar

**hu·bris** \'hyūbrəs\ *n* : excessive pride

**huck·le·ber·ry** \'həkəlˌberē\ *n* **1** : shrub related to the blueberry or its berry **2** : blueberry

**huck·ster** \'həkstər\ *n* : peddler

**hud·dle** \'həd°l\ *vb* **-dled; -dling** **1** : crowd together **2** : confer — **huddle** *n*

**hue** \'hyū\ *n* : color or gradation of color — **hued** \'hyüd\ *adj*

**huff** \'həf\ *n* : fit of pique — **huffy** *adj*

**hug** \'həg\ *vb* **-gg-** **1** : press tightly in the arms **2** : stay close to — **hug** *n*

**huge** \'hyüj\ *adj* **hug·er; hug·est** : very large or extensive — **huge·ly** *adv* — **huge·ness** *n*

**hu·la** \'hülə\ *n* : Polynesian dance

**hulk** \'həlk\ *n* **1** : bulky or unwieldy person or thing **2** : old ship unfit for service — **hulk·ing** *adj*

**hull** \'həl\ *n* **1** : outer covering of a fruit or seed **2** : frame or body of a ship or boat ~ *vb* : remove the hulls of — **hull·er** *n*

**hul·la·ba·loo** \'hələbəˌlü\ *n, pl* **-loos** : uproar

**hum** \'həm\ *vb* **-mm-** **1** : make a prolonged sound like that of the speech sound \m\ **2** : be busily active **3** : run smoothly **4** : sing with closed lips — **hum** *n* — **hum·mer** *n*

**hu·man** \'hyümən, 'yü-\ *adj* **1** : of or relating to the species people belong to **2** : by, for, or like people — **human** *n* — **hu·man·kind** *n* — **hu·man·ly** *adv* — **hu·man·ness** *n*

**hu·mane** \hyü'mān, ,yü-\ *adj* : showing compassion or consideration for others — **hu·mane·ly** *adv* — **hu·mane·ness** *n*

**hu·man·ism** \'hyümə,nizəm, 'yü-\ *n* : doctrine or way of life centered on human interests or values — **hu·man·ist** \-nist\ *n or adj* — **hu·man·is·tic** \,hyümə'nistik, ,yü-\ *adj*

**hu·man·i·tar·i·an** \hyü,manə'terēən, yü-\ *n* : person promoting human welfare — **humanitarian** *adj* — **hu·man·i·tari·an·ism** *n*

**hu·man·i·ty** \hyü'manətē, yü-\ *n, pl* **-ties 1** : human or humane quality or state **2** : the human race

**hu·man·ize** \'hyümə,nīz, 'yü-\ *vb* **-ized; -iz·ing** : make human or humane — **hu·man·iza·tion** \,hyümənə'zā-shən, ,yü-\ *n* — **hu·man·iz·er** *n*

**hu·man·oid** \'hyümə,nóid, 'yü-\ *adj* : having human form — **humanoid** *n*

**hum·ble** \'həmbəl\ *adj* **-bler; -blest 1** : not proud or haughty **2** : not pretentious ~ *vb* **-bled; -bling** : make humble — **hum·ble·ness** *n* — **hum·bler** *n* — **hum·bly** \-blē\ *adv*

**hum·bug** \'həm,bəg\ *n* : nonsense

**hum·drum** \-,drəm\ *adj* : monotonous

**hu·mid** \'hyüməd, 'yü-\ *adj* : containing or characterized by moisture — **hu·mid·i·fi·ca·tion** \hyü,midəfə'kā-shən\ *n* — **hu·mid·i·fi·er** \-'midə,fīər\ *n* — **hu·mid·i·fy** \-,fī\ *vb* — **hu·mid·ly** *adv*

**hu·mid·i·ty** \hyü'midətē, yü-\ *n, pl* **-ties** : atmospheric moisture

**hu·mi·dor** \'hyümə,dòr, 'yü-\ *n* : humidified storage case (as for cigars)

**hu·mil·i·ate** \hyü'milē,āt, yü-\ *vb* **-at·ed; -at·ing** : injure the self-respect of — **hu·mil·i·at·ing·ly** *adv* — **hu·mil·i·ation** \-,milē'āshən\ *n*

**hu·mil·i·ty** \hyü'milətē, yü-\ *n* : humble quality or state

**hum·ming·bird** \'həmiŋ,bərd\ *n* : tiny American bird that can hover

**hum·mock** \'həmək\ *n* : mound or knoll — **hum·mocky** \-məkē\ *adj*

**hu·mor** \'hyümər, 'yü-\ *n* **1** : mood **2** : quality of being laughably ludicrous or incongruous **3** : appreciation of what is ludicrous or incongruous **4**

: something intended to be funny ~ *vb* : comply with the wishes or mood of — **hu·mor·ist** \-ərist\ *n* — **hu·mor·less** *adj* — **hu·mor·less·ly** *adv* — **hu·mor·less·ness** *n* — **hu·mor·ous** \'hyümərəs, 'yü-\ *adj* — **hu·mor·ous·ly** *adv* — **hu·mor·ous·ness** *n*

**hump** \'həmp\ *n* : rounded protuberance — **humped** *adj*

**hump·back** *n* : hunchback — **hump·backed** *adj*

**hu·mus** \'hyüməs, 'yü-\ *n* : dark organic part of soil

**hunch** \'hənch\ *vb* : assume or cause to assume a bent or crooked posture ~ *n* : strong intuitive feeling

**hunch·back** *n* **1** : back with a hump **2** : person with a crooked back — **hunch·backed** *adj*

**hun·dred** \'həndrəd\ *n, pl* **-dreds** or **-dred** : 10 times 10 — **hundred** *adj* — **hun·dredth** \-drədth\ *adj or n*

**¹hung** *past of* HANG

**²hung** *adj* : unable to reach a verdict

**hun·ger** \'həŋgər\ *n* **1** : craving or urgent need for food **2** : strong desire — **hunger** *vb* — **hun·gri·ly** \-grəlē\ *adv* — **hun·gry** *adj*

**hunk** \'həŋk\ *n* : large piece

**hun·ker** \'həŋkər\ *vb* : settle in for a sustained period — used with *down*

**hunt** \'hənt\ *vb* **1** : pursue for food or sport **2** : try to find ~ *n* : act or instance of hunting — **hunt·er** *n*

**hur·dle** \'hərdᵊl\ *n* **1** : barrier to leap over in a race **2** : obstacle — **hurdle** *vb* — **hur·dler** *n*

**hurl** \'hərl\ *vb* : throw with violence — **hurl** *n* — **hurl·er** *n*

**hur·rah** \hù'rä, -'rò\ *interj* — used to express joy or approval

**hur·ri·cane** \'hərə,kān\ *n* : tropical storm with winds of 74 miles per hour or greater

**hur·ry** \'hərē\ *vb* **-ried; -ry·ing** : go or cause to go with haste ~ *n* : extreme haste — **hur·ried·ly** *adv* — **hur·ried·ness** *n*

**hurt** \'hərt\ *vb* **hurt; hurt·ing 1** : feel or cause pain **2** : do harm to ~ *n* **1** : bodily injury **2** : harm — **hurt·ful** \-fəl\ *adj* — **hurt·ful·ness** *n*

**hur·tle** \'hərtᵊl\ *vb* **-tled; -tling** : move rapidly or forcefully

**hus·band** \'həzbənd\ *n* : married man ~ *vb* : manage prudently

**hus·band·ry** \-bəndrē\ n 1 : careful use 2 : agriculture

**hush** \'həsh\ vb : make or become quiet ~ n : silence

**husk** \'həsk\ n : outer covering of a seed or fruit ~ vb : strip the husk from — **husk·er** n

**¹hus·ky** \'həskē\ adj **-ki·er; -est** : hoarse — **hus·ki·ly** adv — **hus·ki·ness** n

**²husky** adj **-ki·er; -est** : burly — **husk·i·ness** n

**³husky** n, pl **-kies** : working dog of the arctic

**hus·sy** \'həsē, -zē\ n, pl **-sies** 1 : brazen woman 2 : mischievous girl

**hus·tle** \'həsəl\ vb **-tled; -tling** 1 : hurry 2 : work energetically — **hustle** n — **hus·tler** \'həslər\ n

**hut** \'hət\ n : small often temporary dwelling

**hutch** \'həch\ n 1 : cupboard with open shelves 2 : pen for an animal

**hy·a·cinth** \'hīə,sinth\ n : bulbous herb grown for bell-shaped flowers

**hy·brid** \'hībrəd\ n : offspring of genetically differing parents — **hybrid** adj — **hy·brid·iza·tion** \,hībrədə'zā-shən\ n — **hy·brid·ize** \'hībrəd,īz\ vb — **hy·brid·iz·er** n

**hy·drant** \'hīdrənt\ n : pipe from which water may be drawn to fight fires

**hy·drau·lic** \hī'dròlik\ adj : operated by liquid forced through a small hole — **hy·drau·lics** \-liks\ n

**hy·dro·car·bon** \,hīdrə'kärbən\ n : organic compound of carbon and hydrogen

**hy·dro·elec·tric** \,hīdrōi'lektrik\ adj : producing electricity by waterpower — **hy·dro·elec·tric·i·ty** \-,lek-'trisətē\ n

**hy·dro·gen** \'hīdrəjən\ n : very light gaseous colorless odorless flammable chemical element

**hydrogen bomb** n : powerful bomb that derives its energy from the union of atomic nuclei

**hy·dro·pho·bia** \,hīdrə'fōbēə\ n : rabies

**hy·dro·plane** \'hīdrə,plān\ n : speedboat that skims the water

**hy·drous** \'hīdrəs\ adj : containing water

**hy·e·na** \hī'ēnə\ n : nocturnal carnivorous mammal of Asia and Africa

**hy·giene** \'hī,jēn\ n : conditions or practices conducive to health — **hygien·ic** \hī'jenik, -'jēn-; ,hījē'enik\ adj — **hy·gien·i·cal·ly** \-iklē\ adv — **hy·gien·ist** \hī'jēnist, -'jen-; 'hī-jēn-\ n

**hy·grom·e·ter** \hī'grämətər\ n : instrument for measuring atmospheric humidity

**hying** pres part of HIE

**hymn** \'him\ n : song of praise esp. to God — **hymn** vb

**hym·nal** \'himnəl\ n : book of hymns

**hype** \'hīp\ vb **hyped; hyp·ing** : publicize extravagantly — **hype** n

**hyper-** prefix 1 : above or beyond 2 : excessively or excessive

**hy·per·bo·le** \hī'pərbəlē\ n : extravagant exaggeration

**hy·per·ten·sion** \'hīpər,tenchən\ n : high blood pressure — **hy·per·ten·sive** \,hīpər'tensiv\ adj or n

**hy·phen** \'hīfən\ n : punctuation mark - used to divide or compound words — **hyphen** vb

**hy·phen·ate** \'hīfə,nāt\ vb **-at·ed; -at·ing** : connect or divide with a hyphen — **hy·phen·ation** \,hīfə'nāshən\ n

**hyp·no·sis** \hip'nōsəs\ n, pl **-no·ses** \-,sēz\ : induced state like sleep in which the subject is responsive to suggestions of the inducer (**hyp·no·tist** \'hipnətist\) — **hyp·no·tism** \'hipnə,tizəm\ n — **hyp·no·tiz·able** \,hipnə'tīzəbəl\ adj — **hyp·no·tize** \'hipnə,tīz\ vb

---

**List of self-explanatory words with the prefix** *hyper-*

| | | |
|---|---|---|
| hyperacid | hyperenergetic | hypersensitive |
| hyperacidity | hyperexcitable | hypersensitiveness |
| hyperactive | hyperfastidious | hypersensitivity |
| hyperacute | hyperintense | hypersexual |
| hyperaggressive | hypermasculine | hypersusceptible |
| hypercautious | hypernationalistic | hypertense |
| hypercorrect | hyperreactive | hypervigilant |
| hypercritical | hyperrealistic | |
| hyperemotional | hyperromantic | |

**hyp·not·ic** \hip'nätik\ *adj* : relating to hypnosis — **hypnotic** *n* — **hyp·not·i·cal·ly** \-iklē\ *adv*

**hy·po·chon·dria** \ˌhīpə'kändrēə\ *n* : morbid concern for one's health — **hy·po·chon·dri·ac** \-drē͵ak\ *adj or n*

**hy·poc·ri·sy** \hip'äkrəsē\ *n, pl* -sies : a feigning to be what one is not — **hyp·o·crite** \'hipə͵krit\ *n* — **hyp·o·crit·i·cal** \ˌhipə'kritikəl\ *adj* — **hyp·o·crit·i·cal·ly** *adv*

**hy·po·der·mic** \ˌhīpə'dərmik\ *adj* : administered or used in making an injection beneath the skin ~ *n* : hypodermic syringe

**hy·pot·e·nuse** \hī'pätə͵nüs, -͵nüz, -͵nyüs, -͵nyüz\ *n* : side of a right=angled triangle opposite the right angle

**hy·poth·e·sis** \hī'päthəsəs\ *n, pl* **-e·ses** \-͵sēz\ : assumption made in order to test its consequences — **hy·poth·e·size** \-͵sīz\ *vb* — **hy·po·thet·i·cal** \ˌhīpə'thetikəl\ *adj* — **hy·po·thet·i·cal·ly** *adv*

**hys·ter·ec·to·my** \ˌhistə'rektəmē\ *n, pl* **-mies** : surgical removal of the uterus

**hys·te·ria** \his'terēə, -tir-\ *n* : uncontrollable fear or outburst of emotion — **hys·ter·i·cal** \-'terikəl\ *adj* — **hys·ter·i·cal·ly** *adv*

**hys·ter·ics** \-'teriks\ *n pl* : uncontrollable laughter or crying

# I

**i** \'ī\ *n, pl* **i's** *or* **is** \'īz\ : 9th letter of the alphabet

**I** \'ī\ *pron* : the speaker

**-ial** *adj suffix* : of, relating to, or characterized by

**-ian** — see -AN

**ibis** \'ībəs\ *n, pl* **ibis** *or* **ibis·es** : wading bird with a down-curved bill

**-ible** — see -ABLE

**ibu·pro·fen** \ˌībyù'prōfən\ *n* : drug used to relieve inflammation, pain, and fever

**-ic** \ik\ *adj suffix* **1** : of, relating to, or being **2** : containing **3** : characteristic of **4** : marked by **5** : caused by

**-i·cal** \ikəl\ *adj suffix* : -ic — **-i·cal·ly** \iklē, -kəlē\ *adv suffix*

**ice** \'īs\ *n* **1** : frozen water **2** : flavored frozen dessert ~ *vb* **iced; ic·ing 1** : freeze **2** : chill **3** : cover with icing

**ice·berg** \'īs͵bərg\ *n* : large floating mass of ice

**ice·box** *n* : refrigerator

**ice·break·er** *n* : ship equipped to cut through ice

**ice cream** *n* : sweet frozen food

**ice–skate** *vb* : skate on ice — **ice skater** *n*

**ich·thy·ol·o·gy** \ˌikthē'äləjē\ *n* : study of fishes — **ich·thy·ol·o·gist** \-jist\ *n*

**ici·cle** \'ī͵sikəl\ *n* : hanging mass of ice

**ic·ing** \'īsiŋ\ *n* : sweet usu. creamy coating for baked goods

**icon** \'ī͵kän\ *n* **1** : religious image **2** : small picture on a computer screen identified with an available function

**icon·o·clast** \ī'känə͵klast\ *n* : attacker of cherished beliefs or institutions — **icon·o·clasm** \-͵klazəm\ *n*

**icy** \'īsē\ *adj* **ic·i·er; -est 1** : covered with or consisting of ice **2** : very cold — **ic·i·ly** *adv* — **ic·i·ness** *n*

**id** \'id\ *n* : unconscious instinctual part of the mind

**idea** \ī'dēə\ *n* **1** : something imagined in the mind **2** : purpose or plan

**ide·al** \ī'dēəl\ *adj* **1** : imaginary **2** : perfect ~ *n* **1** : standard of excellence **2** : model **3** : aim — **ide·al·ly** *adv*

**ide·al·ism** \ī'dēə͵lizəm\ *n* : adherence to ideals — **ide·al·ist** \-list\ *n* — **ide·al·is·tic** \ī͵dēə'listik\ *adj* — **ide·al·is·ti·cal·ly** \-tiklē\ *adv*

**ide·al·ize** \ī'dēə͵līz\ *vb* **-ized; -iz·ing** : think of or represent as ideal — **ide·al·iza·tion** \-͵dēələ'zāshən\ *n*

**iden·ti·cal** \ī'dentikəl\ *adj* **1** : being the same **2** : exactly or essentially alike

**iden·ti·fi·ca·tion** \ī͵dentəfə'kāshən\ *n* **1** : act of identifying **2** : evidence of identity

**iden·ti·fy** \ī'dentə͵fī\ *vb* **-fied; -fy·ing 1** : associate **2** : establish the identity of — **iden·ti·fi·able** \ī͵dentə'fīəbəl\ *adj* — **iden·ti·fi·er** \ī'dentə͵fīər\ *n*

**iden·ti·ty** \ī'dentətē\ *n, pl* **-ties 1** : sameness of essential character **2**

: individuality **3** : fact of being what is supposed

**ide·ol·o·gy** \ˌīdē'äləjē, ˌid-\ *n, pl* **-gies** : body of beliefs — **ide·o·log·i·cal** \ˌīdēə'läjikəl, ˌid-\ *adj*

**id·i·om** \'idēəm\ *n* **1** : language peculiar to a person or group **2** : expression with a special meaning — **id·i·om·at·ic** \ˌidēə'matik\ *adj* — **id·i·om·at·i·cal·ly** \-iklē\ *adv*

**id·io·syn·cra·sy** \ˌidēō'siŋkrəsē\ *n, pl* **-sies** : personal peculiarity — **id·io·syn·crat·ic** \-sin'kratik\ *adj* — **id·io·syn·crat·i·cal·ly** \-'kratiklē\ *adv*

**id·i·ot** \'idēət\ *n* : mentally retarded or foolish person — **id·i·o·cy** \-əsē\ *n* — **id·i·ot·ic** \ˌidē'ätik\ *adj* — **id·i·ot·i·cal·ly** \-iklē\ *adv*

**idle** \'id°l\ *adj* **idler; idlest 1** : worthless **2** : inactive **3** : lazy ~ *vb* **idled; idling** : spend time doing nothing — **idle·ness** *n* — **idler** *n* — **idly** \'idlē\ *adv*

**idol** \'id°l\ *n* **1** : image of a god **2** : object of devotion — **idol·iza·tion** \ˌid°lə'zāshən\ *n* — **idol·ize** \'id°līz\ *vb*

**idol·a·ter, idol·a·tor** \ī'dälətər\ *n* : worshiper of idols — **idol·a·trous** \-trəs\ *adj* — **idol·a·try** \-trē\ *n*

**idyll** \'id°l\ *n* : period of peace and contentment — **idyl·lic** \ī'dilik\ *adj*

**-ier** — see **-ER**

**if** \'if\ *conj* **1** : in the event that **2** : whether **3** : even though

**-i·fy** \ə,fī\ *vb suffix* : -fy

**ig·loo** \'iglü\ *n, pl* **-loos** : hut made of snow blocks

**ig·nite** \ig'nīt\ *vb* **-nit·ed; -nit·ing** : set afire or catch fire — **ig·nit·able** \-'nītəbəl\ *adj*

**ig·ni·tion** \ig'nishən\ *n* **1** : a setting on fire **2** : process or means of igniting fuel

**ig·no·ble** \ig'nōbəl\ *adj* : not honorable — **ig·no·bly** \-blē\ *adv*

**ig·no·min·i·ous** \ˌignə'minēəs\ *adj* **1** : dishonorable **2** : humiliating — **ig·no·min·i·ous·ly** *adv* — **ig·no·mi·ny** \'ignə,minē, ig'nämənē\ *n*

**ig·no·ra·mus** \ˌignə'rāməs\ *n* : ignorant person

**ig·no·rant** \'ignərənt\ *adj* **1** : lacking knowledge **2** : showing a lack of knowledge or intelligence **3** : unaware — **ig·no·rance** \-rəns\ *n* — **ig·no·rant·ly** *adv*

**ig·nore** \ig'nōr\ *vb* **-nored; -nor·ing** : refuse to notice

**igua·na** \i'gwänə\ *n* : large tropical American lizard

**iik** \'ilk\ *n* : kind

**ill** \'il\ *adj* **worse** \'wərs\; **worst** \'wərst\ **1** : sick **2** : bad **3** : rude or unacceptable **4** : hostile ~ *adv* **worse; worst 1** : with displeasure **2** : harshly **3** : scarcely **4** : badly ~ *n* **1** : evil **2** : misfortune **3** : sickness

**il·le·gal** \il'lēgəl\ *adj* : not lawful — **il·le·gal·i·ty** \ili'galətē\ *n* — **il·le·gal·ly** \il'lēgəlē\ *adv*

**il·leg·i·ble** \il'lejəbəl\ *adj* : not legible — **il·leg·i·bil·i·ty** \il,lejə'bilətē\ *n* — **il·leg·i·bly** \il'lejəblē\ *adv*

**il·le·git·i·mate** \ˌili'jitəmət\ *adj* **1** : born of unmarried parents **2** : illegal — **il·le·git·i·ma·cy** \-əməsē\ *n* — **il·le·git·i·mate·ly** *adv*

**il·lic·it** \il'lisət\ *adj* : not lawful — **il·lic·it·ly** *adv*

**il·lim·it·able** \il'limətəbəl\ *adj* : boundless — **il·lim·it·ably** \-blē\ *adv*

**il·lit·er·ate** \il'litərət\ *adj* : unable to read or write — **il·lit·er·a·cy** \-ərəsē\ *n* — **illiterate** *n*

**ill-na·tured** \-'nāchərd\ *adj* : cross — **ill-na·tured·ly** *adv*

**ill·ness** \'ilnəs\ *n* : sickness

**il·log·i·cal** \il'läjikəl\ *adj* : contrary to sound reasoning — **il·log·i·cal·ly** *adv*

**ill-starred** \il'stärd\ *adj* : unlucky

**il·lu·mi·nate** \il'ümə,nāt\ *vb* **-nat·ed; -nat·ing 1** : light up **2** : make clear — **il·lu·mi·nat·ing·ly** \-,nātiŋlē\ *adv* — **il·lu·mi·na·tion** \-,ümə'nāshən\ *n*

**ill-use** \-'yüz\ *vb* : abuse — **ill-use** \-'yüs\ *n*

**il·lu·sion** \il'üzhən\ *n* **1** : mistaken idea **2** : misleading visual image

**il·lu·so·ry** \il'üsərē, -'üz-\ *adj* : based on or producing illusion

**il·lus·trate** \'iləs,trāt\ *vb* **-trat·ed; -trat·ing 1** : explain by example **2** : provide with pictures or figures — **il·lus·tra·tor** \-ər\ *n*

**il·lus·tra·tion** \ˌiləs'trāshən\ *n* **1** : example that explains **2** : pictorial explanation

**il·lus·tra·tive** \il'əstrətiv\ *adj* : designed to illustrate — **il·lus·tra·tive·ly** *adv*

**il·lus·tri·ous** \-trēəs\ *adj* : notably or

brilliantly outstanding — **il·lus·tri·ous·ness** *n*

**ill will** *n* : unfriendly feeling

**im·age** \'imij\ *n* 1 : likeness 2 : visual counterpart of an object formed by a lens or mirror 3 : mental picture ~ *vb* **-aged; -ag·ing** : create a representation of

**im·ag·ery** \'imijrē\ *n* 1 : images 2 : figurative language

**imag·i·nary** \im'ajə,nerē\ *adj* : existing only in the imagination

**imag·i·na·tion** \im,ajə'nāshən\ *n* 1 : act or power of forming a mental image 2 : creative ability — **imag·i·na·tive** \im'ajənətiv, -ə,nātiv\ *adj* — **imag·i·na·tive·ly** *adv*

**imag·ine** \im'ajən\ *vb* **-ined; -in·ing** : form a mental picture of something not present — **imag·in·able** \-'ajənəbəl\ *adj* — **imag·in·ably** \-blē\ *adv*

**im·bal·ance** \im'baləns\ *n* : lack of balance

**im·be·cile** \'imbəsəl, -,sil\ *n* : idiot — imbecile, **im·be·cil·ic** \,imbə'silik\ *adj* — **im·be·cil·i·ty** \-'silətē\ *n*

**im·bibe** \im'bīb\ *vb* **-bibed; -bib·ing** : drink — **im·bib·er** *n*

**im·bro·glio** \im'brōlyō\ *n, pl* **-glios** : complicated situation

**im·bue** \-'byü\ *vb* **-bued; -bu·ing** : fill (as with color or a feeling)

**im·i·tate** \'imə,tāt\ *vb* **-tat·ed; -tat·ing** 1 : follow as a model 2 : mimic — **im·i·ta·tive** \-,tātiv\ *adj* — **im·i·ta·tor** \-ər\ *n*

**im·i·ta·tion** \,imə'tāshən\ *n* 1 : act of imitating 2 : copy — **imitation** *adj*

**im·mac·u·late** \im'akyələt\ *adj* : without stain or blemish — **im·mac·u·late·ly** *adv*

**im·ma·te·ri·al** \,imə'tirēəl\ *adj* 1 : spiritual 2 : not relevant — **im·ma·te·ri·al·i·ty** \-,tirē'alətē\ *n*

**im·ma·ture** \,imə'tùr, -'tyùr\ *adj* : not yet mature — **im·ma·tu·ri·ty** \-ətē\ *n*

**im·mea·sur·able** \im'ezhərəbəl\ *adj* : indefinitely extensive — **im·mea·sur·ably** \-blē\ *adv*

**im·me·di·a·cy** \im'ēdēəsē\ *n, pl* **-cies** : quality or state of being urgent

**im·me·di·ate** \-ēət\ *adj* 1 : direct 2 : being next in line 3 : made or done at once 4 : not distant — **im·me·di·ate·ly** *adv*

**im·me·mo·ri·al** \,imə'mōrēəl\ *adj* : old beyond memory

**im·mense** \im'ens\ *adj* : vast — **im·mense·ly** *adv* — **im·men·si·ty** \-'ensətē\ *n*

**im·merse** \im'ərs\ *vb* **-mersed; -mers·ing** 1 : plunge or dip esp. into liquid 2 : engross — **im·mer·sion** \-'ərzhən\ *n*

**im·mi·grant** \'imigrənt\ *n* : one that immigrates

**im·mi·grate** \'imə,grāt\ *vb* **-grat·ed; -grat·ing** : come into a place and take up residence — **im·mi·gra·tion** \,imə'grāshən\ *n*

**im·mi·nent** \'imənənt\ *adj* : ready to take place — **im·mi·nence** \-nəns\ *n* — **im·mi·nent·ly** *adv*

**im·mo·bile** \im'ōbəl\ *adj* : incapable of being moved — **im·mo·bil·i·ty** \,imō'bilətē\ *n* — **im·mo·bi·lize** \im'ōbəlīz\ *vb*

**im·mod·er·ate** \im'ädərət\ *adj* : not moderate — **im·mod·er·a·cy** \-ərəsē\ *n* — **im·mod·er·ate·ly** *adv*

**im·mod·est** \im'ädəst\ *adj* : not modest — **im·mod·est·ly** *adv* — **im·mod·es·ty** \-əstē\ *n*

**im·mo·late** \'imə,lāt\ *vb* **-lat·ed; -lat·ing** : offer in sacrifice — **im·mo·la·tion** \,imə'lāshən\ *n*

**im·mor·al** \im'ôrəl\ *adj* : not moral — **im·mor·al·i·ty** \,imō'ralətē, ,imə-\ *n* — **im·mor·al·ly** *adv*

**im·mor·tal** \im'ôrt°l\ *adj* 1 : not mortal 2 : having lasting fame ~ *n* : one exempt from death or oblivion — **im·mor·tal·i·ty** \,imôr'talətē\ *n* — **im·mor·tal·ize** \im'ôrt°l,īz\ *vb*

**im·mov·able** \im'üvəbəl\ *adj* 1 : stationary 2 : unyielding — **im·mov·abil·i·ty** \im,üvə'bilətē\ *n* — **im·mov·ably** *adv*

**im·mune** \im'yün\ *adj* : not liable esp. to disease — **im·mu·ni·ty** \im'yünətē\ *n* — **im·mu·ni·za·tion** \,imyənə'zāshən\ *n* — **im·mu·nize** \'imyə,nīz\ *vb*

**im·mu·nol·o·gy** \,imyə'näləjē\ *n* : science of immunity to disease — **im·mu·no·log·ic** \-yən°l'äjik\, **im·mu·no·log·i·cal** \-ikəl\ *adj* — **im·mu·nol·o·gist** \,imyə'näləjist\ *n*

**im·mu·ta·ble** \im'yütəbəl\ *adj* : unchangeable — **im·mu·ta·bil·i·ty** \im,yütə'bilətē\ *n* — **im·mu·ta·bly** *adv*

**imp** \'imp\ *n* 1 : demon 2 : mischievous child

**im·pact** \im'pakt\ *vb* **1** : press close **2** : have an effect on ~ \'im,pakt\ *n* **1** : forceful contact **2** : influence

**im·pact·ed** \im'paktəd\ *adj* : wedged between the jawbone and another tooth

**im·pair** \im'par\ *vb* : diminish in quantity, value, or ability — **im·pair·ment** *n*

**im·pa·la** \im'palə\ *n, pl* **impalas** or **impala** : large African antelope

**im·pale** \im'pāl\ *vb* **-paled; -pal·ing** : pierce with something pointed

**im·pal·pa·ble** \im'palpəbəl\ *adj* : incapable of being felt — **im·pal·pa·bly** *adv*

**im·pan·el** \im'pan°l\ *vb* : enter in or on a panel

**im·part** \-'pärt\ *vb* : give from or as if from a store

**im·par·tial** \im'pärshəl\ *adj* : not partial — **im·par·tial·i·ty** \im,pärshē'alətē\ *n* — **im·par·tial·ly** *adv*

**im·pass·able** \im'pasəbəl\ *adj* : not passable — **im·pass·ably** \-'pasəblē\ *adv*

**im·passe** \'im,pas\ *n* : inescapable predicament

**im·pas·sioned** \im'pashənd\ *adj* : filled with passion

**im·pas·sive** \im'pasiv\ *adj* : showing no feeling or interest — **im·pas·sive·ly** *adv* — **im·pas·siv·i·ty** \,im,pas'ivətē\ *n*

**im·pa·tiens** \im'pāshənz, -shəns\ *n* : annual herb with showy flowers

**im·pa·tient** \im'pāshənt\ *adj* : not patient — **im·pa·tience** \-shəns\ *n* — **im·pa·tient·ly** *adv*

**im·peach** \im'pēch\ *vb* **1** : charge (an official) with misconduct **2** : cast doubt on **3** : remove from office for misconduct — **im·peach·ment** *n*

**im·pec·ca·ble** \im'pekəbəl\ *adj* : faultless — **im·pec·ca·bly** *adv*

**im·pe·cu·nious** \,impi'kyünēəs\ *adj* : broke — **im·pe·cu·nious·ness** *n*

**im·pede** \im'pēd\ *vb* **-ped·ed; -ped·ing** : interfere with

**im·ped·i·ment** \-'pedəmənt\ *n* **1** : hindrance **2** : speech defect

**im·pel** \-'pel\ *vb* **-pelled; -pel·ling** : urge forward

**im·pend** \-'pend\ *vb* : be about to occur

**im·pen·e·tra·ble** \im'penətrəbəl\ *adj* : incapable of being penetrated or understood — **im·pen·e·tra·bil·i·ty** \im,penətrə'bilətē\ *n* — **im·pen·e·tra·bly** *adv*

**im·pen·i·tent** \im'penətənt\ *adj* : not penitent — **im·pen·i·tence** \-təns\ *n*

**im·per·a·tive** \im'perətiv\ *adj* **1** : expressing a command **2** : urgent ~ *n* **1** : imperative mood or verb form **2** : unavoidable fact, need, or obligation — **im·per·a·tive·ly** *adv*

**im·per·cep·ti·ble** \,impər'septəbəl\ *adj* : not perceptible — **im·per·cep·ti·bly** *adv*

**im·per·fect** \im'pərfikt\ *adj* : not perfect — **im·per·fec·tion** *n* — **im·per·fect·ly** *adv*

**im·pe·ri·al** \im'pirēəl\ *adj* **1** : relating to an empire or an emperor **2** : royal

**im·pe·ri·al·ism** \im'pirēə,lizəm\ *n* : policy of controlling other nations — **im·pe·ri·al·ist** \-list\ *n or adj* — **im·pe·ri·al·is·tic** \-,pirēə'listik\ *adj* — **im·pe·ri·al·is·ti·cal·ly** \-tiklē\ *adv*

**im·per·il** \im'perəl\ *vb* **-iled** *or* **-illed; -il·ing** *or* **-il·ling** : endanger

**im·pe·ri·ous** \im'pirēəs\ *adj* : arrogant or domineering — **im·pe·ri·ous·ly** *adv*

**im·per·ish·able** \im'perishəbəl\ *adj* : not perishable

**im·per·ma·nent** \-'pərmənənt\ *adj* : not permanent — **im·per·ma·nent·ly** *adv*

**im·per·me·able** \-'pərmēəbəl\ *adj* : not permeable

**im·per·mis·si·ble** \,impər'misəbəl\ *adj* : not permissible

**im·per·son·al** \im'pərs°nəl\ *adj* : not involving human personality or emotion — **im·per·son·al·i·ty** \im,pərs°n'alətē\ *n* — **im·per·son·al·ly** *adv*

**im·per·son·ate** \im'pərs°n,āt\ *vb* **-at·ed; -at·ing** : assume the character of — **im·per·son·a·tion** \-,pərs°n-'āshən\ *n* — **im·per·son·a·tor** \-'pərs°n,ātər\ *n*

**im·per·ti·nent** \im'pərt°nənt\ *adj* **1** : irrelevant **2** : insolent — **im·per·ti·nence** \-°nəns\ *n* — **im·per·ti·nent·ly** *adv*

**im·per·turb·able** \,impər'tərbəbəl\ *adj* : calm and steady

**im·per·vi·ous** \im'pərvēəs\ *adj* : incapable of being penetrated or affected

**im·pet·u·ous** \im'pechəwəs\ *adj* : impulsive — **im·pet·u·os·i·ty** \im,pechə'wäsətē\ *n* — **im·pet·u·ous·ly** *adv*

**im·pe·tus** \'impətəs\ *n* : driving force

**im·pi·ety** \im'pīətē\ *n* : quality or state of being impious

**im·pinge** \im'pinj\ *vb* **-pinged; -ping·ing** : encroach — **im·pinge·ment** \-mənt\ *n*

**im·pi·ous** \'impēəs, im'pī-\ *adj* : not pious

**imp·ish** \'impish\ *adj* : mischievous — **imp·ish·ly** *adv* — **imp·ish·ness** *n*

**im·pla·ca·ble** \im'plakəbəl, -'plā-\ *adj* : not capable of being appeased or changed — **im·pla·ca·bil·i·ty** \im-͵plakə'bilətē, -͵plā-\ *n* — **im·pla·ca·bly** \im'plakəblē\ *adv*

**im·plant** \im'plant\ *vb* 1 : set firmly or deeply 2 : fix in the mind or spirit ∼ \'im͵plant\ *n* : something implanted in tissue — **im·plan·ta·tion** \͵im-͵plan'tāshən\ *n*

**im·plau·si·ble** \im'plózəbəl\ *adj* : not plausible — **im·plau·si·bil·i·ty** \im-͵plózə'bilətē\ *n*

**im·ple·ment** \'impləmənt\ *n* : tool, utensil ∼ \-͵ment\ *vb* : put into practice — **im·ple·men·ta·tion** \͵implə-mən'tāshən\ *n*

**im·pli·cate** \'implə͵kāt\ *vb* -cat·ed; -cat·ing : involve

**im·pli·ca·tion** \͵implə'kāshən\ *n* 1 : an implying 2 : something implied

**im·plic·it** \im'plisət\ *adj* 1 : understood though only implied 2 : complete and unquestioning — **im·plic·it·ly** *adv*

**im·plode** \im'plōd\ *vb* -plod·ed; -plod·ing : burst inward — **im·plo·sion** \-'plōzhən\ *n* — **im·plo·sive** \-'plōsiv\ *adj*

**im·plore** \im'plōr\ *vb* -plored; -plor·ing : entreat

**im·ply** \-'plī\ *vb* -plied; -ply·ing : express indirectly

**im·po·lite** \͵impə'līt\ *adj* : not polite

**im·pol·i·tic** \im'pälə͵tik\ *adj* : not politic

**im·pon·der·a·ble** \im'pändərəbəl\ *adj* : incapable of being precisely evaluated — **imponderable** *n*

**im·port** \im'pōrt\ *vb* 1 : mean 2 : bring in from an external source ∼ \'im͵pōrt\ *n* 1 : meaning 2 : importance 3 : something imported — **im·por·ta·tion** \͵im͵pōr'tāshən\ *n* — **im·port·er** *n*

**im·por·tant** \im'pōrtənt\ *adj* : having great worth, significance, or influence — **im·por·tance** \-ᵊns\ *n* — **im·por·tant·ly** *adv*

**im·por·tu·nate** \im'pōrchənət\ *adj* : troublesomely persistent or urgent

**im·por·tune** \͵impər'tün, -'tyün; im-'pōrchən\ *vb* -tuned; -tun·ing : urge or beg persistently — **im·por·tu·ni·ty** \͵impər'tünətē, -'tyü-\ *n*

**im·pose** \im'pōz\ *vb* -posed; -pos-

ing 1 : establish as compulsory 2 : take unwarranted advantage of — **im·po·si·tion** \͵impə'zishən\ *n*

**im·pos·ing** \im'pōziŋ\ *adj* : impressive — **im·pos·ing·ly** *adv*

**im·pos·si·ble** \im'päsəbəl\ *adj* 1 : incapable of occurring 2 : enormously difficult — **im·pos·si·bil·i·ty** \im-͵päsə'bilətē\ *n* — **im·pos·si·bly** \im-'päsəblē\ *adv*

**im·post** \'im͵pōst\ *n* : tax

**im·pos·tor, im·pos·ter** \im'pästər\ *n* : one who assumes an identity or title to deceive — **im·pos·ture** \-'päs-chər\ *n*

**im·po·tent** \'impətənt\ *adj* 1 : lacking power 2 : sterile — **im·po·tence** \-pətəns\ *n* — **im·po·ten·cy** \-ənsē\ *n* — **im·po·tent·ly** *adv*

**im·pound** \im'paùnd\ *vb* : seize and hold in legal custody — **im·pound·ment** *n*

**im·pov·er·ish** \im'pävərish\ *vb* : make poor — **im·pov·er·ish·ment** *n*

**im·prac·ti·ca·ble** \im'praktikəbəl\ *adj* : not practicable

**im·prac·ti·cal** \-'praktikəl\ *adj* : not practical

**im·pre·cise** \͵impri'sīs\ *adj* : not precise — **im·pre·cise·ly** *adv* — **im·pre·cise·ness** *n* — **im·pre·ci·sion** \-'sizhən\ *n*

**im·preg·na·ble** \im'pregnəbəl\ *adj* : able to resist attack — **im·preg·na·bil·i·ty** \im͵pregnə'bilətē\ *n*

**im·preg·nate** \im'preg͵nāt\ *vb* -nat·ed; -nat·ing 1 : make pregnant 2 : cause to be filled, permeated, or saturated — **im·preg·na·tion** \͵im-͵preg'nāshən\ *n*

**im·pre·sa·rio** \͵imprə'särē͵ō\ *n, pl* -ri·os : one who sponsors an entertainment

¹**im·press** \im'pres\ *vb* 1 : apply with or produce by pressure 2 : press, stamp, or print in or upon 3 : produce a vivid impression of 4 : affect (as the mind) forcibly

²**im·press** \im'pres\ *vb* : force into naval service — **im·press·ment** *n*

**im·pres·sion** \im'preshən\ *n* 1 : mark made by impressing 2 : marked influence or effect 3 : printed copy 4 : vague notion or recollection — **im·pres·sion·able** \-'preshənəbəl\ *adj*

**im·pres·sive** \im'presiv\ *adj* : making a marked impression — **im·pres·sive·ly** *adv* — **im·pres·sive·ness** *n*

**im·pri·ma·tur** \͵imprə'mä͵túr\ *n* : official approval (as of a publication by a censor)

**im·print** \im'print, 'im,-\ *vb* : stamp or mark by or as if by pressure ~ \'im,-\ *n* : something imprinted or printed

**im·pris·on** \im'priz³n\ *vb* : put in prison — **im·pris·on·ment** \-mənt\ *n*

**im·prob·a·ble** \im'präbəbəl\ *adj* : unlikely to be true or to occur — **im·prob·a·bil·i·ty** \im,präbə'bilətē\ *n* — **im·prob·a·bly** *adv*

**im·promp·tu** \im'prämptü, -tyü\ *adj* : not planned beforehand — **impromptu** *adv or n*

**im·prop·er** \im'präpər\ *adj* : not proper — **im·prop·er·ly** *adv*

**im·pro·pri·ety** \,imprə'prīətē\ *n, pl* **-eties** : state or instance of being improper

**im·prove** \im'prüv\ *vb* **-proved; -proving** : grow or make better — **im·prov·able** \-'prüvəbəl\ *adj* — **im·prove·ment** *n*

**im·prov·i·dent** \im'prävədənt\ *adj* : not providing for the future — **im·prov·i·dence** \-əns\ *n*

**im·pro·vise** \'imprə,vīz\ *vb* **-vised; -vis·ing** : make, invent, or arrange offhand — **im·pro·vi·sa·tion** \im,prävə-'zāshən, ,imprəvə-\ *n* — **im·pro·vis·er, im·pro·vi·sor** \'imprə,vīzər\ *n*

**im·pru·dent** \im'prüd³nt\ *adj* : not prudent — **im·pru·dence** \-³ns\ *n*

**im·pu·dent** \impyədənt\ *adj* : insolent — **im·pu·dence** \-əns\ *n* — **im·pu·dent·ly** *adv*

**im·pugn** \im'pyün\ *vb* : attack as false

**im·pulse** \'im,pəls\ *n* **1** : moving force **2** : sudden inclination

**im·pul·sive** \im'pəlsiv\ *adj* : acting on impulse — **im·pul·sive·ly** *adv* — **im·pul·sive·ness** *n*

**im·pu·ni·ty** \im'pyünətē\ *n* : exemption from punishment or harm

**im·pure** \im'pyúr\ *adj* : not pure — **im·pu·ri·ty** \-'pyùrətē\ *n*

**im·pute** \im'pyüt\ *vb* **-put·ed; -put·ing** : credit to or blame on a person or cause — **im·pu·ta·tion** \,impyə-'tāshən\ *n*

**in** \'in\ *prep* **1** — used to indicate location, inclusion, situation, or manner **2** : into **3** : during ~ *adv* : to or toward the inside ~ *adj* : located inside

**in-** \in\ *prefix* **1** : not **2** : lack of

**in·ad·ver·tent** \,inəd'vərt³nt\ *adj* : unintentional — **in·ad·ver·tence** \-³ns\ *n* — **in·ad·ver·ten·cy** \-³nsē\ *n* — **in·ad·ver·tent·ly** *adv*

**in·alien·able** \in'ālyənəbəl, -'ālēənə-\ *adj* : incapable of being transferred or given up — **in·alien·abil·i·ty** \in-,ālyənə'bilətē, -'ālēənə-\ *n* — **in·alien·ably** *adv*

**inane** \in'ān\ *adj* **inan·er; -est** : silly or stupid — **inan·i·ty** \in'anətē\ *n*

**in·an·i·mate** \in'anəmət\ *adj* : not animate or animated — **in·an·i·mate·ly** *adv* — **in·an·i·mate·ness** *n*

**in·ap·pre·cia·ble** \,inə'prēshəbəl\ *adj* : too small to be perceived — **in·ap·pre·cia·bly** *adv*

**in·ar·tic·u·late** \,inär'tikyələt\ *adj* : without the power of speech or effective expression — **in·ar·tic·u·late·ly** *adv*

**in·as·much as** \,inaz'məchaz\ *conj* : because

**in·at·ten·tion** \,inə'tenchən\ *n* : failure to pay attention

**in·au·gu·ral** \in'ógyərəl, -gərəl\ *adj* : relating to an inauguration ~ *n* **1** : inaugural speech **2** : inauguration

**in·au·gu·rate** \in'ógyə,rāt, -gə-\ *vb* **-rat·ed; -rat·ing** **1** : install in office **2** : start — **in·au·gu·ra·tion** \-,ógyə-'rāshən, -gə-\ *n*

**in·board** \,in,bōrd\ *adv* : inside a vehicle or craft — **inboard** *adj*

**in·born** \'in,bórn\ *adj* : present from birth

**in·bred** \'in,bred\ *adj* : deeply ingrained in one's nature

**in·breed·ing** \'in,brēdiŋ\ *n* : interbreeding of closely related individuals — **in·breed** \-,brēd\ *vb*

**in·cal·cu·la·ble** \in'kalkyələbəl\ *adj*

---

**List of self-explanatory words with the prefix** *in-*

| | | |
|---|---|---|
| inability | inactivity | inadvisable |
| inaccessibility | inadequacy | inapparent |
| inaccessible | inadequate | inapplicable |
| inaccuracy | inadequately | inapposite |
| inaccurate | inadmissibility | inappositely |
| inaction | inadmissible | inappositeness |
| inactive | inadvisability | inappreciative |

: too large to be calculated — **in·cal·cu·la·bly** *adv*

**in·can·des·cent** \ˌinkənˈdesᵊnt\ *adj* **1** : glowing with heat **2** : brilliant — **in·can·des·cence** \-ᵊns\ *n*

**in·can·ta·tion** \ˌin₁kanˈtāshən\ *n* : use of spoken or sung charms or spells as a magic ritual

**in·ca·pac·i·tate** \ˌinkəˈpasəˌtāt\ *vb* -tat·ed; -tat·ing : disable

**in·ca·pac·i·ty** \ˌinkəˈpasətē\ *n, pl* -ties : quality or state of being incapable

**in·car·cer·ate** \inˈkärsəˌrāt\ *vb* -at·ed; -at·ing : imprison — **in·car·cer·a·tion** \inˌkärsəˈrāshən\ *n*

**in·car·nate** \inˈkärnət, -ˌnāt\ *adj* : having bodily form and substance — **in·car·nate** \-ˌnāt\ *vb* — **in·car·na·tion** \-ˌkärˈnāshən\ *n*

**in·cen·di·ary** \inˈsendēˌerē\ *adj* **1** : pertaining to or used to ignite fire **2** : tending to excite — **incendiary** *n*

**in·cense** \ˈin₁sens\ *n* : material burned to produce a fragrant odor or its smoke ∼ \inˈsens\ *vb* -censed; -cens·ing : make very angry

**in·cen·tive** \inˈsentive\ *n* : inducement to do something

**in·cep·tion** \inˈsepshən\ *n* : beginning

**in·ces·sant** \inˈsesᵊnt\ *adj* : continuing without interruption — **in·ces·sant·ly** *adv*

**in·cest** \ˈin₁sest\ *n* : sexual intercourse between close relatives — **in·ces·tu·ous** \inˈseschəwəs\ *adj*

**inch** \ˈinch\ *n* : unit of length equal to ¹⁄₁₂ foot ∼ *vb* : move by small degrees

**in·cho·ate** \inˈkōət, ˈinkəˌwāt\ *adj* : new and not fully formed or ordered

**in·ci·dent** \ˈinsədənt\ *n* : occurrence — **in·ci·dence** \-əns\ *n* — **incident** *adj*

**in·ci·den·tal** \ˌinsəˈdentᵊl\ *adj* **1** : subordinate, nonessential, or attendant **2** : met by chance ∼ *n* **1** : something incidental **2** *pl* : minor expenses that are not itemized — **in·ci·den·tal·ly** *adv*

**in·cin·er·ate** \inˈsinəˌrāt\ *vb* -at·ed;

-at·ing : burn to ashes — **in·cin·er·a·tor** \-ˌrātər\ *n*

**in·cip·i·ent** \inˈsipēənt\ *adj* : beginning to be or appear

**in·cise** \inˈsīz\ *vb* -cised; -cis·ing : carve into

**in·ci·sion** \inˈsizhən\ *n* : surgical cut

**in·ci·sive** \inˈsīsiv\ *adj* : keen and discerning — **in·ci·sive·ly** *adv*

**in·ci·sor** \inˈsīzər\ *n* : tooth for cutting

**in·cite** \inˈsīt\ *vb* -cit·ed; -cit·ing : arouse to action — **in·cite·ment** *n*

**in·ci·vil·i·ty** \ˌinsəˈvilətē\ *n* : rudeness

**in·clem·ent** \inˈklemənt\ *adj* : stormy — **in·clem·en·cy** \-ənsē\ *n*

**in·cline** \inˈklīn\ *vb* -clined; -clin·ing **1** : bow **2** : tend toward an opinion **3** : slope ∼ *n* : slope — **in·cli·na·tion** \ˌinkləˈnāshən\ *n* — **in·clin·er** *n*

**inclose, inclosure** *var of* ENCLOSE, ENCLOSURE

**in·clude** \inˈklüd\ *vb* -clud·ed; -clud·ing : take in or comprise — **in·clu·sion** \inˈklüzhən\ *n* — **in·clu·sive** \-ˈklüsiv\ *adj*

**in·cog·ni·to** \ˌin₁kägˈnētō, inˈkägnə₁tō\ *adv or adj* : with one's identity concealed

**in·come** \ˈin₁kəm\ *n* : money gained (as from work or investment)

**in·com·ing** \ˈin₁kəmiŋ\ *adj* : coming in

**in·com·mu·ni·ca·do** \ˌinkəˌmyünə-ˈkädō\ *adv or adj* : without means of communication

**in·com·pa·ra·ble** \inˈkämpərəbəl\ *adj* : eminent beyond comparison

**in·com·pe·tent** \inˈkämpətənt\ *adj* : lacking sufficient knowledge or skill — **in·com·pe·tence** \-pətəns\ *n* — **in·com·pe·ten·cy** \-ənsē\ *n* — **incompetent** *n*

**in·con·ceiv·able** \ˌinkənˈsēvəbəl\ *adj* **1** : impossible to comprehend **2** : unbelievable — **in·con·ceiv·ably** \-blē\ *adv*

**in·con·gru·ous** \inˈkäŋgrəwəs\ *adj* : inappropriate or out of place — **in·con·gru·i·ty** \ˌinkənˈgrüətē, -ˌkän-\ *n* — **in·con·gru·ous·ly** *adv*

**in·con·se·quen·tial** \ˌin₁känsəˈkwen-

---

inapproachable
inappropriate
inappropriately
inappropriateness
inapt
inarguable
inartistic

inartistically
inattentive
inattentively
inattentiveness
inaudible
inaudibly
inauspicious

inauthentic
incapability
incapable
incautious
incoherence
incoherent
incoherently

chəl\ *adj* : unimportant — **in·con·se·quence** \in'känsə‚kwens\ *n* — **in·con·se·quen·tial·ly** *adv*

**in·con·sid·er·able** \‚inkən'sidərəbəl\ *adj* : trivial

**in·con·sol·able** \‚inkən'sōləbəl\ *adj* : incapable of being consoled — **in·con·sol·ably** *adv*

**in·con·ve·nience**\ ‚inkən'vēnyəns\ *n* **1** : discomfort **2** : something that causes trouble or annoyance ～ *vb* : cause inconvenience to — **in·con·ve·nient** \‚inkən'vēnyənt\ *adj* — **in·con·ve·nient·ly** *adv*

**in·cor·po·rate** \in'kórpə‚rāt\ *vb* -rat·ed; -rat·ing **1** : blend **2** : form into a legal body — **in·cor·po·rat·ed** *adj* — **in·cor·po·ra·tion** \-‚kórpə'rāshən\ *n*

**in·cor·ri·gi·ble** \in'kórəjəbəl\ *adj* : incapable of being corrected or re-formed — **in·cor·ri·gi·bil·i·ty** \in‚kórəjə'bilətē\ *n*

**in·crease** \in'krēs, 'in‚krēs\ *vb* -creased; -creas·ing : make or become greater ～ \'in‚-, in'-\ *n* **1** : enlargement in size **2** : something added — **in·creas·ing·ly** \-'krēsiŋlē\ *adv*

**in·cred·i·ble** \in'kredəbəl\ *adj* : too extraordinary to be believed — **in·cred·i·bil·i·ty** \in‚kredə'bilətē\ *n* — **in·cred·i·bly** \in'kredəblē\ *adv*

**in·cred·u·lous** \in'krejələs\ *adj* : skeptical — **in·cre·du·li·ty** \‚inkri-'dül·ətē, -'dyü-\ *n* — **in·cred·u·lous·ly** *adv*

**in·cre·ment** \'iŋkrəmənt, 'in-\ *n* : increase or amount of increase — **in·cre·men·tal** \‚iŋkrə'ment°l, ‚in-\ *adj*

**in·crim·i·nate** \in'krimə‚nāt\ *vb* -nat·ed; -nat·ing : show to be guilty of a crime — **in·crim·i·na·tion** \-‚krimə-'nāshən\ *n* — **in·crim·i·na·to·ry** \-'krimənə‚tōrē\ *adj*

**in·cu·bate** \'iŋkyə‚bāt, 'in-\ *vb* -bat·ed; -bat·ing : keep (as eggs) under conditions favorable for development — **in·cu·ba·tion** \‚iŋkyə'bāshən,

‚in-\ *n* — **in·cu·ba·tor** \'iŋkyə‚bātər, 'in-\ *n*

**in·cul·cate** \in'kəl‚kāt, 'in‚kəl-\ *vb* -cat·ed; -cat·ing : instill by repeated teaching — **in·cul·ca·tion** \‚in‚kəl-'kāshən\ *n*

**in·cum·bent** \in'kəmbənt\ *n* : holder of an office ～ *adj* : obligatory — **in·cum·ben·cy** \-bənsē\ *n*

**in·cur** \in'kər\ *vb* -rr- : become liable or subject to

**in·cur·sion** \in'kərzhən\ *n* : invasion

**in·debt·ed** \in'detəd\ *adj* : owing something — **in·debt·ed·ness** *n*

**in·de·ci·sion** \‚indi'sizhən\ *n* : inability to decide

**in·deed** \in'dēd\ *adv* : without question

**in·de·fat·i·ga·ble** \indi'fatigəbəl\ *adj* : not tiring — **in·de·fat·i·ga·bly** \-blē\ *adv*

**in·def·i·nite** \in'defənət\ *adj* **1** : not defining or identifying **2** : not precise **3** : having no fixed limit — **in·def·i·nite·ly** *adv*

**in·del·i·ble** \in'deləbəl\ *adj* : not capable of being removed or erased — **in·del·i·bly** *adv*

**in·del·i·cate** \in'delikət\ *adj* : improper — **in·del·i·ca·cy** \in'deləkəsē\ *n*

**in·dem·ni·fy** \in'demnə‚fī\ *vb* -fied; -fy·ing : repay for a loss — **in·dem·ni·fi·ca·tion** \-‚demnəfə'kāshən\ *n*

**in·dem·ni·ty** \in'demnətē\ *n, pl* -ties : security against loss or damage

[1]**in·dent** \in'dent\ *vb* : leave a space at the beginning of a paragraph

[2]**indent** *vb* : force inward so as to form a depression or dent

**in·den·ta·tion** \‚in‚den'tashən\ *n* **1** : notch, recess, or dent **2** : action of indenting **3** : space at the beginning of a paragraph

**in·den·ture** \in'denchər\ *n* : contract binding one person to work for another for a given period — usu. in pl. ～ *vb* -tured; -tur·ing : bind by indentures

**Independence Day** *n* : July 4 observed as a legal holiday in commemoration

---

incombustible
incommensurate
incommodious
incommunicable
incompatibility
incompatible
incomplete

incompletely
incompleteness
incomprehensible
inconclusive
incongruent
inconsecutive
inconsiderate

inconsiderately
inconsiderateness
inconsistency
inconsistent
inconsistently
inconspicuous
inconspicuously

of the adoption of the Declaration of Independence in 1776

**in·de·pen·dent** \‚ində'pendənt\ *adj* **1** : not governed by another **2** : not requiring or relying on something or somebody else **3** : not easily influenced — **in·de·pen·dence** \-dəns\ *n* — **independent** *n* — **in·de·pen·dent·ly** *adv*

**in·de·ter·mi·nate** \‚indi'tərmənət\ *adj* : not definitely determined — **in·de·ter·mi·na·cy** \-nəsē\ *n* — **in·de·ter·mi·nate·ly** *adv*

**in·dex** \'in‚deks\ *n, pl* **-dex·es** *or* **-di·ces** \-də‚sēz\ **1** : alphabetical list of items (as topics in a book) **2** : a number that serves as a measure or indicator of something ～ *vb* **1** : provide with an index **2** : serve as an index of

**index finger** *n* : forefinger

**in·di·cate** \'ində‚kāt\ *vb* **-cat·ed; -cat·ing 1** : point out or to **2** : show indirectly **3** : state briefly — **in·di·ca·tion** \‚ində'kāshən\ *n* — **in·di·ca·tor** \'ində‚kātər\ *n*

**in·dic·a·tive** \in'dikətiv\ *adj* : serving to indicate

**in·dict** \in'dīt\ *vb* : charge with a crime — **in·dict·able** *adj* — **in·dict·ment** *n*

**in·dif·fer·ent** \in'difrənt\ *adj* **1** : having no preference **2** : showing neither interest nor dislike **3** : mediocre — **in·dif·fer·ence** \-'difrəns\ *n* — **in·dif·fer·ent·ly** *adv*

**in·dig·e·nous** \in'dijənəs\ *adj* : native to a particular region

**in·di·gent** \'indijənt\ *adj* : needy — **in·di·gence** \-jəns\ *n*

**in·di·ges·tion** \‚indi'jeschən, -də-\ *n* : discomfort from inability to digest food

**in·dig·na·tion** \‚indig'nāshən\ *n* : anger aroused by something unjust or unworthy — **in·dig·nant** \in'dignənt\ *adj* — **in·dig·nant·ly** *adv*

**in·dig·ni·ty** \in'dignətē\ *n, pl* **-ties 1** : offense against self-respect **2** : humiliating treatment

**in·di·go** \'indi‚gō\ *n, pl* **-gos** *or* **-goes**

**1** : blue dye **2** : deep reddish blue color

**in·di·rect** \‚ində'rekt, -dī-\ *adj* : not straight or straightforward — **in·di·rec·tion** \-'rekshən\ *n* — **in·di·rect·ly** *adv* — **in·di·rect·ness** *n*

**in·dis·crim·i·nate** \‚indis'krimənət\ *adj* **1** : not careful or discriminating **2** : haphazard — **in·dis·crim·i·nate·ly** *adv*

**in·dis·pens·able** \‚indis'pensəbəl\ *adj* : absolutely essential — **in·dis·pens·abil·i·ty** \-‚pensə'bilətē\ *n* — **indispensable** *n* — **in·dis·pens·ably** \-'pensəblē\ *adv*

**in·dis·posed** \-'pōzd\ *adj* : slightly ill — **in·dis·po·si·tion** \in‚dispə'zishən\ *n*

**in·dis·sol·u·ble** \‚indis'älyəbəl\ *adj* : not capable of being dissolved or broken

**in·di·vid·u·al** \‚ində'vijəwəl\ *n* **1** : single member of a category **2** : person — **individual** *adj* — **in·di·vid·u·al·ly** *adv*

**in·di·vid·u·al·ist** \-əwəlist\ *n* : person who is markedly independent in thought or action

**in·di·vid·u·al·i·ty** \-‚vijə'walətē\ *n* : special quality that distinguishes an individual

**in·di·vid·u·al·ize** \-'vijəwə‚līz\ *vb* **-ized; -iz·ing 1** : make individual **2** : treat individually

**in·doc·tri·nate** \in'däktrə‚nāt\ *vb* **-nat·ed; -nat·ing** : instruct in fundamentals (as of a doctrine) — **in·doc·tri·na·tion** \in‚däktrə'nāshən\ *n*

**in·do·lent** \'indələnt\ *adj* : lazy — **in·do·lence** \-ləns\ *n*

**in·dom·i·ta·ble** \in'dämətəbəl\ *adj* : invincible — **in·dom·i·ta·bly** \-blē\ *adv*

**in·door** \'in'dōr\ *adj* : relating to the inside of a building

**in·doors** \in'dōrz\ *adv* : in or into a building

**in·du·bi·ta·ble** \in'dübətəbəl, -'dyü-\ *adj* : being beyond question — **in·du·bi·ta·bly** \-blē\ *adv*

---

**in•duce** \in'düs, -'dyüs\ vb -duced; -duc•ing 1 : persuade 2 : bring about — **in•duce•ment** n — **in•duc•er** n

**in•duct** \in'dəkt\ vb 1 : put in office 2 : admit as a member 3 : enroll (as for military service) — **in•duct•ee** \in-,dək'tē\ n

**in•duc•tion** \in'dəkshən\ n 1 : act or instance of inducting 2 : reasoning from particular instances to a general conclusion

**in•duc•tive** \in'dəktiv\ adj : reasoning by induction

**in•dulge** \in'dəlj\ vb -dulged; -dulg•ing : yield to the desire of or for — **in•dul•gence** \-'dəljəns\ n — **in•dul•gent** \-jənt\ adj — **in•dul•gent•ly** adv

**in•dus•tri•al** \in'dəstrēəl\ adj 1 : relating to industry 2 : heavy-duty — **in•dus•tri•al•ist** \-əlist\ n — **in•dus•tri•al•iza•tion** \-,dəstrēələ'zāshən\ n — **in•dus•tri•al•ize** \-'dəstrēə,līz\ vb — **in•dus•tri•al•ly** adv

**in•dus•tri•ous** \in'dəstrēəs\ adj : diligent or busy — **in•dus•tri•ous•ly** adv — **in•dus•tri•ous•ness** n

**in•dus•try** \'indəstrē\ n, pl -tries 1 : diligence 2 : manufacturing enterprises or activity

**in•ebri•at•ed** \i'nēbrē,ātəd\ adj : drunk — **in•ebri•a•tion** \-,ēbrē'āshən\ n

**in•ef•fa•ble** \in'efəbəl\ adj : incapable of being expressed in words — **in•ef•fa•bly** \-blē\ adv

**in•ept** \in'ept\ adj 1 : inappropriate or foolish 2 : generally incompetent — **in•ep•ti•tude** \in'eptə,tüd, -,tyüd\ n — **in•ept•ly** adv — **in•ept•ness** n

**in•equal•i•ty** \,ini'kwälətē\ n : quality of being unequal or uneven

**in•ert** \in'ərt\ adj 1 : powerless to move or act 2 : sluggish — **in•ert•ly** adv — **in•ert•ness** n

**in•er•tia** \in'ərshə\ n : tendency of matter to remain at rest or in motion — **in•er•tial** \-shəl\ adj

**in•es•cap•able** \,inə'skāpəbəl\ adj : inevitable — **in•es•cap•ably** \-blē\ adv

**in•es•ti•ma•ble** \in'estəməbəl\ adj : incapable of being estimated — **in•es•ti•ma•bly** \-blē\ adv

**in•ev•i•ta•ble** \in'evətəbəl\ adj : incapable of being avoided or escaped — **in•ev•i•ta•bil•i•ty** \in,evətə'bilətē\ n — **in•ev•i•ta•bly** \in'evətəblē\ adv

**in•ex•cus•able** \,inik'skyüzəbəl\ adj : being without excuse or justification — **in•ex•cus•ably** \-blē\ adv

**in•ex•haust•ible** \,inig'zóstəbəl\ adj : incapable of being used up or tired out — **in•ex•haust•ibly** \-blē\ adv

**in•ex•o•ra•ble** \in'eksərəbəl\ adj : unyielding or relentless — **in•ex•o•ra•bly** adv

**in•fal•li•ble** \in'faləbəl\ adj : incapable of error — **in•fal•li•bil•i•ty** \in,falə-'bilətē\ n — **in•fal•li•bly** adv

**in•fa•mous** \'infəməs\ adj : having the worst kind of reputation — **in•fa•mous•ly** adv

**in•fa•my** \-mē\ n, pl -mies : evil reputation

**in•fan•cy** \'infənsē\ n, pl -cies 1 : early childhood 2 : early period of existence

**in•fant** \'infənt\ n : baby

**in•fan•tile** \'infən,tīl, -t'l, -,tēl\ adj 1 : relating to infants 2 : childish

**in•fan•try** \'infəntrē\ n, pl -tries : soldiers that fight on foot

**in•fat•u•ate** \in'fachə,wāt\ vb -at•ed; -at•ing : inspire with foolish love or admiration — **in•fat•u•a•tion** \-,fachə-'wāshən\ n

**in•fect** \in'fekt\ vb : contaminate with disease-producing matter — **in•fec•tion** \-'fekshən\ n — **in•fec•tious** \-shəs\ adj — **in•fec•tive** \-'fektiv\ adj

**in•fer** \in'fər\ vb -rr- : deduce — **in•fer•ence** \'infərəns\ n — **in•fer•en•tial** \,infə'renchəl\ adj

**in•fe•ri•or** \in'firēər\ adj 1 : being lower in position, degree, rank, or

merit **2** : of lesser quality — **inferior**
*n* — **in·fe·ri·or·i·ty** \in,firē'örətē\ *n*

**in·fer·nal** \in'fərn°l\ *adj* : of or like
hell — often used as a general expression of disapproval — **in·fer·nal·ly**
*adv*

**in·fer·no** \in'fərnō\ *n, pl* **-nos** : place
or condition suggesting hell

**in·fest** \in'fest\ *vb* : swarm or grow
in or over — **in·fes·ta·tion** \,in,fes-
'tāshən\ *n*

**in·fi·del** \'infəd°l, -fə,del\ *n* : one who
does not believe in a particular religion

**in·fi·del·i·ty** \,infə'delətē, -fī-\ *n, pl*
**-ties** : lack of faithfulness

**in·field** \'in,fēld\ *n* : baseball field inside the base lines — **in·field·er** *n*

**in·fil·trate** \in'fil,trāt, 'infil-\ *vb* **-trat-
ed; -trat·ing** : enter or become established in without being noticed —
**in·fil·tra·tion** \,infil'trāshən\ *n*

**in·fi·nite** \'infənət\ *adj* **1** : having no
limit or extending indefinitely **2** : vast
— **infinite** *n* — **in·fi·nite·ly** *adv* —
**in·fin·i·tude** \in'finə,tüd, -tyüd\ *n*

**in·fin·i·tes·i·mal** \,in,finə'tesəməl\ *adj*
: immeasurably small — **in·fin·i·tes-
i·mal·ly** *adv*

**in·fin·i·tive** \in'finətiv\ *n* : verb form in
English usu. used with *to*

**in·fin·i·ty** \in'finətē\ *n, pl* **-ties 1**
: quality or state of being infinite **2**
: indefinitely great number or amount

**in·firm** \in'fərm\ *adj* : feeble from age
— **in·fir·mi·ty** \-'fərmətē\ *n*

**in·fir·ma·ry** \in'fərmərē\ *n, pl* **-ries**
: place for the care of the sick

**in·flame** \in'flām\ *vb* **-flamed; -flam-
ing 1** : excite to intense action or
feeling **2** : affect or become affected
with inflammation — **in·flam·ma·to-
ry** \-'flamə,tōrē\ *adj*

**in·flam·ma·ble** \in'flaməbəl\ *adj*
: flammable

**in·flam·ma·tion** \,inflə'māshən\ *n*
: response to injury in which an affected area becomes red and painful
and congested with blood

**in·flate** \in'flāt\ *vb* **-flat·ed; -flat·ing 1**
: swell or puff up (as with gas) **2** : expand or increase abnormally — **in-
flat·able** *adj*

**in·fla·tion** \in'flāshən\ *n* **1** : act of in-
flating **2** : continual rise in prices —
**in·fla·tion·ary** \-shə,nerē\ *adj*

**in·flec·tion** \in'flekshən\ *n* **1** : change
in pitch or loudness of the voice **2**
: change in form of a word — **in·flect**
\-'flekt\ *vb* — **in·flec·tion·al** \-'flek-
shənəl\ *adj*

**in·flict** \in'flikt\ *vb* : give by or as if by
hitting — **in·flic·tion** \-'flikshən\ *n*

**in·flu·ence** \'in,flüəns\ *n* **1** : power or
capacity of causing an effect in indirect or intangible ways **2** : one that
exerts influence ~ *vb* **-enced; -enc-
ing** : affect or alter by influence — **in-
flu·en·tial** \,inflü'enchəl\ *adj*

**in·flu·en·za** \,inflü'enzə\ *n* : acute
very contagious virus disease

**in·flux** \'in,fləks\ *n* : a flowing in

**in·form** \in'förm\ *vb* : give information
or knowledge to — **in·for·mant** \-ənt\
*n* — **in·form·er** *n*

**in·for·mal** \in'förməl\ *adj* **1** : without
formality or ceremony **2** : for ordinary or familiar use — **in·for·mal·i·ty**
\,inför'malətē, -fər-\ *n* — **in·for·mal-
ly** *adv*

**in·for·ma·tion** \,infər'māshən\ *n*
: knowledge obtained from investigation, study, or instruction — **in·for-
ma·tion·al** \-shənəl\ *adj*

**in·for·ma·tive** \in'förmətiv\ *adj* : giving knowledge

**in·frac·tion** \in'frakshən\ *n* : violation

**in·fra·red** \,infrə'red\ *adj* : being, relating to, or using radiation of wavelengths longer than those of red light
— **infrared** *n*

**in·fra·struc·ture** \'infrə,strəkchər\ *n*
: foundation of a system or organization

**in·fringe** \in'frinj\ *vb* **-fringed; -fring-
ing** : violate another's right or privilege — **in·fringe·ment** *n*

**in·fu·ri·ate** \in'fyurē,āt\ *vb* **-at·ed; -at-**

ing : make furious — **in·fu·ri·at·ing·ly** \-ˌātiŋlē\ adv

**in·fuse** \in'fyüz\ vb **-fused; -fus·ing 1** : instill a principle or quality in **2** : steep in liquid without boiling — **in·fu·sion** \-'fyüzhən\ n

¹**-ing** \iŋ\ vb suffix or adj suffix — used to form the present participle and sometimes an adjective resembling a present participle

²**-ing** n suffix **1** : action or process **2** : something connected with or resulting from an action or process

**in·ge·nious** \in'jēnyəs\ adj : very clever — **in·ge·nious·ly** adv — **in·ge·nious·ness** n

**in·ge·nue, in·gé·nue** \'anjə,nü, 'än-; 'aⁿzhə-, 'äⁿ-\ n : naïve young woman

**in·ge·nu·ity** \ˌinjə'nüətē, -'nyü-\ n, pl **-ities** : skill or cleverness in planning or inventing

**in·gen·u·ous** \in'jenyəwəs\ adj : innocent and candid — **in·gen·u·ous·ly** adv — **in·gen·u·ous·ness** n

**in·gest** \in'jest\ vb : eat — **in·ges·tion** \-'jeschən\ n

**in·gle·nook** \'iŋgəl,nu̇k\ n : corner by the fireplace

**in·got** \'iŋgət\ n : block of metal

**in·grained** \in'grānd\ adj : deep-seated

**in·grate** \'in,grāt\ n : ungrateful person

**in·gra·ti·ate** \in'grāshē,āt\ vb **-at·ed; -at·ing** : gain favor for (oneself) — **in·gra·ti·at·ing** adj

**in·gre·di·ent** \in'grēdēənt\ n : one of the substances that make up a mixture

**in·grown** \'in,grōn\ adj : grown in and esp. into the flesh

**in·hab·it** \in'habət\ vb : live or dwell in — **in·hab·it·able** adj — **in·hab·it·ant** \-ətənt\ n

**in·hale** \in'hāl\ vb **-haled; -hal·ing** : breathe in — **in·hal·ant** \-ənt\ n — **in·ha·la·tion** \,inhə'lāshən, ,inə-\ n — **in·hal·er** n

**in·here** \in'hir\ vb **-hered; -her·ing** : be inherent

**in·her·ent** \in'hirənt, -'her-\ adj : be-
ing an essential part of something — **in·her·ent·ly** adv

**in·her·it** \in'herət\ vb : receive from one's ancestors — **in·her·it·able** \-əbəl\ adj — **in·her·i·tance** \-ətəns\ n — **in·her·i·tor** \-ətər\ n

**in·hib·it** \in'hibət\ vb : hold in check — **in·hi·bi·tion** \,inhə'bishən, ,inə-\ n

**in·hu·man** \in'hyümən, -'yü-\ adj : cruel or impersonal — **in·hu·man·i·ty** \-hyü'manətē, -yü-\ n — **in·hu·man·ly** adv — **in·hu·man·ness** n

**in·im·i·cal** \in'imikəl\ adj : hostile or harmful — **in·im·i·cal·ly** adv

**in·im·i·ta·ble** \in'imətəbəl\ adj : not capable of being imitated

**in·iq·ui·ty** \in'ikwətē\ n, pl **-ties** : wickedness — **in·iq·ui·tous** \-wətəs\ adj

**ini·tial** \in'ishəl\ adj **1** : of or relating to the beginning **2** : first ∼ n : 1st letter of a word or name ∼ vb **-tialed** or **-tialled; -tial·ing** or **-tial·ling** : put initials on — **ini·tial·ly** adv

**ini·ti·ate** \in'ishē,āt\ vb **-at·ed; -at·ing 1** : start **2** : induct into membership **3** : instruct in the rudiments of something — **initiate** \-'ishēət\ n — **ini·ti·a·tion** \-,ishē'āshən\ n — **ini·tia·to·ry** \-'ishēə,tōrē\ adj

**ini·tia·tive** \in'ishətiv\ n **1** : first step **2** : readiness to undertake something on one's own

**in·ject** \in'jekt\ vb : force or introduce into something — **in·jec·tion** \-'jekshən\ n

**in·junc·tion** \in'jəŋkshən\ n : court writ requiring one to do or to refrain from doing a specified act

**in·jure** \'injər\ vb **-jured; -jur·ing** : do damage, hurt, or a wrong to

**in·ju·ry** \'injərē\ n, pl **-ries 1** : act that injures **2** : hurt, damage, or loss sustained — **in·ju·ri·ous** \in'ju̇rēəs\ adj

**in·jus·tice** \in'jəstəs\ n : unjust act

**ink** \'iŋk\ n : usu. liquid and colored material for writing and printing ∼ vb : put ink on — **ink·well** \-ˌwel\ n — **inky** adj

**in·kling** \'iŋkliŋ\ n : hint or idea

---

**in·land** \'in,land, -lənd\ *n* : interior of a country — **inland** *adj or adv*

**in–law** \'in,lò\ *n* : relative by marriage

**in·lay** \in'lā, 'in,lā\ *vb* **-laid** \-'lād\; **-lay·ing** : set into a surface for decoration ~ \'in,lā\ *n* **1** : inlaid work **2** : shaped filling cemented into a tooth

**in·let** \'in,let, -lət\ *n* : small bay

**in·mate** \'in,māt\ *n* : person confined to an asylum or prison

**in me·mo·ri·am** \,inmə'mōrēəm\ *prep* : in memory of

**in·most** \'in,mōst\ *adj* : deepest within

**inn** \'in\ *n* : hotel

**in·nards** \'inərdz\ *n pl* : internal parts

**in·nate** \in'āt\ *adj* **1** : inborn **2** : inherent — **in·nate·ly** *adv*

**in·ner** \'inər\ *adj* : being on the inside

**in·ner·most** \'inər,mōst\ *adj* : farthest inward

**in·ner·sole** \,inər'sōl\ *n* : insole

**in·ning** \'iniŋ\ *n* : baseball team's turn at bat

**inn·keep·er** \'in,kēpər\ *n* : owner of an inn

**in·no·cent** \'inəsənt\ *adj* **1** : free from guilt **2** : harmless **3** : not sophisticated — **in·no·cence** \-səns\ *n* — **innocent** *n* — **in·no·cent·ly** *adv*

**in·noc·u·ous** \in'äkyəwəs\ *adj* **1** : harmless **2** : inoffensive

**in·no·va·tion** \,inə'vāshən\ *n* : new idea or method — **in·no·vate** \'inə,vāt\ *vb* — **in·no·va·tive** \'inə,vātiv\ *adj* — **in·no·va·tor** \-,vātər\ *n*

**in·nu·en·do** \,inyə'wendō\ *n, pl* **-dos** *or* **-does** : insinuation

**in·nu·mer·a·ble** \in'ümərəbəl, -'yüm-\ *adj* : countless

**in·oc·u·late** \in'äkyə,lāt\ *vb* **-lat·ed; -lat·ing** : treat with something esp. to establish immunity — **in·oc·u·la·tion** \-,äkyə'lāshən\ *n*

**in·op·por·tune** \in,äpər'tün, -'tyün\ *adj* : inconvenient — **in·op·por·tune·ly** *adv*

**in·or·di·nate** \in'òrd°nət\ *adj* : unusual or excessive — **in·or·di·nate·ly** *adv*

**in·or·gan·ic** \,in,òr'ganik\ *adj* : made of mineral matter

**in·pa·tient** \'in,pāshənt\ *n* : patient who stays in a hospital

**in·put** \'in,pút\ *n* : something put in — **input** *vb*

**in·quest** \'in,kwest\ *n* : inquiry esp. before a jury

**in·quire** \in'kwīr\ *vb* **-quired; -quir·ing** **1** : ask **2** : investigate — **in·quir·er** *n* — **in·quir·ing·ly** *adv* — **in·qui·ry** \'in,kwīrē, in'kwīrē; 'inkwərē, 'in-\ *n*

**in·qui·si·tion** \,inkwə'zishən, ,iŋ-\ *n* **1** : official inquiry **2** : severe questioning — **in·quis·i·tor** \in'kwizətər\ *n* — **in·quis·i·to·ri·al** \-,kwizə-'tōrēəl\ *adj*

**in·quis·i·tive** \in'kwizətiv\ *adj* : curious — **in·quis·i·tive·ly** *adv* — **in·quis·i·tive·ness** *n*

**in·road** \'in,rōd\ *n* : encroachment

**in·rush** \'in,rəsh\ *n* : influx

**in·sane** \in'sān\ *adj* **1** : not sane **2** : absurd — **in·sane·ly** *adv* — **in·san·i·ty** \in'sanətē\ *n*

**in·sa·tia·ble** \in'sāshəbəl\ *adj* : incapable of being satisfied — **in·sa·tia·bil·i·ty** \,sāshə'bilətē\ *n* — **in·sa·tia·bly** *adv*

**in·scribe** \in'skrīb\ *vb* **1** : write **2** : engrave **3** : dedicate (a book) to someone — **in·scrip·tion** \-'skripshən\ *n*

**in·scru·ta·ble** \in'skrütəbəl\ *adj* : mysterious — **in·scru·ta·bly** *adv*

**in·seam** \'in,sēm\ *n* : inner seam (of a garment)

**in·sect** \'in,sekt\ *n* : small usu. winged animal with 6 legs

**in·sec·ti·cide** \in'sektə,sīd\ *n* : insect poison — **in·sec·ti·cid·al** \in,sektə-'sīd°l\ *adj*

**in·se·cure** \,insi'kyùr\ *adj* **1** : uncertain **2** : unsafe **3** : fearful — **in·se·cure·ly** *adv* — **in·se·cu·ri·ty** \-'kyùrətē\ *n*

**in·sem·i·nate** \in'semə,nāt\ *vb* **-nat·ed; -nat·ing** : introduce semen into

---

| | | |
|---|---|---|
| **inflexibility** | **ingratitude** | **inoperable** |
| **inflexible** | **inhumane** | **inoperative** |
| **inflexibly** | **inhumanely** | **insalubrious** |
| **infrequent** | **injudicious** | **insensitive** |
| **infrequently** | **injudiciously** | **insensitivity** |
| **inglorious** | **injudiciousness** | **inseparable** |
| **ingloriously** | **inoffensive** | **insignificant** |

— in·sem·i·na·tion \-ˌsemə'nāshən\ n

in·sen·si·ble \in'sensəbəl\ adj 1 : unconscious 2 : unable to feel 3 : unaware — in·sen·si·bil·i·ty \inˌsensə-'bilətē\ n — in·sen·si·bly adv

in·sen·tient \in'senchənt\ adj : lacking feeling — in·sen·tience \-chəns\ n

in·sert \in'sərt\ vb : put in — insert \'inˌsərt\ n — in·ser·tion \in-'sərshən\ n

in·set \'inˌset\ vb inset or in·set·ted; in·set·ting : set in — inset n

in·shore \'in'shōr\ adj 1 : situated near shore 2 : moving toward shore ~ adv : toward shore

in·side \in'sīd, 'inˌsīd\ n 1 : inner side 2 pl : innards ~ prep 1 : in or into the inside of 2 : within ~ adv 1 : on the inner side 2 : into the interior — inside adj — in·sid·er \in'sīdər\ n

inside of prep : inside

in·sid·i·ous \in'sidēəs\ adj 1 : treacherous 2 : seductive — in·sid·i·ous·ly adv — in·sid·i·ous·ness n

in·sight \'inˌsīt\ n : understanding — in·sight·ful \in'sītfəl-\ adj

in·sig·nia \in'signēə\, in·sig·ne \-ˌnē\ n, pl -nia or -ni·as : badge of authority or office

in·sin·u·ate \in'sinyəˌwāt\ vb -at·ed; -at·ing 1 : imply 2 : bring in artfully — in·sin·u·a·tion \inˌsinyə'wāshən\ n

in·sip·id \in'sipəd\ adj 1 : tasteless 2 : not stimulating — in·si·pid·i·ty \ˌinsə'pidətē\ n

in·sist \in'sist\ vb : be firmly demanding — in·sis·tence \in'sistəns\ n — in·sis·tent \-tənt\ adj — in·sis·tent·ly adv

insofar as \ˌinsō'färaz\ conj : to the extent that

in·sole \'inˌsōl\ n : inside sole of a shoe

in·so·lent \'insələnt\ adj : contemptuously rude — in·so·lence \-ləns\ n

in·sol·vent \in'sälvənt\ adj : unable or insufficient to pay debts — in·sol·ven·cy \-vənsē\ n

in·som·nia \in'sämnēə\ n : inability to sleep — in·som·ni·ac \-nē-ˌak\ n

in·so·much as \ˌinsō'məchaz\ conj : inasmuch as

insomuch that conj : to such a degree that

in·sou·ci·ance \in'süsēəns, aⁿsü'syäⁿs\ n : lighthearted indifference — in·sou·ci·ant \in'süsēənt, aⁿsü'syäⁿ\ adj

in·spect \in'spekt\ vb : view closely and critically — in·spec·tion \-'spekshən\ n — in·spec·tor \-tər\ n

in·spire \in'spīr\ vb -spired; -spir·ing 1 : inhale 2 : influence by example 3 : bring about 4 : stir to action — in·spi·ra·tion \ˌinspə'rāshən\ n — in·spi·ra·tion·al \-'rāshənəl\ adj — in·spir·er n

in·stall, in·stal \in'stól\ vb -stalled; -stall·ing 1 : induct into office 2 : set up for use — in·stal·la·tion \ˌinstə-'lāshən\ n

in·stall·ment \in'stólmənt\ n : partial payment

in·stance \'instəns\ n 1 : request or instigation 2 : example

in·stant \'instənt\ n : moment ~ adj 1 : immediate 2 : ready to mix — in·stan·ta·neous \ˌinstən'tānēəs\ adj — in·stan·ta·neous·ly adv — in·stant·ly adv

in·stead \in'sted\ adv : as a substitute or alternative

instead of prep : as a substitute for or alternative to

in·step \'inˌstep\ n : part of the foot in front of the ankle

in·sti·gate \'instəˌgāt\ vb -gat·ed; -gat·ing : incite — in·sti·ga·tion \ˌinstə'gāshən\ n — in·sti·ga·tor \'instəˌgātər\ n

in·still \in'stil\ vb -stilled; -still·ing : impart gradually

in·stinct \'inˌstiŋkt\ n 1 : natural talent 2 : natural inherited or subconsciously motivated behavior — in·stinc·tive \in'stiŋktiv\ adj — in·stinc·tive·ly adv — in·stinc·tu·al \in'stiŋkchəwəl\ adj

in·sti·tute \'instəˌtüt, -ˌtyüt\ vb -tut-

---

| | | |
|---|---|---|
| insincere | insufficiency | intolerable |
| insincerely | insufficient | intolerably |
| insincerity | insufficiently | intolerance |
| insolubility | insupportable | intolerant |
| insoluble | intangibility | intractable |
| instability | intangible | invariable |
| insubstantial | intangibly | invariably |

ed; -tut·ing : establish, start, or organize ~ n 1 : organization promoting a cause 2 : school

in·sti·tu·tion \ˌinstə'tüshən, -'tyü-\ n 1 : act of instituting 2 : custom 3 : corporation or society of a public character — in·sti·tu·tion·al \-shənəl\ adj — in·sti·tu·tion·al·ize \-ˌīz\ vb — in·sti·tu·tion·al·ly adv

in·struct \in'strəkt\ vb 1 : teach 2 : give an order to — in·struc·tion \in'strəkshən\ n — in·struc·tion·al \-shənəl\ adj — in·struc·tive \in-'strəktiv\ adj — in·struc·tor \in-'strəktər\ n — in·struc·tor·ship n

in·stru·ment \'instrəmənt\ n 1 : something that produces music 2 : means 3 : device for doing work and esp. precision work 4 : legal document — in·stru·men·tal \ˌinstrə-'mentᵊl\ adj — in·stru·men·tal·ist \-ist\ n — in·stru·men·tal·i·ty \ˌinstrəmən'talətē, -ˌmen-\ n — in·stru·men·ta·tion \ˌinstrəmən'tāshən, -ˌmen-\ n

in·sub·or·di·nate \ˌinsə'bȯrdᵊnət\ adj : not obeying — in·sub·or·di·na·tion \-ˌbȯrdᵊn'āshən\ n

in·suf·fer·able \in'səfərəbəl\ adj : unbearable — in·suf·fer·ably \-blē\ adv

in·su·lar \'insülər, -syü-\ adj 1 : relating to or residing on an island 2 : narrow-minded — in·su·lar·i·ty \ˌinsü'larətē, -syü-\ n

in·su·late \'insəˌlāt\ vb -lat·ed; -lating : protect from heat loss or electricity — in·su·la·tion \ˌinsə'lāshən\ n — in·su·la·tor \'insəˌlātər\ n

in·su·lin \'insələn\ n : hormone used by diabetics

in·sult \in'səlt\ vb : treat with contempt ~ \'inˌsəlt\ n : insulting act or remark — in·sult·ing·ly \-iŋlē\ adv

in·su·per·a·ble \in'süpərəbəl\ adj : too difficult — in·su·per·a·bly \-blē\ adv

in·sure \in'shu̇r\ vb -sured; -sur·ing 1 : guarantee against loss 2 : make certain — in·sur·able \-əbəl\ adj — in·sur·ance \-əns\ n — in·sured \in'shu̇rd\ n — in·sur·er n

in·sur·gent \in'sərjənt\ n : rebel — insur·gence \-jəns\ n — in·sur·gen·cy \-jənsē\ n — in·sur·gent adj

in·sur·mount·able \ˌinsər'mau̇ntəbəl\

adj : too great to be overcome — in·sur·mount·ably \-blē\ adv

in·sur·rec·tion \ˌinsə'rekshən\ n : revolution — in·sur·rec·tion·ist n

in·tact \in'takt\ adj : undamaged

in·take \'inˌtāk\ n 1 : opening through which something enters 2 : act of taking in 3 : amount taken in

in·te·ger \'intijər\ n : number that is not a fraction and does not include a fraction

in·te·gral \'intigrəl\ adj : essential

in·te·grate \'intəˌgrāt\ vb -grat·ed; -grat·ing 1 : unite 2 : end segregation of or at — in·te·gra·tion \ˌintə-'grāshən\ n

in·teg·ri·ty \in'tegrətē\ n 1 : soundness 2 : adherence to a code of values 3 : completeness

in·tel·lect \'intᵊlˌekt\ n : power of knowing or thinking — in·tel·lec·tual \ˌintᵊl'ekchəwəl\ adj or n — in·tel·lec·tu·al·ism \-chəwəˌlizəm\ n — in·tel·lec·tu·al·ly adv

in·tel·li·gence \in'teləjəns\ n 1 : ability to learn and understand 2 : mental acuteness 3 : information

in·tel·li·gent \in'teləjənt\ adj : having or showing intelligence — in·tel·ligent·ly adv

in·tel·li·gi·ble \in'teləjəbəl\ adj : understandable — in·tel·li·gi·bil·i·ty \-ˌteləjə'bilətē\ n — in·tel·li·gi·bly adv

in·tem·per·ance \in'tempərəns\ n : lack of moderation — in·tem·per·ate \-pərət\ adj — in·tem·per·ateness n

in·tend \in'tend\ vb : have as a purpose

in·tend·ed \-'tendəd\ n : engaged person — intended adj

in·tense \in'tens\ adj 1 : extreme 2 : deeply felt — in·tense·ly adv — in·ten·si·fi·ca·tion \-ˌtensəfə'kāshən\ n — in·ten·si·fy \-'tensəˌfī\ vb — in·ten·si·ty \in'tensətē\ n — in·tensive \in'tensiv\ adj — in·ten·sive·ly adv

¹in·tent \in'tent\ n : purpose — in·tention \-'tenchən\ n — in·ten·tion·al \-'tenchənəl\ adj — in·ten·tion·al·ly adv

²intent adj : concentrated — in·tent·ly adv — in·tent·ness n

in·ter \in'tər\ vb -rr- : bury

---

inviable
invisibility
invisible

invisibly
involuntarily
involuntary

invulnerability
invulnerable
invulnerably

**inter-** *prefix* : between or among

**in·ter·ac·tion** \ˌintər'akshən\ *n* : mutual influence — **in·ter·act** \-'akt\ *vb* — **in·ter·ac·tive** *adj*

**in·ter·breed** \ˌintər'brēd\ *vb* -**bred** \-'bred\; -**breed·ing** : breed together

**in·ter·ca·late** \in'tərkəˌlāt\ *vb* -**lat·ed**; -**lat·ing** : insert — **in·ter·ca·la·tion** \-ˌtərkə'lāshən\ *n*

**in·ter·cede** \ˌintər'sēd\ *vb* -**ced·ed**; -**ced·ing** : act to reconcile — **in·ter·ces·sion** \-'seshən\ *n* — **in·ter·ces·sor** \-'sesər\ *n*

**in·ter·cept** \ˌintər'sept\ *vb* : interrupt the progress of — **intercept** \'intərˌsept\ *n* — **in·ter·cep·tion** \ˌintər'sepshən\ *n* — **in·ter·cep·tor** \-'septər\ *n*

**in·ter·change** \ˌintər'chānj\ *vb* 1 : exchange 2 : change places ~ \'intərˌchānj\ *n* 1 : exchange 2 : junction of highways — **in·ter·change·able** \ˌintər'chānjəbəl\ *adj*

**in·ter·course** \'intərˌkōrs\ *n* 1 : relations between persons or nations 2 : copulation

**in·ter·de·pen·dent** \ˌintərdi'pendənt\ *adj* : mutually dependent — **in·ter·de·pen·dence** \-dəns\ *n*

**in·ter·dict** \ˌintər'dikt\ *vb* 1 : prohibit 2 : destroy or cut (an enemy supply line) — **in·ter·dic·tion** \-'dikshən\ *n*

**in·ter·est** \'intrəst, -təˌrest\ *n* 1 : right 2 : benefit 3 : charge for borrowed money 4 : readiness to pay special attention 5 : quality that causes interest ~ *vb* 1 : concern 2 : get the attention of — **in·ter·est·ing** *adj* — **in·ter·est·ing·ly** *adv*

**in·ter·face** \'intərˌfās\ *n* : common boundary — **in·ter·fa·cial** \ˌintər'fāshəl\ *adj*

**in·ter·fere** \ˌintər'fir\ *vb* -**fered**; -**fer·ing** 1 : collide or be in opposition 2 : try to run the affairs of others — **in·ter·fer·ence** \-'firəns\ *n*

**in·ter·im** \'intərəm\ *n* : time between — **interim** *adj*

**in·te·ri·or** \in'tirēər\ *adj* : being on the inside ~ *n* 1 : inside 2 : inland area

**in·ter·ject** \ˌintər'jekt\ *vb* : stick in between

**in·ter·jec·tion** \-'jekshən\ *n* : an exclamatory word — **in·ter·jec·tion·al·ly** \-shənəlē\ *adv*

**in·ter·lace** \ˌintər'lās\ *vb* : cross or cause to cross one over another

**in·ter·lin·ear** \ˌintər'linēər\ *adj* : between written or printed lines

**in·ter·lock** \ˌintər'läk\ *vb* 1 : interlace 2 : connect for mutual effect — **interlock** \'intərˌläk\ *n*

**in·ter·lop·er** \ˌintər'lōpər\ *n* : intruder or meddler

**in·ter·lude** \'intərˌlüd\ *n* : intervening period

**in·ter·mar·ry** \ˌintər'marē\ *vb* 1 : marry each other 2 : marry within a group — **in·ter·mar·riage** \-'marij\ *n*

**in·ter·me·di·ary** \ˌintər'mēdēˌerē\ *n*, *pl* -**ar·ies** : agent between individuals or groups — **intermediary** *adj*

**in·ter·me·di·ate** \ˌintər'mēdēət\ *adj* : between extremes — **intermediate** *n*

**in·ter·ment** \in'tərmənt\ *n* : burial

**in·ter·mi·na·ble** \in'tərmənəbəl\ *adj* : endless — **in·ter·mi·na·bly** *adv*

**in·ter·min·gle** \ˌintər'miŋgəl\ *vb* : mingle

**in·ter·mis·sion** \ˌintər'mishən\ *n* : break in a performance

**in·ter·mit·tent** \-'mit³nt\ *adj* : coming at intervals — **in·ter·mit·tent·ly** *adv*

**in·ter·mix** \ˌintər'miks\ *vb* : mix together — **in·ter·mix·ture** \-'mikschər\ *n*

**¹in·tern** \'inˌtərn, in'tərn\ *vb* : confine esp. during a war — **in·tern·ee** \ˌinˌtər'nē\ *n* — **in·tern·ment** *n*

---

**List of self-explanatory words with the prefix *inter-***

| | | |
|---|---|---|
| interagency | intercommunal | interfaculty |
| interatomic | intercommunity | interfamily |
| interbank | intercompany | interfiber |
| interborough | intercontinental | interfraternity |
| intercampus | intercounty | intergalactic |
| interchurch | intercultural | intergang |
| intercity | interdenominational | intergovernmental |
| interclass | interdepartmental | intergroup |
| intercoastal | interdivisional | interhemispheric |
| intercollegiate | interelectronic | interindustry |
| intercolonial | interethnic | interinstitutional |

²in·tern \'in,tərn\ *n* : advanced student (as in medicine) gaining supervised experience ∼ *vb* : act as an intern — **in·tern·ship** *n*

in·ter·nal \in'tərn°l\ *adj* 1 : inward 2 : inside of the body 3 : relating to or existing in the mind — **in·ter·nal·ly** *adv*

in·ter·na·tion·al \,intər'nashənəl\ *adj* : affecting 2 or more nations ∼ *n* : something having international scope — **in·ter·na·tion·al·ism** \-,izəm\ *n* — **in·ter·na·tion·al·ize** \-,īz\ *vb* — **in·ter·na·tion·al·ly** *adv*

In·ter·net \'intər,net\ *n* : network that connects computer networks worldwide

in·ter·nist \'in,tərnist\ *n* : specialist in nonsurgical medicine

in·ter·play \'intər,plā\ *n* : interaction

in·ter·po·late \in'tərpə,lāt\ *vb* -lat·ed; -lat·ing : insert — **in·ter·po·la·tion** \-,tərpə'lāshən\ *n*

in·ter·pose \,intər'pōz\ *vb* -posed; -pos·ing 1 : place between 2 : intrude — **in·ter·po·si·tion** \-pə'zishən\ *n*

in·ter·pret \in'tərprət\ *vb* : explain the meaning of — **in·ter·pre·ta·tion** \in,tərprə'tāshən\ *n* — **in·ter·pre·ta·tive** \-'tərprə,tātiv\ *adj* — **in·ter·pret·er** *n* — **in·ter·pre·tive** \-'tərprətiv\ *adj*

in·ter·re·late \,intəri'lāt\ *vb* : have a mutual relationship — **in·ter·re·lat·ed·ness** \-'lātədnəs\ *n* — **in·ter·re·la·tion** \-'lāshən\ *n* — **in·ter·re·la·tion·ship** *n*

in·ter·ro·gate \in'terə,gāt\ *vb* -gat·ed; -gat·ing : question — **in·ter·ro·ga·tion** \-,terə'gāshən\ *n* — **in·ter·rog·a·tive** \,intə'rägətiv\ *adj or n* — **in·ter·ro·ga·tor** \-'terə,gātər\ *n* — **in·ter·rog·a·to·ry** \,intə'rägə,tōrē\ *adj*

in·ter·rupt \,intə'rəpt\ *vb* : intrude so as to hinder or end continuity — **in·ter·rupt·er** *n* — **in·ter·rup·tion** \-'rəpshən\ *n* — **in·ter·rup·tive** \-'rəptiv\ *adv*

in·ter·sect \,intər'sekt\ *vb* 1 : cut across or divide 2 : cross — **in·ter·sec·tion** \-'sekshən\ *n*

in·ter·sperse \,intər'spərs\ *vb* -spersed; -spers·ing : insert at intervals — **in·ter·per·sion** \-'spərzhən\ *n*

in·ter·stice \in'tərstəs\ *n, pl* -stic·es \-stə,sēz, -stəsəz\ : space between — **in·ter·sti·tial** \,intər'stishəl\ *adj*

in·ter·twine \,intər'twīn\ *vb* : twist together — **in·ter·twine·ment** *n*

in·ter·val \'intərvəl\ *n* 1 : time between 2 : space between

in·ter·vene \,intər'vēn\ *vb* -vened; -ven·ing 1 : happen between events 2 : intercede — **in·ter·ven·tion** \-'venchən\ *n*

in·ter·view \'intər,vyü\ *n* : a meeting to get information — **interview** *vb* — **in·ter·view·er** *n*

in·ter·weave \,intər'wēv\ *vb* -wove \-'wōv\; -wo·ven \-'wōvən\; -weav·ing : weave together — **in·ter·wo·ven** \-'wōvən\ *adj*

in·tes·tate \in'tes,tāt, -tət\ *adj* : not leaving a will

in·tes·tine \in'testən\ *n* : tubular part of the digestive system after the stomach including a long narrow upper part (**small intestine**) followed by a broader shorter lower part (**large intestine**) — **in·tes·ti·nal** \-tən°l\ *adj*

in·ti·mate \'intə,māt\ *vb* -mat·ed; -mat·ing : hint ∼ \'intəmət\ *adj* 1 : very friendly 2 : suggesting privacy 3 : very personal ∼ *n* : close friend — **in·ti·ma·cy** \'intəməsē\ *n* — **in·ti·mate·ly** *adv* — **in·ti·ma·tion** \,intə'māshən\ *n*

in·tim·i·date \in'timə,dāt\ *vb* -dat·ed;

---

interisland
interlibrary
intermolecular
intermountain
interoceanic
interoffice
interparticle
interparty
interpersonal
interplanetary
interpopulation

interprovincial
interracial
interregional
interreligious
interscholastic
intersectional
interstate
interstellar
intersystem
interterm
interterminal

intertribal
intertroop
intertropical
interuniversity
interurban
intervalley
intervillage
interwar
interzonal
interzone

-dat•ing : make fearful — **in•tim•i•da-tion** \-ˌtiməˈdāshən\ n

**in•to** \ˈintü\ prep **1** : to the inside of **2** : to the condition of **3** : against

**in•to•na•tion** \ˌintōˈnāshən\ n : way of singing or speaking

**in•tone** \inˈtōn\ vb **-toned; -ton•ing** : chant

**in•tox•i•cate** \inˈtäkəˌkāt\ vb **-cat•ed; -cat•ing** : make drunk — **in•tox•i•cant** \-sikənt\ n or adj — **in•tox•i•ca•tion** \-ˌtäkəˈkāshən\ n

**in•tra•mu•ral** \ˌintrəˈmyùrəl\ adj : within a school

**in•tran•si•gent** \inˈtransəjənt\ adj : uncompromising — **in•tran•si•gence** \-jəns\ n — **intransigent** n

**in•tra•ve•nous** \ˌintrəˈvēnəs\ adj : by way of the veins — **in•tra•ve•nous•ly** adv

**in•trep•id** \inˈtrepəd\ adj : fearless — **in•tre•pid•i•ty** \ˌintrəˈpidətē\ n

**in•tri•cate** \ˈintrikət\ adj : very complex and delicate — **in•tri•ca•cy** \-trikəsē\ n — **in•tri•cate•ly** adv

**in•trigue** \inˈtrēg\ vb **-trigued; -trigu-ing** **1** : scheme **2** : arouse curiosity of ~ n : secret scheme — **in•trigu-ing•ly** \-iŋlē\ adv

**in•trin•sic** \inˈtrinzik, -sik\ adj : essential — **in•trin•si•cal•ly** \-ziklē, -si-\ adv

**in•tro•duce** \ˌintrəˈdüs, -ˈdyüs\ vb **-duced; -duc•ing** **1** : bring in esp. for the 1st time **2** : cause to be acquainted **3** : bring to notice **4** : put in — **in•tro•duc•tion** \-ˈdəkshən\ n — **in•tro•duc•to•ry** \-ˈdəktərē\ adj

**in•tro•spec•tion** \ˌintrəˈspekshən\ n : examination of one's own thoughts or feelings — **in•tro•spec•tive** \-ˈspektiv\ adj — **in•tro•spec•tive-ly** adv

**in•tro•vert** \ˈintrəˌvərt\ n : shy or reserved person — **in•tro•ver•sion** \ˌintrəˈvərzhən\ n — **introvert** adj — **in•tro•vert•ed** \ˈintrəˌvərtəd\ adj

**in•trude** \inˈtrüd\ vb **-trud•ed; -trud-ing** **1** : thrust in **2** : encroach — **in•trud•er** n — **in•tru•sion** \-ˈtrüzhən\ n — **in•tru•sive** \-ˈtrüsiv\ adj — **in•tru•sive•ness** n

**in•tu•i•tion** \ˌintüˈishən, -tyü-\ n : quick and ready insight — **in•tu•it** \inˈtüət, -ˈtyü-\ vb — **in•tu•i•tive** \-ətiv\ adj — **in•tu•i•tive•ly** adv

**in•un•date** \ˈinənˌdāt\ vb **-dat•ed; -dat-**

ing : flood — **in•un•da•tion** \ˌinən-ˈdāshən\ n

**in•ure** \inˈùr, -ˈyùr\ vb **-ured; -ur•ing** : accustom to accept something undesirable

**in•vade** \inˈvād\ vb **-vad•ed; -vad•ing** : enter for conquest — **in•vad•er** n — **in•va•sion** \-ˈvāzhən\ n

**¹in•val•id** \inˈvaləd\ adj : not true or legal — **in•va•lid•i•ty** \ˌinvəˈlidətē\ n — **in•val•id•ly** adv

**²in•va•lid** \ˈinvələd\ adj : sickly ~ n : one chronically ill

**in•val•i•date** \inˈvaləˌdāt\ vb : make invalid — **in•val•i•da•tion** \inˌvaləˈdāshən\ n

**in•valu•able** \inˈvalyəwəbəl\ adj : extremely valuable

**in•va•sive** \inˈvāsiv\ adj : involving entry into the body

**in•vec•tive** \inˈvektiv\ n : abusive language — **invective** adj

**in•veigh** \inˈvā\ vb : protest or complain forcefully

**in•vei•gle** \inˈvāgəl, -ˈvē-\ vb **-gled; -gling** : win over or get by flattery

**in•vent** \inˈvent\ vb **1** : think up **2** : create for the 1st time — **in•ven-tion** \-ˈvenchən\ n — **in•ven•tive** \-ˈventiv\ adj — **in•ven•tive•ness** n — **in•ven•tor** \-ˈventər\ n

**in•ven•to•ry** \ˈinvənˌtōrē\ n, pl **-ries** **1** : list of goods **2** : stock — **inventory** vb

**in•verse** \inˈvərs, ˈinˌvərs\ adj or n : opposite — **in•verse•ly** adv

**in•vert** \inˈvərt\ vb **1** : turn upside down or inside out **2** : reverse — **in•ver•sion** \-ˈverzhən\ n

**in•ver•te•brate** \inˈvərtəbrət, -ˌbrāt\ adj : lacking a backbone ~ n : invertebrate animal

**in•vest** \inˈvest\ vb **1** : give power or authority to **2** : endow with a quality **3** : commit money to someone else's use in hope of profit — **in•vest•ment** \-mənt\ n — **in•ves•tor** \-ˈvestər\ n

**in•ves•ti•gate** \inˈvestəˌgāt\ vb **-gat•ed; -gat•ing** : study closely and systematically — **in•ves•ti•ga•tion** \-ˌvestə-ˈgāshən\ n — **in•ves•ti•ga•tive** \-ˈvestəˌgātiv\ adj — **in•ves•ti•ga-tor** \-ˈvestəˌgātər\ n

**in•ves•ti•ture** \inˈvestəˌchùr, -chər\ n : act of establishing in office

**in•vet•er•ate** \inˈvetərət\ adj : acting out of habit

**in·vid·i·ous** \in'vidēəs\ *adj* : harmful or obnoxious — **in·vid·i·ous·ly** *adv*

**in·vig·o·rate** \in'vigə,rāt\ *vb* **-rat·ed;** **-rat·ing** : give life and energy to — **in·vig·o·ra·tion** \-,vigə'rāshən\ *n*

**in·vin·ci·ble** \in'vinsəbəl\ *adj* : incapable of being conquered — **in·vin·ci·bil·i·ty** \in,vinsə'bilətē\ *n* — **in·vin·ci·bly** \in'vinsəblē\ *adv*

**in·vi·o·la·ble** \in'vīələbəl\ *adj* : safe from violation or desecration — **in·vi·o·la·bil·i·ty** \in,vīələ'bilətē\ *n*

**in·vi·o·late** \in'vīələt\ *adj* : not violated or profaned

**in·vite** \in'vīt\ *vb* **-vit·ed;** **-vit·ing** 1 : entice 2 : increase the likelihood of 3 : request the presence or participation of 4 : encourage — **in·vi·ta·tion** \,invə'tāshən\ *n* — **in·vit·ing** \in-'vītiŋ\ *adj*

**in·vo·ca·tion** \,invə'kāshən\ *n* 1 : prayer 2 : incantation

**in·voice** \'in,vois\ *n* : itemized bill for goods shipped ~ *vb* **-voiced;** **-voic·ing** : bill

**in·voke** \in'vōk\ *vb* **-voked;** **-vok·ing** 1 : call on for help 2 : cite as authority 3 : conjure 4 : carry out

**in·volve** \in'välv\ *vb* **-volved;** **-volv·ing** 1 : draw in as a participant 2 : relate closely 3 : require as a necessary part 4 : occupy fully — **in·volve·ment** *n*

**in·volved** \-'välvd\ *adj* : intricate

¹**in·ward** \'inwərd\ *adj* : inside

²**inward, in·wards** \-wərdz\ *adv* : toward the inside, center, or inner being

**in·ward·ly** *adv* 1 : mentally or spiritually 2 : internally 3 : to oneself

**io·dide** \'īə,dīd\ *n* : compound of iodine

**io·dine** \'īə,dīn, -əd°n\ *n* 1 : nonmetallic chemical element 2 : solution of iodine used as an antiseptic

**io·dize** \'īə,dīz\ *vb* **-dized;** **-diz·ing** : treat with iodine or an iodide

**ion** \'īən, 'ī,än\ *n* : electrically charged particle — **ion·ic** \ī'änik\ *adj* — **ion·iz·able** \'īə,nīzəbəl\ *adj* — **ion·iza·tion** \,īənə'zāshən\ *n* — **ion·ize** \'īə,nīz\ *vb* — **ion·iz·er** \'īə,nīzər\ *n*

**-ion** *n suffix* 1 : act or process 2 : state or condition

**ion·o·sphere** \ī'änə,sfir\ *n* : layer of the upper atmosphere containing ionized gases — **ion·o·spher·ic** \ī,änə-'sfirik, -'sfer-\ *adj*

**io·ta** \ī'ōtə\ *n* : small quantity

**IOU** \,ī,ō'yü\ *n* : acknowledgment of a debt

**IRA** \ī,är'ā\ *n* : individual retirement savings account

**iras·ci·ble** \ir'asəbəl, ī'ras-\ *adj* : marked by hot temper — **iras·ci·bil·i·ty** \-,asə'bilətē, -,ras-\ *n*

**irate** \ī'rāt\ *adj* : roused to intense anger — **irate·ly** *adv*

**ire** \'īr\ *n* : anger

**ir·i·des·cence** \,irə'des°ns\ *n* : rainbowlike play of colors — **ir·i·des·cent** \-°nt\ *adj*

**iris** \'īrəs\ *n, pl* **iris·es** *or* **iri·des** \'īrə,dēz, 'ir-\ 1 : colored part around the pupil of the eye 2 : plant with long leaves and large showy flowers

**irk** \'ərk\ *vb* : annoy — **irk·some** \-əm\ *adj* — **irk·some·ly** *adv*

**iron** \'īərn\ *n* 1 : heavy metallic chemical element 2 : something made of iron 3 : heated device for pressing clothes 4 : hardness, determination ~ *vb* : press or smooth out with an iron — **iron·ware** *n* — **iron·work** *n* — **iron·work·er** *n* — **iron·works** *n pl*

**iron·clad** \-'klad\ *adj* 1 : sheathed in iron armor 2 : strict or exacting

**iron·ing** \'īərniŋ\ *n* : clothes to be ironed

**iron·wood** \-,wud\ *n* : tree or shrub with very hard wood or this wood

**iro·ny** \'īrənē\ *n, pl* **-nies** 1 : use of words to express the opposite of the literal meaning 2 : incongruity between the actual and the expected result of events — **iron·ic** \ī'ränik\, **iron·i·cal** \-ikəl\ *adj* — **iron·i·cal·ly** \-iklē\ *adv*

**ir·ra·di·ate** \ir'ādē,āt\ *vb* **-at·ed;** **-at·ing** : treat with radiation — **ir·ra·di·a·tion** \-,ādē'āshən\ *n*

**ir·ra·tio·nal** \ir'ashənəl\ *adj* 1 : incapable of reasoning 2 : not based on reason — **ir·ra·tio·nal·i·ty** \ir,ashə-'nalətē\ *n* — **ir·ra·tio·nal·ly** *adv*

**ir·rec·on·cil·able** \ir,ekən'sīləbəl\ *adj* : impossible to reconcile — **ir·rec·on·cil·abil·i·ty** \-,sīlə'bilətē\ *n*

**ir·re·cov·er·able** \,iri'kəvərəbəl\ *adj* : not capable of being recovered — **ir·re·cov·er·ably** \-blē\ *adv*

**ir·re·deem·able** \,iri'dēməbəl\ *adj* : not redeemable

**ir·re·duc·ible** \,iri'düsəbəl, -'dyü-\ *adj* : not reducible — **ir·re·duc·ibly** \-blē\ *adv*

**ir·re·fut·able** \ˌiri'fyütəbəl, ir'refyət-\ *adj* : impossible to refute

**ir·reg·u·lar** \ir'egyələr\ *adj* : not regular or normal — **irregular** *n* — **ir·reg·u·lar·i·ty** \ir,egyə'larətē\ *n* — **ir·reg·u·lar·ly** *adv*

**ir·rel·e·vant** \ir'eləvənt\ *adj* : not relevant — **ir·rel·e·vance** \-vəns\ *n*

**ir·re·li·gious** \ˌiri'lijəs\ *adj* : not following religious practices

**ir·rep·a·ra·ble** \ir'epərəbəl\ *adj* : impossible to make good, undo, or remedy

**ir·re·place·able** \ˌiri'plāsəbəl\ *adj* : not replaceable

**ir·re·press·ible** \-'presəbəl\ *adj* : impossible to repress or control

**ir·re·proach·able** \-'prōchəbəl\ *adj* : blameless

**ir·re·sist·ible** \-'zistəbəl\ *adj* : impossible to successfully resist — **ir·re·sist·ibly** \-blē\ *adv*

**ir·res·o·lute** \ir'ezəlüt\ *adj* : uncertain — **ir·res·o·lute·ly** *adv* — **ir·res·o·lu·tion** \-,ezə'lüshən\ *n*

**ir·re·spec·tive of** \ˌiri'spektiv-\ *prep* : without regard to

**ir·re·spon·si·ble** \ˌiri'spänsəbəl\ *adj* : not responsible — **ir·re·spon·si·bil·i·ty** \-,spänsə'bilətē\ *n* — **ir·re·spon·si·bly** *adv*

**ir·re·triev·able** \ˌiri'trēvəbəl\ *adj* : not retrievable

**ir·rev·er·ence** \ir'evərəns\ *n* 1 : lack of reverence 2 : irreverent act or utterance — **ir·rev·er·ent** \-rənt\ *adj*

**ir·re·vers·ible** \ˌiri'vsərəbəl\ *adj* : incapable of being reversed

**ir·rev·o·ca·ble** \ir'evəkəbəl\ *adj* : incapable of being revoked — **ir·rev·o·ca·bly** \-blē\ *adv*

**ir·ri·gate** \'irə,gāt\ *vb* -gat·ed; -gat·ing : supply with water by artificial means — **ir·ri·ga·tion** \ˌirə'gāshən\ *n*

**ir·ri·tate** \'irə,tāt\ *vb* -tat·ed; -tat·ing 1 : excite to anger 2 : make sore or inflamed — **ir·ri·ta·bil·i·ty** \ˌirətə-'bilətē\ *n* — **ir·ri·ta·ble** \'irətəbəl\ *adj* — **ir·ri·ta·bly** \'irətəblē\ *adv* — **ir·ri·tant** \'irətənt\ *adj or n* — **ir·ri·tat·ing·ly** *adv* — **ir·ri·ta·tion** \ˌirə'tā-shən\ *n*

**is** *pres 3d sing of* BE

**-ish** \ish\ *adj suffix* 1 : characteristic of 2 : somewhat

**Is·lam** \is'läm, iz-, -'lam\ *n* : religious faith of Muslims — **Is·lam·ic** \-ik\ *adj*

**is·land** \'īlənd\ *n* : body of land surrounded by water — **is·land·er** \'īləndər\ *n*

**isle** \'īl\ *n* : small island

**is·let** \'īlət\ *n* : small island

**-ism** \ˌizəm\ *n suffix* 1 : act or practice 2 : characteristic manner 3 : condition 4 : doctrine

**iso·late** \'īsə,lāt\ *vb* -lat·ed; -lat·ing : place or keep by itself — **iso·la·tion** \ˌīsə'lāshən\ *n*

**iso·met·rics** \ˌīsə'metriks\ *n sing or pl* : exercise against unmoving resistance — **isometric** *adj*

**isos·ce·les** \ī'säsə,lēz\ *adj* : having 2 equal sides

**iso·tope** \'īsə,tōp\ *n* : species of atom of a chemical element — **iso·to·pic** \ˌīsə'täpik, -'tō-\ *adj*

**is·sue** \'ishü\ *vb* -sued; -su·ing 1 : go, come, or flow out 2 : descend from a specified ancestor 3 : emanate or result 4 : put forth or distribute officially ~ *n* 1 : action of issuing 2 : offspring 3 : result 4 : point of controversy 5 : act of giving out or printing 6 : quantity given out or printed — **is·su·ance** \'ishəwəns\ *n* — **is·su·er** *n*

**-ist** \ist\ *n suffix* 1 : one that does 2 : one that plays 3 : one that specializes in 4 : follower of a doctrine

**isth·mus** \'isməs\ *n* : narrow strip of land connecting 2 larger portions

**it** \'it\ *pron* 1 : that one — used of a lifeless thing or an abstract entity 2 — used as an anticipatory subject or object ~ *n* : player who tries to catch others (as in a game of tag)

**ital·ic** \ə'talik, i-, ī-\ *n* : style of type with slanting letters — **italic** *adj* — **ital·i·ci·za·tion** \ˌtaləsə'zāshən, i-, ī-\ *n* — **ital·i·cize** \ə'talə,sīz, i-, ī-\ *vb*

**itch** \'ich\ *n* 1 : uneasy irritating skin sensation 2 : skin disorder 3 : persistent desire — **itch** *vb* — **itchy** *adj*

**item** \'ītəm\ *n* 1 : particular in a list, account, or series 2 : piece of news — **item·iza·tion** \ˌītəmə'zāshən\ *n* — **item·ize** \'ītə,mīz\ *vb*

**itin·er·ant** \ī'tinərənt, ə-\ *adj* : traveling from place to place

**itin·er·ary** \ī'tinə,rerē, ə-\ *n, pl* -ar·ies : route or outline of a journey

**its** \'its\ *adj* : relating to it

**it·self** \it'self\ *pron* : it — used reflexively or for emphasis

**-i·ty** \ətē\ *n suffix* : quality, state, or degree

**-ive** \iv\ *adj suffix* : that performs or tends toward an action

**ivo·ry** \ˈīvərē\ *n, pl* **-ries 1** : hard creamy-white material of elephants' tusks **2** : pale yellow color

**ivy** \ˈīvē\ *n, pl* **ivies** : trailing woody vine with evergreen leaves

**-ize** \ˌīz\ *vb suffix* **1** : cause to be, become, or resemble **2** : subject to an action **3** : treat or combine with **4** : engage in an activity

# J

**j** \ˈjā\ *n, pl* **j's** *or* **js** \ˈjāz\ : 10th letter of the alphabet

**jab** \ˈjab\ *vb* **-bb-** : thrust quickly or abruptly ∼ *n* : short straight punch

**jab·ber** \ˈjabər\ *vb* : talk rapidly or unintelligibly — **jabber** *n*

**jack** \ˈjak\ *n* **1** : mechanical device to raise a heavy body **2** : small flag **3** : small 6-pointed metal object used in a game (**jacks**) **4** : electrical socket ∼ *vb* **1** : raise with a jack **2** : increase

**jack·al** \ˈjakəl, -ˌȯl\ *n* : wild dog

**jack·ass** *n* **1** : male ass **2** : stupid person

**jack·et** \ˈjakət\ *n* : garment for the upper body

**jack·ham·mer** \ˈjak,hamər\ *n* : pneumatic tool for drilling

**jack·knife** \ˈjak,nīf\ *n* : pocketknife ∼ *vb* : fold like a jackknife

**jack-o'–lan·tern** \ˈjakə,lantərn\ *n* : lantern made of a carved pumpkin

**jack·pot** \ˈjak,pät\ *n* : sum of money won

**jack·rab·bit** \-,rabət\ *n* : large hare of western No. America

**jade** \ˈjād\ *n* : usu. green gemstone

**jad·ed** \ˈjādəd\ *adj* : dulled or bored by having too much

**jag·ged** \ˈjagəd\ *adj* : sharply notched

**jag·uar** \ˈjag,wär, ˈjagyə-\ *n* : black-spotted tropical American cat

**jai alai** \ˈhī,lī\ *n* : game with a ball propelled by a basket on the hand

**jail** \ˈjāl\ *n* : prison — **jail** *vb* — **jail·break** *n* — **jail·er, jail·or** *n*

**ja·la·pe·ño** \ˌhälə'pān,yō, -ˌpēnō\ *n* : Mexican hot pepper

**ja·lopy** \jə'läpē\ *n, pl* **-lopies** : dilapidated vehicle

**jal·ou·sie** \ˈjaləsē\ *n* : door or window with louvers

**jam** \ˈjam\ *vb* **-mm- 1** : press into a tight position **2** : cause to become wedged and unworkable ∼ *n* **1** : crowded mass that blocks or impedes **2** : difficult situation **3** : thick sweet food made of cooked fruit

**jamb** \ˈjam\ *n* : upright framing piece of a door

**jam·bo·ree** \ˌjambə'rē\ *n* : large festive gathering

**jan·gle** \ˈjaŋgəl\ *vb* **-gled; -gling** : make a harsh ringing sound — **jangle** *n*

**jan·i·tor** \ˈjanətər\ *n* : person who has the care of a building — **jan·i·to·ri·al** \ˌjanə'tōrēəl\ *adj*

**Jan·u·ary** \ˈjanyə,werē\ *n* : 1st month of the year having 31 days

**¹jar** \ˈjär\ *vb* **-rr- 1** : have a harsh or disagreeable effect **2** : vibrate or shake ∼ *n* **1** : jolt **2** : painful effect

**²jar** *n* : wide-mouthed container

**jar·gon** \ˈjärgən, -ˌgän\ *n* : special vocabulary of a group

**jas·mine** \ˈjazmən\ *n* : climbing shrub with fragrant flowers

**jas·per** \ˈjaspər\ *n* : red, yellow, or brown opaque quartz

**jaun·dice** \ˈjȯndəs\ *n* : yellowish discoloration of skin, tissues, and body fluids

**jaun·diced** \-dəst\ *adj* : exhibiting envy or hostility

**jaunt** \ˈjȯnt\ *n* : short pleasure trip

**jaun·ty** \ˈjȯntē\ *adj* **-ti·er; -est** : lively in manner or appearance — **jaun·ti·ly** \ˈjȯntᵊlē\ *adv* — **jaun·ti·ness** *n*

**jav·e·lin** \ˈjavələn\ *n* : light spear

**jaw** \ˈjȯ\ *n* **1** : either of the bony or cartilaginous structures that support the mouth **2** : one of 2 movable parts for holding or crushing ∼ *vb* : talk indignantly or at length — **jaw·bone** \-ˌbōn\ *n* — **jawed** \ˈjȯd\ *adj*

**jay** \ˈjā\ *n* : noisy brightly colored bird

**jay·bird** *n* : jay

**jay·walk** \vb : cross a street carelessly — **jay·walk·er** n

**jazz** \'jaz\ vb : enliven ~ n 1 : kind of American music involving improvisation 2 : empty talk — **jazzy** adj

**jeal·ous** \'jeləs\ adj : suspicious of a rival or of one believed to enjoy an advantage — **jeal·ous·ly** adv — **jeal·ou·sy** \-əsē\ n

**jeans** \'jēnz\ n pl : pants made of durable twilled cotton cloth

**jeep** \'jēp\ n : 4-wheel army vehicle

**jeer** \'jir\ vb 1 : speak or cry out in derision 2 : ridicule ~ n : taunt

**Je·ho·vah** \ji'hōvə\ n : God

**je·june** \ji'jün\ adj : dull or childish

**jell** \'jel\ vb 1 : come to the consistency of jelly 2 : take shape

**jel·ly** \'jelē\ n, pl **-lies** : a substance (as food) with a soft somewhat elastic consistency — **jelly** vb

**jel·ly·fish** \n : sea animal with a saucer⹀shaped jellylike body

**jen·ny** \'jenē\ n, pl **-nies** : female bird or donkey

**jeop·ar·dy** \'jepərdē\ n : exposure to death, loss, or injury — **jeop·ar·dize** \-ər‚dīz\ vb

**jerk** \'jərk\ vb 1 : give a sharp quick push, pull, or twist 2 : move in short abrupt motions ~ n 1 : short quick pull or twist 2 : stupid or foolish person — **jerk·i·ly** adv — **jerky** adj

**jer·kin** \'jərkən\ n : close-fitting sleeveless jacket

**jer·ry–built** \'jerē‚bilt\ adj : built cheaply and flimsily

**jer·sey** \'jərzē\ n, pl **-seys** 1 : plain knit fabric 2 : knitted shirt

**jest** \'jest\ n : witty remark — **jest** vb

**jest·er** \'jestər\ n : one employed to entertain a court

¹**jet** \'jet\ n : velvet-black coal used for jewelry

²**jet** vb **-tt-** 1 : spout or emit in a stream 2 : travel by jet ~ n 1 : forceful rush of fluid through a narrow opening 2 : jet-propelled airplane

**jet–propelled** adj : driven by an engine (**jet engine**) that produces propulsion (**jet propulsion**) by the rearward discharge of a jet of fluid

**jet·sam** \'jetsəm\ n : jettisoned goods

**jet·ti·son** \'jetəsən\ vb 1 : throw (goods) overboard 2 : discard — **jettison** n

**jet·ty** \'jetē\ n, pl **-ties** : pier or wharf

**Jew** \'jü\ n : one whose religion is Judaism — **Jew·ish** adj

**jew·el** \'jüəl\ n 1 : ornament of precious metal 2 : gem ~ vb **-eled** or **-elled; -el·ing** or **-el·ling** : adorn with jewels — **jew·el·er, jew·el·ler** \-ər\ n — **jew·el·ry** \-rē\ n

**jib** \'jib\ n : triangular sail

**jibe** \'jīb\ vb **jibed; jib·ing** : be in agreement

**jif·fy** \'jifē\ n, pl **-fies** : short time

**jig** \'jig\ n : lively dance ~ vb **-gg-** : dance a jig

**jig·ger** \'jigər\ n : measure used in mixing drinks

**jig·gle** \'jigəl\ vb **-gled; -gling** : move with quick little jerks — **jiggle** n

**jig·saw** \n : machine saw with a narrow blade that moves up and down

**jilt** \'jilt\ vb : drop (a lover) unfeelingly

**jim·my** \'jimē\ n, pl **-mies** : small crowbar ~ vb **-mied; -my·ing** : pry open

**jim·son·weed** \'jimsən‚wēd\ n : coarse poisonous weed

**jin·gle** \'jiŋgəl\ vb **-gled; -gling** : make a light tinkling sound ~ n 1 : light tinkling sound 2 : short verse or song

**jin·go·ism** \'jiŋgō‚izəm\ n : extreme chauvinism or nationalism — **jin·go·ist** \-ist\ n — **jin·go·is·tic** \‚jiŋgō'istik\ adj

**jinx** \'jiŋks\ n : one that brings bad luck — **jinx** vb

**jit·ney** \'jitnē\ n, pl **-neys** : small bus

**jit·ters** \'jitərz\ n pl : extreme nervousness — **jit·tery** \-ərē\ adj

**job** \'jäb\ n 1 : something that has to be done 2 : regular employment — **job·hold·er** n — **job·less** adj

**job·ber** \'jäbər\ n : middleman

**jock·ey** \'jäkē\ n, pl **-eys** : one who rides a horse in a race ~ vb **-eyed; -ey·ing** : manipulate or maneuver adroitly

**jo·cose** \jō'kōs\ adj : jocular

**joc·u·lar** \'jäkyələr\ adj : marked by jesting — **joc·u·lar·i·ty** \‚jäkyə'larətē\ n — **joc·u·lar·ly** adv

**jo·cund** \'jäkənd\ adj : full of mirth or gaiety

**jodh·purs** \'jädpərz\ n pl : riding breeches

¹**jog** \'jäg\ vb **-gg-** 1 : give a slight shake or push to 2 : run or ride at a slow pace ~ n 1 : slight shake 2 : slow pace — **jog·ger** n

²**jog** n : brief abrupt change in direction or line

**join** \'join\ vb 1 : come or bring together **2** : become a member of — **join•er** n

**joint** \'jóint\ n **1** : point of contact between bones **2** : place where 2 parts connect **3** : often disreputable place ~ adj : common to 2 or more — **joint•ed** adj — **joint•ly** adv

**joist** \'jóist\ n : beam supporting a floor or ceiling

**joke** \'jōk\ n : something said or done to provoke laughter ~ vb **joked; joking** : make jokes — **jok•er** n — **jok•ing•ly** \'jōkiņlē\ adv

**jol•li•ty** \'jälətē\ n, pl **-ties** : gaiety or merriment

**jol•ly** \'jälē\ adj **-li•er; -est** : full of high spirits

**jolt** \'jōlt\ vb **1** : move with a sudden jerky motion **2** : give a jolt to ~ n **1** : abrupt jerky blow or movement **2** : sudden shock — **jolt•er** n

**jon•quil** \'jänkwəl\ n : narcissus with white or yellow flowers

**josh** \'jäsh\ vb : tease or joke

**jos•tle** \'jäsəl\ vb **-tled; -tling** : push or shove

**jot** \'jät\ n : least bit ~ vb **-tt-** : write briefly and hurriedly  .

**jounce** \'jaúns\ vb **jounced; jouncing** : jolt — **jounce** n

**jour•nal** \'jərn⁰l\ n **1** : brief account of daily events **2** : periodical (as a newspaper)

**jour•nal•ism** \'jərn⁰l‚izəm\ n : business of reporting or printing news — **jour•nal•ist** \-ist\ n — **jour•nal•is•tic** \‚jərn⁰l'istik\ adj

**jour•ney** \'jərnē\ n, pl **-neys** : a going from one place to another ~ vb **-neyed; -ney•ing** : make a journey

**jour•ney•man** \-mən\ n : worker who has learned a trade and works for another person

**joust** \'jaúst\ n : combat on horseback between 2 knights with lances — **joust** vb

**jo•vial** \'jōvēəl\ adj : marked by good humor — **jo•vi•al•i•ty** \‚jōvē'alətē\ n — **jo•vi•al•ly** \'jōvēəlē\ adv

¹**jowl** \'jaúl\ n : loose flesh about the lower jaw or throat

²**jowl** n **1** : lower jaw **2** : cheek

**joy** \'jói\ n **1** : feeling of happiness **2** : source of happiness — **joy** vb — **joyful** adj — **joy•ful•ly** adv — **joy•less** adj — **joy•ous** \'jóiəs\ adj — **joyous•ly** adv — **joy•ous•ness** n

**joy•ride** n : reckless ride for pleasure — **joy•rid•er** n — **joy•rid•ing** n

**ju•bi•lant** \'jübələnt\ adj : expressing great joy — **ju•bi•lant•ly** adv — **ju•bila•tion** \‚jübə'lāshən\ n

**ju•bi•lee** \'jübə‚lē\ n **1** : 50th anniversary **2** : season or occasion of celebration

**Ju•da•ism** \'jüdə‚izəm\ n : religion developed among the ancient Hebrews — **Ju•da•ic** \jü'dāik\ adj

**judge** \'jəj\ vb **judged; judg•ing 1** : form an opinion **2** : decide as a judge ~ n **1** : public official authorized to decide questions brought before a court **2** : one who gives an authoritative opinion — **judge•ship** n

**judg•ment, judge•ment** \'jəjmənt\ n **1** : decision or opinion given after judging **2** : capacity for judging — **judg•men•tal** \‚jəj'mentəl\ adj — **judg•men•tal•ly** adv

**ju•di•ca•ture** \'jüdikə‚chùr\ n : administration of justice

**ju•di•cial** \jü'dishəl\ adj : relating to judicature or the judiciary — **ju•di•cial•ly** adv

**ju•di•cia•ry** \jü'dishē‚erē, -'dishərē\ n : system of courts of law or the judges of them — **judiciary** adj

**ju•di•cious** \jü'dishəs\ adj : having or characterized by sound judgment — **ju•di•cious•ly** adv

**ju•do** \'jüdō\ n : form of wrestling — **judo•ist** n

**jug** \'jəg\ n : large deep container with a narrow mouth and a handle

**jug•ger•naut** \'jəgər‚nòt\ n : massive inexorable force or object

**jug•gle** \'jəgəl\ vb **-gled; -gling 1** : keep several objects in motion in the air at the same time **2** : manipulate for an often tricky purpose — **juggler** \'jəglər\ n

**jug•u•lar** \'jəgyələr\ adj : in or on the throat or neck

**juice** \'jüs\ n **1** : extractable fluid contents of cells or tissues **2** : electricity — **juic•er** n — **juic•i•ly** \'jüsəlē\ adv — **juic•i•ness** \-sēnəs\ n — **juicy** \'jüsē\ adj

**ju•jube** \'jü‚jüb, 'jüjù‚bē\ n : gummy candy

**juke•box** \'jük‚bäks\ n : coin-operated machine for playing music recordings

**ju•lep** \'jüləp\ n : mint-flavored bourbon drink

**Ju•ly** \ju̇ʷlī\ n : 7th month of the year having 31 days

**jum•ble** \'jəmbəl\ vb -bled; -bling : mix in a confused mass — **jumble** n

**jum•bo** \'jəmbō\ n, pl -bos : very large version — **jumbo** adj

**jump** \'jəmp\ vb 1 : rise into or through the air esp. by muscular effort 2 : pass over 3 : give a start 4 : rise or increase sharply ∼ n 1 : a jumping 2 : sharp sudden increase 3 : initial advantage

¹**jump•er** \'jəmpər\ n : one that jumps

²**jumper** n : sleeveless one-piece dress

**jumpy** \'jəmpē\ adj **jump•i•er; -est** : nervous or jittery

**junc•tion** \'jəŋkshən\ n 1 : a joining 2 : place or point of meeting

**junc•ture** \'jəŋkchər\ n 1 : joint or connection 2 : critical time or state of affairs

**June** \'jün\ n : 6th month of the year having 30 days

**jun•gle** \'jəŋgəl\ n : thick tangled mass of tropical vegetation

**ju•nior** \'jünyər\ n 1 : person who is younger or of lower rank than another 2 : student in the next-to-last year ∼ adj : younger or lower in rank

**ju•ni•per** \'jünəpər\ n : evergreen shrub or tree

¹**junk** \'jəŋk\ n 1 : discarded articles 2 : shoddy product ∼ vb : discard or scrap — **junky** adj

²**junk** n : flat-bottomed ship of Chinese waters

**jun•ket** \'jəŋkət\ n : trip made by an official at public expense

**jun•ta** \'hùntə, 'jəntə, 'həntə\ n : group of persons controlling a government

**ju•ris•dic•tion** \ju̇rəs'dikshən\ n 1 : right or authority to interpret and apply the law 2 : limits within which authority may be exercised — **ju•ris•dic•tion•al** \-shənəl\ adj

**ju•ris•pru•dence** \-'prüdᵊns\ n 1 : system of laws 2 : science or philosophy of law

**ju•rist** \'ju̇rist\ n : judge

**ju•ror** \'ju̇rər\ n : member of a jury

**ju•ry** \'ju̇rē\ n, pl -ries : body of persons sworn to give a verdict on a matter

**just** \'jəst\ adj 1 : reasonable 2 : correct or proper 3 : morally or legally right 4 : deserved ∼ adv 1 : exactly 2 : very recently 3 : barely 4 : only 5 : quite 6 : possibly — **just•ly** adv — **just•ness** n

**jus•tice** \'jəstəs\ n 1 : administration of what is just 2 : judge 3 : administration of law 4 : fairness

**jus•ti•fy** \'jəstə‚fī\ vb -fied; -fy•ing : prove to be just, right, or reasonable — **jus•ti•fi•able** adj — **jus•ti•fi•ca•tion** \‚jəstəfə'kāshən\ n

**jut** \'jət\ vb -tt- : stick out

**jute** \'jüt\ n : strong glossy fiber from a tropical plant

**ju•ve•nile** \'jüvə‚nīl, -vənᵊl\ adj : relating to children or young people ∼ n : young person

**jux•ta•pose** \'jəkstə‚pōz\ vb -posed; -pos•ing : place side by side — **jux•ta•po•si•tion** \‚jəkstəpə'zishən\ n

# K

**k** \'kā\ n, pl **k's** or **ks** \'kāz\ : 11th letter of the alphabet

**kai•ser** \'kīzər\ n : German ruler

**kale** \'kāl\ n : curly cabbage

**ka•lei•do•scope** \kə'līdə‚skōp\ n : device containing loose bits of colored material reflecting in many patterns — **ka•lei•do•scop•ic** \-‚līdə'skäpik\ adj — **ka•lei•do•scop•i•cal•ly** \-iklē\ adv

**kan•ga•roo** \‚kaŋgə'rü\ n, pl -roos : large leaping Australian mammal

**ka•o•lin** \'kāələn\ n : fine white clay

**kar•a•o•ke** \‚karē'ōkē\ n : device that plays accompaniments for singers

**kar•at** \'karət\ n : unit of gold content

**ka•ra•te** \kə'rätē\ n : art of self-defense by crippling kicks and punches

**ka•ty•did** \'kātē‚did\ n : large American grasshopper

**kay•ak** \'kī‚ak\ n : Eskimo canoe

**ka•zoo** \kə'zü\ n, pl -zoos : toy musical instrument

**keel** \'kēl\ n : central lengthwise strip

on the bottom of a ship — **keeled**
\'kēld\ *adj*

**keen** \'kēn\ *adj* **1** : sharp **2** : severe **3**
: enthusiastic **4** : mentally alert —
**keen·ly** *adv* — **keen·ness** *n*

**keep** \'kēp\ *vb* **kept** \'kept\; **keep·ing**
**1** : perform **2** : guard **3** : maintain **4**
: retain in one's possession **5** : detain
**6** : continue in good condition **7** : refrain ∼ *n* **1** : fortress **2** : means by
which one is kept — **keep·er** *n*

**keep·ing** \'kēpiŋ\ *n* : conformity

**keep·sake** \'kēp,sāk\ *n* : souvenir

**keg** \'keg\ *n* : small cask or barrel

**kelp** \'kelp\ *n* : coarse brown seaweed

**ken** \'ken\ *n* : range of sight or understanding

**ken·nel** \'ken³l\ *n* : dog shelter — **ken-
nel** *vb*

**ker·chief** \'kərchəf, -,chēf\ *n* : square
of cloth worn as a head covering

**ker·nel** \'kərn³l\ *n* **1** : inner softer part
of a seed or nut **2** : whole seed of a
cereal **3** : central part

**ker·o·sene, ker·o·sine** \'kerə,sēn,
,kerə³-\ *n* : thin flammable oil from
petroleum

**ketch·up** \'kechəp, 'ka-\ *n* : spicy
tomato sauce

**ket·tle** \'ket³l\ *n* : vessel for boiling liquids

**ket·tle·drum** \-,drum\ *n* : brass or copper kettle-shaped drum

¹**key** \'kē\ *n* **1** : usu. metal piece to open
a lock **2** : explanation **3** : lever
pressed by a finger in playing an instrument or operating a machine **4**
: leading individual or principle **5**
: system of musical tones or pitch ∼
*vb* : attune ∼ *adj* : basic — **key·hole**
*n* — **key up** *vb* : make nervous

²**key** *n* : low island or reef

**key·board** *n* : arrangement of keys

**key·note** \-,nōt\ *n* **1** : 1st note of a
scale **2** : central fact, idea, or mood
∼ *vb* **1** : set the keynote of **2** : deliver the major speech

**key·stone** *n* : wedge-shaped piece at the
crown of an arch

**kha·ki** \'kakē, 'käk-\ *n* : light yellowish brown color

**khan** \'kän, 'kan\ *n* : Mongol leader

**kib·butz** \kib'ùts, -'üts\ *n, pl* **-but·zim**
\-,ùt'sēm, -,üt-\ : Israeli communal
farm or settlement

**ki·bitz·er** \'kibətsər, kə'bit-\ *n* : one
who offers unwanted advice — **kib·itz**
\'kibəts\ *vb*

**kick** \'kik\ *vb* **1** : strike out or hit with
the foot **2** : object strongly **3** : recoil
∼ *n* **1** : thrust with the foot **2** : recoil of a gun **3** : stimulating effect —
**kick·er** *n*

**kid** \'kid\ *n* **1** : young goat **2** : child ∼
*vb* **-dd-** **1** : deceive as a joke **2** : tease
— **kid·der** *n* — **kid·ding·ly** *adv*

**kid·nap** \'kid,nap\ *vb* **-napped** *or*
**-naped** \-,napt\; **-nap·ping** *or* **-nap-
ing** : carry a person away by illegal
force — **kid·nap·per, kid·nap·er** *n*

**kid·ney** \'kidnē\ *n, pl* **-neys** : either of
a pair of organs that excrete urine

**kill** \'kil\ *vb* **1** : deprive of life **2** : finish **3** : use up (time) ∼ *n* : act of
killing — **kill·er** *n*

**kiln** \'kil, 'kiln\ *n* : heated enclosure for
burning, firing, or drying — **kiln** *vb*

**ki·lo** \'kēlō\ *n, pl* **-los** : kilogram

**kilo·cy·cle** \'kilə,sīkəl\ *n* : kilohertz

**ki·lo·gram** \'kēlə,gram, 'kilə-\ *n*
: metric unit of weight equal to 2.2
pounds

**ki·lo·hertz** \'kilə,hərts, 'kēlə-, -,herts\
*n* : 1000 hertz

**ki·lo·me·ter** \kil'ämətər, 'kilə,mēt-\
*n* : 1000 meters

**ki·lo·volt** \'kilə,vōlt\ *n* : 1000 volts

**kilo·watt** \'kilə,wät\ *n* : 1000 watts

**kilt** \'kilt\ *n* : knee-length pleated skirt

**kil·ter** \'kiltər\ *n* : proper condition

**ki·mo·no** \kə'mōnō\ *n, pl* **-nos** : loose
robe

**kin** \'kin\ *n* **1** : one's relatives **2** : kinsman

**kind** \'kīnd\ *n* **1** : essential quality **2**
: group with common traits ∼ *vari-
ety* ∼ *adj* **1** : of a sympathetic nature **2** : arising from sympathy —
**kind·heart·ed** *adj* — **kind·ness** *n*

**kin·der·gar·ten** \'kindər,gärt³n\ *n*
: class for young children — **kin·der-
gart·ner** \-,gärtnər\ *n*

**kin·dle** \'kind³l\ *vb* **-dled; -dling** **1**
: set on fire or start burning **2** : stir up

**kin·dling** \'kindliŋ, 'kinlən\ *n* : material for starting a fire

**kind·ly** \'kīndlē\ *adj* **-li·er; -est** : of a
sympathetic nature ∼ *adv* **1** : sympathetically **2** : courteously — **kind-
li·ness** *n*

**kin·dred** \'kindrəd\ *n* **1** : related individuals **2** : kin ∼ *adj* : of a like nature

**kin·folk** \'kin,fōk\, **kinfolks** *n pl* : kin

**king** \'kiŋ\ *n* : male sovereign — **king-**

dom \-dəm\ *n* — **king•less** *adj* — **king•ly** *adj* — **king•ship** *n*

**king•fish•er** \-ˌfishər\ *n* : bright-colored crested bird

**kink** \'kiŋk\ *n* **1** : short tight twist or curl **2** : cramp — **kinky** *adj*

**kin•ship** *n* : relationship

**kins•man** \'kinzmən\ *n* : male relative

**kins•wom•an** \-ˌwùmən\ *n* : female relative

**kip•per** \'kipər\ *n* : dried or smoked fish — **kipper** *vb*

**kiss** \'kis\ *vb* : touch with the lips as a mark of affection — **kiss** *n*

**kit** \'kit\ *n* : set of articles (as tools or parts)

**kitch•en** \'kichən\ *n* : room with cooking facilities

**kite** \'kīt\ *n* **1** : small hawk **2** : covered framework flown at the end of a string

**kith** \'kith\ *n* : familiar friends

**kit•ten** \'kitᵊn\ *n* : young cat — **kit•ten•ish** *adj*

**¹kit•ty** \'kitē\ *n, pl* **-ties** : kitten

**²kitty** *n, pl* **-ties** : fund or pool (as in a card game)

**kit•ty-cor•ner, kit•ty-cor•nered** *var of* CATERCORNER

**ki•wi** \'kē‚wē\ *n* **1** : small flightless New Zealand bird **2** : brownish egg-shaped subtropical fruit

**klep•to•ma•nia** \ˌkleptə'mānēə\ *n* : neurotic impulse to steal — **klep•to•ma•ni•ac** \-nē‚ak\ *n*

**knack** \'nak\ *n* **1** : clever way of doing something **2** : natural aptitude

**knap•sack** \'nap‚sak\ *n* : bag for carrying supplies on one's back

**knave** \'nāv\ *n* : rogue — **knav•ery** \'nāvərē\ *n* — **knav•ish** \'nāvish\ *adj*

**knead** \'nēd\ *vb* **1** : work and press with the hands **2** : massage — **knead•er** *n*

**knee** \'nē\ *n* : joint in the middle part of the leg — **kneed** \'nēd\ *adj*

**knee•cap** \'nē‚kap\ *n* : bone forming the front of the knee

**kneel** \'nēl\ *vb* **knelt** \'nelt\ *or* **kneeled; kneel•ing** : rest on one's knees

**knell** \'nel\ *n* : stroke of a bell

**knew** *past of* KNOW

**knick•ers** \'nikərz\ *n pl* : pants gathered at the knee

**knick•knack** \'nik‚nak\ *n* : small decorative object

**knife** \'nīf\ *n, pl* **knives** \'nīvz\ : sharp blade with a handle ∼ *vb* **knifed; knif•ing** : stab or cut with a knife

**knight** \'nīt\ *n* **1** : mounted warrior of feudal times **2** : man honored by a sovereign ∼ *vb* : make a knight of — **knight•hood** *n* — **knight•ly** *adv*

**knit** \'nit\ *vb* **knit** *or* **knit•ted; knit•ting** **1** : link firmly or closely **2** : form a fabric by interlacing yarn or thread ∼ *n* : knitted garment — **knit•ter** *n*

**knob** \'näb\ *n* : rounded protuberance or handle — **knobbed** \'näbd\ *adj* — **knob•by** \'näbē\ *adj*

**knock** \'näk\ *vb* **1** : strike with a sharp blow **2** : collide **3** : find fault with ∼ *n* : sharp blow — **knock out** *vb* : make unconscious

**knock•er** *n* : device hinged to a door to knock with

**knoll** \'nōl\ *n* : small round hill

**knot** \'nät\ *n* **1** : interlacing (as of string) that forms a lump **2** : base of a woody branch in the stem **3** : group **4** : one nautical mile per hour ∼ *vb* **-tt-** : tie in or with a knot — **knot•ty** *adj*

**know** \'nō\ *vb* **knew** \'nü, 'nyü\; **known** \'nōn\; **know•ing 1** : perceive directly or understand **2** : be familiar with — **know•able** *adj* — **know•er** *n*

**know•ing** \'nōiŋ\ *adj* : shrewdly and keenly alert — **know•ing•ly** *adv*

**knowl•edge** \'nälij\ *n* **1** : understanding gained by experience **2** : range of information — **knowl•edge•able** *adj*

**knuck•le** \'nəkəl\ *n* : rounded knob at a finger joint

**ko•ala** \kō'älə\ *n* : gray furry Australian animal

**kohl•ra•bi** \kōl'rabē, -'räb-\ *n, pl* **-bies** : cabbage that forms no head

**Ko•ran** \kə'ran, -'rän\ *n* : book of Islam containing revelations made to Muhammad by Allah

**ko•sher** \'kōshər\ *adj* : ritually fit for use according to Jewish law

**kow•tow** \kaü'taü, 'kaü‚taü\ *vb* : show excessive deference

**kryp•ton** \'krip‚tän\ *n* : gaseous chemical element used in lamps

**ku•dos** \'kyü‚däs, 'kü-, -ˌdōz\ *n* : fame and renown

**kum•quat** \'kəm‚kwät\ *n* : small citrus fruit

**Kwan•zaa, Kwan•za** \'kwänzə\ *n* : African-American festival held from December 26 to January 1 ∼

# L

**l** \'el\ *n*, *pl* **l's** *or* **ls** \'elz\ : 12th letter of the alphabet

**lab** \'lab\ *n* : laboratory

**la·bel** \'lābəl\ *n* **1** : identification slip **2** : identifying word or phrase ~ *vb* **-beled** *or* **-belled**; **-bel·ing** *or* **-bel·ling** : put a label on

**la·bi·al** \'lābēəl\ *adj* : of or relating to the lips

**la·bor** \'lābər\ *n* **1** : physical or mental effort **2** : physical efforts of childbirth **3** : task **4** : people who work manually ~ *vb* : work esp. with great effort — **la·bor·er** *n*

**lab·o·ra·to·ry** \'labrə,tōrē\ *n*, *pl* **-ries** : place for experimental testing

**Labor Day** *n* : 1st Monday in September observed as a legal holiday in recognition of working people

**la·bo·ri·ous** \lə'bōrēəs\ *adj* : requiring great effort — **la·bo·ri·ous·ly** *adv*

**lab·y·rinth** \'labə,rinth\ *n* : maze — **lab·y·rin·thine** \,labə'rinthən\ *adj*

**lace** \'lās\ *n* **1** : cord or string for tying **2** : fine net usu. figured fabric ~ *vb* **laced**; **lac·ing** **1** : tie **2** : adorn with lace — **lacy** \'lāsē\ *adj*

**lac·er·ate** \'lasə,rāt\ *vb* **-at·ed**; **-at·ing** : tear roughly — **lac·er·a·tion** \,lasə'rāshən\ *n*

**lach·ry·mose** \'lakrə,mōs\ *adj* : tearful

**lack** \'lak\ *vb* : be missing or deficient in ~ *n* : deficiency

**lack·a·dai·si·cal** \,lakə'dāzikəl\ *adj* : lacking spirit — **lack·a·dai·si·cal·ly** \-klē\ *adv*

**lack·ey** \'lakē\ *n*, *pl* **-eys** **1** : footman or servant **2** : toady

**lack·lus·ter** \'lak,ləstər\ *adj* : dull

**la·con·ic** \lə'känik\ *adj* : sparing of words — **la·con·i·cal·ly** \-iklē\ *adv*

**lac·quer** \'lakər\ *n* : glossy surface coating — **lacquer** *vb*

**la·crosse** \lə'krös\ *n* : ball game played with long-handled rackets

**lac·tate** \'lak,tāt\ *vb* **-tat·ed**; **-tat·ing** : secrete milk — **lac·ta·tion** \lak'tāshən\ *n*

**lac·tic** \'laktik\ *adj* : relating to milk

**la·cu·na** \lə'künə, -'kyü-\ *n*, *pl* **-nae** \-,nē\ *or* **-nas** : blank space or missing part

**lad** \'lad\ *n* : boy

**lad·der** \'ladər\ *n* : device with steps or rungs for climbing

**lad·en** \'lād³n\ *adj* : loaded

**la·dle** \'lād³l\ *n* : spoon with a deep bowl **-ladle** *vb*

**la·dy** \'lādē\ *n*, *pl* **-dies** **1** : woman of rank or authority **2** : woman

**la·dy·bird** \'lādē,bərd\ *n* : ladybug

**la·dy·bug** \-,bəg\ *n* : brightly colored beetle

**lag** \'lag\ *vb* **-gg-** : fail to keep up ~ *n* **1** : a falling behind **2** : interval

**la·ger** \'lägər\ *n* : beer

**lag·gard** \'lagərd\ *adj* : slow ~ *n* : one that lags — **lag·gard·ly** *adv*

**la·gniappe** \'lan,yap\ *n* : bonus

**la·goon** \lə'gün\ *n* : shallow sound, channel, or pond near or connecting with a larger body of water

**laid** *past of* LAY

**lain** *past part of* LIE

**lair** \'lar\ *n* : den

**lais·sez-faire** \,les,ā'far\ *n* : doctrine opposing government interference in business

**la·ity** \'lāətē\ *n* : people of a religious faith who are not clergy members

**lake** \'lāk\ *n* : inland body of water

**la·ma** \'lämə\ *n* : Buddhist monk

**lamb** \'lam\ *n* : young sheep or its flesh used as food

**lam·baste, lam·bast** \lam'bāst, -'bast\ *vb* **1** : beat **2** : censure

**lam·bent** \'lambənt\ *adj* : light or bright — **lam·bent·ly** *adv*

**lame** \'lām\ *adj* **lam·er**; **lam·est** **1** : having a limb disabled **2** : weak ~ *vb* **lamed**; **lam·ing** : make lame — **lame·ly** *adv* **-lame·ness** *n*

**la·mé** \lä'mā, la-\ *n* : cloth with tinsel threads

**lame·brain** \'lām,brān\ *n* : fool

**la·ment** \lə'ment\ *vb* **1** : mourn **2** : express sorrow for ~ *n* **1** : mourning **2** : complaint — **lam·en·ta·ble** \'laməntəbəl, lə'mentə-\ *adj* — **lam·en·ta·bly** \-blē\ *adv* — **lam·en·ta·tion** \,lamən'tāshən\ *n*

**lam·i·nat·ed** \'lamə,nātəd\ *adj* : made of thin layers of material — **lam·i·nate** \-,nāt\ *vb* — **lam·i·nate** \-nət\ *n or adj* — **lam·i·na·tion** \,lamə'nā-shən\ *n*

**lamp** \'lamp\ *n* : device for producing light or heat

**lam·poon** \lam'pün\ *n* : satire — **lampoon** *vb*

**lam·prey** \'lamprē\ *n, pl* -**preys** : sucking eellike fish

**lance** \'lans\ *n* : spear ~ *vb* **lanced; lanc·ing** : pierce or open with a lancet

**lance corporal** *n* : enlisted man in the marine corps ranking above a private first class and below a corporal

**lan·cet** \'lansət\ *n* : pointed surgical instrument

**land** \'land\ *n* **1** : solid part of the surface of the earth **2** : country ~ *vb* **1** : go ashore **2** : catch or gain **3** : touch the ground or a surface — **land·less** *adj* — **land·own·er** *n*

**land·fill** *n* : dump

**land·ing** \'landiŋ\ *n* **1** : action of one that lands **2** : place for loading passengers and cargo **3** : level part of a staircase

**land·la·dy** \'land,lādē\ *n* : woman landlord

**land·locked** *adj* : enclosed by land

**land·lord** *n* : owner of property

**land·lub·ber** \-,ləbər\ *n* : one with little sea experience

**land·mark** \-,märk\ *n* **1** : object that marks a boundary or serves as a guide **2** : event that marks a turning point

**land·scape** \-,skāp\ *n* : view of natural scenery ~ *vb* -**scaped; -scap·ing** : beautify a piece of land (as by decorative planting)

**land·slide** \-,slīd\ *n* **1** : slipping down of a mass of earth **2** : overwhelming victory

**land·ward** \'landwərd\ *adj* : toward the land — **landward** *adv*

**lane** \'lān\ *n* : narrow way

**lan·guage** \'laŋgwij\ *n* : words and the methods of combining them for communication

**lan·guid** \'laŋgwəd\ *adj* **1** : weak **2** : sluggish — **lan·guid·ly** *adv* — **lan·guid·ness** *n*

**lan·guish** \'laŋgwish\ *vb* : become languid or discouraged

**lan·guor** \'laŋgər\ *n* : listless indolence — **lan·guor·ous** *adj* — **lan·guor·ous·ly** *adv*

**lank** \'laŋk\ *adj* **1** : thin **2** : limp

**lanky** *adj* **lank·i·er; -est** : tall and thin

**ian·o·lin** \'lan°lən\ *n* : fatty wax from sheep's wool used in ointments

**lan·tern** \'lantərn\ *n* : enclosed portable light

¹**lap** \'lap\ *n* **1** : front part of the lower trunk and thighs of a seated person **2** : overlapping part **3** : one complete circuit completing a course (as around a track or pool) ~ *vb* -**pp**- : fold over

²**lap** *vb* -**pp**- **1** : scoop up with the tongue **2** : splash gently

**lap·dog** *n* : small dog

**la·pel** \lə'pel\ *n* : fold of the front of a coat

**lap·i·dary** \'lapə,derē\ *n* : one who cuts and polishes gems ~ *adj* : relating to gems

**lapse** \'laps\ *n* **1** : slight error **2** : termination of a right or privilege **3** : interval ~ *vb* **lapsed; laps·ing 1** : slip **2** : subside **3** : cease

**lap·top** \'lap,täp\ *adj* : of a size that may be used on one's lap

**lar·board** \'lärbərd\ *n* : port side

**lar·ce·ny** \'lärs°nē\ *n, pl* -**nies** : theft — **lar·ce·nous** \'lärs°nəs\ *adj*

**larch** \'lärch\ *n* : tree like a pine that loses its needles

**lard** \'lärd\ *n* : pork fat

**lar·der** \'lärdər\ *n* : pantry

**large** \'lärj\ *adj* **larg·er; larg·est** : greater than average — **large·ly** *adv* — **large·ness** *n*

**lar·gesse, lar·gess** \lär'zhes, -'jes; 'lär,-\ *n* : liberal giving

**lar·i·at** \'larēət\ *n* : lasso

¹**lark** \'lärk\ *n* : small songbird

²**lark** *vb or n* : romp

**lar·va** \'lärvə\ *n, pl* -**vae** \-,vē\ : wormlike form of an insect — **lar·val** \-vəl\ *adj*

**lar·yn·gi·tis** \,larən'jītəs\ *n* : inflammation of the larynx

**lar·ynx** \'lariŋks\ *n, pl* -**ryn·ges** \lə'rin,jēz\ *or* -**ynx·es** : upper part of the trachea — **la·ryn·ge·al** \,larən 'jēəl, lə'rinjēəl\ *adj*

**la·sa·gna** \lə'zäny°\ *n* : flat noodles baked usu. with tomato sauce, meat, and cheese

**las·civ·i·ous** \lə'sivēəs\ *adj* : lewd — **las·civ·i·ous·ness** *n*

**la·ser** \'lāzər\ *n* : device that produces an intense light beam

¹**lash** \'lash\ *vb* : whip ~ *n* **1** : stroke esp. of a whip **2** : eyelash

²**lash** *vb* : bind with a rope or cord

**lass** \'las\ *n* : girl

**lass·ie** \'lasē\ *n* : girl

**las·si·tude** \'lasə,tüd, -,tyüd\ *n* 1 : fatigue 2 : listlessness

**las·so** \'lasō, la'sü\ *n, pl* **-sos** *or* **-soes** : rope with a noose for catching livestock — **lasso** *vb*

¹**last** \'last\ *vb* : continue in existence or operation

²**last** *adj* 1 : final 2 : previous 3 : least likely ~ *adv* 1 : at the end 2 : most recently 3 : in conclusion ~ *n* : something that is last — **last·ly** *adv* — **at last** : finally

³**last** *n* : form on which a shoe is shaped

**latch** \'lach\ *vb* : catch or get hold ~ *n* : catch that holds a door closed

**late** \'lāt\ *adj* **lat·er; lat·est** 1 : coming or staying after the proper time 2 : advanced toward the end 3 : recently deceased 4 : recent — **late** *adv* — **late·com·er** \-,kəmər\ *n* — **late·ly** *adv* — **late·ness** *n*

**la·tent** \'lāt°nt\ *adj* : present but not visible or expressed — **la·ten·cy** \-°nsē\ *n*

**lat·er·al** \'latərəl\ *adj* : on or toward the side — **lat·er·al·ly** *adv*

**la·tex** \'lā,teks\ *n, pl* **-ti·ces** \'lātə,sēz, 'lat-\ *or* **-tex·es** : emulsion of synthetic rubber or plastic

**lath** \'lath, 'lath\ *n, pl* **laths** *or* **lath** : building material (as a thin strip of wood) used as a base for plaster — **lath** *vb* — **lath·ing** \-iŋ\ *n*

**lathe** \'lāth\ *n* : machine that rotates material for shaping

**lath·er** \'lathər\ *n* : foam ~ *vb* : form or spread lather

**lat·i·tude** \'latə,tüd, -,tyüd\ *n* 1 : distance north or south from the earth's equator 2 : freedom of action

**la·trine** \lə'trēn\ *n* : toilet

**lat·ter** \'latər\ *adj* 1 : more recent 2 : being the second of 2 — **lat·ter·ly** *adv*

**lat·tice** \'latəs\ *n* : framework of crossed strips

**laud** *vb or n* : praise — **laud·able** *adj* — **laud·ably** *adv*

**laugh** \'laf, 'láf\ *vb* : show mirth, joy, or scorn with a smile and explosive sound — **laugh** *n* — **laugh·able** *adj* — **laugh·ing·ly** \-iŋlē\ *adv*

**laugh·ing·stock** \'lafiŋ,stäk, 'láf-\ *n* : object of ridicule

**laugh·ter** \'laftər, 'láf-\ *n* : action or sound of laughing

¹**launch** \'lónch\ *vb* 1 : hurl or send off 2 : set afloat 3 : start — **launch** *n* — **launch·er** *n*

²**launch** *n* : small open boat

**laun·der** \'lóndər\ *vb* : wash or iron fabrics — **laun·der·er** *n* — **laun·dress** \-drəs\ *n* — **laun·dry** \-drē\ *n*

**lau·re·ate** \'lórēət\ *n* : recipient of honors — **laureate** *adj*

**lau·rel** \'lórəl\ *n* 1 : small evergreen tree 2 : honor

**la·va** \'lävə, 'lav-\ *n* : volcanic molten rock

**lav·a·to·ry** \'lavə,tōrē\ *n, pl* **-ries** : bathroom

**lav·en·der** \'lavəndər\ *n* 1 : aromatic plant used for perfume 2 : pale purple color

**lav·ish** \'lavish\ *adj* : expended profusely ~ *vb* : expend or give freely — **lav·ish·ly** *adv* — **lav·ish·ness** *n*

**law** \'ló\ *n* 1 : established rule of conduct 2 : body of such rules 3 : principle of construction or procedure 4 : rule stating uniform behavior under uniform conditions 5 : lawyer's profession — **law·break·er** *n* — **law·giv·er** *n* — **law·less** *adj* — **law·less·ly** *adv* — **law·less·ness** *n* — **law·mak·er** *n* — **law·man** \-mən\ *n* — **law·suit** *n*

**law·ful** \'lófəl\ *adj* : permitted by law — **law·ful·ly** *adv*

**lawn** \'lón\ *n* : grass-covered yard

**law·yer** \'lóyər\ *n* : legal practitioner

**lax** \'laks\ *adj* : not strict or tense — **lax·i·ty** \'laksətē\ *n* — **lax·ly** *adv*

**lax·a·tive** \'laksətiv\ *n* : drug relieving constipation

¹**lay** \'lā\ *vb* **laid** \'lād\; **lay·ing** 1 : put or set down 2 : produce eggs 3 : bet 4 : impose as a duty or burden 5 : put forward ~ *n* : way something lies or is laid

²**lay** *past of* LIE

³**lay** *n* : song

⁴**lay** *adj* : of the laity — **lay·man** \-mən\ *n* — **lay·wom·an** \-,wùmən\ *n*

**lay·er** \'lāər\ *n* 1 : one that lays 2 : one thickness over or under another

**lay·off** \'lā,óf\ *n* : temporary dismissal of a worker

**lay·out** \'lā,aùt\ *n* : arrangement

**la·zy** \'lāzē\ *adj* **-zi·er; -est** : disliking activity or exertion — **la·zi·ly** \'lāzəlē\ *adv* — **la·zi·ness** *n*

**lea** \'lē, 'lā\ *n* : meadow

**leach** \'lēch\ *vb* : remove (a soluble part) with a solvent

¹**lead** \'lēd\ *vb* **led** \'led\; **lead·ing** 1 : guide on a way 2 : direct the activity

of **3** : go at the head of **4** : tend to a definite result ~ *n* : position in front — **lead·er** *n* — **lead·er·less** *adj* — **lead·er·ship** *n*

²**lead** \'led\ *n* **1** : heavy bluish white chemical element **2** : marking substance in a pencil — **lead·en** \'led³n\ *adj*

**leaf** \'lēf\ *n, pl* **leaves** \'lēvz\ **1** : green outgrowth of a plant stem **2** : leaflike thing ~ *vb* **1** : produce leaves **2** : turn book pages — **leaf·age** \'lēfij\ *n* — **leafed** \'lēft\ *adj* — **leaf·less** *adj* — **leafy** *adj* — **leaved** \'lēfd\ *adj*

**leaf·let** \'lēflət\ *n* : pamphlet

¹**league** \'lēg\ *n* : unit of distance equal to about 3 miles

²**league** *n* : association for a common purpose — **league** *vb* — **leagu·er** *n*

**leak** \'lēk\ *vb* **1** : enter or escape through a leak **2** : become or make known ~ *n* : opening that accidentally admits or lets out a substance — **leak·age** \'lēkij\ *n* — **leaky** *adj*

¹**lean** \'lēn\ *vb* **1** : bend from a vertical position **2** : rely on for support **3** : incline in opinion — **lean** *n*

²**lean** *adj* **1** : lacking in flesh **2** : lacking richness — **lean·ness** \'lēnnəs\ *n*

**leap** \'lēp\ *vb* **leapt** *or* **leaped** \'lēpt, 'lept\; **leap·ing** : jump — **leap** *n*

**leap year** *n* : 366-day year

**learn** \'lərn\ *vb* **1** : gain understanding or skill by study or experience **2** : memorize **3** : find out — **learn·er** *n*

**learn·ed** \-əd\ *adj* : having great learning — **learn·ed·ness** *n*

**learn·ing** \-iŋ\ *n* : knowledge

**lease** \'lēs\ *n* : contract transferring real estate for a term and usu. for rent ~ *vb* **leased; leas·ing** : grant by or hold under a lease

**leash** \'lēsh\ *n* : line to hold an animal — **leash** *vb*

**least** \'lēst\ *adj* **1** : lowest in importance or position **2** : smallest **3** : scantiest ~ *n* : one that is least ~ *adv* : in the smallest or lowest degree

**leath·er** \'lethər\ *n* : dressed animal skin — **leath·ern** \-ərn\ *adj* — **leath·ery** *adj*

¹**leave** \'lēv\ *vb* **left** \'left\; **leav·ing** **1** : bequeath **2** : allow or cause to remain **3** : have as a remainder **4** : go away ~ *n* **1** : permission **2** : authorized absence **3** : departure

²**leave** *vb* **leaved; leav·ing** : leaf

**leav·en** \'levən\ *n* : substance for producing fermentation ~ *vb* : raise dough with a leaven

**leaves** *pl of* LEAF

**lech·ery** \'lechərē\ *n* : inordinate indulgence in sex — **lech·er** \'lechər\ *n* — **lech·er·ous** \-chərəs\ *adj* — **lech·er·ous·ly** *adv* — **lech·er·ous·ness** *n*

**lec·ture** \'lekchər\ *n* **1** : instructive talk **2** : reprimand — **lecture** *vb* — **lec·tur·er** *n* — **lec·ture·ship** *n*

**led** *past of* LEAD

**ledge** \'lej\ *n* : shelflike projection

**led·ger** \'lejər\ *n* : account book

**lee** \'lē\ *n* : side sheltered from the wind — **lee** *adj*

**leech** \'lēch\ *n* : segmented freshwater worm that feeds on blood

**leek** \'lēk\ *n* : onionlike herb

**leer** \'lir\ *n* : suggestive or malicious look — **leer** *vb*

**leery** \'lirē\ *adj* : suspicious or wary

**lees** \'lēz\ *n pl* : dregs

**lee·ward** \'lēwərd, 'lüərd\ *adj* : situated away from the wind ~ *n* : the lee side

**lee·way** \'lē,wā\ *n* : allowable margin

¹**left** \'left\ *adj* : on the same side of the body as the heart ~ *n* : left hand — **left** *adv*

²**left** *past of* LEAVE

**leg** \'leg\ *n* **1** : limb of an animal that supports the body **2** : something like a leg **3** : clothing to cover the leg ~ *vb* **-gg-** : walk or run — **leg·ged** \'legəd\ *adj* — **leg·less** *adj*

**leg·a·cy** \'legəsē\ *n, pl* **-cies** : inheritance

**le·gal** \'lēgəl\ *adj* **1** : relating to law or lawyers **2** : lawful — **le·gal·is·tic** \,lēgə'listik\ *adj* — **le·gal·i·ty** \li-'galətē\ *n* — **le·gal·ize** \'lēgə,līz\ *vb* — **le·gal·ly** \-gəlē\ *adv*

**leg·ate** \'legət\ *n* : official representative

**le·ga·tion** \li'gāshən\ *n* **1** : diplomatic mission **2** : official residence and office of a diplomat

**leg·end** \'lejənd\ *n* **1** : story handed down from the past **2** : inscription **3** : explanation of map symbols — **leg·end·ary** \-ən,derē\ *adj*

**leg·er·de·main** \,lejərdə'mān\ *n* : sleight of hand

**leg·ging, leg·gin** \'legən, -iŋ\ *n* : leg covering

**leg·i·ble** \'lejəbəl\ *adj* : capable of being read — **leg•i•bil•i•ty** \ˌlejə-ˈbilətē\ n — **leg•i•bly** \ˈlejəblē\ adv

**le•gion** \ˈlējən\ n 1 : large army unit 2 : multitude 3 : association of former servicemen — **le•gion•ary** \-ˌerē\ n — **le•gion•naire** \ˌlējənˈar\ n

**leg•is•late** \ˈlejəˌslāt\ vb **-lat•ed; -lat•ing** : enact or bring about with laws — **leg•is•la•tion** \ˌlejəˈslāshən\ n — **leg•is•la•tive** \ˈlejəˌslātiv\ adj — **leg•is•la•tor** \-ˌər\ n

**leg•is•la•ture** \ˈlejəˌslāchər\ n : organization with authority to make laws

**le•git•i•mate** \liˈjitəmət\ adj 1 : lawfully begotten 2 : genuine 3 : conforming with law or accepted standards — **le•git•i•ma•cy** \-məsē\ n — **le•git•i•mate•ly** adv — **le•git•i•mize** \-ˌmīz\ vb

**le•gume** \ˈlegˌyüm, liˈgyüm\ n : plant bearing pods — **le•gu•mi•nous** \liˈgyümənəs\ adj

**lei** \ˈlā\ n : necklace of flowers

**lei•sure** \ˈlēzhər, ˈlezh-, ˈlāzh-\ n 1 : free time 2 : ease 3 : convenience — **lei•sure•ly** adj or adv

**lem•ming** \ˈlemiŋ\ n : short-tailed rodent

**lem•on** \ˈlemən\ n : yellow citrus fruit — **lem•ony** adj

**lem•on•ade** \ˌleməˈnād\ n : sweetened lemon beverage

**lend** \ˈlend\ vb **lent** \ˈlent\; **lend•ing** 1 : give for temporary use 2 : furnish — **lend•er** n

**length** \ˈleŋth\ n 1 : longest dimension 2 : duration in time 3 : piece to be joined to others — **length•en** \ˈleŋthən\ vb — **length•wise** adv or adj — **lengthy** adj

**le•nient** \ˈlēnēənt, -nyənt\ adj : of mild and tolerant disposition or effect — **le•ni•en•cy** \ˈlēnēənsē -nyənsē\ n — **le•ni•ent•ly** adv

**len•i•ty** \ˈlenətē\ n : leniency

**lens** \ˈlenz\ n 1 : curved piece for forming an image in an optical instrument 2 : transparent body in the eye that focuses light rays

**Lent** \ˈlent\ n : 40-day period of penitence and fasting from Ash Wednesday to Easter — **Lent•en** \-ᵊn\ adj

**len•til** \ˈlentᵊl\ n : legume with flat edible seeds

**le•o•nine** \ˈlēəˌnīn\ adj : like a lion

**leop•ard** \ˈlepərd\ n : large tawny black-spotted cat

**le•o•tard** \ˈlēəˌtärd\ n : close-fitting garment

**lep•er** \ˈlepər\ n : person with leprosy

**lep•re•chaun** \ˈleprəˌkän\ n : mischievous Irish elf

**lep•ro•sy** \ˈleprəsē\ n : chronic bacterial disease — **lep•rous** \-rəs\ adj

**les•bi•an** \ˈlezbēən\ n : female homosexual — **lesbian** adj — **les•bi•an•ism** \-ˌizəm\ n

**le•sion** \ˈlēzhən\ n : abnormal area in the body due to injury or disease

**less** \ˈles\ adj 1 : fewer 2 : of lower rank, degree, or importance 3 : smaller ~ adv : to a lesser degree ~ n, pl **less** : smaller portion ~ prep : minus — **less•en** \-ᵊn\ vb

**-less** \ləs\ adj suffix 1 : not having 2 : unable to act or be acted on

**les•see** \leˈsē\ n : tenant under a lease

**less•er** \ˈlesər\ adj : of less size, quality, or significance

**les•son** \ˈlesᵊn\ n 1 : reading or exercise to be studied by a pupil 2 : something learned

**les•sor** \ˈlesˌȯr, leˈsȯr\ n : one who transfers property by a lease

**lest** \ˌlest\ conj : for fear that

¹**let** \ˈlet\ n : hindrance or obstacle

²**let** vb **let; let•ting** 1 : cause to 2 : rent 3 : permit

**-let** \lət\ n suffix : small one

**le•thal** \ˈlēthəl\ adj : deadly — **le•thal•ly** adv

**leth•ar•gy** \ˈlethərjē\ n 1 : drowsiness 2 : state of being lazy or indifferent — **le•thar•gic** \lᵊˈthärjik\ adj

**let•ter** \ˈletər\ n 1 : unit of an alphabet 2 : written or printed communication 3 pl : literature or learning 4 : literal meaning ~ vb : mark with letters — **let•ter•er** n

**let•tuce** \ˈletəs\ n : garden plant with crisp leaves

**leu•ke•mia** \lüˈkēmēə\ n : cancerous blood disease — **leu•ke•mic** \-mik\ adj or n

**lev•ee** \ˈlevē\ n : embankment to prevent flooding

**lev•el** \ˈlevəl\ n 1 : device for establishing a flat surface 2 : horizontal surface 3 : position in a scale ~ vb **-eled** or **-elled; -el•ing** or **-el•ling** 1 : make flat or level 2 : aim 3 : raze ~ adj 1 : having an even surface 2 : of the same height or rank — **lev•el•er** n — **lev•el•ly** adv — **lev•el•ness** n

**le•ver** \ˈlevər, ˈlē-\ n : bar for prying or

dislodging something — **le·ver·age** \'levərij, 'lēv-\ n

**le·vi·a·than** \li'vīəthən\ n **1** : large sea animal **2** : enormous thing

**lev·i·ty** \'levətē\ n : unseemly frivolity

**levy** \'levē\ n, pl **lev·ies** : imposition or collection of a tax ∼ vb **lev·ied; levy·ing 1** : impose or collect legally **2** : enlist for military service **3** : wage

**lewd** \'lüd\ adj **1** : sexually unchaste **2** : vulgar — **lewd·ly** adv — **lewd·ness** n

**lex·i·cog·ra·phy** \ˌleksə'kägrəfē\ n : dictionary making — **lex·i·cog·ra·pher** \-fər\ n — **lex·i·co·graph·i·cal** \-kō'grafikəl\, **lex·i·co·graph·ic** \-ik\ adj

**lex·i·con** \'leksəˌkän\ n, pl **-ca** \-sikə\ or **-icons** : dictionary

**li·a·ble** \'līəbəl\ adj **1** : legally obligated **2** : probable **3** : susceptible — **li·a·bil·i·ty** \ˌlīə'bilətē\ n

**li·ai·son** \'lēəˌzän, lē'ā-\ n **1** : close bond **2** : communication between groups

**li·ar** \'līər\ n : one who lies

**li·bel** \'lībəl\ n : action, crime, or an instance of injuring a person's reputation esp. by something written ∼ vb **-beled** or **-belled; -bel·ing** or **-bel·ling** : make or publish a libel — **li·bel·er** n — **li·bel·ist** n — **li·bel·ous, li·bel·lous** \-bələs\ adj

**lib·er·al** \'librəl, 'libə-\ adj : not stingy, narrow, or conservative — **liberal** n — **lib·er·al·ism** \-ˌizəm\ n — **lib·er·al·i·ty** \ˌlibə'ralətē\ n — **lib·er·al·ize** \'librə-ˌlīz, 'libə-\ vb — **lib·er·al·ly** \-rəlē\ adv

**lib·er·ate** \'libəˌrāt\ vb **-at·ed; -at·ing** : set free — **lib·er·a·tion** \ˌlibə'rāshən\ n — **lib·er·a·tor** \'libəˌrātər\ n

**lib·er·tine** \'librərˌtēn\ n : one who leads a dissolute life

**lib·er·ty** \'libərtē\ n, pl **-ties 1** : quality or state of being free **2** : action going beyond normal limits

**li·bi·do** \lə'bēdō, -'bīd-\ n, pl **-dos** : sexual drive — **li·bid·i·nal** \lə'bid°nəl\ adj — **li·bid·i·nous** \-əs\ adj

**li·brary** \'līˌbrerē\ n, pl **-brar·ies 1** : place where books are kept for use **2** : collection of books — **li·brar·i·an** \lī'brerēən\ n

**li·bret·to** \lə'bretō\ n, pl **-tos** or **-ti** \-ē\ : text of an opera — **li·bret·tist** \-ist\ n

**lice** pl of LOUSE

**li·cense, li·cence** \'līs°ns\ n **1** : legal permission to engage in some activity **2** : document or tag providing proof of a license **3** : irresponsible use of freedom — **license** vb — **li·cens·ee** \ˌlīs°n'sē\ n

**li·cen·tious** \lī'senchəs\ adj : disregarding sexual restraints — **li·cen·tious·ly** adv — **li·cen·tious·ness** n

**li·chen** \'līkən\ n : complex lower plant made up of an alga and a fungus

**lic·it** \'lisət\ adj : lawful

**lick** \'lik\ vb **1** : draw the tongue over **2** : beat ∼ n **1** : stroke of the tongue **2** : small amount

**lic·o·rice** \'likərish, -rəs\ n : dried root of a European legume or candy flavored by it

**lid** \'lid\ n **1** : movable cover **2** : eyelid

¹**lie** \'lī\ vb **lay** \'lā\; **lain** \'lān\; **ly·ing** \'līiŋ\ **1** : be in, rest in, or assume a horizontal position **2** : occupy a certain relative position ∼ n : position in which something lies

²**lie** vb **lied; ly·ing** \'līiŋ\ : tell a lie ∼ n : untrue statement

**liege** \'lēj\ n : feudal superior or vassal

**lien** \'lēn, 'lēən\ n : legal claim on the property of another

**lieu·ten·ant** \lü'tenənt\ n **1** : representative **2** : first lieutenant or second lieutenant **3** : commissioned officer in the navy ranking next below a lieutenant commander — **lieu·ten·an·cy** \-ənsē\ n

**lieutenant colonel** n : commissioned officer (as in the army) ranking next below a colonel

**lieutenant commander** n : commissioned officer in the navy ranking next below a commander

**lieutenant general** n : commissioned officer (as in the army) ranking next below a general

**lieutenant junior grade** n, pl **lieutenants junior grade** : commissioned officer in the navy ranking next below a lieutenant

**life** \'līf\ n, pl **lives** \'līvz\ **1** : quality that distinguishes a vital and functional being from a dead body or inanimate matter **2** : physical and mental experiences of an individual **3** : biography **4** : period of existence **5** : way of living **6** : liveliness — **life·less** adj — **life·like** adj

**life·blood** n : basic source of strength and vitality

**life·boat** n : boat for saving lives at sea

**life·guard** n : one employed to safeguard bathers

**life·long** adj : continuing through life

**life-sav-ing** *n* : art or practice of saving lives — **life-sav-er** \-ˌsāvər\ *n*

**life-style** \ˈlīfˌstīl\ *n* : a way of life

**life-time** *n* : duration of an individual's existence

**lift** \ˈlift\ *vb* **1** : move upward or cause to move upward **2** : put an end to — **lift** *n* — **lift-er** *n*

**lift-off** \ˈliftˌȯf\ *n* : vertical takeoff by a rocket

**lig-a-ment** \ˈligəmənt\ *n* : band of tough tissue that holds bones together

**lig-a-ture** \ˈligəˌchu̇r, -chər\ *n* : something that binds or ties

**¹light** \ˈlīt\ *n* **1** : radiation that makes vision possible **2** : daylight **3** : source of light **4** : public knowledge **5** : aspect **6** : celebrity **7** : flame for lighting ~ *adj* **1** : bright **2** : weak in color ~ *vb* **lit** \ˈlit\ *or* **light-ed**; **light-ing 1** : make or become light **2** : cause to burn — **light-er** *n* — **light-ness** *n* — **light-proof** *adj*

**²light** *adj* : not heavy, serious, or abundant — **light** *adv* — **light-ly** *adv* — **light-ness** *n* — **light-weight** *adj*

**³light** *vb* **light-ed** *or* **lit** \ˈlit\; **light-ing** : settle or dismount

**¹light-en** \ˈlīt³n\ *vb* **1** : make light or bright **2** : give out flashes of lightning

**²lighten** *vb* **1** : relieve of a burden **2** : become lighter

**light-heart-ed** \-ˈhärtəd\ *adj* : free from worry — **light-heart-ed-ly** *adv* — **light-heart-ed-ness** *n*

**light-house** *n* : structure with a powerful light for guiding sailors

**light-ning** \ˈlītniŋ\ *n* : flashing discharge of atmospheric electricity

**light-year** \ˈlītˌyir\ *n* : distance traveled by light in one year equal to about 5.88 trillion miles

**lig-nite** \ˈligˌnīt\ *n* : brownish black soft coal

**¹like** \ˈlīk\ *vb* **liked; lik-ing 1** : enjoy **2** : desire ~ *n* : preference — **lik-able** *or* **like-able** \ˈlīkəbəl\ *adj*

**²like** *adj* : similar ~ *prep* **1** : similar or similarly to **2** : typical of **3** : such as ~ *n* : counterpart ~ *conj* : as or as if — **like-ness** *n* — **like-wise** *adv*

**-like** \ˌlīk\ *adj comb form* : resembling or characteristic of

**like-li-hood** \ˈlīklēˌhu̇d\ *n* : probability

**like-ly** \ˈlīklē\ *adj* **-li-er; -est 1** : probable **2** : believable ~ *adv* : in all probability

**lik-en** \ˈlīkən\ *vb* : compare

**lik-ing** \ˈlīkiŋ\ *n* : favorable regard

**li-lac** \ˈlīlək, -ˌlak, -ˌläk\ *n* : shrub with clusters of fragrant pink, purple, or white flowers

**lilt** \ˈlilt\ *n* : rhythmical swing or flow

**lily** \ˈlilē\ *n, pl* **lil-ies** : tall bulbous herb with funnel-shaped flowers

**lima bean** \ˈlīmə-\ *n* : flat edible seed of a plant or the plant itself

**limb** \ˈlim\ *n* **1** : projecting appendage used in moving or grasping **2** : tree branch — **limb-less** *adj*

**lim-ber** \ˈlimbər\ *adj* : supple or agile ~ *vb* : make or become limber

**lim-bo** \ˈlimbō\ *n, pl* **-bos** : place or state of confinement or oblivion

**¹lime** \ˈlīm\ *n* : caustic white oxide of calcium

**²lime** *n* : small green lemonlike citrus fruit — **lime-ade** \-ˌād\ *n*

**lime-light** *n* : center of public attention

**lim-er-ick** \ˈlimərik\ *n* : light poem of 5 lines

**lime-stone** *n* : rock that yields lime when burned

**lim-it** \ˈlimət\ *n* **1** : boundary **2** : something that restrains or confines ~ *vb* : set limits on — **lim-i-ta-tion** \ˌliməˈtāshən\ *n* — **lim-it-less** *adj*

**lim-ou-sine** \ˈliməˌzēn, ˌliməˈ-\ *n* : large luxurious sedan

**limp** \ˈlimp\ *vb* : walk lamely ~ *n* : limping movement or gait ~ *adj* : lacking firmness and body — **limp-ly** *adv* — **limp-ness** *n*

**lim-pid** \ˈlimpəd\ *adj* : clear or transparent

**lin-den** \ˈlindən\ *n* : tree with large heart-shaped leaves

**¹line** \ˈlīn\ *vb* **lined; lin-ing** : cover the inner surface of — **lin-ing** *n*

**²line** *n* **1** : cord, rope, or wire **2** : row or something like a row **3** : note **4** : course of action or thought **5** : state of agreement **6** : occupation **7** : limit **8** : transportation system **9** : long narrow mark ~ *vb* **lined; lin-ing 1** : mark with a line **2** : place in a line **3** : form a line

**lin-e-age** \ˈlinēij\ *n* : descent from a common ancestor

**lin-e-al** \ˈlinēəl\ *adj* **1** : linear **2** : in a direct line of ancestry

**lin-ea-ments** \ˈlinēəmənts\ *n pl* : features or contours esp. of a face

**lin-e-ar** \ˈlinēər\ *adj* **1** : straight **2** : long and narrow

**lin·en** \'linən\ n 1 : cloth or thread made of flax 2 : household articles made of linen cloth

**lin·er** \'līnər\ n 1 : one that lines 2 : ship or airplane belonging to a line

**line-up** \'līn,əp\ n 1 : line of persons for inspection or identification 2 : list of players in a game

**-ling** \liŋ\ n suffix 1 : one linked with 2 : young, small, or minor one

**lin·ger** \'liŋgər\ vb : be slow to leave or act — **lin·ger·er** n

**lin·ge·rie** \,länjə'rā, ,laⁿzhə-, -'rē\ n : women's underwear

**lin·go** \'liŋgō\ n, pl -goes : usu. strange language

**lin·guist** \'liŋgwist\ n 1 : person skilled in speech or languages 2 : student of language — **lin·guis·tic** \liŋ-'gwistik\ adj — **lin·guis·tics** n pl

**lin·i·ment** \'linəmənt\ n : liquid medication rubbed on the skin

**link** \'liŋk\ n 1 : connecting structure (as a ring of a chain) 2 : bond — **link** vb — **link·age** \-ij\ n — **link·er** n

**li·no·leum** \lə'nōlēəm\ n : floor covering with hard surface

**lin·seed** \'lin,sēd\ n : seeds of flax yielding an oil (**linseed oil**)

**lint** \'lint\ n : fine fluff or loose short fibers from fabric

**lin·tel** \'lintᵊl\ n : horizontal piece over a door or window

**li·on** \'līən\ n : large cat of Africa and Asia — **li·on·ess** \'līənəs\ n

**li·on·ize** \'līə,nīz\ vb -ized; -iz·ing : treat as very important — **li·on·iza·tion** \,līənə'zāshən\ n

**lip** \'lip\ n 1 : either of the 2 fleshy folds surrounding the mouth 2 : edge of something hollow — **lipped** \'lipt\ adj — **lip·read·ing** n

**li·po·suc·tion** \'lipə,səkshən, 'lī-\ n : surgical removal of fat deposits (as from the thighs)

**lip·stick** \'lip,stik\ n : stick of cosmetic to color lips

**liq·ue·fy** \'likwə,fī\ vb -fied; -fy·ing : make or become liquid — **liq·ue·fi·er** \'likwə,fīər\ n

**li·queur** \li'kər\ n : sweet or aromatic alcoholic liquor

**liq·uid** \'likwəd\ adj 1 : flowing freely like water 2 : neither solid nor gaseous 3 : of or convertible to cash — **liquid** n — **li·quid·i·ty** \lik'widətē\ n

**liq·ui·date** \'likwə,dāt\ vb -dat·ed; -dat·ing 1 : pay off 2 : dispose of — **liq·ui·da·tion** \,likwə'dāshən\ n

**li·quor** \'likər\ n : liquid substance and esp. a distilled alcoholic beverage

**lisp** \'lisp\ vb : pronounce s and z imperfectly — **lisp** n

**lis·some** \'lisəm\ adj : supple or agile

**¹list** \'list\ n 1 : series of names or items ~ vb 1 : make a list of 2 : put on a list

**²list** vb : tilt or lean over ~ n : slant

**lis·ten** \'lisᵊn\ vb 1 : pay attention in order to hear 2 : heed — **lis·ten·er** \'lisᵊnər\ n

**list·less** \'listləs\ adj : having no desire to act — **list·less·ly** adv — **list·less·ness** n

**lit** \'lit\ past of LIGHT

**lit·a·ny** \'litᵊnē\ n, pl -nies 1 : prayer said as a series of responses to a leader 2 : long recitation

**li·ter** \'lētər\ n : unit of liquid measure equal to about 1.06 quarts

**lit·er·al** \'litərəl\ adj : being exactly as stated — **lit·er·al·ly** adv

**lit·er·ary** \'litə,rerē\ adj : relating to literature

**lit·er·ate** \'litərət\ adj : able to read and write — **lit·er·a·cy** \'litərəsē\ n

**lit·er·a·ture** \'litərə,chùr, -chər\ n : writings of enduring interest

**lithe** \'līth, 'lith\ adj 1 : supple 2 : graceful — **lithe·some** \-səm\ adj

**lith·o·graph** \'lithə,graf\ n : print from a drawing on metal or stone — **li·thog·ra·pher** \lith'ägrəfər, 'lithə,grafər\ n — **lith·o·graph·ic** \,lithə'grafik\ adj — **li·thog·ra·phy** \lith'ägrəfē\ n

**lit·i·gate** \'litə,gāt\ vb -gat·ed; -gat·ing : carry on a lawsuit — **lit·i·gant** \'litigənt\ n — **lit·i·ga·tion** \,litə'gā-shən\ n — **li·ti·gious** \lə'tijəs, li-\ adj — **li·ti·gious·ness** n

**lit·mus** \'litməs\ n : coloring matter that turns red in acid solutions and blue in alkaline

**lit·ter** \'litər\ n 1 : animal offspring of one birth 2 : stretcher 3 : rubbish 4 : material to absorb animal waste ~ vb 1 : give birth to young 2 : strew with litter

**lit·tle** \'litᵊl\ adj lit·tler or less \'les\ or less·er \'lesər\; lit·tlest or least \'lēst\ 1 : not big 2 : not much 3 : not important ~ adv less \'les\; least \'lēst\ 1 : slightly 2 : not often ~ n : small amount — **lit·tle·ness** n

**lit·ur·gy** \'litərjē\ n, pl -gies : rite of

worship — **li·tur·gi·cal** \lə'tərjikəl\
*adj* — **li·tur·gi·cal·ly** \-klē\ *adv* —
**lit·ur·gist** \'litərjist\ *n*

**liv·able** \'livəbəl\ *adj* : suitable for living in or with — **liv·a·bil·i·ty** \ˌlivə-
'bilətē\ *n*

¹**live** \'liv\ *vb* **lived; liv·ing 1** : be alive
**2** : conduct one's life **3** : subsist **4**
: reside

²**live** \'līv\ *adj* **1** : having life **2** : burning **3** : connected to electric power **4**
: not exploded **5** : of continuing interest **6** : involving the actual presence of real people

**live·li·hood** \'līvlē,hůd\ *n* : means of
subsistence

**live·long** \'liv'lòŋ\ *adj* : whole

**live·ly** \'līvlē\ *adj* **-li·er; -est** : full of
life and vigor — **live·li·ness** *n*

**liv·en** \'līvən\ *vb* : enliven

**liv·er** \'livər\ *n* : organ that secretes bile

**liv·ery** \'livərē\ *n, pl* **-er·ies 1** : servant's uniform **2** : care of horses for
pay — **liv·er·ied** \-rēd\ *adj* — **liv·ery-
man** \-mən\ *n*

**lives** *pl of* LIFE

**live·stock** \'liv,stäk\ *n* : farm animals

**liv·id** \'livəd\ *adj* **1** : discolored by
bruising **2** : pale **3** : enraged

**liv·ing** \'liviŋ\ *adj* : having life ~
: livelihood

**liz·ard** \'lizərd\ *n* : reptile with 4 legs
and a long tapering tail

**lla·ma** \'lämə\ *n* : So. American mammal related to the camel

**load** \'lōd\ *n* **1** : cargo **2** : supported
weight **3** : burden **4** : a large quantity
— usu. pl. ~ *vb* **1** : put a load on **2**
: burden **3** : put ammunition in

¹**loaf** \'lōf\ *n, pl* **loaves** \'lōvz\ : mass of
bread

²**loaf** *vb* : waste time — **loaf·er** *n*

**loam** \'lōm, 'lüm\ *n* : soil — **loamy** *adj*

**loan** \'lōn\ *n* **1** : money borrowed at interest **2** : something lent temporarily
**3** : grant of use — *vb* : lend

**loath** \'lōth, 'lōth\ *adj* : very reluctant

**loathe** \'lōth\ *vb* **loathed; loath·ing**
: hate

**loath·ing** \'lōthiŋ\ *n* : extreme disgust

**loath·some** \'lōthsəm, 'lōth-\ *adj* : repulsive

**lob** \'läb\ *vb* **-bb-** : throw or hit in a high
arc **-lob** *n*

**lob·by** \'läbē\ *n, pl* **-bies 1** : public
waiting room at the entrance of a
building **2** : persons lobbying ~ *vb*

**-bied; -by·ing** : try to influence legis-
lators — **lob·by·ist** *n*

**lobe** \'lōb\ *n* : rounded part — **lo·bar**
\'lōbər\ *adj* — **lobed** \'lōbd\ *adj*

**lo·bot·o·my** \lō'bätəmē\ *n, pl* **-mies**
: surgical severance of nerve fibers in
the brain

**lob·ster** \'läbstər\ *n* : marine crustacean with 2 large pincerlike claws

**lo·cal** \'lōkəl\ *adj* : confined to or serving a limited area — **local** *n* — **lo-
cal·ly** *adv*

**lo·cale** \lō'kal\ *n* : setting for an event

**lo·cal·i·ty** \lō'kalətē\ *n, pl* **-ties** : particular place

**lo·cal·ize** \'lōkə,līz\ *vb* **-ized; -iz·ing**
: confine to a definite place — **lo·cal-
i·za·tion** \ˌlōkələ'zāshən\ *n*

**lo·cate** \'lō,kāt, lō'kāt\ *vb* **-cat·ed;
-cat·ing 1** : settle **2** : find a site for **3**
: discover the place of — **lo·ca·tion**
\lō'kāshən\ *n*

¹**lock** \'läk\ *n* : tuft or strand of hair

²**lock** *n* **1** : fastener using a bolt **2** : enclosure in a canal to raise or lower
boats — *vb* **1** : make fast with a lock
**2** : confine **3** : interlock

**lock·er** \'läkər\ *n* : storage compartment

**lock·et** \'läkət\ *n* : small case worn on
a necklace

**lock·jaw** *n* : tetanus

**lock·out** *n* : closing of a plant by an employer during a labor dispute

**lock·smith** \-ˌsmith\ *n* : one who
makes or repairs locks

**lo·co·mo·tion** \ˌlōkə'mōshən\ *n*
: power of moving — **lo·co·mo·tive**
\-'mōtiv\ *adj*

**lo·co·mo·tive** \-'mōtiv\ *n* : vehicle that
moves railroad cars

**lo·co·weed** \'lōkō,wēd\ *n* : western
plant poisonous to livestock

**lo·cust** \'lōkəst\ *n* **1** : migratory
grasshopper **2** : cicada **3** : tree with
hard wood or this wood

**lo·cu·tion** \lō'kyüshən\ *n* : way of
saying something

**lode** \'lōd\ *n* : ore deposit

**lode·stone** *n* : magnetic rock

**lodge** \'läj\ *vb* **lodged; lodg·ing 1**
: provide quarters for **2** : come to rest
**3** : file ~ *n* **1** : special house (as for
hunters) **2** : animal's den **3** : branch
of a fraternal organization — **lodg·er**
\'läjər\ *n* — **lodg·ing** *n* — **lodg-
ment, lodge·ment** \-mənt\ *n*

**loft** \\'lȯft\ *n* **1** : attic **2** : upper floor (as of a warehouse)

**lofty** \\'lȯftē\ *adj* **loft·i·er; -est 1** : noble **2** : proud **3** : tall or high — **loft·i·ly** *adv* — **loft·i·ness** *n*

**log** \\'lȯg, 'läg\ *n* **1** : unshaped timber **2** : daily record of a ship's or plane's progress ∼ *vb* **-gg- 1** : cut (trees) for lumber **2** : enter in a log — **log·ger** \-ər\ *n*

**log·a·rithm** \\'lȯgə,rithəm, 'läg-\ *n* : exponent to which a base number is raised to produce a given number

**loge** \\'lōzh\ *n* : box in a theater

**log·ger·head** \\'lȯgər,hed, 'läg-\ *n* : large Atlantic sea turtle — **at loggerheads** : in disagreement

**log·ic** \\'läjik\ *n* **1** : science of reasoning **2** : sound reasoning — **log·i·cal** \-ikəl\ *adj* — **log·i·cal·ly** *adv* — **lo·gi·cian** \lō'jishən\ *n*

**lo·gis·tics** \lō'jistiks\ *n sing or pl* : procurement and movement of people and supplies — **lo·gis·tic** *adj*

**logo** \\'lōgō, 'lȯg-, 'läg-\ *n, pl* **log·os** \-ōz\ : advertising symbol

**loin** \\'lȯin\ *n* **1** : part of the body on each side of the spine between the hip and lower ribs **2** *pl* : pubic regions

**loi·ter** \\'lȯitər\ *vb* : remain around a place idly — **loi·ter·er** *n*

**loll** \\'läl\ *vb* : lounge

**lol·li·pop, lol·ly·pop** \\'läli,päp\ *n* : hard candy on a stick

**lone** \\'lōn\ *adj* **1** : alone or isolated **2** : only — **lone·li·ness** *n* — **lone·ly** *adj* — **lon·er** \\'lōnər\ *n*

**lone·some** \-səm\ *adj* : sad from lack of company — **lone·some·ly** *adv* — **lone·some·ness** *n*

**long** \\'lȯŋ\ *adj* **lon·ger** \\'lȯŋgər\; **long·est** \\'lȯŋgəst\ **1** : extending far or for a considerable time **2** : having a specified length **3** : tedious **4** : well supplied — used with *on* ∼ *adv* : for a long time ∼ *n* : long period ∼ *vb* : feel a strong desire — **long·ing** \\lȯŋiŋ\ *n* — **long·ing·ly** *adv*

**lon·gev·i·ty** \län'jevətē\ *n* : long life

**long·hand** *n* : handwriting

**long·horn** *n* : cattle with long horns

**lon·gi·tude** \\'länjə,tüd, -,tyüd\ *n* : angular distance east or west from a meridian

**lon·gi·tu·di·nal** \,länjə'tüd°nəl, -'tyüd-\ *adj* : lengthwise — **lon·gi·tu·di·nal·ly** *adv*

**long·shore·man** \\'lȯŋ'shōrmən\ *n* : one who loads and unloads ships

**look** \\'lu̇k\ *vb* **1** : see **2** : seem **3** : direct one's attention **4** : face ∼ *n* **1** : action of looking **2** : appearance of the face **3** : aspect — **look after** : take care of — **look for 1** : expect **2** : search for

**look·out** *n* **1** : one who watches **2** : careful watch

**¹loom** \\'lüm\ *n* : frame or machine for weaving

**²loom** *vb* : appear large and indistinct or impressive

**loon** \\'lün\ *n* : black-and-white diving bird

**loo·ny, loo·ney** \\'lünē\ *adj* **-ni·er; -est** : crazy

**loop** \\'lüp\ *n* **1** : doubling of a line that leaves an opening **2** : something like a loop **-loop** *vb*

**loop·hole** \\'lüp,hōl\ *n* : means of evading

**loose** \\'lüs\ *adj* **loos·er; -est 1** : not fixed tight **2** : not restrained **3** : not dense **4** : slack **5** : not exact ∼ *vb* **loosed; loos·ing 1** : release **2** : untie or relax — **loose** *adv* — **loose·ly** *adv* — **loos·en** \\'lüs°n\ *vb* — **loose·ness** *n*

**loot** \\'lüt\ *n or vb* : plunder — **loot·er** *n*

**lop** \\'läp\ *vb* **-pp-** : cut off

**lope** \\'lōp\ *n* : bounding gait — **lope** *vb*

**lop·sid·ed** \\'läp'sīdəd\ *adj* **1** : leaning to one side **2** : not symmetrical — **lop·sid·ed·ly** *adv* — **lop·sid·ed·ness** *n*

**lo·qua·cious** \lō'kwāshəs\ *adj* : very talkative — **lo·quac·i·ty** \-'kwasətē\ *n*

**lord** \\'lȯrd\ *n* **1** : one with authority over others **2** : British nobleman

**lord·ly** \-lē\ *adj* **-li·er; -est** : haughty

**lord·ship** \-,ship\ *n* : rank of a lord

**Lord's Supper** *n* : Communion

**lore** \\'lōr\ *n* : traditional knowledge

**lose** \\'lüz\ *vb* **lost** \\'lȯst\; **los·ing** \\'lüziŋ\ **1** : have pass from one's possession **2** : be deprived of **3** : waste **4** : be defeated in **5** : fail to keep to or hold **6** : get rid of — **los·er** *n*

**loss** \\'lȯs\ *n* **1** : something lost **2** *pl* : killed, wounded, or captured soldiers **3** : failure to win

**lost** \\'lȯst\ *adj* **1** : not used, won, or claimed **2** : unable to find the way

**lot** \\'lät\ *n* **1** : object used in deciding something by chance **2** : share **3** : fate **4** : plot of land **5** : much

**loth** \\'lōth, 'lōt͟h\ *var of* **LOATH**

**lo·tion** \'lōshən\ *n* : liquid to rub on the skin

**lot·tery** \'lätərē\ *n, pl* **-ter·ies** : drawing of lots with prizes going to winners

**lo·tus** \'lōtəs\ *n* 1 : legendary fruit that causes forgetfulness 2 : water lily

**loud** \'laůd\ *adj* 1 : high in volume of sound 2 : noisy 3 : obtrusive in color or pattern — **loud** *adv* — **loud·ly** *adv* — **loud·ness** *n*

**loud·speak·er** *n* : device that amplifies sound

**lounge** \'laůnj\ *vb* **lounged; loung·ing** : act or move lazily ∼ *n* : room with comfortable furniture

**lour** \'laůər\ *var of* LOWER

**louse** \'laůs\ *n, pl* **lice** \'līs\ : parasitic wingless usu. flat insect

**lousy** \'laůzē\ *adj* **lous·i·er; -est** 1 : infested with lice 2 : not good — **lous·i·ly** *adv* — **lous·i·ness** *n*

**lout** \'laůt\ *n* : stupid awkward person — **lout·ish** *adj* — **lout·ish·ly** *adv*

**lou·ver, lou·vre** \'lüvər\ *n* : opening having parallel slanted slats for ventilation or such a slat

**love** \'ləv\ *n* 1 : strong affection 2 : warm attachment 3 : beloved person ∼ *vb* **loved; lov·ing** 1 : feel affection for 2 : enjoy greatly — **lov·able** \-əbəl\ *adj* — **love·less** *adj* — **lov·er** *n* — **lov·ing·ly** *adv*

**love·lorn** \-,lórn\ *adj* : deprived of love or of a lover

**love·ly** \'ləvlē\ *adj* **-li·er; -est** : beautiful — **love·li·ness** *n* — **lovely** *adv*

¹**low** \'lō\ *vb or n* : moo

²**low** *adj* **low·er; low·est** 1 : not high or tall 2 : below normal level 3 : not loud 4 : humble 5 : sad 6 : less than usual 7 : falling short of a standard 8 : unfavorable ∼ *n* 1 : something low 2 : automobile gear giving the slowest speed — **low** *adv* — **low·ness** *n*

**low·brow** \'lō,braů\ *n* : person with little taste or intellectual interest

¹**low·er** \'laůər\ *vb* 1 : scowl 2 : become dark and threatening

²**low·er** \'lōər\ *adj* : relatively low (as in rank)

³**low·er** \'lōər\ *vb* 1 : drop 2 : let descend 3 : reduce in amount

**low·land** \'lōlənd, -,land\ *n* : low flat country

**low·ly** \'lōlē\ *adj* **-li·er; -est** 1 : humble 2 : low in rank — **low·li·ness** *n*

**loy·al** \'lóiəl\ *adj* : faithful to a country, cause, or friend — **loy·al·ist** *n* — **loy·al·ly** *adv* — **loy·al·ty** \'lóiəltē\ *n*

**loz·enge** \'läz²nj\ *n* : small medicated candy

**lu·bri·cant** \'lübrikənt\ *n* : material (as grease) to reduce friction

**lu·bri·cate** \-,kāt\ *vb* **-cat·ed; -cat·ing** : apply a lubricant to — **lu·bri·ca·tion** \,lübrə'kāshən\ *n* — **lu·bri·ca·tor** \'lübrə,kātər\ *n*

**lu·cid** \'lüsəd\ *adj* 1 : mentally sound 2 : easily understood — **lu·cid·i·ty** \lü-'sidətē\ *n* — **lu·cid·ly** *adv* — **lu·cid·ness** *n*

**luck** \'lək\ *n* 1 : chance 2 : good fortune — **luck·i·ly** *adv* — **luck·i·ness** *n* — **luck·less** *adj* — **lucky** *adj*

**lu·cra·tive** \'lükrətiv\ *adj* : profitable — **lu·cra·tive·ly** *adv* — **lu·cra·tive·ness** *n*

**Lud·dite** \'lə,dīt\ *n* : one who opposes technological change

**lu·di·crous** \'lüdəkrəs\ *adj* : comically ridiculous — **lu·di·crous·ly** *adv* — **lu·di·crous·ness** *n*

**lug** \'ləg\ *vb* **-gg-** : drag or carry laboriously

**lug·gage** \'ləgij\ *n* : baggage

**lu·gu·bri·ous** \lu'gübrēəs\ *adj* : mournful often to an exaggerated degree — **lu·gu·bri·ous·ly** *adv* — **lu·gu·bri·ous·ness** *n*

**luke·warm** \'lük'wórm\ *adj* 1 : moderately warm 2 : not enthusiastic

**lull** \'ləl\ *vb* : make or become quiet or relaxed ∼ *n* : temporary calm

**lul·la·by** \'lələ,bī\ *n, pl* **-bies** : song to lull children to sleep

**lum·ba·go** \,ləm'bāgō\ *n* : rheumatic back pain

**lum·ber** \'ləmbər\ *n* : timber dressed for use ∼ *vb* : cut logs — **lum·ber·man** *n* — **lum·ber·yard** *n*

**lum·ber·jack** \-,jak\ *n* : logger

**lu·mi·nary** \'lümə,nerē\ *n, pl* **-nar·ies** : very famous person

**lu·mi·nes·cence** \,lümə'nes²ns\ *n* : low-temperature emission of light — **lu·mi·nes·cent** \-²nt\ *adj*

**lu·mi·nous** \'lümənəs\ *adj* : emitting light — **lu·mi·nance** \-nəns\ *n* — **lu·mi·nos·i·ty** \,lümə'näsətē\ *n* — **lu·mi·nous·ly** *adv*

**lump** \'ləmp\ *n* 1 : mass of irregular shape 2 : abnormal swelling ∼ *vb* : heap together — **lump·ish** *adj* — **lumpy** *adj*

**lu·na·cy** \'lünəsē\ *n, pl* **-cies** : state of insanity

**lu·nar** \'lünər\ *adj* : of the moon

**lu·na·tic** \'lünə,tik\ *adj* : insane — **lunatic** *n*

**lunch** \'lənch\ *n* : noon meal ∼ *vb* : eat lunch

**lun·cheon** \'lənchən\ *n* : usu. formal lunch

**lung** \'ləŋ\ *n* : breathing organ in the chest — **lunged** \'ləŋd\ *adj*

**lunge** \'lənj\ *n* 1 : sudden thrust 2 : sudden move forward — **lunge** *vb*

**lurch** \'lərch\ *n* : sudden swaying — **lurch** *vb*

**lure** \'lủr\ *n* 1 : something that attracts 2 : artificial fish bait ∼ *vb* **lured; luring** : attract

**lu·rid** \'lủrəd\ *adj* 1 : gruesome 2 : sensational — **lu·rid·ly** *adv*

**lurk** \'lərk\ *vb* : lie in wait

**lus·cious** \'ləshəs\ *adj* 1 : pleasingly sweet in taste or smell 2 : sensually appealing — **lus·cious·ly** *adv* — **luscious·ness** *n*

**lush** \'ləsh\ *adj* : covered with abundant growth

**lust** \'ləst\ *n* 1 : intense sexual desire 2 : intense longing — **lust** *vb* — **lustful** *adj*

**lus·ter, lus·tre** \'ləstər\ *n* 1 : brightness from reflected light 2 : magnificence — **lus·ter·less** *adj* — **lustrous** \-trəs\ *adj*

**lusty** \'ləstē\ *adj* **lust·i·er; -est** : full of vitality — **lust·i·ly** *adv* — **lust·i·ness** *n*

**lute** \'lüt\ *n* : pear-shaped stringed instrument — **lute·nist, lu·ta·nist** \'lüt°nist\ *n*

**lux·u·ri·ant** \,ləg'zhủrēənt, ,lək'shủr-\ *adj* 1 : growing plentifully 2 : rich and varied — **lux·u·ri·ance** \-ēəns\ *n* — **lux·u·ri·ant·ly** *adv*

**lux·u·ri·ate** \-ē,āt\ *vb* **-at·ed; -at·ing** : revel

**lux·u·ry** \'ləkshərē, 'ləgzh-\ *n, pl* **-ries** 1 : great comfort 2 : something adding to pleasure or comfort — **luxu·ri·ous** \,ləg'zhủrēəs, ,lək'shủr-\ *adj* — **lux·u·ri·ous·ly** *adv*

**-ly** \lē\ *adv suffix* 1 : in a specified way 2 : from a specified point of view

**ly·ce·um** \lī'sēəm, 'līsē-\ *n* : hall for public lectures

**lye** \'lī\ *n* : caustic alkaline substance

**lying** *pres part of* LIE

**lymph** \'limf\ *n* : bodily liquid consisting chiefly of blood plasma and white blood cells — **lym·phat·ic** \lim'fatik\ *adj*

**lynch** \'linch\ *vb* : put to death by mob action — **lynch·er** *n*

**lynx** \'liŋks\ *n, pl* **lynx** *or* **lynx·es** : wildcat

**lyre** \'līr\ *n* : ancient Greek stringed instrument

**lyr·ic** \'lirik\ *adj* 1 : suitable for singing 2 : expressing direct personal emotion ∼ *n* 1 : lyric poem 2 *pl* : words of a song — **lyr·i·cal** \-ikəl\ *adj*

# M

**m** \'em\ *n, pl* **m's** *or* **ms** \'emz\ : 13th letter of the alphabet

**ma'am** \'mam\ *n* : madam

**ma·ca·bre** \mə'käb, -'käbər, -'käbrə\ *adj* : gruesome

**mac·ad·am** \mə'kadəm\ *n* : pavement of cemented broken stone — **mac·ad·am·ize** \-,īz\ *vb*

**mac·a·ro·ni** \,makə'rōnē\ *n* : tube-shaped pasta

**mac·a·roon** \,makə'rün\ *n* : cookie of ground almonds or coconut

**ma·caw** \mə'kó\ *n* : large long-tailed parrot

[1]**mace** \'mās\ *n* 1 : heavy spiked club 2

: ornamental staff as a symbol of authority

[2]**mace** *n* : spice from the fibrous coating of the nutmeg

**ma·chete** \mə'shetē\ *n* : large heavy knife

**mach·i·na·tion** \,makə'nāshən, ,mashə-\ *n* : plot or scheme — **mach·i·nate** \'makə,nāt, 'mash-\ *vb*

**ma·chine** \mə'shēn\ *n* : combination of mechanical or electrical parts ∼ *vb* **-chined; -chin·ing** : modify by machine-operated tools — **ma·chin·able** *adj* — **ma·chin·ery** \-ərē\ *n* — **ma·chin·ist** *n*

**mack·er·el** \\'makərəl\\ *n, pl* **-el** *or* **-els** : No. Atlantic food fish

**mack·i·naw** \\'makə,nȯ\\ *n* : short heavy plaid coat

**mac·ra·mé** \\,makrə'mā\\ *n* : coarse lace or fringe made by knotting

**mac·ro** \\'makrō\\ *adj* : very large

**mac·ro·cosm** \\'makrə,käzəm\\ *n* : universe

**mad** \\'mad\\ *adj* **-dd-** **1** : insane or rabid **2** : rash and foolish **3** : angry **4** : carried away by enthusiasm — **mad·den** \\'mad⁾n\\ *vb* — **mad·den·ing·ly** \\'mad⁾niŋlē\\ *adv* — **mad·ly** *adv* — **mad·ness** *n*

**mad·am** \\'madəm\\ *n, pl* **mes·dames** \\mā'däm\\ — used in polite address to a woman

**ma·dame** \\mə'dam, *before a surname also* 'madəm\\ *n, pl* **mes·dames** \\mā'däm\\ — used as a title for a woman not of English-speaking nationality

**mad·cap** \\'mad,kap\\ *adj* : wild or zany — **madcap** *n*

**made** *past of* MAKE

**Ma·dei·ra** \\mə'dirə\\ *n* : amber-colored dessert wine

**ma·de·moi·selle** \\,madmwə'zel, -mə-'zel\\ *n, pl* **ma·de·moi·selles** \\-'zelz\\ *or* **mes·de·moi·selles** \\,mādmwə-'zel\\ : an unmarried girl or woman — used as a title for a woman esp. of French nationality

**mad·house** *n* **1** : insane asylum **2** : place of great uproar or confusion

**mad·man** \\-,man, -mən\\ *n* : lunatic

**mad·ri·gal** \\'madrigəl\\ *n* : elaborate song for several voice parts

**mad·wom·an** \\'mad,wùmən\\ *n* : woman who is insane

**mael·strom** \\'mālstrəm\\ *n* **1** : whirlpool **2** : tumult

**mae·stro** \\'mīstrō\\ *n, pl* **-stros** *or* **-stri** \\-,strē\\ : eminent composer or conductor

**Ma·fia** \\'mäfēə\\ *n* : secret criminal organization

**ma·fi·o·so** \\,mäfē'ōsō\\ *n, pl* **-si** \\-sē\\ : member of the Mafia

**mag·a·zine** \\'magə,zēn\\ *n* **1** : storehouse **2** : publication issued at regular intervals **3** : cartridge container in a gun

**ma·gen·ta** \\mə'jentə\\ *n* : deep purplish red color

**mag·got** \\'magət\\ *n* : wormlike fly larva — **mag·goty** *adj*

**mag·ic** \\'majik\\ *n* **1** : art of using supernatural powers **2** : extraordinary power or influence **3** : sleight of hand — **magic, mag·i·cal** \\-ikəl\\ *adj* — **mag·i·cal·ly** *adv* — **ma·gi·cian** \\mə'jishən\\ *n*

**mag·is·te·ri·al** \\,majə'stirēəl\\ *adj* **1** : authoritative **2** : relating to a magistrate

**mag·is·trate** \\'majə,strāt\\ *n* : judge — **mag·is·tra·cy** \\-strəsē\\ *n*

**mag·ma** \\'magmə\\ *n* : molten rock

**mag·nan·i·mous** \\mag'nanəməs\\ *adj* : noble or generous — **mag·na·nim·i·ty** \\,magnə'nimətē\\ *n* — **mag·nan·i·mous·ly** *adv*

**mag·ne·sia** \\mag'nēzhə, -shə\\ *n* : oxide of magnesium used as a laxative

**mag·ne·sium** \\mag'nēzēəm, -zhəm\\ *n* : silver-white metallic chemical element

**mag·net** \\'magnət\\ *n* **1** : body that attracts iron **2** : something that attracts — **mag·net·ic** \\mag'netik\\ *adj* — **mag·net·i·cal·ly** \\-iklē\\ *adv* — **mag·ne·tism** \\'magnə,tizəm\\ *n*

**mag·ne·tite** \\'magnə,tīt\\ *n* : black iron ore

**mag·ne·tize** \\'magnə,tīz\\ *vb* **-tized;** **-tiz·ing** **1** : attract like a magnet **2** : give magnetic properties to — **mag·ne·tiz·able** *adj* — **mag·ne·ti·za·tion** \\,magnətə'zāshən\\ *n* — **mag·ne·tiz·er** *n*

**mag·nif·i·cent** \\mag'nifəsənt\\ *adj* : splendid — **mag·nif·i·cence** \\-səns\\ *n* — **mag·nif·i·cent·ly** *adv*

**mag·ni·fy** \\'magnə,fī\\ *vb* **-fied; -fy·ing** **1** : intensify **2** : enlarge — **mag·ni·fi·ca·tion** \\,magnəfə'kāshən\\ *n* — **mag·ni·fi·er** \\'magnə,fīər\\ *n*

**mag·ni·tude** \\'magnə,tüd, -,tyüd\\ *n* **1** : greatness of size or extent **2** : quantity

**mag·no·lia** \\mag'nōlyə\\ *n* : shrub with large fragrant flowers

**mag·pie** \\'mag,pī\\ *n* : long-tailed black-and-white bird

**ma·hog·a·ny** \\mə'hägənē\\ *n, pl* **-nies** : tropical evergreen tree or its reddish brown wood

**maid** \\'mād\\ *n* **1** : unmarried young woman **2** : female servant

**maid·en** \\'mād⁾n\\ *n* : unmarried young woman ∼ *adj* **1** : unmarried **2** : first — **maid·en·hood** \\-,hùd\\ *n* — **maid·en·ly** *adj*

**maid·en·hair** \-ˌhar\ *n* : fern with delicate feathery fronds

**¹mail** \ˈmāl\ *n* 1 : something sent or carried in the postal system 2 : postal system ~ *vb* : send by mail — **mail·box** *n* — **mail·man** \-ˌman, -mən\ *n*

**²mail** *n* : armor of metal links or plates

**malm** \ˈmām\ *vb* : seriously wound or disfigure

**main** \ˈmān\ *n* 1 : force 2 : ocean 3 : principal pipe, duct, or circuit of a utility system ~ *adj* : chief — **main·ly** *adv*

**main·frame** \ˈmānˌfrām\ *n* : large fast computer

**main·land** \ˈmānˌland, -lənd\ *n* : part of a country on a continent

**main·stay** *n* : chief support

**main·stream** *n* : prevailing current or direction of activity or influence — **mainstream** *adj*

**main·tain** \mānˈtān\ *vb* 1 : keep in an existing state (as of repair) 2 : sustain 3 : declare — **main·tain·abil·i·ty** \-ˌtānəˈbilətē\ *n* — **main·tain·able** \-ˈtānəbəl\ *adj* — **main·te·nance** \ˈmāntᵊnəns\ *n*

**maî·tre d'hô·tel** \ˌmātrədōˈtel, ˌme-\ *n* : head of a dining room staff

**maize** \ˈmāz\ *n* : corn

**maj·es·ty** \ˈmajəstē\ *n, pl* **-ties** 1 : sovereign power or dignity — used as a title 2 : grandeur or splendor — **ma·jes·tic** \məˈjestik\ *adj* — **ma·jes·ti·cal·ly** \-tiklē\ *adv*

**ma·jor** \ˈmājər\ *adj* 1 : larger or greater 2 : noteworthy or conspicuous ~ *n* 1 : commissioned officer (as in the army) ranking next below a lieutenant colonel 2 : main field of study ~ *vb* **-jored, -jor·ing** : pursue an academic major

**ma·jor-do·mo** \ˌmājərˈdōmō\ *n, pl* **-mos** : head steward

**major general** *n* : commissioned officer (as in the army) ranking next below a lieutenant general

**ma·jor·i·ty** \məˈjorətē\ *n, pl* **-ties** 1 : age of full civil rights 2 : quantity more than half

**make** \ˈmāk\ *vb* **made** \ˈmād\; **mak·ing** 1 : cause to exist, occur, or appear 2 : fashion or manufacture 3 : formulate in the mind 4 : constitute 5 : prepare 6 : cause to be or become 7 : carry out or perform 8 : compel 9 : gain 10 : have an effect — used with *for* ~ *n* : brand — **mak·er** *n* —

**make do** *vb* : get along with what is available — **make good** *vb* 1 : repay 2 : succeed — **make out** *vb* 1 : draw up or write 2 : discern or understand 3 : fare — **make up** *vb* 1 : invent 2 : become reconciled 3 : compensate for

**make-be·lieve** *n* : a pretending to believe ~ *adj* : imagined or pretended

**make·shift** *n* : temporary substitute — **makeshift** *adj*

**make·up** \-ˌəp\ *n* 1 : way in which something is constituted 2 : cosmetics

**mal·ad·just·ed** \ˌmaləˈjəstəd\ *adj* : poorly adjusted (as to one's environment) — **mal·ad·just·ment** \-ˈjəstmənt\ *n*

**mal·adroit** \ˌmaləˈdroit\ *adj* : clumsy or inept

**mal·a·dy** \ˈmalədē\ *n, pl* **-dies** : disease or disorder

**mal·aise** \məˈlāz, ma-\ *n* : sense of being unwell

**mal·a·mute** \ˈmaləˌmyüt\ *n* : powerful heavy-coated dog

**mal·a·prop·ism** \ˈmaləˌsprapˌizəm\ *n* : humorous misuse of a word

**ma·lar·ia** \məˈlerēə\ *n* : disease transmitted by a mosquito — **ma·lar·i·al** \-əl\ *adj*

**mal·ar·key** \məˈlärkē\ *n* : foolishness

**mal·con·tent** \ˌmalkənˈtent\ *n* : discontented person — **malcontent** *adj*

**male** \ˈmāl\ *adj* 1 : relating to the sex that performs a fertilizing function 2 : masculine ~ *n* : male individual — **male·ness** *n*

**mal·e·dic·tion** \ˌmaləˈdikshən\ *n* : curse

**mal·e·fac·tor** \ˈmaləˌfaktər\ *n* : one who commits an offense esp. against the law

**ma·lef·i·cent** \məˈlefəsənt\ *adj* : harmful

**ma·lev·o·lent** \məˈlevələnt\ *adj* : malicious or spiteful — **ma·lev·o·lence** \-ləns\ *n*

**mal·fea·sance** \malˈfēzᵊns\ *n* : misconduct by a public official

**mal·for·ma·tion** \ˌmalforˈmāshən\ *n* : distortion or faulty formation — **mal·formed** \malˈformd\ *adj*

**mal·func·tion** \malˈfəŋkshən\ *vb* : fail to operate properly — **malfunction** *n*

**mal·ice** \ˈmaləs\ *n* : desire to cause pain or injury to another — **ma·li-**

cious \mə'lishəs\ *adj* — **ma·li·cious·ly** *adv*

**ma·lign** \mə'līn\ *adj* **1** : wicked **2** : malignant ∼ *vb* : speak evil of

**ma·lig·nant** \mə'lignənt\ *adj* **1** : harmful **2** : likely to cause death — **ma·lig·nan·cy** \-nənsē\ *n* — **ma·lig·nant·ly** *adv* — **ma·lig·ni·ty** \-nətē\ *n*

**ma·lin·ger** \mə'lingər\ *vb* : pretend illness to avoid duty — **ma·lin·ger·er** *n*

**mall** \'mól\ *n* **1** : shaded promenade **2** : concourse providing access to rows of shops

**mal·lard** \'malərd\ *n, pl* **-lard** *or* **-lards** : common wild duck

**mal·lea·ble** \'malēəbəl\ *adj* **1** : easily shaped **2** : adaptable — **mal·le·a·bil·i·ty** \,malēə'bilətē\ *n*

**mal·let** \'malət\ *n* : hammerlike tool

**mal·nour·ished** \mal'nərisht\ *adj* : poorly nourished

**mal·nu·tri·tion** \,malnù'trishən, -nyù-\ *n* : inadequate nutrition

**mal·odor·ous** \mal'ōdərəs\ *adj* : foul-smelling — **mal·odor·ous·ly** *adv* — **mal·odor·ous·ness** *n*

**mal·prac·tice** \-'praktəs\ *n* : failure of professional duty

**malt** \'mólt\ *n* : sprouted grain used in brewing

**mal·treat** \mal'trēt\ *vb* : treat badly — **mal·treat·ment** *n*

**ma·ma, mam·ma** \'mämə\ *n* : mother

**mam·mal** \'maməl\ *n* : warm-blooded vertebrate animal that nourishes its young with milk — **mam·ma·li·an** \mə'mālēən, ma-\ *adj or n*

**mam·ma·ry** \'mamərē\ *adj* : relating to the milk-secreting glands (**mammary glands**) of mammals

**mam·mo·gram** \'mamə,gram\ *n* : X-ray photograph of the breasts

**mam·moth** \'maməth\ *n* : large hairy extinct elephant ∼ *adj* : enormous

**man** \'man\ *n, pl* **men** \'men\ **1** : human being **2** : adult male **3** : mankind ∼ *vb* **-nn-** : supply with people for working — **man·hood** *n* — **man·hunt** *n* — **man·like** *adj* — **man·li·ness** *n* — **man·ly** *adj or adv* — **man-made** *adj* — **man·nish** *adj* — **man·nish·ly** *adv* — **man·nish·ness** *n* — **man-size, man-sized** *adj*

**man·a·cle** \'manikəl\ *n* : shackle for the hands or wrists — **manacle** *vb*

**man·age** \'manij\ *vb* **-aged; -ag·ing 1** : control **2** : direct or carry on business or affairs **3** : cope — **man·age·abil-**

ity \,manijə'bilətē\ *n* — **man·age·able** \'manijəbəl\ *adj* — **man·age·able·ness** *n* — **man·age·ably** \-blē\ *adv* — **man·age·ment** \'manijmənt\ *n* — **man·ag·er** \'manijər\ *n* — **man·a·ge·ri·al** \,manə'jirēəl\ *adj*

**man·da·rin** \'mandərən\ *n* : Chinese imperial official

**man·date** \'man,dāt\ *n* : authoritative command

**man·da·to·ry** \'mandə,tōrē\ *adj* : obligatory

**man·di·ble** \'mandəbəl\ *n* : lower jaw — **man·dib·u·lar** \man'dibyələr\ *adj*

**man·do·lin** \,mandə'lin, 'mand³lən\ *n* : stringed musical instrument

**man·drake** \'man,drāk\ *n* : herb with a large forked root

**mane** \'mān\ *n* : animal's neck hair — **maned** \'mānd\ *adj*

**ma·neu·ver** \mə'nüvər, -'nyü-\ *n* **1** : planned movement of troops or ships **2** : military training exercise **3** : clever or skillful move or action — **maneuver** *vb* — **ma·neu·ver·abil·i·ty** \-,nüvərə'bilətē, -,nyü-\ *n*

**man·ful** \'manfəl\ *adj* : courageous — **man·ful·ly** *adv*

**man·ga·nese** \'mangə,nēz, -,nēs\ *n* : gray metallic chemical element

**mange** \'mānj\ *n* : skin disease of domestic animals — **mangy** \'mānjē\ *adj*

**man·ger** \'mānjər\ *n* : feeding trough for livestock

**man·gle** \'mangəl\ *vb* **-gled; -gling 1** : mutilate **2** : bungle — **man·gler** *n*

**man·go** \'mangō\ *n, pl* **-goes** : juicy yellowish red tropical fruit

**man·grove** \'man,grōv, 'man-\ *n* : tropical tree growing in salt water

**man·han·dle** *vb* : handle roughly

**man·hole** *n* : entry to a sewer

**ma·nia** \'mānēə, -nyə\ *n* **1** : insanity marked by uncontrollable emotion or excitement **2** : excessive enthusiasm — **ma·ni·ac** \-nē,ak\ *n* — **ma·ni·a·cal** \mə'nīəkəl\ *adj* — **man·ic** \'manik\ *adj or n*

**man·i·cure** \'manə,kyùr\ *n* : treatment for the fingernails ∼ *vb* **-cured; -cur·ing 1** : do manicure work on **2** : trim precisely — **man·i·cur·ist** \-,kyùrist\ *n*

**¹man·i·fest** \'manə,fest\ *adj* : clear to the senses or to the mind ∼ *vb* : make evident — **man·i·fes·ta·tion**

\ˌmanəfəˈstāshən\ n — **man·i·fest·ly** adv

²**manifest** n : invoice of cargo or list of passengers

**man·i·fes·to** \ˌmanəˈfestō\ n, pl **-tos** or **-toes** : public declaration of policy or views

**man·i·fold** \ˈmanəˌfōld\ adj : marked by diversity or variety ~ n : pipe fitting with several outlets for connections

**ma·nila paper** \məˈnilə-\ n : durable brownish paper

**ma·nip·u·late** \məˈnipyəˌlāt\ vb **-lat·ed; -lat·ing** 1 : treat or operate manually or mechanically 2 : influence esp. by cunning — **ma·nip·u·la·tion** \məˌnipyəˈlāshən\ n — **ma·nip·u·la·tive** \-ˈnipyəˌlātiv, -lətiv\ adj — **ma·nip·u·la·tor** \-ˌlātər\ n

**man·kind** \ˈmanˈkīnd\ n : human race

**man·na** \ˈmanə\ n : something valuable that comes unexpectedly

**manned** \ˈmand\ adj : carrying or performed by a man

**man·ne·quin** \ˈmanikən\ n : dummy used to display clothes

**man·ner** \ˈmanər\ n 1 : kind 2 : usual way of acting 3 : artistic method 4 pl : social conduct

**man·nered** \-ərd\ adj 1 : having manners of a specified kind 2 : artificial

**man·ner·ism** \ˈmanəˌrizəm\ n : individual peculiarity of action

**man·ner·ly** \-lē\ adj : polite — **man·ner·li·ness** n — **mannerly** adv

**man–of–war** \ˌmanəˈwȯr, -əvˈwȯr\ n, pl **men–of–war** \ˌmen-\ : warship

**man·or** \ˈmanər\ n : country estate — **ma·no·ri·al** \məˈnȯrēəl\ adj

**man·pow·er** n : supply of people available for service

**man·sard** \ˈmanˌsärd\ n : roof with two slopes on all sides and the lower slope the steeper

**manse** \ˈmans\ n : parsonage

**man·ser·vant** n, pl **men·ser·vants** : a male servant

**man·sion** \ˈmanchən\ n : very big house

**man·slaugh·ter** n : unintentional killing of a person

**man·tel** \ˈmantəl\ n : shelf above a fireplace

**man·tis** \ˈmantəs\ n, pl **-tis·es** or **-tes** \ˈmanˌtēz\ : large green insect-eating insect with stout forelegs

**man·tle** \ˈmantəl\ n 1 : sleeveless

cloak 2 : something that covers, enfolds, or envelops — **mantle** vb

**man·tra** \ˈmantrə\ n : mystical chant

**man·u·al** \ˈmanyəwəl\ adj : involving the hands or physical force ~ n : handbook — **man·u·al·ly** adv

**man·u·fac·ture** \ˌmanyəˈfakchər, ˌmanə-\ n : process of making wares by hand or by machinery ~ vb **-tured; -tur·ing** : make from raw materials — **man·u·fac·tur·er** n

**ma·nure** \məˈnúr, -ˈnyúr\ n : animal excrement used as fertilizer

**manu·script** \ˈmanyəˌskript\ n 1 : something written or typed 2 : document submitted for publication

**many** \ˈmenē\ adj more \ˈmȯr\; most \ˈmōst\ : consisting of a large number — **many** n or pron

**map** \ˈmap\ n : representation of a geographical area ~ vb **-pp-** 1 : make a map of 2 : plan in detail — **map·pa·ble** \-əbəl\ adj — **map·per** n

**ma·ple** \ˈmāpəl\ n : tree with hard light-colored wood

**mar** \ˈmär\ vb **-rr-** : damage

**mar·a·schi·no** \ˌmarəˈskēnō, -ˈshē-\ n, pl **-nos** : preserved cherry

**mar·a·thon** \ˈmarəˌthän\ n 1 : long-distance race 2 : test of endurance — **mar·a·thon·er** \-ˌthänər\ n

**ma·raud** \məˈród\ vb : roam about in search of plunder — **ma·raud·er** n

**mar·ble** \ˈmärbəl\ n 1 : crystallized limestone 2 : small glass ball used in a children's game (**marbles**)

**mar·bling** \-bəliŋ\ n : intermixture of fat and lean in meat

**march** \ˈmärch\ vb : move with regular steps or in a purposeful manner ~ n 1 : distance covered in a march 2 : measured stride 3 : forward movement 4 : music for marching — **march·er** n

**March** n : 3d month of the year having 31 days

**mar·chio·ness** \ˈmärshənəs\ n : woman holding the rank of a marquess

**Mar·di Gras** \ˈmärdēˌgrä\ n : Tuesday before the beginning of Lent often observed with parades and merrymaking

**mare** \ˈmar\ n : female horse

**mar·ga·rine** \ˈmärjərən\ n : butter substitute made usu. from vegetable oils

**mar·gin** \ˈmärjən\ n 1 : edge 2 : spare amount, measure, or degree

**mar·gin·al** \-jənəl\ adj 1 : relating to

or situated at a border or margin **2** : close to the lower limit of acceptability — **mar·gin·al·ly** adv

**mari·gold** \'marə,gōld\ n : garden plant with showy flower heads

**mari·i·jua·na** \,marə'wänə, -'hwä-\ n : intoxicating drug obtained from the hemp plant

**ma·ri·na** \mə'rēnə\ n : place for mooring pleasure boats

**mar·i·nate** \'marə,nāt\ vb **-nat·ed; -nat·ing** : soak in a savory sauce

**ma·rine** \mə'rēn\ adj **1** : relating to the sea **2** : relating to marines ∼ n : infantry soldier associated with a navy

**mar·i·ner** \'marənər\ n : sailor

**mar·i·o·nette** \,marēə'net\ n : puppet

**mar·i·tal** \'marət°l\ adj : relating to marriage

**mar·i·time** \'marə,tīm\ adj : relating to the sea or commerce on the sea

**mar·jo·ram** \'märjərəm\ n : aromatic mint used as a seasoning

**mark** \'märk\ n **1** : something aimed at **2** : something (as a line) designed to record position **3** : visible sign **4** : written symbol **5** : grade **6** : lasting impression **7** : blemish ∼ vb **1** : designate or set apart by a mark or make a mark on **2** : characterize **3** : remark — **mark·er** n

**marked** \'märkt\ adj : noticeable — **mark·ed·ly** \'märkədlē\ adv

**mar·ket** \'märkət\ n **1** : buying and selling of goods or the place this happens **2** : demand for commodities **3** : store ∼ vb : sell — **mar·ket·able** adj

**mar·ket·place** n **1** : market **2** : world of trade or economic activity

**marks·man** \'märksmən\ n : good shooter — **marks·man·ship** n

**mar·lin** \'märlən\ n : large oceanic fish

**mar·ma·lade** \'märmə,lād\ n : jam with pieces of fruit and rind

**mar·mo·set** \'märmə,set\ n : small bushy-tailed monkey

**mar·mot** \'märmət\ n : burrowing rodent

¹**ma·roon** \mə'rün\ vb : isolate without hope of escape

²**maroon** n : dark red color

**mar·quee** \mär'kē\ n : canopy over an entrance

**mar·quess** \'märkwəs\, **mar·quis** \'märkwəs, mär'kē\ n, pl **-quess·es**

or **-quis·es** or **-quis** : British noble ranking next below a duke

**mar·quise** \mär'kēz\ n, pl **mar·quises** \-'kēz, -'kēzəz\ : marchioness

**mar·riage** \'marij\ n **1** : state of being married **2** : wedding ceremony — **mar·riage·able** adj

**mar·row** \'marō\ n : soft tissue in the cavity of bone

**mar·ry** \'marē\ vb **-ried; -ry·ing 1** : join as husband and wife **2** : take or give in marriage — **mar·ried** adj or n

**marsh** \'märsh\ n : soft wet land — **marshy** adj

**mar·shal** \'märshəl\ n **1** : leader of ceremony **2** : usu. high military or administrative officer ∼ vb **-shaled** or **-shalled; -shal·ing** or **-shal·ling 1** : arrange in order, rank, or position **2** : lead with ceremony

**marsh·mal·low** \'märsh,melō, -,malō\ n : spongy candy

**mar·su·pi·al** \mär'süpēəl\ n : mammal that nourishes young in an abdominal pouch — **marsupial** adj

**mart** \'märt\ n : market

**mar·ten** \'märt°n\ n, pl **-ten** or **-tens** : weasellike mammal with soft fur

**mar·tial** \'märshəl\ adj **1** : relating to war or an army **2** : warlike

**mar·tin** \'märt°n\ n : small swallow

**mar·ti·net** \,märt°n'et\ n : strict disciplinarian

**mar·tyr** \'märtər\ n : one who dies or makes a great sacrifice for a cause ∼ vb : make a martyr of — **mar·tyr·dom** \-dəm\ n

**mar·vel** \'märvəl\ vb **-veled** or **-velled; -vel·ing** or **-vel·ling** : feel surprise or wonder ∼ n : something amazing — **mar·vel·ous, mar·vel·lous** \'märvələs\ adj — **mar·vel·ous·ly** adv — **mar·vel·ous·ness** n

**Marx·ism** \'märk,sizəm\ n : political and social principles of Karl Marx — **Marx·ist** \-sist\ n or adj

**mas·cara** \mas'karə\ n : eye cosmetic

**mas·cot** \'mas,kät, -kət\ n : one believed to bring good luck

**mas·cu·line** \'maskyələn\ adj : relating to the male sex — **mas·cu·lin·i·ty** \,maskyə'linətē\ n

**mash** \'mash\ n **1** : crushed steeped grain for fermenting **2** : soft pulpy mass ∼ vb **1** : reduce to a pulpy mass **2** : smash — **mash·er** n

**mask** \'mask\ n : disguise for the face

~ vb **1** : disguise **2** : cover to protect — **mask·er** n

**mas·och·ism** \'masǝ,kizǝm, 'maz-\ n : pleasure in being abused — **mas·och·ist** \-kist\ n — **mas·och·is·tic** \,masǝ'kistik, ,maz-\ adj

**ma·son** \'mās°n\ n : workman who builds with stone or brick — **ma·son·ry** \-rē\ n

**mas·quer·ade** \,maskǝ'rād\ n **1** : costume party **2** : disguise ~ vb **-ad·ed; -ad·ing 1** : disguise oneself **2** : take part in a costume party — **mas·quer·ad·er** n

**mass** \'mas\ n **1** : large amount of matter or number of things **2** : expanse or magnitude **3** : great body of people — usu. pl. ~ vb : form into a mass — **mass·less** \-lǝs\ adj — **massy** adj

**Mass** n : worship service of the Roman Catholic Church

**mas·sa·cre** \'masikǝr\ n : wholesale slaughter — **massacre** vb

**mas·sage** \mǝ'säzh, -'säj\ n : a rubbing of the body — **massage** vb

**mas·seur** \ma'sǝr\ n : man who massages

**mas·seuse** \-'sœēz, -'süz\ n : woman who massages

**mas·sive** \'masiv\ adj **1** : being a large mass **2** : large in scope — **mas·sive·ly** adv — **mas·sive·ness** n

**mast** \'mast\ n : tall pole esp. for supporting sails — **mast·ed** adj

**mas·ter** \'mastǝr\ n **1** : male teacher **2** : holder of an academic degree between a bachelor's and a doctor's **3** : one highly skilled **4** : one in authority ~ vb **1** : subdue **2** : become proficient in — **mas·ter·ful** \-fǝl\ adj — **mas·ter·ful·ly** adv — **mas·ter·ly** adj — **mas·tery** \'mastǝrē\ n

**master chief petty officer** n : petty officer of the highest rank in the navy

**master gunnery sergeant** n : noncommissioned officer in the marine corps ranking above a master sergeant

**mas·ter·piece** \'mastǝr,pēs\ n : great piece of work

**master sergeant** n **1** : noncommissioned officer in the army ranking next below a sergeant major **2** : noncommissioned officer in the air force ranking next below a senior master sergeant **3** : noncommissioned officer in the marine corps ranking next below a master gunnery sergeant

**mas·ter·work** n : masterpiece

**mas·tic** \'mastik\ n : pasty glue

**mas·ti·cate** \'mastǝ,kāt\ vb **-cat·ed; -cat·ing** : chew — **mas·ti·ca·tion** \,mastǝ'kāshǝn\ n

**mas·tiff** \'mastǝf\ n : large dog

**mas·to·don** \'mastǝ,dän\ n : extinct elephantlike animal

**mas·toid** \'mas,tȯid\ n : bone behind the ear — **mastoid** adj

**mas·tur·ba·tion** \,mastǝr'bāshǝn\ n : stimulation of sex organs by hand — **mas·tur·bate** \'mastǝr,bāt\ vb

¹**mat** \'mat\ n **1** : coarse woven or plaited fabric **2** : mass of tangled strands **3** : thick pad ~ vb **-tt-** : form into a mat

²**mat** vb **-tt- 1** : make matte **2** : provide (a picture) with a mat ~ or **matt** or **matte** n : border around a picture

³**mat** var of MATTE

**mat·a·dor** \'matǝ,dȯr\ n : bullfighter

¹**match** \'mach\ n **1** : one equal to another **2** : one able to cope with another **3** : suitable pairing **4** : game **5** : marriage ~ vb **1** : set in competition **2** : marry **3** : be or provide the equal of **4** : fit or go together — **match·less** adj — **match·mak·er** n

²**match** n : piece of wood or paper material with a combustible tip

**mate** \'māt\ n **1** : companion **2** : subordinate officer on a ship **3** : one of a pair ~ vb **mat·ed; mat·ing 1** : fit together **2** : come together as a pair **3** : copulate

**ma·te·ri·al** \mǝ'tirēǝl\ adj **1** : natural **2** : relating to matter **3** : important **4** : of a physical or worldly nature ~ n : stuff something is made of — **ma·te·ri·al·ly** adv

**ma·te·ri·al·ism** \mǝ'tirēǝ,lizǝm\ n **1** : theory that matter is the only reality **2** : preoccupation with material and not spiritual things — **ma·te·ri·al·ist** \-list\ n or adj — **ma·te·ri·al·is·tic** \-,tirēǝ'listik\ adj

**ma·te·ri·al·ize** \mǝ'tirēǝ,līz\ vb **-ized; -iz·ing** : take or cause to take bodily form — **ma·te·ri·al·i·za·tion** \mǝ,tirēǝlǝ'zāshǝn\ n

**ma·té·ri·el, ma·te·ri·el** \mǝ,tirē'el\ n : military supplies

**ma·ter·nal** \mǝ'tǝrn°l\ adj : motherly — **ma·ter·nal·ly** adv

**ma·ter·ni·ty** \mǝ'tǝrnǝtē\ n, pl **-ties 1** : state of being a mother **2** : hospital's childbirth facility ~ adj **1**

: worn during pregnancy **2** : relating to the period close to childbirth

**math** \'math\ n : mathematics

**math·e·mat·ics** \,mathə'matiks\ n pl : science of numbers and of shapes in space — **math·e·mat·i·cal** \-ikəl\ adj — **math·e·mat·i·cal·ly** adv — **math·e·ma·ti·cian** \,mathəmə'tishən\ n

**mat·i·nee, mat·i·née** \,mat°n'ā\ n : afternoon performance

**mat·ins** \'mat°nz\ n : morning prayers

**ma·tri·arch** \'mātrē,ärk\ n : woman who rules a family — **ma·tri·ar·chal** \,mātrē'ärkəl\ adj — **ma·tri·ar·chy** \'mātrē,ärkē\ n

**ma·tri·cide** \'matrə,sīd, 'mā-\ n : murder of one's mother — **ma·tri·cid·al** \,matrə'sīd°l, ,mā-\ adj

**ma·tric·u·late** \mə'trikyə,lāt\ vb -lat-ed; -lat·ing : enroll in school — **ma·tric·u·la·tion** \-,trikyə'lāshən\ n

**mat·ri·mo·ny** \'matrə,mōnē\ n : marriage — **mat·ri·mo·ni·al** \,matrə-'mōnēəl\ adj — **mat·ri·mo·ni·al·ly** adv

**ma·trix** \'mātriks\ n, pl -tri·ces \'mātrə,sēz, 'ma-\ or -trix·es \'mātriksəz\ : something (as a mold) that gives form, foundation, or origin to something else enclosed in it

**ma·tron** \'mātrən\ n 1 : dignified mature woman **2** : woman supervisor — **ma·tron·ly** adj

**matte** \'mat\ adj : not shiny

**mat·ter** \'matər\ n 1 : subject of interest **2** pl : circumstances **3** : trouble **4** : physical substance ~ vb : be important

**mat·tock** \'matək\ n : a digging tool

**mat·tress** \'matrəs\ n : pad to sleep on

**ma·ture** \mə'tùr, -'tyùr, -'chùr\ adj -tur·er; -est **1** : carefully considered **2** : fully grown or developed **3** : due for payment ~ vb -tured; -tur·ing : become mature — **mat·u·ra·tion** \,machə'rāshən\ n — **ma·ture·ly** adv — **ma·tu·ri·ty** \-ətē\ n

**maud·lin** \'mòdlən\ adj : excessively sentimental

**maul** \'mòl\ n : heavy hammer ~ vb 1 : beat **2** : handle roughly

**mau·so·le·um** \,mòsə'lēəm, ,mòzə-\ n, pl -leums or -lea \-'lēə\ : large above-ground tomb

**mauve** \'mōv, 'mòv\ n : lilac color

**ma·ven, ma·vin** \'māvən\ n : expert

**mav·er·ick** \'mavrik\ n 1 : unbranded range animal **2** : nonconformist

**maw** \'mò\ n 1 : stomach **2** : throat, esophagus, or jaws

**mawk·ish** \'mòkish\ adj : sickly sentimental — **mawk·ish·ly** adv — **mawk·ish·ness** n

**max·im** \'maksəm\ n : proverb

**max·i·mum** \'maksəməm\ n, pl -ma \-səmə\ or -mums **1** : greatest quantity **2** : upper limit **3** : largest number — **maximum** adj — **max·i·mize** \-sə,mīz\ vb

**may** \'mā\ verbal auxiliary, past **might** \'mīt\; pres sing & pl **may** **1** : have permission **2** : be likely to **3** — used to express desire, purpose, or contingency

**May** \'mā\ n : 5th month of the year having 31 days

**may·ap·ple** n : woodland herb having edible fruit

**may·be** \'mābē\ adv : perhaps

**may·flow·er** n : spring-blooming herb

**may·fly** n : fly with an aquatic larva

**may·hem** \'mā,hem, 'māəm\ n 1 : crippling or mutilation of a person **2** : needless damage

**may·on·naise** \'māə,nāz\ n : creamy white sandwich spread

**may·or** \'māər, 'mer\ n : chief city official — **may·or·al** \-əl\ adj — **may·or·al·ty** \-əltē\ n

**maze** \'māz\ n : confusing network of passages — **mazy** adj

**ma·zur·ka** \mə'zərkə\ n : Polish dance

**me** \'mē\ pron, objective case of I

**mead** \'mēd\ n : alcoholic beverage brewed from honey

**mead·ow** \'medō\ n : low-lying usu. level grassland — **mead·ow·land** \-,land\ n

**mead·ow·lark** n : songbird with a yellow breast

**mea·ger, mea·gre** \'mēgər\ adj **1** : thin **2** : lacking richness or strength — **mea·ger·ly** adv — **mea·ger·ness** n

**¹meal** \'mēl\ n 1 : food to be eaten at one time **2** : act of eating — **meal·time** n

**²meal** n : ground grain — **mealy** adj

**¹mean** \'mēn\ adj **1** : humble **2** : worthy of or showing little regard **3** : stingy **4** : malicious — **mean·ly** adv — **mean·ness** n

**²mean** \'mēn\ vb meant \'ment\; mean·ing \'mēniŋ\ **1** : intend **2** : serve to convey, show, or indicate **3** : be important

**³mean** n 1 : middle point **2** pl : something that helps gain an end **3** *pl* : material resources **4** : sum of several quantities divided by the number of quantities ~ *adj* : being a mean

**me·an·der** \mē'andər\ *vb* **-dered; -der·ing 1** : follow a winding course **2** : wander aimlessly — **meander** *n*

**mean·ing** \'mēniŋ\ *n* **1** : idea conveyed or intended to be conveyed **2** : aim — **mean·ing·ful** \-fəl\ *adj* — **mean·ing·ful·ly** *adv* — **mean·ing·less** *adj*

**mean·time** \'mēn,tīm\ *n* : intervening time — **meantime** *adv*

**mean·while** \-,hwīl\ *n* : meantime ~ *adv* **1** : meantime **2** : at the same time

**mea·sles** \'mēzəlz\ *n pl* : disease that is marked by red spots on the skin

**mea·sly** \'mēzlē\ *adj* **-sli·er; -est** : contemptibly small in amount

**mea·sure** \'mezhər, 'māzh-\ *n* **1** : moderate amount **2** : dimensions or amount **3** : something to show amount **4** : unit or system of measurement **5** : act of measuring **6** : means to an end ~ *vb* **-sured; -sur·ing 1** : find out or mark off size or amount of **2** : have a specified measurement — **mea·sur·able** \'mezhərəbəl, 'māzh-\ *adj* — **mea·sur·ably** \-blē\ *adv* — **mea·sure·less** *adj* — **mea·sure·ment** *n* — **mea·sur·er** *n*

**meat** \'mēt\ *n* **1** : food **2** : animal flesh used as food — **meat·ball** *n* — **meaty** *adj*

**me·chan·ic** \mi'kanik\ *n* : worker who repairs cars

**me·chan·i·cal** \mi'kanikəl\ *adj* **1** : relating to machines or mechanics **2** : involuntary — **me·chan·i·cal·ly** *adv*

**me·chan·ics** \-iks\ *n sing or pl* **1** : branch of physics dealing with energy and forces in relation to bodies **2** : mechanical details

**mech·a·nism** \'mekə,nizəm\ *n* **1** : piece of machinery **2** : technique for gaining a result **3** : basic processes producing a phenomenon — **mech·a·nis·tic** \,mekə'nistik\ *adj* — **mech·a·ni·za·tion** \,mekənə'zāshən\ *n* — **mech·a·nize** \'mekə,nīz\ *vb* — **mech·a·niz·er** *n*

**med·al** \'medᵊl\ *n* **1** : religious pin or pendant **2** : coinlike commemorative metal piece

**med·al·ist, med·al·list** \'medᵊlist\ *n* : person awarded a medal

**me·dal·lion** \mə'dalyən\ *n* : large medal

**med·dle** \'medᵊl\ *vb* **-dled; -dling** : interfere — **med·dler** \'medᵊlər\ *n* — **med·dle·some** \'medᵊlsəm\ *adj*

**me·dia** \'mēdēə\ *n pl* : communications organizations

**me·di·an** \'mēdēən\ *n* : middle value in a range — **median** *adj*

**me·di·ate** \'mēdē,āt\ *vb* **-at·ed; -at·ing** : help settle a dispute — **me·di·a·tion** \,mēdē'āshən\ *n* — **me·di·a·tor** \'mēdē,ātər\ *n*

**med·ic** \'medik\ *n* : medical worker esp. in the military

**med·i·ca·ble** \'medikəbəl\ *adj* : curable

**med·ic·aid** \'medi,kād\ *n* : government program of medical aid for the poor

**med·i·cal** \'medikəl\ *adj* : relating to medicine — **med·i·cal·ly** \-klē\ *adv*

**medi·care** \'medi,ker\ *n* : government program of medical care for the aged

**med·i·cate** \'medə,kāt\ *vb* **-cat·ed; -cat·ing** : treat with medicine

**med·i·ca·tion** \,medə'kāshən\ *n* **1** : act of medicating **2** : medicine

**med·i·cine** \'medəsən\ *n* **1** : preparation used to treat disease **2** : science dealing with the cure of disease — **me·dic·i·nal** \mə'disᵊnəl\ *adj* — **me·dic·i·nal·ly** *adv*

**me·di·e·val, me·di·ae·val** \,mēdē-'ēval, ,med-, ,mid-; ,mē'dē-, ,me-, ,mi-\ *adj* : of or relating to the Middle Ages — **me·di·eval·ist** \-ist\ *n*

**me·di·o·cre** \,mēdē'ōkər\ *adj* : not very good — **me·di·oc·ri·ty** \-'äkrətē\ *n*

**med·i·tate** \'medə,tāt\ *vb* **-tat·ed; -tat·ing** : contemplate — **med·i·ta·tion** \,medə'tāshən\ *n* — **med·i·ta·tive** \'medə,tātiv\ *adj* — **med·i·ta·tive·ly** *adv*

**me·di·um** \'mēdēəm\ *n, pl* **-diums** or **-dia** \-ēə\ **1** : middle position or degree **2** : means of effecting or conveying something **3** : surrounding substance **4** : means of communication **5** : mode of artistic expression — **medium** *adj*

**med·ley** \'medlē\ *n, pl* **-leys** : series of songs performed as one

**meek** \'mēk\ *adj* **1** : mild-mannered **2** : lacking spirit — **meek·ly** *adv* — **meek·ness** *n*

**meer·schaum** \'mirshəm, -,shȯm\ *n* : claylike tobacco pipe

**¹meet** \'mēt\ *vb* **met** \'met\; **meet·ing**

1 : run into  2 : join  3 : oppose  4 : assemble  5 : satisfy  6 : be introduced to ∼ *n* : sports team competition

²**meet** *adj* : proper

**meet·ing** \'mētiŋ\ *n* : a getting together — **meet·ing·house** *n*

**mega·byte** \'megəbīt\ *n* : unit of computer storage capacity

**mega·hertz** \-ˌhərts, -ˌherts\ *n* : one million hertz

**mega·phone** \'megəˌfōn\ *n* : cone-shaped device to intensify or direct the voice

**mel·an·choly** \'melənˌkälē\ *n* : depression — **mel·an·chol·ic** \ˌmelənˈkälik\ *adj* — **melancholy** *adj*

**mel·a·no·ma** \ˌmeləˈnōmə\ *n, pl* **-mas** : usu. malignant skin tumor

**me·lee** \'māˌlā, māˈlā\ *n* : brawl

**me·lio·rate** \'mēlyəˌrāt, 'mēlēə-\ *vb* **-rat·ed; -rat·ing** : improve — **me·lio·ra·tion** \ˌmēlyəˈrāshən, ˌmēlēə-\ *n* — **me·lio·ra·tive** \'mēlyəˌrātiv, 'mēlēə-\ *adj*

**mel·lif·lu·ous** \meˈliflǝwǝs, mǝ-\ *adj* : sweetly flowing — **mel·lif·lu·ous·ly** *adv* — **mel·lif·lu·ous·ness** *n*

**mel·low** \'melō\ *adj* **1** : grown gentle or mild  **2** : rich and full — **mellow** *vb* — **mel·low·ness** *n*

**melo·dra·ma** \'meləˌdrämə, -ˌdram-\ *n* : overly theatrical play — **melo·dra·mat·ic** \ˌmelədrəˈmatik\ *adj* — **melo·dra·mat·i·cal·ly** \-tiklē\ *adv*

**mel·o·dy** \'melədē\ *n, pl* **-dies 1** : agreeable sound  **2** : succession of musical notes — **me·lod·ic** \mǝˈlädik\ *adj* — **me·lod·i·cal·ly** \-iklē\ *adv* — **me·lo·di·ous** \mǝˈlōdēǝs\ *adj* — **me·lo·di·ous·ly** *adv* — **me·lo·di·ous·ness** *n*

**mel·on** \'melən\ *n* : gourdlike fruit

**melt** \'melt\ *vb* **1** : change from solid to liquid usu. by heat  **2** : dissolve or disappear gradually  **3** : move or be moved emotionally

**mem·ber** \'membər\ *n* **1** : part of a person, animal, or plant  **2** : one of a group  **3** : part of a whole — **mem·ber·ship** \-ˌship\ *n*

**mem·brane** \'memˌbrān\ *n* : thin layer esp. in an organism — **mem·bra·nous** \-brənəs\ *adj*

**me·men·to** \miˈmentō\ *n, pl* **-tos** *or* **-toes** : souvenir

**memo** \'memō\ *n, pl* **mem·os** : memorandum

**mem·oirs** \'memˌwärz\ *n pl* : autobiography

**mem·o·ra·bil·ia** \ˌmemərəˈbilēə, -ˈbilyə\ *n pl* **1** : memorable things  **2** : mementos

**mem·o·ra·ble** \'memərəbəl\ *adj* : worth remembering — **mem·o·ra·bil·i·ty** \ˌmemərəˈbilətē\ *n* — **mem·o·ra·ble·ness** *n* — **mem·o·ra·bly** \-blē\ *adv*

**mem·o·ran·dum** \ˌmeməˈrandəm\ *n, pl* **-dums** *or* **-da** \-də\ : informal note

**me·mo·ri·al** \mǝˈmōrēəl\ *n* : something (as a monument) meant to keep remembrance alive — **memorial** *adj* — **me·mo·ri·al·ize** *vb*

**Memorial Day** *n* : last Monday in May or formerly May 30 observed as a legal holiday in commemoration of dead servicemen

**mem·o·ry** \'memrē, 'memə-\ *n, pl* **-ries 1** : power of remembering  **2** : something remembered  **3** : commemoration  **4** : time within which past events are remembered — **mem·o·ri·za·tion** \ˌmemərəˈzāshən\ *n* — **mem·o·rize** \'meməˌrīz\ *vb* — **mem·o·riz·er** *n*

**men** *pl of* MAN

**men·ace** \'menəs\ *n* : threat of danger ∼ *vb* **-aced; -ac·ing 1** : threaten  **2** : endanger — **men·ac·ing·ly** *adv*

**me·nag·er·ie** \mǝˈnajərē\ *n* : collection of wild animals

**mend** \'mend\ *vb* **1** : improve  **2** : repair  **3** : heal — **mend** *n* — **mend·er** *n*

**men·da·cious** \menˈdāshəs\ *adj* : dishonest — **men·da·cious·ly** *adv* — **men·dac·i·ty** \-ˈdasətē\ *n*

**men·di·cant** \'mendikənt\ *n* : beggar — **men·di·can·cy** \-kənsē\ *n* — **mendicant** *adj*

**men·ha·den** \menˈhād°n, mən-\ *n, pl* **-den** : fish related to the herring

**me·nial** \'mēnēəl, -nyəl\ *adj* **1** : relating to servants  **2** : humble ∼ *n* : domestic servant — **me·ni·al·ly** *adv*

**men·in·gi·tis** \ˌmenənˈjītəs\ *n, pl* **-git·i·des** \-ˈjitəˌdēz\ : disease of the brain and spinal cord

**meno·pause** \'menəˌpöz\ *n* : time when menstruation ends — **meno·paus·al** \ˌmenəˈpözəl\ *adj*

**me·no·rah** \mǝˈnōrǝ\ *n* : candelabrum used in Jewish worship

**men·stru·a·tion** \ˌmenstrəˈwāshən, menˈstrā-\ *n* : monthly discharge of blood from the uterus — **men·stru·al**

\'menstrəwəl\ *adj* — **men·stru·ate**
\'menstrə‚wāt, -‚strāt\ *vb*

**-ment** \mənt\ *n suffix* **1** : result or means
of an action **2** : action or process **3**
: place of an action **4** : state or condition

**men·tal** \'ment³l\ *adj* : relating to the
mind or its disorders — **men·tal·i·ty**
\men'talətē\ *n* — **men·tal·ly** *adv*

**men·thol** \'men‚thȯl, -‚thōl\ *n* : soothing substance from oil of peppermint
— **men·tho·lat·ed** \-thə‚lātəd\ *adj*

**men·tion** \'menchən\ *vb* : refer to —
**mention** *n*

**men·tor** \'men‚tȯr, 'mentər\ *n* : in-
structor

**menu** \'menyü\ *n* **1** : restaurant's list
of food **2** : list of offerings

**me·ow** \mē'aů\ *n* : characteristic cry of
a cat — **meow** *vb*

**mer·can·tile** \'mərkən‚tēl, -‚tīl\ *adj*
: relating to merchants or trade

**mer·ce·nary** \'mərs³n‚erē\ *n, pl* **-nar-
ies** : hired soldier ~ *adj* : serving only
for money

**mer·chan·dise** \'mərchən‚dīz, -‚dīs\
*n* : goods bought and sold ~ *vb*
**-dised; -dis·ing** : buy and sell —
**mer·chan·dis·er** *n*

**mer·chant** \'mərchənt\ *n* : one who
buys and sells

**merchant marine** *n* : commercial ships

**mer·cu·ri·al** \mər'kyůrēəl\ *adj* : unpredictable — **mer·cu·ri·al·ly** *adv* —
**mer·cu·ri·al·ness** *n*

**mer·cu·ry** \'mərkyərē\ *n* : heavy liquid metallic chemical element

**mer·cy** \'mərsē\ *n, pl* **-cies** **1** : show of
pity or leniency **2** : divine blessing —
**mer·ci·ful** \-sifəl\ *adj* — **mer·ci·ful-
ly** *adv* — **mer·ci·less** \-siləs\ *adj* —
**mer·ci·less·ly** *adv* — **mercy** *adj*

**mere** \'mir\ *adj, superlative* **mer·est**
: nothing more than — **mere·ly** *adv*

**merge** \'mərj\ *vb* **merged; merg·ing**
**1** : unite **2** : blend — **merg·er**
\'mərjər\ *n*

**me·rid·i·an** \mə'ridēən\ *n* : imaginary
circle on the earth's surface passing
through the poles — **meridian** *adj*

**me·ringue** \mə'raŋ\ *n* : baked dessert
topping of beaten egg whites

**me·ri·no** \mə'rēnō\ *n, pl* **-nos** **1** : kind
of sheep **2** : fine soft woolen yarn

**mer·it** \'merət\ *n* **1** : praiseworthy
quality **2** *pl* : rights and wrongs of a
legal case ~ *vb* : deserve — **mer·i-
to·ri·ous** \‚merə'tōrēəs\ *adj* —

**mer·i·to·ri·ous·ly** *adv* — **mer·i·to·ri-
ous·ness** *n*

**mer·lot** \mer'lō\ *n* : dry red wine

**mer·maid** \'mər‚mād\ *n* : legendary
female sea creature

**mer·ry** \'merē\ *adj* **-ri·er; -est** : full of
high spirits — **mer·ri·ly** *adv* — **mer-
ri·ment** \'merimənt\ *n* — **mer·ry-
mak·er** \'merē‚mākər\ *n* — **mer·ry-
mak·ing** \'merē‚mākiŋ\ *n*

**merry–go–round** *n* : revolving amusement ride

**me·sa** \'māsə\ *n* : steep flat-topped hill

**mesdames** *pl of* MADAM *or of*
MADAME *or of* MRS.

**mesdemoiselles** *pl of* MADEMOI-
SELLE

**mesh** \'mesh\ *n* **1** : one of the open-
ings in a net **2** : net fabric **3** : working contact — *vb* : fit together
properly — **meshed** \'mesht\ *adj*

**mes·mer·ize** \'mezmə‚rīz\ *vb* **-ized;
-iz·ing** : hypnotize

**mess** \'mes\ *n* **1** : meal eaten by a
group **2** : confused, dirty, or offensive state ~ *vb* **1** : make dirty or untidy **2** : putter **3** : interfere — **messy**
*adj*

**mes·sage** \'mesij\ *n* : news, information, or a command sent by one person to another

**mes·sen·ger** \'mes³njər\ *n* : one who
carries a message or does an errand

**Mes·si·ah** \mə'sīə\ *n* **1** : expected de-
liverer of the Jews **2** : Jesus Christ **3**
*not cap* : great leader

**messieurs** *pl of* MONSIEUR

**Messrs.** *pl of* MR.

**mes·ti·zo** \me'stēzō\ *n, pl* **-zos** : person of mixed blood

**met** *past of* MEET

**me·tab·o·lism** \mə'tabə‚lizəm\ *n* : bio-
chemical processes necessary to life
— **met·a·bol·ic** \‚metə'bälik\ *adj* —
**me·tab·o·lize** \mə'tabə‚līz\ *vb*

**met·al** \'met³l\ *n* : shiny substance that
can be melted and shaped and con-
ducts heat and electricity — **me·tal-
lic** \mə'talik\ *adj* — **met·al·ware** *n*
— **met·al·work** *n* — **met·al·work·er**
*n* — **met·al·work·ing** *n*

**met·al·lur·gy** \'met³l‚ərjē\ *n* : science
of metals — **met·al·lur·gi·cal** \‚met³l-
'ərjikəl\ *adj* — **met·al·lur·gist**
\'met³l‚ərjist\ *n*

**meta·mor·pho·sis** \‚metə'mȯrfəsəs\
*n, pl* **-pho·ses** \-‚sēz\ : sudden and

drastic change (as of form) — **meta-mor·phose** \-ˌfōz, -ˌfōs\ vb

**met·a·phor** \'metə,fòr, -fər\ n : use of a word denoting one kind of object or idea in place of another to suggest a likeness between them — **met·a·phor·i·cal** \ˌmetə'fòrikəl\ adj

**meta·phys·ics** \ˌmetə'fiziks\ n : study of the causes and nature of things — **meta·phys·i·cal** \-'fizikəl\ adj

**mete** \'mēt\ vb **met·ed; met·ing** : allot

**me·te·or** \'mētēər, -ē,òr\ n : small body that produces a streak of light as it burns up in the atmosphere

**me·te·or·ic** \ˌmētē'òrik\ adj 1 : relating to a meteor 2 : sudden and spectacular — **me·te·or·i·cal·ly** \-iklē\ adv

**me·te·or·ite** \'mētēə,rīt\ n : meteor that reaches the earth

**me·te·o·rol·o·gy** \ˌmētēə'räləjē\ n : science of weather — **me·te·o·ro·log·ic** \ˌmētē,òrə'läjik\, **me·te·o·ro·log·i·cal** \-'läjikəl\ adj — **me·te·o·rol·o·gist** \-ēə'räləjist\ n

¹**me·ter** \'mētər\ n : rhythm in verse or music

²**meter** n : unit of length equal to 39.37 inches

³**meter** n : measuring instrument

**meth·a·done** \'methə,dōn\ n : synthetic addictive narcotic

**meth·ane** \'meth,ān\ n : colorless odorless flammable gas

**meth·a·nol** \'methə,nól, -,nōl\ n : volatile flammable poisonous liquid

**meth·od** \'methəd\ n 1 : procedure for achieving an end 2 : orderly arrangement or plan — **me·thod·i·cal** \mə-'thädikəl\ adj — **me·thod·i·cal·ly** \-klē\ adv — **me·thod·i·cal·ness** n

**me·tic·u·lous** \mə'tikyələs\ adj : extremely careful in attending to details — **me·tic·u·lous·ly** adv — **me·tic·u·lous·ness** n

**met·ric** \'metrik\, **met·ri·cal** \-trikəl\ adj : relating to meter or the metric system — **met·ri·cal·ly** adv

**metric system** n : system of weights and measures using the meter and kilogram

**met·ro·nome** \'metrə,nōm\ n : instrument that ticks regularly to mark a beat in music

**me·trop·o·lis** \mə'träpələs\ n : major city — **met·ro·pol·i·tan** \ˌmetrə-'pälət'n\ adj

**met·tle** \'met'l\ n : spirit or courage — **met·tle·some** \-səm\ adj

**mez·za·nine** \'mez'n,ēn, ,mez'n'ēn\ n 1 : intermediate level between 2 main floors 2 : lowest balcony

**mez·zo·so·pra·no** \ˌmetsōsə'pranō, ,medz-\ n : voice between soprano and contralto

**mi·as·ma** \mī'azmə\ n 1 : noxious vapor 2 : harmful influence — **mi·as·mic** \-mik\ adj

**mi·ca** \'mīkə\ n : mineral separable into thin transparent sheets

**mice** pl of MOUSE

**mi·cro** \'mīkrō\ adj : very small

**mi·crobe** \'mī,krōb\ n : disease-causing microorganism — **mi·cro·bi·al** \mī-'krōbēəl\ adj

**mi·cro·bi·ol·o·gy** \ˌmīkrōbī'äləjē\ n : biology dealing with microscopic life — **mi·cro·bi·o·log·i·cal** \ˌmīkrō-,bīə'läjikəl\ adj — **mi·cro·bi·ol·o·gist** \ˌmīkrōbī'äləjist\ n

**mi·cro·com·put·er** \'mīkrōkəm,pyütər\ n : small computer that uses a microprocessor

**mi·cro·cosm** \'mīkrə,käzəm\ n : one thought of as a miniature universe

**mi·cro·film** \-,film\ n : small film recording printed matter — **microfilm** vb

**mi·crom·e·ter** \mī'krämətər\ n : instrument for measuring minute distances

**mi·cro·min·i·a·tur·ized** \ˌmīkrō-'minēəchə,rīzd, -'minichə-\ adj : reduced to a very small size — **mi·cro·min·i·a·tur·iza·tion** \-,minēə,chùrə'zāshən, -,mini,chùr-, -chər-\ n

**mi·cron** \'mī,krän\ n : one millionth of a meter

**mi·cro·or·gan·ism** \ˌmīkrō'òrgə,nizəm\ n : very tiny living thing

**mi·cro·phone** \'mīkrə,fōn\ n : instrument for changing sound waves into variations of an electric current

**mi·cro·pro·ces·sor** \'mīkrō,präsesər\ n : miniaturized computer processing unit on a single chip

**mi·cro·scope** \-,skōp\ n : optical device for magnifying tiny objects — **mi·cro·scop·ic** \ˌmīkrə'skäpik\ adj — **mi·cro·scop·i·cal·ly** adv — **mi·cros·co·py** \mī'kräskəpē\ n

**mi·cro·wave** \'mīkrə,wāv\ n 1 : short radio wave 2 : oven that cooks food using microwaves ~ vb : heat or cook in a microwave oven — **mi·cro·wav·able, mi·cro·wave·able** \ˌmīkrə-ˈwāvəbəl\ *adj*

**mid** \ˈmid\ *adj* : middle — **mid·point** *n* — **mid·stream** *n* — **mid·sum·mer** *n* — **mid·town** *n or adj* — **mid·week** *n* — **mid·win·ter** *n* — **mid·year** *n*

**mid·air** *n* : a point in the air well above the ground

**mid·day** *n* : noon

**mid·dle** \ˈmidᵊl\ *adj* 1 : equally distant from the extremes 2 : being at neither extreme ~ *n* : middle part or point

**Middle Ages** *n pl* : period from about A.D. 500 to about 1500

**mid·dle·man** \-ˌman\ *n* : dealer or agent between the producer and consumer

**mid·dling** \ˈmidliŋ, -lən\ *adj* 1 : of middle or medium size, degree, or quality 2 : mediocre

**midge** \ˈmij\ *n* : very tiny fly

**midg·et** \ˈmijət\ *n* : very small person or thing

**mid·land** \ˈmidlənd, -ˌland\ *n* : interior of a country

**mid·most** *adj* : being nearest the middle — **midmost** *adv*

**mid·night** *n* : 12 o'clock at night

**mid·riff** \ˈmidˌrif\ *n* : mid-region of the torso

**mid·ship·man** \ˈmidˌshipmən, ˌmid-ˈship-\ *n* : student naval officer

**midst** \ˈmidst\ *n* : position close to or surrounded by others — **midst** *prep*

**mid·way** \ˈmidˌwā\ *n* : concessions and amusements at a carnival ~ *adv* : in the middle

**mid·wife** \ˈmidˌwīf\ *n* : person who aids at childbirth — **mid·wife·ry** \midˈwifərē, -ˈwīf-\ *n*

**mien** \ˈmēn\ *n* : appearance

**miff** \ˈmif\ *vb* : upset or peeve

¹**might** \ˈmīt\ *past of* MAY — used to express permission or possibility or as a polite alternative to *may*

²**might** *n* : power or resources

**mighty** \ˈmītē\ *adj* **might·i·er; -est** 1 : very strong 2 : great — **might·i·ly** *adv* — **might·i·ness** *n* — **mighty** *adv*

**mi·graine** \ˈmīˌgrān\ *n* : severe headache often with nausea

**mi·grant** \ˈmīgrənt\ *n* : one who moves frequently to find work

**mi·grate** \ˈmīˌgrāt\ *vb* **-grat·ed; -grating** 1 : move from one place to another 2 : pass periodically from one region or climate to another — **mi-**

**gra·tion** \mīˈgrāshən\ *n* — **mi·gra·to·ry** \ˈmīgrəˌtōrē\ *adj*

**mild** \ˈmīld\ *adj* 1 : gentle in nature or behavior 2 : moderate in action or effect — **mild·ly** *adv* — **mild·ness** *n*

**mil·dew** \ˈmilˌdü, -ˌdyü\ *n* : whitish fungal growth — **mildew** *vb*

**mile** \ˈmīl\ *n* : unit of length equal to 5280 feet

**mile·age** \ˈmīlij\ *n* 1 : allowance per mile for traveling expenses 2 : amount or rate of use expressed in miles

**mile·stone** *n* : significant point in development

**mi·lieu** \mēlˈyü, -ˈyœ̄\ *n, pl* **-lieus** or **-lieux** \-ˈyüz, -ˈyœ̄\ : surroundings or setting

**mil·i·tant** \ˈmilətənt\ *adj* : aggressively active or hostile — **mil·i·tan·cy** \-tənsē\ *n* — **militant** *n* — **mil·i·tant·ly** *adv*

**mil·i·ta·rism** \ˈmilətəˌrizəm\ *n* : dominance of military ideals or of a policy of aggressive readiness for war — **mil·i·ta·rist** \-rist\ *n* — **mil·i·ta·ris·tic** \ˌmilətəˈristik\ *adj*

**mil·i·tary** \ˈmiləˌterē\ *adj* 1 : relating to soldiers, arms, or war 2 : relating to or performed by armed forces — ~ *n* : armed forces or the people in them — **mil·i·tar·i·ly** \ˌmiləˈterəlē\ *adv*

**mil·i·tate** \-ˌtāt\ *vb* **-tat·ed; -tat·ing** : have an effect

**mi·li·tia** \məˈlishə\ *n* : civilian soldiers — **mi·li·tia·man** \-mən\ *n*

**milk** \ˈmilk\ *n* : white nutritive fluid secreted by female mammals for feeding their young ~ *vb* 1 : draw off the milk of 2 : draw something from as if by milking — **milk·er** *n* — **milk·i·ness** \-ēnəs\ *n* — **milky** *adj*

**milk·man** \-ˌman, -mən\ *n* : man who sells or delivers milk

**milk·weed** *n* : herb with milky juice

¹**mill** \ˈmil\ *n* 1 : building in which grain is ground into flour 2 : manufacturing plant 3 : machine used esp. for forming or processing ~ *vb* 1 : subject to a process in a mill 2 : move in a circle — **mill·er** *n*

²**mill** *n* : ¹⁄₁₀ cent

**mil·len·ni·um** \məˈlenēəm\ *n, pl* **-nia** \-ēə\ or **-niums** : a period of 1000 years

**mil·let** \ˈmilət\ *n* : cereal and forage grass with small seeds

**mil·li·gram** \ˈmiləˌgram\ *n* : ¹⁄₁₀₀₀ gram

**mil·li·li·ter** \-ₗlētər\ n : ¹⁄₁₀₀₀ liter

**mil·li·me·ter** \-ₗmētər\ : ¹⁄₁₀₀₀ meter

**mil·li·ner** \'milənər\ n : person who makes or sells women's hats — **mil·li·nery** \'miləₙnerē\ n

**mil·lion** \'milyən\ n, pl **millions** or **million** : 1000 thousands — **million** adj — **mil·lionth** \-yənth\ adj or n

**mil·lion·aire** \ₘmilyə'nar, 'milyəₙnar\ n : person worth a million or more (as of dollars)

**mil·li·pede** \'miləₚpēd\ n : longbodied arthropod with 2 pairs of legs on most segments

**mill·stone** n : either of 2 round flat stones used for grinding grain

**mime** \'mīm\ n 1 : mimic 2 : pantomime — **mime** vb

**mim·eo·graph** \'mimēəₚgraf\ n : machine for making many stencil copies — **mimeograph** vb

**mim·ic** \'mimik\ n : one that mimics ~ vb **-icked; -ick·ing** 1 : imitate closely 2 : ridicule by imitation — **mim·ic·ry** \'mimikrē\ n

**min·a·ret** \ₘminə'ret\ n : tower attached to a mosque

**mince** \'mins\ vb **minced; minc·ing** 1 : cut into small pieces 2 : choose (one's words) carefully 3 : walk in a prim affected manner

**mind** \'mīnd\ n 1 : memory 2 : the part of an individual that feels, perceives, and esp. reasons 3 : intention 4 : normal mental condition 5 : opinion 6 : intellectual ability ~ vb 1 : attend to 2 : obey 3 : be concerned about 4 : be careful — **mind·ed** adj — **mindless** \'mīndləs\ adj — **mind·less·ly** adv — **mind·less·ness** n

**mind·ful** \-fəl\ adj : aware or attentive — **mind·ful·ly** adv — **mind·ful·ness** n

¹**mine** \'mīn\ pron : that which belongs to me

²**mine** \'mīn\ n 1 : excavation from which minerals are taken 2 : explosive device placed in the ground or water for destroying enemy vehicles or vessels that later pass ~ vb **mined; min·ing** 1 : get ore from 2 : place military mines in — **minefield** n — **min·er** n

**min·er·al** \'minərəl\ n 1 : crystalline substance not of organic origin 2 : useful natural substance (as coal) obtained from the ground — **mineral** adj

**min·er·al·o·gy** \ₘminə'räləjē, -'ral-\ n : science dealing with minerals — **min·er·al·og·i·cal** \ₘminərə'läjikəl\ adj — **min·er·al·o·gist** \ₘminə'räləjist, -'ral-\ n

**min·gle** \'miŋgəl\ vb **-gled; -gling** : bring together or mix

**mini-** comb form : miniature or of small dimensions

**min·ia·ture** \'minēəₚchúr, 'miniₚchúr, -chər\ n : tiny copy or very small version — **miniature** adj — **min·ia·tur·ist** \-ₚchúrist, -chər-\ n — **min·ia·tur·ize** \-ēəchəₚrīz, -ichə-\ vb

**mini·bike** \'minēₚbīk\ n : small motorcycle

**mini·bus** \-ₚbəs\ n : small bus

**mini·com·put·er** \-kəmₚpyütər\ n : computer intermediate between a mainframe and a microcomputer in size and speed

**mini·course** \-ₚkōrs\ n : short course of study

**min·i·mal** \'minəməl\ adj : relating to or being a minimum — **min·i·mal·ly** adv

**min·i·mize** \'minəₚmīz\ vb **-mized; -miz·ing** 1 : reduce to a minimum 2 : underestimate intentionally

**min·i·mum** \'minəməm\ n, pl **-ma** \-mə\ or **-mums** : lowest quantity or amount — **minimum** adj

**min·ion** \'minyən\ n 1 : servile dependent 2 : subordinate official

**mini·se·ries** \'minēₚsirēz\ n : television story in several parts

**mini·skirt** \-ₚskərt\ n : very short skirt

**min·is·ter** \'minəstər\ n 1 : Protestant member of the clergy 2 : high officer of state 3 : diplomatic representative ~ vb : give aid or service — **min·is·te·ri·al** \ₘminə'stirēəl\ adj — **min·is·tra·tion** n

**min·is·try** \'minəstrē\ n, pl **-tries** 1 : office or duties of a minister 2 : body of ministers 3 : government department headed by a minister

**mini·van** \'minēₚvan\ n : small van

**mink** \'miŋk\ n, pl **mink** or **minks** : weasellike mammal or its soft brown fur

**min·now** \'minō\ n, pl **-nows** : small freshwater fish

**mi·nor** \'mīnər\ adj 1 : less in size, importance, or value 2 : not serious ~ n 1 : person not yet of legal age 2 : secondary field of academic specialization

**mi·nor·i·ty** \mə'nórətē, mī-\ n, pl

**-ties 1** : time or state of being a minor **2** : smaller number (as of votes) **3** : part of a population differing from others (as in race or religion)

**min·strel** \'minstrəl\ *n* **1** : medieval singer of verses **2** : performer in a program usu. of black American songs and jokes — **min·strel·sy** \-sē\ *n*

**¹mint** \'mint\ *n* **1** : fragrant herb that yields a flavoring oil **2** : mint-flavored piece of candy — **minty** *adj*

**²mint** *n* **1** : place where coins are made **2** : vast sum ~ *adj* : unused — **mint** *vb* — **mint·er** *n*

**min·u·et** \,minyə'wet\ *n* : slow graceful dance

**mi·nus** \'mīnəs\ *prep* **1** : diminished by **2** : lacking ~ *n* : negative quantity or quality

**mi·nus·cule** \'minəs,kyül, min'əs-, min·is·cule \'minəs-\ *adj* : very small

**¹min·ute** \'minət\ *n* **1** : 60th part of an hour or of a degree **2** : short time **3** *pl* : official record of a meeting

**²mi·nute** \mī'nüt, mə-, -'nyüt\ *adj* -**nut·er**; -**est 1** : very small **2** : marked by close attention to details — **mi·nute·ly** *adv* — **mi·nute·ness** *n*

**mir·a·cle** \'mirikəl\ *n* **1** : extraordinary event taken as a sign of divine intervention in human affairs **2** : marvel — **mi·rac·u·lous** \mə'rakyələs\ *adj* — **mi·rac·u·lous·ly** *adv*

**mi·rage** \mə'räzh\ *n* : distant illusion caused by atmospheric conditions (as in the desert)

**mire** \'mīr\ *n* : heavy deep mud ~ *vb* **mired; mir·ing** : stick or sink in mire — **miry** *adj*

**mir·ror** \'mirər\ *n* : smooth surface (as of glass) that reflects images ~ *vb* : reflect in or as if in a mirror

**mirth** \'mərth\ *n* : gladness and laughter — **mirth·ful** \-fəl\ *adj* — **mirth·ful·ly** *adv* — **mirth·ful·ness** *n* — **mirth·less** *adj*

**mis·an·thrope** \'misᵊn,thrōp\ *n* : one who hates mankind — **mis·an·throp·ic** \,misᵊn'thräpik\ *adj* — **mis·an·thro·py** \mis'anthrəpē\ *n*

**mis·ap·pre·hend** \,mis,aprə'hend\ *vb* : misunderstand — **mis·ap·pre·hen·sion** *n*

**mis·ap·pro·pri·ate** \,misə'prōprē,āt\ *vb* : take dishonestly for one's own use — **mis·ap·pro·pri·a·tion** *n*

**mis·be·got·ten** \-bi'gät²n\ *adj* **1** : illegitimate **2** : ill-conceived

**mis·be·have** \,misbi'hāv\ *vb* : behave improperly — **mis·be·hav·er** *n* — **mis·be·hav·ior** *n*

**mis·cal·cu·late** \mis'kalkyə,lāt\ *vb* : calculate wrongly — **mis·cal·cu·la·tion** *n*

**mis·car·ry** \mis'karē, 'mis,karē\ *vb* **1** : give birth prematurely before the fetus can survive **2** : go wrong or be unsuccessful — **mis·car·riage** \-rij\ *n*

**mis·ce·ge·na·tion** \mis,ejə'nāshən, ,misijə'nā-\ *n* : marriage between persons of different races

**mis·cel·la·neous** \,misə'lānēəs\ *adj* : consisting of many things of different kinds — **mis·cel·la·neous·ly** *adv* — **mis·cel·la·neous·ness** *n*

**mis·cel·la·ny** \'misə,lānē\ *n, pl* **-nies** : collection of various things

**mis·chance** \mis'chans\ *n* : bad luck

**mis·chief** \'mischəf\ *n* : conduct esp. of a child that annoys or causes minor damage

**mis·chie·vous** \'mischəvəs\ *adj* **1** : causing annoyance or minor injury **2** : irresponsibly playful — **mis·chie·vous·ly** *adv* — **mis·chie·vous·ness** *n*

**mis·con·ceive** \,miskən'sēv\ *vb* : interpret incorrectly — **mis·con·cep·tion** *n*

**mis·con·duct** \mis'kändəkt\ *n* **1** : mismanagement **2** : bad behavior

**mis·con·strue** \,miskən'strü\ *vb* : misinterpret — **mis·con·struc·tion** *n*

**mis·cre·ant** \'miskrēənt\ *n* : one who behaves criminally or viciously — **miscreant** *adj*

**mis·deed** \mis'dēd\ *n* : wrong deed

**mis·de·mean·or** \,misdi'mēnər\ *n* : crime less serious than a felony

**mi·ser** \'mīzər\ *n* : person who hoards and is stingy with money — **mi·ser·li·ness** \-lēnəs\ *n* — **mi·ser·ly** *adj*

**mis·er·a·ble** \'mizərəbəl\ *adj* **1** : wretchedly deficient **2** : causing extreme discomfort **3** : shameful — **mis·er·a·ble·ness** *n* — **mis·er·a·bly** \-blē\ *adv*

**mis·ery** \'mizərē\ *n, pl* **-er·ies** : suffering and want caused by distress or poverty

**mis·fire** \mis'fīr\ *vb* **1** : fail to fire **2** : miss an intended effect — **mis·fire** \'mis,fīr\ *n*

**mis·fit** \'mis,fit, mis'fit\ *n* : person poorly adjusted to his environment

**mis·for·tune** \mis'fȯrchən\ n **1** : bad luck **2** : unfortunate condition or event

**mis·giv·ing** \mis'giviŋ\ n : doubt or concern

**mis·guid·ed** \mis'gīdəd\ adj : mistaken, uninformed, or deceived

**mis·hap** \'mis,hap\ n : accident

**mis·in·form** \,mis°n'fȯrm\ vb : give wrong information to — **mis·in·for·ma·tion** \,mis,infər'māshən\ n

**mis·in·ter·pret** \,mis°n'tərprət\ vb : understand or explain wrongly — **mis·in·ter·pre·ta·tion** \-,tərprə'tāshən\ n

**mis·judge** \mis'jəj\ vb : judge incorrectly or unjustly — **mis·judg·ment** n

**mis·lay** \mis'lā\ vb -laid; -lay·ing : misplace

**mis·lead** \mis'lēd\ vb -led; -lead·ing : lead in a wrong direction or into error — **mis·lead·ing·ly** adv

**mis·man·age** \mis'manij\ vb : manage badly — **mis·man·age·ment** n

**mis·no·mer** \mis'nōmər\ n : wrong name

**mi·sog·y·nist** \mə'säjənist\ n : one who hates or distrusts women — **mi·sog·y·nis·tic** \mə,säjə'nistik\ adj — **mi·sog·y·ny** \-nē\ n

**mis·place** \mis'plās\ vb : put in a wrong or unremembered place

**mis·print** \'mis,print, mis'-\ n : error in printed matter

**mis·pro·nounce** \,misprə'na٨ns\ vb : pronounce incorrectly — **mis·pro·nun·ci·a·tion** n

**mis·quote** \mis'kwōt\ vb : quote incorrectly — **mis·quo·ta·tion** \,miskwō'tāshən\ n

**mis·read** \mis'rēd\ vb -read; -read·ing : read or interpret incorrectly

**mis·rep·re·sent** \,mis,repri'zent\ vb : represent falsely or unfairly — **mis·rep·re·sen·ta·tion** n

**mis·rule** \mis'rül\ vb : govern badly ~ n **1** : bad or corrupt government **2** : disorder

¹**miss** \'mis\ vb **1** : fail to hit, reach, or contact **2** : notice the absence of **3** : fail to obtain **4** : avoid **5** : omit — **miss** n

²**miss** n : young unmarried woman or girl — often used as a title

**mis·sal** \'misəl\ n : book containing what is said at mass during the year

**mis·shap·en** \mis'shāpən\ adj : distorted

**mis·sile** \'misəl\ n : object (as a stone or rocket) thrown or shot

**miss·ing** \'misiŋ\ adj : absent or lost

**mis·sion** \'mishən\ n **1** : ministry sent by a church to spread its teaching **2** : group of diplomats sent to a foreign country **3** : task

**mis·sion·ary** \'mishə,nerē\ adj : relating to religious missions ~ n, pl **-ar·ies** : person sent to spread religious faith

**mis·sive** \'misiv\ n : letter

**mis·spell** \mis'spel\ vb : spell incorrectly — **mis·spell·ing** n

**mis·state** \mis'stāt\ vb : state incorrectly — **mis·state·ment** n

**mis·step** \'mis,step\ n **1** : wrong step **2** : mistake

**mist** \'mist\ n : particles of water falling as fine rain

**mis·take** \mə'stāk\ n **1** : misunderstanding or wrong belief **2** : wrong action or statement — **mistake** vb

**mis·tak·en** \-'stākən\ adj : having a wrong opinion or incorrect information — **mis·tak·en·ly** adv

**mis·ter** \'mistər\ n : sir — used without a name in addressing a man

**mis·tle·toe** \'misəl,tō\ n : parasitic green shrub with waxy white berries

**mis·treat** \mis'trēt\ vb : treat badly — **mis·treat·ment** n

**mis·tress** \'mistrəs\ n **1** : woman in control **2** : a woman not his wife with whom a married man has recurrent sexual relations

**mis·tri·al** \mis'trīəl\ n : trial that has no legal effect

**mis·trust** \-'trəst\ n : lack of confidence ~ vb : have no confidence in — **mis·trust·ful** \-fəl\ adj — **mis·trust·ful·ly** adv — **mis·trust·ful·ness** n

**misty** \'mistē\ adj mist·i·er; -est **1** : obscured by mist **2** : tearful — **mist·i·ly** adv — **mist·i·ness** n

**mis·un·der·stand** \,mis,əndər'stand\ vb **1** : fail to understand **2** : interpret incorrectly

**mis·un·der·stand·ing** \-'standiŋ\ n **1** : wrong interpretation **2** : disagreement

**mis·use** \mis'yüz\ vb **1** : use incorrectly **2** : mistreat — **mis·use** \-'yüs\ n

**mite** \'mīt\ n **1** : tiny spiderlike animal **2** : small amount

**mi·ter, mi·tre** \'mītər\ n **1** : bishop's headdress **2** : angular joint in wood

~ vb **-tered** or **-tred; -ter·ing** or **-tring** \'mītəriŋ\ : bevel the ends of for a miter joint

**mit·i·gate** \'mitə,gāt\ vb **-gat·ed; -gat·ing** : make less severe — **mit·i·ga·tion** \,mitə'gāshən\ n — **mit·i·ga·tive** \'mitə,gātiv\ adj

**mi·to·sis** \mī'tōsəs\ n, pl **-to·ses** \-,sēz\ : process of forming 2 cell nuclei from one — **mi·tot·ic** \-'tätik\ adj

**mitt** \'mit\ n : mittenlike baseball glove

**mit·ten** \'mit°n\ n : hand covering without finger sections

**mix** \'miks\ vb : combine or join into one mass or group ~ n : commercially prepared food mixture — **mix·able** adj — **mix·er** n — **mix up** vb : confuse

**mix·ture** \'mikschər\ n : act or product of mixing

**mix–up** n : instance of confusion

**mne·mon·ic** \ni'mänik\ adj : relating to or assisting memory

**moan** \'mōn\ n : low prolonged sound of pain or grief — **moan** vb

**moat** \'mōt\ n : deep wide trench around a castle

**mob** \'mäb\ n 1 : large disorderly crowd 2 : criminal gang ~ vb **-bb-** : crowd around and attack or annoy

**mo·bile** \'mōbəl, -,bēl, -,bīl\ adj : capable of moving or being moved ~ \'mō,bēl\ n : suspended art construction with freely moving parts — **mo·bil·i·ty** \mō'bilətē\ n

**mo·bi·lize** \'mōbə,līz\ vb **-lized; -liz·ing** : assemble and make ready for war duty — **mo·bi·li·za·tion** \,mōbələ-'zāshən\ n

**moc·ca·sin** \'mäkəsən\ n 1 : heelless shoe 2 : venomous U.S. snake

**mo·cha** \'mōkə\ n 1 : mixture of coffee and chocolate 2 : dark brown color

**mock** \'mäk, 'mȯk\ vb 1 : ridicule 2 : mimic in derision ~ adj 1 : simulated 2 : phony — **mock·er** n — **mock·ery** \-ərē\ n — **mock·ing·ly** adv

**mock·ing·bird** \'mäkiŋ,bərd, 'mȯk-\ n : songbird that mimics other birds

**mode** \'mōd\ n 1 : particular form or variety 2 : style — **mod·al** \-°l\ adj — **mod·ish** \'mōdish\ adj

**mod·el** \'mäd°l\ n 1 : structural design 2 : miniature representation 3 : something worthy of copying 4 : one who poses for an artist or displays clothes

5 : type or design ~ vb **-eled** or **-elled; -el·ing** or **-el·ling** 1 : shape 2 : work as a model ~ adj 1 : serving as a pattern 2 : being a miniature representation of

**mo·dem** \'mōdəm, -,dem\ n : device by which a computer communicates with another computer over telephone lines

**mod·er·ate** \'mädərət\ adj : avoiding extremes ~ \'mädə,rāt\ vb **-at·ed; -at·ing** 1 : lessen the intensity of 2 : act as a moderator — **moderate** n — **mod·er·ate·ly** adv — **mod·er·ate·ness** n — **mod·er·a·tion** \,mädə-'rāshən\ n

**mod·er·a·tor** \'mädə,rātər\ n : one who presides

**mod·ern** \'mädərn\ adj : relating to or characteristic of the present — **modern** n — **mo·der·ni·ty** \mə-'dərnətē\ n — **mod·ern·i·za·tion** \,mädərnə'zāshən\ n — **mod·ern·ize** \'mädər,nīz\ vb — **mod·ern·iz·er** \'mädər-,nīzər\ n — **mod·ern·ly** adv — **mod·ern·ness** n

**mod·est** \'mädəst\ adj 1 : having a moderate estimate of oneself 2 : reserved or decent in thoughts or actions 3 : limited in size, amount, or aim — **mod·est·ly** adv — **mod·es·ty** \-əstē\ n

**mod·i·cum** \'mädikəm\ n : small amount

**mod·i·fy** \'mädə,fī\ vb **-fied; -fy·ing** 1 : limit the meaning of 2 : change — **mod·i·fi·ca·tion** \,mädəfə'kāshən\ n — **mod·i·fi·er** \'mädə,fīər\ n

**mod·u·lar** \'mäjələr\ adj : built with standardized units — **mod·u·lar·ized** \-lə,rīzd\ adj

**mod·u·late** \'mäjə,lāt\ vb **-lat·ed; -lat·ing** 1 : keep in proper measure or proportion 2 : vary a radio wave — **mod·u·la·tion** \,mäjə'lāshən\ n — **mod·u·la·tor** \'mäjə,lātər\ n — **mod·u·la·to·ry** \-lə,tōrē\ adj

**mod·ule** \'mäjül\ n : standardized unit

**mo·gul** \'mōgəl\ n : important person

**mo·hair** \'mō,har\ n : fabric made from the hair of the Angora goat

**moist** \'mȯist\ adj : slightly or moderately wet — **moist·en** \'mȯis°n\ vb — **moist·en·er** \'mȯis°nər\ n — **moist·ly** adv — **moist·ness** n

**mois·ture** \'mȯischər\ n : small amount of liquid that causes damp-

ness — **mois·tur·ize** \-chə₁rīz\ *vb*
— **mois·tur·iz·er** *n*

**mo·lar** \'mōlər\ *n* : grinding tooth —
**molar** *adj*

**mo·las·ses** \mə'lasəz\ *n* : thick brown
syrup from raw sugar

¹**mold** \'mōld\ *n* : crumbly organic soil

²**mold** *n* : frame or cavity for forming ~
*vb* : shape in or as if in a mold —
**mold·er** *n*

³**mold** *n* : surface growth of fungus ~ *vb*
: become moldy — **mold·i·ness**
\'mōldēnəs\ *n* — **moldy** *adj*

**mold·er** \'mōldər\ *vb* : crumble

**mold·ing** \'mōldiŋ\ *n* : decorative surface, plane, or strip

¹**mole** \'mōl\ *n* : spot on the skin

²**mole** *n* : small burrowing mammal —
**mole·hill** *n*

**mol·e·cule** \'mäli₁kyül\ *n* : small particle of matter — **mo·lec·u·lar**
\mə'lekyələr\ *adj*

**mole·skin** \-₁skin\ *n* : heavy cotton
fabric

**mo·lest** \mə'lest\ *vb* **1** : annoy or disturb **2** : force physical and usu. sexual contact on — **mo·les·ta·tion**
\₁mōl₁es'tāshən, ₁mäl-\ *n* — **mo-
lest·er** *n*

**mol·li·fy** \'mälə₁fī\ *vb* **-fied; -fy·ing**
: soothe in temper — **mol·li·fi·ca-
tion** \₁mäləfə'kāshən\ *n*

**mol·lusk, mol·lusc** \'mäləsk\ *n* : shelled
aquatic invertebrate — **mol·lus·can**
\mə'ləskən\ *adj*

**mol·ly·cod·dle** \'mälē₁käd³l\ *vb* **-dled;
-dling** : pamper

**molt** \'mōlt\ *vb* : shed hair, feathers,
outer skin, or horns periodically —
**molt** *n* — **molt·er** *n*

**mol·ten** \'mōlt³n\ *adj* : fused or lique-
fied by heat

**mom** \'mäm, 'məm\ *n* : mother

**mo·ment** \'mōmənt\ *n* **1** : tiny portion
of time **2** : time of excellence **3** : importance

**mo·men·tar·i·ly** \₁mōmən'terəlē\ *adv*
**1** : for a moment **2** : at any moment

**mo·men·tary** \'mōmən₁terē\ *adj*
: continuing only a moment — **mo-
men·tar·i·ness** *n*

**mo·men·tous** \mō'mentəs\ *adj* : very
important — **mo·men·tous·ly** *adv* —
**mo·men·tous·ness** *n*

**mo·men·tum** \-əm\ *n*, *pl* **-ta** \-ə\ *or*
**-tums** : force of a moving body

**mon·arch** \'mänərk, -₁ärk\ *n* : ruler of

a kingdom or empire — **mo·nar·chi-
cal** \mə'närkikəl\ *adj*

**mon·ar·chist** \'mänərkist\ *n* : believer
in monarchical government — **mon-
ar·chism** \-₁kizəm\ *n*

**mon·ar·chy** \'mänərkē\ *n*, *pl* **-chies**
: realm of a monarch

**mon·as·tery** \'mänə₁sterē\ *n*, *pl* **-ter-
ies** : house for monks

**mo·nas·tic** \mə'nastik\ *adj* : relating
to monasteries, monks, or nuns — **monastic** *n* — **mo·nas·ti·cal·ly** \-tiklē\
*adv* — **mo·nas·ti·cism** \-tə₁sizəm\ *n*

**Mon·day** \'məndā, -dē\ *n* : 2d day of
the week

**mon·e·tary** \'mänə₁terē, 'mən-\ *adj*
: relating to money

**mon·ey** \'mənē\ *n*, *pl* **-eys** *or* **-ies**
\'mənēz\ **1** : something (as coins or
paper currency) used in buying **2**
: wealth — **mon·eyed** \-ēd\ *adj* —
**mon·ey·lend·er** *n*

**mon·ger** \'məŋgər, 'mäŋ-\ *n* : dealer

**mon·gol·ism** \'mäŋgə₁lizəm\ *n* : con-
genital mental retardation — **Mon-
gol·oid** \-gə₁lȯid\ *adj or n*

**mon·goose** \'män₁güs, 'mäŋ-\ *n*, *pl*
**-goos·es** : small agile mammal esp.
of India

**mon·grel** \'mäŋgrəl, 'məŋ-\ *n* : offspring of mixed breed

**mon·i·tor** \'mänətər\ *n* **1** : student assistant **2** : television screen ~ *vb*
: watch or observe esp. for quality

**monk** \'məŋk\ *n* : member of a religious order living in a monastery —
**monk·ish** *adj*

**mon·key** \'məŋkē\ *n*, *pl* **-keys** : small
long-tailed arboreal primate ~ *vb* **1**
: fool **2** : tamper

**mon·key·shines** \-₁shīnz\ *n pl* : pranks

**monks·hood** \'məŋks₁hùd\ *n* : poisonous herb with showy flowers

**mon·o·cle** \'mänikəl\ *n* : eyeglass for
one eye

**mo·nog·a·my** \mə'nägəmē\ *n* **1**
: marriage with one person at a time
**2** : practice of having a single mate
for a period of time — **mo·nog·a-
mist** \mə'nägəmist\ *n* — **mo·nog-
a·mous** \-məs\ *adj*

**mono·gram** \'mänə₁gram\ *n* : sign of
identity made of initials — **mono-
gram** *vb*

**mono·graph** \-₁graf\ *n* : learned trea-
tise

**mono·lin·gual** \₁mänə'liŋgwəl\ *adj*
: using only one language

**mono·lith** \'mänᵊl,ith\ n 1 : single great stone 2 : single uniform massive whole — **mono·lith·ic** \,mänᵊl-'ithik\ adj

**mono·logue** \'mänᵊl,óg\ n : long speech — **mono·logu·ist** \-,ógist\, **mo·no·lo·gist** \mə'näləjist, 'mänᵊl-,ógist\ n

**mono·nu·cle·o·sis** \,mänō,nüklē'ōsəs, -,nyü-\ n : acute infectious disease

**mo·nop·o·ly** \mə'näpəlē\ n, pl **-lies** 1 : exclusive ownership or control of a commodity 2 : one controlling a monopoly — **mo·nop·o·list** \-list\ n — **mo·nop·o·lis·tic** \mə,näpə'listik\ adj — **mo·nop·o·li·za·tion** \-lə-'zāshən\ n — **mo·nop·o·lize** \mə-'näpə,līz\ vb

**mono·rail** \'mänə,rāl\ n : single rail for a vehicle or a vehicle or system using it

**mono·syl·lab·ic** \,mänəsə'labik\ adj : consisting of or using words of only one syllable — **mono·syl·la·ble** \'mänə,siləbəl\ n

**mono·the·ism** \'mänōthē,izəm\ n : doctrine or belief that there is only one deity — **mono·the·ist** \-,thēist\ n — **mono·the·is·tic** \,mänōthē-'istik\ adj

**mono·tone** \'mänə,tōn\ n : succession of words in one unvarying tone

**mo·not·o·nous** \mə'nätᵊnəs\ adj 1 : sounded in one unvarying tone 2 : tediously uniform — **mo·not·o·nous·ly** adv — **mo·not·o·nous·ness** n — **mo·not·o·ny** \-ᵊnē\ n

**mon·ox·ide** \mə'näk,sīd\ n : oxide containing one atom of oxygen in a molecule

**mon·sieur** \məs'yər, məsh-\ n, pl **mes·sieurs** \-yərz, mā'syərz\ : man of high rank or station — used as a title for a man esp. of French nationality

**mon·si·gnor** \män'sēnyər\ n, pl **mon·si·gnors** or **mon·si·gno·ri** \,män-,sēn'yōrē\ : Roman Catholic prelate — used as a title

**mon·soon** \män'sün\ n : periodic rainy season

**mon·ster** \'mänstər\ n 1 : abnormal or terrifying animal 2 : ugly, wicked, or cruel person — **mon·stros·i·ty** \män'sträsətē\ n — **mon·strous** \'mänstrəs\ adj — **mon·strous·ly** adv

**mon·tage** \män'täzh\ n : artistic composition of several different elements

**month** \'mənth\ n : 12th part of a year — **month·ly** adv or adj or n

**mon·u·ment** \'mänyəmənt\ n : structure erected in remembrance

**mon·u·men·tal** \,mänyə'mentᵊl\ adj 1 : serving as a monument 2 : outstanding 3 : very great — **mon·u·men·tal·ly** adv

**moo** \'mü\ vb : make the noise of a cow — **moo** n

**mood** \'müd\ n : state of mind or emotion

**moody** \'müdē\ adj **mood·i·er; -est** 1 : sad 2 : subject to changing moods and esp. to bad moods — **mood·i·ly** \'müdᵊlē\ adv — **mood·i·ness** \-ēnəs\ n

**moon** \'mün\ n : natural satellite (as of earth) — **moon·beam** n — **moon·light** n — **moon·lit** adj

**moon·light** \-,līt\ vb **-ed; -ing** : hold a 2d job — **moon·light·er** n

**moon·shine** n 1 : moonlight 2 : meaningless talk 3 : illegally distilled liquor

¹**moor** \'mùr\ n : open usu. swampy wasteland — **moor·land** \-lənd, -,land\ n

²**moor** vb : fasten with line or anchor

**moor·ing** \-iŋ\ n : place where boat can be moored

**moose** \'müs\ n, pl **moose** : large heavy-antlered deer

**moot** \'müt\ adj : open to question

**mop** \'mäp\ n : floor-cleaning implement ~ vb **-pp-** : use a mop on

**mope** \'mōp\ vb **moped; mop·ing** : be sad or listless

**mo·ped** \'mō,ped\ n : low-powered motorbike

**mo·raine** \mə'rān\ n : glacial deposit of earth and stones

**mor·al** \'mórəl\ adj 1 : relating to principles of right and wrong 2 : conforming to a standard of right behavior 3 : relating to or acting on the mind, character, or will ~ n 1 : point of a story 2 pl : moral practices or teachings — **mor·al·ist** \'mórəlist\ n — **mor·al·is·tic** \,mórə'listik\ adj — **mor·al·i·ty** \mə'ralətē\ n — **mor·al·ize** \'mórə,līz\ vb — **mor·al·ly** adv

**mo·rale** \mə'ral\ n : emotional attitude

**mo·rass** \mə'ras\ n : swamp

**mor·a·to·ri·um** \,mórə'tōrēəm\ n, pl **-ri·ums** or **-ria** \-ēə\ : suspension of activity

**mo·ray** \'mór,ā, mə'rā\ n : savage eel

**mor·bid** \\'mórbəd\ *adj* **1** : relating to disease **2** : gruesome — **mor·bid·i·ty** \mór'bidətē\ *n* — **mor·bid·ly** *adv* — **mor·bid·ness** *n*

**mor·dant** \\'mórd°nt\ *adj* : sarcastic — **mor·dant·ly** *adv*

**more** \\'mōr\ *adj* **1** : greater **2** : additional ∼ *adv* **1** : in addition **2** : to a greater degree ∼ *n* **1** : greater quantity **2** : additional amount ∼ *pron* : additional ones

**mo·rel** \mə'rel\ *n* : pitted edible mushroom

**more·over** \mōr'ōvər\ *adv* : in addition

**mo·res** \\'mór,āz, -ēz\ *n pl* : customs

**morgue** \\'mórg\ *n* : temporary holding place for dead bodies

**mor·i·bund** \\'mórə,bənd\ *adj* : dying

**morn** \\'mórn\ *n* : morning

**morn·ing** \\'mórniŋ\ *n* : time from sunrise to noon

**mo·ron** \\'mōr,än\ *n* **1** : mentally retarded person **2** : very stupid person — **mo·ron·ic** \mə'ränik\ *adj* — **mo·ron·i·cal·ly** *adv*

**mo·rose** \mə'rōs\ *adj* : sullen — **mo·rose·ly** *adv* — **mo·rose·ness** *n*

**mor·phine** \\'mór,fēn\ *n* : addictive painkilling drug

**mor·row** \\'märō\ *n* : next day

**Morse code** \\'mórs-\ *n* : code of dots and dashes or long and short sounds used for transmitting messages

**mor·sel** \\'mórsəl\ *n* : small piece or quantity

**mor·tal** \\'mórt°l\ *adj* **1** : causing or subject to death **2** : extreme — **mortal** *n* — **mor·tal·i·ty** \mór'talətē\ *n* — **mor·tal·ly** \\'mórt°lē\ *adv*

**mor·tar** \\'mórtər\ *n* **1** : strong bowl **2** : short-barreled cannon **3** : masonry material used to cement bricks or stones in place — **mortar** *vb*

**mort·gage** \\'mórgij\ *n* : transfer of property rights as security for a loan — **mortgage** *vb* — **mort·gag·ee** \,mórgi'jē\ *n* — **mort·ga·gor** \,mórgi'jór\ *n*

**mor·ti·fy** \\'mórtə,fī\ *vb* **-fied; -fy·ing** **1** : subdue by abstinence or self-inflicted pain **2** : humiliate — **mor·ti·fi·ca·tion** \,mórtəfə'kāshən\ *n*

**mor·tu·ary** \\'mórchə,werē\ *n, pl* **-ar·ies** : place where dead bodies are kept until burial

**mo·sa·ic** \mō'zāik\ *n* : inlaid stone decoration — **mosaic** *adj*

**Mos·lem** \\'mäzləm\ *var of* MUSLIM

**mosque** \\'mäsk\ *n* : building where Muslims worship

**mos·qui·to** \mə'skētō\ *n, pl* **-toes** : biting bloodsucking insect

**moss** \\'mós\ *n* : green seedless plant — **mossy** *adj*

**most** \\'mōst\ *adj* **1** : majority of **2** : greatest ∼ *adv* : to the greatest or a very great degree ∼ *n* : greatest amount ∼ *pron* : greatest number or part

**-most** \,mōst\ *adj suffix* : most : most toward

**most·ly** \\'mōstlē\ *adv* : mainly

**mote** \\'mōt\ *n* : small particle

**mo·tel** \mō'tel\ *n* : hotel with rooms accessible from the parking lot

**moth** \\'móth\ *n* : small pale insect related to the butterflies

**moth·er** \\'məthər\ *n* **1** : female parent **2** : source ∼ *vb* **1** : give birth to **2** : cherish or protect — **moth·er·hood** \-,hùd\ *n* — **moth·er·land** \-,land\ *n* — **moth·er·less** *adj* — **moth·er·ly** *adj*

**moth·er–in–law** *n, pl* **mothers–in–law** : spouse's mother

**mo·tif** \mō'tēf\ *n* : dominant theme

**mo·tion** \\'mōshən\ *n* **1** : act or instance of moving **2** : proposal for action ∼ *vb* : direct by a movement — **mo·tion·less** *adj* — **mo·tion·less·ly** *adv* — **mo·tion·less·ness** *n*

**motion picture** *n* : movie

**mo·ti·vate** \\'mōtə,vāt\ *vb* **-vat·ed; -vat·ing** : provide with a motive — **mo·ti·va·tion** \,mōtə'vāshən\ *n* — **mo·ti·va·tor** \\'mōtə,vātər\ *n*

**mo·tive** \\'mōtiv\ *n* : cause of a person's action ∼ *adj* **1** : moving to action **2** : relating to motion — **mo·tive·less** *adj*

**mot·ley** \\'mätlē\ *adj* : of diverse colors or elements

**mo·tor** \\'mōtər\ *n* : unit that supplies power or motion ∼ *vb* : travel by automobile — **mo·tor·ist** \-ist\ *n* — **mo·tor·ize** \\'mōtə,rīz\ *vb*

**mo·tor·bike** *n* : lightweight motorcycle

**mo·tor·boat** *n* : engine-driven boat

**mo·tor·car** *n* : automobile

**mo·tor·cy·cle** *n* : 2-wheeled automotive vehicle — **mo·tor·cy·clist** *n*

**mo·tor·truck** *n* : automotive truck

**mot·tle** \\'mät°l\ *vb* **-tled; -tling** : mark with spots of different color

**mot·to** \\'mätō\ *n, pl* **-toes** : brief guiding rule

**mould** \'mōld\ *var of* MOLD

**mound** \'maůnd\ *n* : pile (as of earth)

¹**mount** \'maůnt\ *n* : mountain

²**mount** *vb* 1 : increase in amount 2 : get up on 3 : put in position ~ *n* 1 : frame or support 2 : horse to ride — **mount•able** *adj* — **mount•er** *n*

**moun•tain** \'maůnt³n\ *n* : elevated land higher than a hill — **moun•tain•ous** \'maůnt³nəs\ *adj* — **moun•tain•top** *n*

**moun•tain•eer** \,maůnt³n'ir\ *n* : mountain resident or climber

**moun•te•bank** \'maůnti,baŋk\ *n* : impostor

**mourn** \'mōrn\ *vb* : feel or express grief — **mourn•er** *n* — **mourn•ful** \-fəl\ *adj* — **mourn•ful•ly** *adv* — **mourn•ful•ness** *n* — **mourn•ing** *n*

**mouse** \'maůs\ *n, pl* **mice** \'mīs\ 1 : small rodent 2 : device for controlling cursor movement on a computer display — **mouse•trap** *n or vb* — **mousy, mous•ey** \'maůsē, -zē\ *adj*

**mousse** \'müs\ *n* 1 : light chilled dessert 2 : foamy hair-styling preparation

**mous•tache** \'məs,tash, məs'tash\ *var of* MUSTACHE

**mouth** \'maůth\ *n* : opening through which an animal takes in food ~ \'maůth̲\ *vb* 1 : speak 2 : repeat without comprehension or sincerity 3 : form soundlessly with the lips — **mouthed** \'maůth̲d, 'maůtht\ *adj* — **mouth•ful** \-,fůl\ *n*

**mouth•piece** *n* 1 : part (as of a musical instrument) held in or to the mouth 2 : spokesman

**mou•ton** \'mü,tän\ *n* : processed sheepskin

**move** \'müv\ *vb* **moved; mov•ing** 1 : go or cause to go to another point 2 : change residence 3 : change or cause to change position 4 : take or cause to take action 5 : make a formal request 6 : stir the emotions ~ *n* 1 : act or instance of moving 2 : step taken to achieve a goal — **mov•able, move•able** \-əbəl\ *adj* — **move•ment** *n* — **mov•er** *n*

**mov•ie** \'müvē\ *n* : projected picture in which persons and objects seem to move

¹**mow** \'maů\ *n* : part of a barn where hay or straw is stored

²**mow** \'mō\ *vb* **mowed; mowed** *or* **mown** \'mōn\; **mow•ing** : cut with a machine — **mow•er** *n*

**Mr.** \'mistər\ *n, pl* **Messrs.** \'mesərz\ — conventional title for a man

**Mrs.** \'misəz, -səs, *esp South* 'mizəz, -əs\ *n, pl* **Mes•dames** \mā'däm, -'dam\ — conventional title for a married woman

**Ms.** \'miz\ *n* — conventional title for a woman

**much** \'məch\ *adj* **more** \'mōr\; **most** \'mōst\ : great in quantity, extent, or degree ~ *adv* **more; most** : to a great degree or extent ~ *n* : great quantity, extent, or degree

**mu•ci•lage** \'myüsəlij\ *n* : weak glue

**muck** \'mək\ *n* : manure, dirt, or mud — **mucky** *adj*

**mu•cus** \'myükəs\ *n* : slippery protective secretion of membranes (**mucous membranes**) lining body cavities — **mu•cous** \-kəs\ *adj*

**mud** \'məd\ *n* : soft wet earth — **mud•di•ly** \'məd³lē\ *adv* — **mud•di•ness** \-ēnəs\ *n* — **mud•dy** *adj or vb*

**mud•dle** \'məd³l\ *vb* **-dled; -dling** 1 : make, be, or act confused 2 : make a mess of — **muddle** *n* — **mud•dle•head•ed** \,məd³l'hedəd\ *adj*

**mu•ez•zin** \mü'ez³n, myü-\ *n* : Muslim who calls the hour of daily prayer

¹**muff** \'məf\ *n* : tubular hand covering

²**muff** *vb* : bungle — **muff** *n*

**muf•fin** \'məfən\ *n* : soft cake baked in a cup-shaped container

**muf•fle** \'məfəl\ *vb* **-fled; -fling** 1 : wrap up 2 : dull the sound of — **muf•fler** \'məflər\ *n*

**muf•ti** \'məftē\ *n* : civilian clothes

¹**mug** \'məg\ *n* : drinking cup ~ *vb* **-gg-** : make faces

²**mug** *vb* **-gg-** : assault with intent to rob — **mug•ger** *n*

**mug•gy** \'məgē\ *adj* **-gi•er; -est** : hot and humid — **mug•gi•ness** *n*

**Mu•ham•mad•an** \mō'hamədən, -'häm-; mü-\ *n* : Muslim — **Mu•ham•mad•an•ism** \-,izəm\ *n*

**mu•lat•to** \mü'lätō, -'lat-\ *n, pl* **-toes** *or* **-tos** : person of mixed black and white ancestry

**mul•ber•ry** \'məl,berē\ *n* : tree with small edible fruit

**mulch** \'məlch\ *n* : protective ground covering — **mulch** *vb*

**mulct** \'məlkt\ *n or vb* : fine

¹**mule** \'myül\ *n* 1 : offspring of a male ass and a female horse 2 : stubborn person — **mul•ish** \'myülish\ *adj* — **mul•ish•ly** *adv* — **mu•lish•ness** *n*

²**mule** *n* : backless shoe

**mull** \'məl\ *vb* : ponder

**mul•let** \'mələt\ *n, pl* **-let** *or* **-lets** : marine food fish

**multi-** *comb form* **1** : many or multiple **2** : many times over

**mul•ti•far•i•ous** \ˌməltə'farēəs\ *adj* : diverse

**mul•ti•lat•er•al** \ˌməlti'latərəl, -ˌtī-\ *adj* : having many sides or participants

**mul•ti•lin•gual** \-'liŋgwəl\ *adj* : knowing or using several languages — **mul•ti•lin•gual•ism** \-gwəˌlizəm\ *n*

**mul•ti•na•tion•al** \-'nashənəl\ *adj* **1** : relating to several nations or nationalities **2** : having divisions in several countries — **multinational** *n*

**mul•ti•ple** \'məltəpəl\ *adj* **1** : several or many **2** : various ～ *n* : product of one number by another

**multiple sclerosis** \-sklə'rōsəs\ *n* : brain or spinal disease affecting muscle control

**mul•ti•pli•ca•tion** \ˌməltəplə'kāshən\ *n* **1** : increase **2** : short method of repeated addition

**mul•ti•plic•i•ty** \ˌməltə'plisətē\ *n, pl* **-ties** : great number or variety

**mul•ti•ply** \'məltəˌplī\ *vb* **-plied; -plying 1** : increase in number **2** : perform multiplication — **mul•ti•pli•er** \-ˌplīər\ *n*

**mul•ti•tude** \'məltəˌtüd, -ˌtyüd\ *n* : great number — **mul•ti•tu•di•nous** \ˌməltə'tüd°nəs, -'tyü-\ *adj*

¹**mum** \'məm\ *adj* : silent

²**mum** *n* : chrysanthemum

**mum•ble** \'məmbəl\ *vb* **-bled; -bling** : speak indistinctly — **mumble** *n* — **mum•bler** *n*

**mum•mer** \'məmər\ *n* **1** : actor esp. in a pantomime **2** : disguised merrymaker — **mum•mery** *n*

**mum•my** \'məmē\ *n, pl* **-mies** : embalmed body — **mum•mi•fi•ca•tion** \ˌməmifə'kāshən\ *n* — **mum•mi•fy** \'məmiˌfī\ *vb*

**mumps** \'məmps\ *n sing or pl* : virus disease with swelling esp. of the salivary glands

**munch** \'mənch\ *vb* : chew

**mun•dane** \ˌmən'dān, 'mənˌ-\ *adj* **1** : relating to the world **2** : lacking concern for the ideal or spiritual — **mun•dane•ly** *adv*

**mu•nic•i•pal** \myu̇'nisəpəl\ *adj* : of or relating to a town or city — **mu•nic•i•pal•i•ty** \myu̇ˌnisə'palətē\ *n*

**mu•nif•i•cent** \myu̇'nifəsənt\ *adj* : generous — **mu•nif•i•cence** \-səns\ *n*

**mu•ni•tion** \myu̇'nishən\ *n* : armaments

**mu•ral** \'myu̇rəl\ *adj* : relating to a wall ～ *n* : wall painting — **mu•ra•list** *n*

**mur•der** \'mərdər\ *n* : unlawful killing of a person ～ *vb* : commit a murder — **mur•der•er** *n* — **mur•der•ess**

---

**List of self-explanatory words with the prefix** *multi-*

| | | |
|---|---|---|
| multiarmed | multifunction | multipurpose |
| multibarreled | multifunctional | multiracial |
| multibillion | multigrade | multiroom |
| multibranched | multiheaded | multisense |
| multibuilding | multihospital | multiservice |
| multicenter | multihued | multisided |
| multichambered | multilane | multispeed |
| multichannel | multilevel | multistage |
| multicolored | multimedia | multistep |
| multicounty | multimember | multistory |
| multicultural | multimillion | multisyllabic |
| multidimensional | multimillionaire | multitalented |
| multidirectional | multipart | multitrack |
| multidisciplinary | multipartite | multiunion |
| multidiscipline | multiparty | multiunit |
| multidivisional | multiplant | multiuse |
| multifaceted | multipolar | multivitamin |
| multifamily | multiproblem | multiwarhead |
| multifilament | multiproduct | multiyear |

\-əs\ *n* — **mur·der·ous** \-əs\ *adj* — **mur·der·ous·ly** *adv*

**murk** \'mərk\ *n* : darkness — **murk·i·ly** \'mərkəlē\ *adv* — **murk·i·ness** \-kēnəs\ *n* — **murky** *adj*

**mur·mur** \'mərmər\ *n* **1** : muttered complaint **2** : low indistinct sound — **murmur** *vb* — **mur·mur·er** *n* — **mur·mur·ous** *adj*

**mus·ca·tel** \₁məskə'tel\ *n* : sweet wine

**mus·cle** \'məsəl\ *n* **1** : body tissue capable of contracting to produce motion **2** : strength ~ *vb* -**cled**; -**cling** : force one's way — **mus·cled** *adj* — **mus·cu·lar** \'məskyələr\ *adj* — **mus·cu·lar·i·ty** \₁məskyə'larətē\ *n*

**muscular dystrophy** *n* : disease marked by progressive wasting of muscles

**mus·cu·la·ture** \'məskyələ₁chùr\ *n* : bodily muscles

¹**muse** \'myüz\ *vb* **mused**; **mus·ing** : ponder — **mus·ing·ly** *adv*

²**muse** *n* : source of inspiration

**mu·se·um** \myù'zēəm\ *n* : institution displaying objects of interest

**mush** \'məsh\ *n* **1** : corn meal boiled in water or something of similar consistency **2** : sentimental nonsense — **mushy** *adj*

**mush·room** \'məsh₁rüm, -₁rùm\ *n* : caplike organ of a fungus ~ *vb* : grow rapidly

**mu·sic** \'myüzik\ *n* : vocal or instrumental sounds — **mu·si·cal** \-zikəl\ *adj or n* — **mu·si·cal·ly** *adv*

**mu·si·cian** \myù'zishən\ *n* : composer or performer of music — **mu·si·cian·ly** *adj* — **mu·si·cian·ship** *n*

**musk** \'məsk\ *n* : strong-smelling substance from an Asiatic deer used in perfume — **musk·i·ness** \'məskēnəs\ *n* — **musky** *adj*

**mus·kel·lunge** \'məskə₁lənj\ *n, pl* -**lunge** : large No. American pike

**mus·ket** \'məskət\ *n* : former shoulder firearm — **mus·ke·teer** \₁məskə'tir\ *n*

**musk·mel·on** \'məsk₁melən\ *n* : small edible melon

**musk-ox** \'məsk₁äks\ *n* : shaggy-coated wild ox of the arctic

**musk·rat** \-₁rat\ *n, pl* -**rat** *or* -**rats** : No. American aquatic rodent

**Mus·lim** \'məzləm, 'mùs-, 'mùz-\ *n* : adherent of Islam — **Muslim** *adj*

**mus·lin** \'məzlən\ *n* : cotton fabric

**muss** \'məs\ *n* : untidy state ~ *vb* : disarrange — **muss·i·ly** \'məsəlē\

*adv* — **muss·i·ness** \-ēnəs\ *n* — **mussy** *adj*

**mus·sel** \'məsəl\ *n* : edible mollusk

**must** \'məst\ *vb* — used as an auxiliary esp. to express a command, obligation, or necessity ~ \'məst\ *n* : something necessary

**mus·tache** \'məs₁tash, məs'-\ *n* : hair of the human upper lip

**mus·tang** \'məs₁taŋ\ *n* : wild horse of Western America

**mus·tard** \'məstərd\ *n* : pungent yellow seasoning

**mus·ter** \'məstər\ *vb* **1** : assemble **2** : rouse ~ *n* : assembled group

**musty** \'məstē\ *adj* **mus·ti·er**; -**est** : stale — **must·i·ly** *adv* — **must·i·ness** *n*

**mu·ta·ble** \'myütəbəl\ *adj* : changeable — **mu·ta·bil·i·ty** \₁myütə'bilətē\ *n*

**mu·tant** \'myüt³nt\ *adj* : relating to or produced by mutation — **mutant** *n*

**mu·tate** \'myü₁tāt\ *vb* -**tat·ed**; -**tat·ing** : undergo mutation — **mu·ta·tive** \'myü₁tātiv, 'myütət-\ *adj*

**mu·ta·tion** \myü'tāshən\ *n* : change in a hereditary character — **mu·ta·tion·al** *adj*

**mute** \'myüt\ *adj* **mut·er**; **mut·est** **1** : unable to speak **2** : silent ~ *n* **1** : one who is mute **2** : muffling device ~ *vb* **mut·ed**; **mut·ing** : muffle — **mute·ly** *adv* — **mute·ness** *n*

**mu·ti·late** \'myüt³l₁āt\ *vb* -**lat·ed**; -**lat·ing** : damage seriously (as by cutting off or altering an essential part) — **mu·ti·la·tion** \₁myüt³l'āshən\ *n* — **mu·ti·la·tor** \'myüt³l₁ātər\ *n*

**mu·ti·ny** \'myütənē\ *n, pl* -**nies** : rebellion — **mu·ti·neer** \₁myüt³n'ir\ *n* — **mu·ti·nous** \'myüt³nəs\ *adj* — **mu·ti·nous·ly** *adv* — **mutiny** *vb*

**mutt** \'mət\ *n* : mongrel

**mut·ter** \'mətər\ *vb* **1** : speak indistinctly or softly **2** : grumble — **mut·ter** *n*

**mut·ton** \'mət³n\ *n* : flesh of a mature sheep — **mut·tony** *adj*

**mu·tu·al** \'myüchəwəl\ *adj* **1** : given or felt by one another in equal amount **2** : common — **mu·tu·al·ly** *adv*

**muz·zle** \'məzəl\ *n* **1** : nose and jaws of an animal **2** : muzzle covering to immobilize an animal's jaws **3** : discharge end of a gun ~ *vb* -**zled**; -**zling** : restrain with or as if with a muzzle

**my** \'mī\ *adj* **1** : relating to me or myself **2** — used interjectionally esp. to express surprise

**my·nah, my·na** \'mīnə\ *n* : dark crested Asian bird

**my·o·pia** \mī'ōpēə\ *n* : nearsightedness — **my·o·pic** \-'ōpik, -'äpik\ *adj* — **my·o·pi·cal·ly** *adv*

**myr·i·ad** \'mirēəd\ *n* : indefinitely large number — **myriad** *adj*

**myrrh** \'mər\ *n* : aromatic plant gum

**myr·tle** \'mərt³l\ *n* : shiny evergreen

**my·self** \mī'self\ *pron* : I, me — used reflexively or for emphasis

**mys·tery** \'mistərē\ *n, pl* **-ter·ies** **1** : religious truth **2** : something not understood **3** : puzzling or secret quality or state — **mys·te·ri·ous** \mis-'tirēəs\ *adj* — **mys·te·ri·ous·ly** *adv* — **mys·te·ri·ous·ness** *n*

**mys·tic** \'mistik\ *adj* : mystical or mysterious ~ *n* : one who has mystical experiences — **mys·ti·cism** \-tə₁sizəm\ *n*

**mys·ti·cal** \'mistikəl\ *adj* **1** : spiritual **2** : relating to direct communion with God — **mys·ti·cal·ly** *adj*

**mys·ti·fy** \'mistə₁fī\ *vb* **-fied; -fy·ing** : perplex — **mys·ti·fi·ca·tion** \₁mistəfə'kāshən\ *n*

**mys·tique** \mis'tēk\ *n* : aura of mystery surrounding something

**myth** \'mith\ *n* **1** : legendary narrative explaining a belief or phenomenon **2** : imaginary person or thing — **myth·i·cal** \-ikəl\ *adj*

**my·thol·o·gy** \mith'äləjē\ *n, pl* **-gies** : body of myths — **myth·o·log·i·cal** \₁mithə'läjikəl\ *adj* — **my·thol·o·gist** \mith'äləjist\ *n*

# N

**n** \'en\ *n, pl* **n's** *or* **ns** \'enz\ : 14th letter of the alphabet

**nab** \'nab\ *vb* **-bb-** : seize or arrest

**na·cho** \'nächō\ *n* : tortilla chip topped with a savory mixture and cheese and broiled

**na·dir** \'nā₁dir, 'nādər\ *n* : lowest point

¹**nag** \'nag\ *n* : old or decrepit horse

²**nag** *vb* **-gg-** **1** : complain **2** : scold or urge continually **3** : be persistently annoying ~ *n* : one who nags habitually

**na·iad** \'nāəd, 'nī-, -₁ad\ *n, pl* **-iads** *or* **-ia·des** \-ə₁dēz\ : mythological water nymph

**nail** \'nāl\ *n* **1** : horny sheath at the end of each finger and toe **2** : pointed metal fastener ~ *vb* : fasten with a nail — **nail·er** *n*

**na·ive, na·ïve** \nä'ēv\ *adj* **-iv·er; -est** **1** : innocent and unsophisticated **2** : easily deceived — **na·ive·ly** *adv* — **na·ive·ness** *n*

**na·ive·té** \₁nä₁ēvə'tā, nä'ēvə₁-\ *n* : quality or state of being naive

**na·ked** \'nākəd, 'nekəd\ *adj* **1** : having no clothes on **2** : uncovered **3** : plain or obvious **4** : unaided — **na·ked·ly** *adv* — **na·ked·ness** *n*

**nam·by–pam·by** \₁nambē'pambē\ *adj* : weak or indecisive

**name** \'nām\ *n* **1** : word by which a person or thing is known **2** : disparaging word for someone **3** : distinguished reputation ~ *vb* **named; nam·ing** **1** : give a name to **2** : mention or identify by name **3** : nominate or appoint ~ *adj* **1** : relating to a name **2** : prominent — **name·able** *adj* — **name·less** *adj* — **name·less·ly** *adv*

**name·ly** \'nāmlē\ *adv* : that is to say

**name·sake** \-₁sāk\ *n* : one named after another

**nano·tech·nol·o·gy** \₁nanōtek'näləjē\ *n* : manipulation of materials on an atomic or molecular scale

¹**nap** \'nap\ *vb* **-pp-** **1** : sleep briefly **2** : be off guard ~ *n* : short sleep

²**nap** *n* : soft downy surface — **nap·less** *adj* — **napped** \'napt\ *adj*

**na·palm** \'nä₁pälm, -₁päm\ *n* : gasoline in the form of a jelly

**nape** \'nāp, 'nap\ *n* : back of the neck

**naph·tha** \'nafthə\ *n* : flammable solvent

**nap·kin** \'napkən\ *n* : small cloth for use at the table

**nar·cis·sism** \'närsə₁sizəm\ *n* : self-love — **nar·cis·sist** \-sist\ *n or adj* — **nar·cis·sis·tic** \₁närsə'sistik\ *adj*

**nar•cis•sus** \när'sisəs\ *n, pl* **-cis•sus** *or* **-cis•sus•es** *or* **-cis•si** \-'sis,ī, -,ē\ : plant with flowers usu. borne separately

**nar•cot•ic** \när'kätik\ *n* : painkilling addictive drug — **narcotic** *adj*

**nar•rate** \'nar,āt\ *vb* **nar•rat•ed; nar•rat•ing** : tell (a story) — **nar•ra•tion** \na-'rāshən\ *n* — **nar•ra•tive** \'narətiv\ *n or adj* — **nar•ra•tor** \'nar,ātər\ *n*

**nar•row** \'narō\ *adj* **1** : of less than standard width **2** : limited **3** : not liberal **4** : barely successful ∼ *vb* : make narrow — **nar•row•ly** *adv* — **nar•row•ness** *n*

**nar•row–mind•ed** \,narō'mīndəd\ *adj* : shallow, provincial, or bigoted

**nar•rows** \'narōz\ *n pl* : narrow passage

**nar•whal** \'när,hwäl, 'närwəl\ *n* : sea mammal with a tusk

**nasal** \'nāzəl\ *adj* : relating to or uttered through the nose — **na•sal•ly** *adv*

**nas•tur•tium** \nə'stərshəm, na-\ *n* : herb with showy flowers

**nas•ty** \'nastē\ *adj* **nas•ti•er; -est 1** : filthy **2** : indecent **3** : malicious or spiteful **4** : difficult or disagreeable **5** : unfair — **nas•ti•ly** \'nastəlē\ *adv* — **nas•ti•ness** \-tēnəs\ *n*

**na•tal** \'nāt°l\ *adj* : relating to birth

**na•tion** \'nāshən\ *n* **1** : people of similar characteristics **2** : community with its own territory and government — **na•tion•al** \'nashənəl\ *adj or n* — **na•tion•al•ly** *adv* — **na•tion•hood** *n* — **na•tion•wide** *adj*

**na•tion•al•ism** \'nashənəl,izəm\ *n* : devotion to national interests, unity, and independence — **na•tion•al•ist** \-ist\ *n or adj* — **na•tion•al•is•tic** \,nashənəl'istik\ *adj*

**na•tion•al•i•ty** \,nashə'nalətē\ *n, pl* **-ties 1** : national character **2** : membership in a nation **3** : political independence **4** : ethnic group

**na•tion•al•ize** \'nashənəl,īz\ *vb* **-ized; -iz•ing 1** : make national **2** : place under government control — **na•tion•al•i•za•tion** \,nashənələ'zāshən\ *n*

**na•tive** \'nātiv\ *adj* **1** : belonging to a person at or by way of birth **2** : born or produced in a particular place ∼ *n* : one who belongs to a country by birth

**Na•tiv•i•ty** \nə'tivətē, nā-\ *n, pl* **-ties 1** : birth of Christ **2** *not cap* : birth

**nat•ty** \'natē\ *adj* **-ti•er; -est** : smartly dressed — **nat•ti•ly** \'nat°lē\ *adv*

**nat•u•ral** \'nachərəl\ *adj* **1** : relating to

or determined by nature **2** : not artificial **3** : simple and sincere **4** : lifelike ∼ *n* : one having an innate talent — **nat•u•ral•ness** *n*

**nat•u•ral•ism** \'nachərə,lizəm\ *n* : realism in art and literature — **nat•u•ral•is•tic** \,nachərə'listik\ *adj*

**nat•u•ral•ist** \-list\ *n* **1** : one who practices naturalism **2** : student of animals or plants

**nat•u•ral•ize** \-,līz\ *vb* **-ized; -iz•ing 1** : become or cause to become established **2** : confer citizenship on — **nat•u•ral•i•za•tion** \,nachərələ'zāshən\ *n*

**nat•u•ral•ly** \'nachərəlē\ *adv* **1** : in a natural way **2** : as might be expected

**na•ture** \'nāchər\ *n* **1** : basic quality of something **2** : kind **3** : disposition **4** : physical universe **5** : natural environment

**naught** \'nȯt, 'nät\ *n* **1** : nothing **2** : zero

**naugh•ty** \'nȯtē, 'nät-\ *adj* **-ti•er; -est 1** : disobedient or misbehaving **2** : improper — **naught•i•ly** \'nȯt°lē, 'nät-\ *adv* — **naught•i•ness** \-ēnəs\ *n*

**nau•sea** \'nȯzēə, -shə\ *n* **1** : sickness of the stomach with a desire to vomit **2** : extreme disgust — **nau•seous** \-shəs, -zēəs\ *adj*

**nau•se•ate** \'nȯzē,āt, -zhē-, -sē-, -shē-\ *vb* **-ated; -at•ing** : affect or become affected with nausea — **nau•se•at•ing•ly** \-,ātiŋlē\ *adv*

**nau•ti•cal** \'nȯtikəl\ *adj* : relating to ships and sailing — **nau•ti•cal•ly** *adv*

**nau•ti•lus** \'nȯt°ləs\ *n, pl* **-lus•es** *or* **-li** \-°l,ī, -,ē\ : sea mollusk with a spiral shell

**na•val** \'nāvəl\ *adj* : relating to a navy

**nave** \'nāv\ *n* : central part of a church

**na•vel** \'nāvəl\ *n* : depression in the abdomen

**nav•i•ga•ble** \'navigəbəl\ *adj* : capable of being navigated — **nav•i•ga•bil•i•ty** \,navigə'bilətē\ *n*

**nav•i•gate** \'navə,gāt\ *vb* **-gat•ed; -gat•ing 1** : sail on or through **2** : direct the course of — **nav•i•ga•tion** \,navə'gāshən\ *n* — **nav•i•ga•tor** \'navə,gātər\ *n*

**na•vy** \'nāvē\ *n, pl* **-vies 1** : fleet **2** : nation's organization for sea warfare

**nay** \'nā\ *adv* : no — used in oral voting ∼ *n* : negative vote

**Na•zi** \'nätsē, 'nat-\ *n* : member of a German fascist party from 1933 to 1945 — **Nazi** *adj* — **Na•zism** \'nät-,sizəm, 'nat-\, **Na•zi•ism** \-sē,izəm\ *n*

**near** \'nir\ *adv* : at or close to ~ *prep* : close to ~ *adj* **1** : not far away **2** : very much like ~ *vb* : approach — **near•ly** *adv* — **near•ness** *n*

**near•by** \nir'bī, 'nir‚bī\ *adv or adj* : near

**near•sight•ed** \'nir'sītəd\ *adj* : seeing well at short distances only — **near•sight•ed•ly** *adv* — **near•sight•ed•ness** *n*

**neat** \'nēt\ *adj* **1** : not diluted **2** : tastefully simple **3** : orderly and clean — **neat** *adv* — **neat•ly** *adv* — **neat•ness** *n*

**neb•u•la** \'nebyələ\ *n, pl* **-lae** \-‚lē, -‚lī\ : large cloud of interstellar gas — **neb•u•lar** \-lər\ *adj*

**neb•u•lous** \-ləs\ *adj* : indistinct

**nec•es•sary** \'nesə‚serē\ *n, pl* **-saries** : indispensable item ~ *adj* **1** : inevitable **2** : compulsory **3** : positively needed — **nec•es•sar•i•ly** \‚nesə-'serəlē\ *adv*

**ne•ces•si•tate** \ni'sesə‚tāt\ *vb* **-tat•ed; -tat•ing** : make necessary

**ne•ces•si•ty** \ni'sesətē\ *n, pl* **-ties 1** : very great need **2** : something that is necessary **3** : poverty **4** : circumstances that cannot be changed

**neck** \'nek\ *n* **1** : body part connecting the head and trunk **2** : part of a garment at the neck **3** : narrow part ~ *vb* : kiss and caress — **necked** \'nekt\ *adj*

**neck•er•chief** \'nekərchəf, -‚chēf\ *n, pl* **-chiefs** \-chəfs, -‚chēfs\ : cloth worn tied about the neck

**neck•lace** \'nekləs\ *n* : ornament worn around the neck

**neck•tie** *n* : ornamental cloth tied under a collar

**nec•ro•man•cy** \'nekrə‚mansē\ *n* : art of conjuring up the spirits of the dead — **nec•ro•man•cer** \-sər\ *n*

**ne•cro•sis** \nə'krōsəs, ne-\ *n, pl* **-cro•ses** \-‚sēz\ : death of body tissue

**nec•tar** \'nektər\ *n* : sweet plant secretion

**nec•tar•ine** \‚nektə'rēn\ *n* : smooth-skinned peach

**née, nee** \'nā\ *adj* — used to identify a married woman by maiden name

**need** \'nēd\ *n* **1** : obligation **2** : lack of something or what is lacking **3** : poverty ~ *vb* **1** : be in want **2** : have cause for **3** : be under obligation — **need•ful** \-fəl\ *adj* — **need•less** *adj* — **need•less•ly** *adv* — **needy** *adj*

**nee•dle** \'nēd³l\ *n* **1** : pointed sewing implement or something like it **2** : movable bar in a compass **3** : hollow instrument for injecting or withdrawing material ~ *vb* **-dled; -dling** : incite to action by repeated gibes — **nee•dle•work** \-‚wərk\ *n*

**nee•dle•point** \'nēd³l‚point\ *n* **1** : lace fabric **2** : embroidery on canvas — **needlepoint** *adj*

**ne•far•i•ous** \ni'farēəs\ *adj* : very wicked — **ne•far•i•ous•ly** *adv*

**ne•gate** \ni'gāt\ *vb* **-gat•ed; -gat•ing 1** : deny **2** : nullify — **ne•ga•tion** \-'gāshən\ *n*

**neg•a•tive** \'negətiv\ *adj* **1** : marked by denial or refusal **2** : showing a lack of something suspected or desirable **3** : less than zero **4** : having more electrons than protons **5** : having light and shadow images reversed ~ *n* **1** : negative word or vote **2** : a negative number **3** : negative photographic image — **neg•a•tive•ly** *adv* — **neg•a•tive•ness** *n* — **neg•a•tiv•i•ty** \‚negə'tivətē\ *n*

**ne•glect** \ni'glekt\ *vb* **1** : disregard **2** : leave unattended to ~ *n* **1** : act of neglecting **2** : condition of being neglected — **ne•glect•ful** *adj*

**neg•li•gee** \‚neglə'zhā\ *n* : woman's loose robe

**neg•li•gent** \'neglijənt\ *adj* : marked by neglect — **neg•li•gence** \-jəns\ *n* — **neg•li•gent•ly** *adv*

**neg•li•gi•ble** \'neglijəbəl\ *adj* : insignificant

**ne•go•ti•ate** \ni'gōshē‚āt\ *vb* **-at•ed; -at•ing 1** : confer with another to settle a matter **2** : obtain cash for **3** : get through successfully — **ne•go•tia•ble** \-shəbəl, -shēə-\ *adj* — **ne•go•ti•a•tion** \-‚gōshē'āshən, -shēˈā-\ *n* — **ne•go•ti•a•tor** \-'gōshē‚ātər\ *n*

**Ne•gro** \'nēgrō\ *n, pl* **-groes** *sometimes offensive* : member of the dark-skinned race native to Africa — **Negro** *adj* — **Ne•groid** \'nē‚gròid\ *n or adj, often not cap*

**neigh** \'nā\ *n* : cry of a horse — **neigh** *vb*

**neigh•bor** \'nābər\ *n* **1** : one living nearby **2** : fellowman ~ *vb* : be near or next to — **neigh•bor•hood** \-‚hùd\ *n* — **neigh•bor•li•ness** *n* — **neigh•bor•ly** *adv*

**nei•ther** \'nēthər, 'nī-\ *pron or adj* : not the one or the other ~ *conj* **1** : not either **2** : nor

**nem•e•sis** \'neməsəs\ *n, pl* **-e•ses** \-əˌsēz\ **1 :** old and usu. frustrating rival **2 :** retaliation

**ne•ol•o•gism** \nē'äləˌjizəm\ *n* **:** new word

**ne•on** \'nēˌän\ *n* **:** gaseous colorless chemical element that emits a reddish glow in electric lamps — **neon** *adj*

**neo•phyte** \'nēəˌfīt\ *n* **:** beginner

**neph•ew** \'nefyü, *chiefly Brit* 'nev-\ *n* **:** a son of one's brother, sister, brother-in-law, or sister-in-law

**nep•o•tism** \'nepəˌtizəm\ *n* **:** favoritism shown in hiring a relative

**nerd** \'nərd\ *n* **:** one who is not stylish or socially at ease — **nerdy** *adj*

**nerve** \'nərv\ *n* **1 :** strand of body tissue that connects the brain with other parts of the body **2 :** self-control **3 :** daring **4** *pl* **:** nervousness — **nerved** \'nərvd\ *adj* — **nerve•less** *adj*

**ner•vous** \'nərvəs\ *adj* **1 :** relating to or made up of nerves **2 :** easily excited **3 :** timid or fearful — **ner•vous•ly** *adv* — **ner•vous•ness** *n*

**nervy** \'nərvē\ *adj* **nerv•i•er; -est :** insolent or presumptuous

**-ness** \nəs\ *n suffix* **:** condition or quality

**nest** \'nest\ *n* **1 :** shelter prepared by a bird for its eggs **2 :** place where eggs (as of insects or fish) are laid and hatched **3 :** snug retreat **4 :** set of objects fitting one inside or under another ~ *vb* **:** build or occupy a nest

**nes•tle** \'nesəl\ *vb* **-tled; -tling :** settle snugly (as in a nest)

**¹net** \'net\ *n* **:** fabric with spaces between strands or something made of this ~ *vb* **-tt- :** cover with or catch in a net

**²net** *adj* **:** remaining after deductions ~ *vb* **-tt- :** have as profit

**neth•er** \'ne<u>th</u>ər\ *adj* **:** situated below

**net•tle** \'netᵊl\ *n* **:** coarse herb with stinging hairs ~ *vb* **-tled; -tling :** provoke or vex — **net•tle•some** *adj*

**net•work** *n* **:** system of crossing or connected elements

**neu•ral** \'nürəl, 'nyür-\ *adj* **:** relating to a nerve

**neu•ral•gia** \nü'raljə, nyü-\ *n* **:** pain along a nerve — **neu•ral•gic** \-jik\ *adj*

**neu•ri•tis** \nü'rītəs, nyü-\ *n, pl* **-rit•i•des** \-'ritəˌdēz\ *or* **-ri•tis•es :** inflammation of a nerve

**neu•rol•o•gy** \nü'räləjē, nyü-\ *n* **:** study of the nervous system — **neu•ro•log•i•cal** \ˌnürə'läjikəl, ˌnyür-\, **neu•ro•log•ic** \-ik\ *adj* — **neu•rol•o•gist** \nü'räləjist, nyü-\ *n*

**neu•ro•sis** \nü'rōsəs, nyü-\ *n, pl* **-ro•ses** \-ˌsēz\ **:** nervous disorder

**neu•rot•ic** \nü'rätik, nyü-\ *adj* **:** relating to neurosis ~ *n* **:** unstable person — **neu•rot•i•cal•ly** *adv*

**neu•ter** \'nütər, 'nyü-\ *adj* **:** neither masculine nor feminine ~ *vb* **:** castrate or spay

**neu•tral** \-trəl\ *adj* **1 :** not favoring either side **2 :** being neither one thing nor the other **3 :** not decided in color **4 :** not electrically charged ~ *n* **1 :** one that is neutral **2 :** position of gears that are not engaged — **neu•tral•i•za•tion** \ˌnütrələ'zāshən, ˌnyü-\ *n* — **neu•tral•ize** \'nütrəˌlīz, 'nyü-\ *vb*

**neu•tral•i•ty** \nü'tralətē, nyü-\ *n* **:** state of being neutral

**neu•tron** \'nüˌträn, 'nyü-\ *n* **:** uncharged atomic particle

**nev•er** \'nevər\ *adv* **1 :** not ever **2 :** not in any degree, way, or condition

**nev•er•more** *adv* **:** never again

**nev•er•the•less** *adv* **:** in spite of that

**new** \'nü, 'nyü\ *adj* **1 :** not old or familiar **2 :** different from the former **3 :** recently discovered or learned **4 :** not accustomed **5 :** refreshed or regenerated **6 :** being such for the first time ~ *adv* **:** newly — **new•ish** *adj* — **new•ness** *n*

**new•born** *adj* **1 :** recently born **2 :** born anew ~ *n, pl* **-born** *or* **-borns :** newborn individual

**new•ly** \-lē\ *adv* **:** recently

**news** \'nüz, 'nyüz\ *n* **:** report of recent events — **news•let•ter** *n* — **news•mag•a•zine** *n* — **news•man** \-mən, -ˌman\ *n* — **news•pa•per** *n* — **news•pa•per•man** \-ˌman\ *n* — **news•stand** *n* — **news•wom•an** \-ˌwümən\ *n* — **news•wor•thy** *adj*

**news•cast** \-ˌkast\ *n* **:** broadcast of news — **news•cast•er** \-ˌkastər\ *n*

**news•print** *n* **:** paper made from wood pulp

**newsy** \'nüzē, 'nyü-\ *adj* **news•i•er; -est :** filled with news

**newt** \'nüt, 'nyüt\ *n* **:** small salamander

**New Year** *n* **:** New Year's Day

**New Year's Day** *n* **:** January 1 observed as a legal holiday

**next** \'nekst\ *adj* **:** immediately preceding or following ~ *adv* **1 :** in the time or place nearest **2 :** at the first time yet to come ~ *prep* **:** nearest to

**nex•us** \'neksəs\ *n, pl* **-us•es** \-səsəz\ *or* **-us** \-səs, -ˌsüs\ **:** connection

**nib** \'nib\ *n* : pen point

**nib·ble** \'nibəl\ *vb* **-bled; -bling** : bite gently or bit by bit ~ *n* : small bite

**nice** \'nīs\ *adj* **nic·er; nic·est 1** : fastidious **2** : very precise or delicate **3** : pleasing **4** : respectable — **nice·ly** *adv* — **nice·ness** *n*

**nice·ty** \'nīsətē\ *n, pl* **-ties 1** : dainty or elegant thing **2** : fine detail **3** : exactness

**niche** \'nich\ *n* **1** : recess in a wall **2** : fitting place, work, or use

**nick** \'nik\ *n* **1** : small broken area or chip **2** : critical moment ~ *vb* : make a nick in

**nick·el** \'nikəl\ *n* **1** : hard silver-white metallic chemical element used in alloys **2** : U.S. 5-cent piece

**nick·name** \'nik,nām\ *n* : informal substitute name — **nickname** *vb*

**nic·o·tine** \'nikə,tēn\ *n* : poisonous and addictive substance in tobacco

**niece** \'nēs\ *n* : a daughter of one's brother, sister, brother-in-law, or sister-in-law

**nig·gard·ly** \'nigərdlē\ *adj* : stingy — **nig·gard** *n* — **nig·gard·li·ness** *n*

**nig·gling** \'nigəliŋ\ *adj* : petty and annoying

**nigh** \'nī\ *adv or adj or prep* : near

**night** \'nīt\ *n* **1** : period between dusk and dawn **2** : the coming of night — **night** *adj* — **night·ly** *adj or adv* — **night·time** *n*

**night·clothes** *n pl* : garments worn in bed

**night·club** \-,kləb\ *n* : place for drinking and entertainment open at night

**night crawler** *n* : earthworm

**night·fall** *n* : the coming of night

**night·gown** *n* : gown worn for sleeping

**night·in·gale** \'nīt³n,gāl, -iŋ-\ *n* : Old World thrush that sings at night

**night·mare** \'nīt,mar\ *n* : frightening dream — **nightmare** *adj* — **night·mar·ish** \-,marish\ *adj*

**night·shade** \'nīt,shād\ *n* : group of plants that include poisonous forms and food plants (as the potato and eggplant)

**nil** \'nil\ *n* : nothing

**nim·ble** \'nimbəl\ *adj* **-bler; -blest 1** : agile **2** : clever — **nim·ble·ness** *n* — **nim·bly** \-blē\ *adv*

**nine** \'nīn\ *n* **1** : one more than 8 **2** : 9th in a set or series — **nine** *adj or pron* — **ninth** \'nīnth\ *adj or adv or n*

**nine·pins** *n* : bowling game using 9 pins

**nine·teen** \nīn'tēn\ *n* : one more than 18 — **nineteen** *adj or pron* — **nine·teenth** \-'tēnth\ *adj or n*

**nine·ty** \'nīntē\ *n, pl* **-ties** : 9 times 10 — **nine·ti·eth** \-ēəth\ *adj or n* — **ninety** *adj or pron*

**nin·ny** \'ninē\ *n, pl* **nin·nies** : fool

**¹nip** \'nip\ *vb* **-pp- 1** : catch hold of and squeeze tightly **2** : pinch or bite off **3** : destroy the growth or fulfillment of ~ *n* **1** : biting cold **2** : tang **3** : pinch or bite

**²nip** *n* : small quantity of liquor ~ *vb* **-pp-** : take liquor in nips

**nip·per** \'nipər\ *n* **1** : one that nips **2** *pl* : pincers **3** : small boy

**nip·ple** \'nipəl\ *n* : tip of the breast or something resembling it

**nip·py** \'nipē\ *adj* **-pi·er; -est 1** : pungent **2** : chilly

**nir·va·na** \nir'vänə\ *n* : state of blissful oblivion

**nit** \'nit\ *n* : egg of a parasitic insect

**ni·ter** \'nītər\ *n* : potassium nitrate used in gunpowder or fertilizer or in curing meat

**ni·trate** \'nī,trāt, -trət\ *n* : chemical salt used esp. in curing meat

**ni·tric acid** \'nītrik-\ *n* : liquid acid used in making dyes, explosives, and fertilizers

**ni·trite** \-,trīt\ *n* : chemical salt used in curing meat

**ni·tro·gen** \'nītrəjən\ *n* : tasteless odorless gaseous chemical element

**ni·tro·glyc·er·in, ni·tro·glyc·er·ine** \,nītrō'glisərən\ *n* : heavy oily liquid used as an explosive and as a blood-vessel relaxer

**nit·wit** \'nit,wit\ *n* : stupid person

**no** \'nō\ *adv* **1** — used to express the negative **2** : in no respect or degree **3** : not so **4** — used as an interjection of surprise or doubt ~ *adj* **1** : not any **2** : not a ~ *n, pl* **noes** *or* **nos** \'nōz\ **1** : refusal **2** : negative vote

**no·bil·i·ty** \nō'bilətē\ *n* **1** : quality or state of being noble **2** : class of people of noble rank

**no·ble** \'nōbəl\ *adj* **-bler; -blest 1** : illustrious **2** : aristocratic **3** : stately **4** : of outstanding character ~ *n* : nobleman — **no·ble·ness** *n* — **no·bly** *adv*

**no·ble·man** \-mən\ *n* : member of the nobility

**no·ble·wom·an** \-,wùmən\ *n* : a woman of noble rank

**no·body** \'nōbədē, -,bädē\ *pron* : no person ~ *n, pl* **-bod·ies** : person of no influence or importance

**no–brain·er** \'nō'brānər\ : something that requires a minimum of thought

**noc·tur·nal** \näk'tərn°l\ adj : relating to, occurring at, or active at night

**noc·turne** \'näk,tərn\ n : dreamy musical composition

**nod** \'näd\ vb **-dd- 1** : bend the head downward or forward (as in bowing or going to sleep or as a sign of assent) **2** : move up and down **3** : show by a nod of the head — **nod** n

**node** \'nōd\ n : stem part from which a leaf arises — **nod·al** \-°l\ adj

**nod·ule** \'näjül\ n : small lump or swelling — **nod·u·lar** \'näjələr\ adj

**no·el** \nō'el\ n **1** : Christmas carol **2** cap : Christmas season

**noes** pl of NO

**nog·gin** \'nägən\ n **1** : small mug **2** : person's head

**no·how** \'nō,haú\ adv : in no manner

**noise** \'nóiz\ n : loud or unpleasant sound ∼ vb **noised; nois·ing** : spread by rumor — **noise·less** adj

— **noise·less·ly** adv — **noise·mak·er** n — **nois·i·ly** \'nóizəlē\ adv — **nois·i·ness** \-zēnəs\ n — **noisy** \'nóizē\ adj

**noi·some** \'nóisəm\ adj : harmful or offensive

**no·mad** \'nō,mad\ n : one who has no permanent home — **nomad** adj — **no·mad·ic** \nō'madik\ adj

**no·men·cla·ture** \'nōmən,klāchər\ n : system of names

**nom·i·nal** \'nämən°l\ adj **1** : being something in name only **2** : small or negligible — **nom·i·nal·ly** adv

**nom·i·nate** \'nämə,nāt\ vb **-nat·ed; -nat·ing** : propose or choose as a candidate — **nom·i·na·tion** \,nämə'nāshən\ n

**nom·i·na·tive** \'nämənətiv\ adj : relating to or being a grammatical case marking typically the subject of a verb — **nominative** n

**nom·i·nee** \,nämə'nē\ n : person nominated

**non-** \'nän, ,nän\ prefix **1** : not, reverse of, or absence of **2** : not important

---

**List of self-explanatory words with the prefix non-**

nonabrasive
nonabsorbent
nonacademic
nonaccredited
nonacid
nonaddictive
nonadhesive
nonadjacent
nonadjustable
nonaffiliated
nonaggression
nonalcoholic
nonaligned
nonappearance
nonautomatic
nonbeliever
nonbinding
nonbreakable
noncancerous
noncandidate
non-Catholic
non-Christian
nonchurchgoer
noncitizen
nonclassical
nonclassified
noncombat
noncombatant

noncombustible
noncommercial
noncommunist
noncompliance
nonconflicting
nonconforming
nonconsecutive
nonconstructive
noncontagious
noncontrollable
noncontroversial
noncorrosive
noncriminal
noncritical
noncumulative
noncurrent
nondeductible
nondeferrable
nondegradable
nondelivery
nondemocratic
nondenominational
nondestructive
nondiscrimination
nondiscriminatory
noneducational
nonelastic
nonelected

nonelective
nonelectric
nonelectronic
nonemotional
nonenforcement
nonessential
nonexclusive
nonexistence
nonexistent
nonexplosive
nonfat
nonfatal
nonfattening
nonfictional
nonflammable
nonflowering
nonfunctional
nongovernmental
nongraded
nonhazardous
nonhereditary
nonindustrial
nonindustrialized
noninfectious
noninflationary
nonintegrated
nonintellectual
noninterference

**non•age** \'nänij, 'nōnij\ *n* : period of youth and esp. legal minority

**nonce** \'näns\ *n* : present occasion ~ *adj* : occurring, used, or made only once

**non•cha•lant** \,nänshə'länt\ *adj* : showing indifference — **non•cha•lance** \-'läns\ *n* — **non•cha•lant•ly** *adv*

**non•com•mis•sioned officer** \,nänkə-'mishənd-\ *n* : subordinate officer in the armed forces appointed from enlisted personnel

**non•com•mit•tal** \,nänkə'mit°l\ *adj* : indicating neither consent nor dissent

**non•con•duc•tor** *n* : substance that is a very poor conductor

**non•con•form•ist** *n* : one who does not conform to an established belief or mode of behavior — **non•con•for•mi•ty** *n*

**non•de•script** \,nändi'skript\ *adj* : lacking distinctive qualities

**none** \'nən\ *pron* : not any ~ *adv* : not at all

**non•en•ti•ty** *n* : one of no consequence

**none•the•less** \,nənthə'les\ *adv* : nevertheless

**non•pa•reil** \,nänpə'rel\ *adj* : having no equal ~ *n* **1** : one who has no equal **2** : chocolate candy disk

**non•par•ti•san** *adj* : not influenced by political party bias

**non•per•son** *n* : person without social or legal status

**non•plus** \,nän'pləs\ *vb* -**ss**- : perplex

**non•pre•scrip•tion** *adj* : available without a doctor's prescription

**non•pro•lif•er•a•tion** *adj* : aimed at ending increased use of nuclear arms

**non•sched•uled** *adj* : licensed to carry by air without a regular schedule

**non•sense** \'nän,sens, -səns\ *n* : foolish or meaningless words or actions — **non•sen•si•cal** \nän'sensikəl\ *adj* — **non•sen•si•cal•ly** *adv*

**non•sup•port** *n* : failure in a legal obligation to provide for someone's needs

**non•vi•o•lence** *n* : avoidance of violence esp. in political demonstrations — **non•vi•o•lent** *adj*

---

nonintoxicating
noninvasive
non-Jewish
nonlegal
nonlethal
nonliterary
nonliving
nonmagnetic
nonmalignant
nonmedical
nonmember
nonmetal
nonmetallic
nonmilitary
nonmusical
nonnative
nonnegotiable
nonobjective
nonobservance
nonorthodox
nonparallel
nonparticipant
nonparticipating
nonpaying
nonpayment
nonperformance
nonperishable
nonphysical
nonpoisonous

nonpolitical
nonpolluting
nonporous
nonpregnant
nonproductive
nonprofessional
nonprofit
nonracial
nonradioactive
nonrated
nonrealistic
nonrecurring
nonrefillable
nonrefundable
nonreligious
nonrenewable
nonrepresentative
nonresident
nonresponsive
nonrestricted
nonreversible
nonsalable
nonscientific
nonscientist
nonsegregated
non–self–governing
nonsexist
nonsexual
nonsignificant

nonskier
nonsmoker
nonsmoking
nonspeaking
nonspecialist
nonspecific
nonstandard
nonstick
nonstop
nonstrategic
nonstudent
nonsugar
nonsurgical
nonswimmer
nontaxable
nonteaching
nontechnical
nontoxic
nontraditional
nontransferable
nontropical
nontypical
nonunion
nonuser
nonvenomous
nonverbal
nonvoter
nonwhite
nonworker

**noo•dle** \'nüd³l\ *n* : ribbon-shaped food paste

**nook** \'nuk\ *n* **1** : inside corner **2** : private place

**noon** \'nün\ *n* : middle of the day — **noon** *adj*

**noon•day** \-₁dā\ *n* : noon

**no one** *pron* : no person

**noon•time** *n* : noon

**noose** \'nüs\ *n* : rope loop that slips down tight

**nor** \'nor\ *conj* : and not — used esp. after *neither* to introduce and negate the 2d member of a series

**norm** \'norm\ *n* **1** : standard usu. derived from an average **2** : typical widespread practice or custom

**nor•mal** \'normal\ *adj* : average, regular, or standard — **nor•mal•cy** \-sē\ *n* — **nor•mal•i•ty** \nor'malətē\ *n* — **nor•mal•i•za•tion** \₁normələ'zāshən\ *n* — **nor•mal•ize** \'normə₁līz\ *vb* — **nor•mal•ly** *adv*

**north** \'north\ *adv* : to or toward the north ~ *adj* : situated toward, at, or coming from the north ~ *n* **1** : direction to the left of one facing east **2** *cap* : regions to the north — **north•er•ly** \'northərlē\ *adv or adj* — **north•ern** \-ərn\ *adj* — **North•ern•er** *n* — **north•ern•most** \-₁mōst\ *adj* — **north•ward** \-wərd\ *adv or adj* — **north•wards** \-wərdz\ *adv*

**north•east** \north'ēst\ *n* **1** : direction between north and east **2** *cap* : regions to the northeast — **northeast** *adj or adv* — **north•east•er•ly** \-ərlē\ *adv or adj* — **north•east•ern** \-ərn\ *adj*

**northern lights** *n pl* : aurora borealis

**north pole** *n* : northernmost point of the earth

**north•west** \-'west\ *n* **1** : direction between north and west **2** *cap* : regions to the northwest — **northwest** *adj or adv* — **north•west•er•ly** \-ərlē\ *adv or adj* — **north•west•ern** \-ərn\ *adj*

**nose** \'nōz\ *n* **1** : part of the face containing the nostrils **2** : sense of smell **3** : front part ~ *vb* **nosed; nos•ing** **1** : detect by smell **2** : push aside with the nose **3** : pry **4** : inch ahead — **nose•bleed** *n* — **nosed** \'nōzd\ *adj* — **nose out** *vb* : narrowly defeat

**nose•gay** \-₁gā\ *n* : small bunch of flowers

**nos•tal•gia** \nä'staljə, nə-\ *n* : wistful yearning for something past — **nos•tal•gic** \-jik\ *adj*

**nos•tril** \'nästrəl\ *n* : opening of the nose

**nos•trum** \-trəm\ *n* : questionable remedy

**nosy, nos•ey** \'nōzē\ *adj* **nos•i•er; -est** : tending to pry

**not** \'nät\ *adv* — used to make a statement negative

**no•ta•ble** \'nōtəbəl\ *adj* **1** : noteworthy **2** : distinguished ~ *n* : notable person — **no•ta•bil•i•ty** \nōtə'bilətē\ *n* — **no•ta•bly** \'nōtəblē\ *adv*

**no•ta•rize** \'nōtə₁rīz\ *vb* **-rized; -riz•ing** : attest as a notary public

**no•ta•ry public** \'nōtərē-\ *n, pl* **-ries public** *or* **-ry publics** : public official who attests writings to make them legally authentic

**no•ta•tion** \nō'tāshən\ *n* **1** : note **2** : act, process, or method of marking things down

**notch** \'näch\ *n* : V-shaped hollow — **notch** *vb*

**note** \'nōt\ *vb* **not•ed; not•ing** **1** : notice **2** : write down ~ *n* **1** : musical tone **2** : written comment or record **3** : short informal letter **4** : notice or heed — **note•book** *n*

**not•ed** \'nōtəd\ *adj* : famous

**note•wor•thy** \-₁wərthē\ *adj* : worthy of special mention

**noth•ing** \'nəthin\ *pron* **1** : no thing **2** : no part **3** : one of no value or importance ~ *adv* : not at all ~ *n* **1** : something that does not exist **2** : zero **3** : one of little or no importance — **noth•ing•ness** *n*

**no•tice** \'nōtəs\ *n* **1** : warning or announcement **2** : attention ~ *vb* **-ticed; -tic•ing** : take notice of — **no•tice•able** *adj* — **no•tice•ably** *adv*

**no•ti•fy** \'nōtə₁fī\ *vb* **-fied; -fy•ing** : give notice of or to — **no•ti•fi•ca•tion** \₁nōtəfə'kāshən\ *n*

**no•tion** \'nōshən\ *n* **1** : idea or opinion **2** : whim

**no•to•ri•ous** \nō'tōrēəs\ *adj* : widely and unfavorably known — **no•to•ri•e•ty** \₁nōtə'rīətē\ *n* — **no•to•ri•ous•ly** *adv*

**not•with•stand•ing** \₁nätwith'standin, -with-\ *prep* : in spite of ~ *adv* : nevertheless ~ *conj* : although

**nou•gat** \'nügət\ *n* : nuts or fruit pieces in a sugar paste

**nought** \'not, 'nät\ *var of* NAUGHT

**noun** \'naun\ *n* : word that is the name of a person, place, or thing

**nour•ish** \'nərish\ *vb* : promote the

growth of — **nour·ish·ing** *adj* — **nour·ish·ment** *n*

**no·va** \'nōvə\ *n, pl* **-vas** *or* **-vae** \-,vē, -,vī\ : star that suddenly brightens and then fades gradually

**nov·el** \'nävəl\ *adj* : new or strange ~ *n* : long invented prose story — **nov·el·ist** \-əlist\ *n*

**nov·el·ty** \'nävəltē\ *n, pl* **-ties** 1 : something new or unusual 2 : newness 3 : small manufactured article — usu. pl.

**No·vem·ber** \nō'vembər\ *n* : 11th month of the year having 30 days

**nov·ice** \'nävəs\ *n* 1 : one preparing to take vows in a religious order 2 : one who is inexperienced or untrained

**no·vi·tiate** \nō'vishət, nə-\ *n* : period or state of being a novice

**now** \'naů\ *adv* 1 : at the present time or moment 2 : forthwith ~ *conj* : in view of the fact ~ *n* : present time

**now·a·days** \'naůə,dāz\ *adv* : now

**no·where** \-,hwer\ *adv* : not anywhere — **no·where** *n*

**nox·ious** \'näkshəs\ *adj* : harmful

**noz·zle** \'näzəl\ *n* : device to direct or control a flow of fluid

**nu·ance** \'nü,äns, 'nyü-\ *n* : subtle distinction or variation

**nub** \'nəb\ *n* 1 : knob or lump 2 : gist

**nu·bile** \'nü,bīl, 'nyü-, -bəl\ *adj* 1 : of marriageable condition or age 2 : sexually attractive

**nu·cle·ar** \'nüklēər, 'nyü-\ *adj* 1 : relating to the atomic nucleus or atomic energy 2 : relating to a weapon whose power is from a nuclear reaction

**nu·cle·us** \'nüklēəs, 'nyü-\ *n, pl* **-clei** \-klē,ī\ : central mass or part (as of a cell or an atom)

**nude** \'nüd, 'nyüd\ *adj* **nud·er; nud·est** : naked ~ *n* : nude human figure — **nu·di·ty** \'nüdətē, 'nyü-\ *n*

**nudge** \'nəj\ *vb* **nudged; nudg·ing** : touch or push gently — **nudge** *n*

**nud·ism** \'nüd,izəm, 'nyü-\ *n* : practice of going nude — **nud·ist** \'nüdist, 'nyü-\ *n*

**nug·get** \'nəgət\ *n* : lump of gold

**nui·sance** \'nüs°ns, 'nyü-\ *n* : something annoying

**null** \'nəl\ *adj* : having no legal or binding force — **nul·li·ty** \'nälətē\ *n*

**nul·li·fy** \'nələ,fī\ *vb* **-fied; -fy·ing**

: make null or valueless — **nul·li·fi·ca·tion** \,nələfə'kāshən\ *n*

**numb** \'nəm\ *adj* : lacking feeling — **numb** *vb* — **numb·ly** *adv* — **numb·ness** *n*

**num·ber** \'nəmbər\ *n* 1 : total of individuals taken together 2 : indefinite total 3 : unit of a mathematical system 4 : numeral 5 : one in a sequence ~ *vb* 1 : count 2 : assign a number to 3 : comprise in number — **num·ber·less** *adj*

**nu·mer·al** \'nümərəl, 'nyü-\ *n* : conventional symbol representing a number

**nu·mer·a·tor** \'nümə,rātər, 'nyü-\ *n* : part of a fraction above the line

**nu·mer·i·cal** \nú'merikəl, nyü-\, **nu·mer·ic** \-'merik\ *adj* 1 : relating to numbers 2 : expressed in or involving numbers — **nu·mer·i·cal·ly** *adv*

**nu·mer·ol·o·gy** \,nümə'räləjē, ,nyü-\ *n* : occult study of numbers — **nu·mer·ol·o·gist** \-jist\ *n*

**nu·mer·ous** \'nümərəs, 'nyü-\ *adj* : consisting of a great number

**nu·mis·mat·ics** \,nüməz'matiks, ,nyü-\ *n* : study or collection of monetary objects — **nu·mis·mat·ic** \-ik\ *adj* — **nu·mis·ma·tist** \nü'mizmətist, nyü-\ *n*

**num·skull** \'nəm,skəl\ *n* : stupid person

**nun** \'nən\ *n* : woman belonging to a religious order — **nun·nery** \-ərē\ *n*

**nup·tial** \'nəpshəl\ *adj* : relating to marriage or a wedding ~ *n* : marriage or wedding — usu. pl.

**nurse** \'nərs\ *n* 1 : one hired to care for children 2 : person trained to care for sick people ~ *vb* **nursed; nurs·ing** 1 : suckle 2 : care for

**nurs·ery** \'nərsərē\ *n, pl* **-er·ies** 1 : place where children are cared for 2 : place where young plants are grown

**nursing home** : private establishment providing care for persons who are unable to care for themselves

**nur·ture** \'nərchər\ *n* 1 : training or upbringing 2 : food or nourishment ~ *vb* **-tured; -tur·ing** 1 : care for or feed 2 : educate

**nut** \'nət\ *n* 1 : dry hard-shelled fruit or seed with a firm inner kernel 2 : metal block with a screw hole through it 3 : foolish, eccentric, or crazy person 4 : enthusiast — **nut·crack·er** *n* — **nut·shell** *n* — **nut·ty** *adj*

**nut·hatch** \'nət,hach\ *n* : small bird

**nut·meg** \'nət₁meg, -₁māg\ *n* : nutlike aromatic seed of a tropical tree

**nu·tri·ent** \'nütrēənt, 'nyü-\ *n* : something giving nourishment — **nutrient** *adj*

**nu·tri·ment** \-trəmənt\ *n* : nutrient

**nu·tri·tion** \nú'trishən, nyü-\ *n* : act or process of nourishing esp. with food — **nu·tri·tion·al** \-'trishənəl\ *adj* — **nu·tri·tious** \-'trishəs\ *adj* — **nu·tri·tive** \'nütrətiv, 'nyü-\ *adj*

**nuts** \'nəts\ *adj* **1** : enthusiastic **2** : crazy

**nuz·zle** \'nəzəl\ *vb* **-zled; -zling 1** : touch with or as if with the nose **2** : snuggle

**ny·lon** \'nī₁län\ *n* **1** : tough synthetic material used esp. in textiles **2** *pl* : stockings made of nylon

**nymph** \'nimf\ *n* **1** : lesser goddess in ancient mythology **2** : girl **3** : immature insect

# O

**o** \'ō\ *n, pl* **o's** *or* **os** \'ōz\ **1** : 15th letter of the alphabet **2** : zero

**O** *var of* **OH**

**oaf** \'ōf\ *n* : stupid or awkward person — **oaf·ish** \'ōfish\ *adj*

**oak** \'ōk\ *n, pl* **oaks** *or* **oak** : tree bearing a thin-shelled nut or its wood — **oak·en** \'ōkən\ *adj*

**oar** \'ōr\ *n* : pole with a blade at the end used to propel a boat

**oar·lock** \-₁läk\ *n* : u-shaped device for holding an oar

**oa·sis** \ō'āsəs\ *n, pl* **oa·ses** \-₁sēz\ : fertile area in a desert

**oat** \'ōt\ *n* : cereal grass or its edible seed — **oat·cake** *n* — **oat·en** \-ᵊn\ *adj* — **oat·meal** *n*

**oath** \'ōth\ *n, pl* **oaths** \'ōthz, 'ōths\ **1** : solemn appeal to God as a pledge of sincerity **2** : profane utterance

**ob·du·rate** \'äbdúret, -dyú-\ *adj* : stubbornly resistant — **ob·du·ra·cy** \-rəsē\ *n*

**obe·di·ent** \ō'bēdēənt\ *adj* : willing to obey — **obe·di·ence** \-əns\ *n* — **obe·di·ent·ly** *adv*

**obei·sance** \ō'bēsəns, -'bās-\ *n* : bow of respect or submission

**obe·lisk** \'äbə₁lisk\ *n* : 4-sided tapering pillar

**obese** \ōbēs\ *adj* : extremely fat — **obe·si·ty** \-'bēsətē\ *n*

**obey** \ō'bā\ *vb* **obeyed; obey·ing 1** : follow the commands or guidance of **2** : behave in accordance with

**ob·fus·cate** \'äbfə₁skāt\ *vb* **-cat·ed; -cat·ing** : confuse — **ob·fus·ca·tion** \₁äbfəs'kāshən\ *n*

**obit·u·ary** \ə'bichə₁werē\ *n, pl* **-ar·ies** : death notice

**¹ob·ject** \'äbjikt\ *n* **1** : something that may be seen or felt **2** : purpose **3** : noun or equivalent toward which the action of a verb is directed or which follows a preposition

**²object** \əb'jekt\ *vb* : offer opposition or disapproval — **ob·jec·tion** \-'jekshən\ *n* — **ob·jec·tion·able** \-shənəbəl\ *adj* — **ob·jec·tion·ably** \-blē\ *adv* — **ob·jec·tor** \-'jektər\ *n*

**ob·jec·tive** \əb'jektiv\ *adj* **1** : relating to an object or end **2** : existing outside an individual's thoughts or feelings **3** : treating facts without distortion **4** : relating to or being a grammatical case marking objects ∼ *n* : aim or end of action — **ob·jec·tive·ly** *adv* — **ob·jec·tive·ness** *n* — **ob·jec·tiv·i·ty** \₁äb₁jek'tivətē\ *n*

**ob·li·gate** \'äblə₁gāt\ *vb* **-gat·ed; -gat·ing** : bind legally or morally — **ob·li·ga·tion** \₁äblə'gāshən\ *n* — **oblig·a·to·ry** \ə'bligə₁tōrē, 'äbligə-\ *adj*

**oblige** \ə'blīj\ *vb* **obliged; oblig·ing 1** : compel **2** : do a favor for — **oblig·ing** *adj* — **oblig·ing·ly** *adv*

**oblique** \ō'blēk, -'blīk\ *adj* **1** : lying at a slanting angle **2** : indirect — **oblique·ly** *adv* — **oblique·ness** *n* — **obliq·ui·ty** \-'blikwətē\ *n*

**oblit·er·ate** \ə'blitə₁rāt\ *vb* **-at·ed; -at·ing** : completely remove or destroy — **oblit·er·a·tion** \-₁blitə'rāshən\ *n*

**obliv·i·on** \ə'blivēən\ *n* **1** : state of having lost conscious awareness **2** : state of being forgotten

**obliv·i·ous** \-ēəs\ *adj* : not aware or mindful — with *to* or *of* — **obliv·i·ous·ly** *adv* — **obliv·i·ous·ness** *n*

**ob·long** \'äb₁lòn\ *adj* : longer in one direction than in the other with opposite sides parallel — **oblong** *n*

**ob·lo·quy** \'äbləkwē\ n, pl **-quies** 1 : strongly condemning utterance 2 : bad repute

**ob·nox·ious** \äb'näkshəs, əb-\ adj : repugnant — **ob·nox·ious·ly** adv — **ob·nox·ious·ness** n

**oboe** \'ōbō\ n : slender woodwind instrument with a reed mouthpiece — **obo·ist** \'o͝obōist\ n

**ob·scene** \äb'sēn, əb-\ adj : repugnantly indecent — **ob·scene·ly** adv — **ob·scen·i·ty** \-'senətē\ n

**ob·scure** \äb'skyu̇r, əb-\ adj 1 : dim or hazy 2 : not well known 3 : vague ∼ vb : make indistinct or unclear — **ob·scure·ly** adv — **ob·scu·ri·ty** \-'skyu̇rətē\ n

**ob·se·quies** \'äbsəkwēz\ n pl : funeral or burial rites

**ob·se·qui·ous** \əb'sēkwēəs\ adj : excessively attentive or flattering — **ob·se·qui·ous·ly** adv — **ob·se·qui·ous·ness** n

**ob·ser·va·to·ry** \əb'zərvə₁tōrē\ n, pl **-ries** : place for observing astronomical phenomena

**ob·serve** \əb'zərv\ vb **-served; -serv·ing** 1 : conform to 2 : celebrate 3 : see, watch, or notice 4 : remark — **ob·serv·able** adj — **ob·ser·vance** \-'zərvəns\ n — **ob·ser·vant** \-vənt\ adj — **ob·ser·va·tion** \₁äbsər'vā-shən, -zər-\ n

**ob·sess** \əb'ses\ vb : preoccupy intensely or abnormally — **ob·session** \äb'seshən, əb-\ n — **ob·session·sive** \-'sesiv\ adj — **ob·ses·sive·ly** adv

**ob·so·les·cent** \₁äbsə'les³nt\ adj : going out of use — **ob·so·les·cence** \-³ns\ n

**ob·so·lete** \₁äbsə'lēt, 'äbsə₁-\ adj : no longer in use

**ob·sta·cle** \'äbstikəl\ n : something that stands in the way or opposes

**ob·stet·rics** \əb'stetriks\ n sing or pl : branch of medicine that deals with childbirth — **ob·stet·ric** \-rik\, **stet·ri·cal** \-rikəl\ adj — **ob·ste·tri·cian** \₁äbstə'trishən\ n

**ob·sti·nate** \'äbstənət\ adj : stubborn — **ob·sti·na·cy** \-nəsē\ n — **ob·sti·nate·ly** adv

**ob·strep·er·ous** \əb'strepərəs\ adj : uncontrollably noisy or defiant — **ob·strep·er·ous·ness** n

**ob·struct** \əb'strəkt\ vb : block or impede — **ob·struc·tion** \-'strəkshən\ n — **ob·struc·tive** \-'strəktiv\ adj — **ob·struc·tor** \-tər\ n

**ob·tain** \əb'tān\ vb 1 : gain by effort 2 : be generally recognized — **ob·tain·able** adj

**ob·trude** \əb'trüd\ vb **-trud·ed; -truding** 1 : thrust out 2 : intrude — **ob·tru·sion** \-'trüzhən\ n — **ob·tru·sive** \-'trüsiv\ adj — **ob·tru·sive·ly** adv — **ob·tru·sive·ness** n

**ob·tuse** \äb'tüs, əb-, -'tyüs\ adj 1 : slow-witted 2 : exceeding 90 but less than 180 degrees — **ob·tuse·ly** adv — **ob·tuse·ness** n

**ob·verse** \'äb₁vərs, äb'-\ n : principal side (as of a coin)

**ob·vi·ate** \'äbvē₁āt\ vb **-at·ed; -at·ing** : make unnecessary

**ob·vi·ous** \'äbvēəs\ adj : plain or unmistakable — **ob·vi·ous·ly** adv — **ob·vi·ous·ness** n

**oc·ca·sion** \ə'kāzhən\ n 1 : favorable opportunity 2 : cause 3 : time of an event 4 : special event ∼ vb : cause — **oc·ca·sion·al** \-'kāzhənəl\ n — **oc·ca·sion·al·ly** adv

**oc·ci·den·tal** \₁äksə'dent³l\ adj : western — **Occidental** n

**oc·cult** \ə'kəlt, 'äk₁əlt\ adj 1 : secret or mysterious 2 : relating to supernatural agencies — **oc·cult·ism** \-'kəl₁tizəm\ n — **oc·cult·ist** \-tist\ n

**oc·cu·pan·cy** \'äkyəpənsē\ n, pl **-cies** : an occupying

**oc·cu·pant** \-pənt\ n : one who occupies

**oc·cu·pa·tion** \₁äkyə'pāshən\ n 1 : vocation 2 : action or state of occupying — **oc·cu·pa·tion·al** \-shənəl\ adj — **oc·cu·pa·tion·al·ly** adv

**oc·cu·py** \'äkyə₁pī\ vb **-pied; -py·ing** 1 : engage the attention of 2 : fill up 3 : take or hold possession of 4 : reside in — **oc·cu·pi·er** \-₁pīər\ n

**oc·cur** \ə'kər\ vb **-rr-** 1 : be found or met with 2 : take place 3 : come to mind

**oc·cur·rence** \ə'kərəns\ n : something that takes place

**ocean** \'ōshən\ n 1 : whole body of salt water 2 : very large body of water — **ocean·front** n — **ocean·go·ing** adj — **oce·an·ic** \₁ōshē'anik\ adj

**ocean·og·ra·phy** \₁ōshə'nägrəfē\ n : science dealing with the ocean — **ocean·og·ra·pher** \-fər\ n — **ocean·o·graph·ic** \-nə'grafik\ adj

**oce·lot** \'äsə₁lät, 'ōsə-\ n : medium-sized American wildcat

**ocher, ochre** \'ōkər\ n : red or yellow pigment

**o'-clock** \ə'kläk\ adv : according to the clock

**oc·ta·gon** \'äktə,gän\ n : 8-sided polygon — **oc·tag·o·nal** \äk'tagən²l\ adj

**oc·tave** \'äktiv\ n : musical interval of 8 steps or the notes within this interval

**Oc·to·ber** \äk'tōbər\ n : 10th month of the year having 31 days

**oc·to·pus** \'äktəpəs\ n, pl **-pus·es** or **-pi** \-,pī\ : sea mollusk with 8 arms

**oc·u·lar** \'äkyələr\ adj : relating to the eye

**oc·u·list** \'äkyəlist\ n 1 : ophthalmologist 2 : optometrist

**odd** \'äd\ adj 1 : being only one of a pair or set 2 : not divisible by two without a remainder 3 : additional to what is usual or to the number mentioned 4 : queer — **odd·ly** adv — **odd·ness** n

**odd·i·ty** \'ädətē\ n, pl **-ties** : something odd

**odds** \'ädz\ n pl 1 : difference by which one thing is favored 2 : disagreement 3 : ratio between winnings and the amount of the bet

**ode** \'ōd\ n : solemn lyric poem

**odi·ous** \'ōdēəs\ adj : hated — **odi·ous·ly** adv — **odi·ous·ness** n

**odi·um** \'ōdēəm\ n 1 : merited loathing 2 : disgrace

**odor** \'ōdər\ n : quality that affects the sense of smell — **odor·less** adj — **odor·ous** adj

**od·ys·sey** \'ädəsē\ n, pl **-seys** : long wandering

**o'er** \'ōr\ adv or prep : OVER

**of** \'əv, 'äv\ prep 1 : from 2 : distinguished by 3 : because of 4 : made or written by 5 : made with, being, or containing 6 : belonging to or connected with 7 : about 8 : that is 9 : concerning 10 : before

**off** \'óf\ adv 1 : from a place 2 : unattached or removed 3 : to a state of being no longer in use 4 : away from work 5 : at a distance in time or space ~ prep 1 : away from 2 : at the expense of 3 : not engaged in or abstaining from 4 : below the usual level of ~ adj 1 : not operating, up to standard, or correct 2 : remote 3 : provided for

**of·fal** \'ófəl\ n 1 : waste 2 : viscera and trimmings of a butchered animal

**of·fend** \ə'fend\ vb 1 : sin or act in violation 2 : hurt, annoy, or insult — **of·fend·er** n

**of·fense, of·fence** \ə'fens, 'äf,ens\ n : attack, misdeed, or insult

**of·fen·sive** \ə'fensiv, 'äf,en-\ adj : causing offense ~ n : attack — **of·fen·sive·ly** adv — **of·fen·sive·ness** n

**of·fer** \'ófər\ vb 1 : present for acceptance 2 : propose 3 : put up (an effort) ~ n 1 : proposal 2 : bid — **of·fer·ing** n

**of·fer·to·ry** \'ófər,tōrē\ n, pl **-ries** : presentation of offerings or its musical accompaniment

**off·hand** adv or adj : without previous thought or preparation

**of·fice** \'ófəs\ n 1 : position of authority (as in government) 2 : rite 3 : place where a business is transacted — **of·fice·hold·er** n

**of·fi·cer** \'ófəsər\ n 1 : one charged with law enforcement 2 : one who holds an office of trust or authority 3 : one who holds a commission in the armed forces

**of·fi·cial** \ə'fishəl\ n : one in office ~ adj : authorized or authoritative — **of·fi·cial·dom** \-dəm\ n — **of·fi·cial·ly** adv

**of·fi·ci·ant** \ə'fishēənt\ n : clergy member who officiates at a religious rite

**of·fi·ci·ate** \ə'fishē,āt\ vb **-at·ed; -at·ing** : perform a ceremony or function

**of·fi·cious** \ə'fishəs\ adj : volunteering one's services unnecessarily — **of·fi·cious·ly** adv — **of·fi·cious·ness** n

**off·ing** \'ófiŋ\ n : future

**off·set** \'óf,set\ vb **-set; -set·ting** : provide an opposite or equaling effect to

**off·shoot** \'óf,shüt\ n : outgrowth

**off·shore** adv : at a distance from the shore ~ adj : moving away from or situated off the shore

**off·spring** \'óf,spriŋ\ n, pl **offspring** : one coming into being through animal or plant reproduction

**of·ten** \'ófən, 'óft-\ adv : many times — **of·ten·times, oft·times** adv

**ogle** \'ōgəl\ vb **ogled; ogling** : stare at lustily — **ogle** n — **ogler** \-ələr\ n

**ogre** \'ōgər\ n 1 : monster 2 : dreaded person

**oh** \'ō\ interj 1 — used to express an emotion 2 — used in direct address

**ohm** \'ōm\ n : unit of electrical resistance — **ohm·me·ter** \'ōm,mētər\ n

**oil** \'óil\ n 1 : greasy liquid substance

2 ; petroleum ~ *vb* : put oil in or on — **oil•er** *n* — **oil•i•ness** \'òilēnəs\ *n* — **oily** \'òilē\ *adj*

**oil•cloth** *n* : cloth treated with oil or paint and used for coverings

**oil•skin** *n* : oiled waterproof cloth

**oink** \'òiŋk\ *n* : natural noise of a hog — **oink** *vb*

**oint•ment** \'òintmənt\ *n* : oily medicinal preparation

**OK** *or* **okay** \ō'kā\ *adv or adj* : all right ~ *vb* **OK'd** *or* **okayed; OK'•ing** *or* **okay•ing** : approve ~ *n* : approval

**okra** \'ōkrə, *South also* -krē\ *n* : leafy vegetable with edible green pods

**old** \'ōld\ *adj* 1 : of long standing 2 : of a specified age 3 : relating to a past era 4 : having existed a long time — **old•ish** \'ōldish\ *adj*

**old•en** \'ōldən\ *adj* : of or relating to a bygone era

**old–fash•ioned** \-'fashənd\ *adj* 1 : out-of-date 2 : conservative

**old maid** *n* : spinster

**old–tim•er** \ōld'tīmər\ *n* 1 : veteran 2 : one who is old

**ole•an•der** \'ōlē,andər\ *n* : poisonous evergreen shrub

**oleo•mar•ga•rine** \,ōlēō'märjərən\ *n* : margarine

**ol•fac•to•ry** \äl'faktərē, ōl-\ *adj* : relating to the sense of smell

**oli•gar•chy** \'älə,gärkē, 'ōlə-\ *n, pl* **-chies** 1 : government by a few people 2 : those holding power in an oligarchy — **oli•garch** \-,gärk\ *n* — **oli•gar•chic** \,älə'gärkik, ,ōlə-\, **oli•gar•chi•cal** \-kikəl\ *adj*

**ol•ive** \'äliv, -əv\ *n* 1 : evergreen tree bearing small edible fruit or the fruit 2 : dull yellowish green color

**om•buds•man** \'äm,bùdzmən, äm-'bùdz-\ *n, pl* **-men** \-mən\ : complaint investigator

**om•e•let, om•e•lette** \'ämələt\ *n* : beaten eggs lightly fried and folded

**omen** \'ōmən\ *n* : sign or warning of the future

**om•i•nous** \'ämənəs\ *adj* : presaging evil — **om•i•nous•ly** *adv* — **om•i•nous•ness** *n*

**omit** \ō'mit\ *vb* **-tt-** 1 : leave out 2 : fail to perform — **omis•si•ble** \ō-'misəbəl\ *adj* — **omis•sion** \-'mishən\ *n*

**om•nip•o•tent** \äm'nipətənt\ *adj* : almighty — **om•nip•o•tence** \-əns\ *n* — **om•nip•o•tent•ly** *adv*

**om•ni•pres•ent** \,ämni'prez²nt\ *adj* : ever-present — **om•ni•pres•ence** \-²ns\ *n*

**om•ni•scient** \äm'nishənt\ *adj* : all-knowing — **om•ni•science** \-əns\ *n* — **om•ni•scient•ly** *adv*

**om•niv•o•rous** \äm'nivərəs\ *adj* 1 : eating both meat and vegetables 2 : avid — **om•niv•o•rous•ly** *adv*

**on** \'òn, 'än\ *prep* 1 : in or to a position over and in contact with 2 : at or to 3 : about 4 : from 5 : with regard to 6 : in a state or process 7 : during the time of ~ *adv* 1 : in or into contact with 2 : forward 3 : into operation

**once** \'wəns\ *adv* 1 : one time only 2 : at any one time 3 : formerly ~ *n* : one time ~ *conj* : as soon as ~ *adj* : former — **at once** 1 : simultaneously 2 : immediately

**once–over** *n* : swift examination

**on•com•ing** *adj* : approaching

**one** \'wən\ *adj* 1 : being a single thing 2 : being one in particular 3 : being the same in kind ~ *pron* 1 : certain indefinitely indicated person or thing 2 : a person in general ~ *n* 1 : 1st in a series 2 : single person or thing — **one•ness** *n*

**oner•ous** \'änərəs, 'ōnə-\ *adj* : imposing a burden

**one•self** \,wən'self\ *pron* : one's own self — usu. used reflexively or for emphasis

**one–sid•ed** \-'sīdəd\ *adj* 1 : occurring on one side only 2 : partial

**one•time** *adj* : former

**one–way** *adj* : made or for use in only one direction

**on•go•ing** *adj* : continuing

**on•ion** \'ənyən\ *n* : plant grown for its pungent edible bulb or this bulb

**on•ly** \'ōnlē\ *adj* : alone in its class ~ *adv* 1 : merely or exactly 2 : solely 3 : at the very least 4 : as a result ~ *conj* : but

**on•set** *n* : start

**on•shore** *adj* 1 : moving toward shore 2 : lying on or near the shore — **on•shore** *adv*

**on•slaught** \'än,slòt, 'òn-\ *n* : attack

**on•to** \'òntü, 'än-\ *prep* : to a position or point on

**onus** \'ōnəs\ *n* : burden (as of obligation or blame)

**on•ward** \'ònwərd, 'än-\ *adv or adj* : forward

**on•yx** \'äniks\ *n* : quartz used as a gem

**ooze** \'üz\ *n* : soft mud ~ *vb* **oozed;**
**ooz•ing** : flow or leak out slowly —
**oozy** \'üzē\ *adj*

**opac•i•ty** \ō'pasətē\ *n* : quality or state
of being opaque or an opaque spot

**opal** \'ōpəl\ *n* : gem with delicate colors

**opaque** \ō'pāk\ *adj* **1** : blocking light
**2** : not easily understood **3** : dull-
witted — **opaque•ly** *adv*

**open** \'ōpən\ *adj* **1** : not shut or shut
up **2** : not secret or hidden **3** : frank
or generous **4** : extended **5** : free
from controls **6** : not decided ~ *vb*
**1** : make or become open **2** : make or
become functional **3** : start ~ *n*
: outdoors — **open•er** \-ər\ *n* —
**open•ly** *adv* — **open•ness** *n*

**open•hand•ed** \-'handəd\ *adj* : generous — **open•hand•ed•ly** *adv*

**open•ing** \'ōpəniŋ\ *n* **1** : act or instance of making open **2** : something
that is open **3** : opportunity

**op•era** \'äpərə, 'äprə\ *n* : drama set to
music — **op•er•at•ic** \,äpə'ratik\ *adj*

**op•er•a•ble** \'äpərəbəl\ *adj* **1** : usable
or in working condition **2** : suitable
for surgical treatment

**op•er•ate** \'äpə,rāt\ *vb* **-at•ed; -at•ing**
**1** : perform work **2** : perform an
operation **3** : manage — **op•er•a•tor**
\-,rātər\ *n*

**op•er•a•tion** \,äpə'rāshən\ *n* **1** : act or
process of operating **2** : surgical work
on a living body **3** : military action or
mission — **op•er•a•tion•al** \-shənəl\
*adj*

**op•er•a•tive** \'äpərətiv, -,rāt-\ *adj*
: working or having an effect

**op•er•et•ta** \,äpə'retə\ *n* : light opera

**oph•thal•mol•o•gy** \,äf,thal'mäləjē\ *n*
: branch of medicine dealing with the
eye — **oph•thal•mol•o•gist** \-jist\ *n*

**opi•ate** \'ōpēət, -pē,āt\ *n* : preparation
or derivative of opium

**opine** \ō'pīn\ *vb* **opined; opin•ing**
: express an opinion

**opin•ion** \ə'pinyən\ *n* **1** : belief **2**
: judgment **3** : formal statement by an
expert

**opin•ion•at•ed** \-yə,nātəd\ *adj* : stubborn in one's opinions

**opi•um** \'ōpēəm\ *n* : addictive narcotic
drug that is the dried juice of a poppy

**opos•sum** \ə'päsəm\ *n* : common tree-
dwelling nocturnal mammal

**op•po•nent** \ə'pōnənt\ *n* : one that opposes

**op•por•tune** \,äpər'tün, -'tyün\ *adj*

: suitable or timely — **op•por•tune•ly**
*adv*

**op•por•tun•ism** \-'tü,nizəm, -'tyü-\ *n*
: a taking advantage of opportunities
— **op•por•tun•ist** \-nist\ *n* — **op-
por•tu•nis•tic** \-tü'nistik, -tyü-\ *adj*

**op•por•tu•ni•ty** \-'tünətē, -'tyü-\ *n, pl*
**-ties** : favorable time

**op•pose** \ə'pōz\ *vb* **-posed; -pos•ing**
**1** : place opposite or against something **2** : resist — **op•po•si•tion**
\,äpə'zishən\ *n*

**op•po•site** \'äpəzət\ *n* : one that is opposed ~ *adj* **1** : set facing something that is at the other side or end
: opposed or contrary ~ *adv* : on opposite sides ~ *prep* : across from —
**op•po•site•ly** *adv*

**op•press** \ə'pres\ *vb* **1** : persecute
**2** : weigh down — **op•pres•sion**
\ə'preshən\ *n* — **op•pres•sive**
\-'presiv\ *adj* — **op•pres•sive•ly**
*adv* — **op•pres•sor** \-'presər\ *n*

**op•pro•bri•ous** \ə'prōbrēəs\ *adj* : expressing or deserving opprobrium
— **op•pro•bri•ous•ly** *adv*

**op•pro•bri•um** \-brēəm\ *n* **1** : something that brings disgrace **2** : infamy

**opt** \'äpt\ *vb* : choose

**op•tic** \'äptik\ *adj* : relating to vision or
the eye

**op•ti•cal** \'äptikəl\ *adj* : relating to op-
tics, vision, or the eye

**op•ti•cian** \äp'tishən\ *n* : maker of or
dealer in eyeglasses

**op•tics** \'äptiks\ *n pl* : science of light
and vision

**op•ti•mal** \'äptəməl\ *adj* : most favorable — **op•ti•mal•ly** *adv*

**op•ti•mism** \'äptə,mizəm\ *n* : tendency to hope for the best — **op•ti-
mist** \-mist\ *n* — **op•ti•mis•tic**
\,äptə'mistik\ *adj* — **op•ti•mis•ti-
cal•ly** *adv*

**op•ti•mum** \'äptəməm\ *n, pl* **-ma**
\-mə\ : amount or degree of something most favorable to an end — **op-
timum** *adj*

**op•tion** \'äpshən\ *n* **1** : ability to choose
**2** : right to buy or sell a stock **3** : alternative — **op•tion•al** \-shənəl\ *adj*

**op•tom•e•try** \äp'tämətrē\ *n* : profession of examining the eyes — **op-
tom•e•trist** \-trist\ *n*

**op•u•lent** \'äpyələnt\ *adj* : lavish —
**op•u•lence** \-ləns\ *n* — **op•u•lent•ly**
*adv*

**opus** \'ōpəs\ *n, pl* **opera** \'ōpərə, 'äpə-\ : work esp. of music

**or** \'òr\ *conj* — used to indicate an alternative

**-or** \ər\ *n suffix* : one that performs an action

**or•a•cle** \'òrəkəl\ *n* 1 : one held to give divinely inspired answers or revelations 2 : wise person or an utterance of such a person — **orac•u•lar** \ò'rakyələr\ *adj*

**oral** \'òrəl\ *adj* 1 : spoken 2 : relating to the mouth — **oral•ly** *adv*

**or•ange** \'òrinj\ *n* 1 : reddish yellow citrus fruit 2 : color between red and yellow — **or•ange•ade** \,òrinj'ād\ *n*

**orang•u•tan** \ə'raŋə,taŋ, -,tan\ *n* : large reddish brown ape

**ora•tion** \ə'rāshən\ *n* : elaborate formal speech

**or•a•tor** \'òrətər\ *n* : one noted as a public speaker

**or•a•to•rio** \,òrə'tōrē,ō\ *n, pl* **-ri•os** : major choral work

**or•a•to•ry** \'òrə,tōrē\ *n* : art of public speaking — **or•a•tor•i•cal** \,òrə-'tòrikəl\ *adj*

**orb** \'òrb\ *n* : spherical body

**or•bit** \'òrbət\ *n* : path made by one body revolving around another ~ *vb* : revolve around — **or•bit•al** \-ᵊl\ *adj* — **or•bit•er** *n*

**or•chard** \'òrchərd\ *n* : place where fruit or nut trees are grown — **or•chard•ist** \-ist\ *n*

**or•ches•tra** \'òrkəstrə\ *n* 1 : group of musicians 2 : front seats of a theater's main floor — **or•ches•tral** \òr-'kestrəl\ *adj* — **or•ches•tral•ly** *adv*

**or•ches•trate** \'òrkə,strāt\ *vb* **-trat•ed; -trat•ing** 1 : compose or arrange for an orchestra 2 : arrange or combine for best effect — **or•ches•tra•tion** \,òrkə'strāshən\ *n*

**or•chid** \'òrkəd\ *n* : plant with showy 3-petal flowers or its flower

**or•dain** \òr'dān\ *vb* 1 : admit to the clergy 2 : decree

**or•deal** \òr'dēl, 'òr,dēl\ *n* : severely trying experience

**or•der** \'òrdər\ *n* 1 : rank, class, or special group 2 : arrangement 3 : rule of law 4 : authoritative regulation or instruction 5 : working condition 6 : special request for a purchase or what is purchased ~ *vb* 1 : arrange 2 : give an order to 3 : place an order for

**or•der•ly** \-lē\ *adj* 1 : being in order or tidy 2 : well behaved ~ *n, pl* **-lies** 1 : officer's attendant 2 : hospital attendant — **or•der•li•ness** *n*

**or•di•nal** \'òrdᵊnəl\ *n* : number indicating order in a series

**or•di•nance** \-ᵊnəns\ *n* : municipal law

**or•di•nary** \'òrdᵊn,erē\ *adj* : of common occurrence, quality, or ability — **or•di•nar•i•ly** \,òrdᵊn'erəlē\ *adv*

**or•di•na•tion** \,òrdᵊn'āshən\ *n* : act of ordaining

**ord•nance** \'òrdnəns\ *n* : military supplies

**ore** \'ōr\ *n* : mineral containing a valuable constituent

**oreg•a•no** \ə'regə,nō\ *n* : mint used as a seasoning and source of oil

**or•gan** \'òrgən\ *n* 1 : air-powered or electronic keyboard instrument 2 : animal or plant structure with special function 3 : periodical

**or•gan•ic** \òr'ganik\ *adj* 1 : relating to a bodily organ 2 : relating to living things 3 : relating to or containing carbon or its compounds 4 : relating to foods produced without the use of laboratory-made products — **or•gan•i•cal•ly** *adv*

**or•gan•ism** \'òrgə,nizəm\ *n* : a living thing

**or•gan•ist** \'òrgənist\ *n* : organ player

**or•ga•nize** \'òrgə,nīz\ *vb* **-nized; -niz•ing** : form parts into a functioning whole — **or•ga•ni•za•tion** \,òrgənə-'zāshən\ *n* — **or•ga•ni•za•tion•al** \-shənəl\ *adj* — **or•ga•niz•er** *n*

**or•gasm** \'òr,gazəm\ *n* : climax of sexual excitement — **or•gas•mic** \òr'gazmik\ *adj*

**or•gy** \'òrjē\ *n, pl* **-gies** : unrestrained indulgence (as in sexual activity)

**ori•ent** \'ōrē,ent\ *vb* 1 : set in a definite position 2 : acquaint with a situation — **ori•en•ta•tion** \,ōrēən'tāshən\ *n*

**ori•en•tal** \,ōrē'entᵊl\ *adj* : Eastern — **Oriental** *n*

**or•i•fice** \'òrəfəs\ *n* : opening

**or•i•gin** \'òrəjən\ *n* 1 : ancestry 2 : rise, beginning, or derivation from a source — **orig•i•nate** \ə'rijə,nāt\ *vb* — **orig•i•na•tor** \-ər\ *n*

**orig•i•nal** \ə'rijənəl\ *n* : something from which a copy is made ~ *adj* 1 : first 2 : not copied from something else 3 : inventive — **orig•i•nal•i•ty** *n* — **orig•i•nal•ly** *adv*

**ori•ole** \'òrē,ōl, -ēəl\ *n* : American songbird

**or•na•ment** \'òrnəmənt\ *n* : something

that adorns ∼ vb : provide with ornament — **or·na·men·tal** \ˌȯrnə-ˈment²l\ adj — **or·na·men·ta·tion** \-mənˈtāshən\ n

**or·nate** \ȯrˈnāt\ adj : elaborately decorated — **or·nate·ly** adv — **or·nate·ness** n

**or·nery** \ˈȯrnərē, ˈän-\ adj : irritable

**or·ni·thol·o·gy** \ˌȯrnəˈthäləjē\ n, pl **-gies** : study of birds — **or·ni·tho·log·i·cal** \-thəˈläjikəl\ adj — **or·ni·thol·o·gist** \-ˈthäləjist\ n

**or·phan** \ˈȯrfən\ n : child whose parents are dead — **orphan** vb — **or·phan·age** \-ənij\ n

**or·tho·don·tics** \ˌȯrthəˈdäntiks\ n : dentistry dealing with straightening teeth — **or·tho·don·tist** \-ˈdäntist\ n

**or·tho·dox** \ˈȯrthəˌdäks\ adj 1 : conforming to established doctrine 2 cap : of or relating to a Christian church originating in the Eastern Roman Empire — **or·tho·doxy** \-ˌdäksē\ n

**or·thog·ra·phy** \ȯrˈthägrəfē\ n : spelling — **or·tho·graph·ic** \ˌȯrthəˈgrafik\ adj

**or·tho·pe·dics** \ˌȯrthəˈpēdiks\ n sing or pl : correction or prevention of skeletal deformities — **or·tho·pe·dic** \-ik\ adj — **or·tho·pe·dist** \-ˈpēdist\ n

**-o·ry** \ˌȯrē, ȯrē, ərē\ adj suffix 1 : of, relating to, or characterized by 2 : serving for, producing, or maintaining

**os·cil·late** \ˈäsəˌlāt\ vb **-lat·ed; -lat·ing** : swing back and forth — **os·cil·la·tion** \ˌäsəˈlāshən\ n

**os·mo·sis** \äzˈmōsəs, äs-\ n : diffusion esp. of water through a membrane — **os·mot·ic** \-ˈmätik\ adj

**os·prey** \ˈäsprē, -ˌprā\ n, pl **-preys** : large fish-eating hawk

**os·si·fy** \ˈäsəˌfī\ vb **-fied; -fy·ing** : make or become hardened or set in one's ways

**os·ten·si·ble** \äˈstensəbəl\ adj : seeming — **os·ten·si·bly** \-blē\ adv

**os·ten·ta·tion** \ˌästənˈtāshən\ n : pretentious display — **os·ten·ta·tious** \-shəs\ adj — **os·ten·ta·tious·ly** adv

**os·te·op·a·thy** \ˌästēˈäpəthē\ n : system of healing that emphasizes manipulation (as of joints) — **os·te·o·path** \ˈästēəˌpath\ n — **os·te·o·path·ic** \ˌästēəˈpathik\ adj

**os·te·o·po·ro·sis** \ˌästēōpəˈrōsəs\ n, pl **-ro·ses** \-ˌsēz\ : condition characterized by fragile and porous bones

**os·tra·cize** \ˈästrəˌsīz\ vb **-cized; -ciz**ing : exclude by common consent — **os·tra·cism** \-ˌsizəm\ n

**os·trich** \ˈästrich, ˈȯs-\ n : very large flightless bird

**oth·er** \ˈəthər\ adj 1 : being the one left 2 : alternate 3 : additional ∼ pron 1 : remaining one 2 : different one

**oth·er·wise** adv 1 : in a different way 2 : in different circumstances 3 : in other respects — **otherwise** adj

**ot·ter** \ˈätər\ n : fish-eating mammal with webbed feet

**ot·to·man** \ˈätəmən\ n : upholstered footstool

**ought** \ˈȯt\ verbal auxiliary — used to express obligation, advisability, or expectation

**ounce** \ˈau̇ns\ n 1 : unit of weight equal to about 28.3 grams 2 : unit of capacity equal to about 29.6 milliliters

**our** \ˈär, ˈau̇r\ adj : of or relating to us

**ours** \ˈau̇rz, ˈärz\ pron : that which belongs to us

**our·selves** \är'selvz, au̇r-\ pron : we, us — used reflexively or for emphasis

**-ous** \əs\ adj suffix : having or having the qualities of

**oust** \ˈau̇st\ vb : expel or eject

**oust·er** \ˈau̇stər\ n : expulsion

**out** \ˈau̇t\ adv 1 : away from the inside or center 2 : beyond control 3 : to extinction, exhaustion, or completion 4 : in or into the open ∼ vb : become known ∼ adj 1 : situated outside 2 : absent ∼ prep 1 : out through 2 : outward on or along — **out·bound** adj — **out·build·ing** n

**out·age** \ˈau̇tij\ n : period of no electricity

**out·board** \ˈau̇tˌbōrd\ adv : outside a boat or ship — **outboard** adj

**out·break** \ˈau̇tˌbrāk\ n : sudden occurrence

**out·burst** \-ˌbərst\ n : violent expression of feeling

**out·cast** \-ˌkast\ n : person cast out by society

**out·come** \-ˌkəm\ n : result

**out·crop** \ˈau̇tˌkräp\ n : part of a rock stratum that appears above the ground — **outcrop** vb

**out·cry** \-ˌkrī\ n : loud cry

**out·dat·ed** \au̇tˈdātəd\ adj : out-of-date

**out·dis·tance** vb : go far ahead of

**out·do** \au̇tˈdü\ vb **-did** \-ˈdid\; **-done** \-ˈdən\; **-do·ing** \-ˈdüiŋ\; **-does** \-ˈdəz\ : do better than

**out·doors** \aút'dōrz\ *adv* : in or into the open air ∼ *n* : open air — **out·door** *adj*

**out·er** \'aútər\ *adj* **1** : external **2** : farther out — **out·er·most** *adj*

**out·field** \'aút,fēld\ *n* : baseball field beyond the infield — **out·field·er** \-,fēldər\ *n*

**out·fit** \'aút,fit\ *n* **1** : equipment for a special purpose **2** : group ∼ *vb* **-tt-** : equip — **out·fit·ter** *n*

**out·go** \'aút,gō\ *n, pl* **outgoes** : expenditure

**out·go·ing** \'aút,gōiŋ\ *adj* **1** : retiring from a position **2** : friendly

**out·grow** \aút'grō\ *vb* **-grew** \-'grü\; **-grown** \-'grōn\; **-grow·ing** **1** : grow faster than **2** : grow too large for

**out·growth** \'aút,grōth\ *n* **1** : product of growing out **2** : consequence

**out·ing** \'aútiŋ\ *n* : excursion

**out·land·ish** \aút'landish\ *adj* : very strange — **out·land·ish·ly** *adv*

**outlast** *vb* : last longer than

**out·law** \'aút,lò\ *n* : lawless person ∼ *vb* : make illegal

**out·lay** \'aút,lā\ *n* : expenditure

**out·let** \'aút,let, -lət\ *n* **1** : exit **2** : means of release **3** : market for goods **4** : electrical device that gives access to wiring

**out·line** \'aút,līn\ *n* **1** : line marking the outer limits **2** : summary ∼ *vb* **1** : draw the outline of **2** : indicate the chief parts of

**out·live** \aút'liv\ *vb* : live longer than

**out·look** \'aút,lúk\ *n* **1** : viewpoint **2** : prospect for the future

**out·ly·ing** \'aút,līiŋ\ *adj* : far from a central point

**out·ma·neu·ver** \,aútmə'nüvər, -'nyü,-\ *vb* : defeat by more skillful maneuvering

**out·mod·ed** \aút'mōdəd\ *adj* : out-of-date

**out·num·ber** \-'nəmbər\ *vb* : exceed in number

**out of** *prep* **1** : out from within **2** : beyond the limits of **3** : among **4** — used to indicate absence or loss **5** : because of **6** : from or with

**out—of—date** *adj* : no longer in fashion or in use

**out·pa·tient** *n* : person treated at a hospital who does not stay overnight

**out·post** *n* : remote military post

**out·put** *n* : amount produced ∼ *vb* **-put·ted** *or* **-put; -put·ting** : produce

**out·rage** \'aút,rāj\ *n* **1** : violent or shameful act **2** : injury or insult **3** : extreme anger ∼ *vb* **-raged; -rag·ing 1** : subject to violent injury **2** : make very angry

**out·ra·geous** \aút'rājəs\ *adj* : extremely offensive or shameful — **out·ra·geous·ly** *adv* — **out·ra·geous·ness** *n*

**out·right** *adv* **1** : completely **2** : instantly ∼ *adj* **1** : complete **2** : given without reservation

**out·set** *n* : beginning

**out·side** \aút'sīd, 'aút,-\ *n* **1** : place beyond a boundary **2** : exterior **3** : utmost limit ∼ *adj* **1** : outer **2** : coming from without **3** : remote ∼ *adv* : on or to the outside ∼ *prep* **1** : on or to the outside of **2** : beyond the limits of

**outside of** *prep* **1** : outside **2** : besides

**out·sid·er** \-'sīdər\ *n* : one who does not belong to a group

**out·skirts** *n pl* : outlying parts (as of a city)

**out·smart** \aút'smärt\ *vb* : outwit

**out·source** \'aút,sòrs\ *vb* **-sourced; -sourc·ing** : obtain from an outside supplier

**out·spo·ken** *adj* : direct and open in speech — **out·spo·ken·ness** *n*

**out·stand·ing** *adj* **1** : unpaid **2** : very good — **out·stand·ing·ly** *adv*

**out·strip** \aút'strip\ *vb* **1** : go faster than **2** : surpass

¹**out·ward** \'aútwərd\ *adj* **1** : being toward the outside **2** : showing outwardly

²**outward, out·wards** \-wərdz\ *adv* : toward the outside — **out·ward·ly** *adv*

**out·wit** \aút'wit\ *vb* : get the better of by superior cleverness

**ova** *pl of* OVUM

**oval** \'ōvəl\ *adj* : egg-shaped — **oval** *n*

**ova·ry** \'ōvərē\ *n, pl* **-ries 1** : egg-producing organ **2** : seed-producing part of a flower — **ovar·i·an** \ō'-varēən\ *adj*

**ova·tion** \ō'vāshən\ *n* : enthusiastic applause

**ov·en** \'əvən\ *n* : chamber (as in a stove) for baking

**over** \'ōvər\ *adv* **1** : across **2** : upside down **3** : in excess or addition **4** : above **5** : at an end **6** : again ∼ *prep* **1** : above in position or authority **2** : more than **3** : along, through, or across **4** : because of ∼ *adj* **1** : upper **2** : remaining **3** : ended

**over-** *prefix* **1** : so as to exceed or surpass **2** : excessive or excessively

¹**over·age** \ˌōvər'āj\ *adj* : too old

²**overage** \'ōvərij\ *n* : surplus

**over·all** \ˌōvər'ȯl\ *adj* : including everything

**over·alls** \'ōvərˌȯlz\ *n pl* : pants with an extra piece covering the chest

**over·awe** *vb* : subdue by awe

**over·bear·ing** \-'barin\ *adj* : arrogant

**over·blown** \-'blōn\ *adj* : pretentious

**over·board** *adv* : over the side into the water

**over·cast** *adj* : clouded over — ~ *n* : cloud covering

**over·coat** *n* : outer coat

**over·come** *vb* **-came** \-'kām\; **-come**; **-com·ing** **1** : defeat **2** : make helpless or exhausted

**over·do** *vb* **-did**; **-done**; **-do·ing**; **-does** : do too much

**over·draft** *n* : overdrawn sum

**over·draw** *vb* **-drew**; **-drawn**; **-drawing** : write checks for more than one's bank balance

**over·flow** \ˌōvər'flō\ *vb* **1** : flood **2** : flow over — **overflow** \'ōvərˌflō\ *n*

**over·grow** *vb* **-grew**; **-grown**; **-growing** : grow over

**over·hand** *adj* : made with the hand brought down from above — **overhand** *adv* — **over·hand·ed** \-ˌhandəd\ *adv or adj*

**over·hang** *vb* **-hung**; **-hang·ing** : jut out over ~ *n* : something that overhangs

**over·haul** *vb* **1** : repair **2** : overtake

**over·head** \ˌōvər'hed\ *adv* : aloft ~ \'ōvərˌ-\ *adj* : situated above ~ \'ōvərˌ-\ *n* : general business expenses

**over·hear** *vb* **-heard**; **-hear·ing** : hear without the speaker's knowledge

**over·joyed** *adj* : filled with joy

**over·kill** \'ōvərˌkil\ *n* : large excess

**over·land** \-ˌland, -lənd\ *adv or adj* : by, on, or across land

**over·lap** *vb* : lap over — **overlap** \'ōvərˌlap\ *n*

**over·lay** \ˌōvər'lā\ *vb* **-laid**; **-lay·ing** : lay over or across — **over·lay** \'ōvərˌlā\ *n*

**over·look** \ˌōvər'lúk\ *vb* **1** : look down on **2** : fail to see **3** : ignore **4**

---

**List of self-explanatory words with the prefix** *over-*

overabundance
overabundant
overachiever
overactive
overaggressive
overambitious
overanalyze
overanxiety
overanxious
overarousal
overassertive
overbake
overbid
overbill
overbold
overborrow
overbright
overbroad
overbuild
overburden
overbusy
overbuy
overcapacity
overcapitalize
overcareful
overcautious
overcharge
overcivilized
overclean

overcommit
overcompensate
overcomplicate
overconcern
overconfidence
overconfident
overconscientious
overconsume
overconsumption
overcontrol
overcook
overcorrect
overcritical
overcrowd
overdecorate
overdependence
overdependent
overdevelop
overdose
overdramatic
overdramatize
overdress
overdrink
overdue
overeager
overeat
overeducated
overelaborate
overemotional

overemphasis
overemphasize
overenergetic
overenthusiastic
overestimate
overexaggerate
overexaggeration
overexcite
overexcited
overexercise
overexert
overexertion
overexpand
overexpansion
overexplain
overexploit
overexpose
overextend
overextension
overexuberant
overfamiliar
overfatigued
overfeed
overfertilize
overfill
overfond
overgeneralization
overgeneralize
overgenerous

: pardon **5** : supervise ~ \\'ōvər₁-\\ *n*
: observation point

**over•ly** \\'ōvərlē\\ *adv* : excessively

**over•night** *adv* **1** : through the night **2**
: suddenly — **overnight** *adj*

**over•pass** *n* : bridge over a road

**over•pow•er** *vb* : conquer

**over•reach** \\₁ōvər'rēch\\ *vb* : try or
seek too much

**over•ride** *vb* **-rode; -rid•den; -rid•ing**
: neutralize action of

**over•rule** *vb* : rule against or set aside

**over•run** *vb* **-ran; -run•ning 1** : swarm
or flow over **2** : go beyond ~ *n* : an
exceeding of estimated costs

**over•seas** *adv or adj* : beyond or across
the sea

**over•see** \\₁ōvər'sē\\ *vb* **-saw; -seen;**
**-seeing** : supervise — **over•seer**
\\'ōvər₁siər\\ *n*

**over•shad•ow** *vb* : exceed in importance

**over•shoe** *n* : protective outer shoe

**over•shoot** *vb* **-shot; -shoot•ing**
: shoot or pass beyond

**over•sight** *n* : inadvertent omission or
error

**over•sleep** *vb* **-slept; -sleep•ing** : sleep
longer than intended

**over•spread** *vb* **-spread; -spread•ing**
: spread over or above

**over•state** *vb* : exaggerate — **over•**
**state•ment** *n*

**over•stay** *vb* : stay too long

**over•step** *vb* : exceed

**overt** \\ō'vərt, 'ō₁vərt\\ *adj* : not secret
— **overt•ly** *adv*

**over•take** *vb* **-took; -tak•en; -tak•ing**
: catch up with

**over•throw** \\₁ōvər'thrō\\ *vb* **-threw;**
**-thrown; -throw•ing 1** : upset **2**
: defeat — **over•throw** \\'ōvər₁-\\ *n*

**over•time** *n* : extra working time —
**overtime** *adv*

**over•tone** *n* **1** : higher tone in a complex musical tone **2** : suggestion

**over•ture** \\'ōvər₁chúr, -chər\\ *n* **1**
: opening offer **2** : musical introduction

**over•turn** *vb* **1** : turn over **2** : nullify

**over•view** *n* : brief survey

**over•ween•ing** \\₁ōvər'wēniŋ\\ *adj* **1**
: arrogant **2** : excessive

**over•whelm** \\₁ōvər'hwelm\\ *vb* : overcome completely — **over•whelm•**
**ing•ly** \\-'hwelmiŋlē\\ *adv*

**over•wrought** \\₁ōvər'rȯt\\ *adj* : extremely excited

---

| | | |
|---|---|---|
| overglamorize | overparticular | overserious |
| overgraze | overpay | oversexed |
| overharvest | overpayment | oversimple |
| overhasty | overplay | oversimplify |
| overheat | overpopulated | oversolicitous |
| overidealize | overpraise | overspecialize |
| overimaginative | overprescribe | overspend |
| overimpress | overpressure | overstaff |
| overindebtedness | overprice | overstimulation |
| overindulge | overprivileged | overstock |
| overindulgence | overproduce | overstrain |
| overindulgent | overproduction | overstress |
| overinflate | overpromise | overstretch |
| overinsistent | overprotect | oversubtle |
| overintense | overprotective | oversupply |
| overintensity | overqualified | oversuspicious |
| overinvestment | overrate | oversweeten |
| overladen | overreact | overtax |
| overlarge | overreaction | overtighten |
| overlend | overrefined | overtip |
| overload | overregulate | overtired |
| overlong | overregulation | overtrain |
| overloud | overreliance | overtreat |
| overmedicate | overrepresented | overuse |
| overmodest | overrespond | overutilize |
| overmuch | overripe | overvalue |
| overobvious | oversaturate | overweight |
| overoptimistic | oversell | overwork |
| overorganize | oversensitive | overzealous |

**ovoid** \'ō͵void\, **ovoi·dal** \ō'void°l\ *adj* : egg-shaped

**ovu·late** \'ävyə͵lāt, 'ōv-\ *vb* **-lat·ed; -lat·ing** : produce eggs from an ovary — **ovu·la·tion** \͵ävyə'lāshən, ͵ōv-\ *n*

**ovum** \'ōvəm\ *n, pl* **ova** \-və\ : female germ cell

**owe** \'ō\ *vb* **owed; ow·ing 1** : have an obligation to pay **2** : be indebted to or for

**owing to** *prep* : because of

**owl** \'aủl\ *n* : nocturnal bird of prey — **owl·ish** *adj* — **owl·ish·ly** *adv*

**own** \'ōn\ *adj* : belonging to oneself ∼ *vb* **1** : have as property **2** : acknowl-

edge ∼ *pron* : one or ones belonging to oneself — **own·er** *n* — **own·er·ship** *n*

**ox** \'äks\ *n, pl* **ox·en** \'äksən\ : bovine mammal and esp. a castrated bull

**ox·ide** \'äk͵sīd\ *n* : compound of oxygen

**ox·i·dize** \'äksə͵dīz\ *vb* **-dized; -diz·ing** : combine with oxygen — **ox·i·da·tion** \͵äksə'dāshən\ *n* — **ox·i·diz·er** *n*

**ox·y·gen** \'äksijən\ *n* : gaseous chemical element essential for life

**oys·ter** \'öistər\ *n* : bivalve mollusk — **oys·ter·ing** \-riŋ\ *n*

**ozone** \'ō͵zōn\ *n* : very reactive bluish form of oxygen

# P

**p** \'pē\ *n, pl* **p's** *or* **ps** \'pēz\ : 16th letter of the alphabet

**pace** \'pās\ *n* **1** : walking step **2** : rate of progress ∼ *vb* **paced; pac·ing 1** : go at a pace **2** : cover with slow steps **3** : set the pace of

**pace·mak·er** *n* : electrical device to regulate heartbeat

**pachy·derm** \'paki͵dərm\ *n* : elephant

**pa·cif·ic** \pə'sifik\ *adj* : calm or peaceful

**pac·i·fism** \'pasə͵fizəm\ *n* : opposition to war or violence — **pac·i·fist** \-fist\ *n or adj* — **pac·i·fis·tic** \͵pasə'fistik\ *adj*

**pac·i·fy** \'pasə͵fī\ *vb* **-fied; -fy·ing** : make calm — **pac·i·fi·ca·tion** \͵pasəfə'kāshən\ *n* — **pac·i·fi·er** \'pasə͵fīər\ *n*

**pack** \'pak\ *n* **1** : compact bundle **2** : group of animals ∼ *vb* **1** : put into a container **2** : fill tightly or completely **3** : send without ceremony — **pack·er** *n*

**pack·age** \'pakij\ *n* : items bundled together ∼ *vb* **-aged; -ag·ing** : enclose in a package

**pack·et** \'pakət\ *n* : small package

**pact** \'pakt\ *n* : agreement

**pad** \'pad\ *n* **1** : cushioning part or thing **2** : floating leaf of a water plant **3** : tablet of paper ∼ *vb* **-dd- 1** : furnish with a pad **2** : expand with needless matter — **pad·ding** *n*

**pad·dle** \'pad°l\ *n* : implement with a flat blade ∼ *vb* **-dled; -dling** : move, beat, or stir with a paddle

**pad·dock** \'padək\ *n* : enclosed area for racehorses

**pad·dy** \'padē\ *n, pl* **-dies** : wet land where rice is grown

**pad·lock** *n* : lock with a U-shaped catch — **padlock** *vb*

**pae·an** \'pēən\ *n* : song of praise

**pa·gan** \'pāgən\ *n or adj* : heathen — **pa·gan·ism** \-͵izəm\ *n*

**¹page** \'pāj\ *n* : messenger ∼ *vb* **paged; pag·ing** : summon by repeated calls — **pag·er** *n*

**²page** *n* **1** : single leaf (as of a book) or one side of the leaf **2** : information at a single World Wide Web address

**pag·eant** \'pajənt\ *n* : elaborate spectacle or procession — **pag·eant·ry** \-əntrē\ *n*

**pa·go·da** \pə'gōdə\ *n* : tower with roofs curving upward

**paid** *past of* PAY

**pail** \'pāl\ *n* : cylindrical container with a handle — **pail·ful** \-͵fủl\ *n*

**pain** \'pān\ *n* **1** : punishment or penalty **2** : suffering of body or mind **3** *pl* : great care ∼ *vb* : cause or experience pain — **pain·ful** \-fəl\ *adj* — **pain·ful·ly** *adv* — **pain·kill·er** *n* — **pain·kill·ing** *adj* — **pain·less** *adj* — **pain·less·ly** *adv*

**pains·tak·ing** \'pān₋stākiŋ\ adj : taking pains — **painstaking** n — **pains·tak·ing·ly** adv

**paint** \'pānt\ vb 1 : apply color or paint to 2 : portray esp. in color ~ n : mixture of pigment and liquid — **paint·brush** n — **paint·er** n — **paint·ing** n

**pair** \'par\ n : a set of two ~ vb : put or go together as a pair

**pa·ja·mas** \pə'jäməz, -'jam-\ n pl : loose suit for sleeping

**pal** \'pal\ n : close friend

**pal·ace** \'paləs\ n 1 : residence of a chief of state 2 : mansion — **pa·la·tial** \pə'lāshəl\ adj

**pal·at·able** \'palətəbəl\ adj : agreeable to the taste

**pal·ate** \'palət\ n 1 : roof of the mouth 2 : taste — **pal·a·tal** \-ət²l\ adj

**pa·la·ver** \pə'lavər, -'läv-\ n : talk — **palaver** vb

¹**pale** \'pāl\ adj **pal·er; pal·est** 1 : lacking in color or brightness 2 : light in color or shade ~ vb **paled; pal·ing** : make or become pale — **pale·ness** n

²**pale** n 1 : fence stake 2 : enclosed place

**pa·le·on·tol·o·gy** \₋pālē₋än'täləjē\ n : branch of biology dealing with ancient forms of life known from fossils — **pa·le·on·tol·o·gist** \-₋än'täləjist, -ən-\ n

**pal·ette** \'palət\ n : board on which paints are laid and mixed

**pal·i·sade** \₋palə'sād\ n 1 : high fence 2 : line of cliffs

¹**pall** \'pòl\ n 1 : cloth draped over a coffin 2 : something that produces gloom

²**pall** vb : lose in interest or attraction

**pall·bear·er** n : one who attends the coffin at a funeral

¹**pal·let** \'palət\ n : makeshift bed

²**pallet** n : portable storage platform

**pal·li·ate** \'palē₋āt\ vb **-at·ed; -at·ing** 1 : ease without curing 2 : cover or conceal by excusing — **pal·li·a·tion** \₋palē'āshən\ n — **pal·li·a·tive** \'palē₋ātiv\ adj or n

**pal·lid** \'paləd\ adj : pale

**pal·lor** \'palər\ n : paleness

¹**palm** \'päm, 'pälm\ n 1 : tall tropical tree crowned with large leaves 2 : symbol of victory

²**palm** n : underside of the hand ~ vb 1

: conceal in the hand 2 : impose by fraud

**palm·ist·ry** \'päməstrē, 'pälmə-\ n : reading a person's character or future in his palms — **palm·ist** \'pämist, 'pälm-\ n

**palmy** \'pämē, 'pälmē\ adj **palm·i·er; -est** : flourishing

**pal·o·mi·no** \₋palə'mēnō\ n, pl **-nos** : light-colored horse

**pal·pa·ble** \'palpəbəl\ adj 1 : capable of being touched 2 : obvious — **pal·pa·bly** \-blē\ adv

**pal·pi·tate** \'palpə₋tāt\ vb **-tat·ed; -tat·ing** : beat rapidly — **pal·pi·ta·tion** \₋palpə'tāshən\ n

**pal·sy** \'pòlzē\ n, pl **-sies** 1 : paralysis 2 : condition marked by tremor — **pal·sied** \-zēd\ adj

**pal·try** \'pòltrē\ adj **-tri·er; -est** : trivial

**pam·per** \'pampər\ vb : spoil or indulge

**pam·phlet** \'pamflət\ n : unbound publication — **pam·phle·teer** \₋pamflə'tir\ n

**pan** \'pan\ n : broad, shallow, and open container ~ vb 1 : wash gravel in a pan to search for gold 2 : criticize severely

**pan·a·cea** \₋panə'sēə\ n : remedy for all ills or difficulties

**pan·cake** n : fried flat cake

**pan·cre·as** \'paŋkrēəs, 'pan-\ n : gland that produces insulin — **pan·cre·at·ic** \₋paŋkrē'atik, ₋pan-\ adj

**pan·da** \'pandə\ n : black-and-white bearlike animal

**pan·de·mo·ni·um** \₋pandə'mōnēəm\ n : wild uproar

**pan·der** \'pandər\ n 1 : pimp 2 : one who caters to others' desires or weaknesses ~ vb : act as a pander

**pane** \'pān\ n : sheet of glass

**pan·e·gy·ric** \₋panə'jirik\ n : eulogistic oration — **pan·e·gyr·ist** \-'jirist\ n

**pan·el** \'pan²l\ n 1 : list of persons (as jurors) 2 : discussion group 3 : flat piece of construction material 4 : board with instruments or controls ~ vb **-eled** or **-elled; -el·ing** or **-el·ling** : decorate with panels — **pan·el·ing** n — **pan·el·ist** \-ist\ n

**pang** \'paŋ\ n : sudden sharp pain

**pan·han·dle** \'pan₋hand²l\ vb **-dled; -dling** : ask for money on the street — **pan·han·dler** \-ər\ n

**pan·ic** \\'panik\ *n* : sudden overpowering fright ∼ *vb* **-icked; -ick·ing** : affect or be affected with panic — **pan·icky** \-ikē\ *adj*

**pan·o·ply** \\'panəplē\ *n, pl* **-plies 1** : full suit of armor **2** : impressive array

**pan·o·ra·ma** \,panə'ramə, -'räm-\ *n* : view in every direction — **pan·o·ram·ic** \-'ramik\ *adj*

**pan·sy** \\'panzē\ *n, pl* **-sies** : low-growing garden herb with showy flowers

**pant** \\'pant\ *vb* **1** : breathe with great effort **2** : yearn ∼ *n* : panting sound

**pan·ta·loons** \,pant²l'ünz\ *n pl* : pants

**pan·the·on** \\'panthē,än, -ən\ *n* **1** : the gods of a people **2** : group of famous people

**pan·ther** \\'panthər\ *n* : large wild cat

**pant·ies** \\'pantēz\ *n pl* : woman's or child's short underpants

**pan·to·mime** \\'pantə,mīm\ *n* **1** : play without words **2** : expression by bodily or facial movements ∼ *vb* : represent by pantomime

**pan·try** \\'pantrē\ *n, pl* **-tries** : storage room for food and dishes

**pants** \\'pants\ *n pl* **1** : 2-legged outer garment **2** : panties

**pap** \\'pap\ *n* : soft food

**pa·pa·cy** \\'pāpəsē\ *n, pl* **-cies 1** : office of pope **2** : reign of a pope

**pa·pal** \\'pāpəl\ *adj* : relating to the pope

**pa·pa·ya** \pə'pīə\ *n* : tropical tree with large yellow edible fruit

**pa·per** \\'pāpər\ *n* **1** : pliable substance used to write or print on, to wrap things in, or to cover walls **2** : printed or written document **3** : newspaper — **paper** *adj or vb* — **pa·per·hang·er** *n* — **pa·per·weight** *n* — **pa·pery** \\'pāpərē\ *adj*

**pa·per·board** *n* : cardboard

**pa·pier-mâ·ché** \,pāpərmə'shā, ,pap-,yāmə-, -ma-\ *n* : molding material of waste paper

**pa·poose** \pa'püs, pə-\ *n* : young child of American Indian parents

**pa·pri·ka** \pə'prēkə, pa-\ *n* : mild red spice from sweet peppers

**pa·py·rus** \pə'pīrəs\ *n, pl* **-rus·es** or **-ri** \-,rē, -,rī\ **1** : tall grasslike plant **2** : paper from papyrus

**par** \\'pär\ *n* **1** : stated value **2** : common level **3** : accepted standard or normal condition — **par** *adj*

**par·a·ble** \\'parəbəl\ *n* : simple story illustrating a moral truth

**para·chute** \\'parə,shüt\ *n* : large umbrella-shaped device for making a descent through air — **parachute** *vb* — **para·chut·ist** \-,shütist\ *n*

**pa·rade** \pə'rād\ *n* **1** : pompous display **2** : ceremonial formation and march ∼ *vb* **-rad·ed; -rad·ing 1** : march in a parade **2** : show off

**par·a·digm** \\'parə,dīm, -,dim\ *n* : model

**par·a·dise** \\'parə,dīs, -,dīz\ *n* : place of bliss

**par·a·dox** \\'parə,däks\ *n* : statement that seems contrary to common sense yet is perhaps true — **par·a·dox·i·cal** \,parə'däksikəl\ *adj* — **par·a·dox·i·cal·ly** *adv*

**par·af·fin** \\'parəfən\ *n* : white waxy substance used esp. for making candles and sealing foods

**par·a·gon** \\'parə,gän, -gən\ *n* : model of perfection

**para·graph** \\'parə,graf\ *n* : unified division of a piece of writing ∼ *vb* : divide into paragraphs

**par·a·keet** \\'parə,kēt\ *n* : small slender parrot

**par·al·lel** \\'parə,lel\ *adj* **1** : lying or moving in the same direction but always the same distance apart **2** : similar ∼ *n* **1** : parallel line, curve, or surface **2** : line of latitude **3** : similarity ∼ *vb* **1** : compare **2** : correspond to — **par·al·lel·ism** \-,izəm\ *n*

**par·al·lel·o·gram** \,parə'lelə,gram\ *n* : 4-sided polygon with opposite sides equal and parallel

**pa·ral·y·sis** \pə'raləsəs\ *n, pl* **-y·ses** \-,sēz\ : loss of function and esp. of voluntary motion — **par·a·lyt·ic** \,parə'litik\ *adj or n*

**par·a·lyze** \\'parə,līz\ *vb* **-lyzed; -lyz·ing** : affect with paralysis — **par·a·lyz·ing·ly** *adv*

**para·med·ic** \,parə'medik\ *n* : person trained to provide initial emergency medical treatment

**pa·ram·e·ter** \pə'ramətər\ *n* : characteristic element — **para·met·ric** \,parə'metrik\ *adj*

**par·a·mount** \\'parə,maúnt\ *adj* : superior to all others

**par·amour** \\'parə,múr\ *n* : illicit lover

**para·noia** \,parə'nôiə\ *n* : mental disorder marked by irrational suspicion — **para·noid** \'parə,nȯid\ *adj or n*

**par·a·pet** \'parəpət, -,pet\ *n* : protecting rampart in a fort

**par·a·pher·na·lia** \,parəfə'nālyə, -fər-\ *n sing or pl* : equipment

**para·phrase** \'parə,frāz\ *n* : restatement of a text giving the meaning in different words — **paraphrase** *vb*

**para·ple·gia** \,parə'plējə, -jēə\ *n* : paralysis of the lower trunk and legs — **para·ple·gic** \-jik\ *adj or n*

**par·a·site** \'parə,sīt\ *n* : organism living on another — **par·a·sit·ic** \,parə-'sitik\ *adj* — **par·a·sit·ism** \'parəse-,tizəm, -,sīt,iz-\ *n*

**para·sol** \'parə,sȯl\ *n* : umbrella used to keep off the sun

**para·troops** \-,trüps\ *n pl* : troops trained to parachute from an airplane — **para·troop·er** \-,trüpər\ *n*

**par·boil** \'pär,bȯil\ *vb* : boil briefly

**par·cel** \'pärsəl\ *n* **1** : lot **2** : package ~ *vb* **-celed** *or* **-celled; -cel·ing** *or* **-cel·ling** : divide into portions

**parch** \'pärch\ *vb* : toast or shrivel with dry heat

**parch·ment** \'pärchmənt\ *n* : animal skin prepared to write on

**par·don** \'pärdᵊn\ *n* : excusing of an offense ~ *vb* : free from penalty — **par·don·able** \'pärdᵊnəbəl\ *adj* — **par·don·er** \-ᵊnər\ *n*

**pare** \'par\ *vb* **pared; par·ing 1** : trim off an outside part **2** : reduce as if by paring — **par·er** *n*

**par·e·gor·ic** \,parə'gȯrik\ *n* : tincture of opium and camphor

**par·ent** \'parənt\ *n* : one that begets or brings up offspring — **par·ent·age** \-ij\ *n* — **pa·ren·tal** \pə'rentᵊl\ *adj* — **par·ent·hood** *n*

**pa·ren·the·sis** \pə'renthəsəs\ *n, pl* **-the·ses** \-,sēz\ **1** : word or phrase inserted in a passage **2** : one of a pair of punctuation marks ( ) — **par·en·thet·ic** \,parən'thetik\, **par·en·thet·i·cal** \-ikəl\ *adj* — **par·en·thet·i·cal·ly** *adv*

**par·fait** \pär'fā\ *n* : layered cold dessert

**pa·ri·ah** \pə'rīə\ *n* : outcast

**par·ish** \'parish\ *n* : local church community

**pa·rish·io·ner** \pə'rishənər\ *n* : member of a parish

**par·i·ty** \'parətē\ *n, pl* **-ties** : equality

**park** \'pärk\ *n* : land set aside for recreation or for its beauty ~ *vb* : leave a vehicle standing

**par·ka** \'pärkə\ *n* : usu. hooded heavy jacket

**park·way** \'pärk,wā\ *n* : broad landscaped thoroughfare

**par·lance** \'pärləns\ *n* : manner of speaking

**par·lay** \'pär,lā\ *n* : the risking of a stake plus its winnings — **parlay** *vb*

**par·ley** \'pärlē\ *n, pl* **-leys** : conference about a dispute — **parley** *vb*

**par·lia·ment** \'pärləmənt\ *n* : legislative assembly — **par·lia·men·tar·i·an** *n* — **par·lia·men·ta·ry** \,pärlə-'mentərē\ *adj*

**par·lor** \'pärlər\ *n* **1** : reception room **2** : place of business

**pa·ro·chi·al** \pə'rōkēəl\ *adj* **1** : relating to a church parish **2** : provincial — **pa·ro·chi·al·ism** \-ə,lizəm\ *n*

**par·o·dy** \'parədē\ *n, pl* **-dies** : humorous or satirical imitation — **parody** *vb*

**pa·role** \pə'rōl\ *n* : conditional release of a prisoner — **parole** *vb* — **pa·rol·ee** \-,rō'lē, -'rō,lē\ *n*

**par·ox·ysm** \'parək,sizəm, pə'räk-\ *n* : convulsion

**par·quet** \'pär,kā, pär'kā\ *n* : flooring of patterned wood inlay

**par·ra·keet** *var of* PARAKEET

**par·rot** \'parət\ *n* : bright-colored tropical bird

**par·ry** \'parē\ *vb* **-ried; -ry·ing 1** : ward off a blow **2** : evade adroitly — **parry** *n*

**parse** \'pärs\ *vb* **parsed; pars·ing** : analyze grammatically

**par·si·mo·ny** \'pärsə,mōnē\ *n* : extreme frugality — **par·si·mo·ni·ous** \,pärsə'mōnēəs\ *adj* — **par·si·mo·ni·ous·ly** *adv*

**pars·ley** \'pärslē\ *n* : garden plant used as a seasoning or garnish

**pars·nip** \'pärsnəp\ *n* : carrotlike vegetable with a white edible root

**par·son** \'pärsᵊn\ *n* : minister

**par·son·age** \'pärsᵊnij\ *n* : parson's house

**part** \'pärt\ *n* **1** : one of the units into which a larger whole is divided **2** : function or role ~ *vb* **1** : take leave **2** : separate **3** : go away **4** : give up

**par·take** \pär'tāk, pər-\ *vb* **-took; -tak·en; -tak·ing** : have or take a share — **par·tak·er** *n*

**par·tial** \'pärshəl\ *adj* **1** : favoring one over another **2** : affecting a part only — **par·tial·i·ty** \ˌpärshē'alətē\ *n* — **par·tial·ly** \'pärshəlē\ *adv*

**par·tic·i·pate** \pər'tisəˌpāt, pär-\ *vb* **-pat·ed; -pat·ing** : take part in something — **par·tic·i·pant** \-pənt\ *adj or n* — **par·tic·i·pa·tion** \-ˌtisə'pāshən\ *n* — **par·tic·i·pa·to·ry** \-'tisəpəˌtōrē\ *adj*

**par·ti·ci·ple** \'pärtəˌsipəl\ *n* : verb form with functions of both verb and adjective — **par·ti·cip·i·al** \ˌpärtə'sipēəl\ *adj*

**par·ti·cle** \'pärtikəl\ *n* : small bit

**par·tic·u·lar** \pär'tikyələr\ *adj* **1** : relating to a specific person or thing **2** : individual **3** : hard to please **~** *n* : detail — **par·tic·u·lar·ly** *adv*

**par·ti·san** \'pärtəzən, -sən\ *n* **1** : adherent **2** : guerrilla — **partisan** *adj* — **par·ti·san·ship** *n*

**par·tite** \'pärˌtīt\ *adj* : divided into parts

**par·ti·tion** \pər'tishən, pär-\ *n* **1** : distribution **2** : something that divides — **partition** *vb*

**part·ly** \'pärtlē\ *adv* : in some degree

**part·ner** \'pärtnər\ *n* **1** : associate **2** : companion **3** : business associate — **part·ner·ship** *n*

**part of speech** : class of words distinguished esp. according to function

**par·tridge** \'pärtrij\ *n*, *pl* **-tridge** *or* **-tridg·es** : stout-bodied game bird

**par·ty** \'pärtē\ *n*, *pl* **-ties 1** : political organization **2** : participant **3** : company of persons esp. with a purpose **4** : social gathering

**par·ve·nu** \'pärvəˌnü, -ˌnyü\ *n* : social upstart

**pass** \'pas\ *vb* **1** : move past, over, or through **2** : go away or die **3** : allow to elapse **4** : go unchallenged **5** : transfer or undergo transfer **6** : render a judgment **7** : occur **8** : enact **9** : undergo testing successfully **10** : be regarded **11** : decline **~** *n* **1** : low place in a mountain range **2** : act of passing **3** : accomplishment **4** : permission to leave, enter, or move about — **pass·able** *adj* — **pass·ably** *adv* — **pass·er** *n* — **pass·er·by** *n*

**pas·sage** \'pasij\ *n* **1** : process of passing **2** : means of passing **3** : voyage **4** : right to pass **5** : literary selection — **pas·sage·way** *n*

**pass·book** *n* : bankbook

**pas·sé** \pa'sā\ *adj* : out-of-date

**pas·sen·ger** \'pas³njər\ *n* : traveler in a conveyance

**pass·ing** \'pasiŋ\ *n* : death

**pas·sion** \'pashən\ *n* **1** : strong feeling esp. of anger, love, or desire **2** : object of affection or enthusiasm — **pas·sion·ate** \'pashənət\ *adj* — **pas·sion·ate·ly** *adv* — **pas·sion·less** *adj*

**pas·sive** \'pasiv\ *adj* **1** : not active but acted upon **2** : submissive — **passive** *n* — **pas·sive·ly** *adv* — **pas·siv·i·ty** \pa'sivətē\ *n*

**Pass·over** \'pasˌōvər\ *n* : Jewish holiday celebrated in March or April in commemoration of the Hebrews' liberation from slavery in Egypt

**pass·port** \'pasˌpōrt\ *n* : government document needed for travel abroad

**pass·word** *n* **1** : word or phrase spoken to pass a guard **2** : sequence of characters needed to get into a computer system

**past** \'past\ *adj* **1** : ago **2** : just gone by **3** : having existed before the present **4** : expressing past time **~** *prep or adv* : beyond **~** *n* **1** : time gone by **2** : verb tense expressing time gone by **3** : past life

**pas·ta** \'pästə\ *n* : fresh or dried shaped dough

**paste** \'pāst\ *n* **1** : smooth ground food **2** : moist adhesive **~** *vb* **past·ed; past·ing** : attach with paste — **pasty** *adj*

**paste·board** *n* : cardboard

**pas·tel** \pas'tel\ *n* : light color — **pastel** *adj*

**pas·teur·ize** \'paschəˌrīz, 'pastə-\ *vb* **-ized; -iz·ing** : heat (as milk) so as to kill germs — **pas·teur·i·za·tion** \ˌpaschərə'zāshən, ˌpastə-\ *n*

**pas·time** \'pasˌtīm\ *n* : amusement

**pas·tor** \'pastər\ *n* : priest or minister serving a church or parish — **pas·tor·ate** \-tərət\ *n*

**pas·to·ral** \'pastərəl\ *adj* **1** : relating to rural life **2** : of or relating to spiritual guidance or a pastor **~** *n* : literary work dealing with rural life

**pas·try** \'pāstrē\ *n*, *pl* **-ries** : sweet baked goods

**pas·ture** \'paschər\ *n* : land used for grazing **~** *vb* **-tured; -tur·ing** : graze

**pat** \'pat\ *n* **1** : light tap **2** : small mass

~ vb **-tt-** : tap gently ~ adj or adv **1**
: apt or glib **2** : unyielding

**patch** \'pach\ n **1** : piece used for
mending **2** : small area distinct from
surrounding area ~ vb **1** : mend
with a patch **2** : make of fragments **3**
: repair hastily — **patchy** \-ē\ adj

**patch·work** n : something made of
pieces of different materials, shapes,
or colors

**pate** \'pāt\ n : crown of the head

**pa·tel·la** \pə'telə\ n, pl **-lae** \-'tel,ē,
-,ī\ or **-las** : kneecap

**pa·tent** adj **1** \'pat²nt, 'pāt-\ : obvious
**2** \'pat-\ : protected by a patent ~
\'pat-\ n : document conferring or securing a right ~ \'pat-\ vb : secure
by patent — **pat·ent·ly** adv

**pa·ter·nal** \pə'tərn²l\ adj **1** : fatherly
**2** : related through or inherited from a
father — **pa·ter·nal·ly** adv

**pa·ter·ni·ty** \pə'tərnətē\ n : fatherhood

**path** \'path, 'páth\ n **1** : trodden way
**2** : route or course — **path·find·er** n
— **path·way** n — **path·less** adj

**pa·thet·ic** \pə'thetik\ adj : pitiful —
**pa·thet·i·cal·ly** adv

**pa·thol·o·gy** \pə'thäləjē\ n, pl **-gies 1**
: study of disease **2** : physical abnor-
mality — **path·o·log·i·cal** \,pathə-
'läjikəl\ adj — **pa·thol·o·gist** \pə-
'thäləjist\ n

**pa·thos** \'pā,thäs\ n : element evoking
pity

**pa·tience** \'pāshəns\ n : habit or fact of
being patient

**pa·tient** \'pāshənt\ adj : bearing pain
or trials without complaint ~ n : one
under medical care — **pa·tient·ly** adv

**pa·ti·na** \pə'tēnə, 'patənə\ n, pl **-nas**
\-nəz\ or **-nae** \-,nē, -,nī\ : green
film formed on copper and bronze

**pa·tio** \'patē,ō, 'pät-\ n, pl **-ti·os 1**
: courtyard **2** : paved recreation area
near a house

**pa·tri·arch** \'pātrē,ärk\ n **1** : man
revered as father or founder **2** : ven-
erable old man — **pa·tri·ar·chal**
\,pātrē'ärkəl\ adj — **pa·tri·ar·chy**
\-,ärkē\ n

**pa·tri·cian** \pə'trishən\ n : person of
high birth — **patrician** adj

**pat·ri·mo·ny** \'patrə,mōnē\ n : something inherited — **pat·ri·mo·ni·al**
\,patrə'mōnēəl\ adj

**pa·tri·ot** \'pātrēət, -,ät\ n : one who
loves his or her country — **pa·tri·ot·**

**ic** \,pātrē'ätik\ adj — **pa·tri·ot·i·**
**cal·ly** adv — **pa·tri·o·tism** \'pātrēə-
,tizəm\ n

**pa·trol** \pə'trōl\ n **1** : a going around
for observation or security **2** : group
on patrol ~ vb **-ll-** : carry out a patrol

**pa·trol·man** \-mən\ n : police officer

**pa·tron** \'pātrən\ n **1** : special protector **2** : wealthy supporter **3** : customer

**pa·tron·age** \'patrənij, 'pā-\ n **1**
: support or influence of a patron **2**
: trade of customers **3** : control of
government appointments

**pa·tron·ess** \'pātrənəs, 'pā-\ n : woman
who is a patron

**pa·tron·ize** \'pātrə,nīz, 'pa-\ **-ized;**
**-iz·ing 1** : be a customer of **2** : treat
with condescension

¹**pat·ter** \'patər\ vb : talk glibly or mechanically ~ n : rapid talk

²**patter** vb : pat or tap rapidly ~ n
: quick succession of pats or taps

**pat·tern** \'patərn\ n **1** : model for imitation or for making things **2** : artistic
design **3** : noticeable formation or set
of characteristics ~ vb : form according to a pattern

**pat·ty** \'patē\ n, pl **-ties** : small flat cake

**pau·ci·ty** \'pósətē\ n : shortage

**paunch** \'ponch\ n : large belly —
**paunchy** adj

**pau·per** \'pópər\ n : poor person —
**pau·per·ism** \-pə,rizəm\ n — **pau·**
**per·ize** \-pə,rīz\ vb

**pause** \'póz\ n : temporary stop ~ vb
**paused; paus·ing** : stop briefly

**pave** \'pāv\ vb **paved; pav·ing** : cover
to smooth or firm the surface —
**pave·ment** \-mənt\ n — **pav·ing** n

**pa·vil·ion** \pə'vilyən\ n **1** : large tent
**2** : light structure used for entertainment or shelter

**paw** \'pó\ n : foot of a 4-legged clawed
animal ~ vb **1** : handle clumsily
or rudely **2** : touch or strike with a
paw

**pawn** \'pón\ n **1** : goods deposited
as security for a loan **2** : state of being pledged ~ vb : deposit as a
pledge — **pawn·bro·ker** n — **pawn·**
**shop** n

**pay** \'pā\ vb **paid** \'pād\; **pay·ing 1**
: make due return for goods or services **2** : discharge indebtedness for **3**
: requite **4** : give freely or as fitting **5**
: be profitable ~ n **1** : status of being paid **2** : something paid — **pay-**

able *adj* — **pay•check** *n* — **pay•ee** \pā'ē\ *n* — **pay•er** *n* — **pay•ment** *n*

**PC** \pē'sē\ *n, pl* **PCs** *or* **PC's** : microcomputer

**pea** \'pē\ *n* : round edible seed of a leguminous vine

**peace** \'pēs\ *n* **1** : state of calm and quiet **2** : absence of war or strife — **peace•able** \-əbəl\ *adj* — **peace•ably** \-blē\ *adv* — **peace•ful** \-fəl\ *adj* — **peace•ful•ly** *adv* — **peace•keep•er** *n* — **peace•keep•ing** *n* — **peace•mak•er** *n* — **peace•time** *n*

**peach** \'pēch\ *n* : sweet juicy fruit of a flowering tree or this tree

**pea•cock** \'pē,käk\ *n* : brilliantly colored male pheasant

**peak** \'pēk\ *n* **1** : pointed or projecting part **2** : top of a hill **3** : highest level ~ *vb* : reach a maximum — **peak** *adj*

**peak•ed** \'pēkəd\ *adj* : sickly

**peal** \'pēl\ *n* : loud sound (as of ringing bells) ~ *vb* : give out peals

**pea•nut** \'pē,nət\ *n* : annual herb that bears underground pods or the pod or the edible seed inside

**pear** \'par\ *n* : fleshy fruit of a tree related to the apple

**pearl** \'pərl\ *n* : gem formed within an oyster — **pearly** \'pərlē\ *adj*

**peas•ant** \'pez'nt\ *n* : tiller of the soil — **peas•ant•ry** \-'ntrē\ *n*

**peat** \'pēt\ *n* : decayed organic deposit often dried for fuel — **peaty** *adj*

**peb•ble** \'pebəl\ *n* : small stone — **peb•bly** *adj*

**pe•can** \pi'kän, -'kan\ *n* : hickory tree bearing a smooth-shelled nut or the nut

**pec•ca•dil•lo** \,pekə'dilō\ *n, pl* **-loes** *or* **-los** : slight offense

¹**peck** \'pek\ *n* : unit of dry measure equal to 8 quarts

²**peck** *vb* : strike or pick up with the bill ~ *n* : quick sharp stroke

**pec•tin** \'pektən\ *n* : water-soluble plant substance that causes fruit jellies to set — **pec•tic** \-tik\ *adj*

**pec•to•ral** \'pektərəl\ *adj* : relating to the breast or chest

**pe•cu•liar** \pi'kyülyər\ *adj* **1** : characteristic of only one **2** : strange — **pe•cu•liar•i•ty** \-,kyül'yaretē, -ē'ar-\ *n* — **pe•cu•liar•ly** *adv*

**pe•cu•ni•ary** \pi'kyünē,erē\ *adj* : relating to money

**ped•a•go•gy** \'pedə,gōjē, -,gäj-\ *n* : art or profession of teaching — **ped•a•gog•ic** \,pedə'gäjik, -'gōj-\, **ped•a•gog•i•cal** \-ikəl\ *adj* — **ped•a•gogue** \'pedə,gäg\ *n*

**ped•al** \'ped'l\ *n* : lever worked by the foot ~ *adj* : relating to the foot ~ *vb* : use a pedal

**ped•ant** \'ped'nt\ *n* : learned bore — **pe•dan•tic** \pi'dantik\ *adj* — **ped•ant•ry** \'ped'ntrē\ *n*

**ped•dle** \'ped'l\ *vb* **-dled; -dling** : offer for sale — **ped•dler** \'pedlər\ *n*

**ped•es•tal** \'pedəst'l\ *n* : support or foot of something upright

**pe•des•tri•an** \pə'destrēən\ *adj* **1** : ordinary **2** : walking ~ *n* : person who walks

**pe•di•at•rics** \,pēdē'atriks\ *n* : branch of medicine dealing with children — **pe•di•at•ric** \-trik\ *adj* — **pe•di•a•tri•cian** \,pēdēə'trishən\ *n*

**ped•i•gree** \'pedə,grē\ *n* : line of ancestors or a record of it

**ped•i•ment** \'pedəmənt\ *n* : triangular gablelike decoration on a building

**peek** \'pēk\ *vb* **1** : look furtively **2** : glance — **peek** *n*

**peel** \'pēl\ *vb* **1** : strip the skin or rind from **2** : lose the outer layer ~ *n* : skin or rind — **peel•ing** *n*

¹**peep** \'pēp\ *vb or n* : cheep

²**peep** *vb* **1** : look slyly **2** : begin to emerge ~ *n* : brief look — **peep•er** *n* — **peep•hole** *n*

¹**peer** \'pir\ *n* **1** : one's equal **2** : nobleman — **peer•age** \-ij\ *n*

²**peer** *vb* : look intently or curiously

**peer•less** \-ləs\ *adj* : having no equal

**peeve** \'pēv\ *vb* **peeved; peev•ing** : make resentful ~ *n* : complaint — **peev•ish** \-ish\ *adj* — **peev•ish•ly** *adv* — **peev•ish•ness** *n*

**peg** \'peg\ *n* : small pinlike piece ~ *vb* **-gg-** **1** : put a peg into **2** : fix or mark with or as if with pegs

**peig•noir** \pān'wär, pen-\ *n* : negligee

**pe•jo•ra•tive** \pi'jórətiv\ *adj* : having a negative or degrading effect ~ *n* : a degrading word or phrase — **pe•jo•ra•tive•ly** *adv*

**pel•i•can** \'pelikən\ *n* : large-billed seabird

**pel•la•gra** \pə'lagrə, -'läg-\ *n* : protein-deficiency disease

**pel•let** \'pelət\ *n* : little ball — **pel•let•al** \-'l\ *adj* — **pel•let•ize** \-,īz\ *vb*

**pell–mell** \'pel'mel\ *adv* : in confusion or haste

**pel·lu·cid** \pə'lüsəd\ adj : very clear

**¹pelt** \'pelt\ n : skin of a fur-bearing animal

**²pelt** vb : strike with blows or missiles

**pel·vis** \'pelvəs\ n, pl **-vis·es** \-vəsəz\ or **-ves** \-,vēz\ : cavity formed by the hip bones — **pel·vic** \-vik\ adj

**¹pen** \'pen\ n : enclosure for animals ~ vb **-nn-** : shut in a pen

**²pen** n : tool for writing with ink ~ vb **-nn-** : write

**pe·nal** \'pēn³l\ adj : relating to punishment

**pe·nal·ize** \'pēn³l,īz, 'pen-\ vb **-ized; -iz·ing** : put a penalty on

**pen·al·ty** \'pen³ltē\ n, pl **-ties** 1 : punishment for crime 2 : disadvantage, loss, or hardship due to an action

**pen·ance** \'penəns\ n : act performed to show repentance

**pence** \'pens\ pl of PENNY

**pen·chant** \'penchənt\ n : strong inclination

**pen·cil** \'pensəl\ n : writing or drawing tool with a solid marking substance (as graphite) as its core ~ vb **-ciled** or **-cilled; -cil·ing** or **-cil·ling** : draw or write with a pencil

**pen·dant** \'pendənt\ n : hanging ornament

**pen·dent, pen·dant** \'pendənt\ adj : hanging

**pend·ing** \'pendiŋ\ prep : while awaiting ~ adj : not yet decided

**pen·du·lous** \'penjələs, -dyùləs\ adj : hanging loosely

**pen·du·lum** \-ləm\ n : a hanging weight that is free to swing

**pen·e·trate** \'penə,trāt\ vb **-trat·ed; -trat·ing** 1 : enter into 2 : permeate 3 : see into — **pen·e·tra·ble** \-trəbəl\ adj — **pen·e·tra·tion** \,penə'trāshən\ n — **pen·e·tra·tive** \'penə,trātiv\ adj

**pen·guin** \'pengwən, 'peŋ-\ n : short-legged flightless seabird

**pen·i·cil·lin** \,penə'silən\ n : antibiotic usu. produced by a mold

**pen·in·su·la** \pə'ninsələ, -'ninchə-\ n : land extending out into the water — **pen·in·su·lar** \-lər\ adj

**pe·nis** \'pēnəs\ n, pl **-nes** \-,nēz\ or **-nis·es** : male organ of copulation

**pen·i·tent** \'penətənt\ adj : feeling sorrow for sins or offenses ~ n : penitent person — **pen·i·tence** \-təns\ n — **pen·i·ten·tial** \,penə'tenchəl\ adj

**pen·i·ten·tia·ry** \,penə'tenchərē\ n, pl **-ries** : state or federal prison

**pen·man·ship** \'penmən,ship\ n : art or practice of writing

**pen·nant** \'penənt\ n : nautical or championship flag

**pen·ny** \'penē\ n, pl **-nies** \-ēz\ or **pence** \'pens\ 1 : monetary unit equal to 1/100 pound 2 pl **-nies** : cent — **pen·ni·less** \'peniləs\ adj

**pen·sion** \'penchən\ n : retirement income ~ vb : pay a pension to — **pen·sion·er** n

**pen·sive** \'pensiv\ adj : thoughtful — **pen·sive·ly** adv

**pent** \'pent\ adj : confined

**pent·a·gon** \'pentə,gän\ n : 5-sided polygon — **pen·tag·o·nal** \pen-'tagən³l\ adj

**pen·tam·e·ter** \pen'tamətər\ n : line of verse containing 5 metrical feet

**pent·house** \'pent,haùs\ n : rooftop apartment

**pen·u·ry** \'penyərē\ n 1 : poverty 2 : thrifty or stingy manner — **pe·nu·ri·ous** \pə'nùreəs, -'nyùr-\ adj

**pe·on** \'pē,än, -ən\ n, pl **-ons** or **-o·nes** \pā'ōnēz\ : landless laborer in Spanish America — **pe·on·age** \-ənij\ n

**pe·o·ny** \'pēənē\ n, pl **-nies** : garden plant having large flowers

**peo·ple** \'pēpəl\ n, pl **people** 1 pl : human beings in general 2 pl : human beings in a certain group (as a family) or community 3 pl **peo·ples** : tribe, nation, or race ~ vb **-pled; -pling** : constitute the population of

**pep** \'pep\ n : brisk energy ~ vb **pepped; pep·ping** : put pep into — **pep·py** adj

**pep·per** \'pepər\ n 1 : pungent seasoning from the berry (**peppercorn**) of a shrub 2 : vegetable grown for its hot or sweet fruit ~ vb : season with pepper — **pep·pery** \-ərē\ adj

**pep·per·mint** \-,mint, -mənt\ n : pungent aromatic mint

**pep·per·o·ni** \,pepə'rōnē\ n : spicy beef and pork sausage

**pep·tic** \'peptik\ adj : relating to digestion or the effect of digestive juices

**per** \'pər\ prep 1 : by means of 2 : for each 3 : according to

**per·am·bu·late** \pə'rambyə,lāt\ vb **-lat·ed; -lat·ing** : walk — **per·am·bu·la·tion** \-,rambyə'lāshən\ n

**per•cale** \,pər'kāl, 'pər-,; ,pər'kal\ *n* : fine woven cotton cloth

**per•ceive** \pər'sēv\ *vb* **-ceived; -ceiv•ing 1** : realize **2** : become aware of through the senses — **per•ceiv•able** *adj*

**per•cent** \pər'sent\ *adv* : in each hundred ~ *n, pl* **-cent** *or* **-cents 1** : one part in a hundred **2** : percentage

**per•cent•age** \pər'sentij\ *n* : part expressed in hundredths

**per•cen•tile** \pər'sen,tīl\ *n* : a standing on a scale of 0–100

**per•cep•ti•ble** \pər'septəbəl\ *adj* : capable of being perceived — **per•cep•ti•bly** \-blē\ *adv*

**per•cep•tion** \pər'sepshən\ *n* **1** : act or result of perceiving **2** : ability to understand

**per•cep•tive** \pər'septiv\ *adj* : showing keen perception — **per•cep•tive•ly** *adv*

¹**perch** \'pərch\ *n* : roost for birds ~ *vb* : roost

²**perch** *n, pl* **perch** *or* **perch•es** : freshwater spiny-finned food fish

**per•co•late** \'pərkə,lāt\ *vb* **-lat•ed; -lat•ing** : trickle or filter down through a substance — **per•co•la•tor** \-,lātər\ *n*

**per•cus•sion** \pər'kəshən\ *n* **1** : sharp blow **2** : musical instrument sounded by striking

**pe•remp•to•ry** \pə'remptərē\ *adj* **1** : imperative **2** : domineering — **pe•remp•to•ri•ly** \-tərəlē\ *adv*

**pe•ren•ni•al** \pə'renēəl\ *adj* **1** : present at all seasons **2** : continuing from year to year **3** : recurring regularly ~ *n* : perennial plant — **pe•ren•ni•al•ly** *adv*

**per•fect** \'pərfikt\ *adj* **1** : being without fault or defect **2** : exact **3** : complete ~ \pər'fekt\ *vb* : make perfect — **per•fect•ibil•i•ty** \pər,fektə'bilətē\ *n* — **per•fect•ible** \pər'fektəbəl\ *adj* — **per•fect•ly** *adv* — **per•fect•ness** *n*

**per•fec•tion** \pər'fekshən\ *n* **1** : quality or state of being perfect **2** : highest degree of excellence — **per•fec•tion•ist** \-shənist\ *n*

**per•fid•i•ous** \pər'fidēəs\ *adj* : treacherous — **per•fid•i•ous•ly** *adv*

**per•fo•rate** \'pərfə,rāt\ *vb* **-rat•ed; -rat•ing** : make a hole in — **per•fo•ra•tion** \,pərfə'rāshən\ *n*

**per•force** \pər'fōrs\ *adv* : of necessity

**per•form** \pər'fórm\ *vb* **1** : carry out **2** : do in a set manner **3** : give a performance — **per•form•er** *n*

**per•for•mance** \pər'fór,məns\ *n* **1** : act or process of performing **2** : public presentation

**per•fume** \'pər,fyüm, pər'-\ *n* **1** : pleasant odor **2** : something that gives a scent ~ \pər'-, 'pər,-\ *vb* **-fumed; -fum•ing** : add scent to

**per•func•to•ry** \pər'fəŋktərē\ *adj* : done merely as a duty — **per•func•to•ri•ly** \-tərəlē\ *adv*

**per•haps** \pər'haps\ *adv* : possibly but not certainly

**per•il** \'perəl\ *n* : danger — **per•il•ous** *adj* — **per•il•ous•ly** *adv*

**pe•rim•e•ter** \pə'rimətər\ *n* : outer boundary of a body or figure

**pe•ri•od** \'pirēəd\ *n* **1** : punctuation mark . used esp. to mark the end of a declarative sentence or an abbreviation **2** : division of time **3** : stage in a process or development

**pe•ri•od•ic** \,pirē'ädik\ *adj* : occurring at regular intervals — **pe•ri•od•i•cal•ly** *adv*

**pe•ri•od•i•cal** \,pirē'ädikəl\ *n* : newspaper or magazine

**pe•riph•ery** \pə'rifərē\ *n, pl* **-er•ies** : outer boundary — **pe•riph•er•al** \-ərəl\ *adj*

**peri•scope** \'perə,skōp\ *n* : optical instrument for viewing from a submarine

**per•ish** \'perish\ *vb* : die or spoil — **per•ish•able** \-əbəl\ *adj or n*

**per•ju•ry** \'pərjərē\ *n* : lying under oath — **per•jure** \'pərjər\ *vb* — **per•jur•er** *n*

¹**perk** \'pərk\ *vb* **1** : thrust (as the head) up jauntily **2** : freshen **3** : gain vigor or spirit — **perky** *adj*

²**perk** *vb* : percolate

³**perk** *n* : privilege or benefit in addition to regular pay

**per•ma•nent** \'pərmənənt\ *adj* : lasting ~ *n* : hair wave — **per•ma•nence** \-nəns\ *n* — **per•ma•nent•ly** *adv*

**per•me•able** \'pərmēəbəl\ *adj* : permitting fluids to seep through — **per•me•a•bil•i•ty** \,pərmēə'bilətē\ *n*

**per•me•ate** \'pərmē,āt\ *vb* **-at•ed; -at•ing 1** : seep through **2** : pervade — **per•me•ation** \,pərmē'āshən\ *n*

**per•mis•si•ble** \pər'misəbəl\ *adj* : that may be permitted

**per·mis·sion** \pər'mishən\ n : formal consent

**per·mis·sive** \pər'misiv\ adj : granting freedom esp. to excess — **per·miss·ive·ly** adv — **per·mis·sive·ness** n

**per·mit** \pər'mit\ vb -tt- 1 : approve 2 : make possible ~ \'pər,-, pər'-\ n : license

**per·ni·cious** \pər'nishəs\ adj : very harmful — **per·ni·cious·ly** adv

**per·ox·ide** \pə'räk,sīd\ n : compound (as hydrogen peroxide) in which oxygen is joined to oxygen

**per·pen·dic·u·lar** \,pərpən'dikyələr\ adj 1 : vertical 2 : meeting at a right angle — **perpendicular** n — **per·pen·dic·u·lar·i·ty** \-,dikyə'larətē\ n — **per·pen·dic·u·lar·ly** adv

**per·pe·trate** \'pərpə,trāt\ vb -trat·ed; -trat·ing : be guilty of doing — **per·pe·tra·tion** \,pərpə'trāshən\ n — **per·pe·tra·tor** \'pərpə,trātər\ n

**per·pet·u·al** \pər'pechəwəl\ adj 1 : continuing forever 2 : occurring continually — **per·pet·u·al·ly** adv — **per·pe·tu·ity** \,pərpə'tüətē, -'tyü-\ n

**per·pet·u·ate** \pər'pechə,wāt\ vb -at·ed; -at·ing : make perpetual — **per·pet·u·a·tion** \-,pechə'wāshən\ n

**per·plex** \pər'pleks\ vb : confuse — **per·plex·i·ty** \-ətē\ n

**per·se·cute** \'pərsi,kyüt\ vb -cut·ed; -cut·ing : harass, afflict — **per·se·cu·tion** \,pərsi'kyüshən\ n — **per·se·cu·tor** \'pərsi,kyütər\ n

**per·se·vere** \,pərsə'vir\ vb -vered; -ver·ing : persist — **per·se·ver·ance** \-'virəns\ n

**per·sist** \pər'sist, -'zist\ vb 1 : go on resolutely in spite of difficulties 2 : continue to exist — **per·sis·tence** \-'sistəns, -'zis-\ n — **per·sis·ten·cy** \-tənsē\ n — **per·sis·tent** \-tənt\ adj — **per·sis·tent·ly** adv

**per·son** \'pərsən\ n 1 : human being 2 : human being's body or individuality 3 : reference to the speaker, one spoken to, or one spoken of

**per·son·able** \'pərsənəbəl\ adj : having a pleasing personality

**per·son·age** \'pərsənij\ n : person of rank or distinction

**per·son·al** \'pərsənəl\ adj 1 : relating to a particular person 2 : done in person 3 : affecting one's body 4 : offensive to a certain individual — **per·son·al·ly** adv

**per·son·al·i·ty** \,pərsən'alətē\ n, pl -ties 1 : manner and disposition of an individual 2 : distinctive or well-known person

**per·son·al·ize** \'pərsənə,līz\ vb -ized; -iz·ing : mark as belonging to a particular person

**per·son·i·fy** \pər'sänə,fī\ vb -fied; -fy·ing 1 : represent as a human being 2 : be the embodiment of — **per·son·i·fi·ca·tion** \-,sänəfə'kāshən\ n

**per·son·nel** \,pərsən'el\ n : body of persons employed

**per·spec·tive** \pər'spektiv\ n 1 : apparent depth and distance in painting 2 : view of things in their true relationship or importance

**per·spi·ca·cious** \,pərspə'kāshəs\ adj : showing keen understanding or discernment — **per·spi·cac·i·ty** \-'kasətē\ n

**per·spire** \pər'spīr\ vb -spired; -spir·ing : sweat — **per·spi·ra·tion** \,pərspə'rāshən\ n

**per·suade** \pər'swād\ vb -suad·ed; -suad·ing : win over to a belief or course of action by argument or entreaty — **per·sua·sion** \pər'swāzhən\ n — **per·sua·sive** \-'swāsiv, -ziv\ adj — **per·sua·sive·ly** adv — **per·sua·sive·ness** n

**pert** \'pərt\ adj : flippant or irreverent

**per·tain** \pər'tān\ vb 1 : belong 2 : relate

**per·ti·nent** \'pərtənənt\ adj : relevant — **per·ti·nence** \-əns\ n

**per·turb** \pər'tərb\ vb : make uneasy — **per·tur·ba·tion** \,pərtər'bāshən\ n

**pe·ruse** \pə'rüz\ vb -rused; -rus·ing : read attentively — **pe·rus·al** \-'rüzəl\ n

**per·vade** \pər'vād\ vb -vad·ed; -vad·ing : spread through every part of — **per·va·sive** \-'vāsiv, -ziv\ adj

**per·verse** \pər'vərs\ adj 1 : corrupt 2 : unreasonably contrary — **per·verse·ly** adv — **per·verse·ness** n — **per·ver·sion** \pər'vərzhən\ n — **per·ver·si·ty** \-'vərsətē\ n

**per·vert** \pər'vərt\ vb : corrupt or distort ~ \'pər,-\ n : one that is perverted

**pe·so** \'pāsō\ n, pl -sos : monetary unit (as of Mexico)

**pes·si·mism** \'pesə,mizəm\ n : inclination to expect the worst — **pes·si·mist** \-,mist\ n — **pes·si·mis·tic** \,pesə'mistik\ adj

**pest** \'pest\ n **1** : nuisance **2** : plant or animal detrimental to humans or their crops — **pes·ti·cide** \'pestə‚sīd\ n

**pes·ter** \'pestər\ vb **-tered; -ter·ing** : harass with petty matters

**pes·ti·lence** \'pestələns\ n : plague — **pes·ti·lent** \-lənt\ adj

**pes·tle** \'pesəl, 'pest⁰l\ n : implement for grinding substances in a mortar

**pet** \'pet\ n **1** : domesticated animal kept for pleasure **2** : favorite ~ vb **-tt-** : stroke gently or lovingly

**pet·al** \'pet⁰l\ n : modified leaf of a flower head

**pe·tite** \pə'tēt\ adj : having a small trim figure

**pe·ti·tion** \pə'tishən\ n : formal written request ~ vb : make a request — **pe·ti·tion·er** n

**pet·ri·fy** \'petrə‚fī\ vb **-fied; -fy·ing 1** : change into stony material **2** : make rigid or inactive (as from fear) — **pet·ri·fac·tion** \‚petrə'fakshən\ n

**pe·tro·leum** \pə'trōlēəm\ n : raw oil obtained from the ground

**pet·ti·coat** \'petē‚kōt\ n : skirt worn under a dress

**pet·ty** \'petē\ adj **-ti·er; -est 1** : minor **2** : of no importance **3** : narrow-minded or mean — **pet·ti·ly** \'pet⁰lē\ adv — **pet·ti·ness** n

**petty officer** n : subordinate officer in the navy or coast guard

**pet·u·lant** \'pechələnt\ adj : irritable — **pet·u·lance** \-ləns\ n — **pet·u·lant·ly** adv

**pe·tu·nia** \pi'tünyə, -'tyü-\ n : tropical herb with bright flowers

**pew** \'pyü\ n : bench with a back used in a church

**pew·ter** \'pyütər\ n : alloy of tin used for household utensils

**pH** \‚pē'āch\ n : number expressing relative acidity and alkalinity

**pha·lanx** \'fā‚laŋks\ n, pl **-lanx·es** or **-lan·ges** \fə'lan‚jēz\ **1** : body (as of troops) in compact formation **2** pl phalanges : digital bone of the hand or foot

**phal·lus** \'faləs\ n, pl **-li** \'fal‚ī\ or **-lus·es** : penis — **phal·lic** adj

**phan·tasy** var of FANTASY

**phan·tom** \'fantəm\ n : something that only appears to be real — **phantom** adj

**pha·raoh** \'ferō, 'färō\ n : ruler of ancient Egypt

**phar·ma·ceu·ti·cal** \‚färmə'sütikəl\ adj : relating to pharmacy or the making and selling of medicinal drugs — **pharmaceutical** n

**phar·ma·col·o·gy** \‚färmə'käləjē\ n : science of drugs esp. as related to medicinal uses — **phar·ma·co·log·i·cal** \-ikəl\ adj — **phar·ma·col·o·gist** \-'käləjist\ n

**phar·ma·cy** \'färməsē\ n, pl **-cies 1** : art or practice of preparing and dispensing medical drugs **2** : drugstore — **phar·ma·cist** \-sist\ n

**phar·ynx** \'fariŋks\ n, pl **pha·ryn·ges** \fə'rin‚jēz\ : space behind the mouth into which the nostrils, esophagus, and windpipe open — **pha·ryn·ge·al** \fə'rinjəl, ‚farən'jēəl\ adj

**phase** \'fāz\ n **1** : particular appearance or stage in a recurring series of changes **2** : stage in a process — **phase in** vb : introduce in stages — **phase out** vb : discontinue gradually

**pheas·ant** \'fez⁰nt\ n, pl **-ant** or **-ants** : long-tailed brilliantly colored game bird

**phe·nom·e·non** \fi'nämə‚nän, -nən\ n, pl **-na** \-nə\ or **-nons 1** : observable fact or event **2** pl **-nons** : prodigy — **phe·nom·e·nal** \-'nämən⁰l\ adj

**phi·lan·der·er** \fə'landərər\ n : one who makes love without serious intent

**phi·lan·thro·py** \fə'lanthrəpē\ n, pl **-pies** : charitable act or gift or an organization that distributes such gifts — **phil·an·throp·ic** \‚filən'thräpik\ adj — **phi·lan·thro·pist** \fə'lanthräpist\ n

**phi·lat·e·ly** \fə'lat⁰lē\ n : collection and study of postage stamps — **phi·lat·e·list** \-⁰list\ n

**phi·lis·tine** \'filə‚stēn, fə'listən\ n : one who is smugly indifferent to intellectual or artistic values — **philistine** adj

**phil·o·den·dron** \‚filə'dendrən\ n, pl **-drons** or **-dra** \-drə\ : plant grown for its showy leaves

**phi·los·o·pher** \fə'läsəfər\ n **1** : reflective thinker **2** : student of philosophy

**phi·los·o·phy** \fə'läsəfē\ n, pl **-phies 1** : critical study of fundamental beliefs **2** : sciences and liberal arts exclusive of medicine, law, and theology **3** : system of ideas **4** : sum of personal convictions — **phil·o·soph·ic** \‚filə'säfik\, **phil·o·soph·i-**

**cal** \-ikəl\ adj — **phil·o·soph·i·cal·ly** \-klē\ adv — **phi·los·o·phize** \fə'läsə,fīz\ vb

**phle·bi·tis** \fli'bītəs\ n : inflammation of a vein

**phlegm** \'flem\ n : thick mucus in the nose and throat

**phlox** \'fläks\ n, pl phlox or **phlox·es** : herb grown for its flower clusters

**pho·bia** \'fōbēə\ n : irrational persistent fear

**phoe·nix** \'fēniks\ n : legendary bird held to burn itself to death and rise fresh and young from its ashes

**phone** \'fōn\ n : telephone ~ vb **phoned; phon·ing** : call on a telephone

**pho·neme** \'fō,nēm\ n : basic distinguishable unit of speech — **pho·ne·mic** \fō'nēmik\ adj

**pho·net·ics** \fə'netiks\ n : study of speech sounds — **pho·net·ic** \-ik\ adj — **pho·ne·ti·cian** \,fōnə'tishən\ n

**pho·nics** \'fäniks\ n : method of teaching reading by stressing sound values of syllables and words

**pho·no·graph** \'fōnə,graf\ n : instrument that reproduces sounds from a grooved disc

**pho·ny, pho·ney** \'fōnē\ adj **-ni·er; -est** : not sincere or genuine — **phony** n

**phos·phate** \'fäs,fāt\ n : chemical salt used in fertilizers — **phos·phat·ic** \fäs'fatik\ adj

**phos·phor** \'fäsfər\ n : phosphorescent substance

**phos·pho·res·cence** \,fäsfə'res°ns\ n : luminescence from absorbed radiation — **phos·pho·res·cent** \-°nt\ adj

**phos·pho·rus** \'fäsfərəs\ n : poisonous waxy chemical element — **phos·phor·ic** \-'fōrik, -'fär-\ adj — **phos·pho·rous** \'fäsfərəs, fäs'fōrəs\ adj

**pho·to** \'fōtō\ n, pl **-tos** : photograph — **photo** vb or adj

**pho·to·copy** \'fōtə,käpē\ n : photographic copy (as of a printed page) — **photocopy** vb

**pho·to·elec·tric** \,fōtōi'lektrik\ adj : relating to an electrical effect due to the interaction of light with matter

**pho·to·ge·nic** \,fōtə'jenik\ adj : suitable for being photographed

**pho·to·graph** \'fōtə,graf\ n : picture taken by photography — **photograph** vb — **pho·tog·ra·pher** \fə'tägrəfər\ n

**pho·tog·ra·phy** \fə'tägrəfē\ n : process of using light to produce images on a sensitized surface — **pho·to·graph·ic** \,fōtə'grafik\ adj — **pho·to·graph·i·cal·ly** adv

**pho·to·syn·the·sis** \,fōtō'sinthəsəs\ n : formation of carbohydrates by chlorophyll-containing plants exposed to sunlight — **pho·to·syn·the·size** \-,sīz\ vb — **pho·to·syn·thet·ic** \-sin'thetik\ adj

**phrase** \'frāz\ n **1** : brief expression **2** : group of related words that express a thought ~ vb **phrased; phras·ing** : express in a particular manner

**phrase·ol·o·gy** \,frāzē'äləjē\ n, pl **-gies** : manner of phrasing

**phy·lum** \'fīləm\ n, pl **-la** \-lə\ : major division of the plant or animal kingdom

**phys·i·cal** \'fizikəl\ adj **1** : relating to nature **2** : material as opposed to mental or spiritual **3** : relating to the body ~ n : medical examination — **phys·i·cal·ly** \-klē\ adv

**phy·si·cian** \fə'zishən\ n : doctor of medicine

**physician's assistant** n : person certified to provide basic medical care under a physician's supervision

**phys·i·cist** \'fizəsist\ n : specialist in physics

**phys·ics** \'fiziks\ n : science that deals with matter and motion

**phys·i·og·no·my** \,fizē'ägnəmē\ n, pl **-mies** : facial appearance esp. as a reflection of inner character

**phys·i·ol·o·gy** \,fizē'äləjē\ n : functional processes in an organism — **phys·i·o·log·i·cal** \-ēə'läjikəl\, **phys·i·o·log·ic** \-ik\ adj — **phys·i·ol·o·gist** \-ē'äləjist\ n

**phy·sique** \fə'zēk\ n : build of a person's body

**pi** \'pī\ n, pl pis \'pīz\ : symbol π denoting the ratio of the circumference of a circle to its diameter or the ratio itself

**pi·a·nist** \pē'anist, 'pēənist\ n : one who plays the piano

**pi·ano** \pē'anō\ n, pl **-anos** : musical instrument with strings sounded by hammers operated from a keyboard

**pi·az·za** \pē'azə, -'äz-, -tsə\ n, pl **-zas** or **-ze** \-tsā\ : public square in a town

**pic·a·yune** \,pikē'yün\ adj : trivial or petty

**pic·co·lo** \'pikə,lō\ *n, pl* **-los** : small shrill flute

**¹pick** \'pik\ *vb* **1** : break up with a pointed instrument **2** : remove bit by bit **3** : gather by plucking **4** : select **5** : rob **6** : provoke **7** : unlock with a wire **8** : eat sparingly ~ *n* **1** : act of choosing **2** : choicest one — **pick·er** *n* — **pick up** *vb* **1** : improve **2** : put in order

**²pick** *n* : pointed digging tool

**pick·ax** *n* : pick

**pick·er·el** \'pikərəl\ *n, pl* **-el** *or* **-els** : small pike

**pick·et** \'pikət\ *n* **1** : pointed stake (as for a fence) **2** : worker demonstrating on strike ~ *vb* : demonstrate as a picket

**pick·le** \'pikəl\ *n* **1** : brine or vinegar solution for preserving foods or a food preserved in a pickle **2** : bad state — **pickle** *vb*

**pick·pock·et** *n* : one who steals from pockets

**pick·up** \'pik,əp\ *n* **1** : revival or acceleration **2** : light truck with an open body

**pic·nic** \'pik,nik\ *n* : outing with food usu. eaten in the open ~ *vb* **-nicked**; **-nick·ing** : go on a picnic

**pic·to·ri·al** \pik'tōrēəl\ *adj* : relating to pictures

**pic·ture** \'pikchər\ *n* **1** : representation by painting, drawing, or photography **2** : vivid description **3** : copy **4** : movie ~ *vb* **-tured**; **-tur·ing** : form a mental image of

**pic·tur·esque** \,pikchə'resk\ *adj* : attractive enough for a picture

**pie** \'pī\ *n* : pastry crust and a filling

**pie·bald** \'pī,bold\ *adj* : blotched with white and black

**piece** \'pēs\ *n* **1** : part of a whole **2** : one of a group or set **3** : single item **4** : product of creative work ~ *vb* **pieced**; **piec·ing** : join into a whole

**piece·meal** \'pēs,mēl\ *adv or adj* : gradually

**pied** \'pīd\ *adj* : colored in blotches

**pier** \'pir\ *n* **1** : support for a bridge span **2** : deck or wharf built out over water **3** : pillar

**pierce** \'pirs\ *vb* **pierced**; **pierc·ing** **1** : enter or thrust into or through **2** : penetrate **3** : see through

**pi·ety** \'pīətē\ *n, pl* **-eties** : devotion to religion

**pig** \'pig\ *n* **1** : young swine **2** : dirty or greedy individual **3** : iron casting — **pig·gish** \-ish\ *adj* — **pig·let** \-lət\ *n* — **pig·pen** *n* — **pig·sty** *n*

**pi·geon** \'pijən\ *n* : stout-bodied short-legged bird

**pi·geon·hole** *n* : small open compartment for letters or documents ~ *vb* **1** : place in a pigeonhole **2** : classify

**pig·gy·back** \'pigē,bak\ *adv or adj* : up on the back and shoulders

**pig·head·ed** \-'hedəd\ *adj* : stubborn

**pig·ment** \'pigmənt\ *n* : coloring matter — **pig·men·ta·tion** *n*

**pigmy** *var of* PYGMY

**pig·tail** *n* : tight braid of hair

**¹pike** \'pīk\ *n, pl* **pike** *or* **pikes** : large freshwater fish

**²pike** *n* : former weapon consisting of a long wooden staff with a steel point

**³pike** *n* : turnpike

**pi·laf**, **pi·laff** \pi'läf, 'pē,läf\, **pi·lau** \pi'lō, -'lȯ; 'pēlō, -lȯ\ *n* : dish of seasoned rice

**¹pile** \'pīl\ *n* : supporting pillar driven into the ground

**²pile** *n* : quantity of things thrown on one another ~ *vb* **piled**; **pil·ing** : heap up, accumulate

**³pile** *n* : surface of fine hairs or threads — **piled** *adj*

**piles** \'pīls\ *n pl* : hemorrhoids

**pil·fer** \'pilfər\ *vb* : steal in small quantities

**pil·grim** \'pilgrəm\ *n* **1** : one who travels to a shrine or holy place in devotion **2** *cap* : one of the English settlers in America in 1620

**pil·grim·age** \-grəmij\ *n* : pilgrim's journey

**pill** \'pil\ *n* : small rounded mass of medicine — **pill·box** *n*

**pil·lage** \'pilij\ *vb* **-laged**; **-lag·ing** : loot and plunder — **pillage** *n*

**pil·lar** \'pilər\ *n* : upright usu. supporting column — **pil·lared** *adj*

**pil·lo·ry** \'pilərē\ *n, pl* **-ries** : wooden frame for public punishment with holes for the head and hands ~ *vb* **-ried**; **-ry·ing** **1** : set in a pillory **2** : expose to public scorn

**pil·low** \'pilō\ *n* : soft cushion for the head — **pil·low·case** *n*

**pi·lot** \'pīlət\ *n* **1** : helmsman **2** : person licensed to take ships into and out of a port **3** : guide **4** : one that flies an aircraft or spacecraft ~ *vb* : act as pilot of — **pi·lot·less** *adj*

**pi·men·to** \pə'mentō\ *n, pl* **-tos** *or* **-to 1** : allspice **2** : pimiento

**pi·mien·to** \pə'mentō, -'myen-\ *n, pl* **-tos** : mild red sweet pepper

**pimp** \'pimp\ *n* : man who solicits clients for a prostitute — **pimp** *vb*

**pim·ple** \'pimpəl\ *n* : small inflamed swelling on the skin — **pim·ply** \-pəlē\ *adj*

**pin** \'pin\ *n* **1** : fastener made of a small pointed piece of wire **2** : ornament or emblem fastened to clothing with a pin **3** : wooden object used as a target in bowling ~ *vb* **-nn-** **1** : fasten with a pin **2** : hold fast or immobile — **pin·hole** *n*

**pin·a·fore** \'pinə,fōr\ *n* : sleeveless dress or apron fastened at the back

**pin·cer** \'pinsər\ *n* **1** *pl* : gripping tool with 2 jaws **2** : pincerlike claw

**pinch** \'pinch\ *vb* **1** : squeeze between the finger and thumb or between the jaws of a tool **2** : compress painfully **3** : restrict **4** : steal ~ *n* **1** : emergency **2** : painful effect **3** : act of pinching **4** : very small quantity

**pin·cush·ion** *n* : cushion for storing pins

**¹pine** \'pīn\ *n* : evergreen cone-bearing tree or its wood

**²pine** *vb* **pined; pin·ing** **1** : lose health through distress **2** : yearn for intensely

**pine·ap·ple** *n* : tropical plant bearing an edible juicy fruit

**pin·feath·er** *n* : new feather just coming through the skin

**¹pin·ion** \'pinyən\ *vb* : restrain by binding the arms

**²pinion** *n* : small gear

**¹pink** \'piŋk\ *n* **1** : plant with narrow leaves and showy flowers **2** : highest degree

**²pink** *n* : light red color — **pink** *adj* — **pink·ish** *adj*

**pink·eye** *n* : contagious eye inflammation

**pin·na·cle** \'pinikəl\ *n* : highest point

**pi·noch·le** \'pē,nəkəl\ *n* : card game played with a 48-card deck

**pin·point** *vb* : locate, hit, or aim with great precision

**pint** \'pīnt\ *n* : 1/2 quart

**pin·to** \'pin,tō\ *n, pl* **pintos** : spotted horse or pony

**pin·worm** *n* : small parasitic intestinal worm

**pi·o·neer** \,pīə'nir\ *n* **1** : one that originates or helps open up a new line of thought or activity **2** : early settler ~ *vb* : act as a pioneer

**pi·ous** \'pīəs\ *adj* **1** : conscientious in religious practices **2** : affectedly religious — **pi·ous·ly** *adv*

**pipe** \'pīp\ *n* **1** : tube that produces music when air is forced through **2** : bagpipe **3** : long tube for conducting a fluid **4** : smoking tool ~ *vb* **piped; pip·ing** **1** : play on a pipe **2** : speak in a high voice **3** : convey by pipes — **pip·er** *n*

**pipe·line** *n* **1** : line of pipe **2** : channel for information

**pip·ing** \'pīpiŋ\ *n* **1** : music of pipes **2** : narrow fold of material used to decorate edges or seams

**pi·quant** \'pēkənt\ *adj* **1** : tangy **2** : provocative or charming — **pi·quan·cy** \-kənsē\ *n*

**pique** \'pēk\ *n* : resentment ~ *vb* **piqued; piqu·ing** **1** : offend **2** : arouse by provocation

**pi·qué, pi·que** \pi'kā\ *n* : durable ribbed clothing fabric

**pi·ra·cy** \'pīrəsē\ *n, pl* **-cies** **1** : robbery on the seas **2** : unauthorized use of another's production or invention

**pi·ra·nha** \pə'ranyə, -'ränə\ *n* : small So. American fish with sharp teeth

**pi·rate** \'pīrət\ *n* : one who commits piracy — **pirate** *vb* — **pi·rat·i·cal** \pə'ratikəl, pī-\ *adj*

**pir·ou·ette** \,pirə'wet\ *n* : ballet turn on the toe or ball of one foot — **pirouette** *vb*

**pis** *pl of* PI

**pis·ta·chio** \pə'stashē,ō, -'stäsh-\ *n, pl* **-chios** : small tree bearing a greenish edible seed or its seed

**pis·til** \'pist²l\ *n* : female reproductive organ in a flower — **pis·til·late** \'pistə,lāt\ *adj*

**pis·tol** \'pist²l\ *n* : firearm held with one hand

**pis·ton** \'pistən\ *n* : sliding piece that receives and transmits motion usu. inside a cylinder

**¹pit** \'pit\ *n* **1** : hole or shaft in the ground **2** : sunken or enclosed place for a special purpose **3** : hell **4** : hollow or indentation ~ *vb* **-tt-** **1** : form pits in **2** : become marred with pits

²**pit** *n* : stony seed of some fruits ∼ *vb* **-tt-** : remove the pit from

**pit bull** *n* : powerful compact dog bred for fighting

¹**pitch** \'pich\ *n* : resin from conifers — **pitchy** *adj*

²**pitch** *vb* **1** : erect and fix firmly in place **2** : throw **3** : set at a particular tone level **4** : fall headlong ∼ *n* **1** : action or manner of pitching **2** : degree of slope **3** : relative highness of a tone **4** : sales talk — **pitched** *adj*

¹**pitch•er** \'pichər\ *n* : container for liquids

²**pitcher** *n* : one that pitches (as in baseball)

**pitch•fork** *n* : long-handled fork for pitching hay

**pit•e•ous** \'pitēəs\ *adj* : arousing pity — **pit•e•ous•ly** *adv*

**pit•fall** \'pit,fȯl\ *n* : hidden danger

**pith** \'pith\ *n* **1** : spongy plant tissue **2** : essential or meaningful part — **pithy** *adj*

**piti•able** \'pitēəbəl\ *adj* : pitiful

**piti•ful** \'pitifəl\ *adj* **1** : arousing or deserving pity **2** : contemptible — **piti•ful•ly** *adv*

**pit•tance** \'pit°ns\ *n* : small portion or amount

**pi•tu•i•tary** \pə'tüə,terē, -'tyü-\ *adj* : relating to or being a small gland attached to the brain

**pity** \'pitē\ *n, pl* **pi•ties 1** : sympathetic sorrow **2** : something to be regretted ∼ *vb* **pit•ied; pity•ing** : feel pity for — **piti•less** *adj* — **piti•less•ly** *adv*

**piv•ot** \'pivət\ *n* : fixed pin on which something turns ∼ *vb* : turn on or as if on a pivot — **piv•ot•al** *adj*

**pix•ie, pixy** \'piksē\ *n, pl* **pix•ies** : mischievous sprite

**piz•za** \'pētsə\ *n* : thin pie of bread dough spread with a spiced mixture (as of tomatoes, cheese, and meat)

**piz•zazz, pi•zazz** \pə'zaz\ *n* : glamour

**piz•ze•ria** \,pētsə'rēə\ *n* : pizza restaurant

**plac•ard** \'plakərd, -,ärd\ *n* : poster ∼ *vb* : display placards in or on

**pla•cate** \'plā,kāt, 'plak,āt\ *vb* **-cat•ed; -cat•ing** : appease — **pla•ca•ble** \'plakəbəl, 'plākə-\ *adj*

**place** \'plās\ *n* **1** : space or room **2** : indefinite area **3** : a particular building, locality, area, or part **4** : relative position in a scale or sequence **5** : seat **6** : job ∼ *vb* **placed; plac•ing 1** : put in a place **2** : identify — **place•ment** *n*

**pla•ce•bo** \plə'sēbō\ *n, pl* **-bos** : something inactive prescribed as a remedy for its psychological effect

**pla•cen•ta** \plə'sentə\ *n, pl* **-tas** *or* **-tae** \-,ē\ : structure in a uterus by which a fetus is nourished — **pla•cen•tal** \-'sent°l\ *adj*

**plac•id** \'plasəd\ *adj* : undisturbed or peaceful — **pla•cid•i•ty** \pla'sidətē\ *n* — **plac•id•ly** *adv*

**pla•gia•rize** \'plājə,rīz\ *vb* **-rized; -riz•ing** : use (words or ideas) of another as if your own — **pla•gia•rism** \-,rizəm\ *n* — **pla•gia•rist** \-rist\ *n*

**plague** \'plāg\ *n* **1** : disastrous evil **2** : destructive contagious bacterial disease ∼ *vb* **plagued; plagu•ing 1** : afflict with disease or disaster **2** : harass

**plaid** \'plad\ *n* : woolen fabric with a pattern of crossing stripes or the pattern itself — **plaid** *adj*

**plain** \'plān\ *n* : expanse of relatively level treeless country ∼ *adj* **1** : lacking ornament **2** : not concealed or disguised **3** : easily understood **4** : frank **5** : not fancy or pretty — **plain•ly** *adv* — **plain•ness** \'plānnəs\ *n*

**plain•tiff** \'plāntəf\ *n* : complaining party in a lawsuit

**plain•tive** \'plāntiv\ *adj* : expressive of suffering or woe — **plain•tive•ly** *adv*

**plait** \'plāt, 'plat\ *n* **1** : pleat **2** : braid of hair or straw — **plait** *vb*

**plan** \'plan\ *n* **1** : drawing or diagram **2** : method for accomplishing something ∼ *vb* **-nn- 1** : form a plan of **2** : intend — **plan•less** *adj* — **plan•ner** *n*

¹**plane** \'plān\ *vb* **planed; plan•ing** : smooth or level off with a plane ∼ *n* : smoothing or shaping tool — **plan•er** *n*

²**plane** *n* **1** : level surface **2** : level of existence, consciousness, or development **3** : airplane ∼ *adj* **1** : flat **2** : dealing with flat surfaces or figures

**plan•et** \'planət\ *n* : celestial body that revolves around the sun — **plan•e•tary** \-ə,terē\ *adj*

**plan•e•tar•i•um** \,planə'terēəm\ *n, pl* **-iums** *or* **-ia** \-ēə\ : building or room housing a device to project images of celestial bodies

**plank** \'plaŋk\ *n* **1** : heavy thick board

**2** : article in the platform of a political party — **plank·ing** n

**plank·ton** \'plaŋktən\ n : tiny aquatic animal and plant life — **plank·ton·ic** \plaŋk'tänik\ adj

**plant** \'plant\ vb **1** : set in the ground to grow **2** : place firmly or forcibly ~ n **1** : living thing without sense organs that cannot move about **2** : land, buildings, and machinery used esp. in manufacture

¹**plan·tain** \'plant³n\ n : short-stemmed herb with tiny greenish flowers

²**plantain** n : banana plant with starchy greenish fruit

**plan·ta·tion** \plan'tāshən\ n : agricultural estate usu. worked by resident laborers

**plant·er** \'plantər\ n **1** : plantation owner **2** : plant container

**plaque** \'plak\ n **1** : commemorative tablet **2** : film layer on a tooth

**plas·ma** \'plazmə\ n **1** : watery part of blood **2** : highly ionized gas — **plas·mat·ic** \plaz'matik\ adj

**plasma TV** n : television screen in which cells of plasma emit light upon receiving an electric current

**plas·ter** \'plastər\ n **1** : medicated dressing **2** : hardening paste for coating walls and ceilings ~ vb : cover with plaster — **plas·ter·er** n

**plas·tic** \'plastik\ adj : capable of being molded ~ n : material that can be formed into rigid objects, films, or filaments — **plas·tic·i·ty** \plas'tisətē\ n

**plate** \'plāt\ n **1** : flat thin piece **2** : plated metalware **3** : shallow usu. circular dish **4** : denture or the part of it that fits to the mouth **5** : something printed from an engraving ~ vb **plat·ed; plat·ing** : overlay with metal — **plat·ing** n

**pla·teau** \pla'tō\ n, pl -**teaus** or -**teaux** \-'tōz\ : large level area of high land

**plat·form** \'plat,fȯrm\ n **1** : raised flooring or stage **2** : declaration of principles for a political party

**plat·i·num** \'plat³nəm\ n : heavy grayish-white metallic chemical element

**plat·i·tude** \'platə,tüd, -,tyüd\ n : trite remark — **plat·i·tu·di·nous** \,platə-'tüd³nəs, -'tyüd-\ adj

**pla·toon** \plə'tün\ n : small military unit

**platoon sergeant** n : noncommissioned officer in the army ranking below a first sergeant

**plat·ter** \'platər\ n : large serving plate

**platy·pus** \'platipəs\ n : small aquatic egg-laying mammal

**plau·dit** \'plȯdət\ n : act of applause

**plau·si·ble** \'plȯzəbəl\ adj : reasonable or believeable — **plau·si·bil·i·ty** \,plȯzə'bilətē\ n — **plau·si·bly** \-blē\ adv

**play** \'plā\ n **1** : action in a game **2** : recreational activity **3** : light or fitful movement **4** : free movement **5** : stage representation of a drama ~ vb **1** : engage in recreation **2** : move or toy with aimlessly **3** : perform music **4** : act in a drama — **play·act·ing** n — **play·er** n — **play·ful** \-fəl\ adj — **play·ful·ly** adv — **play·ful·ness** n — **play·pen** n — **play·suit** n — **play·thing** n

**play·ground** n : place for children to play

**play·house** n **1** : theater **2** : small house for children to play in

**playing card** n : one of a set of 24 to 78 cards marked to show its rank and suit and used to play a game of cards

**play·mate** n : companion in play

**play·off** n : contest or series of contests to determine a champion

**play·wright** \-,rīt\ n : writer of plays

**pla·za** \'plazə, 'pläz-\ n **1** : public square **2** : shopping mall

**plea** \'plē\ n **1** : defendant's answer to charges **2** : urgent request

**plead** \'plēd\ vb **plead·ed** \'plēdəd\ or **pled** \'pled\; **plead·ing 1** : argue for or against in court **2** : answer to a charge or indictment **3** : appeal earnestly — **plead·er** n

**pleas·ant** \'plez³nt\ adj **1** : giving pleasure **2** : marked by pleasing behavior or appearance — **pleas·ant·ly** adv — **pleas·ant·ness** n

**pleas·ant·ries** \-³ntrēz\ n pl : pleasant and casual conversation

**please** \'plēz\ vb **pleased; pleas·ing 1** : give pleasure or satisfaction to **2** : desire or intend

**pleas·ing** \'plēziŋ\ adj : giving pleasure — **pleas·ing·ly** adv

**plea·sur·able** \'plezhərəbəl\ adj : pleasant — **plea·sur·ably** \-blē\ adv

**plea·sure** \'plezhər\ n **1** : desire or inclination **2** : enjoyment **3** : source of delight

**pleat** \'plēt\ *vb* : arrange in pleats ~ *n* : fold in cloth

**ple·be·ian** \pli'bēən\ *n* : one of the common people ~ *adj* : ordinary

**pledge** \'plej\ *n* 1 : something given as security 2 : promise or vow ~ *vb* **pledged; pledg·ing** 1 : offer as or bind by a pledge 2 : promise

**ple·na·ry** \'plēnərē, 'plen-\ *adj* : full

**pleni·po·ten·tia·ry** \,plenəpə'tenchərē, -'tenchē,erē\ *n* : diplomatic agent having full authority — **plenipoten-tiary** *adj*

**plen·i·tude** \'plenə,tüd, -,tyüd\ *n* 1 : completeness 2 : abundance

**plen·te·ous** \'plentēəs\ *adj* : existing in plenty

**plen·ty** \'plentē\ *n* : more than adequate number or amount — **plen·ti·ful** \'plentifəl\ *adj* — **plen·ti·ful·ly** *adv*

**pleth·o·ra** \'plethərə\ *n* : excess

**pleu·ri·sy** \'plùrəsē\ *n* : inflammation of the chest membrane

**pli·able** \'plīəbəl\ *adj* : flexible

**pli·ant** \'plīənt\ *adj* : flexible — **pli·an·cy** \-ənsē\ *n*

**pli·ers** \'plīərz\ *n pl* : pinching or gripping tool

¹**plight** \'plīt\ *vb* : pledge

²**plight** *n* : bad state

**plod** \'pläd\ *vb* **-dd-** 1 : walk heavily or slowly 2 : work laboriously and monotonously — **plod·der** *n* — **plod-ding·ly** \-iŋlē\ *adv*

**plot** \'plät\ *n* 1 : small area of ground 2 : ground plan 3 : main story development (as of a book or movie) 4 : secret plan for doing something ~ *vb* **-tt-** 1 : make a plot or plan of 2 : plan or contrive — **plot·ter** *n*

**plo·ver** \'pləvər, 'plōvər\ *n, pl* **-ver** or **-vers** : shorebird related to the sandpiper

**plow, plough** \'plaù\ *n* 1 : tool used to turn soil 2 : device for pushing material aside ~ *vb* 1 : break up with a plow 2 : cleave or move through like a plow — **plow·man** \-mən, -,man\ *n*

**plow·share** \-,sher\ *n* : plow part that cuts the earth

**ploy** \'plòi\ *n* : clever maneuver

**pluck** \'plək\ *vb* 1 : pull off or out 2 : tug or twitch ~ *n* 1 : act or instance of plucking 2 : spirit or courage

**plucky** \'pləkē\ *adj* **pluck·i·er; -est** : courageous or spirited

**plug** \'pləg\ *n* 1 : something for seal-ing an opening 2 : electrical connector at the end of a cord 3 : piece of favorable publicity ~ *vb* **-gg-** 1 : stop or make tight or secure by inserting a plug 2 : publicize

**plum** \'pləm\ *n* 1 : smooth-skinned juicy fruit 2 : fine reward

**plum·age** \'plümij\ *n* : feathers of a bird — **plum·aged** \-mijd\ *adj*

**plumb** \'pləm\ *n* : weight on the end of a line (**plumb line**) to show vertical direction ~ *adv* 1 : vertically 2 : completely ~ *vb* : sound or test with a plumb ~ *adj* : vertical

**plumb·er** \'pləmər\ *n* : one who repairs usu. water pipes and fixtures

**plumb·ing** \'pləmiŋ\ *n* : system of water pipes in a building

**plume** \'plüm\ *n* : large, conspicuous, or showy feather ~ *vb* **plumed; plum·ing** 1 : provide or deck with feathers 2 : indulge in pride — **plumed** \'plümd\ *adj*

**plum·met** \'pləmət\ *vb* : drop straight down

¹**plump** \'pləmp\ *vb* : drop suddenly or heavily ~ *adv* 1 : straight down 2 : in a direct manner

²**plump** *adj* : having a full rounded form — **plump·ness** *n*

**plun·der** \'pləndər\ *vb* : rob or take goods by force (as in war) ~ *n* : something taken in plundering — **plun·der·er** *n*

**plunge** \'plənj\ *vb* **plunged; plung·ing** 1 : thrust or drive with force 2 : leap or dive into water 3 : begin an action suddenly 4 : dip or move suddenly forward or down ~ *n* : act or instance of plunging — **plung·er** *n*

**plu·ral** \'plùrəl\ *adj* : relating to a word form denoting more than one — **plu-ral** *n*

**plu·ral·i·ty** \plù'ralətē\ *n, pl* **-ties** : greatest number of votes cast when not a majority

**plu·ral·ize** \'plùrə,līz\ *vb* **-ized; -iz·ing** : make plural — **plu·ral·i·za·tion** \,plùrələ'zāshən\ *n*

**plus** \'pləs\ *prep* : with the addition of ~ *n* 1 : sign + (**plus sign**) in mathematics to indicate addition 2 : added or positive quantity 3 : advantage ~ *adj* : being more or in addition ~ *conj* : and

**plush** \'pləsh\ *n* : fabric with a long pile ~ *adj* : luxurious — **plush·ly** *adv* — **plushy** *adj* — **plush·ness** *n*

**plu·toc·ra·cy** \plü'täkrəsē\ *n, pl* **-cies**
1 : government by the wealthy 2 : a
controlling class of the wealthy —
**plu·to·crat** \'plütə,krat\ *n* — **plu·to·crat·ic** \,plütə'kratik\ *adj*

**plu·to·ni·um** \plü'tōnēəm\ *n* : radio-active chemical element

¹**ply** \'plī\ *n, pl* **plies** : fold, thickness, or strand of which something is made

²**ply** *vb* **plied; ply·ing** 1 : use or work at 2 : keep supplying something to 3 : travel regularly usu. by sea

**ply·wood** *n* : sheets of wood glued and pressed together

**pneu·mat·ic** \nù'matik, nyù-\ *adj* 1 : moved by air pressure 2 : filled with compressed air — **pneu·mat·i·cal·ly** *adv*

**pneu·mo·nia** \nù'mōnyə, nyù-\ *n* : inflammatory lung disease

¹**poach** \'pōch\ *vb* : cook in simmering liquid

²**poach** *vb* : hunt or fish illegally — **poach·er** *n*

**pock** \'päk\ *n* : small swelling on the skin or its scar — **pock·mark** *n* — **pock·marked** *adj*

**pock·et** \'päkət\ *n* 1 : small open bag sewn into a garment 2 : container or receptacle 3 : isolated area or group ∼ *vb* : put in a pocket — **pock·et·ful** \-,fùl\ *n*

**pock·et·book** *n* 1 : purse 2 : financial resources

**pock·et·knife** *n* : knife with a folding blade carried in the pocket

**pod** \'päd\ *n* 1 : dry fruit that splits open when ripe 2 : compartment on a ship or craft

**po·di·a·try** \pə'dīətrē, pō-\ *n* : branch of medicine dealing with the foot — **po·di·a·trist** \pə'dīətrist, pō-\ *n*

**po·di·um** \'pōdēəm\ *n, pl* **-di·ums** or **-dia** \-ēə\ : dais

**po·em** \'pōəm\ *n* : composition in verse

**po·et** \'pōət\ *n* : writer of poetry

**po·et·ry** \'pōətrē\ *n* 1 : metrical writing 2 : poems — **po·et·ic** \pō'etik\, **po·et·i·cal** \-ikəl\ *adj*

**po·grom** \'pōgrəm, pə'gräm, 'pägrəm\ *n* : organized massacre

**poi·gnant** \'pòinyənt\ *adj* 1 : emotionally painful 2 : deeply moving — **poi·gnan·cy** \-nyənsē\ *n*

**poin·set·tia** \pòin'setēə, -'setə\ *n* : showy tropical American plant

**point** \'pòint\ *n* 1 : individual often essential detail 2 : purpose 3 : particular place, time, or stage 4 : sharp end 5 : projecting piece of land 6 : dot or period 7 : division of the compass 8 : unit of counting ∼ *vb* 1 : sharpen 2 : indicate direction by extending a finger 3 : direct attention to 4 : aim — **point·ed·ly** \-ədlē\ *adv* — **point·less** *adj*

**point-blank** *adj* 1 : so close to a target that a missile fired goes straight to it 2 : direct — **point-blank** *adv*

**point·er** \'pòintər\ *n* 1 : one that points out 2 : large short-haired hunting dog 3 : hint or tip

**poise** \'pòiz\ *vb* **poised; pois·ing** : balance ∼ *n* : self-possessed calmness

**poi·son** \'pòizᵊn\ *n* : chemical that can injure or kill ∼ *vb* 1 : injure or kill with poison 2 : apply poison to 3 : affect destructively — **poi·son·er** *n* — **poi·son·ous** \'pòizᵊnəs\ *adj*

**poke** \'pōk\ *vb* **poked; pok·ing** : prod 2 : dawdle ∼ *n* : quick thrust

¹**pok·er** \'pōkər\ *n* : rod for stirring a fire

²**poker** *n* : card game for gambling

**po·lar** \'pōlər\ *adj* : relating to a geographical or magnetic pole

**po·lar·ize** \'pōlə,rīz\ *vb* **-ized; -iz·ing** 1 : cause to have magnetic poles 2 : break up into opposing groups — **po·lar·i·za·tion** \,pōlərə'zāshən\ *n*

¹**pole** \'pōl\ *n* : long slender piece of wood or metal

²**pole** *n* 1 : either end of the earth's axis 2 : battery terminal 3 : either end of a magnet

**pole·cat** \'pōl,kat\ *n, pl* **polecats** or **polecat** 1 : European carnivorous mammal 2 : skunk

**po·lem·ics** \pə'lemiks\ *n sing or pl* : practice of disputation — **po·lem·i·cal** \-ikəl\ *adj* — **po·lem·i·cist** \-əsist\ *n*

**po·lice** \pə'lēs\ *n, pl* **police** 1 : department of government that keeps public order and enforces the laws 2 : members of the police ∼ *vb* **-liced; -lic·ing** : regulate and keep in order — **po·lice·man** \-mən\ *n* — **po·lice·wom·an** *n*

**police officer** *n* : member of the police

¹**pol·i·cy** \'päləsē\ *n, pl* **-cies** : course of action selected to guide decisions

²**policy** *n, pl* **-cies** : insurance contract — **pol·i·cy·hold·er** *n*

**po·lio** \'pōlē,ō\ *n* : poliomyelitis — **po·lio** *adj*

**po·lio·my·eli·tis** \-,mīə'lītəs\ *n* : acute virus disease of the spinal cord

**pol·ish** \'pälish\ *vb* **1** : make smooth and glossy **2** : develop or refine ∼ *n* **1** : shiny surface **2** : refinement

**po·lite** \pə'līt\ *adj* **-lit·er; -est** : marked by courteous social conduct — **po·lite·ly** *adv* — **po·lite·ness** *n*

**pol·i·tic** \'pälə,tik\ *adj* : shrewdly tactful

**politically correct** *adj* : seeking to avoid offending members of a different group

**pol·i·tics** \'pälə,tiks\ *n sing or pl* : practice of government and managing of public affairs — **po·lit·i·cal** \pə'litikəl\ *adj* — **po·lit·i·cal·ly** *adv* — **pol·i·ti·cian** \,pälə'tishən\ *n*

**pol·ka** \'pōlkə\ *n* : lively couple dance — **polka** *vb*

**pol·ka dot** \'pōkə,dät\ *n* : one of a series of regular dots in a pattern

**poll** \'pōl\ *n* **1** : head **2** : place where votes are cast — usu. pl. **3** : a sampling of opinion ∼ *vb* **1** : cut off **2** : receive or record votes **3** : question in a poll — **poll·ster** \-stər\ *n*

**pol·len** \'pälən\ *n* : spores of a seed plant

**pol·li·na·tion** \,pälə'nāshən\ *n* : the carrying of pollen to fertilize the seed — **pol·li·nate** \'pälə,nāt\ *vb* — **pol·li·na·tor** \-ər\ *n*

**pol·lute** \pə'lüt\ *vb* **-lut·ed; -lut·ing** : contaminating with waste products — **pol·lut·ant** \-'lüt°nt\ *n* — **pol·lut·er** *n* — **pol·lu·tion** \-'lüshən\ *n*

**pol·ly·wog, pol·li·wog** \'pälē,wäg\ *n* : tadpole

**po·lo** \'pōlō\ *n* : game played by 2 teams on horseback using long-handled mallets to drive a wooden ball

**pol·ter·geist** \'pōltər,gīst\ *n* : mischievous ghost

**pol·troon** \päl'trün\ *n* : coward

**poly·es·ter** \'pälē,estər\ *n* : synthetic fiber

**po·lyg·a·my** \pə'ligəmē\ *n* : marriage to several spouses at the same time — **po·lyg·a·mist** \-mist\ *n* — **po·lyg·a·mous** \-məs\ *adj*

**poly·gon** \'päli,gän\ *n* : closed plane figure with straight sides

**poly·mer** \'päləmər\ *n* : chemical compound of molecules joined in long strings — **po·lym·er·i·za·tion** \pə-

,limərə'zāshən\ *n* — **po·lym·er·ize** \pə'limə,rīz\ *vb*

**poly·tech·nic** \,päli'teknik\ *adj* : relating to many technical arts or applied sciences

**poly·the·ism** \'pälithē,izəm\ *n* : worship of many gods — **poly·the·ist** \-,thēist\ *adj or n*

**poly·un·sat·u·rat·ed** \,pälē,ən'sachə-,rātəd\ *adj* : having many double or triple bonds in a molecule

**pome·gran·ate** \'päm,granət, 'pämə-\ *n* : tropical reddish fruit with many seeds

**pom·mel** \'pəməl, 'päm-\ *n* **1** : knob on the hilt of a sword **2** : knob at the front of a saddle ∼ \'pəməl\ *vb* **-meled** *or* **-melled; -mel·ing** *or* **-mel·ling** : pummel

**pomp** \'pämp\ *n* **1** : brilliant display **2** : ostentation

**pomp·ous** \'pämpəs\ *adj* : pretentiously dignified — **pom·pos·i·ty** \päm-'päsətē\ *n* — **pomp·ous·ly** *adv*

**pon·cho** \'pänchō\ *n, pl* **-chos** : blanketlike cloak

**pond** \'pänd\ *n* : small body of water

**pon·der** \'pändər\ *vb* : consider

**pon·der·ous** \'pändərəs\ *adj* **1** : very heavy **2** : clumsy **3** : oppressively dull

**pon·tiff** \'päntəf\ *n* : pope — **pon·tif·i·cal** \pän'tifikəl\ *adj*

**pon·tif·i·cate** \pän'tifə,kāt\ *vb* **-cat·ed; -cat·ing** : talk pompously

**pon·toon** \pän'tün\ *n* : flat-bottomed boat or float

**po·ny** \'pōnē\ *n, pl* **-nies** : small horse

**po·ny·tail** \-,tāl\ *n* : hair arrangement like the tail of a pony

**poo·dle** \'püd°l\ *n* : dog with a curly coat

¹**pool** \'pül\ *n* **1** : small body of water **2** : puddle

²**pool** *n* **1** : amount contributed by participants in a joint venture **2** : game of pocket billiards ∼ *vb* : combine in a common fund

**poor** \'púr, 'pōr\ *adj* **1** : lacking material possessions **2** : less than adequate **3** : arousing pity **4** : unfavorable — **poor·ly** *adv*

¹**pop** \'päp\ *vb* **-pp-** **1** : move suddenly **2** : burst with or make a sharp sound **3** : protrude ∼ *n* **1** : sharp explosive sound **2** : flavored soft drink

²**pop** *adj* : popular

**pop·corn** \'päp,kórn\ *n* : corn whose

kernels burst open into a light mass when heated

**pope** \'pōp\ *n, often cap* : head of the Roman Catholic Church

**pop·lar** \'päplər\ *n* : slender quick-growing tree

**pop·lin** \'päplən\ *n* : strong plain-woven fabric with crosswise ribs

**pop·over** \'päp,ōvər\ *n* : hollow muffin made from egg-rich batter

**pop·py** \'päpē\ *n, pl* **-pies** : herb with showy flowers

**pop·u·lace** \'päpyələs\ *n* **1** : common people **2** : population

**pop·u·lar** \'päpyələr\ *adj* **1** : relating to the general public **2** : widely accepted **3** : commonly liked — **pop·u·lar·i·ty** \,päpyə'larətē\ *n* — **pop·u·lar·ize** \'päpyələ,rīz\ *vb* — **pop·u·lar·ly** \-lərlē\ *adv*

**pop·u·late** \'päpyə,lāt\ *vb* **-lat·ed; -lat·ing** : inhabit or occupy

**pop·u·la·tion** \,päpyə'lāshən\ *n* : people or number of people in an area

**pop·u·list** \'päpyəlist\ *n* : advocate of the rights of the common people — **pop·u·lism** \-,lizəm\ *n*

**pop·u·lous** \'päpyələs\ *adj* : densely populated — **pop·u·lous·ness** *n*

**por·ce·lain** \'pōrsələn\ *n* : fine-grained ceramic ware

**porch** \'pōrch\ *n* : covered entrance

**por·cu·pine** \'pórkyə,pīn\ *n* : mammal with sharp quills

¹**pore** \'pōr\ *vb* **pored; por·ing** : read attentively

²**pore** *n* : tiny hole (as in the skin) — **pored** *adj*

**pork** \'pórk\ *n* : pig meat

**pork barrel** *n* : government projects benefiting political patrons

**por·nog·ra·phy** \pór'nägrəfē\ *n* : depiction of erotic behavior intended to cause sexual excitement — **por·no·graph·ic** \,pórnə'grafik\ *adj*

**po·rous** \'pōrəs\ *adj* : permeable to fluids — **po·ros·i·ty** \pə'räsətē\ *n*

**por·poise** \'pórpəs\ *n* **1** : small whale with a blunt snout **2** : dolphin

**por·ridge** \'pórij\ *n* : soft boiled cereal

**por·rin·ger** \'pórənjər\ *n* : low one-handled metal bowl or cup

¹**port** \'pōrt\ *n* **1** : harbor **2** : city with a harbor

²**port** *n* **1** : inlet or outlet (as in an engine) for a fluid **2** : porthole

³**port** *n* : left side of a ship or airplane looking forward — **port** *adj*

⁴**port** *n* : sweet wine

**por·ta·ble** \'pōrtəbəl\ *adj* : capable of being carried — **portable** *n*

**por·tage** \'pōrtij, pór'tăzh\ *n* : carrying of boats overland between navigable bodies of water or the route where this is done — **portage** *vb*

**por·tal** \'pōrtªl\ *n* : entrance

**por·tend** \pór'tend\ *vb* : give a warning of beforehand

**por·tent** \'pór,tent\ *n* : something that foreshadows a coming event — **por·ten·tous** \pór'tentəs\ *adj*

**por·ter** \'pōrtər\ *n* : baggage carrier

**por·ter·house** \-,haús\ *n* : choice cut of steak

**port·fo·lio** \pōrt'fōlē,ō\ *n, pl* **-lios** **1** : portable case for papers **2** : office or function of a diplomat **3** : investor's securities

**port·hole** \'pōrt,hōl\ *n* : window in the side of a ship or aircraft

**por·ti·co** \'pōrti,kō\ *n, pl* **-coes** *or* **-cos** : colonnade forming a porch

**por·tion** \'pōrshən\ *n* : part or share of a whole ~ *vb* : divide into or allot portions

**port·ly** \'pōrtlē\ *adj* **-li·er; -est** : somewhat stout

**por·trait** \'pōrtrət, -,trāt\ *n* : picture of a person — **por·trait·ist** \-ist\ *n* — **por·trai·ture** \'pōrtrə,chúr\ *n*

**por·tray** \pór'trā\ *vb* **1** : make a picture of **2** : describe in words **3** : play the role of — **por·tray·al** *n*

**por·tu·laca** \,pōrchə'lakə\ *n* : tropical herb with showy flowers

**pose** \'pōz\ *vb* **posed; pos·ing** **1** : assume a posture or attitude **2** : propose **3** : pretend to be what one is not ~ *n* **1** : sustained posture **2** : pretense — **pos·er** *n*

**posh** \'päsh\ *adj* : elegant

**po·si·tion** \pə'zishən\ *n* **1** : stand taken on a question **2** : place or location **3** : status **4** : job — **position** *vb*

**pos·i·tive** \'päzətiv\ *adj* **1** : definite **2** : confident **3** : relating to or being an adjective or adverb form that denotes no increase **4** : greater than zero **5** : having a deficiency of electrons **6** : affirmative — **pos·i·tive·ly** *adv* — **pos·i·tive·ness** *n*

**pos·se** \'päsē\ *n* : emergency assistants of a sheriff

**pos•sess** \pə'zes\ *vb* **1** : have as property or as a quality **2** : control — **pos•ses•sion** \-'zeshən\ *n* — **pos•ses•sor** \-'zesər\ *n*

**pos•ses•sive** \pə'zesiv\ *adj* **1** : relating to a grammatical case denoting ownership **2** : jealous — **possessive** *n* — **pos•ses•sive•ness** *n*

**pos•si•ble** \'päsəbəl\ *adj* **1** : that can be done **2** : potential — **pos•si•bil•i•ty** \ˌpäsə'bilətē\ *n* — **pos•si•bly** *adv*

**pos•sum** \'päsəm\ *n* : opossum

¹**post** \'pōst\ *n* : upright stake serving to support or mark ~ *vb* : put up or announce by a notice

²**post** *vb* **1** : mail **2** : inform

³**post** *n* **1** : sentry's station **2** : assigned task **3** : army camp ~ *vb* : station

**post-** *prefix* : after or subsequent to

**post•age** \'pōstij\ *n* : fee for mail

**post•al** \'pōst³l\ *adj* : relating to the mail

**post•card** *n* : card for mailing a message

**post•date** \ˌpōst'dāt\ *vb* : assign a date to that is later than the actual date of execution

**post•er** \'pōstər\ *n* : large usu. printed notice

**pos•te•ri•or** \pō'stirēər, pä-\ *adj* **1** : later **2** : situated behind ~ *n* : buttocks

**pos•ter•i•ty** \pä'sterətē\ *n* : all future generations

**post•haste** \'pōst'hāst\ *adv* : speedily

**post•hu•mous** \'päschəməs\ *adj* : occurring after one's death — **post•hu•mous•ly** *adv*

**post•man** \'pōstmən, -ˌman\ *n* : mail carrier

**post•mark** *n* : official mark on mail — **postmark** *vb*

**post•mas•ter** *n* : chief of a post office

**post me•ri•di•em** \'pōstmə'ridēəm, -ēˌem\ *adj* : being after noon

**post•mor•tem** \ˌpōst'mórtəm\ *adj* : occurring or done after death ~ *n* **1** : medical examination of a corpse **2** : analysis after an event

**post office** *n* : agency or building for mail service

**post•op•er•a•tive** \ˌpōst'äpərətiv, -'äpəˌrāt-\ *adj* : following surgery

**post•paid** *adv* : with postage paid by the sender

**post•par•tum** \-'pärtəm\ *adj* : following childbirth — **postpartum** *adv*

**post•pone** \-'pōn\ *vb* **-poned; -pon•ing** : put off to a later time — **post•pone•ment** *n*

**post•script** \'pōstˌskript\ *n* : added note

**pos•tu•lant** \'päschələnt\ *n* : candidate for a religious order

**pos•tu•late** \'päschəˌlāt\ *vb* **-lat•ed; -lat•ing** : assume as true ~ *n* : assumption

**pos•ture** \'päschər\ *n* : bearing of the body ~ *vb* **-tured; -tur•ing** : strike a pose

**po•sy** \'pōzē\ *n, pl* **-sies** : flower or bunch of flowers

**pot** \'pät\ *n* : rounded container ~ *vb* **-tt-** : place in a pot — **pot•ful** *n*

**po•ta•ble** \'pōtəbəl\ *adj* : drinkable

**pot•ash** \'pätˌash\ *n* : white chemical salt of potassium used esp. in agriculture

**po•tas•si•um** \pə'tasēəm\ *n* : silver-white metallic chemical element

**po•ta•to** \pə'tātō\ *n, pl* **-toes** : edible plant tuber

---

**List of self-explanatory words with the prefix** *post-*

| | | |
|---|---|---|
| postadolescent | postgraduation | postpuberty |
| postattack | postharvest | postrecession |
| postbaccalaureate | posthospital | postretirement |
| postbiblical | postimperial | postrevolutionary |
| postcollege | postinaugural | postseason |
| postcolonial | postindustrial | postsecondary |
| postelection | postinoculation | postsurgical |
| postexercise | postmarital | posttreatment |
| postflight | postmenopausal | posttrial |
| postgame | postnatal | postvaccination |
| postgraduate | postnuptial | postwar |
| | postproduction | |

**pot•bel•ly** *n* : paunch — **pot•bel•lied** *adj*

**po•tent** \'pōt³nt\ *adj* : powerful or effective — **po•ten•cy** \-³nsē\ *n*

**po•ten•tate** \'pōt³n,tāt\ *n* : powerful ruler

**po•ten•tial** \pə'tenchəl\ *adj* : capable of becoming actual ∼ *n* 1 : something that can become actual 2 : degree of electrification with reference to a standard — **po•ten•ti•al•i•ty** \pə,tenchē'alətē\ *n* — **po•ten•tial•ly** *adv*

**poth•er** \'päthər\ *n* : fuss

**pot•hole** \'pät,hōl\ *n* : large hole in a road surface

**po•tion** \'pōshən\ *n* : liquid medicine or poison

**pot•luck** *n* : whatever food is available

**pot•pour•ri** \,pōpù'rē\ *n* 1 : mix of flowers, herbs, and spices used for scent 2 : miscellaneous collection

**pot•shot** *n* 1 : casual or easy shot 2 : random critical remark

**pot•ter** \'pätər\ *n* : pottery maker

**pot•tery** \'pätərē\ *n, pl* **-ter•ies** : objects (as dishes) made from clay

**pouch** \'paùch\ *n* 1 : small bag 2 : bodily sac

**poul•tice** \'pōltəs\ *n* : warm medicated dressing — **poultice** *vb*

**poul•try** \'pōltrē\ *n* : domesticated fowl

**pounce** \'paùns\ *vb* **pounced; pouncing** : spring or swoop upon and seize

**¹pound** \'paùnd\ *n* 1 : unit of weight equal to 16 ounces 2 : monetary unit (as of the United Kingdom) — **pound•age** \-ij\ *n*

**²pound** *n* : shelter for stray animals

**³pound** *vb* 1 : crush by beating 2 : strike heavily 3 : drill 4 : move along heavily

**pour** \'pōr\ *vb* 1 : flow or supply esp. copiously 2 : rain hard

**pout** \'paùt\ *vb* : look sullen — **pout** *n*

**pov•er•ty** \'pävərtē\ *n* 1 : lack of money or possessions 2 : poor quality

**pow•der** \'paùdər\ *n* : dry material of fine particles ∼ *vb* : sprinkle or cover with powder — **pow•dery** *adj*

**pow•er** \'paùər\ *n* 1 : position of authority 2 : ability to act 3 : one that has power 4 : physical might 5 : force or energy used to do work ∼

*vb* : supply with power — **pow•er•ful** \-fəl\ *adj* — **pow•er•ful•ly** *adv* — **pow•er•less** *adj*

**pow•er•house** *n* : dynamic or energetic person

**pow•wow** \'paù,waù\ *n* : conference

**pox** \'päks\ *n, pl* **pox** *or* **pox•es** : disease marked by skin rash

**prac•ti•ca•ble** \'praktikəbəl\ *adj* : feasible — **prac•ti•ca•bil•i•ty** \,praktikə'bilətē\ *n*

**prac•ti•cal** \'praktikəl\ *adj* 1 : relating to practice 2 : virtual 3 : capable of being put to use 4 : inclined to action as opposed to speculation — **prac•ti•cal•i•ty** \,prakti'kalətē\ *n* — **prac•ti•cal•ly** \'praktiklē\ *adv*

**prac•tice, prac•tise** \'praktəs\ *vb* **-ticed** *or* **-tised; -tic•ing** *or* **-tis•ing** 1 : perform repeatedly to become proficient 2 : do or perform customarily 3 : be professionally engaged in ∼ *n* 1 : actual performance 2 : habit 3 : exercise for proficiency 4 : exercise of a profession

**prac•ti•tio•ner** \prak'tishənər\ *n* : one who practices a profession

**prag•ma•tism** \'pragmə,tizəm\ *n* : practical approach to problems — **prag•mat•ic** \prag'matik\ *adj* — **prag•mat•i•cal•ly** *adv*

**prai•rie** \'prerē\ *n* : broad grassy rolling tract of land

**praise** \'prāz\ *vb* **praised; prais•ing** 1 : express approval of 2 : glorify — **praise** *n* — **praise•wor•thy** *adj*

**prance** \'prans\ *vb* **pranced; pranc•ing** 1 : spring from the hind legs 2 : swagger — **prance** *n* — **pranc•er** *n*

**prank** \'praŋk\ *n* : playful or mischievous act — **prank•ster** \-stər\ *n*

**prate** \'prāt\ *vb* **prat•ed; prat•ing** : talk long and foolishly

**prat•fall** \'prat,fòl\ *n* : fall on the buttocks

**prat•tle** \'prat³l\ *vb* **-tled; -tling** : babble — **prattle** *n*

**prawn** \'pròn\ *n* : shrimplike crustacean

**pray** \'prā\ *vb* 1 : entreat 2 : ask earnestly for something 3 : address God or a god

**prayer** \'prer\ *n* 1 : earnest request 2 : an addressing of God or a god 3 : words used in praying — **prayer•ful** *adj* — **prayer•ful•ly** *adv*

**praying mantis** *n* : mantis

**pre-** *prefix* : before, prior to, or in advance

**preach** \'prēch\ *vb* **1** : deliver a sermon **2** : advocate earnestly — **preach•er** *n* — **preach•ment** *n*

**pre•am•ble** \'prē₁ambəl\ *n* : introduction

**pre•can•cer•ous** \₁prē'kansərəs\ *adj* : likely to become cancerous

**pre•car•i•ous** \pri'karēəs\ *adj* : dangerously insecure — **pre•car•i•ous•ly** *adv* — **pre•car•i•ous•ness** *n*

**pre•cau•tion** \pri'kôshən\ *n* : care taken beforehand — **pre•cau•tion•ary** \-shə₁nerē\ *adj*

**pre•cede** \pri'sēd\ *vb* **-ced•ed; -ced•ing** : be, go, or come ahead of — **pre•ce•dence** \'presədəns, pri'sēd³ns\ *n*

**prec•e•dent** \'presədənt\ *n* : something said or done earlier that serves as an example

**pre•cept** \'prē₁sept\ *n* : rule of action or conduct

**pre•cinct** \'prē₁siŋkt\ *n* **1** : district of a city **2** *pl* : vicinity

**pre•cious** \'preshəs\ *adj* **1** : of great value **2** : greatly cherished **3** : affected

**prec•i•pice** \'presəpəs\ *n* : steep cliff

**pre•cip•i•tate** \pri'sipə₁tāt\ *vb* **-tat•ed; -tat•ing** **1** : cause to happen quickly or abruptly **2** : cause to separate out of a liquid **3** : fall as rain, snow, or hail ∼ *n* : solid matter precipitated from a liquid ∼ \-'sipətət, -ə₁tāt\ *adj* : unduly hasty — **pre•cip•i•tate•ly** *adv* — **pre•cip•i•tate•ness** *n* — **pre•cip•i•tous** \pri'sipətəs\ *adj* — **pre•cip•i•tous•ly** *adv*

**pre•cip•i•ta•tion** \pri₁sipə'tāshən\ *n* **1** : rash haste **2** : rain, snow, or hail

**pré•cis** \prā'sē\ *n, pl* **pré•cis** \-'sēz\ : concise summary of essentials

**pre•cise** \pri'sīs\ *adj* **1** : definite **2** : highly accurate — **pre•cise•ly** *adv* — **pre•cise•ness** *n*

**pre•ci•sion** \pri'sizhən\ *n* : quality or state of being precise

**pre•clude** \pri'klüd\ *vb* **-clud•ed; -clud•ing** : make impossible

**pre•co•cious** \pri'kōshəs\ *adj* : exceptionally advanced — **pre•co•cious•ly** *adv* — **pre•coc•i•ty** \pri-'käsətē\ *n*

**pre•cur•sor** \pri'kərsər\ *n* : harbinger

**pred•a•to•ry** \'predə₁tōrē\ *adj* : preying upon others — **pred•a•tor** \'predətər\ *n*

**pre•de•ces•sor** \'predə₁sesər, 'prēd-\ *n* : a previous holder of a position

**pre•des•tine** \prē'destən\ *vb* : settle beforehand — **pre•des•ti•na•tion** \-₁destə'nāshən\ *n*

**pre•dic•a•ment** \pri'dikəmənt\ *n* : difficult situation

**pred•i•cate** \'predikət\ *n* : part of a sentence that states something about the subject ∼ \'predə₁kāt\ *vb* **-cat•ed; -cat•ing** **1** : affirm **2** : establish — **pred•i•ca•tion** \₁predə-'kāshən\ *n*

**pre•dict** \pri'dikt\ *vb* : declare in advance — **pre•dict•abil•i•ty** \-₁dikte'bilətē\ *n* — **pre•dict•able** \-'diktəbəl\ *adj* — **pre•dict•ably** \-blē\ *adv* — **pre•dic•tion** \-'dikshən\ *n*

**pre•di•lec•tion** \₁pred³l'ekshən, ₁prēd-\ *n* : established preference

**pre•dis•pose** \₁prēdis'pōz\ *vb* : cause to be favorable or susceptible to something beforehand — **pre•dis•po•si•tion** \₁prē₁dispə'zishən\ *n*

**pre•dom•i•nate** \pri'dämə₁nāt\ *vb* : be

---

**List of self-explanatory words with the prefix *pre-***

| | | |
|---|---|---|
| preadmission | prebreakfast | preconception |
| preadolescence | precalculus | preconcert |
| preadolescent | precancel | precondition |
| preadult | precancellation | preconstructed |
| preanesthetic | preclear | preconvention |
| prearrange | preclearance | precook |
| prearrangement | precollege | precool |
| preassembled | precolonial | precut |
| preassign | precombustion | predawn |
| prebattle | precompute | predefine |
| prebiblical | preconceive | predeparture |

superior — **pre·dom·i·nance** \-nəns\ *n* — **pre·dom·i·nant** \-nənt\ *adj* — **pre·dom·i·nant·ly** *adv*

**pre·em·i·nent** \prē'emənənt\ *adj* : having highest rank — **pre·em·i·nence** \-nəns\ *n* — **pre·em·i·nent·ly** *adv*

**pre·empt** \prē'empt\ *vb* **1** : seize for oneself **2** : take the place of — **pre·emp·tion** \-'empshən\ *n* — **pre·emp·tive** \-'emptiv\ *adj*

**preen** \'prēn\ *vb* : dress or smooth up (as feathers)

**pre·fab·ri·cat·ed** \'prē'fabrə,kātəd\ *adj* : manufactured for rapid assembly elsewhere — **pre·fab·ri·ca·tion** \,prē-,fabri'kāshən\ *n*

**pref·ace** \'prefəs\ *n* : introductory comments ~ *vb* **-aced; -ac·ing** : introduce with a preface — **pref·a·to·ry** \'prefə,tōrē\ *adj*

**pre·fect** \'prē,fekt\ *n* : chief officer or judge — **pre·fec·ture** \-,fekchər\ *n*

**pre·fer** \pri'fər\ *vb* **-rr- 1** : like better **2** : bring (as a charge) against a person — **pref·er·a·ble** \'prefərəbəl\ *adj* — **pref·er·a·bly** *adv* — **pref·er·ence** \-ərəns\ *n* — **pref·er·en·tial** \,prefə-'renchəl\ *adj*

**pre·fer·ment** \pri'fərmənt\ *n* : promotion

**pre·fig·ure** \prē'figyər\ *vb* : foreshadow

¹**pre·fix** \'prē,fiks, prē'fiks\ *vb* : place before

²**pre·fix** \'prē,fiks\ *n* : affix at the beginning of a word

**preg·nant** \'pregnənt\ *adj* **1** : containing unborn young **2** : meaningful — **preg·nan·cy** \-nənsē\ *n*

**pre·hen·sile** \prē'hensəl, -,sīl\ *adj* : adapted for grasping

**pre·his·tor·ic** \,prēhis'tôrik\, **pre·his·tor·i·cal** \-ikəl\ *adj* : relating to the period before written history

**prej·u·dice** \'prejədəs\ *n* **1** : damage esp. to one's rights **2** : unreasonable attitude for or against something ~ *vb* **-diced; -dic·ing 1** : damage **2** : cause to have prejudice — **prej·u·di·cial** \,prejə'dishəl\ *adj*

**prel·ate** \'prelət\ *n* : clergy member of high rank — **prel·a·cy** \-əsē\ *n*

**pre·lim·i·nary** \pri'limə,nerē\ *n, pl* **-nar·ies** : something that precedes or introduces — **preliminary** *adj*

**pre·lude** \'prel,üd, -,yüd; 'prā,lüd\ *n* : introductory performance, event, or musical piece

**pre·ma·ture** \,prēmə'tùər, -'tyùr, -'chùr\ *adj* : coming before the usual or proper time — **pre·ma·ture·ly** *adv*

**pre·med·i·tate** \pri'medə,tāt\ *vb* : plan beforehand — **pre·med·i·ta·tion** \-,medə'tāshən\ *n*

**pre·mier** \pri'mir, -'myir; 'prēmēər\ *adj* : first in rank or importance ~ *n* : prime minister — **pre·mier·ship** *n*

**pre·miere** \pri'myer, -'mir\ *n* : 1st performance ~ *vb* **-miered; -mier·ing** : give a 1st performance of

**prem·ise** \'preməs\ *n* **1** : statement made or implied as a basis of argument **2** *pl* : piece of land with the structures on it

**pre·mi·um** \'prēmēəm\ *n* **1** : bonus **2** : sum over the stated value **3** : sum paid for insurance **4** : high value

**pre·mo·ni·tion** \,prēmə'nishən, ,premə-\ *n* : feeling that something is about to happen — **pre·mon·i·to·ry** \pri'mänə,tōrē\ *adj*

**pre·oc·cu·pied** \prē'äkyə,pīd\ *adj* : lost in thought

**pre·oc·cu·py** \-,pī\ *vb* : occupy the attention of — **pre·oc·cu·pa·tion** \prē-,äkyə'pāshən\ *n*

---

| | | |
|---|---|---|
| predesignate | prefight | premarital |
| predetermine | preform | premenopausal |
| predischarge | pregame | premenstrual |
| predrill | preheat | premix |
| preelection | preinaugural | premodern |
| preelectric | preindustrial | premodify |
| preemployment | preinterview | premoisten |
| preestablish | prejudge | premold |
| preexist | prekindergarten | prenatal |
| preexistence | prelaunch | prenotification |
| preexistent | prelife | prenotify |

pre•pare \pri'par\ vb -pared; -par•ing 1 : make or get ready often beforehand 2 : put together or compound — prep•a•ra•tion \,prepə'rāshən\ n — pre•pa•ra•to•ry \pri'parə,tōrē\ adj — pre•pared•ness \-'parədnəs\ n

pre•pon•der•ant \pri'pändərənt\ adj : having great weight, power, importance, or numbers — pre•pon•der•ance \-rəns\ n — pre•pon•der•ant•ly adv

prep•o•si•tion \,prepə'zishən\ n : word that combines with a noun or pronoun to form a phrase — prep•o•si•tion•al \-'zishənəl\ adj

pre•pos•sess•ing \,prēpə'zesiŋ\ adj : tending to create a favorable impression

pre•pos•ter•ous \pri'pästərəs\ adj : absurd

pre•req•ui•site \prē'rekwəzət\ n : something required beforehand — prerequisite adj

pre•rog•a•tive \pri'rägətiv\ n : special right or power

pre•sage \'presij, pri'sāj\ vb -saged; -sag•ing 1 : give a warning of 2 : predict — pres•age \'presij\ n

pres•by•ter \'prezbətər\ n : priest or minister

pre•science \'prēshəns, 'presh-\ n : foreknowledge of events — pre•scient \-ənt\ adj

pre•scribe \pri'skrīb\ vb -scribed; -scrib•ing 1 : lay down as a guide 2 : direct the use of as a remedy

pre•scrip•tion \pri'skripshən\ n : written direction for the preparation and use of a medicine or the medicine prescribed

pres•ence \'prezəns\ n 1 : fact or condition of being present 2 : appearance or bearing

¹pres•ent \'prezᵊnt\ n : gift

²pre•sent \pri'zent\ vb 1 : introduce 2 : bring before the public 3 : make a gift to or of 4 : bring before a court for inquiry — pre•sent•able adj — pre•sen•ta•tion \,prē,zen'tāshən, ,prezᵊn-\ n — pre•sent•ment \pri'zentmənt\ n

³pres•ent \'prezᵊnt\ adj : now existing, in progress, or attending ~ n : present time

pre•sen•ti•ment \pri'zentəmənt\ n : premonition

pres•ent•ly \'prezᵊntlē\ adv 1 : soon 2 : now

present participle n : participle that typically expresses present action

pre•serve \pri'zərv\ vb -served; -serv•ing 1 : keep safe from danger or spoilage 2 : maintain ~ n 1 : preserved fruit — often in pl. 2 : area for protection of natural resources — pres•er•va•tion \,prezər'vāshən\ n — pre•ser•va•tive \pri'zərvətiv\ adj or n — pre•serv•er \-'zərvər\ n

pre•side \pri'zīd\ vb -sid•ed; -sid•ing 1 : act as chairman 2 : exercise control

pres•i•dent \'prezədənt\ n 1 : one chosen to preside 2 : chief official (as of a company or nation) — pres•i•den•cy \-ənsē\ n — pres•i•den•tial \,prezə'denchəl\ adj

press \'pres\ n 1 : crowded condition 2 : machine or device for exerting pressure and esp. for printing 3 : pressure 4 : printing or publishing establishment 5 : news media and esp. newspapers ~ vb 1 : lie against and exert pressure on 2 : smooth with an iron or squeeze with something heavy 3 : urge 4 : crowd 5 : force one's way — press•er n

press•ing adj : urgent

pres•sure \'preshər\ n 1 : burden of distress or urgent business 2 : direct

---

prenuptial
preopening
preoperational
preoperative
preordain
prepackage
prepay
preplan
preprocess
preproduction
preprofessional
preprogram

prepubertal
prepublication
prepunch
prepurchase
prerecorded
preregister
preregistration
prerehearsal
prerelease
preretirement
prerevolutionary
prerinse

presale
preschool
preseason
preselect
preset
preshrink
preshrunk
presoak
presort
prestamp
presterilize
prestrike

application of force — **pressure** *vb* — **pres·sur·i·za·tion** \ˌpreshərə-ˈzāshən\ *n* — **pres·sur·ize** \-ˌīz\ *vb*

**pres·ti·dig·i·ta·tion** \ˌprestəˌdijə'-tāshən\ *n* : sleight of hand

**pres·tige** \pres'tēzh, -'tēj\ *n* : estimation in the eyes of people — **pres·ti·gious** \-'tijəs\ *adj*

**pres·to** \'prestō\ *adv or adj* : quickly

**pre·sume** \pri'züm\ *vb* -**sumed;** -**sum·ing** **1** : assume authority without right to do so **2** : take for granted — **pre·sum·able** \-'züməbəl\ *adj* — **pre·sum·ably** \-blē\ *adv*

**pre·sump·tion** \pri'zəmpshən\ *n* **1** : presumptuous attitude or conduct **2** : belief supported by probability — **pre·sump·tive** \-tiv\ *adj*

**pre·sump·tu·ous** \pri'zəmpchəwəs\ *adj* : too bold or forward — **pre·sump·tu·ous·ly** *adv*

**pre·sup·pose** \ˌprēsə'pōz\ *vb* : take for granted — **pre·sup·po·si·tion** \ˌprēˌsəpə'zishən\ *n*

**pre·tend** \pri'tend\ *vb* **1** : act as if something is real or true when it is not **2** : act in a way that is false **3** : lay claim — **pre·tend·er** *n*

**pre·tense, pre·tence** \'prē,tens, pri'tens\ *n* **1** : insincere effort **2** : deception — **pre·ten·sion** \pri-'tenchən\ *n*

**pre·ten·tious** \pri'tenchəs\ *adj* : overly showy or self-important — **pre·ten·tious·ly** *adv* — **pre·ten·tious·ness** *n*

**pre·ter·nat·u·ral** \ˌprētər'nachərəl\ *adj* **1** : exceeding what is natural **2** : inexplicable by ordinary means — **pre·ter·nat·u·ral·ly** *adv*

**pre·text** \'prē,tekst\ *n* : falsely stated purpose

**pret·ty** \'pritē, 'pùrt-\ *adj* -**ti·er;** -**est** : pleasing by delicacy or attractiveness ∼ *adv* : in some degree ∼ *vb* -**tied;** -**ty·ing** : make pretty — **pret·ti·ly** \'pritə'lē\ *adv* — **pret·ti·ness** *n*

**pret·zel** \'pretsəl\ *n* : twisted thin bread that is glazed and salted

**pre·vail** \pri'vāl\ *vb* **1** : triumph **2** : urge successfully **3** : be frequent, widespread, or dominant

**prev·a·lent** \'prevələnt\ *adj* : widespread — **prev·a·lence** \-ləns\ *n*

**pre·var·i·cate** \pri'varə,kāt\ *vb* -**cat·ed;** -**cat·ing** : deviate from the truth — **pre·var·i·ca·tion** \-ˌvarə-'kāshən\ *n* — **pre·var·i·ca·tor** \-'varə-ˌkātər\ *n*

**pre·vent** \pri'vent\ *vb* : keep from happening or acting — **pre·vent·able** *adj* — **pre·ven·tion** \-'venchən\ *n* — **pre·ven·tive** \-'ventiv\ *adj or n* — **pre·ven·ta·tive** \-'ventətiv\ *adj or n*

**pre·view** \'prē,vyü\ *vb* : view or show beforehand — **preview** *n*

**pre·vi·ous** \'prēvēəs\ *adj* : having gone, happened, or existed before — **pre·vi·ous·ly** *adv*

**prey** \'prā\ *n, pl* **preys 1** : animal taken for food by another **2** : victim ∼ *vb* **1** : seize and devour animals as prey **2** : have a harmful effect on

**price** \'prīs\ *n* : cost ∼ *vb* **priced; pric·ing** : set a price on

**price·less** \-ləs\ *adj* : too precious to have a price

**pric·ey** \'prīsē\ *adj* **pric·i·er;** -**est** : expensive

**prick** \'prik\ *n* **1** : tear or small wound made by a point **2** : something sharp or pointed ∼ *vb* : pierce slightly with a sharp point — **prick·er** *n*

**prick·le** \'prikəl\ *n* **1** : small sharp spine or thorn **2** : slight stinging pain ∼ *vb* -**led;** -**ling** : tingle — **prick·ly** \'priklē\ *adj*

**pride** \'prīd\ *n* : quality or state of being proud ∼ *vb* **prid·ed; prid·ing** : indulge in pride — **pride·ful** *adj*

**priest** \'prēst\ *n* : person having authority to perform the sacred rites of a religion — **priest·hood** *n* — **priest·li·ness** \-lēnəs\ *n* — **priest·ly** *adj*

**priest·ess** \'prēstəs\ *n* : woman who is a priest

**prig** \'prig\ *n* : one who irritates by rigid or pointed observance of proprieties — **prig·gish** \-ish\ *adj* — **prig·gish·ly** *adv*

**prim** \'prim\ *adj* -**mm-** : stiffly formal and proper — **prim·ly** *adv* — **prim·ness** *n*

---

| | | |
|---|---|---|
| presurgery | pretournament | prewar |
| presweeten | pretreat | prewash |
| pretape | pretreatment | prewrap |
| pretelevision | pretrial | |

**pri•mal** \'prīməl\ *adj* **1** : original or primitive **2** : most important

**pri•ma•ry** \'prī,merē, 'prīmərē\ *adj* : first in order of time, rank, or importance ~ *n, pl* **-ries** : preliminary election — **pri•mar•i•ly** \prī'merəlē\ *adv*

**primary school** *n* : elementary school

**pri•mate** *n* **1** \'prī,māt, -mət\ : highest-ranking bishop **2** \-,māt\ : mammal of the group that includes humans and monkeys

**prime** \'prīm\ *n* : earliest or best part or period ~ *adj* : standing first (as in significance or quality) ~ *vb* **primed; prim•ing 1** : fill or load **2** : lay a preparatory coating on

**prime minister** *n* : chief executive of a parliamentary government

¹**prim•er** \'primər\ *n* : small introductory book

²**prim•er** \'prīmər\ *n* **1** : device for igniting an explosive **2** : material for priming a surface

**pri•me•val** \prī'mēvəl\ *adj* : relating to the earliest ages

**prim•i•tive** \'primətiv\ *adj* **1** : relating to or characteristic of an early stage of development **2** : of or relating to a tribal people or culture ~ *n* : one that is primitive — **prim•i•tive•ly** *adv* — **prim•i•tive•ness** *n*

**pri•mor•di•al** \prī'mòrdēəl\ *adj* : primeval

**primp** \'primp\ *vb* : dress or groom in a finicky manner

**prim•rose** \'prim,rōz\ *n* : low herb with clusters of showy flowers

**prince** \'prins\ *n* **1** : ruler **2** : son of a king or queen — **prince•ly** *adj*

**prin•cess** \'prinsəs, -,ses\ *n* **1** : daughter of a king or queen **2** : wife of a prince

**prin•ci•pal** \'prinsəpəl\ *adj* : most important ~ *n* **1** : leading person **2** : head of a school **3** : sum lent at interest — **prin•ci•pal•ly** *adv*

**prin•ci•pal•i•ty** \,prinsə'palətē\ *n, pl* **-ties** : territory of a prince

**prin•ci•ple** \'prinsəpəl\ *n* **1** : general or fundamental law **2** : rule or code of conduct or devotion to such a code

**print** \'print\ *n* **1** : mark or impression made by pressure **2** : printed state or form **3** : printed matter **4** : copy made by printing **5** : cloth with a figure stamped on it ~ *vb* **1** : produce impressions of (as from type)

**2** : write in letters like those of printer's type — **print•able** *adj* — **print•er** *n*

**print•ing** \'printiŋ\ *n* : art or business of a printer

**print•out** \'print,aùt\ *n* : printed output produced by a computer — **print out** *vb*

¹**pri•or** \'prīər\ *n* : head of a religious house — **pri•o•ry** \'prīərē\ *n*

²**prior** *adj* : coming before in time, order, or importance — **pri•or•i•ty** \prī'òrətē\ *n*

**pri•or•ess** \'prīərəs\ *n* : nun who is head of a religious house

**prism** \'prizəm\ *n* : transparent 3-sided object that separates light into colors — **pris•mat•ic** \priz'matik\ *adj*

**pris•on** \'priz³n\ *n* : place where criminals are confined

**pris•on•er** \'priz³nər\ *n* : person on trial or in prison

**pris•sy** \'prisē\ *adj* **-si•er; -est** : overly prim — **pris•si•ness** *n*

**pris•tine** \'pris,tēn, pris'-\ *adj* : pure

**pri•va•cy** \'prīvəsē\ *n, pl* **-cies** : quality or state of being apart from others

**pri•vate** \'prīvət\ *adj* **1** : belonging to a particular individual or group **2** : carried on independently **3** : withdrawn from company or observation ~ *n* : enlisted person of the lowest rank in the marine corps or of one of the two lowest ranks in the army — **pri•vate•ly** *adv*

**pri•va•teer** \,prīvə'tir\ *n* : private ship armed to attack enemy ships and commerce

**private first class** *n* : enlisted person ranking next below a corporal in the army and next below a lance corporal in the marine corps

**pri•va•tion** \prī'vāshən\ *n* : lack of what is needed for existence

**priv•i•lege** \'privəlij\ *n* : right granted as an advantage or favor — **priv•i•leged** *adj*

**privy** \'privē\ *adj* **1** : private or secret **2** : having access to private or secret information ~ *n, pl* **priv•ies** : outdoor toilet — **priv•i•ly** \'privəlē\ *adv*

¹**prize** \'prīz\ *n* **1** : something offered or striven for in competition or in contests of chance **2** : something very desirable — **prize** *adj* — **prize•win•ner** *n* — **prize•win•ning** *adj*

²**prize** *vb* **prized; priz•ing** : value highly

³**prize** *vb* **prized; priz•ing** : pry

**prize·fight** *n* : professional boxing match — **prize·fight·er** *n* — **prize·fight·ing** *n*

¹**pro** \'prō\ *n* : favorable argument or person ∼ *adv* : in favor

²**pro** *n or adj* : professional

**prob·a·ble** \'präbəbəl\ *adj* : seeming true or real or to have a good chance of happening — **prob·a·bil·i·ty** \,präbə'bilətē\ *n* — **prob·a·bly** \'präbəblē\ *adv*

**pro·bate** \'prō,bāt\ *n* : judicial determination of the validity of a will ∼ *vb* **-bat·ed; -bat·ing** : establish by probate

**pro·ba·tion** \prō'bāshən\ *n* **1** : period of testing and trial **2** : freedom for a convict during good behavior under supervision — **pro·ba·tion·ary** \-shə,nerē\ *adj* — **pro·ba·tion·er** *n*

**probe** \'prōb\ *n* **1** : slender instrument for examining a cavity **2** : investigation ∼ *vb* **probed; prob·ing 1** : examine with a probe **2** : investigate

**pro·bi·ty** \'prōbətē\ *n* : honest behavior

**prob·lem** \'präbləm\ *n* **1** : question to be solved **2** : source of perplexity or vexation — **problem** *adj* — **prob·lem·at·ic** \,präblə'matik\ *adj* — **prob·lem·at·i·cal** \-ikəl\ *adj*

**pro·bos·cis** \prə'bäsəs\ *n, pl* **-cis·es** *also* **-ci·des** \-ə,dēz\ : long flexible snout

**pro·ce·dure** \prə'sējər\ *n* **1** : way of doing something **2** : series of steps in regular order — **pro·ce·dur·al** \-'sējərəl\ *adj*

**pro·ceed** \prō'sēd\ *vb* **1** : come forth **2** : go on in an orderly way **3** : begin and carry on an action **4** : advance

**pro·ceed·ing** *n* **1** : procedure **2** *pl* : something said or done or its official record

**pro·ceeds** \'prō,sēdz\ *n pl* : total money taken in

**pro·cess** \'präs,es, 'prōs-\ *n, pl* **-cess·es** \-,esəz, -əsəz, -ə,sēz\ **1** : something going on **2** : natural phenomenon marked by gradual changes **3** : series of actions or operations directed toward a result **4** : summons **5** : projecting part ∼ *vb* : subject to a process — **pro·ces·sor** \-ər\ *n*

**pro·ces·sion** \prə'seshən\ *n* : group moving along in an orderly way

**pro·ces·sion·al** \-'seshənəl\ *n* : music for a procession

**pro·claim** \prō'klām\ *vb* : announce publicly or with conviction — **proc·la·ma·tion** \,präklə'māshən\ *n*

**pro·cliv·i·ty** \prō'klivətē\ *n, pl* **-ties** : inclination

**pro·cras·ti·nate** \prə'krastə,nāt\ *vb* **-nat·ed; -nat·ing** : put something off until later — **pro·cras·ti·na·tion** \-,krastə'nāshən\ *n* — **pro·cras·ti·na·tor** \-'krastə,nātər\ *n*

**pro·cre·ate** \'prōkrē,āt\ *vb* **-at·ed; -at·ing** : produce offspring — **pro·cre·ation** \,prōkrē'āshən\ *n* — **pro·cre·ative** \'prōkrē,ātiv\ *adj* — **pro·cre·ator** \-,ātər\ *n*

**proc·tor** \'präktər\ *n* : supervisor of students (as at an examination) — **proctor** *vb*

**pro·cure** \prə'kyu̇r\ *vb* **-cured; -cur·ing** : get possession of — **pro·cur·able** \-'kyu̇rəbəl\ *adj* — **pro·cure·ment** *n* — **pro·cur·er** *n*

**prod** \'präd\ *vb* **-dd-** : push with or as if with a pointed instrument — **prod** *n*

**prod·i·gal** \'prädigəl\ *adj* : recklessly extravagant or wasteful — **prodigal** *n* — **prod·i·gal·i·ty** \,prädə'galətē\ *n*

**pro·di·gious** \prə'dijəs\ *adj* : extraordinary in size or degree — **pro·di·gious·ly** *adv*

**prod·i·gy** \'prädəjē\ *n, pl* **-gies** : extraordinary person or thing

**pro·duce** \prə'düs, -'dyüs\ *vb* **-duced; -duc·ing 1** : present to view **2** : give birth to **3** : bring into existence ∼ \'präd,üs, 'prōd-, -,yüs-\ *n* **1** : product **2** : agricultural products — **pro·duc·er** \prə'düsər, -'dyü-\ *n*

**prod·uct** \'präd,əkt\ *n* **1** : number resulting from multiplication **2** : something produced

**pro·duc·tion** \prə'dəkshən\ *n* : act, process, or result of producing — **pro·duc·tive** \-'dəktiv\ *adj* — **pro·duc·tive·ness** *n* — **pro·duc·tiv·i·ty** \,prō,dək'tivətē, ,prä-\ *n*

**prof** \'präf\ *n* : professor

**pro·fane** \prō'fān\ *vb* **-faned; -fan·ing** : treat with irreverence ∼ *adj* **1** : not concerned with religion **2** : serving to debase what is holy — **pro·fane·ly** *adv* — **pro·fane·ness** *n* — **pro·fan·i·ty** \prō'fanətē\ *n*

**pro·fess** \prə'fes\ *vb* **1** : declare openly **2** : confess one's faith in — **pro·fessed·ly** \-ədlē\ *adv*

**pro·fes·sion** \prə'feshən\ *n* **1** : open

declaration of belief **2** : occupation requiring specialized knowledge and academic training

**pro·fes·sion·al** \prə'feshənəl\ *adj* **1** : of, relating to, or engaged in a profession **2** : playing sport for pay — **professional** *n* — **pro·fes·sion·al·ism** *n* — **pro·fes·sion·al·ize** *vb* — **pro·fes·sion·al·ly** *adv*

**pro·fes·sor** \prə'fesər\ *n* : university or college teacher — **pro·fes·so·ri·al** \ˌprōfə'sōrēəl, ˌpräfə-\ *adj* — **pro·fes·sor·ship** *n*

**prof·fer** \'präfər\ *vb* **-fered; -fer·ing** : offer — **proffer** *n*

**pro·fi·cient** \prə'fishənt\ *adj* : very good at something — **pro·fi·cien·cy** \-ənsē\ *n* — **proficient** *n* — **pro·fi·cient·ly** *adv*

**pro·file** \'prō,fīl\ *n* : picture in outline — **profile** *vb*

**prof·it** \'präfət\ *n* **1** : valuable return **2** : excess of the selling price of goods over cost ~ *vb* : gain a profit — **prof·it·able** \'präfətəbəl\ *adj* — **prof·it·ably** *adv* — **prof·it·less** *adj*

**prof·i·teer** \ˌpräfə'tir\ *n* : one who makes an unreasonable profit — **prof·iteer** *vb*

**prof·li·gate** \'präfligət, -lə,gāt\ *adj* **1** : shamelessly immoral **2** : wildly extravagant — **prof·li·ga·cy** \-gəsē\ *n* — **profligate** *n* — **prof·li·gate·ly** *adv*

**pro·found** \prə'faûnd\ *adj* **1** : marked by intellectual depth or insight **2** : deeply felt — **pro·found·ly** *adv* — **pro·fun·di·ty** \-'fəndətē\ *n*

**pro·fuse** \prə'fyüs\ *adj* : pouring forth liberally — **pro·fuse·ly** *adv* — **pro·fu·sion** \-'fyüzhən\ *n*

**pro·gen·i·tor** \prō'jenətər\ *n* : direct ancestor

**prog·e·ny** \'präjənē\ *n, pl* **-nies** : offspring

**pro·ges·ter·one** \prō'jestə,rōn\ *n* : female hormone

**prog·no·sis** \präg'nōsəs\ *n, pl* **-no·ses** \-,sēz\ : prospect of recovery from disease

**prog·nos·ti·cate** \präg'nästə,kāt\ *vb* **-cat·ed; -cat·ing** : predict from signs or symptoms — **prog·nos·ti·ca·tion** \-,nästə'kāshən\ *n* — **prog·nos·ti·ca·tor** \-'nästə,kātər\ *n*

**pro·gram** \'prō,gram, -grəm\ *n* **1** : outline of the order to be pursued or the subjects included (as in a performance) **2** : plan of procedure **3** : coded instructions for a computer ~ *vb* **-grammed** *or* **-gramed; -gram·ming** *or* **-gram·ing** **1** : enter in a program **2** : provide a computer with a program — **pro·gram·ma·bil·i·ty** \ˌprō,gramə'bilətē\ *n* — **pro·gram·ma·ble** \'prō,graməbəl\ *adj* — **pro·gram·mer** \'prō,gramər\ *n*

**prog·ress** \'prägrəs, -,res\ *n* : movement forward or to a better condition ~ \prə'gres\ *vb* **1** : move forward **2** : improve — **pro·gres·sive** \-'gresiv\ *adj* — **pro·gres·sive·ly** *adv*

**pro·gres·sion** \prə'greshən\ *n* **1** : act of progressing **2** : continuous connected series

**pro·hib·it** \prō'hibət\ *vb* : prevent by authority

**pro·hi·bi·tion** \ˌprōə'bishən\ *n* **1** : act of prohibiting **2** : legal restriction on sale or manufacture of alcoholic beverages — **pro·hi·bi·tion·ist** \-'bishənist\ *n* — **pro·hib·i·tive** \prō'hibətiv\ *adj* — **pro·hib·i·tive·ly** *adv* — **pro·hib·i·to·ry** \-'hibə,tōrē\ *adj*

**proj·ect** \'präj,ekt, -ikt\ *n* : planned undertaking ~ \prə'jekt\ *vb* **1** : design or plan **2** : protrude **3** : throw forward — **pro·jec·tion** \-'jekshən\ *n*

**pro·jec·tile** \prə'jekt³l\ *n* : missile hurled by external force

**pro·jec·tor** \-'jektər\ *n* : device for projecting pictures on a screen

**pro·le·tar·i·an** \ˌprōlə'terēən\ *n* : member of the proletariat — **proletarian** *adj*

**pro·le·tar·i·at** \-ēət\ *n* : laboring class

**pro·lif·er·ate** \prə'lifə,rāt\ *vb* **-at·ed; -at·ing** : grow or increase in number rapidly — **pro·lif·er·a·tion** \-,lifə'rāshən\ *n*

**pro·lif·ic** \prə'lifik\ *adj* : producing abundantly — **pro·lif·i·cal·ly** *adv*

**pro·logue** \'prō,lòg, -,läg\ *n* : preface

**pro·long** \prə'lòŋ\ *vb* : lengthen in time or extent — **pro·lon·ga·tion** \ˌprō,lòŋ'gāshən\ *n*

**prom** \'präm\ *n* : formal school dance

**prom·e·nade** \ˌprämə'nād, -'näd\ *n* **1** : leisurely walk **2** : place for strolling — **promenade** *vb*

**prom·i·nence** \'prämənəns\ *n* **1** : quality, state, or fact of being readily noticeable or distinguished **2** : something that stands out — **prom·i-**

**nent** \-nənt\ *adj* — **prom·i·nent·ly** *adv*

**pro·mis·cu·ous** \prə'miskyəwəs\ *adj* : having a number of sexual partners — **prom·is·cu·i·ty** \,prämis'kyüətē, ,prō,mis-\ *n* — **pro·mis·cu·ous·ly** *adv* — **pro·mis·cu·ous·ness** *n*

**prom·ise** \'präməs\ *n* **1** : statement that one will do or not do something **2** : basis for expectation — **promise** *vb* — **prom·is·so·ry** \-ə,sōrē\ *adj*

**prom·is·ing** \'präməsiŋ\ *adj* : likely to succeed — **prom·is·ing·ly** *adv*

**prom·on·to·ry** \'prämən,tōrē\ *n, pl* **-ries** : point of land jutting into the sea

**pro·mote** \prə'mōt\ *vb* **-mot·ed; -mot·ing** **1** : advance in rank **2** : contribute to the growth, development, or prosperity of — **pro·mot·er** *n* — **pro·mo·tion** \-'mōshən\ *n* — **pro·mo·tion·al** \-'mōshənəl\ *adj*

¹**prompt** \'prämpt\ *vb* **1** : incite **2** : give a cue to (an actor or singer) — **prompt·er** *n*

²**prompt** *adj* : ready and quick — **prompt·ly** *adv* — **prompt·ness** *n*

**prone** \'prōn\ *adj* **1** : having a tendency **2** : lying face downward — **prone·ness** \'prōnnəs\ *n*

**prong** \'proŋ\ *n* : sharp point of a fork — **pronged** \'prond\ *adj*

**pro·noun** \'prō,naùn\ *n* : word used as a substitute for a noun

**pro·nounce** \prə'naùns\ *vb* **-nounced; -nounc·ing** **1** : utter officially or as an opinion **2** : say or speak esp. correctly — **pro·nounce·able** *adj* — **pro·nounce·ment** *n* — **pro·nun·ci·a·tion** \-,nənsē'āshən\ *n*

**pro·nounced** \-'naùnst\ *adj* : decided

¹**proof** \'prüf\ *n* **1** : evidence of a truth or fact **2** : trial impression or print

²**proof** *adj* : designed for or successful in resisting or repelling

**proof·read** *vb* : read and mark corrections in — **proof·read·er** *n*

**prop** \'präp\ *vb* **-pp-** **1** : support **2** : sustain — **prop** *n*

**pro·pa·gan·da** \,präpə'gandə, ,prōpə-\ *n* : the spreading of ideas or information to further or damage a cause — **pro·pa·gan·dist** \-dist\ *n* — **pro·pa·gan·dize** \-,dīz\ *vb*

**prop·a·gate** \'präpə,gāt\ *vb* **-gat·ed; -gat·ing** **1** : reproduce biologically **2** : cause to spread — **prop·a·ga·tion** \,präpə'gāshən\ *n*

**pro·pane** \'prō,pān\ *n* : heavy flammable gaseous fuel

**pro·pel** \prə'pel\ *vb* **-ll-** : drive forward — **pro·pel·lant, pro·pel·lent** *n or adj*

**pro·pel·ler** \prə'pelər\ *n* : hub with revolving blades that propels a craft

**pro·pen·si·ty** \prə'pensətē\ *n, pl* **-ties** : particular interest or inclination

**prop·er** \'präpər\ *adj* **1** : suitable or right **2** : limited to a specified thing **3** : correct **4** : strictly adhering to standards of social manners, dignity, or good taste — **prop·er·ly** *adv*

**prop·er·ty** \'präpərtē\ *n, pl* **-ties** **1** : quality peculiar to an individual **2** : something owned **3** : piece of real estate **4** : ownership

**proph·e·cy** \'präfəsē\ *n, pl* **-cies** : prediction

**proph·e·sy** \-,sī\ *vb* **-sied; -sy·ing** : predict — **proph·e·si·er** \-,sīər\ *n*

**proph·et** \'präfət\ *n* : one who utters revelations or predicts events — **proph·et·ess** \-əs\ *n* — **pro·phet·ic** \prə'fetik\ *adj* — **pro·phet·i·cal·ly** *adv*

**pro·pin·qui·ty** \prə'piŋkwətē\ *n* : nearness

**pro·pi·ti·ate** \prō'pishē,āt\ *vb* **-at·ed; -at·ing** : gain or regain the favor of — **pro·pi·ti·a·tion** \-,pishē'āshən\ *n* — **pro·pi·tia·to·ry** \-'pishēə,tōrē\ *adj*

**pro·pi·tious** \prə'pishəs\ *adj* : favorable

**pro·po·nent** \prə'pōnənt\ *n* : one who argues in favor of something

**pro·por·tion** \prə'pōrshən\ *n* **1** : relation of one part to another or to the whole with respect to magnitude, quantity, or degree **2** : symmetry **3** : share ~ *vb* : adjust in size in relation to others — **pro·por·tion·al** \-shənəl\ *adj* — **pro·por·tion·al·ly** *adv* — **pro·por·tion·ate** \-shənət\ *adj* — **pro·por·tion·ate·ly** *adv*

**pro·pose** \prə'pōz\ *vb* **-posed; -pos·ing** **1** : plan or intend **2** : make an offer of marriage **3** : present for consideration — **pro·pos·al** \-'pōzəl\ *n*

**prop·o·si·tion** \,präpə'zishən\ *n* : something proposed ~ *vb* : suggest sexual intercourse to

**pro·pound** \prə'paùnd\ *vb* : set forth for consideration

**pro·pri·e·tor** \prə'prīətər\ *n* : owner — **pro·pri·etary** \prə'prīə,terē\ *adj* —

**pro·pri·etor·ship** n — **pro·pri·etress** \-ˈprīətrəs\ n

**pro·pri·ety** \prəˈprīətē\ n, pl **-eties** : standard of acceptability in social conduct

**pro·pul·sion** \prəˈpəlshən\ n **1** : action of propelling **2** : driving power — **pro·pul·sive** \-siv\ adj

**pro·sa·ic** \prōˈzāik\ adj : dull

**pro·scribe** \prōˈskrīb\ vb **-scribed; -scrib·ing** : prohibit — **pro·scrip·tion** \-ˈskripshən\ n

**prose** \ˈprōz\ n : ordinary language

**pros·e·cute** \ˈpräsiˌkyüt\ vb **-cut·ed; -cut·ing 1** : follow to the end **2** : seek legal punishment of — **pros·e·cu·tion** \ˌpräsiˈkyüshən\ n — **pros·e·cu·tor** \ˈpräsiˌkyütər\ n

**pros·e·lyte** \ˈpräsəˌlīt\ n : new convert — **pros·e·ly·tize** \ˈpräsələˌtīz\ vb

**pros·pect** \ˈpräsˌpekt\ n **1** : extensive view **2** : something awaited **3** : potential buyer ∼ vb : look for mineral deposits — **pro·spec·tive** \prəˈspektiv, ˈpräsˌpek-\ adj — **pro·spec·tive·ly** adv — **pros·pec·tor** \-ˌpektər, -ˈpek-\ n

**pro·spec·tus** \prəˈspektəs\ n : introductory description of an enterprise

**pros·per** \ˈpräspər\ vb : thrive or succeed — **pros·per·ous** \-pərəs\ adj

**pros·per·i·ty** \präsˈperətē\ n : economic well-being

**pros·tate** \ˈpräsˌtāt\ n : glandular body about the base of the male urethra — **prostate** adj

**pros·the·sis** \präsˈthēsəs, ˈprästhə-\ n, pl **-the·ses** \-ˌsēz\ : artificial replacement for a body part — **pros·thet·ic** \präsˈthetik\ adj

**pros·ti·tute** \ˈprästəˌtüt, -ˌtyüt\ vb **-tut·ed; -tut·ing 1** : offer sexual activity for money **2** : put to corrupt or unworthy purposes ∼ n : one who engages in sexual activities for money — **pros·ti·tu·tion** \ˌprästəˈtüshən, -ˈtyü-\ n

**pros·trate** \ˈpräsˌtrāt\ adj : stretched out with face on the ground ∼ vb **-trat·ed; -trat·ing 1** : fall or throw (oneself) into a prostrate position **2** : reduce to helplessness — **pros·tra·tion** \präsˈtrāshən\ n

**pro·tag·o·nist** \prōˈtagənist\ n : main character in a drama or story

**pro·tect** \prəˈtekt\ vb : shield from injury — **pro·tec·tor** \-tər\ n

**pro·tec·tion** \prəˈtekshən\ n **1** : act of protecting **2** : one that protects — **pro·tec·tive** \-ˈtektiv\ adj

**pro·tec·tor·ate** \-tərət\ n : state dependent upon the authority of another state

**pro·té·gé** \ˈprōtəˌzhā\ n : one under the care and protection of an influential person

**pro·tein** \ˈprōˌtēn\ n : complex combination of amino acids present in living matter

**pro·test** \ˈprōˌtest\ n **1** : organized public demonstration of disapproval **2** : strong objection ∼ \prəˈtest\ vb **1** : assert positively **2** : object strongly — **pro·tes·ta·tion** \ˌprätəsˈtāshən\ n — **pro·test·er, pro·tes·tor** \ˈprōˌtestər\ n

**Prot·es·tant** \ˈprätəstənt\ n : Christian not of a Catholic or Orthodox church — **Prot·es·tant·ism** \ˈprätəstəntˌizəm\ n

**pro·to·col** \ˈprōtəˌkȯl\ n : diplomatic etiquette

**pro·ton** \ˈprōˌtän\ n : positively charged atomic particle

**pro·to·plasm** \ˈprōtəˌplazəm\ n : complex colloidal living substance of plant and animal cells — **pro·to·plas·mic** \ˌprōtəˈplazmik\ adj

**pro·to·type** \ˈprōtəˌtīp\ n : original model

**pro·to·zo·an** \ˌprōtəˈzōən\ n : single-celled lower invertebrate animal

**pro·tract** \prōˈtrakt\ vb : prolong

**pro·trac·tor** \-ˈtraktər\ n : instrument for drawing and measuring angles

**pro·trude** \prōˈtrüd\ vb **-trud·ed; -trud·ing** : stick out or cause to stick out — **pro·tru·sion** \-ˈtrüzhən\ n

**pro·tu·ber·ance** \prōˈtübərəns, -ˈtyü-\ n : something that protrudes — **pro·tu·ber·ant** adj

**proud** \ˈpraud\ adj **1** : having or showing excessive self-esteem **2** : highly pleased **3** : having proper self-respect **4** : glorious — **proud·ly** adv

**prove** \ˈprüv\ vb **proved; proved** or **prov·en** \ˈprüvən\; **prov·ing 1** : test by experiment or by a standard **2** : establish the truth of by argument or evidence **3** : turn out esp. after trial or test — **prov·able** \ˈprüvəbəl\ adj

**prov·en·der** \ˈprävəndər\ n : dry food for domestic animals

**prov·erb** \ˈprävˌərb\ n : short meaningful popular saying — **pro·ver·bi·al** \prəˈvərbēəl\ adj

**pro·vide** \prə'vīd\ *vb* **-vid·ed; -vid·ing** **1** : take measures beforehand **2** : make a stipulation **3** : supply what is needed — **pro·vid·er** *n*

**pro·vid·ed** *conj* : if

**prov·i·dence** \'prävədəns\ *n* **1** *often cap* : divine guidance **2** *cap* : God **3** : quality of being provident

**prov·i·dent** \-ədənt\ *adj* **1** : making provision for the future **2** : thrifty — **prov·i·dent·ly** *adv*

**prov·i·den·tial** \,prävə'denchəl\ *adj* **1** : relating to Providence **2** : opportune

**pro·vid·ing** *conj* : provided

**prov·ince** \'prävəns\ *n* **1** : administrative district **2** *pl* : all of a country outside the metropolis **3** : sphere

**pro·vin·cial** \prə'vinchəl\ *adj* **1** : relating to a province **2** : limited in outlook — **pro·vin·cial·ism** \-,izəm\ *n*

**pro·vi·sion** \prə'vizhən\ *n* **1** : act of providing **2** : stock of food — usu. in pl. **3** : stipulation ~ *vb* : supply with provisions

**pro·vi·sion·al** \-'vizhənəl\ *adj* : provided for a temporary need — **pro·vi·sion·al·ly** *adv*

**pro·vi·so** \prə'vīzō\ *n, pl* **-sos** or **-soes** : stipulation

**pro·voke** \prə'vōk\ *vb* **-voked; -vok·ing** **1** : incite to anger **2** : stir up on purpose — **prov·o·ca·tion** \,prävə'kāshən\ *n* — **pro·voc·a·tive** \prə-'väkətiv\ *adj*

**prow** \'prau\ *n* : bow of a ship

**prow·ess** \'prauəs\ *n* **1** : valor **2** : extraordinary ability

**prowl** \'praul\ *vb* : roam about stealthily — **prowl** *n* — **prowl·er** *n*

**prox·i·mate** \'präksəmət\ *adj* : very near

**prox·im·i·ty** \präk'simətē\ *n* : nearness

**proxy** \'präksē\ *n, pl* **prox·ies** : authority to act for another — **proxy** *adj*

**prude** \'prüd\ *n* : one who shows extreme modesty — **prud·ery** \'prüdərē\ *n* — **prud·ish** \'prüdish\ *adj*

**pru·dent** \'prüd³nt\ *adj* **1** : shrewd **2** : cautious **3** : thrifty — **pru·dence** \-³ns\ *n* — **pru·den·tial** \prü-'denchəl\ *adj* — **pru·dent·ly** *adv*

**¹prune** \'prün\ *n* : dried plum

**²prune** *vb* **pruned; prun·ing** : cut off unwanted parts

**pru·ri·ent** \'prúrēənt\ *adj* : lewd — **pru·ri·ence** \-ēəns\ *n*

**¹pry** \'prī\ *vb* **pried; pry·ing** : look closely or inquisitively

**²pry** *vb* **pried; pry·ing** : raise, move, or pull apart with a lever

**psalm** \'säm, 'sälm\ *n* : sacred song or poem — **psalm·ist** *n*

**pseu·do·nym** \'süd³n,im\ *n* : fictitious name — **pseu·don·y·mous** \sü'dänəməs\ *adj*

**pso·ri·a·sis** \sə'rīəsəs\ *n* : chronic skin disease

**psy·che** \'sīkē\ *n* : soul or mind

**psy·chi·a·try** \sə'kīətrē, sī-\ *n* : branch of medicine dealing with mental, emotional, and behavioral disorders — **psy·chi·at·ric** \,sīkē'atrik\ *adj* — **psy·chi·a·trist** \sə'kīətrist, sī-\ *n*

**psy·chic** \'sīkik\ *adj* **1** : relating to the psyche **2** : sensitive to supernatural forces ~ *n* : person sensitive to supernatural forces — **psy·chi·cal·ly** *adv*

**psy·cho·anal·y·sis** \,sīkōə'naləsəs\ *n* : study of the normally hidden content of the mind esp. to resolve conflicts — **psy·cho·an·a·lyst** \-'an³list\ *n* — **psy·cho·an·al·yt·ic** \-,an³l'itik\ *adj* — **psy·cho·an·a·lyze** \-'an³l,īz\ *vb*

**psy·chol·o·gy** \sī'käləjē\ *n, pl* **-gies** **1** : science of mind and behavior **2** : mental and behavioral aspect (as of an individual) — **psy·cho·log·i·cal** \,sīkə'läjikəl\ *adj* — **psy·cho·log·i·cal·ly** *adv* — **psy·chol·o·gist** \sī-'käləjist\ *n*

**psy·cho·path** \'sīkə,path\ *n* : mentally ill or unstable person — **psy·cho·path·ic** \,sīkə'pathik\ *adj*

**psy·cho·sis** \sī'kōsəs\ *n, pl* **-cho·ses** \-,sēz\ : mental derangement (as paranoia) — **psy·chot·ic** \-'kätik\ *adj or n*

**psy·cho·so·mat·ic** \,sīkəsə'matik\ *adj* : relating to bodily symptoms caused by mental or emotional disturbance

**psy·cho·ther·a·py** \,sīkō'therəpē\ *n* : treatment of mental disorder by psychological means — **psy·cho·ther·a·pist** \-pist\ *n*

**pto·maine** \'tō,mān\ *n* : bacterial decay product

**pu·ber·ty** \'pyübərtē\ *n* : time of sexual maturity

**pu·bic** \'pyübik\ *adj* : relating to the lower abdominal region

**pub·lic** \'pəblik\ *adj* **1** : relating to the

people as a whole **2** : civic **3** : not private **4** : open to all **5** : well-known ~ *n* : people as a whole — **pub·lic·ly** *adv*

**pub·li·ca·tion** \ˌpəblə'kāshən\ *n* **1** : process of publishing **2** : published work

**pub·lic·i·ty** \pə'blisətē\ *n* **1** : news information given out to gain public attention **2** : public attention

**pub·li·cize** \'pəblə,sīz\ *vb* **-cized; -ciz·ing** : bring to public attention — **pub·li·cist** \-sist\ *n*

**pub·lish** \'pəblish\ *vb* **1** : announce publicly **2** : reproduce for sale esp. by printing — **pub·lish·er** *n*

**puck·er** \'pəkər\ *vb* : pull together into folds or wrinkles ~ *n* : wrinkle

**pud·ding** \'pu̇diŋ\ *n* : creamy dessert

**pud·dle** \'pəd°l\ *n* : very small pool of water

**pudgy** \'pəjē\ *adj* **pudg·i·er; -est** : short and plump

**pu·er·ile** \'pyu̇rəl\ *adj* : childish

**puff** \'pəf\ *vb* **1** : blow in short gusts **2** : pant **3** : enlarge ~ *n* **1** : short discharge (as of air) **2** : slight swelling **3** : something light and fluffy — **puffy** *adj*

**pug** \'pəg\ *n* : small stocky dog

**pu·gi·lism** \'pyüjə,lizəm\ *n* : boxing — **pu·gi·list** \-list\ *n* — **pu·gi·lis·tic** \ˌpyüjə'listik\ *adj*

**pug·na·cious** \ˌpəg'nāshəs\ *adj* : prone to fighting — **pug·nac·i·ty** \-'nasətē\ *n*

**puke** \'pyük\ *vb* **puked; puk·ing** : vomit — **puke** *n*

**pul·chri·tude** \'pəlkrə,tüd, -,tyüd\ *n* : beauty — **pul·chri·tu·di·nous** \ˌpəlkrə'tüd°nəs, -'tyüd-\ *adj*

**pull** \'pu̇l\ *vb* **1** : exert force so as to draw (something) toward or out **2** : move **3** : stretch or tear ~ *n* **1** : act of pulling **2** : influence **3** : device for pulling something — **pull·er** *n*

**pul·let** \'pu̇lət\ *n* : young hen

**pul·ley** \'pu̇lē\ *n, pl* **-leys** : wheel with a grooved rim

**Pull·man** \'pu̇lmən\ *n* : railroad car with berths

**pull·over** \'pu̇l,ōvər\ *adj* : put on by being pulled over the head — **pullover** *n*

**pul·mo·nary** \'pu̇lmə,nerē, 'pəl-\ *adj* : relating to the lungs

**pulp** \'pəlp\ *n* **1** : soft part of a fruit or

vegetable **2** : soft moist mass (as of mashed wood) — **pulpy** *adj*

**pul·pit** \'pu̇l,pit\ *n* : raised desk used in preaching

**pul·sate** \'pəl,sāt\ *vb* **-sat·ed; -sat·ing** : expand and contract rhythmically — **pul·sa·tion** \ˌpəl'sāshən\ *n*

**pulse** \'pəls\ *n* : arterial throbbing caused by heart contractions — **pulse** *vb*

**pul·ver·ize** \'pəlvə,rīz\ *vb* **-ized; -iz·ing** : beat or grind into a powder

**pu·ma** \'pümə, 'pyü-\ *n* : cougar

**pum·ice** \'pəməs\ *n* : light porous volcanic glass used in polishing

**pum·mel** \'pəməl\ *vb* **-meled; -mel·ing** : beat

[1]**pump** \'pəmp\ *n* : device for moving or compressing fluids ~ *vb* **1** : raise (as water) with a pump **2** : fill by means of a pump — with *up* **3** : move like a pump — **pump·er** *n*

[2]**pump** *n* : woman's low shoe

**pum·per·nick·el** \'pəmpər,nikəl\ *n* : dark rye bread

**pump·kin** \'pəŋkən, 'pəmpkən\ *n* : large usu. orange fruit of a vine related to the gourd

**pun** \'pən\ *n* : humorous use of a word in a way that suggests two or more interpretations — **pun** *vb*

[1]**punch** \'pənch\ *vb* **1** : strike with the fist **2** : perforate with a punch ~ *n* : quick blow with the fist — **punch·er** *n*

[2]**punch** *n* : tool for piercing or stamping

[3]**punch** *n* : mixed beverage often including fruit juice

**punc·til·i·ous** \ˌpəŋk'tilēəs\ *adj* : marked by precise accordance with conventions

**punc·tu·al** \'pəŋkchəwəl\ *adj* : prompt — **punc·tu·al·i·ty** \ˌpəŋkchə'walətē\ *n* — **punc·tu·al·ly** *adv*

**punc·tu·ate** \'pəŋkchə,wāt\ *vb* **-at·ed; -at·ing** : mark with punctuation

**punc·tu·a·tion** \ˌpəŋkchə'wāshən\ *n* : standardized marks in written matter to clarify the meaning and separate parts

**punc·ture** \'pəŋkchər\ *n* : act or result of puncturing ~ *vb* **-tured; -tur·ing** : make a hole in

**pun·dit** \'pəndət\ *n* **1** : learned person **2** : expert or critic

**pun·gent** \'pənjənt\ *adj* : having a sharp or stinging odor or taste — **pun·gen·cy** \-jənsē\ *n* — **pun·gent·ly** *adv*

**pun·ish** \'pənish\ *vb* : impose a penalty

on or for — **pun·ish·able** *adj* — **pun·ish·ment** *n*

**pu·ni·tive** \'pyünətiv\ *adj* : inflicting punishment

**pun·kin** *var of* PUMPKIN

¹**punt** \'pənt\ *n* : long narrow flat-bottomed boat ∼ *vb* : propel (a boat) by pushing with a pole

²**punt** *vb* : kick a ball dropped from the hands ∼ *n* : act of punting a ball

**pu·ny** \'pyünē\ *adj* **-ni·er; -est** : slight in power or size

**pup** \'pəp\ *n* : young dog

**pu·pa** \'pyüpə\ *n, pl* **-pae** \-ˌpē, -ˌpī\ *or* **-pas** : insect (as a moth) when it is in a cocoon — **pu·pal** \-pəl\ *adj*

¹**pu·pil** \'pyüpəl\ *n* : young person in school

²**pupil** *n* : dark central opening of the iris of the eye

**pup·pet** \'pəpət\ *n* : small doll moved by hand or by strings — **pup·pe·teer** \ˌpəpə'tir\ *n*

**pup·py** \'pəpē\ *n, pl* **-pies** : young dog

**pur·chase** \'pərchəs\ *vb* **-chased; -chas·ing** : obtain in exchange for money ∼ *n* 1 : act of purchasing 2 : something purchased 3 : secure grasp — **pur·chas·er** *n*

**pure** \'pyur\ *adj* **pur·er; pur·est** : free of foreign matter, contamination, or corruption — **pure·ly** *adv*

**pu·ree** \pyu'rā, -'rē\ *n* : thick liquid mass of food — **puree** *vb*

**pur·ga·to·ry** \'pərgəˌtōrē\ *n, pl* **-ries** : intermediate state after death for purification by expiating sins — **pur·ga·tor·i·al** \ˌpərgə'tōrēəl\ *adj*

**purge** \'pərj\ *vb* **purged; purg·ing** 1 : purify esp. from sin 2 : have or cause emptying of the bowels 3 : get rid of ∼ *n* 1 : act or result of purging 2 : something that purges — **pur·ga·tive** \'pərgətiv\ *adj or n*

**pu·ri·fy** \'pyurəˌfī\ *vb* **-fied; -fy·ing** : make or become pure — **pu·ri·fi·ca·tion** \ˌpyurəfə'kāshən\ *n* — **pu·ri·fi·er** \-ˌfīər\ *n*

**Pu·rim** \'purim\ *n* : Jewish holiday celebrated in February or March in commemoration of the deliverance of the Jews from the massacre plotted by Haman

**pu·ri·tan** \'pyurət²n\ *n* : one who practices or preaches a very strict moral code — **pu·ri·tan·i·cal** \ˌpyurə'tanikəl\ *adj* — **pu·ri·tan·i·cal·ly** *adv*

**pu·ri·ty** \'pyurətē\ *n* : quality or state of being pure

**purl** \'pərl\ *n* : stitch in knitting ∼ *vb* : knit in purl stitch

**pur·loin** \pər'lóin, 'pərˌlóin\ *vb* : steal

**pur·ple** \'pərpəl\ *n* : bluish red color — **pur·plish** \'pərpəlish\ *adj*

**pur·port** \pər'pōrt\ *vb* : convey outwardly as the meaning ∼ \'pərˌpōrt\ *n* : meaning — **pur·port·ed·ly** \-ədlē\ *adv*

**pur·pose** \'pərpəs\ *n* 1 : something (as a result) aimed at 2 : resolution ∼ *vb* **-posed; -pos·ing** : intend — **pur·pose·ful** \-fəl\ *adj* — **pur·pose·ful·ly** *adv* — **pur·pose·less** *adj* — **pur·pose·ly** *adv*

**purr** \'pər\ *n* : low murmur typical of a contented cat — **purr** *vb*

¹**purse** \'pərs\ *n* 1 : bag or pouch for money and small objects 2 : financial resource 3 : prize money

²**purse** *vb* **pursed; purs·ing** : pucker

**pur·su·ance** \pər'süəns\ *n* : act of carrying out or into effect

**pur·suant to** \-'süənt-\ *prep* : according to

**pur·sue** \pər'sü\ *vb* **-sued; -su·ing** 1 : follow in order to overtake 2 : seek to accomplish 3 : proceed along 4 : engage in — **pur·su·er** *n*

**pur·suit** \pər'süt\ *n* 1 : act of pursuing 2 : occupation

**pur·vey** \pər'vā\ *vb* **-veyed; -vey·ing** : supply (as provisions) usu. as a business — **pur·vey·or** \-ər\ *n*

**pus** \'pəs\ *n* : thick yellowish fluid (as in a boil)

**push** \'push\ *vb* 1 : press against to move forward 2 : urge on or provoke ∼ *n* 1 : vigorous effort 2 : act of pushing — **push·cart** *n* — **push·er** \'pushər\ *n*

**pushy** \'pushē\ *adj* **push·i·er; -est** : objectionably aggressive

**pu·sil·lan·i·mous** \ˌpyüsə'lanəməs\ *adj* : cowardly

**pussy** \'pusē\ *n, pl* **puss·ies** : cat

**pus·tule** \'pəschül\ *n* : pus-filled pimple

**put** \'put\ *vb* **put; put·ting** 1 : bring to a specified position or condition 2 : subject to pain, suffering, or death 3 : impose or cause to exist 4 : express 5 : cause to be used or employed — **put off** *vb* : postpone or delay — **put out** *vb* : bother or inconvenience —

**put up** *vb* **1** : prepare for storage **2** : lodge **3** : contribute or pay — **put up with** : endure

**pu·tre·fy** \'pyütrə‚fī\ *vb* **-fied; -fy·ing** : make or become putrid — **pu·tre·fac·tion** \‚pyütrə'fakshən\ *n*

**pu·trid** \'pyütrəd\ *adj* : rotten — **pu·trid·i·ty** \pyü'tridətē\ *n*

**put·ty** \'pətē\ *n, pl* **-ties** : doughlike cement — **putty** *vb*

**puz·zle** \'pəzəl\ *vb* **-zled; -zling 1** : confuse **2** : attempt to solve — **with** *out* or *over* ~ *n* : something that confuses or tests ingenuity — **puz·zle·ment** *n* — **puz·zler** \-ələr\ *n*

**pyg·my** \'pigmē\ *n, pl* **-mies** : dwarf — **pygmy** *adj*

**py·lon** \'pī‚län, -lən\ *n* : tower or tall post

**pyr·a·mid** \'pirə‚mid\ *n* : structure with a square base and 4 triangular sides meeting at a point

**pyre** \'pīr\ *n* : material heaped for a funeral fire

**py·ro·ma·nia** \‚pīrō'mānēə\ *n* : irresistible impulse to start fires — **py·ro·ma·ni·ac** \-nē‚ak\ *n*

**py·ro·tech·nics** \‚pīrə'tekniks\ *n pl* : spectacular display (as of fireworks) — **py·ro·tech·nic** \-nik\ *adj*

**Pyr·rhic** \'pirik\ *adj* : achieved at excessive cost

**py·thon** \'pī‚thän, -thən\ *n* : very large constricting snake

# Q

**q** \'kyü\ *n, pl* **q's** *or* **qs** \'kyüz\ : 17th letter of the alphabet

[1]**quack** \'kwak\ *vb* : make a cry like that of a duck — **quack** *n*

[2]**quack** *n* : one who pretends to have medical or healing skill — **quack** *adj* — **quack·ery** \-ərē\ *n*

**quad·ran·gle** \'kwäd‚raŋgəl\ *n* : rectangular courtyard

**quad·rant** \'kwädrənt\ *n* : 1/4 of a circle

**quad·ri·lat·er·al** \‚kwädrə'latərəl\ *n* : 4-sided polygon

**qua·drille** \kwä'dril, kə-\ *n* : square dance for 4 couples

**quad·ru·ped** \'kwädrə‚ped\ *n* : animal having 4 feet

**qua·dru·ple** \kwä'drüpəl, -'drəp-; 'kwädrəp-\ *vb* **-pled; -pling** \-pliŋ\ : multiply by 4 ~ *adj* : being 4 times as great or as many

**qua·dru·plet** \kwä'drəplət, -'drüp-; 'kwädrəp-\ *n* : one of 4 offspring born at one birth

**quaff** \'kwäf, 'kwaf\ *vb* : drink deeply or repeatedly — **quaff** *n*

**quag·mire** \'kwag‚mīr, 'kwäg-\ *n* : soft land or bog

**qua·hog** \'kō‚hòg, 'kwò-, 'kwō-, -‚häg\ *n* : thick-shelled clam

[1]**quail** \'kwāl\ *n, pl* **quail** *or* **quails** : short-winged plump game bird

[2]**quail** *vb* : cower in fear

**quaint** \'kwānt\ *adj* : pleasingly old-fashioned or odd — **quaint·ly** *adv* — **quaint·ness** *n*

**quake** \'kwāk\ *vb* **quaked; quak·ing** : shake or tremble ~ *n* : earthquake

**qual·i·fi·ca·tion** \‚kwäləfə'kāshən\ *n* **1** : limitation or stipulation **2** : special skill or experience for a job

**qual·i·fy** \'kwälə‚fī\ *vb* **-fied; -fy·ing 1** : modify or limit **2** : fit by skill or training for some purpose **3** : become eligible — **qual·i·fied** *adj* — **qual·i·fi·er** \-‚fīər\ *n*

**qual·i·ty** \'kwälətē\ *n, pl* **-ties 1** : peculiar and essential character, nature, or feature **2** : excellence or distinction

**qualm** \'kwäm, 'kwälm, 'kwȯm\ *n* : sudden feeling of doubt or uneasiness

**quan·da·ry** \'kwändrē\ *n, pl* **-ries** : state of perplexity or doubt

**quan·ti·ty** \'kwäntətē\ *n, pl* **-ties 1** : something that can be measured or numbered **2** : considerable amount

**quan·tum theory** \'kwäntəm-\ *n* : theory in physics that radiant energy (as light) is composed of separate packets of energy

**quar·an·tine** \'kwòrən‚tēn\ *n* **1** : restraint on the movements of persons or goods to prevent the spread of pests or disease **2** : place or period of quarantine — **quarantine** *vb*

**quar·rel** \'kwòrəl\ n : basis of conflict — **quarrel** vb — **quar·rel·some** \-səm\ adj

¹**quar·ry** \'kwòrē\ n, pl -**ries** : prey

²**quarry** n, pl -**ries** : excavation for obtaining stone — **quarry** vb

**quart** \'kwòrt\ n : unit of liquid measure equal to .95 liter or of dry measure equal to 1.10 liters

**quar·ter** \'kwòrtər\ n 1 : 1/4 part 2 : 1/4 of a dollar 3 : city district 4 pl : place to live esp. for a time 5 : mercy ~ vb : divide into 4 equal parts

**quar·ter·ly** \'kwòrtərlē\ adv or adj : at 3-month intervals ~ n, pl -**lies** : periodical published 4 times a year

**quar·ter·mas·ter** n 1 : ship's helmsman 2 : army supply officer

**quar·tet** \kwòr'tet\ n 1 : music for 4 performers 2 : group of 4

**quar·to** \'kwòrtō\ n, pl -**tos** : book printed on pages cut 4 from a sheet

**quartz** \'kwòrts\ n : transparent crystalline mineral

**quash** \'kwäsh, 'kwòsh\ vb 1 : set aside by judicial action 2 : suppress summarily and completely

**qua·si** \'kwä,zī, -sī; 'kwäzē, 'kwäs-; 'kwāzē\ adj : similar or nearly identical

**qua·train** \'kwä,trān\ n : unit of 4 lines of verse

**qua·ver** \'kwāvər\ vb : tremble or trill — **quaver** n

**quay** \'kē, 'kā, 'kwā\ n : wharf

**quea·sy** \'kwēzē\ adj -si·er; -est : nauseated — **quea·si·ly** \-zəlē\ adv — **quea·si·ness** \-zēnəs\ n

**queen** \'kwēn\ n 1 : wife or widow of a king 2 : female monarch 3 : woman of rank, power, or attractiveness 4 : fertile female of a social insect — **queen·ly** adj

**queer** \'kwir\ adj : differing from the usual or normal — **queer·ly** adv — **queer·ness** n

**quell** \'kwel\ vb : put down by force

**quench** \'kwench\ vb 1 : put out 2 : satisfy (a thirst) — **quench·able** adj — **quench·er** n

**quer·u·lous** \'kwerələs, -yələs\ adj : fretful or whining — **quer·u·lous·ly** adv — **quer·u·lous·ness** n

**que·ry** \'kwirē, 'kwer-\ n, pl -**ries** : question — **query** vb

**quest** \'kwest\ n or vb : search

**ques·tion** \'kweschən\ n 1 : something asked 2 : subject for debate 3 : dispute ~ vb 1 : ask questions 2 : doubt or dispute 3 : subject to analysis — **ques·tion·er** n

**ques·tion·able** \'kweschənəbəl\ adj 1 : not certain 2 : of doubtful truth or morality — **ques·tion·ably** \-blē\ adv

**question mark** n : a punctuation mark ? used esp. at the end of a sentence to indicate a direct question

**ques·tion·naire** \ˌkweschə'nar\ n : set of questions

**queue** \'kyü\ n 1 : braid of hair 2 : a waiting line ~ vb **queued; queu·ing** or **queue·ing** : line up

**quib·ble** \'kwibəl\ n : minor objection — **quibble** vb — **quib·bler** n

**quick** \'kwik\ adj 1 : rapid 2 : alert or perceptive ~ n : sensitive area of living flesh — **quick** adv — **quick·ly** adv — **quick·ness** n

**quick·en** \'kwikən\ vb 1 : come to life 2 : increase in speed

**quick·sand** n : deep mass of sand and water

**quick·sil·ver** n : mercury

**qui·es·cent** \kwī'es⁰nt\ adj : being at rest — **qui·es·cence** \-⁰ns\ n

**qui·et** \'kwīət\ adj 1 : marked by little motion or activity 2 : gentle 3 : free from noise 4 : not showy 5 : secluded ~ vb : pacify — **quiet** adv or n — **qui·et·ly** adv — **qui·et·ness** n

**qui·etude** \'kwīə,tüd, -,tyüd\ n : quietness or repose

**quill** \'kwil\ n 1 : a large stiff feather 2 : porcupine's spine

**quilt** \'kwilt\ n : padded bedspread ~ vb : stitch or sew in layers with padding in between

**quince** \'kwins\ n : hard yellow apple-like fruit

**qui·nine** \'kwī,nīn\ n : bitter drug used against malaria

**quin·tes·sence** \kwin'tes⁰ns\ n 1 : purest essence of something 2 : most typical example — **quin·tes·sen·tial** \ˌkwintə'senchəl\ adj — **quin·tes·sen·tial·ly** adv

**quin·tet** \kwin'tet\ n 1 : music for 5 performers 2 : group of 5

**quin·tu·ple** \kwin'tüpəl, -'tyüp-, -'təp-; 'kwintəp-\ adj 1 : having 5 units or members 2 : being 5 times as great or as many — **quintuple** n or vb

**quin·tu·plet** \-plət\ *n* : one of 5 offspring at one birth

**quip** \'kwip\ *vb* **-pp-** : make a clever remark — **quip** *n*

**quire** \'kwīr\ *n* : 24 or 25 sheets of paper of the same size and quality

**quirk** \'kwərk\ *n* : peculiarity of action or behavior — **quirky** *adj*

**quit** \'kwit\ *vb* **quit; quit·ting** 1 : stop 2 : leave — **quit·ter** *n*

**quite** \'kwīt\ *adv* 1 : completely 2 : to a considerable extent

**quits** \'kwits\ *adj* : even or equal with another (as by repaying a debt)

¹**quiv·er** \'kwivər\ *n* : case for arrows

²**quiver** *vb* : shake or tremble — **quiver** *n*

**quix·ot·ic** \kwik'sätik\ *adj* : idealistic to an impractical degree — **quix·ot·i·cal·ly** \-tiklē\ *adv*

**quiz** \'kwiz\ *n, pl* **quiz·zes** : short test ~ *vb* **-zz-** : question closely

**quiz·zi·cal** \'kwizikəl\ *adj* 1 : teasing 2 : curious

**quoit** \'kóit, 'kwóit, 'kwät\ *n* : ring thrown at a peg in a game (**quoits**)

**quon·dam** \'kwändəm, -ˌdam\ *adj* : former

**quo·rum** \'kwôrəm\ *n* : required number of members present

**quo·ta** \'kwōtə\ *n* : proportional part or share

**quotation mark** *n* : one of a pair of punctuation marks " " or ' ' used esp. to indicate the beginning and the end of a quotation

**quote** \'kwōt\ *vb* **quot·ed; quot·ing** 1 : repeat (another's words) exactly 2 : state (a price) — **quot·able** *adj* — **quo·ta·tion** \kwō'tāshən\ *n* — **quote** *n*

**quo·tient** \'kwōshənt\ *n* : number obtained from division

# R

**r** \'är\ *n, pl* **r's** *or* **rs** \'ärz\ : 18th letter of the alphabet

**rab·bet** \'rabət\ *n* : groove in a board

**rab·bi** \'rab,ī\ *n* : Jewish religious leader — **rab·bin·ic** \rə'binik\, **rab·bin·i·cal** \-ikəl\ *adj*

**rab·bin·ate** \'rabənət, -ˌnāt\ *n* : office of a rabbi

**rab·bit** \'rabət\ *n, pl* **-bit** *or* **-bits** : long-eared burrowing mammal

**rab·ble** \'rabəl\ *n* : mob

**ra·bid** \'rabəd\ *adj* 1 : violent 2 : fanatical 3 : affected with rabies — **ra·bid·ly** *adv*

**ra·bies** \'rābēz\ *n, pl* **rabies** : acute deadly virus disease

**rac·coon** \ra'kün\ *n, pl* **-coon** *or* **-coons** : tree-dwelling mammal with a black mask and a bushy ringed tail

¹**race** \'rās\ *n* 1 : strong current of water 2 : contest of speed 3 : election campaign ~ *vb* **raced; rac·ing** 1 : run in a race 2 : rush — **race·course** *n* — **rac·er** *n* — **race·track** *n*

²**race** *n* 1 : family, tribe, people, or nation of the same stock 2 : division of mankind based on hereditary traits — **ra·cial** \'rāshəl\ *adj* — **ra·cial·ly** *adv*

**race·horse** *n* : horse used for racing

**rac·ism** \'rās,izəm\ *n* : discrimination based on the belief that some races are by nature superior — **rac·ist** \-ist\ *n*

**rack** \'rak\ *n* 1 : framework for display or storage 2 : instrument that stretches the body for torture ~ *vb* : torture with or as if with a rack

¹**rack·et** \'rakət\ *n* : bat with a tight netting across an open frame

²**racket** *n* 1 : confused noise 2 : fraudulent scheme — **rack·e·teer** \ˌrakə'tir\ *n* — **rack·e·teer·ing** *n*

**ra·con·teur** \ˌrak,än'tər\ *n* : storyteller

**racy** \'rāsē\ *adj* **rac·i·er; -est** : risqué — **rac·i·ly** *adv* — **rac·i·ness** *n*

**ra·dar** \'rā,där\ *n* : radio device for determining distance and direction of distant objects

**ra·di·al** \'rādēəl\ *adj* : having parts arranged like rays coming from a common center — **ra·di·al·ly** *adv*

**ra·di·ant** \'rādēənt\ *adj* 1 : glowing 2 : beaming with happiness 3 : transmitted by radiation — **ra·di·ance** \-əns\ *n* — **ra·di·ant·ly** *adv*

**ra·di·ate** \'rādē,āt\ *vb* **-at·ed; -at·ing** 1 : issue rays or in rays 2 : spread from a center — **ra·di·a·tion** \ˌrādē'āshən\ *n*

**ra·di·a·tor** \'rādē₁ātər\ *n* : cooling or heating device

**rad·i·cal** \'radikəl\ *adj* **1** : fundamental **2** : extreme ~ *n* : person favoring extreme changes — **rad·i·cal·ism** \-₁izəm\ *n* — **rad·i·cal·ly** *adv*

**radii** *pl of* RADIUS

**ra·dio** \'rādē₁ō\ *n, pl* **-di·os 1** : wireless transmission or reception of sound by means of electric waves **2** : radio receiving set ~ *vb* : send a message to by radio — **radio** *adj*

**ra·dio·ac·tiv·i·ty** \₁rādēō₁ak'tivətē\ *n* : property of an element that emits energy through nuclear disintegration — **ra·dio·ac·tive** \-'aktiv\ *adj*

**ra·di·ol·o·gy** \₁rādē'äləjē\ *n* : medical use of radiation — **ra·di·ol·o·gist** \-jist\ *n*

**rad·ish** \'radish\ *n* : pungent fleshy root usu. eaten raw

**ra·di·um** \'rādēəm\ *n* : metallic radioactive chemical element

**ra·di·us** \'rādēəs\ *n, pl* **-dii** \-ē₁ī\ **1** : line from the center of a circle or sphere to the circumference or surface **2** : area defined by a radius

**ra·don** \'rā₁dän\ *n* : gaseous radioactive chemical element

**raff·ish** \'rafish\ *adj* : flashily vulgar — **raff·ish·ly** *adv* — **raff·ish·ness** *n*

**raf·fle** \'rafəl\ *n* : lottery among people who have bought tickets ~ *vb* **-fled; -fling** : offer in a raffle

**¹raft** \'raft\ *n* : flat floating platform ~ *vb* : travel or transport by raft

**²raft** *n* : large amount or number

**raf·ter** \'raftər\ *n* : beam supporting a roof

**¹rag** \'rag\ *n* : waste piece of cloth

**²rag** *n* : composition in ragtime

**rag·a·muf·fin** \'ragə₁məfən\ *n* : ragged dirty person

**rage** \'rāj\ *n* **1** : violent anger **2** : vogue ~ *vb* **raged; rag·ing 1** : be extremely angry or violent **2** : be out of control

**rag·ged** \'ragəd\ *adj* : torn — **rag·ged·ly** *adv* — **rag·ged·ness** *n*

**ra·gout** \ra'gü\ *n* : meat stew

**rag·time** *n* : syncopated music

**rag·weed** *n* : coarse weedy herb with allergenic pollen

**raid** \'rād\ *n* : sudden usu. surprise attack — **raid** *vb* — **raid·er** *n*

**¹rail** \'rāl\ *n* **1** : bar serving as a guard or barrier **2** : bar forming a track for wheeled vehicles **3** : railroad

**²rail** *vb* : scold someone vehemently — **rail·er** *n*

**rail·ing** \'rāliŋ\ *n* : rail or a barrier of rails

**rail·lery** \'rālərē\ *n, pl* **-ler·ies** : good-natured ridicule

**rail·road** \'rāl₁rōd\ *n* : road for a train laid with iron rails and wooden ties ~ *vb* : force something hastily — **rail·road·er** *n* — **rail·road·ing** *n*

**rail·way** \-₁wā\ *n* : railroad

**rai·ment** \'rāmənt\ *n* : clothing

**rain** \'rān\ **1** : water falling in drops from the clouds **2** : shower of objects ~ *vb* : fall as or like rain — **rain·coat** *n* — **rain·drop** *n* — **rain·fall** *n* — **rain·mak·er** *n* — **rain·mak·ing** *n* — **rain·storm** *n* — **rain·water** *n* — **rainy** *adj*

**rain·bow** \-₁bō\ *n* : arc of colors formed by the sun shining through moisture

**raise** \'rāz\ *vb* **raised; rais·ing 1** : lift **2** : arouse **3** : erect **4** : collect **5** : breed, grow, or bring up **6** : increase **7** : make light ~ *n* : increase esp. in pay — **rais·er** *n*

**rai·sin** \'rāz²n\ *n* : dried grape

**ra·ja, ra·jah** \'räjə\ *n* : Indian prince

**rake** \'rāk\ *n* : garden tool for smoothing or sweeping ~ *vb* **raked; rak·ing 1** : gather, loosen, or smooth with or as if with a rake **2** : sweep with gunfire

**²rake** *n* : dissolute man

**rak·ish** \'rākish\ *adj* : smart or jaunty — **rak·ish·ly** *adv* — **rak·ish·ness** *n*

**ral·ly** \'ralē\ *vb* **-lied; -ly·ing 1** : bring or come together **2** : revive or recover **3** : make a comeback ~ *n, pl* **-lies 1** : act of rallying **2** : mass meeting

**ram** \'ram\ *n* **1** : male sheep **2** : beam used in battering down walls or doors ~ *vb* **-mm- 1** : force or drive in or through **2** : strike against violently

**RAM** \'ram\ *n* : main internal storage area in a computer

**ram·ble** \'rambəl\ *vb* **-bled; -bling** : wander — **ramble** *n* — **ram·bler** \-blər\ *n*

**ram·bunc·tious** \ram'bəŋkshəs\ *adj* : unruly

**ram·i·fi·ca·tion** \₁raməfə'kāshən\ *n* : consequence

**ram·i·fy** \'ramə₁fī\ *vb* **-fied; -fy·ing** : branch out

**ramp** \'ramp\ *n* : sloping passage or connecting roadway

ram·page \'ram͵pāj, ram'pāj\ vb
-paged; -pag·ing : rush about wildly
~ \'ram͵-\ n : violent or riotous action or behavior

ram·pant \'rampənt\ adj : widespread
— ram·pant·ly adv

ram·part \'ram͵pärt\ n : embankment
of a fortification

ram·rod n : rod used to load or clean a
gun ~ adj : strict or inflexible

ram·shack·le \'ram͵shakəl\ adj : shaky

ran past of RUN

ranch \'ranch\ n 1 : establishment for
the raising of cattle, sheep, or horses
2 : specialized farm ~ vb : operate a
ranch — ranch·er n

ran·cid \'ransəd\ adj : smelling or tast-
ing as if spoiled — ran·cid·i·ty \ran-
'sidətē\ n

ran·cor \'rankər\ n : bitter deep-seated
ill will — ran·cor·ous adj

ran·dom \'randəm\ adj : occurring by
chance — ran·dom·ly adv — ran-
dom·ness n — at random : without
definite aim or method

ran·dom·ize \'randə͵mīz\ vb -ized;
-izing : select, assign, or arrange in a
random way

rang past of RING

range \'rānj\ n 1 : series of things in a
row 2 : open land for grazing 3
: cooking stove 4 : variation within
limits 5 : place for target practice 6
: extent ~ vb ranged; rang·ing 1
: arrange 2 : roam at large, freely, or
over 3 : vary within limits

rang·er \'rānjər\ n : officer who manages and protects public lands

rangy \'rānjē\ adj rang·i·er; -est : being slender with long limbs — rang·i-
ness n

¹rank \'rank\ adj 1 : vigorous in growth
2 : unpleasantly strong-smelling —
rank·ly adv — rank·ness n

²rank n 1 : line of soldiers 2 : orderly
arrangement 3 : grade of official
standing 4 : position within a group
~ vb 1 : arrange in formation or according to class 2 : take or have a relative position

rank and file n : general membership

ran·kle \'rankəl\ vb -kled; -kling
: cause anger, irritation, or bitterness

ran·sack \'ran͵sak\ vb : search through
and rob

ran·som \'ransəm\ n : something de-
manded for the freedom of a captive

~ vb : gain the freedom of by paying
a price — ran·som·er n

rant \'rant\ vb : talk or scold violently
— rant·er n — rant·ing·ly adv

¹rap \'rap\ n : sharp blow or rebuke ~
vb -pp- : strike or criticize sharply

²rap vb -pp- : talk freely

ra·pa·cious \rə'pāshəs\ adj 1 : excessively greedy 2 : ravenous — ra·pa-
cious·ly adv — ra·pa·cious·ness n
— ra·pac·i·ty \-'pasətē\ n

¹rape \'rāp\ n : herb grown as a forage
crop and for its seeds (rape·seed)

²rape vb raped; rap·ing : force to have
sexual intercourse — rape n — rap-
er n — rap·ist \'rāpist\ n

rap·id \'rapəd\ adj : very fast — ra·pid-
i·ty \rə'pidətē\ n — rap·id·ly adv

rap·ids \-ədz\ n pl : place in a stream
where the current is swift

ra·pi·er \'rāpēər\ n : narrow 2-edged
sword

rap·ine \'rapən, -͵īn\ n : plunder

rap·port \ra'pōr\ n : harmonious relationship

rapt \'rapt\ adj : engrossed — rapt·ly
adv — rapt·ness n

rap·ture \'rapchər\ n : spiritual or
emotional ecstasy — rap·tur·ous
\-chərəs\ adj — rap·tur·ous·ly adv

¹rare \'rar\ adj rar·er; rar·est : having a
portion relatively uncooked

²rare adj rar·er; rar·est 1 : not dense 2
: unusually fine 3 : seldom met with
— rare·ly adv — rare·ness n — rar-
i·ty \'rarətē\ n

rar·e·fy \'rarə͵fī\ vb -fied; -fy·ing : make
or become rare, thin, or less dense —
rar·e·fac·tion \͵rarə'fakshən\ n

rar·ing \'rarən, -iŋ\ adj : full of enthusiasm

ras·cal \'raskəl\ n : mean, dishonest, or
mischievous person — ras·cal·i·ty
\ras'kalətē\ n — ras·cal·ly \'ras-
kəlē\ adj

¹rash \'rash\ adj : too hasty in decision
or action — rash·ly adv — rash-
ness n

²rash n : a breaking out of the skin with
red spots

rasp \'rasp\ vb 1 : rub with or as if
with a rough file 2 : speak in a grating tone ~ n : coarse file

rasp·ber·ry \'raz͵berē\ n : edible red
or black berry

rat \'rat\ n : destructive rodent larger
than the mouse ~ vb : betray or inform on

**ratch·et** \'rachət\ *n* : notched device for allowing motion in one direction

**rate** \'rāt\ *n* 1 : quantity, amount, or degree measured in relation to some other quantity 2 : rank ~ *vb* **rat·ed; rat·ing** 1 : estimate or determine the rank or quality of 2 : deserve

**rath·er** \'rathər, 'rəth-, 'räth-\ *adv* 1 : preferably 2 : on the other hand 3 : more properly 4 : somewhat

**rat·i·fy** \'ratə₃fī\ *vb* **-fied; -fy·ing** : approve and accept formally — **rat·i·fi·ca·tion** \₃ratəfə'kāshən\ *n*

**rat·ing** \'rātiŋ\ *n* : classification according to grade

**ra·tio** \'rāshēō\ *n, pl* **-tios** : relation in number, quantity, or degree between things

**ra·tion** \'rashən, 'rāshən\ *n* : share or allotment (as of food) ~ *vb* : use or allot sparingly

**ra·tio·nal** \'rashənəl\ *adj* 1 : having reason or sanity 2 : relating to reason — **ra·tio·nal·ly** *adv*

**ra·tio·nale** \₃rashə'nal\ *n* 1 : explanation of principles of belief or practice 2 : underlying reason

**ra·tio·nal·ize** \'rashənə₃līz\ *vb* **-ized; -iz·ing** : justify (as one's behavior or weaknesses) esp. to oneself — **ra·tio·nal·i·za·tion** \₃rashənələ'zāshən\ *n*

**rat·tan** \ra'tan, rə-\ *n* : palm with long stems used esp. for canes and wickerwork

**rat·tle** \'ratᵊl\ *vb* **-tled; -tling** 1 : make a series of clattering sounds 2 : say briskly 3 : confuse or upset ~ *n* 1 : series of clattering sounds 2 : something (as a toy) that rattles

**rat·tler** \'ratlər\ *n* : rattlesnake

**rat·tle·snake** *n* : American venomous snake with a rattle at the end of the tail

**rat·ty** \'ratē\ *adj* **rat·ti·er; -est** : shabby

**rau·cous** \'rókəs\ *adj* : harsh or boisterous — **rau·cous·ly** *adv* — **rau·cous·ness** *n*

**rav·age** \'ravij\ *n* : destructive effect ~ *vb* **-aged; -ag·ing** : lay waste — **rav·ag·er** *n*

**rave** \'rāv\ *vb* **raved; rav·ing** 1 : talk wildly in or as if in delirium 2 : talk with extreme enthusiasm ~ *n* 1 : act of raving 2 : enthusiastic praise

**rav·el** \'ravəl\ *vb* **-eled** *or* **-elled; -el·ing** *or* **-el·ling** 1 : unravel 2 : tangle ~ *n* 1 : something tangled 2 : loose thread

**ra·ven** \'rāvən\ *n* : large black bird ~ *adj* : black and shiny

**rav·en·ous** \'ravənəs\ *adj* : very hungry — **rav·en·ous·ly** *adv* — **rav·en·ous·ness** *n*

**ra·vine** \rə'vēn\ *n* : narrow steep-sided valley

**rav·ish** \'ravish\ *vb* 1 : seize and take away by violence 2 : overcome with joy or delight 3 : rape — **rav·ish·er** *n* — **rav·ish·ment** *n*

**raw** \'ró\ *adj* **raw·er** \'róər\; **raw·est** \'róəst\ 1 : not cooked 2 : not processed 3 : not trained 4 : having the surface rubbed off 5 : cold and damp 6 : vulgar — **raw·ness** *n*

**raw·hide** \'ró₃hīd\ *n* : untanned skin of cattle

**ray** \'rā\ *n* 1 : thin beam of radiant energy (as light) 2 : tiny bit

**ray·on** \'rā₃än\ *n* : fabric made from cellulose fiber

**raze** \'rāz\ *vb* **razed; raz·ing** : destroy or tear down

**ra·zor** \'rāzər\ *n* : sharp cutting instrument used to shave off hair

**re-** \rē, ₁rē, 'rē\ *prefix* 1 : again or anew 2 : back or backward

**reach** \'rēch\ *vb* 1 : stretch out 2 : touch or try to touch or grasp 3 : extend to or arrive at 4 : communicate with ~ *n* 1 : act of reaching 2 : distance one can reach 3 : ability to reach — **reach·able** *adj* — **reach·er** *n*

**re·act** \rē'akt\ *vb* 1 : act in response to some influence or stimulus 2 : undergo chemical change — **re·ac·tive** \-'aktiv\ *adj*

**re·ac·tion** \rē'akshən\ *n* 1 : action or emotion caused by and directly related or counter to another action 2 : chemical change

**re·ac·tion·ary** \-shə₃nerē\ *adj* : relat-

---

**List of self-explanatory words with the prefix re-**

| | | |
|---|---|---|
| reaccelerate | reacquire | readjustment |
| reaccept | reactivate | readmit |
| reacclimatize | reactivation | readopt |
| reaccredit | readdress | reaffirm |
| reacquaint | readjust | realign |

ing to or favoring return to an earlier political order or policy — **reactionary** n

**re-ac-tor** \rē'aktər\ n 1 : one that reacts 2 : device for the controlled release of nuclear energy

**read** \'rēd\ vb **read** \'red\; **read-ing** \'rēdiŋ\ 1 : understand written language 2 : utter aloud printed words 3 : interpret 4 : study 5 : indicate ~ \'red\ adj : informed by reading — **read-a-bil-i-ty** \,rēdə'bilətē\ n — **read-able** adj — **read-ably** adv — **read-er** n — **read-er-ship** n

**read-ing** \'rēdiŋ\ n 1 : something read or for reading 2 : particular version, interpretation, or performance 3 : data indicated by an instrument

**ready** \'redē\ adj **read-i-er**; **-est** 1 : prepared or available for use or action 2 : willing to do something ~ vb **read-ied**; **ready-ing** : make ready ~ n : state of being ready — **read-i-ly** adv — **read-i-ness** n

**re-al** \'rēl\ adj 1 : relating to fixed or immovable things (as land) 2 : genuine 3 : not imaginary ~ adv : very — **re-al-ness** n — **for real** 1 : in earnest 2 : genuine

**real estate** n : property in houses and land

**re-al-ism** \'rēə,lizəm\ n 1 : disposition to deal with facts practically 2 : faithful portrayal of reality — **re-al-ist** \-list\ adj or n — **re-al-is-tic** \,rēə'listik\ adj — **re-al-is-ti-cal-ly** \-tiklē\ adv

**re-al-i-ty** \rē'alətē\ n, pl **-ties** 1 : quality or state of being real 2 : something real

**re-al-ize** \'rēə,līz\ vb **-ized**; **-iz-ing** 1 : make actual 2 : obtain 3 : be aware of — **re-al-iz-able** adj — **re-al-i-za-tion** \,rēələ'zāshən\ n

**re-al-ly** \'rēlē, 'ril-\ adv : in truth

**realm** \'relm\ n 1 : kingdom 2 : sphere

¹**ream** \'rēm\ n : quantity of paper that is 480, 500, or 516 sheets

²**ream** vb : enlarge, shape, or clean with a specially shaped tool (**reamer**)

**reap** \'rēp\ vb : cut or clear (as a crop) with a scythe or machine — **reap-er** n

¹**rear** \'rir\ vb 1 : raise upright 2 : breed or bring up 3 : rise on the hind legs

²**rear** n 1 : back 2 : position at the back of something ~ adj : being at the back — **rear-ward** \-wərd\ adj or adv

**rear admiral** n : commissioned officer in the navy or coast guard ranking next below a vice admiral

**rea-son** \'rēz²n\ n 1 : explanation or justification 2 : motive for action or belief 3 : power or process of thinking ~ vb 1 : use the faculty of reason 2 : try to persuade another — **rea-son-er** n — **rea-son-ing** \'rēz²niŋ\ n

**rea-son-able** \'rēz²nəbəl\ adj 1 : being within the bounds of reason 2 : inexpensive — **rea-son-able-ness** n — **rea-son-ably** \-blē\ adv

**re-as-sure** \,rēə'shūr\ vb : restore one's confidence ~ — **re-as-sur-ance** \-'shūrəns\ n — **re-as-sur-ing-ly** adv

**re-bate** \'rē,bāt\ n : return of part of a payment — **rebate** vb

**reb-el** \'rebəl\ n : one that resists authority ~ \ri'bel\ vb **-belled**; **-bel-ling** 1 : resist authority 2 : feel or exhibit anger — **rebel** \'rebəl\ adj

**re-bel-lion** \ri'belyən\ n : resistance to authority and esp. to one's government

**re-bel-lious** \-yəs\ adj 1 : engaged in rebellion 2 : inclined to resist authority — **re-bel-lious-ly** adv — **re-bel-lious-ness** n

**re-birth** \'rē'bərth\ n 1 : new or second birth 2 : revival

**re-bound** \'rē'baùnd, ri-\ vb 1 : spring back on striking something 2 : recover from a reverse ~ \'rē,-\ n 1 : action of rebounding 2 : reaction to a reverse

**re-buff** \ri'bəf\ vb : refuse or repulse rudely — **rebuff** n

**re-buke** \-'byük\ vb **-buked**; **-buk-ing** : reprimand sharply — **rebuke** n

**re-bus** \'rēbəs\ n : riddle representing syllables or words with pictures

**re-but** \ri'bət\ vb **-but-ted**; **-but-ting** : refute — **re-but-ter** n

**re-but-tal** \-²l\ n : opposing argument

**re-cal-ci-trant** \ri'kalsətrənt\ adj 1 : stubbornly resisting authority 2 : resistant to handling or treatment — **re·cal·ci·trance** \-trəns\ n

**re·call** \ri'kȯl\ vb **1** : call back **2** : remember **3** : revoke ~ \ri'-, 'rē,-\ n **1** : a summons to return **2** : remembrance **3** : act of revoking

**re·cant** \ri'kant\ vb : take back (something said) publicly

**re·ca·pit·u·late** \,rēkə'pichə,lāt\ vb : summarize — **re·ca·pit·u·la·tion** \-,pichə'lāshən\ n

**re·cede** \ri'sēd\ vb **-ced·ed; -ced·ing** **1** : move back or away **2** : slant backward

**re·ceipt** \-'sēt\ n **1** : act of receiving **2** : something (as payment) received — usu. in pl. **3** : writing acknowledging something received

**re·ceive** \ri'sēv\ vb **-ceived; -ceiv·ing** **1** : take in or accept **2** : greet or entertain (visitors) **3** : pick up radio waves and convert into sounds or pictures — **re·ceiv·able** adj

**re·ceiv·er** \ri'sēvər\ n **1** : one that receives **2** : one having charge of property or money involved in a lawsuit **3** : apparatus for receiving radio waves — **re·ceiv·er·ship** n

**re·cent** \'rēs°nt\ adj **1** : having lately come into existence **2** : of the present time or time just past — **re·cent·ly** adv — **re·cent·ness** n

**re·cep·ta·cle** \ri'septikəl\ n : container

**re·cep·tion** \ri'sepshən\ n **1** : act of receiving **2** : social gathering at which guests are formally welcomed

**re·cep·tion·ist** \-shənist\ n : person employed to greet callers

**re·cep·tive** \ri'septiv\ adj : open and responsive to ideas, impressions, or suggestions — **re·cep·tive·ly** adv — **re·cep·tive·ness** n — **re·cep·tiv·i·ty** \,rē,sep'tivətē\ n

**re·cess** \'rē,ses, ri'ses\ n **1** : indentation in a line or surface **2** : suspension of a session for rest ~ vb **1** : make a recess in or put into a recess **2** : interrupt a session for a recess

**re·ces·sion** \ri'seshən\ n **1** : departing procession **2** : period of reduced economic activity

**rec·i·pe** \'resə,pē\ n : instructions for making something

**re·cip·i·ent** \ri'sipēənt\ n : one that receives

**re·cip·ro·cal** \ri'siprəkəl\ adj **1** : affecting each in the same way **2** : so related that one is equivalent to the other — **re·cip·ro·cal·ly** adv — **re·ci·proc·i·ty** \,resə'präsətē\ n

**re·cip·ro·cate** \-,kāt\ vb : make a return for something done or given — **re·cip·ro·ca·tion** \-,siprə'kāshən\ n

**re·cit·al** \ri'sīt°l\ n **1** : public reading or recitation **2** : music or dance concert or exhibition by pupils — **re·cit·al·ist** \-°list\ n

**rec·i·ta·tion** \,resə'tāshən\ n : a reciting or recital

**re·cite** \ri'sīt\ vb **-cit·ed; -cit·ing** **1** : repeat verbatim **2** : recount — **re·cit·er** n

**reck·less** \'rekləs\ adj : lacking caution — **reck·less·ly** adv — **reck·less·ness** n

**reck·on** \'rekən\ vb **1** : count or calculate **2** : consider

**reck·on·ing** n **1** : act or instance of reckoning **2** : settling of accounts

**re·claim** \ri'klām\ vb **1** : change to a desirable condition **2** : obtain from a waste product or by-product **3** : demand or obtain the return of — **re·claim·able** adj — **rec·la·ma·tion** \,reklə'māshən\ n

**re·cline** \ri'klīn\ vb **-clined; -clin·ing** : lean backward or lie down

**rec·luse** \'rek,lüs, ri'klüs\ n : one who leads a secluded or solitary life

**rec·og·ni·tion** \,rekig'nishən\ n : act of recognizing or state of being recognized

**re·cog·ni·zance** \ri'känəzəns, -'käg-\ n : promise recorded before a court

**rec·og·nize** \'rekig,nīz\ vb **1** : identify as previously known **2** : take notice of **3** : acknowledge esp. with appreciation — **rec·og·niz·able** \'rekəg,nīzəbəl\ adj — **rec·og·niz·ably** \-blē\ adv

**re·coil** \ri'kȯil\ vb : draw or spring back ~ \'rē,-, ri'-\ n : action of recoiling

**rec·ol·lect** \,rekə'lekt\ vb : remember

---

reassemble
reassert
reassess
reassessment
reassign

reassignment
reattach
reattain
reawaken
rebalance

rebaptize
rebid
rebind
reborn
rebroadcast

**rec·ol·lec·tion** \ˌrekəˈlekshən\ n 1 : act or power of recollecting 2 : something recollected

**rec·om·mend** \ˌrekəˈmend\ vb 1 : present as deserving of acceptance or trial 2 : advise — **rec·om·mend·able** \-ˈmendəbəl\ adj

**rec·om·men·da·tion** \ˌrekəmənˈdāshən\ n 1 : act of recommending 2 : something recommended or that recommends

**rec·om·pense** \ˈrekəmˌpens\ n : compensation — **recompense** vb

**rec·on·cile** \ˈrekənˌsīl\ vb -ciled; -ciling 1 : cause to be friendly again 2 : adjust or settle 3 : bring to acceptance — **rec·on·cil·able** adj — **rec·on·cile·ment** n — **rec·on·cil·er** n — **rec·on·cil·i·a·tion** \ˌrekənˌsilēˈāshən\ n

**re·con·dite** \ˈrekənˌdīt, riˈkän-\ adj 1 : hard to understand 2 : little known

**re·con·di·tion** \ˌrēkənˈdishən\ vb : restore to good condition

**re·con·nais·sance** \riˈkänəzəns, -səns\ n : exploratory survey of enemy territory

**re·con·noi·ter, re·con·noi·tre** \ˌrēkəˈnóitər, ˌrekə-\ vb -tered or -tred; -ter·ing or -tring : make a reconnaissance of

**re·cord** \riˈkórd\ vb 1 : set down in writing 2 : register permanently 3 : indicate 4 : preserve (as sound or images) for later reproduction ~ \ˈrekərd\ n 1 : something recorded 2 : best performance

**re·cord·er** \riˈkórdər\ n 1 : person or device that records 2 : wind instrument with finger holes

¹**re·count** \riˈkaúnt\ vb : relate in detail

²**re·count** \ˈrēˈ-\ vb : count again — **re·count** \ˈrēˌ-, ˌrēˈ-\ n

**re·coup** \riˈküp\ vb : make up for (an expense or loss)

**re·course** \ˈrēˌkórs, riˈ-\ n : source of aid or a turning to such a source

**re·cov·er** \riˈkəvər\ vb 1 : regain position, poise, or health 2 : recoup — **re·cov·er·able** adj — **re·cov·ery** \-ˈkəvərē\ n

**rec·re·a·tion** \ˌrekrēˈāshən\ n : a refreshing of strength or spirits as a change from work or study — **rec·re·a·tion·al** \-shənəl\ adj

**re·crim·i·na·tion** \riˌkriməˈnāshən\ n : retaliatory accusation — **re·crim·i·nate** vb

**re·cruit** \riˈkrüt\ n : newly enlisted member ~ vb : enlist the membership or services of — **re·cruit·er** n — **re·cruit·ment** n

**rect·an·gle** \ˈrekˌtaŋgəl\ n : 4-sided figure with 4 right angles — **rect·an·gu·lar** \rekˈtaŋgyələr\ adj

**rec·ti·fy** \ˈrektəˌfī\ vb -fied; -fy·ing : make or set right — **rec·ti·fi·ca·tion** \ˌrektəfəˈkāshən\ n

**rec·ti·tude** \ˈrektəˌtüd, -ˌtyüd\ n : moral integrity

**rec·tor** \ˈrektər\ n : pastor

**rec·to·ry** \ˈrektərē\ n, pl -ries : rector's residence

**rec·tum** \ˈrektəm\ n, pl -tums or -ta \-tə\ : last part of the intestine joining the colon and anus — **rec·tal** \-t°l\ adj

**re·cum·bent** \riˈkəmbənt\ adj : lying down

**re·cu·per·ate** \riˈküpəˌrāt, -ˈkyü-\ vb -at·ed; -at·ing : recover (as from illness) — **re·cu·per·a·tion** \-ˌküpə-ˈrāshən, -ˌkyü-\ n — **re·cu·per·a·tive** \-ˈküpərātiv, -ˈkyü-\ adj

**re·cur** \riˈkər\ vb -rr- 1 : return in thought or talk 2 : occur again — **re·cur·rence** \-ˈkərəns\ n — **re·cur·rent** \-ənt\ adj

**re·cy·cle** \rēˈsīkəl\ vb : process (as glass or cans) in order to regain a material for human use — **re·cy·cla·ble** \-kələbəl\ adj

**red** \ˈred\ n 1 : color of blood or of the ruby 2 cap : communist — **red** adj — **red·dish** adj — **red·ness** n

**red·den** \ˈred°n\ vb : make or become red or reddish

**re·deem** \riˈdēm\ vb 1 : regain, free, or rescue by paying a price 2 : atone for 3 : free from sin 4 : convert into something of value — **re·deem·able** adj — **re·deem·er** n

**re·demp·tion** \-ˈdempshən\ n : act of

redeeming — **re•demp•tive** \-tiv\ *adj*
— **re•demp•to•ry** \-tərē\ *adj*

**red•head** \-,hed\ *n* : one having red
hair — **red•head•ed** \-'hedəd\ *adj*

**red•o•lent** \'red°lənt\ *adj* **1** : having a
fragrance **2** : suggestive — **red•o•
lence** \-əns\ *n* — **red•o•lent•ly** *adv*

**re•dou•ble** \rē'dəbəl\ *vb* **1** : make
twice as great in size or amount **2**
: intensify

**re•doubt** \ri'daut\ *n* : small fortification

**re•doubt•able** \-əbəl\ *adj* : arousing
dread

**re•dound** \ri'daund\ *vb* : have an effect

**re•dress** \ri'dres\ *vb* : set right ~ *n* **1**
: relief or remedy **2** : compensation

**red tape** *n* : complex obstructive official
routine

**re•duce** \ri'düs, -'dyüs\ *vb* **1** : lessen
**2** : put in a lower rank **3** : lose weight
— **re•duc•er** *n* — **re•duc•ible**
\-'düsəbəl, -'dyü-\ *adj*

**re•duc•tion** \ri'dəkshən\ *n* **1** : act of
reducing **2** : amount lost in reducing
**3** : something made by reducing

**re•dun•dant** \ri'dəndənt\ *adj* : using
more words than necessary — **re•
dun•dan•cy** \-dənsē\ *n* — **re•dun•
dant•ly** *adv*

**red•wood** *n* : tall coniferous timber tree

**reed** \'rēd\ *n* **1** : tall slender grass of
wet areas **2** : elastic strip that vibrates
to produce tones in certain wind instruments — **reedy** *adj*

**reef** \'rēf\ *n* : ridge of rocks or sand at
or near the surface of the water

**reek** \'rēk\ *n* : strong or disagreeable
fume or odor ~ *vb* : give off a reek

**¹reel** \'rēl\ *n* : revolvable device on
which something flexible is wound or
a quantity of something wound on it
~ *vb* **1** : wind on a reel **2** : pull in by
reeling — **reel•able** *adj* — **reel•er** *n*

**²reel** *vb* **1** : whirl or waver as from a
blow **2** : walk or move unsteadily ~
*n* : reeling motion

**³reel** *n* : lively dance

**re•fer** \ri'fər\ *vb* **-rr-** **1** : direct or send
to some person or place **2** : submit
for consideration or action **3** : have
connection **4** : mention or allude to

something — **re•fer•able** \'refərəbəl,
ri'fərə-\ *adj* — **re•fer•ral** \ri'fərəl\ *n*

**ref•er•ee** \,refə'rē\ *n* **1** : one to whom
an issue is referred for settlement **2**
: sports official ~ *vb* **-eed; -ee•ing**
: act as referee

**ref•er•ence** \'refərəns\ *n* **1** : act of re-
ferring **2** : a bearing on a matter **3**
: consultation for information **4** : person who can speak for one's character
or ability or a recommendation given
by such a person

**ref•er•en•dum** \,refə'rendəm\ *n, pl*
**-da** \-də\ *or* **-dums** : a submitting of
legislative measures for voters' approval or rejection

**re•fill** \,rē'fil\ *vb* : fill again — **re•fill**
\'rē,-\ *n* — **re•fill•able** *adj*

**re•fine** \ri'fīn\ *vb* **-fined; -fin•ing** **1**
: free from impurities or waste matter
**2** : improve or perfect **3** : free or become free of what is coarse or uncouth — **re•fine•ment** \-mənt\ *n* —
**re•fin•er** *n*

**re•fin•ery** \ri'fīnərē\ *n, pl* **-er•ies**
: place for refining (as oil or sugar)

**re•flect** \ri'flekt\ *vb* **1** : bend or cast
back (as light or heat) **2** : bring as a
result **3** : cast reproach or blame **4**
: ponder — **re•flec•tion** \-'flekshən\
*n* — **re•flec•tive** \-tiv\ *adj* — **re•flec•
tor** \ri'flektər\ *n*

**re•flex** \'rē,fleks\ *n* : automatic response to a stimulus ~ *adj* **1** : bent
back **2** : relating to a reflex — **re•
flex•ly** *adv*

**re•flex•ive** \ri'fleksiv\ *adj* : of or relating to an action directed back upon
the doer or the grammatical subject
— **reflexive** *n* — **re•flex•ive•ly** *adv*
— **re•flex•ive•ness** *n*

**re•form** \ri'fôrm\ *vb* : make or become
better esp. by correcting bad habits —
**reform** *n* — **re•form•able** *adj* — **re•
for•ma•tive** \-'fôrmətiv\ *adj* — **re•
form•er** *n*

**re•for•ma•to•ry** \ri'fôrmə,tōrē\ *n, pl*
**-ries** : penal institution for reforming
young offenders

**re•fract** \ri'frakt\ *vb* : subject to refrac-
tion

**re·frac·tion** \-'frakshən\ *n* : the bending of a ray (as of light) when it passes from one medium into another — **re·frac·tive** \-tiv\ *adj*

**re·frac·to·ry** \ri'fraktərē\ *adj* : obstinate or unmanageable

**re·frain** \ri'frān\ *vb* : hold oneself back ~ *n* : verse recurring regularly in a song — **re·frain·ment** *n*

**re·fresh** \ri'fresh\ *vb* **1** : make or become fresh or fresher **2** : supply or take refreshment — **re·fresh·er** *n* — **re·fresh·ing·ly** *adv*

**re·fresh·ment** \-mənt\ *n* **1** : act of refreshing **2** *pl* : light meal

**re·frig·er·ate** \ri'frijə,rāt\ *vb* **-at·ed; -at·ing** : chill or freeze (food) for preservation — **re·frig·er·ant** \-ərənt\ *adj or n* — **re·frig·er·a·tion** \-,frijə-'rāshən\ *n* — **re·frig·er·a·tor** \-'frijə,rātər\ *n*

**ref·uge** \'ref,yüj\ *n* **1** : protection from danger **2** : place that provides protection

**ref·u·gee** \,refyü'jē\ *n* : person who flees for safety

**re·fund** \ri'fənd, 'rē,fənd\ *vb* : give or put back (money) ~ \'rē,-\ *n* **1** : act of refunding **2** : sum refunded — **re·fund·able** *adj*

**re·fur·bish** \ri'fərbish\ *vb* : renovate

**¹re·fuse** \ri'fyüz\ *vb* **-fused; -fus·ing** : decline to accept, do, or give — **re·fus·al** \-'fyüzəl\ *n*

**²ref·use** \'ref,yüs, -,yüz\ *n* : worthless matter

**re·fute** \ri'fyüt\ *vb* **-fut·ed; -fut·ing** : prove to be false — **ref·u·ta·tion** \,refyù'tāshən\ *n* — **re·fut·er** \ri-'fyütər\ *n*

**re·gal** \'rēgəl\ *adj* **1** : befitting a king **2** : stately — **re·gal·ly** *adv*

**re·gale** \ri'gāl\ *vb* **-galed; -gal·ing** **1** : entertain richly or agreeably **2** : delight

**re·ga·lia** \ri'gālyə\ *n pl* **1** : symbols of royalty **2** : insignia of an office or order **3** : finery

**re·gard** \ri'gärd\ *n* **1** : consideration **2** : feeling of approval and liking **3** *pl* : friendly greetings **4** : relation ~ *vb*

**1** : pay attention to **2** : show respect for **3** : have an opinion of **4** : look at **5** : relate to — **re·gard·ful** *adj* — **re·gard·less** *adj*

**re·gard·ing** *prep* : concerning

**regardless of** \ri'gärdləs-\ *prep* : in spite of

**re·gen·er·ate** \ri'jenərət\ *adj* **1** : formed or created again **2** : spiritually reborn ~ \-'jenə,rāt\ *vb* **1** : reform completely **2** : replace (a lost body part) by new tissue growth **3** : give new life to — **re·gen·er·a·tion** \-,jenə'rāshən\ *n* — **re·gen·er·a·tive** \-'jenə,rātiv\ *adj* — **re·gen·er·a·tor** \-,rātər\ *n*

**re·gent** \'rējənt\ *n* **1** : person who rules during the childhood, absence, or incapacity of the sovereign **2** : member of a governing board — **re·gen·cy** \-jənsē\ *n*

**re·gime** \rā'zhēm, ri-\ *n* : government in power

**reg·i·men** \'rejəmən\ *n* : systematic course of treatment or training

**reg·i·ment** \'rejəmənt\ *n* : military unit ~ \-,ment\ *vb* **1** : organize rigidly for control **2** : make orderly — **reg·i·men·tal** \,rejə'ment³l\ *adj* — **reg·i·men·ta·tion** \-mən'tāshən\ *n*

**re·gion** \'rējən\ *n* : indefinitely defined area — **re·gion·al** \'rējənəl\ *adj* — **re·gion·al·ly** *adv*

**reg·is·ter** \'rejəstər\ *n* **1** : record of items or details or a book for keeping such a record **2** : device to regulate ventilation **3** : counting or recording device **4** : range of a voice or instrument ~ *vb* **1** : enter in a register **2** : record automatically **3** : get special care for mail by paying more postage

**reg·is·trar** \-,strär\ *n* : official keeper of records

**reg·is·tra·tion** \,rejə'strāshən\ *n* **1** : act of registering **2** : entry in a register

**reg·is·try** \'rejəstrē\ *n, pl* **-tries** **1** : enrollment **2** : place of registration **3** : official record book

**re·gress** \ri'gres\ *vb* : go or cause to go

---

| | | |
|---|---|---|
| recopy | rededication | rediscover |
| re-create | redefine | rediscovery |
| recross | redeposit | redissolve |
| redecorate | redesign | redistribute |
| rededicate | redevelop | redraft |

back or to a lower level — **re·gres·sion** \-'greshən\ *n* — **re·gres·sive** *adj*

**re·gret** \ri'gret\ *vb* **-tt-** **1** : mourn the loss or death of **2** : be very sorry for ∼ *n* **1** : sorrow or the expression of sorrow **2** *pl* : message declining an invitation — **re·gret·ful** \-fəl\ *adj* — **re·gret·ful·ly** *adv* — **re·gret·ta·ble** \-əbəl\ *adj* — **re·gret·ta·bly** \-blē\ *adv* — **re·gret·ter** *n*

**reg·u·lar** \'regyələr\ *adj* **1** : conforming to what is usual, normal, or average **2** : steady, uniform, or unvarying — **regular** *n* — **reg·u·lar·i·ty** \,regyə-'larətē\ *n* — **reg·u·lar·ize** \'regyələ-,rīz\ *vb* — **reg·u·lar·ly** *adv*

**reg·u·late** \'regyə,lāt\ *vb* **-lat·ed; -lat·ing** **1** : govern according to rule **2** : adjust to a standard — **reg·u·la·tive** \-,lātiv\ *adj* — **reg·u·la·tor** \-,lātər\ *n* — **reg·u·la·to·ry** \-lə,tōrē\ *adj*

**reg·u·la·tion** \,regyə'lāshən\ *n* **1** : act of regulating **2** : rule dealing with details of procedure

**re·gur·gi·tate** \rē'gərjə,tāt\ *vb* **-tat·ed; -tat·ing** : vomit — **re·gur·gi·ta·tion** \-,gərjə'tāshən\ *n*

**re·ha·bil·i·tate** \,rēhə'bilə,tāt\ *vb* **-tat·ed; -tat·ing** **1** : reinstate **2** : make good or usable again — **re·ha·bil·i·ta·tion** \-,bilə'tāshən\ *n*

**re·hears·al** \ri'hərsəl\ *n* : practice session or performance

**re·hearse** \-'hərs\ *vb* **-hearsed; -hears·ing** **1** : repeat or recount **2** : engage in a rehearsal of — **re·hears·er** *n*

**reign** \'rān\ *n* : sovereign's authority or rule ∼ *vb* : rule as a sovereign

**re·im·burse** \,rēəm'bərs\ *vb* **-bursed; -burs·ing** : repay — **re·im·burs·able** *adj* — **re·im·burse·ment** *n*

**rein** \'rān\ *n* **1** : strap fastened to a bit to control an animal **2** : restraining influence ∼ *vb* : direct by reins

**re·in·car·na·tion** \,rē,inkär'nāshən\ *n* : rebirth of the soul — **re·in·car·nate** \,rēin'kär,nāt\ *vb*

**rein·deer** \'rān,dir\ *n* : caribou

**re·in·force** \,rēən'fōrs\ *vb* : strengthen or support — **re·in·force·ment** *n* — **re·in·forc·er** *n*

**re·in·state** \,rēən'stāt\ *vb* : restore to a former position — **re·in·state·ment** *n*

**re·it·er·ate** \rē'itə,rāt\ *vb* : say again — **re·it·er·a·tion** \-,itə'rāshən\ *n*

**re·ject** \ri'jekt\ *vb* **1** : refuse to grant or consider **2** : refuse to admit, believe, or receive **3** : throw out as useless or unsatisfactory ∼ \'rē,-\ *n* : rejected person or thing — **re·jec·tion** \-'jek-shən\ *n*

**re·joice** \ri'jȯis\ *vb* **-joiced; -joic·ing** : feel joy — **re·joic·er** *n*

**re·join** *vb* **1** \rē'jȯin\ : join again **2** \ri'-\ : say in answer

**re·join·der** \ri'jȯindər\ *n* : answer

**re·ju·ve·nate** \ri'jüvə,nāt\ *vb* **-nat·ed; -nat·ing** : make young again — **re·ju·ve·na·tion** \-,jüvə'nāshən\ *n*

**re·lapse** \ri'laps, 'rē,laps\ *n* : recurrence of illness after a period of improvement ∼ \ri'-\ *vb* : suffer a relapse

**re·late** \ri'lāt\ *vb* **-lat·ed; -lat·ing** **1** : give a report of **2** : show a connection between **3** : have a relationship — **re·lat·able** *adj* — **re·lat·er, re·la·tor** *n*

**re·la·tion** \-'lāshən\ *n* **1** : account **2** : connection **3** : relationship **4** : reference **5** *pl* : dealings

**re·la·tion·ship** \-,ship\ *n* : state of being related or interrelated

**rel·a·tive** \'relətiv\ *n* : person connected with another by blood or marriage ∼ *adj* : considered in comparison with something else — **rel·a·tive·ly** *adv* — **rel·a·tive·ness** *n*

**re·lax** \ri'laks\ *vb* **1** : make or become less tense or rigid **2** : make less severe **3** : seek rest or recreation — **re·lax·er** *n*

**re·lax·a·tion** \,rē,lak'sāshən\ *n* **1** : lessening of tension **2** : recreation

**re·lay** \'rē,lā\ *n* : fresh supply (as of horses or people) arranged to relieve others ∼ \'rē,-, ri'-\ *vb* **-layed; -lay·ing** : pass along in stages

**re·lease** \ri'lēs\ *vb* **-leased; -leas·ing** **1** : free from confinement or oppression **2** : relinquish **3** : permit publication, performance, exhibition, or sale **~** *n* **1** : relief from trouble **2** : discharge from an obligation **3** : act of releasing or what is released

**rel·e·gate** \'relə₂gāt\ *vb* **-gat·ed; -gat·ing 1** : remove to some less prominent position **2** : assign to a particular class or sphere — **rel·e·ga·tion** \₂relə-'gāshən\ *n*

**re·lent** \ri'lent\ *vb* : become less severe

**re·lent·less** \-ləs\ *adj* : mercilessly severe or persistent — **re·lent·less·ly** *adv* — **re·lent·less·ness** *n*

**rel·e·vance** \'reləvəns\ *n* : relation to the matter at hand — **rel·e·vant** \-vənt\ *adj* — **rel·e·vant·ly** *adv*

**re·li·able** \ri'līəbəl\ *adj* : fit to be trusted — **re·li·abil·i·ty** \-₂līə'bilətē\ *n* — **re·li·able·ness** *n* — **re·li·ably** \-'līəblē\ *adv*

**re·li·ance** \ri'līəns\ *n* : act or result of relying

**re·li·ant** \ri'līənt\ *adj* : dependent

**rel·ic** \'relik\ *n* **1** : object venerated because of its association with a saint or martyr **2** : remaining trace

**re·lief** \ri'lēf\ *n* **1** : lightening of something oppressive **2** : welfare

**re·lieve** \ri'lēv\ *vb* **-lieved; -liev·ing 1** : free from a burden or distress **2** : release from a post or duty **3** : break the monotony of — **re·liev·er** *n*

**re·li·gion** \ri'lijən\ *n* **1** : service and worship of God **2** : set or system of religious beliefs — **re·li·gion·ist** *n*

**re·li·gious** \-'lijəs\ *adj* **1** : relating or devoted to an ultimate reality or deity **2** : relating to religious beliefs or observances **3** : faithful, fervent, or zealous — **re·li·gious·ly** *adv*

**re·lin·quish** \-'liŋkwish, -'lin-\ *vb* **1** : renounce **2** : let go of — **re·lin·quish·ment** *n*

**rel·ish** \'relish\ *n* **1** : keen enjoyment **2** : highly seasoned sauce (as of pickles) **~** *vb* : enjoy — **rel·ish·able** *adj*

**re·live** \₂rē'liv\ *vb* : live over again (as in the imagination)

**re·lo·cate** \₂rē'lō₂kāt, ₂rēlō'kāt\ *vb* : move to a new location — **re·lo·ca·tion** \₂rēlō'kāshən\ *n*

**re·luc·tant** \ri'ləktənt\ *adj* : feeling or showing doubt or unwillingness — **re·luc·tance** \ri'ləktəns\ *n* — **re·luc·tant·ly** *adv*

**re·ly** \ri'lī\ *vb* **-lied; -ly·ing** : place faith or confidence — often with *on*

**re·main** \ri'mān\ *vb* **1** : be left after others have been removed **2** : be something yet to be done **3** : stay behind **4** : continue unchanged

**re·main·der** \-'māndər\ *n* : that which is left over

**re·mains** \-'mānz\ *n pl* **1** : remaining part or trace **2** : dead body

**re·mark** \ri'märk\ *vb* : express as an observation **~** *n* : passing comment

**re·mark·able** \-'märkəbəl\ *adj* : extraordinary — **re·mark·able·ness** *n* — **re·mark·ably** \-blē\ *adv*

**re·me·di·al** \ri'mēdēəl\ *adj* : intended to remedy or improve

**rem·e·dy** \'remədē\ *n, pl* **-dies 1** : medicine that cures **2** : something that corrects an evil or compensates for a loss **~** *vb* **-died; -dy·ing** : provide or serve as a remedy for

**re·mem·ber** \ri'membər\ *vb* **1** : think of again **2** : keep from forgetting **3** : convey greetings from

**re·mem·brance** \-brəns\ *n* **1** : act of remembering **2** : something that serves to bring to mind

**re·mind** \ri'mīnd\ *vb* : cause to remember — **re·mind·er** *n*

**rem·i·nisce** \₂remə'nis\ *vb* **-nisced; -nisc·ing** : indulge in reminiscence

**rem·i·nis·cence** \-'nis°ns\ *n* **1** : recalling of a past experience **2** : account of a memorable experience

**rem·i·nis·cent** \-°nt\ *adj* **1** : relating to reminiscence **2** : serving to remind — **rem·i·nis·cent·ly** *adv*

**re·miss** \ri'mis\ *adj* : negligent or careless in performance of duty — **re·miss·ly** *adv* — **re·miss·ness** *n*

**re·mis·sion** \ri'mishən\ *n* **1** : act of forgiving **2** : period of relief from or easing of symptoms of a disease

**re·mit** \ri'mit\ *vb* **-tt- 1** : pardon **2** : send money in payment

**re·mit·tance** \ri'mit°ns\ *n* : sum of money remitted

---

**rem·nant** \'remnənt\ *n* : small part or trace remaining

**re·mod·el** \rē'mäd°l\ *vb* : alter the structure of

**re·mon·strance** \ri'mänstrəns\ *n* : act or instance of remonstrating

**re·mon·strate** \ri'män,strāt\ *vb* **-strat·ed; -strat·ing** : speak in protest, reproof, or opposition — **re·mon·stra·tion** \ri,män'strāshən, ,remən-\ *n*

**re·morse** \ri'mòrs\ *n* : distress arising from a sense of guilt — **re·morse·ful** *adj* — **re·morse·less** *adj*

**re·mote** \ri'mōt\ *adj* **-mot·er; -est 1** : far off in place or time **2** : hard to reach or find **3** : acting, acted on, or controlled indirectly or from afar **4** : slight **5** : distant in manner — **re·mote·ly** *adv* — **re·mote·ness** *n*

**re·move** \ri'müv\ *vb* **-moved; -mov·ing 1** : move by lifting or taking off or away **2** : get rid of — **re·mov·able** *adj* — **re·mov·al** \-vəl\ *n* — **re·mov·er** *n*

**re·mu·ner·ate** \ri'myünə,rāt\ *vb* **-at·ed; -at·ing** : pay — **re·mu·ner·a·tion** \-,myünə'rāshən\ *n* — **re·mu·ner·a·tor** \-,rātər\ *n*

**re·mu·ner·a·tive** \ri'myünərətiv, -,rāt-\ *adj* : gainful

**re·nais·sance** \,renə'säns, -'zäns\ *n* : rebirth or revival

**re·nal** \'rēn°l\ *adj* : relating to the kidneys

**rend** \'rend\ *vb* **rent** \'rent\; **rend·ing** : tear apart forcibly

**ren·der** \'rendər\ *vb* **1** : extract by heating **2** : hand over or give up **3** : do (a service) for another **4** : cause to be or become

**ren·dez·vous** \'rändi,vü, -dā-\ *n, pl* **ren·dez·vous** \-,vüz\ **1** : place appointed for a meeting **2** : meeting at an appointed place ~ *vb* **-voused; -vous·ing** : meet at a rendezvous

**ren·di·tion** \ren'dishən\ *n* : version

**ren·e·gade** \'reni,gād\ *n* : deserter of one faith or cause for another

**re·nege** \ri'nig, -'neg, -'nēg, -'nāg\ *vb* **-neged; -neg·ing** : go back on a promise — **re·neg·er** *n*

**re·new** \ri'nü, -'nyü\ *vb* **1** : make or become new, fresh, or strong again **2** : begin again **3** : grant or obtain an extension of — **re·new·able** *adj* — **re·new·al** *n* — **re·new·er** *n*

**re·nounce** \ri'naůns\ *vb* **-nounced; -nounc·ing** : give up, refuse, or resign — **re·nounce·ment** *n*

**ren·o·vate** \'renə,vāt\ *vb* **-vat·ed; -vat·ing** : make like new again — **ren·o·va·tion** \,renə'vāshən\ *n* — **ren·o·va·tor** \'renə,vātər\ *n*

**re·nown** \ri'naůn\ *n* : state of being widely known and honored — **renowned** \-'naůnd\ *adj*

**¹rent** \'rent\ *n* : money paid or due periodically for the use of another's property ~ *vb* : hold or give possession and use of for rent — **rent·al** *n or adj* — **rent·er** *n*

**²rent** *n* : a tear in cloth

**re·nun·ci·a·tion** \ri,nənsē'āshən\ *n* : act of renouncing

**¹re·pair** \ri'par\ *vb* : go

**²repair** *vb* : restore to good condition ~ *n* **1** : act or instance of repairing **2** : condition — **re·pair·er** *n* — **re·pair·man** \-,man\ *n*

**rep·a·ra·tion** \,repə'rāshən\ *n* : money paid for redress — usu. pl.

**rep·ar·tee** \,repər'tē\ *n* : clever replies

**re·past** \ri'past, 'rē,past\ *n* : meal

**re·pa·tri·ate** \rē'pātrē,āt\ *vb* **-at·ed; -at·ing** : send back to one's own country — **re·pa·tri·ate** \-trēət, -trē,āt\ *n* — **re·pa·tri·a·tion** \-,pātrē'āshən\ *n*

**re·pay** \rē'pā\ *vb* **-paid; -pay·ing** : pay back — **re·pay·able** *adj* — **re·pay·ment** *n*

**re·peal** \ri'pēl\ *vb* : annul by legislative action — **repeal** *n* — **re·peal·er** *n*

**re·peat** \ri'pēt\ *vb* : say or do again ~ *n* **1** : act of repeating **2** : something repeated — **re·peat·able** *adj* — **re·peat·ed·ly** *adv* — **re·peat·er** *n*

**re·pel** \ri'pel\ *vb* **-pelled; -pel·ling 1** : drive away **2** : disgust — **re·pel·lent** \-'pelənt\ *adj or n*

**re·pent** \ri'pent\ *vb* **1** : turn from sin **2** : regret — **re·pen·tance** \ri'pent°ns\ *n* — **re·pen·tant** \-°nt\ *adj*

**re·per·cus·sion** \,rēpər'kəshən,

,rep-\ *n* : effect of something done or said

**rep·er·toire** \'repər,twär\ *n* : pieces a company or performer can present

**rep·er·to·ry** \'repər,tōrē\ *n, pl* **-ries** 1 : repertoire 2 : theater with a resident company doing several plays

**rep·e·ti·tion** \,repə'tishən\ *n* : act or instance of repeating

**rep·e·ti·tious** \-'tishəs\ *adj* : tediously repeating — **rep·e·ti·tious·ly** *adv* — **rep·e·ti·tious·ness** *n*

**re·pet·i·tive** \ri'petətiv\ *adj* : repetitious — **re·pet·i·tive·ly** *adv* — **re·pet·i·tive·ness** *n*

**re·pine** \ri'pīn\ *vb* **re·pined; re·pin·ing** : feel or express discontent

**re·place** \ri'plās\ *vb* 1 : restore to a former position 2 : take the place of 3 : put something new in the place of — **re·place·able** *adj* — **re·place·ment** *n* — **re·plac·er** *n*

**re·plen·ish** \ri'plenish\ *vb* : stock or supply anew — **re·plen·ish·ment** *n*

**re·plete** \ri'plēt\ *adj* : full — **re·plete·ness** *n* — **re·ple·tion** \-'plēshən\ *n*

**rep·li·ca** \'replikə\ *n* : exact copy

**rep·li·cate** \'replə,kāt\ *vb* **-cat·ed; -cat·ing** : duplicate or repeat — **rep·li·cate** \-likət\ *n* — **rep·li·ca·tion** \-lə'kāshən\ *n*

**re·ply** \ri'plī\ *vb* **-plied; -ply·ing** : say or do in answer ~ *n, pl* **-plies** : answer

**re·port** \ri'pōrt\ *n* 1 : rumor 2 : statement of information (as events or causes) 3 : explosive noise ~ *vb* 1 : give an account of 2 : present an account of (an event) as news 3 : present oneself 4 : make known to authorities — **re·port·age** \ri'pōrtij, ,repər'täzh, ,rep,ȯr'-\ *n* — **re·port·ed·ly** *adv* — **re·port·er** *n* — **re·por·to·ri·al** \,repər'tōrēəl\ *adj*

**re·pose** \ri'pōz\ *vb* **-posed; -pos·ing** : lay or lie at rest ~ *n* 1 : state of resting 2 : calm or peace — **re·pose·ful** *adj*

**re·pos·i·to·ry** \ri'päzə,tōrē\ *n, pl* **-ries** : place where something is stored

**re·pos·sess** \,rēpə'zes\ *vb* : regain possession and legal ownership of — **re·pos·ses·sion** \-'zeshən\ *n*

**rep·re·hend** \,repri'hend\ *vb* : censure — **rep·re·hen·sion** \-'henchən\ *n*

**rep·re·hen·si·ble** \-'hensəbəl\ *adj* : deserving condemnation — **rep·re·hen·si·bly** *adv*

**rep·re·sent** \,repri'zent\ *vb* 1 : serve as a sign or symbol of 2 : act or speak for 3 : describe as having a specified quality or character — **rep·re·sen·ta·tion** \,repri,zen'tāshən\ *n*

**rep·re·sen·ta·tive** \,repri'zentətiv\ *adj* 1 : standing or acting for another 2 : carried on by elected representatives ~ *n* 1 : typical example 2 : one that represents another 3 : member of usu. the lower house of a legislature — **rep·re·sen·ta·tive·ly** *adv* — **rep·re·sen·ta·tive·ness** *n*

**re·press** \ri'pres\ *vb* : restrain or suppress — **re·pres·sion** \-'preshən\ *n* — **re·pres·sive** \-'presiv\ *adj*

**re·prieve** \ri'prēv\ *n* 1 : a delay in punishment 2 : temporary respite — **re·prieve** *vb*

**rep·ri·mand** \'reprə,mand\ *n* : formal or severe criticism — **reprimand** *vb*

**re·pri·sal** \ri'prīzəl\ *n* : act in retaliation

**re·prise** \ri'prēz\ *n* : musical repetition

**re·proach** \ri'prōch\ *n* 1 : disgrace 2 : rebuke ~ *vb* : express disapproval to — **re·proach·ful** *adj* — **re·proach·ful·ly** *adv* — **re·proach·ful·ness** *n*

**rep·ro·bate** \'reprə,bāt\ *n* : scoundrel — **reprobate** *adj*

**rep·ro·ba·tion** \,reprə'bāshən\ *n* : strong disapproval

**re·pro·duce** \,rēprə'düs, -'dyüs\ *vb* 1 : produce again or anew 2 : produce offspring — **re·pro·duc·ible** \-'düsəbəl, -'dyü-\ *adj* — **re·pro·duc·tion** \-'dəkshən\ *n* — **re·pro·duc·tive** \-'dəktiv\ *adj*

**re·proof** \ri'prüf\ *n* : blame or censure for a fault

**re·prove** \ri'prüv\ *vb* **-proved; -prov·ing** : express disapproval to or of

**rep·tile** \'rept³l, -,tīl\ *n* : air-breathing scaly vertebrate — **rep·til·ian** \rep'tilēən\ *adj or n*

---

**re·pub·lic** \ri'pəblik\ *n* : country with representative government

**re·pub·li·can** \-likən\ *adj* **1** : relating to or resembling a republic **2** : supporting a republic — **republican** *n* — **re·pub·li·can·ism** *n*

**re·pu·di·ate** \ri'pyüdē‚āt\ *vb* **-at·ed; -at·ing** : refuse to have anything to do with — **re·pu·di·a·tion** \-‚pyüdē'ā-shən\ *n*

**re·pug·nant** \ri'pəgnənt\ *adj* : contrary to one's tastes or principles — **re·pug·nance** \-nəns\ *n* — **re·pug·nant·ly** *adv*

**re·pulse** \ri'pəls\ *vb* **-pulsed; -puls·ing** **1** : drive or beat back **2** : rebuff **3** : be repugnant to — **repulse** *n* — **re·pul·sion** \-'pəlshən\ *n*

**re·pul·sive** \-siv\ *adj* : arousing aversion or disgust — **re·pul·sive·ly** *adv* — **re·pul·sive·ness** *n*

**rep·u·ta·ble** \'repyətəbəl\ *adj* : having a good reputation — **rep·u·ta·bly** \-blē\ *adv*

**rep·u·ta·tion** \‚repyə'tāshən\ *n* : one's character or public esteem

**re·pute** \ri'pyüt\ *vb* **-put·ed; -put·ing** : think of as being ~ *n* : reputation — **re·put·ed** *adj* — **re·put·ed·ly** *adv*

**re·quest** \ri'kwest\ *n* : act or instance of asking for something or a thing asked for ~ *vb* **1** : make a request of **2** : ask for — **re·quest·er** *n*

**re·qui·em** \'rekwēəm, 'rāk-\ *n* : Mass for a dead person or a musical setting for this

**re·quire** \ri'kwīr\ *vb* **-quired; -quir·ing** **1** : insist on **2** : call for as essential — **re·quire·ment** *n*

**req·ui·site** \'rekwəzət\ *adj* : necessary — **requisite** *n*

**req·ui·si·tion** \‚rekwə'zishən\ *n* : formal application or demand — **requisition** *vb*

**re·quite** \ri'kwīt\ *vb* **-quit·ed; -quit·ing** : make return for or to — **re·quit·al** \-'kwīt°l\ *n*

**re·scind** \ri'sind\ *vb* : repeal or cancel — **re·scis·sion** \-'sizhən\ *n*

**res·cue** \'reskyü\ *vb* **-cued; -cu·ing** : set free from danger or confinement — **rescue** *n* — **res·cu·er** *n*

**re·search** \ri'sərch, 'rē‚sərch\ *n* : careful or diligent search esp. for new knowledge — **research** *vb* — **re·search·er** *n*

**re·sem·ble** \ri'zembəl\ *vb* **-sem·bled; -sem·bling** : be like or similar to — **re·sem·blance** \-'zembləns\ *n*

**re·sent** \ri'zent\ *vb* : feel or show annoyance at — **re·sent·ful** *adj* — **re·sent·ful·ly** *adv* — **re·sent·ment** *n*

**res·er·va·tion** \‚rezər'vāshən\ *n* **1** : act of reserving or something reserved **2** : limiting condition

**re·serve** \ri'zərv\ *vb* **-served; -serv·ing** **1** : store for future use **2** : set aside for special use ~ *n* **1** : something reserved **2** : restraint in words or bearing **3** : military forces withheld from action or not part of the regular services — **re·served** *adj*

**res·er·voir** \'rezər‚vwär, -‚vwȯr, -‚vȯr, -‚vȯi\ *n* : place where something (as water) is kept in store

**re·side** \ri'zīd\ *vb* **-sid·ed; -sid·ing** **1** : make one's home **2** : be present

**res·i·dence** \'rezədəns\ *n* **1** : act or fact of residing in a place **2** : place where one lives — **res·i·dent** \-ənt\ *adj or n* — **res·i·den·tial** \‚rezə'denchəl\ *adj*

**res·i·due** \'rezə‚dü, -‚dyü\ *n* : part remaining — **re·sid·u·al** \ri'zijəwəl\ *adj*

**re·sign** \ri'zīn\ *vb* **1** : give up deliberately **2** : give (oneself) over without resistance — **res·ig·na·tion** \‚rezig-'nāshən\ *n* — **re·sign·ed·ly** \-'zīnədlē\ *adv*

**re·sil·ience** \ri'zilyəns\ *n* : ability to recover or adjust easily

**re·sil·ien·cy** \-yənsē\ *n* : resilience

**re·sil·ient** \-yənt\ *adj* : elastic

**res·in** \'rez°n\ *n* : substance from the gum or sap of trees — **res·in·ous** *adj*

**re·sist** \ri'zist\ *vb* **1** : withstand the force or effect of **2** : fight against — **re·sist·ible** \-'zistəbəl\ *adj* — **re·sist·less** *adj*

**re·sis·tance** \ri'zistəns\ *n* **1** : act of resisting **2** : ability of an organism to

---

| | | |
|---|---|---|
| reknit | relight | rematch |
| relabel | reline | remelt |
| relandscape | reload | remobilize |
| relaunch | remarriage | remoisten |
| relearn | remarry | remold |

resist disease **3** : opposition to electric current

**re•sis•tant** \-tənt\ adj : giving resistance

**res•o•lute** \'rezə,lüt\ adj : having a fixed purpose — **res•o•lute•ly** adv — **res•o•lute•ness** n

**res•o•lu•tion** \,rezə'lüshən\ n **1** : process of resolving **2** : firmness of purpose **3** : statement of the opinion, will, or intent of a body

**re•solve** \ri'zälv\ vb **-solved; -solv•ing 1** : find an answer to **2** : make a formal resolution ~ n **1** : something resolved **2** : steadfast purpose — **re•solv•able** adj

**res•o•nant** \'rezə°nənt\ adj **1** : continuing to sound **2** : relating to intensification or prolongation of sound (as by a vibrating body) — **res•o•nance** \-əns\ n — **res•o•nant•ly** adv

**re•sort** \ri'zórt\ n **1** : source of help **2** : place to go for vacation ~ vb **1** : go often or habitually **2** : have recourse

**re•sound** \ri'zaùnd\ vb : become filled with sound

**re•sound•ing** \-iŋ\ adj : impressive — **re•sound•ing•ly** adv

**re•source** \'rē,sórs, ri'sórs\ n **1** : new or reserve source **2** pl : available funds **3** : ability to handle situations — **re•source•ful** adj — **re•source•ful•ness** n

**re•spect** \ri'spekt\ n **1** : relation to something **2** : high or special regard **3** : detail ~ vb : consider deserving of high regard — **re•spect•er** n — **re•spect•ful** adj — **re•spect•ful•ly** adv — **re•spect•ful•ness** n

**re•spect•able** \ri'spektəbəl\ adj **1** : worthy of respect **2** : fair in size, quantity, or quality — **re•spect•abil•i•ty** \-,spektə'bilətē\ n — **re•spect•ably** \-'spektəblē\ adv

**re•spec•tive** \-tiv\ adj : individual and specific

**re•spec•tive•ly** \-lē\ adv **1** : as relating to each **2** : each in the order given

**res•pi•ra•tion** \,respə'rāshən\ n : act or process of breathing — **re•spi•ra•to•ry** \'respərə,tōrē, ri'spīrə-\ adj — **re•spire** \ri'spīr\ vb

**res•pi•ra•tor** \'respə,rātər\ n : device for artificial respiration

**re•spite** \'respət\ n : temporary delay or rest

**re•splen•dent** \ri'splendənt\ adj : shining brilliantly — **re•splen•dence** \-dəns\ n — **re•splen•dent•ly** adv

**re•spond** \ri'spänd\ vb **1** : answer **2** : react — **re•spon•dent** \-'spändənt\ n or adj — **re•spond•er** n

**re•sponse** \ri'späns\ n **1** : act of responding **2** : answer

**re•spon•si•ble** \ri'spänsəbəl\ adj **1** : answerable for acts or decisions **2** : able to fulfill obligations **3** : having important duties — **re•spon•si•bil•i•ty** \ri-,spänsə'bilətē\ n — **re•spon•si•ble•ness** n — **re•spon•si•bly** \-blē\ adv

**re•spon•sive** \-siv\ adj : quick to respond — **re•spon•sive•ly** adv — **re•spon•sive•ness** n

**¹rest** \'rest\ n **1** : sleep **2** : freedom from work or activity **3** : state of inactivity **4** : something used as a support ~ vb **1** : get rest **2** : cease action or motion **3** : give rest to **4** : sit or lie fixed or supported **5** : depend — **rest•ful** adj — **rest•ful•ly** adv

**²rest** n : remainder

**res•tau•rant** \'restərənt, -tə,ränt\ n : public eating place

**res•ti•tu•tion** \,restə'tüshən, -'tyü-\ n : act or fact of restoring something or repaying someone

**res•tive** \'restiv\ adj : uneasy or fidgety — **res•tive•ly** adv — **res•tive•ness** n

**rest•less** \'restləs\ adj **1** : lacking or giving no rest **2** : always moving **3** : uneasy — **rest•less•ly** adv — **rest•less•ness** n

**re•store** \ri'stōr\ vb **-stored; -stor•ing 1** : give back **2** : put back into use or into a former state — **re•stor•able** adj — **res•to•ra•tion** \,restə'rāshən\ n — **re•stor•ative** \ri'stōrətiv\ n or adj — **re•stor•er** n

**re•strain** \ri'strān\ vb : limit or keep under control — **re•strain•able** adj — **re•strained** \-'strānd\ adj — **re•strain•ed•ly** \-'strānədlē\ adv — **re•strain•er** n

---

remotivate
rename
renegotiate
reoccupy
reoccur

reoccurrence
reoperate
reorchestrate
reorganization
reorganize

reorient
repack
repave
rephotograph
replan

**restraining order** *n* : legal order directing one person to stay away from another

**re•straint** \-'strānt\ *n* **1** : act of restraining **2** : restraining force **3** : control over feelings

**re•strict** \ri'strikt\ *vb* **1** : confine within bounds **2** : limit use of — **re•stric•tion** \-'strikshən\ *n* — **re•stric•tive•ly** *adv*

**re•sult** \ri'zəlt\ *vb* : come about because of something else ~ *n* **1** : thing that results **2** : something obtained by calculation or investigation — **re•sul•tant** \-'zəlt³nt\ *adj or n*

**re•sume** \ri'züm\ *vb* -**sumed; -sum•ing** : return to or take up again after interruption — **re•sump•tion** \-'zəmpshən\ *n*

**ré•su•mé, re•su•me, re•su•mé** \'rezə,mā, ,rezə'-\ *n* : summary of one's career and qualifications

**re•sur•gence** \ri'sərjəns\ *n* : a rising again — **re•sur•gent** \-jənt\ *adj*

**res•ur•rect** \,rezə'rekt\ *vb* **1** : raise from the dead **2** : bring to attention or use again — **res•ur•rec•tion** \-'rekshən\ *n*

**re•sus•ci•tate** \ri'səsə,tāt\ *vb* -**tat•ed; -tat•ing** : bring back from apparent death — **re•sus•ci•ta•tion** \ri,səsə-'tāshən, ,rē-\ *n* — **re•sus•ci•ta•tor** \-,tātər\ *n*

**re•tail** \'rē,tāl\ *vb* : sell in small quantities directly to the consumer ~ *n* : business of selling to consumers — **retail** *adj or adv* — **re•tail•er** *n*

**re•tain** \ri'tān\ *vb* **1** : keep or hold onto **2** : engage the services of

**re•tain•er** *n* **1** : household servant **2** : retaining fee

**re•tal•i•ate** \ri'talē,āt\ *vb* -**at•ed; -at•ing** : return (as an injury) in kind — **re•tal•i•a•tion** \-,talē'āshən\ *n* — **re•tal•ia•to•ry** \-'talyə,tōrē\ *adj*

**re•tard** \ri'tärd\ *vb* : hold back — **re•tar•da•tion** \,rē,tär'dāshən, ri-\ *n*

**re•tard•ed** \ri'tärdəd\ *adj* : slow or limited in intellectual development

**retch** \'rech\ *vb* : try to vomit

**re•ten•tion** \ri'tenchən\ *n* **1** : state of being retained **2** : ability to retain — **re•ten•tive** \-'tentiv\ *adj*

**ret•i•cent** \'retəsənt\ *adj* : tending not to talk — **ret•i•cence** \-səns\ *n* — **ret•i•cent•ly** *adv*

**ret•i•na** \'ret³nə\ *n, pl* -**nas** *or* -**nae** \-³n,ē\ : sensory membrane lining the eye — **ret•i•nal** \'ret³nəl\ *adj*

**ret•i•nue** \'ret³n,ü, -,yü\ *n* : attendants or followers of a distinguished person

**re•tire** \ri'tīr\ *vb* -**tired; -tir•ing 1** : withdraw for privacy **2** : end a career **3** : go to bed — **re•tir•ee** \ri,tī'rē\ *n* — **re•tire•ment** *n*

**re•tir•ing** \ri'tīrin\ *adj* : shy

**re•tort** \ri'tórt\ *vb* : say in reply ~ *n* : quick, witty, or cutting answer

**re•trace** \,rē'trās\ *vb* : go over again or in reverse

**re•tract** \ri'trakt\ *vb* **1** : draw back or in **2** : withdraw a charge or promise — **re•tract•able** *adj* — **re•trac•tion** \-'trakshən\ *n*

**re•treat** \ri'trēt\ *n* **1** : act of withdrawing **2** : place of privacy or safety or meditation and study ~ *vb* : make a retreat

**re•trench** \ri'trench\ *vb* : cut down (as expenses) — **re•trench•ment** *n*

**ret•ri•bu•tion** \,retrə'byushən\ *n* : retaliation — **re•trib•u•tive** \ri'tribyətiv\ *adj* — **re•trib•u•to•ry** \-yə,tōrē\ *adj*

**re•trieve** \ri'trēv\ *vb* -**trieved; -triev•ing 1** : search for and bring in game **2** : recover — **re•triev•able** *adj* — **re•triev•al** \-'trēvəl\ *n*

**re•triev•er** \-'trēvər\ *n* : dog for retrieving game

**ret•ro•ac•tive** \,retrō'aktiv\ *adj* : made effective as of a prior date — **ret•ro•ac•tive•ly** *adv*

**ret•ro•grade** \'retrə,grād\ *adj* **1** : moving backward **2** : becoming worse

**ret•ro•gress** \,retrə'gres\ *vb* : move backward — **ret•ro•gres•sion** \-'greshən\ *n*

**ret•ro•spect** \'retrə,spekt\ *n* : review of past events — **ret•ro•spec•tion** \,retrə'spekshən\ *n* — **ret•ro•spec•tive** \-'spektiv\ *adj* — **ret•ro•spec•tive•ly** *adv*

---

| | | |
|---|---|---|
| replaster | repressurize | reread |
| replay | reprice | rereading |
| replot | reprint | rerecord |
| repolish | reprocess | reregister |
| repopulate | reprogram | reroof |

**re·turn** \ri'tərn\ *vb* **1** : go or come back **2** : pass, give, or send back to an earlier possessor **3** : answer **4** : bring in as a profit **5** : give or do in return ～ *n* **1** : act of returning or something returned **2** *pl* : report of balloting results **3** : statement of taxable income **4** : profit — **return** *adj* — **return·able** *adj or n* — **re·turn·er** *n*

**re·union** \rē'yünyən\ *n* **1** : act of reuniting **2** : a meeting of persons after a separation

**re·vamp** \ˌrē'vamp\ *vb* : renovate or revise

**re·veal** \ri'vēl\ *vb* **1** : make known **2** : show plainly

**rev·eil·le** \'revəlē\ *n* : military signal sounded about sunrise

**rev·el** \'revəl\ *vb* **-eled** *or* **-elled; -el·ing** *or* **-el·ling** **1** : take part in a revel **2** : take great pleasure ～ *n* : wild party or celebration — **rev·el·er,** **rev·el·ler** \-ər\ *n* — **rev·el·ry** \-rē\ *n*

**rev·e·la·tion** \ˌrevə'lāshən\ *n* **1** : act of revealing **2** : something enlightening or astonishing

**re·venge** \ri'venj\ *vb* : avenge ～ *n* **1** : desire for retaliation **2** : act of retaliation — **re·venge·ful** *adj* — **re·veng·er** *n*

**rev·e·nue** \'revəˌnü, -ˌnyü\ *n* : money collected by a government

**re·ver·ber·ate** \ri'vərbəˌrāt\ *vb* **-at·ed; -at·ing** : resound in a series of echoes — **re·ver·ber·a·tion** \-ˌvərbə'rāshən\ *n*

**re·vere** \ri'vir\ *vb* **-vered; -ver·ing** : show honor and devotion to — **rev·er·ence** \'revərəns\ *n* — **rev·er·ent** \-rənt\ *adj* — **rev·er·ent·ly** *adv*

**rev·er·end** \'revərənd\ *adj* : worthy of reverence ～ *n* : clergy member

**rev·er·ie** \'revərē\ *n, pl* **-er·ies** : daydream

**re·verse** \ri'vərs\ *adj* **1** : opposite to a previous or normal condition **2** : acting in an opposite way ～ *vb* **-versed; -vers·ing** **1** : turn upside down or completely around **2** : change to the contrary or in the opposite direction ～ *n* **1** : something contrary **2**

: change for the worse **3** : back of something — **re·ver·sal** \-səl\ *n* — **re·verse·ly** *adv* — **re·vers·ible** \-'vərsəbəl\ *adj*

**re·vert** \ri'vərt\ *vb* : return to an original type or condition — **re·ver·sion** \-'vərzhᵊn\ *n*

**re·view** \ri'vyü\ *n* **1** : formal inspection **2** : general survey **3** : critical evaluation **4** : second or repeated study or examination ～ *vb* **1** : examine or study again **2** : reexamine judicially **3** : look back over **4** : examine critically **5** : inspect — **re·view·er** *n*

**re·vile** \ri'vīl\ *vb* **-viled; -vil·ing** : abuse verbally — **re·vile·ment** *n* — **re·vil·er** *n*

**re·vise** \-'vīz\ *vb* **-vised; -vis·ing** **1** : look over something written to correct or improve **2** : make a new version of — **re·vis·able** *adj* — **revise** *n* — **re·vis·er, re·vi·sor** \-'vīzər\ *n* — **re·vi·sion** \-'vizhən\ *n*

**re·viv·al** \-'vīvəl\ *n* **1** : act of reviving or state of being revived **2** : evangelistic meeting

**re·vive** \-'vīv\ *vb* **-vived; -viv·ing** : bring back to life or consciousness or into use — **re·viv·er** *n*

**re·vo·ca·tion** \ˌrevə'kāshən\ *n* : act or instance of revoking

**re·voke** \ri'vōk\ *vb* **-voked; -vok·ing** : annul by recalling — **re·vok·er** *n*

**re·volt** \-'vōlt\ *vb* **1** : throw off allegiance **2** : cause or experience disgust or shock ～ *n* : rebellion or revolution — **re·volt·er** *n*

**re·volt·ing** \-iŋ\ *adj* : extremely offensive — **re·volt·ing·ly** *adv*

**rev·o·lu·tion** \ˌrevə'lüshən\ *n* **1** : rotation **2** : progress in an orbit **3** : sudden, radical, or complete change (as overthrow of a government) — **rev·o·lu·tion·ary** \-shəˌnerē\ *adj or n*

**rev·o·lu·tion·ize** \-shəˌnīz\ *vb* **-ized; -iz·ing** : change radically — **rev·o·lu·tion·iz·er** *n*

**re·volve** \ri'välv\ *vb* **-volved; -volv·ing** **1** : ponder **2** : move in an orbit **3** : rotate — **re·volv·able** *adj*

**re·volv·er** \ri'välvər\ *n* : pistol with a revolving cylinder

---

| reroute | resegregate | resew |
| resalable | resell | reshoot |
| resale | resentence | reshow |
| reschedule | reset | resocialization |
| reseal | resettle | resod |

**re•vue** \ri'vyü\ *n* : theatrical production of brief numbers

**re•vul•sion** \ri'vəlshən\ *n* : complete dislike or repugnance

**re•ward** \ri'wȯrd\ *vb* : give a reward to or for ∼ *n* : something offered for service or achievement

**re•write** \‚rē'rīt\ *vb* **-wrote; -writ•ten; -writ•ing** : revise — **rewrite** *n*

**rhap•so•dy** \'rapsədē\ *n, pl* **-dies 1** : expression of extravagant praise **2** : flowing free-form musical composition — **rhap•sod•ic** \rap'sädik\ *adj* — **rhap•sod•i•cal•ly** \-iklē\ *adv* — **rhap•so•dize** \'rapsə‚dīz\ *vb*

**rhet•o•ric** \'retərik\ *n* : art of speaking or writing effectively — **rhe•tor•i•cal** \ri'tȯrikəl\ *adj* — **rhet•o•ri•cian** \‚retə'rishən\ *n*

**rheu•ma•tism** \'rümə‚tizəm, 'rum-\ *n* : disorder marked by inflammation or pain in muscles or joints — **rheu•mat•ic** \rù'matik\ *adj*

**rhine•stone** \'rīn‚stōn\ *n* : a colorless imitation gem

**rhi•no** \'rīnō\ *n, pl* **-no** *or* **-nos** : rhinoceros

**rhi•noc•er•os** \rī'näsərəs\ *n, pl* **-noc•er•os•es** *or* **-noc•er•os** *or* **-noc•eri** \-'näsə‚rī\ : large thick-skinned mammal with 1 or 2 horns on the snout

**rho•do•den•dron** \‚rōdə'dendrən\ *n* : flowering evergreen shrub

**rhom•bus** \'rämbəs\ *n, pl* **-bus•es** *or* **-bi** \-‚bī\ : parallelogram with equal sides

**rhu•barb** \'rü‚bärb\ *n* : garden plant with edible stalks

**rhyme** \'rīm\ *n* **1** : correspondence in terminal sounds **2** : verse that rhymes

∼ *vb* **rhymed; rhym•ing** : make or have rhymes

**rhythm** \'rithəm\ *n* : regular succession of sounds or motions — **rhyth•mic** \'rithmik\, **rhyth•mi•cal** \-mikəl\ *adj* — **rhyth•mi•cal•ly** *adv*

**rhythm and blues** *n* : popular music based on blues and black folk music

**rib** \'rib\ *n* **1** : curved bone joined to the spine **2** : riblike thing ∼ *vb* **-bb- 1** : furnish or mark with ribs **2** : tease — **rib•ber** *n*

**rib•ald** \'ribəld\ *adj* : coarse or vulgar — **rib•ald•ry** \-əldrē\ *n*

**rib•bon** \'ribən\ *n* **1** : narrow strip of fabric used esp. for decoration **2** : strip of inked cloth (as in a typewriter)

**ri•bo•fla•vin** \‚rībə'flāvən, 'rībə‚-\ *n* : growth-promoting vitamin

**rice** \'rīs\ *n, pl* **rice** : starchy edible seeds of an annual cereal grass

**rich** \'rich\ *adj* **1** : having a lot of money or possessions **2** : valuable **3** : containing much sugar, fat, or seasoning **4** : abundant **5** : deep and pleasing in color or tone **6** : fertile — **rich•ly** *adv* — **rich•ness** *n*

**rich•es** \'richəz\ *n pl* : wealth

**rick•ets** \'rikəts\ *n* : childhood bone disease

**rick•ety** \'rikətē\ *adj* : shaky

**rick•sha, rick•shaw** \'rik‚shȯ\ *n* : small covered 2-wheeled carriage pulled by one person

**ric•o•chet** \'rikə‚shā, *Brit also* -‚shet\ *vb* **-cheted** \-‚shād\ *or* **-chet•ted** \-‚shetəd\; **-chet•ing** \-‚shāin\ *or* **-chet•ting** \-‚shetin\ : bounce off at an angle — **ricochet** *n*

**rid** \'rid\ *vb* **rid; rid•ding** : make free of

---

resolidify
restage
restart
restate
restatement
restimulate
restock
restructure
restudy
restyle
resubmit
resupply
resurface
resurvey

resynthesis
resynthesize
retarget
reteach
retell
retest
rethink
retighten
retrain
retranslate
retransmit
retry
retune
retype

reupholster
reusable
reuse
reutilize
revaccinate
revaccination
revisit
rewash
reweave
rewind
rewire
rewrap

something unwanted — **rid·dance**
\'rid°ns\ n
**rid·den** \'rid°n\ adj : overburdened
with — used in combination
¹**rid·dle** \'rid°l\ n : puzzling question ~
vb -**dled; -dling** : speak in riddles
²**riddle** vb -**dled; -dling** : fill full of holes
**ride** \'rīd\ vb **rode** \'rōd\; **rid·den**
\'rid°n\; **rid·ing** \'rīdiŋ\ **1** : be carried along **2** : sit on and cause to
move **3** : travel over a surface **4**
: tease or nag ~ n **1** : trip on an animal or in a vehicle **2** : mechanical device ridden for amusement
**rid·er** n **1** : one that rides **2** : attached
clause or document — **rid·er·less** adj
**ridge** \'rij\ n **1** : range of hills **2** : raised
line or strip **3** : line of intersection of
2 sloping surfaces — **ridgy** adj
**rid·i·cule** \'ridə,kyül\ vb : laugh at or
make fun of — **ridicule** n
**ri·dic·u·lous** \rə'dikyələs\ adj : arousing ridicule — **ri·dic·u·lous·ly** adv —
**ri·dic·u·lous·ness** n
**rife** \'rīf\ adj : abounding — **rife** adv
**riff·raff** \'rif,raf\ n : mob
¹**ri·fle** \'rīfəl\ vb -**fled; -fling** : ransack esp.
with intent to steal — **ri·fler** \-flər\ n
²**rifle** n : long shoulder weapon with spiral grooves in the bore — **ri·fle·man**
\-mən\ n — **ri·fling** n
**rift** \'rift\ n : separation — **rift** vb
¹**rig** \'rig\ vb -**gg**- **1** : fit out with rigging
**2** : set up esp. as a makeshift ~ n **1**
: distinctive shape, number, and
arrangement of sails and masts of a
sailing ship **2** : equipment **3** : carriage with its horse
²**rig** vb -**gg**- : manipulate esp. by deceptive or dishonest means
**rig·ging** \'rigiŋ, -ən\ n : lines that hold
and move the masts, sails, and spars
of a sailing ship
**right** \'rīt\ adj **1** : meeting a standard of
conduct **2** : correct **3** : genuine **4**
: normal **5** : opposite of left ~ n **1**
: something that is correct, just,
proper, or honorable **2** : something to
which one has a just claim **3** : something that is on the right side ~ adv
**1** : according to what is right **2** : immediately **3** : completely **4** : on or to
the right ~ vb **1** : restore to a proper
state **2** : bring or become upright
again — **right·er** n — **right·ness** n —
**right·ward** \-wərd\ adj
**right angle** n : angle whose sides are perpendicular to each other — **right–**

**an·gled** \'rīt'aŋgəld\, **right–an·gle**
\-gəl\ adj
**righ·teous** \'rīchəs\ adj : acting or being in accordance with what is just or
moral — **righ·teous·ly** adv — **righ-
teous·ness** n
**right·ful** \'rītfəl\ adj : lawful — **right-
ful·ly** \-ē\ adv — **right·ful·ness** n
**right·ly** \'rītlē\ adv **1** : justly **2** : properly **3** : correctly
**rig·id** \'rijəd\ adj : lacking flexibility —
**ri·gid·i·ty** \rə'jidətē\ n — **rig·id·ly** adv
**rig·ma·role** \'rigmə,rōl, 'rigə-\ n **1**
: meaningless talk **2** : complicated
often unnecessary procedure
**rig·or** \'rigər\ n : severity — **rig·or·ous**
adj — **rig·or·ous·ly** adv
**rig·or mor·tis** \,rigər'mórtəs\ n : temporary stiffness of muscles occurring
after death
**rile** \'rīl\ vb **riled; ril·ing** : anger
**rill** \'ril\ n : small brook
**rim** \'rim\ n : edge esp. of something
curved ~ vb -**mm**- : border
¹**rime** \'rīm\ n : frost — **rimy** \'rīmē\ adj
²**rime** var of RHYME
**rind** \'rīnd\ n : usu. hard or tough outer
layer
¹**ring** \'riŋ\ n **1** : circular band used as
an ornament or for holding or fastening **2** : something circular **3** : place
for contest or display **4** : group with a
selfish or dishonest aim ~ vb : surround — **ringed** \'riŋd\ adj — **ring-
like** adj
²**ring** vb **rang** \'raŋ\; **rung** \'rəŋ\; **ringing** **1** : sound resonantly when struck
**2** : cause to make a metallic sound by
striking **3** : resound **4** : call esp. by a
bell ~ n **1** : resonant sound or tone
**2** : act or instance of ringing
**ring·er** \'riŋər\ n **1** : one that sounds
by ringing **2** : illegal substitute **3**
: one that closely resembles another
**ring·lead·er** \'riŋ,lēdər\ n : leader esp.
of troublemakers
**ring·let** n : long curl
**ring·worm** n : contagious skin disease
caused by fungi
**rink** \'riŋk\ n : enclosed place for skating
**rinse** \'rins\ vb **rinsed; rins·ing** **1**
: cleanse usu. with water only **2** : treat
(hair) with a rinse ~ n : liquid used
for rinsing — **rins·er** n
**ri·ot** \'rīət\ n **1** : violent public disorder
**2** : random or disorderly profusion —
**riot** vb — **ri·ot·er** n — **ri·ot·ous** adj

**rip** \'rip\ *vb* **-pp-** : cut or tear open ∼ *n* : rent made by ripping — **rip•per** *n*

**ripe** \'rip\ *adj* **rip•er; rip•est** : fully grown, developed, or prepared — **ripe•ly** *adv* — **rip•en** \'rīpən\ *vb* — **ripe•ness** *n*

**rip-off** *n* : theft — **rip off** *vb*

**rip•ple** \'ripəl\ *vb* **-pled; -pling** 1 : become lightly ruffled on the surface 2 : sound like rippling water — **ripple** *n*

**rise** \'rīz\ *vb* **rose** \'rōz\; **ris•en** \'rizᵊn\; **ris•ing** \'rīziŋ\ 1 : get up from sitting, kneeling, or lying 2 : take arms 3 : appear above the horizon 4 : ascend 5 : gain a higher position or rank 6 : increase ∼ *n* 1 : act of rising 2 : origin 3 : elevation 4 : increase 5 : upward slope 6 : area of high ground — **ris•er** \'rīzər\ *n*

**risk** \'risk\ *n* : exposure to loss or injury — **risk** *vb* — **risk•i•ness** *n* — **risky** *adj*

**ris•qué** \ris'kā\ *adj* : nearly indecent

**rite** \'rīt\ *n* 1 : set form for conducting a ceremony 2 : liturgy of a church 3 : ceremonial action

**rit•u•al** \'richəwəl\ *n* : rite — **ritual** *adj* — **rit•u•al•ism** \-,izəm\ *n* — **rit•u•al•is•tic** \,richəwəl'istik\ *adj* — **rit•u•al•is•ti•cal•ly** \-'tiklē\ *adv* — **rit•u•al•ly** \'richəwəlē\ *adv*

**ri•val** \'rīvəl\ *n* 1 : competitor 2 : peer ∼ *vb* **-valed** *or* **-valled; -val•ing** *or* **-val•ling** 1 : be in competition with 2 : equal — **rival** *adj* — **ri•val•ry** \-rē\ *n*

**riv•er** \'rivər\ *n* : large natural stream of water — **riv•er•bank** *n* — **riv•er•bed** *n* — **riv•er•boat** *n* — **riv•er•side** *n*

**riv•et** \'rivət\ *n* : headed metal bolt ∼ *vb* : fasten with a rivet — **riv•et•er** *n*

**riv•u•let** \'rivyələt\ *n* : small stream

**roach** \'rōch\ *n* : cockroach

**road** \'rōd\ *n* : open way for vehicles, persons, and animals — **road•bed** *n* — **road•side** *n or adj* — **road•way** *n*

**road•block** *n* : obstruction on a road

**road•run•ner** *n* : large fast-running bird

**roam** \'rōm\ *vb* : wander

**roan** \'rōn\ *adj* : of a dark color sprinkled with white ∼ *n* : animal with a roan coat

**roar** \'rōr\ *vb* : utter a full loud prolonged sound — **roar** *n* — **roar•er** *n*

**roast** \'rōst\ *vb* 1 : cook by dry heat 2 : criticize severely ∼ *n* : piece of meat suitable for roasting — **roast** *adj* — **roast•er** *n*

**rob** \'räb\ *vb* **-bb-** 1 : steal from 2 : commit robbery — **rob•ber** *n*

**rob•bery** \'räbərē\ *n, pl* **-ber•ies** : theft of something from a person by use of violence or threat

**robe** \'rōb\ *n* 1 : long flowing outer garment 2 : covering for the lower body ∼ *vb* **robed; rob•ing** : clothe with or as if with a robe

**rob•in** \'räbən\ *n* : No. American thrush with a reddish breast

**ro•bot** \'rō,bät, -bət\ *n* 1 : machine that looks and acts like a human being 2 : efficient but insensitive person — **ro•bot•ic** \rō'bätik\ *adj*

**ro•bust** \rō'bəst, 'rō,bəst\ *adj* : strong and vigorously healthy — **ro•bust•ly** *adv* — **ro•bust•ness** *n*

¹**rock** \'räk\ *vb* : sway or cause to sway back and forth ∼ *n* 1 : rocking movement 2 : popular music marked by repetition and a strong beat

²**rock** *n* : mass of hard mineral material — **rock** *adj* — **rocky** *adj*

**rock•er** *n* 1 : curved piece on which a chair rocks 2 : chair that rocks

**rock•et** \'räkət\ *n* 1 : self-propelled firework or missile 2 : jet engine that carries its own oxygen ∼ *vb* : rise abruptly and rapidly — **rock•et•ry** \-ətrē\ *n*

**rod** \'räd\ *n* 1 : straight slender stick 2 : unit of length equal to 5 yards

**rode** *past of* RIDE

**ro•dent** \'rōdᵊnt\ *n* : usu. small gnawing mammal

**ro•deo** \'rōdē,ō, rō'dāō\ *n, pl* **-de•os** : contest of cowboy skills

**roe** \'rō\ *n* : fish eggs

**rogue** \'rōg\ *n* : dishonest or mischievous person — **rogu•ery** \'rōgərē\ *n* — **rogu•ish** \'rōgish\ *adj* — **rogu•ish•ly** *adv* — **rogu•ish•ness** *n*

**roil** \'rȯil\ *vb* 1 : make cloudy or muddy by stirring up 2 : make angry

**role** \'rōl\ *n* 1 : part to play 2 : function

**roll** \'rōl\ *n* 1 : official record or list of names 2 : something rolled up or rounded 3 : bread baked in a small rounded mass 4 : sound of rapid drum strokes 5 : heavy reverberating sound 6 : rolling movement ∼ *vb* 1 : move by turning over 2 : move on wheels 3 : flow in a continuous stream 4 : swing from side to side 5 : shape or be shaped in rounded form 6 : press with a roller

**roll•er** *n* 1 : revolving cylinder 2 : rod on which something is rolled up 3 : long heavy ocean wave

**roller skate** *n* : a skate with wheels instead of a runner — **roller–skate** *vb*

**rol·lick·ing** \'rälikiŋ\ *adj* : full of good spirits

**Ro·man Catholic** \'rōmən-\ *n* : member of a Christian church led by a pope — **Roman Catholic** *adj* — **Roman Catholicism** *n*

**ro·mance** \rō'mans, 'rō͵mans\ *n* **1** : medieval tale of knightly adventure **2** : love story **3** : love affair ~ *vb* **-manced; -manc·ing 1** : have romantic fancies **2** : have a love affair with — **ro·manc·er** *n*

**ro·man·tic** \rō'mantik\ *adj* **1** : visionary or imaginary **2** : appealing to one's emotions — **ro·man·ti·cal·ly** \-iklē\ *adv*

**romp** \'rämp\ *vb* : play actively and noisily — **romp** *n*

**roof** \'rüf, 'rʉf\ *n, pl* **roofs** \'rüfs, 'rʉfs; 'rüvz, 'rʉvz\ : upper covering part of a building ~ *vb* : cover with a roof — **roofed** \'rüft, 'rʉft\ *adj* — **roof·ing** *n* — **roof·less** *adj* — **roof·top** *n*

¹**rook** \'rʉk\ *n* : crowlike bird

²**rook** *vb* : cheat

**rook·ie** \'rʉkē\ *n* : novice

**room** \'rüm, 'rʉm\ *n* **1** : sufficient space **2** : partitioned part of a building ~ *vb* : occupy lodgings — **room·er** *n* — **room·ful** *n* — **roomy** *adj*

**room·mate** *n* : one sharing the same lodgings

**roost** \'rüst\ *n* : support on which birds perch ~ *vb* : settle on a roost

**roost·er** \'rüstər, 'rʉs-\ *n* : adult male domestic chicken

¹**root** \'rüt, 'rʉt\ *n* **1** : leafless underground part of a seed plant **2** : rootlike thing or part **3** : source **4** : essential core ~ *vb* : form, fix, or become fixed by roots — **root·less** *adj* — **root·let** \-lət\ *n* — **root·like** *adj*

²**root** *vb* : turn up with the snout

³**root** \'rüt, 'rʉt\ *vb* : applaud or encourage noisily — **root·er** *n*

**rope** \'rōp\ *n* : large strong cord of strands of fiber ~ *vb* **roped; rop·ing 1** : tie with a rope **2** : lasso

**ro·sa·ry** \'rōzərē\ *n, pl* **-ries 1** : string of beads used in praying **2** : Roman Catholic devotion

**rose** *past of* RISE

¹**rose** \'rōz\ *n* **1** : prickly shrub with bright flowers **2** : purplish red — **rose** *adj* — **rose·bud** *n* — **rose·bush** *n*

**rose·mary** \'rōz͵merē\ *n, pl* **-mar·ies** : fragrant shrubby mint

**ro·sette** \rō'zet\ *n* : rose-shaped ornament

**Rosh Ha·sha·nah** \͵räshhä'shänə, ͵rōsh-\ *n* : Jewish New Year observed as a religious holiday in September or October

**ros·in** \'räz°n\ *n* : brittle resin

**ros·ter** \'rästər\ *n* : list of names

**ros·trum** \'rästrəm\ *n, pl* **-trums** *or* **-tra** \-trə\ : speaker's platform

**rosy** \'rōzē\ *adj* **ros·i·er; -est 1** : of the color rose **2** : hopeful — **ros·i·ly** *adv* — **ros·i·ness** *n*

**rot** \'rät\ *vb* **-tt-** : undergo decomposition ~ *n* **1** : decay **2** : disease in which tissue breaks down

**ro·ta·ry** \'rōtərē\ *adj* **1** : turning on an axis **2** : having a rotating part

**ro·tate** \'rō͵tāt\ *vb* **-tat·ed; -tat·ing 1** : turn about an axis or a center **2** : alternate in a series — **ro·ta·tion** \rō'tāshən\ *n* — **ro·ta·tor** \'rō͵tātər\ *n*

**rote** \'rōt\ *n* : repetition from memory

**ro·tor** \'rōtər\ *n* **1** : part that rotates **2** : system of rotating horizontal blades for supporting a helicopter

**rot·ten** \'rät°n\ *adj* **1** : having rotted **2** : corrupt **3** : extremely unpleasant or inferior — **rot·ten·ness** *n*

**ro·tund** \rō'tənd\ *adj* : rounded — **ro·tun·di·ty** \-'təndətē\ *n*

**ro·tun·da** \rō'təndə\ *n* : building or room with a dome

**roué** \rù'ā\ *n* : man given to debauched living

**rouge** \'rüzh, 'rüj\ *n* : cosmetic for the cheeks — **rouge** *vb*

**rough** \'rəf\ *adj* **1** : not smooth **2** : not calm **3** : harsh, violent, or rugged **4** : crudely or hastily done ~ *n* : rough state or something in that state ~ *vb* **1** : roughen **2** : manhandle **3** : make roughly — **rough·ly** *adv* — **rough·ness** *n*

**rough·age** \'rəfij\ *n* : coarse bulky food

**rough·en** \'rəfən\ *vb* : make or become rough

**rough·neck** \'rəf͵nek\ *n* : rowdy

**rou·lette** \rü'let\ *n* : gambling game using a whirling numbered wheel

¹**round** \'raùnd\ *adj* **1** : having every part the same distance from the center **2** : cylindrical **3** : complete **4** : approximate **5** : blunt **6** : moving in or forming a circle ~ *n* **1** : round or

curved thing **2** : series of recurring actions or events **3** : period of time or a unit of action **4** : fired shot **5** : cut of beef ~ *vb* **1** : make or become round **2** : go around **3** : finish **4** : express as an approximation — **round•ish** *adj* — **round•ly** *adv* — **round•ness** *n*

²**round** *prep or adv* : around

**round•about** *adj* : indirect

**round•up** \'raund,əp\ *n* **1** : gathering together of range cattle **2** : summary — **round up** *vb*

**rouse** \'rauz\ *vb* **roused; rous•ing 1** : wake from sleep **2** : stir up

**rout** \'raut\ *n* **1** : state of wild confusion **2** : disastrous defeat ~ *vb* : defeat decisively

**route** \'rüt, 'raut\ *n* : line of travel ~ *vb* **rout•ed; rout•ing** : send by a selected route

**rou•tine** \rü'tēn\ *n* **1** : regular course of procedure **2** : an often repeated speech, formula, or part — **routine** *adj* — **rou•tine•ly** *adv*

**rove** \'rōv\ *vb* **roved; rov•ing** : wander or roam — **rov•er** *n*

¹**row** \'rō\ *vb* **1** : propel a boat with oars **2** : carry in a rowboat ~ *n* : act of rowing — **row•boat** *n* — **row•er** \'rōər\ *n*

²**row** *n* : number of objects in a line

³**row** \'rau\ *n* : noisy quarrel — **row** *vb*

**row•dy** \'raudē\ *adj* **-di•er; -est** : coarse or boisterous in behavior — **row•di•ness** *n* — **rowdy** *n*

**roy•al** \'roiəl\ *adj* : relating to or befitting a king ~ *n* : person of royal blood — **roy•al•ly** *adv*

**roy•al•ty** \'roiəltē\ *n, pl* **-ties 1** : state of being royal **2** : royal persons **3** : payment for use of property

**rub** \'rəb\ *vb* **-bb- 1** : use pressure and friction on a body **2** : scour, polish, erase, or smear by pressure and friction **3** : chafe with friction ~ *n* : difficulty

**rub•ber** \'rəbər\ *n* **1** : one that rubs **2** : waterproof elastic substance or something made of it — **rubber** *adj* — **rub•ber•ize** \-,īz\ *vb* — **rub•bery** *adj*

**rub•bish** \'rəbish\ *n* : waste or trash

**rub•ble** \'rəbəl\ *n* : broken fragments esp. of a destroyed building

**ru•ble** \'rübəl\ *n* : monetary unit of Russia

**ru•by** \'rübē\ *n, pl* **-bies** : precious red stone or its color — **ruby** *adj*

**rud•der** \'rədər\ *n* : steering device at the rear of a ship or aircraft

**rud•dy** \'rədē\ *adj* **-di•er; -est** : reddish — **rud•di•ness** *n*

**rude** \'rüd\ *adj* **rud•er; rud•est 1** : roughly made **2** : impolite — **rude•ly** *adv* — **rude•ness** *n*

**ru•di•ment** \'rüdəmənt\ *n* **1** : something not fully developed **2** : elementary principle — **ru•di•men•ta•ry** \,rüdə'mentərē\ *adj*

**rue** \'rü\ *vb* **rued; ru•ing** : feel regret for ~ *n* : regret — **rue•ful** \-fəl\ *adj* — **rue•ful•ly** *adv* — **rue•ful•ness** *n*

**ruf•fi•an** \'rəfēən\ *n* : brutal person

**ruf•fle** \'rəfəl\ *vb* **-fled; -fling 1** : draw into or provide with pleats **2** : roughen the surface of **3** : irritate ~ *n* : strip of fabric pleated on one edge — **ruf•fly** \'rəfəlē, -flē\ *adj*

**rug** \'rəg\ *n* : piece of heavy fabric used as a floor covering

**rug•ged** \'rəgəd\ *adj* **1** : having a rough uneven surface **2** : severe **3** : strong — **rug•ged•ly** *adv* — **rug•ged•ness** *n*

**ru•in** \'rüən\ *n* **1** : complete collapse or destruction **2** : remains of something destroyed — usu. in pl. **3** : cause of destruction ~ *vb* **1** : destroy **2** : damage beyond repair **3** : bankrupt

**ru•in•ous** \'rüənəs\ *adj* : causing ruin — **ruin•ous•ly** *adv*

**rule** \'rül\ *n* **1** : guide or principle for governing action **2** : usual way of doing something **3** : government **4** : straight strip (as of wood or metal) marked off in units for measuring ~ *vb* **ruled; rul•ing 1** : govern **2** : give as a decision — **rul•er** *n*

**rum** \'rəm\ *n* : liquor made from molasses or sugarcane

**rum•ble** \'rəmbəl\ *vb* **-bled; -bling** : make a low heavy rolling sound — **rumble** *n*

**ru•mi•nant** \'rümənənt\ *n* : hoofed mammal (as a cow or deer) that chews the cud — **ruminant** *adj*

**ru•mi•nate** \'rümə,nāt\ *vb* **-nat•ed; -nat•ing** : contemplate — **ru•mi•na•tion** \,rümə'nāshən\ *n*

**rum•mage** \'rəmij\ *vb* **-maged; -mag•ing** : search thoroughly

**rum•my** \'rəmē\ *n* : card game

**ru•mor** \'rümər\ *n* **1** : common talk **2** : widespread statement not authenticated — **rumor** *vb*

**rump** \'rəmp\ *n* : rear part of an animal

**rum•ple** \'rəmpəl\ *vb* **-pled; -pling** : tousle or wrinkle — **rumple** *n*

**rum·pus** \'rəmpəs\ *n* : disturbance

**run** \'rən\ *vb* **ran** \'ran\; **run; run·ning**
**1** : go rapidly or hurriedly **2** : enter a
race or election **3** : operate **4** : continue in force **5** : flow rapidly **6** : take
a certain direction **7** : manage **8** : in-
cur ∼ *n* **1** : act of running **2** : brook
**3** : continuous series **4** : usual kind **5**
: freedom of movement **6** : lengthwise ravel

**run·around** *n* : evasive or delaying action esp. in response to a request

**run·away** \'rənə,wā\ *n* : fugitive ∼
*adj* **1** : fugitive **2** : out of control

**run–down** *adj* : being in poor condition

**¹rung** *past part of* RING

**²rung** \'rən\ *n* : horizontal piece of a
chair or ladder

**run·ner** \'rənər\ *n* **1** : one that runs **2**
: thin piece or part on which some-
thing slides **3** : slender creeping
branch of a plant

**run·ner–up** *n, pl* **run·ners–up** : competitor who finishes second

**run·ning** \'rəniŋ\ *adj* **1** : flowing **2**
: continuous

**runt** \'rənt\ *n* : small person or animal
— **runty** *adj*

**run·way** \'rən,wā\ *n* : strip on which
aircraft land and take off

**ru·pee** \rü'pē, 'rü,-\ *n* : monetary unit
(as of India)

**rup·ture** \'rəpchər\ *n* **1** : breaking or
tearing apart **2** : hernia ∼ *vb* **-tured;**
**-tur·ing** : cause or undergo rupture

**ru·ral** \'rürəl\ *adj* : relating to the country or agriculture

**ruse** \'rüs, 'rüz\ *n* : trick

**¹rush** \'rəsh\ *n* : grasslike marsh plant

**²rush** *vb* **1** : move forward or act with
too great haste **2** : perform in a short
time ∼ *n* : violent forward motion
∼ *adj* : requiring speed — **rush·er** *n*

**rus·set** \'rəsət\ *n* **1** : reddish brown
color **2** : a baking potato — **russet** *adj*

**rust** \'rəst\ *n* **1** : reddish coating on exposed iron **2** : reddish brown color —
**rust** *vb* — **rusty** *adj*

**rus·tic** \'rəstik\ *adj* : relating to or suitable for the country or country
dwellers ∼ *n* : rustic person — **rus-**
**ti·cal·ly** *adv*

**rus·tle** \'rəsəl\ *vb* **-tled; -tling 1** : make
or cause a rustle **2** : forage food **3**
: steal cattle from the range ∼ *n*
: series of small sounds — **rus·tler**
\-ələr\ *n*

**rut** \'rət\ *n* **1** : track worn by wheels or
feet **2** : set routine — **rut·ted** *adj*

**ruth·less** \'rüthləs\ *adj* : having no
pity — **ruth·less·ly** *adv* — **ruth·less-**
**ness** *n*

**RV** \,är-'vē\ *n* recreational vehicle

**-ry** \rē\ *n suffix* : -ery

**rye** \'rī\ *n* **1** : cereal grass grown for
grain **2** : whiskey from rye

# S

**s** \'es\ *n, pl* **s's** *or* **ss** \'esəz\ : 19th letter of the alphabet

**¹-s** \s *after sounds* f, k, k̲, p, t, th; əz *af-*
*ter sounds* ch, j, s, sh, z, zh; z *after*
*other sounds*\ — used to form the
plural of most nouns

**²-s** *vb suffix* — used to form the 3d person singular present of most verbs

**Sab·bath** \'sabəth\ *n* **1** : Saturday observed as a day of worship by Jews
and some Christians **2** : Sunday observed as a day of worship by Christians

**sa·ber, sa·bre** \'sābər\ *n* : curved cavalry sword

**sa·ble** \'sābəl\ *n* **1** : black **2** : dark
brown mammal or its fur

**sab·o·tage** \'sabə,täzh\ *n* : deliberate
destruction or hampering ∼ *vb*
**-taged; -tag·ing** : wreck through sab-
otage

**sab·o·teur** \,sabə'tər\ *n* : person who
sabotages

**sac** \'sak\ *n* : anatomical pouch

**sac·cha·rin** \'sakərən\ *n* : low-calorie
artificial sweetener

**sac·cha·rine** \-ərən\ *adj* : nauseatingly
sweet

**sa·chet** \sa'shā\ *n* : small bag with perfumed powder (**sachet powder**)

**¹sack** \'sak\ *n* : bag ∼ *vb* : fire

**²sack** *vb* : plunder a captured place

**sack·cloth** *n* : rough garment worn as a
sign of penitence

**sac·ra·ment** \'sakrəmənt\ n : formal religious act or rite — **sac·ra·men·tal** \ˌsakrə'ment³l\ adj

**sa·cred** \'sākrəd\ adj 1 : set apart for or worthy of worship 2 : worthy of reverence 3 : relating to religion — **sa·cred·ly** adv — **sa·cred·ness** n

**sac·ri·fice** \'sakrəˌfīs\ n 1 : the offering of something precious to a deity or the thing offered 2 : loss or deprivation ~ vb -ficed; -fic·ing : offer or give up as a sacrifice — **sac·ri·fi·cial** \ˌsakrə'fishəl\ adj

**sac·ri·lege** \'sakrəlij\ n : violation of something sacred — **sac·ri·le·gious** \ˌsakrə'lijəs, -'lējəs\ adj

**sac·ro·sanct** \'sakrōˌsaŋkt\ adj : sacred

**sad** \'sad\ adj -dd- 1 : affected with grief or sorrow 2 : causing sorrow — **sad·den** \'sad³n\ vb — **sad·ly** adv — **sad·ness** n

**sad·dle** \'sad³l\ n : seat for riding on horseback ~ vb -dled; -dling : put a saddle on

**sa·dism** \'sāˌdizəm, 'sadˌiz-\ n : delight in cruelty — **sa·dist** \'sādist, 'sad-\ n — **sa·dis·tic** \sə'distik\ adj — **sa·dis·ti·cal·ly** adv

**sa·fa·ri** \sə'färē, -'far-\ n : hunting expedition in Africa

**safe** \'sāf\ adj saf·er; saf·est 1 : free from harm 2 : providing safety ~ n : container to keep valuables safe — **safe·keep·ing** n — **safe·ly** adv

**safe·guard** n : measure or device for preventing accidents — **safeguard** vb

**safe·ty** \'sāftē\ n, pl -ties 1 : freedom from danger 2 : protective device

**saf·flow·er** \'safˌlaůər\ n : herb with seeds rich in edible oil

**saf·fron** \'safrən\ n : orange powder from a crocus flower used in cooking

**sag** \'sag\ vb -gg- : droop, sink, or settle — **sag** n

**sa·ga** \'sägə\ n : story of heroic deeds

**sa·ga·cious** \sə'gāshəs\ adj : shrewd — **sa·gac·i·ty** \-'gasətē\ n

**¹sage** \'sāj\ adj : wise or prudent ~ n : wise man — **sage·ly** adv

**²sage** n : mint used in flavoring

**sage·brush** n : low shrub of the western U.S.

**said** past of SAY

**sail** \'sāl\ n 1 : fabric used to catch the wind and move a boat or ship 2 : trip on a sailboat ~ vb 1 : travel on a ship or sailboat 2 : move with ease or grace — **sail·boat** n — **sail·or** \'sālər\ n

**sail·fish** n : large fish with a very large dorsal fin

**saint** \'sānt, before a name ˌsānt or sənt\ n : holy or godly person — **saint·ed** \-əd\ adj — **saint·hood** \-ˌhůd\ n — **saint·li·ness** n — **saint·ly** adj

**¹sake** \'sāk\ n 1 : purpose or reason 2 : one's good or benefit

**²sa·ke, sa·ki** \'säkē\ n : Japanese rice wine

**sa·la·cious** \sə'lāshəs\ adj : sexually suggestive — **sa·la·cious·ly** adv

**sal·ad** \'saləd\ n : dish usu. of raw lettuce, vegetables, or fruit

**sal·a·man·der** \'saləˌmandər\ n : lizardlike amphibian

**sa·la·mi** \sə'lämē\ n : highly seasoned dried sausage

**sal·a·ry** \'salərē\ n, pl -ries : regular payment for services

**sale** \'sāl\ n 1 : transfer of ownership of property for money 2 : selling at bargain prices 3 sales pl : activities involved in selling — **sal·able, sale·able** \'sāləbəl\ adj — **sales·man** \-mən\ n — **sales·per·son** n — **sales·wom·an** n

**sa·lient** \'sālyənt\ adj : standing out conspicuously

**sa·line** \'sāˌlēn, -ˌlīn\ adj : containing salt — **sa·lin·i·ty** \sā'linətē, sə-\ n

**sa·li·va** \sə'līvə\ n : liquid secreted into the mouth — **sal·i·vary** \'saləˌverē\ adj — **sal·i·vate** \-ˌvāt\ vb — **sal·i·va·tion** \ˌsalə'vāshən\ n

**sal·low** \'salō\ adj : of a yellowish sickly color

**sal·ly** \'salē\ n, pl -lies 1 : quick attack on besiegers 2 : witty remark — **sally** vb

**salm·on** \'samən\ n, pl salmon 1 : food fish with pink or red flesh 2 : deep yellowish pink color

**sa·lon** \sə'län, 'salˌän, sa'lōⁿ\ n : elegant room or shop

**sa·loon** \sə'lün\ n 1 : public cabin on a passenger ship 2 : barroom

**sal·sa** \'sólsə, 'säl-\ n : spicy sauce of tomatoes, onions, and hot peppers

**salt** \'sólt\ n 1 : white crystalline substance that consists of sodium and chlorine 2 : compound formed usu. from acid and metal — **salt** vb or adj — **salt·i·ness** n — **salty** adj

**salt·wa·ter** adj : relating to or living in salt water

**sa·lu·bri·ous** \sə'lübrēəs\ adj : good for health

**sal·u·tary** \'salyə,terē\ *adj* : health=giving or beneficial

**sal·u·ta·tion** \,salyə'tāshən\ *n* : greeting

**sa·lute** \sə'lüt\ *vb* **-lut·ed; -lut·ing** : honor by ceremony or formal movement — **salute** *n*

**sal·vage** \'salvij\ *n* : something saved from destruction ∼ *vb* **-vaged; -vag·ing** : rescue or save

**sal·va·tion** \sal'vāshən\ *n* : saving of a person from sin or danger

**salve** \'sav, 'sàv\ *n* : medicinal ointment ∼ *vb* **salved; salv·ing** : soothe

**sal·ver** \'salvər\ *n* : small tray

**sal·vo** \'salvō\ *n, pl* **-vos** *or* **-voes** : simultaneous discharge of guns

**same** \'sām\ *adj* : being the one referred to ∼ *pron* : the same one or ones ∼ *adv* : in the same manner — **same·ness** *n*

**sam·ple** \'sampəl\ *n* : piece or part that shows the quality of a whole ∼ *vb* **-pled; -pling** : judge by a sample

**sam·pler** \'samplər\ *n* : piece of needlework testing skill in embroidering

**san·a·to·ri·um** \,sanə'tōrēəm\ *n, pl* **-riums** *or* **-ria** \-ēə\ : hospital for the chronically ill

**sanc·ti·fy** \'saŋktə,fī\ *vb* **-fied; -fy·ing** : make holy — **sanc·ti·fi·ca·tion** \,saŋktəfə'kāshən\ *n*

**sanc·ti·mo·nious** \,saŋktə'mōnēəs\ *adj* : hypocritically pious — **sanc·ti·mo·nious·ly** *adv*

**sanc·tion** \'saŋkshən\ *n* **1** : authoritative approval **2** : coercive measure — usu. pl ∼ *vb* : approve

**sanc·ti·ty** \'saŋktətē\ *n, pl* **-ties** : quality or state of being holy or sacred

**sanc·tu·ary** \'saŋkchə,werē\ *n, pl* **-aries** **1** : consecrated place **2** : place of refuge

**sand** \'sand\ *n* : loose granular particles of rock ∼ *vb* : smooth with an abrasive — **sand·bank** *n* — **sand·er** *n* — **sand·storm** *n* — **sandy** *adj*

**san·dal** \'sand°l\ *n* : shoe consisting of a sole strapped to the foot

**sand·pa·per** *n* : abrasive paper — **sandpaper** *vb*

**sand·pip·er** \-,pīpər\ *n* : long-billed shorebird

**sand·stone** *n* : rock made of naturally cemented sand

**sand·wich** \'sand,wich\ *n* : 2 or more slices of bread with a filling between them ∼ *vb* : squeeze or crowd in

**sane** \'sān\ *adj* **san·er; san·est** **1** : mentally healthy **2** : sensible — **sane·ly** *adv*

**sang** *past of* SING

**san·gui·nary** \'saŋgwə,nerē\ *adj* : bloody

**san·guine** \'saŋgwən\ *adj* **1** : reddish **2** : cheerful

**san·i·tar·i·um** \,sanə'terēəm\ *n, pl* **-i·ums** *or* **-ia** \-ēə\ : sanatorium

**san·i·tary** \'sanəterē\ *adj* **1** : relating to health **2** : free from filth or infective matter

**san·i·ta·tion** \,sanə'tāshən\ *n* : protection of health by maintenance of sanitary conditions

**san·i·ty** \'sanətē\ *n* : soundness of mind

**sank** *past of* SINK

**¹sap** \'sap\ *n* **1** : fluid that circulates through a plant **2** : gullible person

**²sap** *vb* **-pp-** **1** : undermine **2** : weaken or exhaust gradually

**sa·pi·ent** \'sāpēənt, 'sapē-\ *adj* : wise — **sa·pi·ence** \-əns\ *n*

**sap·ling** \'saplin\ *n* : young tree

**sap·phire** \'saf,īr\ *n* : hard transparent blue gem

**sap·py** \'sapē\ *adj* **-pi·er; -est** **1** : full of sap **2** : overly sentimental

**sap·suck·er** \'sap,səkər\ *n* : small No. American woodpecker

**sar·casm** \'sär,kazəm\ *n* **1** : cutting remark **2** : ironical criticism or reproach — **sar·cas·tic** \sär'kastik\ *adj* — **sar·cas·ti·cal·ly** *adv*

**sar·coph·a·gus** \sär'käfəgəs\ *n, pl* **-gi** \-,gī, -,jī\ : large stone coffin

**sar·dine** \sär'dēn\ *n* : small fish preserved for use as food

**sar·don·ic** \sär'dänik\ *adj* : disdainfully humorous — **sar·don·i·cal·ly** *adv*

**sa·rong** \sə'röŋ, -'räŋ\ *n* : loose garment worn esp. by Pacific islanders

**sar·sa·pa·ril·la** \,saspə'rilə, ,särs-\ *n* : dried roots of a tropical American plant used esp. for flavoring or a carbonated drink flavored with this

**sar·to·ri·al** \sär'tōrēəl\ *adj* : relating to a tailor or men's clothes

**¹sash** \'sash\ *n* : broad band worn around the waist or over the shoulder

**²sash** *n, pl* **sash** **1** : frame for a pane of glass in a door or window **2** : movable part of a window

**sas·sa·fras** \'sasə,fras\ *n* : No. American tree or its dried root bark

**sassy** \'sasē\ *adj* **sass·i·er; -est** : saucy

**sat** *past of* SIT

**Sa•tan** \'sāt³n\ *n* : devil — **sa•tan•ic** \sə-'tanik, sā-\ *adj* — **sa•tan•i•cal•ly** *adv*

**satch•el** \'sachəl\ *n* : small bag

**sate** \'sāt\ *vb* **sat•ed; sat•ing** : satisfy fully

**sat•el•lite** \'sat³l‚īt\ *n* **1** : toady **2** : body or object that revolves around a larger celestial body

**sa•ti•ate** \'sāshē‚āt\ *vb* **-at•ed; -at•ing** : sate — **sa•ti•ety** \sə'tīətē\ *n*

**sat•in** \'sat³n\ *n* : glossy fabric — **sat•iny** *adj*

**sat•ire** \'sa‚tīr\ *n* : literary ridicule done with humor — **sa•tir•ic** \sə'tirik\, **sa•tir•i•cal** \-ikəl\ *adj* — **sa•tir•i•cal•ly** *adv* — **sat•i•rist** \'satərist\ *n* — **sat•i•rize** \-ə‚rīz\ *vb*

**sat•is•fac•tion** \‚satəs'fakshən\ *n* : state of being satisfied — **sat•is•fac•to•ri•ly** \-'faktərəlē\ *adv* — **sat•is•fac•to•ry** \-'faktərē\ *adj*

**sat•is•fy** \'satəs‚fī\ *vb* **-fied; -fy•ing 1** : make happy **2** : pay what is due to or on — **sat•is•fy•ing•ly** *adv*

**sat•u•rate** \'sachə‚rāt\ *vb* **-rat•ed; -rat•ing** : soak or charge thoroughly — **sat•u•ra•tion** \‚sachə'rāshən\ *n*

**Sat•ur•day** \'satərdā, -dē\ *n* : 7th day of the week

**sat•ur•nine** \'satər‚nīn\ *adj* : sullen

**sa•tyr** \'sātər, 'sat-\ *n* : pleasure-loving forest god of ancient Greece

**sauce** \'sós\ *n* : fluid dressing or topping for food — **sauce•pan** *n*

**sau•cer** \'sósər\ *n* : small shallow dish under a cup

**saucy** \'sasē, 'sósē\ *adj* **sauc•i•er; -est** : insolent — **sauc•i•ly** *adv* — **sauc•i•ness** *n*

**sau•er•kraut** \'sau̇ər‚krau̇t\ *n* : finely cut and fermented cabbage

**sau•na** \'sau̇nə\ *n* : steam or dry heat bath or a room or cabinet used for such a bath

**saun•ter** \'sóntər, 'sänt-\ *vb* : stroll

**sau•sage** \'sósij\ *n* : minced and highly seasoned meat

**sau•té** \sȯ'tā, sō-\ *vb* **-téed** *or* **-téd; -té•ing** : fry in a little fat — **sauté** *n*

**sav•age** \'savij\ *adj* **1** : wild **2** : cruel ~ *n* : person belonging to a primitive society — **sav•age•ly** *adv* — **sav•age•ness** *n* — **sav•age•ry** *n*

¹**save** \'sāv\ *vb* **saved; sav•ing 1** : rescue from danger **2** : guard from destruction **3** : redeem from sin **4** : put aside as a reserve — **sav•er** *n*

²**save** *prep* : except

**sav•ior, sav•iour** \'sāvyər\ *n* **1** : one who saves **2** *cap* : Jesus Christ

**sa•vor** \'sāvər\ *n* : special flavor ~ *vb* : taste with pleasure — **sa•vory** *adj*

¹**saw** *past of* SEE

²**saw** \'só\ *n* : cutting tool with teeth ~ *vb* **sawed; sawed** *or* **sawn;** : cut with a saw — **saw•dust** \-‚dəst\ *n* — **saw•mill** *n* — **saw•yer** \-yər\ *n*

**saw•horse** *n* : support for wood being sawed

**sax•o•phone** \'saksə‚fōn\ *n* : wind instrument with a reed mouthpiece and usu. a bent metal body

**say** \'sā\ *vb* **said** \'sed\; **say•ing** \'sāiŋ\; **says** \'sez\ **1** : express in words **2** : state positively ~ *n, pl* **says** \'sāz\ **1** : expression of opinion **2** : power of decision

**say•ing** \'sāiŋ\ *n* : commonly repeated statement

**scab** \'skab\ *n* **1** : protective crust over a sore or wound **2** : worker taking a striker's job ~ *vb* **-bb- 1** : become covered with a scab **2** : work as a scab — **scab•by** *adj*

**scab•bard** \'skabərd\ *n* : sheath for the blade of a weapon

**scaf•fold** \'skafəld, -‚ōld\ *n* **1** : raised platform for workmen **2** : platform on which a criminal is executed

**scald** \'skóld\ *vb* **1** : burn with hot liquid or steam **2** : heat to the boiling point

¹**scale** \'skāl\ *n* : weighing device ~ *vb* **scaled; scal•ing** : weigh

²**scale** *n* **1** : thin plate esp. on the body of a fish or reptile **2** : thin coating or layer ~ *vb* **scaled; scal•ing** : strip of scales — **scaled** \'skāld\ *adj* — **scaleless** *adj* — **scaly** *adj*

³**scale** *n* **1** : graduated series **2** : size of a sample (as a model) in proportion to the size of the actual thing **3** : standard of estimation or judgment **4** : series of musical tones ~ *vb* **scaled; scal•ing 1** : climb by a ladder **2** : arrange in a graded series

**scal•lion** \'skalyən\ *n* : bulbless onion

**scal•lop** \'skäləp, 'skal-\ *n* **1** : marine mollusk **2** : rounded projection on a border

**scalp** \'skalp\ *n* : skin and flesh of the head ~ *vb* **1** : remove the scalp from **2** : resell at a greatly increased price — **scalp•er** *n*

**scal•pel** \'skalpəl\ *n* : surgical knife

**scamp** \'skamp\ *n* : rascal

**scam·per** \'skampər\ *vb* : run nimbly — **scamper** *n*

**scan** \'skan\ *vb* **-nn-** **1** : read (verses) so as to show meter **2** : examine closely or hastily **3** : examine with a sensing device — **scan** *n* — **scan·ner** *n*

**scan·dal** \'skand°l\ *n* **1** : disgraceful situation **2** : malicious gossip — **scan·dal·ize** *vb* — **scan·dal·ous** *adj*

**scant** \'skant\ *adj* : barely sufficient ∼ *vb* : stint — **scant·i·ly** *adv* — **scanty** *adj*

**scape·goat** \'skāp₁gōt\ *n* : one that bears the blame for others

**scap·u·la** \'skapyələ\ *n, pl* **-lae** \-₁lē\ *or* **-las** : shoulder blade

**scar** \'skär\ *n* : mark where a wound has healed — **scar** *vb*

**scar·ab** \'skarəb\ *n* : large dark beetle or an ornament representing one

**scarce** \'skers\ *adj* **scarc·er; scarc·est** : lacking in quantity or number — **scar·ci·ty** \'skersətē\ *n*

**scarce·ly** \'skerslē\ *adv* **1** : barely **2** : almost not

**scare** \'sker\ *vb* **scared; scar·ing** : frighten ∼ *n* : fright — **scary** *adj*

**scare·crow** \'sker₁krō\ *n* : figure for scaring birds from crops

**scarf** \'skärf\ *n, pl* **scarves** \'skärvz\ *or* **scarfs** : cloth worn about the shoulders or the neck

**scar·let** \'skärlət\ *n* : bright red color — **scarlet** *adj*

**scarlet fever** *n* : acute contagious disease marked by fever, sore throat, and red rash

**scath·ing** \'skāthiŋ\ *adj* : bitterly severe

**scat·ter** \'skatər\ *vb* **1** : spread about irregularly **2** : disperse

**scav·en·ger** \'skavənjər\ *n* **1** : person that collects refuse or waste **2** : animal that feeds on decayed matter — **scav·enge** \'skavənj\ *vb*

**sce·nar·io** \sə'narē₁ō, -'när-\ *n, pl* **-i·os** **1** : plot of a play or movie **2** : possible sequence of events

**scene** \'sēn\ *n* **1** : single situation in a play or movie **2** : stage setting **3** : view **4** : display of emotion — **sce·nic** \'sēnik\ *adj*

**scen·ery** \'sēnərē\ *n, pl* **-er·ies** **1** : painted setting for a stage **2** : picturesque view

**scent** \'sent\ *vb* **1** : smell **2** : fill with odor ∼ *n* **1** : odor **2** : sense of smell **3** : perfume — **scent·ed** \'sentəd\ *adj*

**scep·ter** \'septər\ *n* : staff signifying authority

**scep·tic** \'skeptik\ *var of* SKEPTIC

**sched·ule** \'skejül, *esp Brit* 'shedyül\ *n* : list showing sequence of events ∼ *vb* **-uled; -ul·ing** : make a schedule of

**scheme** \'skēm\ *n* **1** : crafty plot **2** : systematic design ∼ *vb* **schemed; schem·ing** : form a plot — **sche·mat·ic** \ski'matik\ *adj* — **schem·er** *n*

**schism** \'sizəm, 'skiz-\ *n* : split — **schis·mat·ic** \siz'matik, skiz-\ *n or adj*

**schizo·phre·nia** \₁skitsə'frēnēə\ *n* : severe mental illness — **schiz·oid** \'skit₁sòid\ *adj or n* — **schizo·phren·ic** \₁skitsə'frenik\ *adj or n*

**schol·ar** \'skälər\ *n* : student or learned person — **schol·ar·ly** *adj*

**schol·ar·ship** \-₁ship\ *n* **1** : qualities or learning of a scholar **2** : money given to a student to pay for education

**scho·las·tic** \skə'lastik\ *adj* : relating to schools, scholars, or scholarship

**¹school** \'skül\ *n* **1** : institution for learning **2** : pupils in a school **3** : group with shared beliefs ∼ *vb* : teach — **school·boy** *n* — **school·girl** *n* — **school·house** *n* — **school·mate** *n* — **school·room** *n* — **school·teach·er** *n*

**²school** *n* : large number of fish swimming together

**schoo·ner** \'skünər\ *n* : sailing ship

**sci·ence** \'sīəns\ *n* : branch of systematic study esp. of the physical world — **sci·en·tif·ic** \₁sīən'tifik\ *adj* — **sci·en·tif·i·cal·ly** *adv* — **sci·en·tist** \'sīəntist\ *n*

**scin·til·late** \'sint°l₁āt\ *vb* **-lat·ed; -lat·ing** : flash — **scin·til·la·tion** \₁sint°l-'āshən\ *n*

**scin·til·lat·ing** *adj* : brilliantly lively or witty

**sci·on** \'sīən\ *n* : descendant

**scis·sors** \'sizərz\ *n pl* : small shears

**scoff** \'skäf\ *vb* : mock — **scoff·er** *n*

**scold** \'skōld\ *n* : person who scolds ∼ *vb* : criticize severely

**scoop** \'sküp\ *n* : shovellike utensil ∼ *vb* **1** : take out with a scoop **2** : dig out

**scoot** \'süt\ *vb* : move swiftly

**scoot·er** \'skütər\ *n* : child's foot-propelled vehicle

**¹scope** \'skōp\ *n* **1** : extent **2** : room for development

**²scope** *n* : viewing device (as a microscope)

**scorch** \'skorch\ *vb* : burn the surface of

**score** \'skōr\ *n, pl* **scores 1** *or pl* **score** : twenty **2** : cut **3** : record of points made (as in a game) **4** : debt **5** : music of a composition ~ *vb* **scored; scor·ing 1** : record **2** : mark with lines **3** : gain in a game **4** : assign a grade to **5** : compose a score for — **score·less** *adj* — **scor·er** *n*

**scorn** \'skorn\ *n* : emotion involving both anger and disgust ~ *vb* : hold in contempt — **scorn·er** *n* — **scorn·ful** \-fəl\ *adj* — **scorn·ful·ly** *adv*

**scor·pi·on** \'skorpēən\ *n* : poisonous long-tailed animal

**scoun·drel** \'skaundrəl\ *n* : villain

**¹scour** \'skauər\ *vb* : examine thoroughly

**²scour** *vb* : rub in order to clean

**scourge** \'skərj\ *n* **1** : whip **2** : punishment ~ *vb* **scourged; scourg·ing 1** : lash **2** : punish severely

**scout** \'skaut\ *vb* : inspect or observe to get information ~ *n* : person sent out to get information

**scow** \'skau\ *n* : large flat-bottomed boat with square ends

**scowl** \'skaul\ *vb* : make a frowning expression of displeasure — **scowl** *n*

**scrag·gly** \'skraglē\ *adj* : irregular or unkempt

**scram** \'skram\ *vb* **-mm-** : go away at once

**scram·ble** \'skrambəl\ *vb* **-bled; -bling 1** : clamber clumsily around **2** : struggle for possession of something **3** : mix together **4** : cook (eggs) by stirring during frying — **scramble** *n*

**¹scrap** \'skrap\ *n* **1** : fragment **2** : discarded material ~ *vb* **-pp-** : get rid of as useless

**²scrap** *vb* **-pp-** : fight — **scrap** *n* — **scrap·per** *n*

**scrap·book** *n* : blank book in which mementos are kept

**scrape** \'skrāp\ *vb* **scraped; scrap·ing 1** : remove by drawing a knife over **2** : clean or smooth by rubbing **3** : draw across a surface with a grating sound **4** : damage by contact with a rough surface **5** : gather or proceed with difficulty ~ *n* **1** : act of scraping **2** : predicament — **scrap·er** *n*

**scratch** \'skrach\ *vb* **1** : scrape or dig with or as if with claws or nails **2** : cause to move gratingly **3** : delete by or as if by drawing a line through

~ *n* : mark or sound made in scratching — **scratchy** *adj*

**scrawl** \'skrol\ *vb* : write hastily and carelessly — **scrawl** *n*

**scraw·ny** \'skronē\ *adj* **-ni·er; -est** : very thin

**scream** \'skrēm\ *vb* : cry out loudly and shrilly ~ *n* : loud shrill cry

**screech** \'skrēch\ *vb or n* : shriek

**screen** \'skrēn\ *n* **1** : device or partition used to protect or decorate **2** : surface on which pictures appear (as in movies) ~ *vb* : shield or separate with or as if with a screen

**screw** \'skrü\ *n* **1** : grooved fastening device **2** : propeller ~ *vb* **1** : fasten by means of a screw **2** : move spirally

**screw·driv·er** \'skrü,drīvər\ *n* : tool for turning screws

**scrib·ble** \'skribəl\ *vb* **-bled; -bling** : write hastily or carelessly — **scrib·ble** *n* — **scrib·bler** \-ələr\ *n*

**scribe** \'skrīb\ *n* : one who writes or copies writing

**scrimp** \'skrimp\ *vb* : economize greatly

**scrip** \'skrip\ *n* **1** : paper money for less than a dollar **2** : certificate entitling one to something (as stock)

**script** \'skript\ *n* : text (as of a play)

**scrip·ture** \'skripchər\ *n* : sacred writings of a religion — **scrip·tur·al** \'skripchərəl\ *adj*

**scroll** \'skrōl\ *n* **1** : roll of paper for writing a document **2** : spiral or coiled design

**scro·tum** \'skrōtəm\ *n, pl* **-ta** \-ə\ *or* **-tums** : pouch containing the testes

**scrounge** \'skraunj\ *vb* **scrounged; scroung·ing** : collect by or as if by foraging

**¹scrub** \'skrəb\ *n* : stunted tree or shrub or a growth of these — **scrub** *adj* — **scrub·by** *adj*

**²scrub** *vb* **-bb-** : clean or wash by rubbing — **scrub** *n*

**scruff** \'skrəf\ *n* : loose skin of the back of the neck

**scrump·tious** \'skrəmpshəs\ *adj* : delicious

**scru·ple** \'skrüpəl\ *n* : reluctance due to ethical considerations — **scruple** *vb* — **scru·pu·lous** \-pyələs\ *adj* — **scru·pu·lous·ly** *adv*

**scru·ti·ny** \'skrüt°nē\ *n, pl* **-nies** : careful inspection — **scru·ti·nize** \-°n,īz\ *vb*

**scud** \'skəd\ *vb* **-dd-** : move speedily

**scuff** \'skəf\ *vb* : scratch, scrape, or wear away — **scuff** *n*

**scuf·fle** \'skəfəl\ *vb* -**fled**; -**fling 1** : struggle at close quarters **2** : shuffle one's feet — **scuffle** *n*

**scull** \'skəl\ *n* **1** : oar **2** : racing shell propelled with sculls ∼ *vb* : propel a boat by an oar over the stern

**scul·lery** \'skələrē\ *n, pl* -**ler·ies** : room for cleaning dishes and cookware

**sculpt** \'skəlpt\ *vb* : sculpture

**sculp·ture** \'skəlpchər\ *n* : work of art carved or molded ∼ *vb* -**tured**; -**turing** : form as sculpture — **sculp·tor** \-tər\ *n* — **sculp·tur·al** \-chərəl\ *adj*

**scum** \'skəm\ *n* : slimy film on a liquid

**scur·ri·lous** \'skərələs\ *adj* : vulgar or abusive

**scur·ry** \'skərē\ *vb* -**ried**; -**ry·ing** : scamper

**scur·vy** \'skərvē\ *n* : vitamin-deficiency disease

¹**scut·tle** \'skət⁰l\ *n* : pail for coal

²**scuttle** *vb* -**tled**; -**tling** : sink (a ship) by cutting holes in its bottom

³**scuttle** *vb* -**tled**; -**tling** : scamper

**scythe** \'sīth\ *n* : tool for mowing by hand — **scythe** *vb*

**sea** \'sē\ *n* **1** : large body of salt water **2** : ocean **3** : rough water — **sea** *adj* — **sea·coast** *n* — **sea·food** *n* — **sea·port** *n* — **sea·shore** *n* — **sea·wa·ter** *n*

**sea·bird** *n* : bird frequenting the open ocean

**sea·board** *n* : country's seacoast

**sea·far·er** \-,farər\ *n* : seaman — **sea·far·ing** \-,fariŋ\ *adj or n*

**sea horse** *n* : small fish with a horselike head

¹**seal** \'sēl\ *n* : large sea mammal of cold regions — **seal·skin** *n*

²**seal** *n* **1** : device for stamping a design **2** : something that closes ∼ *vb* **1** : affix a seal to **2** : close up securely **3** : determine finally — **seal·ant** \-ənt\ *n* — **seal·er** *n*

**sea lion** *n* : large Pacific seal with external ears

**seam** \'sēm\ *n* **1** : line of junction of 2 edges **2** : layer of a mineral ∼ *vb* : join by sewing — **seam·less** *adj*

**sea·man** \'sēmən\ *n* **1** : one who helps to handle a ship **2** : naval enlisted man ranking next below a petty officer third class — **sea·man·ship** *n*

**seaman apprentice** *n* : naval enlisted man ranking next below a seaman

**seaman recruit** *n* : naval enlisted man of the lowest rank

**seam·stress** \'sēmstrəs\ *n* : woman who sews

**seamy** \'sēmē\ *adj* **seam·i·er**; -**est** : unpleasant or sordid

**sé·ance** \'sā,äns\ *n* : meeting for communicating with spirits

**sea·plane** *n* : airplane that can take off from and land on the water

**sear** \'sir\ *vb* : scorch — **sear** *n*

**search** \'sərch\ *vb* **1** : look through **2** : seek — **search** *n* — **search·er** *n* — **search·light** *n*

**search engine** *n* : computer software used to search for specified information on the World Wide Web

**sea·sick** *adj* : nauseated by the motion of a ship — **sea·sick·ness** *n*

¹**sea·son** \'sēz⁰n\ *n* **1** : division of the year **2** : customary time for something — **sea·son·al** \'sēz⁰nəl\ *adj* — **sea·son·al·ly** *adv*

²**season** *vb* **1** : add spice to (food) **2** : make strong or fit for use — **sea·son·ing** \-⁰niŋ\ *n*

**sea·son·able** \'sēznəbəl\ *adj* : occurring at a suitable time — **sea·son·ably** \-blē\ *adv*

**seat** \'sēt\ *n* **1** : place to sit **2** : chair, bench, or stool for sitting on **3** : place that serves as a capital or center ∼ *vb* **1** : place in or on a seat **2** : provide seats for

**sea·weed** *n* : marine alga

**sea·wor·thy** *adj* : strong enough to hold up to a sea voyage

**se·cede** \si'sēd\ *vb* -**ced·ed**; -**ced·ing** : withdraw from a body (as a nation)

**se·clude** \si'klüd\ *vb* -**clud·ed**; -**cluding** : shut off alone — **se·clu·sion** \si'klüzhən\ *n*

¹**sec·ond** \'sekənd\ *adj* : next after the 1st ∼ *n* **1** : one that is second **2** : one who assists (as in a duel) — **sec·ond, se·cond·ly** *adv*

²**second** *n* **1** : 60th part of a minute **2** : moment

**sec·ond·ary** \'sekən,derē\ *adj* **1** : second in rank or importance **2** : coming after the primary or elementary

**sec·ond·hand** *adj* **1** : not original **2** : used before

**second lieutenant** *n* : lowest ranking commissioned officer of the army, air force, or marines

**se·cret** \'sēkrət\ *adj* **1** : hidden **2**

: kept from general knowledge — **se-cre-cy** \-krəsē\ *n* — **secret** *n* — **se-cre-tive** \'sēkrətiv, si'krēt-\ *adj* — **se-cret-ly** *adv*

**sec-re-tar-i-at** \ˌsekrə'terēət\ *n* : administrative department

**sec-re-tary** \'sekrəˌterē\ *n, pl* **-tar-ies** **1** : one hired to handle correspondence and other tasks for a superior **2** : official in charge of correspondence or records **3** : head of a government department — **sec-re-tari-al** \ˌsekrə-'terēəl\ *adj*

**¹se-crete** \si'krēt\ *vb* **-cret-ed; -cret-ing** : produce as a secretion

**²se-crete** \si'krēt, 'sēkrət\ *vb* **-cret-ed; -cret-ing** : hide

**se-cre-tion** \si'krēshən\ *n* **1** : process of secreting **2** : product of glandular activity

**sect** \'sekt\ *n* : religious group

**sec-tar-i-an** \sek'terēən\ *adj* **1** : relating to a sect **2** : limited in character or scope ~ *n* : member of a sect

**sec-tion** \'sekshən\ *n* : distinct part — **sec-tion-al** \-shənəl\ *adj*

**sec-tor** \'sektər\ *n* **1** : part of a circle between 2 radii **2** : distinctive part

**sec-u-lar** \'sekyələr\ *adj* **1** : not sacred **2** : not monastic

**se-cure** \si'kyu̇r\ *adj* **-cur-er; -est** : free from danger or loss ~ *vb* **1** : fasten safely **2** : get — **se-cure-ly** *adv*

**se-cu-ri-ty** \si'kyu̇rətē\ *n, pl* **-ties** **1** : safety **2** : something given to guarantee payment **3** *pl* : bond or stock certificates

**se-dan** \si'dan\ *n* **1** : chair carried by 2 men **2** : enclosed automobile

**¹se-date** \si'dāt\ *adj* : quiet and dignified — **se-date-ly** *adv*

**²sedate** *vb* **-dat-ed; -dat-ing** : dose with sedatives — **se-da-tion** \si'dāshən\ *n*

**sed-a-tive** \'sedətiv\ *adj* : serving to relieve tension ~ *n* : sedative drug

**sed-en-tary** \'sedᵊnˌterē\ *adj* : characterized by much sitting

**sedge** \'sej\ *n* : grasslike marsh plant

**sed-i-ment** \'sedəmənt\ *n* : material that settles to the bottom of a liquid or is deposited by water or a glacier — **sed-i-men-ta-ry** \ˌsedə'mentərē\ *adj* — **sed-i-men-ta-tion** \-mən'tā-shən, -ˌmen-\ *n*

**se-di-tion** \si'dishən\ *n* : revolution against a government — **se-di-tious** \-əs\ *adj*

**se-duce** \si'düs, -'dyüs\ *vb* **-duced;** **-duc-ing** **1** : lead astray **2** : entice to sexual intercourse — **se-duc-er** *n* — **se-duc-tion** \-'dəkshən\ *n* — **se-duc-tive** \-tiv\ *adj*

**sed-u-lous** \'sejələs\ *adj* : diligent

**¹see** \'sē\ *vb* **saw** \'sȯ\; **seen** \'sēn\; **see-ing** **1** : perceive by the eye **2** : have experience of **3** : understand **4** : make sure **5** : meet with or escort

**²see** *n* : jurisdiction of a bishop

**seed** \'sēd\ *n, pl* **seed** *or* **seeds** **1** : part by which a plant is propagated **2** : source ~ *vb* **1** : sow **2** : remove seeds from — **seed-less** *adj*

**seed-ling** \-liŋ\ *n* : young plant grown from seed

**seedy** \-ē\ *adj* **seed-i-er; -est** **1** : full of seeds **2** : shabby

**seek** \'sēk\ *vb* **sought** \'sȯt\; **seek-ing** **1** : search for **2** : try to reach or obtain — **seek-er** *n*

**seem** \'sēm\ *vb* : give the impression of being — **seem-ing-ly** *adv*

**seem-ly** \-lē\ *adj* **seem-li-er; -est** : proper or fit

**seep** \'sēp\ *vb* : leak through fine pores or cracks — **seep-age** \'sēpij\ *n*

**seer** \'sēər\ *n* : one who foresees or predicts events

**seer-suck-er** \'sirˌsəkər\ *n* : light puckered fabric

**see-saw** \'sēˌsȯ\ *n* : board balanced in the middle — **seesaw** *vb*

**seethe** \'sēth\ *vb* **seethed; seeth-ing** : become violently agitated

**seg-ment** \'segmənt\ *n* : division of a thing — **seg-ment-ed** \-ˌmentəd\ *adj*

**seg-re-gate** \'segriˌgāt\ *vb* **-gat-ed; -gat-ing** **1** : cut off from others **2** : separate by races — **seg-re-ga-tion** \ˌsegri'gāshən\ *n*

**seine** \'sān\ *n* : large weighted fishing net ~ *vb* : fish with a seine

**seis-mic** \'sīzmik, 'sīs-\ *adj* : relating to an earthquake

**seis-mo-graph** \-mə̱ˌgraf\ *n* : apparatus for detecting earthquakes

**seize** \'sēz\ *vb* **seized; seiz-ing** : take by force — **sei-zure** \'sēzhər\ *n*

**sel-dom** \'seldəm\ *adv* : not often

**se-lect** \sə'lekt\ *adj* **1** : favored **2** : discriminating ~ *vb* : take by preference — **se-lec-tive** \-'lektiv\ *adj*

**se-lec-tion** \sə'lekshən\ *n* : act of selecting or thing selected

**se-lect-man** \si'lektˌman, -mən\ *n* : New England town official

**self** \'self\ *n, pl* **selves** \'selvz\ : essential person distinct from others

**self-** *comb form* **1** : oneself or itself **2** : of oneself or itself **3** : by oneself or automatic **4** : to, for, or toward oneself

**self-cen•tered** *adj* : concerned only with one's own self

**self-con•scious** *adj* : uncomfortably aware of oneself as an object of observation — **self-con•scious•ly** *adv* — **self-con•scious•ness** *n*

**self•ish** \'selfish\ *adj* : excessively or exclusively concerned with one's own well-being — **self•ish•ly** *adv* — **self•ish•ness** *n*

**self•less** \'selfləs\ *adj* : unselfish — **self•less•ness** *n*

**self-made** *adj* : having succeeded by one's own efforts

**self-righ•teous** *adj* : strongly convinced of one's own righteousness

**self•same** \'self,sām\ *adj* : precisely the same

**sell** \'sel\ *vb* **sold** \'sōld\; **sell•ing 1** : transfer (property) esp. for money **2**
: deal in as a business **3** : be sold — **sell•er** *n*

**selves** *pl of* SELF

**se•man•tic** \si'mantik\ *adj* : relating to meaning in language — **se•man•tics** \-iks\ *n sing or pl*

**sem•a•phore** \'semə,fōr\ *n* **1** : visual signaling apparatus **2** : signaling by flags

**sem•blance** \'sembləns\ *n* : appearance

**se•men** \'sēmən\ *n* : male reproductive fluid

**se•mes•ter** \sə'mestər\ *n* : half a school year

**semi-** \,semi, 'sem-, -,ī\ *prefix* **1** : half **2** : partial

**semi•co•lon** \'semi,kōlən\ *n* : punctuation mark ;

**semi•con•duc•tor** *n* : substance between a conductor and a nonconductor in ability to conduct electricity — **semi•con•duct•ing** *adj*

**semi•fi•nal** *adj* : being next to the final — **semifinal** *n*

**semi•for•mal** *adj* : being or suitable for an occasion of moderate formality

---

**List of self-explanatory words with the prefix *self-***

| | | |
|---|---|---|
| self–addressed | self–destructive | self–operating |
| self–administered | self–determination | self–pity |
| self–analysis | self–determined | self–portrait |
| self–appointed | self–discipline | self–possessed |
| self–assertive | self–doubt | self–possession |
| self–assurance | self–educated | self–preservation |
| self–assured | self–employed | self–proclaimed |
| self–awareness | self–employment | self–propelled |
| self–cleaning | self–esteem | self–propelling |
| self–closing | self–evident | self–protection |
| self–complacent | self–explanatory | self–reliance |
| self–conceit | self–expression | self–reliant |
| self–confessed | self–fulfilling | self–respect |
| self–confidence | self–fulfillment | self–respecting |
| self–confident | self–governing | self–restraint |
| self–contained | self–government | self–sacrifice |
| self–contempt | self–help | self–satisfaction |
| self–contradiction | self–image | self–satisfied |
| self–contradictory | self–importance | self–service |
| self–control | self–important | self–serving |
| self–created | self–imposed | self–starting |
| self–criticism | self–improvement | self–styled |
| self–defeating | self–indulgence | self–sufficiency |
| self–defense | self–indulgent | self–sufficient |
| self–denial | self–inflicted | self–supporting |
| self–denying | self–interest | self–taught |
| self–destruction | self–love | self–winding |

**sem•i•nal** \'semən°l\ *adj* **1** : relating to seed or semen **2** : causing or influencing later development

**sem•i•nar** \'semə‚när\ *n* : conference or conferencelike study

**sem•i•nary** \'semə‚nerē\ *n, pl* **-nar•ies** : school and esp. a theological school — **sem•i•nar•i•an** \‚semə'nerēən\ *n*

**sen•ate** \'senət\ *n* : upper branch of a legislature — **sen•a•tor** \-ər\ *n* — **sen•a•to•rial** \‚senə'tōrēəl\ *adj*

**send** \'send\ *vb* **sent** \'sent\; **send•ing** **1** : cause to go **2** : propel — **send•er** *n*

**se•nile** \'sēn‚īl, 'sen-\ *adj* : mentally deficient through old age — **se•nil•i•ty** \si'nilətē\ *n*

**se•nior** \'sēnyər\ *adj* : older or higher ranking — **senior** *n* — **se•nior•i•ty** \‚sēn'yórətē\ *n*

**senior chief petty officer** *n* : petty officer in the navy or coast guard ranking next below a master chief petty officer

**senior master sergeant** *n* : noncommissioned officer in the air force ranking next below a chief master sergeant

**sen•sa•tion** \sen'sāshən\ *n* **1** : bodily feeling **2** : condition of excitement or the cause of it — **sen•sa•tion•al** \-shənəl\ *adj*

**sense** \'sens\ *n* **1** : meaning **2** : faculty of perceiving something physical **3** : sound mental capacity ∼ *vb* **sensed; sens•ing** **1** : perceive by the senses **2** : detect automatically — **sense•less** *adj* — **sense•less•ly** *adv*

**sen•si•bil•i•ty** \‚sensə'bilətē\ *n, pl* **-ties** : delicacy of feeling

**sen•si•ble** \'sensəbəl\ *adj* **1** : capable of sensing or being sensed **2** : aware or conscious **3** : reasonable — **sen•si•bly** \-blē\ *adv*

**sen•si•tive** \'sensətiv\ *adj* **1** : subject to excitation by or responsive to stimuli **2** : having power of feeling **3** : easily affected — **sen•si•tive•ness** *n* — **sen•si•tiv•i•ty** \‚sensə'tivətē\ *n*

**sen•si•tize** \'sensə‚tīz\ *vb* **-tized; -tiz•ing** : make or become sensitive

**sen•sor** \'sen‚sòr, -sər\ *n* : device that responds to a physical stimulus

**sen•so•ry** \'sensərē\ *adj* : relating to sensation or the senses

**sen•su•al** \'senchəwəl, -shəwəl\ *adj* **1** : pleasing the senses **2** : devoted to the pleasures of the senses — **sen•su•al•ist** *n* — **sen•su•al•i•ty** \‚senchə-'walətē\ *n* — **sen•su•al•ly** *adv*

**sen•su•ous** \'senchəwəs\ *adj* : having strong appeal to the senses

**sent** *past of* SEND

**sen•tence** \'sent°ns, -°nz\ *n* **1** : judgment of a court **2** : grammatically self-contained speech unit ∼ *vb* **-tenced; -tenc•ing** : impose a sentence on

**sen•ten•tious** \sen'tenchəs\ *adj* : using pompous language

**sen•tient** \'senchēənt\ *adj* : capable of feeling

**sen•ti•ment** \'sentəmənt\ *n* **1** : belief **2** : feeling

**sen•ti•men•tal** \‚sentə'ment°l\ *adj* : influenced by tender feelings — **sen•ti•men•tal•ism** *n* — **sen•ti•men•tal•ist** *n* — **sen•ti•men•tal•i•ty** \-‚men-'talətē, -mən-\ *n* — **sen•ti•men•tal•ize** \-'ment°l‚īz\ *vb* — **sen•ti•men•tal•ly** *adv*

**sen•ti•nel** \'sent°nəl\ *n* : sentry

**sen•try** \'sentrē\ *n, pl* **-tries** : one who stands guard

**se•pal** \'sēpəl, 'sep-\ *n* : modified leaf in a flower calyx

**sep•a•rate** \'sepə‚rāt\ *vb* **-rat•ed; -rat•ing** **1** : set or keep apart **2** : become divided or detached ∼ \'seprət, 'sepə-\ *adj* **1** : not connected or shared **2** : distinct from each other — **sep•a•ra•ble** \'sepərəbəl\ *adj* — **sep•a•rate•ly** *adv* — **sep•a•ra•tion** \‚sepə'rāshən\ *n* — **sep•a•ra•tor** \'sepə‚rātər\ *n*

**se•pia** \'sēpēə\ *n* : brownish gray

**Sep•tem•ber** \sep'tembər\ *n* : 9th month of the year having 30 days

**sep•ul•chre, sep•ul•cher** \'sepəlkər\ *n* : burial vault — **se•pul•chral** \sə'pəlkrəl\ *adj*

**se•quel** \'sēkwəl\ *n* **1** : consequence or result **2** : continuation of a story

**se•quence** \'sēkwəns\ *n* : continuous or connected series — **se•quen•tial** \si-'kwenchəl\ *adj* — **se•quen•tial•ly** *adv*

**se•ques•ter** \si'kwestər\ *vb* : segregate

**se•quin** \'sēkwən\ *n* : spangle

**se•quoia** \si'kwóiə\ *n* : huge California coniferous tree

**sera** *pl of* SERUM

**ser•aph** \'serəf\ *n, pl* **-a•phim** \-ə‚fim\ *or* **-aphs** : angel — **se•raph•ic** \sə'rafik\ *adj*

**sere** \'sir\ *adj* : dried up or withered

**ser•e•nade** \‚serə'nād\ *n* : music sung or played esp. to a woman being courted — **serenade** *vb*

**ser·en·dip·i·ty** \\,serən'dipətē\ n : good luck in finding things not sought for — **ser·en·dip·i·tous** \-əs\ adj

**se·rene** \sə'rēn\ adj : tranquil — **se·rene·ly** adv — **se·ren·i·ty** \sə-'renətē\ n

**serf** \'sərf\ n : peasant obligated to work the land — **serf·dom** \-dəm\ n

**serge** \'sərj\ n : twilled woolen cloth

**ser·geant** \'särjənt\ n : noncommissioned officer (as in the army) ranking next below a staff sergeant

**sergeant first class** n : noncommissioned officer in the army ranking next below a master sergeant

**sergeant major** n, pl **sergeants major** or **sergeant majors** 1 : noncommissioned officer serving as an enlisted adviser in a headquarters 2 : noncommissioned officer in the marine corps ranking above a first sergeant

**se·ri·al** \'sirēəl\ adj : being or relating to a series or sequence ~ n : story appearing in parts — **se·ri·al·ly** adv

**se·ries** \'sirēz\ n, pl **series** : number of things in order

**se·ri·ous** \'sirēəs\ adj 1 : subdued in appearance or manner 2 : sincere 3 : of great importance — **se·ri·ous·ly** adv — **se·ri·ous·ness** n

**ser·mon** \'sərmən\ n : lecture on religion or behavior

**ser·pent** \'sərpənt\ n : snake — **ser·pen·tine** \-pən,tēn, -,tīn\ adj

**ser·rated** \'ser,ātəd\ adj : saw-toothed

**se·rum** \'sirəm\ n, pl **-rums** or **-ra** \-ə\ : watery part of blood

**ser·vant** \'sərvənt\ n : person employed for domestic work

**serve** \'sərv\ vb **served; serv·ing** 1 : work through or perform a term of service 2 : be of use 3 : prove adequate 4 : hand out (food or drink) 5 : be of service to — **serv·er** n

**ser·vice** \'sərvəs\ n 1 : act or means of serving 2 : meeting for worship 3 : branch of public employment or the persons in it 4 : set of dishes or silverware 5 : benefit ~ vb **-viced; -vic·ing** : repair — **ser·vice·able** adj — **ser·vice·man** \-,man, -mən\ n — **ser·vice·wom·an** n

**ser·vile** \'sərvəl, -,vīl\ adj : behaving like a slave — **ser·vil·i·ty** \,sər-'vilətē\ n

**serv·ing** \'sərviŋ\ n : helping

**ser·vi·tude** \'sərvə,tüd, -,tyüd\ n : slavery

**ses·a·me** \'sesəmē\ n : annual herb or its seeds that are used in flavoring

**ses·sion** \'seshən\ n : meeting

**set** \'set\ vb **set; set·ting** 1 : cause to sit 2 : place 3 : settle, arrange, or adjust 4 : cause to be or do 5 : become fixed or solid 6 : sink below the horizon ~ adj : settled ~ n 1 : group classed together 2 : setting for the scene of a play or film 3 : electronic apparatus 4 : collection of mathematical elements — **set forth** : begin a trip — **set off** vb : set forth — **set out** vb : begin a trip or undertaking — **set up** vb 1 : assemble or erect 2 : cause

**set·back** n : reverse

**set·tee** \se'tē\ n : bench or sofa

**set·ter** \'setər\ n : large long-coated hunting dog

**set·ting** \'setiŋ\ n : the time, place, and circumstances in which something occurs

**set·tle** \'set°l\ vb **-tled; -tling** 1 : come to rest 2 : sink gradually 3 : establish in residence 4 : adjust or arrange 5 : calm 6 : dispose of (as by paying) 7 : decide or agree on — **set·tle·ment** \-mənt\ n — **set·tler** \'set°lər\ n

**sev·en** \'sevən\ n : one more than 6 — **seven** adj or pron — **sev·enth** \-ənth\ adj or adv or n

**sev·en·teen** \,sevən'tēn\ n : one more than 16 — **seventeen** adj or pron — **sev·en·teenth** \-'tēnth\ adj or n

**sev·en·ty** \'sevəntē\ n, pl **-ties** : 7 times 10 — **sev·en·ti·eth** \-tēəth\ adj or n — **seventy** adj or pron

**sev·er** \'sevər\ vb **-ered; -er·ing** : cut off or apart — **sev·er·ance** \'sevrəns, -vərəns\ n

**sev·er·al** \'sevrəl, 'sevə-\ adj 1 : distinct 2 : consisting of an indefinite but not large number — **sev·er·al·ly** adv

**se·vere** \sə'vir\ adj **-ver·er; -est** 1 : strict 2 : restrained or unadorned 3 : painful or distressing 4 : hard to endure — **se·vere·ly** adv — **se·ver·i·ty** \-'verətē\ n

**sew** \'sō\ vb **sewed; sewn** \'sōn\ or **sewed; sew·ing** : join or fasten by stitches — **sew·ing** n

**sew·age** \'süij\ n : liquid household waste

[1]**sew·er** \'sōər\ n : one that sews

[2]**sew·er** \'süər\ n : pipe or channel to carry off waste matter

**sex** \'seks\ n 1 : either of 2 divisions

into which organisms are grouped according to their reproductive roles or the qualities which differentiate them **2** : copulation — **sexed** \'sekst\ *adj* — **sex·less** *adj* — **sex·u·al** \'sek-shəwəl\ *adj* — **sex·u·al·i·ty** \ˌsekshə-'walətē\ *n* — **sex·u·al·ly** *adv* — **sexy** *adj*

**sex·ism** \'sekˌsizəm\ *n* : discrimination based on sex and esp. against women — **sex·ist** \'seksist\ *adj or n*

**sex·tant** \'sekstənt\ *n* : instrument for navigation

**sex·tet** \sek'stet\ *n* **1** : music for 6 performers **2** : group of 6

**sex·ton** \'sekstən\ *n* : church caretaker

**shab·by** \'shabē\ *adj* **-bi·er; -est 1** : worn and faded **2** : dressed in worn clothes **3** : not generous or fair — **shab·bi·ly** *adv* — **shab·bi·ness** *n*

**shack** \'shak\ *n* : hut

**shack·le** \'shakəl\ *n* : metal device to bind legs or arms ~ *vb* **-led; -ling** : bind or fasten with shackles

**shad** \'shad\ *n* : Atlantic food fish

**shade** \'shād\ *n* **1** : space sheltered from the light esp. of the sun **2** : gradation of color **3** : small difference **4** : something that shades ~ *vb* **shaded; shad·ing 1** : shelter from light and heat **2** : add shades of color to **3** : show slight differences esp. in color or meaning

**shad·ow** \'shadō\ *n* **1** : shade cast upon a surface by something blocking light **2** : trace **3** : gloomy influence ~ *vb* **1** : cast a shadow **2** : follow closely — **shad·owy** *adj*

**shady** \'shādē\ *adj* **shad·i·er; -est 1** : giving shade **2** : of dubious honesty

**shaft** \'shaft\ *n* **1** : long slender cylindrical part **2** : deep vertical opening (as of a mine)

**shag** \'shag\ *n* : shaggy tangled mat

**shag·gy** \'shagē\ *adj* **-gi·er; -est 1** : covered with long hair or wool **2** : not neat and combed

**shake** \'shāk\ *vb* **shook** \'shuk\; **shak·en** \'shākən\; **shak·ing 1** : move or cause to move quickly back and forth **2** : distress **3** : clasp (hands) as friendly gesture — **shake** *n* — **shak·er** \-ər\ *n*

**shake–up** *n* : reorganization

**shaky** \'shākē\ *adj* **shak·i·er; -est** : not sound, stable, or reliable — **shak·i·ly** *adv* — **shak·i·ness** *n*

**shale** \'shāl\ *n* : stratified rock

**shall** \'shal\ *vb, past* **should** \'shud\; *pres sing & pl* **shall** — used as an auxiliary to express a command, futurity, or determination

**shal·low** \'shalō\ *adj* **1** : not deep **2** : not intellectually profound

**shal·lows** \-ōz\ *n pl* : area of shallow water

**sham** \'sham\ *adj or n or vb* : fake

**sham·ble** \'shambəl\ *vb* **-bled; -bling** : shuffle along — **sham·ble** *n*

**sham·bles** \'shambəlz\ *n* : state of disorder

**shame** \'shām\ *n* **1** : distress over guilt or disgrace **2** : cause of shame or regret ~ *vb* **shamed; sham·ing 1** : make ashamed **2** : disgrace — **shame·ful** \-fəl\ *adj* — **shame·fully** \-ē\ *adv* — **shame·less** *adj* — **shame·less·ly** *adv*

**shame·faced** \'shām'fāst\ *adj* : ashamed

**sham·poo** \sham'pü\ *vb* : wash one's hair ~ *n, pl* **-poos** : act of or preparation used in shampooing

**sham·rock** \'shamˌräk\ *n* : plant of legend with 3-lobed leaves

**shank** \'shaŋk\ *n* : part of the leg between the knee and ankle

**shan·ty** \'shantē\ *n, pl* **-ties** : hut

**shape** \'shāp\ *vb* **shaped; shap·ing** : form esp. in a particular structure or appearance ~ *n* **1** : distinctive appearance or arrangement of parts **2** : condition — **shape·less** \-ləs\ *adj* — **shape·li·ness** *n* — **shape·ly** *adj*

**shard** \'shärd\ *n* : broken piece

**share** \'sher\ *n* **1** : portion belonging to one **2** : interest in a company's stock ~ *vb* **shared; shar·ing** : divide or use with others — **share·hold·er** *n* — **shar·er** *n*

**share·crop·per** \-ˌkräpər\ *n* : farmer who works another's land in return for a share of the crop — **share·crop** *vb*

**shark** \'shärk\ *n* : voracious sea fish

**sharp** \'shärp\ *adj* **1** : having a good point or cutting edge **2** : alert, clever, or sarcastic **3** : vigorous or fierce **4** : having prominent angles or a sudden change in direction **5** : distinct **6** : higher than the true pitch ~ *adv* : exactly ~ *n* : sharp note — **sharp·ly** *adv* — **sharp·ness** *n*

**sharp·en** \'shärpən\ *vb* : make sharp — **sharp·en·er** \-ənər\ *n*

**sharp·shoot·er** *n* : expert marksman — **sharp·shoot·ing** *n*

**shat·ter** \'shatər\ *vb* : smash or burst into fragments — **shat·ter·proof** \-ˌprüf\ *adj*

**shave** \'shāv\ *vb* **shaved; shaved** *or* **shav·en** \'shāvən\; **shav·ing 1** : cut off with a razor **2** : make bare by cutting the hair from **3** : slice very thin ∼ *n* : act or instance of shaving — **shav·er** *n*

**shawl** \'shȯl\ *n* : loose covering for the head or shoulders

**she** \'shē\ *pron* : that female one

**sheaf** \'shēf\ *n, pl* **sheaves** \'shēvz\ : bundle esp. of grain stalks

**shear** \'shir\ *vb* **sheared; sheared** *or* **shorn** \'shōrn\; **shear·ing 1** : trim wool from **2** : cut off with scissorlike action

**shears** \'shirz\ *n pl* : cutting tool with 2 blades fastened so that the edges slide by each other

**sheath** \'shēth\ *n, pl* **sheaths** \'shēthz, 'shēths\ : covering (as for a blade)

**sheathe** \'shēth\ *vb* **sheathed; sheath·ing** : put into a sheath

**shed** \'shed\ *vb* **shed; shed·ding 1** : give off (as tears or hair) **2** : cause to flow or diffuse ∼ *n* : small storage building

**sheen** \'shēn\ *n* : subdued luster

**sheep** \'shēp\ *n, pl* **sheep** : domesticated mammal covered with wool — **sheep·skin** *n*

**sheep·ish** \'shēpish\ *adj* : embarrassed by awareness of a fault

**sheer** \'shir\ *adj* **1** : pure **2** : very steep **3** : very thin or transparent

**sheet** \'shēt\ *n* : broad flat piece (as of cloth or paper)

**sheikh, sheik** \'shēk, 'shāk\ *n* : Arab chief — **sheikh·dom, sheik·dom** \-dəm\ *n*

**shelf** \'shelf\ *n, pl* **shelves** \'shelvz\ **1** : flat narrow structure used for storage or display **2** : sandbank or rock ledge

**shell** \'shel\ *n* **1** : hard or tough outer covering **2** : case holding explosive powder and projectile for a weapon **3** : light racing boat with oars ∼ *vb* **1** : remove the shell of **2** : bombard — **shelled** \'sheld\ *adj* — **shell·er** *n*

**shel·lac** \shə'lak\ *n* : varnish ∼ *vb* **-lacked; -lack·ing 1** : coat with shellac **2** : defeat — **shel·lack·ing** *n*

**shell·fish** *n* : water animal with a shell

**shel·ter** \'sheltər\ *n* : something that gives protection ∼ *vb* : give refuge to

**shelve** \'shelv\ *vb* **shelved; shelv·ing 1** : place or store on shelves **2** : dismiss or put aside

**she·nan·i·gans** \shə'nanigənz\ *n pl* : mischievous or deceitful conduct

**shep·herd** \'shepərd\ *n* : one that tends sheep ∼ *vb* : act as a shepherd or guardian

**shep·herd·ess** \'shepərdəs\ *n* : woman who tends sheep

**sher·bet** \'shərbət\, **sher·bert** \-bərt\ *n* : fruit-flavored frozen dessert

**sher·iff** \'sherəf\ *n* : county law officer

**sher·ry** \'sherē\ *n, pl* **-ries** : type of wine

**shield** \'shēld\ *n* **1** : broad piece of armor carried on the arm **2** : something that protects — **shield** *vb*

**shier** *comparative of* SHY

**shiest** *superlative of* SHY

**shift** \'shift\ *vb* **1** : change place, position, or direction **2** : get by ∼ *n* **1** : loose-fitting dress **2** : an act or instance of shifting **3** : scheduled work period

**shift·less** \-ləs\ *adj* : lazy

**shifty** \'shiftē\ *adj* **shift·i·er; -est** : tricky or untrustworthy

**shil·le·lagh** \shə'lālē\ *n* : club or stick

**shil·ling** \'shiliŋ\ *n* : former British coin

**shil·ly-shal·ly** \'shilē, shalē\ *vb* **-shal·lied; -shally·ing 1** : hesitate **2** : dawdle

**shim·mer** \'shimər\ *vb or n* : glimmer

**shin** \'shin\ *n* : front part of the leg below the knee ∼ *vb* **-nn-** : climb by sliding the body close along

**shine** \'shīn\ *vb* **shone** \-shōn\ *or* **shined; shin·ing 1** : give off or cause to give off light **2** : be outstanding **3** : polish ∼ *n* : brilliance

**shin·gle** \'shiŋgəl\ *n* **1** : small thin piece used in covering roofs or exterior walls — **shingle** *vb*

**shin·gles** \'shiŋgəlz\ *n pl* : acute inflammation of spinal nerves

**shin·ny** \'shinē\ *vb* **-nied; -ny·ing** : shin

**shiny** \'shīnē\ *adj* **shin·i·er; -est** : bright or polished

**ship** \'ship\ *n* **1** : large oceangoing vessel **2** : aircraft or spacecraft ∼ *vb* **-pp- 1** : put on a ship **2** : transport by carrier — **ship·board** *n* — **ship·build·er** *n* — **ship·per** *n* — **ship·wreck** *n or vb* — **ship·yard** *n*

**-ship** \ˌship\ *n suffix* **1** : state, condition, or quality **2** : rank or profession

**3** : skill **4** : something showing a state or quality

**ship·ment** \'ment\ *n* : an act of shipping or the goods shipped

**ship·ping** \'shipiŋ\ *n* **1** : ships **2** : transportation of goods

**ship·shape** *adj* : tidy

**shire** \'shīr, *in place-name compounds* ˌshir, shər\ *n* : British county

**shirk** \'shərk\ *vb* : evade — **shirk·er** *n*

**shirr** \'shər\ *vb* **1** : gather (cloth) by drawing up parallel lines of stitches **2** : bake (eggs) in a dish

**shirt** \'shərt\ *n* : garment for covering the torso — **shirt·less** *adj*

**shiv·er** \'shivər\ *vb* : tremble — **shiver** *n* — **shiv·ery** *adj*

**shoal** \'shōl\ *n* : shallow place (as in a river)

**¹shock** \'shäk\ *n* : pile of sheaves set up in a field

**²shock** *n* **1** : forceful impact **2** : violent mental or emotional disturbance **3** : effect of a charge of electricity **4** : depression of the vital bodily processes ~ *vb* **1** : strike with surprise, horror, or disgust **2** : subject to an electrical shock — **shock·proof** *adj*

**³shock** *n* : bushy mass (as of hair)

**shod·dy** \'shädē\ *adj* **-di·er; -est** : poorly made or done — **shod·di·ly** \'shädᵊlē\ *adv* — **shod·di·ness** *n*

**shoe** \'shü\ *n* **1** : covering for the human foot **2** : horseshoe ~ *vb* **shod** \'shäd\; **shoe·ing** : put horseshoes on — **shoe·lace** *n* — **shoe·ma·ker** *n*

**shone** *past of* SHINE

**shook** *past of* SHAKE

**shoot** \'shüt\ *vb* **shot** \'shät\; **shooting 1** : propel (as an arrow or bullet) **2** : wound or kill with a missile **3** : discharge (a weapon) **4** : drive (as a ball) at a goal **5** : photograph **6** : move swiftly ~ *n* : new plant growth — **shoot·er** *n*

**shop** \'shäp\ *n* : place where things are made or sold ~ *vb* **-pp-** : visit stores — **shop·keep·er** *n* — **shop·per** *n*

**shop·lift** *vb* : steal goods from a store — **shop·lift·er** \-ˌliftər\ *n*

**¹shore** \'shōr\ *n* : land along the edge of water — **shore·line** *n*

**²shore** *vb* **shored; shor·ing** : prop up ~ *n* : something that props

**shore·bird** *n* : bird of the seashore

**shorn** *past part of* SHEAR

**short** \'shȯrt\ *adj* **1** : not long or tall or extending far **2** : brief in time **3**

: curt **4** : not having or being enough ~ *adv* : curtly ~ *n* **1** *pl* : short drawers or trousers **2** : short circuit — **short·en** \-ᵊn\ *vb* — **short·ly** *adv* — **short·ness** *n*

**short·age** \'shȯrtij\ *n* : deficiency

**short·cake** *n* : dessert of biscuit with sweetened fruit

**short·change** *vb* : cheat esp. by giving too little change

**short circuit** *n* : abnormal electric connection — **short–circuit** *vb*

**short·com·ing** *n* : fault or failing

**short·cut** \-ˌkət\ *n* **1** : more direct route than that usu. taken **2** : quicker way of doing something

**short·hand** *n* : method of speed writing

**short–lived** \'shȯrtᵊlivd, -ˌlivd\ *adj* : of short life or duration

**short·sight·ed** *adj* : lacking foresight

**shot** \'shät\ *n* **1** : act of shooting **2** : attempt (as at making a goal) **3** : small pellets forming a charge **4** : range or reach **5** : photograph **6** : injection of medicine **7** : small serving of liquor — **shot·gun** *n*

**should** \'shùd\ *past of* SHALL — used as an auxiliary to express condition, obligation, or probability

**shoul·der** \'shōldər\ *n* **1** : part of the body where the arm joins the trunk **2** : part that projects or lies to the side ~ *vb* : push with or bear on the shoulder

**shoulder blade** *n* : flat triangular bone at the back of the shoulder

**shout** \'shaùt\ *vb* : give voice loudly — **shout** *n*

**shove** \'shəv\ *vb* **shoved; shov·ing** : push along or away — **shove** *n*

**shov·el** \'shəvəl\ *n* : broad tool for digging or lifting ~ *vb* **-eled** *or* **-elled; -el·ing** *or* **-el·ling** : take up or dig with a shovel

**show** \'shō\ *vb* **showed** \'shōd\; **shown** \'shōn\ *or* **showed; showing 1** : present to view **2** : reveal or demonstrate **3** : teach **4** : prove **5** : conduct or escort **6** : appear or be noticeable ~ *n* **1** : demonstrative display **2** : spectacle **3** : theatrical, radio, or television program — **showcase** *n* — **show off** *vb* **1** : display proudly **2** : act so as to attract attention — **show up** *vb* : arrive

**show·down** *n* : decisive confrontation

**show·er** \'shaùər\ *n* **1** : brief fall of rain **2** : bath in which water sprinkles down on the person or a facility for such a bath **3** : party at which someone gets gifts ~ *vb* **1** : rain or fall in a shower **2** : bathe in a shower — **show·er·y** *adj*

**showy** \'shōē\ *adj* **show·i·er; -est** : very noticeable or overly elaborate — **show·i·ly** *adv* — **show·i·ness** *n*

**shrap·nel** \'shrapnᵊl\ *n, pl* **shrapnel** : metal fragments of a bomb

**shred** \'shred\ *n* : narrow strip cut or torn off ~ *vb* **-dd-** : cut or tear into shreds

**shrew** \'shrü\ *n* **1** : scolding woman **2** : mouselike mammal — **shrew·ish** \-ish\ *adj*

**shrewd** \'shrüd\ *adj* : clever — **shrewd·ly** *adv* — **shrewd·ness** *n*

**shriek** \'shrēk\ *n* : shrill cry — **shriek** *vb*

**shrill** \'shril\ *adj* : piercing and high-pitched — **shril·ly** *adv*

**shrimp** \'shrimp\ *n* : small sea crustacean

**shrine** \'shrīn\ *n* **1** : tomb of a saint **2** : hallowed place

**shrink** \'shriŋk\ *vb* **shrank** \'shraŋk\; **shrunk** \'shrəŋk\ *or* **shrunk·en** \'shrəŋkən\; **shrink·ing 1** : draw back or away **2** : become smaller — **shrink·able** *adj*

**shrink·age** \'shriŋkij\ *n* : amount lost by shrinking

**shriv·el** \'shrivəl\ *vb* **-eled** *or* **-elled; -el·ing** *or* **-el·ling** : shrink or wither into wrinkles

**shroud** \'shraud\ *n* **1** : cloth put over a corpse **2** : cover or screen ~ *vb* : veil or screen from view

**shrub** \'shrəb\ *n* : low woody plant — **shrub·by** *adj*

**shrub·bery** \'shrəbərē\ *n, pl* **-ber·ies** : growth of shrubs

**shrug** \'shrəg\ *vb* **-gg-** : hunch the shoulders up in doubt, indifference, or uncertainty — **shrug** *n*

**shuck** \'shək\ *vb* : strip of a shell or husk — **shuck** *n*

**shud·der** \'shədər\ *vb* : tremble — **shudder** *n*

**shuf·fle** \'shəfəl\ *vb* **-fled; -fling 1** : mix together **2** : walk with a sliding movement — **shuffle** *n*

**shuf·fle·board** \'shəfəl,bōrd\ *n* : game of sliding disks into a scoring area

**shun** \'shən\ *vb* **-nn-** : keep away from

**shunt** \'shənt\ *vb* : turn off to one side

**shut** \'shət\ *vb* **shut; shut·ting 1** : bar passage into or through (as by moving a lid or door) **2** : suspend activity — **shut out** *vb* : exclude — **shut up** *vb* : stop or cause to stop talking

**shut–in** *n* : invalid

**shut·ter** \'shətər\ *n* **1** : movable cover for a window **2** : camera part that exposes film

**shut·tle** \'shətᵊl\ *n* **1** : part of a weaving machine that carries thread back and forth **2** : vehicle traveling back and forth over a short route ~ *vb* **-tled; -tling** : move back and forth frequently

**shut·tle·cock** \'shətᵊl,käk\ *n* : light conical object used in badminton

**shy** \'shī\ *adj* **shi·er** *or* **shy·er** \'shīər\; **shi·est** *or* **shy·est** \'shīəst\ **1** : sensitive and hesitant in dealing with others **2** : wary **3** : lacking ~ *vb* **shied; shy·ing** : draw back (as in fright) — **shy·ly** *adv* — **shy·ness** *n*

**sib·i·lant** \'sibələnt\ *adj* : having the sound of the *s* or the *sh* in *sash* — **sibilant** *n*

**sib·ling** \'sibliŋ\ *n* : brother or sister

**sick** \'sik\ *adj* **1** : not in good health **2** : nauseated **3** : relating to or meant for the sick — **sick·bed** *n* — **sick·en** \-ən\ *vb* — **sick·ly** *adj* — **sick·ness** *n*

**sick·le** \'sikəl\ *n* : curved short-handled blade

**side** \'sīd\ *n* **1** : part to left or right of an object or the torso **2** : edge or surface away from the center or at an angle to top and bottom or ends **3** : contrasting or opposing position or group — **sid·ed** *adj*

**side·board** *n* : piece of dining-room furniture for table service

**side·burns** \-,bərnz\ *n pl* : whiskers in front of the ears

**side·long** \'sīd,lȯŋ\ *adv or adj* : to or along the side

**side·show** *n* : minor show at a circus

**side·step** *vb* **1** : step aside **2** : avoid

**side·swipe** \-,swīp\ *vb* : strike with a glancing blow — **sideswipe** *n*

**side·track** *vb* : lead aside or astray

**side·walk** *n* : paved walk at the side of a road

**side·ways** \-,wāz\ *adv or adj* **1** : to or from the side **2** : with one side to the front

**sid·ing** \'sīdiŋ\ *n* **1** : short railroad track **2** : material for covering the outside of a building

**si·dle** \'sīdᵊl\ *vb* **-dled; -dling** : move sideways or unobtrusively

**siege** \'sēj\ *n* : persistent attack (as on a fortified place)

**si·es·ta** \sē'estə\ *n* : midday nap

**sieve** \'siv\ *n* : utensil with holes to separate particles

**sift** \'sift\ *vb* **1** : pass through a sieve **2** : examine carefully — **sift·er** *n*

**sigh** \'sī\ *n* : audible release of the breath (as to express weariness) — **sigh** *vb*

**sight** \'sīt\ *n* **1** : something seen or worth seeing **2** : process, power, or range of seeing **3** : device used in aiming **4** : view or glimpse ∼ *vb* : get sight of — **sight·ed** *adj* — **sight·less** *adj* — **sight–see·ing** *adj* — **sight–seer** \-,sēər\ *n*

**sign** \'sīn\ *n* **1** : symbol **2** : gesture expressing a command or thought **3** : public notice to advertise or warn **4** : trace ∼ *vb* **1** : mark with or make a sign **2** : write one's name on — **sign·er** *n*

**sig·nal** \'sign°l\ *n* **1** : sign of command or warning **2** : electronic transmission ∼ *vb* **-naled** *or* **-nalled; -nal·ing** *or* **-nal·ling** : communicate or notify by signals ∼ *adj* : distinguished

**sig·na·to·ry** \'signə,tōrē\ *n, pl* **-ries** : person or government that signs jointly with others

**sig·na·ture** \'signə,chùr\ *n* : one's name written by oneself

**sig·net** \'signət\ *n* : small seal

**sig·nif·i·cance** \sig'nifikəns\ *n* **1** : meaning **2** : importance — **sig·nif·i·cant** \-kənt\ *adj* — **sig·nif·i·cant·ly** *adv*

**sig·ni·fy** \'signə,fī\ *vb* **-fied; -fy·ing** *n* **1** : show by a sign **2** : mean — **sig·ni·fi·ca·tion** \,signəfə'kāshən\ *n*

**si·lence** \'sīləns\ *n* : state of being without sound ∼ *vb* **-lenced; -lenc·ing** : keep from making noise or sound — **si·lenc·er** *n*

**si·lent** \'sīlənt\ *adj* : having or producing no sound — **si·lent·ly** *adv*

**sil·hou·ette** \,silə'wet\ *n* : outline filled in usu. with black ∼ *vb* **-et·ted; -et·ting** : represent by a silhouette

**sil·i·ca** \'silikə\ *n* : mineral found as quartz and opal

**sil·i·con** \'silikən, -,kän\ *n* : nonmetallic chemical element

**silk** \'silk\ *n* **1** : fine strong lustrous protein fiber from moth larvae (**silk·worms** \-,wərmz\ ) **2** : thread or cloth made from silk — **silk·en** \'silkən\ *adj* — **silky** *adj*

**sill** \'sil\ *n* : bottom part of a window frame or a doorway

**sil·ly** \'silē\ *adj* **sil·li·er; -est** : foolish or stupid — **sil·li·ness** *n*

**si·lo** \'sīlō\ *n, pl* **-los** : tall building for storing animal feed

**silt** \'silt\ *n* : fine earth carried by rivers ∼ *vb* : obstruct or cover with silt

**sil·ver** \'silvər\ *n* **1** : white ductile metallic chemical element **2** : silverware ∼ *adj* : having the color of silver — **sil·very** *adj*

**sil·ver·ware** \-,war\ *n* : eating and serving utensils esp. of silver

**sim·i·lar** \'simələr\ *adj* : resembling each other in some ways — **sim·i·lar·i·ty** \,simə'larətē\ *n* — **sim·i·lar·ly** \'simələrlē\ *adv*

**sim·i·le** \'simə,lē\ *n* : comparison of unlike things using *like* or *as*

**sim·mer** \'simər\ *vb* : stew gently

**sim·per** \'simpər\ *vb* : give a silly smile — **simper** *n*

**sim·ple** \'simpəl\ *adj* **-pler; -plest 1** : free from dishonesty, vanity, or pretense **2** : of humble origin or modest position **3** : not complex **4** : lacking education, experience, or intelligence — **sim·ple·ness** *n* — **sim·ply** \-plē\ *adv*

**sim·ple·ton** \'simpəltən\ *n* : fool

**sim·plic·i·ty** \sim'plisətē\ *n* : state or fact of being simple

**sim·pli·fy** \'simplə,fī\ *vb* **-fied; -fy·ing** : make easier — **sim·pli·fi·ca·tion** \,simpləfə'kāshən\ *n*

**sim·u·late** \'simyə,lāt\ *vb* **-lat·ed; -lat·ing** : create the effect or appearance of — **sim·u·la·tion** \,simyə'lāshən\ *n* — **sim·u·la·tor** \'simyə,lātər\ *n*

**si·mul·ta·ne·ous** \,sīməl'tānēəs\ *adj* : occurring or operating at the same time — **si·mul·ta·ne·ous·ly** *adv* — **si·mul·ta·ne·ous·ness** *n*

**sin** \'sin\ *n* : offense against God ∼ *vb* **-nn-** : commit a sin — **sin·ful** \-fəl\ *adj* — **sin·less** *adj* — **sin·ner** *n*

**since** \'sins\ *adv* **1** : from a past time until now **2** : backward in time ∼ *prep* **1** : in the period after **2** : continuously from ∼ *conj* **1** : from the time when **2** : because

**sin·cere** \sin'sir\ *adj* **-cer·er; -cer·est** : genuine or honest — **sin·cere·ly** *adv* — **sin·cer·i·ty** \-'serətē\ *n*

**si·ne·cure** \'sīni,kyùr, 'sini-\ *n* : well-paid job that requires little work

**sin·ew** \'sinyü\ *n* **1** : tendon **2** : physical strength — **sin·ewy** *adj*

**sing** \'siŋ\ *vb* **sang** \'saŋ\ *or* **sung** \'səŋ\; **sung; sing·ing** : produce musical tones with the voice — **sing·er** *n*

**singe** \'sinj\ *vb* **singed; singe·ing** : scorch lightly

**sin·gle** \'siŋgəl\ *adj* **1** : one only **2** : unmarried ~ *n* : separate one — **single·ness** *n* — **sin·gly** \-glē\ *adv* — **single out** *vb* : select or set aside

**sin·gu·lar** \'siŋgyələr\ *adj* **1** : relating to a word form denoting one **2** : outstanding or superior **3** : queer — **singular** *n* — **sin·gu·lar·i·ty** \ˌsiŋgyə-'larətē\ *n* — **sin·gu·lar·ly** \'siŋgyə-lərlē\ *adv*

**sin·is·ter** \'sinəstər\ *adj* : threatening evil

**sink** \'siŋk\ *vb* **sank** \'saŋk\ *or* **sunk** \'səŋk\; **sunk; sink·ing 1** : submerge or descend **2** : grow worse **3** : make by digging or boring **4** : invest ~ *n* : basin with a drain

**sink·er** \'siŋkər\ *n* : weight to sink a fishing line

**sin·u·ous** \'sinyəwəs\ *adj* : winding in and out — **sin·u·os·i·ty** \ˌsinyə-'wäsətē\ *n* — **sin·u·ous·ly** *adv*

**si·nus** \'sīnəs\ *n* : skull cavity usu. connecting with the nostrils

**sip** \'sip\ *vb* **-pp-** : drink in small quantities — **sip** *n*

**si·phon** \'sīfən\ *n* : tube that draws liquid by suction — **siphon** *vb*

**sir** \'sər\ *n* **1** — used before the first name of a knight or baronet **2** — used as a respectful form of address

**sire** \'sīr\ *n* : father ~ *vb* **sired; sir·ing** : beget

**si·ren** \'sīrən\ *n* **1** : seductive woman **2** : wailing warning whistle

**sir·loin** \'sər,lȯin\ *n* : cut of beef

**sirup** *var of* SYRUP

**si·sal** \'sīsəl, -zəl\ *n* : strong rope fiber

**sis·sy** \'sisē\ *n, pl* **-sies** : timid or effeminate boy

**sis·ter** \'sistər\ *n* : female sharing one or both parents with another person — **sis·ter·hood** \-ˌhu̇d\ *n* — **sis·ter·ly** *adj*

**sis·ter–in–law** *n, pl* **sis·ters–in–law** : sister of one's spouse or wife of one's brother

**sit** \'sit\ *vb* **sat** \'sat\; **sit·ting 1** : rest on the buttocks or haunches **2** : roost **3** : hold a session **4** : pose for a portrait **5** : have a location **6** : rest or fix in place — **sit·ter** *n*

**site** \'sīt\ *n* **1** : place **2** : Web site

**sit·u·at·ed** \'sicha,wātəd\ *adj* : located

**sit·u·a·tion** \ˌsicha'wāshən\ *n* **1** : location **2** : condition **3** : job

**six** \'siks\ *n* : one more than 5 — **six** *adj or pron* — **sixth** \'siksth\ *adj or adv or n*

**six·teen** \siks'tēn\ *n* : one more than 15 — **sixteen** *adj or pron* — **six·teenth** \-'tēnth\ *adj or n*

**six·ty** \'sikstē\ *n, pl* **-ties** : 6 times 10 — **six·ti·eth** \-əth\ *adj or n* — **sixty** *adj or pron*

**siz·able, size·able** \'sīzəbəl\ *adj* : quite large — **siz·ably** \-blē\ *adv*

**size** \'sīz\ *n* : measurement of the amount of space something takes up ~ *vb* : grade according to size

**siz·zle** \'sizəl\ *vb* **-zled; -zling** : fry with a hissing sound — **sizzle** *n*

**skate** \'skāt\ *n* **1** : metal runner on a shoe for gliding over ice **2** : roller skate — **skate** *vb* — **skat·er** *n*

**skein** \'skān\ *n* : loosely twisted quantity of yarn or thread

**skel·e·ton** \'skelət°n\ *n* : bony framework — **skel·e·tal** \-ət°l\ *adj*

**skep·tic** \'skeptik\ *n* : one who is critical or doubting — **skep·ti·cal** \-tikəl\ *adj* — **skep·ti·cism** \-tə,sizəm\ *n*

**sketch** \'skech\ *n* **1** : rough drawing **2** : short story or essay — **sketch** *vb* — **sketchy** *adj*

**skew·er** \'skyüər\ *n* : long pin for holding roasting meat — **skewer** *vb*

**ski** \'skē\ *n, pl* **skis** : long strip for gliding over snow or water — **ski** *vb* — **ski·er** *n*

**skid** \'skid\ *n* **1** : plank for supporting something or on which it slides **2** : act of skidding ~ *vb* **-dd-** : slide sideways

**skiff** \'skif\ *n* : small boat

**skill** \'skil\ *n* : developed or learned ability — **skilled** \'skild\ *adj* — **skill·ful** \-fəl\ *adj* — **skill·ful·ly** *adv*

**skil·let** \'skilət\ *n* : pan for frying

**skim** \'skim\ *vb* **-mm- 1** : take off from the top of a liquid **2** : read or move over swiftly ~ *adj* : having the cream removed — **skim·mer** *n*

**skimp** \'skimp\ *vb* : give too little of something — **skimpy** *adj*

**skin** \'skin\ *n* **1** : outer layer of an animal body **2** : rind ~ *vb* **-nn-** : take the skin from — **skin·less** adj — **skinned** adj — **skin·tight** adj

**skin diving** n : sport of swimming under water with a face mask and flippers

**skin·flint** \'skin,flint\ n : stingy person

**skin·ny** \'skinē\ adj **-ni·er; -est** : very thin

**skip** \'skip\ vb **-pp-** 1 : move with leaps 2 : read past or ignore — **skip** n

**skip·per** \'skipər\ n : ship's master — **skipper** vb

**skir·mish** \'skərmish\ n : minor combat — **skirmish** vb

**skirt** \'skərt\ n : garment or part of a garment that hangs below the waist ~ vb : pass around the edge of

**skit** \'skit\ n : brief usu. humorous play

**skit·tish** \'skitish\ adj : easily frightened

**skulk** \'skəlk\ vb : move furtively

**skull** \'skəl\ n : bony case that protects the brain

**skunk** \'skəŋk\ n : mammal that can forcibly eject an ill-smelling fluid

**sky** \'skī\ n, pl **skies** 1 : upper air 2 : heaven — **sky·line** n — **sky·ward** \-wərd\ adv or adj

**sky·lark** \'skī,lärk\ n : European lark noted for its song

**sky·light** n : window in a roof or ceiling

**sky·rock·et** n : shooting firework ~ vb : rise suddenly

**sky·scrap·er** \-,skrāpər\ n : very tall building

**slab** \'slab\ n : thick slice

**slack** \'slak\ adj 1 : careless 2 : not taut 3 : not busy ~ n 1 : part hanging loose 2 pl : casual trousers — **slack·en** vb — **slack·ly** adv — **slackness** n

**slag** \'slag\ n : waste from melting of ores

**slain** past part of SLAY

**slake** \'slāk\ vb **slaked; slak·ing** : quench

**slam** \'slam\ n : heavy jarring impact ~ vb **-mm-** : shut, strike, or throw violently and loudly

**slan·der** \'slandər\ n : malicious gossip ~ vb : hurt (someone) with slander — **slan·der·er** n — **slan·der·ous** adj

**slang** \'slaŋ\ n : informal nonstandard vocabulary — **slangy** adj

**slant** \'slant\ vb 1 : slope 2 : present with a special viewpoint ~ n : sloping direction, line, or plane

**slap** \'slap\ vb **-pp-** : strike sharply with the open hand — **slap** n

**slash** \'slash\ vb 1 : cut with sweeping strokes 2 : reduce sharply ~ n : gash

**slat** \'slat\ n : thin narrow flat strip

**slate** \'slāt\ n 1 : dense fine-grained layered rock 2 : roofing tile or writing tablet of slate 3 : list of candidates ~ vb **slat·ed; slat·ing** : designate

**slat·tern** \'slatərn\ n : untidy woman — **slat·tern·ly** adj

**slaugh·ter** \'slótər\ n 1 : butchering of livestock for market 2 : great and cruel destruction of lives ~ vb : commit slaughter upon — **slaughterhouse** n

**slave** \'slāv\ n : one owned and forced into service by another ~ vb **slaved; slav·ing** : work as or like a slave — **slave** adj — **slav·ery** \'slāvərē\ n

**sla·ver** \'slavər, 'slāv-\ vb or n : slobber

**slav·ish** \'slāvish\ adj : of or like a slave — **slav·ish·ly** adv

**slay** \'slā\ vb **slew** \'slü\; **slain** \'slān\; **slay·ing** : kill — **slay·er** n

**slea·zy** \'slēzē, 'slā-\ adj **-zi·er; -est** : shabby or shoddy

**sled** \'sled\ n : vehicle on runners — **sled** vb

¹**sledge** \'slej\ n : sledgehammer

²**sledge** n : heavy sled

**sledge·ham·mer** n : heavy long-handled hammer — **sledgehammer** adj or vb

**sleek** \'slēk\ adj : smooth or glossy — **sleek** vb

**sleep** \'slēp\ n : natural suspension of consciousness ~ vb **slept** \'slept\; **sleep·ing** : rest in a state of sleep — **sleep·er** n — **sleep·less** adj — **sleep·walk·er** n

**sleepy** \'slēpē\ adj **sleep·i·er; -est** 1 : ready for sleep 2 : quietly inactive — **sleep·i·ly** \'slēpəlē\ adv — **sleep·i·ness** \-pēnəs\ n

**sleet** \'slēt\ n : frozen rain — **sleet** vb — **sleety** adj

**sleeve** \'slēv\ n : part of a garment for the arm — **sleeve·less** adj

**sleigh** \'slā\ n : horse-drawn sled with seats ~ vb : drive or ride in a sleigh

**sleight of hand** \'slīt-\ : skillful manual manipulation or a trick requiring it

**slen·der** \'slendər\ adj 1 : thin esp. in physique 2 : scanty

**sleuth** \'slüth\ n : detective

**slew** \'slü\ past of SLAY

**slice** \'slīs\ n : thin flat piece ~ vb **sliced; slic·ing** : cut a slice from

**slick** \'slik\ adj 1 : very smooth 2 : clever — **slick** vb

**slick·er** \'slikər\ *n* : raincoat

**slide** \'slīd\ *vb* **slid** \'slid\; **slid·ing** \'slīdiŋ\ : move smoothly along a surface ∼ *n* **1** : act of sliding **2** : surface on which something slides **3** : transparent picture for projection

**slier** *comparative of* SLY

**sliest** *superlative of* SLY

**slight** \'slīt\ *adj* **1** : slender **2** : frail **3** : small in degree ∼ *vb* **1** : ignore or treat as unimportant — **slight** *n* — **slight·ly** *adv*

**slim** \'slim\ *adj* **-mm- 1** : slender **2** : scanty ∼ *vb* **-mm-** : make or become slender

**slime** \'slīm\ *n* : dirty slippery film (as on water) — **slimy** *adj*

**sling** \'sliŋ\ *vb* **slung** \'sləŋ\; **sling·ing** : hurl with or as if with a sling ∼ *n* **1** : strap for swinging and hurling stones **2** : looped strap or bandage to lift or support

**sling·shot** *n* : forked stick with elastic bands for shooting pebbles

**slink** \'sliŋk\ *vb* **slunk** \'sləŋk\; **slink·ing** : move stealthily or sinuously — **slinky** *adj*

**¹slip** \'slip\ *vb* **-pp- 1** : escape quietly or secretly **2** : slide along smoothly **3** : make a mistake **4** : to pass without being noticed or done **5** : fall off from a standard ∼ *n* **1** : ship's berth **2** : sudden mishap **3** : mistake **4** : woman's undergarment

**²slip** *n* **1** : plant shoot **2** : small strip (as of paper)

**slip·per** \'slipər\ *n* : shoe that slips on easily

**slip·pery** \'slipərē\ *adj* **-peri·er; -est 1** : slick enough to slide on **2** : tricky — **slip·peri·ness** *n*

**slip·shod** \'slip,shäd\ *adj* : careless

**slit** \'slit\ *vb* **slit**; **slit·ting** : make a slit in ∼ *n* : long narrow cut

**slith·er** \'slithər\ *vb* : glide along like a snake — **slith·ery** *adj*

**sliv·er** \'slivər\ *n* : splinter

**slob** \'släb\ *n* : untidy person

**slob·ber** \'släbər\ *vb* : dribble saliva — **slobber** *n*

**slo·gan** \'slōgən\ *n* : word or phrase expressing the aim of a cause

**sloop** \'slüp\ *n* : one-masted sailboat

**slop** \'släp\ *n* : food waste for animal feed ∼ *vb* **-pp-** : spill

**slope** \'slōp\ *vb* **sloped; slop·ing** : deviate from the vertical or horizontal ∼ *n* : upward or downward slant

**slop·py** \'släpē\ *adj* **-pi·er; -est 1** : muddy **2** : untidy

**slot** \'slät\ *n* : narrow opening

**sloth** \'slóth, 'slōth\ *n, pl* **sloths** \with ths *or* thz\ **1** : laziness **2** : slow=moving mammal — **sloth·ful** *adj*

**slouch** \'slaúch\ *n* **1** : drooping posture **2** : lazy or incompetent person ∼ *vb* : walk or stand with a slouch

**¹slough** \'slü, 'slaú\ *n* : swamp

**²slough, sluff** \'sləf\ *vb* : cast off (old skin)

**slov·en·ly** \'sləvənlē\ *adj* : untidy

**slow** \'slō\ *adj* **1** : sluggish or stupid **2** : moving, working, or happening at less than the usual speed ∼ *vb* **1** : make slow **2** : go slower — **slow** *adv* — **slow·ly** *adv* — **slow·ness** *n*

**sludge** \'sləj\ *n* : slushy mass (as of treated sewage)

**slug** \'sləg\ *n* **1** : mollusk related to the snails **2** : bullet **3** : metal disk ∼ *vb* **-gg-** : strike forcibly — **slug·ger** *n*

**slug·gish** \'sləgish\ *adj* : slow in movement or flow — **slug·gish·ly** *adv* — **slug·gish·ness** *n*

**sluice** \'slüs\ *n* : channel for water ∼ *vb* **sluiced; sluic·ing** : wash in running water

**slum** \'sləm\ *n* : thickly populated area marked by poverty

**slum·ber** \'sləmbər\ *vb or n* : sleep

**slump** \'sləmp\ *vb* **1** : sink suddenly **2** : slouch — **slump** *n*

**slung** *past of* SLING

**slunk** *past of* SLINK

**¹slur** \'slər\ *vb* **-rr-** : run (words or notes) together — **slur** *n*

**²slur** *n* : malicious or insulting remark

**slurp** \'slərp\ *vb* : eat or drink noisily — **slurp** *n*

**slush** \'sləsh\ *n* : partly melted snow — **slushy** *adj*

**slut** \'slət\ *n* **1** : untidy woman **2** : lewd woman — **slut·tish** *adj*

**sly** \'slī\ *adj* **sli·er** \'slīər\; **sli·est** \'slīəst\ : given to or showing secrecy and deception — **sly·ly** *adv* — **sly·ness** *n*

**¹smack** \'smak\ *n* : characteristic flavor ∼ *vb* : have a taste or hint

**²smack** *vb* **1** : move (the lips) so as to make a sharp noise **2** : kiss or slap with a loud noise ∼ *n* **1** : sharp noise made by the lips **2** : noisy slap

**³smack** *adv* : squarely and sharply

**⁴smack** *n* : fishing boat

**small** \'smól\ *adj* **1** : little in size or

amount **2** : few in number **3** : trivial — **small•ish** adj — **small•ness** n

**small•pox** \'smȯl,päks\ n : contagious virus disease

**smart** \'smärt\ vb **1** : cause or feel stinging pain **2** : endure distress ~ adj **1** : intelligent or resourceful **2** : stylish — **smart** n — **smart•ly** adv — **smart•ness** n

**smash** \'smash\ vb : break or be broken into pieces ~ n **1** : smashing blow **2** : act or sound of smashing

**smat•ter•ing** \'smatəriŋ\ n **1** : superficial knowledge **2** : small scattered number or amount

**smear** \'smir\ n : greasy stain ~ vb **1** : spread (something sticky) **2** : smudge **3** : slander

**smell** \'smel\ vb **smelled** \'smeld\ or **smelt** \'smelt\; **smell•ing 1** : perceive the odor of **2** : have or give off an odor ~ n **1** : sense by which one perceives odor **2** : odor — **smelly** adj

¹**smelt** \'smelt\ n, pl **smelts** or **smelt** : small food fish

²**smelt** vb : melt or fuse (ore) in order to separate the metal — **smelt•er** n

**smile** \'smīl\ n : facial expression with the mouth turned up usu. to show pleasure — **smile** vb

**smirk** \'smərk\ vb : wear a conceited smile — **smirk** n

**smite** \'smīt\ vb **smote** \'smōt\; **smit•ten** \'smit³n\ or **smote; smit•ing** \'smītiŋ\ **1** : strike heavily or kill **2** : affect strongly

**smith** \'smith\ n : worker in metals and esp. a blacksmith

**smithy** \'smithē\ n, pl **smith•ies** : a smith's workshop

**smock** \'smäk\ n : loose dress or protective coat

**smog** \'smäg, 'smȯg\ n : fog and smoke — **smog•gy** adj

**smoke** \'smōk\ n : sooty gas from burning — vb **smoked; smok•ing 1** : give off smoke **2** : inhale the fumes of burning tobacco **3** : cure (as meat) with smoke — **smoke•less** adj — **smok•er** n — **smoky** adj

**smoke•stack** n : chimney through which smoke is discharged

**smol•der, smoul•der** \'smōldər\ vb **1** : burn and smoke without flame **2** : be suppressed but active — **smolder** n

**smooth** \'smüth\ adj **1** : having a surface without irregularities **2** : not jar-

ring or jolting ~ vb : make smooth — **smooth•ly** adv — **smooth•ness** n

**smor•gas•bord** \'smȯrgəs,bōrd\ n : buffet consisting of many foods

**smoth•er** \'sməthər\ vb **1** : kill by depriving of air **2** : cover thickly

**smudge** \'sməj\ vb **smudged; smudg•ing** : soil or blur by rubbing ~ n **1** : thick smoke **2** : dirty spot

**smug** \'sməg\ adj **-gg-** : content in one's own virtue or accomplishment — **smug•ly** adv — **smug•ness** n

**smug•gle** \'sməgəl\ vb **-gled; -gling** : import or export secretly or illegally — **smug•gler** \'sməglər\ n

**smut** \'smət\ n **1** : something that soils **2** : indecent language or matter **3** : disease of plants caused by fungi — **smut•ty** adj

**snack** \'snak\ n : light meal

**snag** \'snag\ n : unexpected difficulty ~ vb **-gg-** : become caught on something that sticks out

**snail** \'snāl\ n : small mollusk with a spiral shell

**snake** \'snāk\ n : long-bodied limbless reptile — **snake•bite** n

**snap** \'snap\ vb **-pp- 1** : bite at something **2** : utter angry words **3** : break suddenly with a sharp sound ~ n **1** : act or sound of snapping **2** : fastening that closes with a click **3** : something easy to do — **snap•per** n — **snap•pish** adj — **snap•py** adj

**snap•drag•on** n : garden plant with spikes of showy flowers

**snap•shot** \'snap,shät\ n : casual photograph

**snare** \'snar\ n : trap for catching game ~ vb : capture or hold with or as if with a snare

¹**snarl** \'snärl\ n : tangle ~ vb : cause to become knotted

²**snarl** vb or n : growl

**snatch** \'snach\ vb **1** : try to grab something suddenly **2** : seize or take away suddenly ~ n **1** : act of snatching **2** : something brief or fragmentary

**sneak** \'snēk\ vb : move or take in a furtive manner ~ n : one who acts in a furtive manner — **sneak•i•ly** \'snēkəlē\ adv — **sneak•ing•ly** adv — **sneaky** adj

**sneak•er** \'snēkər\ n : sports shoe

**sneer** \'snir\ vb : smile scornfully — **sneer** n

**sneeze** \'snēz\ vb **sneezed; sneez•ing**

: force the breath out with sudden and involuntary violence — **sneeze** n

**snick·er** \'snikər\ n : partly suppressed laugh — **snicker** vb

**snide** \'snīd\ adj : subtly ridiculing

**sniff** \'snif\ vb 1 : draw air audibly up the nose 2 : detect by smelling — **sniff** n

**snip** \'snip\ n : fragment snipped off ~ vb -**pp**- : cut off by bits

¹**snipe** \'snīp\ n, pl **snipes** or **snipe** : game bird of marshy areas

²**snipe** vb **sniped; snip·ing** : shoot at an enemy from a concealed position — **snip·er** n

**snips** \'snips\ n pl : scissorslike tool

**sniv·el** \'snivəl\ vb -**eled** or -**elled;** -**el·ing** or -**el·ling** 1 : have a running nose 2 : whine

**snob** \'snäb\ n : one who acts superior to others — **snob·bery** \-ərē\ n — **snob·bish** adj — **snob·bish·ly** adv — **snob·bish·ness** n

**snoop** \'snüp\ vb : pry in a furtive way ~ n : prying person

**snooze** \'snüz\ vb **snoozed; snooz·ing** : take a nap — **snooze** n

**snore** \'snōr\ vb **snored; snor·ing** : breathe with a hoarse noise while sleeping — **snore** n

**snort** \'snȯrt\ vb : force air noisily through the nose — **snort** n

**snout** \'snaut\ n : long projecting muzzle (as of a swine)

**snow** \'snō\ n : crystals formed from water vapor ~ vb : fall as snow — **snow·ball** n — **snow·bank** n — **snow·drift** n — **snow·fall** n — **snow·plow** n — **snow·storm** n — **snowy** adj

**snow·shoe** n : frame of wood strung with thongs for walking on snow

**snub** \'snəb\ vb -**bb**- : ignore or avoid through disdain — **snub** n

¹**snuff** \'snəf\ vb : put out (a candle) — **snuff·er** n

²**snuff** vb : draw forcibly into the nose ~ n : pulverized tobacco

**snug** \'snəg\ adj -**gg**- 1 : warm, secure, and comfortable 2 : fitting closely — **snug·ly** adv — **snug·ness** n

**snug·gle** \'snəgəl\ vb -**gled; -gling** : curl up comfortably

**so** \'sō\ adv 1 : in the manner or to the extent indicated 2 : in the same way 3 : therefore 4 : finally 5 : thus ~ conj : for that reason

**soak** \'sōk\ vb 1 : lie in a liquid 2 : absorb ~ n : act of soaking

**soap** \'sōp\ n : cleaning substance — **soap** vb — **soapy** adj

**soar** \'sōr\ vb : fly upward on or as if on wings

**sob** \'säb\ vb -**bb**- : weep with convulsive heavings of the chest — **sob** n

**so·ber** \'sōbər\ adj 1 : not drunk 2 : serious or solemn — **so·ber·ly** adv

**so·bri·ety** \sə'brīətē, sō-\ n : quality or state of being sober

**soc·cer** \'säkər\ n : game played by kicking a ball

**so·cia·ble** \'sōshəbəl\ adj : friendly — **so·cia·bil·i·ty** \sōshə'bilətē\ n — **so·cia·bly** \'sōshəblē\ adv

**so·cial** \'sōshəl\ adj 1 : relating to pleasant companionship 2 : naturally living or growing in groups 3 : relating to human society ~ n : social gathering — **so·cial·ly** adv

**so·cial·ism** \'sōshə,lizəm\ n : social system based on government control of the production and distribution of goods — **so·cial·ist** \'sōshəlist\ n or adj — **so·cial·is·tic** \sōshə'listik\ adj

**so·cial·ize** \'sōshə,līz\ vb -**ized; -iz·ing** 1 : regulate by socialism 2 : adapt to social needs 3 : participate in a social gathering — **so·cial·i·za·tion** \sōshələ'zāshən\ n

**social work** n : services concerned with aiding the poor and socially maladjusted — **social worker** n

**so·ci·ety** \sə'sīətē\ n, pl -**et·ies** 1 : companionship 2 : community life 3 : rich or fashionable class 4 : voluntary group

**so·ci·ol·o·gy** \sōsē'äləjē\ n : study of social relationships — **so·ci·o·log·i·cal** \-ə'läjikəl\ adj — **so·ci·ol·o·gist** \-'äləjist\ n

¹**sock** \'säk\ n, pl **socks** or **sox** : short stocking

²**sock** vb or n : punch

**sock·et** \'säkət\ n : hollow part that holds something

**sod** \'säd\ n : turf ~ vb -**dd**- : cover with sod

**so·da** \'sōdə\ n 1 : carbonated water or a soft drink 2 : ice cream drink made with soda

**sod·den** \'säd²n\ adj 1 : lacking spirit 2 : soaked or soggy

**so·di·um** \'sōdēəm\ n : soft waxy silver white metallic chemical element

**so·fa** \'sōfə\ n : wide padded chair

**soft** \'sȯft\ adj 1 : not hard, rough, or harsh 2 : nonalcoholic — **soft·en**

\'sófən\ *vb* — **soft•en•er** \-ənər\ *n*
— **soft•ly** *adv* — **soft•ness** *n*

**soft•ball** *n* : game like baseball

**soft•ware** \'sóft,war\ *n* : computer programs

**sog•gy** \'sägē\ *adj* **-gi•er; -est** : heavy with moisture — **sog•gi•ness** \-ēnəs\ *n*

¹**soil** \'sóil\ *vb* : make or become dirty ~ *n* : embedded dirt

²**soil** *n* : loose surface material of the earth

**so•journ** \'sō,jərn, sō'jərn\ *vb* : temporary stay ~ *vb* : reside temporarily

**so•lace** \'säləs\ *n or vb* : comfort

**so•lar** \'sōlər\ *adj* : relating to the sun or the energy in sunlight

**sold** *past of* SELL

**sol•der** \'sädər, 'sód-\ *n* : metallic alloy melted to join metallic surfaces ~ *vb* : cement with solder

**sol•dier** \'sōljər\ *n* : person in military service ~ *vb* : serve as a soldier — **sol•dier•ly** *adj or adv*

¹**sole** \'sōl\ *n* : bottom of the foot or a shoe — **soled** *adj*

²**sole** *n* : flatfish caught for food

³**sole** *adj* : single or only — **sole•ly** *adv*

**sol•emn** \'säləm\ *adj* **1** : dignified and ceremonial **2** : highly serious — **so•lem•ni•ty** \sə'lemnətē\ *n* — **sol•emn•ly** *adv*

**so•lic•it** \sə'lisət\ *vb* : ask for — **so•lic•i•ta•tion** \-,lisə'tāshən\ *n*

**so•lic•i•tor** \sə'lisətər\ *n* **1** : one that solicits **2** : lawyer

**so•lic•i•tous** \sə'lisətəs\ *adj* : showing or expressing concern — **so•lic•i•tous•ly** *adv* — **so•lic•i•tude** \sə'lisə,tüd, -,tyüd\ *n*

**sol•id** \'säləd\ *adj* **1** : not hollow **2** : having 3 dimensions **3** : hard **4** : of good quality **5** : of one character ~ *n* **1** : 3-dimensional figure **2** : substance in solid form — **solid** *adv* — **so•lid•i•ty** \sə'lidətē\ *n* — **sol•id•ly** *adv* — **sol•id•ness** *n*

**sol•i•dar•i•ty** \,sälə'darətē\ *n* : unity of purpose

**so•lid•i•fy** \sə'lidə,fī\ *vb* **-fied; -fy•ing** : make or become solid — **so•lid•i•fi•ca•tion** \-,lidəfə'kāshən\ *n*

**so•lil•o•quy** \sə'liləkwē\ *n, pl* **-quies** : dramatic monologue — **so•lil•o•quize** \-,kwīz\ *vb*

**sol•i•taire** \'sälə,tar\ *n* **1** : solitary gem **2** : card game for one person

**sol•i•tary** \-,terē\ *adj* **1** : alone **2** : secluded **3** : single

**sol•i•tude** \-,tüd, -,tyüd\ *n* : state of being alone

**so•lo** \'sōlō\ *n, pl* **-los** : performance by only one person ~ *adv* : alone — **solo** *adj or vb* — **so•lo•ist** *n*

**sol•stice** \'sälstəs\ *n* : time of the year when the sun is farthest north or south of the equator

**sol•u•ble** \'sälyəbəl\ *adj* **1** : capable of being dissolved **2** : capable of being solved — **sol•u•bil•i•ty** \,sälyə'bilətē\ *n*

**so•lu•tion** \sə'lüshən\ *n* **1** : answer to a problem **2** : homogeneous liquid mixture

**solve** \'sälv\ *vb* **solved; solv•ing** : find a solution for — **solv•able** *adj*

**sol•vent** \'sälvənt\ *adj* **1** : able to pay all debts **2** : dissolving or able to dissolve ~ *n* : substance that dissolves or disperses another substance — **sol•ven•cy** \-vənsē\ *n*

**som•ber, som•bre** \'sämbər\ *adj* **1** : dark **2** : grave — **som•ber•ly** *adv*

**som•bre•ro** \səm'brerō\ *n, pl* **-ros** : broad-brimmed hat

**some** \'səm\ *adj* **1** : one unspecified **2** : unspecified or indefinite number of **3** : at least a few or a little ~ *pron* : a certain number or amount

**-some** \səm\ *adj suffix* : characterized by a thing, quality, state, or action

**some•body** \'səmbədē, -,bäd-\ *pron* : some person

**some•day** \'səm,dā\ *adv* : at some future time

**some•how** \-,haú\ *adv* : by some means

**some•one** \-,wən\ *pron* : some person

**som•er•sault** \'səmər,sólt\ *n* : body flip — **somersault** *vb*

**some•thing** \'səmthiŋ\ *pron* : some undetermined or unspecified thing

**some•time** \'səm,tīm\ *adv* : at a future, unknown, or unnamed time

**some•times** \-,tīmz\ *adv* : occasionally

**some•what** \-,hwət, -,hwät\ *adv* : in some degree

**some•where** \-,hwer\ *adv* : in, at, or to an unknown or unnamed place

**som•no•lent** \'sämnələnt\ *adj* : sleepy — **som•no•lence** \-ləns\ *n*

**son** \'sən\ *n* : male offspring

**so•nar** \'sō,när\ *n* : device that detects and locates underwater objects using sound waves

**so•na•ta** \sə'nätə\ n : instrumental composition

**song** \'soŋ\ n : music and words to be sung

**song•bird** n : bird with musical tones

**son•ic** \'sänik\ adj : relating to sound waves or the speed of sound

**son–in–law** n, pl **sons–in–law** : husband of one's daughter

**son•net** \'sänət\ n : poem of 14 lines

**so•no•rous** \sə'nōrəs, 'sänərəs\ adj 1 : loud, deep, or rich in sound 2 : impressive — **so•nor•i•ty** \sə'nòrətē\ n

**soon** \'sün\ adv 1 : before long 2 : promptly 3 : early

**soot** \'sùt, 'sət, 'süt\ n : fine black substance formed by combustion — **sooty** adj

**soothe** \'süth\ vb **soothed; sooth•ing** : calm or comfort — **sooth•er** n

**sooth•say•er** \'süth,sāər\ n : prophet — **sooth•say•ing** \-iŋ\ n

**sop** \'säp\ n : conciliatory bribe, gift, or concession ~ vb **-pp-** 1 : dip in a liquid 2 : soak 3 : mop up

**so•phis•ti•cat•ed** \sə'fistə,kātəd\ adj 1 : complex 2 : wise, cultured, or shrewd in human affairs — **so•phis•ti•ca•tion** \-,fistə'kāshən\ n

**soph•ist•ry** \'säfəstrē\ n : subtly fallacious reasoning or argument — **sophist** \'säfist\ n

**soph•o•more** \'säf°m,ōr, 'säf,mòr\ n : 2d-year student

**so•po•rif•ic** \,säpə'rifik, ,sōp-\ adj : causing sleep or drowsiness

**so•pra•no** \sə'pranō\ n, pl **-nos** : highest singing voice

**sor•cery** \'sòrsərē\ n : witchcraft — **sor•cer•er** \-rər\ n — **sor•cer•ess** \-rəs\ n

**sor•did** \'sòrdəd\ adj : filthy or vile — **sor•did•ly** adv — **sor•did•ness** n

**sore** \'sōr\ adj **sor•er; sor•est** 1 : causing pain or distress 2 : severe or intense 3 : angry ~ n : sore usu. infected spot on the body — **sore•ly** adv — **sore•ness** n

**sor•ghum** \'sòrgəm\ n : forage grass

**so•ror•i•ty** \sə'ròrətē\ n, pl **-ties** : women's student social group

¹**sor•rel** \'sòrəl\ n : brownish orange to light brown color or an animal of this color

²**sorrel** n : herb with sour juice

**sor•row** \'särō\ n : deep distress, sadness, or regret or a cause of this — **sor•row•ful** \-fəl\ adj — **sor•row•ful•ly** adv

**sor•ry** \'särē\ adj **-ri•er; -est** 1 : feeling sorrow, regret, or penitence 2 : dismal

**sort** \'sòrt\ n 1 : kind 2 : nature ~ vb : classify — **out of sorts** : grouchy

**SOS** \,es,ō'es\ n : call for help

**so–so** \'sō'sō\ adj or adv : barely acceptable

**sot** \'sät\ n : drunkard — **sot•tish** adj

**souf•flé** \sü'flā\ n : baked dish made light with beaten egg whites

**sought** past of SEEK

**soul** \'sōl\ n 1 : immaterial essence of an individual life 2 : essential part 3 : person

**soul•ful** \'sōlfəl\ adj : full of or expressing deep feeling — **soul•ful•ly** adv

¹**sound** \'saùnd\ adj 1 : free from fault, error, or illness 2 : firm or hard 3 : showing good judgment — **sound•ly** adv — **sound•ness** n

²**sound** n 1 : sensation of hearing 2 : energy of vibration sensed in hearing 3 : something heard ~ vb 1 : make or cause to make a sound 2 : seem — **sound•less** adj — **sound•less•ly** adv — **sound•proof** adj or vb

³**sound** n : wide strait ~ vb 1 : measure the depth of (water) 2 : investigate

**soup** \'süp\ n : broth usu. containing pieces of solid food — **soupy** adj

**sour** \'saùər\ adj 1 : having an acid or tart taste 2 : disagreeable ~ vb : become or make sour — **sour•ish** adj — **sour•ly** adv — **sour•ness** n

**source** \'sōrs\ n 1 : point of origin 2 : one that provides something needed

**souse** \'saùs\ vb **soused; sous•ing** 1 : pickle 2 : immerse 3 : intoxicate ~ n 1 : something pickled 2 : drunkard

**south** \'saùth\ adv : to or toward the south ~ adj : situated toward, at, or coming from the south ~ n 1 : direction to the right of sunrise 2 cap : regions to the south — **south•er•ly** \'səthərlē\ adv or adj — **south•ern** \'səthərn\ adj — **South•ern•er** n — **south•ern•most** \-,mōst\ adj — **southward** \'saùthwərd\ adv or adj — **south•wards** \-wərdz\ adv

**south•east** \saùth'ēst, naut saù'ēst\ n 1 : direction between south and east 2 cap : regions to the southeast — **southeast** adj or adv — **south•east-**

**er·ly** *adv or adj* — **south·east·ern** \-ərn\ *adj*

**south pole** *n* : the southernmost point of the earth

**south·west** \saùth'west, *naut* saò-'west\ *n* **1** : direction between south and west **2** *cap* : regions to the southwest — **southwest** *adj or adv* — **south·west·er·ly** *adv or adj* — **southwest·ern** \-ərn\ *adj*

**sou·ve·nir** \'süvə,nir\ *n* : something that is a reminder of a place or event

**sov·er·eign** \'sävərən\ *n* **1** : supreme ruler **2** : gold coin of the United Kingdom ~ *adj* **1** : supreme **2** : independent — **sov·er·eign·ty** \-tē\ *n*

¹**sow** \'saù\ *n* : female swine

²**sow** \'sō\ *vb* **sowed; sown** \'sōn\ or **sowed; sow·ing 1** : plant or strew with seed **2** : scatter abroad — **sow·er** \'sōər\ *n*

**sox** *pl of* SOCK

**soy·bean** \'sòi,bēn\ *n* : legume with edible seeds

**spa** \'spä\ *n* : resort at a mineral spring

**space** \'spās\ *n* **1** : period of time **2** : area in, around, or between **3** : region beyond earth's atmosphere **4** : accommodations ~ *vb* **spaced**; **spac·ing** : place at intervals — **space·craft** *n* — **space·flight** *n* — **space·man** *n* — **space·ship** *n*

**spa·cious** \'spāshəs\ *adj* : large or roomy — **spa·cious·ly** *adv* — **spa·cious·ness** *n*

¹**spade** \'spād\ *n or vb* : shovel — **spade·ful** *n*

²**spade** *n* : playing card marked with a black figure like an inverted heart

**spa·ghet·ti** \spə'getē\ *n* : pasta strings

**spam** \'spam\ *n* : unsolicited commercial e-mail

**span** \'span\ *n* **1** : amount of time **2** : distance between supports ~ *vb* **-nn-** : extend across

**span·gle** \'spangəl\ *n* : small disk of shining metal or plastic — **spangle** *vb*

**span·iel** \'spanyəl\ *n* : small or medium-sized dog with drooping ears and long wavy hair

**spank** \'spank\ *vb* : hit on the buttocks with an open hand

¹**spar** \'spär\ *n* : pole or boom

²**spar** *vb* **-rr-** : practice boxing

**spare** \'spar\ *adj* **1** : held in reserve **2** : thin or scanty ~ *vb* **spared; spar·ing 1** : reserve or avoid using **2** : avoid punishing or killing — **spare** *n*

**spar·ing** \'sparin\ *adj* : thrifty — **spar·ing·ly** *adv*

**spark** \'spärk\ *n* **1** : tiny hot and glowing particle **2** : smallest beginning or germ **3** : visible electrical discharge ~ *vb* **1** : emit or produce sparks **2** : stir to activity

**spar·kle** \'spärkəl\ *vb* **-kled; -kling 1** : flash **2** : effervesce ~ *n* : gleam — **spark·ler** \-klər\ *n*

**spar·row** \'sparō\ *n* : small singing bird

**sparse** \'spärs\ *adj* **spars·er; spars·est** : thinly scattered — **sparse·ly** *adv*

**spasm** \'spazəm\ *n* **1** : involuntary muscular contraction **2** : sudden, violent, and temporary effort or feeling — **spas·mod·ic** \spaz'mädik\ *adj* — **spas·mod·i·cal·ly** *adv*

**spas·tic** \'spastik\ *adj* : relating to, marked by, or affected with muscular spasm — **spastic** *n*

¹**spat** \'spat\ *past of* SPIT

²**spat** *n* : petty dispute

**spa·tial** \'spāshəl\ *adj* : relating to space — **spa·tial·ly** *adv*

**spat·ter** \'spatər\ *vb* : splash with drops of liquid — **spatter** *n*

**spat·u·la** \'spachələ\ *n* : flexible knife-like utensil

**spawn** \'spòn\ *vb* **1** : produce eggs or offspring **2** : bring forth ~ *n* : egg cluster — **spawn·er** *n*

**spay** \'spā\ *vb* : remove the ovaries of (a female)

**speak** \'spēk\ *vb* **spoke** \'spōk\; **spoken** \'spōkən\; **speak·ing 1** : utter words **2** : express orally **3** : address an audience **4** : use (a language) in talking — **speak·er** *n*

**spear** \'spir\ *n* : long pointed weapon ~ *vb* : strike or pierce with a spear

**spear·head** *n* : leading force, element, or influence — **spearhead** *vb*

**spear·mint** *n* : aromatic garden mint

**spe·cial** \'speshəl\ *adj* **1** : unusual or unique **2** : particularly favored **3** : set aside for a particular use — **special** *n* — **spe·cial·ly** *adv*

**spe·cial·ist** \'speshəlist\ *n* **1** : person who specializes in a particular branch of learning or activity **2** : any of four enlisted ranks in the army corresponding to the grades of corporal through sergeant first class

**spe·cial·ize** \'speshə,līz\ *vb* **-ized; -iz·ing** : concentrate one's efforts — **spe·cial·i·za·tion** \,speshələ'zāshən\ *n*

**spe·cial·ty** \'speshəltē\ n, pl **-ties** : area or field in which one specializes

**spe·cie** \'spēshē, -sē\ n : money in coin

**spe·cies** \'spēshēz, -sēz\ n, pl **species** : biological grouping of closely related organisms

**spe·cif·ic** \spi'sifik\ adj : definite or exact — **spe·cif·i·cal·ly** adv

**spec·i·fi·ca·tion** \ˌspesəfə'kāshən\ n **1** : act or process of specifying **2** : detailed description of work to be done — usu. pl.

**spec·i·fy** \'spesəˌfī\ vb **-fied; -fy·ing** : mention precisely or by name

**spec·i·men** \-əmən\ n : typical example

**spe·cious** \'spēshəs\ adj : apparently but not really genuine or correct

**speck** \'spek\ n : tiny particle or blemish — **speck** vb

**speck·led** \'spekəld\ adj : marked with spots

**spec·ta·cle** \'spektikəl\ n **1** : impressive public display **2** pl : eyeglasses

**spec·tac·u·lar** \spek'takyələr\ adj : sensational or showy

**spec·ta·tor** \'spekˌtātər\ n : person who looks on

**spec·ter, spec·tre** \'spektər\ n **1** : ghost **2** : haunting vision

**spec·tral** \'spektrəl\ adj : relating to or resembling a specter or spectrum

**spec·trum** \'spektrəm\ n, pl **-tra** \-trə\ or **-trums** : series of colors formed when white light is dispersed into its components

**spec·u·late** \'spekyəˌlāt\ vb **-lat·ed; -lat·ing** **1** : think about things yet unknown **2** : risk money in a business deal in hope of high profit — **spec·u·la·tion** \ˌspekyə'lāshən\ n — **spec·u·la·tive** \'spekyəˌlātiv\ adj — **spec·u·la·tor** \-ˌlātər\ n

**speech** \'spēch\ n **1** : power, act, or manner of speaking **2** : talk given to an audience — **speech·less** adj

**speed** \'spēd\ n **1** : quality of being fast **2** : rate of motion or performance ~ vb **sped** \'sped\ or **speed·ed; speed·ing** : go at a great or excessive rate of speed — **speed·boat** n — **speed·er** n — **speed·i·ly** \'spēdᵊlē\ adv — **speed·up** \-ˌəp\ n — **speedy** adj

**speed·om·e·ter** \spi'dämətər\ n : instrument for indicating speed

**¹spell** \'spel\ n : influence of or like magic

**²spell** vb **1** : name, write, or print the letters of **2** : mean — **spell·er** n

**³spell** vb : substitute for or relieve (someone) ~ n **1** : turn at work **2** : period of time

**spell·bound** adj : held by a spell

**spend** \'spend\ vb **spent** \'spent\; **spend·ing** **1** : pay out **2** : cause or allow to pass — **spend·er** n

**spend·thrift** \'spendˌthrift\ n : wasteful person

**sperm** \'spərm\ n, pl **sperm** or **sperms** : semen or a germ cell in it

**spew** \'spyü\ vb : gush out in a stream

**sphere** \'sfir\ n **1** : figure with every point on its surface at an equal distance from the center **2** : round body **3** : range of action or influence — **spher·i·cal** \'sfirikəl, 'sfer-\ adj

**spher·oid** \'sfir-\ n : spherelike figure

**spice** \'spīs\ n **1** : aromatic plant product for seasoning food **2** : interesting quality — **spice** vb — **spicy** adj

**spi·der** \'spīdər\ n : small insectlike animal with 8 legs — **spi·dery** adj

**spig·ot** \'spigət, 'spikət\ n : faucet

**spike** \'spīk\ n : very large nail ~ vb **spiked; spik·ing** : fasten or pierce with a spike — **spiked** \'spīkt\ adj

**spill** \'spil\ vb **1** : fall, flow, or run out unintentionally **2** : divulge ~ n **1** : act of spilling **2** : something spilled — **spill·able** adj

**spill·way** n : passage for surplus water

**spin** \'spin\ vb **spun** \'spən\; **spin·ning** **1** : draw out fiber and twist into thread **2** : form thread from a sticky body fluid **3** : revolve or cause to revolve extremely fast ~ n : rapid rotating motion — **spin·ner** n

**spin·ach** \'spinich\ n : garden herb with edible leaves

**spi·nal** \'spīnᵊl\ adj : relating to the backbone — **spi·nal·ly** adv

**spinal cord** n : thick strand of nervous tissue that extends from the brain along the back within the backbone

**spin·dle** \'spindᵊl\ n **1** : stick used for spinning thread **2** : shaft around which something turns

**spin·dly** \'spindlē\ adj : tall and slender

**spine** \'spīn\ n **1** : backbone **2** : stiff sharp projection on a plant or animal — **spine·less** adj — **spiny** adj

**spin·et** \'spinət\ n : small piano

**spin·ster** \'spinstər\ n : woman who has never married

**spi·ral** \'spīrəl\ adj : circling or wind-

ing around a single point or line —
**spiral** *n or vb* — **spi·ral·ly** *adv*

**spire** \'spīr\ *n* : steeple — **spiry** *adj*

**spir·it** \'spirət\ *n* **1** : life-giving force
**2** *cap* : presence of God **3** : ghost **4**
: mood **5** : vivacity or enthusiasm **6**
*pl* : alcoholic liquor ~ *vb* : carry off
secretly — **spir·it·ed** *adj* — **spir·it·
less** *adj*

**spir·i·tu·al** \'spirichəwəl\ *adj* **1** : relating to the spirit or sacred matters **2**
: deeply religious ~ *n* : religious folk
song — **spir·i·tu·al·i·ty** \,spirichə-
'walətē\ *n* — **spir·i·tu·al·ly** *adv*

**spir·i·tu·al·ism** \'spirichəwə,lizəm\ *n*
: belief that spirits communicate with
the living — **spir·i·tu·al·ist** \-list\ *n
or adj*

¹**spit** \'spit\ *n* **1** : rod for holding and
turning meat over a fire **2** : point of
land that runs into the water

²**spit** *vb* **spit** *or* **spat** \'spat\; **spit·ting**
: eject saliva from the mouth ~ *n* **1**
: saliva **2** : perfect likeness

**spite** \'spīt\ *n* : petty ill will ~ *vb* **spit·
ed**; **spit·ing** : annoy or offend —
**spite·ful** \-fəl\ *adj* — **spite·ful·ly** *adv*
— **in spite of** : in defiance or contempt of

**spit·tle** \'spitᵊl\ *n* : saliva

**spit·toon** \spi'tün\ *n* : receptacle for spit

**splash** \'splash\ *vb* : scatter a liquid on
— **splash** *n*

**splat·ter** \'splatər\ *vb* : spatter —
**splatter** *n*

**splay** \'splā\ *vb* : spread out or apart —
**splay** *n or adj*

**spleen** \'splēn\ *n* **1** : organ for maintenance of the blood **2** : spite or anger

**splen·did** \'splendəd\ *adj* **1** : impressive in beauty or brilliance **2** : outstanding — **splen·did·ly** *adv*

**splen·dor** \'splendər\ *n* **1** : brilliance
**2** : magnificence

**splice** \'splīs\ *vb* **spliced**; **splic·ing**
: join (2 things) end to end — **splice** *n*

**splint** \'splint\ *n* **1** : thin strip of wood
**2** : something that keeps an injured
body part in place

**splin·ter** \'splintər\ *n* : thin needlelike
piece ~ *vb* : break into splinters

**split** \'split\ *vb* **split**; **split·ting** : divide
lengthwise or along a grain — **split** *n*

**splotch** \'spläch\ *n* : blotch

**splurge** \'splərj\ *vb* **splurged**; **splurg·
ing** : indulge oneself — **splurge** *n*

**splut·ter** \'splətər\ *n* : sputter — **splut·
ter** *vb*

**spoil** \'spȯil\ *n* : plunder ~ *vb* **spoiled**
\'spȯild, 'spȯilt\ *or* **spoilt** \'spȯilt\;
**spoil·ing** **1** : pillage **2** : ruin **3** : rot
— **spoil·age** \'spȯilij\ *n* — **spoil·er** *n*

¹**spoke** \'spōk\ *past of* SPEAK

²**spoke** *n* : rod from the hub to the rim of
a wheel

**spo·ken** *past part of* SPEAK

**spokes·man** \'spōksmən\ *n* : person
who speaks for others

**spokes·wom·an** \-,wümən\ *n* : woman
who speaks for others

**sponge** \'spənj\ *n* **1** : porous water-
absorbing mass that forms the skeleton
of some marine animals **2** : sponge-
like material used for wiping ~ *vb*
**sponged**; **spong·ing** **1** : wipe with a
sponge **2** : live at another's expense
— **spongy** \'spənjē\ *adj*

**spon·sor** \'spänsər\ *n* : one who assumes responsibility for another or
who provides financial support —
**sponsor** *vb* — **spon·sor·ship** *n*

**spon·ta·ne·ous** \spän'tānēəs\ *adj*
: done, produced, or occurring naturally or without planning — **spon·ta·
ne·i·ty** \,späntən'ēətē\ *n* — **spon·
ta·ne·ous·ly** \spän'tānēəslē\ *adv*

**spoof** \'spüf\ *vb* : make good-natured
fun of — **spoof** *n*

**spook** \'spük\ *n* : ghost ~ *vb* : frighten
— **spooky** *adj*

**spool** \'spül\ *n* : cylinder on which
something is wound

**spoon** \'spün\ *n* : utensil consisting of
a small shallow bowl with a handle —
**spoon** *vb* — **spoon·ful** \-,fúl\ *n*

**spoor** \'spúr, 'spȯr\ *n* : track or trail
esp. of a wild animal

**spo·rad·ic** \spə'radik\ *adj* : occasional
— **spo·rad·i·cal·ly** *adv*

**spore** \spōr\ *n* : primitive usu. one-
celled reproductive body

**sport** \'spōrt\ *vb* **1** : frolic **2** : show off
~ *n* **1** : physical activity engaged in
for pleasure **2** : jest **3** : person who
shows good sportsmanship — **sport·
ive** \-iv\ *adj* — **sporty** *adj*

**sports·cast** \'spōrts,kast\ *n* : broadcast of a sports event — **sports·cast·
er** \-,kastər\ *n*

**sports·man** \-mən\ *n* : one who enjoys
hunting and fishing

**sports·man·ship** \-mən,ship\ *n* : ability to be gracious in winning or losing

**spot** \'spät\ *n* **1** : blemish **2** : distinctive small part **3** : location ~ *vb* **-tt-**
**1** : mark with spots **2** : see or recog-

nize ~ *adj* : made at random or in limited numbers — **spot·less** *adj* — **spot·less·ly** *adv*

**spot·light** *n* **1** : intense beam of light **2** : center of public interest — **spotlight** *vb*

**spot·ty** \'spätē\ *adj* **-ti·er; -est** : uneven in quality

**spouse** \'spaús\ *n* : one's husband or wife

**spout** \'saút\ *vb* **1** : shoot forth in a stream **2** : say pompously ~ *n* **1** : opening through which liquid spouts **2** : jet of liquid

**sprain** \'sprān\ *n* : twisting injury to a joint ~ *vb* : injure with a sprain

**sprat** \'sprat\ *n* : small or young herring

**sprawl** \'sprȯl\ *vb* : lie or sit with limbs spread out — **sprawl** *n*

**¹spray** \'sprā\ *n* : branch or arrangement of flowers

**²spray** *n* **1** : mist **2** : device that discharges liquid as a mist — **spray** *vb* — **spray·er** *n*

**spread** \'spred\ *vb* **spread; spreading 1** : open up or unfold **2** : scatter or smear over a surface **3** : cause to be known or to exist over a wide area ~ *n* **1** : extent to which something is spread **2** : cloth cover **3** : something intended to be spread — **spread·er** *n*

**spread·sheet** \'spred,shēt\ *n* : accounting program for a computer

**spree** \'sprē\ *n* : burst of indulging in something

**sprig** \'sprig\ *n* : small shoot or twig

**spright·ly** \'sprītlē\ *adj* **-li·er; -est** : lively — **spright·li·ness** *n*

**spring** \'spriŋ\ *vb* **sprang** \'spraŋ\ *or* **sprung** \'sprəŋ\; **sprung; springing 1** : move or grow quickly or by elastic force **2** : come from by descent **3** : make known suddenly ~ *n* **1** : source **2** : flow of water from underground **3** : season between winter and summer **4** : elastic body or device (as a coil of wire) **5** : leap **6** : elastic power — **springy** *adj*

**sprin·kle** \'spriŋkəl\ *vb* **-kled; -kling** : scatter in small drops or particles ~ *n* : light rainfall — **sprin·kler** *n*

**sprint** \'sprint\ *n* : short run at top speed — **sprint** *vb* — **sprint·er** *n*

**sprite** \'sprīt\ *n* : elf or elfish person

**sprock·et** \'präkət\ *n* : toothed wheel whose teeth engage the links of a chain

**sprout** \'spraút\ *vb* : send out new growth ~ *n* : plant shoot

**¹spruce** \'sprüs\ *n* : conical evergreen tree

**²spruce** *adj* **spruc·er; spruc·est** : neat and stylish in appearance ~ *vb* **spruced; spruc·ing** : make or become neat

**spry** \'sprī\ *adj* **spri·er** *or* **spry·er** \'spriər\; **spri·est** *or* **spry·est** \'sprīəst\ : agile and active

**spume** \'spyüm\ *n* : froth

**spun** *past of* SPIN

**spunk** \'spəŋk\ *n* : courage — **spunky** *adj*

**spur** \'spər\ *n* **1** : pointed device used to urge on a horse **2** : something that urges to action **3** : projecting part ~ *vb* **-rr-** : urge on — **spurred** *adj*

**spu·ri·ous** \'spyúrēəs\ *adj* : not genuine

**spurn** \'spərn\ *vb* : reject

**¹spurt** \'spərt\ *n* : burst of effort, speed, or activity ~ *vb* : make a spurt

**²spurt** *vb* : gush out ~ *n* : sudden gush

**sput·ter** \'spətər\ *vb* **1** : talk hastily and indistinctly in excitement **2** : make popping sounds — **sputter** *n*

**spy** \'spī\ *vb* **spied; spy·ing** : watch or try to gather information secretly — **spy** *n*

**squab** \'skwäb\ *n, pl* **squabs** *or* **squab** : young pigeon

**squab·ble** \'skwäbəl\ *n or vb* : dispute

**squad** \'skwäd\ *n* : small group

**squad·ron** \'skwädrən\ *n* : small military unit

**squal·id** \'skwäləd\ *adj* : filthy or wretched

**squall** \'skwȯl\ *n* : sudden violent brief storm — **squally** *adj*

**squa·lor** \'skwälər\ *n* : quality or state of being squalid

**squan·der** \'skwändər\ *vb* : waste

**square** \'skwar\ *n* **1** : instrument for measuring right angles **2** : flat figure that has 4 equal sides and 4 right angles **3** : open area in a city **4** : product of number multiplied by itself ~ *adj* **squar·er; squar·est 1** : being a square in form **2** : having sides meet at right angles **3** : multiplied by itself **4** : being a square unit of area **5** : honest ~ *vb* **squared; squar·ing 1** : form into a square **2** : multiply (a number) by itself **3** : conform **4** : settle — **square·ly** *adv*

**¹squash** \'skwäsh, 'skwȯsh\ *vb* **1** : press flat **2** : suppress

**²squash** *n, pl* **squash·es** *or* **squash** : garden vegetable

**squat** \'skwät\ *vb* **-tt-** **1** : stoop or sit on one's heels **2** : settle on land one does not own ~ *n* : act or posture of squatting ~ *adj* **squat·ter; squat·test** : short and thick — **squat·ter** *n*

**squawk** \'skwók\ *n* : harsh loud cry — **squawk** *vb*

**squeak** \'skwēk\ *vb* : make a thin high-pitched sound — **squeak** *n* — **squeaky** *adj*

**squeal** \'skwēl\ *vb* **1** : make a shrill sound or cry **2** : protest — **squeal** *n*

**squea·mish** \'skwēmish\ *adj* : easily nauseated or disgusted

**squeeze** \'skwēz\ *vb* **squeezed; squeez·ing** **1** : apply pressure to **2** : extract by pressure — **squeeze** *n* — **squeez·er** *n*

**squelch** \'skwelch\ *vb* : suppress (as with a retort) — **squelch** *n*

**squid** \'skwid\ *n, pl* **squid** *or* **squids** : 10-armed long-bodied sea mollusk

**squint** \'skwint\ *vb* : look with the eyes partly closed — **squint** *n or adj*

**squire** \'skwīr\ *n* **1** : knight's aide **2** : country landholder **3** : lady's devoted escort ~ *vb* **squired; squir·ing** : escort

**squirm** \'skwərm\ *vb* : wriggle

**squir·rel** \'skwərəl\ *n* : rodent with a long bushy tail

**squirt** \'skwərt\ *vb* : eject liquid in a spurt — **squirt** *n*

**stab** \'stab\ *n* **1** : wound made by a pointed weapon **2** : quick thrust **3** : attempt ~ *vb* **-bb-** : pierce or wound with or as if with a pointed weapon

¹**sta·ble** \'stābəl\ *n* : building for domestic animals ~ *vb* **-bled; -bling** : keep in a stable

²**stable** *adj* **sta·bler; sta·blest** **1** : firmly established **2** : mentally and emotionally healthy **3** : steady — **sta·bil·i·ty** \stə'bilətē\ *n* — **sta·bil·iza·tion** \,stābələ'zāshən\ *n* — **sta·bi·lize** \'stābə,līz\ *vb* — **sta·bi·liz·er** *n*

**stac·ca·to** \stə'kätō\ *adj* : disconnected

**stack** \'stak\ *n* : large pile ~ *vb* : pile up

**sta·di·um** \'stādēəm\ *n* : outdoor sports arena

**staff** \'staf\ *n, pl* **staffs** \'stafs, stavz\ *or* **staves** \'stavz, 'stāvz\ **1** : rod or supporting cane **2** : people assisting a leader **3** : 5 horizontal lines on which music is written ~ *vb* : supply with workers — **staff·er** *n*

**staff sergeant** *n* : noncommissioned of-ficer ranking next above a sergeant in the army, air force, or marine corps

**stag** \'stag\ *n, pl* **stags** *or* **stag** : male deer ~ *adj* : only for men ~ *adv* : without a date

**stage** \'stāj\ *n* **1** : raised platform for a speaker or performers **2** : theater **3** : step in a process ~ *vb* **staged; stag·ing** : produce (a play)

**stage·coach** *n* : passenger coach

**stag·ger** \'stagər\ *vb* **1** : reel or cause to reel from side to side **2** : overlap or alternate — **stagger** *n* — **stag·ger·ing·ly** *adv*

**stag·nant** \'stagnənt\ *adj* : not moving or active — **stag·nate** \-,nāt\ *vb* — **stag·na·tion** \stag'nāshən\ *n*

¹**staid** \'stād\ *adj* : sedate

²**staid** *past of* **STAY**

**stain** \'stān\ *vb* **1** : discolor **2** : dye (as wood) **3** : disgrace ~ *n* **1** : discolored area **2** : mark of guilt **3** : coloring preparation — **stain·less** *adj*

**stair** \'star\ *n* **1** : step in a series for going from one level to another **2** *pl* : flight of steps — **stair·way** *n*

**stair·case** *n* : series of steps with their framework

**stake** \'stāk\ *n* **1** : usu. small post driven into the ground **2** : bet **3** : prize in a contest ~ *vb* **staked; stak·ing** **1** : mark or secure with a stake **2** : bet

**sta·lac·tite** \stə'lak,tīt\ *n* : icicle-shaped deposit hanging in a cavern

**sta·lag·mite** \stə'lag,mīt\ *n* : icicle-shaped deposit on a cavern floor

**stale** \'stāl\ *adj* **stal·er; stal·est** **1** : having lost good taste and quality from age **2** : no longer new, strong, or effective — **stale·ness** *n*

**stale·mate** \'stāl,māt\ *n* : deadlock — **stalemate** *vb*

¹**stalk** \'stók\ *vb* **1** : walk stiffly or proudly **2** : pursue stealthily

²**stalk** *n* : plant stem — **stalked** \'stókt\ *adj*

¹**stall** \'stól\ *n* **1** : compartment in a stable **2** : booth where articles are sold

²**stall** *vb* : bring or come to a standstill unintentionally

³**stall** *vb* : delay, evade, or keep a situation going to gain advantage or time

**stal·lion** \'stalyən\ *n* : male horse

**stal·wart** \'stólwərt\ *adj* : strong or brave

**sta·men** \'stāmən\ *n* : flower organ that produces pollen

**stam·i·na** \'stamənə\ *n* : endurance

**stam·mer** \'stamər\ *vb* : hesitate in speaking — **stammer** *n*

**stamp** \'stamp\ *vb* **1** : pound with the sole of the foot or a heavy implement **2** : impress or imprint **3** : cut out with a die **4** : attach a postage stamp to ~ *n* **1** : device for stamping **2** : act of stamping **3** : government seal showing a tax or fee has been paid

**stam·pede** \stam'pēd\ *n* : headlong rush of frightened animals ~ *vb* **-ped·ed; -ped·ing** : flee in panic

**stance** \'stans\ *n* : way of standing

¹**stanch** \'stónch, 'stänch\ *vb* : stop the flow of (as blood)

²**stanch** *var of* STAUNCH

**stan·chion** \'stanchən\ *n* : upright support

**stand** \'stand\ *vb* **stood** \'stúd\; **standing 1** : be at rest in or assume an upright position **2** : remain unchanged **3** : be steadfast **4** : maintain a relative position or rank **5** : set upright **6** : undergo or endure ~ *n* **1** : act or place of standing, staying, or resisting **2** : sales booth **3** : structure for holding something upright **4** : group of plants growing together **5** *pl* : tiered seats **6** : opinion or viewpoint

**stan·dard** \'standərd\ *n* **1** : symbolic figure or flag **2** : model, rule, or guide **3** : upright support — **standard** *adj* — **stan·dard·i·za·tion** \₁standərdə-'zāshən\ *n* — **stan·dard·ize** \'standərd₁īz\ *vb*

**standard time** *n* : time established over a region or country

**stand·ing** \'standiŋ\ *n* **1** : relative position or rank **2** : duration

**stand·still** *n* : state of rest

**stank** *past of* STINK

**stan·za** \'stanzə\ *n* : division of a poem

¹**sta·ple** \'stāpəl\ *n* : U-shaped wire fastener — **staple** *vb* — **sta·pler** \-plər\ *n*

²**staple** *n* : chief commodity or item — **staple** *adj*

**star** \'stär\ *n* **1** : celestial body visible as a point of light **2** : 5- or 6-pointed figure representing a star **3** : leading performer ~ *vb* **-rr- 1** : mark with a star **2** : play the leading role — **star·dom** \'stärdəm\ *n* — **star·less** *adj* — **star·light** *n* — **star·ry** *adj*

**star·board** \'stärbərd\ *n* : right side of a ship or airplane looking forward — **starboard** *adj*

**starch** \'stärch\ *n* : nourishing carbohydrate from plants also used in adhesives and laundering ~ *vb* : stiffen with starch — **starchy** *adj*

**stare** \'star\ *vb* **stared; star·ing** : look intently with wide-open eyes — **stare** *n* — **star·er** *n*

**stark** \'stärk\ *adj* **1** : absolute **2** : severe or bleak ~ *adv* : completely — **stark·ly** *adv*

**star·ling** \'stärliŋ\ *n* : bird related to the crows

**start** \'stärt\ *vb* **1** : twitch or jerk (as from surprise) **2** : perform or show performance of the first part of an action or process ~ *n* **1** : sudden involuntary motion **2** : beginning — **start·er** *n*

**star·tle** \'stärt°l\ *vb* **-tled; -tling** : frighten or surprise suddenly

**starve** \'stärv\ *vb* **starved; starv·ing 1** : suffer or die from hunger **2** : kill with hunger — **star·va·tion** \stär'vāshən\ *n*

**stash** \'stash\ *vb* : store in a secret place for future use — **stash** *n*

**state** \'stāt\ *n* **1** : condition of being **2** : condition of mind **3** : nation or a political unit within it ~ *vb* **stat·ed; stat·ing 1** : express in words **2** : establish — **state·hood** \-₁húd\ *n*

**state·ly** \'stātlē\ *adj* **-li·er; -est** : having impressive dignity — **state·li·ness** *n*

**state·ment** \'stātmənt\ *n* **1** : something stated **2** : financial summary

**state·room** *n* : private room on a ship

**states·man** \'stātsmən\ *n* : one skilled in government or diplomacy — **states·man·like** *adj* — **states·man·ship** *n*

**stat·ic** \'statik\ *adj* **1** : relating to bodies at rest or forces in equilibrium **2** : not moving **3** : relating to stationary charges of electricity ~ *n* : noise on radio or television from electrical disturbances

**sta·tion** \'stāshən\ *n* **1** : place of duty **2** : regular stop on a bus or train route **3** : social standing **4** : place where radio or television programs originate ~ *vb* : assign to a station

**sta·tion·ary** \'stāshə₁nerē\ *adj* **1** : not moving or not movable **2** : not changing

**sta·tio·nery** \'stāshə₁nerē\ *n* : letter paper with envelopes

**sta·tis·tic** \stə'tistik\ *n* : single item of statistics

**sta·tis·tics** \-tiks\ *n pl* : numerical facts collected for study — **sta·tis·ti·cal**

\-tikəl\ *adj* — **sta·tis·ti·cal·ly** *adv* — **stat·is·ti·cian** \ˌstatə'stishən\ *n*

**stat·u·ary** \'stachəˌwerē\ *n, pl* **-ar·ies** : collection of statues

**stat·ue** \'stachü\ *n* : solid 3-dimensional likeness — **stat·u·ette** \ˌstachə'wet\ *n*

**stat·u·esque** \ˌstachə'wesk\ *adj* : tall and shapely

**stat·ure** \'stachər\ *n* **1** : height **2** : status gained by achievement

**sta·tus** \'stātəs, 'stat-\ *n* : relative situation or condition

**sta·tus quo** \-'kwō\ *n* : existing state of affairs

**stat·ute** \'stachüt\ *n* : law — **stat·u·to·ry** \'stachəˌtōrē\ *adj*

**staunch** \'stȯnch\ *adj* : steadfast — **staunch·ly** *adv*

**stave** \'stāv\ *n* : narrow strip of wood ⁓ *vb* **staved** *or* **stove** \'stōv\; **stav·ing** **1** : break a hole in **2** : drive away

**staves** *pl of* **STAFF**

¹**stay** \'stā\ *n* : support ⁓ *vb* **stayed; stay·ing** : prop up

²**stay** *vb* **stayed** \'stād\ *or* **staid** \'stād\; **stay·ing** **1** : pause **2** : remain **3** : reside **4** : stop or postpone **5** : satisfy for a time ⁓ *n* : a staying

**stead** \'sted\ *n* : one's place, job, or function — **in good stead** : to advantage

**stead·fast** \-ˌfast\ *adj* : faithful or determined — **stead·fast·ly** *adv*

**steady** \'stedē\ *adj* **steadi·er; -est** **1** : firm in position or sure in movement **2** : calm or reliable **3** : constant **4** : regular ⁓ *vb* **stead·ied; steady·ing** : make or become steady — **stead·i·ly** \'sted³lē\ *adv* — **steadi·ness** *n* — **steady** *adv*

**steak** \'stāk\ *n* : thick slice of meat

**steal** \'stēl\ *vb* **stole** \'stōl\; **sto·len** \'stōlən\; **steal·ing** **1** : take and carry away wrongfully and with intent to keep **2** : move secretly or slowly

**stealth** \'stelth\ *n* : secret or unobtrusive procedure — **stealth·i·ly** \-thəlē\ *adv* — **stealthy** *adj*

**steam** \'stēm\ *n* : vapor of boiling water ⁓ *vb* : give off steam — **steam·boat** *n* — **steam·ship** *n* — **steamy** *adj*

**steed** \'stēd\ *n* : horse

**steel** \'stēl\ *n* : tough carbon-containing iron ⁓ *vb* : fill with courage — **steel** *adj* — **steely** *adj*

¹**steep** \'stēp\ *adj* : having a very sharp slope or great elevation — **steep·ly** *adv* — **steep·ness** *n*

²**steep** *vb* : soak in a liquid

**stee·ple** \'stēpəl\ *n* : usu. tapering church tower

**stee·ple·chase** *n* : race over hurdles

¹**steer** \'stir\ *n* : castrated ox

²**steer** *vb* **1** : direct the course of (as a ship or car) **2** : guide

**steer·age** \'stirij\ *n* : section in a ship for people paying the lowest fares

**stein** \'stīn\ *n* : mug

**stel·lar** \'stelər\ *adj* : relating to stars or resembling a star

¹**stem** \'stem\ *n* : main upright part of a plant ⁓ *vb* **-mm-** **1** : derive **2** : make progress against — **stem·less** *adj* — **stemmed** *adj*

²**stem** *vb* **-mm-** : stop the flow of

**stem cell** *n* : undifferentiated cell that may give rise to many different types of cells

**stench** \'stench\ *n* : stink

**sten·cil** \'stensəl\ *n* : printing sheet cut with letters to let ink pass through — **stencil** *vb*

**ste·nog·ra·phy** \stə'nägrəfē\ *n* : art or process of writing in shorthand — **ste·nog·ra·pher** \-fər\ *n* — **steno·graph·ic** \ˌstenə'grafik\ *adj*

**sten·to·ri·an** \sten'tōrēən\ *adj* : extremely loud and powerful

**step** \'step\ *n* **1** : single action of a leg in walking or running **2** : rest for the foot in going up or down **3** : degree, rank, or stage **4** : way of walking ⁓ *vb* **-pp-** **1** : move by steps **2** : press with the foot

**step-** \'step-\ *comb form* : related by a remarriage and not by blood

**step·lad·der** *n* : light portable set of steps in a hinged frame

**steppe** \'step\ *n* : dry grassy treeless land esp. of Asia

**-ster** \stər\ *n suffix* **1** : one that does, makes, or uses **2** : one that is associated with or takes part in **3** : one that is

**ste·reo** \'sterēˌō, 'stir-\ *n, pl* **-reos** : stereophonic sound system — **stereo** *adj*

**ste·reo·phon·ic** \ˌsterēə'fänik, ˌstir-\ *adj* : relating to a 3-dimensional effect of reproduced sound

**ste·reo·type** \'sterēəˌtīp, 'stir-\ *n* : gross often mistaken generalization — **stereotype** *vb* — **ste·reo·typ·i·cal** \ˌsterēə'tipikəl\ *adj* — **ste·reo·typi·cal·ly** *adv*

**ste·reo·typed** \'sterēəˌtīpt, 'stir-\ *adj* : lacking originality or individuality

**ster·ile** \'sterəl\ *adj* **1** : unable to bear fruit, crops, or offspring **2** : free from disease germs — **ste·ril·i·ty** \stə-'rilətē\ *n* — **ster·il·i·za·tion** \,sterələ-'zāshən\ *n* — **ster·il·ize** \-ə,līz\ *vb* — **ster·il·iz·er** *n*

**ster·ling** \'stərliŋ\ *adj* **1** : being or made of an alloy of 925 parts of silver with 75 parts of copper **2** : excellent

**¹stern** \'stərn\ *adj* : severe — **stern·ly** *adv* — **stern·ness** *n*

**²stern** *n* : back end of a boat

**ster·num** \'stərnəm\ *n, pl* **-nums** *or* **-na** \-nə\ : long flat chest bone joining the 2 sets of ribs

**stetho·scope** \'stethə,skōp\ *n* : instrument used for listening to sounds in the chest

**ste·ve·dore** \'stēvə,dōr\ *n* : worker who loads and unloads ships

**stew** \'stü, 'styü\ *n* **1** : dish of boiled meat and vegetables **2** : state of worry or agitation — **stew** *vb*

**stew·ard** \'stüərd, 'styü-\ *n* **1** : manager of an estate or an organization **2** : person on a ship or airliner who looks after passenger comfort — **stew·ard·ship** *n*

**stew·ard·ess** \-əs\ *n* : woman who is a steward (as on an airplane)

**¹stick** \'stik\ *n* **1** : cut or broken branch **2** : long thin piece of wood or something resembling it

**²stick** *vb* **stuck** \'stək\; **stick·ing** **1** : stab **2** : thrust or project **3** : hold fast to something **4** : attach **5** : become jammed or fixed

**stick·er** \'stikər\ *n* : adhesive label

**stick·ler** \'stiklər\ *n* : one who insists on exactness or completeness

**sticky** \'stikē\ *adj* **stick·i·er; -est** **1** : adhesive or gluey **2** : muggy **3** : difficult

**stiff** \'stif\ *adj* **1** : not bending easily **2** : tense **3** : formal **4** : strong **5** : severe — **stiff·en** \'stifən\ *vb* — **stiff·en·er** \-ənər\ *n* — **stiff·ly** *adv* — **stiff·ness** *n*

**sti·fle** \'stīfəl\ *vb* **-fled; -fling** **1** : smother or suffocate **2** : suppress

**stig·ma** \'stigmə\ *n, pl* **-ma·ta** \stig-'mätə, 'stigmətə\ *or* **-mas** : mark of disgrace — **stig·ma·tize** \'stigmə-,tīz\ *vb*

**stile** \'stīl\ *n* : steps for crossing a fence

**sti·let·to** \stə'letō\ *n, pl* **-tos** *or* **-toes** : slender dagger

**¹still** \'stil\ *adj* **1** : motionless **2** : silent

— *vb* : make or become still ∼ *adv* **1** : without motion **2** : up to and during this time **3** : in spite of that ∼ *n* : silence — **still·ness** *n*

**²still** *n* : apparatus used in distillation

**still·born** *adj* : born dead — **still·birth** *n*

**stilt** \'stilt\ *n* : one of a pair of poles for walking

**stilt·ed** \'stiltəd\ *adj* : not easy and natural

**stim·u·lant** \'stimyələnt\ *n* : substance that temporarily increases the activity of an organism — **stimulant** *adj*

**stim·u·late** \-,lāt\ *vb* **-lat·ed; -lat·ing** : make active — **stim·u·la·tion** \,stimyə'lāshən\ *n*

**stim·u·lus** \'stimyələs\ *n, pl* **-li** \-,lī\ : something that stimulates

**sting** \'stiŋ\ *vb* **stung** \'stəŋ\; **sting·ing** **1** : prick painfully **2** : cause to suffer acutely ∼ *n* : act of stinging or a resulting wound — **sting·er** *n*

**stin·gy** \'stinjē\ *adj* **stin·gi·er; -est** : not generous — **stin·gi·ness** *n*

**stink** \'stiŋk\ *vb* **stank** \'staŋk\ *or* **stunk** \'stəŋk\; **stunk; stink·ing** : have a strong offensive odor — **stink** *n* — **stink·er** *n*

**stint** \'stint\ *vb* : be sparing or stingy ∼ *n* **1** : restraint **2** : quantity or period of work

**sti·pend** \'stī,pend, -pənd\ *n* : money paid periodically

**stip·ple** \'stipəl\ *vb* **-pled; -pling** : engrave, paint, or draw with dots instead of lines — **stipple** *n*

**stip·u·late** \'stipyə,lāt\ *vb* **-lat·ed; -lat·ing** : demand as a condition — **stip·u·la·tion** \,stipyə'lāshən\ *n*

**stir** \'stər\ *vb* **-rr-** **1** : move slightly **2** : prod or push into activity **3** : mix by continued circular movement ∼ *n* : act or result of stirring

**stir·rup** \'stərəp\ *n* : saddle loop for the foot

**stitch** \'stich\ *n* **1** : loop formed by a needle in sewing **2** : sudden sharp pain ∼ *vb* **1** : fasten or decorate with stitches **2** : sew

**stock** \'stäk\ *n* **1** : block or part of wood **2** : original from which others derive **3** : farm animals **4** : supply of goods **5** : money invested in a large business **6** *pl* : instrument of punishment like a pillory with holes for the feet or feet and hands ∼ *vb* : provide with stock

**stock•ade** \stä'kād\ n : defensive or confining enclosure

**stock•ing** \'stäkiŋ\ n : close-fitting covering for the foot and leg

**stock•pile** n : reserve supply — **stock•pile** vb

**stocky** \'stäkē\ adj **stock•i•er; -est** : short and relatively thick

**stock•yard** n : yard for livestock to be slaughtered or shipped

**stodgy** \'stäjē\ adj **stodg•i•er; -est 1** : dull **2** : old-fashioned

**sto•ic** \'stōik\, **sto•i•cal** \-ikəl\ adj : showing indifference to pain — **stoic** n — **sto•i•cal•ly** adv — **sto•i•cism** \'stōə̇sizəm\ n

**stoke** \'stōk\ vb **stoked; stok•ing** : stir up a fire or supply fuel to a furnace — **stok•er** n

¹**stole** \'stōl\ past of STEAL

²**stole** n : long wide scarf

**stolen** past part of STEAL

**stol•id** \'stäləd\ adj : having or showing little or no emotion — **stol•id•ly** \'stälədlē\ adv

**stom•ach** \'stəmək, -ik\ n **1** : saclike digestive organ **2** : abdomen **3** : appetite or desire ~ vb : put up with — **stom•ach•ache** n

**stomp** \'stämp, 'stomp\ vb : stamp

**stone** \'stōn\ n **1** : hardened earth or mineral matter **2** : small piece of rock **3** : seed that is hard or has a hard covering ~ vb **stoned; ston•ing** : pelt or kill with stones — **stony** adj

**stood** past of STAND

**stool** \'stül\ n **1** : seat usu. without back or arms **2** : footstool **3** : discharge of feces

¹**stoop** \'stüp\ vb **1** : bend over **2** : lower oneself ~ n **1** : act of bending over **2** : bent position of shoulders

²**stoop** n : small porch at a house door

**stop** \'stäp\ vb **-pp- 1** : block an opening **2** : end or cause to end **3** : pause for rest or a visit in a journey ~ n **1** : plug **2** : act or place of stopping **3** : delay in a journey — **stop•light** n — **stop•page** \-ij\ n — **stop•per** n

**stop•gap** n : temporary measure or thing

**stor•age** \'stōrij\ n : safekeeping of goods (as in a warehouse)

**store** \'stōr\ vb **stored; stor•ing** : put aside for future use ~ n **1** : something stored **2** : retail business establishment — **store•house** n — **store•keep•er** n — **store•room** n

**stork** \'stork\ n : large wading bird

**storm** \'storm\ n **1** : heavy fall of rain or snow **2** : violent outbreak ~ vb **1** : rain or snow heavily **2** : rage **3** : make an attack against — **stormy** adj

¹**sto•ry** \'stōrē\ n, pl **-ries 1** : narrative **2** : report — **sto•ry•tell•er** n

²**story** n, pl **-ries** : floor of a building

**stout** \'staut\ adj **1** : firm or strong **2** : thick or bulky — **stout•ly** adv — **stout•ness** n

¹**stove** \'stōv\ n : apparatus for providing heat (as for cooking or heating)

²**stove** past of STAVE

**stow** \'stō\ vb **1** : pack in a compact mass **2** : put or hide away

**strad•dle** \'stradᵊl\ vb **-dled; -dling** : stand over or sit on with legs on opposite sides — **straddle** n

**strafe** \'strāf\ vb **strafed; straf•ing** : fire upon with machine guns from a low-flying airplane

**strag•gle** \'stragəl\ vb **-gled; -gling** : wander or become separated from others — **strag•gler** \-ələr\ n

**straight** \'strāt\ adj **1** : having no bends, turns, or twists **2** : just, proper, or honest **3** : neat and orderly ~ adv : in a straight manner — **straight•en** \'strātᵊn\ vb

**straight•for•ward** \strāt'fórwərd\ adj : frank or honest

**straight•way** adv : immediately

¹**strain** \'strān\ n **1** : lineage **2** : trace

²**strain** vb **1** : exert to the utmost **2** : filter or remove by filtering **3** : injure by improper use ~ n **1** : excessive tension or exertion **2** : bodily injury from excessive effort — **strain•er** n

**strait** \'strāt\ n **1** : narrow channel connecting 2 bodies of water **2** pl : distress

**strait•en** \'strātᵊn\ vb **1** : hem in **2** : make distressing or difficult

¹**strand** \'strand\ vb **1** : drive or cast upon the shore **2** : leave helpless

²**strand** n **1** : twisted fiber of a rope **2** : length of something ropelike

**strange** \'strānj\ adj **strang•er; strang•est 1** : unusual or queer **2** : new — **strange•ly** adv — **strange•ness** n

**strang•er** \'strānjər\ n : person with whom one is not acquainted

**stran•gle** \'straŋgəl\ vb **-gled; -gling** : choke to death — **stran•gler** \-glər\ n

**stran•gu•la•tion** \ₒstraŋgyə'lāshən\ n : act or process of strangling

**strap** \'strap\ n : narrow strip of flexible material used esp. for fastening ~ vb 1 : secure with a strap 2 : beat with a strap — **strap·less** n

**strap·ping** \'strapiŋ\ adj : robust

**strat·a·gem** \'stratəjəm, -ˌjem\ n : deceptive scheme or maneuver

**strat·e·gy** \'stratəjē\ n, pl -gies : carefully worked out plan of action — **strate·gic** \strə'tējik\ adj — **strat·e·gist** \'stratəjist\

**strat·i·fy** \'stratəˌfī\ vb -fied; -fy·ing : form or arrange in layers — **strat·i·fi·ca·tion** \ˌstratəfə'kāshən\ n

**strato·sphere** \'stratəˌsfir\ n : earth's atmosphere from about 7 to 31 miles above the surface

**stra·tum** \'strātəm, 'strat-\ n, pl -ta \'strātə, 'strat-\ : layer

**straw** \'strȯ\ n 1 : grass stems after grain is removed 2 : tube for drinking ~ adj : made of straw

**straw·ber·ry** \'strȯˌberē\ n : juicy red pulpy fruit

**stray** \'strā\ vb : wander or deviate ~ n : person or animal that strays ~ adj : separated from or not related to anything close by

**streak** \'strēk\ n 1 : mark of a different color 2 : narrow band of light 3 : trace 4 : run (as of luck) or series ~ vb 1 : form streaks in or on 2 : move fast

**stream** \'strēm\ n 1 : flow of water on land 2 : steady flow (as of water or air) ~ vb 1 : flow in a stream 2 : pour out streams

**stream·er** \'strēmər\ n : long ribbon or ribbonlike flag

**stream·lined** \-ˌlīnd, -'līnd\ adj 1 : made with contours to reduce air or water resistance 2 : simplified 3 : modernized — **streamline** vb

**street** \'strēt\ n : thoroughfare esp. in a city or town

**street·car** n : passenger vehicle running on rails in the streets

**strength** \'streŋth\ n 1 : quality of being strong 2 : toughness 3 : intensity

**strength·en** \'streŋthən\ vb : make, grow, or become stronger — **strength·en·er** \'streŋthənər\ n

**stren·u·ous** \'strenyəwəs\ adj 1 : vigorous 2 : requiring or showing energy — **stren·u·ous·ly** adv

**stress** \'stres\ n 1 : pressure or strain that tends to distort a body 2 : relative prominence given to one thing among others 3 : state of physical or mental tension or something inducing it ~ vb : put stress on — **stress·ful** \'stresfəl\ adj

**stretch** \'strech\ vb 1 : spread or reach out 2 : draw out in length or breadth 3 : make taut 4 : exaggerate 5 : become extended without breaking ~ n : act of extending beyond normal limits

**stretch·er** \'strechər\ n : device for carrying a sick or injured person

**strew** \'strü\ vb **strewed; strewed** or **strewn** \'strün\; **strew·ing** 1 : scatter 2 : cover by scattering something over

**strick·en** \'strikən\ adj : afflicted with disease

**strict** \'strikt\ adj 1 : allowing no escape or evasion 2 : precise — **strict·ly** adv — **strict·ness** n

**stric·ture** \'strikchər\ n : hostile criticism

**stride** \'strīd\ vb **strode** \'strōd\; **strid·den** \'strid⁰n\; **strid·ing** : walk or run with long steps ~ n 1 : long step 2 : manner of striding

**stri·dent** \'strīd⁰nt\ adj : loud and harsh

**strife** \'strīf\ n : conflict

**strike** \'strīk\ vb **struck** \'strək\; **struck; strik·ing** \'strīkiŋ\ 1 : hit sharply 2 : delete 3 : produce by impressing 4 : cause to sound 5 : afflict 6 : occur to or impress 7 : cause (a match) to ignite by rubbing 8 : refrain from working 9 : find 10 : take on (as a pose) ~ n 1 : act or instance of striking 2 : work stoppage 3 : military attack — **strik·er** n —

**strike out** vb : start out vigorously —

**strike up** vb : start

**strik·ing** \'strīkiŋ\ adj : very noticeable — **strik·ing·ly** adv

**string** \'striŋ\ n 1 : line usu. of twisted threads 2 : series 3 pl : stringed instruments ~ vb **strung** \'strəŋ\; **string·ing** 1 : thread on or with a string 2 : hang or fasten by a string

**stringed** \'striŋd\ adj : having strings

**strin·gent** \'strinjənt\ adj : severe

**stringy** \'striŋē\ adj **string·i·er; -est** : tough or fibrous

¹**strip** \'strip\ vb **-pp-** 1 : take the covering or clothing from 2 : undress — **strip·per** n

²**strip** n : long narrow flat piece

**stripe** \'strīp\ n : distinctive line or long narrow section ~ vb **striped**

\\'strīpt\\; **strip•ing** : make stripes on — **striped** \\'strīpt, 'strīpəd\\ *adj*

**strive** \\'strīv\\ *vb* **strove** \\'strōv\\; **striv•en** \\'strivən\\ *or* **strived; striv•ing** \\'strīviŋ\\ **1** : struggle **2** : try hard

**strode** *past of* STRIDE

**stroke** \\'strōk\\ *vb* **stroked; strok•ing** : rub gently ~ *n* **1** : act of swinging or striking **2** : sudden action

**stroll** \\'strōl\\ *vb* : walk leisurely — **stroll** *n* — **stroll•er** *n*

**strong** \\'strȯŋ\\ *adj* **1** : capable of exerting great force or of withstanding stress or violence **2** : healthy **3** : zealous — **strong•ly** *adv*

**strong•hold** *n* : fortified place

**struck** *past of* STRIKE

**struc•ture** \\'strəkchər\\ *n* **1** : building **2** : arrangement of elements ~ *vb* **-tured; -tur•ing** : make into a structure — **struc•tur•al** \\-chərəl\\ *adj*

**strug•gle** \\'strəgəl\\ *vb* **-gled; -gling 1** : make strenuous efforts to overcome an adversary **2** : proceed with great effort ~ *n* **1** : strenuous effort **2** : intense competition for superiority

**strum** \\'strəm\\ *vb* **-mm-** : play (a musical instrument) by brushing the strings with the fingers

**strum•pet** \\'strəmpət\\ *n* : prostitute

**strung** *past of* STRING

**strut** \\'strət\\ *vb* **-tt-** : walk in a proud or showy manner ~ *n* **1** : proud walk **2** : supporting bar or rod

**strych•nine** \\'strik,nīn, -nən, -,nēn\\ *n* : bitter poisonous substance

**stub** \\'stəb\\ *n* : short end or section ~ *vb* **-bb-** : strike against something

**stub•ble** \\'stəbəl\\ *n* : short growth left after cutting — **stub•bly** *adj*

**stub•born** \\'stəbərn\\ *adj* **1** : determined not to yield **2** : hard to control — **stub•born•ly** *adv* — **stub•born•ness** *n*

**stub•by** \\'stəbē\\ *adj* : short, blunt, and thick

**stuc•co** \\'stəkō\\ *n, pl* **-cos** *or* **-coes** : plaster for coating outside walls — **stuc•coed** \\'stəkōd\\ *adj*

**stuck** *past of* STICK

**stuck-up** \\'stək'əp\\ *adj* : conceited

**¹stud** \\'stəd\\ *n* : male horse kept for breeding

**²stud** *n* **1** : upright beam for holding wall material **2** : projecting nail, pin, or rod ~ *vb* **-dd-** : supply or dot with studs

**stu•dent** \\'stüd³nt, 'styü-\\ *n* : one who studies

**stud•ied** \\'stədēd\\ *adj* : premeditated

**stu•dio** \\'stüdē,ō, 'styü-\\ *n, pl* **-dios 1** : artist's workroom **2** : place where movies are made or television or radio shows are broadcast

**stu•di•ous** \\'stüdēəs, 'styü-\\ *adj* : devoted to study — **stu•di•ous•ly** *adv*

**study** \\'stədē\\ *n, pl* **stud•ies 1** : act or process of learning about something **2** : branch of learning **3** : careful examination **4** : room for reading or studying ~ *vb* **stud•ied; study•ing** : apply the attention and mind to a subject

**stuff** \\'stəf\\ *n* **1** : personal property **2** : raw or fundamental material **3** : unspecified material or things ~ *vb* : fill by packing things in — **stuff•ing** *n*

**stuffy** \\'stəfē\\ *adj* **stuff•i•er; -est 1** : lacking fresh air **2** : unimaginative or pompous

**stul•ti•fy** \\'stəltə,fī\\ *vb* **-fied; -fy•ing 1** : cause to appear foolish **2** : impair or make ineffective **3** : have a dulling effect on

**stum•ble** \\'stəmbəl\\ *vb* **-bled; -bling 1** : lose one's balance or fall in walking or running **2** : speak or act clumsily **3** : happen by chance — **stumble** *n*

**stump** \\'stəmp\\ *n* : part left when something is cut off ~ *vb* : confuse — **stumpy** *adj*

**stun** \\'stən\\ *vb* **-nn- 1** : make senseless or dizzy by or as if by a blow **2** : bewilder

**stung** *past of* STING

**stunk** *past of* STINK

**stun•ning** \\'stəniŋ\\ *adj* **1** : astonishing or incredible **2** : strikingly beautiful — **stun•ning•ly** *adv*

**¹stunt** \\'stənt\\ *vb* : hinder the normal growth or progress of

**²stunt** *n* : spectacular feat

**stu•pe•fy** \\'stüpə,fī, 'styü-\\ *vb* **-fied; -fy•ing 1** : make insensible by or as if by drugs **2** : amaze

**stu•pen•dous** \\stü'pendəs, styü-\\ *adj* : very big or impressive — **stu•pendous•ly** *adv*

**stu•pid** \\'stüpəd, 'styü-\\ *adj* : not sensible or intelligent — **stu•pid•i•ty** \\stü-'pidətē, styü-\\ *n* — **stu•pid•ly** *adv*

**stu•por** \\'stüpər, 'styü-\\ *n* : state of being conscious but not aware or sensible

**stur•dy** \\'stərdē\\ *adj* **-di•er; -est**

: strong — **stur·di·ly** \\'stərd°lē\\ *adv*
— **stur·di·ness** *n*

**stur·geon** \\'stərjən\\ *n* : fish whose roe is caviar

**stut·ter** \\'stətər\\ *vb or n* : stammer

¹**sty** \\'stī\\ *n, pl* **sties** : pig pen

²**sty, stye** \\'stī\\ *n, pl* **sties** *or* **styes** : inflamed swelling on the edge of an eyelid

**style** \\'stīl\\ *n* **1** : distinctive way of speaking, writing, or acting **2** : elegant or fashionable way of living ~ *vb* **styled; styl·ing 1** : name **2** : give a particular design or style to — **styl·ish** \\'stīlish\\ *adj* — **styl·ish·ly** *adv* — **styl·ish·ness** *n* — **styl·ist** \\-ist\\ *n* — **styl·ize** \\'stīəl̩īz\\ *vb*

**sty·lus** \\'stīləs\\ *n, pl* **-li** \\'stīl̩ī\\ **1** : pointed writing tool **2** : phonograph needle

**sty·mie** \\'stīmē\\ *vb* **-mied; -mie·ing** : block or frustrate

**suave** \\'swäv\\ *adj* : well-mannered and gracious — **suave·ly** *adv*

¹**sub** \\'səb\\ *n or vb* : substitute

²**sub** *n* : submarine

**sub-** \̩səb, 'səb\\ *prefix* **1** : under or beneath **2** : subordinate or secondary **3** : subordinate portion of **4** : with repetition of a process so as to form, stress, or deal with subordinate parts or relations **5** : somewhat **6** : nearly

**sub·con·scious** \̩səb'känchəs\\ *adj* : existing without conscious awareness ~ *n* : part of the mind concerned with subconscious activities — **sub·con·scious·ly** *adv*

**sub·di·vide** \̩səbdə'vīd, 'səbdə̩vīd\\ *vb* **1** : divide into several parts **2** : divide (land) into building lots — **sub·di·vi·sion** \-'vizhən, -̩vizh-\\ *n*

**sub·due** \səb'dü, -'dyü\\ *vb* **-dued;**

**-du·ing 1** : bring under control **2** : reduce the intensity of

**sub·ject** \\'səbjikt\\ *n* **1** : person under the authority of another **2** : something being discussed or studied **3** : word or word group about which something is said in a sentence ~ *adj* **1** : being under one's authority **2** : prone **3** : dependent on some condition or act ~ \səb'jekt\\ *vb* **1** : bring under control **2** : cause to undergo — **sub·jec·tion** \-'jekshən\\ *n*

**sub·jec·tive** \̩səb'jektiv\\ *adj* : deriving from an individual viewpoint or bias — **sub·jec·tive·ly** *adv* — **sub·jec·tiv·i·ty** \-̩jek'tivətē\\ *n*

**sub·ju·gate** \\'səbji̩gāt\\ *vb* **-gat·ed; -gat·ing** : bring under one's control — **sub·ju·ga·tion** \̩səbji'gāshən\\ *n*

**sub·junc·tive** \səb'jəŋktiv\\ *adj* : relating to a verb form which expresses possibility or contingency — **subjunctive** *n*

**sub·let** \\'səb̩let\\ *vb* **-let; -let·ting** : rent (a property) from a lessee

**sub·lime** \sə'blīm\\ *adj* : splendid — **sub·lime·ly** *adv*

**sub·ma·rine** \\'səbmə̩rēn, ̩səbmə'-\\ *adj* : existing, acting, or growing under the sea ~ *n* : underwater boat

**sub·merge** \səb'mərj\\ *vb* **-merged; -merg·ing** : put or plunge under the surface of water — **sub·mer·gence** \-'mərjəns\\ *n* — **sub·mers·ible** \səb-'mərsəbəl\\ *adj or n* — **sub·mer·sion** \-'mərzhən\\ *n*

**sub·mit** \səb'mit\\ *vb* **-tt- 1** : yield **2** : give or offer — **sub·mis·sion** \-'mishən\\ *n* — **sub·mis·sive** \-'misiv\\ *adj*

**sub·nor·mal** \̩səb'nórməl\\ *adj* : falling below what is normal

**sub·or·di·nate** \sə'bórd°nət\\ *adj* : lower

---

**List of self-explanatory words with the prefix *sub-***

| | | |
|---|---|---|
| subacute | subcategory | subdean |
| subagency | subclass | subdepartment |
| subagent | subclassification | subdistrict |
| subarctic | subclassify | subentry |
| subarea | subcommission | subfamily |
| subatmospheric | subcommittee | subfreezing |
| subaverage | subcommunity | subgroup |
| subbase | subcomponent | subhead |
| subbasement | subcontract | subheading |
| subbranch | subcontractor | subhuman |
| subcabinet | subculture | subindex |

in rank $\sim$ *n* : one that is subordinate
$\sim$ \sə'bȯrd°n,āt\ *vb* **-nat·ed; -nat·
ing** : place in a lower rank or class —
**sub·or·di·na·tion** \-,bȯrd°n'āshən\ *n*

**sub·poe·na** \sə'pēnə\ *n* : summons to
appear in court $\sim$ *vb* **-naed; -na·ing**
: summon with a subpoena

**sub·scribe** \səb'skrīb\ *vb* **-scribed;
-scrib·ing 1** : give consent or approval **2** : agree to support or to receive and pay for — **sub·scrib·er** *n*

**sub·scrip·tion** \səb'skripshən\ *n* : order for regular receipt of a publication

**sub·se·quent** \'səbsikwənt, -sə,kwent\
*adj* : following after — **sub·se·quent·
ly** \-,kwentlē, -kwənt-\ *adv*

**sub·ser·vi·ence** \səb'sərvēəns\ *n* : ob-
sequious submission — **sub·ser·vi·ent**
\-ənt\ *adj*

**sub·side** \səb'sīd\ *vb* **-sid·ed; -sid·ing**
: die down in intensity

**sub·sid·iary** \səb'sidē,erē\ *adj* **1** : fur-
nishing support **2** : of secondary importance $\sim$ *n* : company controlled
by another company

**sub·si·dize** \'səbsə,dīz\ *vb* **-dized;
-diz·ing** : aid with a subsidy

**sub·si·dy** \'səbsədē\ *n, pl* **-dies** : gift
of supporting funds

**sub·sist** \səb'sist\ *vb* : acquire the ne-
cessities of life — **sub·sis·tence**
\-'sistəns\ *n*

**sub·stance** \'səbstəns\ *n* **1** : essence
or essential part **2** : physical material
**3** : wealth

**sub·stan·dard** \,səb'standərd\ *adj*
: falling short of a standard or norm

**sub·stan·tial** \səb'stanchəl\ *adj* **1**
: plentiful **2** : considerable — **sub·
stan·tial·ly** *adv*

**sub·stan·ti·ate** \səb'stanchē,āt\ *vb*
**-at·ed; -at·ing** : verify — **sub·stan·
ti·a·tion** \-,stanchē'āshən\ *n*

**sub·sti·tute** \'səbstə,tüt, -,tyüt\ *n* : replacement $\sim$ *vb* **-tut·ed; -tut·ing**
: put or serve in place of another —
**substitute** *adj* — **sub·sti·tu·tion**
\,səbstə'tüshən, -'tyü-\ *n*

**sub·ter·fuge** \'səbtər,fyüj\ *n* : deceptive trick

**sub·ter·ra·nean** \,səbtə'rānēən\ *adj*
: lying or being underground

**sub·ti·tle** \'səb,tīt°l\ *n* : movie caption

**sub·tle** \'sət°l\ *adj* **-tler** \-ər\; **-tlest**
\-ist\ **1** : hardly noticeable **2** : clever
— **sub·tle·ty** \-tē\ *n* — **sub·tly** \-°lē\
*adv*

**sub·tract** \səb'trakt\ *vb* : take away (as
one number from another) — **sub·
trac·tion** \-'trakshən\ *n*

**sub·urb** \'səb,ərb\ *n* : residential area
adjacent to a city — **sub·ur·ban**
\sə'bərbən\ *adj or n* — **sub·ur·ban·
ite** \-bə,nīt\ *n*

**sub·vert** \səb'vərt\ *vb* : overthrow or
ruin — **sub·ver·sion** \-'vərzhən\ *n*
— **sub·ver·sive** \-'vərsiv\ *adj*

**sub·way** \'səb,wā\ *n* : underground
electric railway

**suc·ceed** \sək'sēd\ *vb* **1** : follow
(someone) in a job, role, or title **2** : attain a desired object or end

**suc·cess** \-'ses\ *n* **1** : favorable outcome **2** : gaining of wealth and
fame **3** : one that succeeds — **suc·
cess·ful** \-fəl\ *adj* — **suc·cess·ful·
ly** *adv*

**suc·ces·sion** \sək'seshən\ *n* **1** : order,
act, or right of succeeding **2** : series

**suc·ces·sive** \-'sesiv\ *adj* : following
in order — **suc·ces·sive·ly** *adv*

**suc·ces·sor** \-'sesər\ *n* : one that succeeds another

**suc·cinct** \sək'siŋkt, sə'siŋkt\ *adj*
: brief — **suc·cinct·ly** *adv* — **suc·
cinct·ness** *n*

**suc·cor** \'səkər\ *n or vb* : help

---

| | | |
|---|---|---|
| subindustry | subpolar | substage |
| sublease | subprincipal | subsurface |
| sublethal | subprocess | subsystem |
| sublevel | subprogram | subtemperate |
| subliterate | subproject | subtheme |
| subnetwork | subregion | subtopic |
| suboceanic | subsea | subtotal |
| suborder | subsection | subtreasury |
| subpar | subsense | subtype |
| subpart | subspecialty | subunit |
| subplot | subspecies | subvariety |

**suc·co·tash** \'səkə,tash\ *n* : beans and corn cooked together

**suc·cu·lent** \'səkyələnt\ *adj* : juicy — **suc·cu·lence** \-ləns\ *n* — **succulent** *n*

**suc·cumb** \sə'kəm\ *vb* **1** : yield **2** : die

**such** \'səch\ *adj* **1** : of this or that kind **2** : having a specified quality — **such** *pron or adv*

**suck** \'sək\ *vb* **1** : draw in liquid with the mouth **2** : draw liquid from by or as if by mouth — **suck** *n*

**suck·er** \'səkər\ *n* **1** : one that sucks or clings **2** : easily deceived person

**suck·le** \'səkəl\ *vb* **-led; -ling** : give or draw milk from the breast or udder

**suck·ling** \'səkliŋ\ *n* : young unweaned mammal

**su·crose** \'sü,krōs, -,krōz\ *n* : cane or beet sugar

**suc·tion** \'səkshən\ *n* **1** : act of sucking **2** : act or process of drawing in by partially exhausting the air

**sud·den** \'səd°n\ *adj* **1** : happening unexpectedly **2** : steep **3** : hasty — **sud·den·ly** *adv* — **sud·den·ness** *n*

**suds** \'sədz\ *n pl* : soapy water esp. when frothy — **sudsy** \'sədzē\ *adj*

**sue** \'sü\ *vb* **sued; su·ing 1** : petition **2** : bring legal action against

**suede, suède** \'swād\ *n* : leather with a napped surface

**su·et** \'süət\ *n* : hard beef fat

**suf·fer** \'səfər\ *vb* **1** : experience pain, loss, or hardship **2** : permit — **suf·fer·er** *n*

**suf·fer·ing** \-əriŋ\ *n* : pain or hardship

**suf·fice** \sə'fīs\ *vb* **-ficed; -fic·ing** : be sufficient

**suf·fi·cient** \sə'fishənt\ *adj* : adequate — **suf·fi·cien·cy** \-ənsē\ *n* — **suf·fi·cient·ly** *adv*

**suf·fix** \'səf,iks\ *n* : letters added at the end of a word — **suffix** \'səfiks, sə'fiks\ *vb* — **suf·fix·a·tion** \,səf,ik-'sāshən\ *n*

**suf·fo·cate** \'səfə,kāt\ *vb* **-cat·ed; -cat·ing** : suffer or die or cause to die from lack of air — **suf·fo·cat·ing·ly** *adv* — **suf·fo·ca·tion** \,səfə'kā-shən\ *n*

**suf·frage** \'səfrij\ *n* : right to vote

**suf·fuse** \sə'fyüz\ *vb* **-fused; -fus·ing** : spread over or through

**sug·ar** \'shügər\ *n* : sweet substance ∼ *vb* : mix, cover, or sprinkle with sugar — **sug·ar·cane** *n* — **sug·ary** *adj*

**sug·gest** \sə'jest, səg-\ *vb* **1** : put into someone's mind **2** : remind one by association of ideas — **sug·gest·ible** \-'jestəbəl\ *adj* — **sug·ges·tion** \'jeschən\ *n*

**sug·ges·tive** \-'jestiv\ *adj* : suggesting something improper — **sug·ges·tive·ly** *adv* — **sug·ges·tive·ness** *n*

**sui·cide** \'süə,sīd\ *n* **1** : act of killing oneself purposely **2** : one who commits suicide — **sui·cid·al** \,süə-'sīd°l\ *adj*

**suit** \'süt\ *n* **1** : action in court to recover a right or claim **2** : number of things used or worn together **3** : one of the 4 sets of playing cards ∼ *vb* **1** : be appropriate or becoming to **2** : meet the needs of — **suit·abil·i·ty** \,süta-'bilətē\ *n* — **suit·able** \'sütəbəl\ *adj* — **suit·ably** *adv*

**suit·case** *n* : case for a traveler's clothing

**suite** \'swēt, *for 2 also* 'süt\ *n* **1** : group of rooms **2** : set of matched furniture

**suit·or** \'sütər\ *n* : one who seeks to marry a woman

**sul·fur** \'səlfər\ *n* : nonmetallic yellow chemical element — **sul·fu·ric** \,səl-'fyürik\ *adj* — **sul·fu·rous** \-'fyürəs, 'səlfərəs, 'səlfyə-\ *adj*

**sulk** \'səlk\ *vb* : be moodily silent or irritable — **sulk** *n*

**sulky** \'səlkē\ *adj* : inclined to sulk ∼ *n* : light 2-wheeled horse-drawn cart — **sulk·i·ly** \'səlkəlē\ *adv* — **sulk·i·ness** \-kēnəs\ *n*

**sul·len** \'sələn\ *adj* **1** : gloomily silent **2** : dismal — **sul·len·ly** *adv* — **sul·len·ness** *n*

**sul·ly** \'səlē\ *vb* **-lied; -ly·ing** : cast doubt or disgrace on

**sul·tan** \'səlt°n\ *n* : sovereign of a Muslim state — **sul·tan·ate** \-,āt\ *n*

**sul·try** \'səltrē\ *adj* **-tri·er; -est 1** : very hot and moist **2** : sexually arousing

**sum** \'səm\ *n* **1** : amount **2** : gist **3** : result of addition ∼ *vb* **-mm-** : find the sum of

**su·mac** \'shü,mak, 'sü-\ *n* : shrub with spikes of berries

**sum·ma·ry** \'səmərē\ *adj* **1** : concise **2** : done without delay or formality ∼ *n, pl* **-ries** : concise statement — **sum·mar·i·ly** \sə'merəlē, 'səmərəlē\ *adv* — **sum·ma·rize** \'səmə,rīz\ *vb*

**sum·ma·tion** \sə'māshən\ *n* : a summing up esp. in court

**sum·mer** \'səmər\ *n* : season in which

the sun shines most directly — **sum-mery** *adj*

**sum·mit** \'səmət\ *n* **1** : highest point **2** : high-level conference

**sum·mon** \'səmən\ *vb* **1** : send for or call together **2** : order to appear in court — **sum·mon·er** *n*

**sum·mons** \'səmənz\ *n, pl* **sum-mons·es** : an order to answer charges in court

**sump·tu·ous** \'səmpchəwəs\ *adj* : lavish

**sun** \'sən\ *n* **1** : shining celestial body around which the planets revolve **2** : light of the sun ~ *vb* **-nn-** : expose to the sun — **sun·beam** *n* — **sun·block** *n* — **sun·burn** *n or vb* — **sun·glass·es** *n pl* — **sun·light** *n* — **sun·ny** *adj* — **sun·rise** *n* — **sun·set** *n* — **sun·shine** *n* — **sun·tan** *n*

**sun·dae** \'səndē\ *n* : ice cream with topping

**Sun·day** \'səndā, -dē\ *n* : 1st day of the week

**sun·di·al** \-ˌdīəl\ *n* : device for showing time by the sun's shadow

**sun·dries** \'səndrēz\ *n pl* : various small articles

**sun·dry** \-drē\ *adj* : several

**sun·fish** *n* : perchlike freshwater fish

**sun·flow·er** *n* : tall plant grown for its oil-rich seeds

**sung** *past of* SING

**sunk** *past of* SINK

**sunk·en** \'səŋkən\ *adj* **1** : submerged **2** : fallen in

**sun·spot** *n* : dark spot on the sun

**sun·stroke** *n* : heatstroke from the sun

**sup** \'səp\ *vb* **-pp-** : eat the evening meal

**super** \'süpər\ *adj* : very fine

**super-** \ˌsüpər, 'sü-\ *prefix* **1** : higher in quantity, quality, or degree than **2** : in addition **3** : exceeding a norm **4** : in excessive degree or intensity **5** : surpassing others of its kind **6** : situated above, on, or at the top of **7** : more inclusive than **8** : superior in status or position

**su·perb** \su'pərb\ *adj* : outstanding — **su·perb·ly** *adv*

**su·per·cil·ious** \ˌsüpər'silēəs\ *adj* : haughtily contemptuous

**su·per·fi·cial** \ˌsüpər'fishəl\ *adj* : relating to what is only apparent — **su·per-fi·ci·al·i·ty** \-ˌfishē'alətē\ *n* — **su·per·fi·cial·ly** *adv*

**su·per·flu·ous** \su'pərfləwəs\ *adj* : more than necessary — **su·per·flu·i·ty** \ˌsüpər'flüətē\ *n*

**su·per·im·pose** \ˌsüpərim'pōz\ *vb* : lay over or above something

**su·per·in·tend** \ˌsüpərin'tend\ *vb* : have charge and oversight of — **su·per-in·ten·dence** \-'tendəns\ *n* — **su·per-in·ten·den·cy** \-dənsē\ *n* — **su·per-in·ten·dent** \-dənt\ *n*

**su·pe·ri·or** \su'pirēər\ *adj* **1** : higher, better, or more important **2** : haughty — **superior** *n* — **su·pe·ri·or·i·ty** \-ˌpirē'orətē\ *n*

**su·per·la·tive** \su'pərlətiv\ *adj* **1** : relating to or being an adjective or adverb form that denotes an extreme level **2** : surpassing others — **su-perlative** *n* — **su·per·la·tive·ly** *adv*

**su·per·mar·ket** \'süpərˌmärkət\ *n* : self-service grocery store

---

**List of self-explanatory words with the prefix *super-***

| | | |
|---|---|---|
| superabundance | supergovernment | superport |
| superabundant | supergroup | superpowerful |
| superambitious | superhero | superrich |
| superathlete | superheroine | supersalesman |
| superbomb | superhuman | superscout |
| superclean | superintellectual | supersecrecy |
| supercolossal | superintelligence | supersecret |
| superconvenient | superintelligent | supersensitive |
| supercop | superman | supersize |
| superdense | supermodern | supersized |
| supereffective | superpatriot | superslick |
| superefficiency | superpatriotic | supersmooth |
| superefficient | superpatriotism | supersoft |
| superfast | superplane | superspecial |
| supergood | superpolite | superspecialist |

**su·per·nat·u·ral** \,süpər'nachərəl\ *adj* : beyond the observable physical world — **su·per·nat·u·ral·ly** *adv*

**su·per·pow·er** \'süpər,paůər\ *n* : politically and militarily dominant nation

**su·per·sede** \,süpər'sēd\ *vb* -**sed·ed;** **sed·ing** : take the place of

**su·per·son·ic** \-'sänik\ *adj* : faster than the speed of sound

**su·per·sti·tion** \,süpər'stishən\ *n* : beliefs based on ignorance, fear of the unknown, or trust in magic — **su·per·sti·tious** \-əs\ *adj*

**su·per·struc·ture** \'süpər,strəkchər\ *n* : something built on a base or as a vertical extension

**su·per·vise** \'süpər,vīz\ *vb* -**vised;** -**vis·ing** : have charge of — **su·per·vi·sion** \,süpər'vizhən\ *n* — **su·per·vi·sor** \'süpər,vīzər\ *n* — **su·per·vi·so·ry** \,süpər'vīzərē\ *adj*

**su·pine** \sü'pīn\ *adj* 1 : lying on the back 2 : indifferent or abject

**sup·per** \'səpər\ *n* : evening meal

**sup·plant** \sə'plant\ *vb* : take the place of

**sup·ple** \'səpəl\ *adj* -**pler;** -**plest** : able to bend easily

**sup·ple·ment** \'səpləmənt\ *n* : something that adds to or makes up for a lack — **supplement** *vb* — **sup·ple·men·tal** \,səplə'ment³l\ *adj* — **sup·ple·men·ta·ry** \-'mentərē\ *adj*

**sup·pli·ant** \'səplēant\ *n* : one who supplicates

**sup·pli·cate** \'səplə,kāt\ *vb* -**cat·ed;** -**cat·ing** 1 : pray to God 2 : ask earnestly and humbly — **sup·pli·cant** \-likənt\ *n* — **sup·pli·ca·tion** \,səplə-'kāshən\ *n*

**sup·ply** \sə'plī\ *vb* -**plied;** -**ply·ing** : furnish ~ *n, pl* -**plies** 1 : amount needed or available 2 *pl* : provisions — **sup·pli·er** \-'plīər\ *n*

**sup·port** \sə'pōrt\ *vb* 1 : take sides with 2 : provide with food, clothing, and shelter 3 : hold up or serve as a foundation for — **support** *n* — **sup·port·able** *adj* — **sup·port·er** *n*

**sup·pose** \sə'pōz\ *vb* -**posed;** -**pos-** ing 1 : assume to be true 2 : expect 3 : think probable — **sup·po·si·tion** \,səpə'zishən\ *n*

**sup·pos·i·to·ry** \sə'päzə,tōrē\ *n, pl* -**ries** : medicated material for insertion (as into the rectum)

**sup·press** \sə'pres\ *vb* 1 : put an end to by authority 2 : keep from being known 3 : hold back — **sup·pres·sant** \sə'pres³nt\ *n* — **sup·pres·sion** \-'preshən\ *n*

**su·prem·a·cy** \sù'preməsē\ *n, pl* -**cies** : supreme power or authority

**su·preme** \sù'prēm\ *adj* 1 : highest in rank or authority 2 : greatest possible — **su·preme·ly** *adv*

**Supreme Being** *n* : God

**sur·charge** \'sər,chärj\ *n* 1 : excessive load or burden 2 : extra fee or cost

**sure** \'shùr\ *adj* **sur·er; sur·est** 1 : confident 2 : reliable 3 : not to be disputed 4 : bound to happen ~ *adv* : surely — **sure·ness** *n*

**sure·ly** \'shùrlē\ *adv* 1 : in a sure manner 2 : without doubt 3 : indeed

**sure·ty** \'shùrətē\ *n, pl* -**ties** 1 : guarantee 2 : one who gives a guarantee for another person

**surf** \'sərf\ *n* : waves that break on the shore ~ *vb* : ride the surf — **surf·board** *n* — **surf·er** *n* — **surf·ing** *n*

**sur·face** \'sərfəs\ *n* 1 : the outside of an object 2 : outward aspect ~ *vb* -**faced;** -**fac·ing** : rise to the surface

**sur·feit** \'sərfət\ *n* 1 : excess 2 : excessive indulgence (as in food or drink) 3 : disgust caused by excess ~ *vb* : feed, supply, or indulge to the point of surfeit

**surge** \'sərj\ *vb* **surged; surg·ing** : rise and fall in or as if in waves ~ *n* : sudden increase

**sur·geon** \'sərjən\ *n* : physician who specializes in surgery

**sur·gery** \'sərjərē\ *n, pl* -**ger·ies** : medical treatment involving cutting open the body

**sur·gi·cal** \'sərjikəl\ *adj* : relating to surgeons or surgery — **sur·gi·cal·ly** *adv*

---

| | | |
|---|---|---|
| superspy | superstrong | superthin |
| superstar | supersystem | supertight |
| superstate | supertanker | superweapon |
| superstrength | superthick | superwoman |

**sur·ly** \'sǝrlē\ *adj* **-li·er; -est** : having a rude nature — **sur·li·ness** *n*

**sur·mise** \sǝr'mīz\ *vb* **-mised; -mis·ing** : guess — **surmise** *n*

**sur·mount** \-'maùnt\ *vb* **1** : prevail over **2** : get to or be the top of

**sur·name** \'sǝr,nām\ *n* : family name

**sur·pass** \sǝr'pas\ *vb* : go beyond or exceed — **sur·pass·ing·ly** *adv*

**sur·plice** \'sǝrplǝs\ *n* : loose white outer ecclesiastical vestment

**sur·plus** \'sǝr,plǝs\ *n* : quantity left over

**sur·prise** \sǝ'prīz, sǝr-\ *vb* **-prised; -pris·ing** **1** : come upon or affect unexpectedly **2** : amaze — **surprise** *n* — **sur·pris·ing** *adj* — **sur·pris·ing·ly** *adv*

**sur·ren·der** \sǝ'rendǝr\ *vb* : give up oneself or a possession to another ∼ *n* : act of surrendering

**sur·rep·ti·tious** \,sǝrǝp'tishǝs\ *adj* : done, made, or acquired by stealth — **sur·rep·ti·tious·ly** *adv*

**sur·rey** \'sǝrē\ *n, pl* **-reys** : horse-drawn carriage

**sur·ro·gate** \'sǝrǝgāt, -gǝt\ *n* : substitute

**sur·round** \sǝ'raùnd\ *vb* : enclose on all sides

**sur·round·ings** \sǝ'raùndiŋz\ *n pl* : objects, conditions, or area around something

**sur·veil·lance** \sǝr'vālǝns, -'vālyǝns, -'vāǝns\ *n* : careful watch

**sur·vey** \sǝr'vā\ *vb* **-veyed; -vey·ing** **1** : look over and examine closely **2** : make a survey of (as a tract of land) ∼ \'sǝr,-\ *n, pl* **-veys** **1** : inspection **2** : process of measuring (as land) — **sur·vey·or** \-ǝr\ *n*

**sur·vive** \sǝr'vīv\ *vb* **-vived; -viv·ing** **1** : remain alive or in existence **2** : outlive or outlast — **sur·viv·al** *n* — **sur·vi·vor** \-'vīvǝr\ *n*

**sus·cep·ti·ble** \sǝ'septǝbǝl\ *adj* : likely to allow or be affected by something — **sus·cep·ti·bil·i·ty** \-,septǝ'bilǝtē\ *n*

**sus·pect** \'sǝs,pekt, sǝ'spekt\ *adj* **1** : regarded with suspicion **2** : questionable ∼ \'sǝs,pekt\ *n* : one who is suspected (as of a crime) ∼ \sǝ'spekt\ *vb* **1** : have doubts of **2** : believe guilty without proof **3** : guess

**sus·pend** \sǝ'spend\ *vb* **1** : temporarily stop or keep from a function or job **2** : withhold (judgment) temporarily **3** : hang

**sus·pend·er** \sǝ'spendǝr\ *n* : one of 2 supporting straps holding up trousers and passing over the shoulders

**sus·pense** \sǝ'spens\ *n* : excitement and uncertainty as to outcome — **suspense·ful** *adj*

**sus·pen·sion** \sǝ'spenchǝn\ *n* : act of suspending or the state or period of being suspended

**sus·pi·cion** \sǝ'spishǝn\ *n* **1** : act of suspecting something **2** : trace

**sus·pi·cious** \-ǝs\ *adj* **1** : arousing suspicion **2** : inclined to suspect — **sus·pi·cious·ly** *adv*

**sus·tain** \sǝ'stān\ *vb* **1** : provide with nourishment **2** : keep going **3** : hold up **4** : suffer **5** : support or prove

**sus·te·nance** \'sǝstǝnǝns\ *n* **1** : nourishment **2** : something that sustains or supports

**svelte** \'sfelt\ *adj* : slender and graceful

**swab** \'swäb\ *n* **1** : mop **2** : wad of absorbent material for applying medicine ∼ *vb* **-bb-** : use a swab on

**swad·dle** \'swäd²l\ *vb* **-dled; -dling** \'swäd²liŋ\ : bind (an infant) in bands of cloth

**swag·ger** \'swagǝr\ *vb* **-gered; -ger·ing** **1** : walk with a conceited swing **2** : boast — **swagger** *n*

¹**swal·low** \'swälō\ *n* : small migratory bird

²**swallow** *vb* **1** : take into the stomach through the throat **2** : envelop or take in **3** : accept too easily — **swallow** *n*

**swam** *past of* SWIM

**swamp** \'swämp\ *n* : wet spongy land ∼ *vb* : deluge (as with water) — **swampy** *adj*

**swan** \'swän\ *n* : white long-necked swimming bird

**swap** \'swäp\ *vb* **-pp-** : trade — **swap** *n*

**swarm** \'swórm\ *n* **1** : mass of honeybees leaving a hive to start a new colony **2** : large crowd ∼ *vb* : gather in a swarm

**swar·thy** \'swórthē, -thē\ *adj* **-thi·er; -est** : dark in complexion

**swash·buck·ler** \'swäsh,bǝklǝr\ *n* : swaggering or daring soldier or adventurer — **swash·buck·ling** \-,bǝkliŋ\ *adj*

**swat** \'swät\ *vb* **-tt-** : hit sharply — **swat** *n* — **swat·ter** *n*

**swatch** \'swäch\ *n* : sample piece (as of fabric)

**swath** \'swäth, 'swóth\, **swathe**

\\'swäth, 'swȯth, 'swäth\ *n* : row or path cut (as through grass)

**swathe** \\'swäth, 'swȯth, 'swäth\ *vb* **swathed; swath·ing** : wrap with or as if with a bandage

**sway** \\'swā\ *vb* **1** : swing gently from side to side **2** : influence ∼ *n* **1** : gentle swinging from side to side **2** : controlling power or influence

**swear** \\'swar\ *vb* **swore** \\'swōr\; **sworn** \\'swōrn\; **swear·ing 1** : make or cause to make a solemn statement under oath **2** : use profane language — **swear·er** *n* — **swear·ing** *n*

**sweat** \\'swet\ *vb* **sweat** *or* **sweat·ed; sweat·ing 1** : excrete salty moisture from skin glands **2** : form drops of moisture on the surface **3** : work or cause to work hard — **sweat** *n* — **sweaty** *adj*

**sweat·er** \\'swetər\ *n* : knitted jacket or pullover

**sweat·shirt** \\'swet̩shərt\ *n* : loose collarless heavy cotton jersey pullover

**sweep** \\'swēp\ *vb* **swept** \\'swept\; **sweep·ing 1** : remove or clean by a brush or a single forceful wipe (as of the hand) **2** : move over with speed and force (as of the hand) **3** : move or extend in a wide curve ∼ *n* **1** : a clearing off or away **2** : single forceful wipe or swinging movement **3** : scope — **sweep·er** *n* — **sweep·ing** *adj*

**sweep·stakes** \\'swēp̩stāks\ *n, pl* **sweep·stakes** : contest in which the entire prize may go to the winner

**sweet** \\'swēt\ *adj* **1** : being or causing the pleasing taste typical of sugar **2** : not stale or spoiled **3** : not salted **4** : pleasant **5** : much loved ∼ *n* : something sweet — **sweet·en** \\'swēt³n\ *vb* — **sweet·ly** *adv* — **sweet·ness** *n* — **sweet·en·er** \-³nər\ *n*

**sweet·heart** *n* : person one loves

**sweet potato** *n* : sweet yellow edible root of a tropical vine

**swell** \\'swel\ *vb* **swelled; swelled** *or* **swol·len** \\'swōlən\; **swell·ing 1** : enlarge **2** : bulge **3** : fill or be filled with emotion ∼ *n* **1** : long rolling ocean wave **2** : condition of bulging — **swell·ing** *n*

**swel·ter** \\'sweltər\ *vb* : be uncomfortable from excessive heat

**swept** *past of* SWEEP

**swerve** \\'swərv\ *vb* **swerved; swerv·ing** : move abruptly aside from a course — **swerve** *n*

**¹swift** \\'swift\ *adj* **1** : moving with great speed **2** : occurring suddenly — **swift·ly** *adv* — **swift·ness** *n*

**²swift** *n* : small insect-eating bird

**swig** \\'swig\ *vb* **-gg-** : drink in gulps — **swig** *n*

**swill** \\'swil\ *vb* : swallow greedily ∼ *n* **1** : animal food of refuse and liquid **2** : garbage

**swim** \\'swim\ *vb* **swam** \\'swam\; **swum** \\'swəm\; **swim·ming 1** : propel oneself in water **2** : float in or be surrounded with a liquid **3** : be dizzy ∼ *n* : act or period of swimming — **swim·mer** *n*

**swin·dle** \\'swind³l\ *vb* **-dled; -dling** \-iŋ\ : cheat (someone) of money or property — **swindle** *n* — **swin·dler** \-ər\ *n*

**swine** \\'swīn\ *n, pl* **swine** : short-legged hoofed mammal with a snout — **swinish** \\'swīnish\ *adj*

**swing** \\'swiŋ\ *vb* **swung** \\'swəŋ\; **swing·ing 1** : move or cause to move rapidly in an arc **2** : sway or cause to sway back and forth **3** : hang so as to sway or sag **4** : turn on a hinge or pivot **5** : manage or handle successfully ∼ *n* **1** : act or instance of swinging **2** : swinging movement (as in trying to hit something) **3** : suspended seat for swinging — **swing** *adj* — **swing·er** *n*

**swipe** \\'swīp\ *n* : strong sweeping blow ∼ *vb* **swiped; swip·ing 1** : strike or wipe with a sweeping motion **2** : steal esp. with a quick movement

**swirl** \\'swərl\ *vb* : move or cause to move in a circle — **swirl** *n*

**swish** \\'swish\ *n* : hissing, sweeping, or brushing sound — **swish** *vb*

**switch** \\'swich\ *n* **1** : slender flexible whip or twig **2** : blow with a switch **3** : shift, change, or reversal **4** : device that opens or closes an electrical circuit ∼ *vb* **1** : punish or urge on with a switch **2** : change or reverse roles, positions, or subjects **3** : operate a switch of

**switch·board** *n* : panel of switches to make and break telephone connections

**swiv·el** \\'swivəl\ *vb* **-eled** *or* **-elled; -eling** *or* **-el·ling** : swing or turn on a pivot — **swivel** *n*

**swollen** *past part of* SWELL

**swoon** \\'swün\ *n* : faint — **swoon** *vb*

**swoop** \\'swüp\ *vb* : make a swift diving attack — **swoop** *n*

**sword** \'sȯrd\ *n* : thrusting or cutting weapon with a long blade

**sword•fish** *n* : large ocean fish with a long swordlike projection

**swore** *past of* SWEAR

**sworn** *past part of* SWEAR

**swum** *past part of* SWIM

**swung** *past of* SWING

**syc•a•more** \'sikə,mōr\ *n* : shade tree

**sy•co•phant** \'sikəfənt\ *n* : servile flatterer — **syc•o•phan•tic** \,sikə-'fantik\ *adj*

**syl•la•ble** \'siləbəl\ *n* : unit of a spoken word — **syl•lab•ic** \sə'labik\ *adj*

**syl•la•bus** \'siləbəs\ *n, pl* **-bi** \-,bī\ *or* **-bus•es** : summary of main topics (as of a course of study)

**syl•van** \'silvən\ *adj* **1** : living or located in a wooded area **2** : abounding in woods

**sym•bol** \'simbəl\ *n* : something that represents or suggests another thing — **sym•bol•ic** \sim'bälik\ *adj* — **sym•bol•i•cal•ly** *adv*

**sym•bol•ism** \'simbə,lizəm\ *n* : representation of meanings with symbols

**sym•bol•ize** \'simbə,līz\ *vb* **-ized; -iz•ing** : serve as a symbol of — **sym•bol•i•za•tion** \,simbələ'zāshən\ *n*

**sym•me•try** \'simətrē\ *n, pl* **-tries** : regularity and balance in the arrangement of parts — **sym•met•ri•cal** \sə'metrikəl\ *adj* — **sym•met•ri•cal•ly** *adv*

**sym•pa•thize** \'simpə,thīz\ *vb* **-thized; -thiz•ing** : feel or show sympathy — **sym•pa•thiz•er** *n*

**sym•pa•thy** \'simpəthē\ *n, pl* **-thies 1** : ability to understand or share the feelings of another **2** : expression of sorrow for another's misfortune — **sym•pa•thet•ic** \,simpə'thetik\ *adj* — **sym•pa•thet•i•cal•ly** *adv*

**sym•pho•ny** \'simfənē\ *n, pl* **-nies** : composition for an orchestra or the orchestra itself — **sym•phon•ic** \sim'fänik\ *adj*

**sym•po•sium** \sim'pōzēəm\ *n, pl* **-sia** \-zēə\ *or* **-siums** : conference at which a topic is discussed

**symp•tom** \'simptəm\ *n* : unusual feeling or reaction that is a sign of disease — **symp•tom•at•ic** \,simptə-'matik\ *adj*

**syn•a•gogue, syn•a•gog** \'sinə,gäg, -,gȯg\ *n* : Jewish house of worship

**syn•chro•nize** \'siŋkrə,nīz, 'sin-\ *vb* **-nized; -niz•ing 1** : occur or cause to occur at the same instant **2** : cause to agree in time — **syn•chro•ni•za•tion** \,siŋkrənə'zāshən, ,sin-\ *n*

**syn•co•pa•tion** \,siŋkə'pāshən, ,sin-\ *n* : shifting of the regular musical accent to the weak beat — **syn•co•pate** \'siŋkə,pāt, 'sin-\ *vb*

**syn•di•cate** \'sindikət\ *n* : business association ~ \-də,kāt\ *vb* **-cat•ed; -cat•ing 1** : form a syndicate **2** : publish through a syndicate — **syn•di•ca•tion** \,sində'kāshən\ *n*

**syn•drome** \'sin,drōm\ *n* : particular group of symptoms

**syn•onym** \'sinə,nim\ *n* : word with the same meaning as another — **syn•on•y•mous** \sə'nänəməs\ *adj* — **syn•on•y•my** \-mē\ *n*

**syn•op•sis** \sə'näpsəs\ *n, pl* **-op•ses** \-,sēz\ : condensed statement or outline

**syn•tax** \'sin,taks\ *n* : way in which words are put together — **syn•tac•tic** \sin'taktik\, **syn•tac•ti•cal** \-tikəl\ *adj*

**syn•the•sis** \'sinthəsəs\ *n, pl* **-the•ses** \-,sēz\ : combination of parts or elements into a whole — **syn•the•size** \-,sīz\ *vb*

**syn•thet•ic** \sin'thetik\ *adj* : artificially made — **synthetic** *n* — **syn•thet•i•cal•ly** *adv*

**syph•i•lis** \'sifələs\ *n* : venereal disease

**sy•ringe** \sə'rinj, 'sirinj\ *n* : plunger device for injecting or withdrawing liquids

**syr•up** \'sərəp, 'sirəp\ *n* : thick sticky sweet liquid — **syr•upy** *adj*

**sys•tem** \'sistəm\ *n* **1** : arrangement of units that function together **2** : regular order — **sys•tem•at•ic** \,sistə'matik\ *adj* — **sys•tem•at•i•cal•ly** *adv* — **sys•tem•a•tize** \'sistəmə,tīz\ *vb*

**sys•tem•ic** \sis'temik\ *adj* : relating to the whole body

# T

**t** \ˈtē\ *n, pl* **t's** *or* **ts** \ˈtēz\ : 20th letter of the alphabet

**tab** \ˈtab\ *n* **1 :** short projecting flap **2** *pl* **:** careful watch

**tab•by** \ˈtabē\ *n, pl* **-bies :** domestic cat

**tab•er•na•cle** \ˈtabərˌnakəl\ *n* **:** house of worship

**ta•ble** \ˈtābəl\ *n* **1 :** piece of furniture having a smooth slab fixed on legs **2 :** supply of food **3 :** arrangement of data in columns **4 :** short list — **ta•ble•cloth** *n* — **ta•ble•top** *n* — **ta•ble•ware** *n* — **tab•u•lar** \ˈtabyələr\ *adj*

**tab•leau** \ˈtabˌlō\ *n, pl* **-leaux** \-ˌlōz\ **1 :** graphic description **2 :** depiction of a scene by people in costume

**ta•ble•spoon** *n* **1 :** large serving spoon **2 :** measuring spoon holding 1/2 fluid ounce — **ta•ble•spoon•ful** \-ˌfu̇l\ *n*

**tab•let** \ˈtablət\ *n* **1 :** flat slab suited for an inscription **2 :** collection of sheets of paper glued together at one edge **3 :** disk-shaped pill

**tab•loid** \ˈtabˌlȯid\ *n* **:** newspaper of small page size

**ta•boo** \təˈbü, ta-\ *adj* **:** banned esp. as immoral or dangerous — **taboo** *n or vb*

**tab•u•late** \ˈtabyəˌlāt\ *vb* **-lat•ed; -lat•ing :** put in the form of a table — **tab•u•la•tion** \ˌtabyəˈlāshən\ *n* — **tab•u•la•tor** \ˈtabyəˌlātər\ *n*

**tac•it** \ˈtasət\ *adj* **:** implied but not expressed — **tac•it•ly** *adv* — **tac•it•ness** *n*

**tac•i•turn** \ˈtasəˌtərn\ *adj* **:** not inclined to talk

**tack** \ˈtak\ *n* **1 :** small sharp nail **2 :** course of action ~ *vb* **1 :** fasten with tacks **2 :** add on

**tack•le** \ˈtakəl, *naut often* ˈtāk-\ *n* **1 :** equipment **2 :** arrangement of ropes and pulleys **3 :** act of tackling ~ *vb* **-led; -ling 1 :** seize or throw down **2 :** start dealing with

**[1]tacky** \ˈtakē\ *adj* **tack•i•er; -est :** sticky to the touch

**[2]tacky** *adj* **tack•i•er; -est :** cheap or gaudy

**tact** \ˈtakt\ *n* **:** sense of the proper thing to say or do — **tact•ful** \-fəl\ *adj* — **tact•ful•ly** *adv* — **tact•less** *adj* — **tact•less•ly** *adv*

**tac•tic** \ˈtaktik\ *n* **:** action as part of a plan

**tac•tics** \ˈtaktiks\ *n sing or pl* **1 :** science of maneuvering forces in combat **2 :** skill of using available means to reach an end — **tac•ti•cal** \-tikəl\ *adj* — **tac•ti•cian** \takˈtishən\ *n*

**tac•tile** \ˈtakt$^{ə}$l, -ˌtīl\ *adj* **:** relating to or perceptible through the sense of touch

**tad•pole** \ˈtadˌpōl\ *n* **:** larval frog or toad with tail and gills

**taf•fe•ta** \ˈtafətə\ *n* **:** crisp lustrous fabric (as of silk)

**taf•fy** \ˈtafē\ *n, pl* **-fies :** candy stretched until porous

**[1]tag** \ˈtag\ *n* **:** piece of hanging or attached material ~ *vb* **-gg- 1 :** provide or mark with a tag **2 :** follow closely

**[2]tag** *n* **:** children's game of trying to catch one another ~ *vb* **:** touch a person in tag

**tail** \ˈtāl\ *n* **1 :** rear end or a growth extending from the rear end of an animal **2 :** back or last part **3 :** the reverse of a coin ~ *vb* **:** follow — **tailed** \ˈtāld\ *adj* — **tail•less** *adj*

**tail•gate** \-ˌgāt\ *n* **:** hinged gate on the back of a vehicle that can be lowered for loading ~ *vb* **-gat•ed; -gat•ing :** drive too close behind another vehicle

**tail•light** *n* **:** red warning light at the back of a vehicle

**tai•lor** \ˈtālər\ *n* **:** one who makes or alters garments ~ *vb* **1 :** fashion or alter (clothes) **2 :** make or adapt for a special purpose

**tail•spin** *n* **:** spiral dive by an airplane

**taint** \ˈtānt\ *vb* **:** affect or become affected with something bad and esp. decay ~ *n* **:** trace of decay or corruption

**take** \ˈtāk\ *vb* **took** \ˈtu̇k\; **tak•en** \ˈtākən\; **tak•ing 1 :** get into one's possession **2 :** become affected by **3 :** receive into one's body (as by eating) **4 :** pick out or remove **5 :** use for transportation **6 :** need or make use of **7** : lead, carry, or cause to go to another place **8** : undertake and do, make, or perform ∼ *n* : amount taken — **take•over** *n* — **tak•er** *n* — **take advantage of** : profit by — **take exception** : object — **take off** *vb* **1** : remove **2** : go away **3** : mimic **4** : begin flight — **take over** *vb* : assume control or possession of or responsibility for — **take place** : happen

**take•off** *n* : act or instance of taking off

**talc** \'talk\ *n* : soft mineral used in making toilet powder (**tal•cum powder** \'talkəm-\)

**tale** \'tāl\ *n* **1** : story or anecdote **2** : falsehood

**tal•ent** \'talənt\ *n* : natural mental or creative ability — **tal•ent•ed** *adj*

**tal•is•man** \'taləsmən, -əz-\ *n, pl* **-mans** : object thought to act as a charm

**talk** \'tók\ *vb* **1** : express one's thoughts in speech **2** : discuss **3** : influence to a position or course of action by talking ∼ *n* **1** : act of talking **2** : formal discussion **3** : rumor **4** : informal lecture — **talk•a•tive** \-ətiv\ *adj* — **talk•er** *n*

**tall** \'tól\ *adj* : extending to a great or specified height — **tall•ness** *n*

**tal•low** \'talō\ *n* : hard white animal fat used esp. in candles

**tal•ly** \'talē\ *n, pl* **-lies** : recorded amount ∼ *vb* **-lied; -ly•ing 1** : add or count up **2** : match

**tal•on** \'talən\ *n* : bird's claw

**tam** \'tam\ *n* : tam-o'-shanter

**tam•bou•rine** \,tambə'rēn\ *n* : small drum with loose disks at the sides

**tame** \'tām\ *adj* **tam•er; tam•est 1** : changed from being wild to being controllable by man **2** : docile **3** : dull ∼ *vb* **tamed; tam•ing** : make or become tame — **tam•able, tame•able** *adj* — **tame•ly** *adv* — **tam•er** *n*

**tam-o'-shan•ter** \'tamə,shantər\ *n* : Scottish woolen cap with a wide flat circular crown

**tamp** \'tamp\ *vb* : drive down or in by a series of light blows

**tam•per** \'tampər\ *vb* : interfere so as to change for the worse

**tan** \'tan\ *vb* **-nn- 1** : change (hide) into leather esp. by soaking in a liquid containing tannin **2** : make or become brown (as by exposure to the sun) ∼ *n* **1** : brown skin color induced by the sun **2** : light yellowish brown — **tan•ner** *n* — **tan•nery** \'tanərē\ *n*

**tan•dem** \'tandəm\ *adv* : one behind another

**tang** \'taŋ\ *n* : sharp distinctive flavor — **tangy** *adj*

**tan•gent** \'tanjənt\ *adj* : touching a curve or surface at only one point ∼ *n* **1** : tangent line, curve, or surface **2** : abrupt change of course — **tan•gen•tial** \tan'jenchəl\ *adj*

**tan•ger•ine** \'tanjə,rēn, ,tanjə'-\ *n* : deep orange citrus fruit

**tan•gi•ble** \'tanjəbəl\ *adj* **1** : able to be touched **2** : substantially real — **tan•gi•bly** *adv*

**tan•gle** \'taŋgəl\ *vb* **-gled; -gling** : unite in intricate confusion ∼ *n* : tangled twisted mass

**tan•go** \'taŋgō\ *n, pl* **-gos** : dance of Latin-American origin — **tango** *vb*

**tank** \'taŋk\ *n* **1** : large artificial receptacle for liquids **2** : armored military vehicle — **tank•ful** *n*

**tan•kard** \'taŋkərd\ *n* : tall one-handled drinking vessel

**tank•er** \'taŋkər\ *n* : vehicle or vessel with tanks for transporting a liquid

**tan•nin** \'tanən\ *n* : substance of plant origin used in tanning and dyeing

**tan•ta•lize** \'tant°l,īz\ *vb* **-lized; -liz•ing** : tease or torment by keeping something desirable just out of reach — **tan•ta•liz•er** *n* — **tan•ta•liz•ing•ly** *adv*

**tan•ta•mount** \'tantə,maúnt\ *adj* : equivalent in value or meaning

**tan•trum** \'tantrəm\ *n* : fit of bad temper

**¹tap** \'tap\ *n* **1** : faucet **2** : act of tapping ∼ *vb* **-pp- 1** : pierce so as to draw off fluid **2** : connect into — **tap•per** *n*

**²tap** *vb* **-pp-** : rap lightly ∼ *n* : light stroke or its sound

**tape** \'tāp\ *n* **1** : narrow flexible strip (as of cloth, plastic, or metal) **2** : tape measure ∼ *vb* **taped; tap•ing 1** : fasten with tape **2** : record on tape

**tape measure** *n* : strip of tape marked in units for use in measuring

**ta•per** \'tāpər\ *n* **1** : slender wax candle **2** : gradual lessening of width in a long object ∼ *vb* **1** : make or become smaller toward one end **2** : diminish gradually

**tap•es•try** \'tapəstrē\ *n, pl* **-tries** : heavy handwoven ruglike wall hanging

**tape•worm** *n* : long flat intestinal worm

**tap•i•o•ca** \,tapē'ōkə\ *n* : a granular starch used esp. in puddings

**tar** \'tär\ *n* : thick dark sticky liquid distilled (as from coal) ~ *vb* -**rr**- : treat or smear with tar

**ta·ran·tu·la** \tə'ranchələ, -'rant³lə\ *n* : large hairy usu. harmless spider

**tar·dy** \'tärdē\ *adj* -**di·er; -est** : late — **tar·di·ly** \'tärd³lē\ *adv* — **tar·di·ness** *n*

**tar·get** \'tärgət\ *n* **1** : mark to shoot at **2** : goal to be achieved ~ *vb* **1** : make a target of **2** : establish as a goal

**tar·iff** \'tarəf\ *n* **1** : duty or rate of duty imposed on imported goods **2** : schedule of tariffs, rates, or charges

**tar·nish** \'tärnish\ *vb* : make or become dull or discolored — **tarnish** *n*

**tar·pau·lin** \tär'pólən, 'tärpə-\ *n* : waterproof protective covering

¹**tar·ry** \'tarē\ *vb* -**ried; -ry·ing** : be slow in leaving

²**tar·ry** \'tärē\ *adj* : resembling or covered with tar

¹**tart** \'tärt\ *adj* **1** : pleasantly sharp to the taste **2** : caustic — **tart·ly** *adv* — **tart·ness** *n*

²**tart** *n* : small pie

**tar·tan** \'tärt³n\ *n* : woolen fabric with a plaid design

**tar·tar** \'tärtər\ *n* : hard crust on the teeth

**task** \'task\ *n* : assigned work

**task·mas·ter** *n* : one that burdens another with labor

**tas·sel** \'tasəl, 'täs-\ *n* : hanging ornament made of a bunch of cords fastened at one end

**taste** \'tāst\ *vb* **tast·ed; tast·ing 1** : test or determine the flavor of **2** : eat or drink in small quantities **3** : have a specific flavor ~ *n* **1** : small amount tasted **2** : bit **3** : special sense that identifies sweet, sour, bitter, or salty qualities **4** : individual preference **5** : critical appreciation of quality — **taste·ful** \-fəl\ *adj* — **taste·ful·ly** *adv* — **taste·less** *adj* — **taste·less·ly** *adv* — **tast·er** *n*

**tasty** \'tāstē\ *adj* **tast·i·er; -est** : pleasing to the sense of taste — **tast·i·ness** *n*

**tat·ter** \'tatər\ *n* **1** : part torn and left hanging **2** *pl* : tattered clothing ~ *vb* : make or become ragged

**tat·tle** \'tat³l\ *vb* -**tled; -tling** : inform on someone — **tat·tler** *n*

**tat·tle·tale** *n* : one that tattles

**tat·too** \ta'tü\ *vb* : mark the skin with indelible designs or figures — **tattoo** *n*

**taught** *past of* TEACH

**taunt** \'tónt\ *n* : sarcastic challenge or insult — **taunt** *vb* — **taunt·er** *n*

**taut** \'tót\ *adj* : tightly drawn — **taut·ly** *adv* — **taut·ness** *n*

**tav·ern** \'tavərn\ *n* : establishment where liquors are sold to be drunk on the premises

**taw·dry** \'tódrē\ *adj* -**dri·er; -est** : cheap and gaudy — **taw·dri·ly** \'tódrəlē\ *adv*

**taw·ny** \'tónē\ *adj* -**ni·er; -est** : brownish orange

**tax** \'taks\ *vb* **1** : impose a tax on **2** : charge **3** : put under stress ~ *n* **1** : charge by authority for public purposes **2** : strain — **tax·able** *adj* — **tax·a·tion** \tak'sāshən\ *n* — **tax·pay·er** *n* — **tax·pay·ing** *adj*

**taxi** \'taksē\ *n, pl* **tax·is** \-sēz\ : automobile transporting passengers for a fare ~ *vb* **tax·ied; taxi·ing** *or* **taxy·ing; tax·is** *or* **tax·ies 1** : transport or go by taxi **2** : move along the ground before takeoff or after landing

**taxi·cab** \'taksē,kab\ *n* : taxi

**taxi·der·my** \'taksə,dərmē\ *n* : skill or job of stuffing and mounting animal skins — **taxi·der·mist** \-mist\ *n*

**tea** \'tē\ *n* : cured leaves of an oriental shrub or a drink made from these — **tea·cup** *n* — **tea·pot** *n*

**teach** \'tēch\ *vb* **taught** \'tót\; **teaching 1** : tell or show the fundamentals or skills of something **2** : cause to know the consequences **3** : impart knowledge of — **teach·able** *adj* — **teach·er** *n* — **teach·ing** *n*

**teak** \'tēk\ *n* : East Indian timber tree or its wood

**tea·ket·tle** \'tē,ket³l\ *n* : covered kettle with a handle and spout for boiling water

**teal** \'tēl\ *n, pl* **teal** *or* **teals** : small short-necked wild duck

**team** \'tēm\ *n* **1** : draft animals harnessed together **2** : number of people organized for a game or work ~ *vb* : form or work together as a team — **team** *adj* — **team·mate** *n* — **team·work** *n*

**team·ster** \'tēmstər\ *n* **1** : one that drives a team of animals **2** : one that drives a truck

¹**tear** \'tir\ *n* : drop of salty liquid that moistens the eye — **tear·ful** \-fəl\ *adj* — **tear·ful·ly** *adv*

²**tear** \'tar\ *vb* **tore** \'tōr\; **torn** \'tōrn\; **tear·ing 1** : separate or pull apart by

force **2** : move or act with violence or haste ~ *n* : act or result of tearing

**tease** \'tēz\ *vb* **teased; teas•ing** : annoy by goading, coaxing, or tantalizing ~ *n* **1** : act of teasing or state of being teased **2** : one that teases

**tea•spoon** \'tē,spün\ *n* **1** : small spoon for stirring or sipping **2** : measuring spoon holding 1/6 fluid ounce — **tea•spoon•ful** \-,fül\ *n*

**teat** \'tēt\ *n* : protuberance through which milk is drawn from an udder or breast

**tech•ni•cal** \'teknikəl\ *adj* **1** : having or relating to special mechanical or scientific knowledge **2** : by strict interpretation of rules — **tech•ni•cal•ly** *adv*

**tech•ni•cal•i•ty** \,teknə'kalətē\ *n, pl* **-ties** : detail meaningful only to a specialist

**technical sergeant** *n* : noncommissioned officer in the air force ranking next below a master sergeant

**tech•ni•cian** \tek'nishən\ *n* : person with the technique of a specialized skill

**tech•nique** \tek'nēk\ *n* : manner of accomplishing something

**tech•nol•o•gy** \tek'näləjē\ *n, pl* **-gies** : applied science — **tech•no•log•i•cal** \,teknə'läjikəl\ *adj*

**te•dious** \'tēdēəs\ *adj* : wearisome from length or dullness — **te•dious•ly** *adv* — **te•dious•ness** *n*

**te•di•um** \'tēdēəm\ *n* : tedious state or quality

**tee** \'tē\ *n* : mound or peg on which a golf ball is placed before beginning play — **tee** *vb*

**teem** \'tēm\ *vb* : become filled to overflowing

**teen•age** \'tēn,āj\, **teen•aged** \-,ājd\ *adj* : relating to people in their teens — **teen•ag•er** \-,ājər\ *n*

**teens** \'tēnz\ *n pl* : years 13 to 19 in a person's life

**tee•pee** *var of* TEPEE

**tee•ter** \'tētər\ *vb* **1** : move unsteadily **2** : seesaw — **teeter** *n*

**teeth** *pl of* TOOTH

**teethe** \'tēth\ *vb* **teethed; teeth•ing** : grow teeth

**tele•cast** \'teli,kast\ *vb* **-cast; -cast•ing** : broadcast by television — **tele•cast** *n* — **tele•cast•er** *n*

**tele•com•mu•ni•ca•tion** \'teləkəmyünə-'kāshən\ *n* : communication at a distance (as by radio or telephone)

**tele•gram** \'telə,gram\ *n* : message sent by telegraph

**tele•graph** \-,graf\ *n* : system for communication by electrical transmission of coded signals ~ *vb* : send by telegraph — **te•leg•ra•pher** \tə'legrəfər\ *n* — **tele•graph•ic** \,telə'grafik\ *adj*

**te•lep•a•thy** \tə'lepəthē\ *n* : apparent communication without known sensory means — **tele•path•ic** \,telə-'pathik\ *adj* — **tele•path•i•cal•ly** *adv*

**tele•phone** \'telə,fōn\ *n* : instrument or system for electrical transmission of spoken words ~ *vb* **-phoned; -phon•ing** : communicate with by telephone — **tele•phon•er** *n*

**tele•scope** \-,skōp\ *n* : tube-shaped optical instrument for viewing distant objects ~ *vb* **-scoped; -scop•ing** : slide or cause to slide inside another similar section — **tele•scop•ic** \,telə-'skäpik\ *adj*

**tele•vise** \'telə,vīz\ *vb* **-vised; -vis•ing** : broadcast by television

**tele•vi•sion** \-,vizhən\ *n* : transmission and reproduction of images by radio waves

**tell** \'tel\ *vb* **told** \'tōld\; **tell•ing** **1** : count **2** : relate in detail **3** : reveal **4** : give information or an order to **5** : find out by observing

**tell•er** \'telər\ *n* **1** : one that relates or counts **2** : bank employee handling money

**te•mer•i•ty** \tə'merətē\ *n, pl* **-ties** : boldness

**temp** \'temp\ *n* **1** : temperature **2** : temporary worker

**tem•per** \'tempər\ *vb* **1** : dilute or soften **2** : toughen ~ *n* **1** : characteristic attitude or feeling **2** : toughness **3** : disposition or control over one's emotions

**tem•per•a•ment** \'tempərəmənt\ *n* : characteristic frame of mind — **tem•per•a•men•tal** \,temprə'ment²l\ *adj*

**tem•per•ance** \'temprəns\ *n* : moderation in or abstinence from indulgence and esp. the use of intoxicating drink

**tem•per•ate** \'tempərət\ *adj* : moderate

**tem•per•a•ture** \'tempər,chúr, -prə-,chúr, -chər\ *n* **1** : degree of hotness or coldness **2** : fever

**tem•pest** \'tempəst\ *n* : violent storm — **tem•pes•tu•ous** \tem'peschəwəs\ *adj*

**¹tem•ple** \'tempəl\ *n* : place of worship

**²temple** *n* : flattened space on each side of the forehead

**tem·po** \'tempō\ *n, pl* **-pi** \-ₚpē\ *or* **-pos** : rate of speed

**tem·po·ral** \'tempərəl\ *adj* : relating to time or to secular concerns

**tem·po·rary** \'tempəˌrerē\ *adj* : lasting for a short time only — **tem·po·rar·i·ly** \ˌtempə'rerəlē\ *adv*

**tempt** \'tempt\ *vb* **1** : coax or persuade to do wrong **2** : attract or provoke — **tempt·er** *n* — **tempt·ing·ly** *adv* — **tempt·ress** \'temptrəs\ *n*

**temp·ta·tion** \temp'tāshən\ *n* **1** : act of tempting **2** : something that tempts

**ten** \'ten\ *n* **1** : one more than 9 **2** : 10th in a set or series **3** : thing having 10 units — **ten** *adj or pron* — **tenth** \'tenth\ *adj or adv or n*

**ten·a·ble** \'tenəbəl\ *adj* : capable of being held or defended — **ten·a·bil·i·ty** \ˌtenə'bilətē\ *n*

**te·na·cious** \tə'nāshəs\ *adj* **1** : holding fast **2** : retentive — **te·na·cious·ly** *adv* — **te·nac·i·ty** \tə'nasətē\ *n*

**ten·ant** \'tenənt\ *n* : one who occupies a rented dwelling — **ten·an·cy** \-ənsē\ *n*

**¹tend** \'tend\ *vb* : take care of or supervise something

**²tend** *vb* **1** : move in a particular direction **2** : show a tendency

**ten·den·cy** \'tendənsē\ *n, pl* **-cies** : likelihood to move, think, or act in a particular way

**¹ten·der** \'tendər\ *adj* **1** : soft or delicate **2** : expressing or responsive to love or sympathy **3** : sensitive (as to touch) — **ten·der·ly** *adv* — **ten·der·ness** *n*

**²tend·er** \'tendər\ *n* **1** : one that tends **2** : boat providing transport to a larger ship **3** : vehicle attached to a steam locomotive for carrying fuel and water

**³ten·der** *n* **1** : offer of a bid for a contract **2** : something that may be offered in payment — **tender** *vb*

**ten·der·ize** \'tendəˌrīz\ *vb* **-ized; -iz·ing** : make (meat) tender — **ten·der·iz·er** \'tendəˌrīzər\ *n*

**ten·der·loin** \'tenderˌlȯin\ *n* : tender beef or pork strip from near the backbone

**ten·don** \'tendən\ *n* : cord of tissue attaching muscle to bone — **ten·di·nous** \-dənəs\ *adj*

**ten·dril** \'tendrəl\ *n* : slender coiling growth of some climbing plants

**ten·e·ment** \'tenəmənt\ *n* **1** : house divided into apartments **2** : shabby dwelling

**te·net** \'tenət\ *n* : principle of belief

**ten·nis** \'tenəs\ *n* : racket-and-ball game played across a net

**ten·or** \'tenər\ *n* **1** : general drift or meaning **2** : highest natural adult male voice

**ten·pin** \'tenˌpin\ *n* : bottle-shaped pin bowled at in a game (**tenpins**)

**¹tense** \'tens\ *n* : distinct verb form that indicates time

**²tense** *adj* **tens·er; tens·est** **1** : stretched tight **2** : marked by nervous tension — **tense** *vb* — **tense·ly** *adv* — **tense·ness** *n* — **ten·si·ty** \'tensətē\ *n*

**ten·sile** \'tensəl, -ˌsīl\ *adj* : relating to tension

**ten·sion** \'tenchən\ *n* **1** : tense condition **2** : state of mental unrest or of potential hostility or opposition

**tent** \'tent\ *n* : collapsible shelter

**ten·ta·cle** \'tentikəl\ *n* : long flexible projection of an insect or mollusk — **ten·ta·cled** \-kəld\ *adj* — **ten·tac·u·lar** \ten'takyələr\ *adj*

**ten·ta·tive** \'tentətiv\ *adj* : subject to change or discussion — **ten·ta·tive·ly** *adv*

**ten·u·ous** \'tenyəwəs\ *adj* **1** : not dense or thick **2** : flimsy or weak — **ten·u·ous·ly** *adv* — **ten·u·ous·ness** *n*

**ten·ure** \'tenyər\ *n* : act, right, manner, or period of holding something — **ten·ured** \-yərd\ *adj*

**te·pee** \'tēˌpē\ *n* : conical tent

**tep·id** \'tepəd\ *adj* : moderately warm

**term** \'tərm\ *n* **1** : period of time **2** : mathematical expression **3** : special word or phrase **4** *pl* : conditions **5** *pl* : relations ～ *vb* : name

**ter·mi·nal** \'tərmən°l\ *n* **1** : end **2** : device for making an electrical connection **3** : station at end of a transportation line — **terminal** *adj*

**ter·mi·nate** \'tərməˌnāt\ *vb* **-nat·ed; -nat·ing** : bring or come to an end — **ter·mi·na·ble** \-nəbəl\ *adj* — **ter·mi·na·tion** \ˌtərmə'nāshən\ *n*

**ter·mi·nol·o·gy** \ˌtərmə'näləjē\ *n* : terms used in a particular subject

**ter·mi·nus** \'tərmənəs\ *n, pl* **-ni** \-ˌnī\ *or* **-nus·es** **1** : end **2** : end of a transportation line

**ter·mite** \'tərˌmīt\ *n* : wood-eating insect

**tern** \'tərn\ *n* : small sea bird

**ter·race** \'terəs\ *n* **1** : balcony or patio **2** : bank with a flat top ~ *vb* **-raced; -rac·ing** : landscape in a series of banks

**ter·ra–cot·ta** \ˌterə'kätə\ *n* : reddish brown earthenware

**ter·rain** \tə'rān\ *n* : features of the land

**ter·ra·pin** \'terəpən\ *n* : No. American turtle

**ter·rar·i·um** \tə'rarēəm\ *n, pl* **-ia** \-ēə\ *or* **-i·ums** : container for keeping plants or animals

**ter·res·tri·al** \tə'restrēəl\ *adj* **1** : relating to the earth or its inhabitants **2** : living or growing on land

**ter·ri·ble** \'terəbəl\ *adj* **1** : exciting terror **2** : distressing **3** : intense **4** : of very poor quality — **ter·ri·bly** \-blē\ *adv*

**ter·ri·er** \'terēər\ *n* : small dog

**ter·rif·ic** \tə'rifik\ *adj* **1** : exciting terror **2** : extraordinary

**ter·ri·fy** \'terəˌfī\ *vb* **-fied; -fy·ing** : fill with terror — **ter·ri·fy·ing·ly** *adv*

**ter·ri·to·ry** \'terəˌtōrē\ *n, pl* **-ries** : particular geographical region — **ter·ri·to·ri·al** \ˌterə'tōrēəl\ *adj*

**ter·ror** \'terər\ *n* : intense fear and panic or a cause of it

**ter·ror·ism** \-ˌizəm\ *n* : systematic covert warfare to produce terror for political coercion — **ter·ror·ist** \-ist\ *adj or n*

**ter·ror·ize** \-ˌīz\ *vb* **-ized; -iz·ing** **1** : fill with terror **2** : coerce by threat or violence

**ter·ry** \'terē\ *n, pl* **-ries** : absorbent fabric with a loose pile

**terse** \'tərs\ *adj* **ters·er; ters·est** : concise — **terse·ly** *adv* — **terse·ness** *n*

**ter·tia·ry** \'tərshēˌerē\ *adj* : of 3d rank, importance, or value

**test** \'test\ *n* : examination or evaluation ~ *vb* : examine by a test — **test·er** *n*

**tes·ta·ment** \'testəmənt\ *n* **1** *cap* : division of the Bible **2** : will — **tes·ta·men·ta·ry** \ˌtestə'mentərē\ *adj*

**tes·ti·cle** \'testikəl\ *n* : testis

**tes·ti·fy** \'testəˌfī\ *vb* **-fied; -fy·ing** **1** : give testimony **2** : serve as evidence

**tes·ti·mo·ni·al** \ˌtestə'mōnēəl\ *n* **1** : favorable recommendation **2** : tribute — **testimonial** *adj*

**tes·ti·mo·ny** \'testəˌmōnē\ *n, pl* **-nies** : statement given as evidence in court

**tes·tis** \'testəs\ *n, pl* **-tes** \-ˌtēz\ : male reproductive gland

**tes·ty** \'testē\ *adj* **-ti·er; -est** : easily annoyed

**tet·a·nus** \'tetᵊnəs\ *n* : bacterial disease producing violent spasms

**tête à tête** \ˌtātə'tāt\ *adv* : privately ~ *n* : private conversation ~ *adj* : private

**teth·er** \'tethər\ *n* : leash ~ *vb* : restrain with a leash

**text** \'tekst\ *n* **1** : author's words **2** : main body of printed or written matter on a page **3** : textbook **4** : scriptural passage used as the theme of a sermon **5** : topic — **tex·tu·al** \'tekschəwəl\ *adj*

**text·book** \-ˌbùk\ *n* : book on a school subject

**tex·tile** \'tekˌstīl, 'tekstᵊl\ *n* : fabric

**tex·ture** \'tekschər\ *n* **1** : feel and appearance of something **2** : structure

**than** \'than\ *conj or prep* — used in comparisons

**thank** \'thaŋk\ *vb* : express gratitude to

**thank·ful** \-fəl\ *adj* : giving thanks — **thank·ful·ly** *adv* — **thank·ful·ness** *n*

**thank·less** *adj* : not appreciated

**thanks** \'thaŋks\ *n pl* : expression of gratitude

**Thanks·giv·ing** \thaŋks'giviŋ\ *n* : 4th Thursday in November observed as a legal holiday for giving thanks for divine goodness

**that** \'that\ *pron, pl* **those** \thōz\ **1** : something indicated or understood **2** : the one farther away ~ *adj, pl* **those** : being the one mentioned or understood or farther away ~ *conj or pron* — used to introduce a clause ~ *adv* : to such an extent

**thatch** \'thach\ *vb* : cover with thatch ~ *n* : covering of matted straw

**thaw** \'thò\ *vb* : melt or cause to melt — **thaw** *n*

**the** \thə, *before vowel sounds usu* thē\ *definite article* : that particular one ~ *adv* — used before a comparative or superlative

**the·ater, the·atre** \'thēətər\ *n* **1** : building or room for viewing a play or movie **2** : dramatic arts

**the·at·ri·cal** \thē'atrikəl\ *adj* **1** : relating to the theater **2** : involving exaggerated emotion

**thee** \'thē\ *pron, archaic objective case of* THOU

**theft** \'theft\ *n* : act of stealing

**their** \'ᵵher\ *adj* : relating to them

**theirs** \'ᵵheərz\ *pron* : their one or ones

**the•ism** \'ᵵhē₁izəm\ *n* : belief in the existence of a god or gods — **the•ist** \-ist\ *n or adj* — **the•is•tic** \thē-'istik\ *adj*

**them** \'ᵵhem\ *pron, objective case of* THEY

**theme** \'ᵵhēm\ *n* **1** : subject matter **2** : essay **3** : melody developed in a piece of music — **the•mat•ic** \thi-'matik\ *adj*

**them•selves** \ᵵhəm'selvz, ᵵhem-\ *pron pl* : they, them — used reflexively or for emphasis

**then** \'ᵵhen\ *adv* **1** : at that time **2** : soon after that **3** : in addition **4** : in that case **5** : consequently ~ *n* : that time ~ *adj* : existing at that time

**thence** \'ᵵhens, 'ᵵhens\ *adv* : from that place or fact

**the•oc•ra•cy** \thē'äkrəsē\ *n, pl* **-cies** : government by officials regarded as divinely inspired — **the•o•crat•ic** \₁thēə'kratik\ *adj*

**the•ol•o•gy** \thē'äləjē\ *n, pl* **-gies** : study of religion — **the•o•lo•gian** \₁thēə'lōjən\ *n* — **the•o•log•i•cal** \-'läjikəl\ *adj*

**the•o•rem** \'thēərəm, 'thirəm\ *n* : provable statement of truth

**the•o•ret•i•cal** \₁thēə'retikəl\ *adj* : relating to or being theory — **the•o•ret•i•cal•ly** *adv*

**the•o•rize** \'thēə₁rīz\ *vb* **-rized; -riz•ing** : put forth theories — **the•o•rist** *n*

**the•o•ry** \'thēərē, 'thirē\ *n, pl* **-ries 1** : general principles of a subject **2** : plausible or scientifically acceptable explanation **3** : judgment, guess, or opinion

**ther•a•peu•tic** \₁therə'pyütik\ *adj* : offering or relating to remedy — **ther•a•peu•ti•cal•ly** *adv*

**ther•a•py** \'therəpē\ *n, pl* **-pies** : treatment for mental or physical disorder — **ther•a•pist** \-pist\ *n*

**there** \'ᵵhar\ *adv* **1** : in, at, or to that place **2** : in that respect ~ *pron* — used to introduce a sentence or clause ~ *n* : that place or point

**there•abouts, there•about** \₁ᵵharə-'bauts, 'ᵵharə₁-, -'baut\ *adv* : near that place, time, number, or quantity

**there•af•ter** \ᵵhar'aftər\ *adv* : after that

**there•by** \ᵵhar'bī, 'ᵵhar₁bī\ *adv* **1** : by that **2** : connected with or with reference to that

**there•fore** \'ᵵhar₁fōr\ *adv* : for that reason

**there•in** \ᵵhar'in\ *adv* **1** : in or into that place, time, or thing **2** : in that respect

**there•of** \-'əv, -'äv\ *adv* **1** : of that or it **2** : from that

**there•upon** \'ᵵharə₁pȯn, -₁pän; ₁ᵵharə-'pȯn, -'pän\ *adv* **1** : on that matter **2** : therefore **3** : immediately after that

**there•with** \ᵵhar'wiᵵh, -'wiᵵh\ *adv* : with that

**ther•mal** \'thərməl\ *adj* : relating to, caused by, or conserving heat — **ther•mal•ly** *adv*

**ther•mo•dy•nam•ics** \₁thərmədī-'namiks\ *n* : physics of heat

**ther•mom•e•ter** \thər'mämətər\ *n* : instrument for measuring temperature — **ther•mo•met•ric** \₁thərmə-'metrik\ *adj*

**ther•mos** \'thərməs\ *n* : double-walled bottle used to keep liquids hot or cold

**ther•mo•stat** \'thərmə₁stat\ *n* : automatic temperature control — **ther•mo•stat•ic** \₁thərmə'statik\ *adj* — **ther•mo•stat•i•cal•ly** *adv*

**the•sau•rus** \thi'sȯrəs\ *n, pl* **-sau•ri** \-'sȯr₁ī\ *or* **-sau•rus•es** \-'sȯrəsəz\ : book of words and esp. synonyms

**these** *pl of* THIS

**the•sis** \'thēsəs\ *n, pl* **the•ses** \'thē-₁sēz\ **1** : proposition to be argued for **2** : essay embodying results of original research

**thes•pi•an** \'thespēən\ *adj* : dramatic ~ *n* : actor

**they** \'ᵵhā\ *pron* **1** : those ones **2** : people in general

**thi•a•mine** \'thīəmən, -₁mēn\ *n* : essential vitamin

**thick** \'thik\ *adj* **1** : having relatively great mass from front to back or top to bottom **2** : viscous ~ *n* : most crowded or thickest part — **thick•ly** *adv* — **thick•ness** *n*

**thick•en** \'thikən\ *vb* : make or become thick — **thick•en•er** \-ənər\ *n*

**thick•et** \'thikət\ *n* : dense growth of bushes or small trees

**thick–skinned** \-'skind\ *adj* : insensitive to criticism

**thief** \'thēf\ *n, pl* **thieves** \'thēvz\ : one that steals

**thieve** \'thēv\ *vb* **thieved; thiev•ing** : steal — **thiev•ery** *n*

**thigh** \'thī\ *n* : upper part of the leg

**thigh•bone** \'thī₁bōn\ *n* : femur

**thim•ble** \'thimbəl\ *n* : protective cap

for the finger in sewing — **thim·ble·ful** n

**thin** \'thin\ adj **-nn-** 1 : having relatively little mass from front to back or top to bottom 2 : not closely set or placed 3 : relatively free flowing 4 : lacking substance, fullness, or strength ~ vb **-nn-** : make or become thin — **thin·ly** adv — **thin·ness** n

**thing** \'thiŋ\ n 1 : matter of concern 2 : event or act 3 : object 4 pl : possessions

**think** \'thiŋk\ vb **thought** \'thot\; **think·ing** 1 : form or have in the mind 2 : have as an opinion 3 : ponder 4 : devise by thinking 5 : imagine — **think·er** n

**thin–skinned** adj : extremely sensitive to criticism

**third** \'thərd\ adj : being number 3 in a countable series ~ n 1 : one that is third 2 : one of 3 equal parts — **third**, **third·ly** adv

**third dimension** n : thickness or depth — **third–dimensional** adj

**third world** n : less developed nations of the world

**thirst** \'thərst\ n 1 : dryness in mouth and throat 2 : intense desire ~ vb : feel thirst — **thirsty** adj

**thir·teen** \,thər'tēn\ n : one more than 12 — **thirteen** adj or pron — **thir·teenth** \-'tēnth\ adj or n

**thir·ty** \'thərtē\ n, pl **thirties** : 3 times 10 — **thir·ti·eth** \-ēəth\ adj or n — **thirty** adj or pron

**this** \'this\ pron, pl **these** \'thēz\ : something close or under immediate discussion ~ adj, pl **these** : being the one near, present, just mentioned, or more immediately under observation ~ adv : to such an extent or degree

**this·tle** \'thisəl\ n : tall prickly herb

**thith·er** \'thithər\ adv : to that place

**thong** \'thoŋ\ n : strip of leather or hide

**tho·rax** \'thōr,aks\ n, pl **-rax·es** or **-races** \'thōrə,sēz\ 1 : part of the body between neck and abdomen 2 : middle of 3 divisions of an insect body — **tho·rac·ic** \thə'rasik\ adj

**thorn** \'thorn\ n : sharp spike on a plant or a plant bearing these — **thorny** adj

**thor·ough** \'thərō\ adj : omitting or overlooking nothing — **thor·ough·ly** adv — **thor·ough·ness** n

**thor·ough·bred** \'thərə,bred\ n 1 cap : light speedy racing horse 2 : one of excellent quality — **thoroughbred** adj

**thor·ough·fare** \'thərə,far\ n : public road

**those** pl of THAT

**thou** \'thaù\ pron, archaic : you

**though** \'thō\ adv : however ~ conj 1 : despite the fact that 2 : granting that

**thought** \'thot\ past of THINK n 1 : process of thinking 2 : serious consideration 3 : idea

**thought·ful** \-fəl\ adj 1 : absorbed in or showing thought 2 : considerate of others — **thought·ful·ly** adv — **thought·ful·ness** n

**thought·less** \-ləs\ adj 1 : careless or reckless 2 : lacking concern for others — **thought·less·ly** adv

**thou·sand** \'thaùz°nd\ n, pl **-sands** or **-sand** : 10 times 100 — **thousand** adj — **thou·sandth** \-°nth\ adj or n

**thrash** \'thrash\ vb 1 : thresh 2 : beat 3 : move about violently — **thrash·er** n

**thread** \'thred\ n 1 : fine line of fibers 2 : train of thought 3 : ridge around a screw ~ vb 1 : pass thread through 2 : put together on a thread 3 : make one's way through or between

**thread·bare** adj 1 : worn so that the thread shows 2 : trite

**threat** \'thret\ n 1 : expression of intention to harm 2 : thing that threatens

**threat·en** \'thret°n\ vb 1 : utter threats 2 : show signs of being near or impending — **threat·en·ing·ly** adv

**three** \'thrē\ n 1 : one more than 2 2 : 3d in a set or series — **three** adj or pron

**three·fold** \'thrē,fōld\ adj : triple — **three·fold** \-'fōld\ adv

**three·score** adj : being 3 times 20

**thresh** \'thresh, 'thrash\ vb : beat to separate grain — **thresh·er** n

**thresh·old** \'thresh,ōld\ n 1 : sill of a door 2 : beginning stage

**threw** past of THROW

**thrice** \'thrīs\ adv : 3 times

**thrift** \'thrift\ n : careful management or saving of money — **thrift·i·ly** \'thriftəlē\ adv — **thrifty** adj

**thrill** \'thril\ vb 1 : have or cause to have a sudden sharp feeling of excitement 2 : tremble — **thrill** n — **thrill·er** n — **thrill·ing·ly** adv

**thrive** \'thrīv\ vb **throve** \'thrōv\ or

**thrived; thriv•en** \'thrivən\ **1** : grow vigorously **2** : prosper

**throat** \'thrōt\ *n* **1** : front part of the neck **2** : passage to the stomach — **throat•ed** *adj* — **throaty** *adj*

**throb** \'thräb\ *vb* **-bb-** : pulsate — **throb** *n*

**throe** \'thrō\ *n* **1** : pang or spasm **2** *pl* : hard or painful struggle

**throne** \'thrōn\ *n* : chair representing power or sovereignty

**throng** \'thròŋ\ *n or vb* : crowd

**throt•tle** \'thrät°l\ *vb* **-tled; -tling** : choke ∼ *n* : valve regulating volume of fuel and air delivered to engine cylinders

**through** \'thrü\ *prep* **1** : into at one side and out at the other side of **2** : by way of **3** : among, between, or all around **4** : because of **5** : throughout the time of ∼ \'thrü\ *adv* **1** : from one end or side to the other **2** : from beginning to end **3** : to the core **4** : into the open ∼ *adj* **1** : going directly from origin to destination **2** : finished

**through•out** \thrü'aút\ *adv* **1** : everywhere **2** : from beginning to end ∼ *prep* **1** : in or to every part of **2** : during the whole of

**throve** *past of* THRIVE

**throw** \'thrō\ *vb* **threw** \'thrü\; **thrown** \'thrōn\; **throw•ing 1** : propel through the air **2** : cause to fall or fall off **3** : put suddenly in a certain position or condition **4** : move quickly as if throwing **5** : put on or off hastily — **throw** *n* — **throw•er** \'thrōər\ *n* — **throw up** *vb* : vomit

**thrush** \'thrəsh\ *n* : songbird

**thrust** \'thrəst\ *vb* **thrust; thrust•ing 1** : shove forward **2** : stab or pierce — **thrust** *n*

**thud** \'thəd\ *n* : dull sound of something falling — **thud** *vb*

**thug** \'thəg\ *n* : ruffian or gangster

**thumb** \'thəm\ *n* **1** : short thick division of the hand opposing the fingers **2** : glove part for the thumb ∼ *vb* : leaf through with the thumb — **thumb•nail** *n*

**thump** \'thəmp\ *vb* : strike with something thick or heavy causing a dull sound — **thump** *n*

**thun•der** \'thəndər\ *n* : sound following lightning — **thunder** *vb* — **thun•der•clap** *n* — **thun•der•ous** \'thəndərəs\ *adj* — **thun•der•ous•ly** *adv*

**thun•der•bolt** \-,bōlt\ *n* : discharge of lightning with thunder

**thun•der•show•er** \'thəndər,shaúər\ *n* : shower with thunder and lightning

**thun•der•storm** *n* : storm with thunder and lightning

**Thurs•day** \'thərzdā, -dē\ *n* : 5th day of the week

**thus** \'thəs\ *adv* **1** : in this or that way **2** : to this degree or extent **3** : because of this or that

**thwart** \'thwòrt\ *vb* : block or defeat

**thy** \'thī\ *adj, archaic* : your

**thyme** \'tīm, 'thīm\ *n* : cooking herb

**thy•roid** \'thī,ròid\ *adj* : relating to a large endocrine gland (**thyroid gland**)

**thy•self** \thī'self\ *pron, archaic* : yourself

**ti•ara** \tē'arə, -'är-\ *n* : decorative formal headband

**tib•ia** \'tibēə\ *n, pl* **-i•ae** \-ē,ē\ : bone between the knee and ankle

**tic** \'tik\ *n* : twitching of facial muscles

**¹tick** \'tik\ *n* : small 8-legged bloodsucking animal

**²tick** *n* **1** : light rhythmic tap or beat **2** : check mark ∼ *vb* **1** : make ticks **2** : mark with a tick **3** : operate

**tick•er** \'tikər\ *n* **1** : something (as a watch) that ticks **2** : telegraph instrument that prints on paper tape

**tick•et** \'tikət\ *n* **1** : tag showing price, payment of a fee or fare, or a traffic offense **2** : list of candidates ∼ *vb* : put a ticket on

**tick•ing** \'tikiŋ\ *n* : fabric covering of a mattress

**tick•le** \'tikəl\ *vb* **-led; -ling 1** : please or amuse **2** : touch lightly causing uneasiness, laughter, or spasmodic movements — **tickle** *n*

**tick•lish** \'tiklish\ *adj* **1** : sensitive to tickling **2** : requiring delicate handling — **tick•lish•ness** *n*

**tid•al wave** \'tīd°l-\ *n* : high sea wave following an earthquake

**tid•bit** \'tid,bit\ *n* : choice morsel

**tide** \'tīd\ *n* : alternate rising and falling of the sea ∼ *vb* **tid•ed; tid•ing** : be enough to allow (one) to get by for a time — **tid•al** \'tīd°l\ *adj* — **tide•wa•ter** *n*

**tid•ings** \'tīdiŋz\ *n pl* : news or message

**ti•dy** \'tīdē\ *adj* **-di•er; -est 1** : well ordered and cared for **2** : large or substantial — **ti•di•ness** *n* — **tidy** *vb*

**tie** \'tī\ *n* **1** : line or ribbon for fastening, uniting, or closing **2** : cross support to which railroad rails are fastened **3** : uniting force **4** : equality in score or tally or a deadlocked contest **5** : necktie ~ *vb* **tied; ty·ing** *or* **tie·ing 1** : fasten or close by wrapping and knotting a tie **2** : form a knot in **3** : gain the same score or tally as an opponent

**tier** \'tir\ *n* : one of a steplike series of rows

**tiff** \'tif\ *n* : petty quarrel — **tiff** *vb*

**ti·ger** \'tīgər\ *n* : very large black-striped cat — **ti·ger·ish** \-gərish\ *adj* — **ti·gress** \-grəs\ *n*

**tight** \'tīt\ *adj* **1** : fitting close together esp. so as not to allow air or water in **2** : held very firmly **3** : taut **4** : fitting too snugly **5** : difficult **6** : stingy **7** : evenly contested **8** : low in supply — **tight** *adv* — **tight·en** \-°n\ *vb* — **tight·ly** *adv* — **tight·ness** *n*

**tights** \'tīts\ *n pl* : skintight garments

**tight·wad** \'tīt,wäd\ *n* : stingy person

**tile** \'tīl\ *n* : thin piece of stone or fired clay used on roofs, floors, or walls ~ *vb* : cover with tiles

**¹till** \'til\ *prep or conj* : until

**²till** *vb* : cultivate (soil) — **till·able** *adj*

**³till** *n* : money drawer

**¹till·er** \'tilər\ *n* : one that cultivates soil

**²til·ler** \'tilər\ *n* : lever for turning a boat's rudder

**tilt** \'tilt\ *vb* : cause to incline ~ *n* : slant

**tim·ber** \'timbər\ *n* **1** : cut wood for building **2** : large squared piece of wood **3** : wooded land or trees for timber ~ *vb* : cover, frame, or support with timbers — **tim·bered** *adj* — **tim·ber·land** \-,land\ *n*

**tim·bre** \'tambər, 'tim-\ *n* : sound quality

**time** \'tīm\ *n* **1** : period during which something exists or continues or can be accomplished **2** : point at which something happens **3** : customary hour **4** : age **5** : tempo **6** : moment, hour, day, or year as indicated by a clock or calendar **7** : one's experience during a particular period ~ *vb* **timed; tim·ing 1** : arrange or set the time of **2** : determine or record the time, duration, or rate of — **time·keep·er** *n* — **time·less** *adj* — **time·less·ness** *n* — **time·li·ness** *n* — **time·ly** *adv* — **tim·er** *n*

**time·piece** *n* : device to show time

**times** \'tīmz\ *prep* : multiplied by

**time·ta·ble** \'tīm,tābəl\ *n* : table of departure and arrival times

**tim·id** \'timəd\ *adj* : lacking in courage or self-confidence — **ti·mid·i·ty** \tə'midətē\ *n* — **tim·id·ly** *adv*

**tim·o·rous** \'timərəs\ *adj* : fearful — **tim·o·rous·ly** *adv* — **tim·o·rous·ness** *n*

**tim·pa·ni** \'timpənē\ *n pl* : set of kettledrums — **tim·pa·nist** \-nist\ *n*

**tin** \'tin\ *n* **1** : soft white metallic chemical element **2** : metal food can

**tinc·ture** \'tiŋkchər\ *n* : alcoholic solution of a medicine

**tin·der** \'tindər\ *n* : substance used to kindle a fire

**tine** \'tīn\ *n* : one of the points of a fork

**tin·foil** \'tin,fȯil\ *n* : thin metal sheeting

**tinge** \'tinj\ *vb* **tinged; tinge·ing** *or* **ting·ing** \'tinjiŋ\ **1** : color slightly **2** : affect with a slight odor ~ *n* : slight coloring or flavor

**tin·gle** \'tiŋgəl\ *vb* **-gled; -gling** : feel a ringing, stinging, or thrilling sensation — **tingle** *n*

**tin·ker** \'tiŋkər\ *vb* : experiment in repairing something — **tin·ker·er** *n*

**tin·kle** \'tiŋkəl\ *vb* **-kled; -kling** : make or cause to make a high ringing sound — **tinkle** *n*

**tin·sel** \'tinsəl\ *n* : decorative thread or strip of glittering metal or paper

**tint** \'tint\ *n* **1** : slight or pale coloration **2** : color shade ~ *vb* : give a tint to

**ti·ny** \'tīnē\ *adj* **-ni·er; -est** : very small

**¹tip** \'tip\ *vb* **-pp- 1** : overturn **2** : lean ~ *n* : act or state of tipping

**²tip** *n* : pointed end of something ~ *vb* **-pp- 1** : furnish with a tip **2** : cover the tip of

**³tip** *n* : small sum given for a service performed ~ *vb* : give a tip to

**⁴tip** *n* : piece of confidential information ~ *vb* **-pp-** : give confidential information to

**tip-off** \'tip,ȯf\ *n* : indication

**tip·ple** \'tipəl\ *vb* **-pled; -pling** : drink intoxicating liquor esp. habitually or excessively — **tip·pler** *n*

**tip·sy** \'tipsē\ *adj* **-si·er; -est** : unsteady or foolish from alcohol

**tip·toe** \'tip,tō\ *n* : the toes of the feet ~ *adv or adj* : supported on tiptoe ~ *vb* **-toed; -toe·ing** : walk quietly or on tiptoe

**tip–top** *n* : highest point ~ *adj* : excellent

**ti·rade** \tī'rād, 'tī,-\ *n* : prolonged speech of abuse

**¹tire** \'tīr\ *vb* **tired; tir·ing 1** : make or become weary **2** : wear out the patience of — **tire·less** *adj* — **tire·less·ly** *adv* — **tire·some** \-səm\ *adj* — **tire·some·ly** *adv*

**²tire** *n* : rubber cushion encircling a car wheel

**tired** \'tīrd\ *adj* : weary

**tis·sue** \'tishü\ *n* **1** : soft absorbent paper **2** : layer of cells forming a basic structural element of an animal or plant body

**ti·tan·ic** \tī'tanik, tə-\ *adj* : gigantic

**ti·ta·ni·um** \tī'tānēəm, tə-\ *n* : gray light strong metallic chemical element

**tithe** \'tīth\ *n* : tenth part paid or given esp. for the support of a church — **tithe** *vb* — **tith·er** *n*

**tit·il·late** \'tit²l,āt\ *vb* **-lat·ed; -lat·ing** : excite pleasurably — **tit·il·la·tion** \,tit²l'āshən\ *n*

**ti·tle** \'tīt²l\ *n* **1** : legal ownership **2** : distinguishing name **3** : designation of honor, rank, or office **4** : championship — **ti·tled** *adj*

**tit·ter** \'titər\ *n* : nervous or affected laugh — **titter** *vb*

**tit·u·lar** \'tichələr\ *adj* **1** : existing in title only **2** : relating to or bearing a title

**tiz·zy** \'tizē\ *n, pl* **tizzies** : state of agitation or worry

**TNT** \,tē,en'tē\ *n* : high explosive

**to** \'tü\ *prep* **1** : in the direction of **2** : at, on, or near **3** : resulting in **4** : before or until **5** — used to show a relationship or object of a verb **6** — used with an infinitive ~ *adv* **1** : forward **2** : to a state of consciousness

**toad** \'tōd\ *n* : tailless leaping amphibian

**toad·stool** \-,stül\ *n* : mushroom esp. when inedible or poisonous

**toady** \'tōdē\ *n, pl* **toad·ies** : one who flatters to gain favors — **toady** *vb*

**toast** \'tōst\ *vb* **1** : make (as a slice of bread) crisp and brown **2** : drink in honor of someone or something **3** : warm ~ *n* **1** : toasted sliced bread **2** : act of drinking in honor of someone — **toast·er** *n*

**to·bac·co** \tə'bakō\ *n, pl* **-cos** : broadleaved herb or its leaves prepared for smoking or chewing

**to·bog·gan** \tə'bägən\ *n* : long flat‑bottomed light sled ~ *vb* : coast on a toboggan

**to·day** \tə'dā\ *adv* **1** : on or for this day **2** : at the present time ~ *n* : present day or time

**tod·dle** \'täd²l\ *vb* **-dled; -dling** : walk with tottering steps like a young child — **toddle** *n* — **tod·dler** \'täd²lər\ *n*

**to–do** \tə'dü\ *n, pl* **to–dos** \-'düz\ : disturbance or fuss

**toe** \'tō\ *n* : one of the 5 end divisions of the foot — **toe·nail** *n*

**tof·fee, tof·fy** \'tȯfē, 'tä-\ *n, pl* **toffees** *or* **toffies** : candy made of boiled sugar and butter

**to·ga** \'tōgə\ *n* : loose outer garment of ancient Rome

**to·geth·er** \tə'gethər\ *adv* **1** : in or into one place or group **2** : in or into contact or association **3** : at one time **4** : as a group — **to·geth·er·ness** *n*

**togs** \'tägz, 'tȯgz\ *n pl* : clothing

**toil** \'tȯil\ *vb* : work hard and long — **toil** *n* — **toil·er** *n* — **toil·some** *adj*

**toi·let** \'tȯilət\ *n* **1** : dressing and grooming oneself **2** : bathroom **3** : water basin to urinate and defecate in

**to·ken** \'tōkən\ *n* **1** : outward sign or expression of something **2** : small part representing the whole **3** : piece resembling a coin

**told** *past of* TELL

**tol·er·a·ble** \'tälərəbəl\ *adj* **1** : capable of being endured **2** : moderately good — **tol·er·a·bly** \-blē\ *adv*

**tol·er·ance** \'tälərəns\ *n* **1** : lack of opposition for beliefs or practices differing from one's own **2** : capacity for enduring **3** : allowable deviation — **tol·er·ant** *adj* — **tol·er·ant·ly** *adv*

**tol·er·ate** \'tälə,rāt\ *vb* **-at·ed; -at·ing 1** : allow to be or to be done without opposition **2** : endure or resist the action of — **tol·er·a·tion** \,tälə'rāshən\ *n*

**¹toll** \'tōl\ *n* **1** : fee paid for a privilege or service **2** : cost of achievement in loss or suffering — **toll·booth** *n* — **toll·gate** *n*

**²toll** *vb* **1** : cause the sounding of (a bell) **2** : sound with slow measured strokes ~ *n* : sound of a tolling bell

**tom·a·hawk** \'tämə,hȯk\ *n* : light ax used as a weapon by American Indians

**to·ma·to** \tə'mātō, -'mät-\ *n, pl* **-toes** : tropical American herb or its fruit

**tomb** \'tüm\ *n* : house, vault, or grave for burial

**tom•boy** \'täm₁bòi\ *n* : girl who behaves in a manner usu. considered boyish

**tomb•stone** *n* : stone marking a grave

**tom•cat** \'täm₁kat\ *n* : male cat

**tome** \'tōm\ *n* : large or weighty book

**to•mor•row** \tə'märō\ *adv* : on or for the day after today — **tomorrow** *n*

**tom–tom** \'täm₁täm\ *n* : small-headed drum beaten with the hands

**ton** \'tən\ *n* : unit of weight equal to 2000 pounds

**tone** \'tōn\ *n* **1** : vocal or musical sound **2** : sound of definite pitch **3** : manner of speaking that expresses an emotion or attitude **4** : color quality **5** : healthy condition **6** : general character or quality ~ *vb* : soften or muffle — often used with *down* — **ton•al** \-ᵊl\ *adj* — **to•nal•i•ty** \tō'nalətē\ *n*

**tongs** \'tänz, 'tònz\ *n pl* : grasping device of 2 joined or hinged pieces

**tongue** \'tən\ *n* **1** : fleshy movable organ of the mouth **2** : language **3** : something long and flat and fastened at one end — **tongued** \'tənd\ *adj* — **tongue•less** *adj*

**ton•ic** \'tänik\ *n* : something (as a drug) that invigorates or restores health — **tonic** *adj*

**to•night** \tə'nīt\ *adv* : on this night ~ *n* : present or coming night

**ton•sil** \'tänsəl\ *n* : either of a pair of oval masses in the throat — **ton•sil•lec•to•my** \₁tänsə'lektəmē\ *n* — **ton•sil•li•tis** \-'lītəs\ *n*

**too** \'tü\ *adv* **1** : in addition **2** : excessively

**took** *past of* TAKE

**tool** \'tül\ *n* : device worked by hand ~ *vb* : shape or finish with a tool

**tool•bar** \'tül₁bär\ *n* : strip of icons on a computer display providing quick access to pictured functions

**toot** \'tüt\ *vb* : sound or cause to sound esp. in short blasts — **toot** *n*

**tooth** \'tüth\ *n, pl* **teeth** \'tēth\ **1** : one of the hard structures in the jaws for chewing **2** : one of the projections on the edge of a gear wheel — **tooth•ache** *n* — **tooth•brush** *n* — **toothed** \'tütht\ *adj* — **tooth•less** *adj* — **tooth•paste** *n* — **tooth•pick** *n*

**tooth•some** \'tüthsəm\ *adj* **1** : delicious **2** : attractive

**¹top** \'täp\ *n* **1** : highest part or level of something **2** : lid or covering ~ *vb* **-pp-** **1** : cover with a top **2** : surpass **3** : go over the top of ~ *adj* : being at the top — **topped** *adj*

**²top** *n* : spinning toy

**to•paz** \'tō₁paz\ *n* : hard gem

**top•coat** *n* : lightweight overcoat

**top•ic** \'täpik\ *n* : subject for discussion or study

**top•i•cal** \-ikəl\ *adj* **1** : relating to or arranged by topics **2** : relating to current or local events — **top•i•cal•ly** *adv*

**top•most** \'täp₁mōst\ *adj* : highest of all

**top–notch** \-'näch\ *adj* : of the highest quality

**to•pog•ra•phy** \tə'pägrəfē\ *n* **1** : art of mapping the physical features of a place **2** : outline of the form of a place — **to•pog•ra•pher** \-fər\ *n* — **top•o•graph•ic** \₁täpə'grafik\, **top•o•graph•i•cal** \-ikəl\ *adj*

**top•ple** \'täpəl\ *vb* **-pled; -pling** : fall or cause to fall

**top•sy–tur•vy** \₁täpsē'tərvē\ *adv or adj* **1** : upside down **2** : in utter confusion

**torch** \'tòrch\ *n* : flaming light — **torch•bear•er** *n* — **torch•light** *n*

**tore** *past of* TEAR

**tor•ment** \'tòr₁ment\ *n* : extreme pain or anguish or a source of this ~ *vb* **1** : cause severe anguish to **2** : harass — **tor•men•tor** \-ər\ *n*

**torn** *past part of* TEAR

**tor•na•do** \tòr'nādō\ *n, pl* **-does** or **-dos** : violent destructive whirling wind

**tor•pe•do** \tòr'pēdō\ *n, pl* **-does** : self-propelled explosive submarine missile ~ *vb* : hit with a torpedo

**tor•pid** \'tòrpəd\ *adj* **1** : having lost motion or the power of exertion **2** : lacking vigor — **tor•pid•i•ty** \tòr'pidətē\ *n*

**tor•por** \'tòrpər\ *n* : extreme sluggishness or lethargy

**torque** \'tòrk\ *n* : turning force

**tor•rent** \'tòrənt\ *n* **1** : rushing stream **2** : tumultuous outburst — **tor•ren•tial** \tò'renchəl, tə-\ *adj*

**tor•rid** \'tòrəd\ *adj* **1** : parched with heat **2** : impassioned

**tor•sion** \'tòrshən\ *n* : a twisting or being twisted — **tor•sion•al** \'tòrshənəl\ *adj* — **tor•sion•al•ly** *adv*

**tor•so** \'tòrsō\ *n, pl* **-sos** or **-si** \-₁sē\ : trunk of the human body

**tor•ti•lla** \tòr'tēyə\ *n* : round flat cornmeal or wheat flour bread

**tor·toise** \'tȯrtəs\ *n* : land turtle

**tor·tu·ous** \'tȯrchəwəs\ *adj* **1** : winding **2** : tricky

**tor·ture** \'tȯrchər\ *n* **1** : use of pain to punish or force **2** : agony ~ *vb* **-tured; -tur·ing** : inflict torture on — **tor·tur·er** *n*

**toss** \'tȯs, 'täs\ *vb* **1** : move to and fro or up and down violently **2** : throw with a quick light motion **3** : move restlessly — **toss** *n*

**toss–up** *n* **1** : a deciding by flipping a coin **2** : even chance

**tot** \'tät\ *n* : small child

**to·tal** \'tōtəl\ *n* : entire amount ~ *vb* **-taled** *or* **-talled; -tal·ing** *or* **-tal·ling** **1** : add up **2** : amount to — **total** *adj* — **to·tal·ly** *adv*

**to·tal·i·tar·i·an** \tō,talə'terēən\ *adj* : relating to a political system in which the government has complete control over the people — **totalitarian** *n* — **to·tal·i·tar·i·an·ism** \-ēə,nizəm\ *n*

**to·tal·i·ty** \tō'talətē\ *n, pl* **-ties** : whole amount or entirety

**tote** \'tōt\ *vb* **tot·ed; tot·ing** : carry

**to·tem** \'tōtəm\ *n* : often carved figure used as a family or tribe emblem

**tot·ter** \'tätər\ *vb* **1** : sway as if about to fall **2** : stagger

**touch** \'təch\ *vb* **1** : make contact with so as to feel **2** : be or cause to be in contact **3** : take into the hands or mouth **4** : treat or mention a subject **5** : relate or concern **6** : move to sympathetic feeling ~ *n* **1** : light stroke **2** : act or fact of touching or being touched **3** : sense of feeling **4** : trace **5** : state of being in contact — **touch up** *vb* : improve with minor changes

**touch·down** \'təch,daun\ *n* : scoring of 6 points in football

**touch·stone** *n* : test or criterion of genuineness or quality

**touchy** \'təchē\ *adj* **touch·i·er; -est** **1** : easily offended **2** : requiring tact

**tough** \'təf\ *adj* **1** : strong but elastic **2** : not easily chewed **3** : severe or disciplined **4** : stubborn ~ *n* : rowdy — **tough·ly** *adv* — **tough·ness** *n*

**tough·en** \'təfən\ *vb* : make or become tough

**tou·pee** \tü'pā\ *n* : small wig for a bald spot

**tour** \'tur\ *n* **1** : period of time spent at work or on an assignment **2** : journey with a return to the starting point ~

*vb* : travel over to see the sights — **tour·ist** \'turist\ *n*

**tour·na·ment** \'turnəmənt, 'tər-\ *n* **1** : medieval jousting competition **2** : championship series of games

**tour·ney** \-nē\ *n, pl* **-neys** : tournament

**tour·ni·quet** \'turnikət, 'tər-\ *n* : tight bandage for stopping blood flow

**tou·sle** \'tauzəl\ *vb* **-sled; -sling** : dishevel (as someone's hair)

**tout** \'taut, 'tüt\ *vb* : praise or publicize loudly

**tow** \'tō\ *vb* : pull along behind — **tow** *n*

**to·ward, to·wards** \'tōrd, tə'wȯrd, 'tȯrdz, tə'wȯrdz\ *prep* **1** : in the direction of **2** : with respect to **3** : in part payment on

**tow·el** \'tauəl\ *n* : absorbent cloth or paper for wiping or drying

**tow·er** \'tauər\ *n* : tall structure ~ *vb* : rise to a great height — **tow·ered** \'tauərd\ *adj* — **tow·er·ing** *adj*

**tow·head** \'tō,hed\ *n* : person having whitish blond hair — **tow·head·ed** \-,hedəd\ *adj*

**town** \'taun\ *n* **1** : small residential area **2** : city — **towns·peo·ple** \'taunz-,pēpəl\ *n pl*

**town·ship** \'taun,ship\ *n* **1** : unit of local government **2** : 36 square miles of U.S. public land

**tox·ic** \'täksik\ *adj* : poisonous — **tox·ic·i·ty** \täk'sisətē\ *n*

**tox·in** \'täksən\ *n* : poison produced by an organism

**toy** \'tȯi\ *n* : something for a child to play with ~ *vb* : amuse oneself or play with something ~ *adj* **1** : designed as a toy **2** : very small

¹**trace** \'trās\ *vb* **traced; trac·ing** **1** : mark over the lines of (a drawing) **2** : follow the trail or the development of ~ *n* **1** : track **2** : tiny amount or residue — **trace·able** *adj* — **trac·er** *n*

²**trace** *n* : line of a harness

**tra·chea** \'trākēə\ *n, pl* **-che·ae** \-kē,ē\ : windpipe — **tra·che·al** \-kēəl\ *adj*

**track** \'trak\ *n* **1** : trail left by wheels or footprints **2** : racing course **3** : train rails **4** : awareness of a progression **5** : looped belts propelling a vehicle ~ *vb* **1** : follow the trail of **2** : make tracks on — **track·er** *n*

**track–and–field** *adj* : relating to athletic contests of running, jumping, and throwing events

¹**tract** \'trakt\ *n* **1** : stretch of land **2** : system of body organs

²**tract** *n* : pamphlet of propaganda

**trac·ta·ble** \'traktəbəl\ *adj* : easily controlled

**trac·tion** \'trakshən\ *n* : gripping power to permit movement — **trac·tion·al** \-shənəl\ *adj* — **trac·tive** \'traktiv\ *adj*

**trac·tor** \'traktər\ *n* **1** : farm vehicle used esp. for pulling **2** : truck for hauling a trailer

**trade** \'trād\ *n* **1** : one's regular business **2** : occupation requiring skill **3** : the buying and selling of goods **4** : act of trading ~ *vb* **trad·ed; trad·ing 1** : give in exchange for something **2** : buy and sell goods **3** : be a regular customer — **trades·peo·ple** \'trādz,pēpəl\ *n pl*

**trade–in** \'trād,in\ *n* : an item traded to a merchant at the time of a purchase

**trade·mark** \'trād,märk\ *n* : word or mark identifying a manufacturer — **trademark** *vb*

**trades·man** \'trādzmən\ *n* : shopkeeper

**tra·di·tion** \trə'dishən\ *n* : belief or custom passed from generation to generation — **tra·di·tion·al** \-'dishənəl\ *adj* — **tra·di·tion·al·ly** *adv*

**tra·duce** \trə'düs, -'dyüs\ *vb* -**duced; -duc·ing** : lower the reputation of — **tra·duc·er** *n*

**traf·fic** \'trafik\ *n* **1** : business dealings **2** : movement along a route ~ *vb* : do business — **traf·fick·er** *n* — **traffic light** *n*

**trag·e·dy** \'trajədē\ *n, pl* -**dies 1** : serious drama describing a conflict and having a sad end **2** : disastrous event

**trag·ic** \'trajik\ *adj* : being a tragedy — **trag·i·cal·ly** *adv*

**trail** \'trāl\ *vb* **1** : hang down and drag along the ground **2** : draw along behind **3** : follow the track of **4** : dwindle ~ *n* **1** : something that trails **2** : path or evidence left by something

**trail·er** \'trālər\ *n* **1** : vehicle intended to be hauled **2** : dwelling designed to be towed to a site

**train** \'trān\ *n* **1** : trailing part of a gown **2** : retinue or procession **3** : connected series **4** : group of linked railroad cars ~ *vb* **1** : cause to grow as desired **2** : make or become prepared or skilled **3** : point — **train·ee** *n* — **train·er** *n* — **train·load** *n*

**traipse** \'trāps\ *vb* traipsed; traipsing : walk

**trait** \'trāt\ *n* : distinguishing quality

**trai·tor** \'trātər\ *n* : one who betrays a trust or commits treason — **trai·tor·ous** *adj*

**tra·jec·to·ry** \trə'jektərē\ *n, pl* -**ries** : path of something moving through air or space

**tram·mel** \'traməl\ *vb* -meled *or* -melled; -mel·ing *or* -mel·ling : impede — **trammel** *n*

**tramp** \'tramp\ *vb* **1** : walk or hike **2** : tread on ~ *n* : beggar or vagrant

**tram·ple** \'trampəl\ *vb* -pled; -pling : walk or step on so as to bruise or crush — **trample** *n* — **tram·pler** \-plər\ *n*

**tram·po·line** \,trampə'lēn, 'trampə,-\ *n* : resilient sheet or web supported by springs and used for bouncing — **tram·po·lin·ist** \-ist\ *n*

**trance** \'trans\ *n* **1** : sleeplike condition **2** : state of mystical absorption

**tran·quil** \'traŋkwəl, 'tran-\ *adj* : quiet and undisturbed — **tran·quil·ize** \-kwə,līz\ *vb* — **tran·quil·iz·er** *n* — **tran·quil·li·ty, tran·quil·i·ty** \tran-'kwilətē, traŋ-\ *n* — **tran·quil·ly** *adv*

**trans·act** \trans'akt, tranz-\ *vb* : conduct (business)

**trans·ac·tion** \-'akshən\ *n* **1** : business deal **2** *pl* : records of proceedings

**tran·scend** \trans'end\ *vb* : rise above or surpass — **tran·scen·dent** \-'endənt\ *adj* — **tran·scen·den·tal** \,trans,en'dent³l, -ən-\ *adj*

**tran·scribe** \trans'krīb\ *vb* -scribed; -scrib·ing : make a copy, arrangement, or recording of — **tran·scrip·tion** \trans'kripshən\ *n*

**tran·script** \'trans,kript\ *n* : official copy

**tran·sept** \'trans,ept\ *n* : part of a church that crosses the nave at right angles

**trans·fer** \trans'fər, 'trans,fər\ *vb* -**rr- 1** : move from one person, place, or situation to another **2** : convey ownership of **3** : print or copy by contact **4** : change to another vehicle or transportation line ~ \'trans,fər\ *n* **1** : act or process of transferring **2** : one that transfers or is transferred **3** : ticket permitting one to transfer — **trans·fer·able** \trans'fərəbəl\ *adj* — **trans·fer·al** \-əl\ *n* — **trans·fer·ence** \-əns\ *n*

**trans·fig·ure** \trans'figyər\ *vb* -ured; -ur·ing **1** : change the form or appearance of **2** : glorify — **trans•fig-u•ra•tion** \ˌtransˌfigyə'rāshən\ n

**trans•fix** \trans'fiks\ vb **1** : pierce through **2** : hold motionless

**trans•form** \-'fòrm\ vb **1** : change in structure, appearance, or character **2** : change (an electric current) in potential or type — **trans•for•ma•tion** \ˌtransfər'māshən\ n — **trans•form•er** \trans'fòrmər\ n

**trans•fuse** \trans'fyüz\ vb **-fused; -fus•ing 1** : diffuse into or through **2** : transfer (as blood) into a vein — **trans•fu•sion** \-'fyüzhən\ n

**trans•gress** \trans'gres, tranz-\ vb : sin — **trans•gres•sion** \-'greshən\ n — **trans•gres•sor** \-'gresər\ n

**tran•sient** \'transhənt\ adj : not lasting or staying long — **transient** n — **tran•sient•ly** adv

**tran•sis•tor** \tranz'istər, trans-\ n : small electronic device used in electronic equipment — **tran•sis•tor•ize** \-təˌrīz\ vb

**tran•sit** \'transət, 'tranz-\ n **1** : movement over, across, or through **2** : local and esp. public transportation **3** : surveyor's instrument

**tran•si•tion** \trans'ishən, tranz-\ n : passage from one state, stage, or subject to another — **tran•si•tion•al** \-'ishənəl\ adj

**tran•si•to•ry** \'transəˌtōrē, 'tranz-\ adj : of brief duration

**trans•late** \trans'lāt, tranz-\ vb **-lat-ed; -lat•ing** : change into another language — **trans•lat•able** adj — **trans•la•tion** \-'lāshən\ n — **trans•la•tor** \-'lātər\ n

**trans•lu•cent** \trans'lüs'nt, tranz-\ adj : not transparent but clear enough to allow light to pass through — **trans•lu•cence** \-'ns\ n — **trans•lu•cen•cy** \-'nsē\ n — **trans•lu•cent•ly** adv

**trans•mis•sion** \-'mishən\ n **1** : act or process of transmitting **2** : system of gears between a car engine and drive wheels

**trans•mit** \-'mit\ vb **-tt- 1** : transfer from one person or place to another **2** : pass on by inheritance **3** : broadcast — **trans•mis•si•ble** \-'misəbəl\ adj — **trans•mit•ta•ble** \-'mitəbəl\ adj — **trans•mit•tal** \-'mit'l\ n — **trans•mit•ter** n

**tran•som** \'transəm\ n : often hinged window above a door

**trans•par•ent** \trans'parənt\ adj **1**

: clear enough to see through **2** : obvious — **trans•par•en•cy** \-ənsē\ n — **trans•par•ent•ly** adv

**tran•spire** \trans'pīr\ vb **-spired; -spir-ing** : take place — **tran•spi•ra•tion** \ˌtranspə'rāshən\ n

**trans•plant** \trans'plant\ vb **1** : dig up and move to another place **2** : transfer from one body part or person to another — **transplant** \'transˌ-\ n — **trans•plan•ta•tion** \ˌtransˌplan'tā-shən\ n

**trans•port** \trans'pōrt\ vb **1** : carry or deliver to another place **2** : carry away by emotion ∼ \'transˌ-\ n **1** : act of transporting **2** : rapture **3** : ship or plane for carrying troops or supplies — **trans•por•ta•tion** \ˌtranspər'tā-shən\ n — **trans•port•er** n

**trans•pose** \trans'pōz\ vb **-posed; -pos•ing** : change the position, sequence, or key — **trans•po•si•tion** \ˌtranspə'zishən\ n

**trans•ship** \tran'ship, trans-\ vb : transfer from one mode of transportation to another — **trans•ship•ment** n

**trans•verse** \trans'vərs, tranz-\ adj : lying across — **trans•verse** \'transˌvərs, 'tranz-\ n — **trans•verse•ly** adv

**trap** \'trap\ n **1** : device for catching animals **2** : something by which one is caught unawares **3** : device to allow one thing to pass through while keeping other things out ∼ vb **-pp-** : catch in a trap — **trap•per** n

**trap•door** n : door in a floor or roof

**tra•peze** \tra'pēz\ n : suspended bar used by acrobats

**trap•e•zoid** \'trapəˌzòid\ n : plane 4-sided figure with 2 parallel sides — **trap•e•zoi•dal** \ˌtrapə'zòid'l\ adj

**trap•pings** \'trapinz\ n pl **1** : ornamental covering **2** : outward decoration or dress

**trash** \'trash\ n : something that is no good — **trashy** adj

**trau•ma** \'traùmə, 'trò-\ n : bodily or mental injury — **trau•mat•ic** \trə'matik, trò-, traù-\ adj

**tra•vail** \trə'vāl, 'travˌāl\ n : painful work or exertion ∼ vb : labor hard

**trav•el** \'travəl\ vb **-eled** or **-elled; -el-ing** or **-el•ling 1** : take a trip or tour **2** : move or be carried from point to point ∼ n : journey — often pl. — **trav•el•er, trav•el•ler** n

**tra·verse** \trə'vərs, tra'vərs, 'travərs\ *vb* **-versed; -vers·ing** : go or extend across — **tra·verse** \'travərs\ *n*

**trav·es·ty** \'travəstē\ *n, pl* **-ties** : imitation that makes crude fun of something — **travesty** *vb*

**trawl** \'trȯl\ *vb* : fish or catch with a trawl ∼ *n* : large cone-shaped net — **trawl·er** *n*

**tray** \'trā\ *n* : shallow flat-bottomed receptacle for holding or carrying something

**treach·er·ous** \'trechərəs\ *adj* : disloyal or dangerous — **treach·er·ous·ly** *adv*

**treach·ery** \'trechərē\ *n, pl* **-er·ies** : betrayal of a trust

**tread** \'tred\ *vb* **trod** \'träd\; **trod·den** \'träd°n\ *or* **trod; tread·ing** **1** : step on or over **2** : walk **3** : press or crush with the feet ∼ *n* **1** : way of walking **2** : sound made in walking **3** : part on which a thing runs

**trea·dle** \'tred°l\ *n* : foot pedal operating a machine — **treadle** *vb*

**tread·mill** *n* **1** : mill worked by walking persons or animals **2** : wearisome routine

**trea·son** \'trēz°n\ *n* : attempt to overthrow the government — **trea·son·able** \'trēz°nəbəl\ *adj* — **trea·son·ous** \-°nəs\ *adj*

**trea·sure** \'trezhər, 'trāzh-\ *n* **1** : wealth stored up **2** : something of great value ∼ *vb* **-sured; -sur·ing** : keep as precious

**trea·sur·er** \'trezhərər, 'trāzh-\ *n* : officer who handles funds

**trea·sury** \'trezhərē, 'trāzh-\ *n, pl* **-sur·ies** : place or office for keeping and distributing funds

**treat** \'trēt\ *vb* **1** : have as a topic **2** : pay for the food or entertainment of **3** : act toward or regard in a certain way **4** : give medical care to ∼ *n* **1** : food or entertainment paid for by another **2** : something special and enjoyable — **treat·ment** \-mənt\ *n*

**trea·tise** \'trētəs\ *n* : systematic written exposition or argument

**trea·ty** \'trētē\ *n, pl* **-ties** : agreement between governments

**tre·ble** \'trebəl\ *n* **1** : highest part in music **2** : upper half of the musical range ∼ *adj* : triple in number or amount ∼ *vb* **-bled; -bling** : make triple — **tre·bly** *adv*

**tree** \'trē\ *n* : tall woody plant ∼ *vb*

**treed; tree·ing** : force up a tree — **tree·less** *adj*

**trek** \'trek\ *n* : difficult trip ∼ *vb* **-kk-** : make a trek

**trel·lis** \'treləs\ *n* : structure of crossed strips

**trem·ble** \'trembəl\ *vb* **-bled; -bling** **1** : shake from fear or cold **2** : move or sound as if shaken

**tre·men·dous** \tri'mendəs\ *adj* : amazingly large, powerful, or excellent — **tre·men·dous·ly** *adv*

**trem·or** \'tremər\ *n* : a trembling

**trem·u·lous** \'tremyələs\ *adj* : trembling or quaking

**trench** \'trench\ *n* : long narrow cut in land

**tren·chant** \'trenchənt\ *adj* : sharply perceptive

**trend** \'trend\ *n* : prevailing tendency, direction, or style ∼ *vb* : move in a particular direction — **trendy** \'trendē\ *adj*

**trep·i·da·tion** \ˌtrepə'dāshən\ *n* : nervous apprehension

**tres·pass** \'trespəs, -ˌpas\ *n* **1** : sin **2** : unauthorized entry onto someone's property ∼ *vb* **1** : sin **2** : enter illegally — **tres·pass·er** *n*

**tress** \'tres\ *n* : long lock of hair

**tres·tle** \'tresəl\ *n* **1** : support with a horizontal piece and spreading legs **2** : framework bridge

**tri·ad** \'trīˌad, -əd\ *n* : union of 3

**tri·age** \trē'äzh, 'trēˌäzh\ *n* : system of dealing with cases (as patients) according to priority guidelines intended to maximize success

**tri·al** \'trīəl\ *n* **1** : hearing and judgment of a matter in court **2** : source of great annoyance **3** : test use or experimental effort — **trial** *adj*

**tri·an·gle** \'trīˌaŋgəl\ *n* : plane figure with 3 sides and 3 angles — **tri·an·gu·lar** \trī'aŋgyələr\ *adj*

**tribe** \'trīb\ *n* : social group of numerous families — **trib·al** \'trībəl\ *adj* — **tribes·man** \'trībzmən\ *n* — **tribes·peo·ple** \-ˌpēpəl\ *n pl*

**trib·u·la·tion** \ˌtribyə'lāshən\ *n* : suffering from oppression

**tri·bu·nal** \trī'byün°l, tri-\ *n* **1** : court **2** : something that decides

**trib·u·tary** \'tribyəˌterē\ *n, pl* **-tar·ies** : stream that flows into a river or lake

**trib·ute** \'tribˌyüt\ *n* **1** : payment to acknowledge submission **2** : tax **3** : gift or act showing respect

**trick** \'trik\ n 1 : scheme to deceive 2 : prank 3 : deceptive or ingenious feat 4 : mannerism 5 : knack 6 : tour of duty ~ vb : deceive by cunning — **trick•ery** \-ərē\ n — **trick•ster** \-stər\ n

**trick•le** \'trikəl\ vb -led; -ling : run in drops or a thin stream — **trickle** n

**tricky** \'trikē\ adj **trick•i•er; -est 1** : inclined to trickery 2 : requiring skill or caution

**tri•cy•cle** \'trī₁sikəl\ n : 3-wheeled bicycle

**tri•dent** \'trīd³nt\ n : 3-pronged spear

**tri•en•ni•al** \'trī'enēəl\ adj : lasting, occurring, or done every 3 years — **triennial** n

**tri•fle** \'trīfəl\ n : something of little value or importance ~ vb -fled; -fling 1 : speak or act in a playful or flirting way 2 : toy — **tri•fler** n

**tri•fling** \'trīfliŋ\ adj : trivial

**trig•ger** \'trigər\ n : finger-piece of a firearm lock that fires the gun ~ vb : set into motion — **trigger** adj — **trig•gered** \-ərd\ adj

**trig•o•nom•e•try** \₁trigə'nämətrē\ n : mathematics dealing with triangular measurement — **trig•o•no•met•ric** \-nə'metrik\ adj

**trill** \'tril\ n 1 : rapid alternation between 2 adjacent tones 2 : rapid vibration in speaking ~ vb : utter in or with a trill

**tril•lion** \'trilyən\ n : 1000 billions — **trillion** adj — **tril•lionth** \-yənth\ adj or n

**tril•o•gy** \'triləjē\ n, pl -gies : 3-part literary or musical composition

**trim** \'trim\ vb -mm- 1 : decorate 2 : make neat or reduce by cutting ~ adj -mm- : neat and compact ~ n 1 : state or condition 2 : ornaments — **trim•ly** adv — **trim•mer** n

**trim•ming** \'trimiŋ\ n : something that ornaments or completes

**Trin•i•ty** \'trinətē\ n : divine unity of Father, Son, and Holy Spirit

**trin•ket** \'triŋkət\ n : small ornament

**trio** \'trēō\ n, pl **tri•os 1** : music for 3 performers 2 : group of 3

**trip** \'trip\ vb -pp- 1 : step lightly 2 : stumble or cause to stumble 3 : make or cause to make a mistake 4 : release (as a spring or switch) ~ n 1 : journey 2 : stumble 3 : drug-induced experience

**tri•par•tite** \trī'pär₁tīt\ adj : having 3 parts or parties

**tripe** \'trīp\ n 1 : animal's stomach used as food 2 : trash

**tri•ple** \'tripəl\ vb -pled; -pling : make 3 times as great ~ n : group of 3 ~ adj 1 : having 3 units 2 : being 3 times as great or as many

**trip•let** \'triplət\ n 1 : group of 3 2 : one of 3 offspring born together

**trip•li•cate** \'triplikət\ adj : made in 3 identical copies ~ n : one of 3 copies

**tri•pod** \'trī₁päd\ n : a stand with 3 legs — **tripod**, **tri•po•dal** \'tripəd³l, 'trī₁päd-\ adj

**tri•sect** \'trī₁sekt, trī'-\ vb : divide into 3 usu. equal parts — **tri•sec•tion** \'trī₁sekshən\ n

**trite** \'trīt\ adj **trit•er; trit•est** : commonplace

**tri•umph** \'trīəmf\ n, pl -umphs : victory or great success ~ vb : obtain or celebrate victory — **tri•um•phal** \trī-'əmfəl\ adj — **tri•um•phant** \-fənt\ adj — **tri•um•phant•ly** adv

**tri•um•vi•rate** \trī'əmvərət\ n : ruling body of 3 persons

**triv•et** \'trivət\ n 1 : 3-legged stand 2 : stand to hold a hot dish

**triv•ia** \'trivēə\ n sing or pl : unimportant details

**triv•i•al** \'trivēəl\ adj : of little importance — **triv•i•al•i•ty** \₁trivē'alətē\ n

**trod** past of TREAD

**trodden** past part of TREAD

**troll** \'trōl\ n : dwarf or giant of folklore inhabiting caves or hills

**trol•ley** \'trälē\ n, pl -leys : streetcar run by overhead electric wires

**trol•lop** \'träləp\ n : untidy or immoral woman

**trom•bone** \träm'bōn, 'träm₁-\ n : musical instrument with a long sliding tube — **trom•bon•ist** \-'bōnist, -₁bō-\ n

**troop** \'trüp\ n 1 : cavalry unit 2 pl : soldiers 3 : collection of people or things ~ vb : move or gather in crowds

**troop•er** \'trüpər\ n 1 : cavalry soldier 2 : police officer on horseback or state police officer

**tro•phy** \'trōfē\ n, pl -phies : prize gained by a victory

**trop•ic** \'träpik\ n 1 : either of the 2 parallels of latitude one 23½ degrees north of the equator (**tropic of Cancer** \-'kansər\) and one 23½ degrees south of the equator (**tropic of Cap·ri·corn** \-'kaprə,kȯrn\) **2** *pl* : region lying between the tropics — **tropic, trop·i·cal** \-ikəl\ *adj*

**trot** \'trät\ *n* : moderately fast gait esp. of a horse with diagonally paired legs moving together ~ *vb* **-tt-** : go at a trot — **trot·ter** *n*

**troth** \'träth, 'trȯth, 'trōth\ *n* **1** : pledged faithfulness **2** : betrothal

**trou·ba·dour** \'trübə,dȯr\ *n* : medieval lyric poet

**trou·ble** \'trəbəl\ *vb* **-bled; -bling 1** : disturb **3** : afflict **3** : make an effort ~ *n* **1** : cause of mental or physical distress **2** : effort — **trou·ble·mak·er** *n* — **trou·ble·some** *adj* — **trou·ble·some·ly** *adv*

**trough** \'trȯf\ *n, pl* **troughs** \'trȯfs, 'trȯvz\ **1** : narrow container for animal feed or water **2** : long channel or depression (as between waves)

**trounce** \'traúns\ *vb* **trounced; trounc·ing** : thrash, punish, or defeat severely

**troupe** \'trüp\ *n* : group of stage performers — **troup·er** *n*

**trou·sers** \'traúzərz\ *n pl* : long pants — **trouser** *adj*

**trous·seau** \'trüsō, trü'sō\ *n, pl* **-seaux** \-sōz, -'sōz\ *or* **-seaus** : bride's collection of clothing and personal items

**trout** \'traút\ *n, pl* **trout** : freshwater food and game fish

**trow·el** \'traúəl\ *n* **1** : tool for spreading or smoothing **2** : garden scoop — **trowel** *vb*

**troy** \'trȯi\ *n* : system of weights based on a pound of 12 ounces

**tru·ant** \'trüənt\ *n* : student absent from school without permission — **tru·an·cy** \-ənsē\ *n* — **truant** *adj*

**truce** \'trüs\ *n* : agreement to halt fighting

**truck** \'trək\ *n* **1** : wheeled frame for moving heavy objects **2** : automotive vehicle for transporting heavy loads ~ *vb* : transport on a truck — **truck·er** *n* — **truck·load** *n*

**truck·le** \'trəkəl\ *vb* **-led; -ling** : yield slavishly to another

**tru·cu·lent** \'trəkyələnt\ *adj* : aggressively self-assertive — **tru·cu·lence** \-ləns\ *n* — **tru·cu·lent·ly** *adv*

**trudge** \'trəj\ *vb* **trudged; trudg·ing** : walk or march steadily and with difficulty

**true** \'trü\ *adj* **tru·er; tru·est 1** : loyal

**2** : in agreement with fact or reality **3** : genuine ~ *adv* **1** : truthfully **2** : accurately ~ *vb* **trued; tru·ing** : make balanced or even — **tru·ly** *adv*

**true–blue** *adj* : loyal

**truf·fle** \'trəfəl\ *n* **1** : edible fruit of an underground fungus **2** : ball-shaped chocolate candy

**tru·ism** \'trü,izəm\ *n* : obvious truth

**trump** \'trəmp\ *n* : card of a designated suit any of whose cards will win over other cards ~ *vb* : take with a trump

**trumped–up** \'trəmpt'əp\ *adj* : made-up

**trum·pet** \'trəmpət\ *n* : tubular brass wind instrument with a flaring end ~ *vb* **1** : blow a trumpet **2** : proclaim loudly — **trum·pet·er** *n*

**trun·cate** \'trəŋ,kāt, 'trən-\ *vb* **-cat·ed; -cat·ing** : cut short — **trun·ca·tion** \,trəŋ'kāshən\ *n*

**trun·dle** \'trənd°l\ *vb* **-dled; -dling** : roll along

**trunk** \'trəŋk\ *n* **1** : main part (as of a body or tree) **2** : long muscular nose of an elephant **3** : storage chest **4** : storage space in a car **5** *pl* : shorts

**truss** \'trəs\ *vb* : bind tightly ~ *n* **1** : set of structural parts forming a framework **2** : appliance worn to hold a hernia in place

**trust** \'trəst\ *n* **1** : reliance on another **2** : assured hope **3** : credit **4** : property held or managed in behalf of another **5** : combination of firms that reduces competition **6** : something entrusted to another's care **7** : custody ~ *vb* **1** : depend **2** : hope **3** : entrust **4** : have faith in — **trust·ful** \-fəl\ *adj* — **trust·ful·ly** *adv* — **trust·ful·ness** *n* — **trust·worth·i·ness** *n* — **trust·wor·thy** *adj*

**trust·ee** \,trəs'tē\ *n* : person holding property in trust — **trust·ee·ship** *n*

**trusty** \'trəstē\ *adj* **trust·i·er; -est** : dependable

**truth** \'trüth\ *n, pl* **truths** \'trü<u>th</u>z, 'trüths\ **1** : real state of things **2** : true or accepted statement **3** : agreement with fact or reality — **truth·ful** \-fəl\ *adj* — **truth·ful·ly** *adv* — **truth·ful·ness** *n*

**try** \'trī\ *vb* **tried; try·ing 1** : conduct the trial of **2** : put to a test **3** : strain **4** : make an effort at ~ *n, pl* **tries** : act of trying

**try·out** *n* : competitive test of performance esp. for athletes or actors — **try out** *vb*

**tryst** \'trist, 'trīst\ *n* : secret rendezvous of lovers

**tsar** \'zär, 'tsär, 'sär\ *var of* CZAR

**T–shirt** \'tē,shərt\ *n* : collarless pullover shirt with short sleeves

**tub** \'təb\ *n* **1** : wide bucketlike vessel **2** : bathtub

**tu•ba** \'tübə, 'tyü-\ *n* : large low-pitched brass wind instument

**tube** \'tüb, 'tyüb\ *n* **1** : hollow cylinder **2** : round container from which a substance can be squeezed **3** : airtight circular tube of rubber inside a tire **4** : electronic device consisting of a sealed usu. glass container with electrodes inside — **tubed** \'tübd, 'tyübd\ *adj* — **tube•less** *adj*

**tu•ber** \'tübər, 'tyü-\ *n* : fleshy underground growth (as of a potato) — **tu•ber•ous** \-rəs\ *adj*

**tu•ber•cu•lo•sis** \tů,bərkyə'lōsəs, tyů-\ *n, pl* **-lo•ses** \-,sēz\ : bacterial disease esp. of the lungs — **tu•ber•cu•lar** \-'bərkyələr\ *adj* — **tu•ber•cu•lous** \-ləs\ *adj*

**tub•ing** \'tübiŋ\ *n* : series or arrangement of tubes

**tu•bu•lar** \'tübyələr, 'tyü-\ *adj* : of or like a tube

**tuck** \'tək\ *vb* **1** : pull up into a fold **2** : put into a snug often concealing place **3** : make snug in bed — with *in* ~ *n* : fold in a cloth

**tuck•er** \'təkər\ *vb* : fatigue

**Tues•day** \'tüzdā, 'tyüz-, -dē\ *n* : 3d day of the week

**tuft** \'təft\ *n* : clump (as of hair or feathers) — **tuft•ed** \'təftəd\ *adj*

**tug** \'təg\ *vb* **-gg-** **1** : pull hard **2** : move by pulling ~ *n* **1** : act of tugging **2** : tugboat

**tug•boat** *n* : boat for towing or pushing ships through a harbor

**tug–of–war** \,təgə'wȯr\ *n, pl* **tugs-of–war** : pulling contest between 2 teams

**tu•ition** \tů'ishən, 'tyü-\ *n* : cost of instruction

**tu•lip** \'tüləp, 'tyü-\ *n* : herb with cup-shaped flowers

**tum•ble** \'təmbəl\ *vb* **-bled; -bling** **1** : perform gymnastic feats of rolling and turning **2** : fall or cause to fall suddenly **3** : toss ~ *n* : act of tumbling

**tum•bler** \'təmblər\ *n* **1** : acrobat **2** : drinking glass **3** : obstruction in a lock that can be moved (as by a key)

**tu•mid** \'tüməd, 'tyü-\ *adj* : turgid

**tum•my** \'təmē\ *n, pl* **-mies** : belly

**tu•mor** \'tümər, 'tyü-\ *n* : abnormal and useless growth of tissue — **tu•mor•ous** *adj*

**tu•mult** \'tü,məlt, 'tyü-\ *n* **1** : uproar **2** : violent agitation of mind or feelings — **tu•mul•tu•ous** \tů'məlchəwəs, tyü-\ *adj*

**tun** \'tən\ *n* : large cask

**tu•na** \'tünə, 'tyü-\ *n, pl* **-na** *or* **-nas** : large sea food fish

**tun•dra** \'təndrə\ *n* : treeless arctic plain

**tune** \'tün, 'tyün\ *n* **1** : melody **2** : correct musical pitch **3** : harmonious relationship ~ *vb* **tuned; tuning** **1** : bring or come into harmony **2** : adjust in musical pitch **3** : adjust a receiver so as to receive a broadcast **4** : put in first-class working order — **tun•able** *adj* — **tune•ful** \-fəl\ *adj* — **tun•er** *n*

**tung•sten** \'təŋstən\ *n* : metallic element used for electrical purposes and in hardening alloys (as steel)

**tu•nic** \'tünik, 'tyü-\ *n* **1** : ancient knee-length garment **2** : hip-length blouse or jacket

**tun•nel** \'tən<sup>ə</sup>l\ *n* : underground passageway ~ *vb* **-neled** *or* **-nelled; -nel•ing** *or* **-nel•ling** : make a tunnel through or under something

**tur•ban** \'tərbən\ *n* : wound headdress worn esp. by Muslims

**tur•bid** \'tərbəd\ *adj* **1** : dark with stirred-up sediment **2** : confused — **tur•bid•i•ty** \,tər'bidətē\ *n*

**tur•bine** \'tərbən, -,bīn\ *n* : engine turned by the force of gas or water on fan blades

**tur•bo•jet** \'tərbō,jet\ *n* : airplane powered by a jet engine having a turbine-driven air compressor or the engine itself

**tur•bo•prop** \'tərbō,präp\ *n* : airplane powered by a propeller turned by a jet engine-driven turbine

**tur•bu•lent** \'tərbyələnt\ *adj* **1** : causing violence or disturbance **2** : marked by agitation or tumult — **tur•bu•lence** \-ləns\ *n* — **tur•bu•lent•ly** *adv*

**tu•reen** \tə'rēn, tyů-\ *n* : deep bowl for serving soup

**turf** \'tərf\ *n* : upper layer of soil bound by grass and roots

**tur•gid** \'tərjəd\ *adj* **1** : swollen **2** : too highly embellished in style — **tur•gid•i•ty** \,tər'jidətē\ *n*

**tur·key** \'tərkē\ *n, pl* **-keys** : large American bird raised for food

**tur·moil** \'tər₁mȯil\ *n* : extremely agitated condition

**turn** \'tərn\ *vb* **1** : move or cause to move around an axis **2** : twist (a mechanical part) to operate **3** : wrench **4** : cause to face or move in a different direction **5** : reverse the sides or surfaces of **6** : upset **7** : go around **8** : become or cause to become **9** : seek aid from a source ∼ *n* **1** : act or instance of turning **2** : change **3** : place at which something turns **4** : place, time, or opportunity to do something in order — **turn·er** *n* — **turn down** *vb* : decline to accept — **turn in** *vb* **1** : deliver or report to authorities **2** : go to bed — **turn off** *vb* : stop the functioning of — **turn out** *vb* **1** : expel **2** : produce **3** : come together **4** : prove to be in the end — **turn over** *vb* : transfer — **turn up** *vb* **1** : discover or appear **2** : happen unexpectedly

**turn·coat** *n* : traitor

**tur·nip** \'tərnəp\ *n* : edible root of an herb

**turn·out** \'tərn₁au̇t\ *n* **1** : gathering of people for a special purpose **2** : size of a gathering

**turn·over** *n* **1** : upset or reversal **2** : filled pastry **3** : volume of business **4** : movement (as of goods or people) into, through, and out of a place

**turn·pike** \'tərn₁pīk\ *n* : expressway on which tolls are charged

**turn·stile** \-₁stīl\ *n* : post with arms pivoted on the top that allows people to pass one by one

**turn·ta·ble** *n* : platform that turns a phonograph record

**tur·pen·tine** \'tərpən₁tīn\ *n* : oil distilled from pine-tree resin and used as a solvent

**tur·pi·tude** \'tərpə₁tüd, -₁tyüd\ *n* : inherent baseness

**tur·quoise** \'tər₁kȯiz, -₁kwȯiz\ *n* : blue or greenish gray gemstone

**tur·ret** \'tərət\ *n* **1** : little tower on a building **2** : revolving tool holder or gun housing

**tur·tle** \'tərtᵊl\ *n* : reptile with the trunk enclosed in a bony shell

**tur·tle·dove** *n* : wild pigeon

**tur·tle·neck** *n* : high close-fitting collar that can be turned over or a sweater or shirt with this collar

**tusk** \'təsk\ *n* : long protruding tooth (as of an elephant) — **tusked** \'təskt\ *adj*

**tus·sle** \'təsəl\ *n or vb* : struggle

**tu·te·lage** \'tütᵊlij, 'yüt-\ *n* **1** : act of protecting **2** : instruction esp. of an individual

**tu·tor** \'tütər, 'yü-\ *n* : private teacher ∼ *vb* : teach usu. individually

**tux·e·do** \₁tək'sēdō\ *n, pl* **-dos** or **-does** : semiformal evening clothes for a man

**TV** \₁tē'vē, 'tē₁vē\ *n* : television

**twain** \'twān\ *n* : two

**twang** \'twaŋ\ *n* **1** : harsh sound like that of a plucked bowstring **2** : nasal speech or resonance ∼ *vb* : sound or speak with a twang

**tweak** \'twēk\ *vb* : pinch and pull playfully — **tweak** *n*

**tweed** \'twēd\ *n* **1** : rough woolen fabric **2** *pl* : tweed clothing — **tweedy** *adj*

**tweet** \'twēt\ *n* : chirping note — **tweet** *vb*

**twee·zers** \'twēzərz\ *n pl* : small pincerlike tool

**twelve** \'twelv\ *n* **1** : one more than 11 **2** : 12th in a set or series **3** : something having 12 units — **twelfth** \'twelfth\ *adj or n* — **twelve** *adj or pron*

**twen·ty** \'twentē\ *n, pl* **-ties** : 2 times 10 — **twen·ti·eth** \-ēəth\ *adj or n* — **twenty** *adj or pron*

**twen·ty–twen·ty, 20–20** *adj* : being vision of normal sharpness

**twice** \'twīs\ *adv* **1** : on 2 occasions **2** : 2 times

**twig** \'twig\ *n* : small branch — **twig·gy** *adj*

**twi·light** \'twī₁līt\ *n* : light from the sky at dusk or dawn — **twilight** *adj*

**twill** \'twil\ *n* : fabric with a weave that gives an appearance of diagonal lines in the fabric

**twilled** \'twild\ *adj* : made with a twill weave

**twin** \'twin\ *n* : either of 2 offspring born together ∼ *adj* **1** : born with one another or as a pair at one birth **2** : made up of 2 similar parts

**twine** \'twīn\ *n* : strong twisted thread ∼ *vb* **twined; twin·ing** **1** : twist together **2** : coil about a support — **twin·er** *n* — **twiny** *adj*

**twinge** \'twinj\ *vb* **twinged; twing·ing** or **twinge·ing** : affect with or feel a sudden sharp pain ∼ *n* : sudden sharp stab (as of pain)

**twin·kle** \'twiŋkəl\ *vb* **-kled; -kling**

: shine with a flickering light ~ *n* **1**
: wink **2** : intermittent shining —
**twin·kler** \-klər\ *n*

**twirl** \'twərl\ *vb* : whirl round ~ *n* **1**
: act of twirling **2** : coil — **twirl·er** *n*

**twist** \'twist\ *vb* **1** : unite by winding
(threads) together **2** : wrench **3**
: move in or have a spiral shape **4**
: follow a winding course ~ *n* **1** : act
or result of twisting **2** : unexpected
development

**twist·er** \'twistər\ *n* : tornado

**¹twit** \'twit\ *n* : fool

**²twit** *vb* **-tt-** : taunt

**twitch** \'twich\ *vb* : move or pull with a
sudden motion ~ *n* : act of twitching

**twit·ter** \'twitər\ *vb* : make chirping
noises ~ *n* : small intermittent noise

**two** \'tü\ *n, pl* **twos 1** : one more than
one **2** : the 2d in a set or series **3**
: something having 2 units — **two** *adj*
*or pron*

**two·fold** \'tü,fōld\ *adj* : double — **two·fold** \-'fōld\ *adv*

**two·some** \'tüsəm\ *n* : couple

**-ty** *n suffix* : quality, condition, or degree

**ty·coon** \tī'kün\ *n* : powerful and successful businessman

**tying** *pres part of* TIE

**tyke** \'tīk\ *n* : small child

**tym·pa·num** \'timpənəm\ *n, pl* **-na**
\-nə\ : eardrum or the cavity which it
closes externally — **tym·pan·ic**
\tim'panik\ *adj*

**type** \'tīp\ *n* **1** : class, kind, or group
set apart by common characteristics
**2** : special design of printed letters
~ *vb* **typed; typ·ing 1** : write with a
typewriter **2** : identify or classify as a
particular type

**type·writ·er** *n* : keyboard machine that
produces printed material by striking
a ribbon with raised letters — **type·write** *vb*

**ty·phoid** \'tī,fȯid, tī'-\ *adj* : relating to
or being a communicable bacterial
disease (**typhoid fever**)

**ty·phoon** \tī'fün\ *n* : hurricane of the
western Pacific ocean

**ty·phus** \'tīfəs\ *n* : severe disease with
fever, delirium, and rash

**typ·i·cal** \'tipikəl\ *adj* : having the
essential characteristics of a group —
**typ·i·cal·i·ty** \,tipə'kalətē\ *n* — **typ·i·cal·ly** *adv* — **typ·i·cal·ness** *n*

**typ·i·fy** \'tipə,fī\ *vb* **-fied; -fy·ing** : be
typical of

**typ·ist** \'tīpist\ *n* : one who operates a
typewriter

**ty·pog·ra·phy** \tī'pägrəfē\ *n* **1** : art of
printing with type **2** : style, arrangement, or appearance of printed matter
— **ty·po·graph·ic** \,tīpə'grafik\, **ty·po·graph·i·cal** \-ikəl\ *adj* — **ty·po·graph·i·cal·ly** *adv*

**ty·ran·ni·cal** \tə'ranikəl, tī-\ *adj* : relating to a tyrant — **ty·ran·ni·cal·ly** *adv*

**tyr·an·nize** \'tirə,nīz\ *vb* **-nized; -niz·ing** : rule or deal with in the manner
of a tyrant — **tyr·an·niz·er** *n*

**tyr·an·ny** \'tirənē\ *n, pl* **-nies** : unjust
use of absolute governmental power

**ty·rant** \'tīrənt\ *n* : harsh ruler having
absolute power

**ty·ro** \'tīrō\ *n, pl* **-ros** : beginner

**tzar** \'zär, 'tsär, 'sär\ *var of* CZAR

# U

**u** \'yü\ *n, pl* **u's** *or* **us** \'yüz\ : 21st letter of the alphabet

**ubiq·ui·tous** \yü'bikwətəs\ *adj* : om-
nipresent — **ubiq·ui·tous·ly** *adv* —
**ubiq·ui·ty** \-wətē\ *n*

**ud·der** \'ədər\ *n* : animal sac containing milk glands and nipples

**ug·ly** \'əglē\ *adj* **ug·li·er; -est 1** : offensive to look at **2** : mean or quar-
relsome — **ug·li·ness** *n*

**uku·le·le** \,yükə'lālē\ *n* : small 4-string
guitar

**ul·cer** \'əlsər\ *n* : eroded sore — **ul·cer·ous** *adj*

**ul·cer·ate** \'əlsə,rāt\ *vb* **-at·ed; -at·ing**
: become affected with an ulcer — **ul·cer·a·tion** \,əlsə'rāshən\ *n* — **ul·cer·a·tive** \'əlsə,rātiv\ *adj*

**ul·na** \'əlnə\ *n* : bone of the forearm
opposite the thumb

**ul·te·ri·or** \,əl'tirēər\ *adj* : not revealed

**ul·ti·mate** \'əltəmət\ *adj* : final, maximum, or extreme — **ultimate** *n* — **ul·ti·mate·ly** *adv*

**ul·ti·ma·tum** \ˌəltə'mātəm, -'mät-\ *n,
pl* **-tums** *or* **-ta** \-ə\ : final proposition
or demand carrying or implying a threat

**ul·tra·vi·o·let** \ˌəltrə'vīələt\ *adj* : having a wavelength shorter than visible
light

**um·bi·li·cus** \ˌəmbə'līkəs, ˌəm'bili-\
*n, pl* **-li·ci** \-bə'līˌkī, -ˌsī; -'biləˌkī,
-ˌkē\ *or* **-li·cus·es** : small depression
on the abdominal wall marking the
site of the cord (**umbilical cord**) that
joins the unborn fetus to its mother —
**um·bil·i·cal** \ˌəm'bilikəl\ *adj*

**um·brage** \'əmbrij\ *n* : resentment

**um·brel·la** \ˌəm'brelə\ *n* : collapsible
fabric device to protect from sun or
rain

**um·pire** \'əmˌpīr\ *n* **1** : arbitrator **2**
: sport official — **umpire** *vb*

**ump·teen** \'əmp'tēn\ *adj* : very numerous — **ump·teenth** \-'tēnth\ *adj*

**un-** \ˌən, 'ən\ *prefix* **1** : not **2** : opposite of

**un·ac·cus·tomed** *adj* **1** : not customary **2** : not accustomed

**un·af·fect·ed** *adj* **1** : not influenced or
changed by something **2** : natural and
sincere — **un·af·fect·ed·ly** *adv*

**unan·i·mous** \yu̇'nanəməs\ *adj* **1**
: showing no disagreement **2** : formed
with the agreement of all — **una-
nim·i·ty** \ˌyünə'nimətē\ *n* — **unan-
i·mous·ly** *adv*

**un·armed** *adj* : not armed or armored

**un·as·sum·ing** *adj* : not bold or arrogant

**un·at·tached** *adj* **1** : not attached **2**
: not married or engaged

**un·aware** *adv* : unawares ∼ *adj* : not
aware

**un·awares** \ˌənə'warz\ *adv* **1** : without warning **2** : unintentionally

**un·bal·anced** *adj* **1** : not balanced **2**
: mentally unstable

**un·beat·en** *adj* : not beaten

**un·be·com·ing** *adj* : not proper or suitable — **un·be·com·ing·ly** *adv*

**un·be·liev·able** *adj* **1** : improbable **2**
: superlative — **un·be·liev·ably** *adv*

**un·bend** *vb* **-bent; -bend·ing** : make or
become more relaxed and friendly

**un·bend·ing** *adj* : formal and inflexible

**un·bind** *vb* **-bound; -bind·ing 1** : remove bindings from **2** : release

**un·bolt** *vb* : open or unfasten by withdrawing a bolt

**un·born** *adj* : not yet born

**un·bo·som** *vb* : disclose thoughts or
feelings

**un·bowed** \ˌən'baud\ *adj* : not defeated or subdued

**un·bri·dled** \ˌən'brīd°ld\ *adj* : unrestrained

**un·bro·ken** *adj* **1** : not damaged **2** : not
interrupted

**un·buck·le** *vb* : unfasten the buckle of

**un·bur·den** *vb* : relieve (oneself) of
anxieties

**un·but·ton** *vb* : unfasten the buttons of

**un·called–for** *adj* : too harsh or rude for
the occasion

**un·can·ny** \ˌən'kanē\ *adj* **1** : weird **2**
: suggesting superhuman powers —
**un·can·ni·ly** \-'kan°lē\ *adv*

**un·ceas·ing** *adj* : never ceasing — **un-
ceas·ing·ly** *adv*

**un·cer·e·mo·ni·ous** *adj* : acting without
ordinary courtesy — **un·cer·e·mo·ni-
ous·ly** *adv*

**un·cer·tain** *adj* **1** : not determined,
sure, or definitely known **2** : subject
to chance or change — **un·cer·tain·ly**
*adv* — **un·cer·tain·ty** *n*

---

**List of self-explanatory words with the prefix *un-***

| | | |
|---|---|---|
| unable | unannounced | unbearable |
| unabridged | unanswered | unbiased |
| unacceptable | unanticipated | unbranded |
| unaccompanied | unappetizing | unbreakable |
| unaccounted | unappreciated | uncensored |
| unacquainted | unapproved | unchallenged |
| unaddressed | unarguable | unchangeable |
| unadorned | unarguably | unchanged |
| unadulterated | unassisted | unchanging |
| unafraid | unattended | uncharacteristic |
| unaided | unattractive | uncharged |
| unalike | unauthorized | unchaste |
| unambiguous | unavailable | uncivilized |
| unambitious | unavoidable | unclaimed |

**un·chris·tian** adj : not consistent with Christian teachings

**un·cle** \'əŋkəl\ n 1 : brother of one's father or mother 2 : husband of one's aunt

**un·clean** adj : not clean or pure — **un·clean·ness** n

**un·clog** vb : remove an obstruction from

**un·coil** vb : release or become released from a coiled state

**un·com·mit·ted** adj : not pledged to a particular allegiance or course of action

**un·com·mon** adj 1 : rare 2 : superior — **un·com·mon·ly** adv

**un·com·pro·mis·ing** adj : not making or accepting a compromise

**un·con·cerned** adj 1 : disinterested 2 : not anxious or upset — **un·con·cerned·ly** adv

**un·con·di·tion·al** adj : not limited in any way — **un·con·di·tion·al·ly** adv

**un·con·scio·na·ble** adj : shockingly unjust or unscrupulous — **un·con·scio·na·bly** adv

**un·con·scious** adj 1 : not awake or aware of one's surroundings 2 : not consciously done ~ n : part of one's mental life that one is not aware of — **un·con·scious·ly** adv — **un·con·scious·ness** n

**un·con·sti·tu·tion·al** adj : not according to or consistent with a constitution

**un·con·trol·la·ble** adj : incapable of being controlled — **un·con·trol·la·bly** adv

**un·count·ed** adj : countless

**un·couth** \ˌən'küth\ adj : rude and vulgar

**un·cov·er** vb 1 : reveal 2 : expose by removing a covering

**unc·tion** \'əŋkshən\ n 1 : rite of anointing 2 : exaggerated or insincere earnestness

**unc·tu·ous** \'əŋkchəwəs\ adj 1 : oily 2 : insincerely smooth in speech or manner — **unc·tu·ous·ly** adv

**un·cut** adj 1 : not cut down, into, off, or apart 2 : not shaped by cutting 3 : not abridged

**un·daunt·ed** adj : not discouraged — **un·daunt·ed·ly** adv

**un·de·ni·able** adj : plainly true — **un·de·ni·ably** adv

**un·der** \'əndər\ adv : below or beneath something ~ prep 1 : lower than and sheltered by 2 : below the surface of 3 : covered or concealed by 4 : subject to the authority of 5 : less than ~ adj 1 : lying below or beneath 2 : subordinate 3 : less than usual, proper, or desired

**un·der·age** \ˌəndər'āj\ adj : of less than legal age

**un·der·brush** \'əndərˌbrəsh\ n : shrubs and small trees growing beneath large trees

**un·der·clothes** \'əndərˌklōz, -ˌklōthz\ n pl : underwear

**un·der·cloth·ing** \-ˌklōthiŋ\ n : underwear

**un·der·cov·er** \ˌəndər'kəvər\ adj : employed or engaged in secret investigation

**un·der·cur·rent** \'əndərˌkərənt\ n : hidden tendency or opinion

**un·der·cut** \ˌəndər'kət\ vb **-cut; -cut·ting** : offer to sell or to work at a lower rate than

**un·der·de·vel·oped** \ˌəndərdi'veləpt\ adj : not normally or adequately developed esp. economically

---

| | | |
|---|---|---|
| unclear | unconventionally | undeserving |
| uncleared | unconverted | undesirable |
| unclothed | uncooked | undetected |
| uncluttered | uncooperative | undetermined |
| uncombed | uncoordinated | undeveloped |
| uncomfortable | uncovered | undeviating |
| uncomfortably | uncultivated | undifferentiated |
| uncomplimentary | undamaged | undignified |
| unconfirmed | undated | undisturbed |
| unconsummated | undecided | undivided |
| uncontested | undeclared | undomesticated |
| uncontrolled | undefeated | undrinkable |
| uncontroversial | undemocratic | unearned |
| unconventional | undependable | uneducated |

**un·der·dog** \'əndər₁dȯg\ n : contestant given least chance of winning

**un·der·done** \₁əndər'dən\ adj : not thoroughly done or cooked

**un·der·es·ti·mate** \₁əndər'estə₁māt\ vb : estimate too low

**un·der·ex·pose** \₁əndərik'spōz\ vb : give less than normal exposure to — **un·der·ex·po·sure** n

**un·der·feed** \₁əndər'fēd\ vb -fed; -feed·ing : feed inadequately

**un·der·foot** \₁əndər'fu̇t\ adv 1 : under the feet 2 : in the way of another

**un·der·gar·ment** \'əndər₁gärmənt\ n : garment to be worn under another

**un·der·go** \₁əndər'gō\ vb -went \-'went\; -gone; -go·ing 1 : endure 2 : go through (as an experience)

**un·der·grad·u·ate** \₁əndər'grajəwət\ n : university or college student

**un·der·ground** \₁əndər'grau̇nd\ adv 1 : beneath the surface of the earth 2 : in secret ~ \'əndər₁-\ adj 1 : being or growing under the surface of the ground 2 : secret ~ \'əndər₁-\ n : secret political movement or group

**un·der·growth** \'əndər₁grōth\ n : low growth on the floor of a forest

**un·der·hand** \'əndər₁hand\ adv or adj 1 : with secrecy and deception 2 : with the hand kept below the waist

**un·der·hand·ed** \₁əndər'handəd\ adj or adv : underhand — **un·der·hand·ed·ly** adv — **un·der·hand·ed·ness** n

**un·der·line** \'əndər₁līn\ vb 1 : draw a line under 2 : stress — **underline** n

**un·der·ling** \'əndərliŋ\ n : inferior

**un·der·ly·ing** \₁əndər₁līiŋ\ adj : basic

**un·der·mine** \₁əndər'mīn\ vb 1 : excavate beneath 2 : weaken or wear away secretly or gradually

**un·der·neath** \₁əndər'nēth\ prep : directly under ~ adv 1 : below a surface or object 2 : on the lower side

**un·der·nour·ished** \₁əndər'nərisht\ adj : insufficiently nourished — **un·der·nour·ish·ment** n

**un·der·pants** \'əndər₁pants\ n pl : short undergarment for the lower trunk

**un·der·pass** \-₁pas\ n : passageway crossing underneath another

**un·der·pin·ning** \'əndər₁piniŋ\ n : support

**un·der·priv·i·leged** adj : poor

**un·der·rate** \₁əndər'rāt\ vb : rate or value too low

**un·der·score** \'əndər₁skōr\ vb 1 : underline 2 : emphasize — **underscore** n

**un·der·sea** \₁əndər'sē\ adj : being, carried on, or used beneath the surface of the sea ~ \₁əndər'sē\, **un·der·seas** \-'sēz\ adv : beneath the surface of the sea

**un·der sec·re·tary** n : deputy secretary

**un·der·sell** \₁əndər'sel\ vb -sold; -sell·ing : sell articles cheaper than

**un·der·shirt** \'əndər₁shərt\ n : shirt worn as underwear

**un·der·shorts** \'əndər₁shȯrts\ n pl : short underpants

**un·der·side** \'əndər₁sīd, ₁əndər'sīd\ n : side or surface lying underneath

**un·der·sized** \₁əndər'sīzd\ adj : unusually small

**un·der·stand** \₁əndər'stand\ vb -stood \-'stu̇d\; -stand·ing 1 : be aware of the meaning of 2 : deduce 3 : have a sympathetic attitude — **un·der·stand·able** \-'standəbəl\ adj — **un·der·stand·ably** \-blē\ adv

**un·der·stand·ing** \₁əndər'standiŋ\ n 1 : intelligence 2 : ability to compre-

---

unemotional
unending
unendurable
unenforceable
unenlightened
unethical
unexcitable
unexciting
unexplainable
unexplored
unfair
unfairly
unfairness
unfavorable

unfavorably
unfeigned
unfilled
unfinished
unflattering
unforeseeable
unforeseen
unforgivable
unforgiving
unfulfilled
unfurnished
ungenerous
ungentlemanly
ungraceful

ungrammatical
unharmed
unhealthful
unheated
unhurt
unidentified
unimaginable
unimaginative
unimportant
unimpressed
uninformed
uninhabited
uninjured
uninsured

hend and judge **3** : mutual agreement ~ *adj* : sympathetic

**un·der·state** \ˌəndər'stāt\ *vb* **1** : represent as less than is the case **2** : state with restraint — **un·der·state·ment** *n*

**un·der·stood** \ˌəndər'stud\ *adj* **1** : agreed upon **2** : implicit

**un·der·study** \'əndərˌstədē, ˌəndər'-\ *vb* : study another actor's part in order to substitute — **understudy** \'əndərˌ-\ *n*

**un·der·take** \ˌəndər'tāk\ *vb* **-took; -tak·en; -tak·ing 1** : attempt (a task) or assume (a responsibility) **2** : guarantee

**un·der·tak·er** \'əndərˌtākər\ *n* : one in the funeral business

**un·der·tak·ing** \'əndərˌtākiŋ, ˌəndər'-\ *n* **1** : something (as work) that is undertaken **2** : promise

**under–the–counter** *adj* : illicit

**un·der·tone** \'əndərˌtōn\ *n* : low or subdued tone or utterance

**un·der·tow** \-ˌtō\ *n* : current beneath the waves that flows seaward

**un·der·val·ue** \ˌəndər'valyü\ *vb* : value too low

**un·der·wa·ter** \-'wótər, -'wät-\ *adj* : being or used below the surface of the water — **underwater** *adv*

**under way** *adv* : in motion or in progress

**un·der·wear** \'əndərˌwar\ *n* : clothing worn next to the skin and under ordinary clothes

**un·der·world** \'əndərˌwərld\ *n* **1** : place of departed souls **2** : world of organized crime

**un·der·write** \'əndərˌrīt, ˌəndər'-\ *vb* **-wrote; -writ·ten; -writ·ing 1** : provide insurance for **2** : guarantee financial support of — **un·der·writ·er** *n*

**un·dies** \'əndēz\ *n pl* : underwear

**un·do** *vb* **-did; -done; -do·ing 1** : unfasten **2** : reverse **3** : ruin — **un·do·ing** *n*

**un·doubt·ed** *adj* : certain — **un·doubt·ed·ly** *adv*

**un·dress** *vb* : remove one's clothes ~ *n* : state of being naked

**un·due** *adj* : excessive — **un·du·ly** *adv*

**un·du·late** \'ənjəˌlāt\ *vb* **-lat·ed; -lat·ing** : rise and fall regularly — **un·du·la·tion** \ˌənjə'lāshən\ *n*

**un·dy·ing** *adj* : immortal or perpetual

**un·earth** *vb* : dig up or discover

**un·earth·ly** *adj* : supernatural

**un·easy** *adj* **1** : awkward or embarrassed **2** : disturbed or worried — **un·eas·i·ly** *adv* — **un·eas·i·ness** *n*

**un·em·ployed** *adj* : not having a job — **un·em·ploy·ment** *n*

**un·equal** *adj* : not equal or uniform — **un·equal·ly** *adv*

**un·equaled, un·equalled** *adj* : having no equal

**un·equiv·o·cal** *adj* : leaving no doubt — **un·equiv·o·cal·ly** *adv*

**un·err·ing** *adj* : infallible — **un·err·ing·ly** *adv*

**un·even** *adj* **1** : not smooth **2** : not regular or consistent — **un·even·ly** *adv* — **un·even·ness** *n*

**un·event·ful** *adj* : lacking interesting or noteworthy incidents — **un·event·ful·ly** *adv*

**un·ex·pect·ed** \ˌənik'spektəd\ *adj* : not expected — **un·ex·pect·ed·ly** *adv*

**un·fail·ing** *adj* : steadfast — **un·fail·ing·ly** *adv*

**un·faith·ful** *adj* : not loyal — **un·faith·ful·ly** *adv* — **un·faith·ful·ness** *n*

**un·fa·mil·iar** *adj* **1** : not well known **2** : not acquainted — **un·fa·mil·iar·i·ty** *n*

---

| | | |
|---|---|---|
| unintelligent | unknowing | unmolested |
| unintelligible | unknowingly | unmotivated |
| unintelligibly | unknown | unmoving |
| unintended | unleavened | unnamed |
| unintentional | unlicensed | unnecessarily |
| unintentionally | unlikable | unnecessary |
| uninterested | unlimited | unneeded |
| uninteresting | unlovable | unnoticeable |
| uninterrupted | unmanageable | unnoticed |
| uninvited | unmarked | unobjectionable |
| unjust | unmarried | unobservable |
| unjustifiable | unmerciful | unobservant |
| unjustified | unmercifully | unobtainable |
| unjustly | unmerited | unobtrusive |

**un·fas·ten** *vb* : release a catch or lock

**un·feel·ing** *adj* : lacking feeling or compassion — **un·feel·ing·ly** *adv*

**un·fit** *adj* : not suitable — **un·fit·ness** *n*

**un·flap·pa·ble** \ˌən'flapəbəl\ *adj* : not easily upset or panicked — **un·flap·pa·bly** *adv*

**un·fold** *vb* **1** : open the folds of **2** : reveal **3** : develop

**un·for·get·ta·ble** *adj* : memorable — **un·for·get·ta·bly** *adv*

**un·for·tu·nate** *adj* **1** : not lucky or successful **2** : deplorable — **unfortunate** *n* — **un·for·tu·nate·ly** *adv*

**un·found·ed** *adj* : lacking a sound basis

**un·freeze** *vb* **-froze; -fro·zen; -freez·ing** : thaw

**un·friend·ly** *adj* : not friendly or kind — **un·friend·li·ness** *n*

**un·furl** *vb* : unfold or unroll

**un·gain·ly** *adj* : clumsy — **un·gain·li·ness** *n*

**un·god·ly** *adj* : wicked — **un·god·li·ness** *n*

**un·grate·ful** *adj* : not thankful for favors — **un·grate·ful·ly** *adv* — **un·grate·ful·ness** *n*

**un·guent** \'əŋgwənt, 'ən-\ *n* : ointment

**un·hand** *vb* : let go

**un·hap·py** *adj* **1** : unfortunate **2** : sad — **un·hap·pi·ly** *adv* — **un·hap·pi·ness** *n*

**un·healthy** *adj* **1** : not wholesome **2** : not well

**un·heard–of** \ˌən'hərdəv, -ˌäv\ *adj* : unprecedented

**un·hinge** \ˌən'hinj\ *vb* **1** : take from the hinges **2** : make unstable esp. mentally

**un·hitch** *vb* : unfasten

**un·ho·ly** *adj* : sinister or shocking — **un·ho·li·ness** *n*

**un·hook** *vb* : release from a hook

**uni·cel·lu·lar** \ˌyüni'selyələr\ *adj* : having or consisting of a single cell

**uni·corn** \'yünəˌkȯrn\ *n* : legendary animal with one horn in the middle of the forehead

**uni·cy·cle** \'yüniˌsīkəl\ *n* : pedal= powered vehicle with only a single wheel

**uni·di·rec·tion·al** \ˌyünidə'rekshənəl, -dī-\ *adj* : working in only a single direction

**uni·form** \'yünəˌfȯrm\ *adj* : not changing or showing any variation ∼ *n* : distinctive dress worn by members of a particular group — **uni·for·mi·ty** \ˌyünə'fȯrmətē\ *n* — **uni·form·ly** *adv*

**uni·fy** \'yünəˌfī\ *vb* **-fied; -fy·ing** : make into a coherent whole — **uni·fi·ca·tion** \ˌyünəfə'kāshən\ *n*

**uni·lat·er·al** \ˌyünə'latərəl\ *adj* : having, affecting, or done by one side only — **uni·lat·er·al·ly** *adv*

**un·im·peach·able** *adj* : blameless

**un·in·hib·it·ed** *adj* : free of restraint — **un·in·hib·it·ed·ly** *adv*

**union** \'yünyən\ *n* **1** : act or instance of joining 2 or more things into one or the state of being so joined **2** : confederation of nations or states **3** : organization of workers (**labor union, trade union**)

**union·ize** \'yünyəˌnīz\ *vb* **-ized; -iz·ing** : form into a labor union — **union·iza·tion** \ˌyünyənə'zāshən\ *n*

**unique** \yu̇'nēk\ *adj* **1** : being the only one of its kind **2** : very unusual — **unique·ly** *adv* — **unique·ness** *n*

**uni·son** \'yünəsən, -nəzən\ *n* **1** : sameness in pitch **2** : exact agreement

**unit** \'yünət\ *n* **1** : smallest whole

---

| | | |
|---|---|---|
| unobtrusively | unpleasantness | unproven |
| unofficial | unpopular | unprovoked |
| unopened | unpopularity | unpunished |
| unopposed | unposed | unqualified |
| unorganized | unpredictability | unquenchable |
| unoriginal | unpredictable | unquestioning |
| unorthodox | unpredictably | unreachable |
| unorthodoxy | unprejudiced | unreadable |
| unpaid | unprepared | unready |
| unpardonable | unpretentious | unrealistic |
| unpatriotic | unproductive | unreasonable |
| unpaved | unprofitable | unreasonably |
| unpleasant | unprotected | unrefined |
| unpleasantly | unproved | unrelated |

number **2** : definite amount or quantity used as a standard of measurement **3** : single part of a whole — **unit** *adj*

**unite** \yu̇ˈnīt\ *vb* **unit·ed; unit·ing** : put or join together

**uni·ty** \ˈyünətē\ *n, pl* **-ties 1** : quality or state of being united or a unit **2** : harmony

**uni·ver·sal** \ˌyünəˈvərsəl\ *adj* **1** : relating to or affecting everyone or everything **2** : present or occurring everywhere — **uni·ver·sal·ly** *adv*

**uni·verse** \ˈyünəˌvərs\ *n* : the complete system of all things that exist

**uni·ver·si·ty** \ˌyünəˈvərsətē\ *n, pl* **-ties** : institution of higher learning

**un·kempt** \ˌənˈkempt\ *adj* : not neat or combed

**un·kind** *adj* : not kind or sympathetic — **un·kind·li·ness** *n* — **un·kind·ly** *adv* — **un·kind·ness** *n*

**un·law·ful** *adj* : illegal — **un·law·ful·ly** *adv*

**un·leash** *vb* : free from control or restraint

**un·less** \ənˈles\ *conj* : except on condition that

**un·like** \ˌənˈlīk, ˈənˌlīk\ *adj* **1** : not similar **2** : not equal ∼ *prep* : different from — **un·like·ly** \ənˈlīklē\ *adv* — **un·like·ness** \-nəs\ *n* — **un·like·li·hood** \-lēˌhu̇d\ *n*

**un·load** *vb* **1** : take (cargo) from a vehicle, vessel, or plane **2** : take a load from **3** : discard

**un·lock** *vb* **1** : unfasten through release of a lock **2** : release or reveal

**un·lucky** *adj* **1** : experiencing bad luck **2** : likely to bring misfortune — **un·luck·i·ly** *adv*

**un·mis·tak·able** *adj* : not capable of being mistaken or misunderstood — **un·mis·tak·ably** *adv*

**un·moved** *adj* **1** : not emotionally affected **2** : remaining in the same place or position

**un·nat·u·ral** *adj* **1** : not natural or spontaneous **2** : abnormal — **un·nat·u·ral·ly** *adv* — **un·nat·u·ral·ness** *n*

**un·nerve** *vb* : deprive of courage, strength, or steadiness

**un·oc·cu·pied** *adj* **1** : not busy **2** : not occupied

**un·pack** *vb* **1** : remove (things packed) from a container **2** : remove the contents of (a package)

**un·par·al·leled** *adj* : having no equal

**un·plug** *vb* **1** : unclog **2** : disconnect from an electric circuit by removing a plug

**un·prec·e·dent·ed** *adj* : unlike or superior to anything known before

**un·prin·ci·pled** *adj* : unscrupulous

**un·ques·tion·able** *adj* : acknowledged as beyond doubt — **un·ques·tion·ably** *adv*

**un·rav·el** *vb* **1** : separate the threads of **2** : solve

**un·re·al** *adj* : not real or genuine — **un·re·al·i·ty** *n*

**un·rea·son·ing** *adj* : not using or being guided by reason

**un·re·lent·ing** *adj* : not yielding or easing — **un·re·lent·ing·ly** *adv*

**un·rest** *n* : turmoil

**un·ri·valed, un·ri·valled** *adj* : having no rival

**un·roll** *vb* **1** : unwind a roll of **2** : become unrolled

**un·ruf·fled** *adj* : not agitated or upset

**un·ruly** \ˌənˈrülē\ *adj* : not readily con-

---

| | | |
|---|---|---|
| unreliable | unsatisfactory | unsolved |
| unremembered | unsatisfied | unsophisticated |
| unrepentant | unscented | unsound |
| unrepresented | unscheduled | unsoundly |
| unrequited | unseasoned | unsoundness |
| unresolved | unseen | unspecified |
| unresponsive | unselfish | unspoiled |
| unrestrained | unselfishly | unsteadily |
| unrestricted | unselfishness | unsteadiness |
| unrewarding | unshaped | unsteady |
| unripe | unshaven | unstructured |
| unsafe | unskillful | unsubstantiated |
| unsalted | unskillfully | unsuccessful |
| unsanitary | unsolicited | unsuitable |

trolled or disciplined — **un·rul·i·ness** n

**un·scathed** \ˌən'skāt͟hd\ adj : unharmed

**un·sci·en·tif·ic** adj : not in accord with the principles and methods of science

**un·screw** vb : loosen or remove by withdrawing screws or by turning

**un·scru·pu·lous** adj : being or acting in total disregard of conscience, ethical principles, or rights of others — **un·scru·pu·lous·ly** adv — **un·scru·pu·lous·ness** n

**un·seal** vb : break or remove the seal of

**un·sea·son·able** adj : not appropriate or usual for the season — **un·sea·son·ably** adv

**un·seem·ly** \ˌən'sēmlē\ adj : not polite or in good taste — **un·seem·li·ness** n

**un·set·tle** vb : disturb — **un·set·tled** adj

**un·sight·ly** \ˌən'sītlē\ adj : not attractive

**un·skilled** adj : not having or requiring a particular skill

**un·snap** vb : loosen by undoing a snap

**un·speak·able** \ˌən'spēkəbəl\ adj : extremely bad — **un·speak·ably** \-blē\ adv

**un·sta·ble** adj 1 : not mentally or physically balanced 2 : tending to change

**un·stop** vb 1 : unclog 2 : remove a stopper from

**un·stop·pa·ble** \ˌən'stäpəbəl\ adj : not capable of being stopped

**un·strung** \ˌən'strəŋ\ adj : nervously tired or anxious

**un·sung** \ˌən'səŋ\ adj : not celebrated in song or verse

**un·tan·gle** vb 1 : free from a state of being tangled 2 : find a solution to

**un·think·able** \ˌən'thiŋkəbəl\ adj : not to be thought of or considered possible

**un·think·ing** adj : careless — **un·think·ing·ly** adv

**un·tie** vb -tied; -ty·ing or -tie·ing : open by releasing ties

**un·til** \ˌən'til\ prep : up to the time of ~ conj : to the time that

**un·time·ly** adj 1 : premature 2 : coming at an unfortunate time

**un·to** \ˌən'tü, 'ən-\ prep : to

**un·told** adj 1 : not told 2 : too numerous to count

**un·to·ward** \ˌən'tōrd\ adj 1 : difficult to manage 2 : inconvenient

**un·truth** n 1 : lack of truthfulness 2 : lie

**un·used** adj 1 \ˌən'yüst, -'yüzd\ : not accustomed 2 \-'yüzd\ : not used

**un·well** adj : sick

**un·wieldy** \ˌən'wēldē\ adj : too big or awkward to manage easily

**un·wind** vb -wound; -wind·ing 1 : undo something that is wound 2 : become unwound 3 : relax

**un·wit·ting** adj 1 : not knowing 2 : not intended — **un·wit·ting·ly** adv

**un·wont·ed** adj 1 : unusual 2 : not accustomed by experience

**un·wrap** vb : remove the wrappings from

**un·writ·ten** adj : made or passed on only in speech or through tradition

**un·zip** vb : zip open

**up** \'əp\ adv 1 : in or to a higher position or level 2 : from beneath a surface or level 3 : in or into an upright position 4 : out of bed 5 : to or with greater intensity 6 : into existence, evidence, or knowledge 7 : away 8 — used to indicate a degree of success, completion, or finality 9 : in or

---

unsuitably
unsuited
unsupervised
unsupported
unsure
unsurprising
unsuspecting
unsweetened
unsympathetic
untamed
untanned
untidy
untouched
untrained

untreated
untrue
untrustworthy
untruthful
unusable
unusual
unvarying
unverified
unwanted
unwarranted
unwary
unwavering
unweaned
unwed

unwelcome
unwholesome
unwilling
unwillingly
unwillingness
unwise
unwisely
unworkable
unworthily
unworthiness
unworthy
unyielding

into parts ~ *adj* **1** : in the state of having risen **2** : raised to or at a higher level **3** : moving, inclining, or directed upward **4** : in a state of greater intensity **5** : at an end ~ *vb* **upped** *or in 1* **up; upped; up•ping; ups** *or in 1* **up 1** : act abruptly **2** : move or cause to move upward ~ *prep* **1** : to, toward, or at a higher point of **2** : along or toward the beginning of

**up•braid** \,əp'brād\ *vb* : criticize or scold

**up•bring•ing** \'əp,briŋiŋ\ *n* : process of bringing up and training

**up•com•ing** \,əp'kəmiŋ\ *adj* : approaching

**up•date** \,əp'dāt\ *vb* : bring up to date — **update** \'əp,dāt\ *n*

**up•end** \,əp'end\ *vb* **1** : stand or rise on end **2** : overturn

**up•grade** \'əp,grād\ *n* **1** : upward slope **2** : increase ~ \'əp,-, ,əp'-\ *vb* : raise to a higher position

**up•heav•al** \,əp'hēvəl\ *n* **1** : a heaving up (as of part of the earth's crust) **2** : violent change

**up•hill** \,əp'hil\ *adv* : upward on a hill or incline ~ \'əp,-\ *adj* **1** : going up **2** : difficult

**up•hold** \,əp'hōld\ *vb* **-held; -hold•ing** : support or defend — **up•hold•er** *n*

**up•hol•ster** \,əp'hōlstər\ *vb* : cover (furniture) with padding and fabric (**up•hol•stery** \-stərē\) — **up•hol•ster•er** *n*

**up•keep** \'əp,kēp\ *n* : act or cost of keeping up or maintaining

**up•land** \'əplənd, -,land\ *n* : high land — **upland** *adj*

**up•lift** \,əp'lift\ *vb* **1** : lift up **2** : improve the condition or spirits of — **up•lift** \'əp,-\ *n*

**up•on** \ə'pȯn, -'pän\ *prep* : on

**up•per** \'əpər\ *adj* : higher in position, rank, or order ~ *n* : top part of a shoe

**upper•hand** *n* : advantage

**up•per•most** \'əpər,mōst\ *adv* : in or into the highest or most prominent position — **uppermost** *adj*

**up•pi•ty** \'əpətē\ *adj* : acting with a manner of undue importance

**up•right** \'əp,rīt\ *adj* **1** : vertical **2** : erect in posture **3** : morally correct ~ *n* : something that stands upright — **upright** *adv* — **up•right•ly** *adv* — **up•right•ness** *n*

**up•ris•ing** \'əp,rīziŋ\ *n* : revolt

**up•roar** \'əp,rōr\ *n* : state of commotion or violent disturbance

**up•roar•i•ous** \,əp'rōrēəs\ *adj* **1** : marked by uproar **2** : extremely funny — **up•roar•i•ous•ly** *adv*

**up•root** \,əp'rüt, -'rut\ *vb* : remove by or as if by pulling up by the roots

**up•set** \,əp'set\ *vb* **-set; -set•ting 1** : force or be forced out of the usual position **2** : disturb emotionally or physically ~ \'əp,-\ *n* **1** : act of throwing into disorder **2** : minor physical disorder ~ *adj* : emotionally disturbed or agitated

**up•shot** \'əp,shät\ *n* : final result

**up•side down** \,əp,sīd'daun\ *adv* **1** : turned so that the upper and lower parts are reversed **2** : in or into confusion or disorder — **upside–down** *adj*

**up•stairs** \'əp,starz, ,əp'-\ *adv* : up the stairs or to the next floor ~ *adj* : situated on the floor above ~ *n sing or pl* : part of a building above the ground floor

**up•stand•ing** \,əp'standiŋ, 'əp,-\ *adj* : honest

**up•start** \'əp,stärt\ *n* : one who claims more personal importance than is warranted — **up•start** *adj*

**up•swing** \'əp,swiŋ\ *n* : marked increase (as in activity)

**up•tight** \,əp'tīt\ *adj* **1** : tense **2** : angry **3** : rigidly conventional

**up–to–date** *adj* : current — **up–to–date•ness** *n*

**up•town** \'əp,taun\ *n* : upper part of a town or city — **uptown** *adj or adv*

**up•turn** \'əp,tərn\ *n* : improvement or increase

**up•ward** \'əpwərd\, **up•wards** \-wərdz\ *adv* **1** : in a direction from lower to higher **2** : toward a higher or greater state or number ~ *adj* : directed toward or situated in a higher place — **up•ward•ly** *adv*

**up•wind** \,əp'wind\ *adv or adj* : in the direction from which the wind is blowing

**ura•ni•um** \yu'rānēəm\ *n* : metallic radioactive chemical element

**ur•ban** \'ərbən\ *adj* : characteristic of a city

**ur•bane** \,ər'bān\ *adj* : polished in manner — **ur•ban•i•ty** \,ər'banətē\ *n*

**ur•ban•ite** \'ərbə,nīt\ *n* : city dweller

**ur•chin** \'ərchən\ *n* : mischievous youngster

**-ure** *n suffix* : act or process

**ure•thra** \yu̇'rēthrə\ *n, pl* **-thras** *or* **-thrae** \-ˌthrē\ : canal that carries off urine from the bladder — **ure•thral** \-thrəl\ *adj*

**urge** \'ərj\ *vb* **urged; urging** **1** : earnestly plead for or insist on (an action) **2** : try to persuade **3** : impel to a course of activity ～ *n* : force or impulse that moves one to action

**ur•gent** \'ərjənt\ *adj* **1** : calling for immediate attention **2** : urging insistently — **ur•gen•cy** \-jənsē\ *n* — **ur•gent•ly** *adv*

**uri•nal** \'yu̇rən°l\ *n* : receptacle to urinate in

**uri•nate** \'yu̇rəˌnāt\ *vb* **-nat•ed; -nat•ing** : discharge urine — **uri•na•tion** \ˌyu̇rə'nāshən\ *n*

**urine** \'yu̇rən\ *n* : liquid waste material from the kidneys — **uri•nary** \-əˌnerē\ *adj*

**URL** \ˌyüˌär'el\ *n* : address on the Internet

**urn** \'ərn\ *n* **1** : vaselike or cuplike vessel on a pedestal **2** : large coffee pot

**us** \'əs\ *pron, objective case of* WE

**us•able** \'yüzəbəl\ *adj* : suitable or fit for use — **us•abil•i•ty** \ˌyüzə'bilətē\ *n*

**us•age** \'yüsij, -zij\ *n* **1** : customary practice **2** : way of doing or of using something

**use** \'yüs\ *n* **1** : act or practice of putting something into action **2** : state of being used **3** : way of using **4** : privilege, ability, or power to use something **5** : utility or function **6** : occasion or need to use ～ \'yüz\ *vb* **used** \'yüzd; "used to" usu 'yüstə\; **us•ing** \'yüzin\ **1** : put into action or service **2** : consume **3** : behave toward **4** : to make use of **5** — used in the past tense with *to* to indicate a former practice — **use•ful** \'yüsfəl\ *adj* — **use•ful•ly** *adv* — **use•ful•ness** *n*

— **use•less** \'yüsləs\ *adj* — **use•less•ly** *adv* — **use•less•ness** *n* — **us•er** *n*

**used** \'yüzd\ *adj* : not new

**ush•er** \'əshər\ *n* : one who escorts people to their seats ～ *vb* : conduct to a place

**ush•er•ette** \ˌəshə'ret\ *n* : woman or girl who is an usher

**usu•al** \'yüzhəwəl\ *adj* : being what is expected according to custom or habit — **usu•al•ly** \'yüzhəwəlē\ *adv*

**usurp** \yu̇'sərp, -'zərp\ *vb* : seize and hold by force or without right — **usur•pa•tion** \ˌyüsər'pāshən, -zər-\ *n* — **usurp•er** *n*

**usu•ry** \'yüzhərē\ *n, pl* **-ries 1** : lending of money at excessive interest or the rate or amount of such interest — **usu•rer** \-zhərər\ *n* — **usu•ri•ous** \yu̇'zhu̇rēəs\ *adj*

**uten•sil** \yu̇'tensəl\ *n* **1** : eating or cooking tool **2** : useful tool

**uter•us** \'yütərəs\ *n, pl* **uteri** \-ˌrī\ : organ for containing and nourishing an unborn offspring — **uter•ine** \-ˌrīn, -rən\ *adj*

**util•i•tar•i•an** \yu̇ˌtilə'terēən\ *adj* : being or meant to be useful rather than beautiful

**util•i•ty** \yu̇'tilətē\ *n, pl* **-ties 1** : usefulness **2** : regulated business providing a public service (as electricity)

**uti•lize** \'yüt°lˌīz\ *vb* **-lized; -liz•ing** : make use of — **uti•li•za•tion** \ˌyüt°lə-'zāshən\ *n*

**ut•most** \'ətˌmōst\ *adj* **1** : most distant **2** : of the greatest or highest degree or amount — **utmost** *n*

**uto•pia** \yu̇'tōpēə\ *n* : place of ideal perfection — **uto•pi•an** \-pēən\ *adj or n*

**ut•ter** \'ətər\ *adj* : absolute ～ *vb* : express with the voice — **ut•ter•er** \-ərər\ *n* — **ut•ter•ly** *adv*

**ut•ter•ance** \'ətərəns\ *n* : what one says

# V

**v** \'vē\ *n, pl* **v's** *or* **vs** \'vēz\ : 22d letter of the alphabet

**va•can•cy** \'vākənsē\ *n, pl* **-cies 1** : state of being vacant **2** : unused or unoccupied place or office

**va•cant** \-kənt\ *adj* **1** : not occupied, filled, or in use **2** : devoid of thought or expression — **va•cant•ly** *adv*

**va•cate** \-ˌkāt\ *vb* **-cat•ed; -cat•ing 1** : annul **2** : leave unfilled or unoccupied

**va·ca·tion** \vā'kāshən, və-\ *n* : period of rest from routine — **vacation** *vb* — **va·ca·tion·er** *n*

**vac·ci·nate** \'vaksə,nāt\ *vb* -nat·ed; -nat·ing : administer a vaccine usu. by injection

**vac·ci·na·tion** \,vaksə'nāshən\ *n* : act of or the scar left by vaccinating

**vac·cine** \vak'sēn, 'vak,-\ *n* : substance to induce immunity to a disease

**vac·il·late** \'vasə,lāt\ *vb* -lat·ed; -lat·ing : waver between courses or opinions — **vac·il·la·tion** \,vasə'lāshən\ *n*

**vac·u·ous** \'vakyəwəs\ *adj* 1 : empty 2 : dull or inane — **va·cu·ity** \va-'kyüətē, və-\ *n* — **vac·u·ous·ly** *adv* — **vac·u·ous·ness** *n*

**vac·u·um** \'vak,yüm, -yəm\ *n, pl* **vac·u·ums** *or* **vac·ua** \-yəwə\ : empty space with no air ∼ *vb* : clean with a vacuum cleaner

**vacuum cleaner** *n* : appliance that cleans by suction

**vag·a·bond** \'vagə,bänd\ *n* : wanderer with no home — **vagabond** *adj*

**va·ga·ry** \'vāgərē, və'gerē\ *n, pl* -ries : whim

**va·gi·na** \və'jīnə\ *n, pl* -nae \-,nē\ *or* -nas : canal that leads out from the uterus — **vag·i·nal** \'vajən²l\ *adj*

**va·grant** \'vāgrənt\ *n* : person with no home and no job — **va·gran·cy** \-grənsē\ *n* — **vagrant** *adj*

**vague** \'vāg\ *adj* **vagu·er; vagu·est** : not clear, definite, or distinct — **vague·ly** *adv* — **vague·ness** *n*

**vain** \'vān\ *adj* 1 : of no value 2 : unsuccessful 3 : conceited — **vain·ly** *adv*

**va·lance** \'valəns, 'väl-\ *n* : border drapery

**vale** \'vāl\ *n* : valley

**vale·dic·to·ri·an** \,valə,dik'tōrēən\ *n* : student giving the farewell address at commencement

**vale·dic·to·ry** \-'diktərē\ *adj* : bidding farewell — **valedictory** *n*

**va·lence** \'vāləns\ *n* : degree of combining power of a chemical element

**val·en·tine** \'valən,tīn\ *n* : sweetheart or a card sent to a sweetheart or friend on St. Valentine's Day

**va·let** \'valət, 'val,ā, va'lā\ *n* : male personal servant

**val·iant** \'valyənt\ *adj* : brave or heroic — **val·iant·ly** *adv*

**val·id** \'valəd\ *adj* 1 : proper and legally binding 2 : founded on truth or fact — **va·lid·i·ty** \və'lidətē, va-\ *n* — **val·id·ly** *adv*

**val·i·date** \'valə,dāt\ *vb* -dat·ed; -dat·ing : establish as valid — **val·i·da·tion** \,valə'dāshən\ *n*

**va·lise** \və'lēs\ *n* : suitcase

**val·ley** \'valē\ *n, pl* -leys : long depression between ranges of hills

**val·or** \'valər\ *n* : bravery or heroism — **val·or·ous** \'valərəs\ *adj*

**valu·able** \'valyəwəbəl\ *adj* 1 : worth a lot of money 2 : being of great importance or use — **valuable** *n*

**val·u·a·tion** \,valyə'wāshən\ *n* 1 : act or process of valuing 2 : market value of a thing

**val·ue** \'valyü\ *n* 1 : fair return or equivalent for something exchanged 2 : how much something is worth 3 : distinctive quality (as of a color or sound) 4 : guiding principle or ideal — usu. pl. ∼ *vb* **val·ued; valu·ing** 1 : estimate the worth of 2 : appreciate the importance of — **val·ue·less** *adj* — **val·u·er** *n*

**valve** \'valv\ *n* : structure or device to control flow of a liquid or gas — **valved** \'valvd\ *adj* — **valve·less** *adj*

**vam·pire** \'vam,pīr\ *n* 1 : legendary night-wandering dead body that sucks human blood 2 : bat that feeds on the blood of animals

¹**van** \'van\ *n* : vanguard

²**van** *n* : enclosed truck

**va·na·di·um** \və'nādēəm\ *n* : soft ductile metallic chemical element

**van·dal** \'vand²l\ *n* : person who willfully defaces or destroys property — **van·dal·ism** \-,izəm\ *n* — **van·dal·ize** \-,īz\ *vb*

**vane** \'vān\ *n* : bladelike device designed to be moved by force of the air or water

**van·guard** \'van,gärd\ *n* 1 : troops moving at the front of an army 2 : forefront of an action or movement

**va·nil·la** \və'nilə\ *n* : a flavoring made from the pods of a tropical orchid or this orchid

**van·ish** \'vanish\ *vb* : disappear suddenly

**van·i·ty** \'vanətē\ *n, pl* -ties 1 : futility or something that is futile 2 : undue pride in oneself 3 : makeup case or table

**van·quish** \'vaŋkwish, 'van-\ *vb* 1

: overcome in battle or in a contest **2** : gain mastery over

**van•tage** \'vantij\ *n* : position of advantage or perspective

**va•pid** \'vapəd, 'vāpəd\ *adj* : lacking spirit, liveliness, or zest — **va•pid•i•ty** \va'pidətē\ *n* — **vap•id•ly** \'vapədlē\ *adv* — **vap•id•ness** *n*

**va•por** \'vāpər\ *n* **1** : fine separated particles floating in and clouding the air **2** : gaseous form of an ordinarily liquid substance — **va•por•ous** \-pərəs\ *adj*

**va•por•ize** \'vāpə,rīz\ *vb* -**ized;** -**iz•ing** : convert into vapor — **va•por•i•za•tion** \,vāpərə'zāshən\ *n* — **va•por•iz•er** *n*

**var•i•able** \'verēəbəl\ *adj* : apt to vary — **var•i•abil•i•ty** \,verēə'bilətē\ *n* — **var•i•able** *n* — **var•i•ably** *adv*

**var•i•ance** \'verēəns\ *n* **1** : instance or degree of variation **2** : disagreement or dispute **3** : legal permission to build contrary to a zoning law

**var•i•ant** \-ənt\ *n* : something that differs from others of its kind — **variant** *adj*

**vari•a•tion** \,verē'āshən\ *n* : instance or extent of varying

**var•i•cose** \'varə,kōs\ *adj* : abnormally swollen and dilated

**var•ied** \'verēd\ *adj* : showing variety — **var•ied•ly** *adv*

**var•ie•gat•ed** \'verēə,gātəd\ *adj* : having patches, stripes, or marks of different colors — **var•ie•gate** \-,gāt\ *vb* — **var•ie•ga•tion** \,verēə'gāshən\ *n*

**va•ri•ety** \və'rīətē\ *n, pl* -**et•ies 1** : state of being different **2** : collection of different things **3** : something that differs from others of its kind

**var•i•ous** \'verēəs\ *adj* : being many and unlike — **var•i•ous•ly** *adv*

**var•nish** \'värnish\ *n* : liquid that dries to a hard glossy protective coating ~ *vb* : cover with varnish

**var•si•ty** \'värsətē\ *n, pl* -**ties** : principal team representing a school

**vary** \'verē\ *vb* **var•ied; vary•ing 1** : alter **2** : make or be of different kinds

**vas•cu•lar** \'vaskyələr\ *adj* : relating to a channel for the conveyance of a body fluid (as blood or sap)

**vase** \'vās, 'vāz\ *n* : tall usu. ornamental container to hold flowers

**vas•sal** \'vasəl\ *n* **1** : one acknowledging another as feudal lord **2** : one in

a dependent position — **vas•sal•age** \-əlij\ *n*

**vast** \'vast\ *adj* : very great in size, extent, or amount — **vast•ly** *adv* — **vast•ness** *n*

**vat** \'vat\ *n* : large tub- or barrel-shaped container

**vaude•ville** \'vódvəl, 'väd-, 'vōd-, -,vil, -əvəl, -ə,vil\ *n* : stage entertainment of unrelated acts

¹**vault** \'vólt\ *n* **1** : masonry arch **2** : usu. underground storage or burial room ~ *vb* : form or cover with a vault — **vault•ed** *adj* — **vaulty** *adj*

²**vault** *vb* : spring over esp. with the help of the hands or a pole ~ *n* : act of vaulting — **vault•er** *n*

**veal** \'vēl\ *n* : flesh of a young calf

**veer** \'vir\ *vb* : change course esp. gradually — **veer** *n*

**veg•e•ta•ble** \'vejtəbəl, 'vejə-\ *adj* **1** : relating to or obtained from plants **2** : like that of a plant ~ *n* **1** : plant **2** : plant grown for food

**veg•e•tar•i•an** \,vejə'terēən\ *n* : person who eats no meat — **vegetarian** *adj* — **veg•e•tar•i•an•ism** \-ēə,nizəm\ *n*

**veg•e•tate** \'vejə,tāt\ *vb* -**tat•ed;** -**tat•ing** : lead a dull inert life

**veg•e•ta•tion** \,vejə'tāshən\ *n* : plant life — **veg•e•ta•tion•al** \-shənəl\ *adj* — **veg•e•ta•tive** \'vejə,tātiv\ *adj*

**ve•he•ment** \'vēəmənt\ *adj* : showing strong esp. violent feeling — **ve•he•mence** \-məns\ *n* — **ve•he•ment•ly** *adv*

**ve•hi•cle** \'vē,hikəl, 'vēəkəl\ *n* **1** : medium through which something is expressed, applied, or administered **2** : structure for transporting something esp. on wheels — **ve•hic•u•lar** \vē-'hikyələr\ *adj*

**veil** \'vāl\ *n* **1** : sheer material to hide something or to cover the face and head **2** : something that hides ~ *vb* : cover with a veil

**vein** \'vān\ *n* **1** : rock fissure filled with deposited mineral matter **2** : vessel that carries blood toward the heart **3** : sap-carrying tube in a leaf **4** : distinctive element or style of expression — **veined** \'vānd\ *adj*

**ve•loc•i•ty** \və'läsətē\ *n, pl* -**ties** : speed

**ve•lour, ve•lours** \və'lúr\ *n, pl* **velours** \-'lúrz\ : fabric with a velvetlike pile

**vel•vet** \'velvət\ *n* : fabric with a short soft pile — **velvet** *adj* — **vel•vety** *adj*

**ve·nal** \'vēn°l\ *adj* : capable of being corrupted esp. by money — **ve·nal·i·ty** \vi'nalətē\ *n* — **ve·nal·ly** *adv*

**vend** \'vend\ *vb* : sell — **vend·ible** *adj* — **ven·dor** \'vendər\ *n*

**ven·det·ta** \ven'detə\ *n* : feud marked by acts of revenge

**ve·neer** \və'nir\ *n* **1** : thin layer of fine wood glued over a cheaper wood **2** : superficial display ~ *vb* : overlay with a veneer

**ven·er·a·ble** \'venərəbəl\ *adj* : deserving of respect

**ven·er·ate** \'venə,rāt\ *vb* -**at·ed**; -**at·ing** : respect esp. with reverence — **ven·er·a·tion** \,venə'rāshən\ *n*

**ve·ne·re·al disease** \və'nirēəl-\ *n* : contagious disease spread through copulation

**ven·geance** \'venjəns\ *n* : punishment in retaliation for an injury or offense

**venge·ful** \'venjfəl\ *adj* : filled with a desire for revenge — **venge·ful·ly** *adv*

**ve·nial** \'vēnēəl\ *adj* : capable of being forgiven

**ven·i·son** \'venəsən, -əzən\ *n* : deer meat

**ven·om** \'venəm\ *n* **1** : poison secreted by certain animals **2** : ill will — **ven·om·ous** \-əməs\ *adj*

**vent** \'vent\ *vb* **1** : provide with or let out at a vent **2** : give expression to ~ *n* : opening for passage or for relieving pressure

**ven·ti·late** \'vent°l,āt\ *vb* -**lat·ed**; -**lat·ing** : allow fresh air to circulate through — **ven·ti·la·tion** \,vent°l'āshən\ *n* — **ven·ti·la·tor** \'vent°l,ātər\ *n*

**ven·tri·cle** \'ventrikəl\ *n* : heart chamber that pumps blood into the arteries

**ven·tril·o·quist** \ven'trilə,kwist\ *n* : one who can make the voice appear to come from another source — **ven·tril·o·quism** \-,kwizəm\ *n* — **ven·tril·o·quy** \-kwē\ *n*

**ven·ture** \'venchər\ *vb* -**tured**; -**tur·ing** **1** : risk or take a chance on **2** : put forward (an opinion) ~ *n* : speculative business enterprise

**ven·ture·some** \-səm\ *adj* : brave or daring — **ven·ture·some·ly** *adv* — **ven·ture·some·ness** *n*

**ven·ue** \'venyü\ *n* : scene of an action or event

**ve·rac·i·ty** \və'rasətē\ *n*, *pl* -**ties** : truthfulness or accuracy — **ve·ra·cious** \və'rāshəs\ *adj*

**ve·ran·da**, **ve·ran·dah** \və'randə\ *n* : large open porch

**verb** \'vərb\ *n* : word that expresses action or existence

**ver·bal** \'vərbəl\ *adj* **1** : having to do with or expressed in words **2** : oral **3** : relating to or formed from a verb — **ver·bal·i·za·tion** \,vərbələ'zāshən\ *n* — **ver·bal·ize** \'vərbə,līz\ *vb* — **ver·bal·ly** \-ē\ *adv*

**verbal auxiliary** *n* : auxiliary verb

**ver·ba·tim** \vər'bātəm\ *adv or adj* : using the same words

**ver·biage** \'vərbēij\ *n* : excess of words

**ver·bose** \vər'bōs\ *adj* : using more words than are needed — **ver·bos·i·ty** \-'bäsətē\ *n*

**ver·dant** \'vərd°nt\ *adj* : green with growing plants — **ver·dant·ly** *adv*

**ver·dict** \'vərdikt\ *n* : decision of a jury

**ver·dure** \'vərjər\ *n* : green growing vegetation or its color

**verge** \'vərj\ *vb* **verged**; **verg·ing** : be almost on the point of happening or doing something ~ *n* **1** : edge **2** : threshold

**ver·i·fy** \'verə,fī\ *vb* -**fied**; -**fy·ing** : establish the truth, accuracy, or reality of — **ver·i·fi·able** *adj* — **ver·i·fi·ca·tion** \,verəfə'kāshən\ *n*

**ver·i·ly** \'verəlē\ *adv* : truly or confidently

**veri·si·mil·i·tude** \,verəsə'milə,tüd\ *n* : appearance of being true

**ver·i·ta·ble** \'verətəbəl\ *adj* : actual or true — **ver·i·ta·bly** *adv*

**ver·i·ty** \'verətē\ *n*, *pl* -**ties** : truth

**ver·mi·cel·li** \,vərmə'chelē, -'sel-\ *n* : thin spaghetti

**ver·min** \'vərmən\ *n*, *pl* **vermin** : small animal pest

**ver·mouth** \vər'müth\ *n* : dry or sweet wine flavored with herbs

**ver·nac·u·lar** \vər'nakyələr\ *adj* : relating to a native language or dialect and esp. its normal spoken form ~ *n* : vernacular language

**ver·nal** \'vərn°l\ *adj* : relating to spring

**ver·sa·tile** \'vərsət°l\ *adj* : having many abilities or uses — **ver·sa·til·i·ty** \,vərsə'tilətē\ *n*

**¹verse** \'vərs\ *n* **1** : line or stanza of poetry **2** : poetry **3** : short division of a chapter in the Bible

**²verse** *vb* **versed**; **versing** : make familiar by experience, study, or practice

**ver·sion** \'vərzhən\ *n* **1** : translation of the Bible **2** : account or description from a particular point of view

**ver·sus** \'vərsəs\ *prep* : opposed to or against

**ver•te•bra** \'vərtəbrə\ *n, pl* **-brae** \-,brā, -,brē\ *or* **-bras** : segment of the backbone — **ver•te•bral** \vər'tēbrəl, 'vərtə-\ *adj*

**ver•te•brate** \'vərtəbrət, -,brāt\ *n* : animal with a backbone — **verte•brate** *adj*

**ver•tex** \'vər,teks\ *n, pl* **ver•ti•ces** \'vərtə,sēz\ 1 : point of intersection of lines or surfaces 2 : highest point

**ver•ti•cal** \'vərtikəl\ *adj* : rising straight up from a level surface — **vertical** *n* — **ver•ti•cal•i•ty** \,vərtə-'kalətē\ *n* — **ver•ti•cal•ly** *adv*

**ver•ti•go** \'vərti,gō\ *n, pl* **-goes** *or* **-gos** : dizziness

**verve** \'vərv\ *n* : liveliness or vividness

**very** \'verē\ *adj* **veri•er; -est** 1 : exact 2 : exactly suitable 3 : mere or bare 4 : precisely the same — *adv* 1 : to a high degree 2 : in actual fact

**ves•i•cle** \'vesikəl\ *n* : membranous cavity — **ve•sic•u•lar** \və'sikyələr\ *adj*

**ves•pers** \'vespərz\ *n pl* : late afternoon or evening worship service

**ves•sel** \'vesəl\ *n* 1 : a container (as a barrel, bottle, bowl, or cup) for a liquid 2 : craft for navigation esp. on water 3 : tube in which a body fluid is circulated

¹**vest** \'vest\ *vb* 1 : give a particular authority, right, or property to 2 : clothe with or as if with a garment

²**vest** *n* : sleeveless garment usu. worn under a suit coat

**ves•ti•bule** \'vestə,byül\ *n* : enclosed entrance — **ves•tib•u•lar** \ve'sti-byələr\ *adj*

**ves•tige** \'vestij\ *n* : visible trace or remains — **ves•ti•gial** \ve'stijēəl\ *adj* — **ves•ti•gial•ly** *adv*

**vest•ment** \'vestmənt\ *n* : clergy member's garment

**ves•try** \'vestrē\ *n, pl* **-tries** : church storage room for garments and articles

**vet•er•an** \'vetərən\ *n* 1 : former member of the armed forces 2 : person with long experience — **veteran** *adj*

**Veterans Day** *n* : 4th Monday in October or formerly November 11 observed as a legal holiday in commemoration of the end of war in 1918 and 1945

**vet•er•i•nar•i•an** \,vetərən'erēən\ *n*

: doctor of animals — **vet•er•i•nary** \'vetərən,erē\ *adj*

**ve•to** \'vētō\ *n, pl* **-toes** 1 : power to forbid and esp. the power of a chief executive to prevent a bill from becoming law 2 : exercise of the veto — *vb* 1 : forbid 2 : reject a legislative bill

**vex** \'veks\ *vb* **vexed; vex•ing** : trouble, distress, or annoy — **vex•a•tion** \vek'sāshən\ *n* — **vex•a•tious** \-shəs\ *adj*

**via** \'vīə, 'vēə\ *prep* : by way of

**vi•a•ble** \'vīəbəl\ *adj* 1 : capable of surviving or growing 2 : practical or workable — **vi•a•bil•i•ty** \,vīə'bilətē\ *n* — **vi•a•bly** \'vīəblē\ *adv*

**via•duct** \'vīə,dəkt\ *n* : elevated roadway or railway bridge

**vi•al** \'vīəl\ *n* : small bottle

**vi•brant** \'vībrənt\ *adj* 1 : vibrating 2 : pulsing with vigor or activity 3 : sounding from vibration — **vi•bran•cy** \-brənsē\ *n*

**vi•brate** \'vī,brāt\ *vb* **-brat•ed; -brat•ing** 1 : move or cause to move quickly back and forth or side to side 2 : respond sympathetically — **vi•bra•tion** \vī'brāshən\ *n* — **vi•bra•tor** \'vī-,brātər\ *n* — **vi•bra•tory** \'vībrə-,tōrē\ *adj*

**vic•ar** \'vikər\ *n* : parish clergy member — **vi•car•i•ate** \-ēət\ *n*

**vi•car•i•ous** \vī'karēəs\ *adj* : sharing in someone else's experience through imagination or sympathetic feelings — **vi•car•i•ous•ly** *adv* — **vi•car•i•ous•ness** *n*

**vice** \'vīs\ *n* 1 : immoral habit 2 : depravity

**vice-** \,vīs\ *prefix* : one that takes the place of

**vice admiral** *n* : commissioned officer in the navy or coast guard ranking above a rear admiral

**vice•roy** \'vīs,rȯi\ *n* : provincial governor who represents the sovereign

**vice ver•sa** \,vīsi'vərsə, ,vīs'vər-\ *adv* : with the order reversed

**vi•cin•i•ty** \və'sinətē\ *n, pl* **-ties** : surrounding area

**vi•cious** \'vishəs\ *adj* 1 : wicked 2

---

**List of self-explanatory words with the prefix** *vice-*

| | | |
|---|---|---|
| vice–chancellor | vice presidency | vice presidential |
| vice–consul | vice president | vice–regent |

: savage **3** : malicious — **vi•cious•ly** adv — **vi•cious•ness** n

**vi•cis•si•tude** \və'sisə,tüd, vī-, -,tyüd\ n : irregular, unexpected, or surprising change — usu. used in pl.

**vic•tim** \'viktəm\ n : person killed, hurt, or abused

**vic•tim•ize** \'viktə,mīz\ vb -ized; -iz•ing : make a victim of — **vic•tim•i•za•tion** \,viktəmə'zāshən\ n — **vic•tim•iz•er** \'viktə,mīzər\ n

**vic•tor** \'viktər\ n : winner

**Vic•to•ri•an** \vik'tōrēən\ adj : relating to the reign of Queen Victoria of England or the art, taste, or standards of her time ~ n : one of the Victorian period

**vic•to•ri•ous** \vik'tōrēəs\ adj : having won a victory — **vic•to•ri•ous•ly** adv

**vic•to•ry** \'viktərē\ n, pl -ries : success in defeating an enemy or opponent or in overcoming difficulties

**vict•uals** \'vit³lz\ n pl : food

**vid•eo** \'vidē,ō\ adj : relating to the television image

**vid•eo•cas•sette** \,vidē,ōkə'set\ n : cassette containing videotape

**vid•eo•tape** \'vidēō,tāp\ vb : make a recording of (a television production) on special tape — **videotape** n

**vie** \'vī\ vb vied; vy•ing : contend — **vi•er** \'vīər\ n

**view** \'vyü\ n **1** : process of seeing or examining **2** : opinion **3** : area of landscape that can be seen **4** : range of vision **5** : purpose or object ~ vb **1** : look at **2** : think about or consider — **view•er** n

**view•point** n : position from which something is considered

**vig•il** \'vijəl\ n **1** : day of devotion before a religious feast **2** : act or time of keeping awake **3** : long period of keeping watch (as over a sick or dying person)

**vig•i•lant** \'vijələnt\ adj : alert esp. to avoid danger — **vig•i•lance** \-ləns\ n — **vig•i•lant•ly** adv

**vig•i•lan•te** \,vijə'lantē\ n : one of a group independent of the law working to suppress crime

**vi•gnette** \vin'yet\ n : short descriptive literary piece

**vig•or** \'vigər\ n **1** : energy or strength **2** : intensity or force — **vig•or•ous** \'vigərəs\ adj — **vig•or•ous•ly** adv — **vig•or•ous•ness** n

**vile** \'vīl\ adj vil•er; vil•est : thoroughly bad or contemptible — **vile•ly** adv — **vile•ness** n

**vil•i•fy** \'vilə,fī\ vb -fied; -fy•ing : speak evil of — **vil•i•fi•ca•tion** \,viləfə'kāshən\ n — **vil•i•fi•er** \'vilə,fīər\ n

**vil•la** \'vilə\ n : country estate

**vil•lage** \'vilij\ n : small country town — **vil•lag•er** n

**vil•lain** \'vilən\ n : bad person — **vil•lain•ess** \-ənəs\ n — **vil•lainy** n

**vil•lain•ous** \-ənəs\ adj : evil or corrupt — **vil•lain•ous•ly** adv — **vil•lain•ous•ness** n

**vim** \'vim\ n : energy

**vin•di•cate** \'vində,kāt\ vb -cat•ed; -cat•ing **1** : avenge **2** : exonerate **3** : justify — **vin•di•ca•tion** \,vində'kāshən\ n — **vin•di•ca•tor** \'vində,kātər\ n

**vin•dic•tive** \vin'diktiv\ adj : seeking or meant for revenge — **vin•dic•tive•ly** adv — **vin•dic•tive•ness** n

**vine** \'vīn\ n : climbing or trailing plant

**vin•e•gar** \'vinigər\ n : acidic liquid obtained by fermentation — **vin•e•gary** \-gərē\ adj

**vine•yard** \'vinyərd\ n : plantation of grapevines

**vin•tage** \'vintij\ n **1** : season's yield of grapes or wine **2** : period of origin ~ adj : of enduring interest

**vi•nyl** \'vīn³l\ n : strong plastic

**vi•o•la** \vē'ōlə\ n : instrument of the violin family tuned lower than the violin — **vi•o•list** \-list\ n

**vi•o•late** \'vīə,lāt\ vb -lat•ed; -lat•ing **1** : act with disrespect or disregard of **2** : rape **3** : desecrate — **vi•o•la•tion** \,vīə'lāshən\ n — **vi•o•la•tor** \'vīə,lātər\ n

**vi•o•lence** \'vīələns\ n : intense physical force that causes or is intended to cause injury or destruction — **vi•o•lent** \-lənt\ adj — **vi•o•lent•ly** adv

**vi•o•let** \'vīələt\ n **1** : small flowering plant **2** : reddish blue

**vi•o•lin** \,vīə'lin\ n : bowed stringed instrument — **vi•o•lin•ist** \-nist\ n

**VIP** \,vē,ī'pē\ n, pl **VIPs** \-'pēz\ : very important person

**vi•per** \'vīpər\ n **1** : venomous snake **2** : treacherous or malignant person

**vi•ra•go** \və'rägō, -'rā-; 'virə,gō\ n, pl -goes or -gos : shrew

**vi•ral** \'vīrəl\ adj : relating to or caused by a virus

**vir•gin** \'vərjən\ n **1** : unmarried woman **2** : a person who has never had sexual intercourse ~ *adj* **1** : chaste **2** : natural and unspoiled — **vir·gin·al** \-əl\ *adj* — **vir·gin·al·ly** *adv* — **vir·gin·i·ty** \vər'jinətē\ *n*

**vir·gule** \'vərgyül\ *n* : mark/used esp. to denote "or" or "per"

**vir·ile** \'virəl\ *adj* : masculine — **vi·ril·i·ty** \və'rilətē\ *n*

**vir·tu·al** \'vərchəwəl\ *adj* : being in effect but not in fact or name — **vir·tu·al·ly** *adv*

**vir·tue** \'vərchü\ *n* **1** : moral excellence **2** : effective or commendable quality **3** : chastity

**vir·tu·os·i·ty** \,vərchə'wäsətē\ *n, pl* **-ties** : great skill (as in music)

**vir·tu·o·so** \,vərchə'wōsō, -zō\ *n, pl* **-sos** *or* **-si** \-,sē, -,zē\ : highly skilled performer esp. of music — **virtuoso** *adj*

**vir·tu·ous** \'vərchəwəs\ *adj* **1** : morally good **2** : chaste — **vir·tu·ous·ly** *adv*

**vir·u·lent** \'virələnt, -yələnt\ *adj* **1** : extremely severe or infectious **2** : full of malice — **vir·u·lence** \-ləns\ *n* — **vir·u·lent·ly** *adv*

**vi·rus** \'vīrəs\ *n* **1** : tiny disease-causing agent **2** : a computer program that performs a malicious action (as destroying data)

**vi·sa** \'vēzə, -sə\ *n* : authorization to enter a foreign country

**vis·age** \'vizij\ *n* : face

**vis·cera** \'visərə\ *n pl* : internal bodily organs esp. of the trunk

**vis·cer·al** \'visərəl\ *adj* **1** : bodily **2** : instinctive **3** : deeply or crudely emotional — **vis·cer·al·ly** *adv*

**vis·cid** \'visəd\ *adj* : viscous — **vis·cid·i·ty** \vis'idətē\ *n*

**vis·count** \'vī,kaunt\ *n* : British nobleman ranking below an earl and above a baron

**vis·count·ess** \-əs\ *n* **1** : wife of a viscount **2** : woman with rank of a viscount

**vis·cous** \'viskəs\ *adj* : having a thick or sticky consistency — **vis·cos·i·ty** \vis'käsətē\ *n*

**vise** \'vīs\ *n* : device for clamping something being worked on

**vis·i·bil·i·ty** \,vizə'bilətē\ *n, pl* **-ties** : degree or range to which something can be seen

**vis·i·ble** \'vizəbəl\ *adj* **1** : capable of being seen **2** : manifest or apparent — **vis·i·bly** *adv*

**vi·sion** \'vizhən\ *n* **1** : vivid picture

seen in a dream or trance or in the imagination **2** : foresight **3** : power of seeing ~ *vb* : imagine

**vi·sion·ary** \'vizhə,nerē\ *adj* **1** : given to dreaming or imagining **2** : illusory **3** : not practical ~ *n* : one with great dreams or projects

**vis·it** \'vizət\ *vb* **1** : go or come to see **2** : stay with for a time as a guest **3** : cause or be a reward, affliction, or punishment ~ *n* : short stay as a guest — **vis·it·able** *adj* — **vis·i·tor** \-ər\ *n*

**vis·i·ta·tion** \,vizə'tāshən\ *n* **1** : official visit **2** : divine punishment or favor **3** : severe trial

**vi·sor** \'vīzər\ *n* **1** : front piece of a helmet **2** : part (as on a cap or car windshield) that shades the eyes

**vis·ta** \'vistə\ *n* : distant view

**vi·su·al** \'vizhəwəl\ *adj* **1** : relating to sight **2** : visible — **vi·su·al·ly** *adv*

**vi·su·al·ize** \'vizhəwə,līz\ *vb* **-ized; -iz·ing** : form a mental image of — **vi·su·al·i·za·tion** \,vizhəwələ'zāshən\ *n* — **vi·su·al·iz·er** \'vizhəwə,līzər\ *n*

**vi·tal** \'vītəl\ *adj* **1** : relating to, necessary for, or characteristic of life **2** : full of life and vigor **3** : fatal **4** : very important — **vi·tal·ly** *adv*

**vi·tal·i·ty** \vī'talətē\ *n, pl* **-ties 1** : life force **2** : energy

**vital signs** *n pl* : body's pulse rate, respiration, temperature, and usu. blood pressure

**vi·ta·min** \'vītəmən\ *n* : natural organic substance essential to health

**vi·ti·ate** \'vishē,āt\ *vb* **-at·ed; -at·ing 1** : spoil or impair **2** : invalidate — **vi·ti·a·tion** \,vishē'āshən\ *n* — **vi·ti·a·tor** \'vishē,ātər\ *n*

**vit·re·ous** \'vitrēəs\ *adj* : relating to or resembling glass

**vit·ri·ol** \'vitrēəl\ *n* : something caustic, corrosive, or biting — **vit·ri·ol·ic** \,vitrē'älik\ *adj*

**vi·tu·per·ate** \vī'tüpə,rāt, və-, -'tyü-\ *vb* **-at·ed; -at·ing** : abuse in words — **vi·tu·per·a·tion** \-,tüpə'rāshən, -,tyü\ *n* — **vi·tu·per·a·tive** \-'tüpərətiv, -'tyü-, -pə,rāt-\ *adj* — **vi·tu·per·a·tive·ly** *adv*

**vi·va·cious** \və'vāshəs, vī-\ *adj* : lively — **vi·va·cious·ly** *adv* — **vi·va·cious·ness** *n* — **vi·vac·i·ty** \-'vasətē\ *n*

**viv·id** \'vivəd\ *adj* **1** : lively **2** : bril-

**liant 3** : intense or sharp — **viv·id·ly**
*adv* — **viv·id·ness** *n*

**viv·i·fy** \'vivə,fī\ *vb* **-fied; -fy·ing** : give
life or vividness to

**vivi·sec·tion** \,vivə'sekshən, 'vivə,-\
*n* : experimental operation on a living
animal

**vix·en** \'viksən\ *n* **1** : scolding woman
**2** : female fox

**vo·cab·u·lary** \vō'kabyə,lerē\ *n, pl*
**-lar·ies 1** : list or collection of words
**2** : stock of words used by a person or
about a subject

**vo·cal** \'vōkəl\ *adj* **1** : relating to or
produced by or for the voice **2**
: speaking out freely and usu. emphatically

**vocal cords** *n pl* : membranous folds in
the larynx that are important in making vocal sounds

**vo·cal·ist** \'vōkəlist\ *n* : singer

**vo·cal·ize** \-,līz\ *vb* **-ized; -iz·ing** : give
vocal expression to

**vo·ca·tion** \vō'kāshən\ *n* : regular
employment — **vo·ca·tion·al** \-shən-
əl\ *adj*

**vo·cif·er·ous** \vō'sifərəs\ *adj* : noisy
and insistent — **vo·cif·er·ous·ly** *adv*

**vod·ka** \'vädkə\ *n* : colorless distilled
grain liquor

**vogue** \'vōg\ *n* : brief but intense pop-
ularity — **vogu·ish** \'vōgish\ *adj*

**voice** \'vȯis\ *n* **1** : sound produced
through the mouth by humans and
many animals **2** : power of speaking
**3** : right of choice or opinion ~ *vb*
**voiced; voic·ing** : express in words
— **voiced** \'vȯist\ *adj*

**void** \'vȯid\ *adj* **1** : containing nothing
**2** : lacking — with *of* **3** : not legally
binding ~ *n* **1** : empty space **2**
: feeling of hollowness ~ *vb* **1** : discharge (as body waste) **2** : make (as a
contract) void — **void·able** *adj* —
**void·er** *n*

**vol·a·tile** \'välət°l\ *adj* **1** : readily vapor-
izing at a relatively low temperature
**2** : likely to change suddenly — **vol·a·
til·i·ty** \,välə'tilətē\ *n* — **vol·a·til·ize**
\'välət°l,īz\ *vb*

**vol·ca·no** \väl'kānō\ *n, pl* **-noes** *or*
**-nos** : opening in the earth's crust
from which molten rock and steam
come out — **vol·ca·nic** \-'kanik\ *adj*

**vo·li·tion** \vō'lishən\ *n* : free will —
**vo·li·tion·al** \-'lishənəl\ *adj*

**vol·ley** \'välē\ *n, pl* **-leys 1** : flight of

missiles (as arrows) **2** : simultaneous
shooting of many weapons

**vol·ley·ball** *n* : game of batting a large
ball over a net

**volt** \'vōlt\ *n* : unit for measuring the
force that moves an electric current

**volt·age** \'vōltij\ *n* : quantity of volts

**vol·u·ble** \'välyəbəl\ *adj* : fluent and
smooth in speech — **vol·u·bil·i·ty**
\,välyə'bilətē\ *n* — **vol·u·bly** \'väl-
yəblē\ *adv*

**vol·ume** \'välyəm\ *n* **1** : book **2** : space
occupied as measured by cubic units
**3** : amount **4** : loudness of a sound

**vo·lu·mi·nous** \və'lümənəs\ *adj* : large
or bulky

**vol·un·tary** \'välən,terē\ *adj* **1** : done,
made, or given freely and without ex-
pecting compensation **2** : relating to
or controlled by the will — **vol·un·
tar·i·ly** *adv*

**vol·un·teer** \,välən'tir\ *n* : person who
offers to help or work without expect-
ing payment or reward ~ *vb* **1** : offer
or give voluntarily **2** : offer oneself
as a volunteer

**vo·lup·tuous** \və'ləpchəwəs\ *adj* **1**
: luxurious **2** : having a full and sexually attractive figure — **vo·lup·tu·
ous·ly** *adv* — **vo·lup·tuous·ness** *n*

**vom·it** \'vämət\ *vb* : throw up the contents of the stomach — **vomit** *n*

**voo·doo** \'vüdü\ *n, pl* **voodoos 1** : religion derived from African polythe-
ism and involving sorcery **2** : one
who practices voodoo **3** : charm or
fetish used in voodoo — **voodoo** *adj*
— **voo·doo·ism** \-,izəm\ *n*

**vo·ra·cious** \vȯ'rāshəs, və-\ *adj*
: greedy or exceedingly hungry — **vo·
ra·cious·ly** *adv* — **vo·ra·cious·ness**
*n* — **vo·rac·i·ty** \-'rasətē\ *n*

**vor·tex** \'vȯr,teks\ *n, pl* **vor·ti·ces**
\'vȯrtə,sēz\ : whirling liquid

**vo·ta·ry** \'vōtərē\ *n, pl* **-ries 1** : devoted participant, adherent, admirer,
or worshiper

**vote** \'vōt\ *n* **1** : individual expression
of preference in choosing or reaching
a decision **2** : right to indicate one's
preference or the preference expressed ~ *vb* **vot·ed; vot·ing 1**
: cast a vote **2** : choose or defeat by
vote — **vote·less** *adj* — **vot·er** *n*

**vo·tive** \'vōtiv\ *adj* : consisting of or
expressing a vow, wish, or desire

**vouch** \'vaủch\ *vb* : give a guarantee or
personal assurance

**vouch·er** \'vaủchər\ *n* : written record

or receipt that serves as proof of a transaction

**vouch•safe** \vaùch'sāf\ *vb* **-safed; -saf•ing** : grant as a special favor

**vow** \vaù\ *n* : solemn promise to do something or to live or act a certain way — **vow** *vb*

**vow•el** \'vaùəl\ *n* **1** : speech sound produced without obstruction or friction in the mouth **2** : letter representing such a sound

**voy•age** \'vȯiij\ *n* : long journey esp. by water or through space ～ *vb* **-aged; -ag•ing** : make a voyage — **voy•ag•er** *n*

**vul•ca•nize** \'vəlkə,nīz\ *vb* **-nized; -niz•ing** : treat (as rubber) to make more elastic or stronger

**vul•gar** \'vəlgər\ *adj* **1** : relating to the common people **2** : lacking refinement **3** : offensive in manner or language — **vul•gar•ism** \-,rizəm\ *n* — **vul•gar•ize** \-,rīz\ *vb* — **vul•gar•ly** *adv*

**vul•gar•i•ty** \,vəl'garətē\ *n, pl* **-ties 1** : state of being vulgar **2** : vulgar language or act

**vul•ner•a•ble** \'vəlnərəbəl\ *adj* : susceptible to attack or damage — **vul•ner•a•bil•i•ty** \,vəlnərə'bilətē\ *n* — **vul•ner•a•bly** *adv*

**vul•ture** \'vəlchər\ *n* : large flesh-eating bird

**vul•va** \'vəlvə\ *n, pl* **-vae** \-,vē, -,vī\ : external genital parts of the female

**vying** *pres part of* VIE

# W

**w** \'dəbəl,yü\ *n, pl* **w's** *or* **ws** \-,yüz\ : 23d letter of the alphabet

**wad** \'wäd\ *n* **1** : little mass **2** : soft mass of fibrous material **3** : pliable plug to retain a powder charge **4** : considerable amount ～ *vb* **1** : form into a wad **2** : stuff with a wad

**wad•dle** \'wäd³l\ *vb* **-dled; -dling** : walk with short steps swaying from side to side — **waddle** *n*

**wade** \'wäd\ *vb* **wad•ed; wad•ing 1** : step in or through (as water) **2** : move with difficulty — **wade** *n* — **wad•er** *n*

**wa•fer** \'wāfər\ *n* **1** : thin crisp cake or cracker **2** : waferlike thing

**waf•fle** \'wäfəl\ *n* : crisped cake of batter cooked in a hinged utensil (**waffle iron**) ～ *vb* : vacillate

**waft** \'wäft, 'waft\ *vb* : cause to move lightly by wind or waves — **waft** *n*

¹**wag** \'wag\ *vb* **-gg-** : sway or swing from side to side or to and fro — **wag** *n*

²**wag** *n* : wit — **wag•gish** *adj*

**wage** \'wāj\ *vb* **waged; wag•ing** : engage in ～ *n* **1** : payment for labor or services **2** : compensation

**wa•ger** \'wājər\ *n or vb* : bet

**wag•gle** \'wagəl\ *vb* **-gled; -gling** : wag — **waggle** *n*

**wag•on** \'wagən\ *n* **1** : 4-wheeled ve-

hicle drawn by animals **2** : child's 4-wheeled cart

**waif** \'wāf\ *n* : homeless child

**wail** \'wāl\ *vb* **1** : mourn **2** : make a sound like a mournful cry — **wail** *n*

**wain•scot** \'wānskət, -,skōt, -,skät\ *n* : usu. paneled wooden lining of an interior wall — **wainscot** *vb*

**waist** \'wāst\ *n* **1** : narrowed part of the body between chest and hips **2** : waistlike part — **waist•line** *n*

**wait** \'wāt\ *vb* **1** : remain in readiness or expectation **2** : delay **3** : attend as a waiter ～ *n* **1** : concealment **2** : act or period of waiting

**wait•er** \'wātər\ *n* : person who serves others at tables

**wait•per•son** \'wāt,pərsən\ *n* : a waiter or waitress

**wait•ress** \'wātrəs\ *n* : woman who serves others at tables

**waive** \'wāv\ *vb* **waived; waiv•ing** : give up claim to

**waiv•er** \'wāvər\ *n* : act of waiving right, claim, or privilege

¹**wake** \'wāk\ *vb* **woke** \'wōk\; **wo•ken** \'wōkən\; **wak•ing 1** : keep watch **2** : bring or come back to consciousness after sleep ～ *n* **1** : state of being awake **2** : watch held over a dead body

²**wake** *n* : track left by a ship

**wake·ful** \'wākfəl\ *adj* : not sleeping or able to sleep — **wake·ful·ness** *n*

**wak·en** \'wākən\ *vb* : wake

**wale** \'wāl\ *n* : ridge on cloth

**walk** \'wók\ *vb* **1** : move or cause to move on foot **2** : pass over, through, or along by walking ~ *n* **1** : a going on foot **2** : place or path for walking **3** : distance to be walked **4** : way of living **5** : way of walking **6** : slow 4-beat gait of a horse — **walk·er** *n*

**wall** \'wól\ *n* **1** : structure for defense or for enclosing something **2** : upright enclosing part of a building or room **3** : something like a wall ~ *vb* : provide, separate, surround, or close with a wall — **walled** \'wóld\ *adj*

**wal·la·by** \'wäləbē\ *n, pl* **-bies** : small or medium-sized kangaroo

**wal·let** \'wälət\ *n* : pocketbook with compartments

**wall·flow·er** *n* **1** : mustardlike plant with showy fragrant flowers **2** : one who remains on the sidelines of social activity

**wal·lop** \'wäləp\ *n* **1** : powerful blow **2** : ability to hit hard ~ *vb* **1** : beat soundly **2** : hit hard

**wal·low** \'wälō\ *vb* **1** : roll about in deep mud **2** : indulge oneself excessively ~ *n* : place for wallowing

**wall·pa·per** *n* : decorative paper for walls — **wallpaper** *vb*

**wal·nut** \'wól,nət\ *n* **1** : nut with a furrowed shell and adherent husk **2** : tree on which this nut grows or its brown wood

**wal·rus** \'wólrəs, 'wäl-\ *n, pl* **-rus** or **-rus·es** : large seallike mammal of northern seas having ivory tusks

**waltz** \'wólts\ *n* : gliding dance to music having 3 beats to the measure or the music — **waltz** *vb*

**wam·pum** \'wämpəm\ *n* : strung shell beads used by No. American Indians as money

**wan** \'wän\ *adj* **-nn-** : sickly or pale — **wan·ly** *adv* — **wan·ness** *n*

**wand** \'wänd\ *n* : slender staff

**wan·der** \'wändər\ *vb* **1** : move about aimlessly **2** : stray **3** : become delirious — **wan·der·er** *n*

**wan·der·lust** \'wändər,ləst\ *n* : strong urge to wander

**wane** \'wän\ *vb* **waned; wan·ing** **1** : grow smaller or less **2** : lose power, prosperity, or influence — **wane** *n*

**wan·gle** \'waŋgəl\ *vb* **-gled; -gling** : obtain by sly or devious means

**want** \'wónt\ *vb* **1** : lack **2** : need **3** : desire earnestly ~ *n* **1** : deficiency **2** : dire need **3** : something wanted

**want·ing** \-iŋ\ *adj* **1** : not present or in evidence **2** : falling below standards **3** : lacking in ability ~ *prep* **1** : less or minus **2** : without

**wan·ton** \'wónt³n\ *adj* **1** : lewd **2** : having no regard for justice or for others' feelings, rights, or safety ~ *n* : lewd or immoral person ~ *vb* : be wanton — **wan·ton·ly** *adv* — **wan·ton·ness** *n*

**wa·pi·ti** \'wäpətē\ *n, pl* **-ti** or **-tis** : elk

**war** \'wór\ *n* **1** : armed fighting between nations **2** : state of hostility or conflict **3** : struggle between opposing forces or for a particular end ~ *vb* **-rr-** : engage in warfare — **war·less** \-ləs\ *adj* — **war·time** *n*

**war·ble** \'wórbəl\ *n* **1** : melodious succession of low pleasing sounds **2** : musical trill ~ *vb* **-bled; -bling** : sing or utter in a trilling way

**war·bler** \'wórblər\ *n* **1** : small thrushlike singing bird **2** : small bright-colored insect-eating bird

**ward** \'wórd\ *n* **1** : a guarding or being under guard or guardianship **2** : division of a prison or hospital **3** : electoral or administrative division of a city **4** : person under protection of a guardian or a law court ~ *vb* : turn aside — **ward·ship** *n*

**¹-ward** \wərd\ *adj suffix* **1** : that moves, tends, faces, or is directed toward **2** : that occurs or is situated in the direction of

**²-ward, -wards** *adv suffix* **1** : in a (specified) direction **2** : toward a (specified) point, position, or area

**war·den** \'wórd³n\ *n* **1** : guardian **2** : official charged with supervisory duties or enforcement of laws **3** : official in charge of a prison

**ward·er** \'wórdər\ *n* : watchman or warden

**ward·robe** \'wórd,rōb\ *n* **1** : clothes closet **2** : collection of wearing apparel

**ware** \'war\ *n* **1** : articles for sale — often pl. **2** : items of fired clay

**ware·house** \-,haùs\ *n* : place for storage of merchandise — **warehouse** *vb* — **ware·house·man** \-mən\ *n* — **ware·hous·er** \-,haùzər, -sər\ *n*

**war·fare** \'wòr‚far\ *n* **1** : military operations between enemies **2** : struggle

**war·head** \-‚hed\ *n* : part of a missile holding the explosive material

**war·like** *adj* : fond of, relating to, or used in war

**warm** \'wòrm\ *adj* **1** : having or giving out moderate or adequate heat **2** : serving to retain heat **3** : showing strong feeling **4** : giving a pleasant impression of warmth, cheerfulness, or friendliness ~ *vb* **1** : make or become warm **2** : give warmth or energy to **3** : experience feelings of affection, interest, or competent — **warm·er** *n* — **warm·ly** *adv* — **warm up** *vb* : make ready by preliminary activity

**war·mon·ger** \'wòr‚məngər, -‚män-\ *n* : one who attempts to stir up war

**warmth** \'wòrmth\ *n* **1** : quality or state of being warm **2** : enthusiasm

**warn** \'wòrn\ *vb* **1** : put on guard **2** : notify in advance — **warn·ing** \-iŋ\ *n or adj*

**warp** \'wòrp\ *n* **1** : lengthwise threads in a woven fabric **2** : twist ~ *vb* **1** : twist out of shape **2** : lead astray **3** : distort

**war·rant** \'wòrənt, 'wär-\ *n* **1** : authorization **2** : legal writ authorizing action ~ *vb* **1** : declare or maintain positively **2** : guarantee **3** : approve **4** : justify

**warrant officer** *n* **1** : officer in the armed forces ranking next below a commissioned officer **2** : commissioned officer in the navy or coast guard ranking below an ensign

**war·ran·ty** \'wòrəntē, 'wär-\ *n, pl* **-ties** : guarantee of the integrity of a product

**war·ren** \'wòrən, 'wär-\ *n* : area where rabbits are bred and kept

**war·rior** \'wòryər, 'wòrēər; 'wärē-, 'wäryər\ *n* : man engaged or experienced in warfare

**war·ship** \'wòr‚ship\ *n* : naval vessel

**wart** \'wòrt\ *n* **1** : small projection on the skin caused by a virus **2** : wartlike protuberance — **warty** *adj*

**wary** \'warē\ *adj* **war·i·er; -est** : careful in guarding against danger or deception

**was** *past 1st & 3d sing of* BE

**wash** \'wòsh, 'wäsh\ *vb* **1** : cleanse with or as if with a liquid (as water) **2** : wet thoroughly with liquid **3** : flow along the border of **4** : flow in a stream **5** : move or remove by or as if by the action of water **6** : cover or daub lightly with a liquid **7** : undergo laundering ~ *n* **1** : act of washing or being washed **2** : articles to be washed **3** : surging action of water or disturbed air — **wash·able** \-əbəl\ *adj*

**wash·board** *n* : grooved board to scrub clothes on

**wash·bowl** *n* : large bowl for water for washing hands and face

**wash·cloth** *n* : cloth used for washing one's face and body

**washed–up** \'wòsht'əp, 'wäsht-\ *adj* : no longer capable or usable

**wash·er** \'wòshər, 'wäsh-\ *n* **1** : machine for washing **2** : ring used around a bolt or screw to ensure tightness or relieve friction

**wash·ing** \'wòshiŋ, 'wäsh-\ *n* : articles to be washed

**Washington's Birthday** *n* : the 3d Monday in February or formerly February 22 observed as a legal holiday

**wash·out** *n* **1** : washing out or away of earth **2** : failure

**wash·room** *n* : bathroom

**wasp** \'wäsp, 'wòsp\ *n* : slender-bodied winged insect related to the bees and having a formidable sting

**wasp·ish** \'wäspish, 'wòs-\ *adj* : irritable

**was·sail** \'wäsəl, wä'sāl\ *n* **1** : toast to someone's health **2** : liquor drunk on festive occasions **3** : riotous drinking — **wassail** *vb*

**waste** \'wāst\ *n* **1** : sparsely settled or barren region **2** : act or an instance of wasting **3** : refuse (as garbage or rubbish) **4** : material (as feces) produced but not used by a living body ~ *vb* **wast·ed; wast·ing** **1** : ruin **2** : spend or use carelessly **3** : lose substance or energy ~ *adj* **1** : wild and uninhabited **2** : being of no further use — **wast·er** *n* — **waste·ful** \-fəl\ *adj* — **waste·ful·ly** *adv* — **waste·ful·ness** *n*

**waste·bas·ket** \-‚baskət\ *n* : receptacle for refuse

**waste·land** \-‚land, -lənd\ *n* : barren uncultivated land

**wast·rel** \'wāstrəl, 'wästrəl\ *n* : one who wastes

**watch** \'wäch, 'wòch\ *vb* **1** : be or stay awake intentionally **2** : be on the lookout for danger **3** : observe **4** : keep oneself informed about ~ *n* **1** : act of keeping awake to guard **2** : close observation **3** : one that watches **4** : period of duty on a ship or those on duty during this period **5** : timepiece carried on the person — **watch•er** *n*

**watch•dog** *n* **1** : dog kept to guard property **2** : one that protects

**watch•ful** \-fəl\ *adj* : steadily attentive — **watch•ful•ly** *adv* — **watch•ful•ness** *n*

**watch•man** \-mən\ *n* : person assigned to watch

**watch•word** *n* **1** : secret word used as a signal **2** : slogan

**wa•ter** \'wȯtər, 'wät-\ *n* **1** : liquid that descends as rain and forms rivers, lakes, and seas **2** : liquid containing or resembling water ~ *vb* **1** : supply with or get water **2** : dilute with or as if with water **3** : form or secrete watery matter

**water buffalo** *n* : common oxlike often domesticated Asian buffalo

**wa•ter•col•or** *n* **1** : paint whose liquid part is water **2** : picture made with watercolors

**wa•ter•course** *n* : stream of water

**wa•ter•cress** \-,kres\ *n* : perennial salad plant with white flowers

**wa•ter•fall** *n* : steep descent of the water of a stream

**wa•ter•fowl** *n* **1** : bird that frequents the water **2 waterfowl** *pl* : swimming game birds

**wa•ter•front** *n* : land fronting a body of water

**water lily** *n* : aquatic plant with floating leaves and showy flowers

**wa•ter•logged** \-,lȯgd, -,lägd\ *adj* : filled or soaked with water

**wa•ter•mark** *n* **1** : mark showing how high water has risen **2** : a marking in paper visible under light ~ *vb* : mark (paper) with a watermark

**wa•ter•mel•on** *n* : large fruit with sweet juicy usu. red pulp

**water moccasin** *n* : venomous snake of the southeastern U.S.

**wa•ter•pow•er** *n* : power of moving water used to run machinery

**wa•ter•proof** *adj* : not letting water through ~ *vb* : make waterproof — **wa•ter•proof•ing** *n*

**wa•ter•shed** \-,shed\ *n* : dividing ridge between two drainage areas or one of these areas

**water ski** *n* : ski used on water when the wearer is towed — **wa•ter–ski** *vb* — **wa•ter–ski•er** *n*

**wa•ter•spout** *n* **1** : pipe from which water is spouted **2** : tornado over a body of water

**wa•ter•tight** *adj* **1** : so tight as not to let water in **2** : allowing no possibility for doubt or uncertainty

**wa•ter•way** *n* : navigable body of water

**wa•ter•works** *n pl* : system by which water is supplied (as to a city)

**wa•tery** \'wȯtərē, 'wät-\ *adj* **1** : containing, full of, or giving out water **2** : being like water **3** : soft and soggy

**watt** \'wät\ *n* : unit of electric power — **watt•age** \'wätij\ *n*

**wat•tle** \'wät°l\ *n* **1** : framework of flexible branches used in building **2** : fleshy process hanging usu. about the head or neck (as of a bird) — **wat•tled** \-°ld\ *adj*

**wave** \'wāv\ *vb* **waved; wav•ing** **1** : flutter **2** : signal with the hands **3** : wave to and fro with the hand **4** : curve up and down like a wave ~ *n* **1** : moving swell on the surface of water **2** : wave-like shape **3** : waving motion **4** : surge **5** : disturbance that transfers energy from point to point — **wave•let** \-lət\ *n* — **wave•like** *adj* — **wavy** *adj*

**wave•length** \'wāv,leŋth\ *n* **1** : distance from crest to crest in the line of advance of a wave **2** : line of thought that reveals a common understanding

**wa•ver** \'wāvər\ *vb* **1** : fluctuate in opinion, allegiance, or direction **2** : flicker **3** : falter — **waver** *n* — **wa•ver•er** *n* — **wa•ver•ing•ly** *adv*

**¹wax** \'waks\ *n* **1** : yellowish plastic substance secreted by bees **2** : substance like beeswax ~ *vb* : treat or rub with wax esp. for polishing

**²wax** *vb* **1** : grow larger **2** : become

**wax•en** \'waksən\ *adj* : made of or resembling wax

**waxy** \'waksē\ *adj* **wax•i•er; -est** : made of, full of, or resembling wax

**way** \'wā\ *n* **1** : thoroughfare for travel or passage **2** : route **3** : course of action **4** : method **5** : detail **6** : usual or characteristic state of affairs **7** : condition **8** : distance **9** : progress along a course — **by the way** : in a digression — **by way of 1** : for the purpose of **2** : by the route through — **out of the way** : remote

**way•bill** *n* : paper that accompanies a

shipment and gives details of goods, route, and charges

**way·far·er** \'wā,farər\ *n* : traveler esp. on foot — **way·far·ing** \-,farin\ *adj*

**way·lay** \'wā,lā\ *vb* **-laid** \-,lād\; **-lay·ing** : lie in wait for

**way·side** *n* : side of a road

**way·ward** \'wāwərd\ *adj* **1** : following one's own capricious inclinations **2** : unpredictable

**we** \'wē\ *pron* — used of a group that includes the speaker or writer

**weak** \'wēk\ *adj* **1** : lacking strength or vigor **2** : deficient in vigor of mind or character **3** : of less than usual strength **4** : not having or exerting authority — **weak·en** \'wēkən\ *vb* — **weak·ly** *adv*

**weak·ling** \-lin\ *n* : person who is physically, mentally, or morally weak

**weak·ly** \'wēklē\ *adj* : feeble

**week·ness** \-nəs\ *n* **1** : quality or state of being weak **2** : fault **3** : object of special liking

**wealth** \'welth\ *n* **1** : abundant possessions or resources **2** : profusion

**wealthy** \'welthē\ *adj* **wealth·i·er; -est** : having wealth

**wean** \'wēn\ *vb* **1** : accustom (a young mammal) to take food by means other than nursing **2** : free from dependence

**weap·on** \'wepən\ *n* **1** : something (as a gun) that may be used to fight with **2** : means by which one contends against another — **weap·on·less** *adj*

**wear** \'war\ *vb* **wore** \'wōr\; **worn** \'wōrn\; **wear·ing** **1** : use as an article of clothing or adornment **2** : carry on the person **3** : show an appearance of **4** : decay by use or by scraping **5** : lessen the strength of **6** : endure use ~ *n* **1** : act of wearing **2** : clothing **3** : lasting quality **4** : result of use — **wear·able** \'warəbəl\ *adj* — **wear·er** *n* — **wear out** *vb* **1** : make or become useless by wear **2** : tire

**wea·ri·some** \'wirēsəm\ *adj* : causing weariness — **wea·ri·some·ly** *adv* — **wea·ri·some·ness** *n*

**wea·ry** \'wirē\ *adj* **-ri·er; -est** **1** : worn out in strength, freshness, or patience **2** : expressing or characteristic of weariness ~ *vb* **-ried; -ry·ing** : make or become weary — **wea·ri·ly** *adv* — **wea·ri·ness** *n*

**wea·sel** \'wēzəl\ *n* : small slender flesh-eating mammal

**weath·er** \'wethər\ *n* : state of the atmosphere ~ *vb* **1** : expose to or endure the action of weather **2** : endure

**weath·er-beat·en** *adj* : worn or damaged by exposure to the weather

**weath·er·man** \-,man\ *n* : one who forecasts and reports the weather

**weath·er·proof** *adj* : able to withstand exposure to weather — **weatherproof** *vb*

**weather vane** *n* : movable device that shows the way the wind blows

**weave** \'wēv\ *vb* **wove** \'wōv\ *or* **weaved; wo·ven** \'wōvən\ *or* **weaved; weav·ing** **1** : form by interlacing strands of material **2** : to make as if by weaving together parts **3** : follow a winding course ~ *n* : pattern or method of weaving — **weav·er** *n*

**web** \'web\ *n* **1** : cobweb **2** : animal or plant membrane **3** : network **4** *cap* : WORLD WIDE WEB ~ *vb* **-bb-** : cover or provide with a web — **webbed** \'webd\ *adj*

**web·bing** \'webin\ *n* : strong closely woven tape

**Web site** *n* : group of World Wide Web pages available online

**wed** \'wed\ *vb* **-dd-** **1** : marry **2** : unite

**wed·ding** \'wedin\ *n* : marriage ceremony and celebration

**wedge** \'wej\ *n* : V-shaped object used for splitting, raising, forcing open, or tightening ~ *vb* **wedged; wedg·ing** **1** : tighten or split with a wedge **2** : force into a narrow space

**wed·lock** \'wed,läk\ *n* : marriage

**Wednes·day** \'wenzdā, -dē\ *n* : 4th day of the week

**wee** \'wē\ *adj* : very small

**weed** \'wēd\ *n* : unwanted plant ~ *vb* **1** : remove weeds **2** : get rid of — **weed·er** *n* — **weedy** *adj*

**weeds** *n pl* : mourning clothes

**week** \'wēk\ *n* **1** : 7 successive days **2** : calendar period of 7 days beginning with Sunday and ending with Saturday **3** : the working or school days of the calendar week

**week·day** \'wēk,dā\ *n* : any day except Sunday and often Saturday

**week·end** \-,end\ *n* : Saturday and Sunday ~ *vb* : spend the weekend

**week·ly** \'wēklē\ *adj* : occurring, appearing, or done every week ~ *n, pl* **-lies** : weekly publication — **weekly** *adv*

**weep** \'wēp\ *vb* **wept** \'wept\; **weep-**

ing : shed tears — **weep•er** *n* —
**weepy** *adj*

**wee•vil** \'wēvəl\ *n* : small injurious
beetle with a long head usu. curved
into a snout — **wee•vily, wee•vil•ly**
\'wēvəlē\ *adj*

**weft** \'weft\ *n* : crosswise threads or
yarn in weaving

**weigh** \'wā\ *vb* **1** : determine the heaviness of **2** : have a specified weight **3**
: consider carefully **4** : raise (an anchor) off the sea floor **5** : press down
or burden

**weight** \'wāt\ *n* **1** : amount that something weighs **2** : relative heaviness **3**
: heavy object **4** : burden or pressure
**5** : importance ~ *vb* **1** : load with a
weight **2** : oppress — **weight•less**
\-ləs\ *adj* — **weight•less•ness** *n* —
**weighty** \'wātē\ *adj*

**weird** \'wird\ *adj* **1** : unearthly or mysterious **2** : strange — **weird•ly** *adv* —
**weird•ness** *n*

**wel•come** \'welkəm\ *vb* **-comed;**
**-com•ing** : accept or greet cordially
~ *adj* : received or permitted gladly
~ *n* : cordial greeting or reception

**weld** \'weld\ *vb* : unite by heating,
hammering, or pressing ~ *n* : union
by welding — **weld•er** *n*

**wel•fare** \'wel,far\ *n* **1** : prosperity **2**
: government aid for those in need

¹**well** \'wel\ *n* **1** : spring **2** : hole sunk in
the earth to obtain a natural deposit
(as of oil) **3** : source of supply **4**
: open space extending vertically
through floors ~ *vb* : flow forth

²**well** *adv* **bet•ter** \'betər\; **best** \'best\
**1** : in a good or proper manner **2** : satisfactorily **3** : fully **4** : intimately **5**
: considerably ~ *adj* **1** : satisfactory **2** : prosperous **3** : desirable **4**
: healthy

**well–adjusted** \,welə'jəstəd\ *adj* : well-
balanced

**well–ad•vised** \,weləd'vīzd\ *adj* : prudent

**well–balanced** \'wel'balənst\ *adj* **1**
: evenly balanced **2** : emotionally or
psychologically sound

**well–be•ing** \'wel'bēiŋ\ *n* : state of being happy, healthy, or prosperous

**well–bred** \-'bred\ *adj* : having good
manners

**well–done** *adj* **1** : properly performed
**2** : cooked thoroughly

**well–heeled** \-'hēld\ *adj* : financially
well-off

**well–mean•ing** *adj* : having good inten-
tions

**well–nigh** *adv* : nearly

**well–off** *adj* : being in good condition
esp. financially

**well–read** \-'red\ *adj* : well informed
through reading

**well–round•ed** \-'raundəd\ *adj* : broadly
developed

**well•spring** *n* : source

**well–to–do** \,weltə'dü\ *adj* : prosperous

**welsh** \'welsh, 'welch\ *vb* **1** : avoid
payment **2** : break one's word

**Welsh rabbit** *n* : melted often seasoned
cheese poured over toast or crackers

**Welsh rare•bit** \-'rarbət\ *n* : Welsh
rabbit

**welt** \'welt\ *n* **1** : narrow strip of leather
between a shoe upper and sole **2**
: ridge raised on the skin usu. by a
blow ~ *vb* : hit hard

**wel•ter** \'weltər\ *vb* **1** : toss about **2**
: wallow ~ *n* : confused jumble

**wen** \'wen\ *n* : abnormal growth or cyst

**wench** \'wench\ *n* : young woman

**wend** \'wend\ *vb* : direct one's course

**went** *past of* GO

**wept** *past of* WEEP

**were** *past 2d sing, past pl, or past subjunctive of* BE

**were•wolf** \'wer,wulf, 'wir-, 'wər-\ *n,
pl* **-wolves** \-,wulvz\ : person held to
be able to change into a wolf

**west** \'west\ *adv* : to or toward the west
~ *adj* : situated toward or at or coming from the west ~ *n* **1** : direction
of sunset **2** *cap* : regions to the west
— **west•er•ly** \'westərlē\ *adv or adj*
— **west•ward** \-wərd\ *adv or adj* —
**west•wards** \-wərdz\ *adv*

**west•ern** \'westərn\ *adj* **1** *cap* : of a
region designated West **2** : lying toward or coming from the west —
**West•ern•er** *n*

**wet** \'wet\ *adj* **-tt- 1** : consisting of or
covered or soaked with liquid **2** : not
dry ~ *n* : moisture ~ *vb* **-tt-** : make
or become moist — **wet•ly** *adv* —
**wet•ness** *n*

**whack** \'hwak\ *vb* : strike sharply ~ *n*
**1** : sharp blow **2** : proper working order **3** : chance **4** : try

¹**whale** \'hwāl\ *n, pl* **whales** *or* **whale**
: large marine mammal ~ *vb* **whaled;**
**whal•ing** : hunt for whales — **whale-
boat** *n* — **whal•er** *n*

²**whale** *vb* **whaled; whal•ing** : strike or
hit vigorously

**whale•bone** *n* : horny substance attached to the upper jaw of some large whales (**whalebone whales**)

**wharf** \'hwȯrf\ *n, pl* **wharves** \'hwȯrvz\ : structure alongside which boats lie to load or unload

**what** \'hwät\ *pron* **1** — used to inquire the identity or nature of something **2** : that which **3** : whatever ∼ *adv* : in what respect ∼ *adj* **1** — used to inquire about the identity or nature of something **2** : how remarkable or surprising **3** : whatever

**what•ev•er** \hwät'evər\ *pron* **1** : anything or everything that **2** : no matter what ∼ *adj* : of any kind at all

**what•not** \'hwät,nät\ *pron* : any of various other things that might be mentioned

**what•so•ev•er** \,hwätsō'evər\ *pron or adj* : whatever

**wheal** \'hwēl\ *n* : a welt on the skin

**wheat** \'hwēt\ *n* : cereal grain that yields flour — **wheat•en** *adj*

**whee•dle** \'hwēdᵊl\ *vb* **-died; -dling** : coax or tempt by flattery

**wheel** \'hwēl\ *n* **1** : disk or circular frame capable of turning on a central axis **2** : device of which the main part is a wheel ∼ *vb* **1** : convey or move on wheels or a wheeled vehicle **2** : rotate **3** : turn so as to change direction — **wheeled** *adj* — **wheel•er** *n* — **wheel•less** *adj*

**wheel•bar•row** \-,barō\ *n* : one-wheeled vehicle for carrying small loads

**wheel•base** *n* : distance in inches between the front and rear axles of an automotive vehicle

**wheel•chair** *n* : chair mounted on wheels esp. for the use of disabled persons

**wheeze** \'hwēz\ *vb* **wheezed; wheezing** : breathe with difficulty and with a whistling sound — **wheeze** *n* — **wheezy** *adj*

**whelk** \'hwelk\ *n* : large sea snail

**whelp** \'hwelp\ *n* : one of the young of various carnivorous mammals (as a dog) ∼ *vb* : bring forth whelps

**when** \'hwen\ *adv* — used to inquire about or designate a particular time ∼ *conj* **1** : at or during the time that **2** : every time that **3** : if **4** : although ∼ *pron* : what time

**whence** \'hwens\ *adv or conj* : from what place, source, or cause

**when•ev•er** \hwen'evər\ *conj or adv* : at whatever time

**where** \'hwer\ *adv* **1** : at, in, or to what place **2** : at, in, or to what situation, position, direction, circumstances, or respect ∼ *conj* **1** : at, in, or to what place, position, or circumstance **2** : at, in, or to which place ∼ *n* : place

**where•abouts** \-ə,baùts\ *adv* : about where ∼ *n sing or pl* : place where a person or thing is

**where•as** \hwer'az\ *conj* **1** : while on the contrary **2** : since

**where•by** *conj* : by, through, or in accordance with which

**where•fore** \'hwer,fōr\ *adv* **1** : why **2** : therefore ∼ *n* : reason

**where•in** \hwer'in\ *adv* : in what respect

**where•of** \-'əv, -äv\ *conj* : of what, which, or whom

**where•up•on** \'hwerə,pȯn, -,pän\ *conj* **1** : on which **2** : and then

**wher•ev•er** \hwer'evər\ *adv* : where ∼ *conj* : at, in, or to whatever place or circumstance

**where•with•al** \'hwerwith,ȯl, -with-\ *n* : resources and esp. money

**whet** \'hwet\ *vb* **-tt-** **1** : sharpen by rubbing (as with a stone) **2** : stimulate — **whet•stone** *n*

**whether** \'hwethər\ *conj* **1** : if it is or was true that **2** : if it is or was better **3** : whichever is the case

**whey** \'hwā\ *n* : watery part of sour milk

**which** \'hwich\ *adj* **1** : being what one or ones out of a group **2** : whichever ∼ *pron* **1** : which one or ones **2** : whichever

**which•ev•er** \hwich'evər\ *pron or adj* : no matter what one

**whiff** \'hwif\ *n* **1** : slight gust **2** : inhalation of odor, gas, or smoke **3** : slight trace ∼ *vb* : inhale an odor

**while** \'hwīl\ *n* **1** : period of time **2** : time and effort used ∼ *conj* **1** : during the time that **2** : as long as **3** : although ∼ *vb* **whiled; whil•ing** : cause to pass esp. pleasantly

**whim** \'hwim\ *n* : sudden wish, desire, or change of mind

**whim•per** \'hwimpər\ *vb* : cry softly — **whimper** *n*

**whim•si•cal** \'hwimzikəl\ *adj* **1** : full of whims **2** : erratic — **whim•si•cal•i•ty** \,hwimzə'kalətē\ *n* — **whim•si•cal•ly** *adv*

**whim·sy, whim·sey** \'hwimzē\ *n, pl* **-sies** *or* **-seys** **1** : whim **2** : fanciful creation

**whine** \'hwīn\ *vb* **whined; whin·ing** **1** : utter a usu. high-pitched plaintive cry **2** : complain — **whine** *n* — **whin·er** *n* — **whiny** *adj*

**whin·ny** \'hwinē\ *vb* **-nied; -ny·ing** : neigh — **whinny** *n*

**whip** \'hwip\ *vb* **-pp-** **1** : move quickly **2** : strike with something slender and flexible **3** : defeat **4** : incite **5** : beat into a froth ∼ *n* **1** : flexible device used for whipping **2** : party leader responsible for discipline **3** : thrashing motion — **whip·per** *n*

**whip·cord** *n* **1** : thin tough cord **2** : cloth made of hard-twisted yarns

**whip·lash** *n* : injury from a sudden sharp movement of the neck and head

**whip·per·snap·per** \'hwipər,snapər\ *n* : small, insignificant, or presumptuous person

**whip·pet** \'hwipət\ *n* : small swift dog often used for racing

**whip·poor·will** \'hwipər,wil\ *n* : American nocturnal bird

**whir** \'hwər\ *vb* **-rr-** : move, fly, or revolve with a whir ∼ *n* : continuous fluttering or vibratory sound

**whirl** \'hwərl\ *vb* **1** : move or drive in a circle **2** : spin **3** : move or turn quickly : reel ∼ *n* **1** : rapid circular movement **2** : state of commotion or confusion **3** : try

**whirl·pool** *n* : whirling mass of water having a depression in the center

**whirl·wind** *n* : whirling wind storm

**whisk** \'hwisk\ *n* **1** : quick light sweeping or brushing motion **2** : usu. wire kitchen implement for beating ∼ *vb* **1** : move or convey briskly **2** : beat **3** : brush lightly

**whisk broom** *n* : small broom

**whis·ker** \'hwiskər\ *n* **1** *pl* : beard **2** : long bristle or hair near an animal's mouth — **whis·kered** \-kərd\ *adj*

**whis·key, whis·ky** \'hwiskē\ *n, pl* **-keys** *or* **-kies** : liquor distilled from a fermented mash of grain

**whis·per** \'hwispər\ *vb* **1** : speak softly **2** : tell by whispering ∼ *n* **1** : soft low sound **2** : rumor

**whist** \'hwist\ *n* : card game

**whis·tle** \'hwisəl\ *n* **1** : device by which a shrill sound is produced **2** : shrill clear sound made by a whistle or through the lips ∼ *vb* **-tled; -tling**

**1** : make or utter a whistle **2** : signal or call by a whistle **3** : produce by whistling — **whis·tler** *n*

**whis·tle–blow·er** \'hwisəl,blōər\ *n* : informer

**whis·tle–stop** *n* : brief political appearance

**whit** \'hwit\ *n* : bit

**white** \'hwīt\ *adj* **whit·er; -est** **1** : free from color **2** : of the color of new snow or milk **3** : having light skin ∼ *n* **1** : color of maximum lightness **2** : white part or thing **3** : person who is light-skinned — **white·ness** *n* — **whit·ish** *adj*

**white blood cell** *n* : blood cell that does not contain hemoglobin

**white·cap** \'hwīt,kap\ *n* : wave crest breaking into white foam

**white–col·lar** *adj* : relating to salaried employees with duties not requiring protective or work clothing

**white elephant** *n* : something costly but of little use or value

**white·fish** \'hwīt,fish\ *n* : freshwater food fish

**whit·en** \'hwīt°n\ *vb* : make or become white — **whit·en·er** \'hwīt°nər\ *n*

**white slave** *n* : woman or girl held unwillingly for purposes of prostitution — **white slavery** *n*

**white·tail** \'hwīt,tāl\ *n* : No. American deer

**white·wash** *vb* **1** : whiten with a composition (as of lime and water) **2** : gloss over or cover up faults or wrongdoing — **whitewash** *n*

**whith·er** \'hwithər\ *adv* **1** : to what place **2** : to what situation, position, degree, or end

¹**whit·ing** \'hwītiŋ\ *n* : usu. light or silvery food fish

²**whiting** *n* : pulverized chalk or limestone

**whit·tle** \'hwit°l\ *vb* **-tled; -tling** **1** : pare **2** : shape by paring **3** : reduce gradually

**whiz, whizz** \'hwiz\ *vb* **-zz-** : make a sound like a speeding object — **whiz, whizz** *n*

**who** \'hü\ *pron* **1** : what or which person or persons **2** : person or persons that **3** — used to introduce a relative clause

**who·dun·it** \hü'dənət\ *n* : detective or mystery story

**who·ev·er** \hü'evər\ *pron* : no matter who

**whole** \'hōl\ *adj* **1** : being in healthy or

sound condition **2** : having all its parts or elements **3** : constituting the total sum of ~ *n* **1** : complete amount or sum **2** : something whole or entire — **on the whole 1** : considering all circumstances **2** : in general — **whole·ness** *n*

**whole·heart·ed** \'hōl'härtəd\ *adj* : sincere

**whole number** *n* : integer

**whole·sale** *n* : sale of goods in quantity usu. for resale by a retail merchant ~ *adj* **1** : of or relating to wholesaling **2** : performed on a large scale ~ *vb* -**saled; -sal·ing** : sell at wholesale — **wholesale** *adv* — **whole·sal·er** *n*

**whole·some** \-səm\ *adj* **1** : promoting mental, spiritual, or bodily health **2** : healthy — **whole·some·ness** *n*

**whole wheat** *adj* : made of ground entire wheat kernels

**whol·ly** \'hōlē\ *adv* **1** : totally **2** : solely

**whom** \'hüm\ *pron, objective case of* WHO

**whom·ev·er** \hüm'evər\ *pron, objective case of* WHOEVER

**whoop** \'hwüp, 'hwůp, 'hüp, 'hůp\ *vb* : shout loudly ~ *n* : shout

**whooping cough** *n* : infectious disease marked by convulsive coughing fits

**whop·per** \'hwäpər\ *n* **1** : something unusually large or extreme of its kind **2** : monstrous lie

**whop·ping** \'hwäpiŋ\ *adj* : extremely large

**whore** \'hōr\ *n* : prostitute

**whorl** \'hwȯrl, 'hwərl\ *n* : spiral — **whorled** *adj*

**whose** \'hüz\ *adj* : of or relating to whom or which ~ *pron* : whose one or ones

**who·so·ev·er** \ˌhüsō'evər\ *pron* : whoever

**why** \'hwī\ *adv* : for what reason, cause, or purpose ~ *conj* **1** : reason for which **2** : for which ~ *n, pl* **whys** : reason ~ *interj* — used esp. to express surprise

**wick** \'wik\ *n* : cord that draws up oil, tallow, or wax to be burned

**wick·ed** \'wikəd\ *adj* **1** : morally bad **2** : harmful or troublesome **3** : very unpleasant **4** : very impressive — **wick·ed·ly** *adv* — **wick·ed·ness** *n*

**wick·er** \'wikər\ *n* **1** : small pliant branch **2** : wickerwork — **wicker** *adj*

**wick·er·work** *n* : work made of wickers

**wick·et** \'wikət\ *n* **1** : small gate, door,

or window **2** : frame in cricket or arch in croquet

**wide** \'wīd\ *adj* **wid·er; wid·est 1** : covering a vast area **2** : measured at right angles to the length **3** : having a great measure across **4** : opened fully **5** : far from the thing in question ~ *adv* **wid·er; wid·est 1** : over a great distance **2** : so as to leave considerable space between **3** : fully — **wide·ly** *adv* — **wid·en** \'wid°n\ *vb*

**wide–awake** *adj* : alert

**wide–eyed** *adj* **1** : having the eyes wide open **2** : amazed **3** : naive

**wide·spread** *adj* : widely extended

**wid·ow** \'widō\ *n* : woman who has lost her husband by death and has not married again ~ *vb* : cause to become a widow — **wid·ow·hood** *n*

**wid·ow·er** \'widəwər\ *n* : man who has lost his wife by death and has not married again

**width** \'width\ *n* **1** : distance from side to side **2** : largeness of extent **3** : measured and cut piece of material

**wield** \'wēld\ *vb* **1** : use or handle esp. effectively **2** : exert — **wield·er** *n*

**wie·ner** \'wēnər\ *n* : frankfurter

**wife** \'wīf\ *n, pl* **wives** \'wīvz\ : married woman — **wife·hood** *n* — **wife·less** *adj* — **wife·ly** *adj*

**wig** \'wig\ *n* : manufactured covering of hair for the head

**wig·gle** \'wigəl\ *vb* -**gled; -gling 1** : move with quick jerky or shaking movements **2** : wriggle — **wiggle** *n* — **wig·gler** *n*

**wig·gly** \-əlē\ *adj* **1** : tending to wiggle **2** : wavy

**wig·wag** \'wig,wag\ *vb* : signal by a flag or light waved according to a code

**wig·wam** \'wig,wäm\ *n* : American Indian hut consisting of a framework of poles overlaid with bark, rush mats, or hides

**wild** \'wīld\ *adj* **1** : living or being in a state of nature and not domesticated or cultivated **2** : unrestrained **3** : turbulent **4** : crazy **5** : uncivilized **6** : erratic ~ *n* **1** : wilderness **2** : undomesticated state ~ *adv* : without control — **wild·ly** *adv* — **wild·ness** *n*

**wild·cat** \-ˌkat\ *n* : any of various undomesticated cats (as a lynx) ~ *adj* **1** : not sound or safe **2** : unauthorized

**wil·der·ness** \'wildərnəs\ *n* : uncultivated and uninhabited region

**wild•fire** \'wīld,fīr\ *n* : sweeping and destructive fire

**wild•fowl** *n* : game waterfowl

**wild•life** \'wīld,līf\ *n* : undomesticated animals

**wile** \'wīl\ *n* : trick to snare or deceive ～ *vb* **wiled; wil•ing** : lure

**will** \'wil\ *vb, past* **would** \'wůd\; *pres sing & pl* **will** 1 : wish 2 — used as an auxiliary verb to express (1) desire or willingness (2) customary action (3) simple future time (4) capability (5) determination (6) probability (7) inevitability or (8) a command 3 : dispose of by a will ～ *n* 1 : often determined wish 2 : act, process, or experience of willing 3 : power of controlling one's actions or emotions 4 : legal document disposing of property after death

**will•ful, wil•ful** \'wilfəl\ *adj* 1 : governed by will without regard to reason 2 : intentional — **will•ful•ly** *adv*

**will•ing** \'wiliŋ\ *adj* 1 : inclined or favorably disposed in mind 2 : prompt to act 3 : done, borne, or accepted voluntarily or without reluctance — **will•ing•ly** *adv* — **will•ing•ness** *n*

**will-o'-the-wisp** \,wiləthə'wisp\ *n* 1 : light that appears at night over marshy grounds 2 : misleading or elusive goal or hope

**wil•low** \'wilō\ *n* : quick-growing shrub or tree with flexible shoots

**wil•lowy** \'wiləwē\ *adj* : gracefully tall and slender

**will•pow•er** \'wil,paůər\ *n* : energetic determination

**wil•ly-nil•ly** \,wilē'nilē\ *adv or adj* : without regard for one's choice

**wilt** \'wilt\ *vb* 1 : lose or cause to lose freshness and become limp esp. from lack of water 2 : grow weak

**wily** \'wīlē\ *adj* **wil•i•er; -est** : full of craftiness — **wil•i•ness** *n*

**win** \'win\ *vb* **won** \'wən\; **win•ning** 1 : get possession of esp. by effort 2 : gain victory in battle or a contest 3 : make friendly or favorable ～ *n* : victory

**wince** \'wins\ *vb* **winced; winc•ing** : shrink back involuntarily — **wince** *n*

**winch** \'winch\ *n* : machine for hoisting or pulling with a drum around which rope is wound — **winch** *vb*

**¹wind** \'wind\ *n* 1 : movement of the air 2 : breath 3 : gas in the stomach or intestines 4 : air carrying a scent 5 : intimation ～ *vb* 1 : get a scent of 2 : cause to be out of breath

**²wind** \'wīnd\ *vb* **wound** \'waůnd\; **wind•ing** 1 : have or follow a curving course 2 : move or lie to encircle 3 : encircle or cover with something pliable 4 : tighten the spring of ～ *n* : turn or coil — **wind•er** *n*

**wind•break** \-,brāk\ *n* : trees and shrubs to break the force of the wind

**wind•break•er** \-,brākər\ *n* : light wind-resistant jacket

**wind•fall** \'wind,fòl\ *n* 1 : thing blown down by wind 2 : unexpected benefit

**wind instrument** *n* : musical instrument (as a flute or horn) sounded by wind and esp. by the breath

**wind•lass** \'windləs\ *n* : winch esp. for hoisting anchor

**wind•mill** \'wind,mil\ *n* : machine worked by the wind turning vanes

**win•dow** \'windō\ *n* 1 : opening in the wall of a building to let in light and air 2 : pane in a window 3 : span of time for something 4 : area of a computer display — **win•dow•less** *adj*

**win•dow-shop** *vb* : look at the displays in store windows — **win•dow-shop-per** *n*

**wind•pipe** \'wind,pīp\ *n* : passage for the breath from the larynx to the lungs

**wind•shield** \'-,shēld\ *n* : transparent screen in front of the occupants of a vehicle

**wind•up** \'wīnd,əp\ *n* : end — **wind up** *vb*

**wind•ward** \'windwərd\ *adj* : being in or facing the direction from which the wind is blowing ～ *n* : direction from which the wind is blowing

**windy** \'windē\ *adj* **wind•i•er; -est** 1 : having wind 2 : indulging in useless talk

**wine** \'wīn\ *n* 1 : fermented grape juice 2 : usu. fermented juice of a plant product (as fruit) used as a beverage ～ *vb* : treat to or drink wine

**wing** \'wiŋ\ *n* 1 : movable paired appendage for flying 2 : winglike thing 3 *pl* : area at the side of the stage out of sight 4 : faction ～ *vb* 1 : fly 2 : propel through the air — **winged** *adj* — **wing•less** *adj* — **on the wing** : in flight — **under one's wing** : in one's charge or care

**wink** \'wiŋk\ *vb* 1 : close and open the eyes quickly 2 : avoid seeing or noticing something 3 : twinkle 4 : close and open one eye quickly as a signal or hint ~ n 1 : brief sleep 2 : act of winking 3 : instant — **wink·er** n

**win·ner** \'winər\ n : one that wins

**win·ning** \-iŋ\ n 1 : victory 2 : money won at gambling ~ adj 1 : victorious 2 : charming

**win·now** \'winō\ vb 1 : remove (as chaff) by a current of air 2 : sort or separate something

**win·some** \'winsəm\ adj 1 : causing joy 2 : cheerful or gay — **win·some·ly** adv — **win·some·ness** n

**win·ter** \'wintər\ n : season between autumn and spring ~ adj : sown in autumn for harvest the next spring or summer — **win·ter·time** n

**win·ter·green** \'wintər,grēn\ n : low heathlike evergreen plant with red berries

**win·try** \'wintrē\ adj **win·tri·er; -est** 1 : characteristic of winter 2 : cold in feeling

**wipe** \'wīp\ vb **wiped; wip·ing** 1 : clean or dry by rubbing 2 : remove by rubbing 3 : erase completely 4 : destroy 5 : pass over a surface ~ n : act or instance of wiping — **wip·er** n

**wire** \'wīr\ n 1 : thread of metal 2 : work made of wire 3 : telegram or cablegram ~ vb 1 : provide with wire 2 : bind or mount with wire 3 : telegraph — **wire·less** adj

**wire·less** \-ləs\ n, chiefly Brit : radio

**wire·tap** vb : connect into a telephone or telegraph wire to get information — **wiretap** n — **wire·tap·per** n

**wir·ing** \'wīriŋ\ n : system of wires

**wiry** \'wīrē\ adj **wir·i·er** \'wīrēər\; **-est** 1 : resembling wire 2 : slender yet strong and sinewy — **wir·i·ness** n

**wis·dom** \'wizdəm\ n 1 : accumulated learning 2 : good sense

**wisdom tooth** n : last tooth on each half of each human jaw

¹**wise** \'wīz\ n : manner

²**wise** adj **wis·er; wis·est** 1 : having or showing wisdom, good sense, or good judgment 2 : aware of what is going on — **wise·ly** adv

**wise·crack** n : clever, smart, or flippant remark ~ vb : make a wisecrack

**wish** \'wish\ vb 1 : have a desire 2 : express a wish concerning 3 : request ~ n 1 : a wishing or desire 2 : expressed will or desire

**wish·bone** n : forked bone in front of the breastbone in most birds

**wish·ful** \-fəl\ adj 1 : expressive of a wish 2 : according with wishes rather than fact

**wishy–washy** \'wishē,wòshē, -,wäsh-\ adj : weak or insipid

**wisp** \'wisp\ n 1 : small bunch of hay or straw 2 : thin strand, strip, fragment, or streak 3 : something frail, slight, or fleeting — **wispy** adj

**wis·te·ria** \wis'tirēə\ n : pealike woody vine with long clusters of flowers

**wist·ful** \'wistfəl\ adj : full of longing — **wist·ful·ly** adv — **wist·ful·ness** n

**wit** \'wit\ n 1 : reasoning power 2 : mental soundness — usu. pl. 3 : quickness and cleverness in handling words and ideas 4 : talent for clever remarks or one noted for witty remarks — **wit·less** adj — **wit·less·ly** adv — **wit·less·ness** n — **wit·ted** adj

**witch** \'wich\ n 1 : person believed to have magic power 2 : ugly old woman ~ vb : bewitch

**witch·craft** \'wich,kraft\ n : power or practices of a witch

**witch·ery** \'wichərē\ n, pl **-er·ies** 1 : witchcraft 2 : charm

**witch ha·zel** \'wich,hāzəl\ n 1 : shrub having small yellow flowers in fall 2 : alcoholic lotion made from witch hazel bark

**witch–hunt** n 1 : searching out and persecution of supposed witches 2 : harassment esp. of political opponents

**with** \'with, 'with\ prep 1 : against, to, or toward 2 : in support of 3 : because of 4 : in the company of 5 : having 6 : despite 7 : containing 8 : by means of

**with·draw** \with'drò, with-\ vb **-drew** \-'drü\; **-drawn** \-'dròn\; **-draw·ing** \-'dròiŋ\ 1 : take back or away 2 : call back or retract 3 : go away 4 : terminate one's participation in or use of — **with·draw·al** \-'dròəl\ n

**with·drawn** \with'dròn\ adj : socially detached and unresponsive

**with·er** \'withər\ vb 1 : shrivel 2 : lose or cause to lose energy, force, or freshness

**with·ers** \'withərz\ n pl : ridge between the shoulder bones of a horse

**with·hold** \with'hōld, with-\ vb **-held** \-'held\; **-hold·ing** 1 : hold back 2 : refrain from giving

**with·in** \with'in, with-\ adv 1 : in or into the interior 2 : inside oneself ~

*prep* **1** : in or to the inner part of **2** : in the limits or compass of

**with·out** \with'aut, with-\ *prep* **1** : outside **2** : lacking **3** : unaccompanied or unmarked by — **without** *adv*

**with·stand** \with'stand, with-\ *vb* **-stood** \-'stud\; **-stand·ing** : oppose successfully

**wit·ness** \'witnəs\ *n* **1** : testimony **2** : one who testifies **3** : one present at a transaction to testify that it has taken place **4** : one who has personal knowledge or experience **5** : something serving as proof ~ *vb* **1** : bear witness **2** : act as legal witness of **3** : furnish proof of **4** : be a witness of **5** : be the scene of

**wit·ti·cism** \'witə,sizəm\ *n* : witty saying or phrase

**wit·ting** \'witiŋ\ *adj* : intentional — **wit·ting·ly** *adv*

**wit·ty** \'witē\ *adj* **-ti·er; -est** : marked by or full of wit — **wit·ti·ly** \'wit³lē\ *adv* — **wit·ti·ness** *n*

**wives** *pl of* WIFE

**wiz·ard** \'wizərd\ *n* **1** : magician **2** : very clever person — **wiz·ard·ry** \-ərdrē\ *n*

**wiz·ened** \'wiz³nd\ *adj* : dried up

**wob·ble** \'wäbəl\ *vb* **-bled; -bling** **1** : move or cause to move with an irregular rocking motion **2** : tremble : waver — **wobble** *n* — **wob·bly** \'wäbəlē\ *adj*

**woe** \'wō\ *n* **1** : deep suffering **2** : misfortune

**woe·be·gone** \'wōbi,gȯn\ *adj* : exhibiting woe, sorrow, or misery

**woe·ful** \'wōfəl\ *adj* **1** : full of woe **2** : bringing woe — **woe·ful·ly** *adv*

**woke** *past of* WAKE

**woken** *past part of* WAKE

**wolf** \'wu̇lf\ *n, pl* **wolves** \'wu̇lvz\ : large doglike predatory mammal ~ *vb* : eat greedily — **wolf·ish** *adj*

**wol·fram** \'wu̇lfrəm\ *n* : tungsten

**wol·ver·ine** \,wu̇lvə'rēn\ *n, pl* **-ines** : flesh-eating mammal related to the weasels

**wom·an** \'wu̇mən\ *n, pl* **wom·en** \'wimən\ **1** : adult female person **2** : womankind **3** : feminine nature — **wom·an·hood** \-,hu̇d\ *n* — **wom·an·ish** *adj*

**wom·an·kind** \-,kīnd\ *n* : females of the human race

**wom·an·ly** \-lē\ *adj* : having qualities

characteristic of a woman — **wom·an·li·ness** \-lēnəs\ *n*

**womb** \'wüm\ *n* : uterus

**won** *past of* WIN

**won·der** \'wəndər\ *n* **1** : cause of astonishment or surprise **2** : feeling (as of astonishment) aroused by something extraordinary ~ *vb* **1** : feel surprise **2** : feel curiosity or doubt

**won·der·ful** \'wəndərfəl\ *adj* **1** : exciting wonder **2** : unusually good — **won·der·ful·ly** *adv* — **won·der·ful·ness** *n*

**won·der·land** \-,land, -lənd\ *n* **1** : fairylike imaginary realm **2** : place that excites admiration or wonder

**won·der·ment** \-mənt\ *n* : wonder

**won·drous** \'wəndrəs\ *adj* : wonderful — **won·drous·ly** *adv* — **won·drous·ness** *n*

**wont** \'wȯnt, 'wōnt\ *adj* : accustomed ~ *n* : habit — **wont·ed** *adj*

**woo** \'wü\ *vb* : try to gain the love or favor of — **woo·er** *n*

**wood** \'wu̇d\ *n* **1** : dense growth of trees usu. smaller than a forest — often pl. **2** : hard fibrous substance of trees and shrubs beneath the bark **3** : wood prepared for some use (as burning) ~ *adj* **1** : wooden **2** : suitable for working with wood **3** *or* **woods** \'wu̇dz\ : living or growing in woods — **wood·chop·per** *n* — **wood·pile** *n* — **wood·shed** *n*

**wood·bine** \'wu̇d,bīn\ *n* : climbing vine

**wood·chuck** \-,chək\ *n* : thick-bodied grizzled animal of No. America

**wood·craft** *n* **1** : skill and practice in matters relating to the woods **2** : skill in making articles from wood

**wood·cut** \-,kət\ *n* **1** : relief printing surface engraved on wood **2** : print from a woodcut

**wood·ed** \'wu̇dəd\ *adj* : covered with woods

**wood·en** \'wu̇d³n\ *adj* **1** : made of wood **2** : lacking resilience **3** : lacking ease, liveliness or interest — **wood·en·ly** *adv* — **wood·en·ness** *n*

**wood·land** \-lənd, -,land\ *n* : land covered with trees

**wood·peck·er** \'wu̇d,pekər\ *n* : brightly marked bird with a hard bill for drilling into trees

**woods·man** \'wu̇dzmən\ *n* : person who works in the woods

**wood·wind** \'wu̇d,wind\ *n* : one of a

group of wind instruments (as a flute or oboe)

**wood•work** *n* : work (as interior house fittings) made of wood

**woody** \'wu̇dē\ *adj* **wood•i•er; -est 1** : abounding with woods **2** : of, containing, or like wood fibers — **wood•i•ness** *n*

**woof** \'wu̇f\ *n* : weft

**wool** \'wu̇l\ *n* **1** : soft hair of some mammals and esp. the sheep **2** : something (as a textile) made of wool — **wooled** \'wu̇ld\ *adj*

**wool•en, wool•len** \'wu̇lən\ *adj* **1** : made of wool **2** : relating to the manufacture of woolen products ∼ *n* **1** : woolen fabric **2** : woolen garments — usu. pl.

**wool•gath•er•ing** *n* : idle daydreaming

**wool•ly** \'wu̇lē\ *adj* **-li•er; -est 1** : of, relating to, or bearing wool **2** : consisting of or resembling wool **3** : confused or turbulent

**woo•zy** \'wüzē\ *adj* **-zi•er; -est 1** : confused **2** : somewhat dizzy, nauseated, or weak — **woo•zi•ness** *n*

**word** \'wərd\ *n* **1** : brief remark **2** : speech sound or series of speech sounds that communicates a meaning **3** : written representation of a word **4** : order **5** : news **6** : promise **7** *pl* : dispute ∼ *vb* : express in words — **word•less** *adj*

**word•ing** \'wərdiŋ\ *n* : verbal expression

**word processing** *n* : production of structured and printed documents through a computer program (**word processor**) — **word process** *vb*

**wordy** \'wərdē\ *adj* **word•i•er; -est** : using many words — **word•i•ness** *n*

**wore** *past of* WEAR

**work** \'wərk\ *n* **1** : labor **2** : employment **3** : task **4** : something (as an artistic production) produced by mental effort or physical labor **5** *pl* : place where industrial labor is done **6** *pl* : moving parts of a mechanism **7** : workmanship ∼ *adj* **1** : suitable for wear while working **2** : used for work ∼ *vb* **worked** \'wərkt\ *or* **wrought** \'rȯt\; **work•ing 1** : bring to pass **2** : create by expending labor upon **3** : bring or get into a form or condition **4** : set or keep in operation **5** : solve **6** : cause to labor **7** : arrange **8** : excite **9** : labor **10** : perform work regularly for wages **11** : function according to plan or design **12** : produce a desired effect — **work•bench** *n* — **work•man** \-mən\ *n* — **work•room** *n* — **in the works** : in preparation

**work•able** \'wərkəbəl\ *adj* **1** : capable of being worked **2** : feasible — **work•able•ness** *n*

**work•a•day** \'wərkə,dā\ *adj* **1** : relating to or suited for working days **2** : ordinary

**work•a•hol•ic** \,wərkə'hȯlik, -'häl-\ *n* : compulsive worker

**work•day** \'wərk,dā\ *n* **1** : day on which work is done **2** : period of time during which one is working

**work•er** \'wərkər\ *n* : person who works esp. for wages

**work•horse** *n* **1** : horse used for hard work **2** : person who does most of the work of a group task

**work•house** *n* : place of confinement for persons who have committed minor offenses

**work•ing** \'wərkiŋ\ *adj* **1** : adequate to allow work to be done **2** : adopted or assumed to help further work or activity ∼ *n* : operation — usu. used in pl.

**work•ing•man** \'wərkiŋ,man\ *n* : worker

**work•man•like** \-,līk\ *adj* : worthy of a good workman

**work•man•ship** \-,ship\ *n* **1** : art or skill of a workman **2** : quality of a piece of work

**work•out** \'wərk,au̇t\ *n* : exercise to improve one's fitness

**work out** *vb* **1** : bring about by effort **2** : solve **3** : develop **4** : to be successful **5** : perform exercises

**work•shop** *n* **1** : small establishment for manufacturing or handicrafts **2** : seminar emphasizing exchange of ideas and practical methods

**world** \'wərld\ *n* **1** : universe **2** : earth with its inhabitants and all things upon it **3** : people in general **4** : great number or quantity **5** : class of persons or their sphere of interest

**world•ly** \'wərldlē\ *adj* **1** : devoted to this world and its pursuits rather than to religion **2** : sophisticated — **world•li•ness** *n*

**world•ly–wise** *adj* : possessing understanding of human affairs

**world•wide** *adj* : extended throughout the entire world — **worldwide** *adv*

**World Wide Web** *n* : part of the Internet accessible through a browser

**worm** \'wərm\ *n* **1** : earthworm or a

similar animal **2** *pl* : disorder caused by parasitic worms ~ *vb* **1** : move or cause to move in a slow and indirect way **2** : to free from worms — **wormy** *adj*

**worm·wood** \'wərm,wud\ *n* **1** : aromatic woody herb (as sagebrush) **2** : something bitter or grievous

**worn** *past part of* WEAR

**worn—out** \'wōrn'aut\ *adj* : exhausted or used up by or as if by wear

**wor·ri·some** \'wərēsəm\ *adj* **1** : causing worry **2** : inclined to worry

**wor·ry** \'wərē\ *vb* **-ried; -ry·ing** **1** : shake and mangle with the teeth **2** : disturb **3** : feel or express anxiety ~ *n, pl* **-ries 1** : anxiety **2** : cause of anxiety — **wor·ri·er** *n*

**worse** \'wərs\ *adj, comparative of* BAD *or of* ILL **1** : bad or evil in a greater degree **2** : more unwell ~ *n* **1** : one that is worse **2** : greater degree of badness ~ *adv comparative of* BAD *or of* ILL : in a worse manner

**wors·en** \'wərs°n\ *vb* : make or become worse

**wor·ship** \'wərshəp\ *n* **1** : reverence toward a divine being or supernatural power **2** : expression of reverence **3** : extravagant respect or devotion ~ *vb* **-shiped** *or* **-shipped; -ship·ing** *or* **-ship·ping 1** : honor or reverence **2** : perform or take part in worship — **wor·ship·er, wor·ship·per** *n*

**worst** \'wərst\ *adj, superlative of* BAD *or of* ILL **1** : most bad, evil, ill, or corrupt **2** : most unfavorable, unpleasant, or painful ~ *n* : one that is worst ~ *adv superlative of* ILL *or of* BAD *or* BADLY : to the extreme degree of badness ~ *vb* : defeat

**wor·sted** \'wustəd, 'wərstəd\ *n* : smooth compact wool yarn or fabric made from such yarn

**worth** \'wərth\ *prep* **1** : equal in value to **2** : deserving of ~ *n* **1** : monetary value **2** : value of something measured by its qualities **3** : moral or personal merit

**worth·less** \-ləs\ *adj* **1** : lacking worth **2** : useless — **worth·less·ness** *n*

**worth·while** \-'hwīl\ *adj* : being worth the time or effort spent

**wor·thy** \'wərthē\ *adj* **-thi·er; -est 1** : having worth or value **2** : having sufficient worth ~ *n, pl* **-thies** : worthy person — **wor·thi·ly** *adv* — **wor·thi·ness** *n*

**would** \'wud\ *past of* WILL — used to express (1) preference (2) intent (3) habitual action (4) contingency (5) probability or (6) a request

**would—be** \'wud'bē\ *adj* : desiring or pretending to be

¹**wound** \'wünd\ *n* **1** : injury in which the skin is broken **2** : mental hurt ~ *vb* : inflict a wound to or in

²**wound** \'waund\ *past of* WIND

**wove** *past of* WEAVE

**woven** *past part of* WEAVE

**wrack** \'rak\ *n* : ruin

**wraith** \'rāth\ *n, pl* **wraiths** \'rāths, 'rāthz\ **1** : ghost **2** : insubstantial appearance

**wran·gle** \'rangəl\ *vb or n* : quarrel — **wran·gler** *n*

**wrap** \'rap\ *vb* **-pp- 1** : cover esp. by winding or folding **2** : envelop and secure for transportation or storage **3** : enclose, surround, or conceal wholly **4** : coil, fold, draw, or twine about something ~ *n* **1** : wrapper or wrapping **2** : outer garment (as a shawl)

**wrap·per** \'rapər\ *n* **1** : that in which something is wrapped **2** : one that wraps

**wrap·ping** *n* : something used to wrap an object

**wrath** \'rath\ *n* : violent anger — **wrath·ful** \-fəl\ *adj*

**wreak** \'rēk\ *vb* **1** : inflict **2** : bring about

**wreath** \'rēth\ *n, pl* **wreaths** \'rēthz, 'rēths\ : something (as boughs) intertwined into a circular shape

**wreathe** \'rēth\ *vb* **wreathed; wreathing 1** : shape into or take on the shape of a wreath **2** : decorate or cover with a wreath

**wreck** \'rek\ *n* **1** : broken remains (as of a ship or vehicle) after heavy damage **2** : something disabled or in a state of ruin **3** : an individual who has become weak or infirm **4** : action of breaking up or destroying something ~ *vb* : ruin or damage by breaking up

**wreck·age** \'rekij\ *n* **1** : act of wrecking **2** : remains of a wreck

**wreck·er** \-ər\ *n* **1** : automotive vehicle for removing disabled cars **2** : one that wrecks or tears down and removes buildings

**wren** \'ren\ *n* : small mostly brown singing bird

**wrench** \'rench\ *vb* **1** : pull with violent twisting or force **2** : injure or disable by a violent twisting or straining ∼ *n* **1** : forcible twisting **2** : tool for exerting a twisting force

**wrest** \'rest\ *vb* **1** : pull or move by a forcible twisting movement **2** : gain with difficulty ∼ *n* : forcible twist

**wres•tle** \'resəl, 'ras-\ *vb* **-tled; -tling** **1** : scuffle with and attempt to throw and pin an opponent **2** : compete against in wrestling **3** : struggle (as with a problem) ∼ *n* : action or an instance of wrestling — **wres•tler** \'reslər, 'ras-\ *n*

**wres•tling** \'resliŋ\ *n* : sport in which 2 opponents try to throw and pin each other

**wretch** \'rech\ *n* **1** : miserable unhappy person **2** : vile person

**wretch•ed** \'rechəd\ *adj* **1** : deeply afflicted, dejected, or distressed **2** : grievous **3** : inferior — **wretch•ed•ly** *adv* — **wretch•ed•ness** *n*

**wrig•gle** \'rigəl\ *vb* **-gled; -gling** **1** : twist and turn restlessly **2** : move along by twisting and turning — **wrig•gle** *n* — **wrig•gler** \'rigələr\ *n*

**wring** \'riŋ\ *vb* **wrung** \'rəŋ\; **wring•ing** **1** : squeeze or twist out moisture **2** : get by or as if by twisting or pressing **3** : twist together in anguish **4** : pain — **wring•er** *n*

**wrin•kle** \'riŋkəl\ *n* : crease or small fold on a surface (as in the skin or in cloth) ∼ *vb* **-kled; -kling** : develop or cause to develop wrinkles — **wrin•kly** \-kəlē\ *adj*

**wrist** \'rist\ *n* : joint or region between the hand and the arm

**writ** \'rit\ *n* **1** : something written **2** : legal order in writing

**write** \'rīt\ *vb* **wrote** \'rōt\; **writ•ten** \'rit³n\; **writ•ing** \'rītiŋ\ **1** : form letters or words on a surface **2** : form the letters or the words of (as on paper) **3** : make up and set down for others to read **4** : write a letter to — **write off** *vb* : cancel

**writ•er** \'rītər\ *n* : one that writes esp. as a business or occupation

**writhe** \'rīth\ *vb* **writhed; writh•ing** : twist and turn this way and that

**writ•ing** \'rītiŋ\ *n* **1** : act of one that writes **2** : handwriting **3** : something written or printed

**wrong** \'roŋ\ *n* **1** : unfair or unjust act **2** : something that is contrary to justice **3** : state of being or doing wrong ∼ *adj* **wrong•er** \'roŋər\; **wrong•est** \'roŋəst\ **1** : sinful **2** : not right according to a standard **3** : unsuitable **4** : incorrect ∼ *adv* **1** : in a wrong direction or manner **2** : incorrectly ∼ *vb* **wronged; wrong•ing** **1** : do wrong to **2** : treat unjustly — **wrong•ly** *adv*

**wrong•do•er** \-'düər\ *n* : one who does wrong — **wrong•do•ing** \-'düiŋ\ *n*

**wrong•ful** \-fəl\ *adj* **1** : wrong **2** : illegal — **wrong•ful•ly** *adv* — **wrong•ful•ness** *n*

**wrong•head•ed** \'roŋ'hedəd\ *adj* : stubborn in clinging to wrong opinion or principles — **wrong•head•ed•ly** *adv* — **wrong•head•ed•ness** *n*

**wrote** *past of* WRITE

**wrought** \'rot\ *adj* **1** : formed **2** : hammered into shape **3** : deeply stirred

**wrung** *past of* WRING

**wry** \'rī\ *adj* **wri•er** \'rīər\; **wri•est** \'rīəst\ **1** : turned abnormally to one side **2** : twisted **3** : cleverly and often ironically humorous — **wry•ly** *adv* — **wry•ness** *n*

# X

**x** \'eks\ *n, pl* **x's** *or* **xs** \'eksəz\ **1** : 24th letter of the alphabet **2** : unknown quantity ∼ *vb* **x–ed; x–ing** *or* **x'ing** : cancel with a series of *x*'s — usu. with *out*

**xe•non** \'zē,nän,'zen,än\ *n* : heavy gaseous chemical element

**xe•no•pho•bia** \,zenə'fōbēə, ,zēn-\ *n* : fear and hatred of foreign people and things — **xe•no•phobe** \'zenə-,fōb, 'zēn-\ *n*

**Xmas** \'krisməs\ *n* : Christmas

**x–ra•di•a•tion** *n* **1** : exposure to X rays **2** : radiation consisting of X rays

**x–ray** \'eks,rā\ *vb* : examine, treat, or photograph with X rays

**X ray** *n* **1** : radiation of short wavelength that is able to penetrate solids **2** : photograph taken with X rays — **X-ray** *adj*

**xy·lo·phone** \'zīlə,fōn\ *n* : musical instrument with wooden bars that are struck — **xy·lo·phon·ist** \-,fōnist\ *n*

# Y

**y** \'wī\ *n, pl* **y's** *or* **ys** \'wīz\ : 25th letter of the alphabet

**¹-y** \ē\ *adj suffix* **1** : composed or full of **2** : like **3** : performing or apt to perform an action

**²-y** \ē\ *n suffix, pl* **-ies 1** : state, condition, or quality **2** : activity, place of business, or goods dealt with **3** : whole group

**yacht** \'yät\ *n* : luxurious pleasure boat ~ *vb* : race or cruise in a yacht

**ya·hoo** \'yāhü, 'yä-\ *n, pl* **-hoos** : uncouth or stupid person

**yak** \'yak\ *n* : big hairy Asian ox

**yam** \'yam\ *n* **1** : edible root of a tropical vine **2** : deep orange sweet potato

**yam·mer** \'yamər\ *vb* **1** : whimper **2** : chatter — **yammer** *n*

**yank** \'yaŋk\ *n* : strong sudden pull — **yank** *vb*

**Yank** \'yaŋk\ *n* : Yankee

**Yan·kee** \'yaŋkē\ *n* : native or inhabitant of New England, the northern U.S., or the U.S.

**yap** \'yap\ *vb* **-pp- 1** : yelp **2** : chatter — **yap** *n*

**¹yard** \'yärd\ *n* **1** : 3 feet **2** : long spar for supporting and spreading a sail — **yard·age** \-ij\ *n*

**²yard** *n* **1** : enclosed roofless area **2** : grounds of a building **3** : work area

**yard·arm** \'yärd,ärm\ *n* : end of the yard of a square-rigged ship

**yard·stick** *n* **1** : measuring stick 3 feet long **2** : standard for judging

**yar·mul·ke** \'yäməkə, 'yär-, -məl-\ *n* : a small brimless cap worn by Jewish males in a synagogue

**yarn** \'yärn\ *n* **1** : spun fiber for weaving or knitting **2** : tale

**yaw** \'yo\ *vb* : deviate erratically from a course — **yaw** *n*

**yawl** \'yol\ *n* : sailboat with 2 masts

**yawn** \'yon\ *vb* : open the mouth wide ~ *n* : deep breath through a wide-open mouth — **yawn·er** *n*

**ye** \'yē\ *pron* : you

**yea** \'yā\ *adv* **1** : yes **2** : truly ~ *n* : affirmative vote

**year** \'yir\ *n* **1** : period of about 365 days **2** *pl* : age

**year·book** *n* : annual report of the year's events

**year·ling** \'yirliŋ, 'yərlən\ *n* : one that is or is rated as a year old

**year·ly** \'yirlē\ *adj* : annual — **yearly** *adv*

**yearn** \'yərn\ *vb* **1** : feel desire esp. for what one cannot have **2** : feel tenderness or compassion

**yearn·ing** \-iŋ\ *n* : tender or urgent desire

**yeast** \'yēst\ *n* : froth or sediment in sugary liquids containing a tiny fungus and used in making alcoholic liquors and as a leaven in baking — **yeasty** *adj*

**yell** \'yel\ *vb* : utter a loud cry — **yell** *n*

**yel·low** \'yelō\ *adj* **1** : of the color yellow **2** : sensational **3** : cowardly ~ *vb* : make or turn yellow ~ *n* **1** : color of lemons **2** : yolk of an egg — **yel·low·ish** \'yeləwish\ *adj*

**yellow fever** *n* : virus disease marked by prostration, jaundice, fever, and often hemorrhage

**yellow jacket** *n* : wasp with yellow stripes

**yelp** \'yelp\ *vb* : utter a sharp quick shrill cry — **yelp** *n*

**yen** \'yen\ *n* : strong desire

**yeo·man** \'yōmən\ *n* **1** : attendant or officer in a royal or noble household **2** : small farmer **3** : naval petty officer with clerical duties — **yeo·man·ry** \-rē\ *n*

**-yer** — see -ER

**yes** \'yes\ *adv* — used to express consent or agreement ~ *n* : affirmative answer

**ye·shi·va, ye·shi·vah** \yə'shēvə\ *n, pl* **yeshivas** *or* **ye·shi·voth** \-,shē'vōt, -'vōth\ : Jewish school

**yes-man** \'yes,man\ *n* : person who agrees with every opinion or suggestion of a boss

**yes·ter·day** \'yestərdē\ *adv* **1** : on the

day preceding today **2** : only a short time ago ∼ *n* **1** : day last past **2** : time not long past

**yet** \'yet\ *adv* **1** : in addition **2** : up to now **3** : so soon as now **4** : nevertheless ∼ *conj* : but

**yew** \'yü\ *n* : evergreen tree or shrubs with dark stiff poisonous needles

**yield** \'yēld\ *vb* **1** : surrender **2** : grant **3** : bear as a crop **4** : produce **5** : cease opposition or resistance ∼ *n* : quantity produced or returned

**yo·del** \'yōd°l\ *vb* **-deled** *or* **-delled; -del·ing** *or* **-del·ling** : sing by abruptly alternating between chest voice and falsetto — **yodel** *n* — **yo·del·er** \'yōd°lər\ *n*

**yo·ga** \'yōgə\ *n* : system of exercises for attaining bodily or mental control and well-being

**yo·gi** \'yōgē\ *n* : person who practices yoga

**yo·gurt** \'yōgərt\ *n* : fermented slightly acid soft food made from milk

**yoke** \'yōk\ *n* **1** : neck frame for coupling draft animals or for carrying loads **2** : clamp **3** : slavery **4** : tie or link **5** : piece of a garment esp. at the shoulder ∼ *vb* **yoked; yok·ing 1** : couple with a yoke **2** : join

**yo·kel** \'yōkəl\ *n* : naive and gullible country person

**yolk** \'yōk\ *n* : yellow part of an egg — **yolked** \'yōkt\ *adj*

**Yom Kip·pur** \,yōmki'pùr, ,yäm-, -'kipər\ *n* : Jewish holiday observed in September or October with fasting and prayer as a day of atonement

**yon** \'yän\ *adj or adv* : yonder

**yon·der** \'yändər\ *adv* : at or to that place ∼ *adj* : distant

**yore** \'yōr\ *n* : time long past

**you** \'yü\ *pron* **1** : person or persons addressed **2** : person in general

**young** \'yən\ *adj* **youn·ger** \'yəngər\; **youn·gest** \'yəngəst\ **1** : being in the first or an early stage of life, growth, or development **2** : recently come into being **3** : youthful ∼ *n, pl* **young** : persons or animals that are young — **young·ish** \-ish\ *adj*

**young·ster** \-stər\ *n* **1** : young person **2** : child

**your** \yər, 'yùr, 'yōr\ *adj* : relating to you or yourself

**yours** \'yùrz, 'yōrz\ *pron* : the ones belonging to you

**your·self** \yər'self\ *pron, pl* **your·selves** \-'selvz\ : you — used reflexively or for emphasis

**youth** \'yüth\ *n, pl* **youths** \'yüthz, 'yüths\ **1** : period between childhood and maturity **2** : young man **3** : young persons **4** : state or quality of being young, fresh, or vigorous

**youth·ful** \'yüthfəl\ *adj* **1** : relating to or appropriate to youth **2** : young **3** : vigorous and fresh — **youth·ful·ly** *adv* — **youth·ful·ness** *n*

**yowl** \'yaùl\ *vb* : utter a loud long mournful cry — **yowl** *n*

**yo-yo** \'yō,yō\ *n, pl* **-yos** : toy that falls from or rises to the hand as it unwinds and rewinds on a string

**yuc·ca** \'yəkə\ *n* : any of several plants related to the lilies that grow in dry regions

**yule** \'yül\ *n* : Christmas — **yule·tide** \-,tīd\ *n*

**yum·my** \'yəmē\ *adj* **-mi·er; -est** : highly attractive or pleasing

# Z

**z** \'zē\ *n, pl* **z's** *or* **zs** : 26th letter of the alphabet

**za·ny** \'zānē\ *n, pl* **-nies 1** : clown **2** : silly person ∼ *adj* **-ni·er; -est** : crazy or foolish — **za·ni·ly** *adv* — **za·ni·ness** *n*

**zeal** \'zēl\ *n* : enthusiasm

**zeal·ot** \'zelət\ *n* : fanatical partisan

**zeal·ous** \'zeləs\ *adj* : filled with zeal — **zeal·ous·ly** *adv* — **zeal·ous·ness** *n*

**ze·bra** \'zēbrə\ *n* : horselike African mammal marked with light and dark stripes

**zeit·geist** \'tsīt,gīst, 'zīt-\ *n* : general spirit of an era

**ze·nith** \'zēnəth\ *n* : highest point

**zeph•yr** \'zefər\ *n* : gentle breeze

**zep•pe•lin** \'zepələn\ *n* : rigid airship like a blimp

**ze•ro** \'zērō\ *n, pl* **-ros** **1** : number represented by the symbol 0 or the symbol itself **2** : starting point **3** : lowest point ~ *adj* : having no size or quantity

**zest** \'zest\ *n* **1** : quality of enhancing enjoyment **2** : keen enjoyment — **zest•ful** \-fəl\ *adj* — **zest•ful•ly** *adv* — **zest•ful•ness** *n*

**zig•zag** \'zig,zag\ *n* : one of a series of short sharp turns or angles ~ *adj* : having zigzags ~ *adv* : in or by a zigzag path ~ *vb* **-gg-** : proceed along a zigzag path

**zil•lion** \'zilyən\ *n* : large indeterminate number

**zinc** \'ziŋk\ *n* : bluish white crystaline metallic chemical element

**zing** \'ziŋ\ *n* **1** : shrill humming noise **2** : energy — **zing** *vb*

**zin•nia** \'zinēə, 'zēnyə\ *n* : American herb widely grown for its showy flowers

**¹zip** \'zip\ *vb* **-pp-** : move or act with speed ~ *n* : energy

**²zip** *vb* **-pp-** : close or open with a zipper

**zip code** *n* : number that identifies a U.S. postal delivery area

**zip•per** \'zipər\ *n* : fastener consisting of 2 rows of interlocking teeth

**zip•py** \'zipē\ *adj* **-pi•er; -est** : brisk

**zir•con** \'zər,kän\ *n* : zirconium-containing mineral sometimes used in jewelry

**zir•co•ni•um** \,zər'kōnēəm\ *n* : corrosion-resistant gray metallic element

**zith•er** \'zithər, 'zith-\ *n* : stringed musical instrument played by plucking

**zi•ti** \'zētē\ *n, pl* **ziti** : short tubular pasta

**zo•di•ac** \'zōdē,ak\ *n* : imaginary belt in the heavens encompassing the paths of the planets and divided into 12 signs used in astrology — **zo•di•a•cal** \zō'dīəkəl\ *adj*

**zom•bie** \'zämbē\ *n* : person thought to have died and been brought back to life without free will

**zon•al** \'zōnᵊl\ *adj* : of, relating to, or having the form of a zone — **zon•al•ly** *adv*

**zone** \'zōn\ *n* **1** : division of the earth's surface based on latitude and climate **2** : distinctive area ~ *vb* **zoned; zoning** **1** : mark off into zones **2** : reserve for special purposes — **zo•na•tion** \zō'nāshən\ *n*

**zoo** \'zü\ *n, pl* **zoos** : collection of living animals usu. for public display — **zoo•keep•er** *n*

**zo•ol•o•gy** \zō'äləjē\ *n* : science of animals — **zo•o•log•i•cal** \,zōə'läjikəl\ *adj* — **zo•ol•o•gist** \zō'äləjist\ *n*

**zoom** \'züm\ *vb* **1** : move with a loud hum or buzz **2** : move or increase with great speed — **zoom** *n*

**zuc•chi•ni** \zü'kēnē\ *n, pl* **-ni** *or* **-nis** : summer squash with smooth cylindrical dark green fruits

**zwie•back** \'swēbak, 'swī-, 'zwē-, 'zwī-\ *n* : biscuit of baked, sliced, and toasted bread

**zy•gote** \'zī,gōt\ *n* : cell formed by the union of 2 sexual cells — **zy•got•ic** \zī'gätik\ *adj*

# Abbreviations

Most of these abbreviations have been given in one form. Variation in use of periods, in type, and in capitalization is frequent and widespread (as *mph, MPH, m.p.h., Mph*).

**abbr** abbreviation
**AC** alternating current
**acad** academic, academy
**AD** in the year of our Lord
**adj** adjective
**adv** adverb, advertisement
**advt** advertisement
**AF** air force, audio frequency
**agric** agricultural, agriculture
**AK** Alaska
**aka** also known as
**AL, Ala** Alabama
**alg** algebra
**Alta** Alberta
**a.m., AM** before noon
**Am, Amer** America, American
**amp** ampere
**amt** amount
**anc** ancient
**anon** anonymous
**ans** answer
**ant** antonym
**APO** army post office
**approx** approximate, approximately
**Apr** April
**apt** apartment, aptitude
**AR** Arkansas
**arith** arithmetic
**Ariz** Arizona
**Ark** Arkansas
**art** article, artificial
**assn** association
**assoc** associate, associated, association
**asst** assistant
**ATM** automated teller machine
**att** attached, attention, attorney
**attn** attention
**atty** attorney
**Aug** August
**auth** authentic, author, authorized
**aux, auxil** auxiliary
**av** avoirdupois
**AV** audiovisual
**ave** avenue
**avg** average

**AZ** Arizona
**BA** bachelor of arts
**bal** balance
**bar** barometer, barrel
**bbl** barrel, barrels
**BC** before Christ, British Columbia
**BCE** before Christian Era, before Common Era
**bet** between
**biog** biographer, biographical, biography
**biol** biologic, biological, biologist, biology
**bldg** building
**blvd** boulevard
**BO** backorder, best offer, body odor, box office, branch office
**Brit** Britain, British
**bro** brother, brothers
**bros** brothers
**BS** bachelor of science
**Btu** British thermal unit
**bu** bureau, bushel
**c** carat, cent, centimeter, century, chapter, circa, cup
**C** Celsius, centigrade
**ca** circa
**CA, Cal, Calif** California
**cal** calendar, caliber, calorie
**Can, Canad** Canada, Canadian
**cap** capacity, capital, capitalize, capitalized
**Capt** captain
**CB** citizens band
**CDT** central daylight time
**cen** central
**cert** certificate, certification, certified, certify
**cf** compare
**chap** chapter
**chem** chemistry
**cir** circle, circuit, circular, circumference
**civ** civil, civilian
**cm** centimeter
**co** company, county

**CO** Colorado
**c/o** care of
**COD** cash on delivery, collect on delivery
**col** colonial, colony, color, colored, column, counsel
**Col** colonel, Colorado
**Colo** Colorado
**comp** comparative, compensation, compiled, compiler, composition, compound, comprehensive, comptroller
**cong** congress, congressional
**conj** conjunction
**Conn** Connecticut
**cont** continued
**contr** contract, contraction
**corp** corporal, corporation
**corr** corrected, correction
**cp** compare, coupon
**CPR** cardiopulmonary resuscitation
**cr** credit, creditor
**CSA** Confederate States of America
**CST** central standard time
**ct** carat, cent, count, court
**CT** central time, certified teacher, Connecticut
**cu** cubic
**cur** currency, current
**CZ** Canal Zone
**d** penny
**DA** district attorney
**dag** dekagram
**dal** dekaliter
**dam** dekameter
**dbl** double
**DC** direct current, District of Columbia
**DDS** doctor of dental science, doctor of dental surgery
**DE** Delaware
**dec** deceased, decrease
**Dec** December
**deg** degree
**Del** Delaware
**Dem** Democrat, Democratic
**dept** department
**det** detached, detachment, detail, determine
**dg** decigram
**dia, diam** diameter
**diag** diagonal, diagram
**dict** dictionary
**dif, diff** difference
**dim** dimension, diminished
**dir** director
**disc** discount
**dist** distance, district

**div** divided, dividend, division, divorced
**dl** deciliter
**dm** decimeter
**DMD** doctor of dental medicine
**DOB** date of birth
**doz** dozen
**DP** data processing
**dr** dram, drive, drum
**Dr** doctor
**DST** daylight saving time
**DUI** driving under the influence
**DWI** driving while intoxicated
**dz** dozen
**e** east, eastern, excellent
**ea** each
**ecol** ecological, ecology
**econ** economics, economist, economy
**EDT** eastern daylight time
**e.g.** for example
**EKG** electrocardiogram, electrocardiograph
**elec** electric, electrical, electricity
**elem** elementary
**eng** engine, engineer, engineering
**Eng** England, English
**esp** especially
**EST** eastern standard time
**ET** eastern time
**et al** and others
**etc** et cetera
**ex** example, express, extra
**exec** executive
**f** false, female, feminine
**F, Fah, Fahr** Fahrenheit
**Feb** February
**fed** federal, federation
**fem** female, feminine
**FL, Fla** Florida
**fl oz** fluid ounce
**FPO** fleet post office
**fr** father, friar, from
**Fri** Friday
**ft** feet, foot, fort
**fut** future
**FYI** for your information
**g** gram
**Ga, GA** Georgia
**gal** gallery, gallon
**gen** general
**geog** geographic, geographical, geography
**geol** geologic, geological, geology
**geom** geometric, geometrical, geometry
**gm** gram
**GMT** Greenwich mean time

**GOP** Grand Old Party (Republican)
**gov** government, governor
**govt** government
**GP** general practice, general practitioner
**gr** grade, grain, gram
**gram** grammar, grammatical
**gt** great
**GU** Guam
**hd** head
**hf** half
**hgt** height
**hgwy** highway
**HI** Hawaii
**hist** historian, historical, history
**hon** honor, honorable, honorary
**hr** here, hour
**HS** high school
**ht** height
**HT** Hawaii time
**hwy** highway
**i** intransitive, island, isle
**Ia, IA** Iowa
**ICU** intensive care unit
**ID** Idaho, identification
**i.e.** that is
**IL, Ill** Illinois
**imp** imperative, imperfect
**in** inch
**IN** Indiana
**inc** incomplete, incorporated
**ind** independent
**Ind** Indian, Indiana
**inf** infinitive
**int** interest
**interj** interjection
**intl, intnl** international
**ital** italic, italicized
**Jan** January
**JD** juvenile delinquent
**jour** journal, journeyman
**JP** justice of the peace
**jr, jun** junior
**JV** junior varsity
**Kan, Kans** Kansas
**kg** kilogram
**km** kilometer
**KS** Kansas
**kW** kilowatt
**Ky, KY** Kentucky
**l** late, left, liter, long
**L** large
**La** Louisiana
**LA** Los Angeles, Louisiana
**lat** latitude
**lb** pound
**lg** large, long
**lib** liberal, librarian, library

**long** longitude
**m** male, masculine, meter, mile
**M** medium
**MA** Massachusetts
**Man** Manitoba
**Mar** March
**masc** masculine
**Mass** Massachusetts
**math** mathematical, mathematician
**max** maximum
**Md** Maryland
**MD** doctor of medicine, Maryland
**MDT** mountain daylight time
**Me, ME** Maine
**med** medium
**mg** milligram
**mgr** manager
**MI, Mich** Michigan
**mid** middle
**min** minimum, minor, minute
**Minn** Minnesota
**misc** miscellaneous
**Miss** Mississippi
**ml** milliliter
**mm** millimeter
**MN** Minnesota
**mo** month
**Mo, MO** Missouri
**Mon** Monday
**Mont** Montana
**mpg** miles per gallon
**mph** miles per hour
**MRI** magnetic resonance imaging
**MS** Mississippi
**MST** mountain standard time
**mt** mount, mountain
**MT** Montana, mountain time
**n** neuter, north, northern, noun
**NA** North America, not applicable
**nat** national, native, natural
**natl** national
**naut** nautical
**NB** New Brunswick
**NC** North Carolina
**ND, N Dak** North Dakota
**NE, Neb, Nebr** Nebraska
**neg** negative
**neut** neuter
**Nev** Nevada
**Nfld** Newfoundland
**NH** New Hampshire
**NJ** New Jersey
**NM, N Mex** New Mexico
**no** north, number
**Nov** November
**NR** not rated
**NS** Nova Scotia
**NV** Nevada

**NWT** Northwest Territories
**NY** New York
**NYC** New York City
**O** Ohio
**obj** object, objective
**occas** occasionally
**Oct** October
**off** office, officer, official
**OH** Ohio
**OJ** orange juice
**OK, Okla** Oklahoma
**ON, Ont** Ontario
**opp** opposite
**OR, Ore, Oreg** Oregon
**orig** original, originally
**oz** ounce, ounces
**p** page
**Pa** Pennsylvania
**PA** Pennsylvania, public address
**PAC** political action committee
**par** paragraph, parallel
**part** participle, particular
**pass** passenger, passive
**pat** patent
**PC** percent, politically correct, post-card
**pd** paid
**PD** police department
**PDT** Pacific daylight time
**PE** physical education
**PEI** Prince Edward Island
**Penn, Penna** Pennsylvania
**pg** page
**PIN** personal identification number
**pk** park, peak, peck
**pkg** package
**pl** place, plural
**p.m., PM** afternoon
**PMS** premenstrual syndrome
**PO** post office
**Port** Portugal, Portuguese
**pos** position, positive
**poss** possessive
**pp** pages
**PQ** Province of Quebec
**pr** pair, price, printed
**PR** public relations, Puerto Rico
**prep** preposition
**pres** present, president
**prob** probable, probably, problem
**prof** professor
**pron** pronoun
**prov** province
**PS** postscript, public school
**PST** Pacific standard time
**psych** psychology
**pt** part, payment, pint, point
**PT** Pacific time, physical therapy

**pvt** private
**qr** quarter
**qt** quantity, quart
**Que** Quebec
**quot** quotation
**r** right, river
**rd** road, rod, round
**RDA** recommended daily allowance, recommended dietary allowance
**recd** received
**reg** region, register, registered, regular
**rel** relating, relative, religion
**rep** report, reporter, representative, republic
**Rep** Republican
**res** residence
**rev** reverse, review, revised, revision, revolution
**Rev** reverend
**RFD** rural free delivery
**RI** Rhode Island
**rm** room
**RPM** revolutions per minute
**RR** railroad, rural route
**RSVP** please reply
**rt** right
**rte** route
**s** small, south, southern
**SA** South America
**SASE** self-addressed stamped envelope
**Sask** Saskatchewan
**Sat** Saturday
**SC** South Carolina
**sci** science, scientific
**SD, S Dak** South Dakota
**secy** secretary
**sen** senate, senator, senior
**Sept, Sep** September
**sing** singular
**sm** small
**so** south, southern
**soph** sophomore
**sp** spelling
**spec** special, specifically
**specif** specific, specifically
**SPF** sun protection factor
**sq** square
**sr** senior
**Sr** sister
**SSN** Social Security number
**SSR** Soviet Socialist Republic
**st** street
**St** saint
**std** standard
**subj** subject
**Sun** Sunday

**supt** superintendent
**SWAT** Special Weapons and Tactics
**syn** synonym
**t** teaspoon, temperature, ton, transitive, troy, true
**T** tablespoon
**tbs, tbsp** tablespoon
**TD** touchdown
**tech** technical, technician, technology
**Tenn** Tennessee
**terr** territory
**Tex** Texas
**Th, Thu, Thur, Thurs** Thursday
**TN** Tennessee
**trans** translated, translation, translator
**tsp** teaspoon
**Tu, Tue, Tues** Tuesday
**TX** Texas
**UK** United Kingdom
**UN** United Nations
**univ** universal, university
**US** United States
**USA** United States of America
**USSR** Union of Soviet Socialist Republics

**usu** usual, usually
**UT** Utah
**UV** ultraviolet
**v** verb, versus
**Va, VA** Virginia
**var** variant, variety
**vb** verb
**VG** very good
**VI** Virgin Islands
**vol** volume, volunteer
**VP** vice president
**vs** versus
**Vt, VT** Vermont
**w** west, western
**WA, Wash** Washington
**Wed** Wednesday
**WI, Wis, Wisc** Wisconsin
**wk** week, work
**wt** weight
**WV, W Va** West Virginia
**WY, Wyo** Wyoming
**XL** extra large, extra long
**yd** yard
**yr** year, younger, your
**YT** Yukon Territory